WHERE *to* SKI
AND *Snowboard* 2014

WITHDRAWN

Published in Great Britain by
NortonWood Publishing

tel 0844 9911 123
email w18@wtss.co.uk

Editors Chris Gill and Dave Watts
Assistant editors Sheila Reid, Mandy
Crook, Rebecca Miles, Abi Butcher

Contributors Minty Clinch,
Alan Coulson, Nicky Holford,
James Hooke, Eric Jackson,
Tim Perry, Ian Porter, Adam Ruck,
Helena Wiesner, Fraser Wilkin,
Arnie Wilson

Advertising manager
Dave Ashmore

Design by Val Fox
Production by Guide Editors
Contents photos generally
by Snowpix.com / Chris Gill
Production manager
Sarah Carreck
Map production
Ian Stratford
Proofreader Sally Vince
Printed and bound in Italy
by Lego SpA

10 9 8 7 6 5 4 3 2 1

ISBN-13: 978-0-9558663-5-7

A CIP catalogue entry for this book
is available from the British Library.

Book trade sales are handled by
Faber Factory Plus
Bloomsbury House
74–77 Great Russell Street
London WC1B 3DA

tel 020 7927 3800
bridgetlj@faber.co.uk

WHERE *to* SKI
AND *SnoWboard* 2014

The Definitive Guide
to the 1,000 Best Winter Sports Resorts in the World

Edited by
Chris Gill
and
Dave Watts

NortonWood

 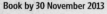

Contents 1

That's the start of it –
turn the page for
the heart of it ...

Family Ski ™

Perfect family skiing holidays in high quality ski chalets with outstanding childcare

+44 (0) 1684 540 333
www.familyski.co.uk
Designed with the family in mind

ABTOT
The Association of Bonded
Travel Organisers Trust Ltd

Contents 2

Resort chapters

ANDORRA 88

Excellent British-oriented ski schools, but charmless villages – and no longer the bargain it once was

FRANCE 202

Unrivalled for big, high, snow-sure ski areas with convenient lodgings – but be prepared for high food and drink prices in the best-known ones

AUSTRIA 98

Charming villages, lively après-ski, friendly locals and modest prices; but many resorts are at low altitudes – a problem in mild weather

ITALY 390

Jolly villages, up-to-the-minute lift systems and snowmaking, and modest prices – but few extensive ski areas to rival those of France

GERMANY 386

Has a great deal in common with Austria, over the border. There is one first-division resort, and dozens of minor ones

Garmisch-Partenkirchen	388

SWITZERLAND 454

Some uniquely cute villages and spectacular scenery; sadly, at current exchange rates, prices are difficult for most Brits to bear

Adelboden	460	Mürren	488
Andermatt	463	Saas-Fee	492
Champéry	465	St Moritz	497
Crans-Montana	468	Val d'Anniviers	504
Davos	470	Verbier	508
Engelberg	477	Villars	519
Grindelwald	479	Wengen	521
Klosters	483	Zermatt	526
Laax	485		

USA 536

Great service, mostly crowd-free slopes, frequent snowfalls and safe ungroomed runs; some costs are very high but food and drink are bearable even at $1.44 to £1

California	**540**	**Utah**	**581**
Heavenly	541	Alta	582
Mammoth	546	Canyons	584
Squaw Valley	551	Deer Valley	586
Colorado	**553**	Park City	588
Aspen	554	Snowbird	593
Beaver Creek	561	**Rest of the West**	**595**
Breckenridge	563	Big Sky	596
Snowmass	568	Jackson Hole	601
Vail	570	**New England**	**606**
Winter Park	577		

CANADA 608

A lot in common with the USA, but with some very distinctive resorts and grand scenery – and less of a culture gap than you find in the USA

Western Canada	**611**
Banff	612
Big White	618
Fernie	621
Kicking Horse	627
Lake Louise	629
Revelstoke	634
Silver Star	637
Sun Peaks	639
Whistler	641
Eastern Canada	**650**

THE REST

SOUTHERN EUROPE

Spain	**651**

SCANDINAVIA

Finland	**653**
Norway	**655**
Sweden	**657**

EASTERN EUROPE

Bulgaria	**658**
Romania	**661**
Slovenia	**662**

UNITED KINGDOM

Scotland	**665**

FAR EAST

Japan	**666**

About this book

Dave Watts

Chris Gill

This is the 18th edition of *Where to Ski and Snowboard* – Britain's only established annual guidebook to ski resorts worldwide. It is the very best resort guide you can buy. Here's why:

- Every edition is the result of a thorough, painstaking process of **checking, updating and reviewing** the book's contents. We visit countless resorts every season – more last season, in fact, than ever before – but even those we can't get to are reconsidered with the same care. In any one year, some chapters change hugely as a result, others hardly at all. But that just reflects what needs to change, and what doesn't.

- The book also benefits enormously from the **hundreds of reports** that readers send in on the resorts they visit. Every year, the 100 best reports are rewarded by a free copy of the book, and one of the readers awarded a book wins a free week in a smart French resort apartment, courtesy of Lagrange Holidays. Read page 12 for more about this.

- By making the most of technology we are able to publish at the right time while going to press very late by conventional book publishing standards – so we can include the late-breaking news that makes the book **up to date for the season ahead**. The earliest editions of this book went to press in June; this year, it's 29 July, only about five weeks ahead of publication day.

- We work hard to make our information **reader-friendly**, with clearly structured text, comparative ratings and no-nonsense verdicts for the main aspects of each resort.

- We don't hesitate to express **critical views**. We learned our craft at Consumers' Association, where Chris became editor of *Holiday Which?* magazine and Dave became editor of *Which?* itself – so a consumerist attitude comes naturally to us.

- Our resort chapters give an **unrivalled level of detail** – including scale plans of each major resort, so that you get a clear idea of size – and all the facts you need.

- We use **colour printing** fully – we include not only piste maps for every major resort but also scores of photographs, carefully chosen so that you can see for yourself what the resorts are like.

Our ability to keep on investing in *Where to Ski and Snowboard* is largely due to the support of our advertisers – many of whom have been with us since the first edition in 1994. We are grateful for that support, and hope you will in turn support our advertisers (and tell them that you saw their ads here: we know advertising in the book works, but advertisers can't be reminded too often).

We are absolutely committed to helping you, our readers, to make an informed choice; and we're confident that you'll find this edition the best yet. Enjoy your skiing and riding this season.

Chris Gill and Dave Watts
Norton St Philip, 29 July 2013

Exclusive reader cash-back offer!

Book your next ski holiday with Alpine Answers, the UK's foremost ski holiday specialist, and save 100s of pounds.*

Why you should use Alpine Answers:
- **21 years** selling ski holidays to discerning skiers
- **Fantastic** user friendly website
- **Great choice** of catered chalets and hotels to suit most budgets
- **Friendly** and **knowledgeable** staff
- **Excellent** customer service

*The cash-back amount ranges from £25 to £50 per person, depending on your holiday spend and group size. For example a group of 10 people will save up to £500.

To register for cash-back, complete our short online form at www.bit.ly/wtss-aa Then, when booking, quote the discount code "WTSS2014" and the email address you used when registering.

Call: 020 7801 1080
www.alpineanswers.co.uk

ABTA
ABTA No.D4050

Win a free week in France with Lagrange

Send us reports on the resorts you visit!

There are too many resorts for us to visit them all every year, and too many hotels, bars and mountain restaurants for us to visit them all. So we are always keen to encourage readers to send in reports on their holiday experiences. Every year, we give 100 copies of the new edition to the writers of the best reports. But now there's an extra incentive: all book winners will automatically be entered for a draw to win a week in a Lagrange apartment.

LAGRANGE

Two of Lagrange's top properties – Les Fermes Emiguy in Les Gets (new in 2011) and Les Chalets de l'Adet in St-Lary ↓

Your resort reports must be based on visits made during the 2013/14 season, and must be received by the end of April 2014. We much prefer to receive reports in digital form. Ideally, we'd like you to use our online form reached via www.wheretoskiandsnowboard.com. If you prefer, you can send an email to reports@wtss.co.uk – but please give your report a clear structure, using the same headings that we use in our resort chapters. If you don't, we'll find it much harder to make much use of your report. And it's vital that you give us the date of your trip, so that we can interpret your report sensibly – plus your postal address, to send your book to if you win one.

The winner of the draw will get a week in a Lagrange residence. The details of the range of options will be made clear on our website. With the exception of Christmas/New Year and the period around February half term, you'll be able to choose your preferred dates (subject to availability).

The editorial

JUST LIKE LONDON BUSES

We wait ages for one, then four come along together. We're not talking about number 9 buses but about major new links between resorts here. This year one of the biggest developments for ages is happening in Austria, with Lech and Zürs being linked by gondola to Warth and Schröcken. (Never heard of them? You should get to know them if you like powder, because they are the snowiest resorts in the Alps. They're covered in our Vorarlberg Bregenzerwald chapter.) The combined ski area will be over 50% bigger than the existing Lech–Zürs terrain, and we are itching to visit in 2014.

Then there are three major new links in Switzerland. There will be a new cable-car link between Grimentz and Zinal (two resorts with great off-piste in the Val d'Anniviers). Verbier will be linked to Bruson by a new gondola from Le Châble. And Arosa and Lenzerheide will be linked by a new cable car to create a ski area with 225km of pistes; we'd be keen to add a chapter on this area, if only Swiss prices were more bearable – more on this later.

ANOTHER VINTAGE SEASON

As we put this edition to bed in late July we were just emerging from the longest heatwave the UK has had for years, and could only daydream about the last fabulous winter and the one to come. Fraser Wilkin, our resident snow geek, sums up last season.

What a winter! Although not everyone saw record-breaking snowfall, nowhere in the Alps (or in most of Europe) did badly and for many 2012/13 was a truly vintage season. By late November most high (and some low) resorts had already established a decent base. December then saw a succession of massive snow storms barrel into the north-western Alps, with the likes of Verbier and Avoriaz reporting near record pre-Christmas depths. The snow fell further east too, but generally in more modest quantities, a theme that was to continue for much of the season.

January remained unsettled with occasional milder interludes bringing rain to some lower resorts. But there was no shortage of snow, particularly at altitude where it continued to pile up in impressive quantities. February was less snowy, but much colder with the best of the sunshine in the southern Alps. It warmed up a little in March, but this was the year that spring never arrived and there were further snowfalls throughout April (and even in May).

Overall, snowfall was above average across the entire western Alps with 7.95m for Val d'Isère, fourth on its all-time list and nearly 3m above average. In Switzerland, Verbier's Ruinettes station (2200m) also impressed with 8.9m, its third highest snowfall ever. Snowiest of all, however, was Avoriaz with a massive 11.8m, second only to 1994/95; its average is 7.6m. Snowfall was more modest further east – 6.9m for Lech is slightly below average – but you wouldn't have known it, such was the regularity with which it fell.

Elsewhere in Europe the big story was in the Pyrenees, where an astonishing 16m fell in Cauterets

13

We've never had to do so much early-morning removal of snow from the editorial motor as we had to do this past season; good thing we have assistants to take care of such things ↓

(at 2000m) and nearby resorts were cut off for days on end. Many US resorts had another modest winter, though things did pick up in Colorado later in the season. Western Canada fared better – Whistler received 10.9m at mid elevations, some 20% above par.

Two countries, two guides, two lunches that figured on our 2013 itinerary. The Austrian guide is maybe marginally better looking, but we'll pass on the dumplings, thanks. Now the paillasse bellevilloise the French guy is looking so smug about ... ↓

SIZE MATTERS

We've been banging on for years about not believing some resorts' claims for the size of their ski area. Is the Grand Massif really twice the size of St Anton–Stuben? Well, now the truth is out: German ski resort expert Christoph Schrahe has done lots of clever stuff with Google Earth and measured the slopes of the major resorts in Europe and North America, and found that most exaggerate their size – claims of over double the measured total are not unusual. Read all about it in our feature on page 28.

NOT SO HAUTE CUISINE

We were chatting with a Tirolean tourist office person last winter about the ongoing competition between France and Austria for British business. 'Of course,' she said, 'the mountain restaurants are one of our big advantages.' The editorial brow furrowed. Is that right? It didn't feel right.

But we were sitting in a lovely, wood-beamed restaurant enjoying efficient and charming service. Why don't we view Austrian mountain restaurants with great enthusiasm? The answer is simple, of course – the food. It's hearty and good value, but in most places it is the same old stuff: gulaschsuppe, dumplings, sausages, Tiroler gröstl and, er ... that's it. In France, the food is more varied, less formulaic. There may be lamb, duck ...

And actually, it isn't just the food. There's another problem for serious lunchers – reservations, lack of. Austrian restaurants are mainly geared to squeezing on to communal tables where reservations are impractical.

MADNESS IN ST ANTON

Another thing we've been banging on about for years is St Anton's acute need for an easy piste to the village other than the massively overcrowded Steissbachtal (aka Happy Valley) and the bumpy blue beneath it. The problem took a new form last season when Happy Valley was closed due to avalanche danger – and when it re-opened there were signs up declaring it temporarily a ski route, and for experienced skiers only. So the only piste down was a black run, and according to reporters there was no advice to intermediates that they could take the gondola down. This is insane. One reporter said: 'Skiers of varied ability were taking the Kandahar black run down; as this was shoulder-to-shoulder, in poor light, with large moguls, it was mayhem. It was a relief to survive without injury.' Come on St Anton: get your act together and get a new piste created.

Outstanding Value French Alpine resort

- ❄ **125km snow-sure pistes**
- ❄ **Prices from £111pp***
- ❄ **Family friendly resort**
- ❄ **Perfect for beginners & intermediates**
- ❄ **Only 1½ hours from Chambéry airport**

AND ON THE SUBJECT OF SKI-ROUTES ...

The Kitzsteinhorn above Kaprun in Austria (covered in our new chapter on Zell am See) appears, at first sight, to be a much more attractive place for experts than it once was, because it has a range of freeride routes marked on its mountain map and on the mountain. Excellent – so you can confidently descend these slopes enjoying unprepared runs without the cost and hassle of arranging guidance, as on most Austrian 'ski routes'.

Or can you? On the slopes, they've set up a Freeride Info Base and Freeride Info Points, where those planning to use these lovely new routes can learn about current avalanche warnings, and check their transceivers. So ... these runs are evidently not made safe against avalanches. In which case they don't represent much of a step forward. Something similar applies on the Stubai glacier where they have even produced a map with descriptions (in German only) of 11 'freeride runs'.

The confusion over the status of unprepared runs – ski routes, itinéraires, freeride runs – is just getting worse. It's particularly bad in Austria because their ski routes are often groomed, even though they are not patrolled. We cannot see the logic of this. Grooming costs serious money. What does a patrol cost a few times a day?

PLANNING AHEAD

A reader was glad last season that he had been advised to stuff the mountain rescue number in to his mobile: 'I ended up using it on the last day, as I came across a guy lying there with a leg in an unnatural shape: there was a crowd, but nobody knew quite what to do. I made the call, and the sled was there in minutes ... but I don't know how long people had been standing around before I got there. Get the mountain rescue number into your phones, people – it's worth the few minutes of effort.' We will, we will.

THE FRENCH GET FRUGAL

We think it started in the Espace Killy when they designated many of their black pistes to be 'Naturides', which means they are never groomed; this is of course a neat way of saving money. Now the concept has expanded to Les Arcs and La Plagne, where they call them Natur' runs. But our readers don't like them. 'I think it would be good if some of the Natur' runs that get baked in the sun were groomed now and again, as they are frequently unpleasant to ski owing to bullet-proof bumps and are deserted as a result,' is a typical comment. We agree – and love skiing freshly groomed blacks at high speed first thing in the morning.

Editor Gill sat out this intense round of Bananagram to give the others a chance to win ↓

WHO NEEDS NIGHTLIFE WHEN THEY'VE GOT BANANAGRAM?

Our one week in a catered chalet last season – a mid-December treat in Ski Amis' lovely old chalet Elliot in La Tania – introduced us to Bananagram, which is a bit like Scrabble but much more lively and suitable for a bunch of semi-inebriated, tired skiers. Just look at the concentration on the faces of our co-inmates. This should have gone into our equipment chapter on page 38 but somehow got overlooked. Recommended.

CALL IT LAND OF THE FREE?

One of the things that annoys us about American resorts are the swanky mountain restaurants that are the preserve of members of an exclusive club with subscriptions running into tens of thousands. The very appealing Beano's Cabin at Beaver Creek is typical – they allow hoi polloi to use it in the evening, when all right-thinking billionaires are eating much more seriously in downtown BC. But at lunchtime, it's members only – as is nearby Zach's and the Game Creek Club in Vail.

Civilized lunching at altitude in American resorts is not easily arranged. So we were dismayed to be told this year that the already limited lunch options on the hill at Mammoth in California have been narrowed further. The pleasant table-service Parallax at mid-mountain is now open only to members of the exclusive Mammoth Black club. We have cut our rating to * as a result.

HOW LONG IS A LONG QUEUE?

Readers who don't spend long hours of the winter surfing around our website may have missed a little thing we did on the site, to see how good people are at estimating how long a queue is, in practice. We came upon the queue in the picture last season. The lift is a standard issue, fast, detachable quad chairlift of the kind that litters the Alps and Rockies. Almost half our readers thought it would take 10 minutes to get through this queue. Another quarter were even more pessimistic, estimating 15 minutes or even 20. In fact, it took

Oh sugar, you think, as you ski round the last bend in the piste. But this queue is probably shorter than you think it is ↓

Where we
Ski and Snowboard

Berner Oberland ✚

just five minutes, which only 22% of readers estimated. Only a very small number of readers under-estimated the time. So, the answer is clearly that most of us have an exaggerated idea of how long queues are. Next season, think positive!

PARTY TIME GOES LARGE IN FRANCE

Not so long ago late afternoon partying up the mountain in France was unheard of; but now it's becoming big business. It all started with the Folie Douce in Val d'Isère (at the top of the gondola from La Daille), which adopted Austrian-style après-ski with live bands and DJs from mid-afternoon onwards. Then the Folie Douce formula was successfully replicated above Val Thorens, and last season another replica opened above Méribel. Next season there'll be one above Alpe-d'Huez. Where will all this end – surely not one in chic Megève? Still, it does seem things are at last looking up for those who like French skiing but hanker for Austrian après.

AND SO DOES MARKETING MADNESS

'Alpe-d'Huez grand domaine Ski'. Trips off the tongue, eh? Believe it or not, that is the name we are now supposed to use for the resort formerly known as Alpe-d'Huez – or, strictly speaking, its ski area. This absurd appellation has all the hallmarks of the marketing consultancy invention. It is too long to be put to practical use, whether in print or in conversation. It uses a bizarre mixture of upper and lower case initial letters that leaves the reader wondering what is going on. It instantly creates confusion with the existing ski area called Grand Domaine – that of Valmorel and St-François-Longchamp – and arguably with Flaine's Grand Massif.

We're amazed to find that lots of websites have adopted this new brand. We'll be ignoring it. Thought you'd like to know. Just as we ignore Val Thorens United (no, it's not a footy team), Campiglio Val Rendena Val di Sole and the abolition of Courchevel 1850.

AVOIDING FRENCH CROWDS

This year we got several complaints of queues and crowds, especially crowds of kids, from reporters who visited French resorts in March. Others who visited in February were delighted by the lack of queues 'even though we were there during the French holidays'. Well, we did warn you. In the introduction to our France section last year we said that you should 'avoid 2 to 17 March' – the fortnight when Paris schools had their hols. This season the whole holiday period runs 15 Feb to 16 March, but the Paris fortnight is at the start. So late February is the time to avoid, at least in the northern resorts. English school holidays seem to be concentrated in the week 16 to 22 Feb. Large parts of Holland are on holiday then too. Avoid.

THE WIND IN YOUR HAIR

Our picture on the facing page shows the world's first open-top cable car, built by Garaventa in 2012 and rising over 1000m vertical to the 1900m

The home slope down to Chaudanne at Méribel at a pretty quiet time of the season. What must it have been like in early March? ↓

Stanserhorn near Lake Lucerne in Switzerland. Imagine one of these on the Grande Motte or Cîme de Caron: that would be an excellent way to clear your head after a late night, would it not?

SWITZERLAND PRICES ITSELF OUT OF THE MARKET

One of our regular reporters who went to Davos on business this year provides a graphic illustration of the impact of exchange rates. 'We were pleasantly surprised by the quality of the skiing,' she says, 'but it is telling that on the weekends either side of the meeting we chose to ski in Austria because of the prices in Switzerland. I doubt we will return to Switzerland for a ski holiday until it becomes better value for money.' The Swiss tourism bodies do try to address the problem by making various offers, but there is not much they can do, really – the problem is the exchange rate. A glance at our Resort Price Index figures in the 'Cutting your costs' chapter shows just how pricey Switzerland is compared with other Alpine countries. North America is even pricier – and the reduced number of reports we now receive on visits to the USA and Canada show that people are voting by taking their ski boots elsewhere.

PROTECTING YOUR MONEY

We occasionally get our ear bent by ski tour operators who are cross about the fact that they have to stump up for a bond or an insurance policy to guarantee the safety of clients' money, whereas other firms get away without it. They get away without it, usually, by not offering a recognisable 'package'. They are not breaking the law; they are making the most of the wriggle room the law allows.

This situation seems nuts – all prepayments should be protected – but it has existed for a very long time and no one seems much interested in changing it. Check the situation with any firm you are booking with, and if they do not offer protection make sure you pay with a credit card, and thus get the protection of Section 75 of the Consumer Credit Act.

THANKS TO YOU

We are grateful to all the hundreds of readers who sent in reports on the resorts they visited last season. These reports are crucial to our annual updating and revision process. As usual, the 100 readers whose reports proved most useful have won a free copy of this edition, and their names have gone into the hat for a free week in a smart Lagrange apartment in the French Alps. And the lucky winner is ... Barry Patrick of Chepstow – many congratulations, Barry. Please send in reports next season – Lagrange is again providing a prize; look at page 12.

We are also indebted to the readers who make up for the inadequacy of resort picture libraries by sending in photos for publication. If we use any of your pics, you get a copy of the book – and the satisfaction of seeing your photos in print, of course. This year we have used countless pictures provided by the faithful Tanya Booth and others from (in no particular order) Stuart McWilliam, Alan Liptrot, David Maxwell-Lees, Simon Medley, Kerry Lewis, Johnathan Scott, Stephen Ashley and Simon Smith.

on Britain's best-selling wintersports magazine

SKI AND SNOWBOARD
YOUR COMPLETE GUIDE TO THE SLOPES

Delivered direct to your door

Subscribe to Ski and Snowboard magazine for just £18. That's a saving of £1.50 every issue!

In-depth resort info
Latest gear
Top technique tips
Great reader offers

What's new?

In this chapter we summarize major developments in ski resorts last season and those planned for 2013/14. Most major resort chapters have a 'News' panel near the start; you'll find many more news items in those panels. To keep up to date with resort developments and regular news items, go to www.wheretoskiandsnowboard.com and sign up for our email newsletters.

ANDORRA

MORE FREERIDE FUN IN SOLDEU
Last season two freeride areas were designated, and snowcat lifts were restored to the bowl below Encampadana.

AUSTRIA

RESTAURANT UPGRADES AT HINTERTUX
The little old Spannagelhaus refuge on the glacier is getting a radical makeover for 2013/14. The much less interesting Tuxer Fernerhaus is also being renovated.

NEW CABLE CAR AT ISCHGL
For 2013/14 the resort is hoping that a new 150-person cable car to Piz Val Gronda will open, opening up a new mountain with a new 3km red piste down.

KITZBÜHEL REPLACES DOUBLE CHAIRS
At Jochberg, the old double chair and a drag are to be replaced by a 10-seater gondola for 2013/14. Last season, on Resterhöhe, the Zweitausender double chair was replaced by an eight-seater and in the Hahnenkamm sector a six-pack replaced the Walde T-bar.

A MAJOR LINK FOR LECH
For 2013/14 a new 10-seat gondola will link Lech with the Warth–Schröcken ski area, adding over 50% in terms of pistes and allowing access to a lot more off-piste in the snowiest region of the Alps. There will be no piste link – you'll ride the gondola both ways.

SIX-PACKS MULTIPLY IN THE ZILLERTAL
Above Mayrhofen, for 2013/14 six-packs will replace the Lämmerbichl double chair on Rastkogel and (with luck) the Ebenwald double chair on Ahorn. Another six-pack is going in at Gerlos, in the Zillertal Arena area. And last season at Zell am Ziller, the Kreuzwiese drag was replaced by a six-pack.

OBERTAUERN OUSTS OUTDATED QUADS
For 2012/13, the Grünwaldkopfbahn quad from below the village was replaced by a chondola hybrid lift. And the Hochalmbahn quad above that was upgraded to a six-pack.

YET MORE SIX-PACKS FOR SAALBACH
Yet another six-pack (heated, with covers) will replace a T-bar on Reiterkogel for 2013/14, and last season a T-bar on Bernkogel was replaced by a six-pack with covers.

A BETTER GONDOLA FOR SCHLADMING
The Gipfelbahn 'pulse' gondola on Hochwurzen is being replaced by a proper 10-seat gondola for next season.

What's new?

Resort news and key links: www.wheretoskiandsnowboard.com

A T-BAR REPLACEMENT AT ST ANTON
The Tanzböden T-bar on Galzig is due to be replaced by a six-pack.

NEW LIFTS AND RUNS FOR THE STUBAI VALLEY
Last season, on the glacier, the Rotadl slow quad was replaced by an eight-seat chair and a new area (Daunjoch) was opened up by a new quad and black run.

MAJOR NEWS AT BREGENZERWALD
A new 10-seat gondola will link the Warth–Schröcken ski area with upmarket Lech–Zürs – almost trebling the size of the ski area in terms of pistes.

UPGRADES AT ZELL AM SEE AND KAPRUN
Next season an eight-seat chair will replace the Glocknerbahn quad and the parallel drag. On Kaprun's Kitzsteinhorn a new black piste, Black Mamba, is to open. Last season the Sonnengratbahn double chair was upgraded to a fast quad.

FRANCE

BETTER FOR BEGINNERS AND APRES-SKI AT ALPE-D'HUEZ
On the main beginner area a chondola will replace the three long Jeux drags next season. And a Folie Douce mountain restaurant, as in Val d'Isère, Val Thorens and Méribel, will open. Last season the Rif Nel chondola was added at Les Bergers.

LES ARCS LODGINGS IMPROVEMENTS
The second phase of the smart new Edenarc development above 1800 opened last season. For 2013/14 a new 4-star hotel is due.

EASIER ACCESS TO AVORIAZ
In 2012/13 the Prodains cable car from the valley below the resort was replaced by a big gondola.

NEW RUNS IN CHATEL
A new green slope is planned for the Linga area, and last season a new blue run, the Chésery, was created in the Plaine Dranse area.

PROGRESS IN COURCHEVEL
Last season at 1850, the Biollay quad was replaced by a six-pack. At 1650, the 3 Vallées chair was replaced by a short gondola for access to the main Ariondaz gondola.

LES DEUX-ALPES REPLACES OLD 'DEVIL' GONDOLA
Last season the Diable gondola at the Venosc end of town was replaced by a six-pack.

NEW LIFTS FOR FLAINE
The Diamant Noir double chair on the upper slopes is to be replaced by a fast quad. In 2012/13 the old four-seat Aup de Veran gondola was replaced by an eight-seater.

QUICKER ACCESS TO REBERTY AT LES MENUIRES
A six-pack replaced the old bucket-lift from the bottom of La Masse to Reberty last season.

MODERN GONDOLAS AND A NEW PARTY VENUE FOR MERIBEL
Last season the first two sections of the Plattières gondola were replaced by a 10-person gondola and the lower stage of the Saulire gondola was upgraded to match the upper stage. A new Folie Douce restaurant (like those in Val d'Isère and Val Thorens) opened near the Saulire gondola mid-station.

Greater capacity at Morzine

For 2013/14 the Pléney gondola is being replaced and will have a much greater capacity. Last season the Troncs chairlift was upgraded to a six-pack.

Lots happening at La Plagne

For 2013/14 the Roche six-pack from near the approach road is due to have its capacity increased by 50%. In 2012/13 the Biolley sector was revamped, with a six-pack replacing the Becoin chair, the Biolley chair and three drags. At the glacier area, the Traversee double chair was replaced by a quad. Phase two of the Plagne-Centre renovation project was completed.

Six-pack for La Rosiere

A six-pack replaced the old quad to Col de la Traversette (for access to La Thuile) last season.

Historic changes at Serre-Chevalier

For 2013/14, the historic cable car from Chantemerle to Serre Ratier is to be replaced by an eight-seat gondola. At Le Monêtier, redevelopment of the base area was completed last season.

Fast lift and new runs for Ste-Foy

The Gran Plan chair out of the village is due to be replaced by a fast quad next season. In 2012/13 three new runs served by the Marquise six-pack opened.

La Tania gets a six-pack

A six-pack is due to replace the Bouc Blanc drag from mid-mountain to Loze next season. Two new slopes are also planned.

Fledgling new village at Tignes

The first phase of the MGM-built Kalinda Village at Tignes 1800 is due to open in December 2013. The rest of the development will open for 2014/15. The Aeroski gondola from Le Lac is to be replaced by a faster 10-seat one with easier access from the slope.

Passes are cheaper in Les Trois Vallees

For 2013/14 a Duo Pass is to be introduced, allowing two people buying lift passes together to get a reduction. Last season a Pass Tribu was introduced, which allowed three or more people buying together to get a reduction. A new family pass enables two adults and two or more children to all pay the child rate.

New six-pack for Val d'Isere

Last season the slow Fontaine Froide quad chairlift on Bellevarde was replaced by a six-pack that starts from the same place but finishes at the top, near the Olympique gondola.

Lots of fast lifts at Val Thorens

Two six-packs are due to replace slow quad chairs: 3 Vallées 1 from the resort towards Méribel and Pyron from Plan Bouchet in the 'fourth valley'. A fast quad is due to replace the slow 3 Vallées 2 chair, which meets 3 Vallées 1 and takes you to the top. And the 2 Lacs fast quad from just below the village is to be rebuilt to increase capacity. In 2012/13, the Péclet gondola was revamped with the addition of nine cabins to increase capacity by 25%.

Germany

Changes at the glacier at Garmisch-Partenkirchen

A six-pack replaced the Wetterwand T-bars last season.

ITALY

NEW RUNS AND PISTES AT MADONNA DI CAMPIGLIO
For 2013/14 a new red piste, Namibino, is to open in the Cinque Laghi sector. Also in that sector, last season saw a new quad chair open up two new pistes, a blue and a black.

SLICKER NURSERY LIFTS AT PASSO TONALE
In 2012/13 the resort's first six-pack was installed on the nursery slopes, replacing two T-bars.

SWIFTER ACCESS TO MARMOLADA GLACIER FROM PARTS OF SELLA RONDA
A new six-pack is being built between Arabba and Passo Pordoi, going up to the Carpazza chair built last year – creating a new way to the lifts towards Marmolada. In Corvara, the Boè gondola was upgraded last season.

MORE CAPACITY AT SELVA
The capacity of the Dantercëpies gondola is to be increased next season, with more parking and better services provided at the base.

SWITZERLAND

ADELBODEN GAINS NEW LIFT AND RUN
A new six/eight-seat chondola is due to replace the existing Hahnenmoos gondola for December 2013. Last year a blue run from Sillerenbühl to Aebi opened, down an otherwise entirely red mountainside.

NEW LODGINGS AT ANDERMATT
The first hotel in the resort's big new development, the Chedi Andermatt, is planned to open in December.

NEW RUNS AND SIX-PACKS AT LAAX
A six-pack from Lavadinas replaced an old double, and another new six-pack now goes from Treis Palas to Crap Masegn. And 15km of new runs were created to go with these two lifts.

GREAT NEW LINK IN VAL D'ANNIVIERS
A 125-person cable car linking Grimentz village to the heart of the Zinal ski area is due to open in 2013/14. Last season at Vercorin, a 10-person gondola replaced an old four-seat one from the village.

NEW LINK AND 5-STAR HOTEL AT VERBIER
A new gondola from Le Châble is due to link to the heart of the Bruson ski area next season, making it much easier to access Bruson from Verbier. In a new development at Médran, a 5-star hotel – W Verbier – is due to open in December 2013, along with upmarket shops, bars and restaurants.

ANCIENT CHAIR REPLACED AT WENGEN
The Wixi double chair has been upgraded to a six-pack with covers.

USA – CALIFORNIA

HALF-PIPE FOR HEAVENLY
Last season a half-pipe was built for the first time in five years.

GOOD NEWS AT MAMMOTH MOUNTAIN
June Mountain, under the same ownership as Mammoth and a 30-minute drive away, is to reopen after being closed last season.

SQUAW VALLEY CHAIR DEVELOPMENT
Last season a triple chair was replaced by a six-pack, Big Blue Express. A rope tow was installed to allow easy access to the Belmont terrain park.

USA – COLORADO

NEW RESTAURANT AND RACE COURSE AT BEAVER CREEK

The restaurant at Red Tail Camp is to be replaced by a new 500-seat place next season, more than doubling the existing capacity. A new women's downhill race course was built last season in the Birds of Prey area, adding 17 acres of new terrain, including a black run.

BRECKENRIDGE EXPANDS TO A NEW PEAK

A new area, Peak 6, is due to open for 2013/14, with 400 acres served by a new six-pack and a quad chair and 143 acres of hike-to terrain. The area will increase the resort's terrain by about 25%.

BIGGER MOUNTAIN RESTAURANT FOR SNOWMASS

At the top of the Elk Camp gondola $13 million has been spent on building a bigger restaurant to replace Cafe Suzanne. And three new gladed black runs opened.

NEW LIFTS FOR VAIL

For 2013/14 a new six-pack is planned to replace the Mountaintop quad at Mid-Vail. A double chair on the nursery slopes at Golden Peak is due to be replaced by a triple. Last season a gondola (with heated seats and Wi-Fi) replaced the Vista Bahn chair from Vail Village to Mid-Vail.

USA – UTAH

DEER VALLEY INSTALLS NEW QUAD

A high-speed quad called Mountaineer Express replaced the slow Deer Crest chair on Little Baldy Peak last season.

TWO DOUBLE CHAIRLIFTS DUMPED AT SNOWBIRD

In 2012/13 the Little Cloud chair was replaced by a fast quad and for 2013/14 the Gad 2 will be too.

USA – REST OF THE WEST

JACKSON HOLE'S LIFT IMPROVEMENTS CONTINUE

In 2012/13, the Casper triple chairlift was replaced by a fast quad.

CANADA – WESTERN CANADA

NEW AND IMPROVED RUNS FOR REVELSTOKE

For 2013/14 the green runs from mid-mountain to the base are to be improved. Two new blue runs and two new tree-skiing areas are planned. Last season the blue run Tumbelina, from mid-mountain to the base, was regraded to provide easier progression.

A SIX-PACK FOR WHISTLER AT LAST

In 2013/14 Whistler will get its first six-pack, planned to replace the queue-prone Harmony chair. The slow Crystal chair on Blackcomb is due to be replaced by a fast quad; the new chair will start lower down, making it more useful.

Piste extent – the truth

You're probably getting less than you are paying for

by **Chris Gill**

Size matters, for skiers and boarders. It is true that you can have the time of your life going up a single lift and down a single slope time after time – particularly if that slope presents challenges of a kind that you relish. But it is also true, for many of us, that once you develop a taste for big ski areas, the variety and sense of travel that they offer becomes irresistible.

So when you're choosing a resort, it's quite likely that you pay some attention to the total length or area of the available runs (generally it's total km in Europe, and total acres in North America). But the numbers come from the resorts – normally from the lift company. Can you trust them? The short answer, in Europe at least, is No.

The long answer follows, drawing heavily on the excellent work of a dedicated German ski resort expert, Christoph Schrahe. He has measured all the big resorts, and found most of them exaggerate the extent of their pistes, and by amounts that may surprise you.

OUR FIGURES

In the margin panels on the facing page we give some examples of ski areas that publish piste totals that closely match those of the Schrahe report, and of areas that exaggerate wildly.

Then we give figures for the biggest areas in the Alps. Saalbach-Hinterglemm would be next on this list if it were not included in the Saints panel.

You may find some of the numbers here don't match the ones we quote in our resort chapter. This is because Christoph Schrahe has focused entirely on linked areas, whereas our figures will often include other local hills that are not linked.

Throughout the time we have been producing this book – perilously close to 20 years, now – we've had trouble accepting the claims of certain resorts. Among those that come to mind are Courmayeur and Monterosa in Italy, Les Deux-Alpes in southern France and the Quatre Vallées area in Switzerland, in which Verbier is the senior partner. As it happens, two of these cases were resolved over a year ago – the two Italian ones.

SOME ITALIAN CONCESSIONS

The Monterosa lift company website is a mine of information, and it includes tables of the lengths of individual runs – so we were able to sit down with detailed topographical maps of the area, to see how the claims matched the maps. We arrived at the view that the run lengths in these tables were about double what you would expect. And after we suggested this, in our 2011 edition, the lift company quietly revised its tables, more or less halving the lengths. Had it just slipped up while doing the sums? We don't know. Bizarrely, it has not yet altered the total it claims.

Then there is the incredible and extreme case of Courmayeur. Since time immemorial, the resort has claimed 100km of pistes; but you can ski the whole area in a morning (provided it's a weekday). Last year the mystery was solved: the lift company told us clearly that 64km of the 100km are off-piste runs; the piste total is 36km. The resort and the lift company are still claiming 100km on their websites and literature.

Clearly, this is bonkers. The inclusion of off-piste runs is inherently misleading, but there is also the fact that you can't measure off-piste in km, because it is by its nature undefined. The situation is compounded (and possibly explained) by the fact that Courmayeur's mountain map shows four 'off-piste itineraries', which would go some way to making up the 64km. That term (itinéraires in France, ski-routes in Austria) normally means marked but unprepared and unpatrolled runs, which we think deserve to be included in a resort's piste total. But these are serious off-piste routes – one goes down the south side of the Mont Blanc massif.

SAINTS

Claimed total /
measured total /
% by which the
resort overstates

Kitzbühel
164 / 164 / 0%
Lech-Zürs
122 / 118 / 3%
St Anton-Stuben
116 / 113 / 3%
Les Saisies etc
185 / 178 / 4%
Saalbach
200 / 187 / 7%

SINNERS

Claimed total /
measured total /
% by which the
resort overstates

Vars
185 / 73 / 152%
Isola 2000
120 / 54 / 123%
4 Valleys
362 / 164 / 120%
Les Sybelles
310 / 141 / 120%

BIG NUMBERS

Claimed total /
measured total /
% by which the
resort overstates

Trois Vallées
600 / 493 / 22%
**Les Arcs-La
Plagne**
425 / 378 / 17%
Sella Ronda
360 / 309 / 17%
Portes du Soleil
(excludes Morzine
and Les Gets)
402 / 263 / 53%
Zermatt-Cervinia
313 / 252 / 24%
Milky Way
400 / 251 / 59%
**Val d'Isère-
Tignes**
300 / 232 / 29%
SkiWelt
270 / 232 / 16%

ENTER HERR SCHRAHE

So far, so amazing. But last year a gigantic spanner was thrown into the works of the ski resort business by German writer and consultant Christoph Schrahe. To our amazement, he announced that by applying the available digital tools he had measured the pistes of the world's 50 biggest ski areas, and was publishing a report on his findings. Naturally, we were first in the queue.

The report makes fascinating reading, for us at least. The first thing that catches the eye is that Schrahe's figures are almost always lower than the resorts' claims, and often by a large margin. But not always: in a small number of cases, Schrahe's measurement and the resort's match closely. Kitzbühel's figure matches Schrahe's 164km exactly. The two linked areas in Austria's Arlberg region, St Anton–St Christoph–Stuben and Lech–Zürs, both claim totals within a few percentage points of Schrahe's figures, as does the French area Espace Diamant (Les Saisies and neighbours). All this suggests to us that his method is probably quite accurate – it does not have an inherent bias towards low results.

In fact, Schrahe tells us that he measures pistes in exactly the way we would (and indeed the way we did when looking into the Monterosa lengths) – down the middle of the piste, following its twists and turns like the white line down the middle of a highway. He calculates the length of the slope on the ground (as opposed to the length you would measure on a map) by taking account of the gradient. This is apparently the way FIS measures race courses. So do the resorts measure in some different way? We'll come back to that in a moment.

There is one resort – Schladming – that actually claims less than the total Schrahe arrives at. We would wager they'll be putting that right real soon. But leaving aside this, and the three close matches mentioned above, Schrahe's report says that the 50 or so other areas where he has made a comparison exaggerate their piste extent by amounts ranging from a negligible 7% to over 150%. And don't be tempted to think that the top figure is some sort of extreme, exceptional case – there are eight other areas making claims that are more than double Schrahe's realistic figure.

WHAT'S GOING ON HERE?

We find it difficult to believe that all these resorts are simply lying or mistaken about the size of their mountains, so we have made some attempts to find out how they arrive at figures that seem to overstate their piste extents.

Coming back to the four resorts about which we have had long-term concerns, one of these makes one of the most outrageous claims – Verbier's 4 Valleys in Switzerland. According to Schrahe the area (leaving aside Bruson) has 164km not the claimed 362km – which means an overstatement by 120%. The commercial director of the lift company tells us that they have hired consultants to re-measure everything and prepare a report. The sort of response you might expect from a government minister.

The fourth resort, Les Deux-Alpes, exaggerates by 70%. When invited to explain, the resort's normally helpful PR people have simply stopped talking to us.

We've attempted to discuss Schrahe's findings with various other resort tourist offices and lift companies. Some promised a response but never gave one. Some just ignored us. One outfit that was very ready for a discussion was the lift company of the Grand Massif (Flaine and neighbours) in the northern French Alps. The published claimed length is an impressive 265km; Schrahe's figure is 172km. We got an admirably clear explanation from the lift company's commercial director. The company measures its pistes in much the same way as Schrahe, and gets an almost identical result – 170km (further support for Schrahe's methodology). But it believes it's more meaningful to publish an estimate of how far a skier actually travels in descending the pistes.

IT'S A MATTER OF TURNS, APPARENTLY

The Grand Massif assumes that you're always making turns – never schussing, and never traversing – and that your track is a continuous series of semicircles. So instead of skiing 10m down the line of the piste, for example, you ski a semicircle with a diameter of 10m; the distance travelled, as any primary school pupil could tell you, is 10 x pi/2. So the piste length is multiplied by pi/2 or 1.57 – ie adding 57%. 170km becomes 267km, rounded down to 265km. Voila!

SORTING OUT THIS MESS

We think inflating the length of runs by making arbitrary assumptions about how skiers behave is ludicrous. But in the end it doesn't matter how pistes are measured. What does matter, clearly, is that resorts should measure their pistes in a standard way, so that you don't get one resort adding nothing to the directly measured length, another adding 57% and a third adding 152%.

We think there is some chance this might come about. Austria's national association of lift companies has issued guidelines about how pistes should be measured, and we expect this to have a major impact. Some resorts have already reduced their claims as a result. The Zillertal resorts have clearly got their act together: the valley as a whole has cut its claim from 666km to 487km; Mayrhofen has cut its claim from 159km to 133km; more radically, Hochzillertal has cut its claim from 181km to 88km.

We have heard from some French resorts that work is going on to arrive at a standard approach in France too, and at least one major resort is expecting to cut its claims for the 2014/15 season.

ACROSS THE POND

One of the interesting side effects of Schrahe's work is the light it sheds on North American resorts, where the lift companies talk about acres of skiable terrain rather than km of pistes. We've struggled with this difference for years, operating two parallel star-rating systems that we have tried to keep in sync by making crude comparisons of topo maps of resorts here and there. Schrahe has measured the major North American areas, so his results have enabled us to check our ratings. Happily, we've needed to make only one or two changes.

According to Schrahe, Whistler is joint number five in the world league table, alongside Zermatt–Cervinia, both with 252km of runs. Vail just pips Big Sky/Moonlight to 10th place (whereas in terms of area the pipping is reversed). There are five other North American ski areas in the top 30 in the world.

Ski resort obsessives can get a copy of Schrahe's report from schrahe@ski-weltweit.de – 99 euros.

We name the resorts where your pound will go further

by **Chris Gill**

RPI	120
lift pass	£220
ski hire	£130
lessons	£135
food & drink	£170
total	**£655**

RPI	100
lift pass	£200
ski hire	£115
lessons	£120
food & drink	£125
total	**£560**

RPI	90
lift pass	£190
ski hire	£90
lessons	£80
food & drink	£120
total	**£480**

FOOD & DRINK

Our budget figure is for six days' modest consumption of food and drink – each day, a cheap pasta or pizza lunch with a quarter-litre of house wine, a small beer, a coke and a large coffee or cappuccino.

By including four different drinks, we have tried to be fair to countries where one kind of drink may be more expensive than others. Bear in mind that if you're not happy with simple lunches day after day, you may spend much more than our budget figure, especially in resorts where the budget figure itself is quite high (ie top French and most Swiss resorts).

Four years back, in response to the declining power of the pound and resulting high cost of staying in a top ski resort, we introduced our Resort Price Index figures, designed to make it simple to see which resorts were affordable, and which were not. Two years back, we extended it to cover not only food and drink but also the costs of lift passes, ski hire and lessons. Our RPI figures are now based on a total of all four costs, but, as you can see from the examples in the margin, we also show the separate costs that feed into the RPI calculation.

The food and drink element of the RPI, as in earlier years, is based on prices noted mainly by our faithful readers. If you find this survey helpful, please contribute to the exercise next season, via our website.

A year ago, we were able to report a 13% increase in the value of the pound against the euro, and a 10% increase against the Swiss franc. Now, in July 2013, a large part of those increases has been reversed. When the euro rate and other rates change differently, our RPIs are of course affected, but this year we have in any case changed the way we work them out. In the past, our RPIs have all been based on the average cost across Europe. Now, with the Swiss market somewhat reduced and prices there typically higher than elsewhere, we've shifted to basing our comparisons on the average cost in the eurozone countries. This has moved the average down, of course, making some resorts look a little more expensive. All in all, we think these new RPIs make better sense.

The margin panels explain exactly what we have included in our 'basket' of items. One particular thing to be aware of is that many people will spend a lot more on food and drink than our modest budget figure – so beware resorts where that figure is high, because yours may be two or three times as big.

In margin boxes in each resort chapter we present these budget figures, and a total. And at the top of the box, we give the resulting RPI. This index compares the total budget for the resort to the average across all eurozone resorts; 100 represents the average resort. Our RPI figures are still colour coded, as shown in the margin on the left, but we've changed the boundaries. Index figures of 120 up are coloured red, and figures of 90 down are green; ones in between are blue. Note that the overall RPI is only part of the picture, though; in particular, the total and RPI don't always reflect the cost of food and drink, which can be swamped by other costs.

LIFT PASSES

Our lift pass figures are for the pass we reckon you're most likely to buy.

In Europe, where a resort sells a pass covering other linked resorts, we have used that pass price.

Where available, in America we have used special passes aimed at the international market (such as the Tri Area Pass, around Park City in Utah).

LESSONS

Our budget figure is half the cost of a four hour private lesson for two people.

Generally, we have taken prices from the main schools. You may pay more at other schools (Brit-run outfits especially) or sometimes less.

Some schools, eg the ESF in France, quote an hourly rate, easily multiplied by four. Where the standard offering is a lesson of 2.5 hours or 3.5 hours or whatever, we scaled the cost up to four hours.

The group of resorts with roughly average blue-coded RPIs (from 95 to 115) is largely French, with quite a few Austrian and some Italian resorts and just two in Switzerland. The green-coded low-cost group has eastern European countries at the bottom, but then includes a healthy mix of resorts in Austria and Italy, with just four in France. The cheapest in the main Alpine countries are Passo Tonale in Italy, a great place to learn to ski on good snow, and Val Cenis in France, back in these pages this year thanks to improving lodgings. The pricey group is dominated by resorts in North America and Switzerland, with just the most fashionable resorts in France and Austria – Courchevel, Méribel and Lech – getting red RPIs. In the top slot are Aspen and Snowmass, closely followed by Vail and Beaver Creek – all in Colorado.

THE PICTURE BY COUNTRY

Swiss prices remain high. Only two Swiss resorts fall outside our high-cost group when you look at the overall RPI. All Swiss resorts are expensive for eating and drinking, with budget figures, even for our very modest 'basket', ranging from £180 to £235 – that is, £30 to £40 a day. You could easily spend £100 a day. For lift passes, too, many resorts are pricey. For lessons and ski hire, the picture is much more mixed. In one of our tables over the page we look at Switzerland in isolation, to identify relative bargains.

All resorts in North America fall well inside the pricey group overall, because of expensive lift passes and lessons (the latter particularly in the US). Ski hire costs are generally high, though there are a few resorts that match Europe in this respect. But the picture is completely different when you come to look at your daily food and drink budget. Most places compare well with Europe, and some are positively cheap. So what you shell out every day is not going to feel too bad. As with Switzerland, we have assembled a table of North American resorts, to identify relative bargains.

Although France doesn't stand out from our overall RPI figures as expensive, compared with Austria and Italy it is way more expensive for food and drink, with nearly all resorts coming in with

WAYS TO KEEP HOLIDAY COSTS UNDER CONTROL

A good way of avoiding the full impact of high resort restaurant prices is to go on a catered chalet holiday. With chalet holidays you get a filling breakfast and afternoon tea, as well as a substantial dinner, so your lunchtime needs can be minimized. Some tour ops offer 'piste picnic' packed lunches for a small extra charge. Crucially, in a chalet you get wine included with dinner – and you can organize your own aperitifs, or buy beer and mixers in the chalet at modest cost.

It's no coincidence that in these difficult times the demand for catered chalet holidays is soaring, and that over recent seasons operators have expanded their programmes to meet that demand. If our records are to be believed, Inghams now operates 95 properties, while sister company Ski Total has almost 130. The total number of chalets we keep tabs on is over 900.

Chalet holidays are not the only way to control costs. A few tour operators such as Ski 2 offer 'all inclusive deal' options, quoting a price that includes half-board, vouchers for lunch at mountain restaurants, lift pass, and more. Inghams now has an all-inclusive deal covering the lift pass, kit hire, a packed lunch and evening drinks. Crystal has two deals in selected resorts, one including ski/ board hire and lift pass, the other including a packed lunch and evening drinks. And yes, you can combine the two. Club Med is a well-established operator of big hotels where everything is included.

And of course there is self-catering. Now that it is so easy to find comfortable apartments with room to prepare meals and a dishwasher to deal with the aftermath – and with attached spas and pools of hotel standard, in many cases – self-catering is more attractive than ever, especially for families.

RPI	Resort	Country	Page	RPI	Resort	Country	Page
45	Poiana Brasov etc	Romania	661	95	Arinsal	Andorra	90
55	Bansko etc	Bulgaria	658	95	Les Carroz	France	231
70	Kranjska Gora etc	Slovenia	662	95	Cervinia	Italy	395
75	Passo Tonale	Italy	426	95	Courmayeur	Italy	406
80	Val Cenis Vanoise	France	363	95	Les Deux-Alpes	France	258
85	Garmisch-Partenkirchen	Germany	388	95	The Pyrenees	France	322
85	Monterosa Ski	Italy	420	95	La Rosière	France	325
85	Rauris	Austria	155	95	Samoëns	France	329
85	Sauze d'Oulx	Italy	428	95	Schladming	Austria	164
85	Ste-Foy-Tarentaise	France	341	95	Serre-Chevalier	France	331
90	Ellmau	Austria	107	95	Zell am See	Austria	198
90	Hintertux / Tux valley	Austria	110	100	Formigal etc	Spain	651
90	Livigno	Italy	411	100	Bad Gastein	Austria	104
90	Mayrhofen	Austria	140	100	Châtel	France	243
90	Montgenèvre	France	297	100	Flaine	France	264
90	Sestriere	Italy	449	100	Les Gets	France	270
90	Söll	Austria	173	100	La Grave	France	272
90	La Thuile	Italy	451	100	Madonna di Campiglio	Italy	415
90	Vars / Risoul	France	383	100	Megève	France	274
90	Alpenregion Bludenz	Austria	195	100	Morzine	France	302
90	Bregenzerwald	Austria	192	100	Obertauern	Austria	152
				100	Saalbach-Hinterglemm	Austria	158

Cutting your costs

33

Build your own shortlist: www.wheretoskiandsnowboard.com

SKI HIRE

Our budget figures are for 'performance' skis that a keen intermediate or advanced skier might choose; not a beginner or top-end demo ski. We looked at several shops.

If you book in advance online, many shops will offer a serious discount.

EUROZONE

In these tables of budget figures for food and drink and for lift passes we show the lowest and highest figures in Austria, France and Italy, and add in a top Swiss resort for comparison.

EXCHANGE RATES

We converted prices to £££ using tourist rates published in July 2012:
€1.11
1.35 Swiss francs
US$1.44
CAN$1.50

SKY HIGH

In these tables we show the lowest and highest RPI figures in Switzerland and North America.

An RPI of 100 is for the eurozone average resort.

---

budget figures of £120 or more – £20 a day – and most of the resorts most popular on the UK market coming in at £135 or more – for very modest consumption, remember.

Both Austria and Italy have more resorts where the costs overall are below average, and have plenty of resorts with below-average food and drink costs. We have put together some food and drink comparisons below.

In Andorra, Soldeu comes in above average, with Arinsal below. Spain costs less than average, and Slovenia appreciably less. But Bulgaria and Romania retain a firm grip on the real budget end of the market.

EUROZONE EXTREMES: FOOD/DRINK

Resort	Country	Budget
LOW		
Monterosa Ski	Italy	£100
Passo Tonale	Italy	£100
Garmisch-Partenk'n	Germany	£105
Alpenregion Bludenz	Austria	£110
Bad Gastein	Austria	£110
Ellmau	Austria	£110
The Pyrenees	France	£110
Rauris	Austria	£110
Saalbach	Austria	£110
Sauze d'Oulx	Italy	£110
Sestriere	Italy	£110
Sölden	Austria	£110
Söll	Austria	£110
HIGH		
Chamonix	France	£145
Megève	France	£145
La Plagne	France	£145
Avoriaz	France	£150
Flaine	France	£150
Lech	Austria	£150
La Tania	France	£150
Tignes	France	£155
Val d'Isère	France	£155
Val Thorens	France	£155
Méribel	France	£175
Courchevel	France	£190

AND A SWISS COMPARISON

Zermatt	Switzerland	£210

EUROZONE EXTREMES: LIFT PASSES

Resort	Country	Budget
LOW		
Val Cenis Vanoise	France	£140
Sauze d'Oulx	Italy	£160
Sestriere	Italy	£160
Alpenregion Bludenz	Austria	£160
Bregenzerwald	Austria	£170
Passo Tonale	Italy	£170
The Pyrenees	France	£170
Rauris	Austria	£170
La Rosière	France	£170
La Thuile	Italy	£170
Vars / Risoul	France	£170
HIGH		
Les Arcs	France	£220
Obergurgl	Austria	£220
La Plagne	France	£220
Sölden	Austria	£220
Cortina d'Ampezzo	Italy	£230
Courchevel	France	£230
Les Menuires	France	£230
Méribel	France	£230
Sella Ronda	Italy	£230
Selva / Val Gardena	Italy	£230
St-Martin-de-B'ville	France	£230
La Tania	France	£230
Val Thorens	France	£230

AND A SWISS COMPARISON

Zermatt	Switzerland	£270

SWISS EXTREMES

Resort	Country	RPI
LOW		
Andermatt	Switzerland	115
Val d'Anniviers	Switzerland	115
Engelberg	Switzerland	120
Villars	Switzerland	120
HIGH		
Davos	Switzerland	135
Saas-Fee	Switzerland	135
Crans-Montana	Switzerland	140
Verbier	Switzerland	140
Zermatt	Switzerland	140
St Moritz	Switzerland	155

NORTH AMERICAN EXTREMES

Resort	Country	RPI
LOW		
Big White	Canada	145
Silver Star	Canada	145
Winter Park	USA	145
Revelstoke	Canada	150
Squaw Valley	USA	150
Sun Peaks	Canada	150
HIGH		
Beaver Creek	USA	180
Vail	USA	180
Aspen	USA	190
Snowmass	USA	190

2014 Winter Olympics

Sochi in Russia is hosting the 2014 Winter Olympics

by **Arnie Wilson**

The palm-fronted Black Sea region of Greater Sochi, 90 miles long, claims to be the longest city in Europe, and is traditionally a summer destination. It was Stalin's favourite holiday location – and the Tsars' before him. Its climate is sub-tropical, yet the mountains that will host most of the Olympic events are just 40 minutes away. An estimated £33 billion (easily a record – the 2010 Vancouver Olympics cost a little over £1 billion) has been spent on preparing for the Games – including building three new ski resorts from scratch to join the existing resort Alpika Service, which opened in the 1990s. Money has been no object for President Putin, who is treating the Winter Olympics as one of his personal projects – both he and the Prime Minister Dmitry Medvedev are keen skiers.

Rosa Khutor	
Resort	560m
	1,840ft
Slopes	940m-2320m
	3,080/7,610ft
Lifts	13
Pistes	72km
	45 miles
Blue	42%
Red	29%
Black	29%

CRYSTAL / CHRIGL LUTHY

Three resorts have been built from scratch for the Olympics ↓

The Winter Olympics will be held 7–23 February 2014 and the Paralympics 7–16 March. All the on-snow events will take place at what is known as the 'mountain cluster' of venues, while the on-ice events will be at Sochi Olympic Park in the 'coastal cluster'.

The Alpine ski and snowboarding events will all take place in Rosa Khutor, by far the biggest of the three new resorts for both accommodation and ski area. Most hotels are in the lower base area of Rosa Valley at 560m, which runs along a river and which you cannot ski back to. From there, a gondola goes to Rosa Plateau at 1170m where the Olympic Village housing the athletes will be. Another gondola goes from the plateau to Rosa Peak, the top of the ski area at 2320m; the lowest lift is at 940m, giving an impressive vertical of 1380m. The resort has around 72km of runs served by 13 lifts (including six gondolas and three six-packs) with some long runs, terrain for all standards and some surprisingly steep black runs. Another five lifts (including two gondolas, a six-pack and a high-speed quad) are planned in time for the Olympics. At Rosa Plateau, the 4-star hotel Park Inn by Radisson is the place to stay, 200m from the gondola up the mountain.

Gornaya Karusel (Mountain Carousel), a favourite resort of the Prime Minister, Dmitry Medvedev, will be the location for the Olympic Media Village. It too has terrain to suit all standards but not much of it at the moment – only around 20km of pistes, served by eight lifts (including three gondolas) – though it has the potential to

Gornaya Karusel	
Resort	960m
	3,150ft
Slopes	960m-2300m
	3,150-7,550ft
Lifts	8
Pistes	20km
	12 miles
Blue	20%
Red	75%
Black	5%

Gazprom Laura	
Resort	950m
	3,120ft
Slopes	950m-1800m
	3,120-5,910ft
Lifts	8
Pistes	15km
	9 miles
Blue	48%
Red	36%
Black	16%

Alpika Service	
Resort	550m
	1,800ft
Slopes	550m-2240m
	1,800-7,350ft
Lifts	6
Pistes	25km
	15 miles
Blue	40%
Red	40%
Black	20%

become Russia's largest ski resort. The off-piste from the peak is the highlight for experts, with some exciting challenges; but most of the pistes are reds and suit intermediates best. There is reportedly an excellent mountain-top restaurant.

President Putin's favourite resort, the sophisticated Gazprom Laura (yup, you guessed it, Gazprom is a gas company majority-owned by the state; and Laura is the name of Editor Gill's daughter, but there's no connection there) will stage the cross-country and biathlon events. In terms of pistes, it is the smallest of the four resorts, with just 15km served by eight lifts (including three gondolas and two fast chairlifts) – but another four lifts (including a gondola and a six-pack) are planned for 2013/14. The slopes suit beginners and intermediates best with nothing very testing. It has the luxurious 5-star Grand Hotel Polyana at the base – with a pool, two spas, three restaurants, three bars, and electric carts to take you the 300m to the gondola if you don't fancy walking.

The original ski area, Alpika Service, will host the bobsleigh and luge events and was closed while the track was being built. It's also the terminal of the newly constructed 36-mile railroad (running parallel with a modernized highway) between Sochi's Adler airport close to the coastal cluster area and the mountain cluster resorts based around the village of Krasnaya Polyana (Red Glade). President Putin took the controls when the first official train made its debut. The area's lifts are ancient. But a big 30-person gondola is planned to span the 5km to Gazprom Laura for 2013/14 – presumably to transport people from the train. The eventual plan is for all four resorts to be linked. But for now you need buses or taxis to get between the rest.

The region is not renowned for reliably good snow-cover, and a poor snow winter would be catastrophic for Russia's first winter Olympics. So, in keeping with the no-expense-spared policy, vast quantities of snow from last winter have been stored in huge refrigerated sites ready for use if needed. This will be backed up by a battery of 446 snow-guns, plus a plant that can allegedly produce snow at temperatures of up to +15ºC.

If you want to ski these resorts, the only UK tour operator

currently offering packages is Crystal, but it says that availability this winter will be limited because of the Olympics and the run-up to them; the best chance of skiing the resorts this season will be in late March. We'd leave it till 2014/15 ourselves. Crystal's packages include overnight flights to Sochi via Istanbul, taking about nine hours. Prices for a four-night B&B package to the Park Inn at Rosa Khutor start at £825; a week's stay costs from £1,137.

↑ Rosa Khutor and Gornaya Karusel have some challenging off-piste terrain; Alpika Service has hosted the Freeride World Tour

CRYSTAL / CHRIGL LUTHY

SECURITY WORRIES

Perhaps because of the VIP guests of the Polyana hotel and because it is Putin's favourite resort, security has been at its most stringent at Gazprom Laura. Getting into the base-area gondolas involves going through airport-style security, with metal detectors and X-ray machines. Terrorism in this sometimes politically troubled Caucasus region is a potential threat, and security measures are likely to be even more strict in all four resorts – plus the venues in the coastal cluster – during the actual Olympics. Security when Messrs Putin and/or Medvedev are in town has always been heightened, with restrictions on rail, road and helicopter transport, which in the past has sometimes led to food and drink supplies being affected, with wine – for example – running out.

GETTING TO SEE THE GAMES

A visa costing from £115 is required for British nationals to visit Russia; see visitrussia.org.uk. The official Olympic UK ticket agent is CoSport (cosport.com), which can also arrange packages including accommodation (but not flights). Applicants will also need to obtain a special spectator pass online, linked with their ticket, to gain admission to the events.

Because most of the accommodation in Sochi and the mountain cluster is being held by the organizing committee, early indications were that accommodation for self-bookers could be hard to come by. The organizers warn that most of the hotel accommodation (particularly the new hotels at the base of Rosa Khutor) will be given to the 'Olympic family' – including the organizers and journalists covering the events. The public will be left to book rooms in guesthouses and small hotels.

TV COVERAGE

After the success of the London 2012 Olympics, the BBC will be investing heavily in Sochi 2014. All events will be shown live either on BBC 2, or interactively via the red button or on BBC online. Sochi is four hours ahead of UK time, which will mean most Alpine ski events will be shown at our breakfast time, and the floodlit snowboard and freestyle events in early evening. There will also be an hour-long highlights programme at 7pm on BBC2. The ski and snowboard events will be presented by the *Ski Sunday* team of Graham Bell and Ed Leigh.

USEFUL WEBSITES

www.olympic.org
www.sochi2014.com
www.teamgb.com
www.cosport.com
www.visitrussia.org.uk
www.crystalski.co.uk

Build your own shortlist: www.wheretoskiandsnowboard.com

New gear for 2014

Skis, boots and gadgets that have impressed us

by **Dave Watts** *and* **Chris Gill**

There is lots of good gear out there to help you enjoy your skiing holiday more. This year we've tested not just all next season's new skis but also some boots and various other bits of kit. Here we report on the stuff we liked, and plan to use.

EDITOR WATTS TRACKS DOWN THE TOP SKIS

Last March I went on a week-long test of all the new skis for 2013/14 in Kühtai, at 2020m one of Austria's highest resorts. The test was organized by the trade body Snowsports Industries of Great Britain, and there were over 800 pairs available.

↑ The ski-test centre with Scott's new Mission, 'The Ski', on display in the foreground

Editor Gill's ski of choice for the last five seasons has been the Scott Mission, and he seems quite happy to carry on using them. He is not alone, and it may be in the hope of weaning people off the Mission that Scott has introduced a colourful replacement called, er, 'The Ski', which comes in four different colour-coded lengths. They did OK in our tests but I suspect Gill will be hanging on to his Missions. Salomon has a new range of freeride skis called 'Q' which did well in our test and is supposed to tie in with their Quest range of 'hike and ride' boots. Dynastar has a new range of Chrome high-performance piste skis and has extended its range of women's skis. Atomic has a new range of Nomad S piste skis with ARC technology, where the bindings are mounted on a plate fixed at the front and rear but not in the middle, so that the skis can flex more naturally – I found this worked very well and created great edge grip and steering power.

My personal favourites on the test included the new Blizzard Brahma freeride ski (which worked amazingly well on piste too) and lots of all-mountain skis including the Salomon Enduro range, the Rossignol Experience 88 (my favourite), the Head Rev 80 (their biggest selling ski worldwide) and the Nordica Steadfast.

THEN FINDS BOOTS THAT REALLY FIT, AT LAST

But the main development in ski hardware for next season comes in boots rather than skis. Salomon's Max Custom Shell boots, where both the shell and inner boot are heated and moulded to your foot, were introduced last season. This year the technology will be extended to a wider range of boots, including women's. I got a pair last November and loved them. It has always taken me a couple of seasons to get new boots to the stage of being really comfortable. But these were amazingly so from day one – I didn't even have to

unclip them at lunchtime. And the lateral support and stability around the ankle and lower shin was extraordinarily firm with no noticeable give at all. That meant that when I rolled my ankle to edge the ski the transmission felt very precise and powerful. I highly recommend them.

↑ Editor Watts relaxes on the first day he wore his new high-performance Salomon boots – so comfy he didn't even unclip them at lunchtime

AND ACHIEVES PERFECT BALANCE IN THOSE BOOTS

At the Kühtai ski test I also tried SkiA's new Sweetspot Ski Trainer – designed to help you improve your balance. Your centre of balance should be near the centre of the arch of your foot not, as many people think, on the balls of your feet. The idea is that the trainer gets you used to balancing correctly, and you then try to replicate the same feeling whenever you are skiing. The trainer comes with blocks that you fix under the centre of your ski boots. You then try to balance on them on a hard surface while making various movements such as bending, stretching and tilting your legs as if edging. It is surprisingly difficult at first, but when you are in balance you can certainly feel the sweet spot. There are four pairs of blocks; you start with the widest and move on to progressively narrower ones. The trainer comes with special exercises designed by Hugh Monney, founder of the British Alpine Ski School – who highly recommends it, as do other leading instructors and race coaches. Go to www.skia.com for more details.

WHILE EDITOR GILL TESTS AN ALTERNATIVE TO RIBBONS

If you've ever lost a ski in deep snow, you'll know how amazingly difficult it can be to find it. The traditional precaution is ribbons fixed to the bindings. But there is now an electronic replacement for this rather crude solution – Resqski. This works a bit like an avalanche transceiver: you fix a little transmitter 'tag' to each ski, and you carry a receiver – credit-card sized, but thicker. This has lights and a beeper to indicate how strong the signal is, and it is directional – so you first establish the direction you need to move

Build your own shortlist: **www.wheretoskiandsnowboard.com**

in, and then detect when you've waded far enough. Each receiver can work with four tags, so a couple could share one receiver.

I attached them to my Missions and got a chum to throw one into deep snow. From quite a distance I found my ski, but I did struggle a bit with the beeper – I had to take my helmet off and hold the gadget quite close to hear it; they need a louder version for the over 50s. The product is claimed to find skis up to 30m away and 1m deep. I haven't tested this claim, but I'm sufficiently convinced to want to carry on using Resqski. The tag mounts are self-adhesive but can be screwed to the ski as well. I'll be screwing mine in place next season – last season one tag fell off (in the car, happily). The basic kit with two ski tags costs £98 from resqski.com.

AND HAS PUT PHONE BATTERY WORRIES BEHIND HIM

If you have an iPhone and use it heavily while skiing (or sailing, or walking ...) get yourself a Mophie Juice Pack Air and forget worries about your battery running down in the afternoon. The JPA snaps on like a hard plastic cover. It adds surprisingly little bulk and weight to your phone – a mere 2.5oz, or 70g. The JPA has a micro-USB port through which you can sync the phone and charge both batteries at the same time. All the other bits and pieces continue to work, of course – the camera, and the little buttons on the side – and with the pack in place the pesky mute switch on the side of the phone is less likely to get accidentally turned to 'mute'. You can put the JPA on standby, so that you know its juice is unused, or use both batteries in parallel. They say you get up to 5 or 6 hours extra use on a 3G network. I have found that you can use your phone as heavily as you like, all day. Recommended. £60 from Apple.

Short break trips to the Alps can give you three refreshing days on the snow and leave you with the feeling of having been away for ages. We love them and frequently take them. Whether you travel independently or as part of a package, short-stay trips are easier to arrange now; the choice of airlines, destination airports and onward transfers is wider than ever. Midweek trips can be even better than weekends: cheaper deals and, depending on the resort, perhaps quieter slopes.

With just a few days to enjoy, you'll need to plan your short break carefully; but that's all part of the fun. We sum up the options here, with a few handy tips to help you to maximize your slope time.

WHERE SHALL WE GO?

Resorts closest to your arrival airport may seem the obvious starting point, but travelling a bit further can avoid any weekend crowds. You could also try smaller resorts that you might not normally bother with for a week's holiday.

Geneva is the classic gateway to the western Alps, with Chamonix just over an hour away, and other major French resorts such as Megève, Flaine and Morzine close by. Allow extra time for the Trois Vallées and the Tarentaise resorts. You could also head into Switzerland and visit Villars or Verbier, or try out the new (for 2013/14) link between Grimentz and Zinal in Val d'Anniviers.

In Italy, Turin is an underused alternative approach to the Aosta Valley, with Courmayeur, Champoluc and La Thuile conveniently reached; Sauze d'Oulx and Montgenèvre in the Milky Way are even nearer.

Further east, in Switzerland, Engelberg and Andermatt are popular options easily accessible from Zürich. So are the Austrian resorts of the Vorarlberg – such as Warth in Bregenzerwald, which will be linked to upmarket Lech for 2013/14. St Anton is easily reached too. Also in Austria, Innsbruck allows you to combine a city break with doorstep skiing. There are lots of resorts surrounding the city, and the Stubai Valley with its reliable glacier is nearby. Similarly Salzburg has lots of resorts within an hour or two.

The Pyrenees offer short-break opportunities too: flights into Pau (where we flew to for two days' skiing recently) and Lourdes put you close to Cauterets, Barèges-La Mongie and St-Lary-Soulan. And for a budget break, you could explore Slovenia very cheaply with flights to Ljubljana – the nearest ski area is just 8km from the airport.

WHERE TO STAY?

The range of short-stay accommodation is improving, but can still be limited in some major resorts – places such as Chamonix, Crans-Montana and Morzine, with big summer or conference business, are easier. From Salzburg or Innsbruck you could take the daily shuttles to different resorts. If you have a rental car, valley towns such as Chur, Sion and Interlaken in Switzerland, Aosta in Italy, Moûtiers and Bourg-St-Maurice in France and Radstadt in Austria are cheaper bases from which you can visit different resorts nearby.

PRICING THE OPTIONS

Costs vary enormously. Tour operators have special deals with hotels and can organize the essentials to save you time.

Around 50% of Ski 2's business is short breaks to Champoluc in Italy's Monterosa ski area. Three nights' B&B in a 3-star hotel, transfers from any of six airports within striking distance (meeting any flight), a three-day lift pass, first-day guiding and lunches costs from £495 (£512 for a half-board package); you book your own flights. Stanford Skiing offers three- and four-night stays in catered chalets or self-catered apartments in Megève; prices for a catered chalet are from £310 excluding flights and transfers.

Ski Weekend is the original short-break ski specialist. A four-night B&B package to Chamonix including flights and transfers costs from £399. Don't confuse them with Skiweekends.com, which offers overnight coach travel or flight options – a four-night half-board coach package (including two nights on the coach) to Brides-les-Bains (for Méribel) giving three days of skiing costs from £299 for most of the season. Momentum offers flights, car hire and three nights' B&B in a 3-star hotel in Courmayeur from £398. STC Ski says three nights half-board in a Kitzbühel 3-star including flights and transfers costs from £359. These companies and Alpine Weekends will tailor-make short breaks to many resorts.

TIPS FOR THE TRIP

Unless booking at short notice, avoid low resorts (where snow may be unreliable) and high, treeless resorts (where slopes may close in bad weather). Go for early or late flights to get the most slope time, but note that Sunday evening traffic can be horrendous with locals going home. Book a transfer or rental car in advance and choose a different car hire company from the one your airline promotes to avoid queuing with others from your flight. Taxis are generally very expensive, and public transport is rarely convenient (though Switzerland has good rail links). Rather than take your skis/board, consider renting: most airlines charge hefty carriage fees.

Smart apartments

Enjoy full independence in comfortable surroundings

by **Dave Watts**

Apartment holidays used to be the budget option for most people – at least on holidays to France. Shoehorn six people into a studio advertised for six and you'd have a cheap but not very comfortable time. Now things have changed, especially in France where lots of plush new apartment blocks ('residences', as the French say – sounds so much better) have been built in recent years. Most have dishwashers, and many share a pool, sauna, steam room and gym to add to the pampering. Some even have comfortable furniture to relax in, too. Sure, the budget option still exists, but now you can have a comfortable apartment holiday with all the other advantages that it brings (see below). We've looked for smart apartments to recommend throughout the Alps and have included them in the resort chapters.

I've been taking my annual ski holiday with my wife and a couple of friends in apartments for over 20 years. That's because we value the freedom an apartment gives you. You don't have to stick to meal times (and meals) dictated by the hotel or chalet staff; you can slob around in whatever clothes you want; you can go out and come back in whenever you choose. And, crucially in our case, you are free to have a big lunch up the mountain without worrying about having to eat a huge meal, which your chalet staff or hotel will have prepared for you, in the evening; if you lack the appetite for a full meal in the evening, you can buy snacks such as oysters, smoked salmon, pâté and local cheeses along with a good bottle of wine or two from the supermarket. If you are hungry, you can go out to a restaurant to eat. Staying in an apartment doesn't mean having to cook big meals – not for us anyway.

When we started this apartment lark, we couldn't find the sort of thing we were looking for in tour operators' brochures – all the apartments were of the 'cram 'em in and make it cheap' variety. So we ended up booking independently. Now, at least in France – the country that used to have the smallest, most sordid apartments – a

SKI COLLECTION

We always look for an apartment with comfortable sofas and chairs and a spacious living room – this is the Télémark in Tignes-le-Lac →

few tour operators (including those advertising in this chapter) offer some really smart and spacious places, mostly with leisure facilities such as pools, saunas and steam rooms. The French smart apartment concept was kick-started by apartments built by or opened in the Montagnettes and MGM names. Now they've been joined by other brands. PV Holidays launched its Pierre & Vacances Premium brand a few winters ago, and it now features 11 residences in nine French resorts. Lagrange has 17 Alpine and six Pyrenean residences in its Prestige range.

So why the sudden change? Xavier Schouller of Peak Retreats and Ski Collection says, 'A lot of smart new residences have been built recently because of tax breaks for people buying them – you get the VAT back if you agree to rent them out for several years, and French residents can set costs against income tax too. This is good news for people wanting to rent an apartment for a holiday – we now have over 200 residences on our books.' And a new classification scheme that came fully into force in July 2012 includes, for the first time, a 5-star rating; but many places that could qualify for 5-star status choose to remain 4-star for various reasons, such as having to charge a higher tourist tax for 5-stars.

Ski Amis is best known as a catered chalet company, but it has moved into apartments in a big way. Instead of offering big

residences such as the companies mentioned opposite do, it offers mostly privately owned apartments and chalets, mainly in the Tarentaise, which includes the Trois Vallées, Paradiski and Espace Killy resorts. It will have a staggering 6,000 to 8,000 available this winter from budget to luxury. Christine Van Zadelhoff, a director of Ski Amis, says, 'They will all be on our website, and you can access a selection by putting in either a budget and the number of people, or more specific requirements such as three bedrooms, dishwasher, Wi-Fi, hot tub. You can book many online.'

Erna Low and Interhome have a lot of apartments available too. And they feature the other Alpine countries as well as France (particularly Switzerland, in the case of Erna Low). Or you can rent independently; as well as contacting local rental agencies there are some good websites to try, such as www.holidaylettings.co.uk and www.homeaway.co.uk.

WHAT TO CHECK BEFORE BOOKING

So what do you need to look for if you're booking what you hope is a smart apartment? Most importantly, you still need to check whether the space is enough to meet your expectations – and whether the number it's advertised for involves anyone sleeping in the living room, in bunk beds, on a mezzanine or in a cabin (which can mean an alcove). Also check the number of bathrooms and toilets. If the leisure facilities such as a pool, sauna, steam room and gym are important to you, check whether there is a charge for using these; sadly, there often is. And while most smart apartments come with a modern design, dishwasher and smartish furniture, we're sometimes disappointed by the lack of really comfy sofas and easy chairs – often because sofas double up as beds and are more comfortable to sleep in than sit on – so check that if you can.

Alpine Answers

No one knows ski holidays like us!

Exclusive reader cash-back offer!

Book your next ski holiday with Alpine Answers, the UK's foremost ski holiday specialist, and save 100s of pounds.*

Why you should use Alpine Answers:
- **21 years** selling ski holidays to discerning skiers
- **Fantastic** user friendly website
- **Great choice** of catered chalets and hotels to suit most budgets
- **Friendly** and **knowledgeable** staff
- **Excellent** customer service

*The cash-back amount ranges from £25 to £50 per person, depending on your holiday spend and group size. For example a group of 10 people will save up to £500.

To register for cash-back, complete our short online form at www.bit.ly/wtss-aa
Then, when booking, quote the discount code "WTSS2014" and the email address you used when registering.

Call: 020 7801 1080
www.alpineanswers.co.uk

ABTA No.D4050

Luxury chalets

Relax and enjoy a comfortable mountain home

by **Dave Watts**

The catered chalet holiday is a uniquely British idea. The deal, in case you're new to it, is that tour operators install their own cooks and housekeepers in chalets for the season and provide half-board plus teatime cake and, usually, travel from the UK. So you get the privacy and relaxed atmosphere of a temporary home in the mountains, without the hassle of self-catering or the cost of eating out in restaurants every night. In the beginning, in the 1960s and 70s, chalet holidays meant creaky old buildings with spartan furniture and paper-thin walls. My, how things have changed. When we first visited Méribel in 1974, en suite bathrooms were unheard of. They are now the norm. Spacious and plush living rooms with log fires are common (but spacious and plush bedrooms are less so). Spa facilities such as a sauna, steam room and hot tub are common too; some chalets even have a swimming pool. And all at prices we ordinary mortals can contemplate paying. It's these chalets that this chapter is about.

SKI TOTAL

Most luxury catered chalets now have big, comfortably furnished living rooms. Some bedrooms can still be a bit poky though – check before you book ↓

Because of the huge number of chalet holidays available, choosing the right one can be difficult. Some very helpful websites have been set up by agents, allowing you to sift out chalets that suit you best; some advertise in this chapter and elsewhere in the book.

The greatest concentration of smart chalets is found – surprise, surprise – in the British skier's favourite French resort, **Méribel**. Ski Total has a wide range of properties here, including two with the firm's top Platinum rating; they have hot tubs, of course – and a cinema and billiard room in the case of chalet Isba. Purple Ski has five top-notch and highly individual chalets – in good positions, with lovely interiors and outdoor hot tubs. Ski Olympic runs the Parc Alpin, formerly a boutique hotel, as a very smart chalet hotel – 12 luxurious rooms with plasma TVs, dinky swimming pool and sauna. Skiworld has the swish Laetitia with hot tub, sauna and cinema room. Inghams has a few smart places with outdoor hot tubs, including Sylvie, new to its programme this year. Other

companies to consider include Consensio, Meriski and VIP.

Over the hill is **Courchevel**, a resort of parts (it has recently renamed these parts – see p249 – but we are using the old names here). 1850 is well established as the 'smartest' resort in France, with the highest prices and the swankiest hotels and chalets. Supertravel has 10 lovely luxurious chalets here including the modern, contemporary and central Eden with pool, steam room and TV room, and their flagship Montana, right on the main piste, built with reclaimed ancient timbers and with a split level living/dining room and a mini wellness centre with steam room, hot tub and monsoon shower. Other operators such as Kaluma, Consensio and Scott Dunn also have lovely properties here, and Ski Total has some bordering on the luxury category.

The big UK chalet centre is 1650, where Le Ski now has 17 chalets, sleeping from 2 to 22; 13 of them have sauna, steam or hot tub. And their flagship Scalottas Lodge has five apartment-chalets with fabulous views, leather armchairs and sofas, solid wooden floors and hi-tech lights and heating. One of Ski Olympic's flagship Gold Collection chalets is here – Monique, with TVs in the bedrooms and an outdoor hot tub. Skiworld has some smart-looking chalets too – the 21-bed Estrella is one of its best, with outdoor hot tub. Down in Le Praz, Mountain Heaven has three chalets, including the very luxurious-looking Edelweiss with outdoor hot tub, and Jardin d'Angele with sauna, steam room, tub.

In **La Tania**, not far away off the road towards Méribel, Ski Amis has seven smart-looking places, all but one with outdoor hot tub and some with its Premium service.

In **Les Menuires** there are smart places on offer in the recently developed areas. Ski Olympic has four with saunas and hot tubs in Reberty; Ski Amis has several chalets with outdoor hot tubs in Les Bruyères and others with hot tubs and saunas in Le Bettex. And in **St-Martin** the Alpine Club has two luxurious chalets in the quiet hamlet of Villarabout, one newly built in traditional style with a

THE CHALET HOLIDAY – A PRIMER

Generally, you can either book a whole chalet (the smallest typically sleep six or eight) or share a larger chalet with others. This works surprisingly well, usually.

In the beginning, the cooking and cleaning was done by your chalet girl – often straight out of college or finishing school, and mainly intent on having a fun season. Chalet girls still exist, but now there are just as many boys, and grown-ups, including couples. It would be an exaggeration to say that service is generally professional, but training standards have certainly improved.

Breakfast is usually a buffet with the option of some cooked items. At teatime, cakes and tea are put out. Often beer and soft drinks are sold at modest prices, on an honesty basis. Dinner is usually a no-choice affair at a communal table, including wine – unlimited in quantity and generally improved in quality since the early days of chalets. In 'luxury' chalets the wine is usually better still and you may be able to pay extra for even higher quality. Once a week the staff have a day off and you're left to your own devices – most people like to dine in a restaurant, but you can buy in a picnic.

In chalet hotels you may have individual tables, or large ones you share with others; there may be a choice of dishes and wines at dinner and there will usually be a bar.

double-height, open-plan living room and the other a beautiful 100-year-old farmhouse with spectacular views.

Val d'Isère is the great rival to Méribel in the French chalet business. The local specialist, YSE, has several very swish places. New to Le Ski's programme for this season is something very different: Angelique, in a back street of La Daille, looks more like a mini stately home than a chalet (and has a steam room and gym). Skiworld's 12 chalets include two of their top properties: Tolima, with sauna and steam room, and Madeleine, with outdoor hot tub. Ski Total has 18 smart places, including four very swanky chalets in their Platinum range – one with outdoor hot tub, two with saunas and, new for this season, one with plunge pool and steam room. Crystal's range includes three of its Finest properties, with saunas. And Inghams has a flagship 24-bed chalet hotel with sauna, steam and hot tub in Le Fornet. Other companies to look at include Scott Dunn, Consensio and Le Chardon Mountain Lodges.

In **Tignes** Skiworld's programme includes some chalets with sauna and hot tub, and a swanky chalet hotel with pool and sauna. Ski Total has some very smart places, lots with outdoor hot tub and sauna, some with pool and two in their top-of-the-market Platinum range. Crystal and Inghams have some smart chalets too.

The other great French mega-area, Paradiski, offers lots of chalets in **La Plagne** and growing numbers at **Peisey-Vallandry**, on the Les Arcs side of the cable car from La Plagne. Few chalets stand out, but Ski Amis has a Premium service chalet in each of these resorts.

There are lots of chalets in **La Rosière**, but few notable ones. Mountain Heaven has two in its Premium range here, both with outdoor hot tubs: the very smart-looking Penthouse with grand

top-floor living space and the renovated farm-style Chez Robert, which is just 30m from the lifts. Ski Olympic has two chalet-apartments in a development with its own pool, sauna, steam room and hot tub. Crystal has a couple of places in its Finest programme with access to a sauna and outdoor hot tub.

Chalets are not common in **Avoriaz**, so it's good to see that Ski Total's handful includes one of its Platinum chalets, with sauna and log fire. In **Alpe-d'Huez**, Ski Total, Skiworld and Inghams all have smart places with outdoor hot tub.

In Switzerland, **Verbier** is the chalet capital. Ski Total has the very smart chalet hotel Montpelier with panoramic pool, sauna and steam room, a separate top-floor chalet within it and another separate smart chalet with floor-to-ceiling windows and a steam room. Another company to look at is Ski Verbier.

Curiously, **Zermatt** has not traditionally been a great chalet resort, but Ski Total now has lots of smart properties there – some with sauna, steam room or hot tub. Skiworld has three very smart chalet-apartments in one building. Supertravel has a big swanky chalet with a pool, sauna and steam room that can be split into four smaller units. Other companies to consider include Scott Dunn and VIP. In nearby **Saas-Fee**, Ski Total's chalet hotel Ambassador is right at the foot of the slopes with indoor pool. And Alpine Life has a lovely looking chalet that we've had very good reports on, with hot tub, sauna and steam room. In cute little **Grimentz** (covered in our Val d'Anniviers chapter), Mountain Heaven has some smart chalets that can be booked on a catered or self-catered basis.

In Austria, **St Anton** is chalet central. Supertravel has nine smart-looking chalets including three newly built apartments, which share an outdoor pool, sauna and steam room and you are driven to/from the slopes each day. Skiworld's flagship Monte Vera has huge bedrooms, sauna and infra-red room. Many of Ski Total's dozen chalets have saunas but none qualify for its top Platinum rating. Crystal has three of its Finest chalets here, including the cool 32-bed Inge, with wellness area and fabulous views. Inghams has several chalets with access to sauna, steam room and pool and, just over the hill in St Christoph, its flagship chalet hotel – ski-in/ski-out, with a sauna and good-sized pool. Ski Total has three smart chalet hotels (all with saunas, one with a pool) in nearby Lech. Others operators to look at are Flexiski, Kaluma and Scott Dunn.

In North America, Skiworld has good chalets in Winter Park, Breckenridge and Vail, and Crystal Finest has one in Breckenridge.

Luxury chalets

51

Build your own shortlist: **www.wheretoskiandsnowboard.com**

Family holidays

Some pointers towards success

by **Chris Gill**

My offer in the last edition to hand over the mantle of 'family skiing expert' at NortonWood Towers to some other literate parent produced a response that was ... well, disappointing; quite poor, really; zilch, actually. So on we go. This year I am going to learn from our readers. I have gone over the reports on successful family holidays we have received in the last two years, to pull out examples of what made those holidays successful. What follows may help you think about what would work for your family trip (tobogganing seems key), and might prompt you to consider resorts you haven't thought about. Do not take this to be a definitive list of the best places to go.

AUSTRIA

Ellmau *Tobogganing* goes down a treat and the Kaiserbad leisure facility provides alternative attractions, including *swimming*.

Obergurgl Most of the big hotels are well geared up for children, with *pools, games rooms and kids' club* facilities – good for when the weather is bad, and after skiing. There is a *toboggan* run, and one of the hotels has a *bowling* alley.

FRANCE

Alpe-d'Huez Excellent *'jungle gym'* at the sports centre. Lots of *gentle early skiing* options. Plenty for the children: *luge run, pools, children's play area, night skiing* – all making it great.

Les Arcs 1950 has lots going on, from *torchlit descent* to local *fun and games*. Easy to get to the cracking little *tobogganing* area up at 2000, just beyond the centre.

Courchevel The range of runs and good lift network is *ideal for a group of mixed ability*. Good *sledging* from 1850 to 1550 is a real bonus. The *secluded kids' area* was safe from the main ski runs. Little ones had *mini roundabouts and pony rides*. Older children could use the *ice rink*, the *bowling* and the *cinema*. There are weekly *firework* displays. Brilliant *Indians-themed run* above 1650 is fantastic – archery, dressing up and 'working wigwam'.

Flaine With *apartments close to the slopes*, carrying kit is kept to a minimum. The *resort nursery* was very good. The *free pass for the beginners' area* allowed us to take our son skiing in short bursts.

Montgenèvre Pizza; *toboggan* runs; pizza; *ski-in/ski-out* lodgings; pizza; tree-lined runs with small *bumps and jumps*; pizza; *short transfer* from Oulx train station; pizza; virtually *no through traffic*; pizza; very *friendly locals*; and did I mention large helpings of *pizza*?

ITALY

Cervinia Kids had a whale of a time at the bottom of the slopes – a play area and *snow tubing, tobogganing* and an *ice rink*.

Livigno *Restaurants by the slopes* at village level makes meeting for lunch easy. Many non-skiing activities on the snow (*tubing* and *riding skidoos*) provided alternatives to skiing.

La Thuile Good place to let *teenagers ski independently*: the pistes are not crowded, the piste map and piste marking were done well. Planibel complex really good – a massive *games room*, a *pool*, a really good *tubing* slope close by, and *no long walks*. *Skating* is available.

Family holidays

53

Build your own shortlist: www.wheretoskiandsnowboard.com

The catered chalet holiday is as popular as ever, especially with families. Since en-suite bathrooms and comfy sofas became the norm rather than the exception, the attractions of the chalet – more private and less formal than hotels – have increased considerably. Now, more people are discovering the merits of the chalet's bigger cousin, the chalet hotel.

Chalet operators have for years set the pace in childcare. It was a natural extension of hiring British gels as cooks and housekeepers to hire a few as nannies, too; then all the operator had to do was identify a suitable room in a suitable chalet, and bingo – a crèche was born. For British parents unable to handle the brutality of French nurseries, the chalet was the obvious solution.

Chalet hotels are a larger version of the same thing, with some additional advantages. Some are purpose-built, but usually they are based on buildings that have operated as proper hotels. As a result, bedrooms typically are more generous than in chalets. Facilities are often better – there is likely to be a bar (with prices below resort norms, if you're lucky), and there may be a swimming pool, spa or gym, for example. There may be a menu choice at dinner.

Two of the most long-established tour operator firms dominate the family chalet hotel market. Esprit Ski was the original family chalet specialist; its programme is still dominated by standard chalets – in total over 50 – but it now also includes seven chalet hotels – five in major French resorts plus one in Gressoney (Monterosa, Italy) and one in Saas-Fee (Switzerland). Mark Warner specializes in chalet hotels, and has crèches in most properties. The editorial Gill family took several successful holidays with these firms in the days when the kids were small.

Strikingly, these firms major on top resorts. They both have chalet hotels with childcare in Courchevel 1850, Méribel, Val d'Isère and La Plagne. Esprit's flagship is the super-cool Deux Domaines at Belle-Plagne, which has a decent pool and spa – young children are not allowed in the latter – and a good ski-in/ski-out location on the lower edge of the village. The other Esprit resort in France is Alpe-d'Huez. Mark Warner also has family-oriented properties in Tignes, Les Deux-Alpes and St Anton (Austria).

SWITZERLAND

Saas-Fee Lots of other activities – *sledging, ice grotto, pool*. Teenager could *find his way around on his own*. The *lack of traffic* (aside from the taxis) is great. There is a *fun park* for first-time skiers. There is a *petting zoo* with marmots, chamois, goats and chickens. Once a week at 5pm there is a *kids' disco* in the square.

WHO TO GO WITH?

You can, of course, have family skiing holidays more or less completely unaided. Or you can call on the support of resort nurseries, and childcare facilities associated with resort ski schools. But huge numbers of British families are wedded to the comfortable childcare arrangements offered by British tour operators.

The firms advertising in this chapter are mostly small, specialized companies going to a small range of resorts that they know inside out (only one resort, in the case of Ski 2). They are basically owner-operated, so you can expect them to be very responsive. Most operate catered chalets (explained in our chapter on luxury chalets). Esprit Ski is a bit different – a chalet operator on a much bigger scale, offering holidays in 10 French resorts plus an interesting sprinkling across the rest of the Alps. And don't forget that there are mainstream operators such as Crystal that operate childcare in some of the many resorts where they sell holidays.

The list on the next page shows who goes to which resorts; it covers the advertisers in this chapter and Crystal, to give you an idea of your options. Note that some of the smaller operators don't have full childcare facilities in every chalet or even every resort.

Family holidays

Build your own shortlist: www.wheretoskiandsnowboard.com

SKI 2 RACING – COACHING FOR YOUR KIDS?

The success of Ryan, Alysha and Charlotte Brown (the children of one of Ski 2's directors) in ski races across Europe is testimony to the expertise of their Italian race coaches. Ski 2 can now offer other youngsters the chance to benefit from the same training routine, while continuing their schooling in Champoluc.

Children joining the Ski 2 Racing programme spend their mornings race training with local coaches and their afternoons furthering their education with two fully trained English teachers. 'House parents' supervise the youngsters at other times, and the Ski 2 resort team offer any other support and guidance the youngsters might need.

Accommodation is in the family-run 3-star Hotel Petit Prince, which offers doorstep skiing at the ski area of Antagnod, close to Champoluc.

Prices – including everything except flights – start at around £1,200 per week, with reductions for longer stays. Short courses are now also available for children holidaying with Ski 2.

In December 2013 the first Ski 2 Winter Games will be held – five days of training and racing in the run-up to Christmas.

WHO GOES WHERE?

Austria
Obergurgl Esprit Ski. **Niederau** Crystal.
Scheffau Crystal. **St Anton** Esprit Ski.
France
Alpe-d'Huez Esprit Ski. **Les Arcs** Esprit Ski, Ski Amis. **Ardent** (Avoriaz) Family Ski. **Les Coches** (La Plagne) Family Ski. **Courchevel** Esprit Ski, Ski Amis, Ski Olympic. **Les Gets** Esprit Ski, Ski Famille. **Les Menuires** Family Ski, Ski Amis, Ski Famille, Ski Olympic. **Méribel** Esprit Ski, Ski Amis, Ski Olympic. **Peisey-Vallandry** (Les Arcs) Esprit Ski, Ski Amis, Ski Olympic. **La Plagne** Crystal, Esprit Ski, Ski Amis, Ski Olympic. **La Rosière** Esprit Ski, Ski Olympic. **St-Martin-de-Belleville** Ski Amis. **La Tania** Ski Amis. **Tignes** Crystal, Esprit Ski, Ski Amis. **Val d'Isère** Esprit Ski, Ski Amis, Ski Olympic. **Val Thorens** Ski Amis.
Italy
Champoluc (Monterosa) Ski 2.
Claviere (Montgenèvre) Crystal.
Gressoney (Monterosa) Esprit Ski.
Selva Esprit Ski. **Val di Fassa** Crystal.
Switzerland
Saas-Fee Esprit Ski.

Buying property

Be quick if you want to buy a new place in Switzerland

by **Dave Watts**

Buying a place in a ski resort is an ambition for lots of keen skiers and snowboarders. The last few years have been difficult times for the Alpine property market because of the economic problems – and for UK buyers it has been made =even more difficult by the weakness of the pound. You can buy in any of the main Alpine countries but now may be your last chance to buy a new property in Switzerland before tough new laws effectively banning the building of second homes in the Swiss Alps mean that construction stops.

In March 2012, the Swiss voted by a wafer-thin majority in a nationwide referendum to restrict the number of second homes in all communes to 20% of the total housing stock. And from now on, no new planning permits for second homes will be granted in most ski resorts (much to the annoyance of locals and many Swiss themselves, because the ban applies not just to foreign-owned second homes but to Swiss-owned ones too). But developments for which permits have already been issued will be allowed to continue to be built.

Simon Malster, managing director of Investors in Property, has been selling property in the Alps for over 25 years. He says, 'The advice to potential buyers must be to move quickly and buy now, as this will be the last opportunity to buy a new ski property in Switzerland.' Prices of Swiss ski resort properties are expected to rise sharply in forthcoming years because the new law means the supply of new properties has effectively been curtailed.

Investors in Property has properties available in the second phase of a very successful new development at the foot of the lifts in Engelberg – easily accessible by car or train from Zürich airport. The first phase has now sold out and is due to be completed in November 2013. A two-bedroom apartment in the second phase

INVESTORS IN PROPERTY

These apartments overlook Lake Brienz near Interlaken and are handy for Wengen, Mürren and Grindelwald ↓

↑ Most new
apartments come
ready-furnished or
with an optional
furniture package.
This development is
in Hollersbach, Austria

INVESTORS IN PROPERTY

will cost from around 650,000 francs and you can choose whether
to put it into a rental pool after reserving weeks for yourself. It also
has properties for sale in villages that link into the Verbier skiing
area – Les Collons and Nendaz (see the end of our Verbier chapter).
And it has some in Grimentz – a lovely old, unspoiled village that
will have a new cable car linking it to neighbouring Zinal for
2013/14 to create a joint ski area with 110km of pistes and lots of
excellent off-piste – see our chapter on Val d'Anniviers.

It also has some beautifully set south-facing apartments
overlooking Lake Brienz near Interlaken in a new car-free 'village'
with restaurants, lakeside leisure centre and its own harbour – great
for summer as well as winter. From there, it's easy to get to
Grindelwald, Wengen and Mürren and a shuttle service will operate
in winter. A two-bedroom apartment costs from 500,000 francs and
it is one of the rare Swiss developments where property can be
bought in the name of a company as well as by individuals.

Investors in Property has been selling an increasing number of
properties in Austria too. In most cases, properties are available to
foreigners as long as they agree to make them available for renting
when not using them personally – this also means that you save up
to 20% VAT on the purchase price. In a few rare cases, some new
properties have 'second-home status' and do not have to be rented
out. Jessica Delaney of Investors in Property says, 'By far our most
popular development has been one on the edge of Bramberg at the
foot of the local Wildkogel ski area (with 55km of pistes) and right
next to a gondola that opened a few seasons ago. The first phase is
virtually all sold and the second phase will be released shortly.' It is
also just three minutes' drive from a gondola into the Kitzbühel ski
area at Hollersbach and within easy reach of many other areas such
as Gerlos/Zell am Ziller and Kaprun (both around 30 minutes);
prices for phase one started at 400,000 euros for two-bedroom
penthouse apartments and around 500,000 euros for three- or four-
bedroom chalets built to order. Investors in Property also has
apartments at Hollersbach near the gondola to the Kitzbühel ski
area that are similarly priced. And it has ski-in/ski-out places in the
old village of Kappl, which currently has 40km of slopes (there are

Build your own shortlist: **www.wheretoskiandsnowboard.com**

↑ Apartments at Bramberg have been selling fast; it has its own ski area and is three minutes' drive from a gondola into Kitzbühel's slopes

INVESTORS IN PROPERTY

CONTACTS

Investors in Property
020 8905 5511
www.investorsin
property.com

Erna Low Property
020 7590 1624
www.ernalowproperty.
co.uk

plans to link it to the Rendl area of St Anton, which will greatly increase Kappl's attraction). It is also just 8km from the Ischgl ski area. Prices start at 600,000 euros for a two-bedroom apartment.

France remains a favourite place for British skiers and boarders to buy property. Joanna Yellowlees-Bound, CEO of Erna Low Property, says: 'We have some great places at the moment. My favourite is in the lovely old village of Tignes-les-Brévières where around 30 very high-quality apartments are being built with excellent spa facilities – a two-bedroom apartment costs from around 300,000 euros.' At a similar price there are also apartments in the much bigger Kalinda Village development at Tignes 1800 (a hotel, huge wellness centre and 350 apartments); an apartment development in Ste-Foy-Tarentaise has two-bedroom places from around 150,000 euros. With both Tignes 1800 and Ste-Foy, you have to agree to your apartment being in a rental pool for most of the season. Erna Low also does a lot of resales of apartments in Arc 1950.

Investors in Property also sells the Tignes 1800 and Ste-Foy developments. And it has many other properties in France – including the former Aspen Park hotel/Club Med building at Rond-Point in Méribel, which is being converted into apartments, and a new development just below the centre of Courchevel-Moriond/1650 – these are both developments of bigger and much pricier apartments at 1.5 to 2.5 million euros for three or four bedrooms.

WHAT TO LOOK FOR WHEN BUYING A HOME IN THE SNOW

First, you need to decide whether you want somewhere just for the skiing or whether you want a place in a resort that is attractive in the summer as well. Many French resorts developed after the 1950s can be deadly dull in summer, whereas others are attractive for summer as well as winter use. Second, if you want the place primarily for skiing and snowboarding, you will want reliable snow. And with climate change likely to continue, that means going for somewhere with access to high, snow-sure slopes and with good snowmaking. Third, if you intend to use the place frequently yourself, you will probably want somewhere within a couple of hours of an easily accessible airport. Fourth, make sure you understand the legal and taxation aspects – buying and running costs, all types of taxes and any resale restrictions. It is highly advisable to get professional advice on these. Fifth, make sure you understand any arrangements that you may be offered for 'sale and leaseback' or 'guaranteed return' from renting it out – these can vary enormously and may enable you to save money on the purchase price in some circumstances. Sixth, if you are intending to rent the property out yourself, don't overestimate the income you will get from it.

Corporate ski trips

A great way to motivate your staff and clients

by **Dave Watts**

Corporate ski trips used to be big business. A few seasons ago we had 13 advertisers in this chapter. Now we have two. Obviously, in difficult economic times, companies cut back on expenditure; and corporate hospitality is an easy target. But the market seems to be recovering and specialist event organizers are reporting increased business.

Amin Momen of Momentum Ski, which does a lot of corporate business, says, 'The market was up 20% for us last season and things are looking good for 2013/14. Our clients realize that for the same price as a hospitality package for Wimbledon or Twickenham they can get three days' valuable time with their staff or customers in the Alps.' Momentum is also running two new events this season. One is a medical conference in the Alps in conjunction with the medical childbirth charity Borne. The other is a Gourmet Ski Experience with Heston Blumenthal, Marcus Waring and other top chefs from the UK and Italy. The emphasis will be on use of local produce and there will be a full programme of skiing as well as dining. It is being held in Courmayeur in Italy, which proudly boasts 'More mountain restaurants than ski lifts'.

Mountain Heaven is a company that has catered chalets and/or self-catering accommodation in five French resorts and in Grimentz in Switzerland. Nick Williams, its MD, says, 'For the last five winters we've pioneered a new concept of great-value corporate trips. A firm of management consultants takes over all our self-catered accommodation in La Plagne Montalbert for its staff. They arrive from all over the world and we organize transfers from whatever airport suits them. They hold a two-day conference midweek but can arrive early or leave late to enjoy time on the slopes – they have the apartments for the whole week. We deliver breakfast daily and fix lunches and dinners – including a dinner up the mountain.'

Roger Walker of Ski 2 (a company that specializes in Champoluc in the Monterosa area of the Italian Alps) says, 'Our corporate clients tend to be different from those of other companies. Most are budget conscious and the whole thing is based more on team bonding than on entertaining clients. Most don't want us to organize meeting facilities either – the trip is more about a bunch of friends who work for the same company going on holiday together, rather than a corporate event. Companies like the fact that we will pick guests up from any of six airports within striking distance – perfect for people arriving from different parts of the world.'

Andrew Peters of STC Ski says, 'We organize a range of different types of trip from companies that simply invite clients for a holiday to those who want full-blown conference facilities. We've recently arranged corporate trips to Zell am See, Kitzbühel and Bad Gastein, for example – Austria offers great value and companies like that.'

HOW TO ORGANIZE IT AND WHERE TO GO

Organizing a corporate trip yourself is a real hassle. People based in different areas of the country are likely to want to fly from different airports and at different times of day. And many hotels in the Alps don't want to take bookings for just a few days, or to provide the

61

number of single rooms that you might want. Numbers are likely to change as people drop out for various reasons. Your group is likely to have skiers and boarders of widely differing abilities and maybe some beginners or non-skiers, so you need to organize ski instructors or guides to lead different groups. You need to organize equipment (and maybe clothing) rental and lift passes. You might want to organize 'jollies' such as dinner up the mountain and a torchlit descent back or a lunchtime BBQ on the piste. And you might need rooms to hold business meetings in. But that's what you use a tour operator or event organizer for – to deal with all the hassle and organize things on your behalf. And the great thing is that they don't charge you any extra for doing all that – it's part of the business to them.

Because corporate trips tend to be short, you'll want to keep the travel time to the minimum. Transfer times from airports to resorts generally range from one to four hours, and you'll probably want to operate at the lower end of that range if you can. That's why resorts such as Courmayeur and Champoluc in Italy (close to Geneva and Turin airports), Engelberg in Switzerland (close to Zürich), Kitzbühel in Austria (close to Salzburg and Innsbruck) and Garmisch in Germany (close to Munich) are popular. All these resorts have hotels that are happy to offer short-break bookings too.

THE MOMENTUM SKI FESTIVAL – CRANS-MONTANA, VALAIS, 13 TO 16 MARCH 2014

The Momentum Ski Festival incorporates the City Ski Championships (now in its 15th year) and a Business Forum run in association with the Financial Times. The Forum is chaired by FT Weekend editor Caroline Daniel and has a panel that discusses current affairs, global issues and the state of the markets. The 2013 panel included Frank Gardner (BBC security correspondent), Marcus Brigstocke (comedian with political attitude) and Jean-Claude Biver (high-flying Swiss watch maker who brought the Hublot brand back from oblivion). The debate was followed by a lively Q&A session.

The festival includes a full programme of après-ski, with stand-up comedy, live bands and big-name DJs. There will be drinks parties hosted by Cavendish Ware and the Valais and dinners with entertainment at different venues, culminating in the prize-giving dinner on the Saturday with trophies presented by sponsors such as Tag Heuer and Swiss International Airlines. Celebrity guests are likely to include Damon Hill, Colin Jackson, Heston Blumenthal, Pink Floyd's Nick Mason, Olympic gold medallist Tommy Moe and UK ski racing figures Graham Bell and Konrad Bartelski.

With the City Ski Championships, two races are held on the Friday: the Radar Trap Challenge (speed skiing) and the Accenture Dual Parallel Slalom. But the main event is the Saturday GS race on the World Cup Piste Nationale with live commentary by the BBC's Matt Chilton. On both days there'll be a Savills Alpine Homes race-side buffet and Snow+Rock will offer ski tuning, boot fitting and demo ski testing.

For more details call 020 7371 9111 or visit www.cityskichampionships.com.

MOMENTUM SKI

Flying to the snow

Flights and transfers for independent travellers

by **Sheila Reid**

There are lots of flights to the Alps and Pyrenees; and you can often avoid the crowds by opting for quieter, queue-free regional airports. But finding your way through the minefield of routes and extra charges is hard work – and the extras can double or triple the basic cost.

So-called budget airlines go to mainstream airports such as Geneva and Milan but also to smaller places, making it easier to get to many resorts in places such as Austria, the Dolomites, the Pyrenees, Slovenia and eastern Europe. You'll find a wide choice of affordable transfers too. National carriers can be competitive, both on cost and destination, so don't ignore them when planning a trip. But note that some winter routes stop operating before the season ends.

THE LEADING GROUP

EasyJet has a big range of flights, many to Geneva, from a broad choice of UK hubs. Other key destination airports include Zürich, Innsbruck, Salzburg, Munich, Turin, Milan and Lyon. From Stansted, Ljubljana is handy for Slovenia and eastern Austria.

Ryanair operates mainly from Stansted, with a few flights from other UK airports. Routes/frequency change regularly, but a wide choice is offered – including Lourdes (for the western and central Pyrenees) and Memmingen (Germany and western Austria). New for 2013/14 are flights to Grenoble three times a week.

Jet2.com has flights to Geneva, Salzburg, Chambéry and Grenoble – mainly from northern England, but also from Edinburgh and Belfast – available through its dedicated ski website.

Flybe serves Geneva, Salzburg, Milan, Chambéry, Nice and, unusually, Stuttgart (handy for Germany and western Austria) – mainly from Southampton but also from Exeter, Birmingham and Glasgow. There are also flights from Newcastle to Bergen, Norway.

British Airways goes to lots of relevant airports, including Innsbruck, from a variety of UK ones. **Swiss** has lots of flights to Zürich and Geneva, some to Basel.

Monarch flies to Grenoble, Innsbruck, Friedrichshafen, Munich, Verona, Venice and Barcelona with some flights from each of Gatwick, Luton, Manchester, Birmingham and Leeds Bradford.

PRICING IT UP …

Charges and rules for baggage and for equipment carriage vary and change frequently, so it's important to check the detail. In July, EasyJet was charging £40 return for one checked bag to Geneva but discounted this to £20 if you booked it in online. Booking in skis online cost another £54 return and gave you 12kg extra weight allowance. Ryanair permits either a standard 15kg for a first bag, priced from £30 return, or 20kg from £50; but skis/board carriage will set you back £100 return. BA effectively charges for skis: one checked-in bag is free up to 23kg; additional bags on European flights cost from £40 return. However, skis can be considered to be your one piece of checked baggage as long as they're packed according to BA guidelines in a proper ski bag weighing no more than 23kg. Swiss and Lufthansa still allow one set of skis and boots

ONLINE BOOKING

Most budget airlines expect you to book online, and many charge less if you book such 'extras' as hold baggage and ski carriage online too. The web addresses of the airlines we list are given as links on our website (click on Directory).

THE EXTRAS

Charges on top of basic flight costs vary between airlines. In July 2013, we looked at three (Jet2, EasyJet and Flybe) for flights to Geneva for a week in February 2014. Basic return fares varied from £66 to £102. Extra charges included:

1 checked-in 20kg bag return.....£20-£36

1 skis/snowboard/boots return..£54-£60

Admin or check-in fee ....£0-£12

Reserve seat return..............£6-£14

Credit card payment fee..........£1.68-£5.44

These can add over £100 to the original cost, and the priciest of our flights worked out at over £217.

Also, you might be offered insurance for, say, £12 (which may not cover winter sports adequately – do check) and missed flight insurance for £9.50. Taking a boot bag counts as a second bag and costs extra – though most airlines allow a boot bag too if you pay for ski carriage.

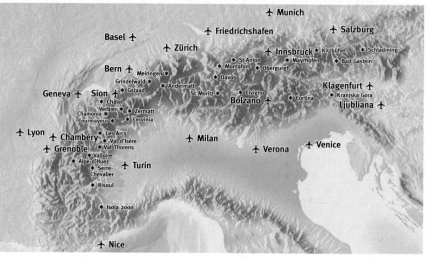

Munich ✈
Friedrichshafen ✈   ✈ Salzburg
Basel ✈
✈ Zürich   Innsbruck ✈ Kitzbühel   ✈ Schladming
                              ✳ St Anton ✳ Mayrhofen
Bern ✈   ✳ Montafon ✳ Obergurgl   ✳ Bad Gastein
Meiringen ✳   ✳ Davos
Grindelwald ✳   ✳ Andermatt
Geneva ✈ Sion ✈ ✳ Gstaad   St Moritz ✳   ✳ Livigno   Klagenfurt ✈
              ✳ Châtel   Bolzano ✈ ✳ Cortina ✳ Kranjska Gora
Chamonix ✳ Verbier ✳ ✳ Zermatt   Ljubliana ✈
Courmayeur ✳   ✳ Cervinia
✈ Lyon   ✳ Les Arcs
     Chambéry ✳ ✳ Val d'Isère   ✈ Milan
✈ Grenoble ✳ Val Thorens
        ✳ Valloire   ✈ Verona   ✈ Venice
   ✳ Alpe-d'Huez
      ✳ Serre-   ✈ Turin
      Chevalier
   ✳ Risoul

✳ Isola 2000

✈ Nice

free in addition to a 23kg bag. There are other extras that inflate the price too (see the margin copy on the previous page). Airport costs such as drop-off and trolley fees can also add to the overall spend. Wizz is now charging for hand baggage on all routes unless it is small and will fit under the seat in front. Let's hope this doesn't catch on (but we fear it might). EasyJet will now only guarantee to allow hand baggage of 50x40x20cm into the cabin. If it's bigger than that up to the maximum 56x45x25cm allowed, then on some busy flights your bag may have to go into the hold – they tell us you are not charged for this.

FROM PLANE TO RESORT

Car rental can be cost-effective for a short break or with a group – but, again, watch for hidden extras.

Most Swiss and Austrian airports have good public transport links to lots of resorts. Special rail passes may be cheaper than return tickets (see page 456) for Swiss passes). In Italy, buses run to the Dolomites from Verona and Innsbruck, and to the Aosta valley from Turin.

Reaching French resorts is slightly trickier, but private minibus transfers are plentiful. Tour operator Ski Amis offers a public shared minibus service from Geneva and Chambéry to the Trois Vallées, La Plagne Montalbert and Peisey-Vallandry on Saturdays. Prices start at £75 per person return. Holiday Taxis (www.holidaytaxis.com) covers over 400 resorts from major airports and some stations. Transfer companies and their relevant links are listed on our website: www.wheretoskiandsnowboard.com (click on Directory).

Travelling by rail

Make tracks to the snow (greener ones)

by **Sheila Reid**

Whether you're an enthusiast or not, rail travel has its advantages for travelling to the snow. As well as the leisurely journey aspect, taking the train rather than flying can avoid overcrowded airports and baggage charges as well as traffic congestion. There are efficient high-speed links between London and Paris, and daytime services to French resorts can take as little as eight hours (with Eurostar direct). Some resorts have their own railway stations and others are easily reached by onward bus or taxi transfers. Here we sum up the main options.

The starting point of most European rail trips is likely to be the Eurostar high-speed train from London St Pancras or from Ashford or Ebbsfleet stations in Kent.

DIRECT SERVICES TO THE FRENCH ALPS
The fastest way to France is Eurostar's direct services to the Tarentaise region – such as to Moûtiers (for the Trois Vallées) and to Bourg-St-Maurice (for Les Arcs, La Rosière, Ste-Foy, Tignes and Val d'Isère). Overnight services allow you eight days on the slopes. Daytime services give you the regular six days, the same as if flying. Generally allow up to an hour or so for onward transfers. We tried the daytime service to Moûtiers last season and thought it brilliant.

Overnight trains will depart from London every Friday evening from 20 December 2013 to 4 April 2014. They leave at 8.09pm and arrive at Bourg at 6.07am. The return service leaves Bourg on Saturday at 10.15pm and arrives in London at 7.16am. There are no special sleeping arrangements – you doze (or not) in your seat. The daytime service will depart from London every Saturday from 21 December 2013 until 5 April 2014. This leaves at 9.39am and arrives in Bourg at 6.51pm. The return service leaves Bourg at 9.44am and arrives in London at 4.11pm.

A Standard adult return costs from £149 (non-flexible). A Standard Premier ticket (non-flexible) – which gets you a bigger seat pitch and meals (hot dinner/continental breakfast for overnight travel and continental breakfast and hot lunch for daytime passengers) – costs from £229. Seats can also be booked as part of a package holiday.

INDIRECT SERVICES TO THE FRENCH ALPS
The French regular rail network (SNCF) can get you to lots of places such as Chambéry, Briançon and Grenoble for onward buses to more southerly resorts. For Chamonix, an overnight train from Paris Austerlitz, via St-Gervais with a connecting train to Chamonix would put you in your resort by 10am the next day; prices started at £150 return. A pre-bookable taxi service to get you between the Paris stations is offered through snowcarbon.co.uk; you ring, email or book online to reserve a place, and the driver will meet your train. It costs 65 euros each way for up to eight people. SNCF has Youth and Senior saver cards. The Youth Card (for 12–27 year olds) costs about £45 and entitles you to 25% to 60% discount, depending on times/days and peak periods. The Senior Card (for over 60s) costs £59 and gets you 25% to 50% discount.

HIGH-SPEED TO SWITZERLAND

On peak dates (21, 28 December 2013; 15, 22 February 2014; 1 March 2014), Eurostar will have a Saturday service, with a change in Lille onto a high-speed Lyria des Neiges TGV train to Brig. This stops at Aigle, Martigny and Visp on the way – allowing easy transfers to resorts such as Villars, Verbier, Crans-Montana, Saas Fee and Zermatt. It leaves London at 6.57am and arrives in Brig at 4.14pm; the return departs Brig at 12.45pm and arrives in London at 9.06pm. A Standard adult return costs from £179, a Standard Premier return from £309 – both fares non-flexible. There are also Lyria des Neiges trains from Paris Gare de Lyon to Brig at weekends. Regular high-speed TGV trains from Paris also serve Geneva, Zürich and Basel, where you can change to connect with most Swiss resorts; lots, such as Andermatt, Davos, Engelberg, Grindelwald, Wengen, Klosters and Zermatt, have convenient local railway stations. It's easy to get to others, such as Saas Fee and Verbier, by a combination of train and post bus. Eurostar has connecting fares to five major Swiss cities, including Geneva, Zürich and Basel; journeys are also bookable (via Rail Europe) from Paris to about 18 other Swiss hubs – such as Chur, Sion and Visp.

AUSTRIA AND GERMANY

Many Austrian resorts also have their own stations or are easy to reach by post bus from a nearby station. City Night Line is part of a large network of European rail services, with weekend sleeper trains departing from Paris and Amsterdam. Winter services from Paris Est include trains direct to Innsbruck or Wörgl (Fridays), arriving late morning; or via Munich (daily). Onward connections can get you to resorts such as St Anton, Zell am See, Mayrhofen and the SkiWelt. From Munich it's an easy hop to Garmisch-Partenkirchen. Typical fares start from £179, including Eurostar to Paris. Check out www.citynightline.de for more details.

THE ITALIAN JOB

Most Italian resorts are hard work to reach by train, but there are exceptions. The Dolomites are close to the line through Trento and Bolzano, reachable from Munich (as an onward connection from the City Night Line – prices to both start at £70 return), from Innsbruck (prices to both start at £34 return), or from Verona to the south (prices start at £38 return to Trento and £47 return to Bolzano). Resorts of the Val di Susa are easily reached via trains from Paris Gare de Lyon to Turin and Milan. These run three times a day and stop at Bardonecchia and Oulx – 15 minutes by bus from Sauze d'Oulx and a bit further from Sestriere. A flexi-return fare from Paris starts at £99. Journeys are bookable through Rail Europe.

PLANNING AND BOOKING

Rail fares have few of the extra charges that you have to watch for with air fares. But the cheapest fares are best secured early. Booking is normally only up to 90 days in advance (but Eurostar's direct service can be booked much earlier). Main sites include: Rail Europe (www.raileurope.co.uk), Eurostar (www.eurostar.com), Swiss railways (www.sbb.ch/en) and Austrian railways (www.oebb.at). Some local lines such as Martigny to Le Châble (for Verbier) and Bex up to Villars may have to be organized separately. Other useful websites include www.seat61.com and www.snowcarbon.co.uk.

Drive to the Alps

And ski where you please

by **Chris Gill** | **Because the Channel gets in the way, and because the British Isles are the centre of the low-cost airline business, we're inclined to travel to the Alps by air whether we are buying a package holiday or travelling independently. The French, the Germans and the Dutch, in contrast, mainly go by car. But for British skiers, too, driving to the Alps can have lots of advantages.**

Even for those going on a pretty standard week in the Alps, many people find driving is less hassle than taking flights. For families (especially those going self-catering), it simplifies the job of moving half the contents of your house to the Alps. If there are four or five people in your party, the cost can be low. If you fancy something a bit more adventurous than a standard week in one resort, taking a car opens up the exciting possibility of visiting several resorts in one trip – maybe even making up your plans as you go, so that you go wherever the snow is looking best.

The experience of driving out can be a pleasant one. Crossing the Channel is slick and painless using the fast and frequent Eurotunnel Le Shuttle trains through the tunnel – read the feature panel below. And although cross-Channel ferries can't compete with Le Shuttle in terms of crossing time, they are faster than they have ever been (as well as more comfortable).

EASY DOES IT WITH EUROTUNNEL LE SHUTTLE

We had a lot of skiing to cram into March 2012, so for the first time for a while we drove out to the Alps, using the tunnel. We'd forgotten just how painless Le Shuttle is – and we've happily used it again for driving trips in 2013.

The terminal at Folkestone is very straightforward to reach. Junction 11A of the M20 takes you directly to the check-in gates. Check-in deadline is half an hour before departure. The check-in system recognizes your number plate and without human intervention prints your boarding pass. After a quick visit to the shops in the terminal to pick up the stuff you've forgotten, it's into the marshalling yard for a few minutes before boarding the train.

If you're at the front of the queue, once on the train you drive the whole length of it before parking – and that will mean a quick exit at the other end. Within minutes you're gliding into the tunnel. If you might want a quick nap while crossing, you might want earplugs.

You can be on the autoroute south of Calais 75 minutes after arrival at Folkestone. Overall, an early start from large parts of southern England can have you in your resorts near Geneva in time for dinner without taking too many liberties with the speed limit.

EUROTUNNEL

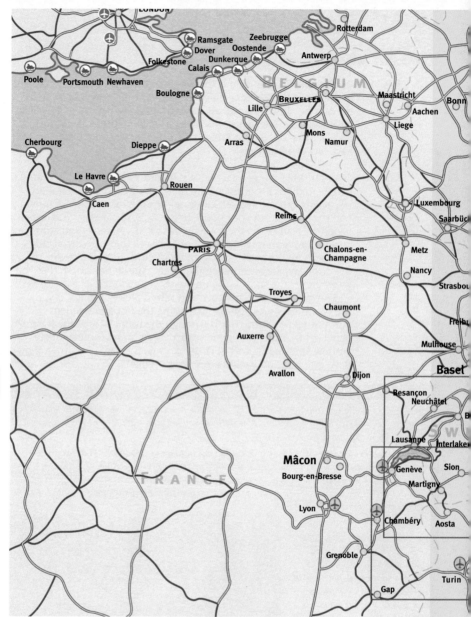

This map should help you plan your route to the Alps, at least in outline. All the main routes from the Channel and all the routes up into the mountains funnel through (or close to) three 'gateways', picked out on the map in larger type – Mâcon in France, Basel in Switzerland and Ulm in Germany.

Decide which gateway suits your destination, and pick a route to it from your planned arrival port at the Channel. Occasionally, using a different Channel port will lead you to use a different gateway.

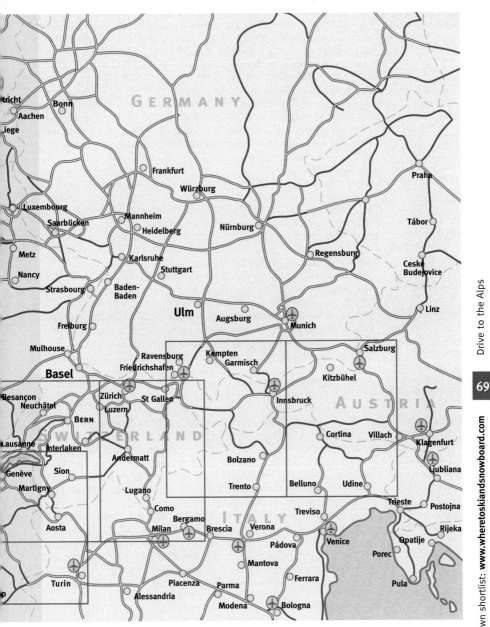

The boxes on the map correspond to the areas covered by the more detailed maps in our introductory chapters on the four main Alpine countries, starting on these pages:

Austria page 98
France page 202
Italy page 390
Switzerland page 454

What's more, the attractions of driving are not confined to the south of England. A reader writes: 'Living in Derbyshire we can be at Hull in just over an hour for a night crossing to Zeebrugge (for French or Swiss alps) or Rotterdam for Austria. After a night in a cabin and a breakfast on-board, we can start the 8-10 hour journey to the Alps at 8.30am fully refreshed'.

Another plus point of driving is that you can easily extend the standard six-day holiday. You can spend a full day on the slopes on the final Saturday (a blissfully quiet day in most resorts) and then drive for a few hours before stopping for the night.

AS YOU LIKE IT

If you fancy visiting several resorts, you can do it in three ways: use one resort as a base and make day trips to others; use a valley town as a base, and make resort visits from there; or go on a tour, moving on every day or two. There are some notable regional lift passes that might form the basis of a trip, in Austria especially.

AROUND THE ALPS IN SEVEN DAYS

The most rewarding approach to exploring the Alps – although the least relaxing – is to go touring, enjoying the freedom of going where you want, when you want. Out of high season there's no need to book accommodation in advance. And a touring holiday doesn't mean you'll be spending more time on the road than on the piste, provided you plan your route carefully. An hour's drive after the lifts have shut is all it need take, normally. It does eat into your après-ski time, of course. The major thing that you have to watch out for with a touring holiday is the cost of accommodation. Checking into a resort hotel for a night or two doesn't come cheap, and can seem a rip-off. But valley hotels can be very good value.

The following chapter has some suggestions for a trip to France. Austria offers lots of possibilities. In the west, you could take in the best skiing the country has to offer, by combining the Arlberg resorts with Ischgl, and maybe Sölden. Further east, it is easy to combine Hintertux and Mayrhofen with the SkiWelt resorts and Kitzbühel. Driving around in Austria is a doddle, because most of the resorts are low, and passes are rarely involved.

In Italy you can stay in the beautiful old city of Aosta and visit a different resort (such as Courmayeur, Cervinia and the Monterosa resorts) each day. Elsewhere in Italy, touring makes more sense.

Switzerland also offers lots of possibilities. In the west, you could combine Verbier with Val d'Anniviers and Crans-Montana. Further east, you could start in Davos/Klosters and end up in Flims.

BE PREPARED

Winter tyres make a big difference to a car's grip on ice and snow. These tyres are compulsory in Austria for the whole winter period. In other Alpine countries, we understand that they are not; but many 'experts' warn that if you go without them and have an incident you could be in trouble. You may still need chains in really deep snow. But winter tyres will keep you going in surprisingly difficult conditions if your car also has traction control, to stop the wheels spinning. This usually forms part of the electronic stability systems now fitted to many new cars (sometimes as an option).

Cars hired in Austria and Switzerland should always be equipped with winter tyres. Cars hired elsewhere may not be.

Drive to the French Alps

To make the most of them

by **Chris Gill** | If you've read the preceding chapter, you'll have gathered that we are pretty keen on driving to the Alps in general. But we're particularly keen on driving to the French Alps. The drive is a relatively short one, whereas many of the transfers to major French resorts from Geneva airport are relatively long.

Of course, the route from the Channel to the French Alps is through France rather than Germany, which for Francophiles like us means it's a pleasant prospect rather than a vaguely off-putting one. Especially if you are using Eurotunnel or a short ferry crossing, rather than a ferry to one of the Normandy ports, the drive is pleasantly low-pressure. Not only because you don't have to tangle with Paris but also because you don't have to use the always-busy Paris–Lyon autoroute.

The French Alps are the number-one destination for British car-borne skiers. The journey time is surprisingly short, at least if you are starting from south-east England. From Calais, for example, you can comfortably cover the 900km/560 miles to Chamonix in about nine hours plus stops – with the exception of the final few miles, the whole journey is on motorways. And except on peak weekends, when half the population of Paris is on the move, the traffic is relatively light, if you steer clear of Paris.

With some exceptions in the southern Alps, all the resorts of the French Alps are within a day's driving range, provided you cross the Channel early in the day (or overnight). Saturday is still the main changeover day for resorts, and Saturday traffic into and out of many resorts can be heavy. This is especially true between Albertville and the Tarentaise resorts (from the Trois Vallées to Val d'Isère). Things are nothing like as bad as they were 25 years ago, before road improvements for the 1992 Olympics removed some of the main bottlenecks; but the resorts have expanded further in that time, and sadly the jams are back – on peak-season Saturdays you can encounter serious queues around Moûtiers. There are traffic lights placed well away from the town, to keep the queues and associated pollution away from Moûtiers.

DAY TRIP BASES

As we explained in the previous chapter, a car opens up different kinds of holiday for the adventurous holidaymaker – day tripping from a base resort, for example.

In the southern French Alps, Serre-Chevalier and Montgenèvre are ideal bases for day tripping. They are within easy reach of one another, and Montgenèvre is at one end of the Milky Way lift network, which includes Sauze d'Oulx and Sestriere in Italy – you can drive on to these resorts, or reach them by lift and piste. On the French side of the border, a few miles south, Vars/Risoul is an underrated area that is well worth a visit for a day. The major resorts of Alpe-d'Huez and Les Deux-Alpes are also within range, as is the cult off-piste resort of La Grave. Getting to them involves crossing the high Col du Lautaret, but it's a major through-route and is not allowed to close for very long in normal winter conditions.

The Chamonix valley is an ideal destination for day tripping. The Mont Blanc Unlimited lift pass covers all the Chamonix areas, plus Courmayeur in Italy (easily reached through the Mont Blanc tunnel) and Verbier in Switzerland (a bit of a trek, even if the intervening passes are open). Megève and Les Contamines are close by, and Flaine and its satellites are fairly accessible. You could stay in a valley town such as Cluses, to escape resort prices – but Chamonix itself is not a wildly expensive town.

In the Tarentaise region, Bourg-St-Maurice is an excellent base for visiting several resorts – Les Arcs is accessible by funicular, and La Plagne is of course linked to Les Arcs. La Rosière is only a short drive away, with a link to La Thuile. Ste-Foy is just up the valley. And at the end of the valley are Val d'Isère and Tignes. We had a great week skiing all of these resorts from a comfortable apartment based in Bourg a couple of seasons ago.

MOVING ON

An alternative approach in the Tarentaise region if you want to include the famous Trois Vallées area is to stay in a series of different resorts for a day or two each, moving on from one to the next in the early evening; this way, you could have the trip of a lifetime (and save a lot on après-ski beers).

GETTING THERE

There are three 'gateways' to the different regions of the French Alps. For the northern Alps – Chamonix valley, Portes du Soleil, Flaine and neighbours – you want to head for Geneva. If coming from Calais or another short-crossing port, you no longer have to tangle with the busy A6 from Paris via Beaune to Mâcon and Lyon. The relatively new A39 autoroute south from Dijon means you can head for Bourg-en-Bresse, well east of Mâcon. For the central Alps – the mega-resorts of the Tarentaise, from Valmorel to Val d'Isère, and the Maurienne valley – you want to head for Chambéry. For the southern Alps – Alpe-d'Huez, Les Deux-Alpes, Serre-Chevalier – you want to head for Grenoble. And for either of these gateways first head for Mâcon and turn left at Lyon.

If you are taking a short Channel crossing, there are plenty of characterful towns for an overnight stop between the Channel and Dijon – Arras (our favourite), St-Quentin, Laon, Troyes, Reims. All have plenty of choice of budget chain hotels, some of them in central locations where you can easily enjoy the facilities of the town (ie the brasseries), others on bleak commercial estates on the outskirts, where at least you can hope to find the compensation of extremely low room rates.

From the more westerly Channel ports of Le Havre or Caen, your route to Geneva or Mâcon sounds dead simple: take the A13 to Paris then the A6 south. But you have to get through or around Paris in the process. The most direct way around the city is the notorious périphérique – a hectic, multi-lane urban motorway close to the centre, with exits every few hundred yards and traffic that is either worryingly fast-moving or jammed solid. If the périphérique is jammed, getting round it takes ages. The more reliable alternative is to take a series of motorways and dual carriageways through the south-west fringes of Greater Paris. The route is not well signed, so it's a great help to have a competent navigator – though it's not as tricky as it once was.

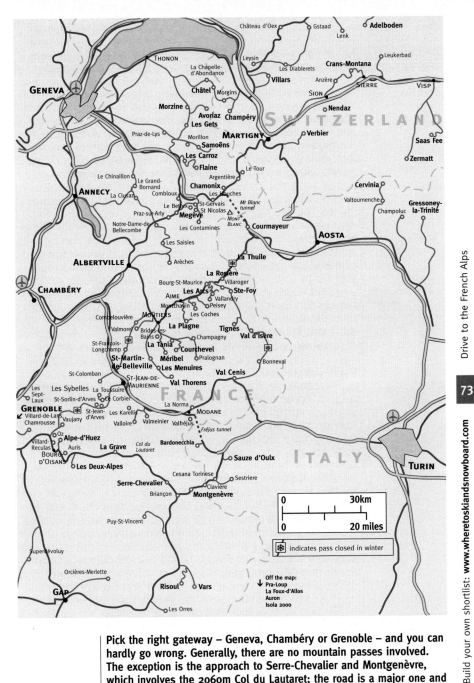

Drive to the French Alps

Build your own shortlist: www.wheretoskiandsnowboard.com

Château d'Oex · Gstaad · Lenk · **Adelboden**

THONON · Leysin · Les Diablerets · **Crans-Montana** · Leukerbad

La Chapelle-d'Abondance · Villars · Anzère · SION · SIERRE · VISP

GENEVA · Châtel · Morgins · Morzine · Avoriaz · Champéry · Nendaz

Les Gets · Praz-de-Lys · Morillon · **MARTIGNY** · Verbier · **Saas Fee**

Samoëns · Les Carroz · SWITZERLAND

Flaine · Le Tour · **Zermatt**

Le Chinaillon · Le Grand-Bornand · Argentière · Cervinia

ANNECY · La Clusaz · Combloux · Chamonix · Les Houches · Valtournenche · Gressoney-la-Trinité

Le Bettex · St-Gervais · Mt Blanc tunnel · Champoluc

Praz-sur-Arly · Megève · St Nicolas · MONT BLANC

Notre-Dame-de-Bellecombe · Les Contamines · Courmayeur · **AOSTA**

Les Saisies · La Thuile

ALBERTVILLE · Arèches · La Rosière

Bourg-St-Maurice · Villaroger

CHAMBÉRY · Les Arcs · Ste-Foy

AIME · Vallandry · Peisey

Combelouvière · Montchavin · Les Coches

MOÛTIERS · La Plagne · Tignes

Valmorel · Brides-les-Bains · Champagny · Val d'Isère

St-François-Longchamp · La Tania · Courchevel

St-Martin-de-Belleville · Méribel · Pralognan · Bonneval

St-Colomban · Les Menuires · Val Cenis

Les Sybelles · La Toussuire · ST-JEAN-DE-MAURIENNE · Val Thorens

Les Sept-Laux · St-Sorlin-d'Arves · Le Corbier · La Norma · FRANCE

GRENOBLE · St-Jean-d'Arves · Les Karellis · MODANE

Villard-de-Lans · Vaujany · Valloire · Valmeinier · Valfréjus · Fréjus tunnel

Chamrousse · Villard-Reculas · Oz · Alpe-d'Huez · Auris · Col du Lautaret · Bardonecchia

BOURG D'OISANS · La Grave · Sauze d'Oulx · ITALY · **TURIN**

Les Deux-Alpes · Cesana Torinese · Sestriere

Serre-Chevalier · Claviere

Briançon · Montgenèvre

Puy-St-Vincent

0		30km
0		20 miles

✳ indicates pass closed in winter

Superdévoluy

Orcières-Merlette

Off the map:
↓ Pra-Loup
La Foux-d'Allos
Auron
Isola 2000

GAP · Risoul · Vars · Les Orres

Pick the right gateway – Geneva, Chambéry or Grenoble – and you can hardly go wrong. Generally, there are no mountain passes involved. The exception is the approach to Serre-Chevalier and Montgenèvre, which involves the 2060m Col du Lautaret; the road is a major one and is ploughed frequently, but we felt the need for chains here on one occasion. Crossing the French–Swiss border between Chamonix and Verbier involves two closure-prone passes – the Montets and the Forclaz. When necessary, one-way traffic runs beside the tracks through the rail tunnel beneath the passes.

Most people get to go skiing or boarding only once or twice a year, so choosing the right resort is crucially important. Chamonix, Châtel and Courchevel are all French resorts, but they are as similar as Cheddar and Camembert. Consider resorts in other countries – Kitzbühel in Austria, say, or Zermatt in Switzerland – and the differences become even more pronounced. For readers with limited experience of different resorts, here is some advice on how to use our information.

Lots of factors need to be taken into account when making your choice. The weight you attach to each of them depends on your own personal preferences, and on the make-up of the group you are going on holiday with. Starting on page 83 you'll find about 20 shortlists of resorts that we rate as outstanding in various key respects. And by now we hope you'll be able to build your own shortlist by going to www.wheretoskiandsnowboard.com.

Minor resorts and regions not widely known in the UK are described in short chapters of two or three pages. Major resorts get more detail, and more pages. Each resort chapter is organized in the same way. This short introduction takes you through the structure and explains what you will find under each heading we use.

GETTING A FEEL FOR THE PLACE

We start each chapter with a two-line verdict, in which we aim to sum up the resort in a few words. If you like the sound of it, you might want to go next to our unique Resort Price Index (RPI), in the margin. Explained fully in the chapter on page 31, this tells you how expensive the resort is, taking account of the prices of lift passes, private lessons, ski hire and simple lunches and drinks; figures around the euro-zone average of 100 are presented in blue, low ones of 90 or less are in green, high ones of 120 or more are in red. The figures that go into the RPI calculation are listed, too.

Then, in the 'Ratings' section, we rate each resort from various points of view – the more stars the better. Longer chapters have a set of 19 ratings, but in shorter chapters we have room for only the 10 most important. Following this chapter, these 10 ratings are set out for all resorts in one chart, so that you can easily track down resorts that might suit you. Still looking at the margin information, in most chapters we have a 'News' section; this is likely to be of most use and interest in resorts you already know from past visits.

The next thing to look at is our list of the main good and bad points about the resort and its slopes, picked out with ➕ and ➖. This is followed by a summary in **bold type**, in which we've aimed to weigh up the pros and cons, coming off the fence and giving our view of who might like the resort. These sections should give you a good idea of whether the resort is likely to suit *you*, and whether it's worth reading our detailed analysis of it.

You'll know by now, for example, whether this is a high, hideous, convenient, purpose-built resort with superb, snow-sure, challenging slopes but absolutely no nightlife; or a pretty, traditional village with gentle wooded slopes, ideal for beginners on the rare occasions when it has some decent snow.

THE RESORT

In this first section of each chapter, we try to sort out the character of the place for you. Later, in the 'Staying there' section, we tell you more about the hotels, restaurants, bars and so on. Resorts vary enormously in some key respects and we have separate sections for each of the following headings. These match our star ratings.

Village charm At the extremes of the range are the handful of really hideous modern apartment-block resorts thrown up in France in the 1960s, and the ancient, captivating mountain villages of which Switzerland has an unfair number. But it isn't simply a question of old versus new. Some purpose-built places can have a much friendlier feel than some long-established resorts with big blocky buildings. Some places are working towns. Some are full of bars, discos and shops; others are peaceful backwaters. Traffic may choke the streets; or the village may be traffic-free.

Convenience This means how easy it is to get around the resort once you are there (not how easy the resort is to get to from the UK). Some places can be remarkably strung out, whereas others are surprisingly compact; our village plans are drawn to a standard scale, to help you gauge this. And of course proximity of lodgings to pistes determines how much walking or bussing you do.

Scenery Mountains are of course generally scenic, but there are differences, from the routinely hilly Colorado to the jaw-droppingly marvellous scenery of the Italian Dolomites and the Swiss Jungfrau region, to name two favourites.

THE MOUNTAINS

Extent of slopes Some mountains and lift networks are vast and complex, while others are much smaller and lacking variety. This year we have a special feature about this aspect on page 28.

Fast lifts Gondolas and fast chairlifts travel at three times the speed of slow chairlifts – cable cars and funicular railways even faster; these lifts offer short ride times, and most also shift queues quickly. We summarize the kinds of lifts you'll spend your time on. On our piste maps, we use a chair symbol to identify only fast chairs; lifts not marked with a symbol are slow chairs or draglifts.

Queues Monster queues are largely a thing of the past, but it still pays to avoid the resorts with the worst queues, especially in high season. Crowding on the pistes is more of a worry in many resorts, and we mention problems of this kind under this heading.

Terrain parks We summarize here the specially prepared fun parks and other terrain features most resorts now arrange for freestylers.

Snow reliability This is a crucial factor for many people, and one that varies enormously. In some resorts you don't have to worry at all about a lack of snow, while others are notorious for treating their paying guests to ice, mud and slush. Whether a resort is likely to have decent snow on its slopes normally depends on the height, the orientation of most of the slopes (north-facing good, south and west facing bad), its snow record and how much snowmaking it has. But bear in mind that in the Alps, high resorts tend to have rocky terrain, where the runs will need more snow than those on the pasture land of lower resorts. In the 'Key facts' section we list the latest amount of snowmaking the resorts claim to have, and comment on it in the snow reliability text.

For experts, intermediates, beginners Most (though not all) resorts have something to offer beginners, but relatively few will keep an expert happy for a week's holiday. As for intermediates, whether a resort will suit you really depends on your skill and inclinations. Places such as Cervinia and Obergurgl are ideal for those who want easy cruising runs, but have little to offer intermediates looking for more challenge. Others, such as Sölden and Val d'Isère, may intimidate the less confident intermediate. Some areas linking several resorts, such as the Trois Vallées and Portes du Soleil, have vast amounts of terrain, so you can cover different ground each day. But some other well-known names, such as Mürren and Courmayeur, have surprisingly small areas.

For boarders In earlier editions we had a special panel in longer chapters but we now deal with boarders' requirements in the main text, commenting on things like flat areas (bad) and the main types of lifts – gondolas, cable cars and chairs (all good) or draglifts (bad).

For cross-country We don't pretend that this is a guide for avid cross-country skiers. But we do try to help.

Mountain restaurants Here's a subject that divides people clearly into two opposing camps. To some, having a decent lunch served at your table in civilized surroundings – either in the sun, contemplating amazing scenery, or in a cosy hut, sheltered from the elements – makes or breaks the holiday. Others regard a long midday stop as a waste of valuable skiing time, as well as valuable spending money. We are firmly in the former camp. We get very disheartened by places with miserable restaurants and miserable food (eg many resorts in America); and there are some resorts that we go to partly because of the cosy huts and the food (eg Zermatt).

Schools and guides This is an area where we rely heavily on readers' reports of their own or their friends' experiences.

For families We sum up the merits of the resort, where possible evaluating the childcare arrangements. Again, to be of real help we need first-hand reports from people whose children have actually used the facilities.

STAYING THERE

Chalets, hotels, apartments Some resorts have few hotels or few catered chalets. Note that we also have feature chapters on notably good chalets and apartments. If there are interesting options for staying in isolation on the slopes above the resort village, or in valley towns below it, we pick them out at the end of this section.

Eating out The range of restaurants varies widely. Even some big resorts have little choice because most visitors dine in their apartments or hotels. Most American resorts offer lots of choice.

Après-ski Tastes and styles vary enormously. Most resorts have pleasant places in which to have an immediate post-skiing beer or hot chocolate. Some then go dead. Others have noisy bars and discos until the early hours.

Off the slopes This is largely aimed at assessing how suitable a resort is for someone who doesn't intend to use the slopes, such as a non-skiing spouse. But of course it is also of interest to anyone who wants some variety of evening entertainment.

Resort ratings at a glance

The RPI figures in the second row for each resort are our Resort Price Index figures, based on a comparison of the costs of food and drink, lift pass, ski hire and a private ski lesson. An average eurozone resort has an RPI of 100.

ANDORRA | AUSTRIA

	Arinsal	Soldeu		Bad Gastein	Ellmau	Hintertux / Tux valley	Ischgl	
Page	90	92		104	107	110	116	
RPI	95	115		100	90	90	110	
Extent	*	***		***	****	***	****	
Fast lifts	**	**		***	****	***	*****	
Queues	***	***		***	****	***	****	
Snow	****	***		***	**	*****	****	
Expert	*	**		***	*	***	****	
Intermediate	**	****		****	****	***	****	
Beginner	****	****		**	****	**	**	
Charm	*	*		***	***	**	***	
Convenience	***	***		**	***	**	***	
Scenery	***	***		***	***	***	***	

	Kitzbühel	Lech	Mayrhofen	Obergurgl	Obertauern	Rauris	Saalbach-Hinterg'm	
Page	123	131	140	146	152	155	158	
RPI	105	125	90	115	100	85	100	
Extent	***	***	***	**	**	*	***	
Fast lifts	*****	****	****	*****	*****	***	*****	
Queues	***	****	*	*****	****	****	****	
Snow	**	****	***	*****	****	***	**	
Expert	***	****	**	**	***	**	**	
Intermediate	****	****	***	***	****	***	****	
Beginner	**	****	**	****	****	***	***	
Charm	****	****	***	****	**	***	****	
Convenience	**	***	*	****	****	***	****	
Scenery	***	***	***	***	***	***	***	

	Schladming	Sölden	Söll	St Anton	Stubai valley	Zell am See	
Page	164	168	173	180	189	198	
RPI	95	105	90	115	105	95	
Extent	***	***	****	***	***	**	
Fast lifts	****	****	****	***	**a*	****	
Queues	****	***	***	***	***	***	
Snow	****	*****	**	****	*****	**	
Expert	**	***	*	*****	***	**	
Intermediate	****	****	****	***	***	***	
Beginner	***	***	**	*	**	***	
Charm	***	**	***	****	****	****	
Convenience	***	**	**	***	**	***	
Scenery	***	***	***	***	****	***	

78

The RPI figures

The figures in the second row for each resort are our Resort Price Index figures, based on a comparison of the costs of food and drink, lift pass, ski hire and a private ski lesson. An average eurozone resort has an RPI of 100.

FRANCE

	Alpe-d'Huez	Les Arcs	Avoriaz	Les Carroz	Chamonix	Chatel	Courchevel
Page	206	216	226	231	233	243	248
RPI	105	105	105	95	110	100	135
Extent	****	***	*****	****	***	*****	*****
Fast lifts	****	****	****	***	***	**	****
Queues	****	***	***	***	**	***	****
Snow	****	****	***	***	****	**	****
Expert	****	*****	***	****	*****	***	****
Intermediate	****	****	****	*****	**	****	*****
Beginner	*****	***	****	****	**	***	****
Charm	**	**	**	****	****	***	**
Convenience	***	****	*****	***	*	**	****
Scenery	****	***	***	****	*****	***	***

	Les Deux-Alpes	Flaine	Les Gets	La Grave	Megeve	Les Menuires	Meribel
Page	258	264	270	272	274	281	287
RPI	95	100	100	95	100	105	125
Extent	***	****	*****	*	*****	*****	*****
Fast lifts	****	***	***		**	****	*****
Queues	**	***	***	****	****	****	****
Snow	****	****	**	***	**	****	***
Expert	****	****	***	*****	**	****	****
Intermediate	**	*****	****	*	****	*****	*****
Beginner	***	*****	****	*	***	***	****
Charm	**	*	****	***	****	**	***
Convenience	***	*****	***	***	**	*****	***
Scenery	****	****	***	****	*****	***	***

	M'tgenevre	Morzine	La Plagne	La Rosiere	Samoens	Serre-Chevalier	Ste-Foy-Tarentaise
Page	297	302	310	325	329	331	341
RPI	90	100	110	95	95	95	85
Extent	**	*****	****	***	****	****	*
Fast lifts	**	***	**	**	***	***	****
Queues	****	***	**	****	****	***	*****
Snow	****	**	****	***	***	***	***
Expert	****	***	****	**	****	***	****
Intermediate	****	****	*****	***	*****	****	***
Beginner	*****	***	****	*****	**	****	**
Charm	***	***	**	***	****	***	***
Convenience	***	**	*****	***	*	***	****
Scenery	***	***	***	****	****	***	***

Want to see the full set?

Major resort chapters in the book have an additional nine ratings shown at the start of each chapter. And you can see the full set of ratings for 200+ resorts on our website.

www.wheretoskiandsnowboard.com

	St-Martin-de-B'ville	La Tania	Tignes	Val Cenis Vanoise	Val d'Isere	Val Thorens	Vars / Risoul
Page	344	347	351	363	366	376	383
RPI	105	115	110	80	110	110	90
Extent	*****	*****	*****	***	*****	*****	***
Fast lifts	****	****	***	***	****	*****	*
Queues	****	****	****	****	****	****	****
Snow	***	***	*****	***	*****	*****	***
Expert	****	****	*****	**	*****	****	**
Intermediate	*****	*****	*****	****	*****	*****	****
Beginner	**	***	**	****	***	****	****
Charm	****	***	*	***	***	**	**
Convenience	***	****	****	***	***	*****	****
Scenery	***	***	***	***	***	***	***

GERMANY   ITALY

	Garmisch-Partenk'n	Cervinia	Cortina d'Ampezzo	Courmayeur	Livigno	Madonna di Campiglio
Page	388	395	401	406	411	415
RPI	85	95	115	95	90	100
Extent	*	***	**	*	**	***
Fast lifts	***	****	***	****	****	****
Queues	***	****	****	****	****	****
Snow	***	*****	***	****	****	***
Expert	****	*	**	***	***	**
Intermediate	***	****	***	****	***	****
Beginner	*	*****	*****	*	****	***
Charm	***	**	****	****	***	****
Convenience	**	***	*	*	**	***
Scenery	****	****	*****	****	***	****

	Monterosa Ski	Passo Tonale	Sauze d'Oulx	Sella Ronda	Selva / Val Gardena	Sestriere	La Thuile
Page	420	426	428	433	442	449	451
RPI	85	75	85	105	105	90	90
Extent	**	**	****	*****	*****	****	***
Fast lifts	*****	****	***	****	****	***	***
Queues	****	****	***	***	***	***	*****
Snow	****	****	**	****	****	****	****
Expert	****	*	**	**	***	***	**
Intermediate	****	***	****	*****	*****	****	****
Beginner	**	*****	*	****	***	***	****
Charm	***	**	**	***	***	*	***
Convenience	***	***	**	***	***	***	***
Scenery	****	***	***	*****	*****	***	***

The RPI figures

The figures in the second row for each resort are our Resort Price Index figures, based on a comparison of the costs of food and drink, lift pass, ski hire and a private ski lesson. An average eurozone resort has an RPI of 100.

SWITZERLAND

	Adelboden	Andermatt	Champery	Crans-Montana	Davos	Engelberg		
Page	460	463	465	468	470	477		
RPI	125	115	125	140	135	120		
Extent	***	**	*****	***	****	**		
Fast lifts	***	**	*	****	****	***		
Queues	***	**	****	***	***	**		
Snow	***	****	**	**	****	***		
Expert	**	****	***	**	****	****		
Intermediate	***	**	****	****	*****	***		
Beginner	****	*	**	***	**	**		
Charm	****	****	****	**	**	**		
Convenience	**	***	*	**	**	*		
Scenery	****	***	****	****	****	****		

	Grindelw'd	Klosters	Laax	Mürren	Saas-Fee	St Moritz		
Page	479	483	485	488	492	497		
RPI	125	130	130	125	135	155		
Extent	***	****	****	*	**	*****		
Fast lifts	****	**	*****	*****	****	****		
Queues	**	**	****	***	****	***		
Snow	**	****	***	***	*****	****		
Expert	**	****	***	***	**	****		
Intermediate	****	*****	*****	***	****	****		
Beginner	***	***	****	***	*****	**		
Charm	****	****	***	*****	*****	**		
Convenience	**	**	***	***	**	*		
Scenery	*****	****	***	*****	****	****		

	Val d'Anniviers	Verbier	Villars	Wengen	Zermatt			
Page	504	508	519	521	526			
RPI	115	140	120	125	140			
Extent	**	*****	***	***	****			
Fast lifts	*	****	**	****	*****			
Queues	****	***	***	***	***			
Snow	****	***	**	**	****			
Expert	****	*****	**	**	****			
Intermediate	***	***	***	****	****			
Beginner	***	**	****	***	**			
Charm	*****	***	***	*****	****			
Convenience	**	**	**	***	**			
Scenery	****	****	***	*****	*****			

Want a shortlist shortcut?

Our website will build a shortlist for you: you specify your priorities, and the system will use our resort ratings to draw up a shortlist – confined to one area or country, if you like.
www.wheretoskiandsnowboard.com

USA

	CALIFORNIA HEAVENLY	MAMMOTH MOUNTAIN	SQUAW VALLEY	COLORADO ASPEN	BEAVER CREEK	BRECKENR'GE	SNOWMASS
Page	541	546	551	554	561	563	568
RPI	165	160	150	190	180	165	190
Extent	★★★	★★★	★★★	★★	★★★	★★★	★★★
Fast lifts	★★★★	★★★★	★★★	★★★★	★★★★★	★★★★	★★★★★
Queues	★★★★	★★★★	★★★★	★★★★	★★★★★	★★★★	★★★★
Snow	★★★★	★★★★	★★★★	★★★★★	★★★★★	★★★★★	★★★★★
Expert	★★★	★★★★	★★★★	★★★★★	★★★★	★★★★	★★★★★
Intermediate	★★★★	★★★★	★★	★★★★★	★★★★	★★★★	★★★★★
Beginner	★★★★	★★★★	★★★★	★★★★★	★★★★★	★★★★★	★★★★★
Charm	★	★★	★★★	★★★★	★★	★★★	★★
Convenience	★	★★	★★★★	★★	★★★★	★★★	★★★★
Scenery	★★★★	★★★	★★★	★★★	★★★	★★★	★★★★

	VAIL	WINTER PARK	UTAH ALTA	CANYONS	DEER VALLEY	PARK CITY	SNOWBIRD
Page	570	577	582	584	586	588	593
RPI	180	145	155	170	175	170	155
Extent	★★★★	★★★	★★★	★★★	★★	★★★	★★★
Fast lifts	★★★★★	★★★★	★★★★	★★★	★★★★	★★★	★★★★★
Queues	★★	★★★★	★★★	★★★★	★★★★	★★★★	★★★
Snow	★★★★★	★★★★★	★★★★★	★★★★	★★★★	★★★★	★★★★★
Expert	★★★★	★★★★	★★★★★	★★★★	★★★	★★★★	★★★★★
Intermediate	★★★★★	★★★★	★★★	★★★★	★★★★	★★★★	★★★
Beginner	★★★	★★★★★	★★★	★★	★★★★	★★★★	★★
Charm	★★★	★★	★★	★★	★★★	★★★	★
Convenience	★★★	★★★	★★★★	★★★★	★★★★	★★	★★★★★
Scenery	★★★	★★★	★★★	★★★	★★★	★★★	★★★

	REST OF THE WEST BIG SKY	JACKSON HOLE					
Page	596	601					
RPI	155	160					
Extent	★★★★	★★★					
Fast lifts	★★	★★★★					
Queues	★★★★★	★★★					
Snow	★★★★★	★★★★					
Expert	★★★★	★★★★★					
Intermediate	★★★★	★★					
Beginner	★★★★★	★★★					
Charm	★★	★★★					
Convenience	★★★★	★★★★					
Scenery	★★★	★★★					

CANADA

	Banff	Big White	Fernie	Kicking Horse	Lake Louise
Page	612	618	621	627	629
RPI	160	145	155	155	165
Extent	***	***	***	***	***
Fast lifts	****	****	**	***	****
Queues	****	*****	****	****	****
Snow	****	*****	****	****	***
Expert	****	***	*****	****	****
Intermediate	****	****	**	**	****
Beginner	***	****	****	***	***
Charm	***	**	**	**	***
Convenience	*	****	****	****	*
Scenery	****	***	***	***	****

	Revelstoke	Silver Star	Sun Peaks	Whistler
Page	634	637	639	641
RPI	150	145	150	170
Extent	***	***	***	****
Fast lifts	*****	****	**	*****
Queues	*****	*****	*****	**
Snow	****	****	****	****
Expert	*****	****	***	*****
Intermediate	**	***	****	*****
Beginner	**	****	****	***
Charm	**	***	***	***
Convenience	***	*****	****	****
Scenery	****	***	***	***

To streamline the job of drawing up your own shortlist, here are some ready-made ones. Many lists we've confined to Europe, because North America has too many qualifying resorts (eg for beginners) or because they do things differently there, making comparisons between here and there invalid (eg for off-piste).

SOMETHING FOR EVERYONE
Everything from good nursery slopes to challenges for experts
Alpe-d'Huez, France 206
Les Arcs, France 216
Aspen, USA 554
Courchevel, France 248
Flaine, France 264
Mammoth Mountain, USA 546
Vail, USA 570
Val d'Isère, France 366
Whistler, Canada 641
Winter Park, USA 577

INTERNATIONAL OVERSIGHTS
Resorts that get less attention than they deserve
Alta, USA 582
Andermatt, Switzerland 463
Bad Gastein, Austria 104
Big Sky, USA 596
Laax, Switzerland 485
Monterosa Ski, Italy 420
Sella Ronda, Italy 433
Sölden, Austria 168
Val d'Anniviers, Switzerland 504
Vars / Risoul, France 383

HIGH-MILEAGE PISTE-BASHING
Extensive intermediate slopes with big, slick lift networks
Alpe-d'Huez, France 206
Les Arcs, France 216
Cervinia, Italy 395
Ellmau, Austria 107
Flaine, France 264
Kitzbühel, Austria 123
Laax, Switzerland 485
La Plagne, France 310
Portes du Soleil, France 321
Sella Ronda, Italy 433
Selva / Val Gardena, Italy 442
Söll, Austria 173
Tignes, France 351
Les Trois Vallées, France 361
Vail, USA 570
Val d'Isère, France 366
Whistler, Canada 641
Zermatt, Switzerland 526

RELIABLE SNOW IN THE ALPS
Alpine resorts where snow is rarely in short supply
Bregenzerwald, Austria 192
Cervinia, Italy 395
Chamonix, France 233
Courchevel, France 248
Les Deux-Alpes, France 258
Hintertux / Tux valley, Austria 110
Lech, Austria 131
Obergurgl, Austria 146
Obertauern, Austria 152
Saas-Fee, Switzerland 492
Sölden, Austria 168
Val d'Isère, France 366
Val Thorens, France 376
Zermatt, Switzerland 526

OFF-PISTE WONDERS
Alpine resorts where you can have the time of your life
Alpe-d'Huez, France 206
Andermatt, Switzerland 463
Chamonix, France 233
Davos, Switzerland 470
La Grave, France 272
Klosters, Switzerland 483
Lech, Austria 131
Monterosa Ski, Italy 420
St Anton, Austria 180
Tignes, France 351
Val d'Isère, France 366
Verbier, Switzerland 508

DRAMATIC SCENERY
Mountains that are spectacularly scenic as well as snowy
Chamonix, France 233
Cortina d'Ampezzo, Italy 401
Courmayeur, Italy 406
Grindelwald, Switzerland 479
Heavenly, USA 541
Lake Louise, Canada 629
Megève, France 274
Mürren, Switzerland 488
Sella Ronda, Italy 433
Selva / Val Gardena, Italy 442
St Moritz, Switzerland 497
Wengen, Switzerland 521
Zermatt, Switzerland 526

BACK-DOOR RESORTS
Cute little Alpine villages linked to big, bold ski areas
Les Brévières (Tignes), France 351
Champagny (La Plagne), France 310
Leogang (Saalbach), Austria 158
Montchavin (La Plagne), France 310
Peisey (Les Arcs), France 216
Le Pré (Les Arcs), France 216
Samoëns (Flaine), France 329
St-Martin (Trois Vallées), France 344
Stuben (St Anton), Austria 180
Vaujany (Alpe-d'Huez), France 206

VILLAGE CHARM
Traditional character – whether villages or towns
Aspen, USA 554
Champéry, Switzerland 465
Courmayeur, Italy 406
Les Gets, France 270
Kitzbühel, Austria 123
Lech, Austria 131
Megève, France 274
Mürren, Switzerland 488
Saas-Fee, Switzerland 492
Samoëns, France 329
Val d'Anniviers, Switzerland 504
Wengen, Switzerland 521
Zermatt, Switzerland 526

BLACK RUNS
Steep, mogully, lift-served slopes, protected from avalanche
Alta, USA 582
Andermatt, Switzerland 463
Aspen, USA 554
Beaver Creek, USA 561
Chamonix, France 233
Courchevel, France 248
Jackson Hole, USA 601
Snowbird, USA 593
Whistler, Canada 641
Winter Park, USA 577
Zermatt, Switzerland 526

POWDER PARADISES
Resorts with the snow and terrain for powder perfection
Alta, USA 582
Andermatt, Switzerland 463
Big Sky, USA 596
Big White, Canada 618
Fernie, Canada 621
La Grave, France 272
Jackson Hole, USA 601
Kicking Horse, Canada 627
Lech, Austria 131
Monterosa Ski, Italy 420
Revelstoke, Canada 634
Snowbird, USA 593
Ste-Foy-Tarentaise, France 341

CHOPAHOLICS
Resorts where you can have a day riding helicopters or cats
Aspen, USA 554
Courmayeur, Italy 406
Fernie, Canada 621
Lech, Austria 131
Monterosa Ski, Italy 420
Revelstoke, Canada 634
La Thuile, Italy 451
Verbier, Switzerland 508
Whistler, Canada 641
Zermatt, Switzerland 526

TOP TERRAIN PARKS
Alpine resorts with the best parks and pipes for freestyle thrills
Les Arcs, France 216
Avoriaz, France 226
Cervinia, Italy 395
Davos, Switzerland 470
Les Deux-Alpes, France 258
Ischgl, Austria 116
Laax, Switzerland 485
Lech, Austria 131
Livigno, Italy 411
Mayrhofen, Austria 140
Méribel, France 287
La Plagne, France 310
Saalbach-Hinterglemm, Austria 158
Saas-Fee, Switzerland 492
St Moritz, Switzerland 497

WEATHERPROOF SLOPES
Fairly snow-sure slopes if the sun shines, trees in case it doesn't
Les Arcs, France 216
Courchevel, France 248
Courmayeur, Italy 406
Laax, Switzerland 485
Schladming, Austria 164
Selva / Val Gardena, Italy 442
Serre-Chevalier, France 331
Sestriere, Italy 449
La Thuile, Italy 451

MOTORWAY CRUISING
Long, gentle, super-smooth pistes to bolster frail confidence
Les Arcs, France 216
Breckenridge, USA 563
Cervinia, Italy 395
Cortina d'Ampezzo, Italy 401
Courchevel, France 248
Megève, France 274
La Plagne, France 310
Snowmass, USA 568
La Thuile, Italy 451
Vail, USA 570

RESORTS FOR BEGINNERS
Gentle, snow-sure nursery slopes and easy long runs to progress to
Alpe-d'Huez, France 206
Cervinia, Italy 395
Courchevel, France 248
Flaine, France 264
Montgenèvre, France 297
Passo Tonale, Italy 426
La Plagne, France 310
La Rosière, France 325
Saas-Fee, Switzerland 492
Soldeu, Andorra 92

SPECIALLY FOR FAMILIES
Where you can easily find lodgings surrounded by snow
Les Arcs, France 216
Avoriaz, France 226
Flaine, France 264
Lech, Austria 131
Les Menuires, France 281
Montchavin, France 310
Mürren, Switzerland 488
La Plagne, France 310
La Rosière, France 325
Saas-Fee, Switzerland 492
Ste-Foy-Tarentaise, France 341
Vars / Risoul, France 383
Wengen, Switzerland 521

SNOW-SURE BUT SIMPATICO
High-rise slopes, but low-rise, traditional-style buildings
Andermatt, Switzerland 463
Arabba, Italy 433
Argentière, France 233
Ischgl, Austria 116
Lech, Austria 131
Monterosa Ski, Italy 420
Obergurgl, Austria 146
Saas-Fee, Switzerland 492
Sella Ronda, Italy 433
Val d'Anniviers, Switzerland 504
Zermatt, Switzerland 526

SPECIAL MOUNTAIN RESTAURANTS
Where satisfying lunches can add something extra to a holiday
Alpe-d'Huez, France 206
Cortina d'Ampezzo, Italy 401
Courmayeur, Italy 406
Kitzbühel, Austria 123
Megève, France 274
La Plagne, France 310
Saalbach-Hinterglemm, Austria 158
Sella Ronda, Italy 433
Selva / Val Gardena, Italy 442
Zermatt, Switzerland 526

MODERN CONVENIENCE
Plenty of slope-side lodgings where you can ski from the door
Les Arcs, France 216
Avoriaz, France 226
Courchevel, France 248
Flaine, France 264
Les Menuires, France 281
Obertauern, Austria 152
La Plagne, France 310
La Tania, France 347
Tignes, France 351
Val Thorens, France 376

LIVELY NIGHTLIFE
Where you'll have no difficulty finding somewhere to boogie
Chamonix, France 233
Ischgl, Austria 116
Kitzbühel, Austria 123
Mayrhofen, Austria 140
Méribel, France 287
Saalbach-Hinterglemm, Austria 158
Sauze d'Oulx, Italy 428
Sölden, Austria 168
St Anton, Austria 180
Val d'Isère, France 366
Verbier, Switzerland 508
Zermatt, Switzerland 526

OTHER AMUSEMENTS
Plenty to divert those not skiing or boarding
Bad Gastein, Austria 104
Chamonix, France 233
Cortina d'Ampezzo, Italy 401
Davos, Switzerland 470
Kitzbühel, Austria 123
Megève, France 274
St Moritz, Switzerland 497

AFFORDABLE FUN
Low in our RPI league table with good, reasonably extensive slopes
Ellmau, Austria 107
Mayrhofen, Austria 140
Monterosa Ski, Italy 420
Montgenèvre, France 297
La Rosière, France 325
Sauze d'Oulx, Italy 428
Schladming, Austria 164
Serre-Chevalier, France 331
Söll, Austria 173
La Thuile, Italy 451
Val Cenis Vanoise, France 363
Vars / Risoul, France 383

Our resort chapters

How to get the best out of them

FINDING A RESORT

The bulk of the book consists of the chapters listed on the facing page, devoted to individual major resorts, plus minor resorts that share the same lift system or pass. Sometimes we devote a chapter to an area not dominated by one resort – then we use the area name (eg Monterosa Ski in Italy, Stubai valley in Austria, Val d'Anniviers in Switzerland).

Chapters are grouped by country: first, the six major European countries (now including Germany); then the US and Canada (where resorts are grouped by states or regions); then minor European countries; and finally Japan. Within each group, resorts are ordered alphabetically. In Austria, the main skiing regions of Vorarlberg, the westernmost 'land', are dealt with under that name.

Short cuts to the resorts that might suit you are provided (on the pages preceding this one) by a table of comparative **star ratings** and a series of **shortlists** of resorts with particular merits.

At the back of the book is an **index** to the resort chapters, combined with a **directory** giving basic information on hundreds of other minor resorts. If the resort you are looking up is covered in a chapter devoted to a bigger resort, the page reference will be to the start of the chapter, not to the exact page on which the minor resort is described.

There's further guidance on using our information in the chapter 'Choosing your resort', on page 74 – designed to be helpful particularly to people with little or no experience of ski resorts, who may not appreciate how big the differences between one resort and another can be.

READING A RESORT CHAPTER

There are various standard items at the start of each resort chapter. In the left margin, **star ratings** summarize our view of the resort, including its suitability for different levels of skill. The more stars, the better. In major resort chapters we give an expanded set of 19 ratings. Then comes our **Resort Price Index** – explained in outline on the facing page and in detail in the feature chapter on page 31.

We give web addresses of the **tourist office** (in North America, the ski lift company) and phone numbers for recommended **hotels**. We give star ratings for hotels – either official ones or ones awarded by major tour operators. The UK tour operators offering **package holidays** in major resorts are listed in the chapter, along with those of minor resorts that are covered in the same chapter.

Our **mountain maps** show the resorts' own classification of runs. On some maps we show black diamonds to mark expert terrain without defined runs. We do not distinguish single-diamond terrain from the steeper double diamond.

We include on the map any lifts definitely expected to be in place for the coming season.

MAJOR LIFTS

On our piste maps we use the following symbols to identify **fast lifts**. Slow chairlifts do not get a chair symbol.

Ⓒ	fast chairlift
Ⓖ	gondola
ⒸⒼ	hybrid chondola
🚡	cable car
🚞	railway/funicular

THE WORLD'S BEST WINTER SPORTS RESORTS

To find a minor resort, or if you are not sure which country you should be looking under, consult the index/directory at the back of the book, which lists all resorts alphabetically.

RESORT PRICE INDEX BOXES

Our RPI figures show how prices in each resort compare with the average euro-zone resort, taking account of food and drink, lift pass, ski hire and lessons. RPIs around the average figure of 100 are in blue boxes. RPIs of 90 or less get a green box. RPIs of 120 or more get a red box. Our price survey is fully explained, and some of the results are summarized, in our chapter on 'Cutting your costs', on page 31.

RPI	90
RPI	100
RPI	120

Our resort chapters

87

Build your own shortlist: www.wheretoskiandsnowboard.com

Andorra

Andorra is a tiny, almost entirely mountainous state sandwiched between France and Spain. It has built its prosperity on the twin pillars of tax-haven status and low-cost tourism – particularly winter tourism, and particularly in the UK market. Andorra used to be seen primarily as a cheap and cheerful holiday destination, attracting singles and young couples looking for a good time in the duty-free bars and clubs, as well as learning to ski or snowboard. But the place has changed radically over the last 25 years and has tried to move upmarket.

LIFT PASSES

Ski Andorra
The Ski Andorra pass covers all Andorran areas and allows skiing at any single one of them each day: €204 for five non-consecutive days

Soldeu, the main resort, is no longer cheap. Our price survey shows it to be as expensive as many high-profile Alpine resorts that have much more appeal. And its popularity has fallen. According to the Crystal Ski Industry Report, a decade ago Andorra's share of the UK ski market was 14%; it has now settled at around 6.5%.

The main resorts – **Soldeu** and **Pas de la Casa** (which share the pretty extensive Grandvalira ski area) and **Arinsal** (linked to **Pal** to form a much more modest area) – are covered in the two chapters that follow this.

The other main ski area is **Arcalis**, tucked away at the head of a long valley with no accommodation at its base. For non-beginners it makes a very worthwhile day trip, particularly from Arinsal and Pal, with which it shares a lift pass. The terrain is varied and scenic, the slopes are usually deserted except at weekends, and the snow is usually the best in Andorra. There is excellent intermediate and beginner terrain, but what marks it out is the expert terrain, including lots of off-piste between the marked runs. 'A real jewel – the boarder in our group was in heaven,' said one reporter.

The capital, **Andorra la Vella**, is choked by traffic and fumes but worth a visit for its duty-free shopping and the splendid Caldea spa at Escaldes-Engordany, just outside the centre, with a fantastic array of pools, baths and treatments.

TOURIST OFFICES

Ski Andorra
www.skiandorra.ad
Arcalis
www.vallnord.com

GRANDVALIRA

← Soldeu in a nutshell: a roadside strip of big hotels facing steep, wooded slopes, with gentle, open runs above (the nursery slopes among them)

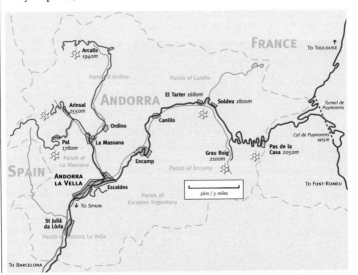

Arinsal

Lively budget base that suits beginners (thanks to an excellent school), with a cable car link to Pal to keep intermediates amused

TOP 10 RATINGS

Extent	★
Fast lifts	★★
Queues	★★★
Snow	★★★★
Expert	★
Intermediate	★★
Beginner	★★★★
Charm	★
Convenience	★★★
Scenery	★★★

RPI

	95
lift pass	£180
ski hire	£110
lessons	£75
food & drink	£120
total	**£485**

NEWS

2012/13: An area exclusively for families opened in the Pedres Blanques II zone of La Caubella in Pal.

VALLNORD

In a fine sunny spot, Far West is at the point where the Arinsal and Pal lift systems meet ↓

+ Lively bars

+ Ski school geared to British needs

+ Cable car link with Pal, and lift pass shared also with Arcalis

+ Pretty, treelined slopes in Pal

− Arinsal slopes are bleak and very confined (though this does mean children can't stray far)

− Linear, dour village with no focus

− Poor bus link to Arcalis

Tour operators are able to tempt British beginners here in large numbers. The Brit-oriented ski school must be the key factor; prices are no longer greatly different from those in more attractive Austrian and Italian resorts.

THE RESORT

Arinsal sits near the head of a steep-sided valley north of Andorra la Vella. Pal has a more open setting in another valley. The two are linked by cable car.

The valley town of La Massana is linked by gondola to Pal's slopes, and makes a better base for those wanting to spend some time at Arcalis (read the Andorra introduction). The Vallnord lift pass covers all of these areas.
Village charm The resort is a long, narrow village of grey, stone-clad buildings. It's no beauty, but the atmosphere is friendly and relaxed, the people 'very friendly and helpful'.
Convenience The village is compact; the main gondola starts from the centre; the alternative is a six-pack 1km away at Cota, with a piste to return. There are free buses linking the lift bases. You can leave kit at the top of the lift.
Scenery Shady valleys and nicely wooded slopes dominate.

THE MOUNTAINS

The slopes of Arinsal are in an open but extremely narrow bowl, facing east. Pal has the most densely wooded slopes in Andorra. Most face east; those down to the link with Arinsal face north. The piste map has lost the ridiculous sepia tint that it acquired some years back, but is still poor, covering distant Arcalis as well as Arinsal and Pal – nuts! Signposting is good though.
Slopes Arinsal's slopes consist essentially of a single, long, narrow bowl above the upper gondola station at Comallempla, served by a network of chairs and drags, including a quad and a six-pack. Almost at the top is the cable car link with Pal. Pal's slopes are widely spread around the mountain, with four main lift bases, all reachable by road. The main one, La Caubella, at the opposite extreme from the Arinsal link, is the arrival point of the gondola from La Massana.
Fast lifts Access is by gondola or fast chairlift. Other fast chairs exist, but there are still many slow lifts too.
Queues Reporters note few problems. But you may meet queues to ride the gondola down, and for the nursery moving carpets. The cable car link with Pal can be closed by high winds.
Terrain parks Arinsal's big freestyle area impressed one 2013 reporter; it has its own lift, rails and jumps, a boardercross, a beginner zone and a chill-out area.
Snow reliability With most runs above 1950m, the easterly orientation and a decent amount of snowmaking, snow is relatively assured. In 2011, for example, the pistes were 'kept in excellent shape', despite the prolonged drought. Grooming is good.

KEY FACTS

Resort	1475m
	4,840ft
Slopes	1550-2560m
	5,090-8,400ft
Lifts	31
Pistes	63km
	39 miles
Green	16%
Blue	36%
Red	38%
Black	10%
Snowmaking	
	296 guns

UK PACKAGES

Crystal, Inghams, Neilson, Skitracer, STC, Thomson

Phone numbers
From abroad use the prefix +376

TOURIST OFFICE

Arinsal and Pal
www.vallnord.com

Experts This isn't a great area for experts, but there is some off-piste around the pistes, and some good tree skiing in Pal. Arcalis has more to offer.

Intermediates Arinsal offers a fair range of difficulty, but competent intermediates will want to explore the much more interesting, varied and extensive Pal slopes, and perhaps make a day trip or two to Arcalis.

Beginners Around half the guests here are beginners. A special pass is available (15.50 euros per day), though we guess most people will book ski/pass/tuition packs from their tour operators. The wide, gentle nursery slopes set apart from the main runs are 'great, exactly what my beginner girlfriend needed'. They can get crowded, though. There are longer easy runs to progress to, as well.

Snowboarding It's a fine place to learn, but over half the lifts are drags and some of them are vicious. There are some flat sections in Pal.

Cross-country There isn't any.

Mountain restaurants These are mainly uninspiring self-service snackeries, and crowded. The Igloo does 'good hearty fare from a varied menu'.

Schools and guides The school is crucial to the appeal of the resort; over half the instructors are native English speakers. A 2013 reporter says: 'All instructors spoke good English and were helpful; rates were good and our daughter thoroughly enjoyed her sessions.'

Families There are themed ski kindergartens for four- to eight-year-olds and nurseries for children aged one to four at both Pal and Arinsal.

STAYING THERE

Hotels The Princesa Parc (736500) is a big, glossy 4-star place near the gondola – 'great value, excellent facilities'; swanky spa (open to non-residents) and a bowling alley. Rooms in the hotel Arinsal (838889) are not large, but the hotel is ideally placed and has a pleasant bar. The 3-star Crest (738020) is at the bottom of the run to Cota, handy for the fast chair up to the slopes – 'spacious apartment, perfectly good meals'. The Husa Xalet Verdú (737140) is a smooth little 3-star – 'great cost-effective base: good-sized room, friendly staff and decent food'. The Micolau (737707) is a characterful stone house near the centre with a jolly, beamed restaurant.

Apartments There is a reasonable choice of places.

Eating out The Surf disco-pub comes highly recommended for 'the best steaks ever'. The Sidreria Pub Herri serves traditional Basque food. Cisco's is a Tex-Mex place in a lovely wood and stone building.

Après-ski Arinsal has plenty of lively bars 'from full-on 18–30 drink fests to great family places'. The hotel Arinsal has good-value pints. The Derby Irish pub 'manages to do great live music and beer while being family-friendly'.

Off the slopes Activities include helicopter rides, dog sledding, snowmobiling, snowshoeing, tobogganing, snow bikes, ice-diving and paragliding. Andorra la Vella is half an hour away by taxi or infrequent bus: 'A shopper's paradise,' says a 2013 visitor.

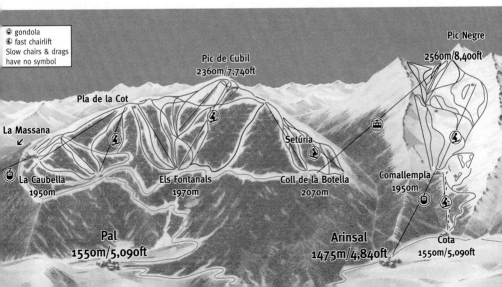

- ⓖ gondola
- ⓕ fast chairlift

Slow chairs & drags have no symbol

Pic Negre
2560m/8,400ft

Pic de Cubil
2360m/7,740ft

Pla de la Cot

La Massana

Setúria

La Caubella
1950m

Els Fontanals
1970m

Coll de la Botella
2070m

Comallempla
1950m

Pal
1550m/5,090ft

Arinsal
1475m/4,840ft

Cota
1550m/5,090ft

SNOWPIX.COM / CHRIS GILL

Soldeu

Our favourite place to stay in Andorra: not an attractive village, but centrally placed in the impressive Grandvalira ski area

RATINGS

The mountains

Extent	★★★
Fast lifts	★★
Queues	★★★
Terrain p'ks	★★★★
Snow	★★★
Expert	★★
Intermediate	★★★★
Beginner	★★★★
Boarder	★★★★
X-country	★
Restaurants	★★
Schools	★★★★★
Families	★★

The resort

Charm	★
Convenience	★★★
Scenery	★★★
Eating out	★★★
Après-ski	★★★★
Off-slope	★

RPI   115

lift pass	£210
ski hire	£150
lessons	£95
food & drink	£140
total	**£595**

NEWS

2013/14: The beginner area above Encamp is due to be further improved.

2012/13: The Aliga slope at El Tarter was revamped, and FIS-approved as a downhill race course. The El Tarter terrain park was expanded. More snow-guns were installed. In the Grau Roig sector, the El Clot lift and the cross-country circuit were improved. Two freeride areas were designated, and snowcat lifts were restored to the bowl below Encampadana. The beginner area at the top of the Encamp gondola got a new slope and lift.

+ Rivals some serious Alpine resorts in terms of size

+ Excellent beginner and early intermediate terrain

+ Ski school has excellent British-run section for English-speaking visitors

− Village is spread along a busy through-road, lacking atmosphere

− Slopes can get very crowded

− Expensive lift pass, and beginners are charged the full cost

− Not much to do off the slopes

If we were planning a holiday in Andorra, it would be in Soldeu (or the isolated hotel at Grau Roig, up the road). It is best placed to explore the extensive Grandvalira area. But the village is a difficult place to like, and beginners be warned: you are forced to buy one of Europe's most pricey passes.

THE RESORT

Soldeu is set on a steep hillside facing the ski area across the valley. It is on the busy road that runs down the valley from France to Andorra la Vella and on to Spain. The Grandvalira ski area is shared with several alternative bases. Chief among them is Pas de la Casa, near the French border; El Tarter, a few miles down the valley from Soldeu, also has both lifts and return pistes. Further down still, Canillo and Encamp have gondolas but no pistes. Outings to other resorts in Andorra are possible – Arcalis in particular is worth the trip, but it's easiest by car. The Ski Andorra pass covers them all.

VILLAGE CHARM ★
An urban ribbon
The village is an ever-growing ribbon of modern hotels, apartments and bars, with the occasional shop; the buildings have traditional stone cladding and mostly chalet-style roofs. Sounds OK, but it isn't; this is not a place to wander about at teatime – there is no focus or atmosphere, and traffic on the through-road can be heavy and sometimes fast.

CONVENIENCE ★★★
Over the river
A steep hillside leads down from the village to the river, and the slopes are on the opposite side. A gondola from village level or a six-pack takes you to the heart of the slopes at Espiolets, and a wide bridge across the river forms the end of the piste home, with elevators to take you up to street level. There are ski lockers at the bottom or top of the gondola. Along

the road down to El Tarter, hotels and apartments are sold by tour operators under the Soldeu banner – so check where your proposed accommodation is if you want to avoid long walks or lots of bus rides. There is a valley bus running fairly frequently.

SCENERY ★★★
Unremarkable
Soldeu sits in a long, quite attractively wooded valley, and from the slopes there are wide mountain views, but they don't include notable drama.

THE MOUNTAINS

Soldeu's main local slopes are on open mountainsides; there are runs in the woods back to Soldeu and El Tarter, but they can be challenging, especially when conditions are not particularly good. Reporters praise signposting, but classification of the runs often overstates difficulty. The piste map is very cramped.

EXTENT OF THE SLOPES ★★★
Pleasantly varied but crowded
The resort claims over 200km of pistes, but the Schrahe report (read our feature on piste extent) suggests that this is a bit of an exaggeration.

The village gondola rises over wooded, north-facing slopes to **Espiolets**, a broad shelf that is virtually a mini-resort – the ski school is based here, and there are extensive nursery slopes. From Espiolets, a gentle run to the east takes you to an area of long, easy runs served by a six-pack. Beyond that is an extensive area of more varied slopes that links with the Pas de la Casa area. Going west from

KEY FACTS

Resort	1800m
	5,910ft

Grandvalira (Soldeu/El Tarter/Pas/Grau Roig)	
Slopes	1710-2560m
	5,610-8,400ft
Lifts	62
Pistes	210km
	130 miles
Green	15%
Blue	38%
Red	28%
Black	19%
Snowmaking	60%

LIFT PASSES

Prices in €

Age	1-day	6-day
under 12	32	160
12 to 17	41	204
18 to 64	44	232
65 plus	23	138

Free Under 6, 70 plus
Beginner Pass €29 per day in Canillo, El Tarter, Grau Roig and Pas de la Casa
Notes Covers all lifts in Soldeu, El Tarter, Canillo, Grau Roig and Pas de la Casa; pedestrian and half-day passes available
Alternative pass The Ski Andorra pass covers all Andorran areas and allows skiing at any single one of them each day; €204 for five non-consecutive days

Espiolets takes you to the open bowl of **Riba Escorxada** and the arrival point of the gondola up from El Tarter. From here, another six-pack serves sunny slopes on Tosa dels Espiolets, and a fourth goes to the high point of Tossal de la Llosada and the link with **El Forn** above Canillo.

FAST LIFTS ★★☆☆☆
Fine access but ...
Most of Grandvalira's key lifts are high-speed chairs or gondolas, but there are a lot of slow lifts too.

QUEUES ★★★☆☆
Some bottlenecks
The lift system generally copes. There can be morning queues for the gondola, but the next-door chair offers a choice. Up the mountain, the chairlifts in both directions out of Grau Roig are the main bottleneck; the quad at Cubil and access to Tosa Espiolets are also 'awful', said a February visitor. You may find crowds on some blue slopes (including lots of school classes snaking along) – the reds and blacks are much quieter.

TERRAIN PARKS ★★★★☆
There are two
The main park – Snowpark El Tarter – above Riba Escorxada has a good reputation, and was extended last season. Features normally include a triple line of kickers, huge gap jump, jib and giant airbag. There's a great selection of rails, including a big rainbow rail and wave-box and two

wall rides. For beginners there are three small jumps, a 5m medium jump and a couple of fun boxes. A half-pipe is built when conditions permit. A draglift serves the park, and a fast quad nearby takes you slightly higher up. The Sunset Park Peretol, above Bordes d'Envalira, opened a couple of years ago and caters for all levels. It now has an intriguing 'street zone' that resembles a village square, they say. It is floodlit in the evenings, with music. A park-only day pass is available.

SNOW RELIABILITY ★★★☆☆
Much better than people expect
Despite its name (Soldeu means Sun God) the slopes generally enjoy reliable snow. Most slopes are north-facing, with a good natural snow record; there's extensive snowmaking, and excellent grooming helps maintain good snow – 'Snow machines and piste-bashers worked wonders,' said a 2012 reporter.

FOR EXPERTS ★★☆☆☆
Hope for good snow off-piste
It's a limited area for experts – on-piste, at least. The Avet black run going directly down to Soldeu deserves its grading, but most of the other blacks do not. The blacks on Tosa dels Espiolets, for example, are indistinguishable from the adjacent (and more direct) red and blue. And don't go looking for moguls – the grooming is too thorough. But there is plenty of off-piste potential, now

GRANDVALIRA

Espiolets, at the top of the gondola from central Soldeu, is a kind of mid-mountain mini-resort →

emphasized by identified freeride zones on the piste map, at Pic Blanc above Pas and in the bowl above Riba Escorxada. Here and above El Forn off-piste routes are shown dotted on the resort piste map and on ours. And we're pleased to hear that the liftless bowl between Riba Escorxada and El Forn is again being served by a snowcat tow. The off-piste remains untouched for days because most visitors are beginners and early intermediates. There's no explanation on the piste map of whether off-piste routes/freeride areas are avalanche controlled, marked or patrolled.

FOR INTERMEDIATES ★★★★
Lots to explore

There is plenty to amuse intermediates. The area east of Espiolets is splendid for building confidence, and those already confident will be able to explore the whole mountain. Riba Escorxada is a fine section for mixed-ability groups. The Canillo/El Forn sector has an easy, little-used blue run along the ridge with excellent views all the way to Pal and Arinsal and an easy black in the valley. Many of the blues and reds have short steeper sections, preceded

by a 'slow' sign and netting in the middle of the piste to slow you down.

FOR BEGINNERS ★★★★
Good, but not ideal

In some respects this is an excellent place to start, particularly because of the school. But it's not ideal: you have to go up the mountain to the nursery slopes, which is not only inconvenient but also expensive. There is no special beginner pass here (unlike other base villages in the area). If you buy a ski pack through your tour operator, you may not care, of course. Soldeu's Espiolets nursery area is vast, and there's a smaller area at Riba Escorxada, above El Tarter – each with a moving carpet. They are relatively snow-sure, and there are numerous easy pistes to move on to (though the crowds can be off-putting). The runs to resort level can be quite challenging because of crowds and snow conditions. Near-beginners are often better off riding a lift down.

FOR BOARDERS ★★★★
Pick of the Pyrenees

Soldeu has become the home of snowboarding in the Pyrenees. This is a perfect place for beginners to learn

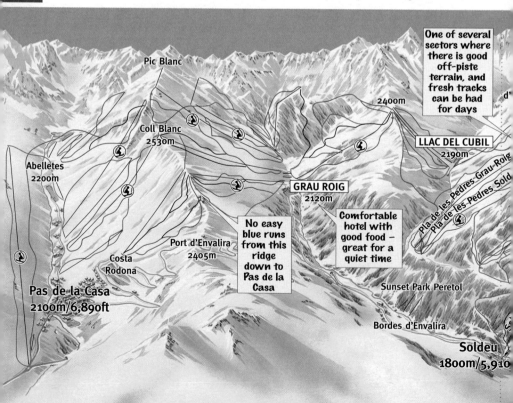

One of several sectors where there is good off-piste terrain, and fresh tracks can be had for days

Pic Blanc

2400m

Coll Blanc
2530m

LLAC DEL CUBIL
2190m

Abelletes
2200m

Pla de les Pedres Grau-Roig
Pla de les Pedres Sold

GRAU ROIG
2120m

Costa Rodona

Port d'Envalira
2405m

No easy blue runs from this ridge down to Pas de la Casa

Comfortable hotel with good food – great for a quiet time

Sunset Park Peretol

Pas de la Casa
2100m/6,890ft

Bordes d'Envalira

Soldeu
1800m/5,910

SCHOOLS

Soldeu
t 735191

Classes
5 3hr-days: from
€124

Private lessons
From €86 for 2hr

CHILDCARE

**Nurseries run by ski
school**
t 753191
Ages 1 to 4

**Snow gardens run by
ski school**
t 753191
Ages 3 to 6

Ski school
Ages 6 to 11

on wide, gentle slopes that are served mainly by chairs, not drags. Just be wary of the plentiful flat spots. For the more advanced, Soldeu offers some good off-piste and the best terrain parks in the Pyrenees. Backcountry enthusiasts should also visit Arcalis, which has the steepest terrain and heli-boarding, and Pal, for the tree runs. Loaded is a snowboard shop run by pro rider Tyler Chorlton.

FOR CROSS-COUNTRY ★★★★★
Head for Grau Roig
The nearest loops are at Grau Roig (read the Pas de la Casa section), reachable by bus.

MOUNTAIN RESTAURANTS ★★★★★
Not a highlight
Restaurants are marked but not named on the piste map. A recent reporter said bluntly: 'Poor – head to the village.' But an earlier reporter enjoyed 'really nice Catalan sausage, roast cod, beef shank and pasta' at various places. The table-service section of Arosseria Pi de Migdia at the top of the El Tarter gondola has been recommended. Not far away, the Riba Escorxada restaurant includes a trattoria-pizzeria with a neat little

terrace. At Espiolets, the Gall de Bosc (steakhouse) has table-service. But the best places are over towards Pas de la Casa – read that section. There is a picnic room at the Espiolets restaurant.

SCHOOLS AND GUIDES ★★★★★
One of the best for Brits
The school is well set up to deal with the huge numbers of beginner Brits, with a dedicated team of mostly native English-speaking instructors led by an Englishman. Reporters are almost all extremely positive (only one mildly dissenting voice in the last few years), and a 2012 visitor said the school was 'brilliant – catered for our mixed ability group well'.

FOR FAMILIES ★★★★★
Unconvincing
Soldeu doesn't strike us as a great place for families, with its busy through-road and remote nursery slopes. Whether skiing or not, children are looked after at the mid-mountain stations. There are nurseries and snow gardens for children aged three to six at various points, and a kids' circuit with themed runs at Riba Escorxada above El Tarter.

Soldeu

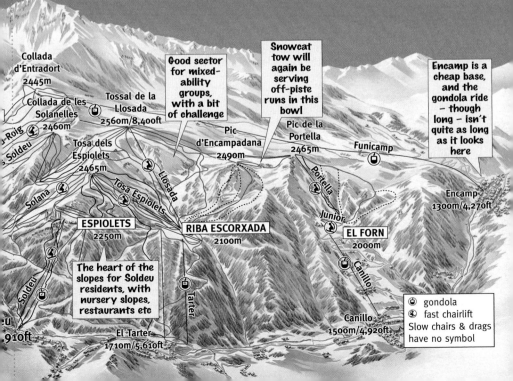

Collada d'Entradort 2445m

Collada de les Solanelles 2460m

Roig

Soldeu

Tosa dels Espiolets 2465m

Solana

Tossal de la Llosada 2560m/8,400ft

Tosa Espiolets

Llosada

Good sector for mixed-ability groups, with a bit of challenge

Pic d'Encampadana 2490m

Snowcat tow will again be serving off-piste runs in this bowl

Pic de la Portella 2465m

Portella

Funicamp

Encamp is a cheap base, and the gondola ride – though long – isn't quite as long as it looks here

Encamp 1300m/4,270ft

ESPIOLETS 2250m

The heart of the slopes for Soldeu residents, with nursery slopes, restaurants etc

Soldeu

U

910ft

RIBA ESCORXADA 2100m

Tarter

Junior

EL FORN 2000m

Canillo

Canillo 1500m/4,920ft

El Tarter 1710m/5,610ft

- ⓖ gondola
- ⓒ fast chairlift
- Slow chairs & drags have no symbol

↑ Llacs de Pessons above Grau Roig is our favourite place for lunch in the whole of Grandvalira; cosy inside on a bad day

GRANDVALIRA

ACTIVITIES

Indoor Spas, pools, hot tubs (in hotels), bowling (at Pas)

Outdoor Helicopter rides, paragliding snowmobiling, dog sledding, ice diving, snowshoeing (not all in Soldeu itself)

GETTING THERE

Air Toulouse 170km/110 miles (2hr45)

Rail L'Hospitalet-Près-L'Andorre (25km/ 16 miles); buses and taxis to Soldeu

UK PACKAGES

Soldeu Absolutely Snow, Crystal, Crystal Finest, Elegant Resorts, Inghams, Lagrange, Neilson, Skitracer, STC, Thomson, Zenith **El Tarter** Interactive Resorts, Neilson **Pas de la Casa** Absolutely Snow, Crystal, Independent Ski Links, Inghams, Lagrange, Neilson, Skitracer, Thomson, Zenith

STAYING THERE

Hotels Beware hotels sold under the Soldeu name that are actually some way out of town.

*****Sport Hotel Hermitage (870670) At the foot of the slopes; all bedrooms are suites with mountain views. A huge spa is part of the hotel.

****Euro Esquí (736666) On road to El Tarter but there is a shuttle. 'Large rooms and good buffet food.'

****Himàlaia (878515) Central, with sauna, steam and hot tub.

****Piolets Park (871787) Beside the gondola, with a pool and spa.

****Sport (870600) Over the road from the other two Sports. Lively, comfortable bar and disco-bar.

****Sport Hotel Village (870500) Right by the Hermitage. Stylish public areas – comfortable chairs and sofas, high ceilings, beams and picture windows.

**Bruxelles (851010) Recommended for its helpful staff and cleanliness; 50m from the lift.

EATING OUT ★★★☆☆
Some atmospheric places

Most of Soldeu's restaurants are hotel-based. But we've enjoyed meals in two atmospheric old restored buildings: Fat Albert's (steaks, fish, burgers) and Borda del Rector (Andorran cuisine), nearer to El Tarter than Soldeu.

APRES-SKI ★★★★☆
No shortage of live music

This traditionally lively resort generates conflicting reports. Some readers seem to have fun, enjoying live music at the Aspen ('great atmosphere') or at Fat Albert's.

OFF THE SLOPES ★☆☆☆☆
Head downhill

Soldeu has lots of sporting activities, including snowmobiling, dog sledding and ice scuba-diving, but is otherwise not great in this respect. The Sport Hotel Hermitage (pricey) and Piolets Park (cheaper) both have excellent spas. Down in Canillo is the Palau de Gel (see below). Andorra la Vella, the capital of Andorra, has good shopping and the Caldea spa – an amazing array of pools, baths and treatments.

LINKED RESORT – 1710m
EL TARTER

El Tarter has grown over recent years and is rather sprawling, with no real centre. It is quiet at night. But it's otherwise a good base for the area. There are two blue runs to the resort, and a black that is now an FIS-approved downhill race course.

LINKED RESORT – 1500m
CANILLO

This acceptably pleasant spot has no runs to valley level, but has a gondola up to El Forn. The impressive Palau de Gel has lots of diversions – an Olympic ice rink plus pool, gym, tennis etc.

LINKED RESORT – 1300m
ENCAMP

Encamp is a traffic-choked town with a long gondola to Cortals, one of the high points of the Soldeu slopes, where there is an improving beginner area, and onward pistes to Soldeu. There is no return piste.

Pas de la Casa 2100m

+ Some conveniently placed hotels
+ Andorra's liveliest nightlife
+ Attractive hotel at Grau Roig

- Village an eyesore and traffic-choked
- Weekend crowds from France
- Few trees for poor-weather days

Pas has the reputation as Andorra's wildest party resort, and we don't doubt it. Having driven through it and skied down to it, we are quite happy to stay over the hill in Soldeu – or, for doorstep access to the Grandvalira slopes, at secluded Grau Roig. So are you, it seems: reports are rarely sighted.

Village charm Pas is a sizeable collection of dreary concrete-box-style apartment blocks and hotels, a product of the late 1960s and early 1970s. The central area at the base of the slopes is traffic-free, but elsewhere traffic and fumes are intrusive. By contrast, the mini-resort of Grau Roig (pronounced 'Rosh') over the ridge from Pas has an isolated hotel in an attractively wooded setting.

Convenience Most accommodation is conveniently placed near the lift base and slopes. There are plenty of shops and bars, as well as a sports centre.

Scenery Pas has a bleak position near the top of a high mountain pass, but there are fine views from the ridges.

THE MOUNTAIN

Slopes The slopes above Pas are all open, and vulnerable to bad weather. But there is some attractively wooded terrain over the ridge in the Grau Roig valley. From there a single lift goes on further west to the rest of the Grandvalira ski area. In the opposite direction out of Pas, a six-pack serving two runs heads towards another ridge and the French border.

Fast lifts Fast chairs exist, but they are outnumbered by slow ones and drags.

Queues Queues are rarely serious during the week, except at key bottlenecks. But at weekends and French school holidays some can develop, especially at Grau Roig.

Terrain parks There's one on the Pas side, together with a boardercross, and another at Grau Roig.

Snow reliability The combination of height and lots of snowmaking means good snow reliability, but we've generally found snow quality to be better in the Soldeu sector.

Experts There are few challenges on-piste, but there seem to be plenty of off-piste slopes inviting exploration – above Grau Roig, in particular.

Intermediates The local slopes suit confident intermediates best – especially those over the ridge, above Grau Roig; more timid intermediates would be better off based in Soldeu.

Beginners There are beginner slopes in Pas and Grau Roig. The Pas area is a short but inconvenient bus ride out of town. Progression to longer runs is easier in the Grau Roig sector.

Snowboarding Boarding is popular with the young crowd that the resort attracts. Drags are usually avoidable.

Cross-country There are 13km of loops near Grau Roig.

Mountain restaurants The Rifugi dels Llacs de Pessons above Grau Roig at the head of the bowl is our favourite: a cosy, beamed table-service place with good local food. There's a photo on the facing page. The Grau Roig hotel is another good option.

Schools and guides The ski school has a high reputation, but a 2012 reporter complains of big classes ('16 in one').

Families There are ski kindergartens at Pas and Grau Roig, and a non-ski one at the latter.

STAYING THERE

Hotels Himàlaia-Pas (735515) is in a good position, with a pool and sauna. The Grau Roig hotel (755556) is in a league of its own; comfortable and smart, with a spa and 'lovely food'.

Apartments Those in the Frontera Blanca are simple, but in pole position at the foot of the slopes.

Eating out It's not a resort for gourmets – but there is a wide enough choice of places to eat. Local tips include Cal Padrí (Catalan food) and KSB (Kamikaze Surf Bar – steakhouse).

Après-ski Après-ski can be very lively, at least at peak holiday times. Popular places include Déjà Beer, a quirky pub with tapas and Wi-Fi, Paddy's Irish Bar and the Underground.

Off the slopes You can go dog sledding, snowmobiling and snowshoeing; otherwise there's visiting the leisure centre, shopping, or taking a trip to Andorra la Vella for more serious and stylish shopping and the impressive Caldea spa.

Central reservations phone number
Call 801074
Phone numbers
From abroad use the prefix +376

TOURIST OFFICE

www.grandvalira.com

Soldeu

Build your own shortlist: www.wheretoskiandsnowboard.com

SKI Bregenzerwald

SKI Bregenzerwald
Thanks to its location on the
northern edge of the Alps, an
above-average amount of snow
falls in the Bregenzerwald – in
the province of Vorarlberg.

**Easy to book your ski holidays –
SKI Bregenzerwald Package:**
4 nights' accommodation,
Sunday to Thursday or 3 nights'
accommodation, Thursday to
Sunday in the accommodation
category of your choice, plus
three-valley ski pass for three
days' varied skiing in all skiing
areas in the Bregenzerwald.

PRICE PER PERSON:
from € 287
in a double room with half-board
from € 215
in a double room with breakfast

BOOKING:
9 January – 6 April 2014
(excl. 27 February – 9 March 2014)

INFORMATION AND BOOKING:
Bregenzerwald Tourismus
T +43 (0)5512 2365
info@bregenzerwald.at
www.bregenzerwald.at/en

Further info on Vorarlberg
www.vorarlberg.travel/en   Austria

VOR
ARL
BERG

Austria

Austria's holiday recipe is quite distinctive. It doesn't suit everybody, but for many holidaymakers nothing else will do; in particular, French resorts will not do. Austria is the land of cute little valley villages clustered around onion-domed churches – there are no monstrous modern apartment blocks here. It's the land of prettily wooded mountains, reassuring to beginners and timid intermediates in a way that bleak snowfields and craggy peaks will never be. It's the land of friendly, welcoming people who speak good English. And it's the land of jolly, alcohol-fuelled après-ski action – in many resorts starting in mid-afternoon with dancing in mountain restaurants, and going on as long as you have the legs for it.

Back in the 1980s, Austria dominated the British skiing market. But gradually the powerful allure of the high, snow-sure French mega-resorts began to exert itself. By 1995 France had taken the lead, and it has kept it ever since. The pendulum is now swinging back: the annual Crystal Ski Industry Report shows that Austria's market share has risen over the last decade or so from 20% to 28%. But for the moment France is still well ahead, at over 34%.

There are three key factors in the revival: lift systems – these days, the most efficient lift systems in Europe are not in France but in Austria; snowmaking, which is now so widespread that you can expect reliable snow-cover even at the low altitudes typical of Austrian villages; and low on-the-spot prices. As our price survey shows, Austrian resorts are generally cheaper than the big French resorts that Brits tend to flock to – and a lot cheaper for eating and drinking.

Being the land of cute valley villages and friendly wooded mountains does have a downside: resorts that conform to this pattern are at low altitude, and as a result don't offer reliably good natural snow. Of course, you may be lucky – and recent seasons have included some bumper natural snow years for much of Austria. But the snowmaking is key; and most low resorts have radically improved their snowmaking in the last decade. In midwinter, especially, lack of snow generally coincides with low night-time temperatures, even at low altitudes, and snowmaking comes into its own. Of course, snow isn't simply a matter of covering the slopes: quality matters too, and it's still the case that low altitude tends to go hand in hand with slushy snow in the middle of the day and icy snow at the start and end of the day.

There are some resorts that don't conform to the Austrian pattern, including some excellent high-altitude ski areas – notably Obergurgl, Ischgl and Obertauern – and some excellent glacier areas, including what we reckon are the world's best, at Hintertux and in the Stubai valley. Western Austria also has areas that get huge amounts of snow – Lech/ Zürs and especially Bregenzerwald, the snowiest corner of the Alps.

THE WORLD'S BEST LIFT SYSTEMS

The improvement in Austrian lift systems over the last decade comes as a surprise to many people. When we invented our 'fast lifts' rating a few years back, we certainly got some surprises. The

Aided by unreasonably early closing of the lifts, many Austrian mountain restaurants go straight from lunch mode into après mode without missing a beat. This is a prime example – Obergurgl's Nederhütte →

SNOWPIX.COM / CHRIS GILL

resorts with the highest proportions of fast lifts in their networks are Saalbach-Hinterglemm and Ischgl, both in Austria. Obergurgl and Obertauern also get five stars. And all four have higher proportions than any other Alpine resort except Monterosa in Italy.

SKI ROUTE CONFUSION

In many resorts you have to deal with chaotic handling of the concept of 'ski routes'. If a resort's piste map explains what a ski route is (and many don't), it often says a ski route is a run that is marked and avalanche controlled but not groomed or patrolled. Officially, we are told, the rule throughout Austria is that a ski route is 'marked, protected against avalanche hazards and can be groomed and patrolled'. In practice, many routes are groomed; they may or may not be patrolled. This is madness. If such a run is groomed *and* patrolled, it is a piste, and should be identified as such so that people skiing solo can confidently go down it. If it is groomed *but not* patrolled, it opens up the insane possibility that people skiing solo might descend it by mistake.

THE PARTY STARTS EARLY

These days, one of the things that annoys us most about Austrian skiing is the strange business of opening hours or, strictly speaking, closing hours. As spring approaches, lift closing times in the rest of the Alps, even for some high-altitude cable cars, drift towards 5pm or even later. In Austria, basically things shut at around 4pm, even if there are three hours of daylight remaining. Nuts.

You're welcome to stay on the mountain drinking, and descend at leisure, and it has crossed our minds that the lift companies may be in the pay of the breweries. Instead of skiing on, people pack into mountain restaurants well before the end of the day and gyrate in their ski boots on the dance floor, on the tables, on the bar, on the roof beams. There are open-air ice bars, umbrella bars and transparent 'igloo' bars in which to shelter from bad weather. Huge quantities of beer and schnapps are drunk, often to the accompaniment of German drinking songs or loud Europop music. In many resorts the bands don't stop playing until after darkness falls, when the happy punters slide off in the general direction of the village to find another watering hole.

After dinner (for those who pause for dinner, that is) the drinking and dancing start again and carry on in town in bars and clubs until the early hours.

Of course, not all resorts conform to this image. 'Exclusive' Lech and Zürs, for example, are full of rich, cool, 'beautiful' people enjoying the comfort of 4- or 5-star hotels. And villages such as Westendorf and Obergurgl are pretty, quiet, family resorts. But lots of big-name places with the best and most extensive slopes are also big party towns – notably St Anton, Saalbach-Hinterglemm, Ischgl and Sölden.

Après-ski is not limited to drinking and dancing. There are lots of floodlit toboggan runs, and UK tour operator reps organize folklore, bowling, fondue, karaoke and other evenings.

GOOD-VALUE, HIGH-QUALITY LODGING

One thing that all Austrian resorts have in common is reliably comfortable accommodation – whether it's in 4- or 5-star hotels with pools, saunas and spas or in great-value, family-run guest houses, of which Austria has thousands. Catered chalets and self-catering apartments are in general much less widely available than in French resorts.

The Germanic aversion to credit cards causes problems for many of our reporters. Many establishments do not accept cards – even quite upmarket hotels, as well as many ski lift companies. So check well in advance, or be prepared to pay in cash.

BUT STILL PUTTING UP WITH SMOKING

As other parts of the Alps have cut out smoking in bars and restaurants, Austria has lagged behind, much to the displeasure of many British visitors. In theory, there is progress. In 'multiple room establishments' the 'main room' now has to be non-smoking. In places with only one room, it's only in small places where you should now have to put up with smoke. But in practice, we find annoying smoke in most bars and some restaurants wherever we go.

GETTING AROUND THE AUSTRIAN ALPS

Austria presents few problems for the car-borne visitor, because practically all the resorts are valley villages, which involve neither steep, winding approach roads nor high-altitude passes.

The motorway along the Inn valley runs from Kufstein via Innsbruck to Landeck and, with one or two breaks, extends to the Arlberg pass and on to Switzerland. This artery is relatively reliable except in exceptionally bad weather – the altitude is low, and the road is a vital link that is kept open in virtually all conditions.

The Arlberg – which divides the Tirol from Vorarlberg, but which

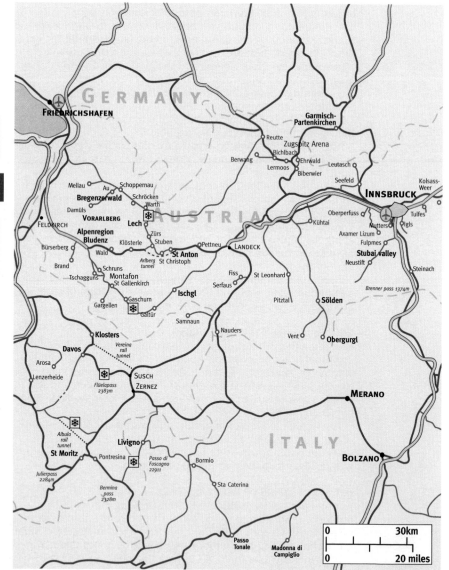

is also the watershed between Austria and Switzerland – is one of the few areas where driving plans are likely to be seriously affected by snow. The east–west Arlberg pass itself has a long tunnel underneath it; this isn't cheap, and you may want to take the pass road when it's clear, through Stuben, St Christoph and St Anton. The Flexen pass road to Zürs and Lech branches off northwards, just to the west of the Arlberg summit; this is often closed by avalanche risk even when the Arlberg pass is open.

All cars must display a motorway toll sticker, available at petrol stations, post offices and newsagents. There's a 10-day one for 8.30 euros and a two-month one for 24.20 euros. From 1 November to 15 April winter tyres must be fitted. Be aware that cars hired in Germany or Italy might not meet this requirement.

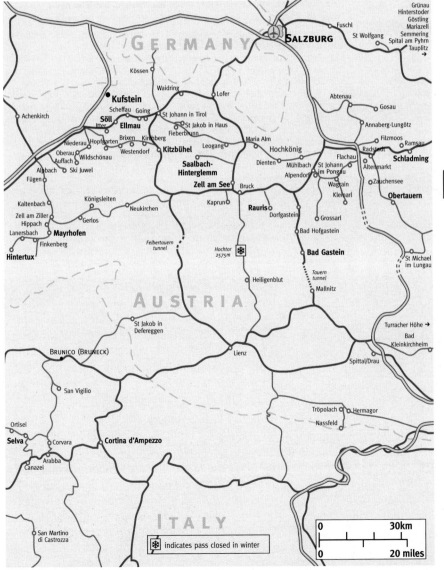

indicates pass closed in winter

Bad Gastein

*If you fancy 'taking the cure', there are few better resorts;
even if you don't, you're likely to be impressed by the slopes*

TOP 10 RATINGS

Extent	★★★
Fast lifts	★★★
Queues	★★★
Snow	★★★
Expert	★★★
Intermediate	★★★★
Beginner	★★
Charm	★★★
Convenience	★★
Scenery	★★★

RPI	100
lift pass	£210
ski hire	£90
lessons	£120
food & drink	£110
total	**£530**

104

➕ Excellent, testing long runs for confident intermediates

➕ Some relatively high slopes

➕ Good mountain restaurants

➕ Excellent thermal spas, but ...

➖ Main resorts are spa towns, lacking the usual Austrian resort ambience

➖ Valley slopes are split into five areas, and having a car helps

➖ Lacks genuinely easy runs

With its essentially red-gradient mountains and spa-town resorts, the Gastein valley is a bit different from Austrian ski resort norms. We prefer spacious Bad Hofgastein to steeply tiered, rather urban Bad Gastein. But little rustic Dorfgastein, down the valley, is our favourite. All three are covered here.

THE RESORT

Bad Gastein is an old spa town near the head of the Gastein valley. At its heart is the original spa area, laid out in a compact horseshoe on steep slopes. Above this, at the level of the railway and the gondola station, is a modern suburb with more lodgings.

The Stubnerkogel slopes above the town link with Bad Hofgastein, down the valley. Beyond that, a separate area of slopes above Dorfgastein links with Grossarl in the next valley. Up the valley is another separate area at Sportgastein. Various ski-bus routes and trains connect the villages and lift stations, and 'run as per timetable' – though many bus services stop earlier than keen après-skiers would wish.

Lots of resorts in this region (including Schladming, which has its own chapter) are covered by the Ski Amadé lift pass and are easily reached by car.
Village charm The core is a curious mix of towny buildings – some grand, some modest. Away from here, the more modern hotels and guest houses have more of a normal ski resort feel.
Convenience The higher part of the resort is handy for the Stubnerkogel gondola, but the resort as a whole spreads widely, and the double chair to the separate Graukogel area is on the opposite side of town.
Scenery The resort is set in virtually a gorge, steeply tiered and wooded. The slopes are higher than many Austrian resorts (particularly at Sportgastein), with wide views as a result.

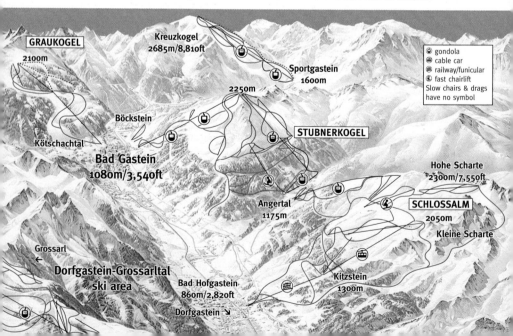

2013/14: Some 3km more snowmaking is planned for Stubnerkogel on the run back to town. A new ski route from Schlossalm to Angertal is planned.

2012/13: Snowmaking was increased on both Stubnerkogel and Schlossalm.

KEY FACTS

Resort	1080m
	3,540ft

The Gastein valley and Grossarl areas

Slopes	840-2685m
	2,760-8,810ft
Lifts	42
Pistes	218km
	135 miles
Blue	26%
Red	60%
Black	14%
Snowmaking	60%

Bad Gastein, Bad Hofgastein, Sportgastein only

Slopes	860-2685m
	2,820-8,810ft
Lifts	25
Pistes	129km
	80 miles

THE MOUNTAINS

Most of the pistes are genuine red runs; this is not a resort for timid intermediates who prefer easy cruising blues. And most are on open slopes; this is a quite exposed region, and wind can affect both the snow and the lifts. Sportgastein is especially vulnerable. Graukogel is wooded. The piste map tries to cover all the areas and so is difficult to follow.

Slopes From the Stubnerkogel gondola a long blue run goes back to base, but most runs head for Angertal, which links with Bad Hofgastein.

Fast lifts There are several gondolas, but also lots of slow chairs and T-bars.

Queues There are few major problems.

Terrain parks There is a 'quiet and well-run' park on Stubnerkogel.

Snow reliability The slopes go a bit higher than many Austrian rivals – Sportgastein much higher – and there is decent snowmaking. Conditions can be better at Dorfgastein–Grossarl than at Stubnerkogel–Schlossalm.

Experts The few black runs are not severe, but many reds are long and satisfying. Graukogel has some of the most testing pistes. There is plenty of good off-piste – by the Jungeralm chair on the shady side of Stubnerkogel, for example. Sportgastein has a ski route from top to bottom.

Intermediates Confident intermediates, will find long, leg-sapping red runs in all sectors. The valley in general and Stubnerkogel in particular are not nearly so good for blue-run skiers. Sportgastein has a good range of runs, up to an easy black.

Beginners There are adequate nursery areas near the gondola station and at Angertal. But progression is awkward – the mountains are essentially steep. The few easy long runs are boring paths. There are no free lifts.

Snowboarding The valley hosts snowboard events, and there is good

STC Ski
Specialists in Tailor-Made Short Breaks & Holidays
01483 771 222
www.stcski.co.uk
ski@stcski.co.uk

freeriding. Draglifts are dotted around.

Cross-country There are 45km of trails in the area, but most are low down.

Mountain restaurants There are lots of pleasant huts doing decent food; but they can get crowded. Reader tips include Bellevuealm, Stubneralm, Waldgasthof and Hirschenhütte.

Schools and guides Past reports on the school have been favourable.

Families Facilities are quite good. Angertal has a snow adventure park.

STAYING THERE

Hotels There are lots of smart 4- and 3-star hotels with spa facilities. The Grüner Baum (25160) is a lovely retreat, but isolated (though they have a shuttle-bus). Reader tips include the quite grand Elizabeth Park (25510) and the quirky, friendly Mozart (26860).

Eating out Choice is reasonable. The traditional Jägerhäusl has been tipped for its lovely food and large portions. The Amici is a good-value Italian.

Après-ski Bars are lively at close of play, evenings more subdued. Silver Bullet and Haeggbloms are among the most popular. Bars for a quiet late drink include Bellini and Ritz. There are a couple of discos and a casino.

Off the slopes The thermal spa/pool facilities are excellent and extensive – but expensive. There's ice climbing, and there are quite a few shops. Excursions to Salzburg are possible.

Bad Gastein

105

Bad Hofgastein 860m

➕ Sunny, spacious setting
➕ Lovely long runs

➖ Lacks ski resort ambience
➖ Funicular from base can be crowded

Bad Hofgastein is a sizeable, spacious, quiet spa town set on flat ground in the widest part of the valley, with funicular access to the slopes.

Village charm The pedestrianized centre is compact and pleasant enough to stroll around, with lots of shops and restaurants. But it does feel like a town; there's little traditional

Austrian rustic charm. There is a sizeable park next to the centre.

Convenience The resort spreads widely; the funicular is an efficient ski-bus ride from many lodgings. It's a

UK PACKAGES

Alpine Answers, Crystal, Crystal Finest, Ski Line, Ski Miquel, STC, White Roc
Bad Hofgastein Crystal, Crystal Finest, Ski Club Freshtracks, Ski Line, Skitracer, STC
Grossarl Inntravel

Phone numbers
From elsewhere in Austria add the prefix 06434 (Bad Gastein), 06432 (Bad Hofgastein), 06433 (Dorfgastein); from abroad use the prefix +43 and omit the initial '0'

TOURIST OFFICE

For all resorts in the Gastein valley:
www.gastein.com

GASTEINERTAL TOURISMUS

Bad Hofgastein sits in a wide, sunny valley with the skiing on the other side – so it's a bus to and from the slopes from most lodgings ↓

longer ski-bus ride to Angertal.
Scenery Good valley views.

THE MOUNTAINS

Schlossalm is a broad, open bowl, with runs through patchy woods both to Bad Hofgastein and Angertal. As at Stubnerkogel, wind can be a problem.
Slopes The funicular to Kitzstein is followed by a cable car to the Schlossalm slopes. These link to Stubnerkogel via Angertal.
Fast lifts Getting up the mountain can be slow, and a few old chairs remain.
Queues The access lifts are queue-prone at peak times – and the cable car can be closed by wind.
Terrain parks There isn't one.
Snow reliability Snowmaking is fairly extensive, but snow-cover down to the bottom is unreliable, especially on the sunny Angertal slopes.
Experts There are no real challenges on the local pistes, but there is ample opportunity to go off-piste.
Intermediates The Schlossalm slopes offer a good range of red runs, from easy to testing; the few blues are not all entirely easy. There are splendid long reds to the valley floor (we loved the away-from-the-lifts Hohe Scharte Nord – 10.4km long, 1440m vertical).
Beginners There is a small nursery area at the funicular station. You have to catch a bus to the bigger nursery area at Angertal. And then you have few options for progression.
Snowboarding Good freeriding. Draglifts are dotted around though.
Cross-country Bad Hofgastein makes a fine base for cross-country when its

lengthy valley-floor trails have snow.
Mountain restaurants A reader favourite is the 'well-organized' self-service Aeroplanstadl. Other tips: the table-service Pyrkerhof, Haitzingalm, Hofgasteinerhaus and Bärsteinalm.
Schools and guides 'Good teaching that pushed us,' says a recent report.
Families See Bad Gastein.

STAYING THERE

Hotels We enjoyed a stay at the 4-star Bismarck (66810) – excellent food, fairly central. Reader tips include the Impuls Tirol (6394) – 'quality five-course dinners and spa' – St Georg (61000) – 200m to lift 'food fine-dining standard' – and Palace (67150).
Apartments The Alpenparks resort is still 'excellent', says a repeat visitor.
Eating out There's plenty of choice. Reader tips include Piccola Italia, Salzburgerhof and Dino's (for pizza).
Après-ski Quiet by Austrian standards. The Aeroplanstadl on the hill and central Piccolo ice bar are popular at close of play. Head to Cafe Weitmoser, a historic little castle, for cakes. There are said to be a couple of disco bars.
Off the slopes The huge Alpen Therme Gastein spa has excellent pools etc. Other amenities include good shops, walking and a full-size ice rink.

DOWN-VALLEY VILLAGE – 830m

DORFGASTEIN

Dorfgastein is a quiet, rustic village. It has its own extensive slopes, shared with Grossarl in the next valley. A two-stage gondola and alternative chairlift start a little way outside the village. There is a nursery slope here, and another at the gondola mid-station. Like the other sectors, the mountain is essentially of red gradient, and best suits confident intermediates. On the front side there is one good long blue, but it doesn't go all the way to the valley. There are pleasant huts. We endorse readers' support for the excellent table-service Wengeralm. A 2013 visitor likes the 'great atmosphere and food' at the Jagahütte and the 'lovely rustic' Harbachhütte. The Gipflstadl and Hochbrandhütte have also been recommended. The ski schools get good reviews. Off-slope amenities are limited, but there's a pool with sauna and steam. Evenings are quiet. Reporters love the 4-star hotel Römerhof (7777) – 'great food, lovely spa, good value'.

Ellmau

A good base on the extensive SkiWelt circuit, combining charm with reasonable convenience – good value, too

TOP 10 RATINGS

Extent	★★★★
Fast lifts	★★★★
Queues	★★★★
Snow	★★
Expert	★
Intermediate	★★★★
Beginner	★★★★
Charm	★★★
Convenience	★★★
Scenery	★★★

RPI 90

lift pass	£190
ski hire	£65
lessons	£110
food & drink	£110
total	**£475**

NEWS

2013/14: Snowmaking facilities are due to be further expanded.

2012/13: Snowmaking was improved. The toboggan run was floodlit.

+ Part of the SkiWelt, Austria's largest linked ski area

+ Excellent nursery slopes

+ Quiet, charming family resort – more appealing than Söll

+ Cheap, even by Austrian standards

+ Snowmaking is now more extensive and well used; even so ...

– Low altitude can mean poor snow

– Main lift a bus or drag from village

– Runs on upper slopes mostly short

– Few challenges on-piste

– Limited range of nightlife

– The slopes can get crowded

– Appallingly inadequate piste map

If you like the sound of the large, undemanding SkiWelt circuit, Ellmau has a lot to recommend it as your base – as does Scheffau, also covered here. But also consider the several resorts covered in the Söll chapter.

THE RESORT

Ellmau sits at the north-eastern corner of the big SkiWelt – Austria's biggest network. Other parts of it are covered in our chapter on Söll. You can also progress (via Brixen) to the slopes of Kitzbühel; these and various other ski areas within reach are covered by the Kitzbüheler Alpen AllStarCard ski pass.

Village charm Although sizeable, the village remains quiet, with traditional chalet-style buildings, welcoming bars and shops, and a pretty church.

Convenience Accommodation is scattered; there is some out by the funicular to the main slopes, but we prefer to stay in the compact centre of the village. There is a frequent bus service, but the buses are very crowded at peak times.

Scenery The village and the slopes enjoy great close-up views of the craggy Wilder Kaiser, across the valley.

THE MOUNTAINS

The piste map is hopelessly over-ambitious in trying to show the whole area in a single view. There's a mix of short runs at altitude and much longer ones to the villages. Lots of trees.

Slopes The funicular railway on the edge of the village takes you up to Hartkaiser, from where a fine long red leads down to Blaiken (Scheffau's lift base station). Here, one of two gondolas takes you up to Brandstadl. Immediately beyond Brandstadl, the

KEY FACTS

Resort	800m
	2,620ft

Entire SkiWelt	
Slopes	620-1890m
	2,030-6,200ft
Lifts	91
Pistes	279km
	173 miles
Blue	44%
Red	46%
Black	10%
Snowmaking	80%

LIFT PASSES

SkiWelt Wilder Kaiser-Brixental

Prices in €

Age	1-day	6-day
under 16	22	105
16 to 17	34	168
18 plus	43	210

Free Under 7
Senior No deals
Beginner Points cards
Notes Ski-bus included; single ascent and part-day options

Alternative pass
Kitzbüheler Alpen AllStarCard covers: Schneewinkel (St Johann), Kitzbühel, SkiWelt, Ski Juwel, Skicircus Saalbach-Hinterglemm and Zell am See-Kaprun

slopes become rather bitty; an array of short runs and lifts link Brandstadl to Zinsberg. From Zinsberg, long, south-facing pistes lead down to Brixen, where a gondola goes up to Choralpe in Westendorf's area. Part-way down to Brixen you can head towards Söll, and if you go up Hohe Salve, you get access to a long run to Hopfgarten.

Ellmau and Going share a pleasant little area of slopes on Astberg, slightly apart from the rest of the area, and well suited to the unadventurous and to families. One piste leads to the funicular for access to the rest of the SkiWelt. The main Astberg chair is midway between Ellmau and Going.

Fast lifts The main access lift is a fast funicular. Fast chairs are increasingly common on the upper slopes.

Queues Lift upgrades have greatly improved this once queue-prone area, and most reporters find few queues. But there are several bottlenecks at slow chairs around the mountain, and when snow is poor the links between Zinsberg and Eiberg get crowded.

Terrain parks Ellmau has its own terrain park, the Kaiserpark, with beginner and expert boxes, rails and kickers, as well as a chill-out zone.

Snow reliability With a low average height, and important links that get a lot of sun, the snowmaking that the SkiWelt has installed is essential; the Ellmau–Going sector now claims 95% of slopes are covered. Snowmaking can, of course, be used only when temperatures are low enough. The north-facing Eiberg area above Scheffau holds its snow well. Grooming is excellent, and reports have praised the snowmaking.

Experts There is a ski route from Brandstadl down to Scheffau and a little mogul field between Brandstadl and Neualm, but the main challenges are in going off-piste.

Intermediates With good snow, the SkiWelt is a paradise for those who love easy cruising. There are lots of blue runs, and many of the reds deserve a blue classification. It is a big area, and you get a feeling of travelling around. In good snow the long red runs to the valley – down the Hartkaiser funicular, for example – are excellent. The main challenge arises when ice and slush can make even gentle lower slopes tricky. For timid intermediates Astberg is handy.

Beginners Ellmau has an array of good nursery slopes covered by snow-guns. The main ones are at the Going end, but there are some by the road to the funicular. The Astberg chair opens up a more snow-sure plateau at altitude. The Brandstadl area has a section of short easy runs.

Snowboarding Ellmau is a good place to learn as its local slopes are easy.

Cross-country The SkiWelt area has a total of 170km of trails, including long and challenging ones, but trails at altitude are lacking.

Mountain restaurants There are many small places providing good-value food in pleasant surroundings. The Rübezahl Alm above Ellmau is one of our favourites – a lovely old hut with good food (the ribs have been recommended) and lots of different rooms and areas that make it very cosy; but it gets very busy. The Tanzbodenalm near Brandstadl above Scheffau is pleasantly woody, serving

UK PACKAGES

Crystal, Neilson, Ski Club Freshtracks, Ski Line, Skitracer, STC, Thomson
Scheffau Crystal, STC, Thomson
Going Inghams, STC

delicious deer stew; 'great service, good food and wide choice'. Other reporter tips include: the Jägerhütte (below Hartkaiser) for 'a lovely atmosphere and good food' before enjoying the home run, and the 'jolly' Hartkaiser ('toilets accessed by escalator!'). The Jochstub'n has a self-service part and a 'cute, lively' bar: 'good for an end of afternoon drink'. The Bergkaiser has 'efficient service, good-value food', and the Blattlalm on Astberg 'super views'. Then there's the Aualm below Zinsberg for cakes and glühwein, the Brandstadl and the 'pleasantly rustic' Neualm above Scheffau, and, a bit lower down, Bavaria – which has a 'lovely comfy bar' and 'great-value lunch specials'.

Schools and guides There are three schools and a specialist boarding school in Ellmau, a couple in Scheffau and another in Going. We have no recent reports.

Families Ellmau is an attractive resort for families: 'Probably the best family resort I have visited – from ski school to alternative attractions,' says a 2012 visitor. Both the Ellmauer and the Top schools have their own fun parks and play areas. The leisure centre and toboggan run are popular.

STAYING THERE

Ellmau is essentially a hotel and guest house resort, though there are apartments that can be booked locally.
Hotels The Bär (2395) is an elegant, relaxed luxury place. The Kaiserhof (2022) is another luxury option. The Sporthotel (3755) is 'incredible for the price', with 'huge five-course meals, gorgeous pool/spa facilities, huge lounge'. The Hochfilzer (2501) is central and well equipped (with outdoor hot tub, indoor pool, sauna, steam); the simpler Pension Claudia is under the same ownership. The Kaiserblick (2230) has good spa facilities and is right by the piste.
Apartments There is a wide variety. The Landhof apartments – with pool, sauna and steam room – have impressed a regular visitor.
Eating out There is quite a wide choice. The jolly Lobewein is a splendid, big, central chalet, with cheerful service in countless rooms. The Ellmauer Alm has been tipped: 'Good service despite being very busy.' A reporter's young children loved the 'no-nonsense food' in the village's Tex-Mex place.

Après-ski Bettina is good for coffee and cakes. Memory is the early-evening riotous party pub. Pub 66 and Ötzy Bar have regular events such as karaoke and 'erotic dancers'. The Ellmauer Alm has live entertainment. Tour operator reps organize events such as sleigh rides and tubing, and bowling and Tirolean folklore evenings in Söll. Ski night and the Instructors' Ball have a party atmosphere each week. The toboggan run from the Astberg lift is also recommended.
Off the slopes A guest card conveys various discounts, including entry to the KaiserBad leisure centre. There's a pool and an ice rink. The many excursions include Innsbruck, Salzburg and Vitipeno. Valley walks may be spoiled by the busy main road.

LINKED RESORT – 745m
SCHEFFAU

Little Scheffau is one of the most attractive of the region's villages and is well placed for quick access to most parts of the SkiWelt area – though the village itself is not convenient for the lifts, which are a short bus ride away. You can ski down to the gondolas at Blaiken, unless of course you opt to leave your kit at the lift station. The village spreads up quite a steep slope. Reporters recommend the 3-star Alpin (85560), the central Gasthof Weberbauer (8115) and the 'well-priced' Waldrand (8158). Après-ski is 'non-existent', says one happy reporter, but there are a couple of bars. The Sternbar, nearest to the gondolas, is lively after the lifts close. There's bowling and tobogganing but little else to do off the slopes.

LINKED RESORT – 775m
GOING

Going is a tiny, attractively rustic village, ideal for families looking for a quiet time. It is well placed for the limited but quiet slopes of the Astberg and for the vast area of nursery slopes shared with Ellmau. Prices are low, but as it's at one extreme end of the SkiWelt, it's not an ideal base for covering the whole of the region on the cheap unless you have a car to speed up access to Scheffau and Söll (or you're happy to take buses). The Lanzenhof (2428) is a cosy central pension, where we have enjoyed an excellent dinner.

Phone numbers
From elsewhere in Austria add the prefix 05358; from abroad use the prefix +43 5358

TOURIST OFFICES

Wilder Kaiser
(Ellmau, Söll, Scheffau, Going)
www.wilderkaiser.info

SkiWelt
www.skiwelt.at

Ellmau

109

Build your own shortlist: **www.wheretoskiandsnowboard.com**

Hintertux / Tux valley

Small, unspoiled, traditional villages, high snow-sure glacier slopes and lots of other areas covered by the valley lift pass

TOP 10 RATINGS

Extent	★★★
Fast lifts	★★★
Queues	★★★
Snow	★★★★★
Expert	★★★
Intermediate	★★★
Beginner	★★
Charm	★★★
Convenience	★★
Scenery	★★★

RPI 90

lift pass	£190
ski hire	£75
lessons	£95
food & drink	£115
total	£475

NEWS

2013/14: The Lämmerbichl double chair on Rastkogel is to be replaced by a six-pack with heated seats and covers. The Tuxer Fernerhaus restaurant on the glacier is to be completely renovated and the little old Spannagelhaus nearby is getting a radical makeover.

2012/13: Snowmaking was increased.

- + Hintertux has one of the best year-round glaciers in the world
- + Lanersbach's slopes form part of an extensive area, linked to Mayrhofen
- + Wide-ranging area lift pass
- + Some excellent off-piste
- + Quiet, traditional villages

- − Not the place for shops and throbbing nightlife
- − Not ideal for beginners or timid intermediates
- − Still some draglifts and slow chairs on the glacier slopes
- − Glacier can be cold and bleak

For guaranteed good snow, Hintertux is simply one of the best places to go. Its glacier is not only extensive; it arguably has the most challenging and interesting runs of any lift-served Alpine glacier area. But the quieter, friendlier, non-glacial slopes down the valley, linked to the slopes of Mayrhofen, are also well worth exploring (check out the Mayrhofen chapter too).

The Tux valley, effectively the top end of the Zillertal, offers a variety of small villages. At the end of the valley, directly below the glacier, is **Hintertux**; a few km down the valley, the major resorts are **Lanersbach** and next-door **Vorderlanersbach**. Lower down still is **Finkenberg**. There is also lodging in Juns and Madseit, which are villages between Hintertux and Lanersbach.

All the major resort villages have gondolas into the local slopes: the Lanersbach one goes to Eggalm, and you can ski to Vorderlanersbach from there; the Vorderlanersbach one goes to Rastkogel, and from there you can ski into Mayrhofen's Penken–Horberg slopes; and the Finkenberg one goes up to Penken, meeting the lifts above Mayrhofen.

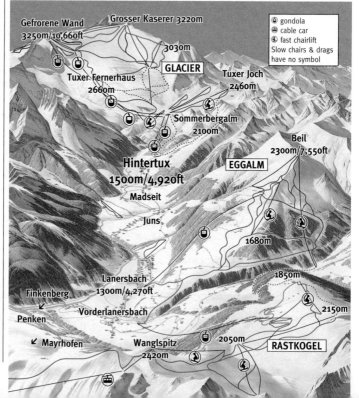

Gefrorene Wand 3250m/10,66oft

Grosser Kaserer 3220m

3030m

GLACIER

☺ gondola
🚡 cable car
🚠 fast chairlift
Slow chairs & drags have no symbol

Tuxer Fernerhaus 2660m

Tuxer Joch 2460m

Sommerbergalm 2100m

Beil 2300m/7,550ft

Hintertux 1500m/4,920ft

EGGALM

Madseit

Juns

1680m

1850m

Lanersbach 1300m/4,270ft

Finkenberg

Vorderlanersbach

2150m

Penken

↙ Mayrhofen

Wanglspitz 2420m

2050m

RASTKOGEL

↑ Sommerbergalm is in the centre of this shot, with Tuxer Joch beyond it and the main glacier slopes off to the left
TVB TUX-FINKENBERG

KEY FACTS

Resort	1500m
	4,920ft

Ziller valley	
Slopes	630-3250m
	2,070-10,660ft
Lifts	161
Pistes	699km
	434 miles
Blue	26%
Red	63%
Black	11%
Snowmaking	75%

Ski and Glacier World Zillertal 3000	
Slopes	630-3250m
	2,070-10,660ft
Lifts	77
Pistes	245km
	152 miles
Blue	26%
Red	58%
Black	16%
Snowmaking	86%

Hintertux only	
Slopes	1500-3250m
	4,920-10,660ft
Lifts	22
Pistes	86km
	53 miles

The higher villages are linked by frequent free ski-buses. A cheap (one euro) night-bus runs until 2.30am. Finkenberg is less well served.

There are some good rustic restaurants and bars and a few places along the valley with discos or live music. But nightlife tends to be quieter than in many Austrian resorts.

The Tux valley and Mayrhofen lifts form what is called the Ski and Glacier World Zillertal 3000. The Superski lift pass also covers other Ziller valley resorts (read the Mayrhofen chapter). The SGWZ3000 piste map is very clear, and names all mountain restaurants.

Hintertux 1500m

➕ Departure point for the excellent high glacier slopes
➕ Liveliest of the villages for après-ski

➖ Quiet later in the evening
➖ Remote setting
➖ Not much to do off the slopes

Life in Hintertux revolves around the glacier; staying at the base gets you up the mountain early, and means you don't have far to stagger after joining in the teatime revelry. But later on, it may feel too quiet for some.

Village charm The resort is little more than a small collection of hotels and guest houses, in traditional style. Well, two collections actually – see below.
Convenience The main village is a 15-minute walk from the lifts, but there are also hotels at the lift base – the obvious place to stay in our view.
Scenery There are fabulous views from the high points of the glacier.

THE MOUNTAINS

Hintertux's slopes are fairly extensive and, for a glacier, surprisingly varied and occasionally challenging. Only the final ski route to the valley is in trees.
Slopes A series of three big twin-cable gondolas go from the base to the top of the glacier in around 30 minutes. The second and third stages are linked by a short slope at Tuxer Fernerhaus. A

second smaller gondola also goes to Tuxer Fernerhaus, and a 10-seat gondola replaced the Gefrorene Wand double chair above it in 2011/12. Above Tuxer Fernerhaus there are further chairs and draglifts with links across to another 1000m-vertical chain of lifts below Grosser Kaserer. Behind Gefrorene Wand is the area's one sunny piste, served by a triple chair.

Descent to the valley involves a short six-pack ride to Sommerbergalm and then a ski route to the base. At Sommerbergalm a fast quad serves short, easy slopes below Tuxer Joch and accesses a second ski route to the base – down a deserted valley.
Fast lifts There are high-capacity gondolas all the way to the top, but the shorter lifts serving most of the slopes are T-bars and slow chairs.

LIFT PASSES

Super-skipass Zillertal

Prices in €

Age	1-day	6-day
under 15	21	97
15 to 18	36	172
19 plus	45	215

Free Under 6
Senior No deals
Beginner No deals
Notes 1-day pass covers Hintertux glacier, Eggalm, Rastkogel and Penken areas; 4-day and over passes include all Ziller valley lifts; part-day passes available

Queues The gondolas make light work of any queues. But the main runs can get crowded, and then it is best to go to the quieter lifts on skier's left.

Terrain parks Europe's highest World Cup half-pipe is on the glacier (a popular summer hang-out), and there is a terrain park for all levels with jumps, fun boxes and rails.

Snow reliability Snow does not come more reliable than this. Even off the glacier, the other slopes are high and face north, making for very reliable snow-cover. The runs from Tuxer Fernerhaus and Tuxer Joch down to Sommerbergalm have snowmaking, as does the longer ski route to the valley – bizarre, for a ski route.

Experts There is more to amuse experts here than on any other glacier, with a proper black run at glacier level and steep slopes beneath. A lot of the off-piste is little used.

Intermediates The area particularly suits good, confident intermediates. The long runs down from Gefrorene Wand and Kaserer are fun. And the ski routes to the valley are very satisfying. Moderate intermediates will love the slopes served by drags up on the glacier, and the Tuxer Joch area.

Beginners There is a short nursery slope at valley level, but then you're riding the gondola up to and back from Sommerbergalm, where there are blue runs served by drags and a chair. You'll need a full lift pass.

Snowboarding There are some great off-piste opportunities, but boarders complain about the number of T-bars.

Cross-country See Lanersbach.

Mountain restaurants For some time our favourite has been Gletscherhütte, at the top of the area – good shielded terraces with BBQ and table-service in parts of the cosy, woody interior.

'Good-value, hearty meals,' says an endorsing 2013 reporter. But the ancient Spannagelhaus refuge lower down is being transformed into 'an inviting table-service restaurant' with 'rustic lounges' and a wide-ranging menu. Yum! There are big self-service places at the main lift junctions: Tuxer Fernerhaus is being renovated; Tuxer Joch Haus has great glacier views.

Schools and guides The three schools serve all the resorts in Tux, but we lack reports. Tux 3000 has guiding, touring and freeriding programmes.

Families Most of the ski schools run classes for children from age four, and lunch is provided. There's a children's fun area on the glacier.

STAYING THERE

Most hotels are large and comfortable and have spa facilities, but there are also more modest pensions.

Hotels We think it makes sense to stay close to the lifts. Closest is the 4-star Neuhintertux (8580) used by our regular reporter ('food not spectacular, but spa very good'); next door is the more intimate Vierjahreszeiten (8525) ('pleasant, good food, smaller spa').

Apartments There are plenty of self-catering apartments.

Eating out Mainly hotel-based.

Après-ski There can be a lively après-ski scene both at mid-mountain (Sommerbergalm) and at the base. The Hohenhaus Tenne has several different bars; the Rindererhof is another popular place to gather, and there are a couple of local bars.

Off the slopes Lots of ice activities on the glacier – climbing, natural ice palace, etc. The hotel spa facilities are excellent, including a thermal pool at the Kirchler, but there are many more options in Mayrhofen.

Lanersbach 1300m

+ Pleasant, compact village
+ Well placed for skiing the glacier and for the Mayrhofen slopes

− Village fairly quiet by Austrian standards
− Few easy local runs for novices

Lanersbach and neighbouring Vorderlanersbach are attractive bases for accessing both the glacier and the valley resorts, with the particular attraction that you can ski home to them from the Eggalm sector.

Village charm Lanersbach is small, attractive, spacious and traditional. The quiet centre near the pretty church is delightfully unspoiled and is bypassed by the busy road up to Hintertux that passes the main lift. Vorderlanersbach is a mini version.

Convenience Lanersbach has everything you need in a resort. The centre is within walking distance of the Eggalm gondola. Vorderlanersbach has its own gondola up to Rastkogel.

Scenery These are attractive villages in a long, pretty and varied valley.

The lift base is out of sight in this shot from the Waldabfahrt itinerary; the village of Hintertux, as you can see, is a little way down the valley – though you can ski to it using the Schwarze Pfanne itinerary →

GETTING THERE

Air Salzburg 195km/120 miles (3hr); Munich 210km/130 miles (3hr30); Innsbruck 90km/55 miles (1hr45)

Rail Local line to Mayrhofen; regular buses from station

UK PACKAGES

Hintertux Snoworks
Lanersbach STC
Finkenberg Crystal, STC

THE MOUNTAINS

Slopes The slopes of Eggalm, accessed by the gondola from Lanersbach, offer a small network of pleasantly varied intermediate pistes, usually delightfully quiet. You can descend on red or blue runs back to the village or to Vorderlanersbach, where a gondola goes up to the higher, open Rastkogel slopes; here, two fast chairlifts serve some very enjoyable long red and blue runs, and link with Mayrhofen's slopes. The linking run has red and black variants; both can get very mogulled, and many people opt to ride the jumbo cable car down; a short rope-tow cuts out the need to hike up to the top station. The lower half of the run back from Rastkogel to Eggalm is a ski route; it is narrow but not steep, and it is served by snowmaking. The alternative is to ride the gondola down to Vorderlanersbach (there are no pistes to the village) and catch the bus to Lanersbach.

Fast lifts 'Great,' was the verdict of a 2012 visitor. Gondolas are the access lifts, and Eggalm and Rastkogel each have two six-packs.

Queues We have no reports of any problems. Indeed, Eggalm can be delightfully quiet.

Terrain parks The nearest parks are at Mayrhofen and Hintertux.

Snow reliability Snow conditions are usually good, at least in early season; by Austrian standards these are high slopes, and snowmaking covers some runs on both Eggalm and Rastkogel. But Rastkogel is excessively sunny. The grooming was 'OK – not great', said a 2012 reporter.

Experts There are no pistes to challenge experts, but there is a fine off-piste route starting a short hike from the top of the Eggalm slopes and finishing at the village.

Intermediates The local slopes suit intermediates best, with some excellent, challenging red runs – and you have Mayrhofen's slopes, too.

Beginners Lanersbach has a nursery slope (as do Madseit and Juns), but there are few ideal progression slopes on Eggalm – most of the easy runs are on the higher lifts of Rastkogel.

Snowboarding The area isn't great for novices – there are draglifts dotted around, some in key places.

Cross-country There are 28km of cross-country trails around Madseit and Vorderlanersbach.

Mountain restaurants There are quite a few rustic places doing simple food, but demand exceeds supply, and self-service is the norm. There are two table-service exceptions on Eggalm. Egger Schialm is tucked away from the main runs, so is less busy – excellent Tirolergröstl, friendly people, good prices. Lattenalm has splendid views of the Tux glacier. On Rastkogel, Heidi's Schistadl also has good views and is the 'best-value hut I've visited', says a 2012 reporter.

Schools and guides There are three schools in the valley, but we lack recent reports on them.

Families The Playarena in Vorderlanersbach nursery takes newborn babies up to teenagers, and most of the schools take children from four upwards. There's a children's snow garden on Eggalm.

STAYING THERE

Both villages are essentially hotel-based resorts.

Hotels The better places tend to be on the main road, but complaints of noise are few. The Lanersbacherof (87256) is a good 4-star with a pool, sauna, steam room and hot tub close to the lifts. The 3-star Pinzger (87541) and Alpengruss (87293) are cheaper alternatives. In Vorderlanersbach the 3-star Kirchlerhof (8560) has been recommended in the past and has a wellness area.

Apartments Quite a lot are available locally.

Eating out Mainly hotel-based, busy, and geared to serving dinner early.

The Forelle is noted for its trout dishes, not surprisingly.

Après-ski Nightlife is generally quiet by Austrian standards. Try the Kleine Tenne or the Bergfriedalm – an old wooden building with traditional Austrian music ('Worth staying in Lanersbach just for this bar,' says a 2012 reporter). Gletscherspalte is a disco ('more commercial and with a younger crowd than Bergfriedalm').

Off the slopes Facilities are fairly good for small resorts, and the bus service throughout the valley is extensive. Some hotels have pools, hot tubs and fitness rooms open to non-residents. Innsbruck and Salzburg are possible excursions.

Finkenberg 840m

- ⊞ Fast lift access to the main slopes
- ⊞ Pleasant, uncrowded village that appeals to families, but ...
- ⊟ Lodging sprawls along a steep and busy main road
- ⊟ No pisted runs to resort level

If you want to ski Mayrhofen's extensive area but avoid the après-ski crowds, Finkenberg makes a quieter alternative – and with direct access to the slopes. But the only way home is an itinerary (not shown on some maps).

Village charm The resort is no more than a collection of traditional-style hotels, bars, cafes and private homes. There is a central pretty area around the church.

Convenience Most of the buildings (and hotels) are spread along the busy, steep, winding main road up to Lanersbach. Beware slippery pavements. Some hotels are within walking distance of the gondola, and many of the more distant ones run their own minibuses; there is also a village minibus service.

Scenery Steep mountains rise up on both sides.

THE MOUNTAIN

Slopes A two-stage gondola gives direct access to the Penken slopes – and in good conditions you can ski back to the village on a ski route (though it is often closed).

Fast lifts See Mayrhofen.

Queues Few problems reported. The gondola to and from the Penken may have queues at peak times.

Terrain parks The Mayrhofen park is easily accessed.

Snow reliability The local slopes are not as well endowed with snowmaking as those on Mayrhofen's side.

Experts Not much challenge, except off-piste and the Harakiri piste (read the Mayrhofen chapter).

Intermediates The whole area opens up from the top of the gondola.

Beginners There are nursery areas at the top of the gondola, on Penken, but Mayrhofen is a better base.

Snowboarding See Mayrhofen.

Cross-country Cross-country skiers have to get a bus up to Lanersbach.

Mountain restaurants Read the Mayrhofen chapter.

Schools and guides The Finkenberg is the main one, but the Sunny and Skipower schools also operate here.

Families The Finkenberg school takes children from age four.

STAYING THERE

Hotels The 5-star Sporthotel Stock (6775 410), owned by the family of downhiller Leonard Stock, has great spa facilities. There are several 4-stars, for example, the Eberl (62667) and the Kristall (62840), which is 150m from the gondola with good wellness/spa facilities. The 3-star B&B hotel Harpfner (62094) has been highly recommended in the past.

Eating out Mainly in hotels, notably the Eberl.

Après-ski The main après-ski spots are the lively Laterndl Pub at the foot of the gondola and Finkennest.

Off the slopes OK for the active: curling, ice skating, swimming and good local walks.

Phone numbers
From elsewhere in Austria use the prefix 05287 (Hintertux, Lanersbach) 05285 (Finkenberg); from abroad use the prefix +43 and omit the initial '0'

TOURIST OFFICE
www.tux.at

Ischgl

Ischgl is unique: high, snow-sure slopes, a superb lift system, and a traditional-style Tirolean village. Perfection? Well, not quite ...

RATINGS

The mountains

Extent	★★★★
Fast lifts	★★★★★
Queues	★★★★
Terrain p'ks	★★★★★
Snow	★★★★
Expert	★★★★
Intermediate	★★★★
Beginner	★★
Boarder	★★★★★
X-country	★★★
Restaurants	★★★★
Schools	★★★
Families	★★

The resort

Charm	★★★
Convenience	★★★
Scenery	★★★
Eating out	★★★★
Après-ski	★★★★★
Off-slope	★★★

RPI   110

lift pass	£190
ski hire	£140
lessons	£115
food & drink	£125
total	**£570**

NEWS

2013/14: The resort hopes that a new 150-person cable car to Piz Val Gronda (at the top of our piste map) will open, together with a new 3km red piste down.

Work is due to start on the new Pardatschgrat gondola ready for the 2014/15 season.

2012/13: The Sattel mountain restaurant at Alp Trida and the Höllboden self-service at the chair of the same name have been refurbished and extended.

➕ Compact, traditional-style village with a traffic-free core

➕ High slopes with reliable snow

➕ Broad area of slopes linked to Samnaun in Switzerland

➕ Superb modern lift system

➕ Après-ski like nowhere else, with an unmatched number of exceptionally lively places

➖ Village is densely developed, and has a rather urban, glitzy feel

➖ Not ideal for beginners or timid intermediates, for various reasons

➖ Few seriously steep runs

➖ Very little wooded terrain

➖ Treks to the gondolas for some

➖ Après-ski can be a bit tacky

Ischgl is at last becoming better known to Brits. It's about time – the mountain is one of Austria's best, and we love it (except in a snowstorm).

The village? We're less convinced. We visited a couple of seasons ago as part of a Tirolean tour and, looking back, Ischgl came in seventh out of seven as a place to stay. Yes, it has clear merits. But it's all a bit high-pressure, with thousands of cars and scores of coaches piling in to its parking lots, and little room to breathe.

THE RESORT

Ischgl is a compact village tucked away south of St Anton in the long, narrow Paznaun valley on the Swiss border; the ski area is shared with Samnaun in Switzerland. The Silvretta ski pass also covers Galtür further up the valley (see the end of this chapter) and Kappl and See down the valley (covered in the resort directory, at the back). All are linked by ski-buses and worth visiting; they make cheaper, quieter bases too. A car makes trips to St Anton viable. But beware: heavy snowfalls can close the valley road for days until avalanche danger is cleared.

VILLAGE CHARM ★★★☆☆
More town than village
The buildings are predominantly in traditional chalet style, with one or two modern exceptions, but this is no

rustic backwater – the narrow streets have a towny feel, and the style is swanky and brash rather than tasteful. There's a selection of lively bars and a better-than-usual selection of fashion shops – 'more luxury shops than Lech', says a reporter. The narrow main street plus a couple of side streets are mostly traffic-free – the valley road up to Galtür bypasses the village.

CONVENIENCE ★★★☆☆
Beware of the bypass
As our village plan suggests, it is not a big place; but it's big enough for some of the lodgings to be a good walk from the nearest lift – beware lodgings on the wrong side of the bypass road. You can leave your kit up at Idalp, Pardatschgrat and at the base lifts. Gondolas go up to mid-mountain from two points about 500m apart. The best location, overall, is on or near the main pedestrian street between the two. The eastern gondola station is separated from the main street by a low hill but is reached by an underground moving walkway.

SCENERY ★★★☆☆
Good at the top
The wooded flanks of the valley rise steeply from the village, which gets almost no sun in January. But above the treeline, the Silvretta range is revealed in all its glory.

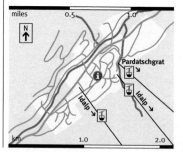

KEY FACTS

Resort	1400m
	4,590ft
Slopes	1400-2870m
	4,590-9,420ft
Lifts	43
Pistes	238km
	148 miles
Blue	20%
Red	64%
Black	16%
Snowmaking	
	1200 guns

This is Ischgl's smaller, quieter, duty-free partner in the ski area – Samnaun in Switzerland ↓

THE MOUNTAINS

Ischgl is a fair-sized, relatively high, snow-sure area. Practically all the slopes are above the treeline, the main exception being the steep lower slopes above the village and a couple of short runs low in the Fimbatal.

The piste map is good. But we have found signposting inadequate and the run numbering confusing: a run may have multiple tributaries, or may split part-way down, with the variants having the same number.

There are two varieties of ski route – plain and 'extreme' – clearly stated to be 'not monitored'.

'Grooming is excellent,' says a 2013 reporter.

EXTENT OF THE SLOPES ★★★★
Extensive cross-border cruising
The sunny **Idalp** plateau, reached by the 24-person Silvrettabahn or the eight-seat Fimbabahn, is the hub of the slopes. It can be very crowded around there. Pardatschgrat, reached by a third gondola, is about 300m higher. From Idalp, lifts radiate to a wide variety of mainly north-west- and west-facing runs and to the Swiss border.

The red runs back down to Ischgl provoke regular complaints. Neither is easy, conditions can be tricky, and countless imbeciles skiing too fast make these runs even more hazardous. Both have final stretches that probably should be black. The wide, quiet piste down the Velilltal

looks better, but turns rather nasty lower down and joins the steep 'black' bottom part of run 1A. Quite a few people choose, very sensibly, to ride the gondolas down.

A short piste brings you from Idalp to the lifts serving the **Höllenkar** bowl, leading up to the area's south-western end and a high point at Palinkopf. Runs of 900m vertical from here lead down to the **Fimbatal**. On the Swiss side, the hub of activity is **Alp Trida**, surrounded by south- and east-facing runs with great views. From here a scenic red run goes down to Compatsch, for buses to Ravaisch (for the cable car back up) and Samnaun. From Palinkopf there is a lovely, long red run down a beautiful valley to Samnaun – not difficult, but very sunny in parts and prone to closure by avalanche risk. There is a long flat stretch at the end.

FAST LIFTS ★★★★★
One of the best
Ischgl is near the top of our fast league table and about 80% of its main lifts are fast – mainly fast chairs. Not surprisingly, reporters praise the lifts – 'best resort I've been to in 20 years', 'superb', say reporters.

QUEUES ★★★★
OK up the mountain
Queues out of the valley are not the problem they once were, since two of the access lifts were upgraded. But peak-time queues still exist. 'Get to the main gondola at 8.30-8.45am to

LIFT PASSES

VIP Skipass

Prices in €

Age	1-day	6-day
under 17	27	128
17 to 59	43	213
60 plus	43	192

Free Under 8

Beginner No deals

Notes Covers Ischgl and Samnaun and local buses; half-day pass and non-skier pass available; family reductions; 2-day-plus pass available only to those with a guest card staying in Ischgl or Mathon

Alternative pass
Regional pass covers Ischgl, Samnaun, Galtür, Kappl and See

avoid them,' says a 2013 visitor. A new jumbo gondola is due to replace the Pardatschgrat one for 2014/15. Crowds on the runs are an issue, especially at Idalp, and on the easier runs on the Swiss side.

TERRAIN PARKS ★★★★★
One of Europe's best
Ischgl is a top place for freestylers. The huge 'excellent' PlayStation Vita park above Idalp is the big draw – 1600m long, and always well maintained.

It has beginner, public and pro lines, revamped each year. Overall, the park obstacles have an impressive creative flair. It has five kickers, 20 elements in a row and an airbag jump. There is another park at Velillscharte and a small park on the Swiss side.

SNOW RELIABILITY ★★★★★
Very good
All the slopes apart from the runs back to the resort are above 1800m, and many on the Ischgl side are north-west-facing. So snow conditions are generally reliable; many reporters comment on excellent early/late season conditions. Snowmaking now covers over half the slopes, including the descents to Ischgl and Samnaun. Reporters praise the grooming.

FOR EXPERTS ★★★★★
Plenty to do
Ischgl can't compare with St Anton for exciting slopes. But by general Tirolean standards it serves experts well. All the blacks are genuine ones and in combination with testing reds offer excellent, challenging descents. Head first for Palinkopf, Greitspitz and Pardatschgrat – piste 4 is a favourite.

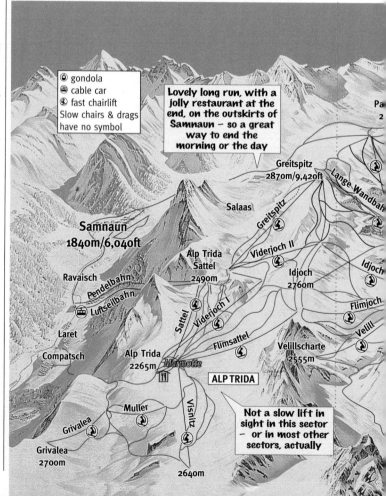

☺ gondola
☺ cable car
☺ fast chairlift
Slow chairs & drags have no symbol

Lovely long run, with a jolly restaurant at the end, on the outskirts of Samnaun – so a great way to end the morning or the day

Greitspitz
2870m/9,420ft

Lange Wandbah

Salaas

Greitspitz

Samnaun
1840m/6,040ft

Viderjoch II

Idjoch

Alp Trida
Sattel
2490m

Idjoch
2760m

Ravaisch

Viderjoch I

Flimjoch

Pendelbahn

Sattel

Velill

Luftseilbahn

Laret

Flimsattel

Velillscharte
2555m

Compatsch

Alp Trida
2265m

Marmotte

ALP TRIDA

Muller

Visnitz

Not a slow lift in sight in this sector – or in most other sectors, actually

Grivalea

Grivalea
2700m

2640m

One of the branches of run 14a on Greitspitz (read our earlier remarks) includes a good steep pitch (70%, they claim). The wooded lower slopes of the Fimbatal are delightful in a storm. There is plenty of off-piste, and powder doesn't get tracked out too quickly, particularly on the Swiss side. We had an excellent day a few seasons ago that included exploration of the shady side of Velilltal. There are also ski routes. Ski route 39 from Palinkopf offers a testing 1000m descent.

FOR INTERMEDIATES ★★★★
Something for everyone
Most of the slopes are wide, forgiving and ideal for intermediates – and there are plenty of them.

At the tough end of the spectrum our favourite runs are those from Palinkopf down to Gampenalp at the edge of the ski area, with great views of virgin slopes. But there are lots of other options on Palinkopf, Greitspitz and Pardatschgrat. The reds down the beautiful Velilltal and the red from Greitspitz into Switzerland are great for quiet, high-speed cruising.

For easier motorway cruising, there is lots of choice, including the runs down around Alp Trida on the Swiss side – but these can get crowded.

FOR BEGINNERS ★★★★★
Up the mountain
Up the mountain at Idalp there are good, sunny, snow-sure nursery slopes served by two moving carpets, drags and two fast chairs, but there are no special deals for beginners – you must buy a full lift pass to reach them. The blue runs on the east side of the bowl offer pleasant progression, and from there it's a small step to Switzerland.

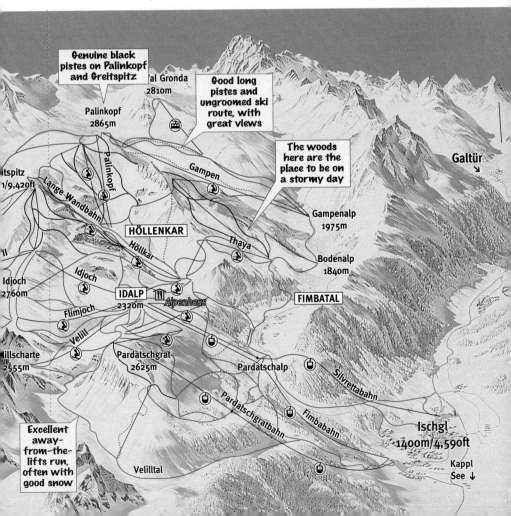

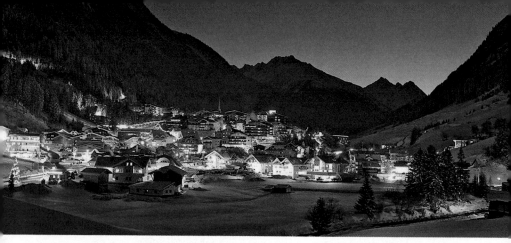

↑ The town looks peaceful and tranquil in this photo – but walk into it and you'll find no shortage of lively bars with loud music and dancing
TVB PAZNAUN-ISCHGL

SCHOOLS

Schneesport-Akademie
t 5257/5404

Classes
5 days (3hr) €180
Private lessons
€115 for 90min; each additional person €25

CHILDCARE

Kindergarten (ski school)
t 5257/5404
Non-skiing children 10am to 4pm; ski-kindergarten for ages 3 to 5

Ski school
From age 5

FOR BOARDERS ★★★★★
Pretty much perfect
Ischgl has long been a popular spot for snowboarders, with its long, wide, well-groomed slopes served by snowboard-friendly gondolas and fast chairlifts. Although the off-piste terrain is less steep than in some other resorts, its above-the-treeline, easily accessible nature and good snow record makes for great riding for most ability levels. Ischgl is home to one of Austria's best terrain parks, and Silvretta Sports and Intersport Mathoy are recommended snowboard shops.

FOR CROSS-COUNTRY ★★★★★
Plenty in the valley
There are 74km of loops in the Ischgl, Galtür and Wirl area. Some trails tend to be shady, especially in early season, and are away from the main slopes, which makes meeting downhillers for lunch inconvenient.

MOUNTAIN RESTAURANTS ★★★★★
Good modern choices
Mountain restaurants generally offer good quality and choice. But they tend to be big and despite this, capacity can be stretched at peak times. They are clearly marked on the piste map.
Editors' choice On the Austrian side at Idalp, the Alpenhaus (6840) is very much a designer place, with both table-service (upstairs) and self-service areas. We're interested only in the former, although service is itself a bit slack. Food is good though, particularly the tarts, and the relaxed ambience is great; a recent reporter confirms our view. On the Swiss side at Alp Trida the Marmotte (+41 81 868 5221) wins no prizes for interior design but does good food in calm

and comfortable surroundings.
Worth knowing about In the Fimbatal the 'lovely' Paznauner Thaya has self-service with famously good pizza, and table-service upstairs for 'fab chicken salad and spicy prawns'; often with live bands or throbbing disco music. Bodenalpe is a bit of a relic but has 'good, simple, cheap food'. At Pardatschgrat, the glass-sided Pardorama complex is impressive, and less crowded than lower places. A recent visitor made it a regular haunt – 'very reasonable prices, excellent rösti'; there's table-service upstairs. A 2013 visitor liked the 'modern' refurbished self-service Höllboden.

On the Swiss side the woody Alp Bella is good value and a consistent favourite with reporters for traditional food and 'old hut' atmosphere. Recent reports on the Alp Trida are enthusiastic. The glass-sided Salaas is very stylish and spacious, but otherwise unremarkable.

SCHOOLS AND GUIDES ★★★★★
No worries
The school meets up at Idalp. Recent reporters have been very happy, with instructors speaking sufficient English and giving 'good advanced lessons'. One visitor's group was smaller than the 10-12 norm. The school also organizes off-piste tours.

FOR FAMILIES ★★★★★
High-altitude options
Children can have lunch with their ski instructor; but small kids would be better off in Galtür or Kappl, where there are good play areas – see the end of this chapter for more on Galtür and the resort directory at the back of the book for more on Kappl.

GETTING THERE

Air Innsbruck 95km/ 60 miles (1hr45); Zürich 240km/150 miles (3hr30); Munich 300km/185 miles (4hr)

Rail Landeck (30km/19 miles); frequent buses from station

UK PACKAGES

Alpine Answers, Crystal, Crystal Finest, Independent Ski Links, Inghams, Interactive Resorts, Kaluma, Mountain Beds, Oxford Ski Co, Ski Bespoke, Ski Expectations, Ski Independence, Ski Solutions, Ski Total, Skitracer, Snow Finders, STC, Zenith
Galtür Crystal, Independent Ski Links, Inghams, Ski Independence, STC

ACTIVITIES

Indoor Silvretta Centre (bowling, billiards, swimming pool, tennis, sauna, solarium, massage), museums, concerts

Outdoor Ice rink, curling, sleigh rides, hiking tours, 7km floodlit toboggan run

STAYING THERE

Chalets Ski Total broke into Ischgl a few seasons ago with the 58-bed chalet hotel Abendrot ('Very pleasant, modern, no noise at night,' says a 2013 reporter), in a central position. A couple of years ago it added the 22-bed Zita, near the Fimbabahn.
Hotels There is a good selection from luxurious and pricey to simple B&Bs.
*****Trofana Royal (600) One of Austria's most luxurious hotels, with prices to match. A celebrity chef runs the kitchen. Sumptuous spa facilities.
****Christine (5346) The best B&B in town? 'Huge rooms, central location, helpful owners, splendid spa.' Pool.
****Elisabeth (5411) Right by the Pardatschgrat gondola, with lively après-ski. Pool, sauna and steam.
****Goldener Adler (5217) Central, traditional ambience but designer rooms; good food. Sauna and spa.
****Gramaser (5293) Near the Trofana Royal. We enjoyed staying here on our last visit; friendly staff, excellent food.
****Jägerhof (5206) Friendly staff, good food, large comfortable rooms. Sauna, steam, spa. 'Food and wine were excellent quality.'
****Lamtana (5609) Near the Silvrettabahn. 'Spacious, modern rooms.' Wellness area.
****Madlein (5226) Convenient, 'terribly chic', modern hotel. 'Excellent' pool, sauna, steam room. Nightclub.
****Post (5232) 'Excellent central position.' Spa.
***Alpenglühn (5294) Convenient, central and good value.
***Arnika (5244) A few minutes' walk from the Fimbabahn gondola. 'Beautiful, gorgeous food, great staff.'
Apartments Some attractive apartments are available. The Golfais by the Pardatschgrat gondola and the apartments in the hotel Solaria (with use of its spa) have been suggested.

EATING OUT ★★★★☆
Plenty of choice
Most restaurants are hotel-based, but not all. We enjoyed excellent, varied meals at the popular Grillalm in hotel Gramaser, which also has the Steakhouse ('very good food and service'). Reporters tip the Salnerhof and Jägerhof ('splendid food and wine') – offering five-course meals and themed evenings. For lighter meals try the Bära Falla ('great pizza and Tirolean food') and Allegra (burgers

etc). The Trofana Alm, which is as much a bar as a restaurant, and the Kitzloch, with its galleries over the dance floor, are best for grills and fondue. For Italian, try the Toscana ('very good') and Salz & Pfeffer.

APRES-SKI ★★★★★
Very lively
Ischgl is the liveliest resort in the Alps, we've concluded after a lot of in-depth research. The fun starts in the early afternoon – mountain restaurants such as Paznauner Thaya slide into après mode directly after lunch – and it doesn't stop; lots of people are still in ski boots late in the evening.

The obvious ports of call in the village are the Trofana Alm near the Silvrettabahn and the Schatzi bar of the hotel Elisabeth by the Pardatschgratbahn – with scantily clad dancing girls ('supremely good fun'). Next door is Freeride, with 'friendly staff, good ski movies and no dancing girls'. Across the river the Kitzloch is one of the places for dancing on the tables in ski boots. Niki's Stadl offers 'surreal madness' thanks to its lively DJs. Feuer & Eis ('great atmosphere') and the basement Kuhstahl are packed all evening – the latter is one reporter's all-time favourite après-bar. The Golden Eagle pub is popular with Brits looking for somewhere to sit ('good music'). We enjoyed a quiet drink at the 'friendly' Kiwi ('weissbier on tap') and cocktails at pricey Guxa.

Later on, we enjoyed dancing to a live band in the huge Trofana Arena, which also has pole dancing, as does the Coyote Ugly. Other nightclubs include Pacha (as in Ibiza and London), Living Room and Posthörndl, with an ancient Rome theme.

OFF THE SLOPES ★★★☆☆
No sun but a nice pool
The village gets little sun in the middle of winter, and the resort is best suited to those keen to hit the slopes. But there's no shortage of off-slope activities. There are lots of maintained paths including many at altitude (the tourist office claims an astonishing 1140km in the valley), a 7km floodlit toboggan run and a splendid sports centre with swimming pool and bowling. And you can browse upmarket shops. It's easy to get around the valley by bus, and the Smuggler Card for pedestrians enables them to use specially selected lifts.

Phone numbers
Calling long-distance
Add the prefix given
below for each resort;
when calling from
abroad use the
country code +43 and
omit the initial '0'
Ischgl
05444
Galtür
05443
Samnaun
(Switzerland)
From elsewhere in
Switzerland add the
prefix 081; from
abroad use the prefix
+41 81

TOURIST OFFICES

Ischgl
www.ischgl.com

Samnaun
(Switzerland)
www.samnaun.ch

Galtür
www.galtuer.com

LINKED RESORT – 1840m

SAMNAUN

Small, quiet duty-free Samnaun is in a corner of Switzerland more easily reached from Austria. We know of no UK tour operators going here, but a recent reporter reckons more Brits are finding their way here.

There are four small components, roughly 1km apart: Samnaun-Dorf, prettily set at the head of the valley and the main focus, with some swanky hotels and duty-free shops; Ravaisch, where the cable car goes up; tiny Plan; and the hamlets of Laret and Compatsch, at the end of the main piste to the valley. We've stayed happily on the edge of Dorf in the Waldpark B&B (8602255), and a recent visitor highly recommends the hotel Montana (8619000) for 'comfy rooms, fab pool, three great restaurants'. Other tips: 4-star Muttler (8618130) (with a good spa and complimentary ski-bus), and Des Alpes (8685273). There's the smart AlpenQuell spa-pool-fitness centre.

The Schmuggler Alm at the bottom of the long run from Palinkopf is a popular lunch and après-ski spot. The Almraus (hotel Cresta) at Compatsch has been recommended for drinks. The school is 'first class', says a reporter.

UP-VALLEY VILLAGE – 1585m

GALTÜR

Galtür is a charming, peaceful, traditional village clustered around a pretty little church, amid impressive mountain scenery at the head of Ischgl's Paznaun valley. Many visitors find the resort very quiet – there are just a few shops, restaurants, and a 'fantastic bakery for coffee and cakes', but a recent visitor 'loved the contrast from bustling Ischgl'.

Sunnier and cheaper than Ischgl, Galtür is a good base for families and mixed-ability groups. Galtür's own slopes rise to 2295m above a lift base at Wirl, a short bus ride from the village. The free buses to Ischgl are regular and quick but overcrowded at peak times even in January; and they stop at around 6pm. Taxis to Ischgl's nightlife are economic if shared. But a recent visitor warns that the roads to both Wirl and Ischgl were closed due to avalanche danger for two days – meaning he was unable to ski.

Galtür's Silvapark ski area has six 'sectors' to help guests make the most of the mountain; there are freestyle and family sectors, for example. The slopes can be bleak in poor weather, and have only 40km of pistes, served by two fast chairs, a gondola and some long draglifts. Queues are rare. The slopes are fairly high, so pretty snow-sure; we had good snow on a warm March visit. Grooming is good.

Most runs are classified red, though some would be blue elsewhere. Run 8 is one of our favourites; a broad, long cruise with great views of the frozen dam below. The main blue piste can get crowded and has a steeper section at the top, but it is a long, pretty cruise to the valley. There are some challenges – reds and a black served by the fast Ballunspitze chair are short and steep. And there are a couple of ski routes to try. The area on the far right of the piste map, served by a slow double chair and a T-bar, is quiet, shady and has some good off-piste in a bowl and among well-spaced trees. There's a terrain park, and a fine nursery area at the lift base.

The school is 'excellent' and offers small classes. Kinderland has its own tow, carousel, moving carpet and cartoon characters. There are 74km of cross-country loops in the Galtür, Ischgl and Wirl area. The cosy, wooden Wieberhimml mountain hut is a lively, sunny spot for drinks. And we had good food at the Panorama Tenne, beside the gondola. The Faulbrunnalm at the top of the gondola is 'never overcrowded'. The Addis Abeba is a hip bar near the Soppalift drag.

There are good hotels. The 'comfortable' 4-star Almhof (8253) has 'excellent evening meals, every course a work of art'. A reporter who stayed at the Alpenhotel Tirol (8206) for the third time in 2013 says it is 'a good family hotel, with food and service second to none'. Flüchthorn (8202) has a 'charming restaurant, traditional Tirol atmosphere', Ballunspitze (8214) and 3-star Alpenrose (8201) have also been recommended in the past.

Off-slope facilities are limited, apart from the impressive Alpinarium, an avalanche-protection structure and exhibition centre built after the avalanche that devastated the village in 1999. Much of the information is in German, but it's worth a visit. There's a sports centre with pool, tennis and squash – and night skiing and tobogganing on Wednesdays.

Kitzbühel

Despite the racy image, the slopes are mostly pretty tame; the town at the base, though, is something special – cute and lively

RATINGS

The mountains

Extent	★★★
Fast lifts	★★★★★
Queues	★★★
Terrain p'ks	★★★
Snow	★★
Expert	★★★
Intermediate	★★★★
Beginner	★★
Boarder	★★
X-country	★★★
Restaurants	★★★★
Schools	★★★★
Families	★

The resort

Charm	★★★★
Convenience	★★
Scenery	★★★
Eating out	★★★★
Après-ski	★★★★
Off-slope	★★★★★

RPI 105

lift pass	£200
ski hire	£115
lessons	£115
food & drink	£120
total	**£550**

NEWS

2013/14: At Jochberg, the old double chair and drag are to be replaced by a 10-seater gondola, the Wagstättbahn.

2012/13: On Resterhöhe the Zweitausender double chair was replaced by an eight-seater. In the Hahnenkamm sector the Walde T-bar was replaced by a six-pack. Snowmaking was increased in several areas.

+ Extensive, attractive, varied slopes offering a sensation of travel

+ Beautiful medieval town centre

+ Vibrant nightlife

+ Lots to do off the slopes

+ Hotels to suit every budget

+ Excellent mountain restaurants

− Low altitude means snow is often poor low down (though snowmaking is fairly extensive)

− Surprisingly few challenges on-piste

− Disappointing resort-level nursery area

− Some crowded pistes

Kitzbühel's Hahnenkamm downhill race course is the most exciting on the World Cup circuit, and race weekend is one of the key dates on the Alpine social calendar. But the place also has powerful attractions for the rest of us.

The lift system has improved hugely in the decade since the massive 3S cross-valley gondola linked Pengelstein to Wurzhöhe, and with a big new gondola at Jochberg this season the area now merits a ★★★★★ rating for fast lifts.

Sadly, it doesn't get the same for snow – for us, the great weakness common to the resorts of the Kitzbüheler Alpen region. It's not a matter of quantity, but of quality. Just once, we arrived in a storm and had good piste conditions to valley level. Normally, as in early March 2013, we find highly variable conditions, with rock-hard pistes in the afternoon. The fact is, Kitzbühel needs more altitude.

The authorities are obviously alert to this, and amazingly have managed to raise the place by a few metres: although topo maps have always shown the centre at a smidge over 760m, these days the resort puts itself at 800m. Very enterprising; but it'll take more than that to do the trick.

THE RESORT

Kitzbühel is a large, animated valley town with its major ski area on one side and its minor one on the other. The major area, spreading south-west from the famous Hahnenkamm directly above the town, is shared with another substantial resort, Kirchberg, covered at the end of the chapter.

The 'still great value' Kitzbüheler Alpen AllStarCard lift pass covers seven separate ski areas in the region

– read 'Lift passes'. One of those – the SkiWelt – is accessible by the Ki-West gondola, a short bus ride from Skirast.

VILLAGE CHARM ★★★★
A historic town

The largely car-free medieval centre is delightful. Many visitors love the upscale, towny ambience and swanky shops and cafes. But the resort spreads widely, and busy roads surround the old town. This is no peaceful little Austrian village.

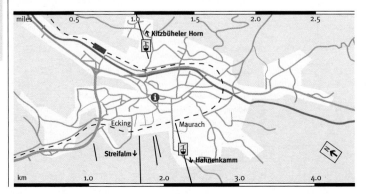

CONVENIENCE ★★★★★
Choose your spot carefully

A gondola from the edge of the town goes up to the Hahnenkamm, start of the main area of slopes. Across town, close to the railway station but some way from the centre, another gondola accesses the much smaller Kitzbüheler Horn sector.

The size of Kitzbühel (compare the map below with other Austrian resorts, such as Ischgl) makes choice of location important. Many visitors prefer to be in the centre of town and close to the Hahnenkamm gondola. Beginners should bear in mind that the Hahnenkamm nursery slopes are often lacking in snow, and then novices are taken up the Horn. Views have varied on the free buses that circle the town. The circular route and high-season crowding have led some recent reporters to walk instead, but a regular visitor rates them 'quick, efficient and uncrowded'. There are ski/boot depots at obvious points.

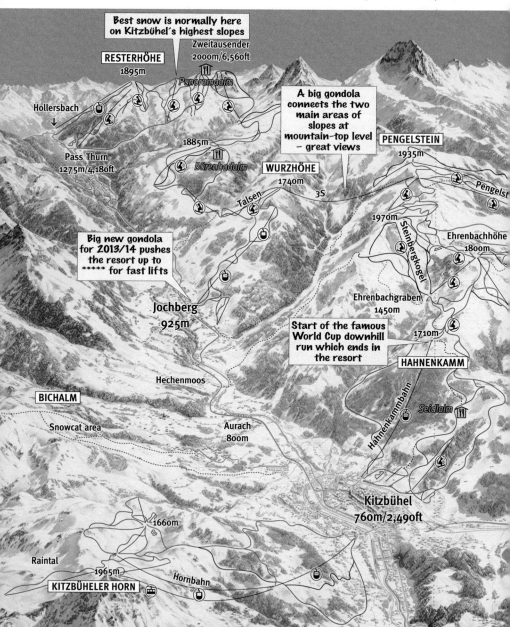

Best snow is normally here on Kitzbühel's highest slopes

RESTERHÖHE 1895m

Zweitausender 2000m/6,56oft

Panoramaalm

Hollersbach

A big gondola connects the two main areas of slopes at mountain-top level – great views

PENGELSTEIN 1935m

1885m

Pengelst

Pass Thurn 1275m/4,18oft

Bärenbadalm

WURZHÖHE 1740m

Talsen

3S

1970m

Steinbergkogel

Ehrenbachhöhe 1800m

Big new gondola for 2013/14 pushes the resort up to ★★★★★ for fast lifts

Jochberg 925m

Ehrenbachgraben 1450m

Start of the famous World Cup downhill run which ends in the resort

1710m

HAHNENKAMM

Hechenmoos

BICHALM

Snowcat area

Aurach 800m

Hahnenkammbahn

Seidlalm

Kitzbühel 760m/2,490ft

1660m

Raintal

1965m

Hornbahn

KITZBÜHELER HORN

SCENERY ★★★☆☆
Attractive valley views

Kitzbühel is set at a junction of broad, pretty valleys, among partly wooded mountains. There are good views from Pengelstein across both valleys (the minor peak of Gr Rettenstein is prominent) and to the SkiWelt. From the Resterhöhe slopes, in particular, there are great panoramic views of the high Alps to the south, including Grossvenediger directly south and Grossglockner slightly east of south.

THE MOUNTAINS

Kitzbühel's extensive slopes – shared with Kirchberg and other villages – offer some open runs higher up but soon run into patchy forest lower down. Most face north-east or north-west. The piste map is pretty clear. Many readers find that run classifications exaggerate difficulty – though not everyone agrees. One reporter reckons the Zweitausender red run at Resterhöhe should still be

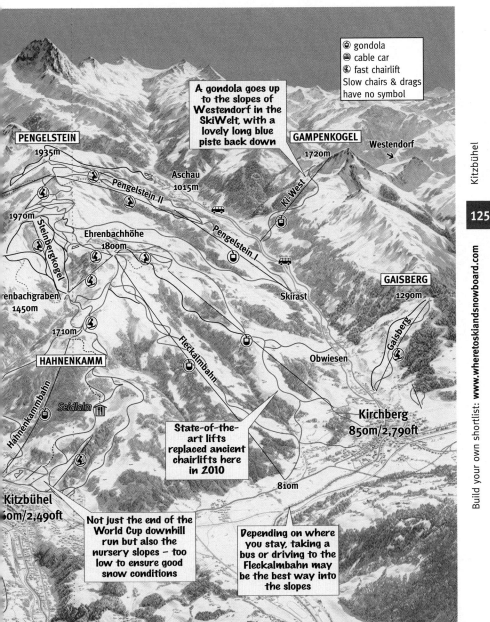

gondola
cable car
fast chairlift
Slow chairs & drags have no symbol

PENGELSTEIN
1935m

A gondola goes up to the slopes of Westendorf in the SkiWelt, with a lovely long blue piste back down

GAMPENKOGEL
1720m

Westendorf

Aschau
1015m

Pengelstein II

Ki West

Pengelstein I

1970m

Steinbergkogel

Ehrenbachhöhe
1800m

GAISBERG
1290m

renbachgraben
1450m

Skirast

Gaisberg

1710m

Fleckalmbahn

Obwiesen

HAHNENKAMM

Seidlalm

Kirchberg
850m/2,790ft

Hahnenkammbahn

State-of-the-art lifts replaced ancient chairlifts here in 2010

810m

Kitzbühel
om/2,490ft

Not just the end of the World Cup downhill run but also the nursery slopes – too low to ensure good snow conditions

Depending on where you stay, taking a bus or driving to the Fleckalmbahn may be the best way into the slopes

classified black. The key thing is the snow. When we were there in early March 2013, that run was like glass in the late afternoon, causing widespread misery. But it is not of black gradient. (Even the black variant is barely of black gradient.)

EXTENT OF THE SLOPES ★★★★★
Big but bitty
The slopes can be divided into several identifiable areas. The **Hahnenkamm** gondola takes you to the bowl of Ehrenbachgraben, a major lift bottleneck in the past but, thanks to new lifts in the last few years, now a place you might want to do laps on the steep slopes of Steinbergkogel.

Beyond is the slightly lower peak of **Pengelstein**, with an eight-pack up to it from the Steinbergkogel area. Long west-facing runs go down to Skirast, where there is a gondola back up, or to Aschau. Ski-buses from these points will take you to the Ki-West gondola towards Westendorf and to Kirchberg.

Pengelstein is also the start of the impressive 30-person cross-valley 3S gondola to **Wurzhöhe** above Jochberg. This peak-to-peak link has fabulous views (especially if you hit the cabin with the partial glass floor).

Further lifts then take you to the **Resterhöhe** sector – well worth the excursion, for better snow and fewer crowds. There is a long, scenic, sunny red run to Breitmoos, mid-station of the gondola up from Hollersbach. Runs are otherwise short, but mostly served by fast chairs.

The **Kitzbüheler Horn** gondola second stage leads to the sunny Trattalm bowl, with an alternative cable car taking you up to the summit of the Horn, from where a fine, solitary piste leads down into the Raintal on the east side. There's a blue piste and two ski routes back towards town.

The separate **Bichlalm** area, which used to offer lift-served off-piste, now offers guided snowcat skiing. The piste map shows a projected replacement lift, but it is not imminent.

FAST LIFTS ★★★★★
Continuing to improve
Lift upgrades saw the resort move from three to four stars three years ago, and the big new gondola at Jochberg lifts it into the five-star category this year. Even so, this is no Saalbach or Ischgl – some problems remain. The trip back from Resterhöhe still involves a slow chair and a drag.

QUEUES ★★★★★
Still some problems
There can still be peak-time queues for the Hahnenkamm gondola out of the town and occasional queues up the hill, especially if good weather at the weekend attracts Germans. The cross-valley gondola to Wurzhöhe has relieved pressure on the slopes closer to town, by encouraging people to use the Resterhöhe slopes, but has created new problems. The Zweitausender chair (unavoidable en route to Resterhöhe) was upgraded to an eight-seater for 2012/13, which dealt with

THE HAHNENKAMM DOWNHILL

KITZBÜHEL TOURISMUS

Kitzbühel's Hahnenkamm Downhill race, held in mid- to late January each year (24 to 26 January in 2014), is the toughest as well as one of the most famous on the World Cup circuit. On the race weekend the town is packed, and there is a real carnival atmosphere, with bands, people in traditional costumes and huge (and loud) cowbells everywhere. The race itself starts with a steep icy section before you hit the famous Mausfalle and Steilhang, where even Franz Klammer used to get worried. The course starts near the top of the Hahnenkamm gondola and drops 860m to finish amid the noise and celebrations right on the edge of town. The course is normally closed from the start of the season until the race is over, but after the race weekend ordinary mortals can try most of the course, if the snow is good enough – it's an unpisted ski route mostly. We found it steep and tricky in parts, even when going slowly – it must be terrifying at race speeds of 80mph or more.

LIFT PASSES

Prices in €

Age	1-day	6-day
under 16	23	113
16 to 18	36	180
19 plus	45	225

Free Under 7

Senior 60+: day pass €36 on Tue & Thu; 80+: season pass €20

Beginner Reduced pass for Gaisberg and Ganslern chairs only; seven free lifts (three in Kitzbühel)

Notes Covers Kitzbühel, Kirchberg, Jochberg, Pass Thurn, Mittersill/Hollersbach; hourly and pedestrian tickets; family reductions; 50% reduction on pool entry; for passes of 2+ days, additional €15 a day to ski in the SkiWelt area

Alternative passes Kitzbüheler Alpen AllStarCard covers Kitzbühel, Schneewinkel (St Johann), SkiWelt, Ski Juwel, Skicircus Saalbach, Zell-Kaprun; Salzburg Super Ski Card covers 22 ski areas in the Salzburg province

that old bottleneck. But the chair and particularly the drag you need to get back from Resterhöhe build queues on busy afternoons.

TERRAIN PARKS ★★★☆☆
Double the fun
The DC Snowpark Hanglalm at Resterhöhe has lots for advanced riders – several kicker lines, from big to huge, as well as advanced rails, a plethora of butter boxes and a visually pleasing wooden obstacle section. Pro riders love the park's centrepiece – a huge gap jump. But it also has an area aimed at beginners and intermediates. The original park on the Kitzbüheler Horn – the Horn-Mini-New-School-Park – is now specifically a beginner area. The park in nearby Westendorf is excellent – well worth the trip.

SNOW RELIABILITY ★★☆☆☆
More snowmaking now
The problem is that Kitzbühel's slopes have one of the lowest average heights in the Alps, and the Horn is also sunny. Even in an exceptionally good snow year some reporters complain of worn patches, ice and slush on the lower slopes. In a normal year, the lower slopes can be very tricky when slushy or more especially when icy (though the snow at the top is often OK). The expansion of snowmaking has improved matters when it's cold enough to make snow – runs down to Kitzbühel, Kirchberg, Klausen and Jochberg are covered. A 2011 visitor found conditions 'better than feared' because of this. But many slopes still remain unprotected. If snow is poor, head for Resterhöhe.

FOR EXPERTS ★★★☆☆
Plan to go off-piste
Steep slopes – pistes and off-piste terrain – are mostly concentrated in the Steinbergkogel–Ehrenbachgraben area, equipped with three fast chairs. Direttissima is seriously steep, but sometimes groomed – fabulous. The other blacks dotted around are easier. There are plenty of long, challenging reds. When conditions allow, there is plenty of gentler off-piste to be found – some of it safely close to pistes, some requiring a guide. And the long ski routes from Pengelstein towards Jochberg and Hechenmoos are delightful in good snow.

FOR INTERMEDIATES ★★★★☆
Lots of alternatives
The Hahnenkamm area is prime terrain but can get crowded. Good intermediates will want to do the World Cup downhill run, of course (see the feature panel earlier in the chapter). And the long blues of around 1000m vertical to Klausen, Kirchberg and Skirast are satisfying. The black to Aschau is not difficult, and a lovely way to end the day (check the bus times first).

The Wurzhöhe runs are good for mixed abilities, and the short, high runs at Resterhöhe are ideal if you are more timid. There are easy reds down to Pass Thurn and Jochberg (but heed our earlier note about the tricky red Zweitausender run). This area tends to be much quieter than Hahnenkamm and Pengelstein. Much of the Horn is good cruising, and the east-facing Raintal is excellent (but, again, it has a slow chair back).

UK PACKAGES

Alpine Answers, Alpine
Weekends, Carrier,
Crystal, Crystal Finest,
Elegant Resorts,
Independent Ski Links,
Inghams, Kaluma,
Momentum, Mountain
Beds, Neilson, Oxford
Ski Co, Ski Line, Ski
Solutions, Skitracer,
Snow Finders,
Snowscape, STC,
Thomson
Kirchberg Crystal,
Inghams, Ski Bespoke,
Snowscape, STC

SNOWPIX.COM / CHRIS GILL

The mountainside
below Steinbergkogel
offers the steepest
slopes around, off-
piste and on the
black Direttissima ↓

FOR BEGINNERS ★★★★★
Not ideal

The Hahnenkamm nursery slopes are
no more than adequate, and prone to
poor snow conditions – but at least
they have some free lifts. There are
nursery areas with free lifts at
Jochberg, Pass Thurn and Aschau, too.
The Horn has a high, sunny, nursery-
like section, and quick learners will
soon be cruising home from there on
the long Hagstein piste. There are
some easy runs to progress to if the
snow is OK. Day and two-day lift
passes just for the Horn slopes are
available. But there are better resorts
to learn in.

FOR BOARDERS ★★★★★
Gaining recognition

Kitzbühel was never known as a
snowboarders' hub, but it is growing
in popularity, year on year. There are
two decent parks and some good off-
piste runs and fun natural obstacles
on the Hahnenkamm and around
Pengelstein. All the major lifts are now
gondolas or chairlifts – so the area
suits beginners well. But a couple of
reporters have drawn attention to the
many flat linking runs, on which
boarders struggle – one versatile chap
ditched his board after a day, and
rented skis instead.

FOR CROSS-COUNTRY ★★★★★
Plentiful but low

There are around 60km of trails
scattered around. Most are at valley
level and prone to lack of snow, but a
2012 reporter who got lots of snow
highly recommends them.

MOUNTAIN RESTAURANTS ★★★★★
A highlight

There are many attractive restaurants,
most offering table-service – one of
the highlights of this resort. Last year
there were two pocket guides in
circulation, but both in German.
Restaurants are named on the piste
map – there are 59 in total.
Editors' choice Bärenbadalm (0664 855
7994), halfway to Resterhöhe, has a
cool, modern bar area with flat-screen
TVs, a roaring log fire and comfy
armchairs and sofas; you can eat there
or in various dining areas with a more
rustic feel. We've had delicious oriental
beef strip salad and crispy pork ribs
here. Endorsed by reporters. But the
terrace is spoiled by the adjacent lift
station – not a criticism you can level
at the Panoramaalm up at Resterhöhe.
This has both a beautiful, intimate
interior and a fine terrace including a
great bar (get there early to bag a
spot). Excellent food. Seidlalm (63135),
right by the lower part of the downhill
course, is quiet and delightfully rustic.
Worth knowing about In the
Hahnenkamm sector we had a jolly
meal at Berghaus Tyrol ('Try the woks,'
says a 2012 visitor). On our 2012 visit
we had a fabulous strudel at the
Sonnbühel – lovely situation, sheltered
and with a good view. One Kitz regular
lists Hahnenkammstüberl among her
favourites ('particularly good gröstl').
Other tips are Hochkitzbühel
('wonderfully light and airy', 'good
menu, food quality and table-service')
and Hochbrunn ('best Gröstl mit Ei').
   On Pengelstein, Usterweis is a nice
woody traditional place that 'neither

SCHOOLS

Rote Teufel
t 62500

Element3
t 72301

Snowsports
t 0664 390 0090

Classes
(Rote Teufel prices)
6 days (2hr am and
pm) €195
Private lessons
From €85 for 1hr

CHILDCARE

There is no non-ski
nursery, but
babysitters and
nannies can be hired

Ski school
From age 3

ACTIVITIES

Indoor Aquarena
centre (pools, slides,
sauna, solarium,
steam baths –
discounted entry with
lift pass); Sportpark
(tennis, bowling,
climbing wall), fitness
studios, beauty
centres, museums,
casino, cinema

Outdoor Ice rink
(curling and skating),
tobogganing,
ballooning, 65km of
cleared walking paths

GETTING THERE

Air Salzburg 75km/
45 miles (1hr30);
Munich 165km/
105 miles (2hr30);
Innsbruck 95km/
60 miles (1hr30)

Rail Mainline station
in resort; post bus
every 15min from
station

enthused nor disappointed' a 2012
visitor; at Gauxerstad'l he found 'a
limited menu but good, friendly
service and mountainous portions'.

At Wurzhöhe/Resterhöhe, try
Hanglalm, Sonnalm, Bruggeralm
('cheap and cheerful with a very
pleasant veranda') or Berggasthaus
Resterhöhe ('wonderful blutwurstgröstl
and so welcoming').

On the Horn, there's the Hornköpfl-
Hütte, and also Gipfelhaus, which is
quieter, with 'super views'. The
Adlerhütte is 'a favourite'.

On the pistes down to Kirchberg
the Fleckalm 'offers better service and
food than some of the smarter places',
reports a 2012 visitor. We can
recommend the meaty gulaschsuppe
at the Maieralm.

They're not very mountainous, but
a reader this year tips the restaurants
in Aschau, at the end of the liftless
black Schwarzkogel run, where you
may have a bit of a wait for a bus.

SCHOOLS AND GUIDES ★★★★
Red Devils rule
The Kitzbühel Rote Teufel (Red Devils)
is the largest. The other schools
emphasize their small scale. Element3
is an adventure company offering ski/
snowboard classes. Reports please.

FOR FAMILIES ★★★★★
Not an ideal choice
It's rather a spread-out resort for
family holiday purposes. Rote Teufel
takes kids from age three.

STAYING THERE

Kitzbühel is essentially a hotel resort.
Chalets Crystal has a 35-bed chalet
close to the Hahnenkamm gondola.
Hotels There is an enormous choice.
★★★★★Schloss Lebenberg (6901)
Modernized 'castle' with smart
wellness centre; inconvenient location
but free shuttle-bus.
★★★★★Tennerhof (63181) Luxurious
former farmhouse, with renowned
restaurant. Beautiful panelled rooms.
Relais & Châteaux.
★★★★Best Western Kaiserhof (75503)
By the Hahnenkamm gondola. Spa,
pool.
★★★★Maria Theresia (64711) Central.
'Food good, rooms well appointed and
staff very helpful.'
★★★★Rasmushof (652520) Right on the
slopes by the race finish area, close to
centre of town.

★★★★Schwarzer Adler (6911) Traditional
hotel turned swanky boutique hotel.
Roof-top pool, spa.
★★★★Tiefenbrunner (66680) Traditional,
family-run. Pool, spa. 'The standards
set by the highly visible owners are
impeccably high, the food is superb
and the facilities faultless.'
★★★Edelweiss (75252) Close to centre.
'Most welcoming hotel we've ever
stayed at; supply bags for you to take
food from breakfast table for lunch.'
★★★Strasshofer (62285) Central. 'Great
location, friendly, good food – hard to
beat for brilliant value,' says a regular.
★★Mühlbergerhof (62835) Small,
friendly pension in good position.
Apartments Many of the best are
attached to hotels.

EATING OUT ★★★★
Something for everyone
There is a wide range of restaurants to
suit all pockets, including pizzerias
and fast-food outlets (even
McDonald's) as well as gourmet dining.

The Neuwirt in the chic Schwarzer
Adler hotel is regarded as the best in
town, and wins awards from food
guides. The Chizzo offers fine dining in
one of the oldest buildings in
Kitzbühel. Good, cheaper places
include the traditional Huberbräu-
Stüberl, Zinnkrug, Eggerwirt and, a
little out of town with great views,
Hagstein (traditional farm food). The
Goldene Gams restaurant in the hotel
Tiefenbrunner has a wide menu. Both
the Centro and the Barrique are
recommended for their pizzas. For
something different take a taxi to
Rosi's Sonnbergstub'n. Choose the
speciality lamb or duck and expect to
be serenaded by Rosi herself.

Seidlalm is the place for a jolly
Tirolean evening on the lower slopes.
On Fridays you can dine at the top of
the Hahnenkamm gondola at the
Hochkitzbühel.

APRES-SKI ★★★★
A main attraction
Nightlife is one of Kitz's attractions, and a 2013 reporter found 'plenty of lively bars for après-ski'. As the lifts close the town is jolly without being much livelier than many other Tirolean resorts. The Streifalm bar at the foot of the slopes is popular. 'The outside bar at Chizzo was great fun,' says a recent reporter whose favourite bar was the Pavillion – 'great staff and a great party atmosphere'. Praxmair and Rupprechter are among the most atmospheric cafes for teatime cakes and pastries. The Centro and the 'quaint' Ursprung are recommended by a 2012 visitor for pre-dinner drinks.

The Lichtl Pub has thousands of lights hanging from the ceiling. The Londoner is a bit of an institution, appealing particularly to young Brits, but a grown-up visiting this year enjoyed it. The heated terrace of the Stamperl, across the road, was doing a roaring trade when we visited last season. La Fonda is 'worth a look' says a 2013 reporter, as 'it's frequented by locals'. The Python, Highways and Take Five are discos.

OFF THE SLOPES ★★★★★
Plenty to do
The lift pass gives a reduction for the pools in the Aquarena centre. There's skating, ice hockey, bowling etc at the Sportpark. There's a museum and a casino. The railway makes excursions easy (eg Salzburg, Innsbruck).

LINKED RESORT – 850m
KIRCHBERG
Kirchberg is a large, busy, spread-out town, with plentiful restaurants and shops and an unremarkable but pleasant centre. The road from Kitzbühel towards Innsbruck bypasses the centre, but traffic is still intrusive.

The slopes it shares with Kitzbühel are accessed via a choice of three gondolas, all requiring the use of 'regular and efficient' ski-buses or affordable taxis (unless you opt to stay at a lift base rather than in the town). The newish Maierlbahn goes from a station 1km from the centre, while the Fleckalmbahn goes up from Klausen beside the road to Kitzbühel about 1.5km out. The third is over 3km out at Skirast. Another 2km on from Skirast is a gondola into Westendorf's slopes. These are linked to the main

SkiWelt slopes via Brixen, which can also easily be reached by train or bus – read the chapter on Söll for more on these. There is a small nursery slope at the bottom of the separate Gaisberg sector, with a free lift, but it's at low altitude, and so prone to poor snow.

The village has a wide choice of lodging; the 4-star Klausen (2128) is convenient for the Klausen gondola, and a 2012 visitor enjoyed the 'cosy' Haus Alpenblick (2234), a five-minute walk from the centre – 'welcoming, good food'. Most restaurants are hotel-based, but there are a couple of pizzerias, a Chinese and a steakhouse.

There is some après action, both at teatime and later on. The restaurants on the home runs do good business as the lifts close. Rohrerstadl, just above Skirast, is tipped for 'animated' après-ski – 'live group; staff very attentive'. We were lucky enough in 2012 to get a dispatch from one of our few après specialists. He reckons the Boomerang is 'the most lively and welcoming bar, with pool table and efficient table-service'. The popular London Pub he rated the most filthy and depressing place he has visited. Several places operate as discos later.

Off the slopes there's floodlit tobogganing on Gaisberg and a leisure centre, and some hotels have pools.

LINKED RESORT – 925m
JOCHBERG
Jochberg – 10km south of Kitzbühel – is not so much a village as a straggle of accommodation along a busy road – it has nothing you could call a centre. There's a church, a bank, a post office, a ski depot, a supermarket, half a dozen restaurants and a couple of bars. But if you're after accommodation close to the lifts, it's worth considering.

Access to the slopes has been greatly improved with a 10-seater gondola replacing an old, slow double chair, and a quite long T-bar above it – a development we guess is not unrelated to the opening in 2011 of the cutting-edge 5-star Kempinski Hotel das Tirol a few metres away.

Most of the other lodgings are small pensions and apartments, but there is also the 4-star Jochbergerhof. Of the restaurants the Alpenland is recommended by a 2012 visitor: 'Good value for money, friendly service, superb food.'

Phone numbers
From elsewhere in Austria add the prefix 05356 for Kitzbühel and 05357 for Kirchberg; from abroad use the prefixes +43 5356 / +43 5357

TOURIST OFFICES
Kitzbühel
www.kitzbuehel.com
Kirchberg
www.kirchberg.at

Lech

Simply one of the best: a captivating village with exceptionally snowy slopes that are set for a big expansion in 2013/14

RATINGS

The mountains

Extent	★★★
Fast lifts	★★★★
Queues	★★★★
Terrain p'ks	★★★★
Snow	★★★★
Expert	★★★★
Intermediate	★★★★
Beginner	★★★★
Boarder	★★★★
X-country	★★★
Restaurants	★★★
Schools	★★★★
Families	★★★★★

The resort

Charm	★★★★
Convenience	★★★
Scenery	★★★
Eating out	★★★
Après-ski	★★★★
Off-slope	★★★

RPI 125

lift pass	£210
ski hire	£165
lessons	£120
food & drink	£150
total	**£645**

NEWS

2013/14: A new 10-seat gondola is planned to link Lech with the Warth-Schröcken ski area (which will also be covered by the Arlberg lift pass and has 68km of runs).

+ Picturesque traditional village
+ Sunny but quite high slopes with excellent snow record
+ Sizeable area of intermediate pistes, plus extensive off-piste
+ Easy access by bus to the slopes of St Anton and other Arlberg resorts
+ Some very smart hotels
+ Lots of lovely heated chairlifts
+ Lively après-ski scene

– Pricey, by Austrian standards
– Surprisingly limited shopping
– Few non-hotel bars or restaurants
– Local traffic intrudes on main street
– Very few challenging pistes
– Nearly all slopes above treeline
– Blue runs back to Lech are rather steep for nervous novices
– Still a few slow, old lifts

We've always loved the ski area that Lech shares with its higher neighbour Zürs for its excellent intermediate pistes and great off-piste in one of the snowiest parts of the Alps. From 2013/14 it is due to get even better with a new link to neighbouring and even snowier Warth–Schröcken – adding 50% more pistes and lots of off-piste. We can't wait to try the newly expanded area in 2014.

Lech and Zürs are the most fashionable resorts in Austria, each able to point to a string of celebrity visitors, and to pull in Porsche-borne Germans by the thousand. Don't worry: we don't feel out of place here in our VWs or Skodas, and neither would you. We always try to stay in Lech with its pretty riverside setting and deeply comfortable hotels; its attraction will be even greater now that it will be in the centre of the new 190km ski area. Zürs has a bleak setting and is spoiled by the through-traffic going to and from Lech. The road to Lech needs to be buried in a tunnel. A whip-round among the owners of the four 5-star hotels should be enough to raise the necessary.

131

THE RESORT

Lech is an old farming village set in a high valley that spent long periods of winter cut off from the outside world until the Flexen Pass road through Zürs was constructed at the end of the 19th century. Even now, the road can be closed for days on end after an exceptional snowfall.

Not far from the centre is the cable car up to Oberlech: a small, traffic-free area of 4-star hotels set on the piste.

Zug is a hamlet 3km from Lech, with a lift into the Lech slopes. It's not ideal for sampling Lech's nightlife, but there is an evening bus service.

Lech is linked by lifts and runs to higher Zürs (described at the end of this chapter) to the south, and from 2013/14 is due to be linked by a new gondola (but not by piste) to Warth and Schröcken to the north (read the feature panel later in this chapter) – adding 50% more pistes.

There is a free and regular – but often very crowded – ski-bus service between Lech and Zürs but the road to Warth and Schröcken is closed in winter because of avalanche danger. Free buses (also crowded) go to Alpe Rauz for the St Anton ski area, which is also covered by the Arlberg pass (see separate chapter). There's also a (less crowded but not free) post bus which runs to St Anton, St Christoph and Stuben. The Sonnenkopf area at Klösterle, reached by free ski-bus from Stuben, is also covered by the Arlberg pass (see the Vorarlberg – Alpenregion Bludenz chapter).

VILLAGE CHARM ★★★★★
Busy main street

The village is attractive, with upmarket hotels built in traditional chalet style, a gurgling river plus bridges, and a high incidence of snow on the streets. But don't expect a rustic idyll: away from the central area the place is fairly ordinary, and the appeal is somewhat dimmed by traffic on the main street, especially at weekends when car-borne German and Austrian visitors arrive and depart.

CONVENIENCE ★★★★★
It's a long village

The heart of the village is a short stretch of the main street beside the river, with most of the main hotels, the main shop (Strolz) and the Rüfikopf cable car, for access to the Zürs slopes. Just across the river are the chairlifts for Lech's main area of slopes. Chalets, apartments and pensions are dotted around the valley, and the village spreads for 2km. Some of the cheaper accommodation is quite a walk from the lifts.

Oberlech is a tiny place with pistes where you would expect streets, and an underground tunnel system linking the hotels and cable car station – used routinely to move baggage, and by guests in bad weather. The cable car works until 1am, allowing access to the nightlife down in Lech.

SCENERY ★★★★★
In a bright spot

Lech is in a fairly sunny position at the junction of two attractive valleys, with adequately impressive scenery, largely thanks to the Omeshorn looming to the south. It is high and open, with very few trees. From the top slopes there are views to the Valluga above St Anton in one direction, and to Warth–Schröcken in the other.

THE MOUNTAINS

Practically all the slopes are treeless, the main exception being the lower runs just above Lech. Most are quite sunny – very few are north-facing.

The toughest runs are called 'ski routes' or 'high-Alpine touring runs'. The touring runs are simply off-piste

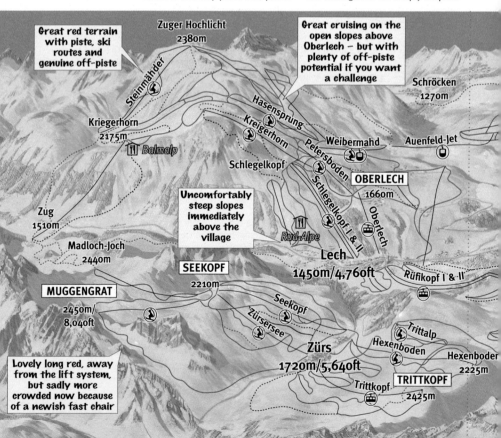

Great red terrain with piste, ski routes and genuine off-piste

Zuger Hochlicht 2380m

Great cruising on the open slopes above Oberlech – but with plenty of off-piste potential if you want a challenge

Schröcken 1270m

Steinmähder

Kriegerhorn 2175m

Balmalp

Hasensprung

Kreigerhorn

Petersboden

Weibermahd

Auenfeld-Jet

Schlegelkopf

OBERLECH 1660m

Schlegelkopf I & II

Oberlech

Zug 1510m

Uncomfortably steep slopes immediately above the village

Rud-Alpe

Madloch-Joch 2440m

Lech 1450m/4,760ft

Rüfikopf I & II

SEEKOPF 2210m

Seekopf

MUGGENGRAT 2450m/ 8,040ft

Zürsersee

Trittalp

Hexenboden

Zürs 1720m/5,640ft

Hexenboder 2225m

Lovely long red, away from the lift system, but sadly more crowded now because of a newish fast chair

Trittkopf

TRITTKOPF 2425m

KEY FACTS

Resort	1450m
	4,760ft

Arlberg region	
Slopes	1075-2650m
	3,530-8,690ft
Lifts	94
Pistes	340km
	210 miles
Blue	43%
Red	41%
Black	16%
Snowmaking	63%

For Lech-Zürs-Warth-Schröcken only	
Slopes	1450-2450m
	4,760-8,040ft
Lifts	47
Pistes	190km
	120 miles
Blue	42%
Red	42%
Black	16%
Snowmaking	40%

runs that would not appear on the piste map at all in most resorts. No problem – if you fancy these, hire a guide. The piste map says the ski routes are marked and avalanche controlled but not groomed or patrolled. We applaud the clear explanation (lacking in many resorts), but we think many of them should be patrolled pistes. Ski routes form the only ways down to Zug and Lech as part of the popular Lech–Zürs–Lech 'White Ring' circuit are treated like pistes, as are several other ski routes. To add to the confusion, some of the routes are sometimes groomed (this happened on our recent visits).

The piste map, which covers the whole of the Arlberg region (including Warth–Schröcken from 2013/14 we understand) in one view, is unclear and misleading in places – particularly around Oberlech and down from Zürs to Zug and Lech. They should really have one piste map for Lech–Zürs–Warth–Schröcken and separate ones for St Anton–St Christoph–Stuben and for Sonnenkopf. There's a smaller separate map that shows the White Ring circuit. Piste marking is OK in general. But, confusingly, the same number is given to several pistes in places. Piste classification understates the difficulty of some pistes.

EXTENT OF THE SLOPES ★★★ ★★
One-way traffic

The main slopes centre on **Oberlech**, 250m above Lech (just below the treeline), and can be reached by cable car or chairlifts. The wide, open pistes above here are perfect intermediate terrain, and there is also lots of off-piste. Zuger Hochlicht, the high point in the sector, gives stunning views. The new gondola to the slopes of **Warth–Schröcken** starts near Oberlech.

The **Rüfikopf** cable car takes Lech residents to the west-facing slopes of Zürs and the start of the Lech–Zürs–Lech circuit, the White Ring, which can be done only in a clockwise direction. This mountainside, with its high point at **Trittkopf**, is a mix of quite challenging intermediate slopes and flat/uphill bits. On the other side of Zürs, the east-facing mountainside is of a more uniform gradient. Chairs go

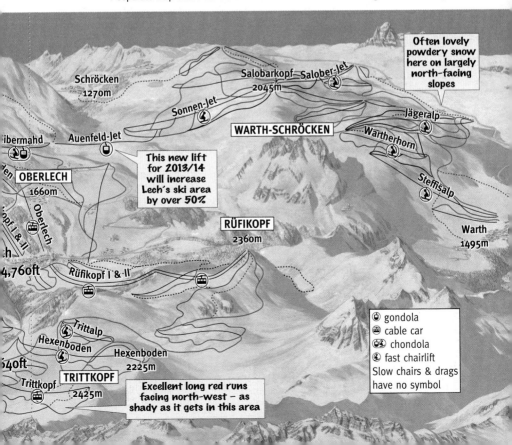

Schröcken
1270m

Salobarkopf — Salober-Jet
2045m

Sonnen-Jet

Often lovely powdery snow here on largely north-facing slopes

ibermahd   Auenfeld-Jet

WARTH-SCHRÖCKEN   Wartherhorn

Jägeralp

This new lift for 2013/14 will increase Lech's ski area by over 50%

OBERLECH
1660m

Oberlech

Steffisalp

RÜFIKOPF
2360m

Warth
1495m

4,76oft   Rüfikopf I & II

Rüfikopf I & II

Trittalp
Hexenboden

Hexenboden
2225m

TRITTKOPF

Trittkopf   2425m

Excellent long red runs facing north-west – as shady as it gets in this area

ⓖ gondola
ⓒ cable car
ⓒⓒ chondola
ⓕ fast chairlift
Slow chairs & drags have no symbol

↑ Lech's traditional chalet-style buildings are prettily set along a river with the Omeshorn looming in the background

LECH-ZÜRS / SEPP MALLAUN

LIFT PASSES

Arlberg

Prices in €

Age	1-day	6-day
under 16	28	137
16 to 19	43	198
20 to 64	47	228
65 plus	43	198

Free No one; day pass €10 if under 8, €20 if over 75

Beginner Points ticket

Notes Covers St Anton, St Christoph, Stuben, Lech, Zürs, Warth and Schröcken lifts, and linking bus between Alpe Rauz and Zürs; also Sonnenkopf (9 lifts) at Klösterle, 7km west of Stuben (bus link); single ascent, half-day and pedestrian options

up to **Seekopf** with intermediate runs back down.

A six-pack goes from near here up to **Muggengrat** (the highest point of the Zürs area). This has a good blue run back under it and the long, scenic, lift-free Muggengrat Täli red run back to Zürs – this used to be delightfully quiet, but we've had reports of crowds since the six-pack arrived. It starts with a choice between a cat track and a mogul field, but develops into a fine, varied red with lots of nearby off-piste options on the way down; at the bottom you can take lifts up the other side or walk through the village to the Zürsersee chair back up to Seekopf.

From Seekopf you can ski down to the Madloch chair – slow and liable to closure by wind – which leads to the long, scenic ski route (often busy, with some tricky sections) back to the fringes of Lech. Or, following the White Ring circuit, you peel off part-way down and take another ski route to Zug and the slow chairlift up to the Kriegerhorn above Oberlech.

FAST LIFTS ★★★★
Hot stuff

A high proportion of lifts are now fast. Seven chairlifts have the luxury bonus of heated seats. But there are still a few slow, old lifts (in particular, the chairs to Madloch-Joch above Zürs and from Zug to Kriegerhorn need modernizing) – Lech–Zürs is still some way behind Austrian pacesetters such as Ischgl and Saalbach in this respect.

QUEUES ★★★★
Still a few bottlenecks

There have been significant lift improvements, and feedback is generally positive, but there are still one or two bottlenecks – the Schlegelkopf fast quad out of Lech and the crucial Madloch double chair mentioned under 'Fast lifts' generate peak-time queues – so can the Rüfikopf cable cars to Zürs. The resort proudly boasts that it limits numbers of day passes sold to 14,000, to ensure a more enjoyable experience – and the slopes certainly seem much quieter than those over the hill in St Anton. We can't imagine that the link with Warth–Schröcken will make them any busier.

TERRAIN PARKS ★★★★
In Lech

The park, beside the Schlegelkopf chairlift, is one of the better terrain parks in Austria and was enjoyed by a recent reporter. The medium and pro lines have kickers, boxes and a 9m-wide wall ride. The rails are also set in lines so you can hit several in a row. There's also a 6m down rail and a rainbow rail. The easy line has a funbox, kickers and rollers and a 4m down rail, great for getting used to air time. There's also a park above Schröcken.

SNOW RELIABILITY ★★★★
One of Austria's best

Lech and Zürs both get a lot of snow. Lech gets an average of almost 8m of

Indoor Sports park (fitness studios, tennis, bowling, climbing wall, sauna), hotel swimming pools, museum, galleries, library, ice rink (in hotel Monzabon)

Outdoor Cleared walking paths, ice rink, curling, toboggan run (from Oberlech), paragliding, horse-drawn sleigh rides

snow each season, almost twice as much as St Anton and three times as much as Kitzbühel; Zürs gets substantially more than Lech; and Warth–Schröcken gets an astonishing 11m. Taken together with good grooming ('perfect' said a recent reporter) and excellent snowmaking, this normally means good snow coverage until late April. But because of the sunny exposure, the lower slopes can suffer and the snow become heavy.

FOR EXPERTS ★★★★
Off-piste is the main attraction

There is only one (very short) black piste on the map, and there is no denying that for the competent skier who prefers to stick to patrolled runs the area is very limited. But the two types of off-piste route explained earlier offer lots to enjoy. There is also plenty of other excellent off-piste, much of it accessed by long traverses, and, in comparison with St Anton, fresh powder lasts well here.

Many of the best runs start from the top of the fast Steinmähder chair, which finishes just below Zuger Hochlicht. Some routes involve a short climb to access bowls of untracked powder. From the Kriegerhorn there are shorter off-piste runs down towards Lech and a very scenic long ski route down to Zug (followed by a slow chair and a rope tow to pull you along a flat area). Most runs, however, are south- or west-facing and can suffer from sun. At the end of the season, when the snow is deep and settled, the off-piste off the shoulder of the Wöstertäli from the top of the Rüfikopf cable car down to Lech can be superb, as can Zuger Hochlicht. There are also good runs from the Trittkopf cable car in the Zürs sector, including a tricky one down to Stuben.

The steeper red runs (notably on Zuger Hochlicht and both sides of Zürs) are well worth a try, as is the lovely away-from-the-lifts Langerzug ski route back to Lech on the Rüfikopf side (steep start, then a gentle cruise, flattish run-out). And you'll want to visit St Anton during your stay (see separate chapter). Heli-skiing is also available on weekdays.

Plus, from 2013/14 there will be the excellent off-piste of Warth–Schröcken to explore.

THE MOST EXCITING NEW LINK IN YEARS

For the 2013/14 season Lech is due to be linked to the neighbouring Warth–Schröcken ski area. This will increase the size of the Lech–Zürs ski area by over 50% in terms of pistes and open up fabulous off-piste. And all this will be on some of Europe's best snow because Warth is the snowiest resort in the Alps, receiving an average of 11m a year – that's way more than the big Colorado resorts, about the same as Jackson Hole and not far off famously snowy Snowbird and Alta in Utah. And Warth's snow stays in good condition because most of the slopes are north-facing. If it's powder you're after this will be the place to be in Europe. It's on our hit list of resorts to visit in 2014 for sure.

The link is by the new 10-seat Auenfeld-Jet gondola, which will start near the Weibermahd chondola (reached from Oberlech). It will take you 2km over flattish land and a cross-country area to just above the bottom station of the Sonnen-Jet six-pack; this goes to the high point of Warth–Schröcken's 68km of slopes at almost 2050m. You'll ride the gondola back too – there are no pistes in either direction.

This is great news for Lech–Zürs residents. And, if you don't mind a quiet time at night and few off-slope diversions, it opens up the chance to stay more cheaply in sleepy little Warth and still ski the slopes of its plush and much pricier neighbours. For more on Warth–Schröcken read our Vorarlberg – Bregenzerwald chapter.

FOR INTERMEDIATES ★★★★
Flattering variety for all
The pistes in the Oberlech area are nearly all immaculately groomed blue runs, the upper ones above the trees, the lower ones in wide swathes cut through them. It is ideal territory for cruisers not wanting surprises. But timid intermediates may find the final blue-run descents to Lech (as opposed to Oberlech) uncomfortably steep.

Strong intermediates will want to do the circuit to Zürs and back. Whether it's wise for less confident intermediates to tackle the red ski routes from Madloch depends on the conditions. They are not steep, and part or all of them may be groomed despite their non-piste status, but parts can be heavily mogulled and busy, and lots of people find the runs a struggle.

More adventurous intermediates will want to spend time on the fast Steinmähder chair on Zuger Hochlicht – a choice of satisfying pistes and ski routes, and from there take the scenic red run all the way to Zug (the latter part on an easy ski route rather than a piste). They may even want to give the Langerzug ski route (see 'For experts') a go. Lech is an excellent place to try skiing deep snow for the first time.

Zürs has many more interesting red runs, on both sides of the village. We like the north-west-facing reds from Trittkopf and the excellent Muggengrat Täli (see 'Extent of the slopes').

Plus, from 2013/14 there will be the excellent intermediate slopes of Warth–Schröcken to explore.

FOR BEGINNERS ★★★★
Easy slopes in all areas
The main nursery slopes are at Oberlech, but there is also a nice dedicated area in Lech. There are good, easy runs to progress to. You can buy a points card rather than a full lift pass.

FOR BOARDERS ★★★★
Easy riders, but mind the flats
Lech's upper-crust image has not stood in the way of its snowboarding development, and it is a popular destination for freeriders. There are few draglifts to deter novices; but beware of the many flat/uphill sections on the west-facing slopes at Zürs.

FOR CROSS-COUNTRY ★★★
Picturesque valley trail
A 21km trail starts from the centre of Lech and leads through the beautiful but shady valley, along the river to Zug and back. There are three other shorter trails. In Zürs there is a 4km track to the Flexen Pass and back.

MOUNTAIN RESTAURANTS ★★★
Still not a strong point
The restaurants of the hotels in Oberlech have traditionally dominated the lunch scene here, but the options are widening. Restaurants are clearly marked on the piste map (except the ones in Oberlech, not surprisingly).

Editors' choice Rud-Alpe (418250) is not far above Lech, but far enough to count as a mountain restaurant – it would be an energetic non-skier who walked up. It's a welcoming, rustic place, lovingly built using timbers from other old huts. We've had excellent gröstl and desserts there, efficiently served in a cosy, wood-built room – 'very good strudel', says a recent report. We and reporters have also enjoyed the modern, woody Balmalp, above Zug: cool music (loud on the terrace, quieter inside); simple food (pasta, pizza, ribs, salad, 'excellent gulaschsuppe'); good views.

Worth knowing about Kriegeralpe above Oberlech is rustic and charming. Above Zürs, Seekopf offers table-service and has been praised for quality and price ('very good pasta'; 'lovely barley soup'). At Oberlech there are several big sunny terraces set prettily around the piste. Quite often you'll find a live band playing outside one. Reader recommendations include Burgwald ('good chicken burgers'), Petersboden ('good pasta and great chicken salad'), Ilga Stüble, the lovely old Alter Goldener Berg ('sheepskins on seats') and the Mohnenfluh.

SCHOOLS AND GUIDES ★★★★
Excellent in parts

The ski schools of Lech, Oberlech and Zürs all have good reputations, and the instructors speak good English. Many instructors are booked every year by regular visitors. We get good reports; one regular visitor has been satisfied for several years and a 2013 visitor had a 'great time' on his off-piste private lesson with the Lech school but warns, 'take your own avalanche gear'. Another reporter says, 'All the kids enjoyed it – lots of piste fun and park action.' Omeshorn Alpincenter and Exklusiv are alternative schools, also with guiding.

FOR FAMILIES ★★★★★
Oberlech's fine, but expensive

Oberlech makes an excellent choice for families who can afford it, particularly as its hotels are so conveniently placed for the slopes. Reporters have praised the family-friendly approach, especially to children using the lifts. There are kids' clubs in Lech, Oberlech and Zürs and Goldener Berg has an in-house kindergarten.

Lech

Build your own shortlist: www.wheretoskiandsnowboard.com

CHILDCARE

Mini-clubs
t 0664 123 9993
Kinderland Lech
From age 3
Kinderland Oberlech
From age 2
Little Zürs
From age 2
Babysitting list
Held by tourist office

Ski school
From 4½ to 12

GETTING THERE

Air Zürich 200km/
125 miles (2hr30);
Innsbruck 120km/
75 miles (1hr30);
Friedrichshafen
130km/80 miles
(1hr45)

Rail Langen (17km/
10 miles); regular
buses from station;
buses connect with
international trains

STAYING THERE

Chalets There are a few chalets run by UK tour ops, including three chalet hotels by Ski Total, one with pool and all three with sauna; and two chalets in Zug by Skiworld, both with sauna.
Hotels There are six 5-stars, over 40 4-stars and countless other places.

LECH
*****Arlberg (21340) Elegantly rustic central chalet, widely thought to be the best in Lech. Pool.
*****Post (22060) Lovely old Relais & Châteaux place on the main street; pool, sauna, steam. One of our favourites.
*****Krone (2551) By the river. Repeatedly tipped. Pool, sauna, steam and spa.
****Filomena (2211) Central aparthotel with rooms and apartments. Breakfast buffet available. Pool, sauna, steam, hot tub, solarium, massage.
****Kristiania (25610) Luxury on outskirts. Free shuttle. 'Gourmet paradise, outstanding service, but expensive.'
****Monzabon (2104) Right by the ski school meeting point. Food, staff and attractive stube have been praised.

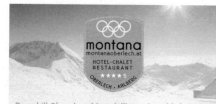

Downhill Olympic gold medallist and world champion Patrick Ortlieb and his family welcome you warmly at deluxe hotel and chalet Montana.

Next to the ski lift, slopes and ski school, making your stay extremely comfortable and unforgettable. A dream holiday comes true!

Pool, steam room, three types of sauna, indoor ice rink.
****Schwarzwand (2469) By the separate nursery slope so perfectly positioned for beginners. Sauna, steam room, solarium. Food, service and value for money are praised.
****Tannbergerhof (22020) Splendidly atmospheric inn on the main street, with outdoor bar. Steam, sauna.
****Plattenhof (25220) A few minutes from the centre; can ski back to hotel. 'Great food, wonderful service, nice pool with waterfalls; four different types of sauna/steam rooms.'
***Lärchenhof (2300) Neat B&B hotel with spa: rooms, breakfast and friendly owners have been praised.
OBERLECH
****Bergkristall (2678) Smart, family-run, good food. Hot tub, steam, sauna, solarium. Own in-house nanny.
****Burg (22910) Smart, with pool, saunas, steam and umbrella bar.
****Montana (2460) Welcoming chalet run by the family of Patrick Ortlieb. Reporters praise food and service. Smart wellness centre with pool, steam room, three types of sauna.
****Pension Sabine (2718) 'Great service and wonderful spa.'
Apartments There are lots available to independent bookers.

EATING OUT ★★★
Mainly hotel-based
There are over 50 restaurants in Lech, but nearly all of them are in hotels. Reporter recommendations include the Krone, Post, Almhof Schneider, Don Enzo Due (Italian) and Fux (Asian fusion). Hûs Nr 8 is one of the best non-hotel restaurants for traditional Austrian food. The Olympia has been suggested for cakes and coffee, and Backstüble for apple strudel. Café Fritz is cosy and relatively good value.
In Zug, the Rote Wand is excellent for traditional Austrian food ('beautiful old fashioned restaurant, attentive but not fussy service'), but pricey. Readers also tip the Alphorn and the Klösterle.

APRES-SKI ★★★★
Good but expensive
At Oberlech, the umbrella bar of the Burg hotel is popular at close of play, as is the champagne bar in hotel Montana. Readers also like the Ilga.
Down in Lech the outdoor bars of hotels Krone (in a lovely, sunny setting by the river) and Tannbergerhof (where there's an afternoon as well as a late-

night disco) are popular. Later on, the K Club (Krone hotel) and Archiv Bar liven up. Readers like the Fux Jazzbar (with live music and a huge wine list).

Zug makes a good night out: you can take a sleigh ride for a meal at the Rote Wand, Klösterle or Auerhahn.

After 7.30pm the free resort bus becomes a pay-for bus (five euros) called James, which runs until 3am.

OFF THE SLOPES ★★★ ★★
At ease

For a resort where many visitors don't ski, the range of shops is surprisingly limited – Strolz's plush emporium (including a champagne bar) right in the centre is the main attraction.

It's easy for pedestrians to get to Oberlech or Zug for lunch. The village outdoor bars are ideal for posing. There are 28km of walking paths – the one along the river to Zug is particularly beautiful; the tourist office produces a good map. There's a sports centre (no pool).

The floodlit sledging run from Oberlech to town is popular with families and is highly recommended (but beware of toboggan theft – one reporter had three stolen).

Phone numbers
From elsewhere in Austria add the prefix 05583; from abroad use the prefix +43 5583

ZÜRS

Some 10 minutes' drive towards St Anton from Lech is Zürs. Austria's first recognizable ski lift was built here in 1937. Zürs is a rare thing: a highly fashionable and expensive resort where the main occupation of visitors is skiing rather than parading. It has some excellent hotels (including four 5-stars); once inside them, all is well with the world. But the village as a whole doesn't have much appeal – it has nothing resembling a centre, few shops and a lot of intrusive traffic to/from Lech on the central through-road. We stayed at the 5-star Zürserhof (25130) and found it excellent – great service, food and spa facilities. There are ten 4-stars, and three 3-stars.

Toni's Einkehr (a rustic hut at the foot of the Trittkopf slopes) is one of the few non-hotel restaurants and has been recommended. Nightlife is quiet: Vernissage is said to be the best spot. There's a disco in the Edelweiss hotel and a piano bar in the Alpenhof.

Many of the local Zürs instructors are booked up for private lessons for the entire season by regular clients.

Lech

Build your own shortlist: **www.wheretoskiandsnowboard.com**

Mayrhofen

Large, lively resort with relatively reliable snow on local slopes and access to other good areas nearby, including a glacier

RATINGS

The mountains

Extent	★★★
Fast lifts	★★★★
Queues	★
Terrain p'ks	★★★★★
Snow	★★★
Expert	★★
Intermediate	★★★
Beginner	★★
Boarder	★★★★
X-country	★★
Restaurants	★★★
Schools	★★★★
Families	★★

The resort

Charm	★★★
Convenience	★
Scenery	★★★
Eating out	★★★
Après-ski	★★★★
Off-slope	★★★★

RPI	90
lift pass	£190
ski hire	£85
lessons	£75
food & drink	£115
total	**£465**

NEWS

2013/14: Swanky six-packs with all mod cons will replace the Lämmerbichl double chair on Rastkogel and (with luck) the Ebenwald double chair on Ahorn. Another smart new six-pack is going in at Gerlos, in the Zillertal Arena area.

2012/13: At Zell am Ziller, the Kreuzwiese drag was replaced by a six-pack.

➕ Good for confident intermediates

➕ High, snow-sure slopes by local standards – plus glacier nearby

➕ Several worthwhile nearby resorts on the same lift pass

➕ Attractive, traditional village with lively après-ski

➕ Excellent children's amenities

➖ Long queues for the main gondola

➖ Slopes can be crowded

➖ Buses are a key feature, and are often oversubscribed

➖ Runs mostly short

➖ Few steep pistes, although they do include Austria's steepest (possibly)

➖ No pistes to the valley locally

Mayrhofen is easy to like – a neat, polished, animated village in a pleasant rural setting – and we always enjoy our visits. But we have the use of a car, so we don't have to mess with the Penken gondola or the complex and often crowded bus services. Without a car, we'd budget for some taxis.

Like so many popular Tirolean resorts, Mayrhofen manages to meet the needs of young people bent on partying and those of families looking for a quieter time. What marks it out from many of its rivals is that its slopes are relatively high, and therefore relatively snow-sure.

Bear in mind that you can access those slopes from quieter villages further up the valley, covered in the Hintertux chapter. Lanersbach and Vorderlanersbach have the merit, rare in these parts, of pistes back to the village.

THE RESORT

Mayrhofen is a fairly large resort sitting in the flat-bottomed, steep-sided Zillertal. Most shops, bars and restaurants are on one long street, with hotels and pensions spread over a wider area.

Free buses and trains linking the Zillertal resorts mean you can easily have an enjoyably varied week visiting different areas on the Ziller valley lift pass, including the excellent glacier at Hintertux (which has its own chapter).

At the end of this chapter we cover the Zillertal Arena area, which starts at Zell am Ziller, a short drive away, and links to Gerlos and Königsleiten. The other major Zillertal area is Hochfügen/Hochzillertal above Kaltenbach, dealt with in the directory at the back of the book. There's a good train service to Salzburg, Innsbruck and Munich.

VILLAGE CHARM ★★★★★
Traditional and spacious

As the village has grown, architecture has been kept traditional, and the place merges with the surrounding fields in a rather charming way. The valley road bypasses the village and the centre is almost, but not quite,

traffic-free. The steep-sided valley makes an attractive setting, but also means the village doesn't get a very long day of sun in midwinter.

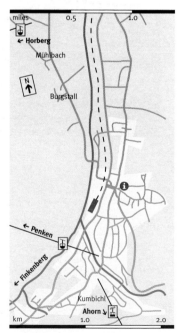

↑ Penken-Horberg has something for everyone, including black runs into the valley between the two mountains
TVB MAYRHOFEN

KEY FACTS

Resort	630m
	2,070ft

Ziller valley	
Slopes	630-3250m
	2,070-10,660ft
Lifts	178
Pistes	485km
	301 miles
Blue	26%
Red	63%
Black	11%
Snowmaking	75%

Mayrhofen-Lanersbach only (ie excluding Hintertux glacier)	
Slopes	630-2500m
	2,070-8,200ft
Lifts	53
Pistes	135km
	84 miles
Snowmaking	100%

CONVENIENCE ★☆☆☆☆
Pick your spot

It's quite a big village, centred on a long main street. The church, the tourist office and the main traditional hotels are at the north end, with the bus/railway station on the nearby bypass; the main lift to the major Penken–Horberg sector of slopes, the Penkenbahn gondola, is 700m away at the south end, with the Ahorn cable car another 200m south, over the river. You can leave equipment at the lift stations (for a fee). Staying close to the Penkenbahn has its attractions, but staying near the station is better for reliable access to buses.

You might want to use the buses to visit other resorts, or just to get to alternatives to the Penkenbahn – particularly the Horbergbahn from Mühlbach, across the valley. The bus services are comprehensive and reliable, but crowded and complex – Finkenberg and Lanersbach are on one service, while Vorderlanersbach and Hintertux are on another, for example. Get the vast timetable leaflet and do some homework. Note that the Finkenberg service runs hourly at best.

SCENERY ★★★☆☆
Views to the glacier

Mayrhofen is set between its two steep-sided mountains. From the top of each there are good views to the high peaks to the south, including the Hintertux glacier.

THE MOUNTAINS

Many of Mayrhofen's slopes are above the treeline, though there are more trees than the piste map suggests in the valley at the heart of the Penken–Horberg sector. Many of the pistes are challenging reds, and some reporters note that the blues are also often relatively tough.

There are two piste maps in circulation, which are easily confused because they are identical on the back side. On the front side, one shows only the linked local slopes; the other shrinks things a bit to include distant Hintertux. Sadly, the designers have managed to make the larger-scale Mayrhofen-only map less clear, particularly in the very complex area at the top of Penken. They have done this by the simple device of plastering it with the names of lifts and restaurants – a masterly display of incompetence. The two maps mark some restaurants in different spots; all very un-Austrian.

Signposting is generally good, but less so in that tricky area on Penken. On one occasion, we very nearly ended up in Finkenberg, with our car waiting in Mühlbach.

As elsewhere in Austria, there are unexplained 'ski routes', including the runs to the valley from Penken–Horberg. You may find some are groomed, but we presume all are unpatrolled. Take care.

LIFT PASSES

Superskipass Zillertal

Prices in €

Age	1-day	6-day
under 15	21	97
15 to 18	36	172
over 19	45	215
Free Under 6		
Senior No deals		
Beginner No deals		

Notes 1-day pass
covers Mayrhofen
areas only; 2-day+
passes include all
Zillertal valley lifts;
part-day passes

AUSTRIA

142

EXTENT OF THE SLOPES ★★★☆☆
Fair-sized but inconvenient

Mayrhofen now measures its pistes in the Austrian standard fashion, and has cut in its claimed total, to 135km. Read our feature on piste extent.

The larger of Mayrhofen's two areas of slopes is **Penken–Horberg**, accessed by the Penkenbahn gondola from one end of town. It is also accessible via the Horbergbahn gondola at Mühlbach and another at Finkenberg, both a bus ride away from the village. If snow cover is good enough (it rarely is), you can ski to Finkenberg or Mühlbach on ski routes (the Finkenberg route is not on one of the two local piste maps).

A big cable car links the Penken area with the **Rastkogel** slopes above Vorderlanersbach, which is in turn linked to **Eggalm** above Lanersbach – read the Hintertux chapter. Getting back to Penken–Horberg from Rastkogel on skis means braving a busy, steep mogul field with red and black variants, but you can avoid it by taking the cable car down.

The **Ahorn** area is pleasant but very small, and tends to be neglected – despite being accessed by Austria's largest cable car (carrying 160) with an eight-pack serving the slopes at the top. There is a lovely, long red run to the valley (about 1300m vertical).

FAST LIFTS ★★★★☆
Capacity is the issue

Look at the map and you'll see that a good proportion of the lifts are fast – gondolas and high-speed chairs. Readers are impressed. But that doesn't help getting people up from town first thing or down at close of play (read 'Queues' below).

QUEUES ★☆☆☆☆
Still a problem

Reporters in 2012 told of waits of 15 to 30+ minutes for the Penkenbahn in the morning, and more queues to ride down in the afternoon, and this year's reporters tell a similar story. One way to deal with them is to stroll over to the queue-free Ahorn cable car and do a few warm-up laps of 1300m vertical on that. Or you can catch a bus to one of four alternative access gondolas. The Horbergbahn, surrounded by car parks, gets a lot of weekend business; here, too, there may be queues to get down as well as up the hill.

Up the mountain, queues are not so much of a problem as overcrowded pistes. One 2012 reporter said, 'Never in 40 years of skiing have I skied on such dangerous, overcrowded pistes.' The run back from Rastkogel, down the jumbo cable-car, is a nightmare at the end of the day.

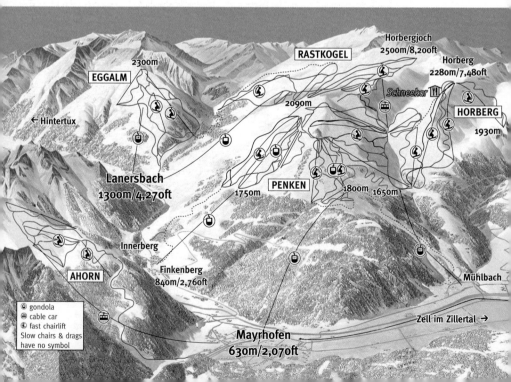

Air Salzburg
175km/110 miles
(2hr15); Munich
195km/120 miles
(2hr45); Innsbruck
70km/45 miles
(1hr15)

Rail Local line through
to resort; regular
buses from station

TERRAIN PARKS ★★★★★
Something for everyone
One of the finest parks in the Alps (www.vans-penken-park.com) lies beneath the Sun-Jet chairlift out of the valley between Penken and Horberg. There's a separate kids' park and intermediate, advanced, fun and pro areas, with a total of 11 kickers, two hips and 36 boxes and rails. The half-pipe is not too big and is perfect for learning the ropes. Experts should bear in mind the World Cup pipe at Hintertux.

SNOW RELIABILITY ★★★
Good by Tirolean standards
The area is better than most Tirolean resorts for snow because the slopes are relatively high – mostly above 1500m. Snowmaking covers the whole Ahorn area, all the main slopes on Penken–Horberg and some on Rastkogel and Eggalm. Hintertux is one of the best glaciers in the world. Grooming is 'impressive'.

FOR EXPERTS ★★
Commit Harakiri
What is claimed to be Austria's steepest piste, called Harakiri, plunges down into the valley between Penken and Horberg. It is certainly steep for a European piste, and does offer a worthwhile challenge, particularly when it is rock-hard. (When we skied it last winter, it had a few cm of fresh on a smooth base, which was delightful.) But we suspect the claimed gradient of 78% (38º) relates to a very limited part of the run. Usually, not surprisingly, it is wonderfully quiet.

The other black runs – 4 just along the mountainside from Harakiri and 17 under the Schneekar chair on Horberg – are not steep. The long ski-route to Mühlbach is quite challenging but rarely has good snow. There is, however, quite a lot of decent off-piste to be found, from the Horbergjoch chair at Rastkogel and under the linking cable car, for example.

FOR INTERMEDIATES ★★★
On the tough side
Most of Mayrhofen's intermediate slopes are on the steep side of the usual range – great for confident intermediates; many of the runs in the main Penken–Horberg area are quite short, though, with verticals in the 300m/400m region. With access to the Lanersbach slopes, there is quite a bit of ground to cover, including lovely quiet runs on Eggalm – read the Lanersbach section of the Hintertux chapter. Don't overlook Ahorn's excellent long, quiet run to the valley.

There are few really gentle blue runs, making the area less than ideal for nervous intermediates or near-beginners. Some of the best are over at Rastkogel; be sure to use the linking cable car to return. The overcrowding on many runs can add to the intimidation factor. Ahorn offers a sanctuary, but is very limited.

FOR BEGINNERS ★★
OK if it works for you
Despite its reputation for teaching, Mayrhofen is not ideal for beginners. You have to ride up the mountain to the nursery slopes, and there are no special lift passes so you'll need the full one. The Ahorn nursery slopes are excellent – high, extensive, sunny and crowd-free. But if you are with non-beginner mates, they will want to be on Penken. There are very few easy blues to progress to.

FOR BOARDERS ★★★★
A popular hangout
Mayrhofen has long been popular with snowboarders. But beginners may have a hard time getting around, as the terrain tends to be relatively steep, the nursery slopes are inconvenient, and the area still has quite a few draglifts. Intermediates and upwards, however, will relish the abundance of good red runs and easily accessible off-piste. The terrain park is one of the best in Europe. The Snowbombing music festival is held here each year, and also – usually – a 5-star TTR event, the Ästhetiker Wängl Tängl, though it didn't happen in 2013.

FOR CROSS-COUNTRY ★★
Head up the valley
There are 28km of trails in the area. Snow in the valley is not reliable but higher Vorderlanersbach has a much more snow-sure trail.

MOUNTAIN RESTAURANTS ★★★
Plenty of them
Most of Penken's many mountain restaurants are attractive and are clearly marked on the piste maps (though as we have noted, the two maps don't always agree). Recent visitors have been impressed with the quality and value for money.

↑ The terrain park, in the valley at the centre of Penken-Horberg, is hugely impressive

TVB MAYRHOFEN / TOM BAUSE

Editors' choice Schneekar (64940) at the top of Horberg is our kind of place – beams and open fire inside, individual bookable tables on the terrace (a very rare thing in Austria), charming service, good view, excellent food. We had a good cheese, onion and bacon tart here.

Worth knowing about The table-service Jausenstation Tappenalm below Horberg has 'great traditional food in bright surroundings'. The modern Panorahma by the draglifts down from the Finkenberg gondola offers 'lovely pizzas' as well as wonderful views and the 'world's best loos'. Christa's Skialm, nearby, is 'self-service but atmospheric with simple Tirolean specialities'. For restaurants in the Rastkogel and Eggalm sectors, read the Hintertux chapter.

SCHOOLS AND GUIDES ★★★★☆
Excellent reputations
Mayrhofen's ski schools have good reputations. Mayrhofen 3000 offered 'very good value and very good instruction' for a 2012 visitor's group. An off-piste guide from the Skimayrhofen.com school provided 'good service and good value'.

FOR FAMILIES ★★☆☆☆
Good but inconvenient
Mayrhofen majors on childcare, and the facilities are excellent. But children have to be bussed around and ferried up and down the mountain.

STAYING THERE

Chalets There are several large places in or approaching the chalet hotel category. Skiworld has the Stoanerhof near the Ahorn cable car. Crystal has the Haus Tirol in the main street, close to the gondola. Inghams has the St Lukas, a short walk from the centre.

Hotels Note that the Penken gondola is 1km from the real centre, so 'central' does not mean 'close to lifts'. There's an ice-hotel on Ahorn.

*****Elisabeth (6767) The only 5-star, slightly out of the centre.

****Gutshof Zillertal (8124) A reporter was delighted to have found this place on the southern outskirts, which offers 'almost free' hire cars. 'Good meals, great deal.' Pool, spa.

****Neue Post (62131) An old favourite, central: 'Spacious but old fashioned bedrooms; excellent breakfasts.' Small pool, sauna, steam.

****Neuhaus (6703) 'Well appointed, comfortable, friendly.'

****Sporthotel Manni (63301) On main street, between station and gondola. 'Large comfortable rooms, good steaks, excellent beer.'

****Strass (6705) By the gondola. Lively bars, disco, wellness centre, pool; but big, with low marks for style, and we've had a complaint of noise keeping people awake.

****Zillertalerhof (62265) 'Excellent food and service, great pool, sauna.' Central.

SCHOOLS
Die Roten Profis
t 63900
SMT
t 63939
Mayrhofen 3000
t 64015
Skimayrhofen.com
t 62829

Classes
(3000 prices)
6 4hr-days €159
Private lessons
From €58 for 1 hour

CHILDCARE
Wuppy's Kinderland
t 63612
Ages 3mnth to 7yr
Crèche (SMT school)
t 63939
From age 2
Babysitting list
at tourist office

Ski school
From ages 4 or 5

ACTIVITIES
Indoor Leisure pool, (pool, sauna, massage), fitness centre

Outdoor Ice rink, curling, 40km of paths, ice climbing, horse-drawn sleigh rides, snowshoeing, paragliding, tobogganing

Phone numbers
From elsewhere in Austria add the prefix 05285 (Mayrhofen), 05282 (Zell), 05284 (Gerlos), 06564 (Königsleiten); from abroad use the prefix +43 and omit the initial '0'

TOURIST OFFICES
Mayrhofen
www.mayrhofen.at

Zillertal Arena
Zell im Zillertal
www.zell.at
Gerlos
www.gerlos.at
Königsleiten
www.wald-koenigsleiten.info

Apartments There are plenty available; Landhaus Gasser is central: 'Modern and well equipped but in traditional style.'

EATING OUT ★★★☆☆
Wide choice
There's a wide range of restaurants, from local specialities to Chinese. We've had good, satisfying meals at the jolly, friendly Tiroler Stuben near the station. Mo's is popular, and 'lively, with good food', American-style. Wirtshaus zum Griena is a lovely rustic old building on the edge of town, with a traditional menu – too much like a mountain restaurant for our taste, but popular with families. The set menu at the Gasthof Brücke was 'excellent quality and value'. A 2013 reporter had the 'best weiner schnitzel ever' in the cafe attached to the Neue Post hotel. Thai Peak is a new restaurant serving, er, Thai food.

APRES-SKI ★★★★☆
Lively
Après-ski is a great selling point – 'unpretentious and friendly, with little of the lager lout mentality that can prevail elsewhere'. At close of play, the bars at the top of the Penkenbahn and Horbergbahn gondolas do good business, while in the village the Ice Bar at the hotel Strass and Brück'n Stadl (Gasthof Brücke) get packed out, the latter proving particularly popular with readers for its great atmosphere. Some of the other bars in the Strass are rocking places later on, including the Speak Easy Arena, with live music and dancing until 4am. Mo's American theme bar is 'lively but not too noisy', has live music and is 'stylish', as is the Hara Kiri bar. Scotland Yard is popular with Brits but 'expensive and tatty', reckoned one visitor. For a quiet drink we head to the bars of the big traditional hotels – the Neuhaus or the Neue Post. Catch the big rugby matches (etc) at the Movie bar.

OFF THE SLOPES ★★★★☆
Good for all
Innsbruck and other resorts are easily reached by train or bus. There are also good walks and sports amenities, including the swimming pool complex – with saunas, steam room and solarium. Pedestrians have no trouble getting up the mountain to meet friends for lunch. 'Several cafes and an ice-cream parlour make just walking

the streets a very pleasant experience,' says a 2012 visitor.

DOWN-VALLEY AREA
ZILLERTAL ARENA
The Zillertal Arena was created in 2000 by linking the slopes of Zell am Ziller, 10km down the valley from Mayrhofen, to those above the villages of Gerlos and Königsleiten. They now share an area about as big as the Mayrhofen–Lanersbach area. The slopes are quite high, as in Mayrhofen, but they also get a lot of sun, so the snow message is a mixed one. The slopes suit intermediates best. You can really get a sense of travelling around: the trip from one end to the other is 17km and takes you over several peaks and ridges. According to a reporter, a return trip is a full day's skiing, with little time to deviate from the main route along the way. Most runs are short – the longest, down to Gerlos, is 4km.

Zell is the main town in the Zillertal, and a real working town rather than just a resort. There are some good hotels, including the 4-star Zapfenhof (2349) on the outskirts (with pool) and the Brau (2313) in the centre. The town is a bus ride from the two gondolas into the ski area. You have to ride these down as well as up. Après-ski centres around a few bars near the base of the gondolas.

Gerlos has the advantage of being centrally situated in the ski area, allowing you to explore in either direction each day. It is a bustling resort that straddles the road up to the Gerlos pass and is a bus ride from the gondola into the slopes. Après-ski is lively and there are several good local hotels, including the 4-star Gaspingerhof (52160) with a very smart spa.

Königsleiten is very spread out, in a scenic wooded setting above a dam, with half a dozen hotels including the 4-star Königsleiten (82160). It has more extensive local slopes than Gerlos, on either side of the Gerlospass road, but less vertical. On the north side (reached by a gondola from the village) the runs are mostly genuine reds, radiating from the peak of Königsleitenspitze (2315m). The lower southern sector has a row of quad chairs serving easier slopes.

Both Gerlos and Königsleiten attract a lot of Dutch visitors.

Mayrhofen

145

Build your own shortlist: www.wheretoskiandsnowboard.com

Obergurgl

A combination of high altitude and traditional Tirolean atmosphere keeps regulars going back, despite the drawbacks

RATINGS

The mountains

Extent	★★
Fast lifts	★★★★★
Queues	★★★★★
Terrain p'ks	★★
Snow	★★★★★
Expert	★★
Intermediate	★★★
Beginner	★★★★
Boarder	★★
X-country	★★
Restaurants	★★★
Schools	★★★★
Families	★★★★

The resort

Charm	★★★★
Convenience	★★★★
Scenery	★★★
Eating out	★★★
Après-ski	★★★★
Off-slope	★★

RPI 115

lift pass	£220
ski hire	£135
lessons	£110
food & drink	£135
total	**£600**

NEWS

2012/13: The terrain park was redesigned and moved beside the Bruggenbodenlift on Hohe Mut. A new ski route was created running from the Rosskarbahn middle station to the Hohe Mut middle station.

KEY FACTS

Resort	1930m
	6,330ft
Slopes	1795-3080m
	5,890-10,100ft
Lifts	24
Pistes	110km
	68 miles
Blue	32%
Red	50%
Black	18%
Snowmaking	99%

➕ Glaciers apart, one of the most snow-sure resorts in the Alps; good for a late-season holiday

➕ Excellent area for beginners, timid intermediates and families

➕ Queue- and crowd-free, with slick lifts in the main

➕ Traditional, quiet, chalet-style village with little traffic

➕ Jolly Tirolean teatime après-ski

➖ Limited area of slopes, with no tough pistes

➖ Exposed setting, with very few sheltered slopes for bad weather

➖ Little to do outside the hotels

➖ Village is fragmented, and lacking a real centre

➖ For a small Austrian resort, hotels are rather expensive

There are, of course, other resorts with reliably good snow, or with uncrowded easy–intermediate pistes, or with traditional chalet-style architecture, or with little or no traffic, or with teatime raves on the slopes. But we're hard pressed to think of other resorts that match all of Obergurgl's attractions.

People go back to Obergurgl time after time, booking the same hotel a year in advance to avoid disappointment, and it's not difficult to see why.

THE RESORT

Obergurgl has grown out of a traditional mountain village, set in a remote spot near the head of its valley – the highest parish in Austria and usually under a blanket of snow.

Although it's a small place, the village is split into three main parts. First you come to a cluster of hotels near the Festkogl gondola. The road then passes another group of hotels set on a little hill (beware steep, sometimes icy walks here). Finally you reach the nearest thing to a centre – a little square with the church, a fountain, the hotel Edelweiss und Gurgl and an underground car park.

Even higher Hochgurgl, linked by a mid-mountain gondola, is little more than a handful of hotels at the foot of its own area of slopes.

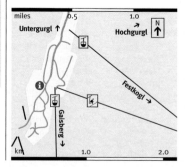

The lift pass is quite pricey, for a small resort. You can make it pricier still by paying 10 euros extra (at the time of buying your main pass) for a day in Sölden, a short bus ride down the valley (buses every half hour).

VILLAGE CHARM ★★★★
On the quiet side
Obergurgl has no through traffic and few day visitors, so the place is calm and relaxed. The village 'centre' is mainly traffic-free, and entirely so at night. It's quite jolly immediately after the slopes close, but rather subdued later; most people stay in their hotels.

CONVENIENCE ★★★★
Lifts at both ends
Obergurgl is a small place, and there are lifts at both ends. The Hohe Mut gondola station is close to the 'centre', and nowhere is a long walk from a lift. But you may need to use the free shuttle-buses (eg to get to ski school), and they are not very frequent. Hochgurgl looks like a convenient ski-in/ski-out resort, but nearly all the hotels are separated from the snow by roads and/or stairs.

SCENERY ★★★
High and bleak
Obergurgl's altitude and position mean fabulous panoramic views from the top of the lifts.

Ski Straight to the Hotel Door!

E&G
EDELWEISS
GURGL
★ ★ ★ ★

Absolutely snow secure from the middle of November till the beginning of May,
on 6,332 feet or almost 2.000 meter above sea level.
Enjoy an <u>outstanding</u> 4 star hotel right at the foot of the slopes.
Top quality skiing – no waiting times at the ski lifts.

Hospitality since 1889 - www.1889.at

Talk to one
of our friendly
holiday experts
right now!
Go to www.1889.at
and press the
live help button!
This service is free
of charge!

Hotel Edelweiss & Gurgl
Ramolweg 5
6456 Obergurgl / Tyrol

info@edelweiss-gurgl.com
P: 0043-(0)5256-6223
F: 0043-(0)5256-6449

www.edelweiss-gurgl.com

LIFT PASSES

Prices in €

Age	1-day	6-day
under 16	30	129
16 to 18	35	179
18 to 59	46	239
60 plus	40	208

Free Under 9

Beginner Limited pass covering nursery lifts

Notes Covers Obergurgl and Hochgurgl, and local ski-bus; part-day passes and non-skier tickets available

THE MOUNTAINS

Most of the slopes are very exposed. Wind and white-outs can shut the lifts, and severe cold can limit enthusiasm, especially in early season. If the weather is bad but not that bad, another problem arises: in our view, and that of many reporters, piste edge marking is dangerously slack – there are huge drop-offs that are not marked, and slopes seem to be marked either on one side only (often the uphill side) or in the middle only. Crazy. The piste map is fine – it's not a complex area. Classification of runs can overstate difficulty.

EXTENT OF THE SLOPES ★★
Limited cruising

The total area of slopes is quite limited. A gondola links the Obergurgl and Hochgurgl ski areas at mid-mountain level. It closes absurdly early at 4pm. There are no piste links.

Obergurgl is the smaller of the two linked areas. It is in two sections, with links at altitude in only one direction. The gondola from the village entrance and the Rosskar fast quad chair go to the higher **Festkogl** section. This is served by a short drag and a longer chair up to 3035m. From here you can head down to the gondola base or – by blue piste or new ski route – over to the **Hohe Mut** sector. This is also reached from the village via a gondola, which goes on to the sector high point at Hohe Mut. Lower down are slopes served by a slow quad and a six-pack.

As well as the new ski route, which a reporter found to be groomed, there

are two other long-standing ones, which we have always found ungroomed. The status of these runs is not explained on the piste map.

The slopes of **Hochgurgl** consist of high, gentle bowls, with fast lifts serving the main slopes above the village, but drags serving the more testing outlying slopes. From the top stations there are spectacular views to the Dolomites. A single run leads down through the woods to Untergurgl.

There's night skiing weekly on 8km of slopes in Obergurgl once a week, and on 3km in Hochgurgl.

FAST LIFTS ★★★★★
Among the best

The system is pretty impressive. Most lifts are now high-capacity gondolas or fast chairs.

QUEUES ★★★★★
Few problems

Queues are rare. 'Fantastic,' say reporters. 'Surprisingly quiet and uncrowded, even in the Easter hols.'

TERRAIN PARKS ★★
Park life moves

The park has moved its jumps, kickers and rails from Festkogl to Hohe Mut.

SNOW RELIABILITY ★★★★★
Excellent

Obergurgl has high slopes and is about the most snow-sure of Europe's non-glacier resorts – even without its snowmaking, which is claimed to cover 99% of the pistes. The resort has a long season. Piste grooming is 'good' say several reporters this year.

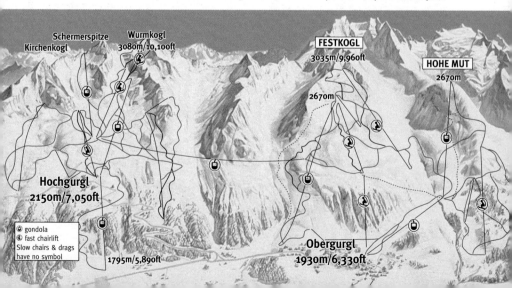

Schermerspitze
Kirchenkogl

Wurmkogl
3080m/10,100ft

FESTKOGL
3035m/9,960ft

HOHE MUT
2670m

2670m

2670m

Hochgurgl
2150m/7,050ft

ⓖ gondola
ⓕ fast chairlift
Slow chairs & drags
have no symbol

1795m/5,890ft

Obergurgl
1930m/6,330ft

↑ It's a simple recipe: cold, dry snow spread across gentle slopes, shared by few people; this is Hochgurgl

ÖTZTAL TOURISMUS

FOR EXPERTS ★★☆☆☆
Not generally recommendable
There are few challenges on-piste – most of the blacks could easily be red, and where genuinely black it's only for short stretches (for example, at the very top of Wurmkogl). The ski routes are more challenging, particularly the one from Hohe Mut when mogulled. There is a lot of easy off-piste to be found – the top school groups often go off-piste when conditions are right. Slopes around the Kirchenkar draglift are good for untracked powder. And there are more serious routes – a reporter last year found 'glorious' untracked powder in the Königstal, on skier's left from Wurmkogl.

FOR INTERMEDIATES ★★★☆☆
Good but limited
There is some perfect intermediate terrain here, made even better by the normally flattering snow conditions. The problem is, there's not much of it. Keen piste-bashers will quickly be itching to catch the bus to Sölden.

Hochgurgl has the bigger area of easy runs, and these make good cruising. For more challenges, head to the Vorderer Wurmkogl lift, on the right as you look at the mountain.

The Obergurgl area has more red than blue runs but most offer no great challenge to a confident intermediate. There is some easy cruising around mid-mountain on Festkogl. The blue run from the top of this sector to the

village, via the Hohe Mut sector, is 1100m vertical. And there's another long enjoyable run down the length of the gondola, with a scenic black run and ski route variant (neither of them very steep) in the adjoining valley.

On Hohe Mut, there are very easy runs in front of Nederhütte and back towards the village. The red from Hohe Mut is narrow and in places winding.

FOR BEGINNERS ★★★★☆
You pays your money
There is one lift that is free only to ski school pupils, and three other beginner lifts (covered by a special day pass) serving adequate slopes, at each end of Obergurgl, and just above Hochgurgl – an awkward walk from most of the hotels, but otherwise satisfactory. After that you require a full lift pass. The gentle run under the gondola from the mid-station of the Hohe Mut gondola to the village is ideal to move on to. The easy broad slopes served by the Bruggenboden chair are also suitable. And then there are good longer slopes to move on to.

FOR BOARDERS ★★☆☆☆
Lacks challenge
Beginners can access most of the slopes without having to ride draglifts. There's some good off-piste potential for more advanced riders; a recent visitor singles out the area around the Steinmann chair in the Hohe Mut sector. There's also a terrain park.

SCHOOLS

Obergurgl
t 6305

Hochgurgl
t 626599

Exclusiv
t 0664 182 6969

Alpinsport
t 6322

Tyrolean
t 0664 422 8370

Classes (Obergurgl prices) 6 days (2hr am and pm) €233

Private lessons
From €136 for 2hr

CHILDCARE

Alpina & Hochfirst hotel kindergartens
From age 3

Bobo Miniclub & Kindergarten (Obergurgl school)
t 6305
From age 3

Ski schools
From age 4

SNOWPIX.COM / CHRIS GILL

Never mind the wurst and chips ... look at the lovely tracks being laid down on the Wasserfallferner; taken from Hohe Mut Alm's busy terrace ↓

FOR CROSS-COUNTRY ★★☆☆☆
Limited but snow-sure
Three small loops, two at Obergurgl and one at Hochgurgl, amount to just 12km of trail. At Hochgurgl 1km is floodlit. All are relatively snow-sure and pleasantly situated but, like the slopes, very exposed in bad weather. Lessons are available.

MOUNTAIN RESTAURANTS ★★★☆☆
Fair choice
Hut choice is limited, but most reports are positive.
Editors' choice Hohe Mut Alm (639632) has table-service, fabulous glacier views from the big terrace, a woody interior, impressively efficient service, and good hearty food on our 2011 visit – endorsed by a reporter. But it gets packed early and doesn't take bookings. The jolly Nederhütte (6425), not far above village level, is hugely popular with readers: 'exceptional food', 'huge, tasty portions', 'modest prices' say this year's crop; 'great atmosphere', 'excellent service' say earlier ones.
Worth knowing about The Top Mountain Star at Wurmkogl looks like an air traffic control tower, has great 360° views, a varied menu but a modern bar ambience. Kirchenkarhütte by contrast is a simple rustic hut – very small, and often crowded.

SCHOOLS AND GUIDES ★★★★☆
Positive reports
We receive positive reports of the Obergurgl school and guides, with good English spoken, a maximum of nine per group except at busy times and excellent organization and lessons. Reporters find the instruction is 'exceptionally good', progression 'genuine' and the standard of teaching 'very high'; 'superb' for children. Demand for private instruction appears to be increasing – a 2013 visitor found the instructors for his kids 'excellent' and the lessons 'surprisingly affordable' – and it is advisable to book ahead during all peak periods.

FOR FAMILIES ★★★★☆
Check out your lodgings
Children's ski classes start at four years and children from age three can either join Bobo Miniclub (outdoor activities) or Bobo Kindergarten (indoor). There's lunchtime supervision for ski school and kindergarten children alike. Many hotels offer childcare of one sort or another (the Alpina has been recommended), and Esprit Ski is a family-specialist UK chalet operator here.

STAYING THERE

Most tour operators feature hotels and pensions. Demand exceeds supply, and for once it is true that you should book early to avoid disappointment.
Chalets Ski Total has a big chalet here, and family-specialist sister company Esprit Ski has two.
Hotels Accommodation is of high quality: most hotels are 4-stars, and none is less than a 3-star.

Build your own shortlist: www.wheretoskiandsnowboard.com

UK PACKAGES

Alpine Answers, Crystal, Crystal Finest, Esprit, Independent Ski Links, Inghams, Interactive Resorts, Momentum, Mountain Beds, Neilson, Oxford Ski Co, Ski Expectations, Ski Monterosa, Ski Solutions, Ski Total, Skitracer, Snow Finders, STC, Thomson
Hochgurgl Crystal Finest, Inghams, Ski Expectations, Skitracer, Snow Finders, Thomson

GETTING THERE

Air Innsbruck 95km/ 60 miles (2hr); Salzburg 285km/ 175 miles (4hr15); Munich 245km/ 150 miles (4hr30)

Rail Train to Ötz; regular buses from station

ACTIVITIES

Indoor Pools, saunas, whirlpools, steam baths and massage in hotels; bowling, indoor golf, indoor horse riding

Outdoor Natural ice rink, curling, snowshoeing, winter hiking paths, tobogganing

Phone numbers
From elsewhere in Austria add the prefix 05256; from abroad use the prefix +43 5256

TOURIST OFFICE

www.obergurgl.com

OBERGURGL

****Alpina de Luxe (6000) Big, smart; excellent children's facilities. 'Wonderful, well-run, traditional hotel with fantastic pool/sauna/spa', 'food even better this year', says a repeat visitor, and a 'Brit-friendly cozzie-on' zone.

****Bergwelt (6274) We stayed here in 2011. Very well run, with excellent food and charming service. Indoor, outdoor pools and spa facilities.

****Edelweiss und Gurgl (6223) The focal hotel; on the central square, near the main lifts. Indoor/outdoor pool, sauna and steam.

****Gotthard-Zeit (62920) Convenient for skiing, but uphill from the village. 'One of the best and friendliest hotels I have stayed in,' says a recent visitor. Pool, sauna, steam and hot tub.

****Hochfirst (63250) Five minutes from gondola. Ski-bus stop outside. Indoor/outdoor pool, spa, hot tub.

****Bellevue (6289) Family-run, new outdoor pool, spa. 'Good service and atmosphere, immaculately clean, professional staff.'

****Josl (6205) Uber-modern, convenient – close to the gondola. Big rooms, lots of storage, glass walls to bathrooms. Top-floor spa. We've stayed here and loved it. But a reporter this year is very critical of the new management. More reports, please.

***Pension Hohenfels (6281) Opposite the Festkogl gondola. Basic, but 'extremely friendly staff, very good breakfasts', says a recent visitor.

HOCHGURGL

*****Top Hotel Hochgurgl (6265) Relais & Châteaux – the only 5-star in the area. Good position.

****Riml (6261) Ski-in/ski-out location. 'Clean, comfortable, good food.'

****Sporthotel Olymp (6491) Near the Grosse Karbahn chair. 'Excellent food and service.'

Apartments The Lohmann residence (6201) is modern and well placed.

EATING OUT ★★★☆☆
Wide choice, limited range

Hotel à la carte dining rooms dominate almost completely. The independent and rustic Krumpn's Stadl (where staff dress in traditional clothing) has a good choice, including rib specials. The Romantika at the hotel Madeleine and the Belmonte are popular pizzerias. For a varied menu, the restaurants in the Edelweiss und Gurgl and the Josl (Austrian, vegetarian) have been recommended. Other tips are the Hexenkuchl in the Jenewein (Austrian food) and the Angerer Alm at Hochgurgl for more of a gourmet offering. Some evenings you can eat on the hill, at Hohe Mut Alm or at David's Skihütte – both popular snowmobile destinations.

APRES-SKI ★★★★☆
Lively early, quiet later

Obergurgl is more animated than you might expect, at least in the early evening. Nederhütte at the Hohe Mut mid-station is the place to be when the lifts close, which in practice means getting there well before then. 'It rocks from the first anthem until the time you want to leave. Schnapps and dancing on your table/chair are obligatory – great fun!' The dancing is often enhanced by live music, said to be 'enjoyed by all age groups'. You ski home afterwards (or ride down on a snowmobile). All the bars at the base of the Rosskar and Hohe Mut lifts are also popular at close of play – try the Pic-Nic ('can get smoky'), or the Hexenkuchl at the Jenewein. The Eisloch (ice dome bar) outside the hotel Alpina is popular.

Later on, the crowded Krumpn's Stadl barn is the liveliest place in town with a DJ most nights. Josl's Keller is popular with all ages – 'good fun'. You can usually find an atmospheric bar at one of the hotels. Reporters have enjoyed the Tuesday ski school display/mountain party/night ski on Festkogl and the 'thoroughly entertaining' night-time tobogganing.

Hochgurgl is very quiet at night except for live music in Toni's Almhütte bar (Sporthotel Olymp).

OFF THE SLOPES ★★☆☆☆
Very limited

There isn't much to do during the day – hardly any shops, limited facilities of other kinds. There is an ice rink. Innsbruck is over two hours away by post bus. Sölden (20 minutes away) has a leisure centre and some shops. There are buses every 15 minutes to Längenfeld (for the thermal spa). Pedestrians can ride gondolas to some of the restaurants for lunch, or walk part-way up the Hohe Mut area; there are 14km of 'pretty' hiking paths. The spas at the Crystal and Bergwelt hotels are open to non-residents at a cost of about 30 euros.

Obertauern

French-style convenience and snow-sure slopes meet Austrian après-ski – an unusual combination; great for a short break

TOP 10 RATINGS

Extent	**
Fast lifts	*****
Queues	****
Snow	****
Expert	***
Intermediate	****
Beginner	****
Charm	**
Convenience	****
Scenery	***

RPI 100

lift pass	£180
ski hire	£100
lessons	£115
food & drink	£125
total	**£520**

NEWS

2012/13: The Grünwaldkopfbahn quad from below the village was replaced by a chondola hybrid lift. And the Hochalmbahn quad above that was upgraded to a six-pack. Two gourmet restaurants, the Freiwild and Steinbock, opened in the village.

152

- ➕ Excellent snow record
- ➕ Quite a lot of ski-in/ski-out lodging
- ➕ Efficient modern lifts
- ➕ Good mountain restaurants
- ➕ Lively but not intrusive après-ski

- ➖ Village not notably charming, and spreads along the pass a long way
- ➖ Slopes limited in extent – and in vertical, in particular
- ➖ Bleak, exposed setting
- ➖ Few off-slope diversions

Obertauern's combination of attractions is unique. If you're hooked on Austrian après-ski but looking for a change from slush and ice, moving up in the world by 1000m or so could be just the ticket. But note the minus points above.

THE RESORT

Obertauern is different from the Austrian norm – a mainly modern development at the top of the Tauern pass. The slopes and lifts form a snow-sure circuit around the village.

Village charm Built in (high-rise) chalet style mixed with stylish modern architecture, the resort is not unattractive and has an upmarket feel to it. Most lodgings are set along the through-road; there is traffic, but it does not intrude greatly. The nearest thing to a central focus is a junction with a side road that has some of the best bars and smart ski shops.

Convenience Lifts go up at various points, and with care you can find ski-in/ski-out lodgings.

Scenery The setting is satisfyingly rugged, with some long views from the high points of the area.

THE MOUNTAINS

Most of the slopes are above the treeline, and bad weather can make skiing impossible (as we found on our last visit). But there are some lightly wooded lower slopes.

Slopes Lifts radiate from the village to form a piste circuit that can be travelled either way in a couple of hours. Runs are short, and vertical is limited – most major lifts are in the 200m to 400m range. There is floodlit skiing twice a week.

Fast lifts Fast chairs dominate, and lifties reportedly manage to fill them.

Queues Crowded pistes can be more of a problem than queues. The Sonnenlift chair can have problems at ski school time.

Terrain parks The Spot is a small park above the Almrausch hut, on the far left on our piste map.

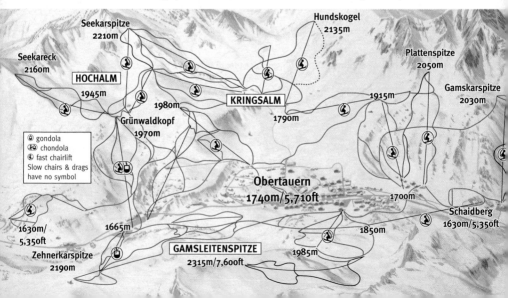

Obertauern.
Where snow is at home!

Official Partner.

It's snowtime in Obertauern from late November to early May.

- Get the fantastic holiday feeling in one of the best skiing resorts of the Alps with a snow guarantee.
- Enjoy perfect winter sports conditions in a romantic atmosphere.
- Ski in – ski out: straight from your hotel onto the slope.

Obertauern at a glance:

100 km of slopes, 26 cable cars and lifts, night skiing, snowkiting school, 5 skiing and snowboarding schools, fun park for snowboarders.

Book online! All accomodation comfortable and easy:
www.obertauern.com

Attractive package periods:
- ▸ **20.11. – 21.12.2013:** Opening weeks
- ▸ **11.01. – 01.02.2014:** Powder Snow Weeks
- ▸ **22.03. – 12.04. / 19.04. – 04.05.2014:** Sun & Fun Weeks

ganz oben
OBERTAUERN.COM

Tourist Association Obertauern | A-5562 Obertauern
Tel. +43(0)6456 / 7252 | info@obertauern.com

↑ On the south side of the village, Zehnerkarspitze rises steeply but has a blue run from the top
TVB OBERTAUERN

KEY FACTS

Resort	1740m
	5,710ft
Slopes	1630-2315m
	5,350-7,600ft
Lifts	26
Pistes	100km
	62 miles
Blue	60%
Red	36%
Black	4%
Snowmaking	90%

UK PACKAGES

Alpine Answers, Crystal Finest, Inghams, Snow Finders, STC, Thomson

Phone numbers
From elsewhere in Austria add the prefix 06456; from abroad use the prefix +43 6456

TOURIST OFFICE

www.obertauern.com

Snow reliability Excellent because of altitude (exceptional, for Austria) and extensive snowmaking.

Experts There are genuinely steep black pistes from the top Gamsleiten chair, but it is prone to closure. The icy race course under the Schaidbergbahn is a challenge. And try the black run from Seekarspitze and the ski route from Hundskogel (flat to start, steep moguls later).

Intermediates Most of the circuit is of intermediate difficulty. Stay low for easier pistes, or try the tougher runs higher up; you can't do the whole circuit without skiing reds.

Beginners There are good nursery slopes in several places, notably by the car parks at the western end of the resort. The Schaidberg chair leads to a high-altitude beginners' slope, and there is an easy run down – and other easy blues to progress to.

Snowboarding Draglifts are optional except for beginners. Blue Tomato is a specialist school.

Cross-country 26km of trails locally.

Mountain restaurants There are lots, but they are often crowded. Readers praise the friendly staff (and the Tiroler gröstl) at the table-service Sonnhof; other tips include Flubachalm ('lovely gulasch soup and gröstl'), and the lively Hochalm.

Schools and guides We have no recent reports of the six schools, but past reviews of both Krallinger and Koch have been positive.

Families The resort isn't particularly family-oriented, and nursery slopes can be inconvenient, but most ski schools do take children. The kindergarten takes babies.

STAYING THERE

Hotels Practically all accommodation is in hotels (mostly 3-star and 4-star) and guest houses. The Steiner (7306) is praised this year: 'Wonderful hotel, faultless, engaging staff, first-class food, extensive spa.' Two others are regularly tipped by readers: the Latschenhof (7334) – 'best food in Austria', 'great spa, 50m from a run' – and the Marietta (7262) – 'friendly, well-run; lovely spa'.

Eating out The choices are mostly hotels (the Latschenhof is highly recommended) though two new gourmet places opened this year (read our News panel). Some of the après-ski bars turn themselves into restaurants – the Almrausch does 'superb food'.

Après-ski Several restaurants above village level get lively as the lifts close – Hochalm and Edelweiss, for example. There are several cute woody chalets at the base that throb at teatime: Latsch'n Alm, Lürzer Alm ('dancing on the tables encouraged'), and Gruber Stadl. WeltcupSchirm is a 'superb' lively umbrella bar; Qu Bar is 'very loud'. The Tauernkönig hotel, hidden away off the 8a home run, has 'a cosy outdoor après area'. Later on, Monkey's Heaven and the People bar have dancing. We had a quiet beer and used the free Wi-Fi in the modern, glass-fronted Mund Werk.

Off the slopes There's an excellent, large sports centre (no pool, but this year you can swim at the Marietta or Kohlmayr hotels). There are marked walks up to Kringsalm and sleigh rides. Salzburg is an easy trip.

Rauris

Little-known Rauris is set amid the beautiful Hohe Tauern National Park and suits those looking for an all-round winter holiday

155

TOP 10 RATINGS

Extent	★
Fast lifts	★★★
Queues	★★★★
Snow	★★★
Expert	★★
Intermediate	★★★
Beginner	★★★
Charm	★★★
Convenience	★★★
Scenery	★★★

RPI	85
lift pass	£170
ski hire	£80
lessons	£80
food & drink	£110
total	**£440**

➕ Slopes best for families, and for beginners and intermediates who don't crave mileage

➕ Lots to do other than ski

➕ Unspoiled picturesque village

➕ Good value

➖ Extent of pistes very limited – not the place for keen piste-bashers

➖ Little for experts except off-piste

➖ Still a few T-bars to cope with

➖ Relatively few village restaurants outside hotels

Rauris is a place to go for an all-round winter holiday. The ski area is small, but there are lots of activities to try other than downhill skiing and boarding, and it is all set within the beautiful Hohe Tauern National Park.

THE RESORT

The Raurisertal is tucked away in the Hohe Tauern National Park between the Gastein valley and Zell am See in Salzburgerland. It was once one of Europe's most important gold-mining areas.

Village charm It's a picturesque village, the centre of which is set off the main valley road, and it has a year-round population of around 3,500.

Convenience A free ski-bus serves the valley lift stations.

Scenery The National Park scenery is spectacular and unspoiled, and there are fine views from the peaks.

THE MOUNTAINS

The lifts are across the main road from the village and take you up slopes that are wooded on the lower part and open higher up, rising to 2175m at Schwarzwand.

Slopes There are two main sectors. A two-stage, six-seat gondola takes you from the main lift base to Hochalm via Heimalm. From just below Hochalm, an eight-seat gondola goes up to the high point.

Three T-bars also serve the top part of the mountain, where there are mainly gentle blue runs. The run down from Heimalm to the valley is classified black, though.

The Hochalm area interconnects with a lower area centred on Kreuzboden and served by a double chairlift from the valley, followed by a T-bar to the high point of 1690m. The main run in this sector is a top-to-bottom red.

Fast lifts There are two gondolas. The other lifts are mainly T-bars.

Queues Rauris doesn't get as crowded as some of the better-known resorts.

Terrain parks The Nuggetpark on Kreuzboden is the place to head for. There's a boardercross too. And for 2013/14 there will be a new fun slope about 600m long, with jumps, tunnels and other fun features.

Snow reliability The slopes face mainly north-east, so they keep their snow well, and 80% of the pistes are covered by snowmaking. The lift company itself produces all the power it needs for the snowmaking, the result being a zero-energy balance

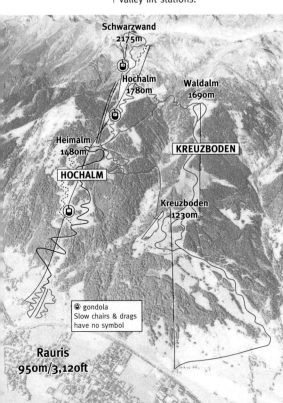

Schwarzwand
2175m

Hochalm
1780m

Waldalm
1690m

Heimalm
1480m

KREUZBODEN

HOCHALM

Kreuzboden
1230m

🚠 gondola
Slow chairs & drags
have no symbol

Rauris
950m/3,120ft

Resort news and key links: www.wheretoskiandsnowboard.com

NEWS

2013/14: A new fun slope with jumps, tunnels and other fun features is planned.

2012/13: At Waldalm a new mountain hut opened, and more snowmaking was installed.

KEY FACTS

Resort	950m
	3,120ft
Slopes	950-2175m
	3,120-7,140ft
Lifts	10
Pistes	30km
	19 miles
Blue	54%
Red	32%
Black	14%
Snowmaking	80%

UK PACKAGES

Crystal, Crystal Finest, Thomson

RAURISER HOCHALMBAHNEN

There's lots of off-piste and good ski touring in the National Park, which has peaks of over 3000m ➔

Phone numbers
From elsewhere in Austria add the prefix 06544; from abroad use the prefix +43 6544

TOURIST OFFICE

www.rauisertal.at

(unique in Austria and qualifying it as the first lift company in Austria to be a Climate Alliance Partner).

Experts There's not much to interest experts as far as piste skiing is concerned. But there's the opportunity for off-piste in bowls at the top and between the pistes. There's also good ski touring nearby in beautiful surroundings amid peaks that go up to over 3000m.

Intermediates Most slopes suit intermediates best. But mileage hungry piste-bashers will find the extent of the pistes very limited.

Beginners The beginner area at the foot of Hochalm is served by two T-bars, and progression is to blue runs at the top of the mountain. There is a limited lift pass for beginners plus a points card.

Snowboarding Snowboarders can enjoy the groomed runs, the freeriding and the terrain park.

Cross-country There are 30km of prepared tracks in the valley.

Mountain restaurants There are five rustic-looking huts to choose from – so you could try a different one virtually every day in a week's stay.

Schools and guides The three schools are Adventure Rauris, Karl Maier and Hohe Tauern.

Families Rauris targets the family market and there's a special area at Hochalm with a wigwam and sledge rides – and where children can meet Tilly the owl, the Rauris mascot. Ski schools take children from age four and there's a private childminding service for non-skiing kids.

STAYING THERE

The tourist office has a good brochure describing the various options.

Hotels The two 4-stars, Kristall (7316) and Rauriserhof (6213), and the 3-star Alpina (6562) all have pools and wellness centres and are close to the chairlift into the slopes. And there are nine more 3-stars as well as B&Bs.

Apartments The 4-star Schönblick Resort has recently built apartments with a good wellness centre and a bar-restaurant. It is close to the gondola.

Eating out There are more than 30 restaurants, mostly in hotels and serving typical Austrian food. Of the individual places Gusto is 4km away in neighbouring Wörth but stands out for quality of cuisine. In town Sonnblick and Pizzeria Italiano both specialize in, er, Italian food and pizzas.

Après-ski It starts up the mountain – try Heimalm or Gamsgart'l at Hochalm. And there's the St Hubertus après-ski bar and Maislau Alm at the bottom of the gondola and Sportalm near the foot of the chairlift. In town try the RockBar or Shakesbeer.

Off the slopes As well as 30km of walking paths you can go snowshoeing in the National Park – including guided tours to Kolm-Saigurn at the end of the valley where there's ice climbing for beginners and experts, a 5km toboggan run, beautiful isolated surroundings and restaurants. You can be towed there on a sled, too. There's also tobaganing (floodlit twice a week) from Kreuzboden. And you can go horse riding or take a sleigh ride.

RAURISER HOCHALMBAHNEN

- ideal for families, beginners and freeriders
- family friendly ski passes, free ski bus
- snow guarantee, climate friendly
- pleasant huts
- lit toboggan run
- winter hiking trails

ACTIVE WINTER
- 7 nights, 6 days ski pass
- 4 days skiing lessons
- from EUR 437,- p.p.

Saalbach-Hinterglemm

Lively, noisy, traditional-style villages and extensive, varied, prettily wooded slopes; pity they are mostly so sunny

RATINGS

The mountains

Extent	★★★
Fast lifts	★★★★★
Queues	★★★★
Terrain p'ks	★★★★
Snow	★★
Expert	★★
Intermediate	★★★★
Beginner	★★★
Boarder	★★★★★
X-country	★★
Restaurants	★★★★
Schools	★★★★
Families	★★★

The resort

Charm	★★★★
Convenience	★★★★
Scenery	★★★
Eating out	★★★
Après-ski	★★★★★
Off-slope	★★

RPI	100
lift pass	£200
ski hire	£110
lessons	£90
food & drink	£110
total	**£510**

158

- ➕ Large, well-linked, intermediate circuit, good for mixed groups
- ➕ Impressive lift system
- ➕ Saalbach is a pleasant, lively village, largely car-free in the centre
- ➕ Dozens of good mountain huts
- ➕ Extensive snowmaking but ...

- ➖ Most slopes are sunny as well as low, and the snow suffers
- ➖ Limited steep terrain
- ➖ Both villages spread widely
- ➖ Both are noisy from 4pm and Saalbach can get rowdy at night

Saalbach-Hinterglemm gets ever closer to completing its mission to abolish the slow lift. Next season, yet another six-pack will replace a T-bar above Hinterglemm. Leaving aside baby drags and the like, only four slow lifts remain, of which only one is unavoidable (if doing the circuit anticlockwise). Amazing.

The valley has a lot going for it in other respects, too. Sadly, good snow isn't one of them. The altitudes are modest, but the bigger problem is that most of the slopes face south. The snowmaking is good enough to make a midwinter visit here a fairly safe bet, but problems can arise as spring approaches.

THE RESORT

Saalbach and Hinterglemm are separate villages, their centres 4km apart, which have expanded along the floor of their dead-end east–west valley. They haven't quite merged, but have adopted a single marketing identity. A 'ski-circus' links the two, with lifts and runs on both sides of the valley. At the eastern end is a link to Leogang, in the next valley.

Saalbach has a justified reputation as a party town – but those doing the partying seem to be a strangely mixed bunch. Big-spending BMW and

Mercedes drivers staying in the smart, expensive hotels that line the main street share the bars with teenagers spending more on alcohol than on their cheap and cheerful pensions.

Hinterglemm is a more diffuse collection of hotels and holiday homes, where prices are lower and less cash is flashed.

Several resorts in Salzburgerland are reachable by road. The nearest are Hochkönig to the north and Zell am See to the south. There are two regional passes to consider – read the 'Lift passes' panel in the margin.

VILLAGE CHARM ★★★★
Very appealing
Saalbach is an attractive, typically Tirolean village, with traditional-style (although mostly modern) buildings huddled together around a classic onion-domed church. Hinterglemm is less cute, with a rather featureless centre spread along a single main street. Both villages are free of through traffic. And both are lively from mid-afternoon until the early hours. Saalbach in particular can get rowdy, with drunken revellers still in their ski boots late in the evening.

CONVENIENCE ★★★★
Lifts near the centre
Saalbach is more convenient than most Austrian villages, with lifts into three sectors of the slopes starting

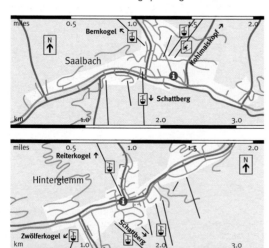

miles 0.5 1.0 1.5 2.0
Bernkogel
Kohlmaiskopf
Saalbach
Schattberg
km 1.0 2.0 3.0

miles 0.5 1.0 1.5 2.0
Reiterkogel
Hinterglemm
Zwölferkogel
Schattberg
km 1.0 2.0 3.0

↑ The Reiterkogel slopes on the left offer nice easy cruising when the snow is good

NEWS

2013/14: Yet another six-pack (heated, with covers) will replace a T-bar on Reiterkogel.

2012/13: The T-bar on Bernkogel that impeded progress from Hinterglemm to Saalbach was replaced by a six-pack with bubbles.

close to the traffic-free village centre; the result, if staying centrally, is near to an ideal blend of Austrian charm with French convenience. Hinterglemm also has lifts and runs close to the centre, and offers quick access to some of the most interesting slopes – and, importantly, to most of the north-facing runs. A few reporters find walking through the villages from one side of the slopes to the other an irritant.

The valley bus service is fine, but not perfect: it finishes early, gets very busy at peak times and doesn't reach hotels or lifts in central Hinterglemm, or hotels set away from the main road. A Nightliner bus runs infrequently between the resorts in the evening.

SCENERY ★★★☆☆
Pleasant rather than dramatic
The villages are flanked by modest, broad mountain ridges. The high points give more dramatic views of the mountains to the north.

THE MOUNTAINS

The runs form a 'circus' almost entirely composed of broad slopes between swathes of forest, so this is a good area in bad weather. The signposting and piste map are good (and consistently praised by reporters). But some say that many of the blues and reds are of much the same gradients.

EXTENT OF THE SLOPES ★★★☆☆
User-friendly circuit
Travelling anticlockwise, you can make a complete circuit of the valley on skis, crossing from one side to the other at Vorderglemm and Lengau – if

you wish you can stick to blues almost the whole way. Going clockwise, you have to do a shorter circuit – there is no lift at Vorderglemm – and there is more red-run skiing to do.

On the south-facing side, five sectors can be identified, each served by a lift from the valley – named on our map. The links across these slopes work well: when traversing the whole hillside you need to descend to the valley floor only once – at Saalbach, where the main street separates Bernkogel from Kohlmaiskopf. The Wildenkarkogel sector connects via Seidl-Alm to the slopes of **Leogang**; a small, high, open area served by fast lifts leads to a long, north-facing slope down to the base of an eight-seat gondola near Hütten, 3km from Leogang village.

Back in the main valley, the north-facing slopes are different in character: two widely separated and steeper mountains, one split into twin peaks. An eight-seat gondola rises from Saalbach to **Schattberg Ost**, where the high, open, sunny slopes behind the peak are served by a fast quad. The slightly higher peak of **Schattberg West** is reached by gondola from Hinterglemm. Another gondola makes the link from Schattberg Ost to Schattberg West. The second north-facing hill is **Zwölferkogel**, served by a two-stage eight-seat gondola from Hinterglemm. A six-pack and draglift serve open slopes on the sunny side of the peak, and a second gondola from the valley provides a link from the south-facing Hochalm slopes.

The Hinterglemm nursery slopes are well used, and floodlit every evening.

KEY FACTS

Resort	1000m
	3,280ft
Slopes	930-2095m
	3,050-6,870ft
Lifts	55
Pistes	200km
	124 miles
Blue	45%
Red	48%
Black	7%
Snowmaking	90%

FAST LIFTS ★★★★★
The world's best

One 2013 visitor remarks: 'One of the best lift systems I've ever used.' And he's quite right: Saalbach-Hinterglemm has the highest proportion of fast lifts of any major resort in the world (90%). The only lifts that aren't fast when doing the circus are the parallel T-bars to the top of Bernkogel when going from Saalbach to Hinterglemm. The resort says replacing these is 'under discussion', but no firm date has been set yet.

QUEUES ★★★★
High season mostly

Given what we say about fast lifts, it's not surprising that the system copes well. The only recent complaints relate to peak season – a '20-minute wait on a sunny day' at Vorderglemm and in the morning peak at Saalbach for the Schattberg gondola.

TERRAIN PARKS ★★★★
Main one has its own gondola

The popular Nightpark just above Hinterglemm is served by its own heated gondola, is floodlit until 9.30pm (except Sundays) and includes Big Air, kickers, wall ride and rails, plus a beginner line. There are other parks below Hochalm and Kl. Asitz towards Leogang, and a boardercross and park for beginners on Bernkogel.

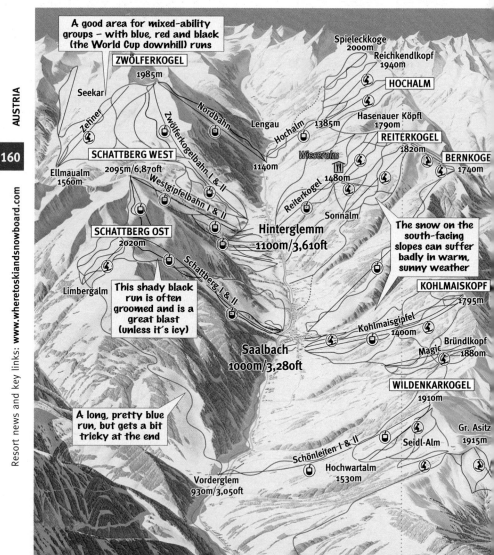

A good area for mixed-ability groups – with blue, red and black (the World Cup downhill) runs

The snow on the south-facing slopes can suffer badly in warm, sunny weather

This shady black run is often groomed and is a great blast (unless it's icy)

A long, pretty blue run, but gets a bit tricky at the end

LIFT PASSES

Prices in €

Age	1-day	6-day
under 16	23	110
16 to 18	34	165
19 plus	45	220

Free Under 6

Senior No deals

Beginner Points card

Notes Covers Saalbach-Hinterglemm and Leogang, and the ski-bus; also Reiterkogel toboggan run at night; part-day and non-skier passes

Alternative passes
Salzburg SuperSkiCard covers 22 ski areas in the Salzburg province; Kitzbüheler Alpen All Star Card covers Kitzbühel, Schneewinkel (St Johann), SkiWelt, Ski Juwel, Skicircus Saalbach, Zell-Kaprun

SNOW RELIABILITY ★★☆☆☆
A tale of two sides

Most slopes are below 1900m and the south-facing slopes are in the majority; they can suffer from the sun and we've often seen strips of machine-made snow amid green and brown fields. The north-facing slopes keep their snow better but can get icy. The long north-facing run to Leogang often has the best snow in the area. Piste maintenance is good and snowmaking covers 90% of the area; but its fundamental problems won't go away.

FOR EXPERTS ★★☆☆☆
Little steep stuff

There are a few challenging slopes on the north-facing side. The long (4km) Nordabfahrt run beneath the Schattberg Ost gondola is a genuine black – a fine fast bash first thing in the morning if it has been groomed and is not icy. The Zwölferkogel Nordabfahrt at Hinterglemm is less consistent, but its classification is justified by a few short, steeper pitches. The World Cup downhill run from Zwölferkogel is interesting, as is the 5km Schattberg West–Hinterglemm red (and its 'ski route' variant). Snow conditions and forest tend to limit the off-piste potential. Given decent snow, however, you can have a good time.

FOR INTERMEDIATES ★★★★☆
Paradise for most

The sunny side of the area is ideal for both the mileage-hungry piste-basher and the more leisurely cruiser, although many of the blues can be quite testing. The otherwise delightful blue run from Bernkogel to Saalbach can get really crowded. For more of a challenge, the long red runs to the valley are good fun.

The north-facing area also has some more challenging runs, with excellent relentless reds from both Schattberg West and Zwölferkogel, and a section of relatively high, open slopes around Zwölferkogel – good for mixed-ability groups wishing to ski together. None of the black runs is beyond an adventurous intermediate, unless icy. The long, pretty blue to Vorderglemm gets right away from lifts – but is a bit steep and tricky towards the end, and probably should be red.

Our favourite intermediate run is the long cruise to Leogang.

FOR BEGINNERS ★★★☆☆
Head for Hinterglemm

Saalbach's two sunny nursery slopes are right next to the village. The upper one is served by a short six-pack but gets a lot of through-traffic. There are short, easy runs to progress to at Bernkogel and Schattberg.

Hinterglemm's spacious nursery area is separate from the main slopes and faces north so lacks sun in midwinter but is more reliable for snow later on. Progression is aided by a gondola serving the blue slope that is also used for night skiing. There are lots of other easy blue runs to move on to, especially on the south-facing side of the valley.

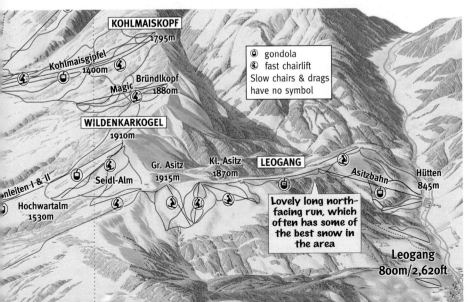

KOHLMAISKOPF
1795m

Kohlmaisgipfel
1400m

Bründlkopf
1880m

Magic

WILDENKARKOGEL
1910m

Gr. Asitz
1915m

Kl. Asitz
1870m

LEOGANG

Asitzbahn

Hütten
845m

Seidl-Alm

...nleiten I & II

Hochwartalm
1530m

⦿ gondola
ⓕ fast chairlift
Slow chairs & drags have no symbol

Lovely long north-facing run, which often has some of the best snow in the area

Leogang
800m/2,620ft

↑ The valley is a tale of two sides: gentler south-facing slopes to the right, steeper north-facing ones to the left
TVB SAALBACH-HINTERGLEMM

SCHOOLS

Saalbach
Fürstauer
t 8444
Snow Academy
t 668256
Zink
t 0664 162 3655
Board.at
t 20047
EasySki
t 0699 111 80010

Hinterglemm
Snow & Fun
t 7511
Activ
t 0676 517 1325
Alpin
t 741 4640
Total
t 560 0669

Classes
(Fürstauer prices)
5 days (4.5hr) from €172
Private lessons
From €139 for 3hr, for 1 or 2 people; extra person €15

CHILDCARE

Several hotels have nurseries

Ski schools
From about age 4

FOR BOARDERS ★★★★★
Good all-rounder
Saalbach is great for boarding. Slopes are extensive, lifts are mainly chairs and gondolas, and there are pistes to appeal to beginners, intermediates and experts alike – with few flats to negotiate. For experienced boarders, there's off-piste terrain between the lifts if snow conditions permit.

FOR CROSS-COUNTRY ★★
Go to Zell am See
In mid-winter the 10km of valley trails get very little sun, and are not very exciting. There is a high trail on the Reiterkogel. But the area beyond nearby Zell am See is better.

MOUNTAIN RESTAURANTS ★★★★
Excellent quality and quantity
The area is liberally scattered with huts – about 40 in total – most of them pleasant, lively, rustic places serving good food. All are marked and named on the piste map.
Editors' choice The Wieseralm (6939), at the heart of the Hinterglemm south-facing slopes, is a welcoming woody chalet doing table-service of satisfying dishes; fine views from the terrace; endorsed by recent reporters.
Worth knowing about Reporters regularly tip the Alte Schmiede above Leogang, a lovely wood hut with table-service, a big fireplace, huge terrace and DJ; 'excellent food, even vegetarian options' says a 2013 reporter; interesting gents' toilet that most reporters comment on. Westernstadl on Bernkogel is 'built around a stable with horses' and has 'great food and friendly service'. Two 2013 reporters tipped Asitzbräu above Leogang ('large' but 'delicious Austrian food and stunning views').
There's a picnic room at the top station of the Schattberg Xpress.

SCHOOLS AND GUIDES ★★★★
More reports would be good ...
There's plenty of choice. A 2013 reporter says the Fürstauer school was 'highly rated' by his group: 'Friendly instructors and good value; our beginner was skiing red runs confidently by the end of the week.'

FOR FAMILIES ★★★
Hinterglemm tries harder
Saalbach doesn't go out of its way to sell itself to families, although it does have a ski kindergarten. Hinterglemm probably makes a better family base, with some good hotel-based nursery facilities – at the Theresia for example. And its nursery slope is better.

STAYING THERE

Chalets Inghams has a chalet hotel (with a sauna), which is right by the Reiterkogel gondola in Hinterglemm.
Hotels Both villages have lots of hotels, mainly 3-star and above. Be aware that some central hotels suffer from disco noise, and front rooms from street noise into the early hours.
SAALBACH
★★★★Alpenhotel (6666) Central with countless bars and restaurants (a 2013 reporter especially enjoyed the Italian), nightclub; small pool, hot tub.
★★★★Kendler (62250) Position second to none, beside the Bernkogel lift. Classy, expensive, good food.
★★★★Kristiana (6253) Near enough to lifts but away from night-time noise. Sauna, steam bath.
★★★★Panther (6227) Central, wellness centre, outdoor pool: 'Excellent food, comfortable room, pleasant staff.'
★★★★Saalbacher Hof (7111) Major central hotel, renovated in 2010, with new restaurants and wellness centre.
★★★Haider (62280) Best-positioned of the 3-stars, right next to the main lifts.

ACTIVITIES

Indoor In hotels: swimming pools, sauna, massage, solarium; tennis, museum, gallery, bowling, casino

Outdoor Ice rink, curling, tobogganing, sleigh rides, snowshoeing, snowmobiling, quad bikes, ice karts, 40km of cleared paths, archery, paragliding

UK PACKAGES

Alpine Answers, Crystal, Crystal Finest, Independent Ski Links, Inghams, Interactive Resorts, Neilson, Ski Club Freshtracks, Ski Expectations, Ski Miquel, Ski Solutions, Skitracer, Snow Finders, Snowscape, STC, Thomson **Leogang** Interactive Resorts, Zenith

GETTING THERE

Air Salzburg 90km/ 55 miles (2hr); Munich 225km/140 miles (3hr30)

Rail Zell am See 19km/12 miles; hourly buses

Phone numbers
From elsewhere in Austria add the prefix 06541 (Saalbach), 06583 (Leogang); from abroad use the prefix +43 and omit the initial '0'

TOURIST OFFICES

Saalbach
www.saalbach.com
Leogang
www.leogang-saalfelden.at

***Peter** (6236) Main street location. Recently renovated.

HINTERGLEMM

****Theresia** (74140) Hinterglemm's top hotel, good for families. On road to Saalbach, but at foot of a red run and close to a draglift into the circus. Superb food and friendly staff, say past reports. Pool and spa.

****Unterschwarzachhof** (6541) Recently refurbished with trendy furnishings and new wellness area, including indoor-outdoor pool, outdoor hot tub; 'great food and spa'.

***Sonnblick** (6408) Convenient and in a quiet location.

Apartments There's a big choice for independent travellers.

At altitude Some mountain restaurants have rooms. One reader greatly enjoyed the 3-star Sonnhof (6295) at the top of the Hochalmbahn, where in the mornings you get two six-packs all to yourself for half an hour.

EATING OUT ★★★☆☆
Wide choice of hotel restaurants
This is essentially a half-board resort, with strikingly few restaurants other than those in hotels. In Saalbach, the Kohlmais Stub'n (Aparthotel Astrid) at the foot of the slopes has friendly service, a warm woody ambience and creative, regional food. The hotel Peter's restaurant, at the top of the main street, is atmospheric and serves excellent meat dishes cooked on hot stones. At the Alpenhotel, we've had good pizza and other dishes at La Trattoria, and its Vitrine will be serving 'organic vegan cuisine' this winter.

APRES-SKI ★★★★★
It rocks from early on
'The best après-ski in the Alps,' claims the resort website, and it is certainly among the best. The site lists over 20 venues. Saalbach, in particular, is very lively from mid-afternoon until the early hours, and can get quite wild.

On the hill above Saalbach, the Berger Hochalm under the Magic chair rocks from early afternoon (with a happy hour from 3pm); 'Banging!' says a 57-year-old reporter. Then it's down to the rustic Hinterhag Alm; an institution – 'Everybody meets here at 4pm' they say, and that's how it seems; live bands ensure a 'totally mental' atmosphere until people start to slide down to the already packed Bauer's Schi-Alm – an old cow shed with attached umbrella bars. Both are

'noisy, drunken places, but good fun'. There are alternatives: Bäckstättstall and the main bar of Berger's Sporthotel have dancing when the lifts close. Bobby's Pub attracts a very young crowd, but is cheap, has bowling, games machines, sport on TVs and serves Guinness. Zum Turm (a converted medieval jail) and Spitzbub (a converted garage) are loud and lively. The Ötzi bar 'is always good for a night out – good prices, friendly staff, dancing on tables'. There are late night clubs under various central hotels, and several pole dancing dives.

We get fewer reports on the après-ski in Hinterglemm, but we enjoyed the Schwarzacher in 2013 and the rustic goat-themed Goasstall just above the village in the past ('the place rocks; one of the great après-ski bars in Austria'). Road King in the hotel Dorfschmiede is a lively Harley-Davidson biker-themed bar. Later on, hit the Tanzhimmel and Hexenhäusl.

OFF THE SLOPES ★★☆☆☆
Surprisingly little to do
The resort is not very entertaining if you're not into winter sports. There are few shops other than supermarkets and ski shops. There are some walking paths, and the gondolas can be used. Many good restaurants are reachable by lift. At Hinterglemm a floodlit treetop walk opened recently. There are long, fun toboggan runs above both Saalbach and Hinterglemm. Excursions to Salzburg are possible.

LINKED RESORT – 800m

LEOGANG

Leogang sits in a pretty valley beneath the impressive Birnhorn. It is quietly attractive but is set on a busy road.

It may seem to offer a good budget base for skiing the slopes of Saalbach-Hinterglemm, but in practice it suits best those who are content with the good, generally quiet local slopes plus the runs at the eastern end of the main circuit; getting to the best slopes beyond Hinterglemm takes quite a time. The nursery slopes are good.

Lodging is widely scattered, but there are good hotels and quiet apartments available. Restaurants are hotel-based. The rustic old chalet Kraller Alm is the focal teatime and evening rendezvous. Activities off the slopes are very limited, but a new 2km long zipwire opened last season.

Schladming

Pleasant old valley town in Styria, with a famous racing hill directly above, links to three other mountains and other areas nearby

RATINGS

The mountains

Extent	★★★
Fast lifts	★★★★
Queues	★★★★
Terrain p'ks	★★★
Snow	★★★★
Expert	★★
Intermediate	★★★★
Beginner	★★★
Boarder	★★★
X-country	★★★★
Restaurants	★★★★
Schools	★★★
Families	★★★★

The resort

Charm	★★★
Convenience	★★★
Scenery	★★★
Eating out	★★★
Après-ski	★★★
Off-slope	★★★

RPI | 95

lift pass	£200
ski hire	£80
lessons	£100
food & drink	£115
total	**£495**

NEWS

2013/14: The Gipfelbahn 'pulse' gondola on Hochwurzen is being replaced by a proper 10-seat gondola.

2012/13: The 2013 Alpine World Ski Championships were held here in February. Two new hotels opened in December 2012 – Planai and Falkensteiner.

➕ Ideal for intermediate cruising

➕ Very sheltered slopes, among trees

➕ Lots of good mountain restaurants

➕ Appealing town with friendly people

➕ Very cheap for meals and drinks

➖ Slopes lack variety

➖ Very little to entertain experts

➖ Nursery slopes not central

➖ Runs to valley level are not easy

One slope may be rather like another here, but with its four linked mountains Schladming offers the keen intermediate a real sense of travelling around on the snow. And its solid, valley-town ambience makes it a pleasant change from the Austrian rustic-village norm. The town had a major injection of investment for last season, thanks to the 2013 Alpine World Ski Championships.

THE RESORT

The old town of Schladming sits at the foot of Planai, one of four linked ski mountains. It has a long skiing tradition: the town has hosted many World Cup races and last season hosted the World Championships, triggering lots of new construction.

At the foot of the next mountain to the west, Hochwurzen, is Rohrmoos – a quiet, scattered satellite village set on an elevated slope that forms a giant nursery area. To the east is the small, attractively rustic village of Haus, at the foot of the highest of the four mountains, Hauser Kaibling.

Timetabled 'efficient' free ski-buses link the villages and lift bases. A night bus runs until 1am (2.5 euros one way); taxis can be more economic.

The Ski Alliance Amadé lift pass also covers many other resorts; trips are feasible to Bad Gastein, Wagrain/Flachau, Zauchensee and Hochkönig (and to Obertauern – not on the pass). A car is useful for these trips.

There are direct trains from Salzburg, so Schladming makes an excellent short break destination.

VILLAGE CHARM ★★★☆☆
Pleasant car-free centre

Most of Schladming's buildings are solid and traditional, and at its heart there's a pleasant, traffic-free main square, prettily lit at night, around which you'll find most of the shops, restaurants, bars and some appealing hotels. The ultra-modern Planet Planai area nearby at the base of the gondola is a complete contrast. The busy main road bypasses the town.

CONVENIENCE ★★★☆☆
Reasonably compact

Much of the accommodation is close to the town centre; the sports centre and tennis halls are five minutes' walk away, as is the gondola to Planai. There is also accommodation out by the Planai–Hochwurzen lift link, and further down the valley (eg Pichl).

SCENERY ★★★☆☆
Four points of view

All four mountains are broadly similar, pleasantly wooded and share decent views along the Ennstal and to the more dramatic Dachsteingruppe, across the valley to the north.

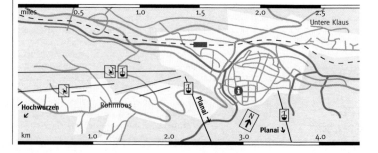

KEY FACTS

Resort	745m
	2,440ft

Schladming's four linked mountains	
Slopes	745-2015m
	2,440-6,610ft
Lifts	45
Pistes	125km
	78 miles
Blue	34%
Red	62%
Black	4%
Snowmaking	99%

THE MOUNTAINS

Most pistes are on the wooded north-facing slopes above the main valley, with some going into the side valleys higher up; there are a few short open slopes above the trees.

Piste maps here can be confusing. The whole four-mountain area is covered on one map, but the individual mountains also do their own maps. These show mountain restaurants, which the main map does not. But they differ from the main map, adding some runs and omitting others. Two of these also show the other mountains – but without restaurants. All a bit messy.

As in many Austrian areas, you may also encounter multiple pistes identified by the same number. Add to this poor signposting, and finding your way around can be tricky.

EXTENT OF THE SLOPES ★★★★★
Four linked sectors
The pistes now total 125km in length – a modest figure, but enough to gain the resort our ★★★ rating. Each of the sectors has a variety of runs to play on and you get a satisfying feeling of travelling around a lot.

Planai is the local mountain, reached directly by gondola from the edge of the town centre. It is linked to **Hauser Kaibling** at altitude via the high, wooded bowl between them. At the base of the mountain, the village of Haus has a cable car and gondola into the slopes. Links to the mountains to the west, **Hochwurzen** and **Reiteralm**, are at valley level (and

the first involves riding a gondola down from Planai). Our favourite area is Reiteralm – a hi-tech lift system and nicely varied terrain, extended down into Preuneggtal in 2010/11 by a new gondola and runs.

Several lower runs go across poorly signposted roads – care is needed.

There are several other separate mountains nearby covered by the local lift pass – including Fageralm (only slow chairlifts and T-bars, but lovely quiet, wide, easy cruising pistes and rustic huts – a very relaxing change of pace), Galsterbergalm, the Dachstein glacier and Stoderzinken.

FAST LIFTS ★★★★
Some neglected links
Each linked sector has gondola access from the car parks at the bases, and there are now lots of fast chairs. But the slow chairlift from Schladming to Hochwurzen, and the one from Pichl to Reiteralm are obvious weaknesses.

QUEUES ★★★★
New lifts helping
Queues for the Planai gondola at peak times are the only issue. We lack February reports this year, but in January and March our reporters had no queue problems.

TERRAIN PARKS ★★★
Three to try
Planai has a park above Larchkogel, with medium and pro kicker lines, jumps, boxes and rails. Reiteralm's park is similarly well equipped; there's also a half-pipe. Hochwurzen's Playground park is floodlit until 10pm.

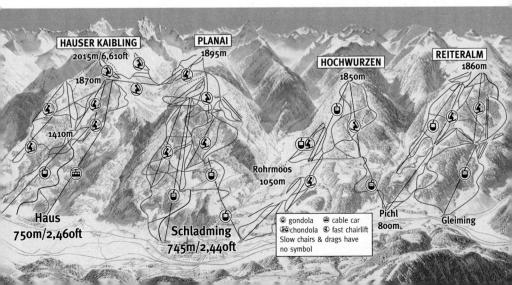

HAUSER KAIBLING 2015m/6,610ft
1870m
1410m
Haus 750m/2,460ft

PLANAI 1895m

HOCHWURZEN 1850m

REITERALM 1860m

Rohrmoos 1050m

Schladming 745m/2,440ft

Pichl 800m

Gleiming

gondola   cable car
chondola   fast chairlift
Slow chairs & drags have no symbol

LIFT PASSES

Ski Amadé

Prices in €

Age	1-day	6-day
under 17	23	107
17 to 19	35	168
20 plus	45	218

Free Under 6
Senior No deals
Beginner No deals

Notes Day-pass price is for Schladming-Dachstein only; part-day tickets available; 2-day-plus passes cover the 860km of pistes and 270 lifts in five regions: Schladming-Dachstein; Gastein; Salzburger Sportwelt; Grossarl; Hochkönig

Alternative pass Salzburg Super Ski Card: all lifts in Salzburgerland, including Zell am See, Kaprun and Saalbach-Hinterglemm

ACTIVITIES

Indoor Swimming pool, sauna, fitness club, bowling, museum, cinema

Outdoor Ice skating, curling, tobogganing, snowshoeing, sleigh rides, 50km of cleared paths

GETTING THERE

Air Salzburg 95km/60 miles (1hr15); Munich 255km/160 miles (3hr30)

Rail Main-line station in resort

SNOW RELIABILITY ★★★★
Excellent in cold weather

The northerly orientation of the slopes helps keep the pistes in good shape. The serious snowmaking operation makes it a good choice for early holidays; coverage is comprehensive and the system is put to good use. But at this altitude poor conditions on the lower slopes are a natural hazard.

FOR EXPERTS ★★
Strictly intermediate stuff

Schladming's status as a racing venue doesn't make it macho. The steep black finish to the Men's Downhill course and the mogul runs at the top of Planai and Hauser Kaibling are the only really challenging slopes there. Reiteralm has two steep black runs (one very short) at the top and some good tree runs. Hauser Kaibling's off-piste is good, but limited; it has two itineraries, not notably steep.

FOR INTERMEDIATES ★★★★
Red runs rule

The area is ideal for intermediate cruising. The majority of runs are red but the gradient of many is similar to the blues. The final section of the red below Rohrmoos is steep though.

New lifts have improved access to more challenging slopes at the top of Planai and Hauser Kaibling, as well as a short but pretty blue from the high point. The black racing pistes in these sectors, and the red alternatives, are ideal for fast cruising but can get very icy and tricky on the lower sections. Hauser Kaibling has a lovely blue running from top to bottom, and Reiteralm has some gentle blues.

FOR BEGINNERS ★★★
Good slopes but poorly sited

The ski schools generally take beginners to the extensive but low-altitude Rohrmoos nursery area – fine if you are based there. For residents of central Schladming, it's a bus ride. There are lots of easy runs to progress to, but getting to them can be tricky.

FOR BOARDERS ★★★
Fine for all but experts

Schladming is popular with boarders. Most lifts on the spread-out mountains are gondolas or chairs, with some short drags around. The area is ideal for beginners and intermediates, except when the lower slopes are icy, though there are few exciting challenges for expert boarders bar the off-piste tree runs. The Blue Tomato snowboard shop runs the 'impressive' specialist snowboard school.

FOR CROSS-COUNTRY ★★★★
Huge network of trails

There are almost 500km of trails in the region, and the World Championships have been held at nearby Ramsau.

MOUNTAIN RESTAURANTS ★★★★
A real highlight

There are plenty of attractive rustic huts, mostly doing table-service and good food. Some of the one-mountain piste maps mark and name them.

On Hauser Kaibling, Schoarlhütte has a real mountain-hut atmosphere and is renowned for its ribs. For 'a very good gröstl', try Krummholzhütte.

On Planai, reporters love Onkel Willy's Hütte – 'very traditional, good service and value', 'great goulash and

TVB SCHLADMING-ROHRMOOS / LANXX / H RAFFALT

Planai is directly above the town; to the right are the slopes of Rohrmoos, at the foot of Hochwurzen →

SCHOOLS

Tritscher
t 22647

Hopl (Hochwurzen-Planai)
t 61525

Blue Tomato (snowboard)
t 20070

Classes (Tritscher prices) 5 days €178

Private lessons
From €104 for 2hr; each additional person €20

CHILDCARE

Mini club (Tritscher school)
t 22647
For ages 3 and 4

Nannies
Details at tourist office

Ski school
From age 4

UK PACKAGES

Alpine Answers, Crystal, Crystal Finest, Rocketski, Skitracer, STC, Zenith

Phone numbers
From elsewhere in Austria add the prefix 03687; from abroad use the prefix +43 and omit the initial '0'

TOURIST OFFICE

www.schladming-dachstein.at
www.skiamade.com

---

the best gröstl of the trip'. Schafalm impressed a 2013 visitor despite being packed on a snowy day.

On Hochwurzen, the 'sweet little' Hochwurzenalm is tipped for rösti and gulaschsuppe. The large self-service Hochwurzenhütte at the top is good, too. Tauernalm, at Rohrmoos, offers 'very good food, cheerful service'.

On Reiteralm the Schnepf'n Alm does 'outstanding food'. Gasselhöh Hütte has been tipped for spare ribs and the Jaga Stüberl has 'impeccable service' and 'delicious crispy pizzas'.

On Fageralm, we've enjoyed the tiny Zeffererhütte, and a reporter had 'superb gröstl' at Unterbergalm.

SCHOOLS AND GUIDES ★★★★★
A choice – how was it for you?
We have a rave review this year of a private lesson with Tritscher: 'Best I've had – corrected things that have dogged me for years; brilliant.'

FOR FAMILIES ★★★★★
Rohrmoos is the place
The extensive gentle slopes of Rohrmoos are ideal for building up confidence. There are Kinderlands on Planai, Reiteralm and Fageralm.

STAYING THERE

Packaged accommodation is in hotels and pensions, but there are plenty of apartments for independent travellers.
Hotels Most lodging is mid-range but a few upmarket places exist.
★★★★Falkensteiner Schladming (214-0) New in 2012. A few minutes from the Planai gondola. Modern wooden interior. Indoor/outdoor pool, sauna.
★★★★Sporthotel Royer (200) Big and comfortable, a few minutes from the Planai gondola. Pool, sauna, steam. We stayed here in 2013; the food was terrific and plentiful.
★★★Aqi (23536) Cool modern place, built in 2008 and supposedly the first of a chain. Opposite Planai gondola. 'Helpful staff, spacious quiet room, good food, breakfast plentiful.'
★★★Kirchenwirt (22435) Off the main square. 'Quaint, rooms a good size, staff friendly and helpful, food was simple but good,' says a 2012 visitor.
★★★Planai (23429) New for 2012/13, big and bright, modern and functional, directly opposite the Planai gondola.
Apartments A reader tips the 'spacious, excellent' Bella Vista apartments.

EATING OUT ★★★★★
Some good places
There's an increasing choice. An experienced reporter brings news that best in town is now the cool Tischlerei – 'Exudes quality: very hospitable team, immensely impressive cooking.' Many of the other good places are in hotels; tips include the 'exceptional' Johann's in the Posthotel – 'very imaginative food, first-class service' – the Kirchenwirt and Neue Post. The small, family-run Friesacher Lanstuberl does 'expertly cooked steaks'. Maria's Mexican does a roaring trade in 'spicy and delicious' Tex-Mex, amid an 'all-round feel-good ambience'. Biochi specializes in organic and vegetarian food. We liked the Lasser Cafe and the Stadttor for coffee and cakes, and the Schwalbenbräu brewery.

APRES-SKI ★★★★★
Hohenhaus gets lively
Some of the mountain huts have live or loud music in the afternoon. On Hochwurzen, Tauernalm at Rohrmoos 'has a good atmosphere'. In town, the focus is the huge Hohenhaus Tenne by the Planai gondola station, the largest après-ski bar in Europe, and 'definitely the hot spot'; fabulous main bar, dance floor and regular live music – 'lively and great fun'. Later on there's a disco and various other bars to entertain. Platzhirsch (with umbrella bar) opposite also gets busy. In the main square, the Posthotel's upmarket umbrella bar Cabalou is lively, with slick service. Many of the central bars stay open until the early hours; but this isn't Ischgl. Cult and Angels are nightclubs.

OFF THE SLOPES ★★★★★
A few things to do
The town has a few shops, museum, pool and an ice rink. Hochwurzen has a floodlit 7km toboggan run. Some mountain restaurants are accessible to pedestrians. Trips to Salzburg are easy.

LINKED RESORT – 750m

HAUS

Haus is a fairly self-contained village, with its own ski schools, kindergartens and railway station. Hotel prices are generally lower here. The user-friendly nursery slopes are between the centre and the gondola. Excursions are easy, but off-slope activities and nightlife are very limited.

Sölden

The resort needs a bypass tunnel, but slopes reaching glacial heights and an impressive lift system offer compensation

FRANK HEUER

+ Excellent snow reliability, with access to two glaciers

+ Fairly extensive network of slopes suited to adventurous intermediates

+ Impressive lift system

+ Wide choice of huts for its size

+ Very lively après-ski/nightlife

– Towny resort is spread along a road that is busy with through-traffic

– You may need a bus to the lifts

– Main runs are almost all above the trees; only a couple are sheltered

– English not universally spoken

– Town centre can get rowdy

'We were very surprised that we were the only people getting off the transfer coach in Sölden, while the other 50 went on to Obergurgl,' said a reporter a couple of years ago. Yes: the resort's low profile in the UK is curious, given the powerful appeal of its snow-sure mountains and (if you like that kind of thing) its very lively après-ski scene. We always enjoy visits here, most recently in 2012, and so do the readers we hear from. And perhaps things are changing: chalet operators Esprit Ski and Skiworld are now well established here.

THE RESORT

Sölden is a long, towny place in the Ötz valley leading up to Obergurgl. Gondolas from opposite ends of town go up to the peak of Gaislachkogl and the lift junction of Giggijoch, with most of the shops, restaurants and hotels in between them. A road winds its way above the town through various hamlets up to Hochsölden – a group of 4-star hotels and little else.

When buying a six-day lift pass you can opt to pay 10 euros extra for a day in nearby Obergurgl (the half-hourly buses are included in the lift pass). You can also get buses down the valley to Längenfeld where there is a big thermal spa. With a car you could make trips to St Anton or Ischgl.

VILLAGE CHARM ★★
Not a strong point
Despite its traditional Tirolean buildings, a pretty church among them, Sölden is no charmer. There's a good selection of shops and bars, but the ambience is towny (prominent ads for strip clubs don't help), and it is strung along the valley road running through it, lacking a central focus. More seriously, the central strip is badly affected by traffic on the road. The place attracts a lively crowd, and the partying can spill into the street. Across the river there's a quieter area, mainly of hotels and guest houses. Hochsölden offers splendid traffic-free isolation up the mountain.

CONVENIENCE ★★
Lifts at either end
It's a long town, and the gondola stations are almost a mile apart. So you may face a good walk to the lifts, or a ride on the free, efficient shuttle-buses. Don't dismiss places over the river from the main street – they aren't necessarily remote from the lifts. Hochsölden is basically ski-in/ski-out.

SCENERY ★★★
Get up on Gaislachkogl
Sölden's top heights offer splendid wide views, especially south to the Italian border.

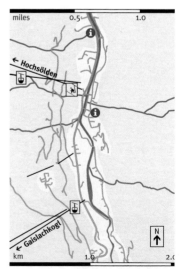

LIFT PASSES

Prices in €

Age	1-day	6-day
under 15	30	130
15 to 19	38	167
20 to 63	47	239
64 plus	40	198

Free Under 5

Senior Min. age for senior women is 59

Beginner No deals

Notes Part-day and pedestrian options

THE MOUNTAINS

Practically all the slopes you spend your days on are above the treeline, though there are red and black runs through trees to the village.

The piste map – published in compact Z-card and a much bigger format – is adequately clear.

EXTENT OF THE SLOPES ★★★★★
Long run network

The ski area is not enormous. The resort claims 150km, but the Schrahe report (read our Piste Extent feature) puts the total at 91km, which sounds much nearer the mark to us. But it does go high. All sectors offer serious vertical and some long runs, which the piste map sets out in juicy (and only occasionally misleading) detail. It's 1880m vertical and a claimed 15km from the top of the glacier to the village; the runs from Gaislachkogl and Hainbachjoch are in the same league.

There are two similar-sized sectors above the town, linked by fast six-packs out of the intervening Rettenbachtal. At the south end of town, a newish gondola leads up to an impressive three-cable gondola to **Gaislachkogl**. The terrain above the mid-station is served by slow chairs. There are links south towards Gaislachalm and north towards Rettenbachtal. Another gondola from the north end of the resort goes to **Giggijoch**. Fast lifts from here serve wide, open slopes below Rotkogljoch, from where a series of fast chairs and gondolas (one a cross-valley affair with no piste beneath it) leads to the glaciers – first the **Rettenbach**, and then the **Tiefenbach**. It may be a long journey (at least five lifts to reach the top) but with luck the reward will be quiet slopes with excellent powdery winter snow. Below Giggijoch, and reached by red and black runs, is Hochsölden, which has now lost its antique single chair from the village.

FAST LIFTS ★★★★★
Well-linked system

There are still some slow lifts around – including (avoidable) T-bars on the glaciers, but most of the area is very well served by fast chairs and gondolas, and the resort hovers on the brink of a 5-star rating.

QUEUES ★★★★★
Giggijoch's not so great

The Giggijoch gondola at one end of town still generates big queues in the morning peak. By contrast, the Gaislachkogl gondola seems to be relatively queue-free. A 2013 visitor says it's worth taking the bus to catch it to avoid the Giggijoch queues. Key

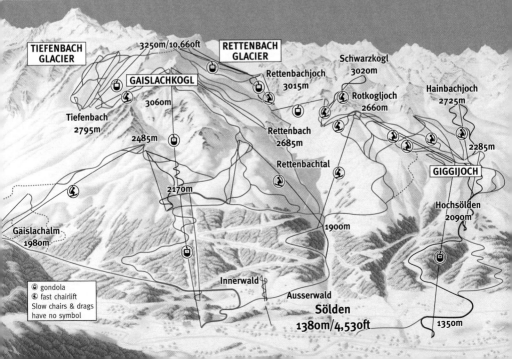

ACTIVITIES

Indoor Freizeit Arena (swimming, sauna, fitness centre, bowling, indoor tennis, climbing wall)

Outdoor Ice rink, sleigh rides, snowshoeing, 30km of walking trails, tobogganing, paragliding

lifts to and from the glacier, such as the Einzeiger chair and Seiterkar chair, get busy. Both chairs to Rotkogljoch (gateway to the glaciers) are queue-prone but shift crowds fast. The slopes above Giggijoch get very busy. There is a weekend influx.

TERRAIN PARKS ★★★
Sufficiently equipped
The Almdudier (formerly Swatch) Snowpark above Giggijoch is well-established and regularly upgraded. As well as beginner, intermediate and pro kickers, there are rails and various types of boxes. There's also a chill-out zone. There's snowcross on blue run 15 and just off it the BMW timed slalom. The Tiefenbach glacier has an early-season park.

SNOW RELIABILITY ★★★★★
Rarely a problem
The slopes are high and roughly east-facing; and there are two extensive glaciers. Snowmaking covers 67% of the area, including all slopes on Giggijoch. Grooming is thorough, and reportedly goes on during the day, which is unusual these days. Even in a generally poor season, such as 2011, you can usually count on coverage to resort level.

FOR EXPERTS ★★★
Off-piste challenges
None of the black pistes dotted around Sölden's map is serious, and some are silly. One reader this year was distressed by the grooming of blacks, and consequent lack of moguls. There are quite a few non-trivial reds, notably on Gaislachkogl – with some steeper pitches above the mid-station – and the length and vertical of some of the runs present their own challenges. There are extensive off-piste possibilities, eg into Rettenbachtal.

FOR INTERMEDIATES ★★★★
Serious verticals
Most of Sölden's main slopes are genuine red runs ideal for adventurous intermediates; there are several easy blacks, too. Keen piste-bashers will love the serious verticals and long runs to be done (notably the one from Gaislachkogl) – but after a couple of days will agree that the claimed extent of 150km is optimistic.

There are two obvious targets for less confident intermediates. The long, quiet run above Gaislachalm, now reclassified blue, is great for cruising, and below it a gentle blue through the trees offers by far the most friendly return to the resort. And the blues above Giggijoch offer gentler gradients; but crowds, too.

The glaciers are accessible to blue-run skiers, and are almost entirely of blue-run gradient – the red runs down the Seiterkar chair offer a bit of a challenge. But it's best to return via the linking gondola to the Giggijoch slopes – the busy blue run down the Rettenbachtal is narrow (it's a road), and eventually turns into a tricky red.

FOR BEGINNERS ★★★
Crowded nursery slopes
The beginners' slopes, served by a pair of parallel draglifts, are situated just above the village at Innerwald and are reached by a free shuttle-lift. Progression to longer runs usually means the blues at Giggijoch; these are wide and gentle, but very busy in places. Hochsölden is on a steep slope – avoid at all costs.

FOR BOARDERS ★★★★
Long, wide runs
Sölden is quite popular with boarders. The nursery slope involves drags, but after that draglifts can be avoided and you'll enjoy the wide, open blue runs above Giggijoch. Intermediates will relish the long runs and open terrain, and there's great freeriding for experienced boarders. There are some flat sections of piste in the Rettenbachtal and on the runs to the resort. There's a decent terrain park.

FOR CROSS-COUNTRY ★
Little to entertain
There are a couple of loops by the river to Hof (back end of town), another 5km trail to Rechenau and a 7km trail at Zwieselstein, between Sölden and Obergurgl.

This is skiing with altitude: Giggijoch (2285m) is in the centre; Hochsölden (2090m) is at the bottom left ↓

MOUNTAIN RESTAURANTS ★★★☆☆
Few notable places

There are 30 huts listed, all usefully marked on the piste map and summarized in a separate leaflet. Most offer traditional food. But those in the main area can get crowded.

We like the rustic Gampe Thaya – simple food, table-service, lovely terrace, cosy interior; a 2011 visitor warmly agrees. We've also enjoyed good käsespätzle at the peaceful Heidealm above Gaislachalm. Both places have fabulous views up the Oetztal towards Obergurgl. Hühnersteign in the Rettenbachtal is 'cosy' and famous for its chicken (Hühner!), and the Stabele just below it is equally famous for its gigantic burgers. At Giggijoch the Wirthaus table-service option has 'food of a high standard though the service is leisurely', and the 'quaint' Eugen's Obstlerhütte is recommended for its 'beautifully presented traditional food'. Below Hochsölden, a reader preferred the Panorama Alm, which is bright, with 'excellent food'.

SCHOOLS AND GUIDES ★★★☆☆
Wide choice, lacking feedback

Sölden has five schools; all restrict class sizes. We lack recent reports, though past feedback has been positive. The Ötztal school provides specialist race training.

FOR FAMILIES ★★☆☆☆
Few special facilities

Sölden does not go out of its way to cater for families. The intrusive main road traffic and possibly lengthy walks make it less attractive. But there are kindergartens at two schools and children aged four to seven pay a euro per day to use all the slopes.

STAYING THERE

Chalets Skiworld has a 30-bed chalet a short walk from the Giggijoch lift and the town centre: a 2013 visitor praises the 'excellent staff, large rooms and the excellent, quality food'. Ski Total has its chalet hotel Hermann above the village; two 2013 reporters were very happy with the food, wine, staff and the chalet itself, but a 2012 visitor was less happy with its location.

Hotels There is one 5-star hotel but most are good 3- or 4-stars. Take care if looking at very central places – there are noisy bars.

★★★★★Central Spa (22600) Fairly central but also the biggest and best in town – the only 5-star; warmly welcoming; major spa, fitness room, pool.

★★★★Bergland (22400) Hip, recently built place next to the shuttle-lift to Innerwald, with big fifth-floor spa, outdoor hot tub and decent pool.

★★★★Erhart (2020) Across the river 500m from the Gaislachkogl gondola.

Sölden

171

↑ The two major sectors are separated by the deep, steep Rettenbachtal, and the lifts to the glaciers go from the top of it
WENDY-JANE KING

GETTING THERE

Air Innsbruck 85km/ 55 miles (1.15hr); Zürich 275km/170 miles (3.45hr); Munich 285km/175 miles (3hr)

Rail Train to Innsbruck or Öetz (30km/19 miles); buses from station

UK PACKAGES

Alpine Weekends, Crystal, Crystal Finest, Independent Ski Links, Interactive Resorts, Momentum, Neilson, Ski Solutions, Ski Total, Skitracer, Skiworld, Snow Finders, Snowscape, STC

Phone numbers Except for the tourist office, from elsewhere in Austria add the prefix 05254; from abroad use the prefix +43 5254

TOURIST OFFICE

www.soelden.com

'Excellent location, superb food,' says a 2011 reporter. Spa/fitness facilities. ****Grauer Bär (2564) Near the Gaislachkogl lift. Spa area. ****Stefan (2237) By the Giggijoch gondola. We've stayed happily here – good food. Fair-sized wellness area. ****Valentin (2267) Next to the Gaislachkogl lift. 'Reasonable prices; good food, small spa, no pool,' says a 2011 visitor. **Apartments** The Gaislachkogl apartments (2246) are close to the gondola, with wellness facilities. Guests also get free entry to the Freizeitarena leisure centre.

EATING OUT ★★★☆☆
A reasonable choice
Many of the hotels have à la carte restaurants, serving traditional Austrian food. And there are various pizzerias – Gusto is praised this year for its 'huge, good-quality, good-value pizzas' – and a steakhouse – Joe's Höhle in hotel Castello was recommended last year. We usually end up in the Tavola in the hotel Rosengarten (because it doesn't take reservations) and haven't been disappointed. S'Pfandl, above the town at Ausserwald, makes a jolly outing for traditional Tirolean food.

APRES-SKI ★★★★★
Throbbing until late
Sölden's après-ski is justly famous. It starts up the mountain, notably at Giggijoch at the 'cosy' Eugen's

Obsterhütte, or at Bubi's Schihütte on Gaislachkogl ('men come round the tables with accordions singing Austrian songs') and progresses (possibly via Philipp's Eisbar at Innerwald) to packed bars in and around the main street. The hotel Liebe Sonne's Schirmbar is 'the place to be': 'The best après in town,' says a seasonaire – lively and packed, usually overflowing into the road. Fire and Ice is a two-storey glass-fronted place that parties from 3pm to 3am (theoretically). There are countless other places, with live bands at, er, Live, and throbbing discos, some with table dancing and/or striptease – Katapult has go-go dancers and guest DJs. And if you've any energy left, Kuhstall 'parties till 5–6am.' Reader tips for quieter places include Grizzly's ('rustic interior, intimate seating, open fire') and Die Alm ('traditional music on Sundays').

OFF THE SLOPES ★★☆☆☆
Disappointing for its size
There's a leisure centre with a swimming pool and an ice rink, and ice climbing at Längenfeld. There's also a 5km floodlit toboggan run. A recent reporter enjoyed the Wednesday-night ski show on Gaislachkogl. Trips to Innsbruck are possible. Aqua Dome is a 'beautiful' thermal spa centre at Längenfeld, now reached by regular buses. There are sleigh rides up the valley at Vent.

SÖLL TOURIST OFFICE

Söll

The ski area is big, but the attractive village is surprisingly small and intimate; shame it is not set right by the lifts

+ Part of the SkiWelt, Austria's largest linked ski and snowboard area

+ Local slopes are north-facing, so they keep their snow relatively well

+ Pretty village with lively après-ski

+ Cheap, even by Austrian standards

+ Snowmaking is now very extensive and well used; even so ...

− Low altitude can mean poor snow

− Long walk or inadequate bus service from the village to the lifts

− Runs on upper slopes mostly short

− Few challenges except Hohe Salve

− Not ideal for beginners

− The SkiWelt slopes can get crowded

− Appallingly inadequate piste map

Söll has long been popular with British beginners and intermediates, attracting both youths and families looking for fun of different kinds. The resort is in fact far from ideal for beginners, but the SkiWelt can be a great area for intermediate cruising. Whether it is depends on the snow. If the weather is coming from Russia, this area can have the best snow in the Alps; but usually it isn't, and the snow may suffer from afternoon thaws and night-time frost.

Many visitors are surprised by the small size of the village (in particular, there aren't many shops) and the long trek out to the slopes. You may prefer to stay near the lifts and trek into the village in the evening. Or you may prefer, like us, to stay in one of the other SkiWelt resorts – Ellmau along the valley (which has its own chapter) or Brixen or Westendorf over the hill (covered at the end of this chapter), which have quicker access to the Kitzbühel slopes.

THE RESORT

Söll is a pleasant, friendly village, bypassed by the main valley road; although its chalet-style buildings spread quite widely, the core is compact – you can explore it on foot thoroughly in a few minutes.

The resort is part of the vast SkiWelt area, with a claimed 279km of slopes – Austria's largest area, and one of the largest in the Alps. You can also progress (via Brixen) to the slopes of Kitzbühel; these and various other ski areas within easy reach, such as Waidring, Fieberbrunn and St Johann, are covered by the Kitzbüheler Alpen AllStarCard ski pass.

VILLAGE CHARM ★★★☆☆
Follows tradition
Söll is quite attractive, with chalet-style buildings and a huge church near the centre (its graveyard prettily lit by candles at night).

CONVENIENCE ★★☆☆☆
Not for the slopes
The slopes are well outside the village, on the other side of a busy road crossed by a pedestrian tunnel. You can leave your equipment at the bottom of the gondola for a small charge. There is some accommodation out near the lifts, but most is in or around the village centre. From there, it's the ski-bus or a 15-minute walk to the lifts. A base on the far side of the village may mean that you can board the bus before it gets too crowded. But the bus does not serve every corner of the community.

SCENERY ★★★☆☆
Head for Hohe Salve
Söll sits in a woody valley, below the distinctive dome-shaped peak of Hohe Salve. From the top, there are good views to the whole SkiWelt and the craggy Wilder Kaiser ridges.

miles · 0.5 · 1.0 · 1.5

N

↙ Hohe Salve

km · 1.0 · 2.0 · 3.0

THE MOUNTAINS

Although there are some open slopes high up, and the prominent high-point of Hohe Salve is noticeably bare, most of the slopes are heavily wooded.

The piste map is better than it was, using arrows to show which way runs go where that is in doubt. We stick to the view, though, that it is hopelessly over-ambitious in trying to show the whole area in a single view; the result is simply inadequate for route finding, especially on the Zinsberg side of Hohe Salve and between Eiberg and Brandstadl. What's needed are separate maps for the main sectors.

Signposting is also criticized by readers, but we found it OK once you realize that the signs point out the direction to the next lift you want and that the signs use the number of the lift to indicate the colour of the run.

EXTENT OF THE SLOPES ★★★★
Short run network

The SkiWelt will easily keep an average intermediate amused for a week. The peaks are not high – with the exception of Hohe Salve they are all under 1700m. In good snow there are long red runs to be done to the valley, but most of the skiing is on the upper slopes where most runs are very short (often less than 300m vertical).

A gondola takes all but complete beginners up to the mid-mountain shelf of Hochsöll, where there are a couple of short lifts and connections in several directions. These include an eight-seat gondola to the high point of Hohe Salve. From here there are runs down to Kälbersalve, Rigi and Hopfgarten. Rigi can also be reached by chairs and runs without going to Hohe Salve – to which it is itself linked by chairs. Rigi is also the start

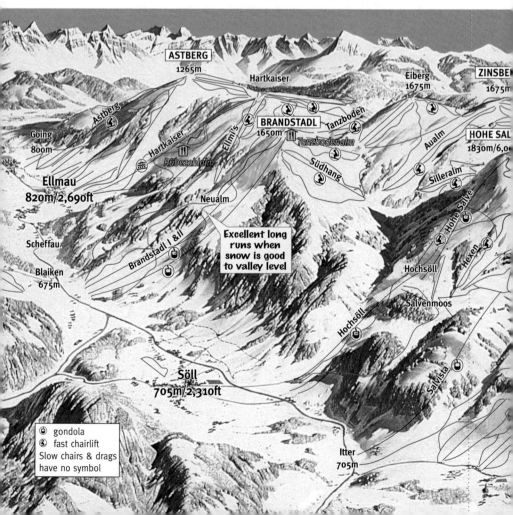

GETTING THERE

Air Salzburg 90km/
55 miles (1hr30);
Innsbruck 80km/
50 miles (1hr15);
Munich 260km/160
miles (3hr45)

Rail Wörgl (13km/
8 miles) or Kufstein
(15km/9 miles); bus
to resort

of runs down to Itter and to
Hopfgarten. From Kälbersalve you can
head down south-facing runs to Brixen
or up to Zinsberg and on towards
Ellmau. From Brixen, a gondola goes
up to Choralpe in Westendorf's area
and a lovely north-facing red piste
comes back down. From Choralpe you
can also head off towards Kitzbühel.

FAST LIFTS ★★★★☆
Gradual improvement
Lifts from the valley are mainly
gondolas, with a growing number of
fast chairs on the upper slopes. But
there are still plenty of slow lifts.

QUEUES ★★★☆☆
Some high-season waits
Lift upgrades have greatly improved
this once queue-prone area. In peak
season getting out of Söll at ski-
school time in the mornings remains a

problem, and there are still some
bottlenecks on the mountain. When
snow is poor, the links between
Zinsberg and Eiberg get crowded.

TERRAIN PARKS ★★★☆☆
Local and floodlit
Söll has its own park below Hochsöll
with beginner and expert lines;
features include boxes, frames and
rails. It's floodlit for night riding.

SNOW RELIABILITY ★★☆☆☆
Erratic – but has artificial help
The SkiWelt has had some good
seasons of late, with several reporters
experiencing good fresh powder for
much of their holidays. But it is not
always like that, and with a low
average height, and important links
that get a lot of sun, the snow can
suffer badly in warm weather. So the
snowmaking that the SkiWelt has

↑ Westendorf's
Gampenkogel, seen
from Brechhornhaus,
is the start of the
lovely long blue run
to the short bus link
with the Kitzbühel lifts
SNOWPIX.COM / CHRIS GILL

LIFT PASSES

SkiWelt Wilder Kaiser-Brixental

Prices in €

Age	1-day	6-day
under 16	22	105
16 to 17	34	168
18 plus	43	210

Free Under 7

Senior No deals

Beginner Points cards

Notes Ski-bus included; single ascent and part-day options; family discounts; 6-day pass can be transferred between parents

Alternative pass
Kitzbüheler Alpen AllStarCard covers: Schneewinkel (St Johann), Kitzbühel, SkiWelt, Ski Juwel, Skicircus Saalbach-Hinterglemm and Zell am See-Kaprun

installed is essential. At 225km and covering about 80% of the area's pistes, it is Austria's biggest snowmaking installation. Reporters have been impressed by its use and by the grooming. We were there one January before any major snowfalls, and snowmaking was keeping the links open well. Warm weather is a more serious problem.

FOR EXPERTS ★☆☆☆☆
Not a lot
The black runs from Hohe Salve are challenging pistes, the steepest of them including a short pitch that locals claim is steeper than Mayrhofen's Harakiri. The black run alongside the Brixen gondola also deserves respect. Those runs apart, the main challenges are gentle off-piste routes – from Brandstadl down to Söll, for example.

FOR INTERMEDIATES ★★★★☆
Mainly easy runs
When blessed with good snow the SkiWelt is a paradise for those who love easy cruising and don't mind short runs. It is a big area, and you really get a feeling of travelling around. There are lots of blue runs and many of the reds could be blue. In general the most difficult slopes are those from the mid-stations to the valleys – to Blaiken, Brixen and Söll, for example. For more challenging reds

head for Westendorf (and don't miss the excellent red down to Brixen).

FOR BEGINNERS ★★☆☆☆
Not ideal
The big area of nursery slopes between the main road and the gondola station is fine when snow is good – gentle, spacious, uncrowded and free from good skiers whizzing past. But it can get icy or slushy. In poor snow the Hochsöll area may be used. None of the lifts is free, but points cards are available. Progression to longer runs is likely to be awkward – there aren't many blue runs in this part of the SkiWelt. One is the narrow blue from Hochsöll, on which fast learners can get home.

FOR BOARDERS ★★☆☆☆
Great cruising
Söll is a good place to try out boarding: slopes are gentle and there are plenty of gondolas and chairs. And it has its own terrain park. For competent boarders it's more limited – the slopes of the SkiWelt are tame.

FOR CROSS-COUNTRY ★★★☆☆
Neighbouring villages are better
Söll has 30km of local trails, but they are less interesting than those between Hopfgarten and Kelchsau and around and beyond Ellmau. There is a total of 170km in the SkiWelt area. Lack of snow-cover can be a problem.

SCHOOLS

Söll-Hochsöll
t 5454
Knolin
t 0676 64 85060
Black Sheep Ski
t 06991 712871

Classes (Söll prices)
5 4hr-days: €160
Private lessons
€58 for 1hr; each
additional person €25

CHILDCARE

Mini-club Hexenstube
t 0664 589 2107
Ages 6mnth to 4yr
**Monti's Kinderwelt
(Bambinis)**
t 5454
Ages 3 to 5

Ski school
From age 5

ACTIVITIES

Indoor Swimming
pool with sauna,
solarium and
massage; bowling,
squash
Outdoor Natural ice
rink (skating, curling),
sleigh rides, 3km of
floodlit toboggan
runs, walks,
snowshoeing, snow
tubing, paragliding

MOUNTAIN RESTAURANTS ★★★
Good, but crowded
There are quite a few jolly little
chalets. Our favourites in the SkiWelt
are covered in the Ellmau chapter –
Tanzbodenalm near Brandstadl, and
Rübezahlalm above Ellmau.

At the lower corner of the Hochsöll
slopes, the atmospheric converted cow
shed Stöcklalm is an excellent spot.
The highly rated Hohe Salve (top of
the gondola) offers a large revolving
terrace and good views (from the
toilets as well, say reporters). Other
reporter recommendations include the
Stoagrub'nhütte above Hopfgarten.
Read the Ellmau chapter, too.

SCHOOLS AND GUIDES ★★★
Reports please
Söll-Hochsöll and Knolin are the main
schools but we lack recent reports. A
visitor had a 'very good' carving clinic
with Black Sheep Ski a few years ago.

FOR FAMILIES ★★★
A range of options
Söll has fairly wide-ranging facilities –
the focus is the Söll-Hochsöll school's
Monti's Kinderwelt (and day care) at
the gondola mid-station, which takes
children from age three. It is well
equipped with play areas and nursery
slopes. There's a special kids-only drag
and slope on the opposite side of the
village to the main lifts. Parents can
buy one pass between them, which
either can use while the other minds
the kids.

STAYING THERE

Chalets Crystal has two big ones.
Hotels There is a wide choice of
simple gasthofs, pensions and B&Bs,
plus better-quality hotel
accommodation – mainly 3-star.
****Alpenpanorama** (5309) Far from
lifts but with own bus stop; wonderful
views; pleasant rooms.
****Bergland** (5454) Well placed
between the village and lifts.
Apartments as well as rooms.
****Greil** (5289) Attractive, but out of
the centre and far from the lifts.
Indoor pool.
****Postwirt** (5081) A reader favourite
– attractive, central, traditional, with
stube; outdoor pool.
***Eggerwirt** (5236) Between centre
and main road, bus stop outside.
***Feichter** (5228) Renovated in 2011.
Spa.

***Feldwebel** (5224) Central,
recommended for food and value.
***Hexenalm** (5544) Close to the lifts,
with a popular après-ski bar.
Apartments The central Aparthotel
Schindlhaus has nice accommodation.
Some of the best apartments in town
are in the Bergland hotel.

EATING OUT ★★
A fair choice
Some of the best restaurants are in
hotels – those in the Postwirt and the
Feldwebel are recommended by
reporters. Dorf Stub'n offers traditional
dishes and steaks, and the Venezia is
a pizzeria.

APRES-SKI ★★★★
Still some very loud bars
Söll is not as raucous as it used to be,
but it's still very lively and a lot of
places have live music.

At teatime the bars at the gondola
base are lively. Moonlight 'has dancing
on the tables even when it's not busy',
and the Hexenalm bar, just down from
the gondola, seems to have been
revived after a period when it fell from
favour. The Salvenstadl (Cow Shed) on
the edge of the village is a good all-
rounder, recommended by reporters.

Later on, the large, central Whisky-
Mühle disco can get 'wild', especially
after the bars close. The hotel Austria
bar is 'boisterous', with pool tables
and quiz evenings. Rossini is good for
cocktails and live music.

OFF THE SLOPES ★★
Not bad for a small village
Sadly, the Panoramabad pool, closed
for some time, is apparently to be
demolished. There's a 3.5km toboggan
run from the top of the gondola that's
floodlit until 10.30 every night. The
large baroque church is worth a visit.
Coach excursions go to Salzburg,
Innsbruck and even Vipiteno, in Italy.

LINKED RESORT – 705m

ITTER

Itter is a tiny village half-way between
Söll and Hopfgarten, with a gondola
starting some way outside the village
that goes up to mid-mountain. There's
a hotel and half a dozen gasthofs and
B&Bs. The school has a rental shop,
and there are nursery slopes close to
hand but few easy longer runs to
progress to locally. Here, as elsewhere,
the home run is red.

UK PACKAGES

Crystal, Independent Ski Links, Inghams, Neilson, Ski Line, Ski Solutions, Skitracer, STC, Thomson, Zenith **Hopfgarten** Contiki, Rocketski, STC **Westendorf** Crystal, Inghams, Interactive Resorts, STC, Thomson **Itter** Crystal

---

LINKED RESORT – 620m

HOPFGARTEN

Hopfgarten is an unspoiled, friendly, traditional resort set off the main Kitzbühel-Innsbruck road at the western extremity of the SkiWelt and with a two-stage gondola (largely queue-free, to judge by reports) from the village to the top of Hohe Salve.

When snow is good, the runs down to Hopfgarten are some of the best in the SkiWelt, but they get the damaging afternoon sun. There is a beginners' slope in the village, but it is sunny as well as low. Hopfgarten is one of the best cross-country bases in the area. There are fine trails to Kelchsau (7km) and the Itter–Bocking loop (15km) starts nearby.

Cheap and cheerful gasthofs, pensions and little private B&Bs are the norm, and most are within five minutes' walk of the gondola. Restaurants are mostly hotel-based, but there is a Chinese and a pizzeria. Après-ski is generally quiet. There's a reasonable range of off-slope activities, and trains run to Kitzbühel and Innsbruck (or Salzburg).

LINKED RESORT – 800m

BRIXEN IM THALE

Brixen im Thale spreads a long way along the valley running along the south side of the SkiWelt area. It is not particularly cute, but it is traditional in style and is pretty quiet now that it is bypassed by the main valley road. From the skiing point of view it has a great location, with lifts going up both sides of the valley. On the north side, a gondola goes to Hochbrixen and the main SkiWelt slopes; lifts diverge for Hohe Salve and Söll, or Astberg and Ellmau. In the opposite direction, a gondola goes up to Choralpe above Westendorf, which links (via a short bus-ride) to the slopes of Kitzbühel. The local slopes suit confident intermediates best, on both sides of the valley. The nursery area is secluded, but a bus ride away.

There are plenty of hotels and pensions but not many restaurants – most are hotel-based. Après-ski is not a highlight though there are two or three bars by the gondola station. Brixen is on the same railway line as Hopfgarten.

Westendorf 800m

➕ Pleasant, traditional village
➕ Challenging local slopes
➕ Good local beginner slopes but ...

➖ Local slopes not ideal territory for progression from the nursery slopes
➖ Getting to main SkiWelt takes time

Westendorf is a quiet, attractive village with good local slopes for confident intermediates; it is slightly off the main SkiWelt circuit, but has easy access to Kitzbühel's area – so it is an appealing base if you plan to spend time on both.

Village charm The village is small with traditional buildings, including an attractive onion-domed church. It has a relaxed, rustic atmosphere. The quite lively late-night scene can mean a bit of noise in the streets.

Convenience The centre is close to the nursery slopes, and a five-minute walk or free ski-bus ride from the main lift. There are also regular buses to the lifts at Brixen, for quick access to the SkiWelt circuit.

Scenery The slopes here offer a bit more drama than some of the other hills nearby, and the views include the craggy Wilder Kaiser to the north.

THE MOUNTAIN

Westendorf's local slopes are separated by one valley from the main SkiWelt circuit to the north and by another valley from the Kitzbühel slopes to the east. There's a pleasant mix of open and wooded slopes.

Slopes A two-stage gondola goes to Talkaser, one of the four minor peaks that make up the local area. From there, you can head for Choralpe and Brixen (via a splendid 5.5km-long red run of over 1000m vertical), or for Fleiding and Gampenkogel. All the local peaks have short east- or west-facing runs. A longer blue run of around 800m vertical goes from Gampenkogel to the Kitzbühel connection (which involves a short shuttle-bus ride to the Pengelstein gondola at Skirast).

Fast lifts The two gondolas make for good access but once up the mountain there are still a lot of slow lifts on the local slopes.

Queues We have no reports of any significant problems with queues.

Terrain parks There's an excellent park with something for all levels including

Phone numbers
From elsewhere in
Austria add the prefix
05358 (Wilder Kaiser),
05333 (Söll), 05332
(Hohe Salve), 05335
(Hopfgarten, Itter),
05334 (Brixen,
Westendorf); from
abroad use the prefix
+43 and omit the
initial '0'

TOURIST OFFICES

WILDER KAISER
(Söll, Scheffau, Going,
Ellmau)
www.wilderkaiser.
info

HOHE SALVE
(Hopfgarten, Itter)
www.hohe-salve.com

KITZBÜHELER ALPEN
(Brixen, Westendorf)
www.kitzbuehel-alpen.
com

SKIWELT
www.skiwelt.at

SNOWPIX.COM / CHRIS GILL

Hochsöll is a great
asset to the resort – a
friendly area of slopes
facing north and
south, 450m higher
than the village
nursery slopes ↓

jumps, boxes, kickers, rails and a half-pipe (www.boardplay.com).

Snow reliability Not a strong point of the region, because of the low altitude. But snowmaking is extensive and grooming excellent.

Experts The pistes are among the most testing in the SkiWelt area, and there is off-piste to be explored.

Intermediates Great for confident intermediates: nearly all Westendorf's terrain is genuinely red in gradient.

Beginners The village nursery slopes are extensive and excellent. There are a couple of genuine blues to progress to on the lower mountain, but further progression can be challenging.

Snowboarding Most lifts are chairs and gondolas, and the park is great. But some runs have tedious flat sections.

Cross-country There are lots of trails, but snow-cover is unreliable.

Mountain restaurants There are good table- and self-service places. On our 2012 visit we particularly liked Ki-West – good location, atmosphere and food. Alpenrosenhütte, Brechhornhaus and the Gassnerwirt are popular. A 2012 visitor found the self-service Talkaser busy at peak times.

Schools and guides There are three schools: Westendorf ('Very good,' says a 2012 visitor), Top and Snow&Co.

Families Westendorf sells itself as a family resort. The ski school kindergartens take children from the age of three.

STAYING THERE

There are plentiful hotels and guest houses, both near the village centre and further afield.

Hotels 4-star places tipped by readers include the Jakobwirt (6245) – 'food of a very high standard, plenty of choice' – and Schermer (6268); the 3-star Post (6202) is 'basic and friendly' with 'good food'. Pension Cafe Elisabeth (8940) is central and recommended as 'very hospitable'. The small Glockenstuhl (6175) is a short walk away with a good spa. There are places out near the gondola.

Apartments The Schermerhof apartments are of good quality.

Eating out Most of the best restaurants are in hotels. The Wastlhof, Klinglers and Berggasthof Stimmlach (a taxi ride out) are other possibilities.

Après-ski There are more lively spots than you might expect in a small, cute village. The Liftstüberl and Gerry's Inn are packed at close of play. Bruchstall 'caters for kids too'. The Kibo bar near the bottom of the nursery slopes is 'friendly' with 'a great atmosphere'. In's Moment (aka Campbell's Bar) in the basement of the Jakobwirt hotel is 'terrific', with Mr Campbell himself described as 'a very genial host'. The funky Moskito Cafe Bar has live music. Karat is a smart lounge bar.

Off the slopes There are excursions to Innsbruck and Salzburg, plus pretty walks and sleigh rides.

St Anton

If what you seek is dumps, bumps, boozing and bopping, there's nowhere quite like it – and with a neat. Tirolean town as a bonus

RATINGS

The mountains

Extent	★★★
Fast lifts	★★★
Queues	★★★
Terrain p'ks	★★★
Snow	★★★★
Expert	★★★★★
Intermediate	★★★
Beginner	★
Boarder	★★★★
X-country	★★
Restaurants	★★★
Schools	★★★
Families	★★★★

The resort

Charm	★★★★
Convenience	★★★
Scenery	★★★
Eating out	★★★★
Après-ski	★★★★★
Off-slope	★★

RPI	115
lift pass	£210
ski hire	£140
lessons	£120
food & drink	£135
total	£605

NEWS

2013/14: The Tanzböden T-bar on Galzig is due to be replaced by a six-pack.

Nearby Lech (covered by the local ski pass) is due to be linked by a new gondola to two other resorts, increasing the size of the ski area by over 50 per cent – see Lech chapter.

180

+ Varied terrain for experts and adventurous intermediates

+ Heavy snowfalls, lots of snow-guns

+ Car-free village centre retains solid traditional charm

+ Very lively après-ski

+ Improved lift system has cut queues from the base areas, but ...

– Some pistes dangerously crowded

– Slopes can be tough for near-beginners and timid intermediates

– Most tough runs are unpatrolled

– Snow quality can suffer from sun

– Resort sprawls, with long treks from some lodgings to key lifts and bars

– Centre can be noisy at night

St Anton is one of the world's best resorts for competent skiers and riders, particularly those with the energy to après-ski as hard as they ski. If you want to, you can party from 3pm to 3am. Good luck!

But the place doesn't suit everyone. If you are thinking of trying an Austrian change from a major French resort, or of going up a gear from Kitzbühel or Söll, be sure that you are not going to get thrown by blues that get heavily mogulled, reds that might be black and runs that are dangerously crowded. We have been saying for years that the resort urgently needs to create an alternative piste to the busy blue run down from its main mountain. The need was highlighted last season when part of this run was closed due to avalanche danger and then re-opened as a ski route – the only piste down was a black.

THE RESORT

St Anton is the western extremity of the Tirol, at the foot of the road up to the Arlberg pass. It is at one end of a lift network that spreads across to St Christoph and over the pass to Stuben. These two tiny villages are described at the end of the chapter.

The resort is a long, sprawling place, almost a town rather than a village, squeezed into a narrow valley. As it spreads down the valley, it thins out before broadening again to form the suburb of Nasserein.

Development spreads up the hill to the west, towards the Arlberg pass – first to Oberdorf, then Gastig, 10 minutes' walk from the centre.

The ski pass covers Lech and Zürs and Warth–Schröcken (see the Vorarlberg – Bregenzerwald chapter), which is due to be linked to Lech for

2013/14. It also covers the Sonnenkopf area above Klösterle (see the Vorarlberg – Alpenregion Bludenz chapter). Lech and Zürs can be reached by regular free ski-buses from Alpe Rauz, where the slopes meet the Arlberg pass road. But these buses can get very crowded; the post bus offers a less crowded alternative and means you can start or end your outing in St Anton, but it is not free. Taxis can be economic if shared. Klösterle can be reached by free ski-buses from Stuben. Serfaus, Ischgl and Sölden are feasible outings by car.

VILLAGE CHARM ★★★★
Traditional but lively
Although it is crowded and commercialized, St Anton is full of character, its traffic-free main street lined by traditional-style buildings. It is an attractively bustling place, day

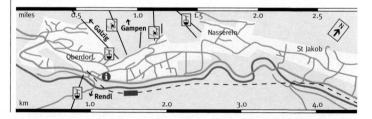

HOTEL MAIENSEE

FAR AWAY FROM EVERYDAY

HOTEL MAIENSEE

FAR AWAY FROM EVERYDAY

6580 ST. CHRISTOPH AM ARLBERG · AUSTRIA
+43(0) 5446 2804 · STAY@MAIENSEE.COM

WWW.MAIENSEE.COM

base stations of the lifts to Gampen (a fast quad chair), to Galzig and to Rendl (modern gondolas). Staying on or close to this main street is ideal to keep treks to the lifts short.

Nasserein has an eight-seater gondola up to Gampen, and makes an appealing base for a quiet time. The nightlife action is a short bus ride or 15-minute walk away. Staying between the centre and Nasserein is fairly convenient, too, as the Fang chairlift gives access to all the base lifts.

and night. Its shops meet everyday needs well – a well-stocked Spar, for example, and an excellent bookshop that sells good numbers of this book.

CONVENIENCE ★★★★★
Not bad for a large resort
The hub of the resort is at the western end of the main street, close to the

SCENERY ★★★★★
Head for the Valluga
St Anton squeezes into a narrow, partly wooded valley. The scenery becomes more impressive as you ride up the lifts, either towards the dramatic Valluga, or across the valley up to Rendl, which opens up a splendid panorama.

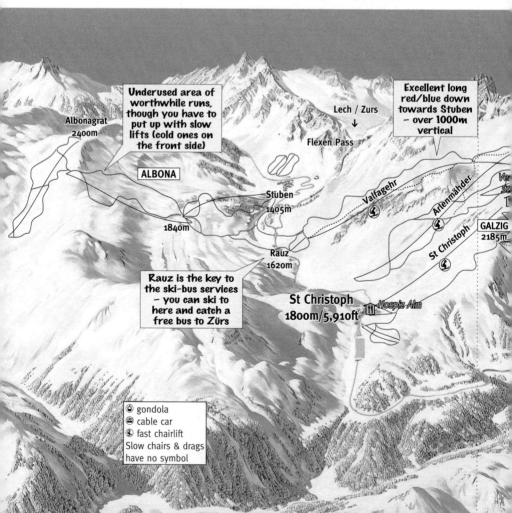

Albonagrat
2400m

**Underused area of
worthwhile runs,
though you have to
put up with slow
lifts (cold ones on
the front side)**

ALBONA

Lech / Zurs ↓

Flexen Pass

**Excellent long
red/blue down
towards Stuben
– over 1000m
vertical**

Stuben
1405m

Valfagehr

Arlenmähder

1840m

St Christoph

GALZIG
2185m

Rauz
1620m

**Rauz is the key to
the ski-bus services
– you can ski to
here and catch a
free bus to Zürs**

St Christoph
1800m/5,910ft

Hospiz Alm

🚠 gondola
🚡 cable car
🚠 fast chairlift
Slow chairs & drags
have no symbol

GETTING THERE

Air Innsbruck 95km/
60 miles (1hr15);
Zürich 210km/
130 miles (2hr45);
Friedrichshafen
135km/85 miles
(1hr45); Munich
210km/130 miles
(3hr)

Rail Main-line station
in resort

THE MOUNTAINS

The main slopes are essentially open: only the lower Gampen runs and the run from Rendl to the valley offer much shelter from bad weather.

St Anton vies with Val d'Isère for the title of 'resort with most underclassified slopes'. Many blue runs would be better classified as red; there are also plenty of reds that could be black. But paradoxically, none of the blacks are seriously steep; this is because the toughest runs are called 'ski routes' or 'high-alpine touring runs'. The touring runs (at Rendl and Stuben) are simply off-piste runs that would not appear on the piste map at all in most resorts – if you want to try these, hire a guide.

The piste map says the ski routes are marked and avalanche controlled but not groomed or patrolled. We applaud the clear explanation (lacking in many resorts), but we think many of these runs should be patrolled pistes. In several areas (notably Schindler Spitze and Rendl) they are popular runs, treated like pistes. To add to the confusion, some of the routes are sometimes groomed.

The piste map is designed for marketing rather than navigation, covering the whole of the Arlberg region in one view (including Warth-Schröcken for 2013/14). It is unclear and misleading in places and provokes complaints from reporters (as does the signposting): 'we had to backtrack a couple of times', 'we went wrong more than once'. What's needed is one piste map for St Anton–St Christoph–Stuben and separate ones for Lech–Zürs–Warth–Schröcken and for Sonnenkopf. The local TV shows the state of the pistes and queues – very useful.

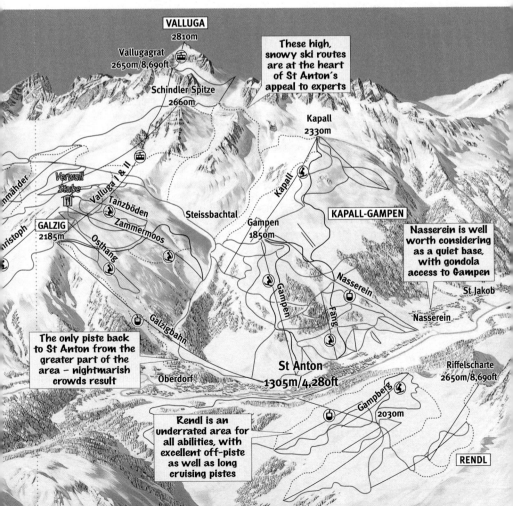

VALLUGA
2810m

Vallugagrat
265om/8,690ft

Schindler Spitze
2660m

These high, snowy ski routes are at the heart of St Anton's appeal to experts

Kapall
2330m

Verwall
Stube

Valluga I & II

Tanzböden

Steissbachtal

Zammermoos

Gampen
1850m

KAPALL-GAMPEN

GALZIG
2185m

Osthang

Nasserein is well worth considering as a quiet base, with gondola access to Gampen

St Jakob

Nasserein

Fang

Galzigbahn

The only piste back to St Anton from the greater part of the area – nightmarish crowds result

Oberdorf

St Anton
1305m/4,280ft

Gampberg

Riffelscharte
265om/8,690ft

2030m

Rendl is an underrated area for all abilities, with excellent off-piste as well as long cruising pistes

RENDL

AUSTRIA

KEY FACTS

Resort	1305m
	4,280ft

Arlberg region	
Slopes	1075-2650m
	3,530-8,690ft
Lifts	94
Pistes	340km
	211 miles
Blue	43%
Red	41%
Black	16%
Snowmaking	63%

St Anton, St Christoph and Stuben	
Slopes	1305-2650m
	4,280-8,690ft
Lifts	38
Pistes	120km
	75 miles
Blue	45%
Red	35%
Black	20%

TVB ST ANTON AM ARLBERG

The traffic-free main
street is an attractive
place to stroll through
and the main lifts are
at one end of it ↓

EXTENT OF THE SLOPES ★★★☆☆
Don't ignore Stuben and Rendl

St Anton's slopes fall into four main sectors, three of them linked. The major sector is that beneath the local high spot, the **Valluga**, accessed by the jumbo gondola to Galzig, then a cable car. The tiny top stage of the cable car to the Valluga summit is mainly for sightseeing – you can take skis or a board up only if you have a guide to lead you down the tricky off-piste run to Zürs. The first stage of the cable car ends at Valluga Grat and gives access to St Anton's famous high, sunny bowls, and to the long, beautiful red/blue run to Alpe Rauz. From there there's a six-pack, the Valfagehr, to return, or you can go on to explore the rather neglected slopes of **Stuben**, described at the end of the chapter. The run to Alpe Rauz and the high Valluga runs can also be accessed by riding the Schindlergrat triple chair, though some also involve a hike. Other runs from Galzig go to St Christoph and into the Steissbachtal.

Beyond this valley, with lift and piste links in both directions, is the

Kapall–Gampen sector, reachable by chairlift from central St Anton or gondola from Nasserein. From Gampen at mid-mountain, pistes lead back to St Anton and Nasserein. Or you can ride a six-pack on up to Kapall to ski the treeless upper mountain.

Rendl is a separate mountain, reached by a gondola from the centre of town. A handful of lifts serve the west-facing upper runs, and there's a good north-facing piste to the valley.

FAST LIFTS ★★★☆☆
Fast access, patchy higher up

Access from the village is by smart gondolas or fast chairs. But while the Gampen and Galzig sectors have a lot of fast chairs higher up, Rendl and Stuben still have a lot of slow ones.

QUEUES ★★★☆☆
Much improved, but ...

Queues are not the problem they once were, and 2013 reporters had few problems. But there can be queues for key lifts, including the Valluga cable car from Galzig ('15-minute wait seemed the norm,' said a 2013 report), the alternative Schindlergrat chair to Schindler Spitze, the Zammermoos chair out of the Steissbachtal and the gondola from Nasserein first thing.

But more of a worry than queues are the crowded pistes – see the feature panel later in this chapter.

TERRAIN PARKS ★★★☆☆
Small, but perfectly formed

The 320m-long Stanton park on Rendl, just below the top of the gondola, has been vastly improved by Q-Parks (www.qparks.com). While it doesn't match Lech's park for quantity, it has lots of quality – a jib line, intermediate and pro lines, beginner area, all including jumps, kickers, boxes and rails, plus fun-cross for the kids, chill area and daily maintenance. And you get a great view of all the action from the restaurant terrace above.

SNOW RELIABILITY ★★★★☆
Generally very good cover

If the weather is coming from the west or north-west (as it often is), the Arlberg region gets it first, and as a result St Anton gets heavy falls of snow – and neighbouring Lech, Zürs, Warth and Schröcken get even more. These resorts often have much better conditions than other resorts of a similar height, and we've had great

The Arlberg region has lots of very varied off-piste. Here are just a few of the huge number of possibilities you could explore with a guide.

Runs from Rendl

An easy first venture away from the pistes is to go beyond the furthest lift to the rolling powder bowls of Rossfall. More serious routes take you well away from all lifts. The North Face, accessed from the Gampberg chair, offers challenging terrain for a confident off-piste skier. The Riffel chairlifts access the imposing Hinter Rendl – a gigantic bowl with a huge descent to St Anton, often in deep powder. A variant involves a climb to Rendl Scharte and a testing descent with sections of 35° to Pettneu.

Runs from Albona, above Stuben

Stuben's outstanding terrain is suited to the more experienced off-piste skier. The open treelines of the Langen forest, where the powder is regularly knee to waist deep, provide fabulous tree skiing. A 30-minute climb from Albonagrat to Maroikopfe opens up runs westwards down undulating open slopes to Langen, or eastwards down steep 40° slopes to Verwalltal ending at an old hunting lodge.

Runs from the Valluga

The runs from the summit cable car of the Valluga will make your pulse race as you trace a steep line between cliff bands in the breathtaking scenery of the Pazieltal, leading down to Zürs. Here, at the top of the Madloch chairlift and after a short climb, you can be roped down into the steep Valhalla Couloir, accessing 1200m vertical of open slopes ending at Zug, near Lech.

TVB ST ANTON AM ARLBERG / JOSEF MALLAUN

LIFT PASSES

Arlberg

Prices in €

Age	1-day	6-day
under 16	28	137
16 to 19	43	198
20 to 64	47	228
65 plus	43	198

Free No one; day pass €10 if under 8, €20 if over 75

Beginner Points ticket

Notes Covers St Anton, St Christoph, Stuben, Lech, Zürs, Warth and Schröcken lifts, and linking bus between Alpe Rauz and Zürs; also Sonnenkopf (9 lifts) at Klösterle, 7km west of Stuben (bus link); single ascent, half-day and pedestrian options

fresh powder here as late as mid-April. But many slopes face south or south-east, causing icy or heavy conditions at times. As spring approaches, in particular, it's vital to time descents of the steeper runs off the Valluga to get decent conditions. The lower runs are well equipped with snowmaking, which generally ensures the home runs remain open. Grooming is good.

FOR EXPERTS ★★★★★
One of the world's great areas

St Anton vies with Chamonix, Val d'Isère and a handful of other resorts for the affections of experts. There are countless opportunities for going off-piste; see the feature panel above for some of them. The runs in the huge bowls below the Valluga are justifiably world-famous, and immediately after a fresh snowfall you can see tracks going all over the mountain; there are ski routes in the bowls too. Lower down, there are challenging runs in many directions from both Galzig and Kapall–Gampen. These lower runs can be doubly tricky if the snow has been hit by the sun.

Don't overlook the Rendl area, which has plenty of open space served by the top lifts, and several quite challenging runs. This is a great area for a mixed group and usually quieter

than the main sector. The Sonnenkopf area, down-valley from Stuben, is even quieter and has several ski routes – and more serious off-piste, including an 'excellent' route to Langen. Read the Stuben section, too.

FOR INTERMEDIATES ★★★★★
Some real challenges

St Anton is well suited to good, adventurous intermediates. As well as lots of testing pistes, they will be able to try some of the ski routes in the Valluga bowls. The run from Schindler Spitze to Rauz is very long (over 1000m vertical), varied and ideal for good intermediates. Alternatively, turn off from this part-way down and take the Steissbachtal to the lifts back to Galzig or Gampen. The Kapall–Gampen section is also interesting, with sporty bumps among trees on the lower half. Good intermediates may enjoy the men's downhill run from the top of this sector to the town.

Timid intermediates will find St Anton less to their taste. There are few easy cruising pistes; most blue runs here would be red in most other resorts, and get bumpy, especially if there is fresh snow (the blue 1 home run often has testing moguls at the end of the day). The gentlest cruisers are the short blues on Galzig and the

UK PACKAGES

Alpine Answers, Alpine Elements, Alpine Weekends, Bramble Ski, Carrier, Crystal, Crystal Finest, Elegant Resorts, Erna Low, Esprit, Flexiski, Friendship Travel, Independent Ski Links, Inghams, Interactive Resorts, Kaluma, Mark Warner, Momentum, Mountain Beds, Neilson, Oxford Ski Co, Powder White, Scott Dunn, Ski Bespoke, Ski Club Freshtracks, Ski Expectations, Ski Independence, Ski Line, Ski Solutions, Ski Total, Ski-Val, Skitracer, Skiweekends.com, Skiworld, Snow Finders, Snoworks, Snowscape, STC, Supertravel, Thomson, VIP, White Roc
Stuben Alpine Answers, Kaluma, Ski Solutions, STC
St Christoph Alpine Answers, Carrier, Crystal Finest, Flexiski, Inghams, Jeffersons, Kaluma, Momentum, Powder Byrne, Scott Dunn, Ski Bespoke, STC, Thomson

Steissbachtal, but they get extremely crowded. The blue from Kapall to Gampen is wide and cruisy.

The underrated Rendl area has a variety of trails suitable for good and moderate intermediates, including the long and genuinely blue Salzböden. The long treelined run to the valley (over 1000m vertical from the top) is the best run in the area when visibility is poor, but it has some awkward sections and can get very busy at the end of the day. You should take the bus to Lech–Zürs at least once during a week's stay.

FOR BEGINNERS ★
Far from ideal
The best bet for beginners is to start at Nasserein, where the nursery slope is less steep than the one close to the main lifts. There are further slopes up at Gampen and a short, gentle blue run at Rendl, served by an easy draglift. But there are no other easy, uncrowded runs for beginners to progress to. A mixed party including novices would be better off staying in Lech or Zürs; those who want to could take the bus to explore St Anton.

FOR BOARDERS ★★★★
Freeriding heaven
For many, St Anton is the Mecca of Austrian freeriding and expert boarders flock here. The terrain is far from ideal for beginners, but there are few T-bars to contend with.

FOR CROSS-COUNTRY ★★
A decent amount
Trails total around 40km, and snow conditions are usually good.

MOUNTAIN RESTAURANTS ★★★
Lots of options
Editors' choice The Verwallstube at Galzig (2352501) is in a class of its own – an expensive table-service place

with splendid views. We've had seriously good lunches here a couple of times. We often lunch on the fringe of St Christoph at the atmospheric Hospiz Alm (3625), famed for its slide down to the toilets as well as its satisfying table-service food and amazing wine cellar. Service gets stretched at times, and it can be expensive. Recent visitors approve: 'The ribs are great to share.'
Worth knowing about The Rodelalm on Gampen is not marked on the piste map, but is beside black run 25 on the way to Nasserein. It has a lovely beamed interior, and we had good traditional food here; a reader enjoyed 'terrific roasted chicken'. On Galzig, the Ulmer Hütte, near the top of the Arlenmähder chair, has a 'fantastic queuing system for quick snacks'. Just above the village, the après-ski bars (Mooserwirt, Griabli, Heustadl and Krazy Kanguruh) serve typical Austrian food and burgers. On Rendl, we've had good stir fry cooked to order at the spacious self-service Rendl restaurant; and the terrace (aka Rendl Beach) has great views of the terrain park action. Or head down the valley run to the small, rustic Bifang-Alm.

SCHOOLS AND GUIDES ★★★
Good reports
The St Anton and the Arlberg schools are under the same ownership but operate separately. Recent reports have been positive, and a reporter had an 'excellent private lesson with a patient and careful instructor'. Piste to Powder is a specialist off-piste outfit run by British guide Graham Austick. A 2013 visitor says, 'they are part of the reason I keep going back'. But we've had reports that ability levels can vary too much. St Anton Classic is a private instruction/guiding outfit.

FOR FAMILIES ★★★★
Nasserein 'ideal'
The youth centre attached to the Arlberg school is excellent, and the special slopes both for toddlers (at the bottom) and bigger children (at Gampen) are well done. Children's instruction is reportedly very good. At Nasserein there is a moving carpet on the baby slope. There's also a good children's area by the Gampen fast quad. Nasserein makes a good base, and family chalet specialist Esprit has its own facilities here.

SCHOOLS

Arlberg
t 3411

St Anton
t 3563

Alpine Faszination
t 0676 630 2136

St Anton Classic
t 3311

Classes (Arlberg prices) 6 days (2hr am and 2hr pm) €247

Private lessons
€174 for 2hr; each additional person €20

GUIDES

Piste to Powder
t 0664 174 6282

CHILDCARE

Kindergartens (run by ski schools)
t 2526 / 3563
From age 30mnth;
must be toilet trained

Ski schools
From age 5

STAYING THERE

There's a wide range of places to stay, from quality hotels to cheap and cheerful pensions and apartments, and a good choice of chalets.

Chalets This is by a wide margin Austria's catered chalet capital; some places are quite luxurious with sauna, steam or hot tub. Chalet operators include Ski Total with a dozen places ranging from six to 26 beds; Supertravel has nine smart-looking chalets including three newly built apartments that share an outdoor pool, sauna and steam room and you are driven to and from the slopes each day. Skiworld has 12 places including the flagship Monte Vera with huge bedrooms, sauna and infra-red room; Crystal has half a dozen properties including the cool 32-bed Inge; Inghams has eight, several with access to sauna, steam room and pool; family specialist Esprit has three big chalets in Nasserein, one next to the gondola.

Hotels There are dozens of 4- and 3-star places.

****Bergschlössl (2220) Charming 10-room B&B right by lifts. 'Beautifully furnished, excellent value.'

****Best Western Alte Post (2553) Atmospheric with lively après-ski bar.

****Galzig (42770) Cool modern place by the lifts, tipped by a regular visitor.

****Pepi's Skihotel (283060) Stylish, modern B&B right by the Rendl lift.

****Post (2213) Ancient place bang in the centre, with good spa and pool.

****Schwarzer Adler (22440) Centuries-old inn on main street. Varying bedrooms. Nice pool.

****Fahrner (22360) Up the hill. 'Unpretentious, clean rooms, friendly, first-rate food, good wine cellar.'

***Parseierblick (3374) In Nasserein. 'Loved it; next to lift; apartment fantastic for a family.'

***Nassereinerhof (3366) Close to the Nasserein gondola; sauna, steam room. 'Very pleasant, with good food.'

**Steffeler (2872) Central B&B. Simple but welcoming; good breakfasts.

Haus Olympia (2520) 'Comfortable' guest house five minutes from the town centre. 'Good breakfasts.'

At altitude The cool 4-star Mooser (2644) opened two seasons ago next to the Moserwirt après-ski bar, with stylish restaurant and bar, three types of sauna and an outdoor pool.

Apartments There are plenty available, but few package deals. Past tips include the Bachmann apartments in Nasserein and Haus Rali at the western end of St Anton.

EATING OUT ★★★★
Some excellent spots
There's a lot of half-board lodging in St Anton, so the restaurant scene is not huge. Our standard port of call for a drink or two and a relaxed meal is the cool Hazienda (a part of the M3 hotel) – a basement place in the main street, with a wide-ranging menu. For more of a blowout, it's up the hill to the village museum's restaurant –

BEWARE OF DANGEROUSLY OVERCROWDED PISTES

We have been saying for years that some of St Anton's pistes are often dangerously overcrowded – especially (but not only) the Steissbachtal (aka Happy Valley) and the home run below it. Bravos going recklessly fast add to the danger. So acute is this problem that several reporters have preferred to catch a bus home from Alpe Rauz or St Christoph. Other alternatives are to ride the gondola down from Galzig or to use the quite testing ski route beneath it. Our picture shows just one of several runs that feed into the home piste.

The run to Rauz can get very busy too; indeed Editor Watts once abandoned skiing for the day because this piste was so crowded with reckless skiers that he felt he needed to look over his shoulder before making each turn – wing mirrors would have been handy.

We get a continual flow of similar complaints from visitors: 'Happy Valley was a frightening experience', 'dangerously crowded', 'reckless skiers', 'people, people and, er, people everywhere', 'very crowded at the end of the day with reckless skiers and lots of moguls'. We could go on …

If this was North America, the mountain would have been planned with enough pistes to cope with the people the lifts can carry, and there would be high-profile staff on duty to give reckless skiers a dressing down (or worse). Why not here?

A KÄRKKÄINEN

ACTIVITIES

Indoor Swimming pool (also hotel pools open to the public, with sauna and massage), fitness centre, tennis, squash, bowling, climbing wall, museum, library

Outdoor Cleared walking paths, natural ice rink (skating, curling), sleigh rides, snowshoeing, tobogganing, climbing, paragliding

BOOKSHOP

Bookshop (Anton Eiter)
Dorfstrasse 28
6580 St Anton
t +43 676 5859 152
On the main street and stocks this guidebook

Phone numbers
From elsewhere in Austria add the prefix 05446 (St Anton and St Christoph), 05582 (Stuben); from abroad use the prefix +43 and omit the initial '0'

TOURIST OFFICES

St Anton
www.stantonamarlberg.com

St Christoph
www.tiscover.com/st.christoph

Stuben
www.stuben.com

excellent, sophisticated food served in elegant panelled rooms. Reader tips: Underground on the Piste ('great steaks, great music, great night out'), Fuhrmannstube ('traditional food, friendly service, you share tables'), Pomodoro ('tasty pizzas'), Fahrnerstube up the hill in Oberdorf ('pretty decor, good hearty food'), Tenne in Nasserein ('good Austrian food').

APRES-SKI ★★★★★
Throbbing till late
St Anton's bars rock from mid-afternoon until the early hours. It all starts in a collection of bars on the slopes above the village. The Krazy Kanguruh now takes second place to the Mooserwirt, which is packed inside and out every afternoon. It fills up as soon as the lunch trade finishes – and reputedly dispenses more beer than any other bar in Austria. Griabli, opposite, is quieter, and the terrace gives you a good view of the goings-on at the Mooserwirt; we enjoyed a live band there. The Heustadl is still the place for 'great German cover bands'. The Sennhütte also has 'a great atmosphere'. All this is followed by a slide down the piste in the dark.

The bars in town are in full swing by 4pm, too. Most are lively, with loud music; sophisticates looking for a quieter time are less well provided for. Pub 37 is recommended by a couple of reporters for a 'quiet drink'. And we like the Bodega tapas bar for pre-dinner drinks and, er, tapas. Base Camp is a lot of fun and 'attracts a mixed crowd and ski instructors'. Underground on the Piste has a 'great live band'. Later on, the Piccadilly and Bar Cuba are popular clubs. Other tips: Scotty's (in Mark Warner's chalet hotel Rosanna), Kandahar and, in Nasserein, the Fang House.

OFF THE SLOPES ★★☆☆☆
Some entertainment
We and reporters love the excellent, but pricey Arlberg-well.com, a leisure centre with great indoor and outdoor pools – including one with jets that propel you around at lightning speed – plus three types of sauna and a huge steam room. A separate sports centre has an indoor climbing wall and an outdoor ice climbing wall. The village is lively during the day, but has few diverting shops. Getting to the other Arlberg resorts by bus is easy, as is visiting Innsbruck by train. Some of

the better mountain huts are accessible by lift or bus. There are 70km of walking trails. The ski museum opens at 3pm.

ST CHRISTOPH

St Christoph is a small collection of smart hotels, restaurants and bars just down from the summit of the Arlberg pass. There are decent beginner slopes served by draglifts and a fast quad chairlift to the heart of St Anton's slopes at Galzig, but the blue back down is not an easy run to progress to. St Christoph is quiet at night. You can't miss the huge 5-star Arlberg-Hospiz (2611). A more affordable but still excellent place is the 4-star Maiensee (2804), right on the slopes by the chair up to Galzig, with health and spa facilities and treatments. We've had good reports of Inghams' flagship 136-bed chalet hotel here – ski-in/ski-out, with good-sized pool and sauna ('comfortable, good food').

STUBEN

Stuben is linked by lift and piste over the Arlberg pass to St Anton. It's a tiny, unspoiled village with an old church and a few hotels, bars and shops. Heavy snowfalls add to the charm.

The Albona area makes a welcome change from the busy slopes of St Anton. The shady slow old chair from the village can be a cold ride, but blankets are available. The reward is north-facing slopes that hold powder well and some deserted off-piste.

Stuben has sunny nursery slopes separate from the main slopes, but a lack of easy runs to progress to makes it unsuitable for beginners. We've had good reports of the school.

The Albonaberg at the very top is a simple hut serving simple food. Lower down, the Albona self-service place gets packed, even on a quiet day, but serves 'good food'. Reporters recommend heading back to the village for lunch at Willi's (pizza, ribs) or the Post hotel ('really good Wiener schnitzl' and 'good value and service').

Evenings are quiet, but several places have a pleasant atmosphere. The charming old Post (761) and Albona (712) are very comfortable. The Hubertushof (7710) is 'welcoming, efficient; excellent food and facilities'.

TOURISM ASSOCIATION NEUSTIFT

Stubai valley

Austria's biggest glacier area, they say, and certainly one of the best; down the valley, a string of appealing village bases

TOP 10 RATINGS	
Extent	★★★
Fast lifts	★★★
Queues	★★★
Snow	★★★★★
Expert	★★★
Intermediate	★★★
Beginner	★★
Charm	★★★★
Convenience	★★
Scenery	★★★★

RPI	105
lift pass	£210
ski hire	£115
lessons	£95
food & drink	£120
total	£540

KEY FACTS

Resorts	935-1000m
	3,070-3,280ft
Slopes	935-3210m
	3,070-10,530ft
Lifts	45
Pistes	147km
	91 miles
Blue	40%
Red	31%
Black	29%
Snowmaking	87%

➕ High, snow-sure glacier slopes plus lower bad-weather options

➕ Quiet, pretty Tirolean villages

➖ A lot of shuttling up and down the valley to and from the glacier

➖ Few challenging pistes

The Stubaier Gletscher ranks alongside Hintertux as one of the most extensive and rewarding glacier ski areas in the Alps. Neustift is the nearest major village, 20km away. But another 5km down valley, livelier Fulpmes is at the base of the Stubaital's best low-altitude area, Schlick 2000.

The 30km-long Stubai valley lies a short drive south of Innsbruck (there's also an antique tram to Fulpmes). The glacier is of course at the head of the valley. There is simple accommodation to be had in hamlets like Falbeson (10km from the glacier) or Krössbach (15km). But three bigger villages – Neustift, Fulpmes and Mieders – have wooded ski areas, covered along with the glacier (and linking buses) by the Stubai Super Skipass. These resorts, described over the page, amount to a sizeable area of mostly intermediate terrain. All have impressive toboggan runs – the valley has 11 in total.

The Stubaier Gletscher offers an extensive area of runs between 3200m and 2300m. Two gondolas go up from the huge car park at Mutterberg to a mid station at Fernau, and then to the two mid-mountain stations of Eisgrat and Gamsgarten. A third gondola from Eisgrat goes to the top of the slopes. Elsewhere, there is a mix of ancient and modern chairlifts (including a new eight-pack added in 2012/13) and the usual glacier drag lifts.

The slopes are broken up by rocky peaks giving more sense of variety than is normal on a glacier. There are lots of fabulous long blue and red cruising runs. The two short black pistes are very much at the easy end of the spectrum. But there are also ski routes ('only with ski instructor or Alpine experience' says the piste map in German). Much the toughest is the 4km Fernau-Mauer at the eastern extremity of the area – after the gentlest and widest of starts this drops steeply towards the Fernau mid-station. There is also a lovely 10km ski route (Wilde Grub'n) from Gamsgarten to the valley – start with a cruise from the top of the glacier for a total of 1450m vertical. And there's proper off-piste to be explored – new for 2012/13 was a map with 11 freeride runs shown (and described in German). There are good beginner slopes at Eisgrat and Gamsgarten, where there is also a major children's area with childcare.

The area is popular with snowboarders. There are lots of natural hits and kickers across the mountain, and a big terrain park.

Queues are not a serious problem. The access gondolas and Eisjoch six-pack can get busy at weekends.

Gamsgarten has a huge self-service place, and excellent food in the table-service Zur Goldenen Gams. Eisgrat has a cool building including a serious table-service section, Schaufelspitz. At Jochdohle, Austria's highest restaurant (3150m) gives good views. The Dresdner Hütte is a proper climbing refuge. There are picnic rooms at Eisgrat and Gamsgarten.

Après-ski starts up the mountain in the lively Gamsgarten bar and Ice Cube bar at Fernau.

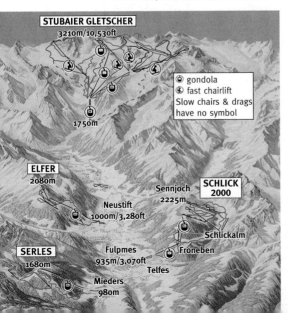

STUBAIER GLETSCHER
3210m/10,530ft

🚠 gondola
🚡 fast chairlift
Slow chairs & drags have no symbol

1750m

ELFER
2080m

Sennjoch
2225m

SCHLICK 2000

Neustift
1000m/3,280ft

Schlickalm

SERLES
1680m

Fulpmes
935m/3,070ft

Froneben

Telfes

Mieders
980m

Pretty Neustift is the nearest major village to the glacier, 20km away →

TVB STUBAI TIROL

NEWS

2013/14: On the glacier, the Gamsgarten area is due to be revamped. At Schlick 2000 two new chairlifts are planned, but when we went to press there were no details.

2012/13: On the glacier, the Rotadl slow quad was replaced by an eight-seat chair. A new area (Daunjoch) has been opened up by a new quad and black run. There's now a special map showing 11 off-piste runs.

UK PACKAGES

Neustift Crystal, Crystal Finest, Momentum, Snowscape, STC, Zenith **Fulpmes** Crystal, Snowscape

Phone numbers
From elsewhere in Austria add the prefix 05226; from abroad use the prefix +43 5226

TOURIST OFFICE

www.stubai.at

1000m
NEUSTIFT

Neustift is the major village closest to the glacier, 20km away. It's an attractive, traditional Tirolean village, with limited local slopes at Elfer.

The slopes at Elfer consist of a narrow chain of runs and lifts from Elferhütte at 2080m down to the village. The pistes are all red, and it is a quiet place for intermediates to practise. This area is north-east-facing; there is a sunny nursery slope at village level and some 40km of cross-country trails.

There is a big 5-star Relais & Châteaux hotel, and lots of 4-stars and 3-stars spread around the area. In the outlying hamlet of Neder, the glacier lift company runs the family-oriented 4-star Happy Stubai (2611).

Nightlife is focused on the Dorf and Bierfassl bars and the Nachtkastl and Scala Club discos. Most restaurants are hotel-based. The big leisure centre has two pools, saunas and bowling.

935m
FULPMES

Fulpmes (with its satellite village of Telfes) sits at the foot of Schlick 2000, the most extensive of the lower ski areas. It is an attractive, sizeable working village not dominated by skiing. The glacier is 25km away.

Uphill from the village a two-stage gondola takes you to Kreuzjoch (2135m), opening up excellent views across the Stubaital and across the Schlick slopes to the dramatic Kalkkogel range. Most of the skiing is below the top gondola station – essentially a single open slope centred on a quad chair rising 580m, with draglifts serving the outermost runs. It is north-facing, so keeps snow well, and grooming is good. There are about five different pistes down, mostly of red difficulty with some easier blue options. There is also a ski-route – challenging at the best of times, very much so if snow is poor. And there is a fair amount of off-piste – 'relatively safe', notes a regular.

Below the main slopes is a long easy run-out to the gondola mid-station at Froneben (1365m). This is the location of the nursery slopes, including Big Ron's Kinderland, with moving carpets and fun features, and a couple of thumping après-ski bars. The blue run winding through woods to the village from here is good fun or tricky, depending on conditions and your competence. There is a terrain park. Queues are rare but the gondola gets busy at peak times.

There are some good huts, with table-service options at the top of the gondola and at Zirmachalm ('great gulaschsuppe'). You can be towed by snowcat to Galtalm, in woods below Kreuzjoch, for 'great food and views'.

There's a good choice of 3- and 4-star hotels, most with pools and spa facilities. The 4-star Stubaierhof (62266) is central. Café Dorfkrug has 'good quality food, friendly service and a great Austrian folk band'.

The nearest leisure centre is in Neustift, but Fulpmes has ice skating, snowshoeing and tobogganing.

980m
MIEDERS

Mieders is near the entrance to the Stubai valley, 15 minutes' drive from Innsbruck. It's an unspoiled village with a few hotels and gust houses and a tiny area of 7km of slopes.

A gondola takes you up the Serles ski area to Kopponeck at 1680m, where a couple of T-bars serve the upper runs. There are a couple of mountain huts and 45km of cross-country tracks above 1600m.

Vorarlberg

The Vorarlberg, west of the Arlberg pass above St Anton, is the snowiest region in the Alps and home to several skiing regions

Ski from St Anton to Stuben, and you cross over the Arlberg pass, moving from the Tirol to the province of Vorarlberg. Here, the melting snow drains into the Rhine, not the Inn and the Danube. It's a famously snowy area, catching the full force of storms sweeping in across the Bodensee. Fashionable and expensive Lech and Zürs are the resorts that are well known internationally, but there are small family resorts elsewhere that deserve attention too.

Vorarlberg is small – the smallest 'land' in the Austrian federation (unless you count the city of Vienna). Its capital is Bregenz, down on the shores of the Bodensee.

Lech, Vorarlberg's best-known resort internationally, gets full coverage in its own chapter a few pages back, which also covers its linked close neighbour **Zürs**.

But there are several other skiing regions too. The first two mentioned below have their own chapters following this introductory one.

Bregenzerwald, to the north-west of the Arlberg, is a delightfully unspoiled area with two small resorts, Damüls and Warth, which vie for the title of snowiest resort in the Alps. Warth is linked to Schröcken and for 2013/14 is due to be linked to Lech to form an area with 190km of slopes. Three seasons ago, Damüls was linked to Mellau. The briefly named village of Au and next-door Schoppernau share the third-biggest ski area, Diedamskopf.

The **Alpenregion Bludenz**, west of the Arlberg, is based around the medieval town of Bludenz. Close to the Swiss border is one of the region's two main ski areas, Brandnertal, shared by the neighbouring resorts of Brand and Bürserberg. Its other main ski area, Sonnenkopf, above Klösterle, is further east and covered by the Arlberg lift pass, so it's a popular outing from the Arlberg resorts.

Then there are three other areas with skiing to offer. By far the biggest is the **Montafon** valley, to the south-west of the Arlberg. The biggest lift-linked ski area (with 155km of pistes and a top height of 2395m) is Silvretta Montafon, shared by Gaschurn, St Gallenkirch and Schruns. It was created two seasons ago when a new gondola opened from St Gallenkirch into the area above Schruns. Golm, above Vandans, is popular with families. Gargellen is a bit of a backwater but usually has the best snow in the valley. At the head of the valley is famously good ski touring terrain. In total, the valley has 243km of slopes served by over 60 lifts.

In the north-east corner of the province is a real curiosity. **Kleinwalsertal** is cut off from the rest of Austria, at the head of a German valley. It is close to one of the main German resorts, Oberstdorf, and is described briefly in the introduction to our section on Germany.

Finally, the **Bodensee–Vorarlberg** area in the north-west corner of Vorarlberg has some small areas. The largest, Laterns, has six lifts and 27km of runs, and a top height of 1780m.

191

Vorarlberg – Bregenzerwald

An unspoiled region that is hardly heard of on the British market,
with a lot of relatively small ski areas covered on one big pass

RPI	90
lift pass	£170
ski hire	£85
lessons	£105
food & drink	£115
total	**£475**

NEWS

2013/14: At Warth a new 10-seat gondola will link the Warth-Schröcken ski area with Lech-Zürs. There will be no piste link – you'll need to ride the gondola both ways.

2012/13: At Warth on the Wannenkopf run you can be videoed and watch it later online. A 'funslope' with waves, curves and boxes was built nearby. At Mellau, the Hubertus hotel has been upgraded to a 4-star.

Bregenzerwald is tucked away between Germany and Switzerland at the western end of Austria, in Vorarlberg. Skirted by all the major road and rail links, it has remained remarkably unspoiled and is still primarily a farming community famous for its cheeses. But it is also the snowiest region in the Alps and has over 270km of pistes served by almost 100 lifts in 15 skiing areas. There is some seriously good skiing here, especially for intermediates. The area is well worth considering for a quiet holiday exploring several different ski areas or for a family holiday. And prices are lower than in many better-known, more fashionable resorts. The resort of Warth, in particular, will be a much more compelling place to stay from 2013/14 when a new gondola should open, linking its ski area to that of plush and pricey Lech and Zürs.

Skiing began in Bregenzerwald in 1894 when the parish priest, Father Johann Müller, sent away to Norway for some newfangled 'Hickoryskis' and then careered down the slopes garbed in his flowing robes, amazing the local farmers. Until then, if you absolutely had to get around in winter, you wore a type of snowshoe. Father Johann established a trend that has transformed the region's economy.

This transformation has been greatly aided by abundant snowfall. One resort in the region, Warth, is supposed to have the best annual average snowfall in the Alps. Another, Damüls, is supposed to be the most snow-sure resort in the world. Eh? Let's just say the whole region gets huge amounts of snow. To put it in perspective: about four times as much as Kitzbühel, three times as much as Chamonix and twice as much as St Anton and Val d'Isère.

There is a ski lift in almost every village. But few of the ski areas are large. They are all covered by the 3-Valley ski pass, which also covers areas outside Bregenzerwald. The pass is valid in 28 ski areas and covers around 340km of slopes served by around 140 lifts. Having a car is useful: getting around on buses is time consuming. There are some excellent deals for families, and nearly all the resorts offer activities other than skiing, with lots of cleared paths, tobogganing and cross-country skiing.

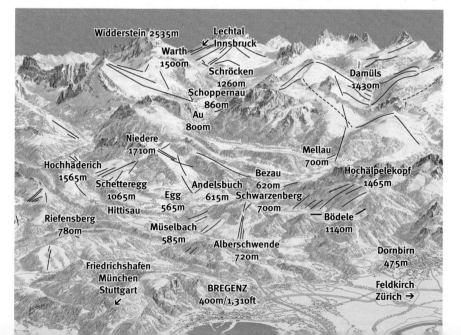

↑ There are great views from the Diedamskopf ski area near Au and Schoppernau

BREGENZERWALD TOURISMUS / DIETMAR WALSER / ARCHIV BERGBAHNEN DIEDAMSKOPF

THE BIGGEST SKI AREAS

Damüls and **Mellau** share the biggest ski area entirely in Bregenzerwald, with 109km of runs. Just under half are red runs, around a quarter blue, and the rest are blacks and ski routes. And there's a good terrain park in Damüls. Altogether there are 31 lifts – these include two gondolas and 14 chairs (with six six-packs and a fast quad).

Damüls is quite high (the base area is at 1430m), and the sunny but snow-sure slopes go up to 2000m. Most runs are quite short, above the treeline and of genuine red steepness, and some of the blues are quite narrow, so it's best for adventurous rather than timid intermediates. On our visit, all of the ski routes we tried had been groomed and were of red run steepness – and some were busier than the pistes. Damüls has 14km of cross-country tracks and 15km of winter walking trails.

Mellau's ski area is reached by an old gondola from the edge of the village and is on the more shady side of the mountain (most slopes are north-facing). There's a steep black run that deserves its classification, as do the reds, and a ski route that is short but enjoyable. Most of the blues have fairly steep sections at the top – not good for timid intermediates. There's a long red through the trees right back to the village – enjoyable but narrow (it's a summer road for much of the way) – plus 20km of walking trails and 43km of cross-country tracks.

Damüls has no real village centre – it is a series of small collections of hotels (six 4-stars, eight 3-stars), inns and gasthofs, scattered along the edge of the slopes, mostly ski-in/ski-out.

Mellau, on the other hand, is much lower (690m), but a proper little village that's quiet and peaceful (it's bypassed by the valley road). There's little more to it than a few 3- and 4-star hotels, some gasthofs and a couple of bars. We enjoyed our stay at the 4-star Sonne Lifestyle (5518 20100) – modern, minimalist, spacious rooms, good food and spa facilities.

Warth and **Schröcken** are at opposite ends of their shared 68km of slopes, which are mainly between 1500m and 2000m and served by 15 lifts, including five fast chairs. But things should be transformed for 2013/14 by a new gondola link to the Lech–Zürs ski area (see Lech chapter) – forming a joint area with 190km of slopes. Warth is only a few kilometres along the valley from Lech but the road between the villages is closed in winter because of avalanche danger.

Thanks to the exceptional snowfall record (11m a year on average) and the north-facing aspect of most slopes, the local pistes are almost always in excellent condition, and the off-piste powder gets tracked out much less quickly than in better-known resorts – let's hope that doesn't change after the new link with Lech opens (reports please). Reporters all mention the quality and quantity of the off-piste.

The marked runs include several easy blacks and ski routes as well as reds and blues, and there's a terrain park with three lines from easy to pro, plus a new 'funslope' that sounds like a boardercross. Most of the pistes are ideal for high-speed cruising and were very quiet on our January visit. Queues are rare (and hopefully will remain so despite the new link). Piste marking and grooming are good.

A regular visitor says the Warth school is excellent for adults' and children's lessons, off-piste guiding and race training.

There are 20km of walking trails, 21km of cross-country and 'brilliant' tobogganing two evenings a week.

The villages are small, pretty and unspoiled. There are six 4-star hotels, two 3-stars and one 2-star, plus inns and gasthofs. In Warth, reporters recommend the Sporthotel Steffisalp (5583 3699) with 'excellent rooms, food and service and a superb spa', an après-ski hut and an umbrella bar; and the Lechtalerhof (5583 2677), which is 'super-friendly and excellent value, with good food, large rooms, lovely pool and spa'. Both are 4-star and right by the pistes and the main lift. Schröcken can be reached on skis only by a ski route, and there are no lifts there – you have to drive or catch a bus to the Hochtannberg pass, where a six-pack whisks you into the centre of the ski area. The Gasthof Tannberg (5519 268) in Schröcken was 'a real find: amazing food, good service and value', says a recent visitor.

Au and **Schoppernau** are neighbouring villages sharing the **Diedamskopf** ski area, which boasts Bregenzerwald's highest lift station (reached by a two-stage gondola) at 2060m and fabulous 360° views from the top (and the Panorama restaurant). The sunny slopes (most face south or south-west) also have good views of the surrounding peaks and are popular with families. The eight lifts serve 40km of slopes, of which two-thirds are blue or red. The terrain park is the biggest in Bregenzerwald. There's night skiing twice a week.

The slopes suit good intermediates best; the blacks are quite serious, and some of the blues should be classified red, especially the blue from the top chair (which had moguls on it the afternoon we skied it). On the other hand, the reds in the Breitenalpe sector were easy and should really be classified blue. The runs are short, except for the 10km runs back to the valley station at 820m, which have a vertical of over 1200m. The lower section of this is served only by one red run and a ski route (the route was closed on our visit and the lowest section of the red run was stony; many people take the gondola down from mid-station). The rest of the pistes are above 1470m.

At the top of the mountain, the Kids Adventure Land takes children aged three to eight years old.

Cross-country enthusiasts will find over 60km of trails. There are 40km of cleared walks and a natural ice rink.

Au and Schoppernau between them have 12 4-star and four 3-star hotels, plus gasthofs and plenty of dining options. Both are a ski-bus ride or drive from the ski area and are rather spread out. We preferred Schoppernau, which is off the main road, on the same side as the slopes, and has nice snow-covered lanes and chalets.

SMALLER SKI AREAS

Andelsbuch and **Bezau** share the local **Niedere** ski area with eight lifts (including a smart newish cable car from Bezau) serving three short blue runs, a 7km-long red, a short black and several ski routes – 15km in total. It's a family ski area, and, given good snow, the ski routes offer more experienced skiers a challenge too. The top height is 1715m, and there's a panoramic restaurant at the top of the cable car. Andelsbuch has a 3-star inn plus a few gasthofs, and Bezau has four 4-star hotels and one 3-star.

Alberschwende has 18km of runs, served by a chairlift and six T-bars, and is popular with beginners. There are 16km of cross-country tracks and an ice rink. The village has a 4-star hotel, a 3-star, plus a few gasthofs.

Riefensberg has the tiny **Hochlitten** ski area, with just 5km of easy blue and red runs and four T-bars. It shares with neighbouring **Hittisau** the **Hochhäderich** ski area. This has 9km of runs (mainly blue and red but with a couple of blacks) served by four T-bars and a quad chair. It has 16km of cross-country tracks at altitude and 12km of walking paths. Hittisau has one 4-star hotel and one 3-star, while Riefensberg has two 2-star inns.

Egg is the biggest village in Bregenzerwald, with around 3,500 inhabitants and a small ski area at **Schetteregg**, with six lifts and 10km of easy blue and red runs between 1100m and 1400m. There are 15km of cleared walks, a 3-star hotel, and six inns.

Schwarzenberg's local **Bödele** mountain has 24km of runs (mainly easy blues and reds) served by nine lifts (nearly all draglifts). There are also 10km of cross-country tracks and 35km of walking trails. Schwarzenberg has one 4-star and two 3-star hotels.

Vorarlberg – Alpenregion Bludenz

Two small, family-friendly ski areas set either side of a medieval town – with easy access to several other nearby ski areas

RPI	90
lift pass	£160
ski hire	£85
lessons	£115
food & drink	£110
total	**£470**

NEWS

2012/13: In Brandnertal several hotels were refurbished, including the 4-star Schillerkopf in Bürserberg and the 3-star Lün (which was almost completely rebuilt in a smart modern style) in Brand.

Alpenregion Bludenz is centred on the medieval mountain town of Bludenz, in the west of Austria, and the region borders on to Switzerland. It has two main ski areas: Brandnertal to the west and Sonnenkopf in the Klostertal to the east. The latter is covered by the Arlberg ski pass (which covers St Anton, Lech–Zürs and Warth–Schröcken) as well as having its own pass.

Getting to the Bludenz region is easy by train or car after flying in to Zürich (155km) or Innsbruck (135km). And if you base yourself in Bludenz, it's easy to ski both the local main ski areas plus the Arlberg, Montafon and Bregenzerwald resorts. Both Brandnertal and Sonnenkopf are popular with families.

BRANDNERTAL

Two separate villages with their own ski areas that are linked by a cable car at altitude.

Brand (1040m) is strung along the valley floor near the head (the south-western end) of the Brandnertal. Eight-seat gondolas (served by free ski-buses) go up from each end of town into the bigger part of the ski area it shares with Bürserberg (890m), which is down the valley to the north-east and has a double chairlift into its own smaller area of slopes. The two areas were linked at altitude in 2007 when the Panoramabahn cable car opened.

You can ski on an easy blue run from the Bürserberg area to the Brand area and catch the cable car the other way.

The area above Brand is served by two recently built six-packs, a couple of short draglifts and an old double chair. One of the six-packs reaches the area's high point of 2000m. Above Bürserberg, the area is served by a couple of old chairs and a couple of drags, one of which takes you to the blue piste linking the two areas.

Most of the runs are red, though there are a few blues and ski routes, and a solitary black run (above Bürserberg); there's a newish terrain park and a half-pipe above Brand (see www.backyards.at). In total there are 55km of mainly east-facing pistes that suit intermediates best; 75% of the pistes are covered by snowmaking. The area is well supplied with huts.

There's excellent cross-country here, with 42km of prepared tracks including some at the top of Bürserberg and a glorious 15km circular route at 1250m.

195

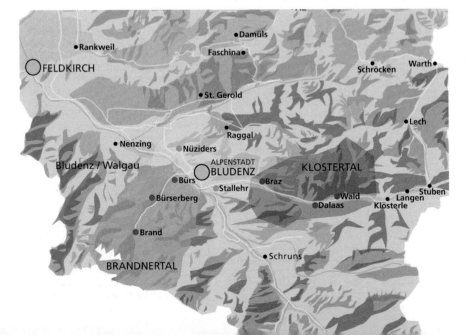

↑ Brandnertal and Sonnenkopf are both prettily set with slopes that suit intermediates and families best

ALPENREGION BLUDENZ

There's also snowshoeing and extensive winter walking trails that go right to the top of Bürserberg, plus ice skating on natural rinks.

The area goes out of its way to be family-friendly, and there's a special Kinderland area in the middle of Brand village where the two ski schools teach three- to five-year-olds. Children aged five and under ski free, and there are discounts up to age 18. When staying at certain hotels between 15 and 28 March 2014 you get a free lift pass through the Märzenslust scheme. There are two good toboggan runs, one 6km long above Brand and a 1.4km one above Bürserberg. And the area is big on dog sledding; you can learn to mush huskies (including a special course for children) and take excursions (including one where you camp overnight on the mountain).

Hotels range from several 4-stars to family-run pensions, and some have a special 'Family Friendly' accreditation. Apartments are plentiful too.

SONNENKOPF

A small family-friendly ski area set off the road between Bludenz and St Anton. You can buy the local lift pass or the Arlberg lift pass, which covers the better-known resorts of St Anton and Lech–Zürs (plus Warth–Schröcken from the 2013/14 season).

The Klostertal has various small villages lining the road to the Arlberg pass, and a roadside eight-person gondola with big car parks nearby goes up to its Sonnenkopf ski area from near the village of Wald (see map on the previous page). This has 31km of pistes served by nine lifts and suits beginners, intermediates and families best; it is often very quiet here when nearby St Anton and Lech are packed. Children under eight ski free.

At the top of the gondola is a restaurant, a good beginner area, a children's area and gentle blue runs served by T-bars and a quad chair. At the top of the chair is a table-service restaurant with a big sun terrace.

Two of the T-bars lead you down to the bigger sector of pistes, which are served by a fast quad and two double chairs, one of which leads to the area's high point of 2300m. This sector has mainly red runs plus a couple of ski routes and a solitary, seriously steep, 1.5km black run. A 2013 visitor found signposting poor in this area. One of the reds goes all the way back to the valley and to either the village of Klösterle or back to the base of the gondola. There's also good off-piste to be explored with a guide.

The 1.8km-long toboggan run goes from the top to the mid-station of the gondola. There's 25km of cross-country on the valley floor and glorious winter walking trails at altitude, including one up to Muttjöchle (2075m).

There is good-value accommodation in villages along the valley floor and two highly regarded restaurants – the 3-star Gasthof Rössle and 4-star Traube Braz, both in Braz.

Zell am See

A real one-off, this: a summer resort town in a lovely lakeside setting, with varied local slopes and an excellent glacier nearby

TOP 10 RATINGS

Extent	★★
Fast lifts	★★★★
Queues	★★★
Snow	★★
Expert	★★
Intermediate	★★★
Beginner	★★★
Charm	★★★★
Convenience	★★★
Scenery	★★★

RPI 95

lift pass	£200
ski hire	£80
lessons	£100
food & drink	£115
total	£495

NEWS

2013/14: An eight-seat chair will replace the Glocknerbahn quad and the parallel drag. A new funslope (a bit like a beginner terrain park) is to be built. On Kaprun's Kitzsteinhorn a new black piste, Black Mamba, is to open.

2012/13: The Sonnengratbahn double chair was upgraded to a fast quad.

UK PACKAGES

Crystal, Crystal Finest, Erna Low, Inghams, Lagrange, Mountain Beds, Neilson, Ski Club Freshtracks, Ski Line, Skitracer, Skiweekends. com, Snow Finders, Snowscape, STC, Thomson, Zenith **Kaprun** Crystal, Crystal Finest, Inghams, Interactive Resorts, Ski Line, Skitracer, Snow Finders, Snowscape, Solos, STC, Thomson, Zenith

➕ Varied, wooded slopes with fine views down to the lake

➕ Charming summer resort town with lots to do off the slopes

➕ Excellent Kaprun glacier nearby

➖ Sunny, low-altitude slopes

➖ Limited local slopes, especially when snow low down is poor

➖ Some hotels are distant from the lifts; buses can be crowded

Like St Moritz, Zell is a town beside a lake (frozen if you're lucky). The similarities end there; but towny Zell makes a change from the Austrian norm of rustic chalet-style villages. From the skiing point of view, the appeal is greatly strengthened by having Kaprun's excellent glacier just down the road.

THE RESORT

Zell is a year-round resort town set between a large lake and the unusual, horseshoe-shaped mountain. About 3km south of Zell is the suburb of Schüttdorf. It's a short bus ride to the glacier slopes of Kaprun, on the lift pass and covered in this chapter. Saalbach is easily reached by bus.
Village charm Zell has a charming, traffic-free medieval centre. The major through-road is buried in a tunnel, but there is still quite a bit of traffic passing close to the centre.
Convenience There are lodgings close to each of the access gondolas – from the edge of town, from Schüttdorf, or from Schmittental, in the heart of the horseshoe-shaped mountain. There are buses for those based further away.
Scenery Zell am See enjoys a pretty lakeside setting and the mountain offers good views south to Kaprun's distinctive Kitzsteinhorn.

THE MOUNTAINS

Zell's mountain is open at the top, mostly densely wooded lower down.
Slopes Above the lifts out of Zell and Schüttdorf a final gondola goes to Schmittenhöhe, meeting the gondola from Schmittental. The several lifts on the back of the hill and on the sunny slopes of the northern arm of the horseshoe mountain are accessed via Schmittenhöhe or by cable car from Schmittental. Black runs descend from various points to Schmittental; easier runs go down the southern arm to Zell and Schüttdorf. The slopes steepen – it's a red run to Schüttdorf, a black to Zell, or a winding blue.
Fast lifts Only the sunny Sonnkogel sector now relies on slow lifts.

Queues Away from peak season there are no problems. But we lack recent high-season reports.
Terrain parks Schmittenhöhe has a half-pipe by the Glocknerbahn chairlift, and this season will have a fun park by the Hochmaisbahn.
Snow reliability Many of Zell's slopes get a lot of sun and, although there is full snowmaking, at these altitudes there is still a danger of slush and ice.
Experts Zell has several black runs, but they are not seriously steep and are usually groomed. Off-piste terrain is limited, but there is a nice 'glade' area on the back of the hill.
Intermediates Good intermediates have a couple of fine, long runs, but this is not a place for high mileage. The wide Sonnkogel runs are relatively quiet – great for carving. The timid can cruise the southern ridge blues.
Beginners A reporter with novice kids advises that the nursery slopes at Schüttdorf are better than those at Schmittental. There are lovely long easy runs to progress to.
Snowboarding Most lifts are chairs, gondolas or cable cars. Snowboard Academy is a specialist school.
Cross-country There's a total of 35km, some lit at night, and more at Kaprun.
Mountain restaurants Zell has quite a few welcoming huts, though some can get very crowded. They are named on the piste map. Breiteckalm and Blaickner's Sonnalm are readers' favourites. Pinzgauer Hütte is away from the piste; you get a skidoo tow back – fun, but may involve queuing.
Schools and guides There is a choice of schools; reports are positive.
Families Staying in Schüttdorf means you have direct gondola access to the Areitalm snow-kindergarten.

KEY FACTS

Resort	755m
	2,480ft

Zell and Kaprun

Slopes	755-3030m
	2,480-9,940ft
Lifts	53
Pistes	138km
	86 miles
Blue	34%
Red	43%
Black	23%
Snowmaking	100%

Zell (Schmittenhöhe) only

Slopes	755-2000m
	2,480-6,560ft
Lifts	26
Pistes	77km
	48 miles
Snowmaking	100%

Kaprun only

Slopes	785-3030m
	2,580-9,940ft
Lifts	22
Pistes	61km
	38 miles
Snowmaking	100%

STAYING THERE

Hotels There is a broad range of hotels and guest houses. Of the many 4-stars, Schloss Prielau (729110) is a converted castle on the outskirts of town, with a shuttle to the slopes: 'Super hotel, fantastic building,' says a reporter. The St Georg (768) is 200m from the CityXPress lift – 'great staff', 'sumptuous food'; the 'exceptionally friendly' Heizmann (72152) is also close to the lifts.

Apartments There are lots of options bookable locally.

Eating out Zell has quite a few non-hotel options. 'Kumpfkessel, Arts and Giuseppe's all good,' says a reporter. Mayer's out at Schloss Prielau has two Michelin stars – 'amazing', says a reader.

Après-ski There are plenty of cafes and bars. Start at the top of the slopes at the Berghotel – where the bar has a good vibe, live music and dancing. In town, Pinzgauer Diele club rocks too. O'Flannigan's is the main sports bar, with all that that entails, and one reader prefers A Little Bit of Irish. Ginhouse is good for a quiet drink, particularly, er, gin. Villa Crazy Daisy is 'a jumping place with a great atmosphere'; live music often.

Off the slopes There is plenty to do. You can often walk across the frozen lake; there are marked paths up at Schmittenhöhe, too. Plus there are good sports facilities, Alpine flights and you can watch ice hockey. Trips to Salzburg and Kitzbühel are possible.

OUTLYING RESORT – 785m

KAPRUN

Kaprun is a pleasant and quite lively village, with a pretty church, and it's bypassed by the road up to the lifts to its Kitzsteinhorn glacier. However, it sprawls over a considerable area, so it's worth picking your spot with care.

There is a small area of easy intermediate slopes on the outskirts of the village on the low hill of Maiskogel. But most people will want to spend their time on the glacier.

This is reached by a two-stage gondola to Alpincenter at 2450m, with other lifts in parallel. A cable car then goes up to the top of the area at over 3000m. The main slopes are in a big bowl above Alpincenter, served by a quad chair, two six-packs and lots of T-bars. There are also runs down to the mid-station of the gondola.

There are three 'excellent' terrain parks on the glacier including one for novices, and a super-pipe.

The high black runs present no challenge to experts (they used to be red), but this season a new black piste

Most pistes are mainly gentle blues and reds – great easy cruising for intermediates. One particularly entertaining red goes down to the gondola mid-station, away from the lifts. For beginners there are nursery slopes next to the village and gentle blues to progress to, both at Maiskogel and on the glacier.

The 18km of cross-country trails on the Kaprun golf course are good, but at altitude there is just one short loop.

There's a decent choice of mountain restaurants on the glacier. One of the best is the Gletschermühle near the Alpincenter. The Krefelder Hütte below it is a genuine mountain refuge. Häuslalm near the gondola mid-station has a 'good atmosphere'.

Crystal and Inghams both have big chalets here. There's a decent choice of hotels. The 4-star Sonnblick (8301) has been recommended, as has the 3-star Mitteregger (8207). There are of course restaurants and bars, but we lack recent reports. There's a sports centre, bowling at the Sportsbar, sleigh rides and a motor museum.

Phone numbers
From elsewhere in Austria add the prefix 06542 (Zell), 06547 (Kaprun); from abroad use the prefix +43 and omit the initial '0'

TOURIST OFFICE

Zell am See/Kaprun
www.zellamsee-kaprun.com

will be added lower down, going to the gondola mid-station, with a claimed gradient of 32° – a proper black. In that same area, the resort now operates a set of similarly steep itineraries – mostly with verticals of around 500m. Sadly, these runs are apparently not avalanche protected, so you still need full off-piste kit and experience to use them. This is a strange and undesirable setup.

Zell am See

201

Build your own shortlist: www.wheretoskiandsnowboard.com

France

Around a third of British skiers and snowboarders choose France for their holidays – that's more than any other country. It's not difficult to see what attracts us to France. The country has the biggest lift and piste networks in the world. Most of these big areas are also at high altitude, ensuring good snow for a long season. The best of them have state-of-the-art lift systems, too – but it's a myth that all French lift systems are wonderfully efficient. Another myth is that French resort villages are all soulless, purpose-built service stations, thrown up without concern for appearance during the 1960s and 1970s.

Many French resorts are now distinctly lively in the evening – a great change over the last 20 years. And some even have the on-mountain afternoon party scene that is so common in Austria, mainly thanks to the Folie Douce chain that started several years ago in Val d'Isère and has expanded to Méribel, Val Thorens and, from 2013/14, Alpe-d'Huez.

Although most French resorts are not expensive overall compared to their main Alpine rivals (as shown by our RPI figures), many are especially expensive for eating and drinking – including major resorts such as Courchevel, Méribel, Val d'Isère and Val Thorens. This leads to many complaints from readers (along with complaints about the ludicrous practice of some mountain restaurants charging customers to use the loos). But UK tour operators do a great job in keeping catered chalet holidays affordable, with lots of food and wine included in the price. Sadly, local prices have become almost 10% more expensive in terms of £s in the last year because of exchange rate changes.

KEEPING COSTS DOWN

Chalet holidays are not the only way of economizing, of course. Renting one of the new generation of genuinely comfortable and stylish apartments and catering for yourself is an attractive option – see our smart apartments chapter on page 43. Other ideas include staying in a relatively cheap valley town such as Bourg-St-Maurice or Brides-les-Bains and packing lunches to eat on the mountain.

ANY STYLE OF RESORT YOU LIKE

The main drawback to France, hinted at above, is the nature of some of the high-altitude purpose-built resorts. It's partly that the worst of them look hideous, but it's also that they were designed to cram in the maximum number of beds (and shops – we really hate the claustrophobic indoor malls) and that they are holiday camps rather than real communities. But even the worst places have learned from past mistakes, and newer developments are being built in a traditional chalet style. And the later generation of purpose-built resorts, such as La Rosière, La Tania and Arc 1950, are built in a much more sympathetic style.

If you prefer, there are genuinely old mountain villages to stay in, linked directly to the big lift networks. These are not usually as convenient for the slopes, but they give you a feel of being in France rather than in a winter-holiday factory. Examples include Montchavin or Champagny for La Plagne, Vaujany for Alpe-d'Huez and St-Martin-de-Belleville for the Trois Vallées. There are also old villages with their own slopes that have developed as resorts while

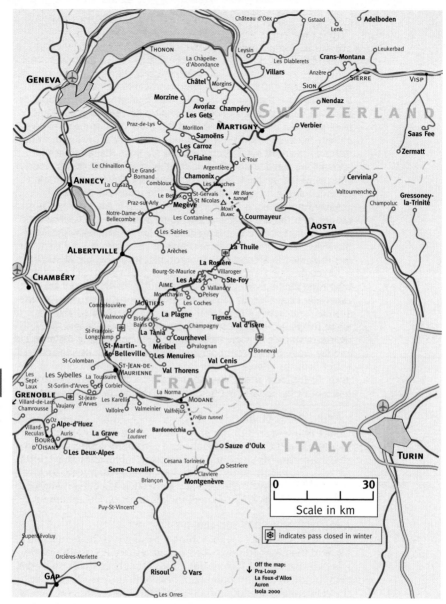

Château d'Oex · Gstaad · Adelboden
Lenk
THONON · Leysin · Crans-Montana · Leukerbad
La Chapelle-d'Abondance · Les Diablerets
GENEVA · Châtel · Morgins · Villars · Anzère · SIERRE · VISP
Morzine · SION
Avoriaz · Champéry · Nendaz
Praz-de-Lys · Les Gets · MARTIGNY · Verbier · Saas Fee
Morillon · Samoëns · SWITZERLAND
Les Carroz · Zermatt
Flaine · Le Tour
Le Chinaillon · Le Grand-Bornand · Argentière
ANNECY · La Clusaz · Combloux · Chamonix · Les Houches · Cervinia
Le Bettex · St-Gervais · Mt Blanc tunnel · Valtournenche · Gressoney-la-Trinité
Praz-sur-Arly · Megève · St Nicolas · MONT BLANC · Champoluc
Notre-Dame-de-Bellecombe · Les Contamines · Courmayeur
Les Saisies · AOSTA
ALBERTVILLE · Arêches · La Thuile
La Rosière
CHAMBÉRY · Bourg-St-Maurice · Villaroger
Les Arcs · Ste-Foy
AIME · Vallandry
Montchavin · Peisey
Combelouvière · MOÛTIERS · Les Coches
Valmorel · Brides-les-Bains · La Plagne · Tignes
St-François-Longchamp · Champagny · Val d'Isère
La Tania
St-Martin-de-Belleville · Courchevel · Pralognan · Bonneval
Méribel · Les Menuires
St-Colomban · ST-JEAN-DE-MAURIENNE · Val Cenis
Les Sept-Laux · Les Sybelles · La Toussuire · Val Thorens
GRENOBLE · St-Sorlin-d'Arves · Corbier · La Norma
Villard-de-Lans · St-Jean-d'Arves · Les Karellis · MODANE
Chamrousse · Vaujany · Valloire · Valmeinier · Valfréjus · Fréjus tunnel
Oz · Alpe-d'Huez
Villard-Reculas · Auris · La Grave · Col du Lauteret · Bardonecchia
D'OISANS · Les Deux-Alpes · Sauze d'Oulx · ITALY · TURIN
Cesana Torinese · Sestriere
Serre-Chevalier · Claviere
Briançon · Montgenèvre
Puy-St-Vincent

0		30

Scale in km

❋ indicates pass closed in winter

Superdévoluy

Orcières-Merlette
Off the map:
↓ Pra-Loup
Risoul · Vars · La Foux-d'Allos
GAP · Auron
Isola 2000
Les Orres

Getting around the French Alps

Pick the right gateway city as your initial Continental target – Geneva, Chambéry or Grenoble – and you can hardly go wrong. The only high pass you need worry about is on the approach to Serre-Chevalier and Montgenèvre – the 2060m Col du Lauteret; but even here the road is a major one, and kept clear of snow or reopened quickly after a fall (or you can fly to Turin and avoid that pass). Crossing the French–Swiss border between Chamonix and Verbier involves two closure-prone passes – the Montets and the Forclaz. When necessary, one-way traffic runs beside the tracks through the rail tunnel beneath the passes.

retaining at least some rustic ambience – such as Serre-Chevalier.

Two other resorts deserve a special mention. Megève is an exceptionally charming little town combining rustic style with sophistication. And then there is Chamonix, a big, bustling town sitting literally in the shadow of Mont Blanc, Europe's highest peak, and the centre of the most radical off-piste terrain in the Alps.

SKI SCHOOL COMPETITION GOOD BUT CLAMPDOWN ON GUIDING BAD

Gone are the days when the ESF was the only school in town. Most resorts now have lots of competing schools, and many are run and staffed by highly qualified British instructors – examples are New Generation and BASS, both of which have branches in several resorts and both of which reporters speak highly of. But last season a French court ruled that ski guiding/hosting by British tour operators, where a member of staff shows you around the pistes, was illegal unless the staff member held the highest ski instructor qualification. Le Ski, the tour operator being prosecuted, is appealing the decision – but until that appeal is decided, most tour operators have suspended their ski hosting programmes in France.

EASY PISTES

France remains unusual among European countries in rating pistes on a four-point scale. The very easiest runs are classified green; except in Val d'Isère, they are reliably gentle. This is a genuinely helpful system that ought to be used more widely. Some French resorts, sadly, make little use of it – notably Les Arcs and La Plagne.

PLAT DU JOUR

Despite the prices, France has advantages in the gastronomic stakes. Table-service in mountain restaurants is common, and most places do food – often including a plat du jour – that is in a different league from what you'll find in Austria or North America. In the evening, most resorts have restaurants serving good traditional French food and regional specialities.

DRIVING AMBITION?

The French Alps are easy to get to by car. Starting on page 71 there is a chapter on driving to the French Alps. Driving is still popular, despite the growth of budget airlines; for self-caterers it has the advantage of being able to stock up in good-value valley supermarkets.

AVOID THE CROWDS

French school holidays mean crowded slopes, so they are worth avoiding. The country is divided into three zones, with fortnight holidays staggered between 15 February and 16 March 2014. Avoid 15 Feb to 2 March in particular, when Paris is on holiday.

Alpe-d'Huez

Impressive and sunny slopes above a hotchpotch of a purpose-built village, but with attractive alternative bases

RATINGS

The mountains

Extent	★★★★
Fast lifts	★★★★
Queues	★★★★
Terrain p'ks	★★★
Snow	★★★★
Expert	★★★★
Intermediate	★★★★
Beginner	★★★★★
Boarder	★★★★
X-country	★★★
Restaurants	★★★★
Schools	★★★★
Families	★★★

The resort

Charm	★★
Convenience	★★★
Scenery	★★★★
Eating out	★★★★
Après-ski	★★★★
Off-slope	★★★★

RPI   105

lift pass	£200
ski hire	£125
lessons	£80
food & drink	£135
total	**£540**

KEY FACTS

Resort	1860m
	6,100ft
Slopes	1100-3330m
	3,610-10,920ft
Lifts	80
Pistes	250km
	155 miles
Green	31%
Blue	26%
Red	31%
Black	12%
Snowmaking	35%

206

➕ Extensive, high, sunny slopes, split interestingly into different sectors, with some very long runs

➕ Vast, gentle, sunny nursery slopes

➕ Efficient access lifts from villages

➕ Livelier than many French resorts

➕ Good, traditional alternative bases

➖ Some main intermediate runs get badly overcrowded in high season

➖ Many runs get too much sun, so slush and ice are hazards

➖ Many tough runs are high, and exposed – very few woodland runs

➖ Spread-out resort village

There are few single resorts to rival Alpe-d'Huez for extent and variety of terrain – in wintery conditions it's one of our favourites. But as the season progresses the effects of the strong southern sun become more and more of a problem.

If you don't like the look of the village, think about the smaller bases described at the end of this chapter – especially Vaujany and Villard-Reculas.

THE RESORT

Alpe-d'Huez is a large, modern resort on a high, open, sunny plateau east of Grenoble. It was developed for skiing, but consists mainly of large numbers of undistinguished small buildings rather than monolithic blocks.

The resort spreads down a gentle slope in a triangular shape from the main lift station at the top corner. The main village is divided into three named 'quarters'; Vieil Alpe includes the original chalet-style part of the village, at the lower end. Outside the central triangle there are four satellite 'quarters'. The major one is Les Bergers, a second major lift base at the eastern corner of the resort; it has a chalet suburb spreading uphill.

A blue piste descends from the west side of the resort to the original (but much expanded) village of Huez, where there is lodging (and a lift to the main resort).

The lift pass gives days in some other resorts. There are buses twice a week to Les Deux-Alpes, but the proper thing to do is go by helicopter – we agree with readers that this is 'fantastic fun' (from 65 euros). The merits of a cross-valley lift are being carefully considered.

VILLAGE CHARM ★★★★★
Bit of a hotchpotch
The central buildings come in all styles; on the fringes there are more sizeable, modern buildings, and areas of chalets. Vieil Alpe has a trace of charm, and as a whole the resort is not unpleasant. The central Avenue des Jeux is a kind of focus, with the ice rink, indoor-outdoor swimming pool, and many of the shops, bars and restaurants.

CONVENIENCE ★★★★★
Choose your spot with care
Very few lodgings are ski-in/ski-out. Staying near one of the two major lift bases is the best plan – or in one of the chalets uphill of Les Bergers. The place is too big to get around on foot. There's a slow bucket-lift (with a piste beneath it) running in daytime through the centre to the main lifts. This opens a bit late (8.45am) and builds queues at peak times. There are also chairlifts across the bottom of the resort up to Les Bergers. The free ski-bus service around the resort usually runs to its timetable, but reporters find the 20-minute interval between buses too long, and capacity inadequate.

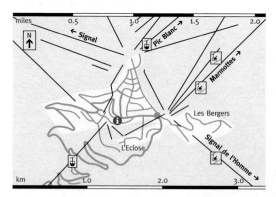

2013/14: On the main beginner area a chondola will replace the three long Jeux drags. The Lac Blanc drag nearby will also be removed. A Folie Douce mountain restaurant, as in Val d'Isère etc, will open. A new multi-activity space is to open, with airbag, ice tower and tubing slope.

2012/13: The Rif Nel chondola was added at Les Bergers. The ultra-modern Signal 2108 restaurant opened at the top of Signal. In Vaujany, a new ice rink and a bowling alley opened.

SNOWPIX.COM / CHRIS GILL

The mountainside above Oz is not natural blue-run terrain; but Chevreuils has been improved in recent years ↓

The satellite quarters are a bit of a trek from the centre – and a reader points out that there are no proper footways – but they have their own lifts, bars and restaurants.

SCENERY ★★★★
Splendid panoramic views
The resort has a fabulous high setting on a sunny plateau. There are splendid views of the Ecrins peaks.

THE MOUNTAINS

Practically all the slopes are above the treeline, and so there may be little to do when a storm socks in or the wind picks up. Piste classification is rather unreliable. There are certainly some tough blues; but readers' views seem to be complicated by snow conditions, which in such a sunny resort are naturally very variable. The piste map works well enough; some reporters find signposting less than ideal.

EXTENT OF THE SLOPES ★★★★
Several well-linked areas
Alpe-d'Huez is a big-league resort, with impressively extensive and varied slopes. It offers many long runs, with big verticals. But its claim of 250km of pistes is an exaggeration. The lift company has told us that it adds

Mega-resort skiing from a quiet base? Check out Vaujany p215.

around 25% to its fall-line piste lengths, to allow for your turns. The Schrahe report, discussed in our piste extent feature, puts the total at 176km, which points to an addition of more like 40%.

The slopes divide into four sectors, with good connections between them.

The biggest sector is directly above the village, on the slopes of **Pic Blanc**. The huge two-stage Grandes Rousses gondola – aka the DMC (a reference to its technology) and marked on the piste map just as 'first stage' and 'second stage' – goes from the top of the village. The first stage to 2100m is now duplicated by a state-of-the-art chondola (3,900 people an hour).

Above the DMC, a cable car goes up to 3330m on Pic Blanc itself – the top of the small Sarenne glacier and start of the longest piste in the Alps (read our feature panel). The glacier is also reached via the Marmottes six-pack, then a two-stage gondola (the first stage of which also serves lower runs from Clocher de Macle).

The alternative from Pic Blanc is to take a 300m tunnel through the ridge to the front face, where a west-facing black mogul field awaits you.

The epic Sarenne black run ends in a gorge that separates the main resort area from **Signal de l'Homme**. It is crossed by a down-and-up fast chairlift from the Bergers part of the village. From the top you can take excellent north-facing slopes towards the gorge, or head south to Auris or west to tiny Chatelard/La Garde.

On the other side of town from Signal de l'Homme is the small **Signal** sector, which is reached by draglifts next to the main gondola or by a couple of chairs lower down. Runs go down the other side of the hill to Villard-Reculas. One blue run back to Alpe-d'Huez is floodlit twice a week.

The **Vaujany-Oz** sector consists largely of north-west-facing slopes, reached from Alpe-d'Huez via red runs. (There is blue-run access too if you are prepared to do a short stretch of easy red.) At the heart of this sector is L'Alpette, the mid-station of the cable car from Vaujany; it can also be reached by a gondola from Oz. Beyond L'Alpette, the slopes around Montfrais are blue, with the notable exception of

the shady black La Fare, which plunges down to L'Enversin, just below Vaujany. The descent from Pic Blanc to L'Enversin is 2230m vertical – the second biggest in the world (beaten, as it happens, by near-neighbour Les Deux-Alpes). The links back to Alpe-

d'Huez are by cable car from L'Alpette, or a second gondola from Oz. You can also reach Oz from the mid-station of the DMC at 2100m, down an excellent red with blue variant most of the way.

FAST LIFTS ★★★★☆
Pretty efficient overall

Gondolas and fast chairs are the main access lifts and serve most areas adequately – and this year the new chondola going the full length of the main nursery area replaces no less than five old draglifts. But there are still some old chairs and draglifts.

QUEUES ★★★★☆
Mainly at village level

We have considered cutting our rating to ★★★ after a couple of years of rising complaints, but two of the main

Excellent varied runs on the home slopes of Vaujany

Giant two-stage cable car can shift the entire population of Vaujany in about 90 minutes

Dôme des Petites Rousses 2800m

Pic

Lac-Blanc

2700m

Montfrais

L'Alpette 2050m

Alpette-Rousses

Chalet du Lac Besson

2100m

La Villette-Montfrais

Vaujany-Alpette

Alpette

VAUJANY/OZ

Marmotte

Vaujany 1250m

Oz Station 1350m

Poutran I & II

Jeux

DMC I & II

Oz-en-Oisans

L' Enversin d'Oz 1100m/3,610ft

SIGNAL 2115m

Rifnel

Romains

Alpe-d'Huez
1860m/
6,100ft

Les Bergers

Le Villarais

Above the village, what must be the world's biggest expanse of genuinely green beginner slopes

Televillage

Huez 1500m

Villard-Reculas 1500m

🚡 gondola
🚠 cable car
🚡 chondola
⬤ fast chairlift
Slow chairs & drags have no symbol

troublespots will be relieved this season by the lengthening of the Romains chair from Les Bergers so that it reaches mid-mountain (relieving pressure on the Marmottes I chair) and the replacement of the Jeux drags by a state-of-the-art chair in parallel with the DMC gondola. Even with these improvements, though, we suspect ski school start periods will need to be avoided, morning and afternoon. The village bucket-lift is said to generate lengthy queues first thing. There can also be waits for the cable car up to Pic Blanc.

Over much of the area a greater problem than lift queues is that some pistes can be unbearably crowded. The Chamois and Couloir runs from the top of the DMC gondola are among the most crowded we've seen, anywhere,

Mega-resort skiing from a quiet base? Check out Vaujany p215.

despite the laudable efforts of the lift company to divert skiers coming up the Vaujany cable car on to the Belvedere and excellent Bartavelles runs. Crowds can also make life miserable on the red Rousses to Vaujany and Poutrans to Oz – 'carnage all the way', said one recent reporter.

In contrast, the slopes at Auris are 'lovely and quiet – excellent skiing'.

TERRAIN PARKS ★★★☆☆
Big and varied

A big park stretches almost all the way down the first stage of the DMC. One of our keen 'park rat' reporters says, 'It is definitely the best-placed and

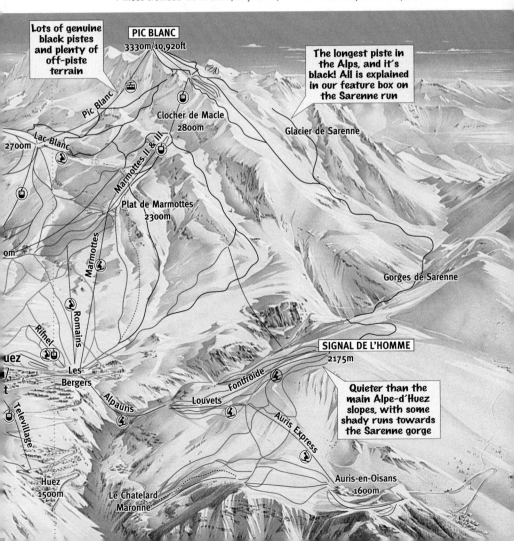

> Lots of genuine black pistes and plenty of off-piste terrain

PIC BLANC
3330m/10,920ft

> The longest piste in the Alps, and it's black! All is explained in our feature box on the Sarenne run

Pic Blanc

Clocher de Macle
2800m

Glacier de Sarenne

Lac Blanc

2700m

Marmottes II & III

Plat de Marmottes
2300m

om

Marmottes

Gorges de Sarenne

Romains

Rifnel

SIGNAL DE L'HOMME
2175m

uez

Les Bergers

Fontfroide

> Quieter than the main Alpe-d'Huez slopes, with some shady runs towards the Sarenne gorge

Alpauris

Louvets

Auris Express

Televillage

Auris-en-Oisans
1600m

Huez
1500m

Le Chatelard
Maronne

It's no surprise that most ski runs that are seriously steep are also seriously short. The really long runs in the Alps tend to be classified blue, or red at the most. The Parsenn runs above Klosters, for example – typically 12km to 15km long – are manageable in your first week on skis. So you could be forgiven for being sceptical about the 'black' Sarenne run from the Pic Blanc: even with an impressive vertical of 2000m, a run 16km long has an average gradient of only 11% – typical of a blue run.

But the Sarenne is a run of two halves. The bottom half is virtually flat (boarders beware), but the top half is a genuine black if you take the direct route – a demanding and highly satisfying run (with stunning views) that any keen, competent and fit skier will enjoy. The steep mogul field near the top can be avoided by taking an easier option (or by using the Marmottes III gondola). The run gets a lot of sun, so snow conditions are highly variable; pick your time with care – there's nothing worse than a sunny run with no sun. Occasionally during the season you can ski the Sarenne by moonlight or wearing a head torch: take the last lift up, have a 'simple meal', then ski down with guides. Last season the cost was 65 euros per person.

possibly the best-designed park I've seen. It has everything from an easy beginner line to enormous jumps and an airbag, with lots of rails too.' Other 2012 reporters praised it as well. There's a half-pipe and 'fast, aggressive' boardercross too. There's also a beginners' park above Vaujany.

SNOW RELIABILITY ★★★★
Affected by the sun
Alpe-d'Huez is unique among major purpose-built resorts in the Alps in having mainly south- or south-west-facing slopes. The strong southern sun can affect piste conditions even in January, and late-season conditions may alternate between slush and ice on most runs. One March 2013 visitor would have liked to have seen some runs closed, so tricky was the ice. There are shady slopes above Vaujany and at Signal de l'Homme. The glacier area is small. Snowmaking is not comprehensive, but is now quite extensive, covering the main runs above Alpe-d'Huez, Vaujany and Oz.

FOR EXPERTS ★★★★
Plenty of blacks and off-piste
There are long and challenging pistes as well as some serious off-piste.

The black slope beneath the Pic Blanc cable car will be on your agenda. Despite improvements to the tunnel exit, the start of the actual slope is often awkward. The slope is of ordinary black steepness, but can be very hard in the mornings because it gets the afternoon sun. Get information on its condition. The long Sarenne run on the back of Pic Blanc is described in the panel above. The black Fare piste to L'Enversin is good – varied, and well away from the lifts

but not steep; it faces west, and relies heavily on artificial snow.

The Marmottes II gondola serves genuine black runs and a red from Clocher de Macle; Balcons is steep and quiet, often with good snow; Clocher de Macle is easier but busier; don't miss the beautiful, long, lonely Combe Charbonnière (but there's a fairly long traverse on moderately steep ground at the start). The Lièvre Blanc chairlift serves further testing slopes – Balme, looping away from the lifts, is a black, and one or two mogully reds would be classified black in many resorts. In good snow conditions, the steep La Fuma run down to Le Chatelard (open as a piste only in good snow) is worth trying. And the Col de Cluy from Signal de l'Homme is long and gets away from all the lifts.

The off-piste possibilities are immense, and some are described in our feature panel. Some of these routes away from the lifts are shady, in contrast to the main slopes.

FOR INTERMEDIATES ★★★★
Fine selection of runs
Good intermediates have a fine selection of runs all over the area. In good snow conditions the variety of runs is difficult to beat.

Every section has some challenging red runs to test the adventurous intermediate. The Canyon run is one of the most challenging. There are lovely long runs down to Oz – the Champclotury blue from the mid-station of the gondola above Oz is a lovely, gentle run and usually quiet – and to Vaujany, with space for some serious carving. The Villard-Reculas and Signal de l'Homme sectors also have long challenging reds. Those at

SNOWPIX.COM / CHRIS GILL

There are excellent slopes above Villard-Reculas – west facing so excessively sunny, but fabulous in the morning after an overnight dump ➔

Signal de L'Homme are quieter, so they keep their snow better. The Chamois red from the top of the gondola down to the mid-station is quite narrow, and miserable when busy and icy and/or heavily mogulled. Fearless intermediates should enjoy the super-long Sarenne black run.

For less ambitious intermediates, there are usually blue alternatives, except on the upper part of the mountain. The main Couloir blue from the top of the big gondola is a lovely run, well served by snowmaking, but like the red Chamois it does get scarily crowded at times.

There are some great cruising runs above Vaujany; but the red runs between Vaujany and Alpe-d'Huez can be too much for early intermediates. You can travel via Oz on gondolas if you are that keen to get around.

Unreliable piste classification (read 'The mountains') can complicate life for early intermediates.

FOR BEGINNERS ★★★★★
Good facilities

The large networks of green runs immediately above the village and above the Les Bergers area form nursery areas as good as you will find anywhere. And these slopes carry a lot of fast through-traffic, despite being declared low-speed zones. In each area two short beginner lifts are free, and a special lift pass covers more lifts to progress to.

FOR BOARDERS ★★★★
Suits the adventurous

The resort suits experienced boarders well – the extent and variety of the

---

Mega-resort skiing from a quiet base? Check out Vaujany p215.

mountains mean that there's a lot of good freeriding to be had; the off-piste is vast and varied and well worth checking out with a guide. The terrain park is good, too. There are quite a few flat areas to beware of though. The nursery slopes are excellent and now have fast chairlifts bottom to top. Planète Surf is the main shop.

FOR CROSS-COUNTRY ★★★
High-level and convenient

There are 50km of trails, with six loops of varying degrees of difficulty, all at around 2000m and consequently relatively snow-sure.

MOUNTAIN RESTAURANTS ★★★★
Some excellent rustic huts

There are more rustic places with table-service than is usual in high French resorts, and almost all readers are impressed – 'it's why we come here' is one emphatic view. But the restaurants in the more obvious positions get over-busy, and some charge for the loos. The piste map does not identify restaurants. The resort's pocket guide covers 15 places, marked on a tiny piste map.

The big news this year is that the unloved Marmottes has been put out of its misery. In its place is a branch of the ever-expanding Folie Douce franchise, complete with dairy-style restaurant La Fruitière. Reports please! **Editors' choice** The cosy little Chalet du Lac Besson (0476 806537) is an oasis of calm – tucked away on the

CHILDCARE

Les Intrépides
t 0476 112161
Ages 3mnth to 4yr

Chalet des Enfants (ESF)
t 0476 803169
From age 2½

Tonton Mayonnaise (Easyski)
t 0476 804277
Ages 2½ to 3½

Ski schools
From 4 to 12

cross-country loops north of the 2100m mid-station of the DMC gondola (and reached by a special access piste, the Boulevard des Lacs). Food and service are excellent. It's repeatedly endorsed by reporters. **Worth knowing about** Immediately above the resort, the best option (apart from the new Fruitière) is Plage des Neiges, at the top of the Babars chair – favourite of several reporters: 'lovely rustic bustling place', 'creamy rich tartiflette', 'very friendly'. We await reports on Signal 2018, the glass-walled, pyramid-shaped place opened last year at Signal; it includes a smooth table-service section. On the back of the hill, the 'cosy' Bergerie above the Villard-Reculas lift base has impressed some readers.

Combe Haute, at the foot of the Chalvet chair towards the end of the Sarenne run, serves 'lovely' food in 'charming, rustic surroundings'. Up on Signal de l'Homme, L'Hermine is 'good value, with cheerful service'. Lower down in the woods on the fringe of this area, the little Forêt de Maronne hotel at Chatelard (aka La Garde) is 'excellent value' with 'charming staff'.

We had a very satisfactory lunch last season at Perce Neige, just below the Oz-Poutran gondola mid-station. It has a wood-burning stove and a 'great snug atmosphere', and does 'terrific salads and a lovely chocolate cake'. Near the Alpette lift station, La Grange pleases readers. Down the hill slightly, Auberge de l'Alpette (aka Chez

Passoud) is an unpretentious place doing good food. Further down, Airelles is a rustic hut built into the rock, with a roaring log fire; we get consistently good reports – 'excellent tartiflette', 'lovely food, friendly staff'.

SCHOOLS AND GUIDES ★★★★
Plenty of choice
Reports on the ESF this year are all positive: 'very happy with the tuition'; 'excellent again'; 'a good well-paced week'. British instructor Stuart Adamson's outfit Masterclass provided 'inspiring tuition' for one 2013 reporter. A 2012 visitor made 'good progress' in boarding lessons with ESI.

FOR FAMILIES ★★★
Positive reports
There's Les Intrépides day care centre for children aged three months to four years. From last season, the ESF is running the Chalets des Enfants for children aged over two and a half years: it combines ski lessons with activities in a new day care centre. Family specialist Esprit operates here (read 'Chalets' in the next section).

STAYING THERE

There's quite a good range of options of all kinds of lodging. There is a Club Med in the Bergers quarter – highly recommended by a 2013 repeat visitor. **Chalets** Skiworld leads the pack with nine chalets including some with hot tub and sauna and one 30-bed

OFF-PISTE FOR ALL STANDARDS

There are vast amounts of off-piste terrain in Alpe-d'Huez, from fairly tame to seriously adventurous. Here we pick out just a few of the many runs to be explored – always with guidance, of course.

*There are lots of off-piste variants on both sides of the Sarenne run that are good for making your first turns off-piste. The **Combe du Loup**, a beautiful south-facing bowl with views over the Meije, has a black-run gradient at the top, and you end up on long, gentle slopes leading back to the Sarenne gorge. **La Chapelle Saint Giraud**, which starts at Signal de l'Homme, includes a series of small, confidence-boosting bowls, interspersed with gentle rolling terrain.*

*For more experienced and adventurous off-piste skiers, the **Grand Sablat** is a classic that runs through a magnificently wild setting on the eastern face of the Massif des Grandes Rousses. This descent of 2000m vertical includes glacial terrain and some steep couloirs. You can either ski down to the village of Clavans, where you can take a pre-booked helicopter or taxi back, or traverse above Clavans back to the Sarenne gorge. In the **Signal** sector, there are various classic routes down towards the village of Huez or to Villard-Reculas.*

*The north-facing Vaujany sector is particularly interesting for experienced off-piste enthusiasts. Route finding can be very tricky, and huge cliffs and rock bands mean this is not a place in which to get lost. From the top of Pic Blanc, a 40-minute hike takes you to Col de la Pyramide at 3250m, the starting point for the classic route **La Pyramide** with a vertical of over 2000m. Once at the bottom of the long and wide Pyramide snowfield, you can link into the Vaujany pistes.*

SCHOOLS

ESF
t 0476 803169

Easyski International
t 0476 804277

Masterclass
t 0679 673456

Stance
t 0680 755572

Classes (ESF prices)
6 days (3hr am and
2½hr pm) €230

Private lessons
€45 for 1hr, for 1 or 2
people

GUIDES

Mountain guide office
t 0476 804255

ACTIVITIES

Indoor Sports centre
(tennis, gym, squash,
aerobics, swimming,
shooting range,
climbing wall,
adventure trail),
sauna, cinemas,
concerts, theatre,
library, museum

Outdoor Ice rink,
curling, cleared
walking paths,
tobogganing, dog
sledding,
snowshoeing,
snowmobiling,
microlight flights,
sightseeing flights, ice
cave, skijoring, off-
road vehicle tours,
hang-gliding,
paragliding, ice-
driving school, snow
kiting

Phone numbers
From abroad use the
prefix +33 and omit
the initial '0' of the
phone number

TOURIST OFFICE

www.alpedhuez.com

property. Crystal has a central 34-bed chalet hotel plus four chalets ('Basic en-suite rooms, but good food and attentive staff,' says a 2013 visitor to one of them). Ski Total has five chalets, most with sauna and one with outdoor hot tub. Inghams has two chalets (one with outdoor hot tub, one with sauna) plus a 70-bed chalet hotel ('excellent staff, good natured, good little bar'). The VIP chalets near the main lifts are also 'excellent'. Family specialist Esprit has a 60-bed chalet hotel in the old village: 'Childcare top-notch, location perfect; staff were troopers,' said a 2012 reporter.

Hotels There are more than in most high French resorts – mainly 3-star.

****Alpenrose (0427 042804) New in 2011. On the fringe of Les Bergers – 'possible to ski back, but a hike up to Marmottes I', says a reporter.

****Au Chamois d'Or (0476 803132) Good facilities, modern rooms, one of the best restaurants in town and well placed for the main gondola.

***Pic Blanc (0476 114242) Across the car park from the lifts at Les Bergers. Comfortable; on a recent visit we stayed in a big ('superior') room.

***Royal Ours Blanc (0476 803550) Heart of the village; pool, sauna, steam, hot tub. 'Good food, nice staff,' said a 2012 reporter.

Apartments There are lots available, though few are notable. Among the smartest are those in CGH's residence Cristal de l'Alpe with pool, hot tubs, fitness stuff etc, and a prime central location. The Pierre & Vacances residence Ours Blanc is 'newly refurbished to a high standard', but is not ideally located. Ski Collection offers these properties. One of Skiworld's chalets is available on a 'flexible catering' basis. The supermarket at Les Bergers is reported to be the best in town.

EATING OUT ★★★★
Good value
Alpe-d'Huez has dozens of restaurants, some of high quality; many offer good value by ski resort standards.

Widely thought to be about the best is Au P'tit Creux, although we lack recent reports. Readers' recommendations include: Smithy's Tavern ('great place for reasonably priced food' – Tex-Mex) and Au Trappeur ('super pizza'). A reporter who worked his way round the resort rated the set menu at the Grenier

'fantastic value'. Other reader tips include: Alaska ('great pizzas and beer'), Edelweiss ('great Savoyard dishes, tables tight but excellent atmosphere') and Pinocchio pizzeria.

APRES-SKI ★★★★
Plenty going on
The idea is that you now end your afternoon dancing on the tables at the new Folie Douce. (Please don't do it unless the terrace is packed – it looks really sad.) In the village there's a wide range of bars, some of which get fairly lively later on. There are several British-run bars in chalet hotels. One is the Underground under the Chamois hotel in Vieil Alpe – 'open mike nights and live music'. Smithy's Tavern is 'great fun, lots of dancing around – gets very hot'. Other places tipped by reporters include O'Bar ('beer really cheap') and the Etalon ('nice chilled-out bar run by friendly staff'). There are reportedly three late-night places: the Sporting (pricey though – '10 euros for a beer'), the Igloo ('fun') and the Caves de l'Alpe. Les Bergers 'was completely dead', says a reporter.

OFF THE SLOPES ★★★★
Good by high-resort standards
There is a wide range of facilities, praised by recent non-skiers, including a big and very popular indoor-outdoor pool ('warm, with friendly staff'), an Olympic-size ice rink – plus an indoor pool and a splendid sports centre. Note that a six-day-plus lift pass now gets you only one free visit to each of these activities (it used to give unlimited access). There's also an ice-driving school and a toboggan run, and you can try paragliding and snowmobiling. A visit to the Ice Cave at the top of the DMC gondola is highly recommended by reporters. Shopping is not impressive. The helicopter excursion to Les Deux-Alpes is exciting. There are 35km of well-marked local walkers' trails (map available); the lifts 'cope well with pedestrians', and there's a special lift pass. The better mountain restaurants are widely spread, so meetings with skiing friends may not work well. There are 'good' weekly organ concerts in the 'interesting church', and there's a museum.

Stylish chalets and serious skiing? Check out p258.

LINKED RESORT – 1500m

VILLARD-RECULAS

Villard-Reculas is a tiny unspoilt village just over the hill (Signal) from Alpe-d'Huez, and set on a small shelf between open snowfields above and tree-filled hillsides below. A fast quad takes you up to Signal from V-R, but the return lifts are slow.

V-R is the tiniest resort we have stayed in: one restaurant, one shop-cum-restaurant, one 2-star hotel (currently out of action), two sports shops. If you don't like ski resorts, this is just the place. On the other hand, a reporter this year calls it 'the most boring resort I have been to'.

Although the village is small, its chalets are spread widely, and practically everyone needs transport to the lifts. There is a shuttle-bus 'with a friendly driver', but 'it's a tight squeeze and a jump when getting off'.

Accommodation is mainly self-catering, booked either through the tourist office or La Source – an English-run agency. We were impressed by the little apartment we stayed in last season, owned by the community.

La Source also runs an eponymous catered chalet – a carefully converted stone building with a lovely, spacious, vaulted living room at the bottom opening on to a terrace (complete with hot tub) giving knockout views. It is warmly furnished with armchairs and sofas, and a wood-burning stove. Food is excellent, and there's a minibus to the lifts. We have had several good reports from readers, too.

The local slopes have something for everyone. For beginners, it may seem near-ideal, with several lifts serving green runs at village level. Sadly, these runs are mostly of blue gradient; a reporter this year who agrees with that assessment also points out that they get icy (from afternoon sun). The blue runs in both directions from Signal are also not entirely easy, especially when icy. So V-R is less than ideal for novices. For confident intermediates, it's fine. And there is challenging skiing on and off the Forêt black piste from Signal. The tiny branch of the ESF gave one 2013 visitor 'good' lessons.

LINKED RESORT – 1350m

OZ-EN-OISANS STATION

The small purpose-built ski station above the old village of the same name has been built in an attractive style, with much use of wood and stone, and has nursery slopes, skating rink, bars, restaurants, supermarket and two mid-range hotels. The pool in the Villages Club du Soleil is open to all. But nightlife is quiet.

The slopes above Oz are about the best in the area when snow is falling. Two gondolas whisk you out of the resort: one goes to L'Alpette, above Vaujany; the other goes in two stages to the mid-station of the DMC above Alpe-d'Huez.

The smart Chalet des Neiges apartments have a pool, sauna, fitness area, bar and restaurant. Available via Peak Retreats, Lagrange and Erna Low.

Phone numbers
From abroad use the prefix +33 and omit the initial '0' of the phone number

TOURIST OFFICES

Villard-Reculas
www.villard-reculas.com

Oz-en-Oisans
www.oz-en-oisans.com

Auris-en-Oisans
www.auris-en-oisans.com

Vaujany
www.vaujany.com

LINKED RESORT – 1250m

VAUJANY

Vaujany is a quiet, rapidly growing village, perched on a sunny hillside opposite its own sector of the domain. Hydroelectricity riches have financed huge investment in infrastructure.

A giant 160-person two-stage cable car whisks you up into the heart of the Alpe-d'Huez lift system. Alternatively, a two-stage gondola takes you less dramatically to the local slopes at Montfrais via a mid-station below the tiny hamlet of La Villette.

As you enter the village, you come to a couple of small, simple hotels. The Rissiou is well run by British tour operator Ski Peak: 'Friendly communal atmosphere, good food but also some single rooms and independence when you want it.' Ski Peak also has half a dozen luxurious catered chalets in Vaujany and La Villette plus nine 5-star apartments. It runs a minibus service for guests. Peak Retreats (no relation) has a wide choice of apartments.

Once past the Rissiou, you come to a recently built complex around a small pedestrian square, Place Centre Village, with spacious, mid-range apartments built in traditional style. There's a good ski shop, restaurants, food shops, a cafe/bar and a cavernous underground car park – and an escalator down to the nearby cable car and gondola stations. An elevator takes you further down the hill to the 'extraordinarily large' sports centre with a pool with a big slide, and a new ice rink and bowling alley.

An impressive enclosed escalator goes up the hillside past chalets and farm buildings to the top of the village, where sizeable apartment buildings are grouped around the Place de la Fare – a small car-free zone with a small supermarket, a food shop, a couple of bars and a couple of restaurants. Since most of the visitor beds are up here, it is naturally the focus of evening activity.

There are no slopes leading directly to the village. But there is a 'pulse' gondola up from L'Enversin, below the village, where the Fare black run finishes (a great run and not steep – read 'For experts' earlier in this chapter), or you can take a blue to the mid-station of the Montfrais gondola and ride down the lower stage.

Beginner children are taken to a gentle roped-off area at the top of the gondola and adult beginners to the nursery slope at Alpette, the cable car mid-station. There's a self-service restaurant with sunny terrace right by the children's learning area. The children's ski school has been praised ('well organized by a local Brit'), as has the nursery ('as good as it gets, good English spoken, not expensive').

LINKED RESORT – 1600m

AURIS-EN-OISANS

Auris-en-Oisans is another small, purpose-built ski station – a series of wood-clad, chalet-style apartment blocks with a few shops, bars and restaurants set just above the treeline. Quite appealing to families.

SNOWPIX.COM / CHRIS GILL

Les Arcs

Three first-generation purpose-built villages plus a couple of attractive alternatives set among varied and extensive slopes

RATINGS

The mountains
Extent	★★★
Fast lifts	★★★★
Queues	★★★
Terrain p'ks	★★★★
Snow	★★★★
Expert	★★★★★
Intermediate	★★★★
Beginner	★★★
Boarder	★★★★
X-country	★★
Restaurants	★★★
Schools	★★★★
Families	★★★★

The resort
Charm	★★
Convenience	★★★★
Scenery	★★★
Eating out	★★★
Après-ski	★★
Off-slope	★

RPI   105
lift pass	£220
ski hire	£120
lessons	£85
food & drink	£135
total	**£560**

KEY FACTS
Resort	1600-2120m
	5,250-6,960ft
Slopes	1200-3225m
	3,940-10,580ft
Lifts	51
Pistes	200km
	124 miles
Green	1%
Blue	50%
Red	32%
Black	17%
Snowmaking	
	333 guns

Paradiski area	
Slopes	1200-3250m
	3,940-10,660ft
Lifts	141
Pistes	425km
	264 miles
Green	5%
Blue	52%
Red	28%
Black	15%
Snowmaking	
	793 guns

+ Varied slopes – on and off-piste
+ Lots of genuinely challenging skiing
+ Some excellent woodland runs
+ Car-free, mainly convenient villages, including cute 1950
+ Some quiet alternative bases
+ Fast cable car link to La Plagne

− Original village centres lack charm, and aren't the most convenient
− Fairly quiet nightlife
− Lots of flat linking runs
− Accommodation in high villages is nearly all in apartments

We've always liked Les Arcs' slopes: they offer long descents, plenty of steep stuff, plenty to keep intermediates happy plus woods to head to in a storm. And for those who really like to travel on skis, the link to La Plagne takes the extent into the Trois Vallées league.

We've never been keen on the functional main villages. We're aware that their various architectural styles are highly regarded by some; we're not among them, but our real objection is to their dreary, depressing mall-style shopping centres. Newer Arc 1950 is something else: a resort that's not only more pleasant to inhabit than the others, but also very conveniently arranged. And Peisey-Vallandry is a quiet, attractive and convenient base for exploring the La Plagne ski area as well.

THE RESORT

Les Arcs is made up of four modern resort units, all purpose-built, traffic-free and apartment-dominated.

Arcs 1600 and 1800 stand a couple of km apart, roughly at the treeline on a broad, steepish mountainside overlooking the town of Bourg-St-Maurice (covered at the end of this chapter). Both consist mainly of large apartment blocks sitting below their slopes, with some development beside the slopes. 1600 was the first Arc, built at the top of a funicular up from Bourg. 1800 is much the largest Arc.

Arc 2000 is quite separate – on the far side of the mountain ridge, at the bottom of a high, treeless bowl. It consists of half a dozen huge, linked apartment blocks, plus more recently built chalet-style blocks. Just below Arc 2000 and linked to it by a short gondola, the newish mini-village of Arc 1950 is built in traditional style – read the margin panel later in the chapter.

The numbers in the village names relate only loosely to their altitudes. 'Arc 2000' was dreamt up in the 60s to evoke the millennium – the future; its altitude is actually over 2100m.

At the southern end of the area is Peisey-Vallandry, from where a cable car links with La Plagne, covered by the Paradiski passes. Even from Arc 1950 you can be at the cable car in 20 minutes. At the northern end of the ski area, at much lower altitude, is the rustic hamlet of Villaroger. These

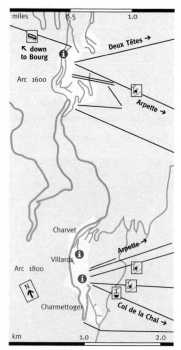

2013/14: A new
4-star hotel at 1800,
the Chalets de
l'Aiguille Grive, is due
to open.

2012/13: The second
phase of the smart
new Edenarc
development above
1800 opened.

OT LES ARCS / S LEON

Arc 1600 was the first
to be built and
opened in 1968. It can
be reached by road or
by funicular from
Bourg-St-Maurice ↓

outlying villages are described at the
end of the chapter.

Day trips by car to Val d'Isère–
Tignes are possible. La Rosière and
Ste-Foy-Tarentaise are closer. Be
warned: you have to pay for parking
at Arcs 1950 and 2000 – the only free
parking is throughout 1600 and before
the entrance to 1800.

VILLAGE CHARM ★★★★★
Head for 1950

Reporters repeatedly comment on the
friendliness of the locals.

The apartment blocks of Arcs 1600
and 1800 are low-rise, and not hugely
intrusive when seen from the slopes.
Arc 1600 is set in the trees and has a
friendly, small-scale atmosphere.
Bigger Arc 1800 has three main parts.
Le Charvet and Les Villards are
focused on small shopping centres,
mostly open-air but still seeming
claustrophobic. Big apartment blocks
run across and down the mountain.
Charmettoger has apartment blocks,
too, but also smaller, wood-clad
buildings. Le Charvet has spread up
the hill in recent years, and now has
an identifiable suburb, Le Chantel. At
the very top, the new Edenarc
development has opened.

Arc 2000 consists of futuristic large
blocks with swooping roof lines, plus
some large chalet-style blocks.

Arc 1950 has been designed to be
cute; its smaller apartment buildings
have been finished in traditional style,
and they are clustered around a
pleasant, traffic-free square and street
– quite lively at close of play.

CONVENIENCE ★★★★★
Generally very good

Arcs 1600 and 1800 offer some very
convenient lodgings, a few yards from
the lifts, but also some that are less
convenient than they look – you can
walk miles within the apartment
buildings to get to (and from) the
snow. The central area in Arc 1600 is
good for families: uncrowded,
compact, and set on even ground. Arc
1800 is more spread out, and some
lodging is further up the hill, well
above the village itself. The main lifts
depart from Les Villards. A 2013 visitor
found 'the 1600/1800 buses run to a
pretty strict timetable, and are
generally efficient, linking with the
funicular etc'.

Arc 2000 and Arc 1950 are compact,
ski-in/ski-out places, with lifts starting
below them as well as above. But
getting around Arc 2000 on foot can
be quite an effort and we've had
reports of antiquated elevators out of
action frequently. All the bits of Arc
1950 we've looked at are genuinely
ski-in/ski-out. You park directly under
the apartment buildings, which is a
rare bonus at the start and end of
your stay.

SCENERY ★★★★★
Attractively varied

Arcs 1600 and 1800, and the slopes,
enjoy views across the valley to Mont
Blanc. The lower villages enjoy good
views along the Nancroix valley and to
La Plagne's splendid north face of
Bellecôte. Higher up, Arc 2000 and Arc
1950 sit beneath the Aiguille Rouge,
high-point of the slopes – great views
from the top.

Les Arcs

THE MOUNTAINS

Les Arcs' terrain is notably varied; it has a good mixture of high, open, snow-sure slopes and lower woodland runs (notably above Peisey-Vallandry).

EXTENT OF THE SLOPES ★★★
Well planned and varied

Our rating relates to just the Les Arcs area; the whole Paradiski area easily scores five stars.

Arc 1600 and Arc 1800 share a west-facing mountainside laced with runs down to one or other village. At the southern end is an area of woodland runs above Peisey-Vallandry.

From various points on the ridge above 1600 and 1800 you can head down into the wide Arc 2000 bowl. From there, lifts take you to the high points of the area, the Aiguille Rouge and the Grand Col. As well as a variety of steep runs back to Arc 2000, the Aiguille Rouge is the start of an epic run (over 2000m vertical and 7km

long) down to the tiny unspoiled village of Villaroger.

The resort identifies nine black runs and one red as Natur' (never groomed) – not popular with reporters (see 'Snow reliability'). On the lower half of the Aiguille Rouge is a speed-skiing run, sometimes open to the public.

On Thursdays outside high season the First Tracks scheme (10 euros) allows you up the mountain an hour early to have breakfast and ski deserted pistes.

FAST LIFTS ★★★★
Generally good

Each of the four main villages and Peisey-Vallandry have fast chair or gondola access to the slopes. The main irritants now are the three successive chairs up from Villaroger and the two chairs up in different directions from Pré-St-Esprit.

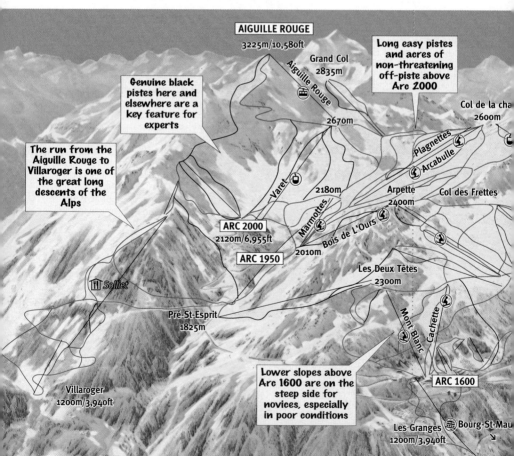

AIGUILLE ROUGE
3225m/10,58oft

Grand Col
2835m

Aiguille Rouge

2670m

Long easy pistes
and acres of
non-threatening
off-piste above
Arc 2000

Col de la cha
2600m

Genuine black
pistes here and
elsewhere are a
key feature for
experts

Plagnettes

Arcabulle

The run from the
Aiguille Rouge to
Villaroger is one of
the great long
descents of the
Alps

Varet

2180m

Arpette
2400m

Col des Frettes

Marmottes

Bois de L'Ours

ARC 2000
2120m/6,955ft

2010m

ARC 1950

Les Deux Têtes
2300m

Solliet

Mont Blanc

Cachette

Pré-St-Esprit
1825m

Villaroger
1200m/3,940ft

Lower slopes above
Arc 1600 are on the
steep side for
novices, especially
in poor conditions

ARC 1600

Les Granges
1200m/3,940ft

Bourg-St-Mau

QUEUES ★★★☆☆
Not without problems

Queues aren't generally an issue in low season, and peak-time queues are improving. But the lifts above Arc 2000 present problems, especially on sunny days. The Varet gondola to the shoulder of the Aiguille Rouge is always busy but shifts its queue quickly because it has lifties pulling people out of the queue to fill the cabins – excellent. Queues for the cable car to the top can be serious in clear weather ('40 minutes at noon in March' said a 2013 report); it dates from 1981, holds only 70 people and desperately needs replacing. The Arcabulle chair has the potential for 'five-to-ten-minute waits'. At 1800 the Transarc gondola is queue prone, especially late in the day. At Plan-Peisey, morning queues for the Peisey chair (and for the Derby above it) are not unknown, partly because of

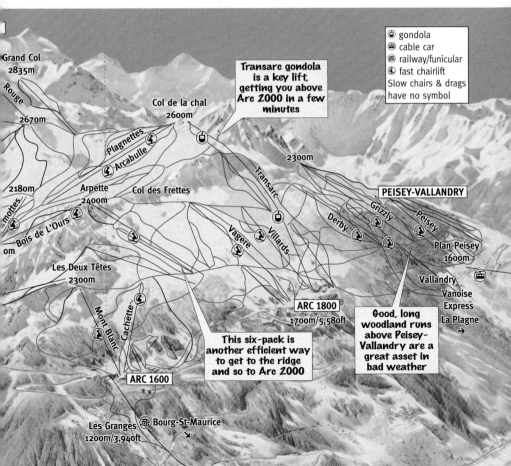

○ gondola
⊕ cable car
⊜ railway/funicular
Ⓕ fast chairlift
Slow chairs & drags
have no symbol

Grand Col 2835m
Rouge
2670m
Plagnettes
Arcabulle
Col de la chal 2600m

Transarc gondola is a key lift, getting you above Arc 2000 in a few minutes

2300m
Transarc

PEISEY-VALLANDRY

Grizzly
Derby
Peisey

Plan-Peisey 1600m

2180m
Arpette 2400m
Col des Frettes
mottes
Bois de L'Ours
om

Vagere
Villards

Les Deux Têtes 2300m

Vallandry
Vanoise Express
La Plagne →

Mont Blanc
Cachette

ARC 1800
1700m/5,580ft

This six-pack is another efficient way to get to the ridge and so to Arc 2000

Good, long woodland runs above Peisey-Vallandry are a great asset in bad weather

ARC 1600

Les Granges 1200m/3,940ft
Bourg-St-Maurice

LIFT PASSES

Les Arcs / Peisey-Vallandry

Prices in €

Age	1-day	6-day
under 14	35	167
14 to 64	46	223
65 plus	35	167

Free Under 6
Beginner Points card for one lift in each of Arcs 1600/1800/2000
Senior 72 plus: 1-15 days €7
Notes Les Arcs areas; half-day pass; family reductions; one-day Paradiski extension

Paradiski Découverte

Prices in €

Age	6-day
under 14	186
14 to 64	247
65 plus	186

Free Under 6
Beginner No deals
Notes Les Arcs areas with one day in Paradiski

Paradiski Unlimited

Prices in €

Age	1-day	6-day
under 14	39	197
14 to 64	51	263
65 plus	39	197

Free Under 6
Beginner No deals
Senior 72 plus: 1-15 days €10
Notes Les Arcs areas and La Plagne areas; family reductions; with 5+ passes one day in Three Valleys and Espace Killy, and reduced rate in Ste-Foy, La Rosière and La Thuile

arrivals on the Vanoise Express from La Plagne; and a March 2013 reporter waited 25 minutes for the Vanoise Express itself.

At peak periods dangerously crowded pistes can be a problem.

TERRAIN PARKS ★★★★
One excellent park
The Apocalypse Parc is between Arcs 1600 and 1800, and is served by a snowboarder-friendly J-bar lift. For years, this has been one of the most advanced parks in the Alps – on a par with the main park at Avoriaz. Three kicker lines are in place for all levels. There is a good rail and box line, a big wall ride, a spine jump and a large gap jump, plus towards the end of the season a water jump is introduced – variety and fun for all.

There are boardercross runs below Col de la Chal and above Plan-Peisey.

SNOW RELIABILITY ★★★★
Good – plenty of high runs
A high percentage of the runs are above 2000m, and when necessary you can stay high by using lifts that start around that altitude. Most of the slopes face roughly west, which is not ideal. Those from the Col de la Chal and the long runs down to Villaroger are north-facing, and the blacks on the Aiguille Rouge are shady enough to keep their snow well. Snowmaking is limited.

Grooming is generally good but most reporters think the Natur' runs should be groomed sometimes and say they are often deserted due to their condition.

FOR EXPERTS ★★★★★
Challenges on- and off-piste
Les Arcs has a lot to offer experts – at least when the high lifts are open (the Aiguille Rouge cable car, in particular, is often shut in bad weather).

Most black runs are now Natur' runs, become huge mogul fields and are often deserted – a huge shame. The lack of many groomed blacks means that the steeper groomed reds can get very busy. One of the quieter reds (and one of our favourites) is the lower part of the epic Aiguille Rouge–Villaroger run, which has remarkably varying terrain – the start is a narrow black shelf, which can be awkward (but this can be avoided by taking the Lanchettes chair from Arc 2000).

There is also a great deal of off-piste potential. There are steep pitches on the front face of the Aiguille Rouge and secluded runs on the back side, towards Villaroger. A short climb to the Grand Col accesses several routes, including a quite serious couloir and an easier option. From Col de la Chal there is an easy route down towards Nancroix. The wooded slopes above 1600 are another attractive possibility and there are open slopes beside the pistes all over the place.

FOR INTERMEDIATES ★★★★
Plenty for all abilities
One strength of the area is that most main routes have easy and more difficult alternatives, making it good for mixed-ability groups. An exception is the solitary Comborcière black from Les Deux Têtes down to Pré-St-Esprit, which has no nearby alternatives. This long mogul-field justifies its classification and can be great fun for strong intermediates. Malgovert, from the same point towards Arc 1600, is a red Natur' piste and is tricky – it is narrow, as well as mogulled.

The woodland runs at either end of the domain, above Peisey-Vallandry and Villaroger, and the bumpy Cachette red down to 1600, also include some challenges. We especially like the Peisey-Vallandry area: its well-groomed, tree-lined runs have a very

Arc 1950, just below Arc 2000, is a self-contained mini-resort that was built in the last decade. It is high and relatively snow-sure, traffic-free (you park under your apartment building) and laid out very conveniently, with genuinely ski-in/ski-out lodgings. It is attractively built, with wood and stone chalet-style buildings grouped around a central square and street.

The accommodation is in apartments, spacious and well furnished by French standards – a reporter notes the Radisson is 'particularly spacious, with saunas and outdoor pools'.

There are just enough restaurants to get you through a week, such as Hemingway's ('very good meat'), plus a reasonable choice of après-ski bars, a tiny but well-stocked supermarket, a bakery, a gift shop, a crêperie, ski school and ski and board equipment shops.

friendly feel and are remarkably uncrowded much of the time, allowing great fast cruising. Good intermediates can enjoy the run to Villaroger.

The lower half of the mountainside above 1600/1800 is great for mixed-ability groups, with a choice of routes through the trees. The red runs from Arpette and Col des Frettes towards 1800 are quite steep but usually well groomed (except Clair Blanc).

Cautious intermediates have plenty of blue cruising terrain. Many of the runs around 2000 are rather bland and prone to overcrowding. Edelweiss is more interesting, with a short red alternative, and takes you to Arc 1950 from Col des Frettes. The blues above 1800 are attractive but also crowded. A blue favourite of ours is Renard, high above Vallandry – usually with excellent snow.

And, of course, you have the whole of La Plagne's slopes to explore.

FOR BEGINNERS ★★★
No long greens
There are 'ski tranquille' beginner zones at each of the three main Arcs, and up the hill on the treeline above Vallandry and Plan-Peisey. Around 10 of the beginner lifts are free to use (in 1800, 2000 and Villaroger – but not 1600, strangely). A chairlift in Peisey-Vallandry is free at weekends as are additional chairs in 1600, 1800 and 2000 – you can buy a points card to use them during the week. Sadly, the resort does not use the valuable green run classification common to most other French resorts. In all sectors there are long, wide blue runs to move on to, and some are gentle enough to be green – eg Forêt down to Vallandry.

FOR BOARDERS ★★★★
A pioneering place
Ever since 1983 when Regis Rolland introduced the sport in the cult film Apocalypse Snow, Les Arcs has been a hot spot for snowboarders. It offers excellent freeriding, including steeps, gullies, trees, natural jibs and hits. And there are plenty of wide-open rolling slopes for intermediates and beginners too, especially at Vallandry and 1800. The terrain park is great and is served by a snowboarder-friendly draglift. Most other lifts are chairs and gondolas. But beware of some long flat areas – especially at Arc 2000 and some linking blue runs (you may find it easier to take the wider reds).

FOR CROSS-COUNTRY ★★
Very boring locally
Short trails, mostly on roads, is all you can expect, but the pretty Nancroix valley's 40km of pleasant trails are accessible by free bus.

MOUNTAIN RESTAURANTS ★★★
OK if you choose the right place
Editors' choice Solliet (0668 960407) above Villaroger is a charming woody chalet with a warm ambience, table- or self-service and great views from the terrace. We've had excellent lunches here and readers agree ('staff were friendly and welcoming, and the food was excellent, if only all the restaurants were as good!'; 'long been one of my favourites').
Worth knowing about Chalets de l'Arc, just above Arc 2000, is a rustic place built in wood and stone. We were great fans in its early days, but standards slipped for a while. Recent reports suggest it's back on song: 'excellent', 'service getting a bit friendlier', 'excellent plat du jour'.

The busy Cordée, just above Plan-Peisey, was endorsed again in 2013: 'top notch food and service' and 'good value set menus'. The Crèche at Col de la Chal has been tipped in the past but this year was found to be 'a disappointment – quite expensive for a self-service'.

The little Blanche Murée below the Transarc mid-station is a simple table-service place in a chalet-style setting and highly praised as the 'best value' and for serving 'wild boar with gratin dauphinois – yum!'. The Arpette, above 1800, has table- and self-service sections and a 2013 reporter enjoyed 'a fab special burger' but complained of slow service. The Enfants Terribles above Peisey serves 'fantastic buckets of hot chocolate' and is 'a wonderful restaurant to hide away in during overcast days – great furs and pictures of polar bears'. The tiny Bulle hut, near the Arcabulle chair above 2000, is 'a good student place for pizza etc', says a 2013 visitor.

The other good options are not very mountainous. At Pré-St-Esprit below Arc 2000, the 500-year-old Belliou la Fumée is set beside a car park; but it is charmingly rustic, and we've had good meals here – 'it's not

Hot chalets beneath glacial slopes? Check out p258.

SCHOOLS

ESF Arc 1600
t 0479 074309

ESF Arc 1800
t 0479 074031

ESF Arc 1950 & 2000
t 0479 074752

Arc Aventures 1800
t 0479 076000

Evolution 2 Arc 2000
t 0479 078553

New Generation
t 0479 010318
0844 770 4733 (UK)
www.skinewgen.com

Privilège Arc 1800
t 0479 072338

Spirit 1950
t 0479 042572

Classes (ESF prices)
6 3hr-days €162

Private lessons
From €40 for 1hr

GUIDES

Bureau des Guides
t 0479 077119

as expensive as you would expect for the quality', found a 2013 visitor. Over the years we and reporters have enjoyed excellent meals at the Ferme at Villaroger. If you want a top-notch meal and don't mind returning to 1600, go to Chalet de l'Arcelle (see 'Eating out').

SCHOOLS AND GUIDES ★★★★
Several, including a Brit school
British school New Generation is consistently recommended: 'Worth every cent – excellent instructor who was good at analysing our skiing and suggested improvements that really made a difference'; 'Fourth year we have used them for private lessons, outstanding each time'. A 2013 visitor was thrilled with the ESF lessons (booked through tour op Esprit) for her son: 'The instructor made it both fun and instructive, and we were delighted with his ability when we skied with him.' But an Arc 2000 ESF instructor had 'poor English'. Arc Aventures (International school – ESI) has been noted as 'good value' for an off-piste guide, while Spirit in 1950 has been tipped for 'friendly teachers and not too big groups'.

FOR FAMILIES ★★★★
Convenient choices
Les Arcs is a good choice for families wanting convenience. There is a children's area at 1800, complete with moving carpets, tobogganing and a climbing wall. There are also a couple of discovery pistes, at 1800 and 1600, for children to find out about flora and fauna of the Alps. The Club Mini Arc 1800 facilities have received favourable reports. Arc 1950 is particularly family-friendly – Spirit 1950 there reportedly provides good care for smaller children, returning them well fed and rested. Comments on kids' ski classes have been positive. The Garderie in 2000 'impressed' last year – 'the two girls loved it'.

Family specialist tour op Esprit has ten chalets in Arc 2000 and six in Peisey-Vallandry (see end of chapter).

STAYING THERE

Most resort beds are in apartments. There is a long-established Club Med presence in Arc 2000 and there's a smarter one at Peisey-Vallandry.
Chalets There are lots of catered chalets in the Peisey-Vallandry area – covered at the end of this chapter. There are also lots of chalet-apartments in smart résidences with pools in Arc 2000 – operators include Ski Total, Inghams, Crystal, Skiworld and family specialist Esprit. Skiworld also has a couple of proper individual chalets above 1800.
Hotels The choice of hotels in Les Arcs is gradually widening but reports are not very positive, so we've dropped a couple of recommendations this year.
★★★★Mercure (1800) (0479 076500) Previously the Grand Paradiso. 80 comfortable rooms and suites, sauna.
★★★Arcadien (1600) (0479 041600) 'Very reasonable, rooms relatively big.'
★★★Cachette (1600) (0479 077050) Recommended, but expect lots of kids – 1600's childcare facilities are here. 'Spotlessly clean, helpful staff, very good food, themed evenings.'
Apartments Beware – there are still plenty of unbearably cramped apartments in the older resort units. But there are now lots of good, modern apartments available, including the brand new Edenarc development above Arc 1800, and several residences at Arc 1950. You'll find lots via companies such as Erna Low, Lagrange, Pierre & Vacances, Ski

CHILDCARE

La Cachette (1600)
t 0479 077050
Ages 4mnth to 12yr
Club mini (1800)
t 0479 074031
Ages 3 to 8
Le Cariboo (1950)
t 0479 070557
Ages 9mnth to 3yr
Garderie 2000
t 0479 076425
Ages 18mnth to 6yr

Ski school
Generally from age 3

OT LES ARCS

Arc 1950 is the newest Arc 'village' and its traditional-style architecture is a huge contrast with the original purpose-built 'villages' ↓

Collection, Ski Amis, Crystal, Ski Independence, Skiworld and Skitracer. In Arc 2000 the Chalet des Neiges, Chalet Altitude and Cimes des Arcs have above-average apartments. The Alpages de Chantel above Arc 1800 (a Pierre & Vacances premium property) is attractive and comfortable, with pools, saunas and gyms. It is very convenient for skiing, but a bit isolated. The Roc Belle Face development in central Arc 1600, built in tiers down the hillside, is a Lagrange Prestige property. The Ruitor apartments, set between Charmettoger and Villards (in 1800), are 'excellent'.

EATING OUT ★★★☆☆
Mostly uninspiring

An ad-based (therefore not comprehensive) guide is given away locally. The choice is generally uninspiring. One of the best places is Chalet de l'Arcelle on the fringe of Arc 1600; it has a warm, quirky wood-and-stone interior and a mouth-watering carte – 'near Michelin one-star quality' said a recent reporter. Also in 1600, the Cairn is 'wood-panelled, with prompt, friendly service' and serves Italian as well as Savoyard dishes.

Arc 1800 has about 15 restaurants but as a regular visitor with an apartment there says, 'they are pretty similar and won't excite anyone'.

In Arc 2000, Chez Eux is our reporters' favourite: 'warm woody interior, friendly staff, excellent roast pork, delicious pizzas'.

Arc 1950 has a reasonable choice for a small place but gets very busy. La Table des Lys ('excellent food, super wines') and Chalet de Luigi ('good selection of pastas') have been recommended. Hemingway's started a new tapas and all-you-can-eat buffet menu last season.

APRES-SKI ★★☆☆☆
Arc 1800 is the place to be

Nightlife is not lively and mainly revolves around the bars. 1800 is the liveliest; some places have regular live music. The cosy Etranger is 'the place to go' and is popular with instructors says a Les Arcs regular. Chez Boubou at Charvet is more British and shows Premiership football matches. The Golf hotel's jazz bar is 'the place to go for an early evening drink'. The J.O. bar is open until the early hours and has a friendly atmosphere. Reporters like the friendly Red Hot Saloon for bar games.

Although it's quieter, there are several options in 1600. The Abreuvoir, with live music and pool, is one reporter's 'favourite ski resort bar' with frequent live bands and pool tables. In Arc 2000 the Whistler's Dream and Crazy Fox 'were the only busy bars but full of boozed-up Brits', says a 2013 reporter. At 1950, O'Chaud was a recent reporter's bar of choice, 'and a favourite with the Russian oligarchs, judging by the number of champagne bottles drunk'.

Les Arcs

ACTIVITIES

Indoor Squash (1800), saunas, solaria, multi-gym (1800), museums, cinemas, bowling (1800, 2000)

Outdoor Ice rinks (1800, 2000), dog sledding, cleared paths, tobogganing, snowshoeing, paragliding, horse riding, skijoring, snowmobiling, ice grotto

GETTING THERE

Air Geneva 160km/100 miles (3hr); Lyon 215km/135 miles (3hr); Chambéry 130km/80 miles (2hr)

Rail Bourg-St-Maurice; frequent buses and direct funicular to resort

OFF THE SLOPES ★☆☆☆☆
Very limited

Les Arcs is not the place for an off-the-slopes holiday, however several of the newer apartment blocks have pools, and there are spa facilities at Arc 1950. There's bowling at 1800 and skating at 1800 and 2000. The cinemas have English films weekly. You can visit the Beaufort cheese dairy and go shopping in Bourg-St-Maurice, and there are walks.

LINKED RESORT – 1600m

PEISEY-VALLANDRY

Plan-Peisey and Vallandry are small ski stations built in a traditional chalet style above the old village of Peisey, which has a bucket-lift up to Plan-Peisey. They sell themselves as Peisey-Vallandry, but the local cluster of villages, including one called Nancroix, is collectively known as Peisey-Nancroix. So that's clear then, eh?

Both resorts have good nursery slopes high up the hill on the tree-line, reached by chairlift. Of course, this means paying to get up there.

The cable car to La Plagne starts from **Plan-Peisey** – one hotel, a few shops, bars and restaurants but no real focus other than the lift station. A six-pack takes you to the local slopes.

UK operator Ski Amis has a 'premium service' chalet here with a hot tub (it also has several self-catered chalets and apartments here). Family specialist operator Esprit has six neat chalets, each with outdoor hot tub and sauna or steam room – 'brilliant location, very comfortable', said a 2013 reporter. The hotel Vanoise (0479 079219) has a good location, a pool and a fitness room: 'Staff were very friendly despite our appalling French, and the food was much better than expected,' says a recent visitor. The Arollaie is a smart apartment development, with a small pool, hot tub, sauna and steam room – available through Peak Retreats.

Of the restaurants, we'd head down to the Ancolie at Nancroix – a fabulous traditional auberge with welcoming hosts and excellent food. (Be aware that taxi drivers may rip you off for the short journey if you're not careful.) Of the local places, reporters like the Vache ('small and friendly, English run') and Chez Felix ('super food, popular with locals'). The Solan is nicely rustic and was recommended in the past, but a 2013 reporter had a bad experience there – more reports please, Après-ski is very quiet, but a 2013 visitor liked L'Armoise in Peisey ('a quiet little French bar') and Au

---

Phone numbers
From abroad use the prefix +33 and omit the initial '0' of the phone number

Planté du bâton in Plan-Peisey ('a great fun quiz night and happy hour').

There is lodging down the hill in the characterful old village of Peisey, complete with fine baroque church. The other, mostly old, buildings include a few shops and a couple of bars and restaurants – a reader enjoyed the Ormelune. UK tour operator Mountain Heaven has a renovated old farm building run as a catered chalet with six en-suite rooms; there are three more in an annex, plus a sauna. A 2013 reader stayed at The Goat Shed, a 'simple but welcoming' catered chalet on the outskirts of Peisey run by a British couple, with minibus service to and from the slopes.

Vallandry is a few hundred metres away from Plan-Peisey and linked by shuttle-bus. A fast quad takes you into the slopes. There are lots of chalets and a small pedestrian-only square at the foot of the slopes with a small supermarket and a ski shop.

Ski Olympic's big piste-side chalet hotel La Forêt has 'outstanding food, good rooms, fabulous views, friendly and helpful staff'. Orée des Cimes is a luxury apartment development right by the Grizzly chairlift and with a pool, saunas, steam rooms, hot tubs and massages. Orée des Neiges is another luxury apartment development with free use of the Cimes' pool etc, 1.3km away. Both developments are available through Peak Retreats, Ski Collection and Ski Independence.

There are several restaurants. The Calèche does 'large portions of Savoyard classics'. The Mont Blanc bar has 'friendly staff', a 'good atmosphere' and table football, and is one of the cheaper options for lunch.

LINKED RESORT – 1200m
VILLAROGER

Villaroger is a charming, quiet, rustic little hamlet with three successive slow chairlifts going up to a point above Arc 2000; its slopes are not suitable for beginners. It has a couple of small bar-restaurants.

DOWN-VALLEY RESORT – 850m
BOURG-ST-MAURICE

With a funicular railway link to Arc 1600, Bourg-St-Maurice is marketed as part of Les Arcs, and does make a viable cheaper alternative to staying on the hill. But it is very different – not a ski resort, but a real valley town, with proper everyday shops and sizeable supermarkets. It is at the end of the TGV railway line, and therefore is very appealing to rail travellers.

The funicular station is a walkable distance from the TGV platforms, but a drive or bus ride from most parts of Bourg. The advertised travel time is seven minutes, but that's for non-stop services, which in our experience are rare. In practice, staying in Bourg rather than Les Arcs costs you an hour a day in extra travelling time.

The plus side, of course, is that everything from accommodation to beer is cheaper. Depending on the time of the season and the exact comparison you make, you can rent an apartment for 30% to 60% less than the cost of a similar apartment on the hill. If you plan to ski Les Arcs (and La Plagne), you need to balance the cost savings against that lost hour a day.

But if you fancy a bit more variety, the appeal of Bourg-St-Maurice becomes clear. We spent a week here a few years back and had a fab time skiing a different resort every day, from La Plagne to Val d'Isère. The more remote resorts are best accessed by car, though there are buses. But you can easily ski La Rosière (and linked La Thuile in Italy) by taking a bus to the chairlift above Séez, which goes up into the slopes of La Rosière.

Built several seasons ago, the Coeur d'Or apartments with pool, hot tub, sauna and steam are available through Peak Retreats, Ski Collection and Ski Independence. Close to the two major supermarkets, they are a walk from the town but a drive (or free shuttle-bus ride) from the funicular.

A reporter has recommended the hotel Angival (0479 072797), centrally set in a quiet back street, and the Petite Auberge (0479 070586), on the outskirts and run by an English couple.

There are some good, unpretentious restaurants. The Refuge in the main street was recommended this year by a reliable reporter: 'Delicious, great service, always packed – reservation essential.' We've had excellent meals at the Tsabio (also in the main street) and the Arssiban (just outside the centre). Bar Martin (which doubles as a fishing tackle shop) was recommended for a pre-dinner beer this year.

Avoriaz

Arguably the definitive purpose-built resort: conveniently arranged, usually snowy, uncompromisingly traffic-free

RATINGS

The mountains

Extent	★★★★★
Fast lifts	★★★★
Queues	★★★
Terrain p'ks	★★★★★
Snow	★★★
Expert	★★★
Intermediate	★★★★
Beginner	★★★★
Boarder	★★★★★
X-country	★★★
Restaurants	★★★★
Schools	★★★
Families	★★★★

The resort

Charm	★★
Convenience	★★★★★
Scenery	★★★
Eating out	★★★
Après-ski	★★★
Off-slope	★

RPI	105
lift pass	£200
ski hire	£120
lessons	£70
food & drink	£150
total	**£540**

KEY FACTS

Resort	1800m
	5,910ft

Portes du Soleil	
Slopes	950-2275m
	3,120-7,460ft
Lifts	195
Pistes	650km
	404 miles
Green	12%
Blue	43%
Red	36%
Black	9%
Snowmaking	
	900 guns

Avoriaz only	
Slopes	1100-2275m
	3,610-7,460ft
Lifts	34
Pistes	75km
	47 miles
Green	10%
Blue	51%
Red	27%
Black	12%

226

➕ Good position on the Portes du Soleil circuit, and good local slopes

➕ Very successful design – car-free, with ski-in/ski-out lodgings

➕ Good children's facilities

➕ Snow generally good and sometimes superb, but ...

➖ Low altitudes and exposure to westerlies means some risk of poor snow lower down, and rain

➖ Architecture doesn't suit everyone

➖ Lacks a slick bag-delivery system

➖ Can get very crowded at weekends

➖ Hardly any hotels

Of the many purpose-built resorts thrown up in France in the 1960s, Avoriaz is probably the best designed. From most points of view, it works. One particularly neat trick is that the resort is sunny but most of the local slopes are shady.

Avoriaz missed out on the smart apartment developments that transformed French self-catering a decade ago, but it has recently more than caught up, with some fabulous new places. Now, how about a few more hotels?

THE RESORT

Avoriaz is a purpose-built resort perched on a sloping shelf above a dramatic high cliff a few km from lower, long-established Morzine.

It is entirely free of wheeled traffic; cars are left in paid-for parks at the edge of the village – book a space underground to avoid a chaotic departure if it snows. ('It's well worth the 10 euros,' says a 2013 visitor.)

Avoriaz is on the main lift circuit of the Portes du Soleil – for an overview, look at our separate chapter. It has links to Châtel in one direction and to Champéry in Switzerland, in the other. It is linked by gondola (but not by piste) to Morzine, which shares a separate area of slopes with Les Gets. All four of these linked resorts get their own chapters, and are covered by the Portes du Soleil pass.

The hamlets of Ardent and Les Prodains are on the fringes of the Avoriaz ski area with lifts into it. Both are described in this chapter. Car trips to Flaine and Chamonix are possible.

VILLAGE CHARM ★★★★★
One of the best modern places
The village is all angular, dark, wood-clad, high-rise buildings – almost all apartments. It's not what you would call charming, but it is at least designed coherently. What's more, the snow-covered paths and pistes give the place a friendly Alpine feel, and both we and reporters have enjoyed the ambience, both day and night.

Family-friendly events are laid on all season. A floodlit cliff behind the resort adds to its nocturnal charm. The lifties have been noted as friendly.

CONVENIENCE ★★★★★
Ready to drag that bag?
As our scale plan suggests, it's a compact place (turn to the Chamonix chapter for a stark contrast). While you are resident, it all works well. Mostly, you can ski from close to the door, and no door is more than 500m from the central shops and bars. Although the upper part of the village is set on a steep slope, escalators and elevators (not entirely reliable) inside the buildings help you get around.

But arrival day and (particularly) departure day are something else.

If you are staying in the new Amara development, you can park your car in the basement (assuming you can face the charges). And if you are staying in the Falaise quarter, near the reception building, you can drag your luggage to your apartment on a borrowed sled.

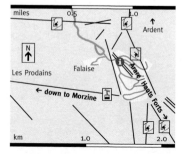

NEWS

2012/13: The Prodains cable car from Morzine has been replaced by a gondola. A new aquatic centre – the Aquariaz – opened in July 2012, with pools, water slides, river rapids, a climbing wall above a plunge pool, outdoor hot tub and lots of tropical plants and trees. The second phase of the Amara apartments opened, as well as the Atria-Crozats residence. Two new restaurants, the 66 and Grand Café, and a new bar, the Lodge, opened.

JOHN SCOTT

Avoriaz wakes up; this early morning shot looks south-west across the reception building and the Falaise quarter to the slopes of Morzine ↓

If you are staying elsewhere, it isn't so simple. Compact though it is, lodgings are up to 800m from the drop-off point, which is a long way to drag your bags, especially if you hit deep, soft snow as we did last winter. So you are probably going to need a ride on a snowcat or a horse-drawn sleigh, for which demand can exceed supply, particularly on departure day.

SCENERY ★★★☆☆
Cliff-top panorama

The village is high, and its position on a sunny balcony gives good views down across Morzine. From the high points there are great views of the Dents Blanches and the Dents du Midi.

THE MOUNTAINS

The slopes closest to Avoriaz are bleak and treeless, but fairly snow-sure.

Five runs – a blue, two reds and two blacks – are called 'snowcross' runs. We understand these are signed, patrolled and avalanche controlled but ungroomed. This is an appealing idea. But the concept of red and blue runs that are never groomed is unique to Avoriaz, and the maps distributed in other PdS resorts show these runs as ordinary pistes. We have reports of people expecting a defined, prepared piste, and finding themselves on a wide, ill-defined mogul field instead.

Another interesting innovation is

Fine chalets in a fun French village? Check out p258.

that the Avoriaz slopes are divided into four sectors – beginner, family, forest and expert. With most of the snowcross runs falling in the family sector, we're not sure this works.

The local piste map is admirably clear, and has a tolerable map of the whole Portes du Soleil on the back.

EXTENT OF THE SLOPES ★★★★★
360° choice

The village has lifts and pistes fanning out in all directions. Facing the village are the slopes of **Arare-Hauts Forts**, and when snow is good, there are long, steep runs to Les Prodains, way below the resort, where a big new gondola brings you back. To the left, lifts go off to the **Chavanette** sector on the Swiss border – a broad, undulating bowl. At the border is the infamous Swiss Wall – now an itinéraire. It's a long, steep mogul slope with a tricky start, but not the terror it is cracked up to be unless it's icy. You can ride the chair down. At the bottom is the open, gentle terrain of Champéry.

From the ridge behind Avoriaz you can descend into the prettily wooded **Lindarets-Brocheaux** valley, from where lifts go over to Châtel's Linga sector or up to Pointe de Mossettes, another way into Switzerland.

FAST LIFTS ★★★★
Good system here and at Linga

In the Avoriaz sector the lifts are impressively modern. And on the nearby Linga slopes, on the way to Châtel, you'll again be mainly riding fast lifts. But beyond Châtel, and in the opposite direction beyond Champéry, skiing the Portes du Soleil circuit is like stepping back 20 years. Maybe 30.

QUEUES ★★★
Still some problems

One long-standing problem – the queue to get up from Les Prodains, below the resort, when snow attracts crowds from Morzine – was tackled last season by the replacement of the old cable car by a big gondola (and we mean big: cabins with 35 seats). But high-season reports in 2013 – as in earlier years – speak of queues for the chairlifts from Les Lindarets (the valley between Avoriaz and Châtel) back to Avoriaz. You may also meet congestion on the runs down to Les Lindarets in the morning, especially when deep snow slows everyone down. Peak-time crowds on the pistes around the village can be hazardous, too; one reporter found the concentration of kids during French holidays 'just foul'.

TERRAIN PARKS ★★★★★
Still leading the way

Avoriaz built the first terrain park in France, in 1993. It is still leading the way, and there are five parks and a super-pipe, all 'very well' maintained. Check www.snowparkavoriaz.com for details. Park lift passes are available.

The expert park is at Arare, and the kicker and rail lines are superbly designed and shaped. It also has an airbag jump – 'the most fun I had all trip', says a recent visitor. Beginners and intermediates should head to La Chapelle – a 500m-long park littered with jumps of all sizes and fun little boxes and rails. Parkway is great for beginners and kids. It has mini-jumps and ride-on boxes, with traffic lights for safety. The Stash, in the Lindarets valley, is a great innovation imported from California – routes cut through the forest, and wooden and natural elements bringing all-mountain riding and freestyle together; great fun. The fifth park is the Lil'Stash – a mini version for younger kids. Just above the village is a good super-pipe. And there's a boardercross too.

SNOW RELIABILITY ★★★
High resort, low slopes

Although Avoriaz itself is high, its slopes don't go much higher – and some parts of the Portes du Soleil circuit are much lower. But it has a good snow record; last season it got the most in the Alps – a staggering 11.8m (that's 465in, for comparison with places like Utah). And considering their altitude, the north-west-facing slopes below Hauts Forts and Chavanette hold snow well – much better than over the border on the sunnier Swiss slopes. But when snow is sparse, the smooth, grassy slopes of lower Morzine–Les Gets can deliver better conditions than the rocky ones around Avoriaz.

FOR EXPERTS ★★★
Several challenging runs

Tough terrain is scattered about. The challenging runs down from Hauts Forts to Les Prodains (including a World Cup downhill) are excellent. There is a tough red and several long, truly black runs, including one of the 'snowcross' runs we've talked about. Snow conditions on the lower runs can be poor, but there is snowmaking. The Swiss Wall at Chavanette will naturally be on your agenda, and Châtel's Linga

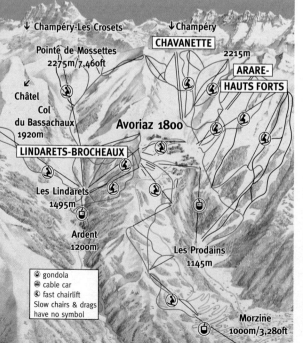

↓ Champéry-Les Crosets   ↓ Champéry

Pointe de Mossettes   **CHAVANETTE**
2275m/7,46oft   2215m

↙   **ARARE-**
Châtel   **HAUTS FORTS**
Col
du Bassachaux   **Avoriaz 1800**
1920m

LINDARETS-BROCHEAUX

Les Lindarets
1495m

Ardent
1200m

Les Prodains
1145m

⊙ gondola
⊜ cable car
④ fast chairlift
Slow chairs & drags
have no symbol

Morzine
1000m/3,28oft

LIFT PASSES

Portes du Soleil

Prices in €

Age	1-day	6-day
under 16	34	169
16 to 19	41	203
20 to 64	45	225
65 plus	41	203

Free Under 5
Beginner Special pass
€24 a day
Notes Family
discounts; 5hr pass
Alternative pass
Avoriaz only

GETTING THERE

Air Geneva 90km/
55 miles (2hr); Lyon
215km/135 miles
(3hr30)

Rail Cluses (42km/
26 miles) or Thonon
(45km/28 miles); bus
and cable car to
resort

ACTIVITIES

Indoor Altiform fitness
centre (sauna, gym,
hot tub), Aquariaz fun
swimming pool,
squash, cinema,
bowling
Outdoor Ice rink, dog
sledding,
tobogganing,
mountain biking on
snow, ice diving,
walking, snowshoeing,
ski jöring, paragliding,
snowmobiling, sleigh
rides, helicopter
flights, segway,
'yooner' tobogganing,
caving

UK PACKAGES

Alpine Answers, Club
Med, Crystal, Erna Low,
Independent Ski Links,
Inghams, Interactive
Resorts, Lagrange,
Neilson, Pierre &
Vacances, PowderBeds,
Powder White, Rude
Chalets, Ski Collection,
Ski France, Ski
Independence, Ski
Solutions, Ski Total,
Skitracer, Skiweekends.
com, STC, Thomson,
White Roc, Zenith
Ardent Family Ski
Company

sector is well worth a trip. The black
runs off the Swiss side of Mossettes
and Pointe de l'Au are worth trying,
and one reporter had a 'very good'
day here off-piste with a guide.

FOR INTERMEDIATES ★★★★
Virtually the whole area
Although some sections lack variety,
the Portes du Soleil circuit through
Châtel, Morgins and Champéry is
excellent for all grades of
intermediates, provided snow is in
good supply on the lower slopes.
Timid types not worried about pretty
surroundings need not leave the
Avoriaz sector: there are quiet and
scenic blues to Les Prodains and the
Arare and Chavanette sectors are
gentle, spacious, above-the-treeline
bowls. The Lindarets area is also easy,
with pretty runs through the trees, but
there are some long flat sections.
   Further afield, Champoussin has a
lot of easy runs, reached without too
much difficulty via Les Crosets and
Pointe de l'Au. Better intermediates
have virtually the whole area at their
disposal. The runs down to Pré-la-Joux
and L'Essert on the way to Châtel, and
those either side of Morgins, are
particularly attractive – as are the long
runs down to Grand-Paradis near
Champéry when snow conditions
allow. Pointe de Mossettes offers a
less challenging route to Switzerland
than the Swiss Wall itinéraire at
Chavanette.

FOR BEGINNERS ★★★★
Convenient, but you pay
The nursery slopes seem small in
relation to the size of the resort, but
appear to cope. The slopes are sunny,
yet good for snow, and link well to
longer, easy runs. Our reservations are
that the pistes can be busy, and that
there are no free lifts. Why not?

FOR BOARDERS ★★★★★
Plenty to keep you busy all week
Avoriaz is great for expert riders. As
well as state-of-the-art 'conventional'
parks, there's The Stash. For safe
freeriding after a dump, head for the
'snowcross' runs. For something more
extreme, the long cliff band accessed
from the Arare lift is perfect for cliff
drops of all sizes. It is well worth
hiring a guide to exploit the off-piste
riding. There are some flat sections,
especially in the Lindarets valley but
very few draglifts, making this a good
choice for novices too.

FOR CROSS-COUNTRY ★★★★★
Varied, with some blacks
There are 45km of trails, mainly
between Avoriaz and Super-Morzine,
plus Lindarets and Montriond.

MOUNTAIN RESTAURANTS ★★★★
Good choice over the hill
There are some good places, marked
but not named on the piste map.
Editors' choice The hamlet of Les
Lindarets in the next valley consists of
countless rustic restaurants – it is a
popular tourist spot in summer. On a
good day it's difficult to beat the
terrace of the, er, Terrasse (0450
741617) – a recent reporter agrees
('fine cooking, friendly efficient
service'). We've enjoyed the jolly
Crémaillière (0450 741168) too, but
new reports would be welcome.
Worth knowing about A 2012 reporter
raves about Les Alpages, just above
Les Lindarets – 'ate there at least three
times – huge and tasty steak with
pepper sauce; such friendly service'. In
the same area are the 'friendly'
Barmettes with 'tasty crêpes and
friendly service' and Mamo's Café –
'very good soup', 'delicious crêpe
forestière'. On the Super-Morzine
slopes, we can confirm that L'Passage
is 'cosy, friendly, with great service'.

SCHOOLS

ESF
t 0450 740565

Evolution 2
t 0450 740218

Alpine (AASS)
t 0450 383491

Classes (ESF prices)
6 (4.75hr) days €185

Private lessons
From €42 for 1hr, for
1 or 2 people

CHILDCARE

Les P'tits Loups
t 0450 740038
3mnth to 5yr

Children's Village Annie Famose
t 0450 740446
From age 3

Ski schools
Ages 4 to 12

Phone numbers
From abroad use the
prefix +33 and omit
the initial '0' of the
phone number

TOURIST OFFICE

www.avoriaz.com

SCHOOLS AND GUIDES ★★★☆☆
Positive reports

We lack new reports on group lessons, but a 2012 visitor has often booked the ESF for three days of 'great' private off-piste lessons. One visitor had 'inspirational' snowboard lessons with former pro Angélique Corrèze-Hubert through Evolution 2. The Avoriaz Alpine Ski School has British instructors and has been highly recommended.

FOR FAMILIES ★★★★☆
Very appealing

With snow everywhere and not a wheeled vehicle to be seen, Avoriaz has obvious appeal. Then there's the Village des Enfants, which takes children from age three. Its facilities are excellent. Check out Ardent.

STAYING THERE

Alternatives to apartments are few.
Chalets Inghams has a chalet for 12. Ski Total has four neighbouring chalets including Marie in its Platinum range. All are ski-in/ski-out. For family-oriented places, check out Ardent.
Hotels There is not much choice.
★★★Dromonts (0450 740811) Owned by a celebrity chef and in the *Hip Hotels* guidebook. Reports welcome.
Apartments Pierre & Vacances' smart new Amara development is an exciting addition, and the obvious place to stay if your budget will cope. It's almost a self-contained mini-resort, with its own shops, restaurants, spa, pool and underground parking (80 euros a week). The main lobby has a spacious lounge/bar, and a big terrace with great views. The apartments are stylish, and spacious by French standards. You can ski from the door to the Proclou fast chair. The Atria Crozats apartments are not quite in the same league, but are smartly furnished. For convenience, you might prefer the 'very comfortable' Saskia Falaise apartments, 'nicely renovated in Alpine wood style.' Agencies such as Ski Collection, Inghams, PowderBeds and Crystal offer these residences.

EATING OUT ★★★☆☆
A few interesting options

There about 25 restaurants, offering adequate variety; but demand can exceed supply. We had an excellent dinner last season at the Alpine-cool Bistro – good menu, excellent braised veal; live jazz sax when we were there. The Table du Marché in hotel Dromonts is ambitious and pricey. The cute, cosy old Chalet d'Avoriaz (aka Chez Lenvers) pleased one reporter this year: 'Excellent omelette, nice staff, good value.' A couple of bars are worth noting: Chapka ('great tapas'), Tavaillon ('the best burgers in town') and Intrêts ('well-priced steak').

APRES-SKI ★★★☆☆
The bars are fun

A few bars have a good atmosphere, particularly in happy hour. There's DJ-fuelled action on the terrace of the Chalet d'Avoriaz at close of play. Other top tips are Tavaillon for sports TV ('very popular, spectacular cocktail of the day') and Shooters. Chapka is a hip bar with TV, live music and pool ('nice atmosphere'). For late-night dance action, the Place has bands.

OFF THE SLOPES ★☆☆☆☆
Not much at the resort

There's not a lot to keep non-skiers interested – few shops, and pedestrians are not allowed to ride the chairlifts. The big news last year was the smart new Aquariaz – a big leisure pool complex with lush vegetation from Cambodia, and all sorts of features to amuse children, in particular. We've only toured it, but a reporter who got immersed rates it 'excellent'. The Altiform fitness centre has steam, saunas and hot tubs. A recent reporter enjoyed bowling.

LINKED RESORT – 1200m
ARDENT

Ardent is a very quiet little place at the foot of the gondola up to Les Lindarets. It has the basics of life, including a bar and a ski shop. It seems ideal for families, and the Family Ski Company has eight chalets here, none more than a short stroll from the gondola station.

LINKED RESORT – 1145m
LES PRODAINS

Les Prodains is at the foot of the cliffs on which Avoriaz sits, with a big new gondola up the cliffs. There are some chalets and small hotels. The 3-star **Lans** (0450 790090) is a traditional family-run place, 300m from the lift – 'simple rooms, exceptional food, helpful patronne, good value'.

Les Carroz

A friendly family resort that makes a more compelling base than Flaine (or Samoëns) for the impressive Grand Massif area

TOP 10 RATINGS

Extent	★★★★☆
Fast lifts	★★★☆☆
Queues	★★★☆☆
Snow	★★★☆☆
Expert	★★★★☆
Intermediate	★★★★★
Beginner	★★★★☆
Charm	★★★★☆
Convenience	★★★☆☆
Scenery	★★★★☆

RPI   95

lift pass	£190
ski hire	£100
lessons	£65
food & drink	£135
total	**£490**

NEWS

2013/14: A new spa/sports centre with outdoor pool will open.

KEY FACTS

Resort	1120m
	3,670ft

Grand Massif ski area (Les Carroz and all linked resorts)	
Slopes	700-2480m
	2,300-8,140ft
Lifts	68
Pistes	265km
	165 miles
Green	11%
Blue	46%
Red	33%
Black	10%
Snowmaking	
	218 guns

Massif ski area (excluding Flaine)	
Slopes	700-2120m
	2,300-6,700ft
Lifts	45
Pistes	125km
	78 miles

Great views of the Chaîne des Aravis from the slopes directly above Les Carroz →

Grand Massif area highlights

+ Part of the big, varied Grand Massif
+ Pleasant, traditional village in a lovely balcony setting
+ Wooded slopes good in a storm

- Still lots of slow old chairlifts
- Village and local slopes are at modest altitudes
- Nightlife not a highlight

You pass through Les Carroz on the drive up to Flaine. You're welcome to carry on up, if you like; these days, we prefer to pull off at the lower village. Not only is it a much more pleasant place to spend time, it also makes more sense as a skiing base. In bad weather, you can ski the local slopes; when the sun comes out you can head off to more exposed slopes elsewhere in the Grand Massif.

THE RESORT

Les Carroz is a traditional village that has spread widely across a sunny, wooded shelf. It claims an altitude of 1200m, but only the top fringes of the village are that high – the centre is at about 1120m. It is linked to Morillon, Samoëns and Flaine; the latter two get their own chapters.

Village charm Les Carroz has the lived-in feel of a real village, where life revolves around the neat central square, with its small shops, cafes and restaurants. Traffic on the through-road to Flaine intrudes only at weekends.

Convenience Your lodgings may be some distance from the gondola or from the centre, or both; there are free ski-buses on five lines; you may find you need to use a timetable, though.

Scenery There are good views from the upper village, and the partly wooded valleys between here and Flaine are very scenic.

THE MOUNTAINS

The slopes directly above the village are densely wooded, but there are lots of open slopes towards Flaine. Some blue runs involved in the trip to Flaine have tricky steep sections.

Slopes Read the Flaine chapter for news on the extent of the Grand Massif pistes. The village gondola rises 600m, serving blue runs and launching you towards the other linked resorts.

Fast lifts Outside the Flaine bowl, there are lots of slow chairs – Tête des Saix has a spectacular gathering of five of them. Investment is needed.

Queues In high season the gondola may have 15-minute morning queues; and you can expect delays and crowded pistes on the way to Flaine – and very crowded runs on the way back at the end of the day. Read the Flaine chapter for more pointers.

Terrain parks The nearest is in Flaine.

Snow reliability The Les Carroz runs are west-facing and low, and can suffer from strong afternoon sun; but a few runs have snowmaking. The slopes of Morillon and Samoëns are north-facing, and the latter are a bit higher, too – so snow keeps better.

Experts There are some proper black pistes above Samoëns and in the next-door Molliets valley, but the main interest is the extensive off-piste in various sectors, including the Molliets and Vernant valleys between Les Carroz and Flaine. Don't miss Flaine's Combe de Gers.

PISTE MAP

Les Carroz is covered on the Flaine map

UK PACKAGES

360 Sun and Ski, AmeriCan Ski, Crystal Finest, Erna Low, Lagrange, Peak Retreats, Pierre & Vacances, Powder White, PowderBeds, Ski France, Ski Independence, Skiology.co.uk, STC, Zenith

Phone numbers
From abroad use the prefix +33 and omit the initial '0' of the phone number

TOURIST OFFICE

www.lescarroz.com

Intermediates As our ★★★★★ rating suggests, this is a great area, whether you like a challenge or not. Most people can get around the whole area, although there are some tricky blues to contend with.

Beginners Pretty good: the village nursery slopes may be excessively sunny, but there are also green and easy blue runs at the top of the gondola. There are excellent longer blue runs to progress to.

Snowboarding Some of the linking runs at altitude are almost flat. But there are few draglifts to deal with.

Cross-country There are extensive tracks between Morillon and Les Carroz, some quite challenging.

Mountain restaurants They are marked but not named on the resort piste map. Read the Flaine and Samoëns chapters too. The 'lovely rustic' Chalet les Molliets at the bottom of the Molliets chair is well liked. 2013 visitors liked the food (and the loos) at the Anfionne on the Plein Soleil home run. Above Morillon, we've had an excellent plat du jour at the rustic Igloo – 'busy, but efficient and friendly', 'awesome salads'. Reporters continue to rate Chalet d'Clair – 'good vibe, cosy, wide menu, great burgers', 'best hot chocolate ever'.

Schools and guides There is regular praise for the ESF: 'The best we've encountered,' says a 2013 visitor. And recent visitors praise the ESI: 'Kids enjoyed it and progressed well.'

Families Pick lodgings near the lifts, would be our advice. The ESF runs a kindergarten for infants, and the Loupiots club offers off-slope activities for children aged 3 to 12.

STAYING THERE

Hotels There are half a dozen hotels, including two at the top of the village, beside the Timalets red home run (with a link to the gondola). Servages d'Armelle (0450 900162) is a lovely little 4-star, housed in two old chalets. The nearby Milkhotel (0617 777023) has been highly recommended: 'friendly staff', 'good set menu'.

Apartments Les Chalets de Jouvence is an excellent CGH low-rise residence in an ideal location next to the Telecarroz draglift (for access to the gondola); we had a very spacious apartment here last season; readers were impressed too – 'lovely pool'. Les Fermes du Soleil is a similar Pierre & Vacances Premium residence with pool, hot tubs etc, close to the centre. Both are available through Peak Retreats.

Eating out Best in town is Aux Petits Oignons, a cosy place run by a charming couple; we had excellent meals here in 2012 and 2013. The very appealing Bistrot-Grill du Gron was booked out when we visited, but is 'a carnivore delight'. Hotel les Airelles has a cosy restaurant. Other reader tips are Spatule, Piccolo and Agora.

Après-ski On the slopes, the Anfionne is a good spot for a quiet beer on the way home. In the village there is some animation at close of play. The Marlow pub has 'a bit of a buzz'; Cave 59 is a wine bar; Pointe Noire and Carpe Diem are other options.

Off the slopes Outdoors there's ice skating, snowshoeing, dog sledding and skijoring. There's a cinema. A new sports/spa centre with outdoor pool is expected to open for next winter.

Chamonix

HQ of French and arguably European mountaineering, with a magnetic attraction for tourists and off-piste thrill seekers alike

RATINGS

The mountains

Extent	★★★
Fast lifts	★★★
Queues	★★
Terrain p'ks	★★★
Snow	★★★★
Expert	★★★★★
Intermediate	★★
Beginner	★★
Boarder	★★★
X-country	★★★
Restaurants	★★
Schools	★★★★★
Families	★★

The resort

Charm	★★★★
Convenience	★
Scenery	★★★★★
Eating out	★★★★★
Après-ski	★★★★
Off-slope	★★★★★

RPI — 110

lift pass	£200
ski hire	£110
lessons	£110
food & drink	£145
total	**£565**

NEWS

2013/14: A new 4-star hotel, the Heliopic, is due to open at the foot of the Aiguille du Midi cable car.

2012/13: The 4-star Mont-Blanc hotel was refurbished and reopened as a 5-star. At Balme, a new mountain restaurant opened, the Ecuries de Charamillon. The Mont Blanc wing of the Aiguille du Midi top station has been renovated and fitted with panoramic windows. At Les Houches, new signposting has been installed on the slopes and a new toboggan run and boardercross built. Snowmaking was installed on the Col de Voz red.

+ A lot of very tough terrain, especially off-piste

+ Amazing cable car to the Aiguille du Midi, for the famous Vallée Blanche

+ Stunning views wherever you are

+ Other resorts covered on extended lift pass, notably sunny Courmayeur

+ Town steeped in Alpine tradition

+ Lots of affordable hotels – and many will take short bookings

− Several separate mountains, widely separated; bad for mixed abilities

− Inadequate bus services

− Bad weather can shut the best runs

− Still some old lifts, and serious queues in key spots

− It's a busy town, with lots of road traffic; not a relaxing place

− Shady and cold in midwinter

Chamonix could not be more different from the archetypal high-altitude, purpose-built French resort. It hasn't been designed to deliver the smoothest possible experience to the widest possible market. It hasn't been designed. You don't have to be an expert to enjoy the place – Editor Gill once took his blue-run-skiing wife and novice kids for a week here, and lived to tell the tale. But it is the expert and the adventurous would-be expert who really must give Chamonix a permanent place on their shortlist, despite its serious drawbacks.

THE RESORT

Chamonix is a long-established, year-round tourist town that spreads for miles along the valley in the shadow of Mont Blanc.

On either side of the centre, just within walking distance, are base stations of the cable car to the Aiguille du Midi (for the famous Vallée Blanche glacier run) and a gondola to Le Brévent. A third high-altitude area, La Flégère, is reached by cable car from the nearby village of Les Praz. There are then three other major ski areas.

At the top of the valley are the villages of Le Tour, at the foot of the Balme slopes (with an alternative base at Vallorcine), and Argentière, beneath the Grands Montets. These villages are described at the end of the chapter, but their slopes are taken in to the main part of the chapter.

Down the valley is Les Houches, with the most sheltered slopes in the valley. This is wholly described at the end of the chapter; its lifts are not covered by the normal Chamonix pass.

Free ski-buses link all these points but can get very crowded – 'even in January it was impossible to get around'. Don't expect additional buses to meet varying demand (eg when everyone wants to get to Les Houches in bad weather). There are also hourly trains along the valley, free with a guest card, and usually recommended by reporters – but one reporter this year found the services suspended.

The Mont Blanc Unlimited lift pass covers not only Les Houches but also Verbier in Switzerland and Courmayeur in Italy. The first is a major expedition; the second is of more practical use, not least because the weather can be good in Italy when it is lousy in

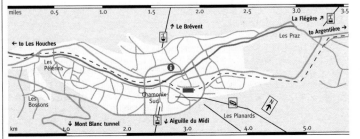

Hot chalets beneath glacial slopes? Check out p258.

Chamonix. And there are buses (free with the Mont Blanc lift pass) through the Mont Blanc tunnel several times daily. Having a car is useful in lots of ways, and makes that outing to Verbier a more practical proposition.

VILLAGE CHARM ★★★★
Lots of atmosphere
It's a bustling place, with scores of hotels and restaurants and shops selling everything from tacky souvenirs to high-tech climbing gear. The car-free centre is full of atmosphere, with cobbled streets and squares, beautiful old buildings, a fast-running river and pavement cafes. Away from the centre, there are lots of apartment blocks. There are some disused buildings, and traffic clogs the streets at times.

CONVENIENCE ★☆☆☆☆
You don't come here for that
The obvious place to stay for the full experience is close to the centre, where you can be a short walk from the gondola to Brévent. Or you adapt to life on the buses or trains.

SCENERY ★★★★★
As dramatic as it gets
The mountains above Chamonix are not just high – the mighty Mont Blanc is the highest in Western Europe –

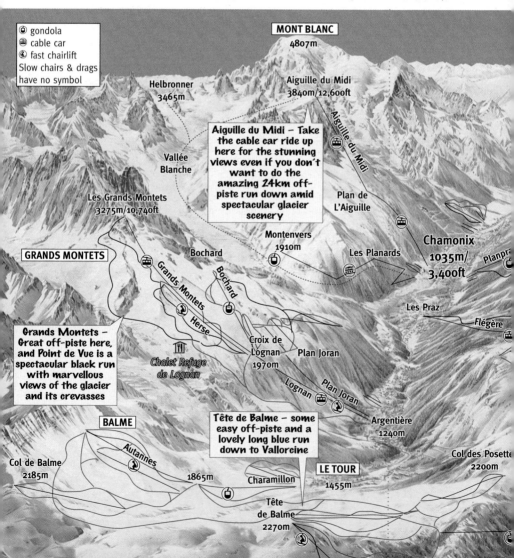

gondola
cable car
fast chairlift
Slow chairs & drags have no symbol

MONT BLANC
4807m

Helbronner
3465m

Aiguille du Midi
3840m/12,600ft

Aiguille du Midi

Aiguille du Midi – Take the cable car ride up here for the stunning views even if you don't want to do the amazing 24km off-piste run down amid spectacular glacier scenery

Vallée Blanche

Plan de L'Aiguille

Les Grands Montets
3275m/10,740ft

Montenvers
1910m

Chamonix
1035m/
3,400ft

Planpr

GRANDS MONTETS

Bochard

Les Planards

Les Praz

Grands Montets

Bochard

Bochard

Flégère

Herse

Grands Montets – Great off-piste here, and Point de Vue is a spectacular black run with marvellous views of the glacier and its crevasses

Chalet Refuge de Lognan

Croix de Lognan
1970m

Plan Joran

Plan Joran

Lognan

Argentière
1240m

BALME

Autannes

Tête de Balme – some easy off-piste and a lovely long blue run down to Vallorcine

Col des Posette
2200m

Col de Balme
2185m

1865m

Charamillon

LE TOUR
1455m

Tête de Balme
2270m

KEY FACTS

Resort	1035m
	3,400ft
Slopes	1035-3840m
	3,400-12,600ft
Lifts	42
Pistes	115km
	71 miles
Green	12%
Blue	42%
Red	31%
Black	15%
Snowmaking	
	125 guns

they are also truly spectacular. The ride up to the Aiguille du Midi is breathtaking in every sense (we've known people need to lie down for a while when they get to the top).

THE MOUNTAINS

Practically all the slopes – with the notable exception of Les Houches – are above the treeline; there are some runs through woods to the valley, but the black ones from Brévent and Flégère, in particular, are often closed, and can be unpleasantly tricky if open.

There is a booklet with separate piste maps for each individual area. We have had mixed reports on signposting and piste marking. In sectors other than Balme, the classification of runs often understates difficulty – in particular, some of the blues would be classified as reds in other resorts.

EXTENT OF THE SLOPES ★★★
Very fragmented

The gondola for **Brévent** departs a short, steep walk or bus ride from the centre. There are runs on open slopes below the arrival point, and a cable car goes on to the summit. There is a lift link to **Flégère**, also accessible via an inadequate old cable car from the village of Les Praz. These sunny areas give stunning views of Mont Blanc.

Up the valley at Argentière a cable car or a chairlift takes you up to the

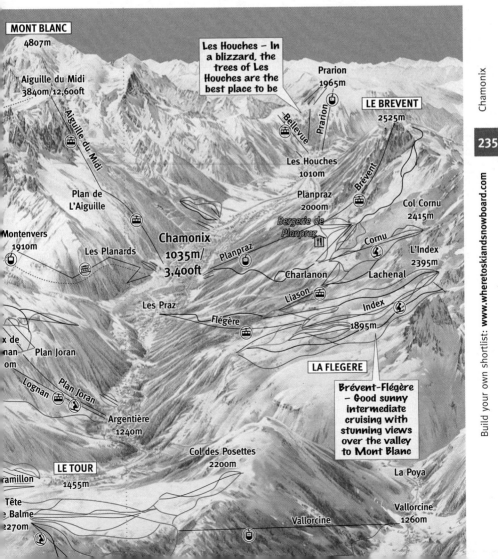

high slopes of **Les Grands Montets**. Chairs and a gondola serve open terrain above mid-mountain, but much of the best terrain is accessed by a further cable car of relatively low capacity, not covered by the standard lift pass (read 'Lift passes'). This shady area can be very cold in early season.

A little way further up the valley, the secluded village of Le Tour sits at the foot of the broad **Balme** area. A gondola goes up to mid-mountain, with a mix of drags and chairs above. There is also a lift up from Vallorcine.

Plus there are several low beginner areas dotted along the valley.

FAST LIFTS ★★★
Not enough
Cable cars and gondolas serve each sector, but many need upgrading. The handful of fast chairs are widely scattered. 'The lifts generally let the place down,' said a 2012 reporter.

QUEUES ★★
Ancient lifts, serious queues
Access to Brévent was transformed by the gondola upgrade a few years ago. But the valley has several other problem lifts. The ancient Flégère cable car can generate queues of an hour or more – to go down as well as up. The lifts out of Argentière build queues: a 2013 visitor found long queues 30 minutes before the cable car opened, and the alternative

chairlift appears to be on its last legs – it no longer operates from the main station, but starts a short way up the slope. At mid-mountain, the top cable car is a famous bottleneck – a 2013 reporter found 45-minute queues in February. You can book slots in advance (on the spot or online), preferably the day before, or join the 'standby' queue, which we've found to be an effective alternative. There may be queues for the lift up to Balme at La Tour, too; it can be quicker to take the train to Vallorcine.

Crowded pistes and skiers travelling too fast for the conditions can also be a problem in places – most notably on parts of the Grands Montets.

TERRAIN PARKS ★★★
A couple of options
The Summit Park on Grands Montets incorporates features for all levels and includes kickers, rails, jumps, a step-up/step-down feature and a boardercross. We have diverging views from reporters this year on its merits. You can check the latest details at www.h05park.com. At Brévent there are five rails and an airbag jump.

SNOW RELIABILITY ★★★★
Good high up; poor low down
The top runs on the north-facing Grands Montets slopes above Argentière generally have good snow, and the season normally lasts well

LIFT PASSES

Chamonix Le Pass

Prices in €

Age	1-day	6-day
under 16	33	185
16 to 64	44	218
65 plus	33	185

Free Under 4
Beginner No deals
Senior 75 plus: 50% of adult price

Notes Covers Brévent, Flégère, Balme, Grands Montets except top cable car, plus four small beginner areas; family reductions

Alternative pass
Mont Blanc Unlimited (MBU) covers all the above plus Les Houches, Aiguille du Midi and Helbronner cable cars, Montenvers train, Lognan-Grands Montets cable car, and the Verbier (Switzerland) and Courmayeur (Italy) ski areas

GETTING THERE

Air Geneva 85km/ 55 miles (1hr15); Lyon 215km/ 135 miles (2hr45)

Rail Station in resort, on the St Gervais-Le Fayet/Vallorcine line. Direct TGV link from Paris on Friday evenings and at weekends

into May. The risk of finding the top lift shut because of bad weather is more of a worry. There's snowmaking on the busy Bochard piste and the run to the valley. Balme has a snowy location, a good late-season record and snowmaking on the run down to the valley at Le Tour. The largely south-facing slopes of Brévent and Flégère suffer in warm weather, and the steep black runs to the resort are often closed. Don't be tempted to try these unless you know they are in good condition – they can be very tricky. Snowmaking was increased at Flégère two seasons ago to improve the link to Brévent. Some of the low beginners' areas have snowmaking. Piste grooming is generally OK – 'very good on Flegère', says a reporter.

FOR EXPERTS ★★★★★
One of the great resorts
Chamonix is renowned for its extensive steep terrain and deep snow. To get the best out of the area you really need to have a local guide. There is also lots of excellent terrain for ski-touring on skins. Read the feature panel for more off-piste possibilities.

The Grands Montets cable car offers stunning views from the observation platform above the top station – if you've got the legs and lungs to climb the 121 steep metal steps. (But beware: it's 200 more slippery steel steps down from the cable car before you hit the snow.) The ungroomed black pistes from here – Point de Vue and Pylones – are long and exhilarating. The former sails right by some dramatic sections of glacier, with marvellous views of the crevasses.

The Bochard gondola serves a challenging red back to Lognan and a black to either Plan Roujon or the chairlift below. Shortly after you have made a start down the black, you can head off-piste down the Combe de la Pendant bowl.

At Brévent there's more to test experts than the piste map suggests – there are a number of variations on the runs down from the summit. These are very steep and prone to ice. The red and black runs in Combe de la Charlanon are quiet, and there is excellent off-piste if the snow is good.

At Flégère there are further challenging slopes – in the Combe Lachenal, crossed by the linking cable car, say – and a tough run back to the village when the snow permits. The

short draglift above L'Index opens up a couple of good steep runs (a red and a black) plus a good area of off-piste.

Balme boasts little tough terrain on-piste, but there are off-piste routes from the high points to Le Tour, towards Vallorcine or into Switzerland.

FOR INTERMEDIATES ★★★★★
Plenty of better resorts
Chamonix is far from ideal for intermediates unless they relish challenging slopes and trying off-piste. If what you want is mile after mile of lift-linked cruisy pistes, go elsewhere.

For less confident intermediates, the Balme area above Le Tour is good for cruising and usually free from crowds. There are excellent shady, steeper runs, wooded lower down, on the north side of Tête de Balme, served by a fast quad. A lovely blue run goes on down to Vallorcine, but it is prone to closure.

The other areas have some blue and red runs. Even the Grands Montets has an area of blues at mid-mountain. The step up to the red terrain higher up is quite pronounced, however.

If the snow and weather are good, confident intermediates can join a guided group and do the Vallée Blanche (read our feature panel).

FOR BEGINNERS ★★★★★
Head for Balme
Chamonix is far from ideal for beginners, too – there are countless better resorts in which to learn. There are limited but adequate nursery slopes either side of the town – Savoy, at the bottom of Brévent, and Les Planards, on the opposite side (dark and cold in midwinter). Moving on to longer runs means taking a lift up to Brévent or Flégère. La Vormaine, at Le Tour, is a much better bet: extensive, relatively high, sunny and connected to the slopes of the Balme area, where there are easy long runs to progress to. But it's 12km from Chamonix itself.

FOR BOARDERS ★★★★★
Leave it to the experts
The undisputed king of freeride resorts, Chamonix is a haven for advanced snowboarders who relish the steep and wild terrain, especially on the Grands Montets. This means, however, that in peak season it's crowded, and fresh snow gets tracked out very quickly. The rough and rugged nature of the slopes means it

237

THE BEST OFF-PISTE SKIING IN THE WORLD?

Chamonix is renowned as an extreme sports Mecca, with arguably some of the best off-piste skiing in the world. And while thrill seekers and off-piste specialists are spoiled for choice, there is plenty for those looking for their first powder experience, too.

Les Houches and **Balme**, *at opposite ends of the Chamonix Valley, are ideal for a first taste off the beaten track. The forested slopes of Les Houches are easy to navigate on bad-weather days, with gentle blue runs bringing you back to the valley. Balme's open slopes are perfect for a foray into deep snow in between the pistes, with firmer ground just a few reassuring metres away.*

Snowboarders flock to **Flégère** *after a snowfall, its array of boulders and drop-offs turning it into a massive terrain park. The open bowl of Combe Lachenal is easily accessed from the top of the Index lift, and the south-facing slopes of this ski area provide excellent spring skiing.*

From the top of **Les Grands Montets** *(3275m) skiing is mostly off-piste and on glacial terrain. The vast north-facing slope of the main face offers countless ways down, satisfyingly steep without being intimidating, with snow conditions that are often among the best in the valley. Off the back, there are several rewarding ways down to the Glacier d'Argentière. In the opposite direction you have access to the steep Pas de Chèvre run. Skiing under the colossal granite spire of Le Dru, with views of the Vallée Blanche, is an unforgettable experience. The Couloir du Dru and the Rectiligne are also on this face, reserved for the adventurous – with some slopes of 40/45°.*

These are just some of the options, but the possibilities are endless. Together with heli-skiing on the Italian side of Mont Blanc and in neighbouring Switzerland, the wealth of off-piste on offer could keep you skiing for a lifetime.

THE LONGEST RUN MOST OF US WILL EVER DO – THE VALLEE BLANCHE

This is a trip you do for the stunning scenery. The views of the glacier and the spectacular rock spires beyond are simply mind-blowing. The standard run, although exceptionally long, is not steep – mostly gliding down gentle slopes (in places a bit too flat for snowboarders) with only the occasional steeper, choppy section to deal with. In the right conditions, it is well within the capability of a confident, fit intermediate. If snow is sparse, as it often is in early season, the run can be very tricky, with patches of sheet ice and exposed rocks, and narrow snow bridges over gaping crevasses. If fresh snow is abundant, different challenges may arise. Go in a guided group and check conditions before signing up at the Maison de la Montagne or other ski school offices. The trip is popular – on a busy day 2,500 people do it. To miss the crowds, go very early on a weekday, or in the afternoon if you are a good skier and can get down quickly.

The cable car takes you to 3840m and the 3842 cafeteria (claimed to be Europe's highest restaurant) – check out the amazing view of Mont Blanc from here while you adjust to the dizzying altitude. Be prepared for extreme cold, too. A tunnel delivers you to the infamous ridge-walk down to the start of the run. Except at the start of the season, the walk is well prepared, with regular steps cut in the snow and fixed ropes to hang on to. If you have a backpack capable of carrying your skis, and crampons to give some grip, it's no problem; ask for them when you book your guide. Without those items, it can be tiring and worrying. Many parties rope up to their guides.

There are variants on the classic route, of varying difficulty and danger; on our last descent we did a mixture of the Petit Envers du Plan and the Vrai Vallée Blanche in 20cm of fresh snow under a blue sky with few other people around – it was absolutely magical, with hundreds of fresh-track turns among all that stunning scenery. Lack of snow often rules out the full 24km run down to Chamonix; a steep stairway (be warned: 311 steps) leading to a slow gondola links the glacier to the station at Montenvers, for the half-hour mountain railway ride down to the town.

SNOWPIX.COM / CHRIS GILL

SCHOOLS

ESF
t 0450 532257

BASS
t 0845 468 1003 (UK)

Evolution 2
t 0450 555357

Ski Sensations
t 0682 105922

Summits
t 0450 535014

Classes (ESF prices)
6 half days: €158

Private lessons
€122 for 2hr, for 1 or 2 people

GUIDES

Compagnie des Guides
t 0450 530088

Chamonix Experience
t 0977 485869

CHILDCARE

Panda Club (Evolution 2)
t 0450 555357
From age 3

Piou Piou (ESF)
0450 532257
From age 3

Babysitter list
At tourist office

Ski schools
Ages 3 to 12

is not best suited for beginners but for more experienced adventurous riders willing to try true all-mountain riding. The easiest terrain is at the Balme area, though there are quite a few difficult drags here (you can avoid these if you can hack the cat tracks to take you to other lifts, says a reporter). Most lifts elsewhere are cable cars, gondolas and chairs. If you do the Vallée Blanche, be warned: the usual route is flat in places. Check out former British champion Neil McNab's excellent extreme backcountry camps at: www.mcnabsnowboarding.com.

FOR CROSS-COUNTRY ★★★★★
A decent network of trails
Most of the 42km of prepared trails lie at valley level in and between Chamonix and Argentière – very much rated by a 2013 visitor. All the trails are shady and often icy in midwinter, and they fade fast in the spring sun. Catch the bus rather than ski between the Chamonix and Argentière areas, suggests a reporter, as the link is by 'steep and difficult trails'.

MOUNTAIN RESTAURANTS ★★★★★
Mainly dull, lacking choice
Editors' choice On Brévent the Bergerie de Planpraz (0450 530542) is a wood and stone building with self- and table-service sections and good food; but it gets very busy. On the Grands Montets the tiny, rustic Chalet-Refuge de Lognan (0688 560354), off the Variante Hôtel run to the valley, has marvellous views and satisfying, simple food. Recent reporters agree. **Worth knowing about** On the Grands Montets, one regular visitor rates Plan Joran 'probably the best in the valley'; it has table- and self-service, and a big terrace. There is a picnic room at Lognan by Le Spot snack bar. Tucked away in the woods to skier's right of the home run, the Crémerie du Glacier is a cosy spot for a croûte.

On Brévent the little Panoramic at the top enjoys amazing views over to Mont Blanc, and the food is fine. On Flégère the recently renovated table-service Adret is 'not outstanding, but definitely pretty good'. The Chavanne is one reader's favourite despite the 'small choice' of food – 'amazing view'. At Balme, at the top of the gondola from Le Tour, there's an adequate self-service and a picnic area. Ecuries de Charamillon opened for 2012/13 in a renovated farmhouse.

SCHOOLS AND GUIDES ★★★★★
The place to try something new
The schools here are particularly strong in specialist fields – off-piste, glacier and couloir skiing, ski touring, snowboarding and cross-country. English-speaking instructors and mountain guides are plentiful.

At the Maison de la Montagne are the main ESF office and the HQ of the Compagnie des Guides, which is highly rated (we and reporters have had very good guides from here) and has taken visitors to the mountains for 150 years. Both organizations offer week-long 'tours' taking clients to a different mountain or resort each day.

Powderama is run by British instructor Simon Halliwell and offers five-day and weekend courses plus, at peak holiday times, specialized one-day clinics (off-piste, piste, moguls). A 2013 reporter found her Evolution 2 instructor 'excellent', giving 'her a new confidence to tackle steeper slopes'.

FOR FAMILIES ★★★★★
Very limited
Childcare is available from some of the ski schools. Evolution 2's Panda Club is used by quite a few British visitors; reports have been enthusiastic but the Argentière base can be inconvenient. Les Houches has better facilities, with a day care centre and children's club.

STAYING THERE

There is all sorts of accommodation, and lots of it.
Chalets Many chalets are run by small specialist operators. Inghams now runs the 60-bed Sapinière – overlooking the nursery slope at the bottom of Brévent and not far from the centre – as a chalet hotel: 'Comfortable, well placed, run to a very high standard,' said a 2012 reporter.
Hotels There's wide choice, many modestly priced, the majority with no more than 30 rooms or so. Bookings for short stays are no problem – the peak season is summer. Momentum can fix whatever you want. Ski Weekends specialize in, er, weekends and offer Le Vert (see below) among others. Club Med has three linked buildings near the centre. Out at Le Lavancher is the 'hameau hôtelier' Les Chalets de Philippe (0607 231726) – a secluded cluster of lovingly furnished wooden chalets, most sleeping no more than three or four, with meals

UK PACKAGES

taken either in your own chalet or in a small central dining room.
*****Hameau Albert 1er (0450 530509) Smart, 100-year-old chalet-style Relais & Châteaux hotel with farmhouse annexe. Restaurant with two Michelin stars. Pool.
*****Auberge du Bois Prin (0450 533351) A small modern chalet with a big reputation; great views; bit of a hike into town (closer to Brévent).
*****Mont-Blanc (0450 530564) Grand 19th-century place in a central location. Refurbished and reopened in 2013 with spa and pool
****Jeu de Paume (Lavancher) (0450 540376) Alpine satellite of a chic Parisian hotel: a beautifully furnished modern chalet halfway to Argentière.
****Morgane (0450 535715) Cool modern style; excellent restaurant, Michelin-starred; good location near Aiguille de Midi cable car; pool, sauna.
***Alpina (0450 534777) Striking modern place just north of centre. Much the biggest in town – 138 rooms, most with balconies and mountain views. Sauna, hot tub.
***Croix-Blanche (0450 530011) Small, simple hotel and brasserie in centre.
***Lanchers (0450 534719) Near Flégère. Recently refurbished and extended by its British owner. Tipped again by a return visitor for quality food and friendly service.
***Mercure (0450 530756) Next to the station. 'Comfortable rooms, friendly service, nothing too much trouble.' Has its own ski hire facilities.
***Oustalet (0450 555499) In Chamonix Sud. 'Spacious, spotless, well-fitted rooms.'
***Prieuré (0450 532072) Mega-chalet on northern ring-road – handy for drivers, quite close to centre. Sauna, hot tub. 'Friendly, comfortable, good food, excellent dessert buffet'.
Clubhouse (0450 984220) Boutique hotel in an art deco mansion, with a wide choice of ultra-modern rooms.
Le Vert (0450 531358) In Le Gailland, a mile from Chamonix, with en suite rooms for one to six people. Lively bar, top DJs, pool table, Sunday roast.
Apartments Many properties in UK package brochures are in convenient blocks in Chamonix Sud but are rather cramped if you fill them to capacity. The Ginabelle is different – a Pierre & Vacances Premium residence near the station, with pool and fitness facilities, also available through Peak Retreats and Skitracer.

EATING OUT ★★★★★
Plenty of quality places
The top hotels all have excellent restaurants, and there are many other good places. One or two advertising-based guides are distributed locally.

It's some years since we ate at the hotel Morgane's Bistrot; it was excellent then, and it has had a Michelin star since 2007. The Impossible is a favourite with us and with readers – a rustic chalet a short walk out of the centre with a varied menu – 'superb food, excellent value set menu, great wine list, friendly staff'. And we always enjoy the intimate Atmosphère, by the river, despite its two-sitting system. According to a regular reporter the Panier des 4 Saisons is 'very possibly the best restaurant in Chamonix' with its inventive modern regional French cuisine. The 'cosy' Monchu does good Savoyard food and service at reasonable prices. The Calèche gets booked up well ahead and is short on space but does 'excellent' traditional and more adventurous dishes.

Chamonix offers more variety than is normal in French resorts. Café de l'Arve is fairly new at the hotel de l'Arve, offering a modern, creative menu. Munchie offers a mix of French and Scandinavian cooking that makes a refreshing change.

Value-oriented reader tips include Pitz and Neopolis (both pizza), La Flambée ('good pizza, pasta, steak and local dishes') and the Poele ('no frills, good basic food, good value').

APRES-SKI ★★★★
You have to know where to go
Chamonix attracts a lot of young Brits and Scandis – blokes, mainly – wanting to après-ski hard after skiing hard. But it is not Austria, or even Méribel, where you can hear the noise from the top village bar as you ski home. It's a big town, and you have to know where to go. One exception is an obvious place at Flégère – the Rhododendrons, which has live music ('great atmosphere').

In the town, the teatime après zone that we hear most about is beside the train station. The Swedish-run Chambre Neuf offers 'good covers band playing, pitchers of beer and even some dancing on the tables – great fun'. Elevation 1904, opposite, is a bit quieter.

Towards the river in Rue Whymper,

ACTIVITIES

Indoor Sports complex (swimming pool, sauna, steam room, tennis, squash, ice rink, fitness room, climbing wall), museums, library, cinemas

Outdoor Ice rink, snowshoeing, walking paths, tobogganing, dog sledding, paragliding

Argentière is not a picture-postcard village, but it'll do ↓

the Lapin Agile is a relaxed wine bar doing Italian-style appetizers. Over the river is the central square with La Terrasse ('head upstairs – really characterful old high-ceilinged place'). To the left is Rue du Dr Paccard. The Pub gets packed with Brits ('on Burns night they piped in the haggis'). Or turn right for the key Rue des Moulins. Bar'dUp is a small, relaxed place with live music and DJs. Mix is a 'wicked' cool DJ bar. Top tip for grown-ups is Privilege, a relaxed, woody, rustic-chic place with table service and live acoustic music. Soul Food is 'cool, French'. In the suburb of Chamonix Sud, Monkey Bar is frequented by 'those in the know'.

Just outside the centre, MBC is a Canadian-run microbrewery, often with live bands – 'good ambience, great beer and apparently reasonable food'.

There's a variety of nightclubs and discos. The Garage claims to be the biggest. The Cantina throbs into the early hours, too. As presumably does the new White Hub, open from 11pm to 7am (free entry for the first couple of hours). Real action enthusiasts may want to look at getting out of town to Le Vert ('hippest nightspot in town').

OFF THE SLOPES ★★★★★
An excellent choice

There's more off-slope activity here than in many resorts. Everyone other than those with medical issues should ride the Aiguille du Midi cable car. Excursion possibilities are endless. The Alpine Museum is 'very interesting but all in French', the library has some English language books and there's a good sports centre with a pool, ice skating and ice hockey matches.

OUTLYING VILLAGE – 1240m
ARGENTIERE

This old village is in an impressive setting towards the head of the valley, 9km from Chamonix. There's a fair bit of modern development, and the road through to Le Tour, Vallorcine and Switzerland gets uncomfortably busy, but it still has a rustic appeal.

The lifts to the Grands Montets are about 600m from the slightly elevated centre of the village. It's a fair hike, but there are buses. Readers like two central hotels: the Couronne, now a 3-star (0450 540002) – 'great, with lots of character' – and the 2-star Dahu (0450 540155) – 'good room,

UK PACKAGES

Argentière Action Outdoors, Adventure Base, Alpine Answers, AmeriCan Ski, Bigfoot Chamonix, Collineige, Crystal, Crystal Finest, Erna Low, Lagrange, Marmotte Mountain, Mountain Beds, Peak Retreats, PowderBeds, Ski Club Freshtracks, Ski France, Ski Independence, Ski Weekend, White Roc
Les Houches Adventure Base, Alpine Answers, AmeriCan Ski, Erna Low, Lagrange, Peak Retreats, Pierre & Vacances, PowderBeds, Ski Collection, Ski Expectations, Ski France, Ski Independence, Zenith
Vallorcine Erna Low, Peak Retreats, PowderBeds, Ski Independence

Phone numbers
From abroad use the prefix +33 and omit the initial '0' of the phone number

TOURIST OFFICES

Chamonix/Argentière
www.chamonix.com
Les Houches
www.leshouches.com

excellent breakfast'. Out near the lifts are the 4-star Grands-Montets (0450 540666), with pool, and the 3-star Montana (0450 541499). Reports SVP.

Le Cristal d'Argentière is a smart Lagrange Prestige residence, between the centre and the lifts, with a decent pool (available through Peak Retreats).

There's a reasonable choice of inexpensive, unpretentious restaurants and bars in the central area. An old favourite is the Office, offering a traditional Brit-pub atmosphere and menu although now reportedly run by 'a great Aussie called Dave'; 'good burgers and steak,' 'very lively until 3am'. The two central hotels mentioned above both have attractive restaurants. Reader recommendations include the P'tite Verte ('brilliant-value set menu'), the 'reasonably priced' Rusticana and the Stone ('excellent pizzas, pasta and steak'). Other tipped bars are the Savoy ('relaxed, cheapest around') and the slalom for 'tapas and good wine'.

OUTLYING VILLAGE – 1455m
LE TOUR

Le Tour is a charming, unspoiled little village 12km from Chamonix at the foot of the Balme area. The valley's best nursery slopes are next to the village, at La Vormaine. A gondola from the edge of the village serves the Balme slopes, an area of mainly easy runs also reachable from Vallorcine.

OUTLYING VILLAGE – 1260m
VALLORCINE

Vallorcine is a small, but developing, traditional mountain village over the Col des Montets, near the Swiss border and 16km from Chamonix. The village shares with Le Tour the main valley's Balme area.

A gondola and a chairlift take you to Tête de Balme. A gentle blue run leads back to the village, but it is prone to closure. There's a separate small area of local slopes at La Poya.

Accommodation is mainly in apartments. The 4-star L'Ours Bleu, with pool and spa facilities, is featured by Peak Retreats and Erna Low. There's a limited choice of restaurants and bars. The Buvette at the station is a rustic restaurant with decent food and good for drinks while waiting for the train back to Chamonix (it takes 20 minutes).

OUTLYING VILLAGE – 1010m
LES HOUCHES

Les Houches is 6km down the valley from Chamonix. The wooded slopes are popular when bad weather closes other areas, but are not covered by the standard Chamonix pass. It has great views of the Mont Blanc massif.

It's a pleasant village, with an old core around a pretty church, but modern developments in chalet style have spread along the road at the foot of the slopes (to an extent a visitor returning after some years' absence found 'incredible'). Some developments are quite a way from the widely separated lifts going to opposite ends of the slopes – a gondola and a queue-prone cable car. On the mountain, all the lifts are slow though there are plans to replace a couple of drags with a fast quad for 2014/15. There are some awkward links in the network.

There are nursery slopes and open, gentle runs at the top of the main lifts, with long, worthwhile runs back towards the village – blue, red and a token black that is Chamonix's World Cup Downhill course – a fine intermediate run. There is a decent terrain park. But there are lots of draglifts and flat areas for boarders to avoid. The ESF gets good reports for children's classes – 'helpful, sensitive to needs', 'flexible'.

Beyond the summit ridge is a very gentle area with cross-country loops and below that some sunny woodland runs with views across to Megève.

In good weather the slopes are quiet, and the views superb from several attractive restaurants. The Vieilles Luges gets an avalanche of rave reports this year – 'fantastic', 'excellent choice', 'wonderful, smoky-fire cooking'. Snow-cover on the lower slopes is not reliable, but there is a fair amount of snowmaking.

The village is quiet, but there are some pleasant bars and restaurants. Reporters have recommended the 3-star Hotel du Bois (0450 545035). Granges d'En Haut (0450 546536) consists of luxury chalets where you could self-cater but there is also a smart restaurant; spa, small pool.

There are some good apartments with pools, including the 4-star Hameau de Pierre Blanche (available through Peak Retreats) and Pierre & Vacances' Hauts de Chavants.

Châtel

A distinctively French base in an ideal position for exploring the huge Portes du Soleil circuit which spans the French–Swiss border

RATINGS

The mountains

Extent	★★★★★
Fast lifts	★★
Queues	★★★
Terrain p'ks	★★★
Snow	★★
Expert	★★★
Intermediate	★★★★
Beginner	★★★
Boarder	★★
X-country	★★★
Restaurants	★★★
Schools	★★★
Families	★★★

The resort

Charm	★★★
Convenience	★★
Scenery	★★★
Eating out	★★★
Après-ski	★★★
Off-slope	★★

RPI 100

lift pass	£200
ski hire	£110
lessons	£75
food & drink	£130
total	**£515**

NEWS

2013/14: A new green slope is planned for the Linga area. Work has started on an aquatic centre, the Forme d'O, which will include an indoor pool and outdoor hot tub and be ready for 2014/15.

2012/13: Seven more snow-guns were installed in the Smoothpark and the blue run beside it. A new blue run, the Chésery, was created in the Plaine Dranse area.

+ Very extensive, pretty, intermediate terrain on Portes du Soleil circuit, with good local slopes

+ Wide range of cheap and cheerful, good-value accommodation

+ Pleasant, lively, French-dominated village, still quite rustic in parts

− Traffic congestion can be a problem at weekends and in peak season

− Low altitude and exposure to westerlies means some risk of rain and poor snow

− Some main lifts a bus ride away

Châtel offers an attractive blend of qualities much like that of Morzine – another valley village in the Portes du Soleil. Châtel (with a claimed 30 working farms) is a bit more rustic and down to earth. But its key advantage is that it is part of the main Portes du Soleil circuit. There is a gap in the circuit at Châtel, filled by buses; but this is more of an irritant to those passing through than for Châtel residents, who get used to the excellent local bus services. On busy days it's worth trying the uncrowded slopes of nearby La Chapelle-d'Abondance.

THE RESORT

Châtel is a much expanded village near the head of the wooded Dranse valley, at the north-eastern limit of the huge French–Swiss Portes du Soleil ski circuit. It has two separate sectors of slopes, one linked to its French neighbour – high, purpose-built Avoriaz – and the other linked to two resorts in Switzerland: Morgins (which is on the Portes du Soleil circuit) and Torgon (which is not on the circuit).

A few kilometres down the valley is rustic La Chapelle-d'Abondance, with lifts into the Torgon slopes – covered at the end of this chapter.

VILLAGE CHARM ★★★
Rustic style, urban traffic
Châtel is still an attractive village, despite the inevitable expansion, and reporters remark on the friendly locals. Modern, unpretentious chalet-style hotels and apartments rub shoulders with old farms where cattle still live in winter. But it is no rustic idyll: life revolves around two streets that are far from traffic-free: lots of visitors take cars, and they can clog the centre – especially at weekends.

CONVENIENCE ★★
No perfect position
Although there is a definite centre, the village sprawls along the road in from Lake Geneva and the diverging roads up the hillside towards Morgins and along the valley towards the Linga and

Pré-la-Joux lifts. There is an excellent, frequent, though sometimes crowded, free bus service linking the sectors. Staying centrally helps with catching the ski-bus to the outlying lifts before it gets very crowded, and simplifies après-ski outings – the night bus finishes at 8pm most nights. But there is accommodation near the Linga lift, if first tracks are the priority.

SCENERY ★★★
Lots of variety
Châtel's broad valley setting is very scenic, with Linga providing a splendid backdrop and pleasantly woody slopes

243

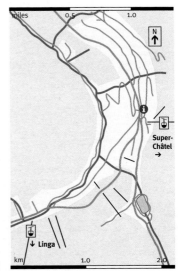

KEY FACTS

Resort	1200m
	3,940ft

Portes du Soleil	
Slopes	950-2275m
	3,120-7,460ft
Lifts	195
Pistes	650km
	404 miles
Green	12%
Blue	43%
Red	36%
Black	9%
Snowmaking	
	900 guns

Châtel only	
Slopes	1100-2205m
	3,610-7,230ft
Lifts	44
Pistes	83km
	52 miles
Green	22%
Blue	37%
Red	31%
Black	10%

curving in both directions. The lifts above Torgon give great views over Lake Geneva. As you travel around the Portes du Soleil circuit the dramatic Dents du Midi are constantly coming into view.

THE MOUNTAINS

Châtel sits between two sectors of the main Portes du Soleil circuit, each offering a mix of open and wooded slopes. For notes on the circuit read our special chapter on it. The local piste map is clear, not least because it doesn't try to show everything in a single view. Pause for applause.

EXTENT OF THE SLOPES ★★★★★
Two sectors to choose between
Châtel has a worthwhile amount of local skiing, in two separate sectors.

Directly above the village is **Super-Châtel** – an area of easy, open and lightly wooded slopes that is accessed by a gondola or a two-stage chair. From here you can embark on a clockwise Portes du Soleil circuit by heading to the Swiss resort of Morgins. Or you can head north for the slopes straddling a different bit of the Swiss border, above **Torgon** (with fab views of Lake Geneva).

An anticlockwise tour of the Portes du Soleil circuit starts outside the village with a lift into the **Linga** sector – a gondola from Villapeyron followed by a six-pack to Tête du Linga or a choice of fast chairs from Pré-la-Joux. The faster way to Avoriaz is via Pré-la-Joux. There is night skiing at Linga on Thursdays.

FAST LIFTS ★★
Luxurious Linga
Linga and the Plaine Dranse area are well served now that the Rochassons double has been replaced by a six-pack – but in the Super-Châtel sector the lifts beyond the access gondola are almost entirely slow chairs and drags, whether you head for Morgins or for Torgon. Hence our rating.

QUEUES ★★★
Bottlenecks have been eased
In recent years queues have been eased throughout the Portes du Soleil by the installation of several fast new chairlifts. But queues form for the gondola to Super-Châtel when school parties gather, and you can also face queues to get down again if the sunny home slope is shut because of poor snow. The slow Morclan chair at Super-Châtel has queues at busy times. Reporters have also found lengthy queues at the Tour de Don and Chermeu draglifts at certain times of the day.

TERRAIN PARKS ★★★
One size suits all
The Smoothpark at Super-Châtel has lines to suit both beginners and experienced freestylers, and they include rails, kickers, boxes, hips and boardercross.

SNOW RELIABILITY ★★
The main drawback
The main drawback of the Portes du Soleil as a whole is that it is low, and exposed to mild weather from the west, so snow quality can suffer when

↑ Altitude and orientation: the village, at a lowly 1200m, gets the afternoon sun; the run you're looking from faces due north
SIMON SMITH

Build your own shortlist: www.wheretoskiandsnowboard.com

LIFT PASSES

Portes du Soleil

Prices in €

Age	1-day	6-day
under 16	34	169
16 to 19	41	203
20 to 64	45	225
65 plus	41	203

Free Under 5

Beginner Lesson, rental and lift deal

Notes Family discounts; 5hr pass

Alternative pass Châtel only

it's warm. But a lot of snowmaking has been installed at Super-Châtel and on runs down to resort level. Linga and Pré-la-Joux are mainly north-facing and generally have the best local snow. The pistes to Morgins and towards Avoriaz get full sun.

FOR EXPERTS ★★★★★
Some challenges
The best steep runs – on- and off-piste – are in the Linga and Pré-la-Joux area. Beneath the Linga gondola and chair there's a pleasant mix of open and wooded ground, which follows the fall line fairly directly. And there's a serious mogul field between Cornebois and Plaine Dranse. Two pistes from the Rochassons ridge are steep and kept well groomed. On the way to Torgon from Super-Châtel, the Barbossine black run is long, steep and quite narrow and tricky at the top. There's plenty of good lift-served off-piste to be explored with a guide: on a recent visit we did a great run from Tête du Linga over into the next (deserted) valley of La Leiche – read the special off-piste feature panel in our Morzine chapter.

FOR INTERMEDIATES ★★★★★
Some great local terrain
When conditions are right the Portes du Soleil is an intermediates' paradise. Good intermediates need not go far from Châtel to find amusement; Linga and Plaine Dranse have some of the best red runs on the circuit. The moderately skilled can do the Portes du Soleil circuit without problem, and will particularly enjoy runs around Les Lindarets and Morgins. Even timid

types can do the circuit, provided they take one or two short cuts and ride chairs down the trickier bits. But some blues are difficult when conditions are poor – in particular, one reporter witnessed skiers 'in tears' on the way down to Morgins from Châtel.

Visits to Avoriaz for the Hauts Forts runs and the ungroomed snowcross run are worthwhile for competent intermediates. And note that the runs back to Plaine Dranse are real reds, and the Rochassons piste, especially, can get extremely busy at the end of the day.

Don't overlook the Torgon sector, which has some excellent slopes, including challenging ones.

FOR BEGINNERS ★★★★★
Three possible options
There are good beginners' areas at Pré-la-Joux (a bus ride away) and at Super-Châtel (a gondola ride above the village). And there are nursery slopes at village level if there is snow there. Reporters have praised the Super-Châtel slopes and lifts, which 'allow the beginner to progress' and 'safely practise' on gentle gradients away from the main runs. Getting up to them is a bit of an effort, though. The home run from Super-Châtel can be tricky – narrow, busy, steep at the end and often icy at the end of the day. The Pré-la-Joux slopes are less varied, with some steeper draglifts. There will be a new green there for 2013/14.

Stylish chalets and serious skiing? Check out p258.

CHILDCARE

Mouflets Garderie
t 0450 813819
Ages 3mnth to 6yr

Piou Piou (Village des Marmottons)
t 0450 732264
Ages 3 to 6

Les Pitchounes
t 0450 813251
Ages 3 and 4

Ski schools
Generally from age 5

GETTING THERE

Air Geneva 80km/ 50 miles (2hr)

Rail Thonon les Bains (40km/25 miles)

FOR BOARDERS ★★
Best for beginners – beware drags
Avoriaz is the hard-core destination in the Portes du Soleil. Châtel is not a bad place to learn or to go to as a budget option. But many lifts in the Super-Châtel sector are drags, and reporters warn they can be a 'painful experience'. The Linga area has good, varied slopes and off-piste possibilities and more boarder-friendly chairlifts.

FOR CROSS-COUNTRY ★★★
Pretty, if low, trails
There are pretty trails (12km) along the river and through the woods on the lower slopes of Linga, but snow-cover can be a problem. When combined with La Chapelle-d'Abondance's trails, the total is 40km. The tourist office produces good maps.

MOUNTAIN RESTAURANTS ★★★
Some quite good local huts
Restaurants are marked but not named on the piste map. A cluster of cosy huts can be found at Plaine Dranse. We get regular reports from a devotee of the 'hyper-twee' Vieux Chalet, aka Chez Babeth – 'food is excellent but increasingly pricey, Babeth the owner absolutely barking'. In the Linga area the Ferme des Pistes is a lovely cosy old barn (complete with stable-door) that pleased a reporter with 'a huge plateful of spud, ham and cheese'. The

chapter on Avoriaz has several tips at Les Lindarets, in the valley between the resorts.

There are picnic rooms at Plaine Dranse and the tops of the gondolas in the Super-Châtel and Linga sectors.

SCHOOLS AND GUIDES ★★★
Plenty of choice
There are seven schools in Châtel, including a branch of BASS (British Alpine Ski & Snowboard School), of which we lack reports. The International school has been recommended by reporters, including visitors who had a private lesson that was 'one of our best ever' and a recent visitor's grandson who had 'so much more fun' than in previous lessons with the ESF. But the ESF has also been praised, with comments such as 'very helpful and customer-focused'.

FOR FAMILIES ★★★
Some good facilities
The ESF-run Marmottons nursery has good facilities, including toboggans, painting, music and videos, and children (from three to six) are reportedly happy there. Ski Sensations has its own nursery area with a draglift and chalet at Linga.

OT CHATEL / JEAN-FRANCOIS VUARAND

Super-Châtel is an excellent area for novices, with easy progression to longer runs ↓

SCHOOLS

ESF
t 0450 732264

ESI Pro Skiing
t 0450 733192

Henri Gonon
t 0450 732304

Sensations
t 0450 813251

BASS
t 020 3286 3661 (UK)

Ecole Ski Academy
t 0681 665280

Classes (ESF prices)
6 half-days (2¼hr am)
€128

Private lessons
€39 for 1hr for 1 or 2
people

UK PACKAGES

Absolute Alps, Connick,
Interactive Resorts,
Lagrange, Mountain
Beds, Oxford Ski Co,
Peak Retreats,
PowderBeds, Ski
Addiction, Ski France,
Ski Line, Skialot, Snow
Finders, Snowfocus,
Susie Ward
**La Chapelle-
d'Abondance** Chalet Le
Dragon, Ski Addiction,
Ski La Cote

ACTIVITIES

Indoor Spas in hotels,
cinemas, library,
bowling

Outdoor Ice rink,
walks, cheese factory
visits, ice diving, ice
fishing, snowshoeing,
paragliding,
airboarding, 'snake-
glisse', 'yooner'
tobogganing

Phone numbers
From abroad use the
prefix +33 and omit
the initial '0' of the
phone number

TOURIST OFFICES

Châtel
www.chatel.com

**La Chapelle-
d'Abondance**
www.lachapelle74.
com

STAYING THERE

This is emphatically a French resort.
No big tour operators feature it.
Hotels Practically all the hotels are
2-stars, mostly friendly chalets,
wooden or at least partly wood-clad.
But there are some smarter places.
****Macchi** (0450 732412) Smart,
modern chalet, spacious comfortable
rooms, 'excellent food'; small pool,
spa; central.
***Fleur de Neige** (0450 732010)
Woody chalet near centre; spa; pool;
Grive Gourmande restaurant is one of
the best in town.
***Belalp** (0450 732439) Simple
chalet, small rooms, but 'very good
food'.
***Kandahar** (0450 733060) One for
peace lovers: a Logis by the river, a
walkable distance from the centre.
****Choucas** (0450 732257) Central
location. 'Friendly owner.'
****Lion d'Or** (0450 813440) In centre.
Fairly basic with a 'good atmosphere'.
****Roitelet** (0450 732479) 'Basic, good
location, four-course dinner, made to
feel part of the family.'
****Tremplin** (0450 732306) 'Excellent,
good value. Owner cooks well but
speaks no English.'
Apartments Peak Retreats offers two
recently built properties that set a new
standard for Châtel, both with pools
and various spa facilities – CGH's
Chalets d'Angèle, and Grand Lodge.
Châtel's village supermarkets are
reported to be small and overcrowded,
but there is a large supermarket out in
the direction of Chapelle-d'Abondance.

EATING OUT ★★★☆☆
Fair selection

There is an adequate number and
range of restaurants. The Macchi and
Fleur de Neige hotels both have
ambitious restaurants. We've also
enjoyed the Table d'Antoine restaurant
of the hotel Chalet d'Alizée, though it's
a few years ago. The rustic Vieux Four
does ambitious dishes alongside
Savoyard specialities and is approved
by readers ('good value and the best
food we had all week'). The Poya does
'a blend of traditional and
contemporary cuisine'. The Pierrier and
the Fiacre ('mains/pizzas good value')
are more modest, everyday
restaurants, good for families.
It's worth a trip to the eccentric
hotel Cornettes in La Chapelle-
d'Abondance (described on the right).

APRES-SKI ★★★☆☆
All down to bars

The Tunnel bar is very popular with
the British and has a DJ or live music
every night. The Avalanche is a very
popular English-style pub with a 'good
atmosphere and live music'. The
Godille – close to the Super-Châtel
gondola and crowded when everyone
descends at close of play – has a
more French feel. The 'small and cosy'
Isba is the locals' choice, and shows
extreme-sports videos. The bowling
alley has a good bar.

OFF THE SLOPES ★★☆☆☆
Less than ideal

Those with a car can easily visit places
such as Geneva, Thonon and Evian.
There are pleasant walks and sleigh
rides; you can visit the cheese factory
or the two cinemas, or join in daily
events organized by the tourist office.
The Portes du Soleil as a whole is
less than ideal for non-skiers who like
to meet their more active friends for
lunch: they are likely to be at some
distant resort – maybe in another
country – at lunchtime, and even if
they are not, very few lifts are
accessible to pedestrians.

DOWN-VALLEY VILLAGE – 1010m

LA CHAPELLE-D'ABONDANCE

This unspoiled, rustic farming
community, complete with old church
and friendly locals, is 5km down the
valley from Châtel. It has its own quiet
little north-facing area of easy wooded
runs, and a gondola starting on the
outskirts links it to slopes between
Torgon in Switzerland and Super-
Châtel, and so to the Portes du Soleil
circuit. The Mousseron hut, near the
Braitaz chairlift, is 'well worth a visit'.
Nightlife is virtually non-existent –
just a few quiet bars, a cinema and
torchlit descents. The Fer Rouge is a
popular microbrewery, with live music.
The hotel Cornettes (0450 735024)
is an amazing 3-star with 4-star
facilities, including an indoor pool, a
sauna, a steam room and hot tubs. It
has an atmospheric bar and an
excellent restaurant with good-value
menus. The hotel has been run by the
Trincaz family since 1894. Look out for
the showcases displaying their
collections of puppets and dolls and
for other eccentric touches, such as
ancient doors that unexpectedly slide
open automatically.

Courchevel

Arguably the best of the half-dozen resorts that make up the famous Trois Vallées – with a choice of four different villages

248

RATINGS

The mountains

Extent	★★★★★
Fast lifts	★★★★
Queues	★★★★
Terrain p'ks	★★
Snow	★★★★
Expert	★★★★
Intermediate	★★★★★
Beginner	★★★★
Boarder	★★★★
X-country	★★★★
Restaurants	★★★
Schools	★★★★
Families	★★★★

The resort

Charm	★★
Convenience	★★★★
Scenery	★★★
Eating out	★★★★★
Après-ski	★★★★
Off-slope	★★★

RPI	135
lift pass	£230
ski hire	£145
lessons	£135
food & drink	£190
total	**£700**

KEY FACTS

Resort	1260-1850m
	4,130-6,070ft

Trois Vallées

Slopes	1260-3230m
	4,130-10,600ft
Lifts	173
Pistes	600km
	373 miles
Green	16%
Blue	40%
Red	34%
Black	10%
Snowmaking	50%

Courchevel/
La Tania only

Slopes	1260-2740m
	4,130-8,990ft
Lifts	62
Pistes	150km
	93 miles
Green	19%
Blue	31%
Red	40%
Black	10%

- ➕ Extensive, varied slopes
- ➕ Impressive snowmaking and piste grooming, and a decent lift system
- ➕ Partly wooded setting
- ➕ Choice of four very different villages
- ➕ Some great restaurants and top-notch hotels

- ➖ 1850 and 1550 lacking in charm
- ➖ Very high prices in 1850 and in mountain restaurants generally
- ➖ The French feel has been lost, with huge numbers of foreign visitors
- ➖ Not great for the indolent non-skier unless glitzy shops are your thing

Courchevel's ski area is the most compelling sector of the famous Trois Vallées, the biggest linked ski area in the world; if we're heading for the 3V, more often than not we'll head for Courchevel.

But it's not one destination, it's four. Swanky 1850 catches the headlines, with its airstrip, ritzy hotels and six Michelin-starred restaurants. The other villages have none of 1850's pretensions and high prices. There are plenty of affordable catered chalet holidays on sale here, even (thanks to the miracles worked by UK tour ops) in 1850. Sadly, there are few affordable lunches.

The resort quietly rebranded all the villages a couple of years ago. But the new branding is a shambles – for more on that see below and opposite.

THE RESORT

In 2011, the local council decided to rebrand its villages. But the result is a shambles so we are sticking with the old names, as are most of the locals – see the feature panel opposite.

Courchevel 1850 was one of the first French resorts to be purpose-built in the years immediately after World War 2. The other villages were developed later, although they already existed as old hamlets.

The lowest village is Le Praz, next is 1550 (new name: Village), then 1650 (new name: Moriond) and finally 1850 (new name: Courchevel).

1850 is big enough to have several distinguishable quarters. The main lift base and the central area around it is La Croisette; the resort spreads a long way up the hillside on the left through the chalet-filled suburbs of Cospillot and Nogentil to the Altiport, the resort's famously hazardous little airstrip. Part of these suburbs is the Jardin Alpin, a forested area with some of the swankiest hotels (and more modest chalets and apartments), served by its own gondola. On the opposite, right-hand side of La Croisette is another little 'downtown' area, with the suburbs of Chenus above it and Plantret below.

The other resort villages are smaller

and simpler. The main part of 1650 has grown up along the road that links the resorts (though traffic is not intrusive); and the centre, around the lift base area, has been attractively developed and is lined with good local shops, restaurants and bars. Opposite the main gondola (reached by an

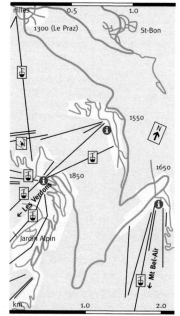

2013/14: A new mountain restaurant, the Cave des Creux, is due to be built near the top of the slow Gravelles chair from Praméruel. A new 5-star hotel, the Apogée, will open in December 2013 at the Jardin Alpin. A new Duo Pass will allow two people buying lift passes together to get a reduction. There are plans to replace the ancient Forêt gondola from Le Praz with a six-pack, and at 1650 the gondola is due to be replaced and rerouted and a new chairlift built to replace the existing drag from the base – but none of these will happen before 2014/15.

2012/13: At 1850, the Biollay quad was replaced by a six-pack, increasing capacity by around a third. At 1650, the 3 Vallées chair from near the top of the village has been removed, and a short gondola takes people to a spot from where they can ski to the main Ariondaz gondola. A Pass Tribu was introduced – allowing three or more people buying lift passes together to get a reduction. And with the new family pass two adults and two or more children now all pay the child rate.

escalator) individual chalets spread down the hill and are served by another (much longer) three-stage covered escalator. Then there is another area of chalet development spreading up the slopes to an area known as Belvedère. 1650 has its own distinct sector of slopes, connected to 1850. It also has a great Intersport rental shop right opposite the main gondola that has excellent demo skis.

1550 is a bit of a backwater, with a few blocks and many more individual properties, directly below 1850. Le Praz is an old village on a plateau at the bottom of wooded slopes.

With a car, Champagny (linked to La Plagne's slopes) is easily reached.

VILLAGE CHARM ★★☆☆☆
Not a strong point

Courchevel 1850 has most of the smart hotels and shops, and you would expect it to be a pretty smooth place in general. The reality is a let-down; when compared with other smart resorts, 1850 does not impress.

The approach has been smartened up but at the hub of the resort, La Croisette, you are confronted by the back side of the main lift station building, complete with garage entrances. Past this point, things improve again: the streets are lined by smart shops and jolly restaurants. But the nearest thing to a central focus is where a hairpin bend on the busy road through the resort to the affluent suburbs touches the slopes. The areas above the centre are more pleasant – in places, peacefully rustic.

Central 1650 is more attractive and has a friendly traditional feel; Editor Watts has had his annual holiday here for the last two seasons. 1550 is a pleasantly quiet, spacious mini-resort, bypassed by the road to 1850. Le Praz suffers from through-traffic, but away from the road is a low-key rustic place, with a friendly atmosphere, relatively unspoilt despite expansion for the

Hot chalets beneath glacial slopes? Check out p258.

Hot chalets beneath glacial slopes? Check out p258.

1992 Olympics – the ski jump is a prominent legacy.

All the villages get a lot of international visitors, and on our March 2013 trip French visitors seemed to be well outnumbered by foreigners.

CONVENIENCE ★★★★☆
Varies – research your location

The villages all have lifts into the slopes, with much of the lodging close by, but in all cases you need to be careful about location if you want to avoid walks. 1850 has several pistes running through it, and a high proportion of ski-in/ski-out lodgings. Central 1650 lodging is a short walk to the lifts, with some ski-in/ski-out places up the hill and the handy covered escalator serving many places down the hill. 1550 is arranged along the bottom of the slopes, with lifts immediately above most of the lodgings. In Le Praz the lifts start a short walk outside the village. Frequent free buses link the villages.

SCENERY ★★★☆☆
Some good views

Most of the villages enjoy a pretty woodland setting, and from parts of them and from the slopes above there are good views to Mont Blanc and over the valley to Champagny and Bellecôte (in the La Plagne ski area).

THE MOUNTAINS

Although there are plenty of trees around the villages, most of the slopes are essentially open, with the notable exception of the runs down to 1550 and to 1300, and the valley between 1850 and 1650.

We have few complaints about the piste map or general signposting. They have stopped handing out maps of

Courchevel

249

NAME CHANGES FOR THE COURCHEVEL VILLAGES

On the advice of a marketing agency, the local town council changed the names of its villages in autumn 2011. Its flagship Courchevel 1850 is now called just Courchevel (an insane move because it means there's no way of distinguishing 1850 from the collective name for all the villages or the valley as a whole). 1650 reverted to the name of the old village it is based on and is now Courchevel Moriond. 1550 became Courchevel Village. Le Praz (sometimes called 1300) is Courchevel Le Praz.

The signs have been changed on the roads. The piste map gives the new names and the altitudes. But most signs on the mountain still refer to the old names of 1850, 1650 and 1550 alone (as do most of the locals). All in all, it's a mess. We're going with the locals and sticking to the old names.

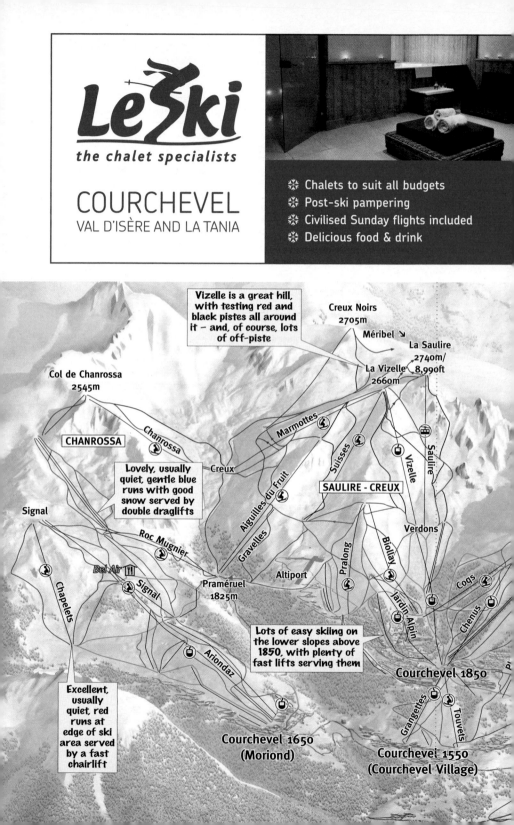

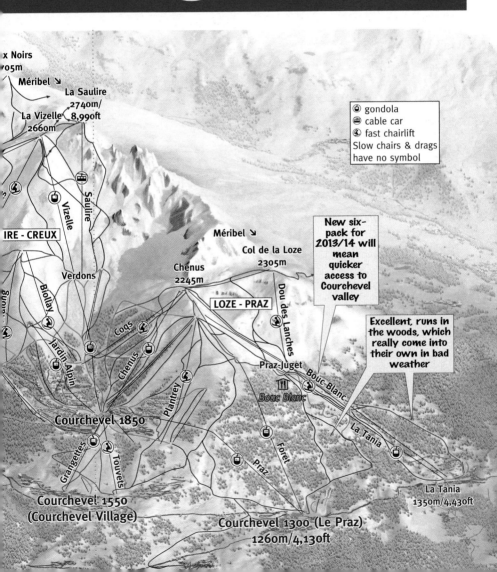

x Noirs
705m

Méribel ↘

La Saulire
2740m/
8,99oft

La Vizelle
266om

IRE - CREUX

Vizelle

Saulire

🚡 gondola
🚠 cable car
🚡 fast chairlift
Slow chairs & drags
have no symbol

Méribel ↘

Col de la Loze
2305m

Chénus
2245m

LOZE - PRAZ

Dou des Lanches

New six-
pack for
2013/14 will
mean
quicker
access to
Courchevel
valley

Excellent, runs in
the woods, which
really come into
their own in bad
weather

Verdons

Biollay

Jardin-Alpin

Cosps

Chénus

Plantrey

Praz-Juget

Bouc Blanc

Bouc Blanc

La Tania

Courchevel 1850

Grangettes

Touvets

Foret

Praz

La Tania
1350m/4,43oft

Courchevel 1550
(Courchevel Village)

Courchevel 1300 (Le Praz)
126om/4,13oft

which pistes have been groomed but you can now get this information on the Trois Vallées smartphone app and it appears in small notices posted in lift stations. They also list 'pistes du jour' (recommended runs that were groomed last night and usually include a black) – a fab idea that we took advantage of every day on our stay.

EXTENT OF THE SLOPES ★★★★★
Huge variety to suit everyone
A network of lifts and pistes spreads out from 1850. The main axis is the **Verdons** gondola, leading to a second gondola to La Vizelle and a nearly parallel cable car up to La Saulire. These high points of the **Saulire–Creux** sector give access to a wide range of terrain above Courchevel and to Méribel and thus the whole of the Trois Vallées. Next to the Verdons gondola is the Jardin Alpin gondola, which serves the hotels until 8pm and also links to lifts and pistes beyond.

To the right looking up, the Chenus gondola goes towards the **Loze–Praz** sector, which forms a second link with Méribel. Runs also go back from here to 1850, and through the woods to La Tania, Le Praz and 1550.

The main gondola from 1650 goes to Bel Air and further lifts on into the **Chanrossa** sector. This sector has links to Saulire–Creux at two points – Praméruel and Creux.

FAST LIFTS ★★★★
Plenty of them
You will occasionally find yourself on a slow chair, but there are only a couple of places where slow lifts are not avoidable. The piste map makes the distinction between slow and fast chairs, which helps. Many of the chairs are now equipped with a 'Magnestick' system where the safety bar is held down automatically until very near the top – this can be quite scary when you first encounter it.

SNOWPIX.COM / CHRIS GILL
The run back to 1850 from Verdons is easy and wooded – with good views over the valley to the La Plagne ski area above Champagny ↓

Courchevel's image is of upmarket luxury and pampered piste skiing. But it is a great resort for off-piste too (always go with a guide). Manu Gaidet is a Courchevel mountain guide and a ski instructor with the Courchevel ESF. He is also one of the world's top freeriders, and won the Freeride World Championship three years running. We asked him to pick out a few of the best runs.

For a first experience off-piste, the Tour du Rocher de l'Ombre is great. Access is easy from the left of the Combe de la Saulire piste, and you are never far from it. It is very quiet, the slope is very broad and easy and you get a real sense of adventure as you plan your way between the rocks. And the view of the Croix des Verdons is impressive. Keep to the left for the best snow.

The Chanrossa chairlift opens up several routes. Les Avals is one of my favourites, involving a short climb to the ridge to the south. This run is not technically difficult and is particularly beautiful in spring conditions. Another possibility is to traverse towards the Aiguille du Fruit, and pick your spot to start skiing down to Creux. And there is Plan Mugnier, a shady run with normally very good snow, but more difficult. It's for experienced off-piste skiers only and starts with a 20-minute hike.

Le Curé is in the Saulire area: this narrow gully starts under a towering rock and offers a steady 35° slope; it is only for expert skiers who don't mind climbing to the Doigt du Curé starting point.

LIFT PASSES

Trois Vallées

Prices in €

Age	1-day	6-day
under 13	42	208
13 to 64	53	260
65 plus	48	234

Free Under 5, 75 plus

Beginner Limited pass

Notes Covers Courchevel, La Tania, Méribel, Val Thorens, Les Menuires and St-Martin; reductions for families and groups of 3+; pedestrian and half-day passes

Alternative passes Courchevel/La Tania + 3V extension; Courchevel 1650 only

QUEUES ★★★★
Not a problem

The lift system is impressive, and even in peak season queues are minimal. But there can be a build-up at 1850 as the ski school gets going. The Biollay chair is very popular with the ski school and was upgraded to a six-pack last season. Despite this, one reporter found queues at New Year and two had to wait '10 to 15 minutes' this March. At 1650, the gondola may have peak-time queues; an upgrade is due for 2014/15. A 2012 visitor found 10-minute waits in mid-February at beginner drags at 1650.

TERRAIN PARKS ★★
Freestyle for all the family

The Family Park below Verdons is now the main park and has lines to suit different levels, with a variety of jumps, rails, tables and obstacles including, at certain times, an airbag jump; there's also a boardercross. There are two smaller 'fun zones' above 1650: Snake Park has boardercross and Fun Park has large bumps. The Wood Park above 1550 has, er, wooden rails and tables.

SNOW RELIABILITY ★★★★
Very good

The combination of Courchevel's northerly orientation, its height, an abundance of snowmaking and excellent grooming usually guarantees good snow down to at least 1850 and 1650. The snow is usually much better than in Méribel, where the slopes get more sun. The runs to 1300 are prone to closure in warm weather.

FOR EXPERTS ★★★★
Entertaining pistes, and ...

There is plenty to interest experts, even without considering the rest of the Trois Vallées. The most obvious expert runs are the shady couloirs you can see on the right near the top of the Saulire cable car. All three main couloirs were once black pistes (some of the steepest in Europe), but only the Grand Couloir remains a piste – the widest and easiest of the three, but reached by a narrow, bumpy, precipitous access ridge.

The shady slopes of La Vizelle and Creux Noirs are not seriously steep, but all the runs – tough reds and not-tough blacks – offer a worthwhile challenge. If you like groomed blacks in the early morning, keep an eye on the grooming notices at lift bases/ticket offices to see when Suisses or M is groomed. Chanrossa often has the most serious bumps. The blacks above Le Praz can be great fun, too – again, they are not seriously steep, but offer a vertical of almost 1000m.

There is a huge amount of off-piste terrain, including lots next to the pistes. The runs off Dou des Lanches through the trees down to La Tania and off the top of Creux Noir (via a little walk) down to join up with the Creux piste are recommended. The wooded areas in general are great for bad weather.

In good snow conditions you can ski all the way down (around 2000m vertical) from La Saulire to Bozel.

There is plenty of other off-piste terrain in this valley to try with a guide – see the feature panel above.

Courchevel

253

Build your own shortlist: www.wheretoskiandsnowboard.com

ACTIVITIES

Indoor Bowling, climbing wall, exhibitions, concerts, cinemas, cookery courses, library; in hotels: health and fitness centres (swimming pools, saunas, steam room, hot tub, water therapy, weight training, massage)

Outdoor Hang-gliding, helicopter flights, paragliding, flying lessons, snowshoeing, snowmobile rides, ballooning, walking on cleared paths, tobogganing, ice climbing, dog sledding

FOR INTERMEDIATES ★★★★★
Paradise for red-run skiers
For confident intermediates, Courchevel's local slopes are simply fabulous. Every sector has long, testing red runs and easy blacks, and there is abundant easy off-piste to experiment in. There are too many excellent runs to list; every high point – Signal, Chanrossa, Vizelle, Creux Noirs, Saulire, Chenus, Loze – offers one, two, three, four notable descents.

For timid intermediates, we're not so enthusiastic. The red runs from Vizelle and Saulire can be quite testing, especially late in the day. But there are some excellent sectors to focus on. The long, narrow sector of blue slopes above 1650 is superb, and there is an array of excellent blue slopes above and below 1850 – the Biollay and Pralong fast chairs are the ones to head for here. On the ridge separating 1850 from La Tania, the Crêtes run and chair offer a great quiet area to build confidence on good snow. The runs on down to La Tania from here are long, rolling cruises, but how easy they are depends crucially on snow conditions.

FOR BEGINNERS ★★★★
Great graduation runs
There are excellent nursery slopes above both 1650 and 1850. At 1650, there are short drags right above the village. At 1850 there is a small but good beginner area in the Jardin Alpin, reachable by the gondola, and an excellent bigger one at Pralong, near the airstrip. Absolute beginners have to get to this by road. Altogether there are nine free beginner lifts – at least one in each village and five in 1850. 1550 and 1300 have small nursery areas; but the former is quite steep. There are some excellent long runs to progress to.

FOR BOARDERS ★★★★
Upmarket all-rounder
Despite being an upmarket resort, Courchevel has always been popular with snowboarders. There are miles of well-groomed pistes, good freeride terrain and the lifts are in general very modern and quick, with few drags. The resort's freestyle facilities are not what you would call hard-core, though.

FOR CROSS-COUNTRY ★★★★
Long wooded trails
Courchevel has around 60km of trails. Le Praz is the best village, with trails through the woods towards 1550, 1850 and Méribel. Given enough snow, there are also loops around the village.

MOUNTAIN RESTAURANTS ★★★
Fine if you can afford them
Mountain restaurants are plentiful and pleasant, but uncomfortably pricey. Fortunately, the local lift pass permits lunch above La Tania; of course the 3V pass gets you to Les Menuires. The piste map does not name restaurants. **Editors' choice** The Bel Air (0479 080093), above 1650, has always stood out for its warm welcome, efficient service, good food, splendid tiered terrace, nice woody interior and (by local standards) reasonable beer and cheap house wine (14 euros a bottle). But even here the food is unpleasantly pricey (25 euros for the plat du jour including a big salad). It and the cheaper Bouc Blanc (see the La Tania chapter) are our firm favourites in the area – and we enjoyed good meals at both in 2013. **Worth knowing about** We've had good lunches at Verdons at the top of the gondola – try for the atmospheric woody upstairs room tucked away off the first room you come to. Good food, very efficient service, reasonably priced pichets but pricey food and bottles of wine; fun conjuror to keep kids amused last time we were there, and live music and dancing on the terrace. We've also enjoyed Pilatus, just below the Altiport: good service and huge portions ('good tartiflette' says a 2013 reporter). The self-service Chenus offers 'reasonable choice and value, very friendly staff, a great steak hâché'. The Courcheneige on the Bellecôte slope is a long-standing reader favourite and was tipped again this year for 'its excellent-value 29 euro three-course lunch', 'the quantity of food has to be seen to be

SCHOOLS

ESF in 1850
t 0479 080772

ESF in 1650
t 0479 082608

ESF in 1550
t 0479 082107

Supreme
t 0479 082787
(UK: 01479 810800)

New Generation
t 0479 010318
0844 770 4733 (UK)
www.skinewgen.com

Magic
t 0479 010181

Oxygène
t 0479 419958

BASS
t 0629 827812

RTM
t 0615 485904

Classes
(ESF 1850 prices)
6 5hr-days €337

Private lessons
From €105 for 1½hr

GUIDES

Bureau des Guides
t 0623 924612

believed'. The Soucoupe at Loze is a traditional place and has 'a wonderful grill with a real fire in its centre' – very expensive though. Chalet de Pierres, between Verdons and 1850, is famously pricey, but we confess to calling in for an occasional treat.

SCHOOLS AND GUIDES ★★★★
Plenty of choice

The many positive reports we have received on New Generation (run by top British instructors) are endorsed this year: 'Really good, excellent English from a French instructor who was really patient with our little terrorist.' Reporters also praise another Brit-based outfit, RTM Snowboarding: 'Great backcountry coaching. Provided split boards and skins for free, extended the four-hour session to all day for free, did a lot of serious backcountry hiking'. A 2013 visitor recommends Magic: 'Our learner had two two-hour private lessons. She went from beginner to a black run; her confidence was sky high.' BASS and Supreme are other Brit-run schools.

The Bureau des Guides runs all-day off-piste excursions.

FOR FAMILIES ★★★★
Lots of suitable options

Courchevel is a good choice for families; there is lots of convenient lodging and gentle slopes. A variation of the 'Magnestick' system (see 'Fast lifts'), using a magnet in the back of a special bib to hold children securely on chairlifts, has been fitted to many fast lifts. The ESF Club des Piou-Piou at 1650, for kids aged three to five, is reportedly 'very well run'. Several UK chalet operators run nurseries. Family specialist Esprit Ski operates in 1850 – read 'Chalets', next. The Indiens blue above 1650 with an 'exciting natural half-pipe and Indian village' was a hit with a 2013 reporter and family.

STAYING THERE

Chalets There are lots available – specialist agents list dozens of them.

1650 is UK chalet central. Le Ski, which celebrated its 30th year there in 2013, now has 17 chalets in 1650 (more than any other operator has in the whole Courchevel valley), sleeping from 2 to 22; 13 of them have sauna, steam or hot tub. Its flagship Scalottas Lodge has five apartment-chalets and

CHILDCARE

Village des Enfants (1850)
t 0479 080847
Ages 18mnth to 3yr

Les Petits Pralins de Moriond (1650)
t 0479 063472
Ages 6mnth to 6yr

Maison des Enfants (1550)
t 0479 082107
Ages from 18mnth

Ski schools
Most offer lessons from age 3 or 4

we've stayed in two of them, both with fabulous views, leather armchairs and sofas, solid wooden floors, a jacuzzi bath and hi-tech lights and heating.

Ski Olympic is also a 1650 specialist, with the central Avals chalet hotel (complete with Rocky's bar) plus two large chalets. Skiworld has four chalets in 1650, including the traditional but smooth Estrella, with hot tub, and two in 1550.

Down in Le Praz, Mountain Heaven has three chalets, including the very luxurious-looking Edelweiss with outdoor hot tub and Jardin d'Angele with sauna, steam room and hot tub. Crystal also has a 14-person chalet in Le Praz and an 8-person one in 1650.

Inghams has five chalets and the very central 30-bedroomed chalet hotel Anémones in 1850, and two chalets with access to a hot tub, sauna and steam room in 1650.

Ski Total has a chalet hotel bang in the centre of 1650 and five chalets and a central 60-bed chalet hotel in 1850. Also in 1850, family specialist Esprit Ski has a chalet hotel with a good pool, sauna and hot tub right next to the lifts at Pralong. We've had glowing reports on its childcare and service – three in 2013 ('our kids had a terrific time') and three in 2012.

Supertravel has 10 very luxurious chalets in 1850 – liberally endowed with saunas, hot tubs, steam rooms and one with a pool. Other luxury operators in 1850 include Consensio, Kaluma and Scott Dunn.

Hotels There are more than 40 hotels,

mostly at 1850 and many of them very swanky. Two were awarded the new 'Palace' rating two years ago – the Cheval Blanc and the Airelles – to distinguish them from the 5-star standard invented only a few years back; 14 now hold 5-star status with a new one due to open in December 2013. The prices of the top places give new meaning to the word 'exorbitant' – it is possible to pay £1,000 per person per night without too much difficulty, though you can of course pay a lot less.

COURCHEVEL 1850

*****Sivolière** (0479 080833) Set among pines on the western edge of the village, with a reputation for friendly service despite the stars.

*****Lana** (0479 080110) Bottom of the Bellecôte piste. Pool, sauna, steam, hot tub, spa. 'Good restaurant, excellent wine list, very good service, rooms are quite small though comfortable,' says a 2013 visitor.

****Bellecôte** (0479 081019) A bit of Alpine atmosphere as well as luxury. Close to the Bellecôte piste.

****Chabichou** (0479 080055) Distinctive white building, right on the slopes; family-run, friendly and rustic, with very good food plus the option of a restaurant with two Michelin stars.

****Courcheneige** (0479 080259) On the Bellecôte piste, with a rustic restaurant. 'Food and service extremely good, but the bedrooms a bit tired.'

COURCHEVEL 1650

*****Manali** (0479 080707) Smart and welcoming; slope-side, just above the gondola, with terrace; spa and pool.

Selected chalets in Courchevel

Alpine Answers, Alpine Weekends, Carrier, Consensio, Crystal, Crystal Finest, Elegant Resorts, Erna Low, Esprit, Flexiski, Friendship Travel, Independent Ski Links, Inghams, Inspired to Ski, Interactive Resorts, Jeffersons, Kaluma, Lagrange, Le Ski, Luxury Chalet Collection, Mark Warner, Momentum, Mountain Beds, Neilson, Oxford Ski Co, Pierre & Vacances, Powder White, PowderBeds, Scott Dunn, Silver Ski, Ski Amis, Ski Bespoke, Ski Bluebird, Ski Collection, Ski Expectations, Ski France, Ski Independence, Ski Line, Ski Olympic, Ski Solutions, Ski Total, Ski Weekend, Skitracer, Skiweekends.com, Skiworld, Snow Finders, Snoworks, STC, Supertravel, Thomson, White Roc
Le Praz Mountain Heaven, Ski Deep

GETTING THERE

Air Geneva 150km/
95 miles (2hr15);
Lyon 195km/
120 miles (2hr30);
Chambéry 110km/
70 miles (1hr30)

Rail Moûtiers (24km/
15 miles); transfer by
bus or taxi

Phone numbers
From abroad use the
prefix +33 and omit
the initial '0' of the
phone number

TOURIST OFFICE

www.courchevel.com

****Portetta** (0479 080147) Neat place at foot of slopes, with steam, hot tub, spa, good restaurant.
***Seizena** (0479 082636) Stylish and central (over road from the gondola).
COURCHEVEL 1550
***Flocons** (0479 080270) Handsome chalet-style building near the Tovets six-pack and the piste from 1850.
COURCHEVEL LE PRAZ
***Peupliers** (0479 084147)
Traditional, smart, good restaurant.
Apartments If you want to self-cater in real style, take a look at the chalets in the resort literature. Ski Amis has privately owned apartments in several parts of the resort, and Skiworld has 'flexible catered chalets' where you can choose what catering (if any) you want. Mountain Heaven has two apartments in Le Praz. The best big residences are the Montagnettes Chalets de la Mouria in 1650 (we stayed there happily in 2013) with sauna, steam and hot tub that you book privately for just your group, and the renovated Chalets du Forum in central 1850 – a Pierres & Vacances Premium residence. Ski Collection features both these. Skitracer is an apartment specialist.

EATING OUT ★★★★★
Pick your price
You can eat very well here, but you have more choice if you have a fat wallet. A non-comprehensive pocket guide is distributed. In 1850 there are no fewer than five places with two Michelin stars and one with one star. A regular visitor recommends Chabotté ('very good food, not that expensive') – owned by, next to and much cheaper than the two Michelin-starred Chabichou. For the budget conscious, the Passage serves 'yummy pizzas' at 'affordable prices'. La Luge also does 'decent burgers and salads'. More reports on affordable places, please.

In 1650 two places which both do pizza, pasta and Savoyard dishes have been recommended again by 2013 reporters – the Petit Savoyard ('good food, friendly and professional staff') and La Table de Marie ('great atmosphere, reasonably priced').

At 1550 the Oeil de Boeuf at the foot of the Tovets run is 'excellent, great steaks cooked on an open fire'.

In Le Praz, the small and unpretentious Michelin-starred Azimut is much more affordable than equivalent places in 1850 (three-course

menus from 28 euros), and we had a delicious meal there in 2012. The Table de Mon Grand-Père has 'superb food and atmosphere' but prices approaching 1850 levels. Bistrot du Praz is also expensive but worth it, say reporters. Cave de Lys is an atmospheric vaulted wine bar that serves tapas-style snacks.

APRES-SKI ★★★★
The choice is yours
At close of play there are bars around the Croisette that are good for a relaxing drink; we like the Tremplin (but not its prices: 12 euros for a half litre of beer). Kudeta is 'good value at happy hour' and later its disco pumps until 4am, as does the Grange – a Moroccan-style place. There are some exclusive nightclubs, such as Caves. The Mangeoire piano bar gets going late and has live music. The Tremplin has karaoke. The P'tit Drink specializes in wine and tapas. The bar of hotel Olympic has 'pints for 3 euros'.

In 1650 there are several lively bars within a few yards of each other. The Bubble and Rocky's are Brit-run, and the Bubble and the Boulotte fill up with chalet staff letting their hair down. We like the Schuss for a quiet drink as the lifts close (great views over 1550 from the windows of the rear tables). The lively Funky Fox has pool, live music or DJs, and the Clinik disco stays open late.

In 1550 there are a handful of bars that can develop a lively atmosphere – the Caterail has DJs and live music.

OFF THE SLOPES ★★★
Not ideal
There is quite a bit to do, but the emphasis is very much on physical activities. A guide to walks is available from the tourist office. A pedestrian lift pass for the gondolas and buses in Courchevel and Méribel makes it easy for non-skiers to get up the mountain to meet others for lunch. There is no public pool, and although some hotel pools are open to non-residents the prices are astronomical. Cinemas in 1850 and 1650 show English-speaking films. Snowshoeing among the trees and 'seriously awesome' tobogganing from 1850 to 1550 are popular. And you can take joyrides from the Altiport. There is a guide listing fashion and jewellery shops in 1850 – the prices in these shops are stratospheric and the customers mostly rich Russians.

Les Deux-Alpes

Sprawling resort with a high, narrow ski area that will disappoint many intermediates; popular for summer skiing and boarding

258

RATINGS

The mountains

Extent	★★★
Fast lifts	★★★★
Queues	★★
Terrain p'ks	★★★★★
Snow	★★★★
Expert	★★★★
Intermediate	★★
Beginner	★★★
Boarder	★★★★
X-country	★★
Restaurants	★★★
Schools	★★★
Families	★★★★

The resort

Charm	★★
Convenience	★★★
Scenery	★★★★
Eating out	★★★★
Après-ski	★★★★
Off-slope	★★

RPI	95
lift pass	£190
ski hire	£105
lessons	£75
food & drink	£135
total	**£505**

NEWS

2012/13: The Diable gondola at the Venosc end of town was replaced by a six-pack. The Crêtes ski-tow for beginners was replaced with a covered moving carpet.

+ High, snow-sure, varied slopes, including an extensive glacier

+ Lots of good off-piste terrain

+ Stunning views of the Ecrins peaks

+ Wide choice of affordable hotels

− Piste network modest by big resort standards, and congested in places

− Home runs are either steep and icy or dangerously overcrowded

− Virtually no woodland runs

Les Deux-Alpes is a big resort, with a tall mountain. But it doesn't come from the standard major resort mould: it is not at all swanky, and good-value hotels are not hard to find. Its mountain is unusual, too: tall and long, offering a splendid Alpine feel, but narrow, with pistes limited in total extent.

We've been complaining since 1994 about the dangerous home runs here. We were told two years ago that the resort was planning a blue alternative to the icy blacks and hideously crowded green. It hasn't materialized, although the piste map suggests that a red run now has. We look forward to trying it.

THE RESORT

Les Deux-Alpes is a long, narrow village sitting on a high col. It is modern, but gives the impression that its development has been unplanned.

Four sectors can be identified. As you enter from the north you pass through an area centred on the tourist office; from here, roads go off left up to Les 2 Alpes 1800; go straight on instead, and you come to the effective centre, with the major gondola stations, outdoor ice rink and lots of shops and restaurants; at this point you enter a long one-way system, and finally come to Alpe de Venosc.

The six-day pass covers La Grave and gives two days in Alpe-d'Huez and days in Serre-Chevalier (an hour away) and other resorts. A car would be handy to make the most of these options. There are day-trip buses twice a week to Alpe-d'Huez, but a better plan is to splash out 70 euros on the splendid helicopter day trip.

VILLAGE CHARM ★★
Lively, but that's all

The village is a long, sprawling collection of apartments, hotels, bars and shops, most lining the two streets that form the one-way traffic system. There is a wide range of building styles, from old chalets through 1960s blocks to more sympathetic recent buildings. Alpe de Venosc has the most character and the best shops. The resort's buildings looks better as you leave than as you arrive – all the balconies face south. The place has quite a buzz in the early evening.

CONVENIENCE ★★★
Fine if you pick your spot

It's a long village – well over 2km end to end – but lifts are dotted fairly evenly along it, and it's not difficult to find lodgings within walking distance of one of the major ones. We'd go for Alpe de Venosc and the new Diable chair. Les 2 Alpes 1800 is inconvenient for shopping and nightlife. A free shuttle-bus links all parts of the resort every 15 minutes.

SCENERY ★★★★
High southern peaks

The resort sits high among the southern Alps, with great views from the upper slopes of the Ecrins peaks.

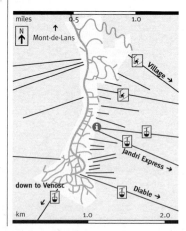

KEY FACTS

Resort	1650m
	5,410ft
Slopes	1300-3570m
	4,270-11,710ft
Lifts	53
Pistes	203km
	126 miles
Green	21%
Blue	45%
Red	22%
Black	12%
Snowmaking	
	211 guns

There are lots of fun features in Freestyle Land at mid-mountain – which in Les Deux-Alpes means at over 2600m ↓

THE MOUNTAINS

The main slopes are all above the treeline, though there are trees directly above the village.

The piste map is very unusual for the Alps in breaking the slopes down into several separate maps. It's a good idea, but poorly executed – the map is still unclear around mid-mountain. We remain unimpressed by the apparently logical scheme of naming runs after the lift they lead to.

A few blue runs have short steep sections, and some runs are different colours on the map and the mountain.

EXTENT OF THE SLOPES ★★★☆☆
Surprisingly small
For a big resort, Les Deux-Alpes has a disappointingly small area of pistes. The main area goes high and stretches a long way – almost 8km from top to bottom – but it is very narrow.

Since our 2000 edition we have been querying the claimed extent. It turns out that the stated figure on the piste map of 225km includes 20km of cross-country loops. But even 205km feels like an exaggeration, and it is. The Schrahe report discussed in our piste extent feature puts the total at 134km. To us, even that feels too high. One reason is that the slopes just above the village don't usually figure in your day – one side is too sunny to offer reliable conditions, and the other side is not well connected.

The morning-sun side of Les Deux-

Alpes, now branded **Vallée Blanche**, is served by lifts at either end of town. It is relatively low (the top is 2100m) so has only short pistes back to town.

On the broad, gentle slope east of the resort are about 10 beginner lifts, and above them a steep slope rising to the ridge of **Les Crêtes**. Lifts go up to the ridge from four points spread along the village. To get back to base you have a choice of a long, winding, narrow green run, often very crowded (and sometimes closed), or three short black runs. The blacks are usually mogulled, and often icy at the end of the day (they get the afternoon sun). Many visitors ride down.

The resort has been promising for years to construct an alternative blue run to the village. We are still waiting – but the piste map now shows a new red run down the Diable chair. When we visited last season our guide from the tourist office didn't include it in our whistle-stop one-day tour, so it may be imaginary.

The ridge has lifts and gentle runs along it, and behind it lies the deep, steep Combe de Thuit. Lifts span the combe to the mid-mountain station at **Toura**, at the heart of the slopes. We seem to spend a lot of time on three key fast chairlifts in this area – Bellecombes, at the top of the Combe; Glaciers, carrying on towards the glacier; and Fée, on its own slightly separate hill. The section of the mountain around and below Toura is very narrow – there is one main way

down, and it gets crowded in the afternoon; but there are now three ways to avoid the worst of the crowds, so they are much less problematic than they once were.

The top **Glacier du Mont de Lans** section has long, easy runs with great views, served by an underground funicular and draglifts. There are steeper slopes off to the north, served by chairs. From the top you can descend all the way to Mont-de-Lans – a descent of 2270m that we believe is the world's biggest on-piste vertical. In the opposite direction, a walk (or snowcat tow) takes you to the famously challenging slopes of La Grave (read our separate chapter).

FAST LIFTS ★★★★☆
Main lifts OK, but …
Les Deux-Alpes has some impressive lifts, with fast chair alternatives to the gondolas. But there are still a few draglifts and slow chairs around.

QUEUES ★★☆☆☆
Problems remain
The village is large, and queues for the gondolas in the morning can be serious. The new Diable chair has improved the total lift capacity out of the village, and to judge by 2013 reports is itself not queue-prone. But

the big Jandri gondola still attracts crowds – it offers a more direct way to the high slopes than the Diable, and is more convenient if you are not staying at the south end of the village. We have reports of 20-minute waits in the mornings even in January last season. The lifts at the junction of the two sectors, at the north end of the village, are also reported to build queues.

Up the mountain there may be queues in late season for the lifts to the glacier, and the Crêtes area gets busy in peak season. The top lifts are prone to closure if it's windy, putting pressure on the lower lifts. There may be queues for the gondolas back to the village when snow is poor.

TERRAIN PARKS ★★★★★
Europe's biggest summer park
The winter terrain park is located above Toura. It is well maintained, and features a slope-style line with three tables, rails, hips and boxes, a big air jump, a half-pipe, a kids-only mini park, a beginner zone and a rail zone, as well as a boardercross and a BBQ area. There's a 120m 4.5m-radius half-pipe. All in all 'possibly the best I have seen' is the view of one reporter.

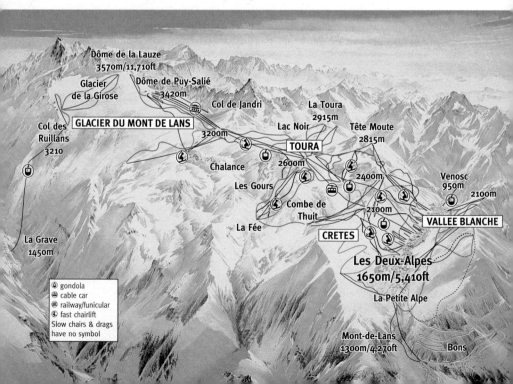

Dôme de la Lauze
3570m/11,710ft

Glacier de la Girose

Dôme de Puy-Salié
3420m

Col de Jandri

La Toura
2915m

Col des Ruillans
3210

GLACIER DU MONT DE LANS

3200m

Lac Noir

Tête Moute
2815m

Chalance

2600m

TOURA

Les Gours

2400m

Venosc
950m

2100m

Combe de Thuit

2100m

VALLEE BLANCHE

La Fée

CRETES

2100m

La Grave
1450m

Les Deux-Alpes
1650m/5,410ft

La Petite Alpe

gondola
cable car
railway/funicular
fast chairlift
Slow chairs & drags have no symbol

Mont-de-Lans
1300m/4,270ft

Bons

The off-piste routes in Les Deux-Alpes are numerous, and varied in difficulty. But never try them without the right equipment and a qualified guide.

*Both sides off the **Bellecombes** piste offer a wide range of varying terrain; it's important to take care here – there are several small cliff faces. For those keen to tackle couloirs, this descent offers small ones that are ideal for your first attempts; they can be avoided, though.*

*Traversing across the top of the black Grand Couloir piste leads to the **North Rachas** area, with off-piste faces that normally offer good snow conditions all winter. The first large valley leads to three couloirs – one fairly broad and easy, the others much narrower and steeper. Traversing further leads to a much wider descent that avoids the three couloirs.*

*Strong skiers will enjoy the famous **Chalance** run (our favourite), which starts just below the glacier and descends 1000m to join the Fée 1 piste; there are several variations, mixing wide open slopes and rocky pitches. These faces are at times subject to quite a high avalanche risk.*

*Traversing above the north face of the Chalance leads to the couloir **Pylone Electrique** – a steep, narrow 200m-long couloir with the reward below it of an excellent wide powder field of moderate gradient. A rest on the Thuit chairlift is a must after this adrenalin-charged descent.*

*As well as these routes within the local lift network, there is a renowned descent to **St-Christophe** (you get a taxi back), and the famous **La Grave** terrain (see separate chapter) is easily accessed.*

LIFT PASSES

Prices in €

Age	1-day	6-day
under 13	34	168
13 to 64	43	211
65 plus	34	168

Free Under 5, 72 plus
Beginner Five free lifts
Notes Family rates; half-day and pedestrian passes; 6-day pass includes entry to swimming pool and ice rink and access to La Grave, and two days in Alpe-d'Huez and one day in Serre-Chevalier, Puy-St-Vincent, Montgenèvre and Sestriere (in Italy)
Alternative pass
Ski Sympa – covers 21 lifts

GETTING THERE

Air Lyon 160km/ 100 miles (2hr45); Grenoble 110km/ 70 miles (2hr15); Chambéry 135km/ 85 miles (2hr15); Geneva 220km/ 135 miles (3hr30)

Rail Grenoble (70km/43 miles); four daily buses from station

SNOW RELIABILITY ★★★★☆
Excellent on higher slopes
The snow on the higher slopes is normally very good, even in a poor winter. On a tour in March 2012 that involved skiing crud in most resorts, we enjoyed packed powder most of the day here. Above 2200m most of the runs are north-facing, and the top glacier section guarantees good snow. But the runs just above the village from Les Crêtes face west, so they get afternoon sun and are often icy. Snowmaking covers some of the lower slopes – apparently including the home green run, at last.

When we visited in 2012, some runs were kept closed in the morning because they were dangerously hard, and opened only once they had softened. This is an excellent scheme.

FOR EXPERTS ★★★★☆
Off-piste is the main attraction
The area offers excellent off-piste – read the panel above. In the past, five routes (including Chalance, described above) were identified as itinéraires, but they are no longer on the map.

There are a few black pistes. The run down the Bellecombes chair is a genuine black, with the best chance of good snow. Fée 6 from above Toura has one steep pitch at the end. Fée 5 isn't much more testing than the adjacent red. The runs down to the resort often have poor snow. The short black higher up served by the Super Diable chairlift is among the steepest.

FOR INTERMEDIATES ★★☆☆☆
Limited cruising
Les Deux-Alpes can disappoint keen intermediates because of the limited extent of the pistes. Avid piste-bashers will cover the pistes in a couple of days. A lot of the runs are either rather tough – some of the blues could be reds – or boringly bland. The runs higher up generally have good snow, and there is some great fast cruising, especially from the glacier to Toura and on the mainly north-facing pistes served by the chairlifts off to the sides. You can often pick gentle or steeper terrain in these bowls as you wish. The chairlifts at the glacier serve great carving pistes. The Vallée Blanche area apparently has quite testing red runs.

Less confident intermediates will love the quality of the snow and the gentle runs on the upper mountain.

FOR BEGINNERS ★★★☆☆
Good slopes
The nursery slopes beside the village are spacious and gentle, and seven lifts are free. The runs along the ridge above them are excellent, too, except when crowded at the end of the day. The glacier also has a fine array of long, very easy slopes.

FOR BOARDERS ★★★★☆
Big appeal
Les Deux-Alpes has become a snowboard Mecca over the past few years in summer when the pros

261

ACTIVITIES

Indoor Swimming pool, hot tub, sauna, sports centres (Club Forme, Acqua Center), squash, cinemas, games rooms, bowling, museums, library

Outdoor Ice rink, snowmobiling, paragliding, quad bikes, snowshoeing, ice climbing, tobogganing, ice gliding, sleigh rides

descend en masse. In the winter, the limited pisted slopes aren't as off-putting to boarders as to skiers. In town there are good trampoline facilities and a huge airbag to get a feeling of what air-time is all about. Although the focus is on the terrain park, the freeriding is not to be underestimated, with plenty of steep challenging terrain. Beginners will find the narrow, flat crowded areas mid-mountain and the routes down to the village intimidating. Most of the lifts on the higher slopes are chairs.

FOR CROSS-COUNTRY ★★
Needs very low-altitude snow
There are small, widely dispersed areas. Given good snow, Venosc, reached by a gondola down, has the only worthwhile picturesque ones. Total trail length is 20km.

MOUNTAIN RESTAURANTS ★★★
A few good places
The restaurants at the major lift junctions are generally unremarkable. Happily there are exceptions.
Editors' choice Diable au Coeur (0476 799950) at the top of the Diable lift has excellent food (delicious confit de

canard on our last visit) and service. Readers agree ('we ate there 3 times in a week it was so good'). The terrace gives good views, but sit as far as you can from the noisy adjacent chairlift machinery. The bigger Chalet la Toura (0671 920768), in a fine position with a big terrace at Toura in the middle of the slopes, is pleasantly woody, and serves good food.
Worth knowing about The Pano, also at Toura, has 'a wide range of daily specials' but is notable mainly for its (brief) après session. There is a small table-service restaurant attached to the big self-service at the bottom of the glacier at 3200m. The Bergerie on the Pied Moutet slopes has been recommended in the past.
   There are picnic rooms at the Toura lift junction, and at the glacier near the top of the cable car.

SCHOOLS AND GUIDES ★★★
Fair selection to choose from
A 2012 reporter was pleased with his son's progress with the ESF. There are plenty of other schools to choose from but we lack recent reports. Freeride Attitude is a free off-piste safety course that sounds well organized.

SCHOOLS

ESF
t 0476 792121

**International
St-Christophe**
t 0476 790421

European
t 0476 797455

Evolution 2
t 0695 978220

Classes (ESF prices)
6 days €238

Private lessons
From €43 for 1hr for
1 or 2 people

GUIDES

Bureau des guides
t 0476 113629

CHILDCARE

**Crèche du Bonhomme
de Neige**
t 0476 790262
Ages 6mnth to 2yr

**Garderie le
Bonhomme de Neige**
t 0476 790677
Ages 2 to 6

Ski schools
Snow gardens for
ages 3 to 6; classes
for ages 6 to 12

UK PACKAGES

Action Outdoors, Alpine
Answers, AmeriCan Ski,
Club Med, Crystal, Erna
Low, Friendship Travel,
Independent Ski Links,
Inghams, Interactive
Resorts, Lagrange,
Mark Warner, Neilson,
Peak Retreats, Pierre &
Vacances, Powder
White, PowderBeds,
Rocketski, Ski
Collection, Ski
Expectations, Ski
France, Ski Ici, Ski
Independence, Ski Line,
Ski Power, Ski
Solutions, Ski Supreme,
Ski Total, Skitracer,
Skiworld, Snoworks,
STC, Thomson, Zenith

Phone numbers
From abroad use the
prefix +33 and omit
the initial '0' of the
phone number

TOURIST OFFICE

www.les2alpes.com

FOR FAMILIES ★★★★
Fine facilities
The village nursery takes kids from six months to two years, the kindergarten from two to six years, and there are chalet-based alternatives run by UK tour operators.

STAYING THERE
The resort has that rarity in high French resorts, an abundance of affordable hotels. There is a Club Med.
Chalets Several UK tour operators run catered chalets or chalet hotels. Ski Total, new to the resort this year, has two newly built chalets well placed at the Venosc end of the resort, with the unusual facility of a mini pool (5m long) on the terrace. Skiworld has four varied chalets including one with outdoor hot tub. Crystal has four, again one or two with hot tubs. Nielson has four. Mark Warner runs a chalet hotel with pool up near 1800.
Hotels There are about 30 hotels, of which the majority are 2-star or below.
★★★★Chalet Mounier (0476 805690) Smartly modernized. Good reputation for food. Pool, steam, sauna, hot tub. At the Venosc end of the resort.
★★★Côte Brune (0476 805489) Transformed in recent years, now a charming woody chalet. On the snow, near Jandri Express. We stayed here in 2012: comfortable rooms, good food.
★★Lutins (0476 792152) Central, basic, convenient, clean and friendly.
Apartments There are plenty of large apartment blocks, but most are notable chiefly for the value they offer. Pierre & Vacances, for example, has three of its value-oriented Maeva residences. Peak Retreats offers some attractive properties ranging from flats in the newly refurbished residence Ours Blanc through the mid-sized Cortina to cute four-bedroom chalets.
Out of resort Close to the final ascent to Les Deux-Alpes are two small hotels, near-ideal for anyone planning to visit Alpe-d'Huez, La Grave and Serre-Chevalier as well as Les Deux-Alpes – the Cassini (0476 800410) at Le Freney, and Panoramique (0476 800625) at Mizoën. An alternative is to stay in the Venosc valley, in a hamlet close to the gondola.

EATING OUT ★★★★
Plenty of choice
There are about 50 restaurants, including lots of simple places such as crêperies. The P'tit Polyte restaurant in the hotel Chalet Mounier has a high reputation. Reader tips include La Grange, Alisier, Patate, Cloche, Crêpes à Gogo ('sounds dreadful but actually a lovely Alpine bar with nice snack food'), Eli's ('good steak, duck etc'), Smokey Joes (Tex-Mex) and Etable. You can get a relatively cheap meal at Bleuets bar, and the Vetrata.

APRES-SKI ★★★★
Hit by exchange rate blues?
Les Deux-Alpes has traditionally been one of the liveliest of French resorts, but reports seem to suggest that it has become quieter in recent years.
On the mountain, an attempt is made to deliver Austrian-style afternoon après action at the Pano at Toura ('very lively') and at Diable au Coeur. We can't see the latter taking off until the long-awaited blue run to the village is in place.
There are still plenty of places to try in the village – the resort website lists about 25. Among the bars favoured by reporters are Pub le Windsor – a smaller, quieter place popular with locals; and the Polar Bear Pub – 'the pick for the 30s English crowd, with just enough space for a dance later on'. Smokey Joes is a popular central sports bar and the Secret has live music and a wide choice of beers. The Red Frog has a big-screen TV and shows sports. The main bar at 1800 is O'Brians; Smithy's Tavern and Mini Bar 'attract the younger crowd and the seasonaires'.
The Avalanche is the main nightclub ('crushingly busy') at the Venosc end of town.

OFF THE SLOPES ★★★★★
Limited options
The pretty valley village of Venosc is worth a visit by gondola, and you can take a scenic helicopter flight to Alpe-d'Huez. There are lots of walks, a big outdoor pool and the Acqua Center has an indoor pool, sauna, steam and hot tub. There's an outdoor artificial ice rink, and three toboggan runs. Several mountain restaurants are accessible to pedestrians. The White Cruise is a snowcat ride across the glacier, providing wonderful views. There is now an ice cave in the glacier, complete with ice sculptures. The resort has a simulator that lets you experience what it's like to be caught in an avalanche. Can't wait.

Flaine

Uncompromisingly modern, high-altitude resort sharing a big, broad area of varied slopes with more rustic alternatives

RATINGS

The mountains

Extent	★★★★
Fast lifts	★★★
Queues	★★★
Terrain p'ks	★★★
Snow	★★★★
Expert	★★★★
Intermediate	★★★★★
Beginner	★★★★★
Boarder	★★★
X-country	★★
Restaurants	★★
Schools	★★★
Families	★★★★

The resort

Charm	★
Convenience	★★★★★
Scenery	★★★★
Eating out	★★
Après-ski	★
Off-slope	★

RPI 100

lift pass	£190
ski hire	£110
lessons	£70
food & drink	£150
total	**£520**

NEWS

2013/14: The Diamant Noir double chair on the upper slopes will be replaced by a fast quad. The pool and spa at the smart new Centaure residence will open.

2012/13: The old four-seat Aup de Veran gondola was replaced by an eight-seater. A new CGH residence opened in the middle of Forum – Le Centaure – and a new restaurant at the bottom of the Almandine run opened – the Pente à Jules.

+ Big, varied area of slopes

+ Reliable snow in the main bowl

+ Compact, convenient, mainly car-free village, plus traditional villages on the lower fringes of the area

+ Excellent facilities for children

− Still some slow old chairlifts

− Austere 1960s buildings

− Bad weather can close main Flaine bowl and links to outer sectors

− Nightlife very quiet

− Little to do off the slopes

Flaine is best known as a convenient resort catering particularly well for families, but it has a much broader appeal than that. The Grand Massif is an excellent and extensive area, with plenty to amuse anyone.

Apartments rule here. There are some very good ones, though; and there are wider lodging options in the outlying traditional villages – Samoëns and Les Carroz (which have their own chapters) and Morillon (covered here).

THE RESORT

Flaine was built from scratch in the 1960s at the foot of a big snowy bowl. It's high, but not super-high (it is set among trees); the road in from Les Carroz actually involves a final descent from a col some 250m higher. The architecture of the main village is distinctive and uncompromising; it has its admirers, not including us.

The road in passes two satellite mini-resorts: Hameau de Flaine – lots of small chalets and the residence Refuge du Golf – and Montsoleil, developed by Intrawest. The main resort is tiny, as our plan shows. There are two parts: Forum, centred on a square blending with the slopes, and bigger Forêt – up the hillside, linked by two lifts (vulnerable to snow, we hear), with its own bars and shops.

Flaine is linked with the lower, traditional villages mentioned above. A car gives you the option of visiting the Portes du Soleil, Megève or Chamonix.

VILLAGE CHARM ★
Not to our taste
The concrete Bauhaus-style blocks that form the core of Flaine were supposed to exhibit 'the principle of shadow and light'. They look shocking from the approach road; from the slopes they are less obtrusive, blending into the rocky grey hillside.

As a place to inhabit, Flaine has an austere feel, and some buildings are now looking tatty. In contrast, the Hameau de Flaine is built in a traditional chalet style, as is

Montsoleil. The resort is mainly traffic-free, and the heart of Forum certainly is, but roads do penetrate the village for access to the residences.

CONVENIENCE ★★★★★
A fine example
The main resort is compact and convenient. Hameau de Flaine is about 1km from the main village, and has one shop, one bar, one restaurant. Montsoleil is much nearer to the mother ship (a few hundred metres' walk) and it has linking pistes. There's a 'very good' free bus service around the village including these areas; in the evening, we are told it is replaced by a free bookable taxi service.

SCENERY ★★★★
Good all around the Massif
The scenery within the area is quite varied, with rocky ridges and partly wooded hillsides – the views from the dividing ridges across the Vernant and Molliets valleys are particularly lovely. To the south-west, the Aravis chain looks dramatic, while there are great views of the Mont Blanc massif from the high-points.

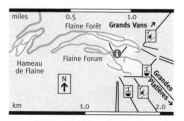

KEY FACTS

Resort	1600m
	5,250ft

Grand Massif (Flaine, Les Carroz, Morillon, Samoëns, Sixt)	
Slopes	700-2480m
	2,300-8,140ft
Lifts	68
Pistes	265km
	165 miles
Green	11%
Blue	46%
Red	33%
Black	10%
Snowmaking	
	218 guns

For Flaine only	
Slopes	1600-2480m
	5,250-8,140ft
Lifts	23
Pistes	140km
	87 miles

SNOWPIX.COM / CHRIS GILL

With snow on the roofs and a dusting on the trees, maybe it doesn't look so bad ... or are we just mellowing a bit? ↓

THE MOUNTAINS

The slopes in the Flaine bowl are mainly open, but the lowest slopes are wooded. Outside the bowl, above the other villages, it's the opposite – most of the runs are below the treeline.

The latest piste map is a vast improvement on the previous version, with a better attempt to define the individual bowls; but it is still difficult to read, and sometimes misleading. Piste classification is generally accurate, but the blue Tourmaline is an exception – distinctly tough.

EXTENT OF THE SLOPES ★★★★
A big white playground
Grand Massif is an impressive area; but its claimed 265km of pistes is an exaggeration – measured down the fall line the total is only 170km. Read our feature on piste extent at the front of the book. A large part of the domain lies outside the main Flaine bowl; the links are vulnerable to bad weather.

The **Grandes Platières** jumbo gondola speeds you in a single stage up the north-west-facing Flaine bowl to the high-point of the Grand Massif. Both the Aup de Veran gondola and the Tête des Verds fast chair offer alternatives on the upper mountain. There are essentially four or five main ways down the largely treeless, rolling terrain back to Flaine. On skier's right, the Cascades blue run leads away from the lift system behind the Tête

Pelouse down to the outskirts of Sixt, dropping over 1700m in its exceptional 14km length. The gentle/flat top half is hard work, especially for boarders, and the run is scenic rather than exciting. At the end you can get a bus (often crowded) to the lifts at Samoëns.

On the near side of the Tête Pelouse, a broad catwalk leads to the experts-only **Gers** bowl.

Back at Platières, an alternative is to head left down the lovely long red Méphisto to a quieter area of slopes beneath Tête des Lindars.

The eight-seat Grand Vans chair gives access to the extensive slopes of **Les Carroz**, **Morillon** and **Samoëns** via the wide Vernant bowl. This and the adjacent Molliets bowl have lift bases with car parks on the road between Les Carroz and Flaine.

FAST LIFTS ★★★
Gradual progress
Replacement of the Diamant Noir double chair for the coming season is very welcome, and effectively opens up an additional fast route to the top. But there are still some frustrating lifts inside and (especially) outside the Flaine bowl. Read the chapters on Les Carroz and Samoëns.

QUEUES ★★★
Still some problems
Despite improvements, the system still can't cope with high-season crowds. The main gondola to Platières is prone to queues despite the alternative

routes; at least it has a singles line. The new Diamant Noir chair at mid-mountain should help, by encouraging people to use the Aup de Veran gondola to get up the hill. In French school holidays all the major lifts can build queues at peak times of the day. Queues in the bowl are particularly likely at weekends if the lifts out of the bowl are shut by wind or if the lower resorts have poor snow.

Some of the blue runs forming links between the resorts get seriously crowded, especially at the beginning and end of the day – Silice and Tourmaline on the way from Samoëns to Flaine, and Perce-Neige at Tête des Saix on the way to Morillon and Les Carroz.

TERRAIN PARKS ★★★☆☆
Cater for kids to experts
The main JamPark Pro (Jam = Jib and Air Maniacs) has a table, rails, kickers, a hip, a 'very good' skicross course and a chill-out zone – 'great variety', said a 2012 reporter. The park is on the edge of the area, served by the Aujon draglift, which also serves some popular blue runs, so it can build queues at busy times.

SNOW RELIABILITY ★★★★☆
Usually keeps its whiteness
Most of the main bowl faces north-west, and keeps snow well. There is snowmaking on many of the lower runs. The slopes outside the bowl are lower. Grooming is excellent.

The 14km-long, lift-free Cascades run to Sixt

Long, tricky draglift that serves a steep black run with great off-piste both sides

GERS

Grand Va 2205m

Tête des Saix 2120m

Vernants

1600m

Chariande Express

This six-pack above Samoëns 1600 has made Samoëns a more appealing base

SAMOENS

1500m

Grand Massif 1600m

Saix

Sairon

Les Esserts

Sixt 800m

Good runs down the old gondola from Vercland, none down the newer one from close to Samoëns

1100m

Samoëns 720m/2,360ft

Morillon 700m/2,300ft

Morillon

MORILLON

Great easy cruising above Morillon – good in bad weather

LIFT PASSES

Grand Massif

Prices in €

Age	1-day	6-day
under 16	31	162
16 to 64	42	216
65 plus	40	205

Free Under 5, 75 plus

Beginner Three free lifts

Notes Family discounts

Alternative pass Flaine area only

FOR EXPERTS ★★★★☆
Great fun with guidance

Flaine has some seriously challenging terrain. But much of it is off-piste, and although some looks temptingly safe this impression is mistaken. The Flaine bowl is riddled with rock crevasses and potholes, and should be treated with glacier-style caution.

All the black pistes are genuine. The Diamant Noir, close to the line of the main gondola, is tricky because of moguls, narrowness and other people, rather than great steepness; the first pitch is the steepest. To skier's left of Diamant Noir are several short, steep off-piste routes through the crags.

The Lindars Nord chair serves a worthwhile slope that often has the best snow in the area.

The Gers draglift, outside the main bowl, serves great on- and off-piste expert terrain in a north-facing bowl (of about 550m vertical) that normally has good snow top to bottom. The Onyx piste is a proper black and nearby off-piste slopes reach 45°. There are more adventurous ways in from the Grand Vans and Véret lifts. Further serious black pistes go down from Tête des Saix towards Samoëns. A reader recommends the Corbalanche piste and the off-piste bowl to skier's right, above the little Airon lake.

Fine chalets in a fun French village? Check out p258.

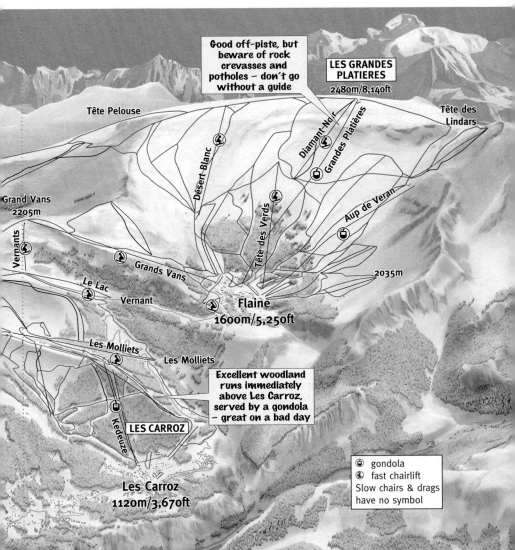

Good off-piste, but beware of rock crevasses and potholes – don't go without a guide

LES GRANDES PLATIERES
248om/8,140ft

Tête Pelouse

Tête des Lindars

Désert-Blanc

Diamant-Noir

Grandes Platières

Grand Vans
2205m

Aup de Veran

Vernants

Tête-des-Verds

2035m

Grands Vans

Le Lac

Vernant

Flaine
1600m/5,250ft

Les Molliets

Les Molliets

Excellent woodland runs immediately above Les Carroz, served by a gondola – great on a bad day

Kedeuze

LES CARROZ

Les Carroz
1120m/3,670ft

☺ gondola
☻ fast chairlift
Slow chairs & drags have no symbol

SCHOOLS

ESF
t 0450 908100

Internationale
t 0450 908441

Moniteurs Indépendants
t 0450 937978

Master Class
t 0450 908716

Ski Clinic
t 0666 139281

Freecimes
t 0664 118329

François Simond
t 0450 908097

Bruno Uyttenhove
t 0610 183082

Mountain Experience
t 0603 294486

Classes (ESF prices)
6 3hr-days €152

Private lessons
From €43 for 1hr

GUIDES

Mountain guide
t 0450 900655

CHILDCARE

Les Petits Loups
t 0450 908782
6mnth to 3yr

Rabbit Club (ESF)
t 0450 908100
From 3yr

La Souris Verte (ESI)
t 0450 908441
3yr to 5yr

Hotel MMV Le Flaine
t 0492 126262
18mnth to 14yr

Ski school
Ages 3 to 11; English-speaking tuition:
Catherine Pouppeville
(0609 266008)

FOR INTERMEDIATES ★★★★★
Something for everyone
Flaine is ideal for confident intermediates, with a great variety of pistes (and usually the bonus of good snow, at least above Flaine itself). The diabolically named reds that dominate the Flaine bowl tend to gain their status from short steep sections rather than overall difficulty. The relatively direct Faust is great carving territory and Méphisto is popular with lots of reporters. There are gentler cruises from the top – Cristal, taking you to the Désert Blanc chair, and Serpentine all the way home. The blues beneath Tête des Lindars are excellent for confidence building, but the drag serving them is not.

The connection with the slopes outside the main bowl is a blue run that can be tricky because of crowds, narrowness or poor snow. Once the connection has been made, however, all intermediates will enjoy the long tree-lined runs down to Les Carroz, as long as the snow is good. (The Perce-Neige run along the ridge to get to them is a bit narrow and exposed, though.) The long runs down to Morillon 1100 slopes are also excellent easy-intermediate terrain.

FOR BEGINNERS ★★★★★
Fairly good
There are excellent nursery slopes below Forum and across the hill from Forêt, served by free lifts which make a pass unnecessary until you are ready to go higher up the mountain. The major Fôret area is being revamped for next season, with a new Petit Balacha lift specially designed to make life easy for novices. There are some gentle blues to progress to on skier's right of the main bowl, beneath Tête Pelouse. An alternative is to get the bus over the hill to the Vernant valley where a fast chair serves the long, gentle, quiet Arolle green run.

FOR BOARDERS ★★★☆☆
Beware the draglifts
Flaine suits boarders quite well – there's lots of varied terrain and plenty of off-piste with interesting nooks and crannies, including woods outside the main bowl. The key lifts are now chairs or gondolas (but beware the draglifts marked as difficult on the piste map plus the Aujon draglift). Black Side is the local specialist shop, with a cafe and bar in the central Forum.

FOR CROSS-COUNTRY ★★☆☆☆
Very fragmented
The Grand Massif claims 64km of tracks but only about 13km of that is around Flaine itself.

MOUNTAIN RESTAURANTS ★★☆☆☆
Few options in the bowl
The piste map marks restaurants but does not name them.

Editors' choice We had an excellent lunch last season (fine burger, good salad, giant tartiflette) at the new Pente à Jules, a new chalet in a fine position where the Faust and Almandine red runs meet, near the bottom of the woods. Even in January and in its first season, it was packed.

Worth knowing about We've also eaten well at the rustic Blanchot (table-service section, naturally) just above the treeline on skier's right. There is a self-service place at the top of the main gondola. At the upper nursery slopes, the Bissac is tipped this year. At Forum level, across the piste from the gondola, are two attractive, woody chalets – the Michet and the fast-food-oriented Eloge. You can of course eat in the village, at places very close to the gondola.

Outside the Flaine bowl, we confirmed last season our affection for the remote Gîte du Lac de Gers (0450 895514 – book in advance and use the piste-side phone to ring for a snowcat to tow you up from the Cascades run) – simple, hearty food in a cosy chalet, splendid isolation. Be aware that you have to ski on down to Sixt, and then ski back to Flaine via the Samoëns lift system. Other places outside the bowl are covered in the Samoëns and Les Carroz chapters.

There are picnic rooms dotted around the Grand Massif, clearly marked on the piste map.

SCHOOLS AND GUIDES ★★★☆☆
Mixed reports
A 2010 reporter who used the ESF got 'the best instructor we've ever had'. We've had good reports on the International school and the Moniteurs Indépendants this year.

FOR FAMILIES ★★★★☆
Parents' paradise?
Flaine prides itself on being a family resort, and the number of English-speaking children around is a bonus. The schools offer classes for children from the age of three.

ACTIVITIES

Indoor Climbing wall, gym, bowling, cinema, cultural centre with art gallery and library

Outdoor Ice rink, snowshoeing, dog sledding, walking, snowmobiling, paragliding, helicopter rides, quad bikes, ice driving, snow kiting

GETTING THERE

Air Geneva 80km/ 50 miles (1hr30)

Rail Cluses (30km/ 19 miles); regular bus service

UK PACKAGES

Action Outdoors, Alpine Answers, Classic Ski, Crystal, Crystal Finest, Erna Low, Independent Ski Links, Inghams, Lagrange, Neilson, Pierre & Vacances, Powder White, PowderBeds, Ski Club Freshtracks, Ski Collection, Ski France, Ski Independence, Skitracer, Ski Weekend, Thomson, Zenith **Morillon** Alps Accommodation, AmeriCan Ski, Erna Low, Lagrange, Peak Retreats, PowderBeds, STC **Sixt** AmeriCan Ski, Peak Retreats

Phone numbers
From abroad use the prefix +33 and omit the initial '0' of the phone number

TOURIST OFFICES

Flaine
www.flaine.com
Morillon
www.ot-morillon.fr

STAYING THERE

Accommodation is overwhelmingly in self-catering apartments.

Hotels B&B is available at the Cascade restaurant (0450 908766), up the hill.

Apartments For a combination of comfort and ski convenience, the new CGH 4-star residence Centaure, a few metres from the gondola, takes some beating – and this season its spa and 25m pool will open. The apartments are cleverly designed so that all have a south view. But you may prefer the 5-star Montsoleil/Terrasses d'Eos residence – a Pierre & Vacances Premium property, in a ski-in/ski-out position slightly outside the village: comfortable, good outdoor pool, sauna, steam, hot tub. In Flaine Forêt, P&V also has the Forêt. Lagrange has several properties, including attractive chalets out at Hameau – also the location of the recently built Refuge du Golf, with pool. All these options are available through Ski Collection.

EATING OUT ★★☆☆☆
Limited choice
The choice is adequate, no more. We get most reports on the Brasserie les Cîmes in Forum: 'Great value, simple but well-cooked food, good portions, caters very well for families.' The tiny Grain de Sel is 'friendly, excellent value'. The Sucré Salé at Forêt does 'excellent, filling and healthy food at good prices'. Other reader tips include the Grange, and the Ancolie in Hameau – 'excellent food', 'friendly staff and very comfortable bar'. They will ferry you to and from your residence.

APRES-SKI ★☆☆☆☆
Take your Kindle
'Don't go to Flaine for nightlife,' says a reporter who spent two months there. You don't have much choice of venue: 'Only two main bars really get going,' says a 2013 reporter: the Dutch-run Flying Dutchman in Forêt ('lively venue full of students singing Dutch songs; good-value drinks') and the White Pub, which has a big-screen TV, rock music and a happy hour; live music some nights. The Perdrix Noire also has an English pub atmosphere. The bar at the bowling alley is popular with families (and stays open until 3am). The Caves is a nightclub.

OFF THE SLOPES ★☆☆☆☆
Curse of the purpose-built
Flaine is not great for people who don't want to hit the slopes. But there is a fine ice-driving circuit where you can take a spin in your car or in theirs. Snowmobiling and dog sledding are popular, and there's a cinema and a gym. The pool and spa at the Centaure residence will be open to everyone. Shopping is extremely limited.

LINKED RESORT – 700m
MORILLON

Morillon is a small, quiet, traditional old village, with a few cafes, restaurants, bars, supermarket and shops spread out along the road through. Newer buildings are in chalet style and quite attractive. There's a 3-star hotel, the Morillon (0450 901032). A gondola goes up to the mid-mountain mini-resort of Morillon 1100 (aka Les Esserts), with slope-side apartments at the foot of wide, gentle and tree-lined slopes. A choice of red and blue runs go to the valley. These low runs are not reliable, although the area as a whole is north-facing.

Morillon 1100 has the essentials of life – two ski schools, three ski shops, a bakery, a supermarket, a couple of restaurants, and the Madison pub with 'live music and quizzes'. Recent reporters have been impressed by the ZigZag school.

Build your own shortlist: **www.wheretoskiandsnowboard.com**

Les Gets

Traditional-style village with a very French feel, providing serious competition for its more established linked neighbour, Morzine

TOP 10 RATINGS

Extent	★★★★★
Fast lifts	★★★
Queues	★★★
Snow	★★
Expert	★★★
Intermediate	★★★★
Beginner	★★★★
Charm	★★★★
Convenience	★★★
Scenery	★★★

RPI 100

lift pass	£200
ski hire	£115
lessons	£70
food & drink	£135
total	**£520**

NEWS

2012/13: A video park was created at the bottom of the Perrières chairlift. You're filmed as you ski a slalom course and then watch the result on a giant screen or on the internet later on. Ski lockers, to be operated with the lift pass, were built at Chavannes. The Quatre Saisons, a gastronomic restaurant, opened in the town.

270

➕ Good-sized, varied and lightly wooded slopes shared with Morzine

➕ Attractive chalet-style village

➕ Few queues or crowds locally unless good weekend weather attracts a weekend influx

➕ Part of the vast Portes du Soleil ski pass region, but ...

➖ It's quite a long way to the main Portes du Soleil circuit at Avoriaz

➖ Low altitude and exposure to westerlies means some risk of rain and poor snow

➖ Few challenging pistes

➖ Slow, old chairs in some sectors

➖ Weekend crowds

Les Gets is an attractive, small, family-friendly resort with a very French feel to it, partly because of appetizing food and wine shops lining the main street. The area of slopes that it shares with slightly lower Morzine offers the most extensive local network in the region, and in some respects Les Gets is the better base for that shared area.

Think about whether you intend to visit the main Portes du Soleil circuit repeatedly. If you have a car, you could quite easily access it by driving to the gondola at Ardent. If you don't, the circuit is much more easily accessed from Morzine, with its quicker access to Avoriaz.

THE RESORT

Les Gets is an attractive, sunny village of traditional chalet-style buildings, on the low pass leading to Morzine. The main road over the pass bypasses the village centre.

The local pass saves a fair bit on a Portes du Soleil pass, and makes a lot of sense for many visitors.

Village charm The village has a quiet ambience that appeals to families, though it does liven up at weekends. The main street is lined with attractive food shops, other shops and restaurants. The centre is fairly pedestrian-friendly, too, and a popular outdoor ice rink adds to the charm.

Convenience Although the village has a scattered appearance, most facilities are close to the main lift station. Depending on where you stay, you may have long walks, but there is a road-train shuttle that appeals mainly to families, and also free conventional buses around the village. Buses to Morzine cost 1.5 euros per journey. You can store skis and boots at the Perrières ski shop. And there are now ski lockers at Chavannes.

Scenery There are good views from the high points: from Mont Chéry, in particular, you get a great panorama of the village and slopes, with Mont Blanc beyond.

Extent rating
This relates to the whole Portes du Soleil area.

Piste map
The whole local area is covered by the map in the Morzine chapter.

THE MOUNTAINS

Slopes The main local slopes – accessed by a gondola and a fast chairlift from the nursery slopes beside the village – are shared with Morzine, and are mainly described in that chapter. On the opposite side of Les Gets is Mont Chéry, accessed by a gondola followed by a chair or drag. The slopes here include some of the most challenging in the area, and are usually very quiet. Both sectors offer wooded and open slopes. Signage is considered 'very good'.

Fast lifts The village lifts are gondolas, but there are a lot of slow chairs both on Mont Chéry and in some sectors of the slopes shared with Morzine.

Queues Read the Morzine chapter. Mont Chéry is crowd-free.

Snow reliability The nursery slopes benefit from a slightly higher elevation than Morzine, but otherwise our general reservations about the lack of altitude apply. You may get rain. The runs to the resort have snowmaking. The front slopes of Mont Chéry face south-east – bad news at this altitude (and in poor snow years they can be closed for much of the time); but the other two flanks are shadier. Grooming is good. ('Pisteurs worked wonders; could ski back to resort in March in a poor snow year and warm

KEY FACTS

Resort	1170m
	3,840ft

Portes du Soleil	
Slopes	950-2275m
	3,120-7,460ft
Lifts	195
Pistes	650km
	404 miles
Green	12%
Blue	43%
Red	36%
Black	9%
Snowmaking	
	900 guns

Morzine-Les Gets only	
Slopes	1000-2010m
	3,280-6,590ft
Lifts	49
Pistes	120km
	75 miles
Snowmaking	
	130 guns

UK PACKAGES

Alpine Answers, Alpine Elements, Alpine Inspirations, AmeriCan Ski, Consensio, Crystal, Esprit, Ferme de Montagne, Hugski, Independent Ski Links, Lagrange, Luxury Chalet Collection, Mountain Beds, Oxford Ski Co, Peak Retreats, PowderBeds, Reach4theAlps, Ski Expectations, Ski Famille, Ski France, Ski Independence, Ski Solutions, Ski Total, Skitracer, Ski Weekend, Skiweekends.com, Snow Finders, STC, VIP, Zenith

Phone numbers
From abroad use the prefix +33 and omit the initial '0' of the phone number

TOURIST OFFICE

www.lesgets.com

LES GETS
Handpicked self-catering accommodation
peakretreats.co.uk/Les_Gets

ABTA
ABTA No. W5537

peak retreats

temperatures,' said a 2011 visitor.) The grassy slopes don't need much snow-cover, and in a sparse snow year you may do better here than in higher, rockier resorts such as Avoriaz.

Terrain parks There's a boardercross on Chavannes plus a jib park with boxes and rails and the small Cross District park for beginners. Mont Chéry has a larger park and airbag.

Experts Black runs on the flank and back of Mont Chéry are quite steep and often bumped. In good snow there's plenty to do off-piste, including some excellent wooded areas.

Intermediates High-mileage piste-bashers might prefer direct access to the main Portes du Soleil circuit, but the local slopes have a lot to offer, with excellent reds on Mont Chéry.

Beginners The village nursery slopes are convenient. At Chavannes there is a bigger and more snow-sure area with four free lifts. There are lots of easy runs to progress to – including the Bleuets on Chavannes.

Snowboarding The local slopes are good for beginners and intermediates.

Cross-country There are 12km of good, varied loops locally.

Mountain restaurants Read the Morzine chapter for places on the shared slopes. There are two restaurants on Mont Chéry giving great views. At the top is the Grande Ourse, run by an English family, offering snacks and table-service lunches rated 'very friendly and fun, with good atmosphere' by a reporter this year. At mid-mountain there's the Belvedère – and a picnic room.

Schools and guides There's a choice of schools, including at least two that are British-run; our most recent report judged Les Gets Snowsports 'excellent'. And a reporter was impressed with the English-speaking instructors at Ecole de Ski 360 who got her six-year-old daughter cruising

down the main slopes on day two.

Families This is a good resort for families. There are comprehensive facilities, including an American Indian-themed trail area on Chavannes with teepees, activities and a warpaint workshop – called the Grand Cry Territory – and major British family-specialist tour operators Esprit Ski and Ski Famille offer catered chalet holidays here.

STAYING THERE

There is a good selection of chalets and mid-range hotels.

Chalets Families have a wide choice: Ski Famille has eight chalets here, including the 'very comfortable' Chalet Marjorie, and Esprit Ski has four in one building (along with its own crèche). Ski Total has four, including Chalet Monet (two sharing an outdoor hot tub). VIP's Altitude chalet is 'beautifully finished and furnished' and has a hot tub. Private catered Chalet le Frene has been praised.

Hotels Of the 3-stars, the Crychar (0450 758050), at the foot of the slopes, is one of the best. The similarly convenient 4-star Marmotte (0450 758033) added eight lovely wood-panelled rooms over its spa last year and is being renovated for the 2013/14 season. In 2012 we stayed happily in the pleasant 2-star Stella (0450 758040).

Apartments Lagrange has two prestige properties – the central Sabaudia apartments and Les Fermes Emiguy (both with pool, hot tub, sauna etc). Peak Retreats offers the latter plus other apartments and several self-catered chalets (some luxurious).

Eating out The Tourbillon and Choucas ('fabulous house red') have been recommended. Try the Tyrol for pizza, the rustic Vieux Chêne for Savoyard specialities. A new gastronomic brasserie, the Quatre Saisons, opened this year.

Après-ski Après-ski is quiet, especially on weekdays. But there are half a dozen bars; the obvious first target is the Irish Pub and the Black Bear above it. The Igloo disco is popular.

Off the slopes There's an outdoor ice rink and bowling. There are quite a few shops, a cinema and an intriguing Mechanical Music Museum. Husky sleigh rides, snowshoeing and parapenting are possible. It's feasible to visit Geneva, Lausanne and Montreux from here, too.

La Grave

A world apart: an unspoiled mountain village beneath high, untamed off-piste slopes, some of them extreme and hazardous

TOP 10 RATINGS

Extent	★
Fast lifts	
Queues	★★★★
Snow	★★★
Expert	★★★★★
Intermediate	★
Beginner	★
Charm	★★★
Convenience	★★★
Scenery	★★★★

RPI   95

lift pass	£200
ski hire	£95
lessons	£90
food & drink	£100
total	**£485**

NEWS

La Grave does not change much, and that is half the charm of the place.

+ Legendary off-piste mountain
+ Usually crowd-free
+ Usually good snow conditions
+ Link to Les Deux-Alpes
+ Easy access by car to other resorts

− Poor weather means closure
− As a holiday base, suitable for experts only
− Through-traffic detracts from Alpine village atmosphere
− Little to do off the slopes

La Grave enjoys cult status among experts. It has around 500 visitor beds and just one serious lift serving a high, wild and almost entirely off-piste mountainside. The result: an exciting, usually crowd-free area. Strictly, you ought to have a guide, but in good weather many people go it alone.

THE RESORT

La Grave is a small, unspoiled village built along the road up to the Col du Lautaret. A car is useful for access to Les Deux-Alpes down the valley and Serre-Chevalier over the pass.
Village charm The centre has a rustic feel, some welcoming hotels and friendly inhabitants. But it is a bit plain, and traffic on the through-road can be intrusive.
Convenience The single serious lift starts a short walk below the centre.
Scenery La Grave is set on a steep hillside facing the impressive glaciers of majestic La Meije. Great views.

THE MOUNTAINS

A slow two-stage 'pulse' gondola (with an extra station at a pylon (P1) half-way up the lower stage) ascends into the slopes and finishes at 3200m. Above that, you are towed by a piste machine to access a drag serving a blue run on a glacier slope of about 350m vertical. From the top (after a walk) you can ski to Les Deux-Alpes. But the reason that people come here is to explore the legendary slopes back towards La Grave.

The slopes can be closed by bad weather or avalanche danger. A reader recommends going to the tiny resort of Le Chazelet, which has short sunny pistes served by several lifts, and easy off-piste. If the Col du Lautaret is open, we would head for the lovely woods of Serre-Chevalier.
Slopes The main slopes offer no defined, patrolled, avalanche-protected pistes – but there are two marked itinéraires (with several variations). Neither is particularly steep. The Chancel route passes the eponymous refuge, and descends 1400m to the P1 station; it involves a long traverse through trees, which may consist of 'energy-sapping icy moguls'. The Vallons de la Meije offers several variants, one going the full 1750m vertical to the valley, another ending at the bottom of the upper gondola. People do take these routes without a guide or avalanche equipment, but we couldn't possibly recommend it.

There are many more demanding routes, including couloirs that range from the straightforward to the seriously hazardous, and long descents from the glacier to the valley

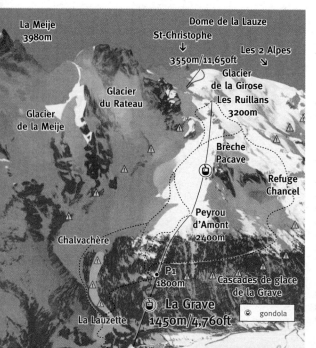

La Meije
3980m

Dome de la Lauze
St-Christophe
↓
3550m/11,650ft ↘
Les 2 Alpes

Glacier de la Girose
Les Ruillans
3200m

Glacier du Rateau

Glacier de la Meije

Brèche Pacave

Refuge Chancel

Peyrou d'Amont
2400m

Chalvachère

P1
1800m

Cascades de glace de la Grave

La Grave
1450m/4,760ft   ○ gondola

La Lauzette

Hello La Grave
Self Catered
Apartments
Ski Coaching
+ Ski Touring
Snowshoe
Adventures
Winter Skills

eurekaski
MORE FROM YOUR MOUNTAIN HOLIDAY
eurekaski.com/lagrave

KEY FACTS

Resort	1450m
	4,760ft
Slopes	1450-3550m
	4,760-11,650ft
Lifts	4
Pistes	5km
	3 miles
Green/Blue	100%

The figures relate
only to pistes;
practically all the
skiing – at least 90%
– is off-piste

Snowmaking	none

UK PACKAGES

Alpine Answers,
EurekaSki, Mountain
Tracks, Pure Powder,
Ski Club Freshtracks,
Ski Weekend

Phone numbers
From abroad use the
prefix +33 and omit
the initial '0' of the
phone number

TOURIST OFFICE

www.lagrave-lameije.
com

OT LA GRAVE LA MEIJE

He or she must have
been on the first lift
→

---

road below the village, with return by taxi, bus, or strategically parked car. The dangers are considerable (people die here every year), and good guidance is essential. On this mountain, blindly following tracks is dangerous. You can also descend a 'spectacular' valley southwards to St-Christophe, returning by taxi or bus and the lifts of Les Deux-Alpes.

Fast lifts There aren't any, and there's no need for any.

Queues The lift can build queues if conditions are very good, especially on March weekends. If there's a queue at the bottom, don't ski down to P1.

Terrain parks There aren't any.

Snow reliability The chances of powder snow on the high, north-facing slopes are good.

Experts La Grave's uncrowded off-piste slopes have earned it cult status among hard-core skiers. Only experts should contemplate a stay here.

Intermediates The itinéraires get tracked into a piste-like state, and adventurous intermediates could tackle them.

Beginners Novices tricked into coming here can go up the sunny side of the valley to the easy slopes at Le Chazelet, which has a fast quad and two snow-guns.

Snowboarding There are no special facilities for boarders, but advanced freeriders will be in their element on the open off-piste powder.

Cross-country There is a total of 20km of loops in the area.

Mountain restaurants Surprisingly, there are three. The excellent, tiny Refuge Chancel, where supplies and

waste are backpacked in and out, is the pucka La Grave experience; call in during the morning to see what's cooking, and book. Les Ruillans at the top is reportedly good, too.

Schools and guides There are claimed to be 30 or so guides, offering a wide range of services through their bureau. 'Excellent' is the usual verdict. Serre-Chevalier-based New Generation ski school is offering two-day ProXplore off-piste guiding for 2013/14. See also 'Hotels' below.

Families Not really a family resort, but nearby Le Chazelet is more geared up. The tourist office knows of babysitters.

STAYING THERE

There are very few choices.

Hotels There are several simple options. The Brit-run 3-star Edelweiss (0476 799093) has quite basic rooms but does 'excellent' food and has a 'legendary' wine list. The Skiers Lodge/ Hotel des Alpes (0476 110318) offers all-inclusive week-long packages including guiding. A past reporter had an excellent week.

Apartments Bookable through the tourist office. New for 2013/14, EurekaSki offers a selection.

Eating out Most people eat in hotels. The Vieux Guide serves the 'best food' in the resort, says a 2013 visitor.

Après-ski The Cafe des Glaciers and the Castillan are the standard teatime venues. The bars of the Edelweiss and Skiers Lodge have live music. The 'lively' Bois du Fees is tipped.

Off the slopes This isn't a resort for non-skiers, unless you are keen on ice-climbing.

La Grave

273

Megève

One of the traditional old winter holiday towns; best for those who enjoy relaxed cruising and spectacular views

RATINGS

The mountains

Extent	★★★★★
Fast lifts	★★
Queues	★★★★
Terrain p'ks	★★★
Snow	★★
Expert	★★
Intermediate	★★★★
Beginner	★★★
Boarder	★★
X-country	★★★★
Restaurants	★★★★
Schools	★★★
Families	★★★

The resort

Charm	★★★★
Convenience	★★
Scenery	★★★★★
Eating out	★★★★
Après-ski	★★
Off-slope	★★★★

RPI   100

lift pass	£180
ski hire	£120
lessons	£75
food & drink	£145
total	**£520**

NEWS

2013/14: More snowmaking is planned for another 6km of runs.

2012/13: A new bus service now runs between Rochebrune and Le Jaillet; also horse-drawn sleighs between the centre and Le Jaillet. In St-Gervais, a new museum about the ascent of Mont Blanc opened. There's also a new crêperie in town, Café Rodolphe.

- ➕ Extensive easy, scenic slopes
- ➕ Charming old town centre
- ➕ Some very smart hotels and shops
- ➕ Some special mountain restaurants
- ➕ Good for weekend trips
- ➕ Great when it snows – woodland runs with no one on them
- ➕ Plenty to do off the slopes

- ➖ Low altitude of slopes means a risk of poor snow, though the grassy terrain does not need deep cover
- ➖ Lots of slow, old lifts remain
- ➖ Three separate mountains
- ➖ Few challenging pistes
- ➖ Very muted après-ski scene
- ➖ Meals and drinks pricey

Megève has a medieval heart but it was, in a way, the original purpose-built French ski resort – developed in the 1920s as a response to Switzerland's irritatingly swanky St Moritz. Although Courchevel long ago took over as France's top resort, Megève's smart hotels still attract the old money. Happily, the rest of us can enjoy it, too. And just look at that list of plus points above.

This is one of our favourite places to be in falling snow, when Megève regulars take one look and retreat to their duvets. But when the sun's out and we want to zip around the pistes, we get very frustrated by the number of slow lifts. The resort still has a lot to learn from St Moritz (never mind Saalbach).

THE RESORT

Megève is in a lovely sunny setting and has a beautifully preserved, partly medieval centre. Visitors are mainly well-heeled French people, who come here for an all-round holiday.

The skiing divides into three sectors. One is directly accessible by lifts from close to the centre and from the southern edge of town, another from an elevated suburb or from an out-of-town lift base. The third involves buses, for most people.

There are several alternative bases (which offer some good-value lodging) on the fringes of the area. St-Gervais and Le Bettex above it (described at the end of this chapter) have gondola access to the main sector. But beware slow access lifts from otherwise attractive spots. The slopes also link with La Giettaz; this has interesting local terrain, but is out on a limb and is not a sensible base.

The Evasion Mont Blanc lift pass also covers Les Contamines. Plans to create a link with this resort have existed for ages, and now the Megève piste map has been redrawn to include it. Don't hold your breath.

A car is handy for outings like that, and for using the Princesse gondola, slightly out of town.

VILLAGE CHARM ★★★★
Old France at its best

Megève's charming old centre is car-free and comes complete with open-air ice rink, horse-drawn sleighs, cobbled streets and a fine church. Lots of smart clothing, jewellery, antique, gift and food shops add to the chic atmosphere. The main Albertville road bypasses the centre, and there are expensive underground car parks. But people arrive here mainly by car, and the resulting traffic can be a problem at times, particularly if you are based outside the very centre. 'Seems to get worse every year,' notes a reporter.

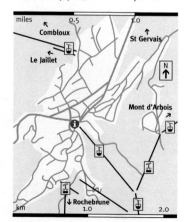

KEY FACTS	
Resort	1100m
	3,610ft
Slopes	850-2355m
	2,790-7,730ft
Lifts	88
Pistes	325km
	202 miles
Green	19%
Blue	29%
Red	39%
Black	13%
Snowmaking	
485 guns + 67 for 2013/14 season	

CONVENIENCE ★★★★★
Stay close to a lift
Unless you have a car, staying close to one of the main lifts makes a lot of sense. Some of the best hotels are above the centre, close to the Mont d'Arbois gondola. But many lodgings depend on the free ski-buses, which are not super-frequent. A 2013 reporter found the new horse-drawn sleigh service from Le Jaillet to the centre 'a great way to finish off the day'.

SCENERY ★★★★★
Beautiful town, beautiful views
The slopes are prettily wooded, but what earns Megève its five stars is the view of Mont Blanc from many of the runs – especially the red Epaule run.

THE MOUNTAINS

On a day like this, in January 2013, the area is very seductive. This is Mont Joux and Mont d'Arbois from the excellent Grande Epaule run ↓

The slopes are largely below the treeline – this is a great resort in poor weather – though there are extensive open areas, particularly higher up in the Mont d'Arbois sector.

Piste classification frequently exaggerates difficulty. The piste map has been redrawn, but not improved.

It is designed mainly for marketing purposes, clearly, and does not deal well with Mont d'Arbois, in particular.

EXTENT OF THE SLOPES ★★★★★
More than enough for a week
Each of the three mountains has a worthwhile amount of terrain, and they add up to a great deal of skiing.

The town is most directly linked with the **Rochebrune** sector – a gondola goes up from the centre of town, and a cable car from the southern edge. A network of gentle, wooded, north-east-facing slopes, served by drags and mainly slow chairlifts, leads to the high point of Côte 2000, which often has the best snow. The minor peak of Alpette was the starting point for Megève's historic downhill course, now abandoned.

At just above resort level the Rocharbois cable car goes across the valley to link Rochebrune to the gondola for the bigger **Mont d'Arbois** sector, starting from an elevated suburb of the resort. The Princesse gondola starting a couple of miles north of the town (with extensive free car parking) offers another way up.

Megève

275

A two-stage gondola comes up from St-Gervais via Le Bettex. You can work your way over to Mont Joux and up to the small Mont Joly area – Megève's highest slopes. And from there you can go to the backwater village of St-Nicolas-de-Véroce (preferably via the splendid Epaule ridge run, with wonderful views of Mont Blanc).

The third area is **Le Jaillet**, accessed by gondola from just outside the north-west edge of town, or from the separate village of Combloux. The high point of Le Christomet is linked to the slopes of tiny **La Giettaz** – worth the trip, not least for spectacular views.

FAST LIFTS ★★★★★
Still too many slow ones
Megève continues to lag behind its rivals in the uplift business. Gondolas and cable cars provide the main access, and fast chairs are dotted around – but overall three out of four lifts are slow. Two seasons ago one more slow lift was replaced, but the chair added on Le Jaillet is slow.

QUEUES ★★★★★
Few weekday problems
Megève is relatively queue-free during the week, mostly. But school holidays and sunny weekends can mean some delays. The long, steep Lanchettes and Roche Fort drags between Côte 2000 and the rest of the Rochebrune slopes can have 'ridiculously long waits' – as can the cable car linking the two mountains. A 2013 reporter found long queues at the Epaule chair on a sunny Saturday. Crowded pistes at Mont Joux and Mont d'Arbois can also be a

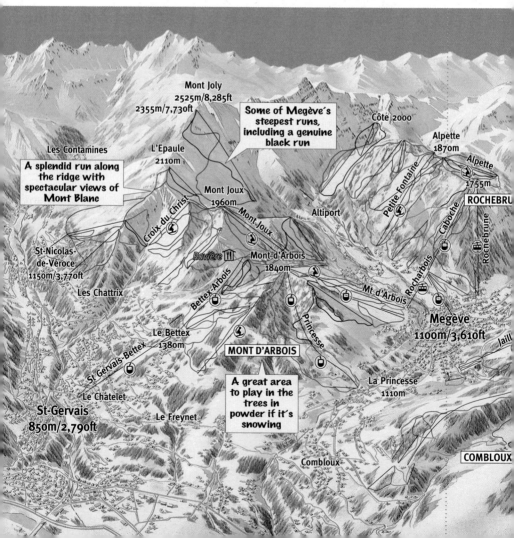

Mont Joly
2525m/8,285ft
2355m/7,730ft

Côte 2000

Les Contaminés

Some of Megève's steepest runs, including a genuine black run

Alpette
1870m

Alpette

1755m

L'Epaule
2110m

A splendid run along the ridge with spectacular views of Mont Blanc

Mont Joux
1960m

Mont-Joux

Altiport

Petite Fontaine

Caboche

Rochaïbois

Rochebrune

ROCHEBRU

St-Nicolas-de-Véroce
1150m/3,770ft

Croix du Christ

Ravière

Mont-d'Arbois
1840m

Mt d'Arbois

Megève
1100m/3,610ft

Les Chattrix

Bettex-Arbois

Princesse

Le Bettex
1380m

MONT D'ARBOIS

St Gervais-Bettex

Le Châtelet

Le Freynet

A great area to play in the trees in powder if it's snowing

La Princesse
1110m

Jaill

St-Gervais
850m/2,790ft

Combloux

COMBLOUX

problem. On a snowy day the slopes can be delightfully quiet as the Parisians stay in bed, leaving the powder to you and us.

TERRAIN PARKS ★★★
Four, surprisingly
The park near the bottom of Rochebrune was designed particularly for beginners. There is a 500m-long boardercross course and a freestyle airbag nearby. There is also a park on Mont d'Arbois, with a good line of jumps for all ability levels. Plus a host

of rails and boxes and a boardercross. Combloux also has a park and La Giettaz a smaller park, albeit with a real multitude of jump sizes and a few rails. Both have boardercross.

SNOW RELIABILITY ★★
The area's main weakness
The slopes are low, with very few runs above 2000m, and quite sunny – the Megève side of Mont d'Arbois gets the afternoon sun. So in a poor snow year, or in a warm spell, snow on the lower slopes can suffer badly. Fortunately,

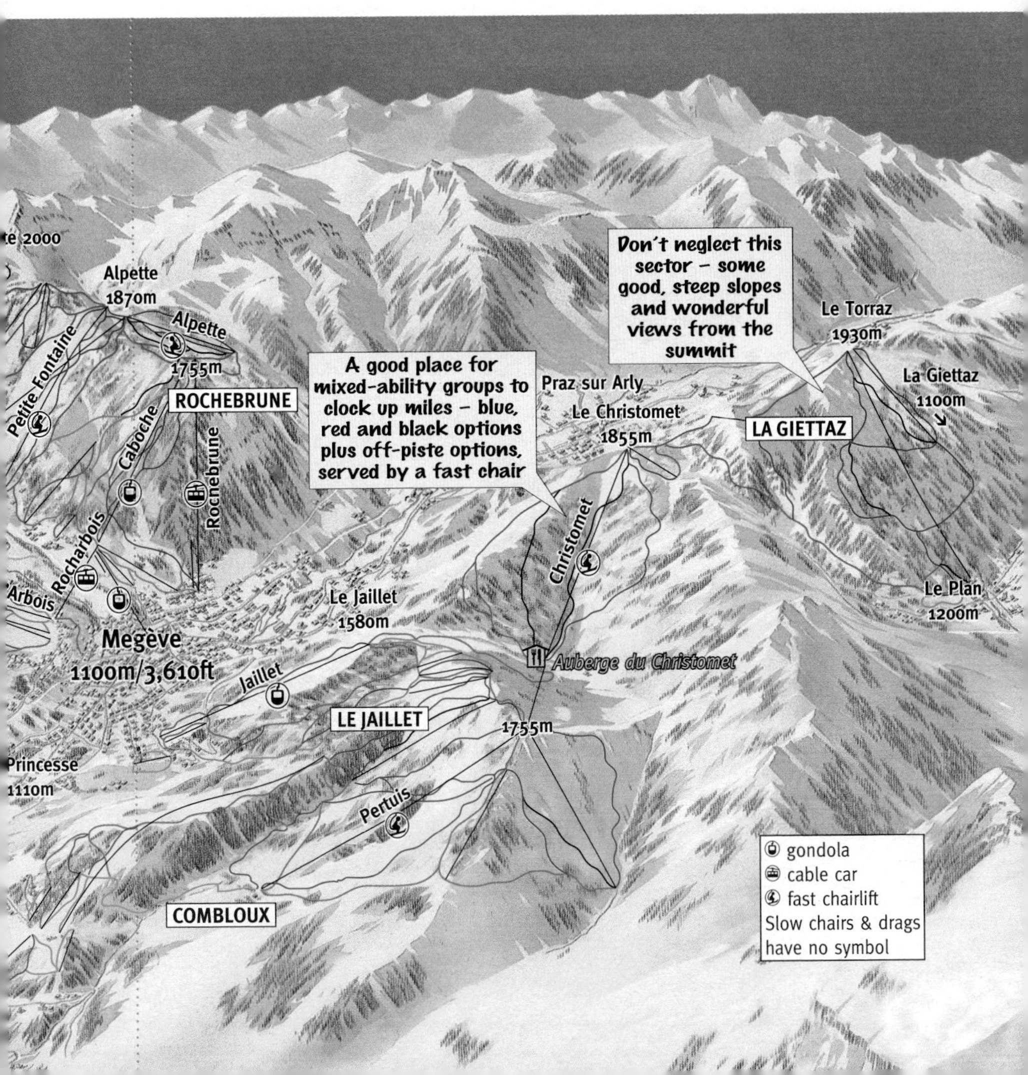

te 2000

Alpette
1870m

Alpette

Petite Fontaine

1755m

ROCHEBRUNE

Caboche

Rochaibois

Rochebrune

Arbois

Megève
1100m/3,610ft

Jaillet

Princesse
1110m

Le Jaillet
1580m

LE JAILLET

Jaillet

Pertuis

COMBLOUX

1755m

> A good place for mixed-ability groups to clock up miles – blue, red and black options plus off-piste options, served by a fast chair

Praz sur Arly

Le Christomet
1855m

Christomet

🍴 *Auberge du Christomet*

> Don't neglect this sector – some good, steep slopes and wonderful views from the summit

Le Torraz
1930m

La Giettaz
1100m

LA GIETTAZ

Le Plan
1200m

🚠 gondola
🚡 cable car
🚏 fast chairlift
Slow chairs & drags
have no symbol

LIFT PASSES

Evasion Mont Blanc

Prices in €

Age	1-day	6-day
under 15	33	157
15 to 64	42	195
65 plus	38	176

Free Under 5, over 80

Beginner Three free lifts; Rochebrune pass covers 6 lifts; three other limited passes, each covering one or two lifts

Notes Megève pass resorts (list below) plus Les Contamines; family discounts

Alternative passes Megève (Megève, La Giettaz, Combloux, St-Gervais and St-Nicolas); Jaillet-Combloux-Giettaz only pass; pedestrian pass

ACTIVITIES

Indoor Sports centre (tennis, ice rink, curling, climbing wall, swimming pool, sauna, solarium, gym), beauty treatments, health and fitness centres, museum, cinemas, casino, language courses, concerts and exhibitions, bridge, painting courses

Outdoor Cleared paths, snowshoeing, tobogganing, ice rink, horse-drawn carriage rides, ice climbing, adventure park, dog sledding, sightseeing flights, paragliding, ballooning

the grassy slopes don't need much depth of snow. There is extensive snowmaking, but that can't work in warm weather. Grooming seems to be good but read 'For experts', below.

FOR EXPERTS ★★
Off-piste is the main attraction
One of Megève's great advantages for expert skiers is that there is not much competition for the powder – many days after a fresh dump you can often make first tracks on good slopes. The resort now leaves about 20 runs ungroomed after a snowfall (they don't say for how long), so you get to enjoy the powder for a bit, and then the moguls. (Given the nature of Megève's clientele, a cynic might wonder if this is more about saving money than meeting a demand for 'ski sauvage'.)

The Mont Joly and Mont Joux sections offer the steepest slopes. The top chair here serves a genuinely black run, with some serious off-piste off the back of the hill; and the slightly lower Epaule chair has some steep runs back down and also accesses some good off-piste, as well as pistes, down to St-Nicolas. The steep area beneath the second stage of the Princesse gondola can be a play area of powder runs among the trees. Côte 2000 has a small section of steep runs, including good off-piste.

The terrain under the Christomet chair can be a good spot to develop off-piste technique, given decent snow – and a reporter recommends the extensive woods at La Giettaz.

FOR INTERMEDIATES ★★★★
Superb if the snow is good
Good intermediates will enjoy the whole area – there is so much choice it's difficult to single out any particular sectors. Keen skiers are likely to want to focus on the fast lifts, and happily several of these serve excellent terrain: the Princesse and Bettex gondolas on Mont d'Arbois, the Fontaine and Alpette chairs on Rochebrune and the Christomet chair in the Le Jaillet sector. But don't confine yourself to those – there are lots of other interesting areas, including the shady north-east-facing slopes on the back of Mont d'Arbois and Mont Joux and the front of Rochebrune, and the genuinely red/

Stylish chalets and serious skiing? Check out p258.

black slopes of La Giettaz. The slopes above Combloux are well worth exploring, particularly the quiet reds and black served by the Jouty chairlift.

Megève is also a great area for the less confident. There are long, easy blue runs in all sectors. A number of gentle runs lead down to Le Bettex and La Princesse from Mont d'Arbois, while nearby Mont Joux accesses long, easy runs to St-Nicolas. Alpette and Côte 2000 are also suitable. As is most of Le Jaillet, especially the long easy runs down to Combloux.

FOR BEGINNERS ★★★
Good choice of nursery areas
There are beginner slopes at valley level, and more snow-sure ones at altitude on each of the main mountains. There are also plenty of very easy green runs to progress to.

FOR BOARDERS ★★
Beginner friendly
Boarding doesn't really fit with Megève's rather staid, upmarket image – there are no specialist schools – and there are quite a few flat linking runs to deal with. But freeriders will love it after snowfalls. It's a good place to try snowboarding for the first time, with plenty of fairly wide, quiet, gentle runs and a lot of chairlifts and gondolas. The draglifts are generally avoidable.

FOR CROSS-COUNTRY ★★★★
An excellent area
There are 40km of varied trails spread throughout the area. Some are at altitude, making meeting with Alpine skiers for lunch simple.

MOUNTAIN RESTAURANTS ★★★★
Something for all budgets
Megève has some chic, expensive, gourmet places, but plenty of cheaper options too. Stanford Skiing's website has an absolutely essential guide to download. The piste map marks restaurants but does not name them. The tourist office restaurant guide includes hosts; it is not comprehensive.

Editors' choice The Auberge du Christomet (0450 211134) has a lovely setting at the foot of the Christomet chair on Le Jaillet with fabulous views and a cosy rustic interior. Readers continue to endorse the place – 'wonderful', 'superb' – but they (and we) are not impressed by the ever-increasing focus on fur-coated customers who drive up to fill the new

SCHOOLS

ESF
t 0450 210097

Evolution 2
t 0450 555357

International
t 0450 587888

Freeride
t 0680 306898

Summits
t 0450 933521

Agence de Ski
t 0699 185200

BASS
t 0845 468 1003 (UK)

Revolution Glisse
t 0667 608964

Ski Pros
t 0681 610615

Powderama
t 0616 871853

Ski Technique
t 0616 766 948

Classes (ESF prices)
5 2.5hr-days €153
Private lessons
€43 for 1hr

GUIDES

Bureau des Guides
t 0450 215511

CHILDCARE

P'tites Frimrousses
t 0450 211869
Ages 1 to 3
Club Piou-Piou
t 0450 589765
Ages 3 to 4

Ski schools
From age 5

GETTING THERE

Air Geneva 90km/
55 miles (1hr15);
Lyon 180km/
110 miles (2hr30)

Rail Sallanches
(12km/7 miles);
regular buses from
station

Stanford Skiing - The Megève Specialist
chalets - hotels - apartments - short breaks - ski guiding
flexible travel - family run - friendly knowledgeable staff
01603 477471   www.stanfordskiing.co.uk

---

car park. On Mont d'Arbois, La Ravière (0450 931571), tucked away in the woods near the Croix chair, is a stark contrast: a tiny rustic hut that does a set meal; booking is essential.
Worth knowing about Mont d'Arbois is well endowed. The famously expensive Idéal 1850 is said to be excellent. There are several modest, small places worth seeking out. We liked Sous les Freddy's, near the Arbois chair; very good meat platter and home-made desserts. Gouet, on the Gouet piste, offers 'friendly family service with great mountain fare'. The tiny Refuge de Porcherey above St-Nicolas offers 'lovely food and ambience' and a 'delicious white vin chaud'; beware – the kitchen closes early (1.30 when we failed to get lunch last season). The Espace at Mont Joux is 'friendly'.
On Rochebrune/Côte 2000 the Alpette is the prestige place – 'good for a blowout'. We had a satisfying lunch in 2012 at Javen d'en Haut. Radaz serves 'well-presented generous portions of food' in several small rooms. Auberge de la Côte 2000 does 'lovely food with good service'. Super Megève at the top of the cable car is 'pricey but good', with 'great atmosphere and attentive service'. On the back of the hill, Chalet le Forestier is an atmospheric hut with 'reliable plat du jour'. For those who need to watch the budget, Petite Fontaine is a '4-star good-value snack bar'.
On Le Jaillet, Face au Mont Blanc does a great fixed-price buffet. A regular rates the Auberge Bonjournal towards La Giettaz – 'good menu, fair value, great views', 'friendly staff, nice ambience'. Two reporters rave about the tiny self-service Balcons de Lydie – 'fair prices', 'best view in Megève'.

SCHOOLS AND GUIDES ★★★
Good private lessons
The ESF is of course the major school. A reporter noted huge class sizes ('up to 20') even in January. Happily, it has lots of competition here, not only from the International school but also from smaller French schools and some British-run outfits. Powderama, based in Chamonix, started offering private

lessons here in 2012/13.
Heli-skiing (in Italy) and expeditions to the Vallée Blanche (in Chamonix) can be arranged, and mountain guides are available (we've had a great morning powder skiing in the trees with Alex Périnet: 0685 428339).

FOR FAMILIES ★★★
Language problems
The kindergartens offer a wide range of activities. But lack of English-speaking staff could be a drawback. The slopes are family-friendly and the schools rated by reporters. There are snow gardens in the main sectors.

STAYING THERE

There is an impressive range of accommodation in the area.
Chalets Stanford is the Megève specialist; for a cheap and cheerful base, you won't do better than its Sylvana – a creaky old hotel, between the Rochebrune cable car and the centre, endorsed by a 2013 visitor – 'good food'. Right in the centre, the Rond-Point is another old hotel. Stanford also has a smarter 10-bed chalet, les Clochettes.
Hotels Megève offers a range of exceptionally stylish hotels, mainly quite small and built in chalet style. Six lovely but very pricey places have now been elevated to 5 stars.
★★★★★Fer à Cheval (0450 213039) Now a 5-star, it's rustic-chic at its best, with a lovely wood interior. Spa and pool.
★★★★★Flocons de Sel (0450 214999) Food-oriented eight-room place in a cluster of chalets secluded a few km out. 'Pampering as good as it gets, amazing staff, best food ever,' says a reporter. Three Michelin stars. Spa.
★★★★Chalet St Georges (0450 930715) Central, close to the gondola. Warmly welcoming, with 24 rooms and suites. Read 'Eating out', below.
★★★Coin du Feu (0450 210494) Mid-sized chalet between Rochebrune and Chamois lifts.
★★Gai Soleil (0450 210070) Simple Logis de France place. 'Good location, excellent breakfast, wonderful staff', says a discriminating reporter.

UK PACKAGES

Alpine Answers, Alpine Weekends, AmeriCan Ski, Carrier, Erna Low, Flexiski, Independent Ski Links, Inghams, Kaluma, Lagrange, Luxury Chalet Collection, Momentum, Mountain Beds, Oxford Ski Co, Peak Retreats, Pierre & Vacances, PowderBeds, Scott Dunn, Simon Butler Skiing, Ski Bespoke, Ski Collection, Ski Expectations, Ski France, Ski Independence, Ski Solutions, Ski Weekend, Snow Finders, Stanford Skiing, STC, White Roc **St Gervais** AmeriCan Ski, Erna Low, Holiday in Alps, Inghams, Lagrange, Peak Retreats, PowderBeds, Ski Club Freshtracks, Ski France, Ski Weekend, Snowcoach, Zenith **Combloux** Erna Low, Peak Retreats

Phone numbers
From abroad use the prefix +33 and omit the initial '0' of the phone number

TOURIST OFFICES

Megève
www.megeve.com

St-Gervais
www.st-gervais.net

Apartments Loges Blanches is central and smart, with pool and restaurant; bookable via Ski Collection. Pierre & Vacances and Lagrange each offer one or two properties. Stanford also has an apartment and an eight-bed self-catering chalet.

EATING OUT ★★★★
Very French
The tourist office produces a pocket guide with photos. There are lots of upmarket restaurants, many of them in the better hotels. The gastro guide favourites – the Michelin-starred Roches Fleuries and the Flocons de Sel (read 'Hotels') – are a drive out of town. The Flocons has a more modest branch, Flocons Villages, that is popular with locals and got two rave reports from readers last year – 'beautifully presented, outstanding value', 'miraculous lamb and veal, wonderful desserts, exceptional bread'.

Meat, 'beautifully cooked', is a speciality at the 'superb' Table du Trappeur in the Chalet St Georges hotel. The Brasserie Centrale does precisely what brasseries were invented to do – 'good entrecôte-frites and crème brûlée'. The 'very French and friendly' Chamois is the place for cheesy specialities.

APRES-SKI ★★☆☆
Strolling and jazz
Megève is a pleasant place to stroll around after the lifts close, but exciting it isn't. If there are lively bars for a post-piste beer, they have so far eluded us. And those looking for loud disco-bars later may be disappointed, too. The 5 Rues is our choice – a very popular jazz club-cum-cocktail bar, open all evening, that gets some big-name musicians. It's pricey, but cocktail measures are large, so 'one per hour is enough', a reporter notes. The Cocoon is a Brit favourite, with live music and British sports TV. The casino is more slot machines than blackjack tables. Palo Alto has two discos.

OFF THE SLOPES ★★★★
Lots to do
There is a 'fantastic' sports centre with a new spa, fitness room, pool and indoor ice rink, an outdoor ice rink, cinemas and a market on Fridays. Shopping is a serious business, aided by a tourist office pocket guide (combined with the restaurant guide).

Trips to Annecy and Chamonix are possible. Walks are excellent, with 50km of marked classified paths, though a picky reporter tells us the marking is not super-clear. Meeting friends on the slopes for lunch is easy.

LINKED RESORT – 850m
ST-GERVAIS

St-Gervais is a handsome 19th-century spa town set in a narrow river gorge, with access to the slopes shared with Megève by a gondola from the fringes.

Although definitely a town, it's a pleasant place, with interesting food shops, cosy and sophisticated bars (we liked the trendy Pur bar for cocktails and posh nibbles), thermal baths and an Olympic ice rink. Prices are noticeably lower than in Megève. The resort has a train station and there are efficient bus services.

The lodgings are mostly modest – there are four 2-star hotels, and four 3-stars. Two hotels convenient for the gondola are the Liberty Mont Blanc (0450 934521), a pleasantly traditional non-classified place with pool and sauna, and the 3-star Carlina (0450 934110), with a small pool and sauna. The unclassified Féline Blanche (0450 965870) is a hip boutique place with just 10 rooms done up in black and white. The basic 2-star Val d'Este (0450 936591) has one of the best restaurants in town (Le Sérac).

Fermes de St Gervais is a smart Lagrange Prestige residence with a pool, a mile out of town. These and other properties are available through Peak Retreats.

The gondola from the edge of town goes to Le Bettex, a mid-mountain area of restaurants, conveniently placed hotels and excellent nursery slopes. The gondola above Le Bettex serves a green run, making this an attractive base for beginners. We enjoyed staying recently at the 3-star Arbois-Bettex (0450 931222), with pool, spa and good restaurant; and dining at the lovely rustic Chalet Rémy – friendly service.

On the opposite side of St-Gervais is a rack-and-pinion railway, which in 1904 was intended to go all the way to the top of Mont Blanc. It was never completed, and terminates at the top of the ski area of Les Houches (described in the Chamonix chapter); but sadly there are no lift pass sharing arrangements.

AGENCE NUTS

Les Menuires

The bargain base for the Trois Vallées – with increasing amounts of stylish accommodation as well as the original dreary blocks

NEWS

2013/14: A 1200m long roller-coaster-style ride on rails is due to be built. A new Duo Pass will allow two people buying lift passes together to get a reduction.

2012/13: A six-pack replaced the old bucket-lift from the bottom of La Masse to Reberty. A camera and screen has been set up on the BK Park so riders can be filmed then see their efforts. The Pass Tribu was introduced – allowing three or more people buying lift passes together to get a reduction. And with the new family pass two adults and two or more children now all pay the child rate.

+ Speedy, mostly queue-free access to the huge Trois Vallées area

+ Lots of slope-side accommodation, with traffic well separated

+ Low prices by local standards

+ French atmosphere

− Big, dreary blocks and gloomy indoor shopping malls in centre

− Main intermediate and beginner slopes get a lot of sun

− Some slopes can get very crowded

Les Menuires arguably has the best position in the Trois Vallées, and we've warmed to it as better (and better-looking) lodgings have continued to be built. As our RPI shows, it is much more affordable than more upmarket Courchevel and Méribel and we now view Les Menuires as a very attractive proposition – especially the traditional-style bits we've christened 'Belles-Menuires'.

THE RESORT

Les Menuires is a purpose-built resort, dominated by large apartment blocks, with about 60% of the visitors French. It has excellent links to Val Thorens in the same valley and to the Méribel valley. The core of the resort is La Croisette, a horseshoe of 1960s- and 1970s-built apartment blocks plus a claustrophobic underground shopping mall right by a gondola and fast chairlift into the heart of the Trois Vallées slopes.

Recent development has added various suburbs to the original core, and a second lift base across the mountainside at Les Bruyères.

VILLAGE CHARM ★★★★★
Much improved

The original buildings that surround the main lift base are among the most brutal examples of the monolithic architecture of the 1960s and 1970s. They still dominate the centre of the resort; but more recent developments in the suburbs have been built in much more attractive chalet style in stone and wood, and many UK tour operators have their accommodation there. Read our Belles-Menuires feature later in the chapter.

SNOWPIX.COM / CHRIS GILL

This is the original part of Les Menuires – now there are much more attractive chalet-style developments in the suburbs ↓

SKI AMIS

Catered Chalets in Superb Locations

020 3411 5439
www.skiamis.com

A couple of the original buildings have been demolished (as we advised way back in the 1990s), and they have been replaced by attractive chalet-style blocks. And the 'front de neige' has been smartened up.

CONVENIENCE ★★★★★
Easy to get around on skis
For most visitors, the resort is very conveniently arranged for skiing – a great deal of the accommodation is ski-in, and much of it ski-out.

If you stay in the central area, nothing is more than a short stroll away. If you stay in some of the outposts, it may be different. They have their own shops and bars, but if you want more choice, you are reliant on buses that are scheduled to run every 20 minutes until 8pm, less frequently after that. In the mornings, too, you may have some hiking to do

if you want to start from a lift other than the nearest one.

SCENERY ★★★☆☆
Go up high
The scenery can be rather bleak, but there are grand views from the peaks of the ski area on both sides, especially from La Masse.

THE MOUNTAINS
Les Menuires is set on the treeline, with almost all the slopes above it. Piste map and signposting are good.

EXTENT OF THE SLOPES ★★★★★
Part of the huge Trois Vallées
Les Menuires is well positioned for exploring the whole Trois Vallées. The major part of the local area spreads across the west-facing mountainside between Les Menuires and St-Martin, with links to the Méribel valley at four points and to Val Thorens at the southern end. A gondola and fast chair go up from La Croisette, and the same from Les Bruyères. A gondola to the separate sector of La Masse, across the valley, starts below the village.

FAST LIFTS ★★★★☆
Good all over
The major lifts up to the peaks are now powerful gondolas or fast chairs. The main slow ones left affect Le Bettex residents and beginners only.

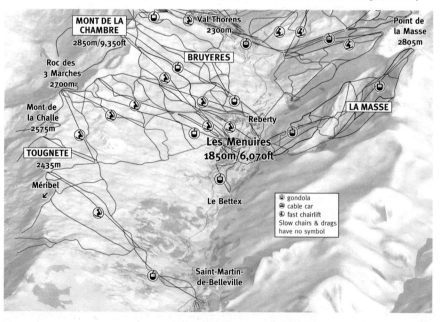

MONT DE LA CHAMBRE 2850m/9,350ft

Val Thorens 2300m

Point de la Masse 2805m

Roc des 3 Marches 2700m

BRUYERES

Mont de la Challe 2575m

LA MASSE

Reberty

TOUGNETE 2435m

Les Menuires 1850m/6,070ft

Méribel

Le Bettex

gondola
cable car
fast chairlift
Slow chairs & drags have no symbol

Saint-Martin-de-Belleville

There's lots of excellent terrain to explore locally – as well as easy access to the rest of the Trois Vallées →

KEY FACTS

Resort	1800m
	5,910ft

Trois Vallées	
Slopes	1260-3230m
	4,130-10,600ft
Lifts	173
Pistes	600km
	373 miles
Green	16%
Blue	40%
Red	34%
Black	10%
Snowmaking	50%

Les Menuires / St-Martin only	
Slopes	1400-2850m
	4,590-9,350ft
Lifts	34
Pistes	160km
	99 miles
Green	15%
Blue	47%
Red	30%
Black	8%

ACTIVITIES

Indoor Centre Sportif (swimming pool, sauna, steam, fitness, squash), library

Outdoor Tobogganing, outdoor pool (Bruyères), cleared paths, snowshoeing, paragliding, snowmobiling, mountain biking on snow

GETTING THERE

Air Geneva 150km/ 95 miles (2hr15); Lyon 190km/120 miles (2hr30); Chambéry 115km/ 70 miles (2hr)

Rail Moûtiers (25km/15 miles)

QUEUES ★★★★
Very slight
Queues are not usually a problem; most reporters comment that there are few. But the Bruyères gondola (for access to Val Thorens) is consistently mentioned by reporters ('15-minute queues at opening time'), and the Mont de la Chambre chair may get busy at peak times. Crowded slopes are more of a problem in general, particularly those leading down to the resort centre.

TERRAIN PARKS ★★★
Family-friendly
The BK park near the top of the Becca chair has blue and red lines of jumps and rails plus a boardercross. And there's the Acticross below it for kids. On La Masse there's the newish Walibi Gliss slalom and boardercross area. There's a big airbag jump at the foot of the Slalom area.

SNOW RELIABILITY ★★★★
Coverage good, quality variable
La Masse's height and northerly orientation ensure good snow for a long season. The main west-facing slopes obviously get lots of strong afternoon sun. They have lots of snowmaking, but the snow lower down is often icy in the morning and slushy later on. Of course, you're close to snow-sure Val Thorens.

FOR EXPERTS ★★★★
Head for La Masse
The upper slopes of La Masse, served by the second stage of a fast jumbo gondola, are virtually all of stiff red or easy black steepness – great fast cruises when groomed, of almost 660m vertical, and with some of the best snow in the Trois Vallées. They are also usually very quiet compared with the rest of the slopes near here because La Masse is set off the busy Trois Vallées 'circuit', and most people doing the circuit from Méribel, Courchevel and Val Thorens don't make the detour.

There is also a huge amount of off-piste, including the wide, sweeping, not-too-steep Vallon du Lou off the back of La Masse towards Val Thorens (this used to be a marked itinéraire and was one of our favourite runs in the whole Trois Vallées).

Read the other Trois Vallées resort chapters too.

FOR INTERMEDIATES ★★★★★
600km of pistes to choose from
With good snow, the slopes above the village on the west-facing side, virtually all blue and red, have a lot to offer. Don't miss La Masse as well – see 'For experts' above.

But the real attraction is the easy access to the rest of the Trois Vallées and its 600km of pistes, most of which are ideal intermediate terrain. There are lifts to four different points from which you can drop into the Méribel valley, and you can be at the far end of the Courchevel ski area in

Stylish chalets and serious skiing? Check out p258.

Les Belles-Menuires

La Plagne has its Belle-Plagne – why shouldn't Les Menuires have its Belles-Menuires? Or should it be Beaux-Menuires? Whatever ... We've made up this name to represent the attractive, chalet-style suburbs of Les Menuires – places where Méribel habitués might be happy.

These suburbs aren't simply built in chalet style – they also contain actual chalets. Most of them are operated by British tour operators that advertise on

DOWN THE HILL

Below the main resort centre in Le Bettex, Ski Amis has a cluster of smart chalets with outdoor hot tubs and saunas, 150m from the piste and the Bettex chairlift. A blue piste from the top of that takes you to the Tortollet chair to get up to Les Menuires and the Rocher Noir chair for La Masse. Absolutely Snow has two adjoining chalets in Le Bettex with in-house bar, sauna and outdoor hot tub.

this spread, and are marked, approximately, on our map. They are concentrated up the slope in Reberty 2000, or down in Les Bruyères, a micro-resort complete with ice rink and swimming pool – and a major lift, the Bruyères gondola. The area shown also has the resort's best hotels, some smart apartment residences (read the margin panel), and an excellent slope-side restaurant, the Ferme.

Down the valley, on the opposite side of the resort centre, are further traditional-style, small-scale, relatively upmarket developments (read the left margin panel).

Reberty, Les Bruyères, Le Bettex

In Reberty 2000, the Chalets du Soleil is an offshoot of the next-door 4-star hotel Kaya. In the same area and ownership is Chalet Julietta, with its own sauna and steam room. Residents of both can use the Kaya's facilities, such as spa and restaurant.

Slightly lower down, Alpages de Reberty is a Pierre & Vacances Premium residence with pool, sauna etc.

La Sapinière includes the Montagnettes residence Hameau de la Sapinière, with sauna, steam room and hot tub, and a restaurant – and a local supermarket will deliver free of charge.

Down in Les Bruyères, Les Chalets du Mont Vallon have a pool, gym, sauna and a serious restaurant.

Several tour operators including French apartment specialists Ski Collection offer these and other residences.

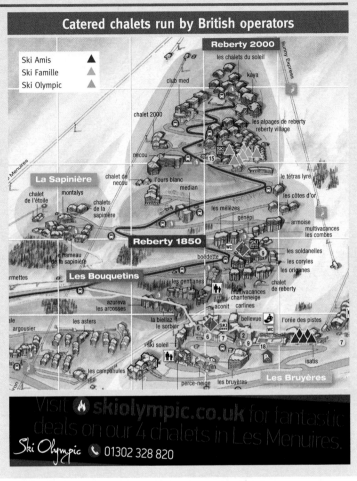

Catered chalets run by British operators

Ski Amis
Ski Famille
Ski Olympic

Reberty 2000
les chalets du soleil
club med
kaya
Sunny Express
chalet 2000
les alpages de reberty
reberty village
necou
SKI 15
chalet de necou
l'ours blanc
le tétras lyre
La Sapinière
median
montalys
le tétras lyre
chalet de l'étoile
chalets de la sapinière
les côtes d'or
les mélèzes
génépi
armoire
multivacances les combes
Reberty 1850
le hameau de la sapinière
boëdette
SKI 9
les soldanelles
les coryles
les origanes
rmettes
Les Bouquetins
les gentianes
multivacances chanteneige
chalet de reberty
azureva les arcosses
aconit carlines
ale
argousier
les asters
la biellaz le sorbier
bellevue
l'orée des pistes
SKI
6 7
ski soleil
9 18
P.
isatis
les campanules
perce-neige les bruyères
Les Bruyères

1650 in around 90 minutes if you don't get distracted on the way. To get to Val Thorens, there's an easy blue run from the top of the Montaulever draglift that is quieter than the main runs down from the top of the Bruyères gondola.

Read the other Trois Vallées resort chapters too.

FOR BEGINNERS ★★★
Snow quality a concern
The resort has improved its nursery areas – now with six moving carpets and one drag that are free – but snow quality here remains a concern because of the sunny aspect. A special lift pass is available for beginners, and there is a green run to the village from the Roc des 3 Marches gondola, and

lots of easy blues to progress to, but they are prone to crowds.

FOR BOARDERS ★★★★
Beware flat parts
Slushy snow on the west-facing slopes won't worry boarders as it does skiers. But you'll still want to escape and explore the vast amount of terrain elsewhere in the Trois Vallées. The local terrain park is far from hard core, but Méribel's two great parks are easy to reach. Locally, there are few draglifts but beware some flattish sections of piste.

FOR CROSS-COUNTRY ★★★
Limited and low
The 28km of trails are along the valley between St-Martin and Les Menuires.

Resort news and key links: www.wheretoskiandsnowboard.com

SCHOOLS

ESF
t 0479 006143

Ski School
t 0667 586777

Prosneige
t 0479 041835

Snowbow
t 0479 419403

Classes (ESF prices)
6 5hr-days €195

Private lessons
€49 for 1hr

CHILDCARE

Les Piou Piou (ESF)
t 0479 006379
Ages 3 to 30mnth

Mini club (ESF)
t 0479 006379
Ages 31mnth to 5yr

Ski school
From age 3 or 4 to 12

Phone numbers
From abroad use the
prefix +33 and omit
the initial '0' of the
phone number

TOURIST OFFICE

www.lesmenuires.com

MOUNTAIN RESTAURANTS ★★★★★
Affordable fare
There are some good places charging
affordable prices.
Editors' choice The Grand Lac (0479
082578) is a big chalet in a fine spot
at the bottom of the Granges chair
where we've always had very good
service and food. Reporters agree.
Worth knowing about Way across the
hill, the Alpage is consistently praised
and we had a good meal there in
2013. The Sonnailles, off the valley-
bottom Cumin run, is another
favourite. Two 2013 visitors like the
self-service Roc des Trois Marches
('great value, delicious walnut flan'). In
the almost-a-mountain-restaurant
category, the Ferme, piste-side at
Reberty 2000, is excellent, while
Maison de Savoy, opposite the bottom
of the Sunny Express chairlift in
Reberty 1850, is singled out by visitors
this year: 'Our new favourite.' Consider
the slope-side hotel terraces in
Reberty, too, particularly the Ours
Blanc, where we had a top-notch meal
in 2013. On the La Masse side, Roches
Blanches at the top of the first
gondola has 'impressive food and
service' and 'good, fresh pizzas'.

SCHOOLS AND GUIDES ★★★★★
Try the Ski School
The ESF gets mixed reviews; it seems
to do a lot of off-piste stuff. A group of
instructors operating here and in
St-Martin under the startling name of
Ski School offer only private lessons
and are said to be 'really good'.

FOR FAMILIES ★★★★★
Lots of options
Good facilities. There are kids'
'villages' with indoor and outdoor
facilities at both La Croisette and Les
Bruyères. Ski Famille is a family
specialist with three chalets in Reberty
and its own childcare arrangements.

STAYING THERE
La Croisette consists mainly of large
apartment blocks. Reberty/Les
Bruyères has hotels and chalets too.
Chalets See our Belles-Menuires
feature earlier in the chapter.
Hotels There are good places on the
slopes at Reberty/Les Bruyères.
★★★★Kaya (0479 414200) Smart and
modern with good spa and restaurant.
★★★★Ours Blanc (0479 006166) Chalet
style, sauna, steam, tub, good food.
★★★Isatis (0479 004545) In chalet
style, right at the Bruyères gondola –
17 suites, all with hot tubs.
Apartments There are lots of new
developments in chalet style, most of
them covered by our Belles-Menuires
feature. In the suburb of Preyerand,
just below the main resort centre, is
the chalet-style 4-star residence Les
Clarines, with spa and pool, and
featured by Ski Collection. Ski Amis
has units in all parts of the resort.

EATING OUT ★★★★★
Mix of gourmet and Savoyard
We had very good traditional and
gourmet meals at the Cocon des
Neiges (hotel Isatis). Up the slope in
Reberty, the K (hotel Kaya) is a good
gourmet option. Consider some of the
places mentioned in 'Mountain
restaurants' too – the Ferme, Maison
de Savoy and Ours Blanc. Other recent
tips include the Chouette ('efficient,
jolly', 'great crêpes') and the Vieux
Grenier ('great atmosphere, huge
portions but slow service').

APRES-SKI ★★★★★
Not a lot of choice
It's pretty quiet in the evening. A
reporter favourite for close-of-play
beers is the Chouette at Les Bruyères.
There is no shortage of bars in La
Croisette, but those in the dreadfully
claustrophobic mall are ruled out for
us. The cabaret at Medz'é-ry is
entertaining, we're told. There are
discos at Croisette and Bruyères.

OFF THE SLOPES ★★★★★
Great sports centre
There is an impressive sports/spa/pool/
fitness centre, the new roller-coaster, a
4km-long toboggan run, mountain
biking on snow, snowmobiling,
evening snowshoe outings and
paragliding. But this is basically a
destination for skiers and boarders,
and not very appealing for others.

Méribel

A sprawling but comfortable, upmarket chalet-style resort in the centre of the incomparable Trois Vallées

RATINGS

The mountains

Extent	★★★★★
Fast lifts	★★★★★
Queues	★★★★
Terrain p'ks	★★★★
Snow	★★★
Expert	★★★★
Intermediate	★★★★★
Beginner	★★★★
Boarder	★★★★
X-country	★★★
Restaurants	★★★
Schools	★★★★
Families	★★★

The resort

Charm	★★★
Convenience	★★★
Scenery	★★★
Eating out	★★★★
Après-ski	★★★★★
Off-slope	★★★

RPI   125

lift pass	£230
ski hire	£125
lessons	£110
food & drink	£175
total	**£640**

KEY FACTS

Resort	1400-1700m
	4,590-5,580ft

Trois Vallées	
Slopes	1260-3230m
	4,130-10,600ft
Lifts	173
Pistes	600km
	373 miles
Green	16%
Blue	40%
Red	34%
Black	10%
Snowmaking	50%

Méribel only	
Slopes	1400-2950m
	4,590-9,680ft
Lifts	41
Pistes	150km
	93 miles
Green	9%
Blue	44%
Red	37%
Black	10%

➕ Central to the Trois Vallées, the biggest lift network in the world

➕ Pleasant chalet-style architecture

➕ Impressive lift system

➕ Very lively après-ski scene

➕ Excellent piste maintenance and snowmaking; nevertheless ...

➖ Snow on the west-facing side suffers from afternoon sun

➖ Sprawling main village

➖ Expensive, particularly for food and drink

➖ Full of Brits

➖ Some pistes can get crowded

A loyal band of regular visitors just love Méribel, and it's not difficult to see why. For keen piste-bashers who like to rack up the miles but dislike tacky post-war resorts, it's difficult to beat: unlike other modern purpose-built resorts, Méribel has always insisted on chalet-style architecture.

Other 3V resorts have the edge in some respects. For better snow opt for Courchevel or Val Thorens; for lower prices, Les Menuires or St-Martin.

THE RESORT

Méribel was founded in 1938 by a Brit, Peter Lindsay, and has retained a strong British presence and influence ever since. It occupies the central valley of the Trois Vallées network and consists of two main resort villages.

The original resort is built on a steepish west-facing hillside with the home piste running down beside it to the main lift stations in the valley bottom, slightly below the village centre. The resort now spreads widely away from the centre and the piste; various quarters can be identified – among them Mussillon, beside the road in to the resort, where many individual chalets are located.

A road winds up from the centre to the top of the main village. From there, one road goes on through woods to the outpost of Altiport (a snow-covered airstrip) while another goes under the home piste to a more recently developed area, Belvedere.

The satellite resort of Méribel-Mottaret, a mile or two up the valley, is centrally placed in the Trois Vallées ski area, offering quicker access to Val Thorens in particular. The hamlet of Méribel-Village, on the road from Méribel to Courchevel, has developed into a pleasant, quiet micro-resort. It is at the bottom of a blue run from Altiport, with a fast quad giving access to the other slopes.

You can stay in the valley below Méribel, in the spa town of Brides-les-Bains – see the end of this chapter – or in the village of Les Allues at a mid-station of the gondola from Brides.

A car is useful for outings to other resorts in the Tarentaise such as Les Arcs, Val d'Isère, Tignes and La Rosière; you can access La Plagne via Champagny.

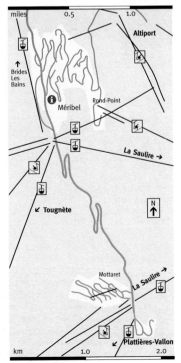

VILLAGE CHARM ★★★☆☆
Built with style

Méribel is one of the most tastefully designed of French purpose-built resorts. The buildings are wood-clad, chalet-style and mainly low-rise, and they include a lot of individual chalets as well as big chalet-shaped blocks of apartments. Mottaret lacks these smaller chalets, and looks more block-like as a result, despite wood cladding on its apartment buildings. Even so, it's more attractive than many other resorts built for slope-side convenience. It has far fewer shops and bars and much less après-ski than Méribel itself, and nothing like the feel of a village.

CONVENIENCE ★★★☆☆
Shuttle to the slopes, usually

Although some lodgings are right on the piste beside the village, many depend on using free (and now 'excellent') public buses which run until midnight or private minibuses to and from the slopes. There are collections of shops and restaurants at a couple of points on the road through the resort – Altitude 1600 and Plateau de Morel.

Méribel-Village is a small place; it has some luxury chalets and apartments, but very limited amenities – a good bread shop, a small supermarket, a bar, a pizzeria and a couple of restaurants.

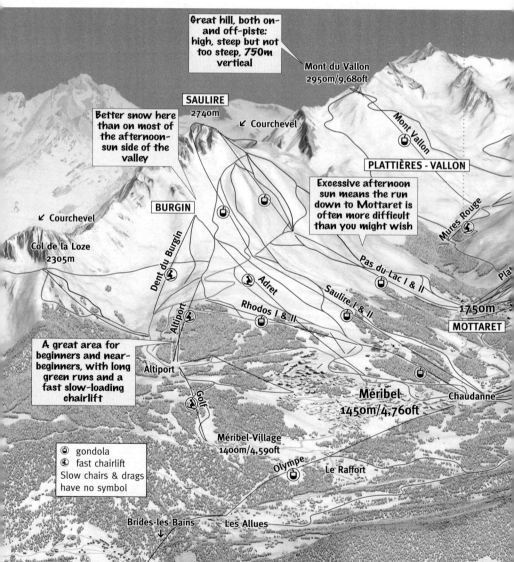

Great hill, both on- and off-piste: high, steep but not too steep, 750m vertical

Mont du Vallon
2950m/9,680ft

SAULIRE
2740m

↙ Courchevel

Better snow here than on most of the afternoon-sun side of the valley

Mont Vallon

PLATTIÈRES - VALLON

BURGIN

Excessive afternoon sun means the run down to Mottaret is often more difficult than you might wish

Mures Rouge

↙ Courchevel

Col de la Loze
2305m

Dent du Burgin

Adret

Pas du Lac I & II

Saulire I & II

1750m

Rhodos I & II

Altiport

MOTTARET

A great area for beginners and near-beginners, with long green runs and a fast slow-loading chairlift

Altiport

Golf

Méribel
1450m/4,760ft

Chaudanne

Ⓖ gondola
Ⓕ fast chairlift
Slow chairs & drags have no symbol

Méribel-Village
1400m/4,590ft

Olympe

Le Raffort

Brides-les-Bains   **Les Allues**

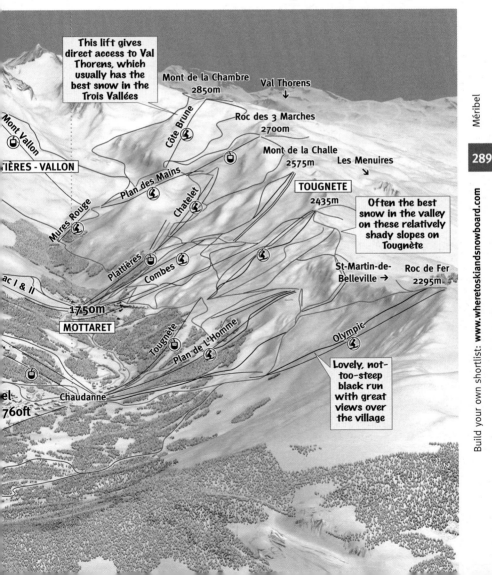

Mottaret has spread up both steep sides of the valley, though most of the blocks are on the east-facing side. Many lodgings are ski-in/ski-out, but not all. Both sides are served by lifts for pedestrians – but the gondola up the east-facing slope stops at 7.30 and it's a long, tiring walk up.

SCENERY ★★★☆☆
Head for Vallon
The village is attractively set in woodland, below long craggy ridges – a satisfying although unspectacular scene. But there are wonderful glacial views from Mont du Vallon at the head of the valley.

Hot chalets beneath glacial slopes? Check out p258.

THE MOUNTAINS

Most of the slopes are above the treeline, but there are some sheltered runs for bad-weather days. Piste classification is not always reliable – a problem compounded by exposure of many slopes to the sun. Signposting is excellent. The piste map is adequate; but it could be so much better if it covered the two sides of the valley separately. They have stopped handing out maps of which pistes have been groomed but you can now get this

---

This lift gives direct access to Val Thorens, which usually has the best snow in the Trois Vallées

Mont de la Chambre
2850m

Val Thorens ↓

Roc des 3 Marches
2700m

Mont de la Challe
2575m

Les Menuires ↘

Mont Vallon

IÈRES - VALLON

Côte Brune

Plan des Mains

Chatelet

Mures Rouge

TOUGNETE
2435m

Often the best snow in the valley on these relatively shady slopes on Tougnète

Plattières

Combes

ac I & II

St-Martin-de-Belleville →

Roc de Fer
2295m

1750m

MOTTARET

Tougnète

Plan de l'Homme

Olympic

el

76oft

Chaudanne

Lovely, not-too-steep black run with great views over the village

information on the Trois Vallées smartphone app and it appears on small notices posted at various places.

EXTENT OF THE SLOPES ★★★★★
Centre of a huge area

Leaving aside the rest of the Trois Vallées, this is a big area. Lifts go up to nine high points on the ridges above the resort: two entry points to the Courchevel valley, no fewer than six entry points to the Belleville valley (shared by St-Martin, Les Menuires and Val Thorens) and one to Mont du Vallon, a very worthwhile cul-de-sac.

On the morning-sun side, chairs go up to the first two links with St-Martin, and some relatively quiet slopes back towards Méribel. To the left, a gondola and then a six-pack go from Méribel to **Tougnète**, for both Les Menuires and St-Martin. You can also head down to

Mottaret from here. From there, a fast chair then a drag take you to Belleville entry point number four.

South of Mottaret are some of the best slopes in the valley, in the **Plattières-Vallon** sector at the head of the valley. The top stage of the old Plattières gondola (the first two stages were replaced by a 10-seater for 2012/13) ends at the fifth entry point to the Belleville valley. To the east of this is the big stand-up gondola to the top of Mont du Vallon. The Côte Brune fast quad from near this area goes up to Mont de la Chambre, the sixth link with the next valley, and the only one giving direct access to Val Thorens.

On the afternoon-sun side, gondolas leave both Méribel and Mottaret for **Saulire**, the main link to Courchevel. The other is from Altiport, via a slow chairlift to Col de la Loze.

FRANCE

290

OT MERIBEL / JM GOUEDARD

Méribel is chalet city, with them spreading far and wide. The ridge on the far side is the junction with the slopes of Les Menuires and St-Martin-de-Belleville ↓

Trois Vallées

Prices in €

Age	1-day	6-day
under 13	42	208
13 to 64	53	260
65 plus	48	234

Free Under 5, 75 plus
Beginner Mini pass

Notes Covers Courchevel, La Tania, Méribel, Val Thorens, Les Menuires and St-Martin; reductions for family and groups of 3+; pedestrian and half-day passes

Alternative passes Méribel and Méribel-Mottaret only + 3V extension

FAST LIFTS ★★★★★
Highly efficient system
Modern chairs and gondolas serve both sides of the valley, with good links into the rest of the Trois Vallées.

QUEUES ★★★★☆
3V traffic a persistent problem
The area is generally queue-free most of the time but there are a few bottlenecks. More singles lines are appearing – but the lift company could achieve a lot by employing lifties to usher people into half-empty cabins and onto chairs, North American style.

We and reporters alike have found that the six-pack above the Tougnète gondola is a serious bottleneck – it comes nowhere near coping with the combination of people coming up the gondola and people descending the four good pistes above.

The new Plattières gondola has cut queues at Mottaret but put more pressure on the old gondola third stage (which remains in place) and the Côte Brune chair from people heading onward to Val Thorens. The new gondola from Méribel to La Saulire shifts a lot of people quickly – but leads to overcrowding at the top where it meets the cable car from Courchevel on quite a narrow patch of snow.

In this central valley the most serious problems result from the tidal flows of people passing through in the morning (when the tide coincides with the start of ski school) and in the late afternoon, when crowds on the runs to Mottaret can also be a problem.

Most people returning from Val Thorens form a queue for the Plan des Mains chair so as to avoid the flat start of the 'blue' Ours valley run. Confident skiers should use our trick instead: by-pass Plan des Mains by traversing above it, off-piste.

TERRAIN PARKS ★★★★☆
Two great areas
Méribel has two big parks. Moonpark at mid-mountain on Tougnète and served by the Arpasson draglift covers over 25 acres. In charge are the respected Ho5 crew. There are kickers, tables, rails and boxes plus bio rails and boxes made of wood with beginner, intermediate and expert lines, a boardercross and a 'chill and grill' BBQ zone. You can be filmed and watch the results on a big screen.

Under the new Plattières gondola, the Area 43 park was massively expanded a couple of seasons ago to be 1200m long with lots of features, lines for different abilities, 200m of rails, a half-pipe, boardercross and air bag jump. You can have your run recorded and play it back online.

Kids get their own mini-boardercross courses, P'tit Moon and Acticross, plus an animal-themed piste in the forest – all on the west-facing slopes.

SNOW RELIABILITY ★★★☆☆
Not the best in the Trois Vallées
Méribel's slopes aren't the highest in the Trois Vallées, and they mainly face roughly east or west; the latter (the runs down from Courchevel) get the full force of the afternoon sun. In late season you soon get into the habit of avoiding this side in the morning, when it is still rock-hard having frozen overnight. Skiers coming over from Courchevel can get a real shock. The run down from Saulire to Mottaret is a particular problem – often like concrete for its whole 1000m vertical; in our countless visits over many years, we've only once found this run enjoyable. The slopes above Altiport get less direct sun and generally have decent snow. And the morning-sun side (the Tougnète side of the valley) can be excellent. At the southern end of the valley, a lot of runs are north-facing and keep their snow well, as do the runs on Mont du Vallon.

Snowmaking has been increased to the point where the lower runs have substantial cover. Lack of snow is rarely a problem. Grooming is good.

FOR EXPERTS ★★★★☆
Exciting choices
The size of the Trois Vallées means experts are well catered for. In the Méribel valley, Mont du Vallon has lots to offer. The long, steep Combe Vallon run here is classified red; it's a wonderful, long, fast cruise when groomed (which it normally is), but presents plenty of challenge when moguled. And there's a beautiful off-piste run in the next valley to the main pistes, leading back to the bottom of the gondola.

A good mogul run is down the side of the double Roc de Tougne draglift which leads up to Mont de la Challe. And there are steep, unrelenting runs from Tougnète back to Méribel – the upper Ecureuil piste is a black and the

Méribel has a lot of very good off-piste to discover. Here, we pick out some of the best runs for skiers with at least some off-piste experience. Don't tackle them without guidance.

The run from near Roc de Fer to Le Raffort, a mid-station on the gondola from Brides-les-Bains, is an adventure with exceptional views. You ride the Olympic chairlift, go along the ridge, then ski a gentle bowl to finish among the trees.

The wide, west-facing slope above Altiport is enjoyable when the snow is fresh – varied terrain, from average to steep, some open some wooded, reached from the Tétras black run.

There are lots of runs suitable for more accomplished off-piste skiers. One is the Cairn, from the Mouflon piste at the top of the Plattières 3 gondola; it starts in a fairly steep couloir and becomes wider, with a consistent pitch, until you reach the Sittelle piste.

The Roc de Tougne draglift accesses some challenging runs. To the right of the Lagopéde red piste is an area guides call the Spot – a rather technical and steep descent to the Sittelle piste. Alternatively, a 15-minute hike brings you to the Couloir du Serail, leading to the Mouflon red piste – a favourite because of the vertical, the constant pitch and the quality of snow.

Some of the best routes in the Méribel valley are accessed from the other valleys. The Col du Fruit is a classic, far away from the lifts and resorts. You ride the Creux Noirs chairlift in Courchevel, then walk along the ridge for 15 minutes before descending through the national park to Lac de Tueda and the cross-country tracks ... 800m of flat ground from the Mottaret lifts. Some of the best snow is accessed from the 3 Vallées 2 chairlift at Val Thorens. Ducking the rope at the top takes you into varied terrain mixing couloirs and gentle slopes, with exposures from north-east to north-west. Eventually you join the red Lac de la Chambre piste.

ACTIVITIES

Indoor Parc Olympique (ice rink, swimming pool, climbing wall), fitness centres, bowling, library, cinemas, museum, heritage tours

Outdoor Flying lessons, snowmobiles, snowshoeing, ice climbing, sleigh rides, cleared paths, paragliding

adjacent Combe Tougnète is a red. At the north end of the valley the Face run was created for the women's downhill race in the 1992 Olympics; served by a fast quad, it's a splendid cruise when freshly groomed (with great views over the village).

Nothing on the Saulire side is as steep as on the other side of the valley. The Mauduit red run is quite challenging, though – it used to be classified black. Throughout the area there are good off-piste opportunities – read our feature panel above, and the other Trois Vallées resort chapters.

FOR INTERMEDIATES ★★★★★
Paradise found
Méribel and the rest of the Trois Vallées form something close to paradise for intermediate skiers and riders; there are few other resorts where a keen piste-basher can cover so many miles so easily and with such satisfaction. Virtually every slope in the region has a good intermediate run down it, and to describe them all would take a book in itself.

For less adventurous intermediates, the Sittelle blue run from the top of the new Plattières gondola back down towards Mottaret is an ideal cruise – gentle and generally in good condition because of its north-facing aspect. But it can get very crowded and the lower

part can get bumpy and slushy later in the day. The red run into Mottaret on the other side of the valley gets dangerously crowded too (and can be very icy).

Even early intermediates should find the runs over into the other valleys well within their capabilities, opening up further vast amounts of intermediate terrain. In Courchevel or Val Thorens you also get the bonus of better snow.

Virtually all the pistes on both sides of the Méribel valley will suit more advanced intermediates. Few of the reds are easy.

FOR BEGINNERS ★★★★
Strengths and weaknesses
Méribel continues to improve its appeal to beginners. At the core of this appeal is an excellent long green slope – gentle, wide, tree-lined – at Altiport (where one of the editors of this book learned to ski, [cough] years ago). This is a lift or bus-ride above the resort, which is not ideal. But the slope is served by a free draglift (and by a fast chair going higher, which is not free). And there are green runs from the top and bottom of the drag back to Rond-Point, at the top of the village, where there is another free drag (beginners should take a lift or bus down from there as the blue run

lower down is not easy). And now a green run goes from the mid-station of the Saulire gondola so that novices are able to ski from that point. The Mini lift pass gives access to a limited number of gentler slopes.

There is a small nursery slope at Rond-Point which is mainly used by the children's ski school.

At Mottaret, facilities are less impressive. There is an enclosed beginner area beside the village with a magic carpet; you can graduate from there to an almost flat green along the valley to the main Méribel lifts (though there may be speeding skiers racing past you).

FOR BOARDERS ★★★★
Good all round
The terrain is good and varied, with a worthwhile number of tree runs. Mont du Vallon has some very good steep freeriding that stays relatively untracked. There are lots of red runs here for intermediates and gentle blues and greens for beginners. The two terrain parks are top-notch too. Most lifts are chairs or gondolas, but

beware of flat sections on the main routes to and from Val Thorens – and avoid the Ours blue run down to Mottaret from Mont du Vallon, which is very hard work. Specialist shops include Avalon Rider (which is in central Méribel).

FOR CROSS-COUNTRY ★★★
Scenic routes
There are about 33km in the Méribel valley. The main area is in the forest near Altiport and is great for trying cross-country for the first time. There's also a loop around Lake Tueda, in the nature reserve at Mottaret, and for the more experienced a 12km itinéraire from Altiport to Courchevel.

MOUNTAIN RESTAURANTS ★★★
A disappointing choice
There are few places worth singling out here, and there aren't enough restaurants to meet the demand, so many places get crowded. The self-service Folie Douce and table-service Fruitière were welcome additions for 2012/13. Restaurants are not named on the piste map.

Méribel

293

SNOWPIX.COM / CHRIS GILL

In the afternoon the sun bakes the west-facing slopes down from La Saulire so that they are often rock hard in the morning ➔

CHILDCARE

Les Saturnins
t 0479 086690
Ages 18mnth to 3yr

Les Piou Piou
t 0479 086031
Ages 3 to 5

Childminder list
Available from the
tourist office

Ski school
Ages 5 to 13

We've had a good lunch in the table-service part of Plan des Mains, and we're told the self-service has improved, but we would welcome more reports. The Chardonnet, mid-station of the Pas du Lac gondola, is popular for its steak tartare prepared at the table, says a recent visitor. The Crêtes, on the Tougnète ridge has a fine position and rustic interior: the 'menu is limited but the food is divine', says a 2013 reporter. The Coeur de Cristal, low down beside the Adret chair, 'is lovely with nice washrooms' and has 'interesting and well-presented food'. The Rhododendrons, at the top of the Altiport drag and Rhodos gondola, is a popular spot for its large terrace but it gets mixed reviews.

This is one of the few resorts where we can be persuaded to descend to resort level for lunch on one of three slope-side hotel terraces – the Adray Télébar, the Allodis or the Altiport. All these are thoroughly excellent. Above Mottaret, the Grain de Sel gets a reader's vote for 'the best burger and chips – we went out of our way to visit twice'. The Martagon at Le Raffort serves 'tasty food and has fair prices'.

SCHOOLS AND GUIDES ★★★★
Some excellent British schools
New Generation, a British school that operates in 10 resorts including Méribel, gets excellent reports – for example, 'progressed quickly', 'all excellent instructors', 'the perfect amount of jokes, drills, talks and brilliant skiing'.

BASS is also Brit-run and a 2013 visitor is full of praise for the 'friendly instructors who took six of a group aged 8 to 45 together – all improved massively'.

Magic Snowsports Academy is run by an Anglo-French team and has a number of native English-speaking instructors.

FOR FAMILIES ★★★
A popular chalet choice
Méribel is a sensible choice for families wanting a chalet holiday. What it lacks in convenience it gains in an impressive area, with gentle beginner slopes and a couple of fun family areas (Acticross with whoops, a tunnel, banked turns and slaloms, and Moon Wild nature trail through the woods – both above Altiport). 'Magnestick' child safety systems have now been fitted to fast chairlifts in the area to prevent them opening until near the end of the ride. But we rarely get reports on childcare facilities – no doubt many readers use the facilities of chalet operators. Family specialist Esprit operates here – see 'Chalets'.

STAYING THERE

Chalets Méribel has more catered chalets than any other resort. Many of them are recently built luxury places with saunas, hot tubs, steam rooms and more. Some are well located, but many rely on minibus services.

The widest choice is from Ski Total, with 13 properties in the mid-to-large size range. Two deservedly get Total's top Platinum rating. Hot tubs, of course, and cinema and billiard room in the case of chalet Isba. Skiworld has 9 chalets of various sizes, including one swanky place with sauna and cinema room.

Purple Ski has five top-notch and highly individual chalets – in good positions, with lovely interiors, and hot tubs.

Ski Olympic has two properties at 1600: the smooth Parc Alpin with 12 luxurious rooms (all with plasma

SCHOOLS

ESF Méribel
t 0479 086031
ESF Méribel-Mottaret
t 0479 004949
Magic
t 0479 085336
New Generation
t 0479 010318
0844 770 4733 (UK)
www.skinewgen.com
Parallel Lines
t 0844 811 2779 (UK)
Snow Systems
t 0479 004022
BASS
t 0679 512405
Snow D'Light
t 0664 816010

Classes (ESF prices)
5 half-days (2.5hr per
day): from €140
Private lessons
From €81 for 1.5hr
for up to 4 people

GUIDES

Mountain guide office
t 0479 003038

GETTING THERE

Air Geneva 140km/
90 miles (2hr15);
Lyon 190km/120
miles (2hr30);
Chambéry 100km/
60 miles (1hr30)

Rail Moûtiers
(18km/11 miles);
regular buses

---

screen TVs), dinky swimming pool and sauna; and Charlotte with eight rooms (and no children allowed).

Family specialist Esprit has a 60-bed chalet hotel in a good slope-side position, up at Rond-Point – 'excellent; childcare beyond exemplary', says a recent guest.

Inghams has seven chalets including the smart chalet Sylvie which is new to their programme this season and has an outdoor hot tub, plus a 60-bed chalet hotel in a prime spot near the lifts at Chaudanne. Crystal has three chalets.

Hotels Méribel doesn't compete with Courchevel in the fancy hotel stakes, although a 5-star, the Kaïla (0479 088903), opened for 2012/13, and it has some other excellent places. Of course, they're not cheap.

****Grand Coeur (0479 086003) Our favourite almost-affordable hotel in Méribel. Just above the village centre. Welcoming, mature building with plush lounge. Huge hot tub, sauna etc.

****Mont-Vallon (0479 004400) The best hotel at Mottaret; good food, pool, sauna, squash, fitness room etc.

****Allodis (0479 005600) Out of town at Belvedere, but ski-in/ski-out and excellent in every other way. Seriously good restaurant, superb service, pool, sauna, nice terrace.

****Altiport (0479 005232) Smart and luxurious hotel, isolated at the foot of the Altiport lifts.

***Arolles (0479 004040) On the piste at the top of Mottaret, with the 'best ever staff, food from good to superb, lovely lounge'. Pool and sauna.

***Merilys (0479 086900) At Rond-

Point. B&B hotel plus apartments. Recommended by a regular reporter: 'Very nice room, excellent breakfast.'

***Adray Télébar (0479 086026) Welcoming piste-side chalet with pretty rooms and restaurant with good food and popular lunch terrace.

Apartments The two most impressive larger residences are Pierre & Vacances Premium properties: Les Fermes de Méribel is a classic tasteful MGM development of six large chalets with the usual good pool, gym, sauna, steam in Méribel-Village; Les Crêts is a big residence up at Mottaret. These (and others) are also available through various agents, including Ski Collection (which also has a very swanky chalet for eight in Les Allues). Ski Amis has a good range of apartments in various areas. Skiworld has apartments plus a flexible catered chalet in Mottaret where you choose what catering (if any) you want.

EATING OUT ★★★★
Some good places to try
There is a reasonable selection of restaurants, from ambitious French cuisine to pizza and pasta. For the best food, in plush surroundings, you won't beat the top hotels – we've had top-notch meals at the Grand Coeur and Allodis. The Zinc brasserie and Escale gourmet restaurant are at the highly regarded Altiport hotel. We've also enjoyed the Kouisena, with its very rustic, intimate interior and open-fire cooking of good meat. For the 'all French' experience and fine food, the Orée du Bois has been suggested. In Mottaret, tucked away near the

---

Selected chalets in Méribel   ADVERTISEMENT

PURPLE SKI *www.purpleski.com*   **T 01885 488799**

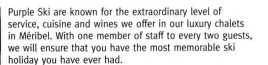

Purple Ski are known for the extraordinary level of service, cuisine and wines we offer in our luxury chalets in Méribel. With one member of staff to every two guests, we will ensure that you have the most memorable ski holiday you have ever had.

* Professional chefs
* Personal service
* On tap Veuve Clicquot
* Domain bottled wines
* En-suite bedrooms
* Private minibus service and transfers
* Hot tubs, saunas, Sky TV and wi-fi internet access

email: michael@purpleski.com

↑ This run down from Rond-Point to the lift base at Chaudanne was one of the first of Editor Watts' skiing career – there were far fewer chalets then of course

OT MERIBEL / DAVID ANDRE

Phone numbers
From abroad use the prefix +33 and omit the initial '0' of the phone number

Plattières lift, Zig Zag is a good cheaper option.

Just outside Méribel-Village, the Plantin is a lovely chalet doing a wide range of dishes. In the village, the unpretentious Brit-run Lodge du Village (pasta, Tuscany specials) was the 'food highlight of the season – Friday dish of the day was fish and chips', says a 2013 visitor; prices are modest by local standards.

APRES-SKI ★★★★★
Méribel rocks – loudly
We checked out the new Folie Douce by the mid-station of the Saulire gondola and it was packed and rocking at 4pm on a sunny March afternoon. It makes a welcome rival to the long-standing afternoon hot spot of Rond-Point at the top of the village. We're told the Arpasson hut (Tougnète) now has 'blaring music' too.

In town, try Jack's, not far from the main lift stations. The ring of bars on the main square do good business at teatime. The Doron attracts a younger crowd for videos, pool and live bands. The Poste injects a bit of French cool into the scene ('good drinks, nice young crowd'). Later on, Dick's Tea Bar is the focus – with a gastro-pub (The Den) next door. But they're away from

the centre and slopes. Aviatic is a bar/ club at the Altiport hotel.

In Mottaret the bars at the foot of the pistes get packed at teatime.

In Méribel-Village, the bar at Lodge du Village has live music at teatime a couple of nights a week.

OFF THE SLOPES ★★★☆☆
Quite a bit to do
The Olympic Centre has the ice rink where the Olympic events were held in 1992 and where you can watch regular hockey matches. It also has bowling, a climbing wall, a gym, a good public pool and a spa – these last two irritatingly separate, a reporter points out. You can take joyrides in the little planes that operate from the altiport. There are 25km of pleasant marked walks in several areas – eg between Méribel and the altiport area; down through hamlets to Les Allues (return by bus or gondola); and at Plan de Tueda, beyond Mottaret – 'gorgeous'. There's a good map of them, says a reporter. There is a pedestrian's lift pass, and accessible restaurants to meet friends for lunch. Mottaret has a cinema. There are few shops other than ski shops, even in Méribel itself.

DOWN-VALLEY TOWN – 600m
BRIDES-LES-BAINS

Brides-les-Bains is an old spa town way down in the valley. For the Méribel events in the 1992 Olympics the competitors were accommodated here and ferried up on a newly built gondola. It offers a quieter, cheaper alternative base, with some simple hotels, good-value apartments, and adequate shops and restaurants. Skiweekends.com runs a chalet hotel here. The 3-star hotel Amelie (0479 553015) is near the spa and gondola ('spacious rooms, popular happy hour, but dinner hit and miss'). There is a casino and cinema, but evenings are distinctly quiet. We have reports of one lively bar. The gondola ride to and from Méribel is supposed to take 25 minutes, but may take 40. It arrives at a point irritatingly short of the main lifts up the mountain. It also closes irritatingly early, at 5pm. But in good conditions you can ski off-piste to one or other of the mid-stations at the end of the day (or in exceptional conditions, down to Brides itself). Given a car, Brides makes a viable base for visiting other resorts.

Montgenèvre

Once a bit of a backwater, this famously snowy resort is developing nicely, but urgently needs to find the cash for more new lifts

RATINGS

The mountains

Extent	★★
Fast lifts	★★
Queues	★★★★
Terrain p'ks	★★★
Snow	★★★★
Expert	★★★★
Intermediate	★★★★
Beginner	★★★★★
Boarder	★★★
X-country	★★★
Restaurants	★★
Schools	★★★
Families	★★★★

The resort

Charm	★★★
Convenience	★★★
Scenery	★★★
Eating out	★★
Après-ski	★★
Off-slope	★

RPI   90

lift pass	£180
ski hire	£90
lessons	£80
food & drink	£115
total	**£465**

NEWS

2013/14: An area for novice boarders is to be created in the beginner area. A leisure and wellness centre is being built next to the Durance drag, which has been moved and extended to allow for this.

2012/13: The Montgenèvre lift pass was extended to include ten slopes above Claviere (over the border in Italy). The promised fast chair on Le Chalvet failed to materialize.

+ Good snow record means local snow is often the best in the Milky Way area

+ All bases covered: excellent nursery slopes, plenty of cruising and good off-piste terrain that is under-used

+ A lot of accommodation close to the slopes, and some right on them

+ Great potential for car drivers to explore other nearby resorts, but ...

− Italian Milky Way resorts such as Sauze d'Oulx are not easy to explore without road transport

− Lots of slow lifts throughout the Montgenèvre slopes, seriously undermining its appeal for some

− Little to challenge experts on-piste

− Limited range of restaurants and après-ski places

Montgenèvre is set on a minor pass between France and Italy, a position that delivers snow whichever way the wind is blowing. It is at one end of the big cross-border Milky Way network. But it's a time-consuming trek from here to Italian Sestriere and Sauze d'Oulx at the far end, so unless you have a car it's best to focus on the local slopes shared with Claviere (also in Italy, but covered here – and an attractive alternative base).

The resort has made big strides in recent years, banishing through-traffic and developing modern upscale lodgings. But it now needs to prioritize investment in fast lifts – our day on the pistes in 2012 was a painfully slow-motion affair. When we went back in 2013 for a day off the pistes, the lifts seemed less important; and the skiing was fabulous.

THE RESORT

Montgenèvre is a small village sitting on a high east–west road pass only 2km from the Italian border. The village is set on the sunny slope above the main street (the through-road is now buried in a tunnel) looking over the nursery slopes at the foot of the north-facing slopes of Les Gondrans. Behind the village are the south-facing slopes of Le Chalvet. Both sectors have piste links with Claviere, just over the Italian border and gateway to the other Italian resorts of the Milky Way – Sansicario, Sestriere and Sauze d'Oulx. But it takes ages to get to those resorts on skis; best to drive or join a group going by bus.

There are lift pass sharing arrangements with Serre-Chevalier and

Puy-St-Vincent, easily reached by car, and with rather less easily reached Les Deux-Alpes and Alpe-d'Huez, which involve going over the Col du Lautaret – high, but not usually a problem.

VILLAGE CHARM ★★★
Rustic and quiet
Cheap and cheerful cafes, bars and restaurants line the street running along the bottom of the nursery slopes, now carrying only local traffic. And a couple of narrow parallel streets with a few bars and restaurants and a church lie behind it. The old buildings give it a rustic and lived-in feel. Friendly natives and generally good snow add to the charm factor. The smart Hameau de l'Obélisque development at the eastern end of the village is wood-clad in chalet style and easy on the eye, too.

CONVENIENCE ★★★
Never far from a lift
It's a compact village – most of the lodgings are less than five minutes from a lift. But the main gondolas are at opposite ends of the village, and if you want to get from one end to the other on skis it can take ages. Some

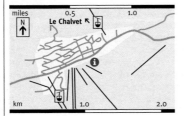

KEY FACTS

Resort	1850m
	6,070ft

Montgenèvre-Monts de la Lune (Claviere)

Slopes	1760-2630m
	5,770-8,630ft
Lifts	32
Pistes	110km
	68 miles
Green	10%
Blue	27%
Red	45%
Black	18%
Snowmaking	55%

Milky Way

Slopes	1390-2825m
	4,560-9,270ft
Lifts	72
Pistes	400km
	249 miles
Blue	25%
Red	55%
Black	20%
Snowmaking	60%

of the newer lodgings in Hameau de l'Obélisque are right on the slopes and thanks to the recently added little draglift there, ski-out as well as ski-in. The free bus service worked well for us on our recent visits, but many reporters haven't needed to use it.

SCENERY ★★★☆☆
Look north or south
The area is broken up by rocky outcrops and woods, with good views from the higher slopes on both sides of the pass.

THE MOUNTAINS

The slopes offer lots of variety – some high and open, some wooded lower down. Run classification on the local map, the Milky Way map and on the mountain are not reliably consistent. And many of the run classifications exaggerate difficulty; the black runs are not steep. Signposting is mainly adequate. The local piste map is admirably clear.

EXTENT OF THE SLOPES ★★☆☆☆
Nicely varied
Our stars are based on the local slopes; the Milky Way as a whole easily gets a ★★★★★ rating, although the Schrahe report discussed in our piste extent feature makes it clear that it is not quite as big as we thought.

The north-facing slopes above Montgenèvre and Claviere divide into three sectors. The high, open slopes of **Les Gondrans** are reached by the Chalmettes chondola from the west end of the village; a green run brings you back. From the same gondola or by riding a chairlift to the lower, steeper wooded peak of Le Prarial you can access the sector of **l'Aigle**, which has links at valley level and at altitude via Colletto Verde to the **Monti della Luna** slopes of Claviere.

The sunny sector behind the village of Montgenèvre – **Le Chalvet** – has long been accessed by a gondola from the east end of the village. A more recently added alternative access is the Serre Thibaud chondola, starting halfway between Montgenèvre and Claviere. This chondola has opened up new blue and black runs into the main Chalvet bowl and into the valley beyond the Col de l'Alpet. The Chalvet runs are mainly on open slopes above the gondola; there are blue and green runs back to Montgenèvre, and a blue run to Claviere (it's a long slog across the village to get up the other side).

FAST LIFTS ★★☆☆☆
A persistent weakness
The main lifts out of the village are a chondola and a gondola. But slow chairs and drags predominate on the upper slopes; this is a real weakness of the resort, and a regular cause of complaints from reporters. And there is little sign of improvement: the upgrade of the chairlift on Le Chalvet, announced a year ago (which we confidently added to our own piste map), has not happened, and it's not clear when it will. The resort's piste map appears to identify fast chairlifts, but actually fails to do so reliably.

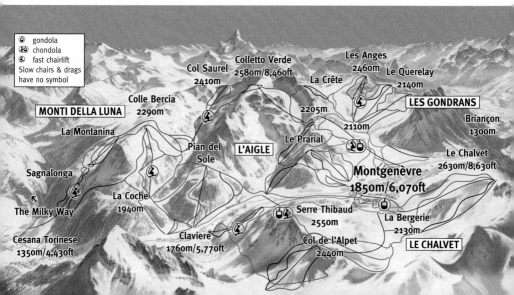

LIFT PASSES

Montgenèvre + Monts de la Lune

Prices in €

Age	1-day	6-day
under 15	30	159
15 to 59	38	200
60 plus	35	180

Free Under 6; 75 plus
Beginner Free lift in beginner area; lesson and lift deals
Notes Montgenèvre and Claviere; 6-day-plus pass allows one day in the Milky Way, Alpe-d'Huez, Serre-Che, Puy-St-Vincent, Deux-Alpes; family reductions
Alternative passes Montgenèvre (now includes 10 Italian slopes); Voie Lactée (Milky Way) area

GETTING THERE

Air Turin 100km/ 60 miles (1hr30); Grenoble 170km/ 105 miles (3hr); Lyon 235km/145 miles (3hr)

Rail Briançon (12km/ 7 miles) or Oulx (15km/9 miles); buses available from both five times a day

QUEUES ★★★★☆
Not a problem
Recent reporters have found the area pretty queue-free, even in peak season – a February 2013 visitor found 'none of any significance', and we had much the same experience.

TERRAIN PARKS ★★★☆☆
Various facilities
There's a half-pipe and a jump with an airbag to cushion landings on the lower slopes of the Gondrans sector and boardercross runs in both main sectors – 'great fun', says a reporter. There's a beginner snow park in the Chalvet sector, and a regular park at Claviere – 'well maintained', but 'really needs its own short lift'.

SNOW RELIABILITY ★★★★☆
Excellent locally
Montgenèvre has a generally excellent snow record, receiving dumps from storms funnelling up the valleys to the east and west. The high north-facing slopes naturally keep their snow better than the south-facing area. Snow-guns now cover 55% of the area, including most lower slopes; 'snow management is excellent', says a 2013 reporter.

FOR EXPERTS ★★★★☆
Some excellent off-piste
The local pistes offer few challenges – the Tetras piste on Le Chalvet is steep, but the other blacks are not. There is, however, ample off-piste terrain and it is wonderfully neglected. On the Gondrans side, there's a small 'freeride zone' of ungroomed slopes that are avalanche controlled, but the real interest lies elsewhere.

We had a great day with a guide here in February 2013, getting fresh tracks down the lovely, lightly wooded east face of Serre Thibaud from the eponymous chondola, then more down Combe de Grand Charvia, accessed by a short hike from the long, slow Rocher d'Aigle chair. After lunch, a run of 1000m vertical off the back of Les Gondrans took us down the Vallon de la Vachette to the bottom of the Montgenèvre pass. On none of these runs did we see anyone else.

The Rocher de l'Aigle chair offers lots of other options, too. In addition to off-piste variants on the red runs it serves on both sides of Colletto Verde, it accesses the classic off-piste run that everybody does, with and without guidance – the Vallon de la Douare,

leading down towards the Brousset chair. If you're prepared to hike, there are further slopes on La Plane, overlooking Claviere, and on Le Chenaillet, next to Les Gondrans. There are further good powder areas accessed from the top lifts on the Italian side.

Back on the Chalvet side, the remote north-east-facing bowl beyond the Col de l'Alpet is superb in good snow and has black pistes, too. Heli-skiing can be arranged in Italy.

FOR INTERMEDIATES ★★★★☆
Plenty of cruising terrain
The overclassified blacks (mainly concentrated in the Chalvet sector) are just right for adventurous intermediates, and there are some excellent reds – such as the pleasantly narrow tree-lined runs to Claviere from Pian del Sole, and both the runs from Colletto Verde. Average intermediates can confidently explore the whole area – few of the reds are particularly challenging. Timid intermediates have some lovely long runs on which to build confidence on both the Gondrans and Chalvet sectors – the Phare is a particularly fine long blue on the latter. Getting around the area as a whole would be easier if the easiest reds were classified blue – key runs from Colle Bercia and from Pian del Sole, for example. The runs down to the village are easy cruises.

The only real drawback of the area is the slow lifts noted above.

FOR BEGINNERS ★★★★★
One of the best
'Perfect' was the verdict of one reporter this year, and he is not far off target. There is a near-perfect nursery slope area at the foot of the Gondrans sector – large, gentle, with a moving carpet and draglift, fenced off so that you don't get speeding skiers going

↑ Underneath the goggles, our guide Matthieu is looking pretty pleased with himself. 24 hours on from a snowfall, and still making fresh tracks on Serre Thibaud

SNOWPIX.COM / CHRIS GILL

SCHOOLS

ESF
t 0492 219046
A-Peak
t 0492 244997

Classes (ESF prices)
6 5hr-days €240
Private lessons
From €41 for 1hr

CHILDCARE

Mini-club (ESF)
t 0492 219046
Ages 6mnth to 5

Ski school
For ages 5 to 14

through it. The moving carpet and a draglift outside the nursery area are free to use, so a full pass is not needed for complete beginners. Progression to longer runs could not be easier, with long, very easy green runs just up the hill at Les Gondrans. Le Chalvet also has the long, easy Phare blue run.

FOR BOARDERS ★★★
Something for everyone
There's plenty to attract boarders to Montgenèvre. There are good local beginner slopes and long runs on varied terrain for intermediates. The only real drawback is that a fair number of the lifts are drags and there are some flat sections (especially getting to and from Sestriere). There are some excellent off-piste areas with a few natural hits for more advanced boarders and a dedicated freeride area in the Gondrans sector. Snowbox is a specialist shop.

FOR CROSS-COUNTRY ★★★
Travel to the best of it
The 17km of local trails offer ample variety. But the best area is the 60km of trails in the unspoiled Clarée valley, starting an 8km drive away in Les Alberts at the bottom of the pass road's winding ascent from Briançon.

> Fine chalets in a fun French village? Check out p258.

MOUNTAIN RESTAURANTS ★★★★★
Head for Italy
A distinct weakness. In the Chalvet sector there's the table-service Bergerie at les Gondrans and the 'very acceptable' self-service les Anges. But most people eat in the village, or head over the border where there are some pleasant simple huts; all agree that Baita La Coche is about the best. It is essentially self-service but if it's quiet the cheerful family that run it will serve you at your table. Last season we enjoyed good pasta dishes and, to our enduring amazement, a good bottle of Barbera d'Asti for 10 euros – a bargain we don't expect to beat. The nearby Chalet Montsoleil is a much smoother operation, tipped by one reporter this year.

SCHOOLS AND GUIDES ★★★★★
Encouraging reports
Reports on the ESF are positive. A reporter who was among those praising the school in 2012 returned in 2013, and was not disappointed: 'The most efficient school I have come across; tuition good, firm and friendly.' A skier who tried boarding with A-Peak in 2012 was 'very impressed'.

FOR FAMILIES ★★★★★
Hugely improved
With the intrusive main road traffic banished to a tunnel, Montgenèvre is now a fine family resort – 'perfect', in the view of one reporter this year, thanks largely to the family-oriented

ACTIVITIES

Indoor Cinema

Outdoor Natural ice rink, snowshoeing, snowmobiling, walking, tobogganing, tubing, yooner tobogganing

Phone numbers
From abroad use the prefix +33 and omit the initial '0' of the phone number

TOURIST OFFICES

Montgenèvre
www.montgenevre.com

Claviere
www.claviere.it

activities available off the slopes. The beginner area has the Mini-club Les Marmottes and a snow garden for young children. There is also a childcare centre. Le Chalvet has a play area at the top station of the gondola.

STAYING THERE

Development of Hameau de l'Obélisque, at the east end of the resort, has introduced a bit of class. **Chalets** Zenith has three catered chalets here, one right by the Chalmettes lift. Crystal's 'economy' chalet Ourson (one of two chalets here) is approved by a reader ('clean, quiet, well located, very good friendly staff'), as is Ski Miquel's chalet hotel Ours Blanc ('high-quality food, a nice bar and lounge with open fire'). Pot de Miel is a B&B run on chalet lines (with optional dinners) by an Australian and her ski instructor husband.
Hotels There are now two smart places in Hameau de l'Obélisque – the first two entries below.
****Chalet Blanc** (0492 442702) Very comfortable, lovely soft duvets and pillows, smart bathrooms. Spa. We enjoyed our 2011 stay here.
***Anova** (0492 544804) Cool, relaxed, comfortable, good food. Pool, spa. We stayed here happily in 2012.
Alpis Cottia (0492 215000) Budget B&B place over the Graal cafe and in the same ownership. Discouraging back-street entrance up steep steps, but that apart we stayed here happily in 2013, in spacious rooms with weirdly tiny showers.
Apartments There are some smart 4-star developments with pool and spa at Hameau de l'Obélisque. We have had enthusiastic reports on the ski-in/ski-out Hameau des Airelles ('spacious apartments', 'well equipped', 'good lounge with fire'). This and the CGH-operated residence Chalet des Dolines are available through Peak Retreats. A major work in progress is the residence Napoléon, being built by MGM in a prime location on the main street. It may be partly open for 2013/14.

EATING OUT ★★★★★
Mainly no-frills
With about 10 no-frills places in the village, the choice is no more than adequate. La Cloche, reputedly the gourmet place, has changed hands. We had excellent pizzas last season at

the Capitaine, which aims to corner the Italian market. We and readers have also enjoyed the Estable, a locals' favourite. Reader tips: Graal ('good basic food'), Caesar ('superb', 'lively vibe'), Rafale ('nice food, great fire, really friendly') and Refuge ('atmospheric and friendly').

APRÈS-SKI ★★★★★
A few bars
The range is limited – it is a quiet village. The Refuge and the Jamy are popular cafe-bars at teatime. The Graal is a friendly, lively place with big TVs (and free Wi-Fi); the Ca del Sol is a cosy place with an open fire ('best chocolate'). The Chaberton has pool tables, and is 'lively later on'.

OFF THE SLOPES ★★★★★
Limited
The Monty Express 1400m-long two-seater monorail 'toboggan' run is said to be France's longest: 'Good fun and not for the faint-hearted.' A bus trip down to the beautiful old town of Briançon is possible.

LINKED RESORT – 1760m

CLAVIERE

Claviere is a small, traditional village just down the road from Montgenèvre, and a metre or two over the Italian border. It is not chocolate-box pretty but, even more than Montgenèvre, it has been transformed by removal of through-traffic. Its single main street, lined by a few shops, restaurants and hotels, was once ruined by traffic but is now a positively charming place to wander about.

The two main lifts – both slow quads – are conveniently close. Getting to the new Montquitaine chair is a slight uphill hike. The nursery slope is right next to the village, with a magic carpet. We continue to receive glowing reports on the ski school's handling of kids: 'Wonderful – could not have wished for a better start.'

Readers tip several restaurants: the Kilt ('excellent pizzas, sensible prices, very friendly'), and Gran Bouc ('good food and service, but a bit pricey'). Après-ski is very quiet; Baita La Coche mountain hut 'can do hot chocolates and crêpes in the evening and lay on snowcat transport'. The bar at the Roma hotel 'has good prices and Sky Sports'. Pub Gallo can be lively later on, they say.

Morzine

A large, lively, year-round resort with its own attractive slopes and linked by lift to the main Portes du Soleil circuit

302

RATINGS

The mountains

Extent	★★★★★
Fast lifts	★★★
Queues	★★★
Terrain p'ks	★★
Snow	★★
Expert	★★★
Intermediate	★★★★
Beginner	★★★
Boarder	★★★★
X-country	★★★★
Restaurants	★★★★
Schools	★★★
Families	★★★★

The resort

Charm	★★★
Convenience	★★
Scenery	★★★
Eating out	★★★
Après-ski	★★★★
Off-slope	★★★

RPI · 100

lift pass	£200
ski hire	£95
lessons	£95
food & drink	£135
total	**£525**

NEWS

2013/14: The Pléney gondola is being replaced and will have a much greater capacity.

2012/13: The Troncs chairlift, a key lift for getting back to Morzine once you go beyond Pléney, is now a six-pack. The Prodains cable car up to Avoriaz has been replaced by a big gondola.

Extent rating
This relates to the whole Portes du Soleil area

- ✚ Good-sized, varied, lightly wooded slopes shared with Les Gets
- ✚ Good nightlife by French standards
- ✚ Quite attractive chalet-style town, popular in summer
- ✚ Few crowds on weekdays, but ...

- ▬ Sunshine brings weekend crowds
- ▬ Just off the Portes du Soleil circuit
- ▬ Some lodgings remote from lifts
- ▬ Low altitude and exposure to westerlies means some risk of rain and poor snow
- ▬ Few tough pistes

Morzine is a long-established year-round resort that's easy to like. With its gentle wooded slopes, it's a good place to be in a snowstorm. For keen piste-bashers wanting to do multiple tours of the Portes du Soleil circuit it's not ideally positioned. But that doesn't seem to deter readers: we got a record number of reports on the resort this year, all from satisfied customers.

THE RESORT

Morzine is a well-established mountain resort, as popular in summer as in winter, sprawling along both sides of a river gorge – though with the centre emphatically on the west side, at the foot of the local slopes. These are shared with slightly higher Les Gets (covered in a separate chapter). Across town a gondola forming the link with Avoriaz on the Portes du Soleil circuit.

Our view that the resort suits car drivers is widely shared. But the roads are busy and the one-way system takes some getting used to. Car trips to Flaine and Chamonix are feasible.

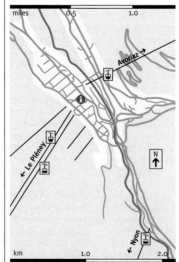

VILLAGE CHARM ★★★
Quietly attractive
The resort consists of chalet-style buildings, mostly small or mid-sized; they look cute under snow, and as that snow disappears towards spring, the village quickly takes on a spruce appearance. Morzine is a family resort, and village ambience tends to be fairly subdued; but there are plenty of bars that get busy as the lifts close.

CONVENIENCE ★★
It's a big resort ...
Morzine is a town where getting from A to B can be tricky. The best plan is to stay in or near the centre of town, a short walk from one or both of the gondolas. Restaurants and bars line the streets up to the lifts to Le Pléney, where a busy one-way street runs along the foot of the slopes. Accommodation is widely scattered; a multi-route bus service (including two electric buses) links all parts of the town to the lifts, including those for Avoriaz; there is a circular route, but only one way, which doesn't always suit your purposes. There are also buses to Les Gets, and to Ardent, which has a lift into the Portes du Soleil circuit, missing out busy Avoriaz.

SCENERY ★★★
Quite good from the tops
Despite their modest top heights, the local peaks of Pointe de Nyon and Chamossière are not without drama (or impressive views, including Mont Blanc), and the slopes below them are attractively wooded.

Pléney has trees right to the top, from which you will deduce, rightly, that it isn't very high; other peaks in the area do creep over 2000m though →

KEY FACTS

Resort	1000m
	3,280ft

Portes du Soleil	
Slopes	950-2275m
	3,120-7,460ft
Lifts	195
Pistes	650km
	404 miles
Green	12%
Blue	43%
Red	36%
Black	9%
Snowmaking	
	900 guns

Morzine-Les Gets only	
Slopes	1000-2010m
	3,280-6,590ft
Lifts	49
Pistes	120km
	75 miles
Snowmaking	70%

LIFT PASSES

Portes du Soleil

Prices in €

Age	1-day	6-day
under 16	34	169
16 to 19	41	203
20 to 64	45	225
65 plus	41	203

Free Under 5
Beginner Lessons and lift pass packages
Notes Family discounts; 5hr pass
Alternative pass Morzine-Les Gets only

ACTIVITIES

Indoor Swimming pool, ice rink, fitness centre (sauna, hot tub), library, cinemas

Outdoor Ice rink, snowshoeing, helicopter flights, snowmobiles, tobogganing, paragliding, skijoring, 'yooner' tobogganing, segway riding

THE MOUNTAINS

The local slopes are mainly wooded, with some open areas higher up. The piste map is fine, and signposting and classification are both 'good'.

EXTENT OF THE SLOPES ★★★★★
Good local area, plus the PdS
Our rating is for the whole Portes du Soleil linked area, the bulk of which is reached via Avoriaz. The local area – shared with Les Gets – is a fair size.

A gondola (being upgraded for the coming season) rises from the edge of central Morzine to **Le Pléney**. Several routes return to the valley, including a run down to Les Fys – a quiet lift junction at the foot of the **Nyon–Chamossière** sector where the area's most challenging slopes are; Chamossière is served by a six-pack, but Nyon still has a slow chair. This sector can also be accessed by a cable car starting a bus ride from Morzine. A slow chair from Les Fys along with a fast one from Le Grand Pré (further up the valley) connect with the sector of **Les Chavannes**, above Les Gets. At the far end of this sector, the bowl beneath Le Ranfoilly has no fewer than five radiating chairlifts together.

Beyond Les Gets, **Mont Chéry** is notably quiet, and well worth a visit.

Across town from the Le Pléney sector is a gondola leading (via another couple of lifts and runs) to Avoriaz and the main Portes du Soleil circuit. You take the gondola down at the end of the day – there's no piste. Alternatives are a bus ride or a short drive to either Les Prodains – for the new gondola to Avoriaz or a chair into the **Hauts Forts** slopes above it – or to Ardent, where a gondola accesses Les Lindarets for lifts towards Châtel, Avoriaz or Champéry. There's floodlit skiing every Thursday and a torchlit descent every Tuesday.

FAST LIFTS ★★★
More fast chairs needed
The main access lifts are gondolas, cable cars or fast chairs, but higher up things are not so good: some areas are equipped with fast chairs, but others rely on slow chairs and drags.

QUEUES ★★★
Peak season problems
The single biggest problem with Morzine's lifts is being rectified this year, in theory at least: the Pléney gondola is being upgraded to a much more powerful lift with 10-seat cabins. Another problem was dealt with last season – mid-season, a big new gondola replaced the inadequate cable car out at Les Prodains, one of the routes to Avoriaz. Doubtless this will to some extent relieve pressure on the other main route, the Super-Morzine gondola from the village. Afternoon logjams at Le Grand Pré when returning to Morzine from Les Gets seem to have been dealt with by the new Troncs chair, a six-pack.

TERRAIN PARKS ★★
Lots to choose from
There is a park below Pointe de Nyon, and parks and a boardercross in Les Gets. Or you can try one of the five excellent terrain parks in Avoriaz.

GETTING THERE

Air Geneva 95km/ 60 miles (1hr30); Lyon 215km/ 135 miles (3hr)

Rail Cluses or Thonon (30km/19 miles); regular bus connections to resort

SNOW RELIABILITY ★★✩✩✩
A weakness at resort level

Morzine has a very low average height, and it can rain here when it is snowing higher up (almost every year some reporters mention days of rain). The grassy slopes don't need much snow-cover and in a sparse snow year you may do better here than in higher,

rockier resorts such as Avoriaz. Snowmaking has been increased, most noticeably on the home runs. Grooming has improved, as several reporters were impressed this year.

FOR EXPERTS ★★★✩✩
A few possibilities

The runs from Pointe de Nyon and Chamossière are quite challenging, as are the black runs down the back of Mont Chéry and the Hauts Forts blacks at Avoriaz. In bad weather the medium-altitude, lightly wooded Ranfoilly bowl is a good place to head for. There is plenty of serious off-piste scope – see feature panel overleaf.

FOR INTERMEDIATES ★★★★✩
Something for everyone

Good intermediates will enjoy the fine, challenging red and black down from Chamossière. Aigle Rouge on Pointe de

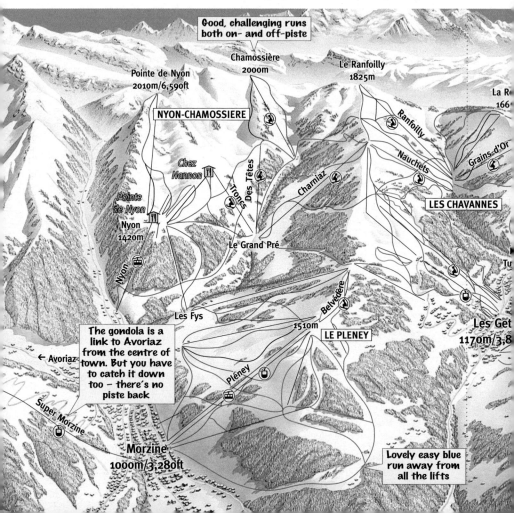

Good, challenging runs both on- and off-piste

Chamossière 2000m

Le Ranfoilly 1825m

La R 166

Pointe de Nyon 2010m/6,590ft

NYON-CHAMOSSIERE

Ranfoilly

Nauchets

Grains-d'Or

Chez Nannon

Des Têtes

Tronc

Charniaz

LES CHAVANNES

Pointe de Nyon

Nyon 1420m

Le Grand Pré

Nyon

Tu

Les Fys

Belvédère

Les Get 1170m/3,8

← Avoriaz

The gondola is a link to Avoriaz from the centre of town. But you have to catch it down too – there's no piste back

1510m

LE PLENEY

Pléney

Super Morzine

Morzine 1000m/3,280ft

Lovely easy blue run away from all the lifts

Nyon is not steep but quite narrow, with great views. Mont Chéry, on the other side of Les Gets, has some fine steepish runs that are usually very quiet. Those looking for something less challenging have a great choice. Le Pléney has a compact network of pistes that are ideal for groups with mixed abilities: there are blue and red options from every lift. One of the easiest cruises on Le Pléney is a great away-from-it-all blue (Piste B) from the top to the valley. Heading from Le Ranfoilly to Le Grand Pré on the blue is also a nice cruise.

The slopes down to Les Gets from Le Pléney are easy when conditions are right (the slopes face south). The Ranfoilly and Rosta sectors have easy blacks and cruisy reds served by fast chairs. And, of course, there is the whole of the Portes du Soleil circuit to explore via Avoriaz.

Stylish chalets and serious skiing? Check out p258.

FOR BEGINNERS ★★★☆☆
Good for novices and improvers
The wide village nursery slopes are convenient, and benefit from snow-guns, though crowds are reported to be a problem ('insanely busy in French holiday weeks – 10-minute queues for the magic carpet'). There are excellent progression runs on Le Pléney, at Nyon, and at Super-Morzine.

FOR BOARDERS ★★★★☆
Great for park and ride
Morzine is very popular with boarding seasonaires because of the extensive slopes, proximity to the excellent terrain parks in Avoriaz and the lower prices here. The slopes in Morzine are great for all abilities and have very

Morzine

305

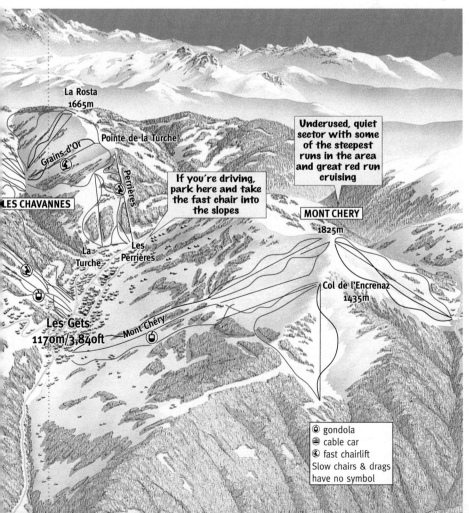

La Rosta
1665m

Pointe de la Turche

Grains-d'Or

Perrières

LES CHAVANNES

If you're driving, park here and take the fast chair into the slopes

Underused, quiet sector with some of the steepest runs in the area and great red run cruising

MONT CHERY
1825m

La Turche

Les Perrières

Col de l'Encrenaz
1435m

Les Gets
1170m/3,840ft

Mont Chéry

⬤ gondola
⬤ cable car
⬤ fast chairlift
Slow chairs & drags have no symbol

Absolutely Snow France

MORZINE
Portes du Soleil
absolutelysnow.co.uk
01248 712567

SCHOOLS

ESF
t 0450 791313

Easy2Ride (E2SA)
t 0450 790516

Snow School
t 0486 688840

BASS
t 0871 780 1500 (UK)

Synergie
t 0686 004189

Adrénaline
t 0686 688840

Mint Snowboard
t 0450 841388

Classes (ESF prices)
6 half days €144
Private lessons
From €42 for 1hr for
1 to 2 people

GUIDES

Bureau des Guides
t 0450 759665

---

few draglifts. But a reporter complained of irritating flat areas. Plenty of tree-lined runs make for scenic and interesting snowboarding, and the more adventurous should hire a guide to explore off-piste.

FOR CROSS-COUNTRY ★★★★
Good variety
There are around 70km of varied cross-country trails, not all at valley level. The best section is in the pretty Vallée de la Manche beside the Nyon mountain up to the Lac de Mines d'Or, where there is a good restaurant. The Pléney-Chavannes loop is pleasant and relatively snow-sure.

MOUNTAIN RESTAURANTS ★★★★
Some excellent huts
There is no shortage of good places, offering table-service in welcoming surroundings; restaurants are marked but not named on the piste map.
Editors' choice We have had several very enjoyable Savoyard lunches at the rustic Chez Nannon (0450 792115), between Nyon and Chamossière – cosy inside and a nice terrace. A regular visitor endorses this again in 2013: 'A little nugget of delights.' The nearby Pointe de Nyon (0450 044564) is a lovely spacious place where we had excellent duck salad and ribs in 2012.
Worth knowing about La Païka, near the top of La Rosta, is a 'rustic gem' doing wood-fired grills; serious wine list; endorsed by a 2013 reporter.

Nearby Café la Rosta is 'really good value'. The Wetzet at Ranfoilly 'is very welcoming' for a mid-morning chocolate. The Vaffieu above the Folliets chair 'can have slow service but the food is worth the wait'. A 2011 visitor raved about Lhottys at the top of the Nauchets chairlift for its 'peasant-style mountain soup – to die for'. The Croix Blanche at Chavannes is 'bustling' and does a great 'salade paysanne'. Les Mouilles, at the top of the Crusaz chair on Pléney, does 'a fine carbonara', with a 'cracking view'.

SCHOOLS AND GUIDES ★★★
Good reports of most
This year (as in most other years) we have a positive report on the local ESF: 'We were thoroughly happy; they did a first-class job with my five-year-old, and she came on in leaps and bounds.' A reporter last year was very happy with Easy2Ride ('Small group size, excellent, experienced instructor with fluent English – despite being nervous, we all progressed well').

FOR FAMILIES ★★★★
A fine family choice
Morzine caters well for families. On the mountain there are gentle, sheltered slopes and play areas. And there are plenty of other activities. Club des Piou Piou is run by the ESF school and takes children from three years old. 'Excellent – my children, six and three, were happy,' said a recent visitor.

OFF-PISTE RUNS IN THE PORTES DU SOLEIL AREA

The Portes du Soleil offers a lot of great lift-served off-piste. Here is a small selection. Like all serious off-piste runs, these should not be undertaken without a guide.

Morzine – Nyon/Chamossière area
From the Chamossière chairlift, heading north brings you to two runs – one on the same north-west slope as the pistes, the other via a col down the north-east slope to the Nyon cable car in the Vallée de La Manche – a wild area, with a great view of Mont Blanc at first.

Avoriaz area – two suggestions
From the Fornet chairlift on the Swiss border, you head west to descend a beautiful, unspoiled bowl leading down to the village of L'Erigné. In powder snow you descend the west-facing slopes of the bowl; when there is spring snow, you traverse right to descend the south-facing slopes. Medium-pitch slopes, for skiers and snowboarders.

From the top of the Machon chairlift you traverse west, beneath the peaks of Les Hauts Forts, across Les Crozats de la Chaux – a steep, north-facing slope. You then turn north to descend through the forest to the cable car station at Les Prodains. Testing terrain, for very good skiers. And be aware that the traverse can be dangerous following a snowfall.

Châtel area
From the top of the Linga chair, head north-west to cross the ridge on your right at a col and then head down the La Leiche slope to the draglift of the same name. It's a north-facing slope, starting in a white wilderness, taking you through trees back to civilization. Steep slopes – for good skiers only.

CHILDCARE

L'Outa nursery
t 0450 792600
Ages 3mnth to 5yr

Piou Piou (ESF)
t 0450 791313
From age 3

Cheeky Monkeys
t 0450 750548
From 3mnth

Jack Frost's
t 07817 138678 (UK)
From 3mnth

Ski school
From age 4

UK PACKAGES

Absolutely Snow, Adventure Base, Aiglon de Morzine, Alpine Answers, Alpine Elements, Alpine Weekends, AmeriCan Ski, Boutique Chalet Company, Chalet Chocolat, Chalet Entre Deux Eaux, Classic Ski, Crystal, Erna Low, Host Savoie, Independent Ski Links, Inghams, Inspired to Ski, Interactive Resorts, Lagrange, Momentum, Mountain Beds, Mountain Heaven, Oxford Ski Co, Peak Retreats, Powder White, PowderBeds, Reach4theAlps, Ride & Slide, Rude Chalets, Ski Expectations, Ski France, Ski Independence, Ski Line, Ski Morzine, Skiology. co.uk, Ski Solutions, Skitracer, Ski Weekend, Skiweekends.com, Snow Finders, Star Ski Chalets, STC, Sugar Mountain, Thomson, VIP, White Roc, Zenith

Phone numbers
From abroad use the prefix +33 and omit the initial '0' of the phone number

TOURIST OFFICE

www.morzine-avoriaz.
com

STAYING THERE

You can arrange affordable short breaks here through Ski Weekends.
Chalets There's a wide choice, widely spread. Mountain Heaven has a premium chalet with outdoor hot tub close to the Nyon cable car. Inghams has six chalets, three new for 2013/14, and at least one of those newly built in fine style. Its 12-bed Nomis is reportedly 'a lovely place'. Absolutely Snow has two chalets, and VIP has several. Ski Weekends runs the 'no-frills' chalet hotel Gourmets. A reader strongly recommends the chalet hotel Dents Blanches, operated by Alpine Encounters, and another Chery du Meuniers operated by Host Savoie.
Hotels Part of a general drift in France, many hotels have moved up the stars scale in the past few years. There are now seven 4-stars; 3-stars dominate.
****Bergerie (0450 791369) Rustic B&B chalet, in centre. Friendly staff. Outdoor pool, sauna, massage.
****Airelles (0450 747121) Central, close to Pléney lifts. Recent upgrade to 4-star. Good pool, 'great food', hot tub.
***Alpenroc (0450 757 543) 'Friendly, convenient, comfortable.'
***Tremplin (0450 791231) At the foot of Pléney slopes. 'Comfortable, very friendly staff, free parking.'
***Equipe (0450 791143) Long been a 2-star tip, now a 3-star; next to the Pléney lift with decent food and 'tiny' pool. Takes short-stay bookings.
Apartments. Aiglon de Morzine has 12 luxury units and is central.

EATING OUT ★★★★★
A reasonable choice
There is a fair choice, including some fine hotel restaurants. Best in town is probably the Atelier in the hotel Samoyède, which offers traditional and modern cuisine; approved by a reader this year. For value you will not beat the unpretentious Etale with its 'huge' pizzas and equally generous Savoyard dishes. The Flamme has been highly rated in the past. The Tyrolien 'serves hearty portions to groups of British skiers'. The Combe à Zorre does 'excellent lamb,' but can get over-busy at weekends. A 2013 visitor liked the 'stylish' Chamade for its 'tasty and beautifully presented meal', but warns that service can be slow. Le Coup de Coeur is a crowded wine bar in the same ownership doing good tapas,

pizza etc. The Grillion is praised this year – 'a mean tartiflette, good service'.
L'Alpage is 'a new concept' – you arrive in a traditional kitchen and proceed to dine at communal tables; the food sounds a bit cheesy.

APRES-SKI ★★★★★
One of the livelier French resorts
Morzine's après-ski is good by French resort standards. Several places around the base area get busy as the slopes empty – the Tremplin apparently has a DJ and a 'good party atmosphere'. The Crépu is a sports bar, pleasantly quiet early on but livening up later. Other options include the long-established bar Robinson and the Dixie ('good atmosphere, popular with seasonaires'), with sport on TV, a cellar bar and some live music. Between the slopes and the centre, and all in the same building are several spots: the Cavern, which is popular with seasonaires; the Coyote for arcade games and DJ; and the 'lively' Tibetan (formerly the Boudha), with Asian decor and 'often a band'. The Opéra and Laury's are late-night haunts.

OFF THE SLOPES ★★★★★
Quite good; excursions possible
There are two cinemas, an excellent ice rink, a newish indoor pool, lots of pretty walks ('booklet available from tourist office, but some walks are difficult to find and some cross pistes, which can be dangerous') and tobogganing – a 2013 visitor's daughter found it 'exhilarating'. Visitors have enjoyed trips to the cheese factory and watching ice hockey. Morzine has a reasonable range of shops, relatively glitz-free. Buses run to Thonon for more shopping, and car owners can drive to Geneva, Annecy or Montreux.

Paradiski

Les Arcs and La Plagne are pretty impressive resorts individually; the ability to explore both is just the icing on the cake

Ten years after its opening, the 200-person double-decker Vanoise Express cable car – which crosses a wooded valley to link Les Arcs and La Plagne, and thus form Paradiski – remains the world's biggest, as far as we know. When it opened, we were a bit sceptical. Sure, it was one of the biggest ski areas in the Alps, but weren't the two resorts quite big enough individually? Well, no. We're now quite used to staying in Arc 1950 and having lunch above Champagny. We might do it only once or twice in a week, but we always do it.

The Vanoise Express cable car spans the 2km-wide valley between Plan-Peisey (on the edge of the Les Arcs area) and a point 300m above Montchavin (on the edge of the La Plagne area).

The linking of these two major resorts is A Good Thing for the great British piste-basher who likes to cover as much ground as possible. For those who like a bit of a challenge, getting from your home base to both far-flung outposts of the area – Villaroger in Les Arcs and Champagny in La Plagne – would make quite a full day.

The link is also good for experts. Those based in either resort can more easily tackle the north face of La Plagne's Bellecôte, finishing the run in Nancroix. Those based in La Plagne who are finding the piste skiing a bit tame can easily get across to Les Arcs' excellent Aiguille Rouge.

If you want to make the most of the link it's sensible to stay near one of the cable car stations. But it's easily accessible from many other bases too.

On the Les Arcs side, **Plan-Peisey** and nearby **Vallandry** are in pole position. They are basically small, low-rise, modern developments, built in a much more sympathetic style than the original Les Arcs resorts. They are quiet but expanding and quite a few UK operators have chalets and apartments in them. You can also stay in the unspoiled old village of **Peisey**, 300m below and linked by bucket-lift to Plan-Peisey. These places are covered at the end of the Les Arcs chapter.

It's easy to get to the cable car station at Plan-Peisey from the main resort parts of Les Arcs. One lift and one run is all it takes to get there from **Arc 1800**, which is the biggest of the main resort units. From quieter **Arc 1600**, along the mountainside from 1800, it takes two lifts. **Arc 2000** and the stylish **Arc 1950** development seem further away, over the ridge that separates them from 1600 and 1800; but all it takes is one fast chair to the ridge and one long run down the other side. In the valley bottom beyond Arc

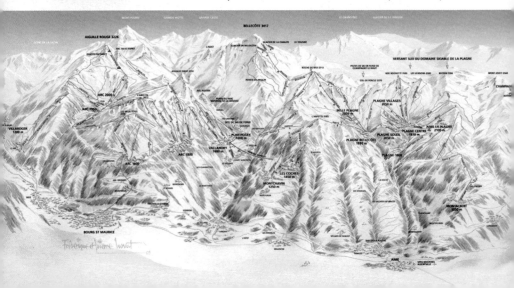

OT LA PLAGNE

The double-decker
200-person Vanoise
Express cable car
spans the 2km wide
valley between Les
Arcs and La Plagne,
and the journey takes
just four minutes ➜

2000, the hamlet of Villaroger is not an ideal starting point.

On the La Plagne side, the obvious place to stay is **Montchavin**, which is below the Vanoise Express station. Montchavin is a carefully developed old village with modern additions built in traditional style. **Les Coches**, across the mountain from the station, is most easily reached with the help of a lift. It is entirely modern, but built in a traditional style. From either village, one lift brings you to the Vanoise Express cable car.

The other parts of La Plagne are some way from the cable car. But one long lift is all it takes to get from monolithic **Plagne-Bellecôte** up to L'Arpette, from which point it's a single long descent. The most attractive of the resort villages, **Belle-Plagne**, is only a short run above Plagne-Bellecôte. From the villages further across the bowl – **Plagne-Villages**, **Plagne-Soleil**, dreary **Plagne-Centre**, futuristic **Aime-la-Plagne** – you have to ride a lift to get to Plagne-Bellecôte. From **Plagne 1800**, below the bowl, add another lift. From the villages beyond the bowl – rustic, sunny **Champagny-en-Vanoise** and expanding **Montalbert** – it's going to be pretty hard work, but it's certainly possible.

RIDING THE VANOISE EXPRESS
The cable car ride from one resort to the other takes less than four minutes. The system is designed to be able to operate in high winds, so the risk of getting stranded miles from home is low. It can shift 2,000 people an hour, and although end-of-the-day crowds could be a snag in theory, they don't seem to be a problem in practice.

The lift company offers a six-day pass covering the whole Paradiski region, perhaps most likely to appeal to people based in the villages close to the lift. It's not cheap. But there is also a pass (Paradiski Découverte) that includes just one day in the other resort during the validity of the pass. Alternatively, you can buy a one-day extension to a Les Arcs or a La Plagne six-day lift pass, as and when you fancy the outing.

Paradiski

309

La Plagne

Villages from the rustic to the futuristic, spread over a vast area of intermediate terrain – mainly high and snow-sure

RATINGS

The mountains

Extent	****
Fast lifts	**
Queues	**
Terrain p'ks	****
Snow	****
Expert	****
Intermediate	*****
Beginner	****
Boarder	***
X-country	****
Restaurants	****
Schools	***
Families	****

The resort

Charm	**
Convenience	*****
Scenery	***
Eating out	***
Après-ski	***
Off-slope	*

RPI	110
lift pass	£220
ski hire	£115
lessons	£100
food & drink	£145
total	**£580**

KEY FACTS

Resort	1800-2100m
	5,900-6,890ft

La Plagne only

Slopes	1250-3250m
	4,100-10,660ft
Lifts	90
Pistes	225km
	140 miles
Green	8%
Blue	53%
Red	25%
Black	14%
Snowmaking	
	460 guns

Paradiski area

Slopes	1200-3250m
	3,940-10,660ft
Lifts	141
Pistes	425km
	264 miles
Green	5%
Blue	52%
Red	28%
Black	15%
Snowmaking	
	793 guns

310

- Extensive and varied intermediate pistes, plus excellent off-piste
- Good nursery slopes
- High and fairly snow-sure
- Wide choice of resort villages: high or low, convenient or cute
- Wooded runs of lower satellite resorts are great in poor weather
- Cable car link to Les Arcs

- Few steep pistes
- Still lots of slow old chairlifts
- Serious high-season queues
- Pistes get very crowded in places
- Lower villages can have poor snow, especially sunny Champagny
- Brutal architecture in some villages
- No long green runs
- Upscale accommodation still rare

With 225km of its own slopes, of which almost 80% are blue or red, La Plagne is an intermediate's paradise, even if you don't use the link to Les Arcs. For experts, it has the attraction that the huge area of off-piste doesn't get skied out too quickly. But the shortage of challenging pistes is a definite drawback, and it's sad to note that two of the most rewarding black pistes (dropping 800m vertical from the glacier) were wiped from the map a few seasons ago.

Plagne-Bellecôte, effectively the hub of the lift and piste network, has had serious lift queues as long as we can remember; when snow is poor lower down, so has the Bellecôte gondola to (and from) the glacier. A solution to these problems is way overdue, but there is no sign of one. At least the resort is renovating the dire shopping malls of Plagne-Centre.

THE RESORT

La Plagne consists of no fewer than 11 separate 'villages'. Each is a self-sufficient mini-resort, though they vary widely in character. They divide basically into two groups: seven units purpose-built at altitude in a broad bowl, on or above the treeline; and four real villages, adapted and expanded for skiing, at lower altitude on the fringes of the area.

At the heart of the high-altitude area, Plagne-Centre is aptly named: it is the focal point for shops and après-ski. Directly below Centre is the chalet-filled suburb of Plagne 1800, spread across a steep hillside. A short lift ride away from Centre are the slightly higher units of Aime-la-Plagne, Plagne-Soleil and Plagne-Villages. Over a low ridge, beyond the last two, are Plagne-Bellecôte and Belle-Plagne above it.

Outside the main bowl, at the northern edge of the area, are Les Coches and Montchavin. At the southern edge is rustic Champagny. Beyond Aime-la-Plagne, at the western edge, is growing Montalbert. These are described later in the chapter.

A cable car from Montchavin links to Les Arcs via Peisey-Vallandry. Day trips by car to Val d'Isère–Tignes or the Trois Vallées resorts are possible. Staying in Champagny means quick access by car or taxi to Courchevel.

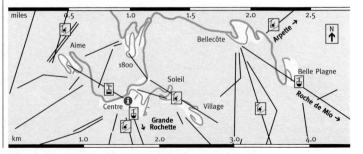

2013/14: The Roche six-pack from near the approach road is due to have its capacity increased by 50%. The Coqs quad chair above here may be moved to Les Bauches at the end of the black run from the glacier, but the resort was still waiting for this to be authorized when we went to press. A new toboggan run will be created at Plagne-Bellecôte.

2012/13: The Biolley sector was revamped, with a six-pack replacing the Becoin chair, the Biolley chair and three drags. The pistes have been modified in front of Plagne-Centre and the slalom stadium, and a new beginner zone has been created. The bottom station of the Colorado lift was lowered to make it easier to access.

The Traversee double chair, which accesses the red run on the glacier area, was replaced by a quad. Phase two of the Plagne-Centre renovation project was completed.

Most of the slopes in the main bowl are above the treeline and they reach glacier level →

VILLAGE CHARM ★★☆☆☆
Take your pick
The high-altitude villages vary quite a lot in character; our rating relates to Belle-Plagne and Plagne 1800, where most Brits go.

The first unit to be built, in the 1960s, was Plagne-Centre. Typical of its time, it has ugly square blocks and dreary indoor 'malls' that house shops, bars and restaurants. A three-year project is into its final stages to improve these malls, though we doubt they will manage to make them any less claustrophobic.

More recent developments are more stylish, but they can't compete with Centre in terms of facilities. Plagne 1800 is all in chalet style, so is visually inoffensive. Aime-la-Plagne, in stark contrast, is a group of monolithic blocks given a bold chalet-roof shape. Plagne-Soleil and Plagne-Villages mainly consist of small-scale apartment buildings finished in chalet style. The apartment buildings of Plagne-Bellecôte form a gigantic wall at the foot of the slopes leading down to it. By contrast, Belle-Plagne just above it is built in a pleasant chalet style, and has a mini-resort centre, though few shops.

CONVENIENCE ★★★★★
No worries at altitude
The high-altitude villages are mostly ski-in/ski-out – but much of Plagne 1800 presents challenges because of its steep setting, which has to be negotiated on foot. At Plagne-Bellecôte you'll walk further inside your apartment building than outside. Belle-Plagne is now quite large, and spread over a steepish hillside that provokes the odd complaint from our easily tired readers. Readers find Plagne-Soleil works well.

A free bus system between the core villages within the bowl runs until 1am, and readers seem happy with it.

SCENERY ★★★☆☆
Look to the horizon
The scenery makes an attractive and varied backdrop to the less attractive core villages. Mont Blanc looms big on the horizon, especially from Montchavin and Les Coches. And there are good views over to Courchevel from the Champagny sector.

The majority of the slopes in the main bowl are above the treeline, though there are trees scattered around most of the resort centres. The slopes outside the bowl are open at the top but descend into woodland – and are the best place to be in bad weather. So there is something to be said for choosing a base outside the bowl.

Some runs are more difficult than their classification suggests, while others are easier – note our warning in 'For intermediates'. Piste names and classification seem to alter regularly. Signposting is fine though piste marking can be a bit vague. The piste map is tricky to follow in places.

EXTENT OF THE SLOPES ★★★★☆
Multi-centred; can be confusing
Our rating relates to just the La Plagne area; the whole Paradiski area easily scores five stars.

La Plagne's pistes are spread over a wide area that can be broken down into seven sectors. From Plagne-Centre you can take a lift up to **Le Biolley**, from where you can head back to Centre, to Aime-la-Plagne or progress to **Montalbert**. But the main lift out of Plagne-Centre leads up to **La Grande**

La Plagne

Rochette. From here there are good sweeping runs back down and an easier one over to Plagne-Bellecôte, or you can drop over into the sunny **Champagny** sector, for excellent long runs and great views of Courchevel.

From Plagne-Bellecôte and Belle-Plagne, you can head up to **Roche de Mio**, and have the choice of a gondola or two successive fast chairs (the first of which also accesses Champagny). From Roche de Mio, runs spread out in all directions – towards La Plagne, Champagny or **Montchavin/Les Coches**. This sector can also be reached by taking an eight-seat chair from Plagne-Bellecôte to L'Arpette. From Roche de Mio you can also take a gondola down then up to the **Bellecôte glacier**. It is prone to closure by high winds or poor weather. The top chair is often shut in winter – but if open, it offers excellent snow and stunning views.

The black piste below Col de la Chiaupe (new a few seasons ago) means that you can descend from the glacier on-piste to the Les Bauches chairlift without riding the gondola back up to Roche de Mio; if you go all the way to Montchavin (be warned: it gets very flat, not recommended for snowboarders), it's 2000m vertical.

This black piste is one of six now marked on the piste map as Natur' (never groomed) – not popular with reporters (see 'Snow reliability'). The map also marks three draglifts (in the Montalbert/Biolley sectors) as 'difficult', and they are.

FAST LIFTS ★★
Slow progress
Many key lifts are fast, and the Montchavin/Les Coches sector is pretty much sorted, but once you start to really explore other sectors of the slopes you find lots of old chairs and draglifts – Inversens at Roche de Mio, all three lifts above Les Bauches and the lifts above Montalbert and out of 1800, for example. There is progress, even if it is slow.

QUEUES ★★
Serious bottlenecks remain
La Plagne's lift and piste network has some fundamental flaws. In particular, moving across the area often involves passing through Plagne-Bellecôte. This is now one of the worst bottlenecks in the Alps – long queues ('horrendous', 'worst in years') build in high season. The Roche de Mio gondola is especially bad ('it looked like half an hour – we took a different route' and '20 minutes is a standard wait most mornings' say 2013 reporters), and the chairs from Bellecôte towards Centre and Montchavin are not queue-free either ('20 minutes for the Coloses chair' was another 2013 comment). What's needed is some lifts from Belle-Plagne, higher up.

The gondola to the glacier is queue-prone when snow is poor lower down – to get back up to Roche de Mio as well as to the glacier (we found huge queues to get back at the end of the day on our most recent visit).

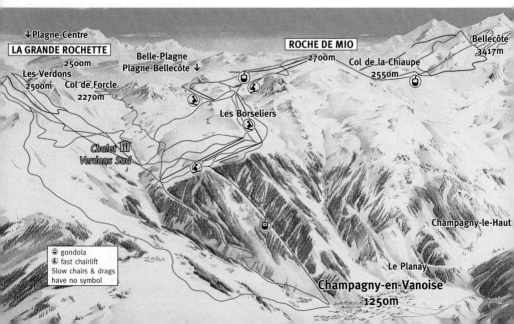

La Plagne

Build your own shortlist: **www.wheretoskiandsnowboard.com**

LIFT PASSES

La Plagne

Prices in €

Age	1-day	6-day
under 14	35	167
14 to 64	46	223
65 plus	35	167

Free Under 6
Beginner 10 free lifts
Senior 72 plus: 1-15 days €7
Notes La Plagne area; half-day passes; Paradiski extension

Alternative passes
Champagny only, Montchavin only, Montalbert only

Paradiski Découverte

Prices in €

Age	6-day
under 14	186
14 to 64	247
65 plus	186

Free Under 6
Beginner No deals
Notes La Plagne areas with one day in Paradiski

Paradiski

Prices in €

Age	1-day	6-day
under 14	39	197
14 to 64	51	263
65 plus	39	197

Free Under 6
Beginner No deals
Senior 72 plus: 1-15 days €10
Notes Les Arcs areas and La Plagne areas; family reductions; with 5+ passes one day in the Trois Vallées and Espace Killy, and reduced rate in Ste-Foy, La Rosière and La Thuile

Plagne-Centre also has problems; the Bergerie six-pack builds queues (but they move quickly) and the Grand Rochette is 'a classic bun fight'.

In the Champagny sector, the upgrade of the Verdons Sud chair to a six-pack two seasons ago has of course relieved that bottleneck.

Crowds on the pistes are now as much of a problem as lift queues. The worst-affected area is from Roche de Mio where a single blue piste takes all the pressure. In the afternoon, this run can be handling traffic from four lifts – maybe 6,000 skiers an hour, or 100 a minute. The Trieuse and Arpette pistes to Bellecôte and some runs to Centre get badly crowded too. Slopes outside the main bowl are quieter, except runs to Montchavin late in the day.

TERRAIN PARKS ★★★★
Lots of choices

With no fewer than four terrain zones, freestylers are well catered for. There is a 90m long, 3m high half-pipe at Plagne-Bellecôte (plus an FIS-approved super-pipe, which hosts the World Cup but isn't open to the public). Belle-Plagne is home to the big park, split into three levels from beginner to more advanced zones, with a mix of jumps, boxes, rails, tables and other obstacles, plus an airbag. There's also a small park with beginner and progression obstacles above Montalbert. Then there are three boardercross courses dotted around.

SNOW RELIABILITY ★★★★
Generally good except low down

Most of La Plagne's runs are snow-sure, being at altitudes between 2000m and 2700m on the largely north-facing open slopes above the purpose-built centres. The two sunny runs to Champagny are something else – one is often closed, the other (Les Bois) is kept open as much as

possible with lots of artificial snow. Snowmaking on runs to all the villages is being improved. On our March 2011 visit we found most of the pistes in great condition, despite the lack of natural snowfall. Grooming is good but most reporters think the 'Natur' runs should be groomed sometimes.

FOR EXPERTS ★★★★
Few steep pistes; good off-piste

The two long black runs from Bellecôte to the Chalet chairlift below Col de la Chiaupe were returned to off-piste status a few years back – not surprising, given that they were rarely open, but a shame all the same. The piste linking this area to Les Bauches and Montchavin doesn't really deserve its black status, but the Crozets black that meets it, from the bottom of the Inversens chair, is a good run.

Up on the glacier, Chiaupe merits its black status for a short stretch, but really the tough piste skiing is now confined to the Biolley sector. On the back of the hill, the Coqs and Morbleu blacks are seriously steep, Palsembleu less so. From the very top of this sector, Etroits owes its black status to a quite short pitch that is both steep and narrow, but is otherwise harmless. The long Emile Allais red down to the La Roche chair is north-facing, often quiet and great fun in good snow.

But experts will get the best out of La Plagne if they hire a guide and explore the vast off-piste potential – which takes longer to get tracked out than in more 'macho' resorts. The glacier and Biolley sectors have some excellent terrain and there are good runs from the glacier to Les Bauches (a drop of over 1400m). For the more experienced, the north face of Bellecôte presents a splendid challenge with usually excellent snow at the top. You can descend to Peisey-Nancroix (a drop of 2000m), enjoy a

good lunch at the charming, rustic
Ancolie (a real favourite of ours) and
then catch a taxi or free bus to the
Vanoise Express cable car. Another
beautiful and out-of-the-way run starts
with a climb and goes over the Cul du
Nant glacier to Champagny-le-Haut.

FOR INTERMEDIATES ★★★★★
Great variety

Virtually the whole of La Plagne's area
is a paradise for intermediates, with
blue and red runs wherever you look.

The main drawback is that many of
them get overcrowded at times.

For early intermediates there are
plenty of gentle blue motorway pistes
in the main La Plagne bowl, and a
long, interesting (but often very
crowded) run from Roche de Mio to
Belle-Plagne called the Tunnel (going
through, er, a tunnel). The blue runs
either side of Arpette, on the
Montchavin side of the main bowl, are
glorious cruises – but beware, the
blues further down towards

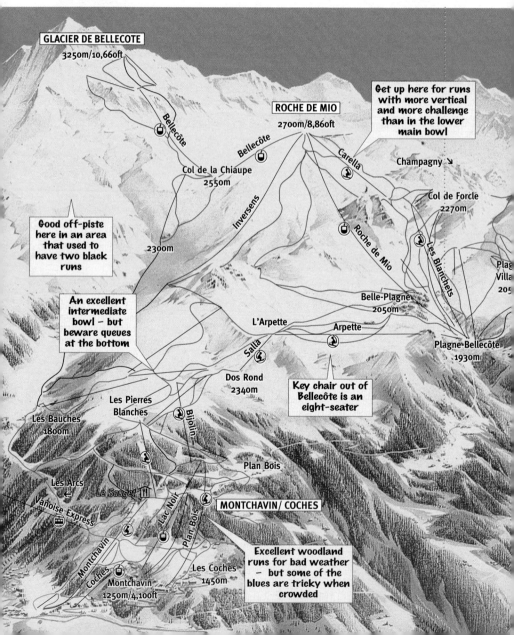

GLACIER DE BELLECOTE
3250m/10,66oft

Bellecôte

ROCHE DE MIO
2700m/8,86oft

Bellecôte

Carella

Champagny ↘

Col de la Chiaupe
2550m

Inversens

Col de Forcle
2270m

Roche de Mio

Les Blanchets

Plag
Villa
205

2300m

Get up here for runs
with more vertical
and more challenge
than in the lower
main bowl

Belle-Plagne
2050m

Good off-piste
here in an area
that used to
have two black
runs

L'Arpette

Arpette

Plagne-Bellecôte
1930m

An excellent
intermediate
bowl – but
beware queues
at the bottom

Salla

Dos Rond
2340m

Key chair out of
Bellecôte is an
eight-seater

Les Pierres
Blanches

Bijolin

Les Bauches
1800m

Plan Bois

Les Arcs
←

Le Sauget

Lac Noir

Plan Bois

MONTCHAVIN / COCHES

Vanoise Express

Excellent woodland
runs for bad weather
– but some of the
blues are tricky when
crowded

Montchavin

Cochés

Les Coches
1450m

Montchavin
1250m/4,10oft

gondola
cable car
fast chairlift
Slow chairs & drags
have no symbol

A new six-pack for 2012/13 speeded access to the serious black runs and good off-piste off the back of this sector

Champagny ↘

Col de Forcle
2270m

LA GRANDE ROCHETTE
2500m

Les Verdons
2500m

2350m

le Mio

Les Blanchets

LE BIOLLEY

le-Plagne
2050m

Plagne-Villages
2050m

Grande-Rochette

Colorado

Plagne-Centre
1970m/
6,460ft

Telemetro

Aime-la-Plagne
2100m

Plagne-Soleil
2050m

Plagne-Bellecôte
1930m

Plagne 1800

La Roche

Le Fornelet
1970m

The main bowl offers mainly easy runs of limited vertical

MONTALBERT

Le Forperet

Montalbert

Plagne-Montalbert
1350m

Longefoy
1170m

The resort is very spread out with no fewer than 11 different 'villages' →

OT LA PLAGNE / ELINA SIRPARANTA

Montchavin are quite challenging. The easiest way to and from Champagny is from the Roche de Mio–Col de Forcle area. Warning: the Mira piste from Grande Rochette and the Lanche Ronde up at Roche de Mio have steep pitches that will upset many blue-run skiers, although Mira has been widened at the top and you can avoid the moguls on the steepest section says a reporter. Verdons, nearby, is a great cruise, too.

Better intermediates have lots of delightful long red runs to try. There are challenging red mogul pitches down from Roche de Mio to Les Bauches (a drop of 900m) – the first half is a fabulous varied run with lots of off-piste diversions possible; the second half, Les Crozats, is classified black, and can be tricky if snow is less than ideal. The Sources red to Belle-Plagne is a good run, too.

The Champagny sector has a couple of tough reds – Kamikaze and Hara-Kiri – leading from Grande Rochette. And the long blue cruise Bozelet has one surprisingly steep section. The long Mont de la Guerre red, with 1250m vertical from Les Verdons to Champagny, is often closed because of its south-facing exposure; but when open, it's a fine away-from-all-lifts run with a decent red-gradient stretch half-way down, but long flattish tracks at the start and finish. There are further excellent red slopes in the other outlying areas.

FOR BEGINNERS ★★★★
Comprehensive facilities
La Plagne is a good place to learn, with 18 free lifts in the whole area; each village has at least one. There are good facilities for beginners, provided you go to the right bits, and generally good snow. There are beginner areas in Centre, 1800, Soleil, Aime and Bellecôte; and in (and above) Montchavin, Les Coches and Montalbert. But there are no long green runs to progress to from the nursery slopes. Although a lot of the blue slopes are easy, you can't count on that; some, as we note above, are quite testing.

FOR BOARDERS ★★★
Something for everyone
With such a huge amount of terrain, there is something for everyone: 'One of the best for boarding,' says a recent visitor. Expert freeriders should hire a guide to explore the off-piste. Although this is a great place for beginners and intermediates, with huge wide-open rolling pistes, there are one or two flattish areas – for example getting across Plagne-Centre, the middle of the Tunnel run and the blue run linking Les Bauches to Montchavin. Most draglifts have been replaced, and others can be avoided; the more difficult ones are marked on the piste map. The park caters for all levels and there are three boardercross runs – see 'Terrain parks'.

SCHOOLS

ESF (Belle)
t 0479 090668
Schools in all centres
Oxygène
t 0479 090399
El Pro (Belle)
t 0479 091162
Reflex (1800)
t 0613 808056
Antenne (2000)
t 0479 091380
Evolution 2
(Montchavin-Coches)
t 0479 078185

Classes (ESF prices)
6 days from €217
Private lessons
From €90 for 2hr for
1-2 people

FOR CROSS-COUNTRY ★★★★
Open and wooded trails
There are 80km of prepared cross-country trails scattered around. The most beautiful of these are the 22km of winding track set out in the sunny valley around Champagny-le-Haut. The north-facing areas have more wooded trails that link the various centres.

MOUNTAIN RESTAURANTS ★★★★
An enormous choice
Mountain restaurants are an attraction of the area: numerous and varied – and crowded only in peak periods. But all our favourites are outside the main bowl, above the satellite villages.
Editors' choice We've had excellent meals at Chalet des Verdons Sud (0621 543924) above Champagny; reporters agree – appetizing food and 'friendly' service, on a terrace with a fine view or in the woody interior with a big fire. Above Montalbert, the Forperet (0479 555127) is an old farm, doing super 'very traditional, beautifully presented' home-made dishes. We had an excellent tartiflette there (as did a reporter). The rustic Sauget (0479 078351), above Montchavin, is a great place to hole up in poor weather for some highly traditional dishes.
Worth knowing about Readers' tips include the 'lovely' Plein Soleil at Plan Bois ('a bit cramped inside but large terrace and excellent food', 'best omelette and chips on the mountain'), Roc des Blanchets above Champagny ('great views, extensive menu'), Borseliers above Champagny ('a long-standing favourite, suitable for good

Fine chalets in a fun French village? Check out p258.

or bad weather'), Bergerie above Plagne-Villages ('what a wonderful atmosphere, with the patron wearing his big beret, such smiling friendly staff and a varied menu'), Chalet des Glaciers on the, er, glacier ('tiny hut with hearty soup in a bread bowl; outside seating only'). Pierres Blanches ('friendly, nice plat du jour and lovely wood-burning stove with both table- and self-service') and Plan Bois ('excellent food with an Austrian influence') both above Les Coches.
There's a picnic room ('sac hors sac') in Plagne-Centre.

SCHOOLS AND GUIDES ★★★
Reports are mixed
Each centre has its own ESF school, and we had a positive report in 2013 of Montchavin: 'My brother loved his two private lessons – instructor was polite, patient, top-notch.' But also in 2013, an 11-year-old boy was unimpressed by the ESF in Plagne 1800: 'The usual follow-the-leader and poor communication.' We've had good reports for Champagny: 'Great day's off-piste guiding; he found us powder all day'; 'for the near-beginner in our group, the lessons were fun'. In Belle-Plagne (arranged by Ski Esprit): 'My four-year-old had positive and encouraging instructors, and progressed well.' The Oxygène school in Plagne-Centre is 'wholly recommended for anyone looking for

La Plagne

Build your own shortlist: **www.wheretoskiandsnowboard.com**

TRY THE OLYMPIC BOBSLEIGH RUN – YOU CAN EVEN DO IT SOLO

If the thrills of a day on the slopes aren't enough, you can round it off by having a go on the bobsleigh run built for the 1992 Olympic Winter Games, based in Albertville. The floodlit 1.5km run has 19 bends, generating forces as high as 3g.

You can go in a driverless bob-raft (40 euros) reaching 50mph, which most people find quite exciting

enough. Then there's the solo mono-bob (107 euros), which reaches 55mph; we found this a great thrill – we had to close our eyes on the sharper bends. Fastest of all is the racing-bob (114 euros), where three of you are wedged in a real four-man bob behind the driver – at speeds of over 60mph. Be sure your physical state is up to the ride; there are minimum age limits. The run is open on certain days only – book ahead. Additional insurance is available. One visitor loved the ride, but thought the staff rude: 'They rushed us through, despite the fact that we were early.'

OT LA PLAGNE / J FAVRE

introductory snowboard instruction' by one 2013 reporter, while another 'had 14 people in the group despite the website claiming they had a maximum of 8 to 10'. Reflex based in 1800 and Evolution 2 based in Montchavin have had good past reviews. Antenne Handicap offers private lessons for skiers with any kind of disability.

FOR FAMILIES ★★★★
Good facilities

Several UK chalet operators run childcare services – see below for more on the Esprit chalet hotel here – and the Family Ski Company is in Les Coches. There are nurseries in most of the villages. One or two reporters were concerned by the crowded pistes.

STAYING THERE

Chalets There are lots of catered chalets. Many are in apartments, but there are lots of proper little chalets in 1800, which is where most large UK tour operators have places. Crystal has about a dozen, mostly in 1800. Inghams has five. Mountain Heaven has three mid-sized places. Skiworld has 11 chalets dotted around several parts of the resort. Family specialist Esprit has its flagship chalet hotel at Belle-Plagne, the exceptionally cool Deux Domaines – in a great position, with good pool and spa ('top quality, well run, excellent childcare' said a 2013 reporter). Ski Olympic has a chalet hotel on the piste overlooking Plagne-Centre ('great team, service and

CHILDCARE

P'tits Bonnets (Centre)
t 0479 090083
Marie-Christine
(Centre)
t 0479 091181
18mnth to 6yr
ESF nurseries (from
18 mnth or 2yr):
Aime 0479 090475
Belle 0479 090668
Snow gardens run by
ESF: ages from 3 to 5

Ski schools
3yr to 13yr or 16yr
depending on village

GETTING THERE

Air Geneva 200km/
125 miles (3hr); Lyon
195km/120 miles
(2hr45); Chambéry
120km/75 miles
(1hr45)
Rail Aime (18km/
11 miles) and Bourg-
St-Maurice (35km/
22 miles) (Eurostar
service available);
frequent buses from
stations

food'; 'good value and wonderful views but a bit tatty in places'). Ice and Fire has a ski-in/ski-out place at Plagne-Villages, and another with a sauna at 1800. See also our descriptions of lower villages.
Hotels There are very few.
****Carlina (0479 097846) Beside the piste below Belle-Plagne. Pleasant rooms, good restaurant, pool and spa centre. Family-friendly. We've enjoyed our stays here. Endorsed by another satisfied reader this year.
***Araucaria (0479 092020) Very modern 3-star at Plagne-Centre. Sauna, spa.
***Balcons (0479 557655) 3-star at Belle-Plagne. Pool.
Apartments There is a wide choice, including lots of smart new properties, most with pools, available through companies such as Ski Collection, Peak Retreats, Ski Amis, Pierre & Vacances, Ski Independence, Lagrange, Inghams, Crystal and Erna Low.
  In Belle-Plagne there are two good Montagnettes residences, Le Vallon and Les Cîmes. In Plagne-Soleil the Granges du Soleil is very comfortable, with pool, spa and excellent views. Up at Aime is the Pierre & Vacances Premium residence Les Hauts Bois ('spacious apartments, hotel-standard spa facilities'). Lagrange has two Prestige residences: Aspen in Plagne-Villages and Chalets Edelweiss (seven chalet-style buildings sharing a pool) – right by the lift out of 1800. And Skiworld has a 'flexible catered chalet', where you can choose what catering (if any) you want, in 1800.

EATING OUT ★★★☆☆
A reasonable choice
There is a decent range of casual restaurants including pizzerias and traditional Savoyard places. In Belle-Plagne, the Face Nord is recommended for 'excellent local cuisine and service'. The Matafan served up a hearty meal of grilled meats and good desserts on our recent visit and we enjoyed a very tasty three-course meal at the hotel Carlina's restaurant, which is also recommended for lunch and is highly rated by readers. La Cloche served an 'excellent côte de boeuf'. In Bellecôte, the Ferme has been recommended for Savoyard dishes.
  Reader recommendations in Plagne-Centre include the Métairie and Le Chaudron for traditional food. The Refuge is one of the oldest restaurants

in La Plagne ('good food and value, space-age loos').
  In Plagne-Villages, the Casa de l'Ours does pizzas and steaks. In Plagne-Soleil, Monica's is 'excellent and good value'.
  In Plagne 1800, we had a good evening at Petit Chaperon Rouge – friendly, cosy atmosphere in a wooden chalet that serves local specialities at reasonable prices; the Loup Blanc is popular for steaks and pizza.
  At Aime-la-Plagne, the rustic old chalet Au Bon Vieux Temps on the slopes is open in the evening and is highly praised ('mainly French clientele, excellent mushroom ravioli and tarte tatin – yummy'). The 'casual, family-friendly' Montana does pizza and the 'usual Savoyard suspects'. The Mont Blanc is also recommended.

APRES-SKI ★★★☆☆
Bars, bars, bars
Though fairly quiet during low season, La Plagne has plenty of bars, catering particularly for the younger crowd.
  In Belle-Plagne, the Tête Inn and the Cheyenne are the main bars. In Plagne-Centre, the Igloo has 'icy white decor' but 'is horribly expensive'. The PlanJA is popular and has English cider, apparently. Scotty's has been known to be 'lively' but a March 2013 visitor found it often closed early, and Mouth is also tipped. The Mine is the focal point in Plagne 1800 – complete with old train and mining artefacts. Mama Mia's is a fun spot, and the Bobsleigh Bar is recommended. Plagne-Soleil has Monica's pub. Aime-la-Plagne is quiet. There are discos at Plagne-Centre, Belle-Plagne and at Plagne-Bellecôte.

OFF THE SLOPES ★☆☆☆☆
OK for the active
As well as the sports and fitness facilities, there are plenty of winter

ACTIVITIES

Indoor Sauna and solarium in most centres, squash (1800), fitness centres (Belle-Plagne, 1800, Centre, Bellecôte), library (Centre), climbing wall, bowling

Outdoor Heated swimming pool (Bellecôte), bobsleigh, marked walks, tobogganing, paragliding, helicopter rides, snowmobiles, ice climbing, ice rink, ice karting, snow quad bikes, snowshoeing, dog sledding, air boarding, zip slide

Phone numbers
From abroad use the prefix +33 and omit the initial '0' of the phone number

TOURIST OFFICES

La Plagne
www.la-plagne.com

Montchavin-Les Coches
www.montchavin-lescoches.com

Champagny
www.champagny.com

walks along marked trails. It's also easy to get up the mountain on the gondolas, both of which have restaurants at the top. There's an ice grotto on the glacier. Plagne 1800 has bowling and tubing, and Plagne-Centre has a toboggan run (as should Bellecôte for 2013/14). The Olympic bobsleigh run is a popular evening activity (see feature box). There are cinemas at Aime, Bellecôte and Plagne-Centre. Excursions are limited.

LINKED RESORT – 1250m
MONTCHAVIN

Montchavin is based on an old farming hamlet and has an attractive traffic-free centre. There are adequate shops, a kindergarten and a ski school. The local slopes have quite a bit to offer – pretty, sheltered runs, well endowed with snowmaking, with nursery slopes at village level, attractively surrounded by chalets and restaurants.

The main blue home runs from Dos Rond can be quite tricky (though you can take a more roundabout route via Les Bauches). Après-ski is quiet, but the village doesn't lack atmosphere and has a couple of nice bars (a 2013 reporter recommends the Dos Rond bar-restaurant), a nightclub, cinema, night skiing, ice rink, and a new swimming pool and the Espace Paradisio spa complex. Hotel Bellecôte (0479 078330) is convenient for the slopes. Restaurant recommendations include La Ferme de César ('amazing steaks') and Le Moulin à Poivre ('classic dishes').

LINKED RESORT – 1450m
LES COCHES

Les Coches is a little way above Montchavin, across the hillside, and shares the same slopes. It is a sympathetically designed, quiet, modern mini-resort with a traffic-free centre. The hillside setting makes for some steep walks. There are nursery slopes across the mountainside, linked by bucket-lift. It has a kindergarten, but Family Ski Company may be a better bet, with two piste-side chalets close to the village centre. Ice and Fire has a smart-looking 24-bed chalet on the piste with a sauna. Chalets de Wengen are comfortable chalet-style apartment buildings sharing a pool, sauna, steam room – available through Peak Retreats.

Dining out options approved by readers include the Poze (pizza), the Savoy'art, and Taverne du Monchu.

LINKED RESORT – 1350m
MONTALBERT

Montalbert is a traditional but much expanded village with a nice little 'front de neige' area, with a choice of restaurant terraces. The lift out of the village is a fast one but the one after that is slow, and your progress to the main bowl depends on two further slow ones, so it takes quite a time to get to Centre. The local slopes are easy and wooded. Restaurant choice is adequate: Abreuvoir has 'reasonable prices in happy hour', Fiftys Legend has 'prompt service', Tourmente is a popular pub with a pool table, and the Code is a 'racy but rocking' nightclub. Ski Amis has a central, all en suite, seven-room chalet with all the trimmings here, and various self-catering options. Mountain Heaven has self-catering apartments in several modern developments; the best of the apartments are notably spacious by French standards, and well furnished.

LINKED RESORT – 1250m
CHAMPAGNY

Champagny is a small, charming village in a pretty, wooded, sunny setting, with its modern expansion done sensitively. It has drawbacks: it is remote from the link to Les Arcs, its local slopes are exposed to full sun, and the red run to the village that is most reliably open is rather steep and narrow for nervous intermediates (though you can ride the gondola down). It is well placed for an outing by taxi or car to Courchevel.

There is a beginner area with free lifts at the top of the gondola, and a boardercross higher up beside the Rossa chairlift.

The Glières (0479 550552) is a rustic old hotel with varied rooms, a friendly welcome and good food ('good set menus and classic dishes, always brilliant'). The Ancolie (0479 550500) is smarter, with modern facilities. The Alpages de Champagny has 'generous-sized apartments', a pool, sauna and steam room. The Club Alpina apartments next to the gondola have also been recommended.

The village is quiet in the evenings, but there is a cinema.

Portes du Soleil

Low-altitude, largely intermediate circuit of slopes straddling the French–Swiss border, with a choice of contrasting resorts

Slopes	950-2275m
	3,120-7,460ft
Lifts	195
Pistes	650km
	404 miles
Green	12%
Blue	43%
Red	36%
Black	9%
Snowmaking	
	900 guns

Pierre & Vacances

Largest
Choice of Ski apartments
in France

From **£55**
per person per week

0870 0267 144
www.pv-holidays.com

The Portes du Soleil vies with the Trois Vallées for the title 'World's Largest Ski Area', but its slopes are very different from those of Méribel, Courchevel, Val Thorens and neighbours. The central attraction is an extensive circular tour, straddling the French–Swiss border, taking you through one or two French resorts and several small Swiss ones – great for keen intermediates who like a sensation of travel. You can travel the circuit in either direction, and longer or shorter variations are possible.

We have separate chapters on all the major Portes du Soleil resorts. On the French side, high, purpose-built **Avoriaz** usually has the best snow around, and it is well placed to make the most of the slopes of Châtel and Champéry, as well as its own. There's a break in the circuit at the lower, traditional village of **Châtel** – you take a bus to bridge the gap.

On the Swiss side, **Champéry** is a classic, charming mountain village with a broad area of slopes spreading across the mountainside above the tiny, purpose-built satellite stations of Champoussin and Les Crosets. Then in a separate valley there is the larger, traditional village of Morgins.

Back in France are two further traditional resorts, off the main circuit but linked by lift to Avoriaz – **Morzine** and **Les Gets**. They share the biggest area of local slopes in the region.

The lifts you ride doing the circuit vary widely. In the Avoriaz sector and in the Linga sector of Châtel the lifts are mainly modern and fast. On the far side of Châtel and on the Swiss side of the network, drags and old chairlifts dominate, and progress is slow.

The slopes are low by French standards, with top heights in the range 2000m to 2275m, and low points where snow may be particularly poor in Morgins and Châtel (1200m). In general, you can expect better snow on the north-facing French side of the circuit than on the sunnier Swiss side, particularly around Avoriaz/Champéry.

In the distant past there was a booklet-style map covering the whole of the Portes du Soleil. But now each resort has a map showing local lifts and pistes – you have to pick these up as you go. There's an overview map of the circuit on the back of each one.

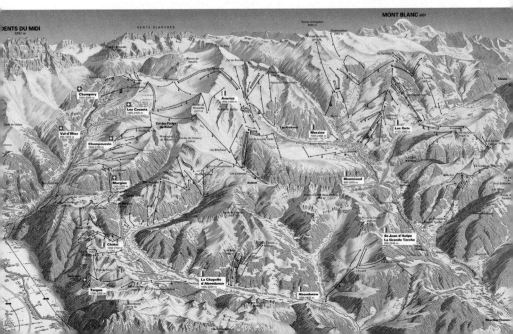

The Pyrenees

An underrated region with decent skiing and boarding at lower prices than the Alps, and villages that remain distinctly French

RPI	95
lift pass	£170
ski hire	£120
lessons	£90
food & drink	£110
total	£490

322

It is certainly true that ski areas in the French Pyrenees can't compete in terms of extent with the mega resorts of the Alps. But don't dismiss them: they have considerable attractions, including price – hotels and apartments can cost half as much as in the French Alps, and meals and drinks are cheaper. Provided the snow is good and you're not in search of steep mogul fields and wild après-ski, there is a surprising amount of variety packed into some of these smaller areas.

The Pyrenees are serious mountains, with dramatic, picturesque scenery, and are worth considering for beginners, intermediates and quiet family holidays at a lower cost. The resorts are attractively French, and many are old mountain villages that double up as spa towns. You'll also find charmless purpose-built satellites.

Access has improved, with low-cost airlines using Toulouse, Pau and Lourdes airports.

The locals (including lots of Spanish) like to visit at weekends, so the slopes can get busy. Queues are rare outside peak holidays though, and a lot of locals do cross-country rather than downhill. British visitors are still relatively few, and English is less widely spoken than in the Alps.

Cauterets

➕ Charming, old spa town
➕ Serious cross-country trails
➖ Downhill slopes very limited
➖ Long gondola ride to/from slopes

Cauterets is good for a short break; it's a relaxing old town, easy to reach, and its small downhill ski area suits a couple of days – try the cross-country too.

Many of Cauterets' buildings are well-preserved examples from the 19th century, and the thermal spas are a popular attraction for visitors.

There is a wide choice of hotels. The town's position at the head of a wide, sunny valley means traffic is rarely a problem, despite its appeal as a large year-round tourist destination.

The skiing takes place in a high, open and treeless bowl, the Cirque du Lys, reached by a long gondola from town; you have to ride it down as well as up. There is parking up at Le Courbet (1360m), from where a short gondola departs for the slopes.

The 36km of varied slopes radiate around the bowl, between 1730m and 2415m. The area just above the gondola top station is ideal for children and beginners. There are some gentle blue runs for progression with a new one planned for 2013/14. But the area does get busy at weekends, as does the main restaurant – a self-service. The Oakley terrain park had a new O-Rail installed for 2012/13.

Cauterets' jewel, though, is its 36.5km of cross-country, a short bus ride from town at Pont d'Espagne. It's one of the best areas we've seen, amid beautiful scenery and waterfalls. There are also 6km of snowshoe trails.

KEY FACTS

Resort	935m
	3,070ft
Slopes	1730-2415m
	5,680-7,920ft
Lifts	12
Pistes	36km
Snow-guns	Some

TOURIST OFFICE

www.cauterets.com

KEY FACTS

Resort	830m
	2,720ft
Slopes	1700-2515m
	5,580-8,250ft
Lifts	28
Pistes	100km
Snow-guns	45%

TOURIST OFFICE
www.saintlary.com

St-Lary-Soulan

- ⊞ One of the biggest Pyrenean areas
- ⊞ Attractive, traditional village
- ▬ Few challenges on-piste
- ▬ No runs back to the valley village

St-Lary combines an attractive, traditional village with one of the largest ski areas in the French Pyrenees – fine for intermediates wanting a sense of travel.

If you stay in the village, you ride a cable car or gondola both ways. Or you can stay up at purpose-built St-Lary 1700 (Pla-d'Adet).
Village charm St-Lary is pleasant with a narrow main street lined with wood and stone buildings.
Convenience Accommodation spreads from the centre along a river towards the hamlet of Soulan. Staying close to one of the two lifts is best.
Scenery The rocky ridges and open slopes give fine views including the Pyrenees National Park.

THE MOUNTAIN
The slopes cover three main sectors and most runs are above the treeline.
Slopes A cable car and gondola go up to an area of short slopes at St-Lary 1700. From there you can head for 1900 and a gondola towards a more extensive area of intermediate slopes.
Fast lifts Apart from the three above,

there are three fast chairs; all other lifts are slow chairs and drags.
Queues 'No problem outside school holidays,' says a recent visitor, who was told weekends can be busy.
Terrain parks There's a park and a boardercross.
Snow reliability Reasonable; many slopes are north-east facing and almost half have snowmaking.
Experts The few black runs are not very challenging but there's off-piste at Courne Blanque and Soum de Matte.
Intermediates Most runs are gentle cruises, with a few more challenging red runs. Best for early intermediates.
Beginners Good nursery slopes, with two covered moving carpets at 1700 and a special lift pass for 1700 only.
Snowboarding There are good cruising runs, though still some old draglifts.
Cross-country Not the best choice.
Mountain restaurants L'Oule, by a lake, is an old refuge with decent self-service food. Rustic Les 3 Guides above 1900 ('excellent charcuterie, local wine by the pichet') and tiny La Cabane on the edge of 1700 do friendly table-service.
Schools and guides The four schools offer the usual options, though good spoken English cannot be guaranteed.
Families St-Lary is a good family resort, with kids' snow gardens, mini terrain park, a family fun area and tobogganing. The day care centre at 1700 takes children from 18 months to six years old.

STAYING THERE
Hotels The 4-star Mercure is linked to the spa and is near the gondola; we enjoyed a recent stay there. The 3-star Pergola is charming with a good restaurant.
Apartments 4-stars with pool, sauna, steam and hot tub include l'Ardoisière (800m from the gondola) and Cami Real (central). Pierre & Vacances has the 4-star Rives de l'Aure (near the cable car). Lagrange has the 3-star Chalets de l'Adet with pool (on the slopes). Ski Collection and Zenith have a good selection of places.
Eating out There's a fair choice, from pizzerias to grills. Our favourite is the

The Pyrenees

Build your own shortlist: **www.wheretoskiandsnowboard.com**

Grange (local gourmet dishes). Other tips: the Gros Minet, Maison du Cassoule, Pergola (in old village); Myrtilles, La Cabane (at 1700).
Après-ski Nightlife is quiet, but there are a few bars. Try the Fitzroy (Irish pub), Balthazar (modern wine bar) or, at 1700, Top Ski (music and tapas).
Off the slopes There's a big spa (with pools, sauna, steam and treatments), snowmobiling, snowshoeing, dog sledding and ice skating.

La Mongie / Barèges

KEY FACTS

La Mongie-Barèges

Resort	1250-1800m
	4,100-5,910ft
Slopes	1400-2500m
	4,590-8,200ft
Lifts	34
Pistes	100km
Snow-guns	239 guns

TOURIST OFFICE

Domaine Tourmalet
uk.n-py.com
www.grand-tourmalet.com

+ One of the biggest Pyrenean areas
+ Contrasting villages but ...

− Purpose-built La Mongie lacks charm
− Lots of slow chairs and drags

Nicely varied slopes and good off-piste shared by two hugely contrasting resorts – one purpose-built, the other a centuries-old spa town.

La Mongie is a purpose-built, modern resort on one side of the high Col du Tourmalet pass (closed in winter). On the other side is Barèges, with which it shares the Grand Tourmalet ski area. The slopes span four valleys and are nicely varied with open bowls above La Mongie and a friendly tree-lined area above Barèges – all suitable for intermediates. The black runs are considered some of the toughest in the French Pyrenees and there is a lot of excellent off-piste including from the Pic du Midi Observatory (where you can stay the night), reached by cable car from La Mongie. There are few huts, but we loved the tiny wood-panelled Etape du Berger above La

Mongie – where most food comes from the owner's farm and you choose your own meat – and the rustic Chez Louisette above Barèges.

La Mongie has little charm but is convenient, with lifts and pistes on its doorstep and good restaurant terraces from which to gaze at the scenery. On our 2012 visit we enjoyed our stay at a catered chalet in Barèges run by an English couple (see www.mountainbug.com); they also have the recently renovated 3-star Hotel du Tourmalet there. Barèges is a small, atmospheric old spa village (with a great modern addition to its traditional old spa building) with a narrow main street a free bus ride from the slopes.

Font-Romeu

KEY FACTS

Resort	1775m
	5,820ft
Slopes	1715-2215m
	5,630-7,270ft
Lifts	23
Pistes	43km
Snow-guns	83%

TOURIST OFFICE

www.font-romeu.fr

+ High, fairly snow-sure slopes
+ Popular family resort

− Limited in extent, with shortish runs
− Weekend crowds

With Font-Romeu you can choose from a delightful old village or a purpose-built station at the foot of the woody, cruisy slopes. Beginners are well catered for.

The old village, complete with 12th-century church and contrasting modern National Scientific Research Centre, is linked to the slopes by a gondola that you ride both ways. You can also stay at Pyrenees 2000 – a purpose-built development at the foot of the lifts, and a short bus ride away.

The slopes span three partly

wooded hills, with a good mix of runs, a terrain park and a boardercross. There are a couple of free beginner lifts and good progression to gentle greens. There is a local lift pass, but the Neiges Catalan pass also covers Les Angles (see below) and six other resorts in the region. There are 111km of cross-country tracks.

Les Angles

KEY FACTS

Resort	1650m
	5,410ft
Slopes	1650-2375m
	5,410-7,790ft
Lifts	19
Pistes	50km
Snow-guns	70%

TOURIST OFFICE

www.lesangles.com

+ Sheltered, tree-lined slopes
+ Good, gentle beginner terrain but ...

− English less widely spoken here
− Shortish runs that lack challenge

Les Angles is a small but charming stone village, complete with old church. The slopes are limited but relatively snow-sure and family-friendly.

Les Angles offers high but mainly wooded slopes that cover a broad hillside. Most runs are short and intermediate; over half are classified red, but there is a good proportion of gentler terrain. There are nursery

slopes at village level and at 1800m – reached by free ski-bus. There is a decent terrain park and 36km of cross-country trails. Font-Romeu is 16km away. Off-slope diversions are few, but dog sledding is possible.

La Rosière

A friendly, family-oriented little resort in a panoramic setting; the link to La Thuile in Italy adds much-needed interest to the skiing

TOP 10 RATINGS

Extent	★★★
Fast lifts	★★
Queues	★★★★
Snow	★★★
Expert	★★
Intermediate	★★★
Beginner	★★★★★
Charm	★★★
Convenience	★★★
Scenery	★★★★

RPI — 95

lift pass	£170
ski hire	£100
lessons	£90
food & drink	£125
total	**£485**

NEWS

2012/13: A six-pack replaced the slow Fort quad to Col de la Traversette.

A new luxury apartment complex, the 4-star Lodge Hemera, with indoor pool, sauna, steam and hot tubs, opened in the village centre.

KEY FACTS

Resort	1850m
	6,070ft

Espace San Bernardo (La Rosière and La Thuile)

Slopes	1175-2610m
	3,850-8,560ft
Lifts	38
Pistes	160km
	99 miles
Green	10%
Blue	31%
Red	40%
Black	19%
Snowmaking	25%

➕ Pleasant, compact, friendly resort in a sunny setting: good for families

➕ Fair-sized area of slopes if you include linked La Thuile in Italy

➕ Good beginner slopes

➕ Exceptionally good branch of ESF

➕ Heli-skiing in Italy from the border

➕ Fine panoramic views

➕ Big dumps of snow when storms sock in from the west, but ...

➖ When storms do sock in, both local slopes and the Italian link can be bleak or closed – few trees

➖ Sunny slopes are affected by sun as the season progresses

➖ Mainly slow old lifts

➖ Local pistes rather limited and lacking variety

➖ Limited village diversions

La Rosière is very different from its famous neighbours such as Val d'Isère–Tignes and Les Arcs – much smaller, quieter and sunnier. Many reporters are more impressed than we are by the skiing, which mainly consists of several runs down a single (admittedly very wide) open slope. But the link with La Thuile over the border in Italy adds another dimension.

THE RESORT

La Rosière has been developed in traditional chalet style high up on the road that climbs from Bourg-St-Maurice towards the Petit-St-Bernard pass to Italy. In winter the road ends at a car park at the top of La Rosière, just below the main lifts. The resort has several identifiable parts, but the key distinction is between the main village and the developing satellite of Les Eucherts, a short bus ride – or a floodlit forest walk – to the east. This is more or less self-sufficient, but offers less choice of everything than the main village.

Village charm The resort is attractively built in traditional styles; it is quiet, with a few shops and friendly locals; don't expect much lively nightlife. It is centred on the road through to the lift station car park; so although there is no real through-traffic, the centre is far from traffic-free.

Convenience It's a small place, where you may have only a short stroll to a lift, but big enough for many locations to require use of an 'efficient' free ski-bus. The satellite of Les Eucherts has its own fast chair into the slopes.

Scenery La Rosière's sunny home slopes offer panoramic views over the Isère valley to Les Arcs and beyond.

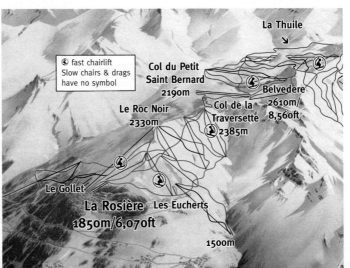

La Thuile

④ fast chairlift
Slow chairs & drags have no symbol

Col du Petit Saint Bernard
2190m

Belvedere
2610m/
8,560ft

Le Roc Noir
2330m

Col de la Traversette
2385m

Le Gollet

La Rosière
1850m/6,070ft

Les Eucherts

1500m

SNOWPIX.COM / CHRIS GILL

The chalets of Les Eucherts enjoy a particularly fine view south to Mont Pourri, with the Aiguille Rouge above Les Arcs at its shoulder ↓

THE MOUNTAINS

La Rosière and La Thuile in Italy share a big area of slopes called Espace San Bernardo. The link with Italy's slopes is a bit prone to closure because of high winds or heavy snow. There are few tree-lined runs. Amazingly, the two resorts produce separate maps showing the whole area; and yes, naturally, they differ. La Rosière's is slightly easier to follow.

Slopes Two fast chairs, one at the main village and one at Les Eucherts, take you into the slopes; then a series of parallel lifts allows progress across the mountain to a six-pack to Col de la Traversette, departure point for Italy. West of the village is a separate sector with red and black runs descending through woods to the Ecudets chair – and a blue on down to the village of Seez when snow is good.

Fast lifts The six-pack to Col de la Traversette (new for 2012/13) is very welcome, and tips the resort into our ** category. Just. There are fast chairs at village level, but the rest are slow.

Queues Reporters stress the lack of queues, even at peak times. In good weather, expect some afternoon queues on the way back from Italy.

Terrain parks The main Poletta park has green, blue, red and expert lines, including a funbox, bumps, rails and a big airbag. There's also a boardercross course.

Snow reliability The slopes get a lot of snow from storms coming up the valley from the south-west, but conditions can be badly affected by sun or wind. Reporters all agree that the grooming is 'superb'.

Experts There are a couple of short, easy but worthwhile black runs – we particularly like Ecudets, down the eponymous chairlift. And there are a couple of ungroomed, avalanche-controlled freeride zones (called, confusingly, 'Snowcross' areas) marked on the map. There is more serious, easily accessed off-piste terrain just outside the lift network. And there's heli-skiing over the Italian border.

Intermediates The main area is a broad open mountainside offering straightforward red pistes, mostly at the easy end of the spectrum and mostly short, with verticals in the range 300m to 450m. The exception is the Marmotte red, dropping over 800m to the chairlift below Les Eucherts. More interesting than anything on the main slope is the lovely wooded Fontaine Froide red, dropping 750m to the Ecudets chair. Keen intermediates will want to make multiple trips to the more varied terrain of La Thuile.

UK PACKAGES

Alpine Answers, Crystal, Crystal Finest, Erna Low, Esprit, Independent Ski Links, Interactive Resorts, Lagrange, Mountain Beds, Mountain Heaven, Peak Retreats, Pierre & Vacances, PowderBeds, Ski Beat, Ski Collection, Ski Expectations, Ski France, Ski Independence, Ski Olympic, Ski Solutions, Skitracer, Skiworld, Snow Finders, SnowCrazy

Blue-run skiers are effectively confined to the pistes near the village. Not surprisingly, they get quite busy. The longer blues running diagonally across the main slope are just tracks from A to B, so not of much interest.

The outing to Italy involves a red run at the start, but it is not especially tricky. The two draglifts that follow are almost 3km in length – miserable in a north or east wind.

Beginners There are good nursery slopes and short lifts near the main village (three are free to use) and near Les Eucherts. The blue runs above the village are pretty good for progression, although some people find them a bit on the steep side, apparently.

Snowboarding Most lifts are chairs, making the place good for novices. And the sunny slopes are good for gentle freeriding in soft snow.

Cross-country There are 5km of trails.

Mountain restaurants There are only two, both self-service (plus a kiosk at Col de la Traversette). Plan du Repos, in the heart of the slopes, is pleasant enough, with 'pretty good grub'. Expect queues in peak season.

Schools and guides We have had consistently good reports over many years of the ESF (run, amazingly, by a Brit, with a special English-language section). 'Thoroughly recommend them,' says a reporter this year, a view shared by many other families our reporter talked to. A recent reporter praises her Evolution 2 instructor for being 'knowledgeable and patient'. Elite Ski is a British school offering clinics and private lessons.

Families The resort caters well for children: 'A great family resort,' says a 2012 visitor. Family specialist Esprit has its own childcare facilities here and Crystal has its own private nanny service. There is a lift pass that offers big savings to families with teenagers.

STAYING THERE

Chalets This is now a major chalet resort. Many chalets are located in Les Eucherts. The biggest operator is family specialist Esprit Ski, with 14 chalets ranging from 5 to 32 beds, plus its usual comprehensive childcare ('staff were brilliant'). Mountain Heaven has a splendid-looking penthouse, with six en-suite rooms and an outdoor hot tub, and five other smart chalets. Ski Olympic has four chalets (including two with access to a

French self-catering operators have properties here. Lagrange, Skiworld and Crystal feature the Cîmes Blanches residences – smart, with pool, hot tub, sauna and steam room. Peak Retreats and Ski Collection also feature them plus the luxurious Lodge Hemera (new last season) and a couple of other places. Pierre & Vacances has the simpler Vanoise. For those who don't take self-catering literally, Montagne Saveurs will deliver gourmet food.

Eating out 'Not one bad meal,' says a reporter. Out of the dozen or so restaurants, readers' current favourites are the MacKinley ('charming with Savoie favourites and a log fire'), Genépi ('best steaks under 20 euro'), the 'cosy' Ancolie in Les Eucherts, the 'atmospheric' Grange, and the Kitzbühel ('excellent burgers').

Après-ski Confined to a few bars in the village. The 'brilliant' Petit Danois has 'a fantastic band some evenings'. The Moobar in the Balcons residences at Les Eucherts is also tipped.

Off the slopes It's improving, but there's not a huge amount to amuse the non-skier – cleared walks, snowshoeing and paragliding, with ten-pin bowling and ice skating at Les Eucherts. There is a cinema. Lunch with skiing friends will have to be in the village. But when keen skiers go off to La Thuile, they won't be coming back for lunch.

pool, sauna, steam and hot tub) with from 5 to 20 rooms: 'A wonderful holiday experience,' said a 2012 reporter. Skiworld has three smart mid-sized chalet apartments in the same building. Crystal has a cluster of four chalets in Les Eucherts. A 2013 visitor rated one of its 'Finest' properties, Cervinia, 'good value; good service'. Ski Beat has several chalets.

Hotels There are a couple of 2-star hotels in the village, and more lower down the hill. Chalet Matsuzaka (0479 075313) is a Japanese-influenced 10-room 4-star at Les Eucherts.

Apartments Many of the best places are in Les Eucherts. Ski Amis has a range of properties from one to four bedrooms. Mountain Heaven has a few, including a smart-looking penthouse apartment. The major

---

Selected chalets in La Rosière

Samoëns

Characterful and charming base for the extensive and varied Grand Massif area, with its own excellent shady slopes

TOP 10 RATINGS

Extent	★★★★
Fast lifts	★★★
Queues	★★★★
Snow	★★★
Expert	★★★★
Intermediate	★★★★★
Beginner	★★
Charm	★★★★
Convenience	★
Scenery	★★★★

RPI 95

lift pass	£190
ski hire	£100
lessons	£65
food & drink	£135
total	**£490**

NEWS

2013/14: An all-suite chalet-style boutique hotel, Le Grand Cerf, is due to open.

PISTE MAP

Samoëns is covered on the Flaine map

SIMON SMITH

The beginner area at 1600 is excellent, if you don't mind the hassle and cost of getting to it ↓

+ Lovely historic village, with traffic-free centre and weekly market

+ Part of the big, varied Grand Massif

+ Glorious views from top heights

− Main access lift is way outside the village, and has no return piste

− Not the best base for beginners

− Limited nightlife

The impressive Grand Massif area is chiefly associated in Britain with high, purpose-built Flaine; but there are also lower, traditional village bases. And the cutest of these, if not the most convenient for skiing, is Samoëns.

THE RESORT

Samoëns is an attractive village – once a thriving centre for stonemasons, with their work much in evidence.
Village charm The resort has a small traffic-free centre of narrow streets lined by appealing food shops, and a pretty square (sadly not traffic-free) with a stone fountain, an ancient linden tree, a fine church and other medieval buildings. Also nearby is a nominally car-free area of modern development. The place as a whole retains the feel of 'real' rural France and makes a compelling base for families. There is a Wednesday market for your cheese supplies.
Convenience The village itself is compact, but as a skiing base it is not convenient. There are two gondolas into the slopes, both a drive or 'reliable and frequent' ski-bus ride from the village: an old one way across the valley at Vercland and a

newer and nearer one. You can ski down to Vercland, but only on red and black runs that can be tricky or closed; there are no runs to the new one. So at the end of the day it's a gondola then a bus; or ski to Sixt or Morillon, for a longer bus-ride from there.
Scenery The village has a pretty valley setting, with attractively woody ridges and glorious views from the tops.

THE MOUNTAINS

Most of the skiing directly above Samoëns is on shady open slopes beneath the peak of Tête des Saix.
Slopes Read the Flaine chapter for news on the extent of the Grand Massif pistes. The two gondolas from the valley arrive at separate points on the hilly balcony of Samoëns 1600 (also reachable by road). A six-pack whisks you up to Tête des Saix, from which point you can proceed towards Flaine via a narrow, crowded piste followed by a fast chair in the Vernant bowl. Or you can turn right to the slopes around Morillon or Les Carroz.
Fast lifts Mountain access is now respectably quick, but the area as a whole has many slow lifts still.
Queues The local lifts don't seem to present problems, but in high season you can expect delays and crowded pistes on the way to Flaine. Read that chapter for more pointers.
Terrain parks The main park is in Flaine.
Snow reliability The slopes above Samoëns face due north, so above 1600 snow is fairly reliable. There is snowmaking around 1600, but one January visitor in 2011 was appalled by the state of the blue run from Tête des Saix, which lacked snowmaking and as a result was 'icy, with lots of stones'.
Experts The upper pistes on Tête des Saix are among the most testing in the

Grand Massif, and there is lots of good off-piste in the region. Don't miss Flaine's Combe de Gers.

Intermediates Samoëns normally makes a satisfactory base for all but the most timid intermediates, who might be better off in Morillon. From Tête des Saix you have a choice of good long runs in various directions. In good snow the valley runs down to Vercland are highly enjoyable – the black is little steeper than the red, and is used less so can be easier.

Beginners Beginners buy a special pass and go up to 1600, where they will find gentle, snow-sure slopes – excellent when not crowded – but no long green runs to progress to. Morillon is a better bet in this respect, with its long winding green run. And the nursery slopes at Sixt are quiet.

Snowboarding Not a big boarding resort, partly perhaps because there are quite a few flat linking runs.

Cross-country There are trails on the valley floor around Samoëns, and tougher ones up the valley beyond Sixt and up at Col de Joux Plane.

Mountain restaurants There are several options at Samoëns 1600. We enjoyed friendly service and good food at Lou Caboëns, a small, woody place endorsed by a 2012 reporter. Mimy's is tipped for its 'massive burger in a lovely crusty roll'. There are some excellent spots covered in the chapters on Les Carroz and Flaine. There's a picnic room at the bottom of the Marmotte piste at 1600, and several others in the Grand Massif, marked on the piste map.

Schools and guides We've had good reports of all three alternatives to the ESF – ZigZag, 360 International and Skisession.

Families The Loupiots nursery takes kids from three months to five years old, and ski lessons are available. ZigZag does multi-activity courses.

STAYING THERE

Chalets The glowing reports of owner-run chalet Bezière continue this year: 'absolutely recommend', 'light and airy', 'good restaurant-standard food', 'great overall impression'.

Hotels There are several 2-star and 3-star places. We and readers have enjoyed the 3-star Neige et Roc (0450 344072), a walk from the centre. The Glaciers (0450 344006) offers 'great location, friendly staff'.

Apartments Self-catering is mostly in small-scale developments, and quite a lot of it in individual chalets. Among many attractive options available through French specialist agency Peak Retreats are the Fermes de Samoëns, a smart Lagrange Prestige residence (with pool), the CGH residence La Reine des Prés and the Ferme des Fontany. Alps Accommodation is a British-run Samoëns specialist.

Eating out A good selection of places. Table de Fifine, a short drive out, is a fine spot for a proper dinner, with a beautiful wooden interior – 'welcoming and comfortable', says a 2013 reporter. Monde à l'Envers offers 'great atmosphere, food and service'. A 2013 reporter endorses the Bois de Lune: 'friendly service, great food'. The Louisiane has 'great' pizzas.

Après-ski Pré d'Oscar up at 1600 is a handy spot for a drink at the end of the day. Nightlife is quiet and there is little choice of bars; Irish pub Covey's ('still the liveliest') and the 'more sophisticated and laid back' Savoie are the reader favourites.

Off the slopes Samoëns offers quite a range of activities. We've enjoyed snowmobiling up at Samoëns 1600, which is wilder than is usual in the Alps. There's dog sledding, and a reader recommends snowshoeing at Sixt. There is an outdoor, covered ice rink, and a sports and cultural centre.

SNOWPIX.COM / CHRIS GILL

Serre-Chevalier

One on its own, this – more character and less swank than you expect in a big French resort, and more woodland runs

RATINGS

The mountains

Extent	★★★★
Fast lifts	★★★
Queues	★★★
Terrain p'ks	★★★
Snow	★★★
Expert	★★★
Intermediate	★★★★
Beginner	★★★★
Boarder	★★★★
X-country	★★★
Restaurants	★★★★
Schools	★★★★
Families	★★★

The resort

Charm	★★★
Convenience	★★★
Scenery	★★★
Eating out	★★★★
Après-ski	★★
Off-slope	★★★

RPI	95
lift pass	£190
ski hire	£100
lessons	£80
food & drink	£130
total	**£500**

NEWS

2013/14: The historic cable car from Chantemerle to Serre Ratier is to be replaced by an eight-seat gondola. Chalet Club Grand Aigle is due to be upgraded to a 4-star hotel and a new 4-star with pool and sauna, the Ice Lodge, is due to be built.

2012/13: More snowmaking (five guns) was installed. In Le Monêtier, redevelopment of the base area was completed.

➕ Big, varied mountain offering a sense of travel as you ski

➕ Lots of good woodland runs

➕ Based on old villages with character

➕ Good-value and atmospheric old hotels, restaurants and chalets

➕ Very friendly and welcoming locals

➖ Busy road through the resorts, and through the heart of Le Monêtier

➖ A lot of indiscriminate new building took place in the 1960s and 70s

➖ Still too many drags and slow chairlifts at altitude

➖ Limited nightlife

This is one of our favourite places. The modern buildings of the main resort areas are off-putting, but get into the original villages and you find the kind of ambience you might look for on a summer holiday – a sort of Provence in the snow, with small family-run hotels and restaurants in old stone buildings.

And the slopes are equally distinctive, with the trees reaching appreciably higher altitudes than the Alpine norm. This is a great place to be in falling snow, as we confirmed during a quick visit last February.

THE RESORT

Serre-Chevalier is made up of a string of villages set on a valley floor, linked by a busy road.

The valley runs roughly north-west to south-east, below the north-east-facing slopes of the mountain range that gives the resort its name. From the north-west – coming over the Col du Lautaret from Grenoble – the three main villages are spread over a distance of 8km – Le Monêtier (or Serre-Che 1500), Villeneuve (1400) and Chantemerle (1350). Finally, at the extreme south-eastern end of the valley, is Briançon (1200) – not a village but a town (the highest in France). As well as the main villages there are nine smaller villages, some of which give their names to the communes: Villeneuve, for example, is in the commune of little old La Salle les Alpes. Confusing? Sure is.

The resort is not at all fashionable, and is only now developing 4-star hotels. But Serre-Che has more hotels here in the modestly priced Logis de France 'club' than any other ski resort.

This is a family resort, and it gets especially busy in the February/March French school holidays.

A six-day area pass (or rather your receipt for that pass) covers a day in each of Les Deux-Alpes, Alpe-d'Huez, Puy-St-Vincent, Montgenèvre/the Milky Way and Sestriere. All of these outings are possible by bus, but are easier by car. From Grenoble you use the Col du Lautaret, which can be closed.

VILLAGE CHARM ★★★
Some quaint old parts
Each of the parts of Serre-Chevalier is based on a simple old village, with narrow cobbled streets lined by small shops, cosy bars, hotels and traditional restaurants that give each village a very French feel. Around these older parts there is a lot more modern development ranging in style from brutal to sympathetic. It is not a smart resort in any sense; even the older parts are roughly rustic rather than chocolate-box pretty. (A ban on corrugated iron roofs would help.) But when blanketed by snow the older villages and hamlets do have an

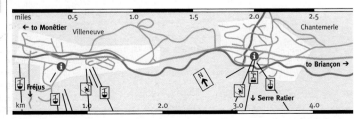

KEY FACTS	
Resort	1200-1500m
	3,940-4,920ft
Slopes	1200-2735m
	3,940-8,970ft
Lifts	62
Pistes	250km
	155 miles
Green	23%
Blue	27%
Red	37%
Black	13%
Snowmaking	
	154 hectares

unpretentious charm, and we find the place as a whole easy to like.

Le Monêtier is the smallest, quietest and most unspoiled of the main villages, with new building mostly in sympathetic style. The heart of the old village is bisected by the road to Grenoble, which skirts the cute parts of the other villages. We find the traffic intrusive, but reporters don't seem to mind it. And if you are based away from the centre, you may be largely unaffected by it.

Because the resort as a whole is so spread out, the impact of cars and buses is difficult to escape, even if you're able to manage without them yourself. But reporters seem happy to put up with the road and its traffic.

Briançon's 17th-century fortified old town is a delight, with its traditional auberges, pâtisseries and restaurants; it is a World Heritage Site. By contrast, the modern area around the lift station, including good-value lodging and a casino, has little character.

Every year reporters stress how friendly and welcoming the locals are – hardly the norm in France.

CONVENIENCE ★★★ ★★
Good access but expect a walk

All four main resort villages have lift access, by gondola, cable car or fast chairs, to different parts of the ski area. Briançon has a gondola from the bottom of the town; your hotel could be next to it, or miles from it. In Chantemerle the old village is quite close to the lifts, as is a lot of new accommodation; but there is still a lot further away across the busy main road. Villeneuve has quite a few lodgings close to its multiple access lifts, but the old village is across the valley; if you want to combine character with convenience in this part of the valley, consider the nearby hamlet of Le Bez – set between two gondolas. At the top of the valley, Le Monêtier has one main access lift, reached from the centre by bus or a 10-minute walk (downhill in the morning, uphill at the end of the day and tricky when ice is around). You can leave your gear at the lift base.

Local ski-buses circulate around the villages, and there are valley buses that link all the villages (running until

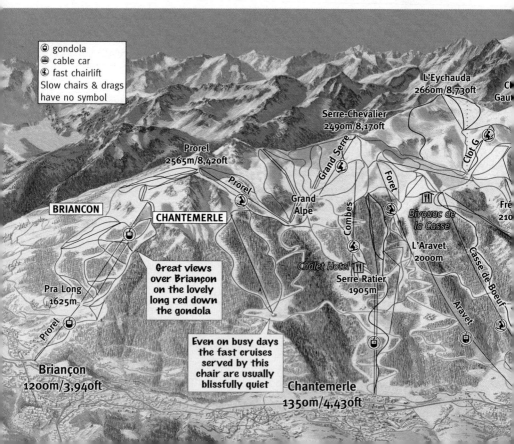

gondola
cable car
fast chairlift
Slow chairs & drags
have no symbol

L'Eychauda
2666m/8,730ft

Serre-Chevalier
2490m/8,170ft

Prorel
2565m/8,420ft

Grand Serre

Prorel

Foret

Clot G

BRIANCON

CHANTEMERLE

Grand
Alpe

Combes

Bivouac de
la Casse

Fré
210

Casse de Boeuf

L'Aravet
2000m

Pra Long
1625m

Great views
over Briançon
on the lovely
long red down
the gondola

Chalet Hotel

Serre Ratier
1905m

Prorel

Aravet

Briançon
1200m/3,940ft

Even on busy days
the fast cruises
served by this
chair are usually
blissfully quiet

Chantemerle
1350m/4,430ft

11.30pm). But a reporter points out that these valley buses do not visit the lift bases of Chantemerle or Villeneuve, though they stop nearby.

SCENERY ★★★☆☆
Great views from the tops
The Serre-Chevalier range is not notably dramatic seen from the valley, though there are great views from Briançon's old town. From the area's high points there are fine views of the rugged 4000m-high Ecrins massif.

THE MOUNTAINS

Trees cover almost two-thirds of the mountain, providing some of France's best bad-weather terrain (we once had a great day here when all the upper lifts were closed by high winds).

Reporters are very impressed by the improved piste signposting – 'much clearer than most resorts', said a 2013 reporter. The map is not ideal, but it is reasonably clear. Piste classification tends to exaggerate difficulty, most of our recent reporters agree.

Hot chalets beneath glacial slopes? Check out p258.

EXTENT OF THE SLOPES ★★★★☆
Interestingly varied and pretty
Serre-Chevalier claims to have 250km of pistes; but the Schrahe report, discussed in our piste extent feature, reveals that the total when measured down the fall line is only 156km. The lift company, which is part of the dominant Compagnie des Alpes, is now reviewing how it calculates its piste extent. Watch this space.

The slopes are spread across four main sectors above the four main villages, and you get a real feeling of travel as you move around.

The sector above **Villeneuve** is the most extensive, reaching back a good way into the mountains and spreading over four or five identifiable bowls. The main mid-station is Fréjus. This sector is linked at altitude and mid-mountain to the slightly smaller **Chantemerle** sector. The onward link from Chantemerle to **Briançon** is over a high, exposed col via a six-pack. In the

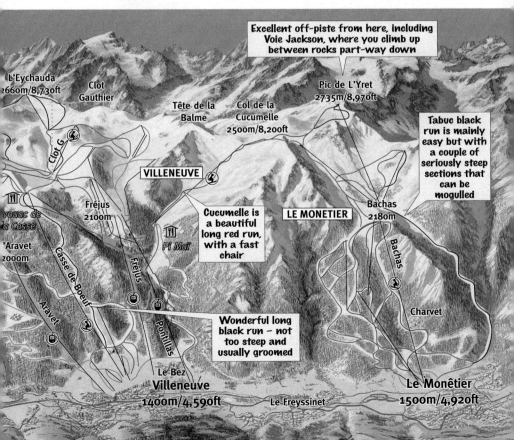

Excellent off-piste from here, including Voie Jackson, where you climb up between rocks part-way down

L'Eychauda 2266m/8,730ft

Clot Gauthier

Tête de la Balme

Col de la Cucumelle 2500m/8,200ft

Pic de L'Yret 2735m/8,970ft

Tabuc black run is mainly easy but with a couple of seriously steep sections that can be mogulled

VILLENEUVE

LE MONETIER

Bachas 2180m

Fréjus 2100m

vouac de a Casse

'Aravet 2000m

Cucumelle is a beautiful long red run, with a fast chair

Pi Maï

Bachas

Casse de Boeuf

Charvet

Aravet

Pontillas

Wonderful long black run – not too steep and usually groomed

Le Bez

Villeneuve 1400m/4,590ft

Le Freyssinet

Le Monêtier 1500m/4,920ft

↑ The Serre Ratier cable car from Chantemerle is being retired, and replaced by a big gondola

SNOWPIX.COM / BEN RILEY

LIFT PASSES

Prices in €

Age	1-day	6-day
under 12	36	171
12 to 64	45	214
65 plus	40	193

Free Under 6, over 75

Beginner Limited pass in each area: eg Villeneuve €17

Notes Briançon, Villeneuve, Chantemerle and Le Monêtier; 6+ days give one day in Les Deux-Alpes, Alpe-d'Huez, Puy-St-Vincent, Sestriere and Montgenèvre; reductions for families

Alternative passes Individual areas of Serre-Chevalier

opposite direction, the link between Villeneuve and **Le Monêtier** was greatly improved in 2010 by the Vallons six-pack up the Cucumelle valley. Skiing from Le Monêtier to Villeneuve involves the red run down this valley, so timid skiers may prefer to use the bus service.

FAST LIFTS ★★★
Improvements, but slowly

A range of big lifts gets you out of the valley, including a new gondola replacing the ancient cable car from Chantemerle for 2013/14, and progress has been made in upgrading some of the higher lifts. But there are still many old, slow lifts at altitude that hinder progress. In particular, the trio of slow chairs from Bachas at mid-mountain above Le Monêtier lead to complaints, though one view is that they keep the Villeneuve crowds away.

QUEUES ★★★
Still some bottlenecks

There are few problems getting out of the villages now, but there can be queues further up. Bottlenecks can include the Fréjus chair above the Pontillas gondola from Villeneuve, the Crêtes draglift it links with and the Côte Chevalier chair from the Villeneuve bowl to Chantemerle. But reporters rarely found queues last season no matter what month they went. The recession bites?

When the resort gets busy in the French school holidays, head for the slow Aiguillette chair at Chantemerle (see 'For intermediates'). And consider riding the gondolas down to avoid busy home runs.

TERRAIN PARKS ★★★
Fully featured

The main parks are easily reached from both Chantemerle and Villeneuve. Legendary ripper Guillaume Chastagnol and the Serre Che Brigade have been improving the parks for several years. The Serre Che snowpark is under the Forêt chair (but has a dedicated draglift). It incorporates about 23 different features (plus chill-out and BBQ area) – clearly marked out in three zones for all levels, including 12 tables, wall ride, rails, boxes and hip jumps. A major focus has been placed on the fabulous beginner area – 'My kids had a great time,' says a 2012 reporter. There's a video zone where your riding is filmed, you watch it on a screen and can download it later. A boardercross accessible by the Grande Serre or Combes lifts is 'good, fast and flowing', says a reporter. The innovative Mélèzone, beside the Champcella draglift features various fun jibs built from larch wood in a wooded setting. There's also a small, fun boardercross near the Rocher Blanc chair.

SNOW RELIABILITY ★★★
Good – especially upper slopes

Most slopes face north or north-east and so hold the snow well, especially high up (there are lots of lifts starting at altitudes above 2000m). The slopes above Le Monêtier are high and shady, and often have the best snow. The weather is different from that of the northern Alps, and even that of Les Deux-Alpes or Alpe-d'Huez, over the col to the west. Some upper lifts may be prone to closure by high winds.

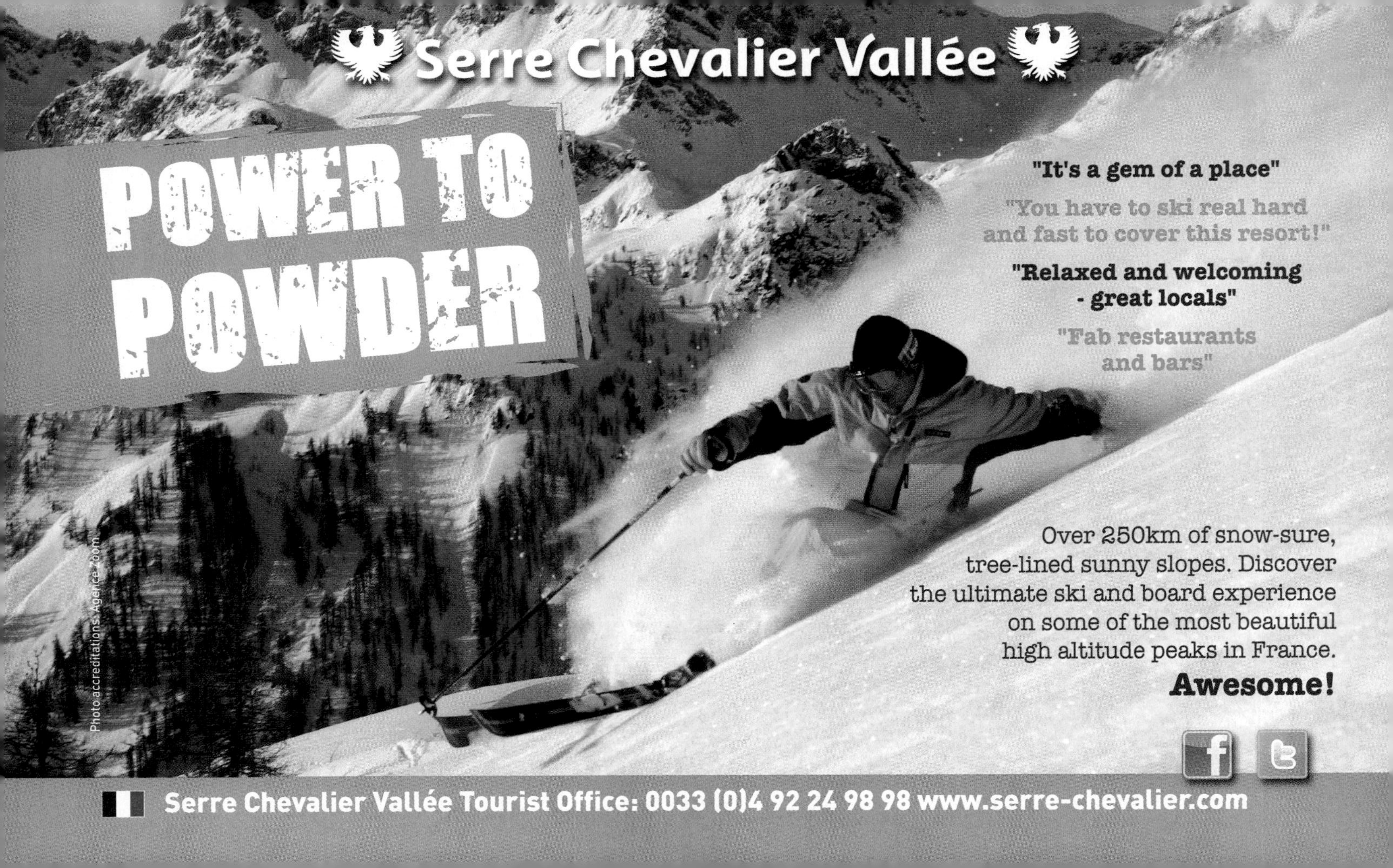
Serre Chevalier Vallée
POWER TO POWDER
"It's a gem of a place"
"You have to ski real hard and fast to cover this resort!"
"Relaxed and welcoming - great locals"
"Fab restaurants and bars"
Over 250km of snow-sure, tree-lined sunny slopes. Discover the ultimate ski and board experience on some of the most beautiful high altitude peaks in France.
Awesome!
Photo accreditations: Agence Zoom
Serre Chevalier Vallée Tourist Office: 0033 (0)4 92 24 98 98 www.serre-chevalier.com

Snowmaking covers 75% of the pistes, including long runs down to each village. Piste grooming is generally excellent.

FOR EXPERTS ★★★★★
Deep, not notably steep
There is plenty to amuse experts – except those wanting extreme steeps. Seven slopes – basically, black runs left ungroomed – are identified as 'brut de neige' areas.

The broad black runs down to Villeneuve (Casse du Boeuf – our favourite) and Chantemerle (Luc Alphand) are only just black in steepness. They are regularly groomed, and are great fun for a fast blast, with their gradient sustained over an impressive vertical of around 800m. Last season we had a fab run on Luc Alphand in largely untracked shin-deep powder. But one or the other may be closed for days on end for racing or training. The rather neglected Tabuc run, sweeping around the mountain away from the lifts to Le Monêtier, has a couple of genuinely steep pitches (which may be heavily mogulled) but is mainly a cruise; great in falling snow, when it is even quieter than usual. For other steepish runs, look higher up the mountain to slopes served by the two top lifts above Le Monêtier and the two above Villeneuve. The runs beside these lifts – on- and off-piste – form a great playground in good snow.

There are huge amounts of off-piste terrain throughout the area – both high-up and in the trees above Villeneuve and Chantemerle. We've enjoyed the Voie Jackson run accessed from the Yret chair above Le Monêtier, which includes a short climb between rocks to a deserted open bowl. The Cucumelle valley at the western side of the Villeneuve sector offers a huge area of gentle off-piste.

There are plenty of more serious off-piste expeditions, including: Tête de Grand Pré to Villeneuve or Le Monêtier, and Couloir de Roche Corneille to Le Monêtier (both a climb from Cucumelle); off the back of L'Eychauda to Puy-St-André (isolated, beautiful, taxi ride home); l'Yret to Le Monêtier via Vallons de la Montagnolle; Tabuc also to Le Monêtier (steep at the start in a big bowl, very beautiful).

FOR INTERMEDIATES ★★★★★
Ski wherever you like
Serre-Chevalier's slopes ideally suit intermediates, who can buzz around without worrying about nasty surprises on the way. On the trail map red runs far outnumber blues – but most reds are at the easy end of the scale. The broad, open bowls above Grande Alpe and Fréjus offer lots of options. The runs on skier's right on the lower slopes of Le Monêtier are gentle, quiet and wind prettily through the woods.

There's plenty for more adventurous intermediates, though. Cucumelle on the edge of the Villeneuve sector is a beautiful long red served by the Vallons fast chairlift, with opportunities to experiment off-piste on easy slopes beside it. The red runs off the little-used slow Aiguillette chair in the Chantemerle sector are worth seeking out – quiet, enjoyable fast cruises. Other favourites include Le Monêtier's Aya and Clos Gaillard, and the wonderful long run from the top to the bottom of the gondola at Briançon (with great views of the town).

If the reds are starting to seem a bit tame, there is plenty more to progress to. Unless ice towards the bottom is a problem, the usually well-groomed blacks on the lower mountain should be on the agenda; try them early in the day when they are uncrowded and freshly groomed.

ACTIVITIES

Indoor Swimming pools, sauna, fitness centres, thermal baths, bowling, museums, cinemas, casino, libraries

Outdoor Ice rinks, cleared paths, dog sledding, snowshoeing, skijoring, ice driving, snowmobiling, snow kites, ballooning, paragliding

FOR BEGINNERS ★★★★
All four areas OK

All four sectors have their own nursery areas, and cheap daily lift passes covering a handful of lifts, including access to mid-mountain where appropriate. At Chantemerle you generally go up to Serre Ratier – rated as good by a beginner reporter. At Villeneuve there are several slopes at valley level – all 'lovely' according to a skier having a first go at boarding last year – but also slopes up the Aravet gondola. At Le Monêtier the slopes are at the lift base – tipped by past reporters for 'better snow and fewer people' than elsewhere. There are also easy high runs to progress to in each sector – the best are probably the green runs above the Fréjus gondola from Villeneuve. There are green paths from mid-mountain to Chantemerle and Villeneuve, though these may not be enjoyable late in the day when the runs become hard and others are speeding past.

FOR BOARDERS ★★★★
Plenty of scope for experts

The resort attracts a lot of boarders. The term 'natural playground' could quite easily have been coined in Serre-Chevalier. The slopes are littered with natural obstacles that seem made for confident snowboarders. Try the Cucumelle slope and the areas around the Rocher Blanc lift at Prorel for such terrain. For less expert boarders, the many draglifts can be a problem, as can the flat areas. There's a good terrain park for all abilities and ESI Generation in Chantemerle is a school that offers everything from beginners' lessons to freestyle courses.

FOR CROSS-COUNTRY ★★★
Excellent if the snow is good

There are 35km of tracks along the valley floor, mainly following the gurgling river between Le Monêtier and Villeneuve and going on up towards the Col du Lautaret.

MOUNTAIN RESTAURANTS ★★★★
Some good places

Mountain restaurants are quite well distributed; they are marked on the piste map, but not named.

Editors' choice At Serre Ratier, Chalet Hotel de Serre Ratier (0492 205288) has a delightful large terrace and pretty dining room, good service and

↑ There are huge amounts of accessible off-piste on the higher slopes above Villeneuve

TANYA BOOTH

SCHOOLS

ESF In all centres
t 0492 241741

ESI Generation
(Chantemerle)
t 0492 242151

ESI Evasion
(Chantemerle)
t 0492 240241

ESI Monêtier
t 0683 670642

ESI Buissonnière
(Villeneuve)
t 0492 247866

New Generation
t 0479 010318
0844 770 4733 (UK)
www.skinewgen.com

Insight
t 0679 068683

Ski Connections
(Villeneuve)
t 0492 462832

Classes (ESF prices)
6 days from €318

Private lessons
From €47 for 1hr

delicious food. Two other options are more expensive. Just above the Casse du Boeuf quad from Villeneuve, the Bivouac de la Casse (0492 248772) is an attractive chalet with both self- and table-service (inside and out). We have twice been impressed by both the food and service, and recent reporters endorse our view. Shame about the plastic chairs on the terrace though. Pi Maï (0492 248363) in the hamlet of Fréjus is cosy on a bad day and charming on a sunny day, and it offers excellent food such as steaks and tartiflette and 'wholesome soup'.

Worth knowing about In the Briançon sector, the Pra Long chalet at the gondola mid-station has good views and good food in both table- and self-service sections. The little Chalet de Serre Blanc, just down from the top of Prorel, has superb views; it gets mixed reports – but 'it's cheap and you get a coffee thrown in'.

Above Chantemerle, we and a 2012 visitor loved the small table-service Troll – great, good-value food and very jolly service. Cafe du Soleil became one reader's regular haunt last season. Grand Alpe self-service is spacious, and a bit cheaper than most places.

Above Villeneuve, we and readers have enjoyed the Echaillon, slightly off-piste from the blue run from Casse du Boeuf to Clot Gauthier – a lofty chalet with open fire and a table-service section: 'Quiche and salad just perfect.' The Bercail, near the top of

the Aravet lift, has impressed one discerning reporter ('best of the week') despite using the Italian system of taking orders at the bar for delivery to your table. The Aravet in the same area does 'deliciously thin and crispy pizzas – very, very good'.

Above Le Monêtier the enlarged but still tiny Peyra Juana near the bottom was a 'winner' with a 2013 visitor: 'Fantastic, hearty, generous, good food. We went there every day.' The self-service Chapka at mid-mountain does 'simple, tasty food' and has a 'welcoming central fire'. Both get packed on bad-weather days. There's plenty of room at the newish Flocon, near the Chapka. We had an excellent table-service lunch on the terrace a couple of seasons ago, but we've since had mixed reports.

SCHOOLS AND GUIDES ★★★★
Choice of good outfits
You are spoilt for choice here. The Serre-Che branch of New Generation, run by Gavin Crosby (formerly of EurekaSki) gets unstinting praise from readers – 'superb', 'good teachers and competitively priced', 'our Italian teacher Simone really helped us progress'. Classes have a maximum size of six. We've skied with Gavin a couple of times, and have been greatly impressed. For 2013/14 Gavin will offer off-piste coaching from first-time to expert levels. Meanwhile, Gavin's wife Mel offers a kind of concierge service for visitors under the EurekaSki name – see 'Staying there'.

We've also had positive reports on another British-run school, Ski Connections: 'The perfect combination of fun, challenge and learning.' And on private lessons with Brit Darren Turner of Insight: 'Changed our skiing dramatically – well worth the money.'

We have received lots of reports on the Ecole de Ski Buissonnière over the years – most of them full of praise.

And the ESF does a good job, too – 'excellent', 'very accommodating'. We've had positive feedback on the Internationale school, but we lack recent reports.

FOR FAMILIES ★★★
Facilities at each village
Serre Chevalier is popular with French families and there are good family-friendly events and activities. For childcare, Les Schtroumpfs in Villeneuve (nine months to five years

Serre-Chevalier

Build your own shortlist: **www.wheretoskiandsnowboard.com**

GUIDES

Montagne Aventure
(Villeneuve)
t 0492 247440

Bureau des Guides
t 0492 247590

Office des Guides
(Villeneuve)
t 0492 247320

Montagne et Ski
(Le Monêtier)
t 0492 244681

CHILDCARE

Les Schtroumpfs
t 0492 247095
9mnth to 5yr

Les P'tits Loup
t 0492 490086
3mnth to 6yr

Les Poussins
t 0492 240343
From 8mnth

Les Eterlous
t 0492 554246
6mnth to 6yr

EurekaSki
t 0679 462484
from 3mnth, private nannies

Ski school
From age 5

old) has been praised in the past. There is a micro-crèche (Les P'tits Loup) in Villeneuve too, taking children from three months to six years. EurekaSki can arrange childcare and private nannies.

STAYING THERE

There is a wide choice of lodging but very little of it has any claim to luxury.

EurekaSki and Chez Serre Chevalier are local British-run operations that can fix more or less any aspect of a holiday in Serre-Che – not only accommodation of various kinds but also such things as transfers, catering, childcare, equipment, coaching and discounted lift passes.

Chalets Several operators offer catered chalets. In Villeneuve, Zenith has four chalets, including the ski-in/ski-out Ridon, and Crystal has two. Inghams is introducing two mid-sized places in good positions here. Chez Serre Chevalier and EurekaSki both have chalets with and without catering.

Hotels A feature of the resort is the range of simple family-run hotels – many members of the generally reliable Logis de France consortium.

But there are some 4-stars in the pipeline – read our News panel.

LE MONÊTIER
****Auberge de Choucas (0492 244273) Smart but small wood-clad rooms; serious restaurant. We have enjoyed a stay there.
***Alliey (0492 244002) Charming place with well-regarded restaurant – 'Excellent food and service.'
**Europe (0492 244003) Simple well-run Logis in heart of old village.

VILLENEUVE
***Christiania (0492 247633) Civilized, family-run hotel on main road.
*Chatelas (0492 247474) Prettily decorated simple chalet by river.
Maison du Bez (0492 248696) Ski-in/ski-out, 'quirky, with cosy lounge'.

CHANTEMERLE
***Boule de Neige (0492 240016) In the old centre. Good past reports. Under new management.
Marmottes (0492 241117) 'Extremely welcoming' renovated old house where Anglo-French couple offer B&B with the option of 'wonderful' dinners.

Apartments EurekaSki makes something of a speciality of self-catering chalets and apartments with pools and saunas. Chez Serre

GETTING THERE

Air Turin 120km/ 75 miles (1hr45); Grenoble 150km/ 95 miles (2hr45); Lyon 200km/125 miles (3hr15)

Rail Briançon (6km/ 4 miles); regular buses from station

UK PACKAGES

Action Outdoors, Alpine Answers, Alpsholiday, AmeriCan Ski, Chalet Chez Bear, Chez Serre Chevalier, Club Med, Crystal, Erna Low, EurekaSki, Hannibals, Independent Ski Links, Inghams, Interactive Resorts, Lagrange, Neilson, Peak Retreats, Pierre & Vacances, PowderBeds, Rocketski, Ski Expectations, Ski France, Ski-in.co.uk, Ski Independence, Ski Miquel, Ski Solutions, Skitopia, Skitracer, Snow Finders, Snowed Inn Chalets, Thomson, Zenith

Briançon AmeriCan Ski, BoardnLodge, Peak Retreats

Phone numbers
From abroad use the prefix +33 and omit the initial '0' of the phone number

TOURIST OFFICE

www.serre-chevalier. com

Chevalier has a wide range of properties in the resorts, too.

There is an increasing supply of high-quality residences. By the slopes in Chantemerle is the 'comfortable and very well-equipped' Hameau du Rocher Blanc, in the Lagrange Prestige range (pool, gym, sauna, steam); bookable through Peak Retreats. 300m from the lifts, with small indoor-outdoor pool, L'Adret is approved by two reporters this year – 'lived up to its 4-star rating', 'excellent, well equipped'. In Villeneuve, Pierre & Vacances' well-placed residence Alpaga has been approved by reporters. In Le Monêtier the Arts et Vie is modern, right on the slopes and good value. The hotel Alliey has apartments too.

At altitude Two mountain restaurants have rooms: Pi Maï (0492 248363) and the Chalet Hotel de Serre Ratier (0492 205288).

EATING OUT ★★★★☆
Unpretentious and traditional
In Le Monêtier, there are several good hotel-based options. At the upper end, the Maison Alliey (hotel Alliey) has a good reputation, and a reporter last year rated it 'excellent'. We've had an excellent dinner at the Auberge du Choucas. The hotel Europe has reliable cooking at more modest prices. Reporter tips include the popular Aquisana and the 'very friendly' Kawa ('excellent confit de canard; we ate there four times'). Up the valley at Le Casset, Chez Finette offers trips in a horse-drawn sleigh before dinner – 'An excellent find,' says a reporter.

In Villeneuve, two 2011 reporters recommended the 'atmospheric little' Refuge where the Alps Bell (cooking meat on a hot cast-iron bell) is popular. And two recent visitors have raved about Eau Petit Pont – 'best French meal in 40 years', 'steaks to die for'. Mojo is a small, welcoming Brit-run bar-restaurant doing a good range of satisfying food at good prices.

In Chantemerle, we had an excellent dinner last season at 34 – a cool spot with a short but wide-ranging menu. We've also enjoyed the Loup Blanc – 'Good food well presented,' says a reporter. Reporters also like the 'cool' Triptyque (traditional French dishes, 'fabulous burgers and crumble to die for'). For fish and chips, there's the Station.

In Briançon, there are several highly regarded places in the charming old town. A local tips Plaisir d'Ambré for a 'special night out', and Pied de la Gargouille for open-fire grills. A reporter recommends Valentin ('four good courses for 26 euros'). Just outside the old town, Italian-run Mamma Mia has 'a fantastic menu and superb prices'.

APRES-SKI ★★☆☆☆
Quiet streets and few bars
Nightlife seems to revolve around bars, scattered through the various villages, and some reporters complain that the resort is too quiet.

In Le Monêtier the British-run Bar de l'Alpen is 'about the only place to go', say two separate reports; it has live music, sports TV, free nibbles and welcoming staff. In Villeneuve, head for the Grotte at the foot of the slopes (live music, happy hour and 'good bar food' – later on it 'doubles up as a nightclub'). Loco Loco in the old village is 'a funky little bar' that gets lively too. The Frog is popular with Brits, while the Cocoon has 'a good local atmosphere'. In Chantemerle the Brit-run Station at the foot of the pistes is popular with Brits and 'seems to have the après all sewn up' – Sky Sports and 'sells bottled real ale'; 'live entertainment' every evening; 'pub food is good'. The 'smart' Piano Bar and Tonneau on the main road get a mention. In Briançon, there's a lively teatime scene (assisted by a happy hour) at the bar next to the gondola.

OFF THE SLOPES ★★★☆☆
Try the hot baths
The old town of Briançon is well worth a visit. The Parc 1326 leisure complex has pools (25m and fun options), sauna, hot tub and steam room. There is a full-size ice-rink, and Briançon has an ice hockey team – their games make 'a good night out'. In Le Monêtier reporters enjoy the large thermal spa complex, Les Grands Bains ('superb tonic for tired limbs'), with indoor and outdoor pools, saunas, steam rooms, a 'chill-out' music grotto and a waterfall (some areas only for the over-18s). The hotel Alliey has a pool and spa. There is a public swimming pool in Villeneuve and bowling in Chantemerle. Each of the villages has a cinema and an ice rink, and there is good walking on 25km of 'well-prepared trails'. You can learn to drive a piste-basher. Hot air ballooning is available.

Ste-Foy-Tarentaise

Tasteful, modern mini-resort appealing to families and experts – and to motorists as a base for expeditions to nearby mega-resorts

TOP 10 RATINGS

Extent	★
Fast lifts	★★★★
Queues	★★★★★
Snow	★★★
Expert	★★★★
Intermediate	★★★
Beginner	★★
Charm	★★★
Convenience	★★★★
Scenery	★★★

RPI 85

lift pass	£140
ski hire	£100
lessons	£90
food & drink	£125
total	**£455**

NEWS

2013/14: The Gran Plan chair out of the village is due to be replaced by a fast quad. A new mountain restaurant is to be built at the foot of the Marquise six-pack (on the left on our piste map).

2012/13: Three new runs served by the Marquise six-pack opened – two reds and a blue. The long run back to the resort from the top of the first chairlift was reclassified from green to blue. A new ungroomed red bumps run was created beneath the lower part of the second chairlift up the mountain.

➕ Safe untracked powder within the lift system, and epic runs outside it

➕ Good base for visits to Val d'Isère/Tignes, Les Arcs

➕ Great value (and the cheapest lift pass of any resort in this book)

➕ Quiet, even in peak periods, but …

➖ Too quiet for some visitors; very little après-ski action and very few restaurants

➖ Very limited piste network, despite a few being added for 2012/13

➖ Still two (out of four) slow chairlifts, despite a new fast quad planned for 2013/14

Ste-Foy is a small, attractive, unpretentious resort built in the past 10 years or so, at the foot of what started life as a cult off-piste mountain. It remains excellent for experts but now attracts many others, including families. Keen piste-bashers will want to travel to big resorts nearby – easily done by car.

THE RESORT

Ste-Foy itself is a village straddling the busy road up from Bourg-St-Maurice to Val d'Isère. Its slopes start at Ste-Foy-Station (aka Bonconseil), which is set 4km off the main road. With a car you can visit some excellent restaurants close by and explore nearby resorts – Val d'Isère, Tignes, Les Arcs, La Plagne and La Rosière. Some tour ops organize excursions too. With a Ste-Foy lift pass for five days or more you can buy day passes for these resorts at 25 euros a day.

Village charm Ste-Foy-Station is a complete resort in miniature, with a limited choice of bars and restaurants and a small supermarket; and these are surrounded by a cluster of chalets and chalet-style apartment blocks, all built in the traditional Savoyard style of wood and stone but without a real central focus. Lots of properties have been bought by Brits and Dutch: 'The atmosphere is very British,' says a recent reporter.

Convenience No accommodation is far from the lifts or nursery slopes.

Scenery The Tarentaise mountains give a dramatic backdrop to Ste-Foy's pleasant setting among the trees.

THE MOUNTAINS

There is an attractive mix of wooded slopes above the village and open slopes higher up.

Slopes A new fast quad chair out of the village is planned for 2013/14. This goes to a mid-mountain station with

341

OT STE-FOY / A ROYER

The village has been built in the last 10 years or so and is small, attractive and convenient →

KEY FACTS

Resort	1550m
	5,090ft
Slopes	1550-2620m
	5,090-8,600ft
Lifts	6
Pistes	40km
	25 miles
Green	5%
Blue	25%
Red	60%
Black	10%
Snowmaking	10 guns

SAINTE-FOY TARENTAISE

Ski-in ski-out 4★ self-catering apartments with pool

peakretreats.co.uk/Sainte_Foy

peak retreats

two small restaurants at Plan Bois and is followed by two successive slow quad chairs which take you to the top of the ski area. The first goes to the treeline and the second to the high point of Col de l'Aiguille at 2620m. From here there are slopes of over 1000m vertical, almost 600m of it above the treeline.

The two marked ungroomed black runs here form the basis of two special off-piste zones that are marked but not explained on the piste map; we're told they are avalanche controlled and closed when conditions aren't right. Slightly further down the hill is a less steep off-piste zone, Shaper's Paradise, which has a new marked ungroomed black run and natural jumps; people can also build their own kickers here.

The two lower chairs serve a few pleasant runs through trees and back to the base station. The Marquise six-pack (on the left of our piste map) serves a blue run that goes into a forested area, three reds and a black.

The red and blue pistes are 'immaculately groomed', say reporters.

Fast lifts The new high-speed quad planned for 2013/14 means two out of the four chairlifts on the mountain will be fast – increasing our fast lifts rating to ★★★★.

Queues Despite all the new building, reporters rarely find queues at Ste-Foy ('Hardly any, even in half-term week,' says a recent reporter).

Terrain parks There isn't one. But in the Shaper's Paradise area you are encouraged to build kickers and other features.

Snow reliability The slopes face roughly north-west. Snow reliability can suffer on the sunnier bits, but the resort has 10 snowmaking guns that it uses on the blue and red runs down to the resort.

Experts Experts can have great fun on and between Ste-Foy's black and red runs, exploring lots of easily accessible off-piste and trees, including the special zones mentioned earlier. The lack of crowds means you can still make fresh tracks days after a storm.

There's more serious off-piste on offer too, for which you need a guide. There are wonderful runs from the top of the lifts down through deserted old villages, either to the road up to Val d'Isère (you can get a bus back) or back to the base (via the deserted hamlet of Le Monal). And there's a splendid route down the north face of Foglietta in the next valley to the tiny village of Le Crot. The ESF runs group off-piste trips, with transport back to base and perhaps with lunch in the

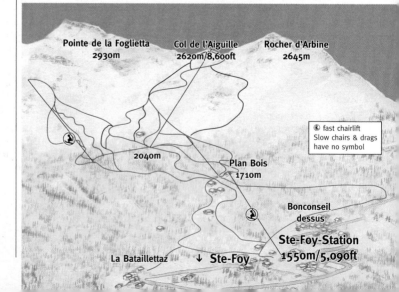

Pointe de la Foglietta
2930m

Col de l'Aiguille
2620m/8,600ft

Rocher d'Arbine
2645m

2040m

④ fast chairlift
Slow chairs & drags have no symbol

Plan Bois
1710m

Bonconseil dessus

Ste-Foy-Station
1550m/5,090ft

La Bataillettaz   ↓ Ste-Foy

↑ Ste-Foy's pistes are very limited in extent and keen piste-bashers will want to visit nearby resorts such as Tignes and Les Arcs as well

OT STE-FOY / MARK JUNAK

UK PACKAGES

Alpine Answers, Alpine Weekends, AmeriCan Ski, Chalet One, Erna Low, Inspired to Ski, Lagrange, Mountain Tracks, Oxford Ski Co, Peak Retreats, PowderBeds, Première Neige, Richmond Holidays, Ski Bespoke, Ski Club Freshtracks, Ski Collection, Ski France, Ski Independence, Ski Weekend

Phone numbers
From abroad use the prefix +33 and omit the initial '0' of the phone number

TOURIST OFFICE

www.saintefoy.net

village of Le Miroir (see 'Eating out'). Heli-skiing in Italy can be arranged, including a route that also brings you back to near Le Miroir.

Intermediates The piste skiing is limited in extent and keen piste-bashers will want to visit nearby resorts too. But you can enjoy 900m vertical of uncrowded reds and blues on the upper slopes above the top of the first chairlift. The red from the Col de l'Aiguille is a superb test for confident intermediates, who would also be up to some of the off-piste routes, especially the one back to base via Le Monal.

Beginners There are good fenced-off nursery slopes with free moving carpets in the village. You can progress to a long, easy blue run (that was classified green until 2012/13) off the new high-speed quad, then to steeper blues higher up.

Snowboarding It's a great freeriding area, with lots of trees and powder between the pistes to play in, plus the Shaper's Paradise area for building kickers and other features.

Cross-country Go elsewhere. There are no prepared trails here.

Mountain restaurants There are two 'rustic and charming' restaurants near the top of the first chair. Tiny Les Brevettes is cosy but cramped with good food ('great omelettes and ravioli; new loos') – while Chez Léon is much more spacious (and 'improving'

says a Ste-Foy regular). Another is due to open at the foot of the Marquise six-pack for 2013/14. Many people head back to the base, where the Maison à Colonnes gets good reports.

Schools and guides A 2013 visitor found his private off-piste lessons with the ESF 'wonderful'. Evolution 2 and K Spirit are alternative schools. The guides from the Bureau des Guides are 'totally great with huge knowledge of the area', says a recent reporter. Tarentaise Tours also specializes in off-piste. All the schools and guides can arrange heli-skiing.

Families Les P'tits Trappeurs takes children from age 3 to 11. UK tour operator Première Neige also runs a nursery.

STAYING THERE

Hotels Recommended places: the smart Monal (0479 069007) down in Ste-Foy village, and Auberge sur la Montagne (0479 069583) near the bottom of the access road to Ste-Foy station.

Chalets and apartments Première Neige has a handful of luxurious-looking catered chalets (all with outdoor hot tubs) and lots of smart self-catered apartments and chalets. Peak Retreats has apartments in the smart Etoile des Cîmes and Fermes de Ste-Foy (both with pool, hot tub, sauna, steam, fitness). Ski Collection also has Fermes de Ste-Foy plus La Ruitor apartments, quietly set at the edge of the resort 400m from the centre (with a free shuttle-bus to the lifts and a pool, sauna and steam).

Eating out In Ste-Foy-Station the Bergerie does excellent food, the 'atmospheric' Maison à Colonnes is highly rated and L'à Coeur does 'a fantastic côte de boeuf, dinosaur size', says a 2013 visitor. In the village of Le Miroir, Chez Merie is excellent (for lunch as well as dinner) – 'the best in the Tarentaise', says a frequent visitor. In Ste-Foy village, the restaurant of the Monal hotel and La Grange next door are both highly rated.

Après-ski Pretty quiet. Reporters have enjoyed the Iceberg piano bar. The Pitchouli is the place to go for a drink later on. The bar of the hotel Monal in Ste-Foy village can get busy, too; tastings are held in the cellar wine bar there.

Off the slopes There's little to do off the slopes, but snowshoeing and dog sledding are available.

St-Martin-de-Belleville

Explore the Trois Vallées from a traditional old village – and so avoid the Méribel crowds who descend on it for lunch

TOP 10 RATINGS

Extent	★★★★★
Fast lifts	★★★★
Queues	★★★★
Snow	★★★
Expert	★★★★
Intermediate	★★★★★
Beginner	★★
Charm	★★★★
Convenience	★★★
Scenery	★★★

RPI 105

lift pass	£230
ski hire	£115
lessons	£75
food & drink	£140
total	**£560**

KEY FACTS

Resort	1400m
	4,590ft

Trois Vallées	
Slopes	1260-3230m
	4,130-10,600ft
Lifts	173
Pistes	600km
	373 miles
Green	16%
Blue	40%
Red	34%
Black	10%
Snowmaking	50%

Les Menuires / St-Martin only	
Slopes	1400-2850m
	4,590-9,350ft
Lifts	34
Pistes	160km
	99 miles
Green	15%
Blue	47%
Red	30%
Black	8%

- ➕ Attractively developed traditional village with pretty church
- ➕ Access to the whole Trois Vallées
- ➕ Long, easy intermediate runs on rolling local slopes
- ➕ Extensive snowmaking keeps runs open in poor conditions, but ...

- ➖ Snow on runs to the resort suffers from afternoon sun, and altitude
- ➖ No green runs for novices
- ➖ Some lodging a long trek from the lifts – transport needed
- ➖ Limited village facilities and diversions

St-Martin is a lived-in, unspoiled village with an old church (prettily lit at night), small square and buildings of wood and stone, a few miles down the valley from Les Menuires. As a quiet, relatively inexpensive, attractive base for exploration of the Trois Vallées it's unbeatable. But it is quiet.

THE RESORT

St-Martin was a backwater farming village until the 1980s, when chairlifts linked it to the slopes of Méribel and Les Menuires.

Village charm St-Martin is a pleasant old village, set on a steep slope, with its extensive modern developments all in traditional style. The main feature remains the lovely 16th-century church – prettily floodlit at night.

Convenience The village core is small, but some lodgings are quite a way from the lifts. The main lift is above the centre, but a draglift from the village square accesses it. There are some good local shops and a few 'touristy' ones.

Scenery St-Martin has one of the more attractive locations in the valley, set among quiet, lightly wooded slopes.

THE MOUNTAINS

The whole of the Trois Vallées can easily be explored from here.

Slopes A gondola followed by a very long fast quad (a cold ride in the mornings) take you to a ridge from which you can access Méribel on one side and Les Menuires on the other.

Fast lifts The main local lifts are both fast – as are most key lifts in the Trois Vallées.

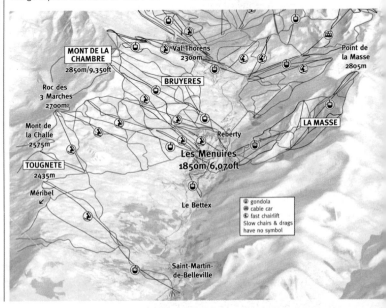

2013/14: A new Duo Pass will allow two people buying lift passes together to get a reduction.

2012/13: The Pass Tribu was introduced – allowing three or more people buying lift passes together to get a reduction. And with the new family pass two adults and two or more children now all pay the child rate.

OT LES MENUIRES / G LANSARD

The village is small and unspoiled with new buildings in traditional style and a lovely 16th-century church ↓

Queues Queues at the village gondola are not unknown.

Terrain parks None locally, but you can get to those above Les Menuires and Méribel relatively easily.

Snow reliability The local slopes get the full force of the afternoon sun, and the village is quite low. The home run is kept open by snowmaking to the bottom, but conditions are often poor.

Experts Locally there are large areas of gentle and often deserted off-piste. The descent from Roc de Fer to the village of Béranger is recommended. Head to La Masse for steep slopes.

Intermediates The local slopes are pleasant blues and reds, mainly of interest to intermediates. One of our favourite runs in the Trois Vallées is the rolling, wide, usually quiet Jerusalem red down to the top of the gondola from the ridge shared with Méribel. The Verdet blue from Roc de Fer is a lovely easy cruise and also usually quiet. Then, of course, there's the whole of the Trois Vallées to explore.

Beginners Not ideal – there's a small nursery slope but no long green runs to progress to. The blue run down the gondola is fairly gentle, though.

Snowboarding There is some great local off-piste freeriding available.

Cross-country There are 28km of trails in the Belleville valley.

Mountain restaurants Reporters love the Grand Lac (read the Les Menuires chapter). There are three atmospheric old places to try lower on the home run: the reliable Loy ('lovely lamb casserole, great service'), Chardon Bleu ('excellent plat du jour') and the small, woody Corbeleys. Just above the village is the Ferme de la Choumette (read 'Eating out').

Schools and guides A regular reporter's husband was 'very satisfied' with his lesson with British-run New

St-Martin-de-Belleville

345

Build your own shortlist: www.wheretoskiandsnowboard.com

UK PACKAGES

Phone numbers
From abroad use the prefix +33 and omit the initial '0' of the phone number

TOURIST OFFICE

www.st-martin-belleville.com

Generation, which recently opened a branch here. Reports on the ESF are generally positive. A potential problem is that when demand is low you may have to go to Les Menuires to find a class of the right level. Instructors operating here and in Les Menuires under the startling name of Ski School offer private lessons only in English, and are reported to be 'really good'.

Families One of our regular reporters on St-Martin has five children and seems to find it near-ideal, not least because it is so small and safe. Piou Piou club at the ESF takes children from 18 months to five years old. The tourist office has a list of babysitters.

STAYING THERE

For a small village there's a good variety of accommodation.

Chalets The Brit-run Alpine Club (not really a club) has two luxurious chalets in the quiet hamlet of Villarabout, one newly built in traditional style with a double-height, open-plan living room and the other a beautifully converted, 100-year-old farmhouse with spectacular views. They get rave reviews ('delicious food', 'fabulous service') and there's a minibus service until 10pm daily.

Hotels There are several 3-stars, on which we lack recent reports. The Alp hotel (0479 089282) is in pole position by the gondola.

Apartments The stylish residence Chalets du Gypse is well placed beside the piste above the village, with a smart pool, hot tubs etc; available through Peak Retreats (which also has an apartment in the village centre and a luxurious chalet in the next village of

St-Marcel with hot tub and minibus transfers to and from the slopes). Ski Amis has an appetizing range of properties, mostly very central.

Eating out There is a good choice for a small village, no doubt due in part to the healthy lunchtime trade. The Montagnard, on the snow, is an atmospheric converted barn doing a good range of dishes. The Lachenal is a simple hotel that suffers from changing hands quite frequently (but does 'excellent lamb', says a reporter). The Voûte is still recommended for pizza and more serious dishes ('a faultless steak au poivre'). The Eterlou does 'great grills'. The Billig is a crêperie that also does 'very good value and tasty food'. The Ferme de la Choumette, slightly out of the village, is a working farm and cheesery and is often recommended. The Ferme Auberge Chantacoucou in Le Chatelard is similar, but we're told it's 'even better'. The Bouitte, up the road in St-Marcel, has two Michelin stars; we and a reporter had splendid meals there a couple of years back; yes, it is very expensive.

Après-ski Choice is limited. The Dahlia, at the bottom of the gondola, is popular for après-ski drinks. Pourquoi Pas? has some live music sessions. Or try Bar Joker or Billig.

Off the slopes Options are limited. The village has a sports hall, an 'excellent' museum with 'comprehensive audio guide in English' and free concerts in the church. And there's dog sledding, snowshoe trips, pleasant walks and a torchlit tour of the village. Pedestrians can ride lifts to and from Méribel.

La Tania

A well-placed budget base for the slopes of Courchevel and Méribel – and a pleasant place, with a good choice of catered chalets

TOP 10 RATINGS	
Extent	★★★★★
Fast lifts	★★★★
Queues	★★★★
Snow	★★★
Expert	★★★★
Intermediate	★★★★★
Beginner	★★★
Charm	★★★
Convenience	★★★★
Scenery	★★★

RPI	115
lift pass	£230
ski hire	£125
lessons	£95
food & drink	£150
total	**£600**

- ➕ Part of the Trois Vallées, with good access to Courchevel and Méribel
- ➕ Long runs through woods to the village: a great place in a storm
- ➕ Attractive, small, traffic-free village
- ➕ Much improved snowmaking, but ...

- ➖ At this altitude, snowmaking is vital in most seasons
- ➖ Limited village facilities
- ➖ Village nursery slope gets through-traffic (but higher one does not)

La Tania is a good-value, family-friendly base from which to explore the slopes of its swanky neighbours, Courchevel and Méribel. The resort was built for the 1992 Winter Olympics, and at 1350m is about the lowest purpose-built French resort you'll find; its wood-clad buildings sit comfortably in a pretty woodland setting – quite a contrast to the bleakness of most French ski stations.

THE RESORT

La Tania is set just off the minor road linking Le Praz to Méribel. Free buses go to Courchevel and there's now an infrequent service to Méribel.
Village charm The village has grown into a quiet, attractive, car-free collection of mainly ski-in/ski-out chalets and apartments. There are a few lively bars and restaurants, but nightlife is still relatively low-key.
Convenience It's a small place – you can walk around the village in a couple of minutes – but big enough to have all the basic amenities (except a pharmacy). A gondola from one end of the village leads up into the slopes, and you should be able to ski back to a point close to your doorstep. And the lower nursery slope is central.
Scenery The resort is prettily set among the trees.

THE MOUNTAINS

The slopes immediately above both La Tania and nearby Le Praz are wooded, and about the best place in the whole Trois Vallées to be in bad weather. Above mid-mountain, the slopes are open.
Slopes The gondola out of the village goes to Praz-Juget. From just below here a new six-pack (replacing a draglift for 2013/14) goes on up to the slopes above Courchevel 1850, and a fast quad goes to the link with Méribel via Col de la Loze. From all these points, varied, interesting intermediate runs can take you back into the La Tania sector.
Fast lifts Our rating is for the whole Courchevel area lift system. The lifts above La Tania will be improved for 2013/14 by the new six-pack. But the gondola is not super-quick, and there

NEWS

2013/14: A new six-pack is due to replace the Bouc Blanc drag from mid-mountain to Loze, so speeding up the link with Courchevel. Two new slopes are also planned. A new Duo Pass will allow two people buying lift passes together to get a reduction.

2012/13: The Pass Tribu was introduced – allowing three or more people buying lift passes together to get a reduction. And with the new family pass two adults and two or more children now all pay the child rate.

will still be a couple of long draglifts labelled 'difficile'.

Queues The slopes above La Tania are relatively crowd-free and not really on the main Trois Vallées 'circuit'. But there may be morning queues for the gondola out of the village in peak season. The problem seems to be that it opens just in time for the ski school to pour on to it through their priority couloir, leaving everyone else waiting ('up to 30 minutes', said a February visitor).

Terrain parks There is no local terrain park or half-pipe, but you can get to Courchevel's 'Family Park' fairly easily.

Snow reliability Good snow-cover down to Praz-Juget is usual all season. Snowmaking covers the green run and the whole of the blue run back to the village; if, despite this, the runs are icy in the afternoon, you have the option of riding the gondola down.

Experts The mountainside above La Tania is steep enough to be interesting without being scary. The Dou des Lanches chairlift serves a lot of good

off-piste terrain as well as an easy black piste. The Jean Blanc and Jockeys blacks from Loze to Le Praz are challenging more because of length than gradient.

Intermediates There are three lovely, long, undulating intermediate runs back through the trees to La Tania. There's little difference in gradient between the blue and the red and even the green Plan Fontaine is great fun and popular. The red Murettes run to Le Praz is of genuine red steepness, winding and interesting. On the higher slopes both the red Lanches and the black Dou des Lanches pistes are excellent and challenging (the latter is often groomed and makes a great fast cruise when it is). The gentle Crêtes blue run (with associated slow chair) is underused and excellent, for building confidence – high, sunny, with good snow.

Beginners There is a good beginner area and lift right in the village, and children are well catered for. But there's a lot of through-traffic on the main slope. There's now a more snow-sure area at the top of the gondola (Praz-Juget). But the Plan Fontaine green run to the village is not an ideal progression run – fairly narrow, not all that gentle, winding and popular with better skiers whizzing down it. And the step up to the blue run back to the village is quite a big one.

Snowboarding It's easy to get around on boarder-friendly gondolas and chairlifts, avoiding drags.

Cross-country There are 66km of trails in the Courchevel/La Tania area, many

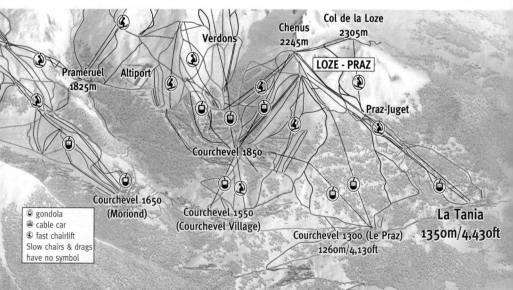

- ⬡ gondola
- ⬡ cable car
- ⬡ fast chairlift
- Slow chairs & drags have no symbol

Praméruel 1825m

Altiport

Verdons

Chenus 2245m

Col de la Loze 2305m

LOZE - PRAZ

Praz-Juget

Courchevel 1850

Courchevel 1650 (Moriond)

Courchevel 1550 (Courchevel Village)

Courchevel 1300 (Le Praz) 1260m/4,130ft

La Tania 1350m/4,430ft

La Tania is an attractive village in a pretty woodland setting →

KEY FACTS

Resort	1350m
	4,430ft

Trois Vallées

Slopes	1260-3230m
	4,130-10,600ft
Lifts	173
Pistes	600km
	373 miles
Green	16%
Blue	40%
Red	34%
Black	10%
Snowmaking	50%

Courchevel/
La Tania only

Slopes	1260-2740m
	4,130-8,990ft
Lifts	55
Pistes	150km
	93 miles
Green	19%
Blue	31%
Red	40%
Black	10%

of them through the woods.

Mountain restaurants Bouc Blanc (0479 088026), near the top of the gondola out of La Tania, is one of our favourites in the whole Trois Vallées – and much cheaper than Courchevel alternatives. It has friendly table-service in two wood-clad dining rooms, good food (reliable plat du jour) and wine (good-value pichets) and a big terrace. We've had our editorial team Christmas lunches there two years running, and Editor Watts had two excellent meals there in March 2013. Reporters endorse our view, but occasionally find service stretched. The tiny Roc Tania, up at Col de la Loze, is very pretty inside but pricey.

Schools and guides Highly regarded British school New Generation gets excellent reports of its La Tania branch: '10/10: our instructor was the best I have come across. Attention to detail was superb – puts my experiences with ESF to shame,' enthuses a recent visitor. Another says: 'Absolutely fabulous – progressed from almost a beginner to lessons on a black.' A 2013 reporter found Ski Excel (private lessons only) 'good' for his daughter who 'learnt a lot'. Magic Snowsports delivered the goods for a family a few seasons ago: 'Kids loved the lessons, and they changed the groups over the first two days to make sure they were of a similar standard.'

Families La Tania is popular with families looking for a quiet and convenient base, and a child-friendly atmosphere – 'excellent for our three-family group of 14, which included all ability levels'. La Tanière des Croës

La Tania

Build your own shortlist: **www.wheretoskiandsnowboard.com**

Stylish chalets and serious skiing? Check out p258.

350

Resort news and key links: www.wheretoskiandsnowboard.com

UK PACKAGES

Alpine Action, Alpine Answers, Alpine Elements, Crystal, Erna Low, Family Friendly Skiing, Independent Ski Links, Interactive Resorts, Lagrange, Le Ski, Mountain Beds, Nick Ski, Oxford Ski Co, Peak Retreats, Pierre & Vacances, PowderBeds, Silver Ski, Ski Amis, Ski Beat, Ski Dazzle, Ski Deep, Ski Expectations, Ski France, Ski Hame, Ski Independence, Ski Line, Ski Magic, Ski Power, Ski Solutions, Ski Weekend, Skitracer, Snoworks, Thomson

Phone numbers
From abroad use the prefix +33 and omit the initial '0' of the phone number

TOURIST OFFICE

www.latania.com

(formerly Chez Nounours) kindergarten takes both skiing and non-skiing children from four months to five years old. UK tour operator Le Ski runs its own nursery. A list of babysitters (for children over six months old) is available from the tourist office. New Generation ski school takes children from the age of four.

STAYING THERE

Chalets There are lots of catered chalets here, mostly dotted around in the woods above the resort centre. Ski Amis has seven chalets sleeping from 8 to 28 and all except one with outdoor hot tubs – we have stayed in the premium service Chalets Elliot (East and West) twice and loved them. Major Courchevel operator Le Ski runs three chalets here; a small one in a great piste-side location, and two largish ones that are particularly child-friendly, with family rooms – and they run a large crèche. Crystal has a 15-bed chalet. Alpine Elements now runs the former 3-star, 170-bed hotel

Montana near the gondola with pool, sauna and hot tub.

Apartments There are plenty of options from the major French specialist agencies – Peak Retreats and Lagrange. Ski Amis has a broad range of properties. Pierre & Vacances has three residences including the recently refurbished Christiania and Britania. There is a deli, bakery and small supermarket.

Eating out There's no doubt that the favourite restaurant among our reporters is the Taïga, over the road from the main village: 'wonderful food'; 'popular, busy, very good'; 'fish soup outstanding'; 'friendly'; 'reasonably priced'. The Ski Lodge does good-value fast food. We've had an excellent meal at the Michelin-starred Farçon, but the bill was a bit shocking. It feels a bit out of place here, frankly.

Après-ski It's quite lively at close of play, but again the choice is limited. The Ski Lodge has long been the focal après-ski place and has live bands – 'lively', 'friendly'. The Chrome bar has regular live music.

Off the slopes The place is very small and limited. However, tobogganing, snowshoeing, dog sledding, snowmobiling and paragliding are possibilities. There are some cleared paths and snowshoe routes. Non-skiers can go up the gondola or take the bus to Courchevel to meet skiing friends for lunch.

Selected chalets in La Tania

Tignes

Stark apartment blocks and a bleak, treeless setting are the prices you pay for the high, snow-sure slopes and varied terrain

RATINGS

The mountains

Extent	★★★★★
Fast lifts	★★★
Queues	★★★★
Terrain p'ks	★★★
Snow	★★★★★
Expert	★★★★★
Intermediate	★★★★★
Beginner	★★
Boarder	★★★★★
X-country	★★★
Restaurants	★★★
Schools	★★★★
Families	★★★

The resort

Charm	★
Convenience	★★★★
Scenery	★★★
Eating out	★★★★
Après-ski	★★★
Off-slope	★★

RPI — 110

lift pass	£210
ski hire	£115
lessons	£90
food & drink	£155
total	**£570**

NEWS

2013/14: The first phase of the MGM Kalinda village at Tignes 1800 is due to open in December 2013. The rest of the development will open for 2014/15. The Aeroski gondola from Le Lac is being replaced by a faster 10-seat one with easier access from the slope.

Tignespace, a sports hall/conference centre/concert hall in Le Lac, reopened this summer after a revamp. The Suites du Nevada hotel is due to be upgraded to a 5-star.

+ Good snow guaranteed for a long season; about the best Alpine bet

+ One of the best areas in the world for lift-served off-piste runs

+ Huge amount of varied terrain, with swift access to Val d'Isère

+ Lots of accommodation close to the slopes

+ Efforts to make the resort villages more welcoming are paying off

− Resort architecture not to everyone's taste (including ours)

− Bleak, treeless setting with many lifts prone to closure in bad weather

− Still a few long, slow chairlifts

− Beginners need an area pass to get to long green runs

− Limited, but improving, après-ski

The appeal of Tignes is simple: good snow, spread over a wide area of varied terrain shared with Val d'Isère. The altitude of Tignes is crucial: a forecast of 'rain up to 2000m' means 'fresh snow down to village level in Tignes' (or at least to Tignes 2100, as they are now trying to rebrand the main resort).

We prefer to stay in Val, which is a more human place. But in many ways Tignes 2100 makes the better base: appreciably higher, more convenient, surrounded by intermediate terrain, with quick access to the Grande Motte glacier. And the case gets stronger as the resort tries to make the place more attractive and as more traditional chalet-style buildings appear.

The lift system has improved, too, with a burst of fast chairs on the western side of the Tignes bowl a few years ago. But investment has stalled since then, and there are still a few key links that need upgrading.

THE RESORT

Tignes was created before the French discovered the benefits of making purpose-built resorts look acceptable. But things are improving, and the villages are gradually acquiring a more traditional look and feel.

Tignes-le-Lac is the hub of the resort and is itself split into two sub-resorts: Le Rosset and Le Bec-Rouge. It's at the point where these two meet – a snowy pedestrian area, with valley traffic passing through a tunnel beneath – that the lifts are concentrated: a powerful gondola towards Tovière and Val d'Isère, and a fast six-pack up the western slopes. There is also a suburb built on the lower slopes known as Les Almes. A nursery slope separates Le Rosset from the fourth component part, the group of apartment blocks called Le Lavachet, below which there are good fast lifts up both sides.

Val Claret is 2km up the valley, beyond the lake. From there, fast chairs head up towards Val d'Isère, up the western slopes opposite and to the Grande Motte. An underground funicular also accesses the Grande Motte.

Beside the road along the valley to the lifts is a ribbon of development in traditional style, named Grande Motte (after the peak). Val Claret is built on two levels, which are linked by a couple of (unreliable) indoor elevators,

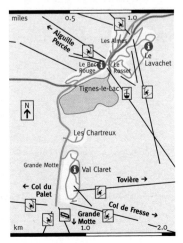

KEY FACTS	
Resort	2100m
	6,890ft
Espace Killy	
Slopes	1550-3455m
	5,090-11,340ft
Lifts	79
Pistes	300km
	186 miles
Green	14%
Blue	44%
Red	25%
Black	17%
Snowmaking	
	974 guns
Tignes only	
Slopes	1550-3455m
	5,090-11,340ft
Lifts	36
Pistes	150km
	93 miles

stairs and hazardous paths.

Down the valley from the main villages (which are becoming known as Tignes 2100) are two smaller places. Tignes 1800 (which used to be called Tignes-les-Boisses) – set in the trees beside the road up – is in the process of a 150-million-euro redevelopment, with a new MGM development called Kalinda Village being built. The first stage is due to open in December 2013, and the development is due to be complete by the end of 2014. Tignes-les-Brévières is a renovated old village at the lowest point of the slopes – a favourite lunch spot, and a friendly place to stay (but there's no bus service to the other Tignes 'villages'). Big gondolas from both these villages arrive at the same point on the slopes.

VILLAGE CHARM ✱✩✩✩✩
Functional, not fancy

Some of Tignes-le-Lac's smaller original eyesore buildings in the central part have been successfully revamped in chalet style. And some attractive new buildings have been added, both in the centre and on the fringes. But the blocks overlooking the lake from Le Bec-Rouge will remain monstrous until

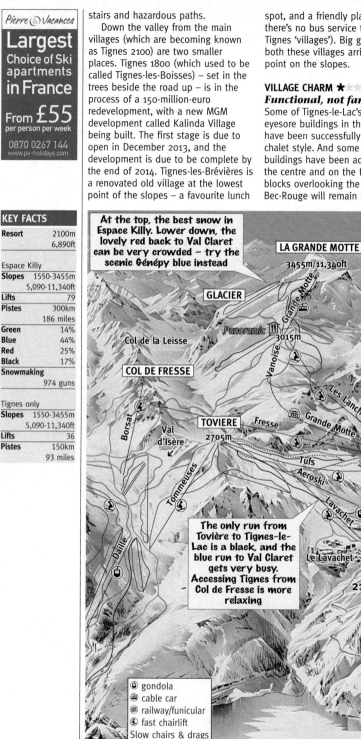

At the top, the best snow in Espace Killy. Lower down, the lovely red back to Val Claret can be very crowded – try the scenic Génépy blue instead

LA GRANDE MOTTE
3455m/11,340ft

GLACIER

Panoramic 3015m

Col de la Leisse

COL DE FRESSE

Vanoise

Les Lanches

Grande Motte

TOVIERE
2705m

Fresse

Borsat

Val d'Isère

Tommeuses

Tufs

Aeroski

Bollin

Val Claret

Tichot

Lavachet

Tignes-le-Lac

Daille

The only run from Tovière to Tignes-le-Lac is a black, and the blue run to Val Claret gets very busy. Accessing Tignes from Col de Fresse is more relaxing

Le Lavachet

Tignes
2100m/6,890ft

○ gondola
○ cable car
○ railway/funicular
○ fast chairlift
Slow chairs & drags have no symbol

the day they are demolished. The main part of Val Claret (Centre) is an uncompromisingly 1960s-style development on a shelf above the valley floor.

So, if it's more charm you seek, stay in Les Brévières or 1800.

CONVENIENCE ★★★★☆
Good all rounder
Location isn't crucial, as a regular, free, 24-hour bus service (praised by reporters) connects all the villages except Les Brévières – but during the day the route runs along the bottom of Val Claret, leaving Val Claret Centre

residents with a climb.

A lift or ski run is never more than a few minutes' walk away in Le Lac. 'Convenience was the main reason we chose to go to Tignes for our holiday this year, and we were not disappointed,' said a recent reporter.

SCENERY ★★★☆☆
Great from the glacier
Tignes is in a high, bleak, treeless bowl; when the sun shines, the rugged mountain terrain is splendid, especially from the glacial heights of the Grande Motte.

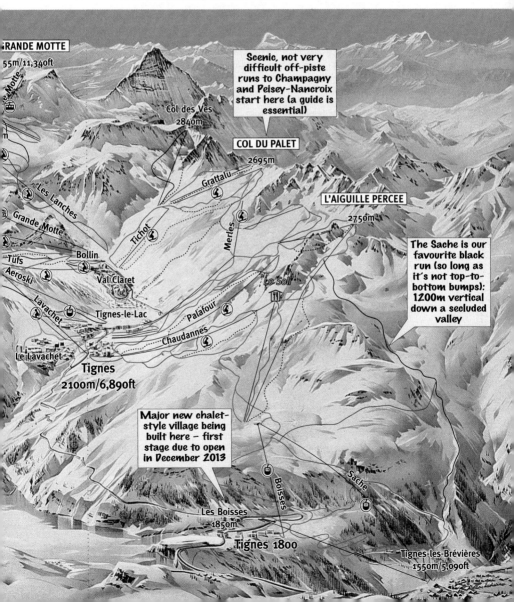

GRANDE MOTTE
55m/11,340ft

Col des Ves
2840m

Scenic, not very difficult off-piste runs to Champagny and Peisey-Nancroix start here (a guide is essential)

COL DU PALET
2695m

Grattalu

Les Lanches

Tichot

Merles

L'AIGUILLE PERCEE
2750m

Grande Motte

Bollin

Tufs
Aeroski

Val Claret

La Sol

The Sache is our favourite black run (so long as it's not top-to-bottom bumps): 1200m vertical down a secluded valley

Lavachet

Tignes-le-Lac

Palafour

Le Lavachet

Chaudannes

Tignes
2100m/6,890ft

Major new chalet-style village being built here – first stage due to open in December 2013

Boisses

Sache

Les Boisses
1850m

Tignes 1800

Tignes-les-Brévières
1550m/5,090ft

LIFT PASSES

Espace Killy

Prices in €

Age	1-day	6-day
under 14	38	188
14 to 64	47	235
65 plus	38	188

Free Under 5, over 75
Beginner Five free lifts
Notes Covers Tignes and Val d'Isère; half-day and pedestrian passes; family discounts; 5-day+ passes valid for a day in the Three Valleys and a day in Paradiski (La Plagne-Les Arcs); 2-day+ pass gives free access to pool and ice rink
Alternative pass Tignes only

THE MOUNTAINS

The area's great weakness is that it can become unusable in bad weather. There are no woodland runs except immediately above Tignes 1800 and Tignes-les-Brévières. Heavy snow produces widespread avalanche risk, and wind closes the higher chairs.

Piste classification here isn't perfect, but it is more reliable than in Val d'Isère, and signposting is clear – 'extremely helpful during poor visibility'. But we've had complaints that lift and piste closing time information is unreliable (and that sometimes information at the lift doesn't match the piste map).

EXTENT OF THE SLOPES ★★★★★
High, snow-sure and varied
Tignes and Val d'Isère share a huge area of slopes known as L'Espace Killy. Locally, Tignes' biggest asset is the **Grande Motte** – and the runs from, as well as on, the glacier. An underground funicular from Val Claret whizzes you up to over 3000m in seven minutes. There are blue, red and black runs to play on up here, as well as beautiful long runs back to the resort.

The main lifts towards Val d'Isère are efficient: a high-capacity gondola from Le Lac to **Tovière**, and a fast chair from Val Claret to **Col de Fresse**. You can head back to Tignes from either lift: the return from Tovière to Tignes-le-Lac is via a steep black run, but there are easier blue runs to Val Claret.

Going up the opposite side of the valley takes you to a quieter area of predominantly east-facing slopes split into two main sectors, linked in both directions – **Col du Palet** and the **Aiguille Percée**. Several years ago, this whole mountainside was at last given some of the fast lifts it had needed for years – but investment has stalled and some chairs still need modernizing. You can descend from the Aiguille

Percée to Tignes-les-Brévières or Tignes 1800 on blue, red or black runs. There are efficient gondolas back.

FAST LIFTS ★★★★★
Improved but not good enough
Fast chairs and gondolas get you up the mountain from most parts of the resort. And there are some fast chairs higher up, too. But a few key slow ones remain that could do with being upgraded, including the Col des Ves chair at the south end of the Col du Palet sector and the one to the Aiguille Percée above Tignes-le-Lac. The chairs above Tignes-les-Brévières and Tignes 1800 are also old and slow, and much in need of upgrading.

QUEUES ★★★★★
Very few
Recent reporters have experienced very few queues, even in February half-term. But if snow low down is poor, the Grande Motte funicular can generate queues; the fast chairs in parallel with it are often quicker, despite the longer ride time. These lifts jointly shift a lot of people, with the result that the red run down to Val Claret can be unpleasantly crowded (the roundabout Génépy blue is a much quieter option). The worst queues now are for the cable car on the glacier – half-hour waits are common. Of course, if higher lifts are closed by heavy snow or high winds, the lifts on the lower slopes have big queues. Otherwise there are usually very few problems; crowded pistes can be more of an issue.

TERRAIN PARKS ★★★★★
X Games standard but ...
Tignes was one of the first French resorts to build a terrain park, and it will be hosting its fifth successive European Winter X Games from 19 to 21 March 2014. The Swatch Snowpark is beneath the Grattalu chair on Col du Palet and has rails and kickers split into green, blue and red levels, plus a black kicker, a boardercross course and an airbag jump. Shoot my Ride is back – check your airbag jump on a giant screen and download it later. In the summer the park doubles in size and moves up to the Grande Motte for freestyle camps. The 120m-long winter half-pipe is right at the bottom of the mountain in Val Claret, which means if it's open and you have the energy to hike, you can ride it for free. There is

↑ An aerial view of Tignes-le-Lac. The new Kalinda Village is down by the dam creating the lake on the left
OT TIGNES / MONICA DALMASSO

also the Gliss park at town level in Le Lac with airbag and mini boardercross, so a day's freestyle for free is definitely an option.

Despite (or maybe because of) hosting the X Games, we've had reader criticism of facilities ('there weren't many rails open and it's not very big – the better park is in Val d'Isère').

SNOW RELIABILITY ★★★★★
Difficult to beat
Tignes has all-year-round runs (barring brief closures in spring or autumn) on its Grande Motte glacier. And the resort height of 2100m generally means good snow-cover right back to base for most of the long winter season – November to May. The west-facing runs down from Col de Fresse and Tovière to Val Claret suffer from the afternoon sun, although they have serious snowmaking. Some of the lower east-facing and south-east-facing slopes on the other side of the valley can suffer late in the season, too. Grooming is excellent – in 2011's challenging conditions 'a lot of wonderful work was done to keep pistes open and in good condition'.

FOR EXPERTS ★★★★★
An excellent choice
Tignes has converted many of its black runs into 'naturides', which means they are never groomed (a neat way of saving money!), but they are marked,

patrolled and avalanche protected. Many of them are not especially steep (eg the Ves run – promoted from red status and renamed after the local freeride hero Guerlain Chicherit). Perhaps the most serious challenge is the long black run from Tovière to Tignes-le-Lac, with steep, usually heavily mogulled sections (the top part, Pâquerettes, is now a naturide, but the bottom part, Trolles, is a normal black). Parts of this run get a lot of afternoon sun. Our favourite black run (still a 'normal' black) is the Sache, from the Aiguille Percée down a secluded valley to Tignes-les-Brévières. It can become very heavily mogulled, especially at the bottom – you can avoid this section by taking the red Arcosses piste option part-way down.

But it is the off-piste possibilities that make Tignes such a draw for experts, and the schools organize off-piste groups. See the feature panel later in the chapter for a few of the off-piste runs. The bizarre French form of heli-skiing is available here: mountaintop drops are forbidden, but from Tovière you can ski down towards the Lac du Chevril to be retrieved by chopper.

Fine chalets in a fun French village? Check out p258.

↑ Tignes-le-Lac on the left, Val Claret in the centre and the Grande Motte above it – and not a tree in sight
OT TIGNES / MONICA DALMASSO

GETTING THERE

Air Geneva 225km/140 miles (3hr30); Lyon 230km/ 145 miles (3hr15); Chambéry 145km/ 90 miles (2hr15)

Rail Bourg-St-Maurice (30km/19 miles); regular buses or taxi from station

FOR INTERMEDIATES ★★★★★
One of the best

For keen intermediate piste-bashers who like varied terrain and lots of it, the Espace Killy is one of the world's best areas.

Tignes' local slopes are ideal intermediate terrain. The runs on the Grande Motte glacier nearly always have superb snow. The runs from the top of the cable car are bizarrely classified red and black, but they are wide and mostly easy on usually fabulous snow, and could easily be blues. The Leisse run down to the chairlift of the same name is classified black and can get very mogulled, but usually has good snow. The red run all the way back to town is a delightful long cruise – though often crowded. The roundabout blue (Génépy) is much gentler and quieter.

From Tovière, the blue Henri (formerly 'H') run to Val Claret is an enjoyable cruise and generally well groomed. But, again, it can get very crowded.

There's lots to do on the other side of the valley too, and the runs down from the Aiguille Percée to Tignes 1800 and Les Brévières are both scenic and fun. There are red and blue options, and adventurous intermediates shouldn't miss the beautiful Sache black run. The runs from the Aiguille Percée to Tignes Le Lac are gentle, wide blues.

FOR BEGINNERS ★★★★★
Good nursery slopes, but …

The nursery slopes of Tignes-le-Lac and Le Lavachet (which meet at the top) are excellent – convenient, snow-sure, gentle, free of through-traffic and served by a slow chair and a drag. The ones at Val Claret are less appealing: an unpleasantly steep slope within the village served by a drag, and a less convenient slope served by the fast Bollin chair. All of these lifts are free.

Although there are some fairly easy blues on the west side of Tignes, for long green runs you have to go over to the Val d'Isère sector. You need an Espace Killy pass to use them, and to get back to Tignes you have a choice between the blue run from Col de Fresse (which has a tricky start) or riding the gondola down from Tovière. And in poor weather, the high Tignes valley is an intimidatingly bleak place – enough to make any wavering beginner retreat to a bar with a book.

FOR BOARDERS ★★★★★
One of the best

Tignes has always been a popular destination for snowboarders. Lots of easily accessible off-piste and lower prices than Val d'Isère are the main attractions, and quite a few top UK snowboarders make this their winter home. There are a few flat areas (avoid Génépy and Myrtilles), but the lift system relies more on chairs and gondolas than drags. There are long, wide pistes to blast down, such as

Grattalu, Carline and Henri, with acres of powder between them to play in. And the backside of Col de Fresse in Val d'Isère is a natural playground. There are two specialist snowboard schools (Snocool and Alliance) and a Welsh-run snowboarder chalet (www.dragonlodge.com). Go to the Snowpark shop in Tignes-le-Lac for all your equipment needs.

FOR CROSS-COUNTRY ★★★★★
Interesting variety
The Espace Killy has 44km of cross-country trails, including 20km of tracks on the frozen Lac de Tignes, along the valley between Val Claret and Tignes-le-Lac, at Tignes 1800 and Les Brévières and up on the Grande Motte.

MOUNTAIN RESTAURANTS ★★★★★
A couple of good places
The mountain restaurants are not a highlight – a regular hazard of high, purpose-built resorts, where it's easy to go back to the village for lunch. The 'biggest rip-off' for a 2012 reporter was being charged 50c for the toilets in almost all the restaurants.

Editors' choice Lo Soli (0479 069863) at the top of the Chaudannes chair is

a clear favourite. From its terrace there's a superb view (shared with the adjacent self-service Alpage) of the Grande Motte . Reporters endorse our opinion: 'excellent food, ambience and service'; 'one of the cheaper vins chauds'; 'did us proud, with epic hot chocolate and enjoyable tartiflette'. The table-service bit of the Panoramic (0479 064721) at the top of the funicular competes: 'wonderful views, very good spaghetti bolognese (enough to share), excellent puddings'.
Worth knowing about On the nursery slope above Val Claret, the Chalet du Bollin has been recommended as a pricier option. The pizzas at the self-service at the top of Tovière were recommended by a 2013 reporter ('big enough to share'); there's a good-looking table-service section too, but it was closed on our December 2012 visit. The big Panoramic self-service at the top of the funicular gets crowded, but has great views from its huge terrace and does 'burger and chips for just eight euros'.

There are lots of easily accessible places for lunch in the resorts. One ski-to-the-door favourite of ours in Le Lac is the hotel Montana, on the left as you descend from the Aiguille Percée. Others are the Ferme des 3 Capucines, a short walk down from the bottom of the Chaudannes and Paquis chairs, and the Arbina (see 'Eating out' for more on these two). The Jam Bar is a 'tiny cafe with brilliant, freshly made pasta sauces, great bruschetta and the best coffee'. In Val Claret the Pignatta has been recommended for quality and value, but we lack recent reports; the Aspen Cafe does 'big American-diner style portions for reasonable prices', and Carline is 'not fancy but convenient and quick'.

At the extremity of the lift system, Les Brévières makes an obvious lunch stop. A short walk round the corner into the village brings you to places much cheaper than the two by the piste. Sachette, for example, is crammed with artefacts from mountain life and is 'a must-go place'. The Armailly is recommended for its 'fantastic food' and 'varied menu that didn't break the bank'.

SCHOOLS AND GUIDES ★★★★★
Plenty of choice
There are over half-a-dozen schools, including two specialist snowboard schools, plus various independent

Tignes

Build your own shortlist: **www.wheretoskiandsnowboard.com**

Tignes is renowned for offering some of the best lift-served off-piste skiing in the world. There is a tremendous choice, with runs to suit all levels, from intermediate skiers to fearless freeriders and off-piste experts. Here's just a small selection. Don't go without a guide.

For a first experience of off-piste, **Lognan** *is ideal. These slopes – down the mountainside between the pistes to Le Lac and the pistes to Val Claret – are broad and not very difficult.*

One of our favourite routes is the **Tour de Pramecou***. After a few minutes' walking at the bottom of the Grande Motte glacier, you pass around a big rock called Pramecou. There is then a multitude of possibilities, varying in difficulty – so routes can be found for skiers of different abilities.*

Petite Balme *is a run for good skiers only – access is easy but it leads to quite challenging north-facing slopes in real high-mountain terrain, far from the pistes.*

To ski **Oreilles de Mickey** *(Mickey's Ears) you start from Tovière and walk north along the ridge to the peak of Lavachet, where you get a great view of Tignes. The descent involves three long couloirs, narrow and pretty steep, that bring you back to Le Lavachet.*

The best place to find good snow is the **Chardonnet** *couloirs – they never get the sun. The route involves a 20-minute walk from the top of the Merles chairlift.*

The **Vallons de la Sache** *is one of the most famous routes – a descent of 1200m vertical down a breathtaking valley in the heart of the National Park, overlooked by the magnificent Sache glacier. Starting from the Aiguille Percée you enter a different world, high up in the mountains, far away from the ski lifts. You arrive down in Les Brévières, below the Tignes dam.*

One of the big adventures is to go away from the Tignes ski area and all signs of civilization, starting from the Col du Palet. From there you can head for **Champagny** *(linked to La Plagne's area) or* **Peisey-Nancroix** *(linked to Les Arcs' area) – both very beautiful runs, and not too difficult.*

FRANCE

358

Resort news and key links: www.wheretoskiandsnowboard.com

CHILDCARE

Les Marmottons
t 0479 065167
From 30mnth

Piou Piou
t 0479 063028
Ages 3 to 5

Ski schools
From age 4

instructors. Reporters advise that at busy times pre-booking is essential.

ESF gets mixed reviews: one recent reporter's group abandoned their group lessons midway through the week because they were so bad; but another had a 'fantastic' day's guiding.

Another reporter had an 'excellent' one-on-one private lesson with New Generation – a British-run school with branches in several other resorts – in which she improved her mogul and off-piste skills 'hugely' and came away 'very happy'. We have had glowing reports of a British-run snowboarding outfit, Alliance: 'tuition was appropriate to our requirements, and very passionate and sincere'; 'we improved our confidence and skills

greatly'; 'excellent instruction'.

333 got a glowing report a couple of years back: 'Best we've ever had, all gaining in confidence after a couple of hours.' Ultimate Snowsports was also praised for 'making the lessons fun and challenging for the children in our group'. Reports on Evolution 2 have been consistently positive: 'had a fantastic instructor who challenged everyone in the group – we all advanced our technique and she had us on reds by day three, blacks on day four'; 'very happy with the children's lessons, booked through Esprit Ski'.

Ali Ross Skiing Clinics (pre-booking required) have been praised: 'a great character who achieved results'.

ACTIVITIES

Indoor Wellness and fitness centres (pools, saunas, Turkish baths, hot tub, spa and beauty treatments, weight training), multi-sports hall, yoga, climbing wall, cinema, library, bowling, multimedia centre

Outdoor Dog sledding, mountaineering, ice climbing, ice driving, ice diving, ice rink, paragliding, snowmobiling, snowshoeing, biking on snow, helicopter flights, snow kiting

FOR FAMILIES ★★★☆☆
Good reports
We have had good reports on the Marmottons kindergarten. British-run t4Nanny (www.t4nanny.com) has been recommended – 'flexible and terrific'. Family specialist tour operator Esprit Ski runs chalets and comprehensive childcare here.

STAYING THERE

All three main styles of lodgings are available through tour operators. More luxury options are appearing.
Chalets Catered chalets run by UK tour operators are mainly in Le Lac. Skiworld has eight chalets (some with sauna/steam room/hot tub) and the swanky 42-bed Ski Lodge Aigle with pool and sauna. Ski Total has a chalet hotel and 16 chalets, including some very smart places, lots with sauna and outdoor hot tub, some with pool, and two in their top-of-the-market Platinum range. Its Chalet Anne-Marie was 'strongly recommended' by a reporter. Family specialist Esprit has nine chalets here, including the smart, 24-person Corniche, with sauna, steam room, hot tub and lifts to all floors. Crystal has seven places from smart to budget, including two in its 'Finest' range. Inghams has four chalets (one with hot tub and sauna) and a 30-bed chalet hotel. A regular reporter has recommended Chalet Chardon, available through Snowstar: 'Used to be Robert Maxwell's private apartment; lovely large lounge with floor-to-ceiling windows and a great view of the lake.' And Mountainsun's chalet hotel Melezes in Tignes 1800 has been recommended for good food and as a place for big groups to stay.
Hotels The few hotels are small and concentrated in Le Lac.
★★★★Campanules (0479 063436) Smartly rustic chalet in upper Le Lac, with good restaurant.

★★★★Village Montana (0479 400144) Stylishly woody, on the east-facing slopes above Le Lac. Outdoor pool, sauna, steam, hot tub. 'Not cheap but first-class with accommodating staff.'
★★★Arbina (0479 063478) Well-run place close to the lifts in Le Lac, with lunchtime terrace, crowded après-ski bar and one of the best restaurants.
★★★Diva (0479 067000) Biggest in town (121 rooms). On lower level of Val Claret, a short walk from lifts. Comfortable rooms and excellent meals. Sauna, steam.
★★★Gentiana (0479 065246) In Le Lac. Friendly, pool, sauna, steam, hot tub. We stayed here happily last season.
★★★Lévanna (0479 063294) Piste side in Le Lac. Comfortable; big hot tub.
★★★Marais (0479 064006) Prettily furnished, simple hotel in Tignes 1800.
★★★Refuge (0479 063664) Oldest hotel in Tignes (Le Lac). 'Well run.'
Génépy (0479 065711) Simple, Dutch-run; in Les Brévières.
Apartments There are lots of apartments in all price ranges. Ski Collection, Ski Amis and Skitracer have a range of options. The growing number of smart places include Jhana, Ferme du Val Claret, Nevada and Pierre & Vacances' Ecrin des Neiges in Val Claret, and Télèmark, and Residence Village Montana in Le Lac. In Les Brévières, the Belvédère has very smart large apartments and chalets with three to six bedrooms. All the above have access to pool, sauna etc, but at extra cost in some cases. The Chalet Club in Val Claret is a collection of simple studios, but it has a free indoor pool, sauna and a restaurant and bar. Skiworld has 'flexible catered chalets' where you can choose what catering (if any) you want.
A new option for 2013/14 is Kalinda Village at Tignes 1800, built by MGM and opening in December – smart apartments, pool, saunas, steam, hot tub. If you have a car, it's easy to drive

Tignes

Build your own shortlist: **www.wheretoskiandsnowboard.com**

← The acceptable face of Tignes-le-Lac with chalet-style buildings and good mountain views – the monstrous Bec-Rouge block is out of shot
SNOWPIX.COM / CHRIS GILL

In Val Claret the Caveau is recommended for a special treat. Pepe 2000 has 'friendly staff' and 'lovely pizzas'. The Aspen Coffee Shop is 'cheap and cheerful' and does 'big portions at reasonable prices'.

APRES-SKI ★★★
Hidden away
Reporters agree that there is plenty going on if you know where to find it. Val Claret has some early-evening atmosphere and popular happy hours. The Drop Zone has live music, 'a good atmosphere and a dance floor that fills up pretty quickly'. Grizzly's is 'very cool' but pricey. The Couloir has a whisky lounge. A recent reporter always ended the night in the 'decidedly nice' Melting Pot.

Le Lac is a natural focus for après-ski drinks. The lively Loop has 'friendly staff', 'good' live bands and a happy hour from 4pm to 6pm which 'kept the beer at a reasonable price', while the Embuscade is 'very friendly'. The bar of the hotel Arbina is our kind of spot – cosy with friendly service. It's a great place to sit outside and people-watch. The Alpaka Lodge bar is popular with Brits and 'a pleasant spot, especially if you manage to grab one of the sofas by the fire'. Bagus Bar is 'rocking'. Jack's is a popular late haunt.

Vincents in Les Brévières is 'lively, with lots of drinking, singing and sometimes live music'.

OFF THE SLOPES ★★
Good leisure centre
Tignes is not a resort for those who do not want to use the slopes. And some activities get booked up quickly – a reporter said it was impossible to find a free dog sledding slot in April. The ice skating on the lake includes a 500m circuit as well as a conventional rink. This and the pools of the Lagon leisure centre (various pools, slides, wellness and fitness facilities, and praised by reporters) are free to use with a lift pass for two days or more. A reporter's kids 'really enjoyed' the bowling at Tignes-le-Lac.

UK PACKAGES
Action Outdoors, Alpine Answers, Alpine Elements, Carrier, Club Med, Crystal, Crystal Finest, Erna Low, Esprit, Flexiski, Friendship Travel, Independent Ski Links, Inghams, Inspired to Ski, Interactive Resorts, Lagrange, Mark Warner, Mountain Beds, Mountainsun, Neilson, Oxford Ski Co, Peak Retreats, Pierre & Vacances, Powder White, PowderBeds, Richmond Holidays, Ski Amis, Ski Bespoke, Ski Club Freshtracks, Ski Collection, Ski Expectations, Ski France, Ski Ici, Ski Independence, Ski Line, Ski Solutions, Ski Supreme, Ski Total, Ski Weekend, Skitracer, Skiweekends.com, Skiworld, Snow Finders, Snowchateaux, Snoworks, Snowpod, STC, Thomson

Phone numbers
From abroad use the prefix +33 and omit the initial '0' of the phone number

TOURIST OFFICE
www.tignes.net

to Val d'Isère as well as take the gondola into the Tignes slopes. Available through Peak Retreats and Ski Collection.

The supermarket at Le Lac is reported to be 'comprehensive but very expensive' – 'stock up in Bourg'.

EATING OUT ★★★★
Good places scattered about
The options in Le Lavachet are rather limited. Our favourite there is Ferme des 3 Capucines where we had a great dinner last season – lovely food, reasonably priced, good service, nice rustic surroundings. And we have very positive reports of the good-value, British-run Brasero. Finding anywhere with some atmosphere is difficult in Le Lac, though the food in some of the better hotels is good, particularly the Chaumière in the Village Montana. The upstairs restaurant at the Arbina is regularly recommended: 'very good service and excellent food'; 'the three-course fixed menu is good value'. We had an enjoyable dinner last season in the simpler ground-floor brasserie. The 'atmospheric' Escale Blanche is popular, with 'great food', but reporters disagree over its value. Repeated visitors have enjoyed 'traditional' food at the Eterlou, but service 'went downhill after we complained about the house wine'.

Les Trois Vallées

With the swankiest resort in the Alps at one end, and the highest at the other: the biggest lift-linked ski area in the world

Despite competing claims, notably from the Portes du Soleil, in practical terms the Trois Vallées cannot be beaten for sheer quantity of lift-linked terrain. The Schrahe report (read our feature on 'Piste Extent' at front of book) confirms this. There is nowhere like it for a keen skier or boarder who wants to cover as much mileage as possible while rarely taking the same run repeatedly. It has a lot to offer everyone, from beginner to expert. And its resorts offer a wide range of alternatives – from the big-name mega-resorts to much smaller places.

What's more, the area undersells itself. It should actually be known as the Quatre Vallées because it expanded south into the Maurienne before the first edition of this book was published almost 20 years ago.

The Trois Vallées area is dealt with in six chapters. The four major resorts are Courchevel, Méribel, Les Menuires and Val Thorens, but we also give chapters to St-Martin-de-Belleville (near Les Menuires) and La Tania (between Courchevel and Méribel).

None of the resorts is cheap, but of the major resorts **Les Menuires** is cheapest. The centre of the resort is an eyesore, but new developments have been built in chalet style, and two of the original buildings have been demolished to make way for new ones – something we suggested back in the 1990s. Les Menuires has an excellent position for exploration of the Trois Vallées as a whole.

Down the valley from Les Menuires is **St-Martin-de-Belleville**, a charming traditional village that has been expanded sympathetically. It has good-value accommodation and lift links towards Les Menuires and Méribel.

Up rather than down the Belleville

valley from Les Menuires, at 2300m, **Val Thorens** is the highest resort in the Alps, and at 3230m the top of its slopes is the high point of the Trois Vallées. The snow in this area is almost always good, and it includes two glaciers where good snow is guaranteed. But the setting is bleak, and the lifts are vulnerable to closure in bad weather. It's a purpose-built resort and very convenient – and visually it is not comparable to Les Menuires, thanks to the smaller-scale buildings and more traditional styles.

Méribel is a multi-part resort. The highest component, **Méribel-Mottaret**, is about the best placed of all the resorts for getting to any part of the Trois Vallées system. **Méribel** itself, 200m lower, is a British favourite. It is the most attractive of the main Trois Vallées resorts, built in chalet style on a steep hillside. Parts of the resort are very convenient for the slopes and the village centre; parts are not. The

Courchevel is at one end of the Trois Vallées, the world's biggest lift-linked ski area →
STUART MCWILLIAM

growing hamlet of **Méribel-Village** has its own chairlift into the system. You can also stay down in the valley town of **Brides-les-Bains**.

Courchevel has four parts, which have recently been rebranded. Courchevel (the new name for what was formerly 1850) is among the most fashionable and expensive resorts in the Alps. The other parts – Le Praz (formerly 1300), Courchevel-Village (formerly 1550) and Moriond (formerly 1650) – are much less expensive. Many people rate the slopes around here the best in the Trois Vallées, with runs to suit all standards.

La Tania was built for the 1992 Olympics, just off the minor road linking Courchevel to Méribel. It has now grown into an attractive, car-free collection of chalets and apartment blocks set among the trees, and is popular with families. It has good nursery slopes and good intermediate runs in the woods above.

Val Cenis Vanoise

A fair-sized mountain above an unspoiled valley, with a row of unpretentious base villages offering attractively low prices

363

TOP 10 RATINGS

Extent	★★★
Fast lifts	★★★
Queues	★★★★
Snow	★★★
Expert	★★
Intermediate	★★★★
Beginner	★★★★
Charm	★★★
Convenience	★★★
Scenery	★★★

RPI	80
lift pass	£140
ski hire	£90
lessons	£65
food & drink	£120
total	**£415**

NEWS

2012/13: A Snow Zone was created, offering snow tubing and big air-bag activities.

OT HAUTE MAURIENNE VANOISE
One of the great attractions of Lanslevillard is the extent of the green slopes next to the village ↓

- ➕ Prices well below the French norm
- ➕ Varied slopes with fairly reliable snow; most slopes face north
- ➕ Some high-quality apartments at attractive rates

- ➖ Still some slow old lifts
- ➖ Little to amuse experts on piste
- ➖ One sector of slopes is a bit separate from the other two
- ➖ Quiet at night

Val Cenis Vanoise is the ski area shared by three quiet, traditional villages in the remote and unspoiled Haute Maurienne valley. It's a modest-sized area, but packs in a lot of variety. There's no shortage of comfortable apartments, in particular, and prices are very low by French standards.

THE RESORT

This is one of those confusing areas that seem to be a French speciality. The Haute Maurienne is the high eastern end of the great curving valley of the Arc, south of the Massif de la Vanoise, which contains so many big-name resorts. Its villages are marketed under the name Haute Maurienne Vanoise. Two of those villages work under the name Val Cenis. And the ski area they share with Termignon is called Val Cenis Vanoise. And that's just the start.

There are six main lift bases: the first resort you come to is Termignon; 6km on is Lanslebourg; then there's Les Champs, a cluster of new residences with a lift and the other necessities of life; then Lanslevillard, which has one main lift base on the outskirts and another nearer the

centre; and finally, its suburb Le Haut, which has the sixth lift.

If you fancy taking a peek at the other side of the French skiing coin, 40km down the road at Orelle is a gondola into the slopes of Val Thorens, part of the Trois Vallées.

Village charm The villages are not chocolate-box pretty but solidly traditional. Lanslebourg is spread along the RN6 road, with no real focus. Lanslevillard is more captivating – less regularly arranged and with more character. The valley doesn't get a lot of sun in midwinter.

Convenience It's not difficult to find lodgings that are more-or-less ski-in, even if they are plod-out. From Les Champs you can walk to the villages either side, but it's along the road.

Scenery The slopes are attractively wooded, and the Haute Maurienne gives a sense of unspoiled wilderness.

VAL CENIS
Superb 4★ self-catering apartments at the foot of the slopes
peakretreats.co.uk/Val_Cenis

ABTA
ABTA No. W5537

peak retreats

KEY FACTS

Resort	1300-1460m
	4,270-4,790ft
Slopes	1300-2800m
	4,270-9,190ft
Lifts	27
Pistes	125km
	78 miles
Green	21%
Blue	23%
Red	42%
Black	14%
Snowmaking	
	200 guns

THE MOUNTAINS

There are half a dozen descents on the prettily wooded lower slopes, but most pistes are on the open upper slopes. Reporters agree that piste classification is generally accurate, but that some blues are tough in parts.

Slopes From each of the lift bases there are fast lifts up to the treeline at mid-mountain. There are three identifiable sectors. The main network of runs on the upper slopes is above Lanslevillard. There are high-altitude links between this sector and the slopes around Col du Mont Cenis, above Lanslebourg. A long fast chair then links this sector to the slopes above Termignon. There is a winding blue piste back, but it is a pretty tedious affair, and downloading on the same chair is more attractive.

Fast lifts Not a strong point: most of the lifts out of the valley are fast, but many upper ones are not.

Queues We lack recent high-season reports, but visitors in January, March and April had few problems.

Terrain parks There are two snowparks. Reports welcome.

Snow reliability Most of the runs are north-facing, and there is snowmaking on the protected tree runs back to each of the base stations.

Experts There are few challenges on-piste. From the top station there is a good black. But there is a lot to do off-piste – routes from virtually all the upper lifts, some staying within the lift system, some ending up outside it.

Intermediates There are intermediate runs all over the mountain, allowing for some top-to-bottom cruises of up to 1400m vertical. To get the best out of the area you have to be prepared to handle some long draglifts on the upper slopes, especially at Termignon.

Beginners Termignon and Lanslevillard have good nursery slopes next to the villages – and the latter has the spectacularly attractive feature of green runs down the length of the gondola from Le Haut. Another feature is the splendid green from the Col du Mont Cenis to the valley, down the hairpins of the summer road to Italy.

Snowboarding Beginners should stay in Lanslevillard to avoid some long drags on the upper slopes.

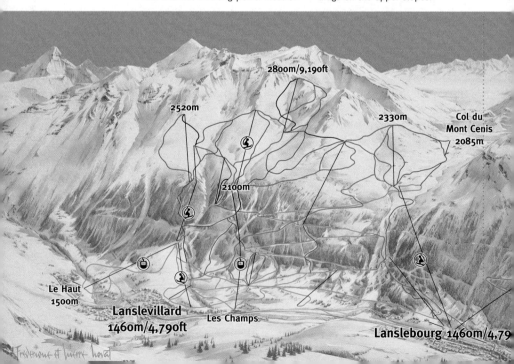

2800m/9,190ft

2520m

2330m

Col du Mont Cenis 2085m

2100m

Le Haut 1500m

Lanslevillard 1460m/4,790ft

Les Champs

Lanslebourg 1460m/4,79

Phone numbers
From abroad use the prefix +33 and omit the initial '0' of the phone number

TOURIST OFFICE

www.valcenis.com

Cross-country There are short trails locally, but real enthusiasts will want to head 10km up the valley for the fabulous 130km of trails at Bessans.

Mountain restaurants There are just enough places, mostly at the mid-mountain lift junctions, marked but not named on the resort piste map. 'More friendly and hospitable than in most French resorts,' says one reporter whose favourite was the Arolle, above Termignon. Another reporter favours the Relais du Col, at Col du Mont Cenis – 'delicious lunch'.

Schools and guides We have generally good reports on the local branch of the ESF, though there are dissenting voices. Not surprisingly in a resort that still has a low international profile, lack of good spoken English is one of the occasional problems.

Families 'A good resort,' says a reporter whose children particularly enjoyed the bowling in Lanslevillard.

STAYING THERE

Chalets We don't know of any.

Hotels The best in principle is the 3-star Moulin de Marie in Lanslebourg (0479 059420). It shares its restaurant with the next-door sister hotel, the 2-star Clé des Champs (0479 059410), apparently housed in a converted sheep barn – 'friendly, good service, plain but good food'. The pair are a 'not too bad' 250m from the lift in the

morning. There are half a dozen other 2-stars to choose from.

Apartments There is an excellent range of self-catering lodgings. Top of that range is the CGH residence Les Chalets de Flambeau, built by MGM two years ago at Les Champs, midway between the main villages, and stylishly furnished. Highly recommended by a reporter who has stayed twice – 'very comfortable, lovely view from the balconies, friendly staff'. 'Fantastic' pool, paddling pool, hot tubs, sauna and fitness. Another reader rates the Balcons du Village, within walking distance of Lanslevillard and the Le Haut gondola – 'great location at the base of the slopes; comfortable, spacious and great value'. Peak Retreats offers these and three other attractive residences.

Eating out There is a limited but adequate range of options. A repeat visitor speaks highly of L'Arcelle in Lanslevillard – 'good range of delicious food, from fondue to duck with bilberry sauce'.

Après-ski Après-ski is quiet, but there are 'some nice bars', says one reporter.

Off the slopes Lanslevillard has all the key facilities – a pool/spa complex, an artificial outdoor ice rink, a popular bowling alley with a lively bar, and a toboggan run down the length of the gondola at Le Haut.

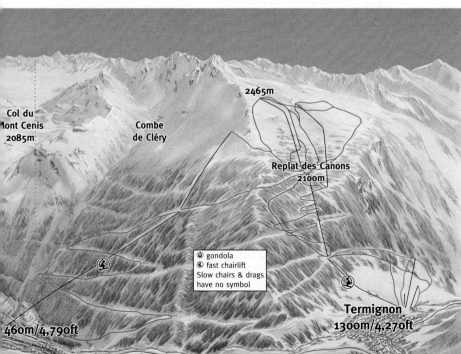

Val d'Isère

One of the great high mega-resorts, particularly (though not only) for experts – with an attractive town at the base

RATINGS

The mountains

Extent	*****
Fast lifts	****
Queues	****
Terrain p'ks	***
Snow	*****
Expert	*****
Intermediate	*****
Beginner	***
Boarder	****
X-country	*
Restaurants	***
Schools	*****
Families	****

The resort

Charm	***
Convenience	***
Scenery	***
Eating out	*****
Après-ski	****
Off-slope	**

RPI	110
lift pass	£210
ski hire	£120
lessons	£80
food & drink	£155
total	**£565**

KEY FACTS

Resort	1850m
	6,070ft

Espace Killy	
Slopes	1550-3455m
	5,090-11,340ft
Lifts	78
Pistes	300km
	186 miles
Green	15%
Blue	42%
Red	26%
Black	17%
Snowmaking	
	974 guns

Val d'Isère only	
Slopes	1785-3300m
	5,860-10,830ft
Lifts	43
Pistes	150km
	93 miles

+ Huge area shared with Tignes, with lots of runs for all abilities

+ One of the great resorts for lift-served off-piste runs

+ Once the snow has fallen, high altitude of slopes keeps it good

+ Wide choice of schools, especially for off-piste lessons and guiding

+ For a high Alpine resort, the town is attractive, is lively at night, and offers a good range of restaurants

+ Wide range of package holidays, including some comfortable chalets

– Some green and blue runs are too challenging, and all runs back to the village are tricky

– You're quite likely to need buses at the start and end of the day (but they are very frequent and efficient)

– Many lifts and slopes are liable to close when the weather is bad

– At times it seems more British than French, especially in low season

– Expensive eating and drinking; it's one of the priciest resorts in France for this – and readers complain

Val d'Isère is one of the world's best resorts for experts – who are attracted by the extent of lift-served off-piste – and for confident, mileage-hungry intermediates. You don't have to be particularly adventurous to enjoy the resort; but it would be much better for novices and timid intermediates if the piste classifications were more reliable.

The drawbacks listed above are mainly not serious complaints, whereas most of the plus-points weigh heavily in the balance. For a combination of seriously impressive skiing and very pleasant village ambience, there are few places we'd rather go.

THE RESORT

Val d'Isère spreads along a remote valley that is a dead end in winter. The road in from Bourg-St-Maurice brings you dramatically through a rocky defile to La Daille – a convenient but hideous slope-side apartment complex and the base of lifts into the major Bellevarde sector of the slopes.

Carry on into the centre of town and turn right, and you drive under the nursery slopes and major lifts up to both the Bellevarde and Solaise sectors to a lot of new development. Continue up the main valley instead, and you come first to Le Laisinant, a peaceful little outpost with a fast lift into the slopes, and then to Le Fornet, the fourth major lift station.

The developments up the side valley beyond the main lift station – in Le Châtelard and La Legettaz – are mainly attractive, and some offer ski-in/ski-out convenience. La Daille and Le Fornet have their (quite different) attractions for those less concerned about nightlife. A car is of no great value around the resort.

VILLAGE CHARM ***
Developing nicely

The outskirts of Val proper are dreary, but as you approach the centre, the improvements put in place over the past 20 or so years – mainly wood- and stone-cladding culminating in the tasteful pedestrian-only Val Village complex – become evident. Many first-time visitors find the resort much more

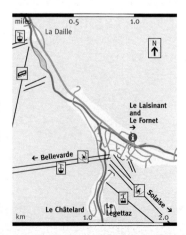

2013/14: The four-star Grand Paradis hotel is due to be upgraded to a 5-star. More snowmaking is planned for the red Josery run back to town on Bellevarde.

2012/13: The slow Fontaine Froide quad chairlift on Bellevarde was replaced by a six-pack that starts from the same place but finishes at the top near the Olympique gondola. Kids Park, a new terrain park for children, was opened under the Borsat chair on Bellevarde with jumps, rails and a natural half-pipe. More snow-guns were installed on the blue Magard run down to Le Fornet.

L'Atelier d'Edmond restaurant at Le Fornet gained a Michelin star.

The main part of the village, seen from Solaise, with La Daille in the distance ↓

pleasant than they expected – 'Val has a lovely atmosphere and charm about it that surprised me,' said a first-timer.

CONVENIENCE ★★★★★
Mostly fine
There is a lot of traffic around, but the resort has worked hard to get cars under control and has made the centre more pedestrian-friendly. The location of your accommodation isn't crucial, unless you want to ski from the door or be close to a nursery slope. The main lift stations are served by very efficient and amazingly frequent free shuttle-buses; but in peak periods you may have to let a few full ones pass before there's space to board. After 8pm they run every 30 minutes until 2.45am.

SCENERY ★★★★★
Valley deep, mountain high
The resort sprawls along a steep-sided river valley, beneath a series of high and partly-wooded mountain ridges. There are splendid views from the Pissaillas glacier.

THE MOUNTAINS
Although there are wooded slopes above the village on all sectors, in practice most of the runs here are on open slopes above the treeline, and a lot of lifts can close in bad weather. Several visitors confirm that piste grooming and signposting are good.

> **Stylish chalets and serious skiing? Check out p258.**

But Val d'Isère vies with St Anton for the title of 'resort with most under-classified slopes'. Many blue and some green runs (including runs to the valley) are simply too steep, narrow and even bumpy; in other resorts they would be reds, or even blacks; we have a hefty file of complaints from readers (including nearly all our 2013 reporters) who agree with our judgement. The piste map has 'quiet skiing' zones marked on it. The local radio (96.1 FM) carries weather reports in English as well as in French.

EXTENT OF THE SLOPES ★★★★★
Vast and varied
Val d'Isère's slopes divide into three main sectors, two reachable from the village. Bellevarde is the mountain that is home to Val d'Isère's two famous downhill courses: the OK piste that is used for the World Cup every December and the Face piste that was used for the 1992 Winter Olympics and the 2009 World Championships. You can reach Bellevarde quickly by underground funicular from La Daille or the powerful Olympique gondola from near the centre of town. From the top you can descend to the valley, play on a variety of drags and chairs at altitude or take a choice of lifts to Tignes' slopes (see separate chapter).

Solaise is the other mountain accessible directly from the village. The Solaise fast quad takes you a few metres higher than the parallel cable car. Once up, a short drag or rope tow takes you over a plateau and down to a variety of chairs that serve this very sunny area of predominantly gentle pistes. From near the top of this area you can catch the fast Leissières chair (which climbs over a ridge and down the other side) to the third main area, in the valley running up to the Col de l'Iseran. This area can also be reached by the fast chair from Le Laisinant or by cable car from Le Fornet. At the top here is the **Glacier de Pissaillas**.

FAST LIFTS ★★★★★
Access all areas
High-capacity lifts provide good access from the valley and there are lots of fast chairs higher up. But there are still a few slow chairs and draglifts around.

Val d'Isère

Build your own shortlist: **www.wheretoskiandsnowboard.com**

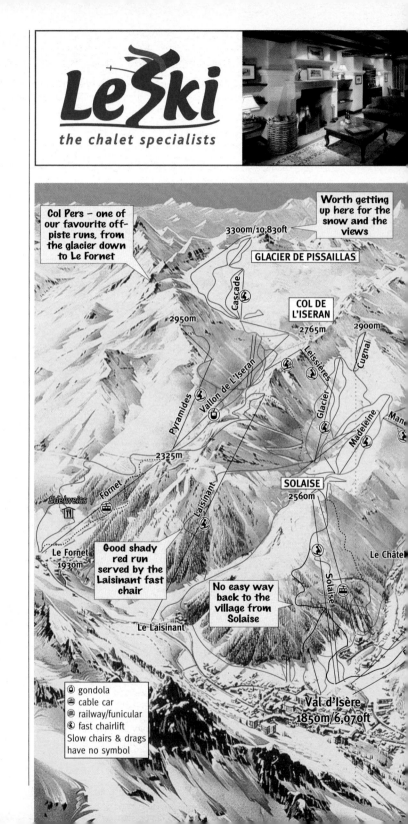

Le Ski the chalet specialists

Col Pers – one of our favourite off-piste runs, from the glacier down to Le Fornet

Worth getting up here for the snow and the views

3300m/10,830ft

GLACIER DE PISSAILLAS

Cascade

2950m

COL DE L'ISERAN
2765m

2900m

Leissières

Cugnai

Vallon de l'Iseran

Pyramides

Glacier

Madeleine

Mane

2325m

SOLAISE
2560m

Edelweiss

Fornet

Laisinant

Le Châte

Le Fornet
1930m

Good shady red run served by the Laisinant fast chair

Solaise

No easy way back to the village from Solaise

Le Laisinant

Val d'Isère
1850m/6,070ft

🍥 gondola
🚡 cable car
🚋 railway/funicular
🚠 fast chairlift
Slow chairs & drags have no symbol

ISSAILLAS

Good area of varied intermediate runs at altitude, with a couple of fast chairs

DE
ERAN
55m

2900m

Cugnai

Excellent runs down to the Manchet chair – though affected by sun later in the season

Madeleine

Manchet

Le Manchet
1940m

issières

Glacier

Lots of long, high easy runs – but also lots of slow old lifts

Grand Pte

The blue from here is the easiest and least crowded intermediate route to Tignes

Glacier de la
Grande Motte

COL DE FRESSE
2770m

Borsat

Tignes
Fresse

TOVIERE
2705m

BELLEVARDE
2705m

Fontaine Froid

Marmottes

SE
m

Loyes

Le Châtelard

Solaise

L'Olympique

Funival

Bellevarde

Tommeuses

The world's trickiest green run – narrow in parts and crowded and mogulled at the end of the day

Daille

The 1992 Winter Olympic men's downhill course is now a genuine black run and often mogulled from top to bottom

Val d'Isère
50m/6,07oft

La Daille
1785m/5,86oft

QUEUES ★★★★★
Few problems

Queues to get out of the resort have been kept in check by lift upgrades and additions – but there can be a short wait at the Olympique gondola up Bellevarde. On Solaise the slow Lac chair back up to the Tête Solaise can generate queues, but a recent reporter praises the 'good queueing systems', with 'each chair filled to capacity'. Crowded pistes in high season is a more common complaint than queues.

TERRAIN PARKS ★★★★★
Beginners and experts welcome

Above the La Daille gondola and served by the Mont Blanc chairlift lies the Valpark (www.valdisere-snowpark. com). Maintenance can be a bit hit or miss – but a recent April visitor said:

'My son really enjoyed messing about in the park which, all credit to those responsible, was kept open and maintained as well as possible in warm conditions.' There are lots of table jumps, boxes and rails of all shapes and sizes plus a large hip, 3m wall ride and four kicker lines, with up to five jumps in a row ranging from 3m in the blue line to 20m in the pro line. There's also a cool zone in the middle of the park, where you can just sit back and enjoy the show, and a boardercross nearby. New last season was the Kids Park, where all ages can learn to ride, with small jumps, wide rails and a natural half-pipe. But head to Tignes for a proper half-pipe.

SNOW RELIABILITY ★★★★★
One of the best

In years when lower resorts have suffered, Val d'Isère has rarely been short of snow. Even in a poor snow year such as 2010/11, decent skiing was still available right until the end of the season. Once a big dump of snow has fallen, the resort's height means you can almost always get back to the village. But what's even more important is that in each sector there are lots of lifts and runs above mid-mountain, between about 2300m and 2900m. Many of the slopes face roughly north. And there is access to

---

THE BEST LIFT-SERVED OFF-PISTE IN THE WORLD?

Few resorts can rival the extent of lift-served off-piste skiing in Val d'Isère. Here is a selection of what's on offer. But don't try any of it without a guide and essential safety equipment.

Some runs are ideal for adventurous intermediates looking to try off-piste for the first time. The **Tour du Charvet** *was Editor Watts' first-ever off-piste run; it goes through glorious scenery from the top of the Grand Pré chairlift on the back of Bellevarde. For most of the way it is very gentle, with only a few steeper pitches. It ends up at the bottom of the Manchet chair up to the Solaise area. The* **Pays Désert** *is an easy run with superb views on the Pissaillas glacier, high above Le Fornet and reached by traversing from the top of the lift system. You end up at the Pays Désert draglift.*

For more experienced off-piste skiers, **Col Pers** *is one of our favourite runs. Again, it starts with a traverse from the Pissaillas glacier. You go over a pass into a big, fairly gentle bowl with glorious views and endless ways down. If there is enough snow, you drop down into the Gorges de Malpasset and ski over the frozen Isère river back to the Fornet cable car. If not, you can take a higher route.*

Cugnai *is a wide, secluded bowl reached from the chair of the same name at the top of the Solaise sector. A steep (37 degree) slope at the far end descends beneath a sheer black rock wall and then narrows into a gully to the valley floor, leading to the Manchet chair.*

Banane *is reached via the Face de Bellevarde piste and is a long and impressive run (37 to 40 degrees) with spectacular views over the Manchet valley. For a real challenge intrepid experts should try the* **Couloir des Pisteurs,** *which requires a 20-minute climb from the Tour de Charvet. The view from the top is simply stunning. A very narrow steep couloir (44 degrees) bounded by rock faces brings you out on to a wide open slope above Le Grand Pré, right opposite Bellevarde.*

Then there's the whole of Tignes' extensive off-piste to explore, of course.

LIFT PASSES

Espace Killy

Prices in €

Age	1-day	6-day
under 14	38	188
14 to 64	47	235
65 plus	38	188

Free under 5, over 75
Beginner five free lifts on nursery slopes;

Notes
Covers Tignes and Val d'Isère; half-day and pedestrian passes; family discounts; 5-day-plus passes valid for a day in the Three Valleys and a day in Paradiski (La Plagne-Les Arcs); 2+ day pass gives one free entry to pool at Aqua Sports Centre

Alternative pass
Val d'Isère only

ACTIVITIES

Indoor Sports centre (with pools, climbing wall, fitness, gym, sauna, steam, squash, climbing wall), fitness and health clubs, cinema

Outdoor Ice rink, walking, snowshoeing, ice climbing, dog sledding, ice driving, paragliding, microlight flights, helicopter flights

glaciers at Pissaillas or over in Tignes. There's snowmaking too.

FOR EXPERTS ★★★★★
One of the world's best
Val d'Isère is one of the top resorts in the world for experts. The main attraction is the huge range of beautiful off-piste possibilities – see the feature panel opposite.

There may be better resorts for really steep pistes – there are certainly lots in North America – but there is plenty of on-piste action to amuse most experts, despite the small number of blacks on the piste map. And some of these have been converted to 'naturides', which means they are never groomed (a neat way of saving money!) but they are marked, patrolled and avalanche protected. Many reds and blues are also steep enough to get mogulled.

On Bellevarde the famous Face run is the main attraction – often mogulled from top to bottom, but not worryingly steep and it's a wonderful blast if it's been groomed. Epaule is the sector's other black run; where the moguls are hit by long exposure to sun it can be slushy or rock hard (it is prone to closure for these reasons too). Most of the blacks on Solaise and above Le Fornet are now naturides (and the proper black from Solaise to the valley is no steeper than the alternative red).

Wayne Watson of off-piste school Alpine Experience puts a daily diary of off-piste snow conditions and runs on the web at www.alpineexperience.com.

FOR INTERMEDIATES ★★★★★
Quantity and quality
Val d'Isère has just as much to offer intermediates as experts. There's enough here to keep you interested for several visits – though pistes can be crowded in high season, and the less experienced should be aware that

many runs are underclassified.

The Solaise sector has a network of gentle blue runs, ideal for building confidence. And there are a couple of beautiful runs from here through the woods to Le Laisinant – ideal in bad weather, though prone to closure in times of avalanche danger.

Most of the runs in the Col de l'Iseran sector are even easier – ideal for early and hesitant intermediates. Those marked blue at the top of the glacier could really be classified green.

Bellevarde has a huge variety of runs ideally suited to intermediates of all levels. From Bellevarde itself there is a choice of green, blue and red runs of varying pitch. The World Cup downhill OK piste is a wonderful rolling cruise when groomed. The wide runs from Tovière normally offer the choice of groomed piste or moguls.

A snag for early intermediates is that runs back to the valley can be challenging. The easiest way is down to La Daille on a green run that would be classified blue or red in most resorts. It gets very crowded and mogulled by the end of the day. None of the runs from Bellevarde and Solaise back to Val itself is easy. Many early intermediates ride the lifts down.

FOR BEGINNERS ★★★★★
OK if you know where to go
The nursery slope right by the centre of town is 95% perfect; it's just a pity that the very top is unpleasantly steep. The lifts serving it are free.

Once off the nursery slopes, you have to know where to find easy runs; many of the greens should be blue, or even red. One local instructor admits: 'We have to have green runs on the map, even if we don't have so many green slopes – otherwise beginners wouldn't come to Val d'Isère.'

A good place for your first real runs off the nursery slopes is the Madeleine

SCHOOLS

Alpine Experience
t 0479 062881

BASS
t 0679 512405

ESF
t 0479 060234

Evolution 2
t 0479 007729

iSki
t 0646 186413

Misty Fly
t 0479 073267

Mountain Masters
t 0479 060514

New Generation
t 0479 010318
0844 770 4733 (UK)
www.skinewgen.com

Oxygène
t 0479 419958

Progression
t 0621 939380

Pro Snowboarding
t 0632 285803

Ski Concept
t 0479 401919

Ski-lesson.com
t 0615 207108

Snow Fun
t 0479 061979

TDC
t 0615 553156

Top Ski
t 0479 061480

Classes (ESF prices)
6 days (3hr am, 2½hr pm) from €404

Private lessons
From €45 for 1hr

GUIDES

Mountain guides
t 0687 528503

Tetra
t 0631 499275

green run on Solaise (a 'quiet skiing' zone served by a six-pack). The Col de l'Iseran runs are also gentle and wide, and not overcrowded. There is good progression terrain (and a big 'quiet skiing' zone) on Bellevarde, too – though getting to it can be tricky. From all sectors, it's best to take a lift back down to the valley.

FOR BOARDERS ★★★★
Watch out for flats
Val d'Isère's more upmarket profile attracts a different kind of holiday boarder from Tignes; the resort is, perhaps, seen as Tignes' less hard-core cousin. But the terrain here is great for freeriders. The easier slopes are suitable for beginners, and there are very few draglifts. But there are quite a few flat areas where you'll end up scooting or walking. Specialist snowboard shops are Orage by Misty Fly and Quiksilver.

FOR CROSS-COUNTRY ★
Limited
There are a couple of loops in each of three areas – towards La Daille, on Solaise and out past Le Laisinant – totalling 20km. More picturesque is the loop going from Le Châtelard (on the road past the main cable car station) to the Manchet chair. But keen cross-country enthusiasts should go elsewhere.

MOUNTAIN RESTAURANTS ★★★
Acceptable – but expensive
For such an upmarket resort, there are surprisingly few enjoyable places to eat on the mountain. The major places are self-service and at the top of lifts. Everywhere gets busy and high-season service can be poor. And in nearly every report we get there are remarks on how 'hideously' expensive they are. The saving grace, says one reporter, is that portions are generally 'too large' and can be shared to cut the costs. Reporters' other major gripe is that in many mountain restaurants, even if you are eating there, you have to pay to use the loos.

Editors' choice The wood-and-stone Edelweiss (0610 287064), above Le Fornet, is our favourite for the best food and ambience. We've eaten there several times and had delicious lamb, duck and fish; reporters regularly send us rave reviews too ('Echo all you say; duck burger with foie gras is to die for,' says a recent visitor). It's a bit

cramped inside, and if it's a nice day, we prefer the sunny terrace.

Worth knowing about On Bellevarde, the Fruitière at the top of the La Daille gondola is kitted out with stuff from a dairy. It crams in too many people, but we had succulent duck there in 2012, and a 2013 reporter says, 'Never fails to impress, great interesting food, quick and friendly service.' The busy table-service Trifollet halfway down the OK run 'always has a good plat du jour' that is 'very reasonable compared to others'. The Marmottes, near the base of the chair of the same name, is consistently recommended by readers and one of the cheapest places to eat – an efficient self-service with a big sunny terrace, helpful staff and good food ('decent goulash and spag bol without requiring a second mortgage'). And the Tanière (popular with locals), set between the two chairs going up Face de Bellevarde, has been recommended.

On Solaise, reader tips include Tête de Solaise self-service at the top of the Solaise chair ('good choice and big portions'); there's a table-service section too, which a regular visitor recommends. The Datcha at the bottom of the Glacier Express has a small table-service section – 'all the dishes were tasty and reasonably priced by Val d'Isère standards'; 'great range of fresh salads including tuna and salmon'. The Bar de L'Ouillette, at the base of the Madeleine chairlift, has a fun terrace with artificial palm trees and deck chairs, is 'friendly' and 'advertises its free loos', but the queue at its tiny self-service counter may be slow-moving.

Above Le Fornet, the Signal at the top of the cable car has self- and table-service sections and a take-away snack bar – recent reporters recommend all three. You'll find us upstairs in the table-service section ('imaginative food, nicely presented', 'pricey but not bad value'). The snack bar served 'huge baguettes big enough to share'.

Of course there are lots of places in the resort villages. Arolay at Le Fornet does 'a sizzling tartiflette, a lovely place for a relaxed late lunch', and the Michelin-starred Atelier d'Edmond (decorated like a carpenter's workshop and opposite the Fornet cable car) is 'serious (expensive) dining with impeccable service, good for a treat'. The terrace of hotel Brussel's in Val d'Isère, right by the nursery slopes, has 'good food and excellent service'. The Sun Bar at the base of the Olympique cable car is 'surprisingly good value', as is the Tartine, used by many ski instructors. In town, the Perdrix Blanche is 'good for a treat', and the coffee shop in the Quiksilver store serves fresh smoothies and '17 different types of burger' – and gets packed on bad-weather days.

SCHOOLS AND GUIDES ★★★★★
A very wide choice
There is a huge choice of schools, guides and private instructors – just look at the list in the margin opposite. But as they all get busy, at peak periods it's best to book in advance. Practically all the schools run off-piste groups as well as on-piste lessons.

New Generation, a British-run school that operates in 10 resorts, has a branch here that is consistently highly praised: 'Excellent progress made with my nervous beginner, er, intermediate wife. A week of group lessons with only five in the group – can't praise them enough!' said a recent reporter; 'The morning we had was one of the highlights of our holiday – lots of fun and we learned a lot too,' said another. The Development Centre (TDC) is a group of British instructors that offers intensive clinics for all levels and has been recommended: 'I fully appreciated the back to basics approach – it made a massive difference to my control on steeps.'

We've also heard this year from satisfied clients of Evolution 2 ('kids' lessons good'), Oxygène ('friendly instructors for the kids') and Pro Snowboarding ('good mix of instruction and off-piste adventure').

Alpine Experience and Top Ski specialize in guided off-piste groups – an excellent way to get off-piste safely without the cost of hiring a guide as an individual. We have had great mornings out with both; reporters recommend both, too. iSki is also recommended for off-piste guiding. Heli-skiing trips can be arranged.

Henry's Avalanche Talks are now on demand at various venues – see www. henrysavalanchetalk.com for 2013/14 details – and are 'very engaging and interesting', says a reporter.

CHILDCARE

Le Village des Enfants
t 0479 400981
Ages 18mnth to 13yr

Le Petit Poucet
t 0479 061397
Ages from 3

Babysitter list
Contact tourist office

Ski schools
Most offer classes for ages 5 up

GETTING THERE

Air Geneva 230km/
145 miles (3hr30);
Lyon 240km/
150 miles (3hr15);
Chambéry 145km/
90 miles (2hr15)

Rail Bourg-St-Maurice
(30km/19 miles);
regular buses from
station

FOR FAMILIES ★★★★★
Good tour op possibilities

Many people prefer to use the facilities of UK tour operators such as family specialist Esprit Ski. But there's a 'children's village' for children from 18 months to 13 years, with supervised indoor and outdoor activities on the village nursery slopes. And Petit Poucet takes children from age three and will pick them up and take them home at any time during the day. However, a reporter who is a policeman says families need to be aware that the resort exudes a 'lager lout' feel at times.

STAYING THERE

More British tour operators go to Val (and Méribel) than anywhere else. Val d'Isère à la Carte specializes in arranging tailor-made holidays there.
Chalets This is Planet Chalet, with properties at every level of the market. Many of the most impressive are in the side valley running south from the village – some in the elevated enclave of Les Carats. YSE is a Val d'Isère specialist, with 21 varied chalets – from swanky apartments for four or six to proper big chalets. Le Ski has eight chalets, including six splendid all-en-suite places grouped together just up from the main street with free pick-up and drop-off service and a big outdoor hot tub. And new for 2013/14 is their luxury Chalet Angelique for 12 in a back street of La Daille that looks more like a mini-stately home than a chalet (with steam room and gym). Skiworld has 12 varied chalets from smart to budget, plus a smart 33-bedroomed chalet hotel with sauna, steam, hot tub. Ski Total has 18 smart places, including four very swanky ones in their Platinum range – one with outdoor hot tub, two with saunas, and new for this year one with

plunge pool and steam – plus a chalet hotel sleeping 80 at La Daille. Crystal has six chalets, including three smart central ones with saunas in their Finest range. Inghams has four chalets (one right on the nursery slope) and their flagship 24-bed chalet hotel with sauna, steam and hot tub in Le Fornet. Ski Olympic has an eight-bed chalet apartment near the centre. Esprit, the family specialist, has a central chalet hotel with 31 bedrooms.

There are some genuinely luxurious chalets from operators like Consensio and Scott Dunn.
Hotels There are over 30, with increasing numbers at the luxury end: six 5-stars and four 4-stars.
★★★★★Avenue Lodge (0479 006767) Central and fairly new. 'Very modern decor, comfortable rooms.'
★★★★★Barmes de L'Ours (0479 413700) The best in town. Close to slopes and centre. Rooms are in a different style on each floor. Excellent pool.
★★★★★Blizzard (0479 060207) Central. Comfortable. Indoor-outdoor pool and sauna. Good food and lively bar.
★★★★★Christiania (0479 060825) Big chalet. Chic but friendly. Pool, sauna.
★★★★Aigle des Neiges (0479 061888) Highly rated refurbished version of former Latitudes. Central. Sauna.
★★★★Auberge St Hubert (0479 060645) On main street. A recent reporter praises it – 'very friendly family hotel'.
★★★★Tsanteleina (0479 061213) Central on main street. Pool, hot tub, two steam rooms, sauna.
★★★Kandahar (0479 060239) Smart building above Taverne d'Alsace on main street.
★★★Samovar (0479 061351) In La Daille. Traditional, with good food.
★★★Sorbiers (0479 062377) Modern but cosy chalet, not far out.
★★Danival (0479 060065) B&B, piste-side location.
★★Galise (0479 060504) Central,

Phone numbers
From abroad use the prefix +33 and omit the initial '0' of the phone number

www.valdisere.com

family-run B&B. 'Comfortable, quiet.'
Forêt (0479 060040) Central, recently refurbished. 'Basic rooms, very friendly staff, outstanding food.'
Apartments There are thousands of apartments available. Among the best are Chalets du Jardin Alpin at the foot of Solaise, Chalets du Laisinant (at Le Laisinant) and Pierre & Vacances' Balcons de Bellevarde at La Daille and Chalets de Solaise (with outdoor pool) close to the centre. Ski Collection, Ski Amis, Ski Independence, Erna Low, Skitracer and local agency Val d'Isère Agence (0479 067350) have good selections. Skiworld has a central, flexible catered chalet where you can choose what catering (if any) you want, plus apartments. The supermarkets have been praised for 'enticing pre-cooked food'.

EATING OUT ★★★★★
Plenty of good places
The 70-odd restaurants offer a wide variety of cuisines; there's a free Guide Pratique (winter guide) booklet covering some, but many worthwhile places are missing.

At the top end, two places have a Michelin star: L'Atelier d'Edmond at Le Fornet (see 'Mountain restaurants') and La Table de l'Ours, in the Barmes de l'Ours hotel. The Grande Ourse, by the nursery slope, also serves top-notch meals ('superb food and charming service'). The rustic Vieille Maison ('excellent, good value') behind the main road at La Daille, hotel Aigle des Neiges' restaurants and Arolay at Le Fornet (see 'Mountain restaurants') are rated highly by locals.

There are plenty of pleasant mid-priced places. We always enjoy the unchanging Taverne d'Alsace. Bar Jacques is regularly recommended for its excellent food and set menu. Casserole and Pré d'Aval have both been recommended for their good-value set menus. Corniche has a 'lovely traditional ambience', 'good service and a range of well-cooked food'. A local says the Perdix Blanche is 'back on track with good service and a great menu; I went several times and it was always excellent'.

Other reporter tips: Chez Paolo is a 'good choice for family dining'; Casa Scara has 'good food'; The Grand Cocor has 'nice pizza'. Bar 1789 does 'great snails and fab ribbed beef'. Canyon has a new owner and 'should be good next year' says a local.

APRES-SKI ★★★★★
Not as lively as it was?
A couple of reporters last year remarked that après-ski was quieter than they expected. But there are lots of bars, many with happy hours and then music and dancing later on.

The Folie Douce, at the top of the La Daille gondola, has become an institution, with mega-loud music, DJs, packed crowds and dancing on tables on the terrace every afternoon; you can ride the gondola down. It has now been replicated in three other French resorts. The Tipi bar on the Glacier run on Solaise is a 'nice place to stop for an afternoon drink – open air with rug-covered loungers'.

At La Daille the bar at the Samovar hotel is a good spot for a quiet beer after skiing. In downtown Val, Blue Note (opposite the ESF) has a 'great low-key atmosphere' and 'offers free après-ski nibbles and a warm welcome'. Café Face is popular, with loud music. The Moris pub (live music at teatime and later) and Saloon (under hotel Brussel's) fill up as the slopes close; Boubou and Bar Jacques are popular with locals. The Pacific Bar has sport on big-screen TVs. The basement Taverne d'Alsace is quiet and relaxing, as are Bar XV, the first-floor bar of the hotel Blizzard, and Wine Not (with a 'great choice' of wines by the glass). The burger/coffee shop in the Quiksilver store serves fresh smoothies and attracts a 'cool young crowd'. The 'great fun' Grand Marnier serves 'tempting cocktails'.

Later on, Dick's Tea Bar is the main disco (go early evening for Val's 'best-value drinking', says a reporter). Doudoune is 'more expensive but nicer'. Graal is 'usually good'.

OFF THE SLOPES ★★★★★
A reasonable amount to do
The sports centre (with two pools, sauna, steam, gym, climbing wall) is consistently praised by reporters; a lift pass for two days or more gets you one free swim. There's an outdoor ice rink and ice driving, and the range of shops is better than in most high French resorts. There are a few mountain restaurants that are easy for pedestrians to get to. A reporter says the nature walk from Le Fornet to Pont St Charles in late season is fascinating, and 2013 reporters enjoyed the January 'polo on snow' tournament despite the –25ºC temperatures.

Val Thorens

Europe's highest resort, with guaranteed good snow – and other attractions, stylish lodgings and good restaurants among them

RATINGS

The mountains

Extent	★★★★★
Fast lifts	★★★★★
Queues	★★★★
Terrain p'ks	★★★★
Snow	★★★★★
Expert	★★★★
Intermediate	★★★★★
Beginner	★★★★
Boarder	★★★★
X-country	★
Restaurants	★★★★
Schools	★★★
Families	★★★

The resort

Charm	★★
Convenience	★★★★★
Scenery	★★★
Eating out	★★★★
Après-ski	★★★★
Off-slope	★★

RPI 110

lift pass	£230
ski hire	£120
lessons	£80
food & drink	£155
total	**£585**

KEY FACTS

Resort	2300m
	7,550ft

Trois Vallées	
Slopes	1260-3230m
	4,130-10,600ft
Lifts	173
Pistes	600km
	373 miles
Green	16%
Blue	40%
Red	34%
Black	10%
Snowmaking	50%

Val Thorens-Orelle only	
Slopes	1800-3230m
	5,900-10,600ft
Lifts	32
Pistes	150km
	93 miles
Green	14%
Blue	37%
Red	39%
Black	10%

376

- Extensive slopes for all abilities,
- The highest resort in the Alps, and one of the most snow-sure
- Fastest lift system in France
- Compact, with ski-in/out lodgings
- Convenient, gentle nursery slopes
- Decent range of hotels and some very smart apartments

- Not a tree in sight
- Away from the 'front de neige', not an attractive place to walk around
- Not ideal for non-skiers
- Some very crowded pistes and dangerous intersections
- Queues for the justifiably popular Cîme de Caron cable car

For the enthusiast looking for the best snow available and fast lifts to whizz you around, it's difficult to beat Val Thorens. For a late trip, in particular, it's the best base in the wonderful Trois Vallées. But we normally prefer a cosier base lower down. That way, if a storm socks in, we can play in the woods; if the sun is scorching, we have the option of setting off for Val Thorens.

THE RESORT

Val Thorens is a classic purpose-built resort, high above the treeline at the head of the valley it shares with Les Menuires and St-Martin. Buses to/from Les Menuires are supposed to carry just pedestrians and cross-country skiers, not downhillers – crazy!

VILLAGE CHARM ★★★★★
Functional but pleasantly so
Seen from the slopes, the resort is not as ugly as many of its rivals, and it has quite a lively ski resort buzz. Buildings are mainly medium-rise and wood-clad; some are distinctly stylish. But many are designed with their smart 'fronts' facing the slopes, and look very dreary from behind – the walk up the road to the centre from plush lodging in the lower part of the village is very dull. The streets are supposedly traffic-free except for loading. But workers' cars generate traffic and Saturdays can be mayhem. You're advised to book parking in advance; we prefer lodgings with an underground garage.

CONVENIENCE ★★★★★
Ski through the centre
It's a compact village with lots of ski-in/ski-out lodging. At its heart is the snowy Place de Caron, on the slope side rather than the street side of the central buildings, where pedestrians mix with skiers and boarders. Many of the shops and restaurants are here, along with some nice hotels; the sports and leisure centres are nearby.
The resort is divided in two by a little slope (with a moving carpet lift) that leads down from here to the broad nursery slope running the length of the village (also served by moving carpets). The upper half of the village is centred on the Place de Péclet, where there is one of two shopping malls. A road runs across the hillside from here to the chalet-style Plein Sud area, where many of the catered chalets run by UK tour operators are located. You can ski to and from some of these places, but it's often very tricky – walking can be too (we've had complaints of icy, uncleared paths).
The lower end of the village has some of the plushest lodgings, including 5-star places.
A free ski-bus runs every half hour on two separate routes.

SCENERY ★★★★★
Panoramas on high
The resort sits on a sunny, west-facing slope. The views are good from the village, fabulous from the high point at Cîme de Caron.

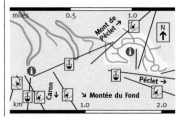

2013/14: Two six-packs are due to replace slow quad chairs: 3 Vallées 1 from the resort towards Méribel and Pyron from Plan Bouchet in the 'fourth valley'. A fast quad is due to replace the slow 3 Vallées 2 chair which meets 3 Vallées 1 and takes you to the top. And the 2 Lacs fast quad from just below the village is to be rebuilt to increase capacity. A new Duo Pass will allow two people buying lift passes together to get a reduction.

A new luxury hotel and residence, the Koh-i-Nor, is due to open.

2012/13: The Péclet gondola was revamped with the addition of nine cabins to increase capacity by 25%. The 4-star Hameau du Kashmir residence opened. The hut at the top of the Cîme de Caron changed hands and became the Freeride Cafe with funkier decor and food. A Pass Tribu was introduced – allowing three or more people buying lift passes together to get a reduction. And with the new family pass two adults and two or more children now all pay the child rate.

The main disadvantage of Val Thorens is the lack of trees. Heavy snowfalls or high wind can shut practically all the lifts and slopes, and even if they don't close, poor visibility can be a problem. Some blue runs are pretty tough.

EXTENT OF THE SLOPES ★★★★★
High and snow-sure
The resort has a wide piste going right down the front of it, leading down to a number of different lifts. The big **Péclet** gondola heads more or less east from the resort and rises 700m to the Péclet glacier, with a choice of red runs or a blue down. Two of these link across to a wide area of runs beneath the ridge directly south of the resort, the high point of which is the **Pointe de Thorens**. Lifts go up to three other points on the ridge. You can take very sunny red or blue runs into the 'fourth valley', the Maurienne, from the Col de Rosaël on the ridge, served by the Grand Fond jumbo gondola.

Above **Orelle** in the Maurienne valley a new six-pack due for 2013/14 followed by a slow quad go up to 3230m on the flanks of Pointe du Bouchet, the highest lift-served point in the Trois Vallées – stunning views. The former black run off the back here is now off-piste because of crevasse and avalanche danger.

The 150-person cable car to **Cîme de Caron** is one of the great lifts of the Alps, rising 900m in no time at all. It can be reached by skiing across from mid-mountain, or via the Caron

gondola that starts below the village. From the top there is a choice of red and black pistes down the front, or a black into the Maurienne. Nearby, the relatively low **Boismint** sector is underused, but it is a very respectable hill with a total vertical of 860m.

Chairlifts heading north from the resort serve sunny slopes above the village and also lead to the link to the Méribel valley. Les Menuires can be reached via these lifts; the alternative Boulevard Cumin along the valley is nearly flat, and can be hard work.

FAST LIFTS ★★★★★
France's fastest lift system
Recent investment means the lift system is impressive, with jumbo gondolas and fast chairs in most of the key places. The three new fast chairs for 2013/14 will mean that 75% of all major lifts are fast – many more than any other French resort.

QUEUES ★★★★
Mainly for the Cîme de Caron
Serious peak-time queues for the Cîme de Caron cable car are the norm. We think it's time a ticket system was operated here, so that you can ski while you wait. Reporters also mention short queues for the Plein Sud chair back towards Méribel and for the Deux Lacs chair further down the slope; but both these should be eased by 2013/14 lift improvements.

Crowded pistes, especially around the village, are a bigger problem than queues – compounded by people going too quickly. We have noticed

Val Thorens

377

Being Europe's highest resort means reliably good snow. But the lack of trees means it can be bleak in bad weather ➔

this on recent visits, and lots of reporters have commented on it, too. We agree with a recent reporter who suggests that it is time the resort imposed slow skiing zones around the village – and policed them.

TERRAIN PARKS ★★★★
Well designed

The terrain park on the 'Plateau' has been improving year-on-year. It is accessible via various chairlifts, is served by a dedicated draglift and has a nice open layout. There are different areas that range from beginner to pro, with all sorts of tables, rails and box combinations, plus an airbag jump.

The hip/corner jump is excellent. The whole park is well maintained, and new obstacles are often built for local competitions. Riders can be filmed and then see their exploits on a big screen. A separate boardercross lower down has some great banked turns.

SNOW RELIABILITY ★★★★★
One of the best

Few resorts can rival Val Thorens for reliably good snow-cover, thanks to its altitude and generally north-facing slopes. Snowmaking covers a lot of the key pistes, including the crowded south- and west-facing runs on the way back from the Méribel valley and

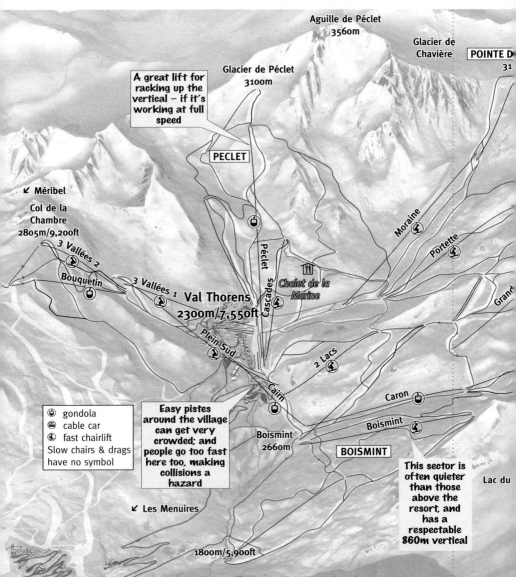

Aguille de Péclet
3560m

Glacier de Chavière

POINTE D

31

Glacier de Péclet
3100m

A great lift for racking up the vertical – if it's working at full speed

PECLET

↙ Méribel

Col de la Chambre
2805m/9,200ft

3 Vallées 2

Bouquetin

3 Vallées 1

Péclet

Cascades

Chalet de la Marine

Moraine

Portette

Grand

Val Thorens
2300m/7,550ft

Plein Sud

2 Lacs

Cairn

Caron

Boismint

BOISMINT

Boismint
2666m

Easy pistes around the village can get very crowded; and people go too fast here too, making collisions a hazard

gondola
cable car
fast chairlift
Slow chairs & drags have no symbol

↙ Les Menuires

This sector is often quieter than those above the resort, and has a respectable 860m vertical

Lac du

1800m/5,900ft

in the Orelle sector. But the terrain is rocky and needs a lot of snow for good coverage – we have found the higher runs patchy in some early season visits when snow throughout the Alps has been slow to arrive, and at times like that the off-piste terrain is obviously hazardous.

FOR EXPERTS ★★★★☆
Lots to do off-piste
Val Thorens' local pistes are primarily intermediate terrain; many of the blacks could easily be classified red instead. The fast Cascades chair serves a short but steep black run that quickly gets mogulled. The pistes down from the Cîme de Caron cable car are challenging, but not seriously steep, and there's a good, sunny black run off the back into the fourth valley.

The Falaise and Variante runs from the Grand Fond gondola can get heavily mogulled and be challenging. The sunny Goitshel run, one of the routes from the Méribel valley, is one of the easiest blacks we've seen, but it can be icy in the morning and slushy in the afternoon.

There is a huge amount of very good off-piste terrain to explore with a guide; read our feature panel overleaf. But it does require good snowfall – note our remarks in 'Snow reliability'.

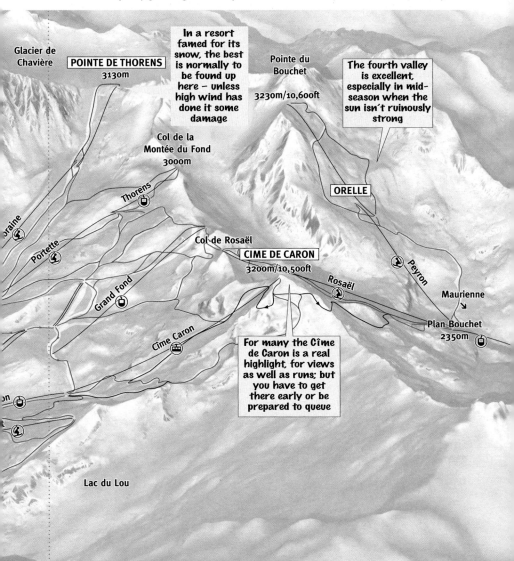

Glacier de Chavière

POINTE DE THORENS
3130m

In a resort famed for its snow, the best is normally to be found up here – unless high wind has done it some damage

Pointe du Bouchet

3230m/10,600ft

The fourth valley is excellent, especially in mid-season when the sun isn't ruinously strong

Col de la Montée du Fond
3000m

Thorens

ORELLE

Col de Rosaël

CIME DE CARON
3200m/10,500ft

Portette

Rosaël

Peyron

Grand Fond

Maurienne

Plan Bouchet
2350m

Cîme Caron

For many the Cîme de Caron is a real highlight, for views as well as runs; but you have to get there early or be prepared to queue

Lac du Lou

LIFT PASSES

Trois Vallées

Prices in €

Age	1-day	6-day
under 13	42	208
13 to 64	53	260
65 plus	48	234

Free Under 5, 75 plus

Beginner Access to Cairn, 2 Lacs and Caron lifts for 50% of Val Thorens rate; free access to one draglift and four magic carpets

Notes Covers Courchevel, La Tania, Méribel, Val Thorens, Les Menuires and St-Martin; reductions for family and groups of 3+; pedestrian and half-day passes

Alternative passes
Val Thorens-Orelle only; Vallée de Belleville only

FOR INTERMEDIATES ★★★★★
Great in good weather

The scope for intermediates in the Trois Vallées is enormous. A keen intermediate can get to Courchevel 1650 at the far end in only 90 minutes or so, if not distracted on the way.

The local slopes in Val Thorens are some of the best intermediate terrain in the region. Most of the pistes are easy reds and blues (steeper on the top half of the mountain than the bottom) and made even more enjoyable by the excellent snow.

The snow on the red Col run is normally some of the best around. The blue Moraine below it is gentle and popular with the schools. The Grand Fond gondola serves a good variety of blue and red runs. The red and blue runs from the Péclet gondola are excellent. The Pluviomètre from the Trois Vallées chair is a glorious varied run, away from the lifts. Adventurous intermediates shouldn't miss the Cîme de Caron runs: the black here is very wide, usually has good snow, and is a wonderful fast cruise when freshly groomed (though reports suggest this is less likely than it was). Don't

neglect the excellent, quiet Boismint area next door to Caron, either.

Blue-run skiers can now venture to the fourth valley, with the return run improved a few years back to become a blue (though not an easy one).

FOR BEGINNERS ★★★★
Good late-season choice

The slopes at the foot of the resort are very gentle and provide convenient, snow-sure nursery slopes, with moving carpet lifts and green runs. These are free, and there is a cheap pass for three serious lifts on the lower slopes – an excellent package. There are no long green runs to progress to, but the blues immediately above the village are easy. The resort's height and bleakness make it cold in midwinter, and intimidating in bad weather.

FOR BOARDERS ★★★★
Reliable all season

Val Thorens has always been popular with snowboarders; it is the highest and most snow-sure of the Trois Vallées resorts, and has a younger feel compared with Courchevel and Méribel – though it's almost as pricey. Being far above the treeline, the slopes are rather bleak; however, there are great steep runs, gullies and groomed pistes for all levels. The terrain park is worth a visit. The lifts are mainly chairs and gondolas.

FOR CROSS-COUNTRY ★
Go to Les Menuires

There are no cross-country trails in Val Thorens. Your best bet is the 28km link between Les Menuires and St-Martin-de-Belleville.

FABULOUS OFF-PISTE IN VAL THORENS

Val Thorens offers a huge choice of off-piste to be explored with a guide. And because of the high altitude, the snow stays powdery longer here than in lower parts of the Trois Vallées.

For those with little off-piste experience, the Pierre Lory Pass run is ideal. It is a wide and gentle slope, reached by an easy traverse on the Chavière glacier from the top of the Col chairlift and with breathtaking views of the Aiguilles d'Arves in the Maurienne valley from the top. You then ski down the glacier du Bouchet, rejoining the lift system at Plan Bouchet.

For those with more off-piste experience, the Lac du Lou is a famous off-piste run of 1400m vertical that is easily accessible via various routes from the Cîme de Caron. Because many of the slopes face north or north-west it is not unusual to find good powder most of the ski season, even in late April. The views are stunning and you'll notice the quietness and vastness of the whole valley. La Combe sans Nom in the fourth valley is also accessible from the Cîme de Caron and is excellent for late season spring skiing conditions.

For the more adventurous there are many options, including hiking up from the Col chairlift to a long run over the Gébroulaz glacier down to Méribel-Mottaret.

SCHOOLS

ESF
t 0479 000286
Ski Cool
t 0479 000492
Prosneige
t 0479 010700
Attitude
t 0479 065772

Classes (ESF prices)
6 days €219
Private lessons
from €42 for 1hr for
1-2 people

CHILDCARE

Nurseries/mini-clubs (ESF)
t 0479 000286
Ages from 3mnth

Ski school
Ages 4 and over

GETTING THERE

Air Geneva 160km/
100 miles (2hr30);
Lyon 200km/
125 miles (2hr45);
Chambéry 120km/
75 miles (2hr15)

Rail Moûtiers
(37km/23 miles);
regular buses from
station

MOUNTAIN RESTAURANTS ★★★★☆
Lots of choice

For a high modern resort, the choice of restaurants is good, and improving. The piste map names the restaurants – unlike the maps of the other valleys. It's such a simple thing ...

Editors' choice We've had several good lunches in the rustic table-service section of the Chalet de la Marine (0479 000186). It has a big terrace with 'funky' music. The self-service section below is also good and has a wide choice. And the loos are 'the best on the piste'. The self-service Folie Douce and table-service Fruitière are modelled on the Val d'Isère originals, the latter with an interesting menu, well executed when we lunched there. Reporters in 2012 confirm that the après-lunch party is 'mental' – 'not to be missed'.

Worth knowing about The rustic Chalet des 2 Lacs is a reader favourite, and we had a good lunch here last season – warm, welcoming, log fire, good food. The Chalet des 2 Ours is repeatedly recommended for food ('great home-made pasta'), service and views; we visited when it was very quiet and had a good tarte tatin. The Aiguilles de Péclet 'serves massive portions'.

The piste map shows picnic areas.

SCHOOLS AND GUIDES ★★★☆☆
Good reports

Prosneige is a small school that limits class sizes to 10 and gets very good reports. A recent reporter used then two years running and 'could not praise them enough – they really brought the children's skiing on across a wide range of ability'. The ESF offers a wide choice of private and group classes, including freestyle and freeride courses. One reporter who was very pleased with their Club Med ESF teacher one year had a bad experience the next when put into an 'English-speaking ghetto' group where 'the instructor didn't do any teaching'. There are several guiding outfits.

FOR FAMILIES ★★★☆☆
Some facilities

There is a children's area, Espace Junior, beside the 2 Lacs chairlift, and a good family toboggan run. The tourist office produces a handy family guide to weekly activities. We lack reports on the ESF nursery.

Hot chalets beneath glacial slopes? Check out p258.

STAYING THERE

Accommodation is of a higher standard than in many purpose-built resorts – more comfortable and stylish.
Chalets Most catered chalets are apartments in quite big developments, mainly relatively new ones above the resort centre. This has the advantage that you often have the use of a pool, sauna, etc in the residence. There are no notably swanky places. Skiworld has 16 units, Crystal nine, Inghams six.

Ski Total has five that are more like actual chalets – two units in one, three in another, all with shared saunas. And it has a stand-alone chalet for 24 with use of the pool and sauna at a nearby residence. All look very smart.
Hotels Unusually for a high, purpose-built resort, there are plenty of hotels, and there's a Club Med, too.
★★★★★Altapura (0457 747474) This stylish 5-star with indoor/outdoor pool etc opened two seasons ago. A reporter liked its 'unfussy atmosphere with tip-top food and service' but found it 'ferociously expensive'.
★★★★Fitz Roy (0479 000478) Smart, with good service and lovely rooms. Good restaurant with flexible half-board menu. Pool, sauna, steam. Well placed at the heart of things.
★★★★Val Thorens (0479 000433) Next door to Fitz Roy. Was renovated for 2012/13 and upgraded to 4-star.
★★★Sherpa (0479 000070) Highly recommended by past reporters. Cosy, lots of wood. Ski-in/ski-out.
★★★Val Chavière (0479 000033) 'Friendly, fab position, good set menu,' says a recent reporter.
Apartments Val Thorens now has lots of smart chalet-style developments. These and many other residences are offered by UK operators and agents including Ski Collection, Ski Amis, Pierre & Vacances, Lagrange, Skiworld, Ski Independence and Skitracer.

In the Plein Sud area, above the main village, there are several chalet-style residences. Among the best are Chalet Altitude and Chalet Val 2400, sharing a pool. The Balcons de Val Thorens has a 'fantastic' spa with pool. The new luxury Koh-i-Nor is due to open for 2013/14. Many properties up here claim to be ski-in and possibly ski-out, but a couple of reporters have confirmed our own suspicion that access can be tricky.

Lower down near the entrance to the resort are some more very smart places, all with pool, sauna etc, including the Hameau du Kashmir (new for last season – we stayed there and found it comfortable and convenient, but a bit cramped), Montana Plein Sud, and Oxalys with a superb restaurant (see 'Eating out'). Skiworld has three 'flexible catered chalets' where you can choose what catering (if any) you want.

EATING OUT ★★★★
Star quality
The resort's 'Holiday Guide' is very helpful, with photos and some idea of the cuisine and prices.

Top of the range is the restaurant in the Oxalys, with two Michelin stars. We had a delicious and very inventive meal here; expensive, but worth it. The Fitz Roy and Val Thorens hotels also have serious restaurants. The Epicurien has gastro ambitions, too.

There are plenty of more modest places. A 2013 reader tips the Chamois d'Or ('superb, varied menu, became a regular'). Others liked the Petite Ferme ('decent food and prices, good pizzas'). For Savoyard stuff there's the Fondue ('friendly, intimate'), Auberge des Balcons, Chaumière and Cabane. The Vieux Chalet has a varied menu, including seafood and duck. The Steak Club found favour with a reporter who 'went three times – excellent pasta, steaks, burgers'. The Blanchot is a wine bar with a simple carte.

APRES-SKI ★★★★
Livelier than you might expect
Val Thorens is more lively than most high-altitude ski stations. The action now starts up the hill at the Folie Douce (see 'Mountain restaurants') or on the terrace of Club Med in the

village. The Red Fox up at Balcons is crowded at close of play, with karaoke. The Frog and Roastbeef at the top of the village is a long-established British ghetto. The Downunder and the Saloon are lively. Quieter bars include the cosy Rhum Box Cafe (aka Mitch's). Later on, the Malaysia cellar bar rocks from 11pm until the early hours with 'top quality' live bands and dancing.

OFF THE SLOPES ★★
Could be worse
Val Thorens is not ideal for non-skiers. But there's a sports centre with a small pool, saunas, hot tubs, gym etc and a leisure centre with bowling (pricey) and pool tables. Free weekly concerts are held in the church (recommended by a reporter), and there are twice-weekly street markets, a small cinema and an ice-driving course. The toboggan run (the longest in France) is 'great fun'. There are four walking trails marked on the reverse of the piste map. A pedestrian lift pass covers nine lifts, allowing access to some mountain restaurants and the Cîme de Caron (don't miss the panorama from there). Buses to St-Martin and Les Menuires run five times a day except Saturdays.

OUTLYING RESORT – 900m
ORELLE

Set at the foot of the gondola from the fourth valley (there's no piste down), Orelle isn't a recognizable resort, but offers good accommodation at a bargain price. A couple of hairpins up the hill from the lift base (there's a frequent ski-bus) is Hameau des Eaux, a smart complex of 200 apartments in eight chalet-style buildings, sharing a spa with decent pool – available through Peak Retreats and Zenith. It includes a small convenience store and a restaurant.

Vars / Risoul

Two high, purpose-built resorts in an attractive setting, with a traditional French atmosphere and a big linked area of slopes

TOP 10 RATINGS

Extent	★★★
Fast lifts	★
Queues	★★★★
Snow	★★★
Expert	★★
Intermediate	★★★★
Beginner	★★★★
Charm	★★
Convenience	★★★★
Scenery	★★★

RPI 90

lift pass	£170
ski hire	£90
lessons	£80
food & drink	£120
total	**£460**

NEWS

2012/13: In Vars a video park has been installed at the Eyssina park. Your riding is filmed and you get to watch how you perform later on the internet.

➕ Attractive, family-friendly resorts

➕ Fair-sized, uncrowded area of slopes

➕ High resorts, reasonably snow-sure, but with lots of tree-lined runs

➕ Among the cheapest resorts in the French Alps

➖ Still mainly draglifts and slow old chairs, though a few fast ones

➖ Few on-piste challenges for expert skiers and boarders

➖ Little to do off the slopes

➖ Fairly remote location

Were they nearer Geneva, Vars and its linked neighbour Risoul might be as well known as Les Arcs and Flaine. The slopes of their shared Forêt Blanche area are equally extensive, and the villages are more attractive than either. We went back a few seasons ago and loved it, despite the seriously flawed lift system.

Vars and Risoul are the most southerly French resorts to get a chapter in this book. Their shared ski area is distinguished in various other ways, too. The lift system is probably the most antiquated in these pages – hence the 1-star rating for fast lifts.

And the claimed 185km of pistes is one of the wildest exaggerations you will find anywhere, according to the Schrahe report discussed in our piste extent feature. Schrahe puts the total at a modest 73km, meaning that the resorts overstate it by 152%.

Vars 1850m

Vars includes several small, old villages on or near the approach road, chief among them Vars-Ste-Marie. There are lifts on the fringe of this village, but the focus for most visitors is higher, purpose-built Vars-les-Claux.

Village charm Vars-les-Claux has a lot of flat-roofed apartment blocks that look worse from up the mountain than from within the village. Reporters like the pleasant, relaxed atmosphere: 'A little gem,' says a reporter this year. Consider 'cosy' Ste-Marie, too.
Convenience It's a small place, but spread along a winding, quite steep road, with two main clusters of shops,

bars, restaurants and lodgings: the original focus at the base of the main gondola, and Point Show 10 minutes' walk up the hill. Each has nursery slopes and fast lifts into the slopes. Buildings spread beyond these points, varying in convenience.
Scenery Pretty wooded slopes surround the village, and Pic de Chabrières has fine views.

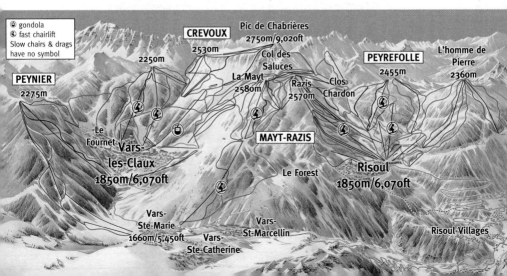

↑ Risoul's more recent developments are in something like chalet style, and the resort enjoys a fine setting
OT RISOUL

THE MOUNTAINS

There are slopes on both sides of the valley, linked by pistes and by slow double chairlifts at the lower end of Vars-les-Claux.

Some reporters have found piste classification variable and the map unclear on the links between resorts.

Slopes The wooded, west-facing Peynier area is the smaller sector, and reaches only 2275m. The main slopes are in an east-facing bowl with links to the Risoul slopes at three points. There's also a speed-skiing course. Beneath it are easy runs, open at the top but dropping into trees.

Fast lifts After the three fast lifts out of the village it's draglifts and slow chairs unless you head down to Vars-Ste-Marie or over to Risoul.

Queues Queues are rare outside the French holidays, and even then Vars is not as busy as most family resorts. But a January 2012 visitor was concerned about crowding on the slopes, with lots of eastern Europeans and Russians about.

Terrain parks There are six freestyle areas, including two newish ones – the Girly and Kid parks. Your riding can be filmed at the Eyssina park.

Snow reliability Not bad: the altitudes are quite high, the orientation mostly easterly, and snowmaking is plentiful.

Experts There is little to challenge experts on-piste, but there is plenty of off-piste terrain (and great off-piste tree skiing in Risoul, too).

Intermediates These are fine

intermediate slopes, with a good mix of decent reds and easy blues. Jas du Boeuf from La Mayt is a gentle cruise. The Olympique red run from the top of La Mayt to Ste-Marie delights most reporters and is a very respectable 920m vertical. If you can face the slow chairlifts and tricky drags, there are good tree-lined runs in the separate Peynier sector, including an easy black.

Beginners There are three free lifts on good slopes in central Vars, with lots of progression runs throughout the area. Quick learners will be able to get over to Risoul by the end of the week.

Snowboarding There is good freeriding, but beginners might find the number of draglifts a problem.

Cross-country There are 10km of trails.

Mountain restaurants Most places are self-service. But the revamped Chal Heureux table-service place is 'good, with acceptable food and prices'.

Schools and guides A recent reporter had 'great' private lessons with ESF.

Families The ski school runs a nursery for children from two years old, and there is a ski kindergarten.

STAYING THERE

Hotels The Ecureuil (0492 465072) is an attractive, modern B&B chalet. Ste-Marie has a Logis de France – the Vallon (0492 465472).

Apartments Ski Collection features five apartment complexes. Pierre & Vacances has two, including the 4-star Albane – liked by a reporter.

Eating out There is a choice of simple,

Vars / Risoul

KEY FACTS

Resort	1850m
	6,070ft

The entire Forêt Blanche ski area

Slopes	1660-2750m
	5,450-9,020ft
Lifts	52
Pistes	185km
	115 miles
Green	17%
Blue	39%
Red	35%
Black	9%
Snowmaking	
	116 guns

UK PACKAGES

Vars Crystal, Erna Low, Lagrange, Pierre & Vacances, PowderBeds, Ski Collection, Ski France
Risoul Crystal, Lagrange, PowderBeds, Rocketski, Ski Collection, Ski France, Skitracer, Thomson, Zenith

Phone numbers
From abroad use the prefix +33 and omit the initial '0' of the phone number

TOURIST OFFICES

Vars
www.vars-ski.com
Risoul
www.risoul.com

good-value places. The Après Ski at Point Show is worth a look, as is the Chaudron in Ste-Marie.

Après-ski Après-ski is animated at teatime. Later on, nightlife revolves around one or two bars.

Off the slopes There's tobogganing, ice skating, 34km of walking paths, cinema, snowmobiling, snowshoeing and dog sledding.

Risoul 1850m

Risoul 1850 is a modern ski station, purpose-built from the late 1970s onwards at the top of a winding road up from the original village of Risoul. It is a quiet, apartment-based resort, popular with families – but not exclusively so.

Village charm Many of the original resort buildings are bulky eight- or nine-storey buildings, but wood-clad with some traditional style. Newer developments are attractive and chalet-style, made of wood and stone. The busy little main street, with a small range of shops, bars and restaurants, is far from traffic-free. But the locals offer a friendly welcome.

Convenience The village meets the mountain in classic French purpose-built style, with sunny restaurant terraces facing the slopes and a compact centre. But some lodgings are a short but 'knackering' uphill walk away if you miss the last lift.

Scenery Risoul has a pleasantly woody setting beneath its slopes; reporters often comment on great views.

THE MOUNTAINS

The upper slopes are open, but those back to Risoul are prettily wooded, and good for bad-weather days.

Slopes The slopes, mainly north-facing, spread over several minor peaks and bowls, and connect with neighbouring Vars at two points.

Fast lifts There are three fast chairs accessing a good number of runs, but still lots of tricky 'difficile' draglifts.

Queues Queues are rare. But see the comment under Vars about crowds.

Terrain parks Since 2012/13 there has been only White Park for beginners, with easy jumps and rails and a boardercross but no half-pipe.

Snow reliability Snow reliability is reasonably good; the slopes are all above 1850m and mostly north-facing. Snowmaking is fairly extensive.

Experts Risoul's main top stations access a couple of steepish descents. And there's some good off-piste terrain – including excellent, widely spaced tree skiing on not very steep slopes and areas accessed through gates that are closed when there's an avalanche risk (though these are not marked or explained on the piste map).

Intermediates There are decent reds and blues in all sectors. Almost all Risoul's runs return to the village, making it difficult to get lost.

Beginners Three free lifts serve good, convenient nursery slopes. There are lots of easy pistes to move on to.

Snowboarding There is a lot of good freeriding to be done throughout the area, although beginners might not like the large proportion of draglifts.

Cross-country There are 15km of trails.

Mountain restaurants Choice is limited. The Homme de Pierre 'brings you decent dishes cooked to order', says a 2012 visitor. And the self-service Tetras is a small, attractive hut.

Schools and guides Reports on the ESF have been positive, and we had an excellent ESF guide on our visit.

Families Risoul is very much a family resort. The ESF operates a ski kindergarten slightly above the village and reached by a child-friendly lift.

STAYING THERE

Most visitors stay in apartments.

Hotels The Chardon Bleu (0492 460727) is right on the slopes. You can also stay overnight up at the Tetras mountain refuge (0492 452831).

Apartments We enjoyed the 4-star Balcons de Sirius units – good pool, hot tub and sauna; Antarés is similar. Ski Collection has these.

Eating out There's a decent choice offering fairly good value. Readers' tips: Chérine (pizza, pasta), Marmite and Entre Pot. We tried L'Extrad, which served huge portions of hearty food.

Après-ski Nightlife is livelier than most people are expecting. There are several bars and the Relex nightclub. Try the Babao and the Chalet or Eterlou for a quieter drink.

Off the slopes Limited. We enjoyed the guided night-time snowmobiling on adventurous and varied terrain. There's also tobogganing, snowshoeing, skating and a cinema. Excursions to Briançon are possible.

Germany

Germany isn't a big destination for UK-based skiers. Over the page is a chapter on Garmisch-Partenkirchen, by far the most important downhill resort in Germany – famously the venue for the 1936 Olympics (when downhill racing was introduced, and Adolf Hitler got the facilities built on time). Seventy-five years later it hosted the 2011 World Championships. On this page is a non-comprehensive tour of the country's main skiing regions.

THE ALPS

Allgäu This region claims 300km of downhill runs and an amazing 800km of cross-country trails. The main lift systems operate under the regional name Das Hoechste. Highest of all is Nebelhorn (2225m) reached from the nice little town of **Oberstdorf** by a two-stage cable car to the main slopes (served by two chairs), with a third stage to the top for Germany's longest piste (7.5km). Oberstdorf is probably best known as the resort that kicks off the annual Four Hills ski jumping tournament held over each New Year period. The Post hotel has been praised for 'good, substantial, reasonably priced' meals. South of Oberstdorf you enter **Kleinwalsertal**, which belongs to Austria, strangely. The Kanzelwand slopes link with Fellhorn to form Germany's biggest area, with three six-packs, two gondolas and nine other lifts. Ifen and Walmendingerhorn are smaller areas in the valley, and the Allgäu has lots of other resorts such as Oberjoch and Pfronten.

Bavarian Alps Garmisch-Partenkirchen is covered over the page. **Mittenwald** (915m) is a cute town in a spectacular setting. The cable car to Karwendel accesses an epic ski route dropping 1300m in 6km. Across the valley seven lifts serve modest slopes up to 1350m.

The other resorts are on the fringes of the Alps, with less dramatic scenery. **Oberammergau** (835m and famous for its once-a-decade Passion Play) is another cute town, with a gondola to Laber (1685m) that accesses a long ski route and a direct black piste; across town a chairlift serves Kolbensattel (1270m). There are more extensive slopes on Brauneck above **Lenggries** (680m) – 34km of pistes with a top height of 1710m, and 18 lifts including a gondola.

There are other small resorts, some near the infamous Berchtesgaden.

THE REST

Black Forest In the south-west corner: a lot of cross-country, but downhill too. Feldberg reaches 1500m with 31 lifts and 55km of pistes.

Harz A low mountain range, south of Hanover. A handful of small resorts, the biggest being Braunlage.

Sauerland Low mountains east of Düsseldorf. Some 500km of cross-country. Winterberg has 24 lifts, Willingen a gondola and seven drags.

Saxony On the border with the Czech Republic: a handful of low, small resorts, the most compelling at Fichtelberg above Oberwiesenthal.

Thüringer Wald North-east of Frankfurt: extensive cross-country, and a bit of easy downhill. The best-known resort is Oberhof.

387

BAYERISCHE ZUGSPITZBAHN BERGBAHN AG

← Life is hard on the glacier at Garmisch-Partenkirchen

WEBSITES

Allgäu
www.allgaeu.info
www.das-hoechste.de

Bavarian Alps
www.karwendelbahn.de
www.laber-bergbahn.de
www.brauneck-bergbahn.de

Black Forest
www.blackforest-tourism.com

Harz
www.harzinfo.de

Sauerland
www.wintersport-arena.de

Saxony
www.oberwiesenthal.com
www.fichtelberg-ski.de

Thüringer Wald
www.oberhof.de

Garmisch-Partenkirchen

Twin resort towns sprawling at the foot of Germany's highest mountain, reaching glacial heights on the Austrian border

TOP 10 RATINGS

Extent	★
Fast lifts	★★★
Queues	★★★
Snow	★★★
Expert	★★★★
Intermediate	★★★
Beginner	★
Charm	★★★
Convenience	★★
Scenery	★★★★

RPI 85

lift pass	£180
ski hire	£95
lessons	£75
food & drink	£105
total	£455

NEWS

2012/13: A six-pack replaced the Wetterwand T-bars on the glacier, starting lower down near the bottom of the Sonnenkar chair but ending at the same place as the T-bars did. Two new freeride information boards were installed.

➕ Weather-proof combination of a fair-sized glacier area and wooded slopes lower down

➕ Some spectacular views

➕ Some excellent, challenging runs

➕ Good-value hotels, cheap for eating and drinking, good for short breaks

➖ Except on the glacier, very few long easy runs; beginners and timid intermediates beware

➖ Many of the best runs descend to low altitude, where conditions are rarely good

➖ Glacier access takes time

Garmisch is Germany's leading ski resort. It has two separate ski areas: one at low altitude with mainly tough runs, the other on a glacier with gentler terrain. It has plenty to amuse confident skiers for a couple of days, and with short transfers from Munich it makes a good short-break destination. We're getting few reports from readers; if you go, do let us know what you think.

THE RESORT

Garmisch and Partenkirchen are separate towns that have merged as they have spread to fill the broad, flat valley bottom beneath the Zugspitze, while keeping their centres distinct.

There are smaller resorts on the Austrian side of the Zugspitze. These and the Garmisch ski areas are covered by the Top Snow Card.

Village charm Each half of the resort is a sizeable town – spacious and pleasant but not notably captivating.

Convenience You'll need to use trains, buses or cars at both ends of the day. The Zugspitze railway starts next to the main station, more or less between the two town centres; it goes to the glacier via the other lift bases.

Scenery The Wetterstein massif, of which the Zugspitze is the peak, is impressive, and there are great panoramic views from the top – plus some dramatic scenery lower down.

THE MOUNTAINS

The glacier is quite separate from the lower slopes, which the resort calls the 'Classic' area. In fact, that area also divides into two parts, awkwardly linked – a higher, almost treeless part (Alpspitz) and a lower, heavily wooded part (Hausberg-Kreuzeck).

Slopes The **Hausberg-Kreuzeck** sector directly above the resort is accessed by two gondolas; these start a few km out of town and are served by the railway. These lower lifts have decent verticals and serve long runs; the lifts higher up are all much shorter. An inconspicuous narrow path and a rope tow form the link between this sector and the base of the higher **Alpspitz** sector, more directly reached via the Alpspitz cable car. Although the altitude is modest, this sector feels like high-mountain terrain, with dramatic scenery – Dolomite-like on the isolated Osterfelder and Bernadein runs, on skier's right.

There are two routes to the glacier: there's the railway from town that serves the Classic area lift bases, which goes on to tunnel slowly through the mountain, emerging at the glacier; or there's the cable car from Eibsee that climbs 1950m to the Zugspitze – from there you have to ride another cable car down to the slopes. Although the Zugspitze is not notably high (2960m), its isolated position gives great views.

Above the main lift junction are typical blue glacier slopes served by multiple drags. Below it and spreading across the bowl is a range of good red runs and some good off-piste terrain served by two six-packs (one new for 2012/13) and two drags. None of these lifts rises more than 400m vertical, but in other respects it's a good area.

Fast lifts Access lifts are fast, but after that it's mainly drags and slow chairs.

Queues Fine weekends attract crowds from Munich; but at other times we don't expect problems.

Terrain parks The park seems to be closed for the moment.

Snow reliability The glacier area is small and remote, so conditions lower down are important. The lower main

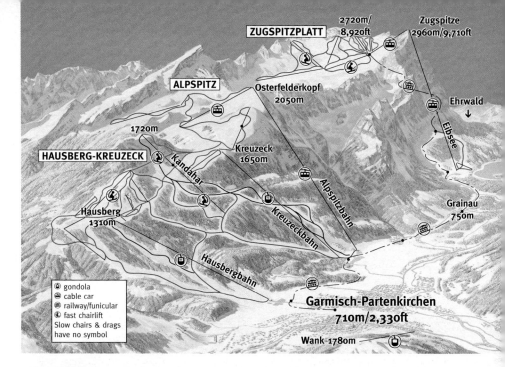

Garmisch-Partenkirchen
710m/2,330ft

Wank 1780m

Key to map
- ⊚ gondola
- ☒ cable car
- ⊜ railway/funicular
- ⊕ fast chairlift
- Slow chairs & drags have no symbol

KEY FACTS

Resort	710m
	2,330ft
Slopes	720-2720m
	2,360-8,920ft
Lifts	27
Pistes	62km
	39 miles
Blue	25%
Red	70%
Black	5%
Snowmaking	47%

UK PACKAGES

Momentum

Phone numbers
From elsewhere in Germany add the prefix 08821. From abroad use the prefix +49 and delete the initial '0'

TOURIST OFFICE

www.gapa.de

area is shady, but some of the best runs descend to valley level – ie to 720m. Despite comprehensive snowmaking, conditions at these altitudes can be poor even when there's great snow higher up, as we confirmed one January visit.

Experts The long runs to the valley are challenging enough to amuse most experts, particularly the excellent Kandahar downhill race course. The final pitch of this takes real bottle when icy at the end of the day. Higher up, there are off-piste opportunities in the Alpspitz sector and on the glacier.

Intermediates For confident skiers it's fine, but this is not a hill where timid intermediates can build confidence.

Beginners Learn elsewhere. The nursery slopes are fine, but they're up the mountain and there is no beginner pass. And the only easy runs to move on to are busy links between Kreuzeck and Hausberg (or on the glacier).

Snowboarding There are drags in all sectors, though many can be avoided.

Cross-country There are 28km of trails along the valleys, of varying difficulty.

Mountain restaurants The glass-sided Gletschergarten on the glacier has a roof that can open on sunny days. Hochalm below Alpspitz in the Classic area does Bavarian fare. The Bayernhaus is worth a stop on the gentle blue run 6 from Hausberg.

Schools and guides There are several schools, but we lack reports.

Families The Kinderland centre at Hausberg looks good, with magic carpet and snow sculptures. There are family discounts on the lift pass.

STAYING THERE

Hotels There is one 5-star – Reindl's Partenkirchner Hof (943870), well placed for the rail stations – and lots of 4-stars and 3-stars. Tips are the 3-star Garmischer Hof (9110) and Atlas Post (7090), and the 4-star Zugspitze (9010). Rates are low in Alpine terms.

Apartments Can be booked via the tourist office.

Eating out Plenty of choice. Gasthof Fraundorfer and the upscale Alpenhof do hearty Bavarian food. Spago – in the Hotel Obermühle – is an Italian.

Après-ski There are bars at the lift bases where you can enjoy waiting for the next train home, and in town there are lots of cosy bars such as Zirbel Stube. Peaches is a lively bar.

Off the slopes There's lots to do, both outdoors and indoors. Walks include one through the Partnachklamm gorge and paths on the lift-served hill that is across town from the slopes – called Wank. There's an ice rink and toboggan runs – including a 5km run at Mount Hausberg that is floodlit twice a week.

Italy

Italy has a lot going for it as a destination: it offers great value for money (over half the Italian resorts we cover have price index figures in our green category – the cheapest); the atmosphere is jolly; it offers reliably good food and wine; the scenery, especially in the Dolomites and Val d'Aosta, is simply stunning; the lift systems include some of the most modern in Europe; the snowmaking is state-of-the-art (and they use it well); and the grooming is top-notch.

Italian resorts vary as widely in their characteristics as they do in location – and they are spread along the full length of the Italian border, from Sauze d'Oulx in the west to the Dolomites. There are quaint backwater villages, fashionable towns, bleak ski stations – the choice is yours.

WEEKDAY PEACE, WEEKEND CROWDS

Many Italians based in the northern cities go skiing at weekends, and it's very noticeable that many resorts are busy only then, and become peaceful once the weekend invaders retreat. It's a great advantage for those of us who are there for the whole week, and probably skiing only one day at the weekend.

This pattern is especially noticeable at chic resorts such as Cortina, Courmayeur and Madonna, and resorts that have not yet found international fame such as those in the Monterosa region. The clearest example is La Thuile, in the Aosta valley. Even at February half-term, the pistes here can be semi-deserted on weekdays. In parts of the Dolomites (such as Val Gardena) that are dominated by German visitors, the Sunday evening exodus doesn't happen – like Brits, the Germans tend to go for a week.

We may be wrong, but we also think we have detected, over the last season or two, an appreciable drop in the numbers of Italian skiers – perhaps related to the economic difficulties. Cortina last February offered delightfully empty pistes.

THE LONG LUNCH LIVES

Many Italians don't take their skiing or boarding too seriously. A late start, a long lunch and an early finish are common – leaving the slopes delightfully quiet for the rest of us. Mountain restaurants are reasonably priced, and there are welcoming places almost everywhere, encouraging leisurely lunching. A persistent drag, though, is the ludicrous system in many self-service places where you have to queue to pay at the cash desk and then queue again at the counter to acquire your food or drink. Italy is also the home of the hybrid-service restaurant, where you order at the bar but are served at your table. Rather like most British pubs.

AND THE LONG EVENING

We've spent a lot of time in Italy in the last couple of years, and we've started to get the hang of Italian après-ski. In its pure form it revolves around the aperitivo – the cocktail or prosecco taken in a cool bar immediately before dinner – normally accompanied by some delicious antipasti to nibble. You need to be in your evening

← Good restaurants with fab views are a key part of Italy's appeal, particularly in the Dolomites – this is Cortina's Faloria

finery by then, of course, and with a visit to the spa to fit in as well, there isn't much time for a protracted Austrian-style drinking session at close of play.

And yet ... Austrian-style après is growing in the Italian Alps too. It may be just the eastern Alps, where the Austrian/German influence is strong, but there are increasing numbers of bars doing a good teatime trade both on the mountain and in the villages.

WHO NEEDS REAL SNOW?

One thing that Italian resorts do have to contend with is erratic snowfall. While the snow in the northern Alps tends to come from the west, Italy's snow tends to come from storms arriving from the south. So Italy can have great conditions when other countries are suffering; or vice versa. And vice versa tends to apply a lot of the time. As a result, Italian resorts got into snowmaking early, and have learnt how to do it well – and our observation is that they tend to use it more effectively than other Alpine countries.

A lot of Italian runs seem flatteringly easy. This is partly because grooming is immaculate and partly because piste classification often seems to overstate difficulty. Nowhere is this clearer than in the linked slopes of La Thuile (in Italy) and La Rosière (in France), where a couple of lift rides take you from Italian motorways classified red to French mogul fields classified blue.

The classification of easy runs as reds creates a real problem. In many areas – Monterosa springs to mind – the red category also includes runs that actually are a bit challenging, and precious few

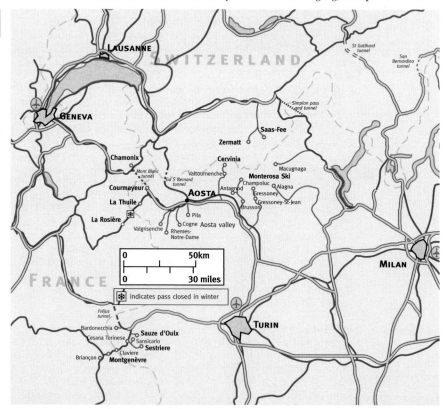

runs are classed as blue. For a nervous intermediate, this is bad news – you can't know which runs you'll be comfortable on, and which ones to avoid.

OFF-PISTE CONFUSION
Many Italian areas declare it illegal to go off-piste near their pistes, or to go off-piste at all, or to go off-piste outside defined routes or without a guide or without transceiver, shovel and probe. We've tried to get to the bottom of these developments; but a prompt, clear, accurate response to a slightly technical question such as this is not a speciality of Italian tourist bodies.

Some resorts tell us there are national laws; others, that it's a regional matter; others, that it's a local matter. Of course, there is then the matter of whether the law is applied and how it is policed. Where we have a clear view of the situation in a given resort, we include that in the relevant chapter. Thankfully, we have no evidence of any interference in off-piste skiing in the Aosta valley, which is Italy's off-piste/heli-skiing HQ.

In our last edition we explained that Livigno had overturned its blanket ban on off-piste skiing by designating half a dozen slopes in one sector as freeride routes – marking them on the piste map and guarding them with entry gates equipped with gadgets to check that your avalanche bleepers are working. Excellent, we thought. But it now turns out that you are not supposed to ski these routes without a guide. The routes have been set up just to stimulate business for the guides. Bonkers.

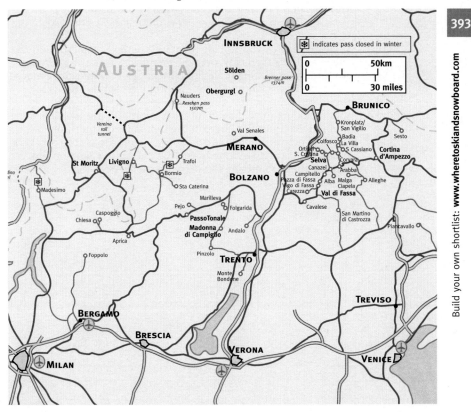

DRIVING IN THE ITALIAN ALPS

There are four main geographical groupings of Italian resorts, widely separated. Getting to some of these resorts is a very long haul, and moving from one area to another can involve very long drives (though the extensive motorway network is a great help).

The handful of resorts to the west of Turin – Bardonecchia, Sauze d'Oulx, Sestriere and neighbours in the Milky Way region – are easily reached from France via the Fréjus tunnel, or via the good road over the pass that the French resort of Montgenèvre sits on.

Further north, and somewhat nearer to Turin than Milan, are the resorts of the Aosta valley – Courmayeur, Cervinia, La Thuile and the Monterosa area are the best known. These (especially Courmayeur) are the easiest of all Italian resorts to reach from Britain or from Geneva airport (via the Mont Blanc tunnel from Chamonix in France). The Aosta valley can also be reached from Switzerland via the Grand St Bernard tunnel. The approach is high and may require chains. The road down the Aosta valley is a major thoroughfare, but the roads up to some of the other resorts are quite long, winding and (in the case of Cervinia) high.

To the east is a string of scattered resorts, most close to the Swiss border, many in isolated and remote valleys involving long drives up from the nearest Italian cities, or high-altitude drives from Switzerland. The links between Switzerland and Italy are more clearly shown on our larger-scale map at the beginning of the Switzerland section of the book than on the map of the Italian Alps included here. The major routes are the St Gotthard tunnel between Göschenen (near Andermatt) and Airolo – the main route between Basel and Milan – and the San Bernardino tunnel a little way to the east, reached via Chur.

Finally, further east still are the resorts of the Dolomites. Getting there from Austria is easy, over the Brenner motorway pass from Innsbruck. But getting there from Britain is a very long drive indeed – allow at least a day and a half. We wouldn't lightly choose to drive there and back for a week's skiing, except as part of a longer tour including some time in Austrian resorts. It's also worth bearing in mind that once you arrive in the Dolomites, getting around the intricate network of valleys on narrow, winding roads can be a slow business – it's often quicker to get from village to village on skis. Impatient Italian driving can make it a bit stressful, too.

Cervinia

One of a kind, this: for extensive, snow-sure, sunny, easy skiing, there is nowhere to match Cervinia. Good for late season holidays

RATINGS

The mountains

Extent	★★★
Fast lifts	★★★★
Queues	★★★★
Terrain p'ks	★★★★
Snow	★★★★★
Expert	★
Intermediate	★★★★
Beginner	★★★★★
Boarder	★★★★
X-country	★
Restaurants	★★★
Schools	★★★★
Families	★★

The resort

Charm	★★
Convenience	★★★
Scenery	★★★★
Eating out	★★★★
Après-ski	★★
Off-slope	★

RPI 95

lift pass	£180
ski hire	£110
lessons	£85
food & drink	£120
total	**£495**

KEY FACTS

Resort	2050m
	6,730ft

Cervinia/Valt'nenche	
Slopes	1525-3480m
	5,000-11,420ft
Lifts	21
Pistes	160km
	100 miles
Blue	30%
Red	59%
Black	11%
Snowmaking	50%

Cervinia/ Valt'nenche/ Zermatt combined	
Slopes	1525-3820m
	5,000-12,530ft
Lifts	54
Pistes	360km
	224 miles
Blue	22%
Red	60%
Black	18%
Snowmaking	61%

➕ Miles of long, consistently gentle runs; ideal for intermediates wary of steep slopes or bumps

➕ Slopes are sunny, but high and pretty snow-sure

➕ Spectacular setting beneath the towering Matterhorn

➕ Excellent village nursery slope

➕ Valuable link with Zermatt in Switzerland, but ...

➖ Bad weather can close not only the Zermatt link but most of the higher lifts, severely limiting your options

➖ Very little to interest those looking for challenges

➖ Not a notably attractive village

➖ Few off-slope amenities

➖ Steep climb to the main gondola, although there is a more convenient chairlift alternative

If there is a better resort than Cervinia for those who like cruising on motorways in spring sunshine, we have yet to find it. And then there's the easiest of Zermatt's slopes just over the Swiss border.

And for the rest of us? Well, to be frank, the rest of us are better off elsewhere. In particular, those with an eye on bumps or powder over in Zermatt should stay there, not here – access to its best slopes is still time-consuming.

The village was branded Cervinia when it was developed for skiing, but these days harks back to its mountaineering roots by prefixing that with its original name, Breuil. Ever heard of that? No, quite. So we'll stick with Cervinia.

THE RESORT

Cervinia is on the Italian side of the Matterhorn (or Monte Cervino), at the head of a long valley off the Aosta valley. The resort gets a lot of Italian weekend business, and quite a lot of Russian January business. We get a good flow of reports from mainly satisfied British visitors, possibly boosted recently by Inghams' expanding programme here.

The slopes link to Valtournenche further down the valley (covered by the lift pass) and at high altitude to Zermatt in Switzerland (covered by a daily supplement, or a more expensive weekly pass). Take your passport.

Day trips by car to Courmayeur, La Thuile and the Monterosa Ski resorts

of Champoluc and Gressoney are not easy, but possible. A six-day Cervinia Valtournenche pass covers two days in these other resorts. Or you can buy an Aosta Valley pass for the week and optionally add two days in Zermatt.

VILLAGE CHARM ★★
Getting smarter?

The old climbing village grew into a ski resort (around the time of WW2) in a haphazard way, and subsequent development is no better. The result is neither pleasing to the eye nor French-style hideous. We sense a gradual smartening up of the centre, with wood and stone taking over from concrete. The cobbled main street is traffic-free, and the place is pleasant enough to walk around in the evening. The river separating the main strip from the nursery slopes adds some charm. But ugly apartment blocks and hotels spoil the views from the slopes.

CONVENIENCE ★★★
Up or down

As our plan makes clear, this is not a big place, but location is still worth considering carefully. What used to be the main lift from the village, a gondola to Plan Maison, starts a hike up from the south end of the village –

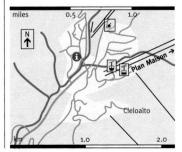

LIFT PASSES

Prices in €

Age	1-day	6-day
under 13	28	123
13 to 64	39	204
65 plus	32	164

Free Under 8 and 80+

Beginner Limited day pass €16

Notes Covers all lifts on the Italian side, including Valtournenche; half-day passes; includes Aosta Valley extension from 3 days

Alternative passes
Valtournenche only; International (includes Zermatt)

irritating for some, 'truly awful' for others. The alternative of successive six-packs from the nursery slopes, next to the village centre, make this the obvious place to stay.

There are also developments above the main village, some of them closer to the gondola. Some hotels run shuttles, and an efficient public bus serves the Cieloalto complex, high up to the south of the main village.

You may have to deal with icy, tricky footpaths.

SCENERY ★★★★
Monte Cervino rules
The Matterhorn is less special seen from the Italian rather than from the Swiss side, but Cervinia's setting close to the mountain is very impressive by normal standards, with the peak towering above the village. Driving up in the late afternoon last season, we were forced to stop and stare. There are fine views from the slopes.

THE MOUNTAINS

Cervinia's main slopes are high, open, sunny and mostly west-facing. It's an unpleasant place when the weather is bad, and the link with Zermatt is often closed by wind (sometimes for days), especially early in the season.

The piste map – which also covers Zermatt – and piste marking are up to scratch, and piste grooming is generally good. The high number of red runs on the map is misleading: most of them could be classified blue.

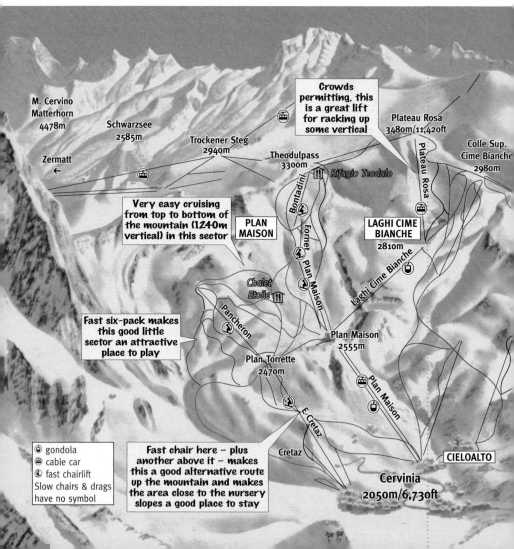

Crowds permitting, this is a great lift for racking up some vertical

Very easy cruising from top to bottom of the mountain (1240m vertical) in this sector

Fast six-pack makes this good little sector an attractive place to play

Fast chair here – plus another above it – makes this a good alternative route up the mountain and makes the area close to the nursery slopes a good place to stay

M. Cervino
Matterhorn
4478m

Schwarzsee
2585m

Trockener Steg
2940m

Zermatt
←

Theodulpass
3300m

Rifugio Teodulo

Plateau Rosa
3480m/11,420ft

Colle Sup.
Cime Bianche
298om

Bontadini

Fornet

Plan Maison

PLAN
MAISON

LAGHI CIME
BIANCHE
2810m

Laghi Cime Bianche

Chalet
Etoile

Pancheron

Plan Maison
2555m

Plan Torrette
2470m

E Cretaz

Plan Maison

Cretaz

CIELOALTO

Cervinia
2050m/6,730ft

⊚ gondola
⊜ cable car
④ fast chairlift
Slow chairs & drags have no symbol

GETTING THERE

Air Turin 120km/
75 miles (2hr);
Geneva 185km/
115 miles (2hr45)

Rail Châtillon
(27km/17 miles);
regular buses from
station

EXTENT OF THE SLOPES ★★★☆☆
High, wide and easy

Cervinia has the biggest, highest, most snow-sure area of easy, well-groomed pistes we've come across. The area has Italy's highest pistes and some of its longest. At the top you are 6km as well as 1400m vertical from the village.

A deep gorge splits the slopes into two main sectors. Looking up the hill, the lifts from the village take you into the bigger left-hand sector at first.

A gondola takes you to the mid-mountain base of **Plan Maison**. We've rarely seen the parallel cable car working. A more convenient alternative for many is the six-pack from the village nursery slopes to Plan Torrette, where another six-pack serves the good slopes under the Matterhorn –

and gives quick access to Plan Maison.

Above Plan Maison, a chain of three fast quads goes on up to Theodulpass, slightly the lower of two links with the slopes of Zermatt. From Plan Maison you can instead take a gondola across to **Laghi Cime Bianche**, and the right-hand sector. From there a big cable car goes up to Plateau Rosa, the other link with Zermatt. This is also the start of the splendid, wide Ventina run back to the cable car station (or on down to the village).

Part-way down you can branch off left for **Valtournenche**. The slopes here are served by three chairlifts above a modern gondola from the village – but the final lift towards Cervinia is still a long draglift with some tricky steep sections. From top to bottom the run

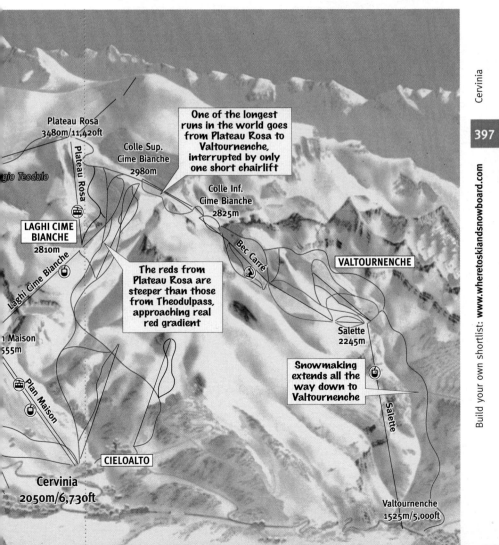

Plateau Rosa
3480m/11,420ft

Colle Sup.
Cime Bianche
2980m

Colle Inf.
Cime Bianche
2825m

gio Teodulo

Plateau Rosa

LAGHI CIME
BIANCHE
2810m

Laghi Cime Bianche

Bec Carré

VALTOURNENCHE

> One of the longest runs in the world goes from Plateau Rosa to Valtournenche, interrupted by only one short chairlift

> The reds from Plateau Rosa are steeper than those from Theodulpass, approaching real red gradient

Salette
2245m

1 Maison
555m

Plan Maison

> Snowmaking extends all the way down to Valtournenche

Salette

CIELOALTO

Cervinia
2050m/6,730ft

Valtournenche
1525m/5,000ft

SCHOOLS

Cervino
t 0166 948744

Breuil
t 0166 940960

Matterhorn-Cervinia
t 0166 949523

Classes
(Cervino prices)
6 days (2hr 45min per
day) €160

Private lessons
From €38 for 1hr for
1 person

GUIDES

Guide del Cervino
t 0166 948169

CHILDCARE

Club Biancaneve
t 0166 940201
Ages from 0 to 10

Ski school
From age 5

to the valley is not far short of 2000m
vertical and a claimed 13km in length,
interrupted only by a very short quad
chairlift part-way.

There is also the very small, little-
used **Cieloalto** area at the bottom of
the Ventina run, served by a slow old
chair to the south of the village. This
has some of Cervinia's steeper pistes,
and the only trees in the area.

FAST LIFTS ★★★★
Few slow lifts left
Most of Cervinia's main lifts are fast
and efficient. The few slow ones left
are in and around the Valtournenche
sector and at Cieloalto.

QUEUES ★★★★
Very few problems
In general, neither we nor readers
have complaints about queues in the
main area of slopes, though the chair
above Plan Maison does still get busy.
Of course, the lower lifts may be busy
when upper lifts are shut by wind. The
gondola station at Valtournenche has
a big car park that fills up at
weekends, and the lifts above the
gondola can then be busy.

TERRAIN PARKS ★★★★
One of Italy's best
The 'Indian' terrain park by the fast
Fornet chair is one of the best parks in
Italy. Run by *Snowboard Italy*'s former
editor, it is said to be over 400m long
and 100m wide. There are three jump
courses of different difficulty. There are
various kickers, rails and walls.
Helmets are compulsory. There is no
half-pipe, but Zermatt's pipe is only
just over the border.

The resort doesn't mention it or
mark it on the piste map, but last
season there was also a small park
near the village that some of our
readers enjoyed, especially with their
children.

SNOW RELIABILITY ★★★★★
A question of altitude
This is not a notably snowy corner of
the Alps, and the slopes get the
afternoon sun. But snow is usually
good from early to late season thanks
to altitude (these slopes are among
the highest in the Alps), good
grooming and snowmaking on most
key runs from top to bottom – down
to Valtournenche as well as Cervinia.

FOR EXPERTS ★★★★★
Forget it
This is not a resort for experts. There
are a few black runs scattered here
and there, but they are not reliably
open and most of them would be
classified red elsewhere; we have only
one sighting of moguls – on the black
above Plan Torrette. Accessible off-
piste terrain is limited, and high winds
can play havoc with fresh snow. But of
course there is some off-piste – above
Plan Torrette for example – and of
course conditions can be brilliant, and
you then have the advantage that the
snow can remain untracked for ages.
Heli-skiing can be arranged.

You can head over to Zermatt for
more challenging slopes – look at the
'Zermatt connection' box in the margin.

FOR INTERMEDIATES ★★★★★
Miles of long, flattering runs
Virtually the whole area can be
covered comfortably by early
intermediates. From top to bottom
there are wide, gentle, smooth runs.
Strong intermediates can find
amusement at the extreme left and
right of the area. The Ventina red is a
particularly good fast cruise. You can
use the cable car to do the top part
repeatedly. The runs served by the
Pancheron chair at Plan Torrette tend
to be attractively quiet. But you'll soon
be itching to be off to Zermatt.

The runs towards Valtournenche are
great cruises and very popular with
reporters. The 13km run all the way
down is very satisfying, through
splendid rocky scenery.

A reader notes that access to
Zermatt via Theodulpass involves a
tricky start – so early intermediates
might want to go via Plateau Rosa.

FOR BEGINNERS ★★★★★
Gentle progress
A limited day pass covers the good
village nursery slope, with its long
moving carpet, and the adjacent

Cervinia

THE ZERMATT CONNECTION

Getting to Zermatt's classic Rothorn/ Stockhorn sectors is much quicker than it once was, thanks to the Furi–Riffelberg gondola. But don't expect to spend very long on those Triftji moguls. On the way back you may meet long queues. Allow plenty of time – and beware closure of the top lifts by wind.

SNOWPIX.COM / CHRIS GILL

Monte Cervino lacks the fantastic shape we associate with the Matterhorn, but it towers over Cervinia; seen from the Saint Hubertus hotel ↓

chairlift. Complete beginners start there and graduate to the fine flat area around Plan Maison and the gentle blue runs above. Fast learners will be going from top to bottom of the mountain in a few days. But a 2012 visitor found many blues 'quite crowded', especially at weekends.

FOR BOARDERS ★★★★
Easy cruising
The wide, gentle and well-groomed slopes, generally good snow and lack of many draglifts make Cervinia pretty much ideal for beginner and early intermediate boarders. But there are some long, flat parts to beware of (notably around Plan Maison). Serious boarders will enjoy the terrain park, and there's a special pass (27 euros a day last season) that covers two chairlifts that access the park plus return trips on the Plan Maison gondola; there's also heli-boarding.

FOR CROSS-COUNTRY ★★★★★
Hardly any
There are only two short trails (both 3km or so).

MOUNTAIN RESTAURANTS ★★★★★
OK if you know where to go
There are some good places if you know where to go. They are marked but not identified on the resort piste map. Toilet facilities are a traditional cause of complaints, but several have now been improved.

Editors' choice Chalet Etoile (0166 940220), amid the blue runs above Plan Maison, is an old favourite. It's best on a sunny day; on a bad day it gets ridiculously crowded inside – though the atmosphere is all the jollier as a result. The food is excellent – we had fab fish soup last season. There's an improved self-service section too. The much simpler Rifugio Teodulo (0166 949400) on the border at Theodulpass is another good option – excellent pasta.

Worth knowing about Recent reporters tip Plan Torrette ('very good food', 'old skiing artefacts on the wall'), with self- and table-service sections. The small, cosy Rifugio Guide del Cervino at Plateau Rosa is tipped for 'desserts to die for' as well as the best view from a loo you will ever see. A new entrant this year is the Gran Sometta on run 39 – 'nice atmosphere, good service, excellent food'.

The restaurants are cheaper and less crowded in the Valtournenche sector. The new Foyer des Guides on the red run to the valley is 'brilliant – lovely friendly service and excellent value'. Tips above Salette include Motta and Lo Baracon dou Tene.

There's a picnic room at the Plan Maison cable car station – used regularly by a 2012 reporter.

SCHOOLS AND GUIDES ★★★★★
Generally positive reports
Cervinia has three main schools. Most reports are on the Cervino school, and are positive: 'Seemed organized. Instructors spoke decent English and worked hard on technique; my compatriot came on in leaps and bounds,' said a 2012 reporter.

FOR FAMILIES ★★★★★
No recent reports
The Cervino ski school runs a mini club. And there's a kindergarten area at Plan Maison.

ACTIVITIES

Indoor Swimming pool, sauna, fitness centre, climbing wall, museum (at Plateau Rosa)

Outdoor Natural ice rink, hiking, snow-biking, snowmobiling, airboarding, mountaineering, snowshoeing, ice karting, ice climbing, kite skiing, tubing (at Valtournenche) paragliding

UK PACKAGES

Alpine Answers, Carrier, Club Med, Crystal, Crystal Finest, Elegant Resorts, Erna Low, Independent Ski Links, Inghams, Interactive Resorts, Momentum, Mountain Beds, Ski Bespoke, Ski Line, Ski Solutions, Skitracer, Ski Weekend, STC, Thomson, Zenith

Phone numbers
From abroad use the prefix +39 (and do **not** omit the initial '0' of the phone number)

TOURIST OFFICE

www.cervinia.it

STAYING THERE

Chalets We know of no small chalets, but Inghams has the chalet hotel Dragon and has added another, Des Guides; both are in great positions close to the nursery slopes. And Crystal operates the Petit Palais, up the hill near the gondola station.

Hotels There are almost 50 hotels, mostly 2- or 3-stars. Choose your location with care, or look for a place with its own shuttle-bus. The Club Med was highly praised by a 2012 reporter.

*****Hermitage (0166 948998) Small, luxurious Relais & Châteaux place just out of the village on the road to Cieloalto. Pool. Minibus to the lifts. Great views from some rooms. Excellent staff and 'top food'.

****Saint Hubertus (0166 545916) Lovely, stylish apart-hotel next to the Hermitage and in related management. Dinner served in your apartment except at weekends when the restaurant is open. We stayed here in 2013 and were very impressed – excellent food, impeccable service.

****Europa (0166 948660) Well placed near nursery slope, with good past reports. Pool.

***Breuil (0166 949537) Central modern place. 'Sedate, but very good rooms, food and staff.'

***Edelweiss (0166 949078) At south end of village. Quirky and creaky place, but 'couldn't have better hosts'.

***Miravidi (0166 948097) Central and recently updated hotel. 'Looked after us superbly,' says a recent visitor.

***Serenella (0166 949041) Very Italian feel (and food), good location, friendly, good value.

Apartments There are many apartments, but few are available via UK tour ops.

EATING OUT ★★★★☆
Plenty to choose from

Cervinia's 50 or so restaurants offer plenty of choice. The established reader favourite is the Copa Pan bar's basement restaurant ('imaginative food perfectly cooked, impeccable service'). A close second is the Falcone ('fine place with good pizza', 'cosy, welcoming, informal'). Lino's at the ice rink is also 'particularly good' for pizza and pasta. Belle Epoque has been tipped for 'very good fish and seafood'. Previous tips include: Matterhorn (varied menu, including vegetarian), La Grotta ('friendly,

extensive menu, delicious food'), Jour et Nuit (restricted menu, good steaks). Dinner at Baita Cretaz, just above the village, makes a change ('pleasant service, good food').

APRES-SKI ★★☆☆☆
Some jolly bars

It's not a particularly lively village. 'Take a good book,' said one reporter. At teatime you can do worse than to try the cakes at the Samovar. The hotel Grivola's bars are attractively woody, friendly and lively, with free nibbles. The 'cosy' Copa Pan is lively (starting with a happy hour), with music. The bars in Inghams' two chalet hotels, the Dragon and Des Guides, are different, but both are deservedly popular. The Yeti is popular too (another happy hour) and serves 'great free nibbles with drinks'. As usual in Italy, discos liven up at weekends.

OFF THE SLOPES ★☆☆☆☆
Little attraction

There is little to do for those who don't plan to hit the slopes. Amenities include hotel pools, a fitness centre and a natural ice rink. There are few diverting shops. The walks are not great. Few mountain restaurants are reachable by gondola or cable car, and most of these are not special.

LINKED RESORT – 1525m

VALTOURNENCHE

Some 9km down the access road and 500m below Cervinia, Valtournenche offers lower prices and a rather more traditional style, and is therefore worth considering as an alternative base unless you are planning multiple trips to Zermatt, which takes time to reach – just to get to the Swiss border involves four lifts, of which two are slow. The village spreads along the busy, steep road up to Cervinia; traffic intrudes, particularly at weekends. The resort is reported to be 'not so much quiet as dead' in the evening.

A gondola leaves from a station below the village (with a big car park). The epic run back from Plateau Rosa on the Swiss border is a great way to end the day – and now has snowmaking right to the bottom

There's a fair selection of simple hotels; some have shuttles to the lift. The 3-star Bijou (0166 92109) has been recommended in the past.

Cortina d'Ampezzo

A captivating town in a truly spectacular setting; do long lunches and side trips, and you won't worry about the rather limited slopes

RATINGS

The mountains

Extent	★★
Fast lifts	★★★
Queues	★★★★
Terrain p'ks	★★
Snow	★★★
Expert	★★
Intermediate	★★★
Beginner	★★★★★
Boarder	★★★
X-country	★★★★★
Restaurants	★★★★
Schools	★★★
Families	★★

The resort

Charm	★★★★
Convenience	★
Scenery	★★★★★
Eating out	★★★★★
Après-ski	★★★
Off-slope	★★★★★

RPI 115

lift pass	£230
ski hire	£120
lessons	£115
food & drink	£130
total	**£595**

NEWS

2013/14: Inghams will be running the central Parc Hotel Victoria as a chalet-hotel.

KEY FACTS

Resort	1225m
	4,020ft
Slopes	1225-2930m
	4,020-9,610ft
Lifts	34
Pistes	115km
	71 miles
Blue	50%
Red	35%
Black	15%
Snowmaking	95%

➕ Magnificent Dolomite setting

➕ Marvellous for novices

➕ Sella Ronda area within reach

➕ Attractive, very Italian town

➕ Lots of off-slope diversions

➕ No crowds or queues

➖ Modest extent of slopes split into several separate areas

➖ Erratic snow record

➖ Expensive by Italian standards

➖ Still quite a few slow lifts

➖ Few tough runs

There is nowhere quite like Cortina. A famous racing town and host of the 1956 Olympics, it certainly has some serious skiing. But it is Italy's most fashionable resort, and many visitors take their lunching and early-evening parading/shopping more seriously than their skiing. The result is that pressure on the slopes is low. No queues, no crowds, few pistes reduced to boilerplate by heavy traffic. In February 2013 we had about the best piste skiing of our season here.

The scenery is just jaw-droppingly wonderful. The town is ringed by dramatic limestone spires and cliffs tinged pink at dawn and dusk. Every time we go back the memory has faded, and our jaws drop once again.

Like all such swanky resorts, Cortina actually attracts few skiers driving Ferraris and many driving Fords (although not many Cortinas). We and our readers find it a friendly place; as a change from standard high-pressure ski resorts, we love it. This season Inghams will be running a chalet-hotel right on the focal Corso Italia. Sounds like we need to start planning a return visit already.

THE RESORT

Cortina is a sizeable town spread across a wide, impossibly scenic bowl. Although it runs World Cup races, it is not a hard-core ski resort – 70% of all Italian visitors don't step on to the slopes. By 5pm everybody is cruising the Corso Italia in smart gear and laden with big bags containing additional supplies of smart gear.

Cortina is pure Italy. The Veneto region has none of the Germanic culture that you'll find in parts of the Südtirol, only a few miles away.

San Cassiano is a short drive to the west, with links into the Sella Ronda – all on the extensive Superski pass.

VILLAGE CHARM ★★★★
Bella Italia

The heart of Cortina is the cobbled, traffic-free Corso Italia – traffic is banished to the roads parallel to the Corso, forming a busy one-way ring-road system that struggles to cope at weekends. The Corso is lined by chic shops selling designer clothes, jewellery, antiques, art and furs. There is also an excellent co-op department store, but proper ski shops are to be found on the ring road, or the streets leading to it. The picturesque church campanile adds to the atmosphere.

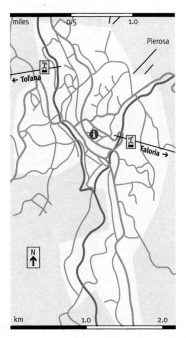

miles · 0.5 · 1.0

Pierosa

← Tofana

Faloria →

N ↑

km · 1.0 · 2.0

SNOWPIX.COM / CHRIS GILL

Not at all your typical
ski resort. Corso Italia,
thronged in the early
evening, is quiet mid-
morning ↓

CONVENIENCE ★☆☆☆☆
Widely scattered

Cortina is the antithesis of the modern ski-in/ski-out resort. The skiing is fragmented, and walks, buses and taxis are just part of life here. Relax, and you'll get used to it. It's probably best to stay close to the Corso and the Faloria cable car, so that some days, at least, you won't need a bus. Or stay in one of the swanky hotels in the suburbs that operate shuttles. Happily, the town bus service is efficient, and 'very punctual' too; it is free to ski pass holders.

A car can be useful, especially for getting to the outlying ski areas and to make the most of other areas on the Dolomiti Superski pass.

SCENERY ★★★★★
Stand and admire

Cortina is surrounded by some of the most stunning mountain scenery in the skiing world – the Dolomite mountains are magnificent, with cliffs and peaks rising up from pretty wooded valleys, and tinged pink at dawn and dusk.

THE MOUNTAINS

There is a good mixture of slopes above and below the treeline. The three major unlinked areas are operated by different companies. We have been struck by the chaotic signing in one sector, Pomedes.

EXTENT OF THE SLOPES ★★☆☆☆
They add up ...

With 115km of pistes (including various outlying areas) Cortina's skiing is modest in extent. When planning the day we find it helpful to identify several small sectors.

A two-stage cable car from the east side of town – about 200m from the Corso – goes up to the shady, partly wooded **Faloria** area. From here you can head down to Rio Gere, and plod across the Passo Tre Croci road to reach chairlifts leading up into the limited but dramatic, sunny runs beneath **Cristallo**. Rio Gere is also reachable by bus from the town.

The town's other access lift – another cable car – starts well to the north of the centre, near the Olympic ice rink. This goes up to **Col Drusciè**, where a second stage goes on to Ra Valles and a sector of very high, shady slopes beneath **Tofana**. There is a third stage to Tofana itself, but not for skiing purposes.

A blue piste from Col Drusciè and a panoramic black one from Ra Valles lead to the largest but least clearly identified sector. We've always called it **Pomedes**, the name of the top station (and restaurant). The resort map calls it Pocol, after a hamlet on the edge of the sector; a more sensible alternative would be Lacedel, the bottom of the sector and arrival point of buses from town. It is a sector of two halves – serious reds and blacks at the top that get the morning sun, glorious super-easy blues at the bottom, sunny most of the day.

On the north-east fringes of the town is the tiny and rather neglected **Mietres** area.

From a point near Son del Prade, on skier's right of the Pomedes area, a bus service takes you up the road west towards Passo Falzarego and delivers you to the small but scenic **Cinque Torri** area, with slopes on both sunny and shady sides of a ridge. On the sunny side, a short double chair accesses a run linking to the tiny, shady **Col Gallina** area. (After a red start, this is mostly a schuss or a walk – boarders be warned.) From here you can take a blue back to Cinque Torri or a cable car from Passo Falzarego up to **Lagazuoi** – the start of a good red run back to the base station and of the famous 'hidden valley' run (more on this in the Sella Ronda chapter).

FAST LIFTS ★★★☆☆
Some in each sector
The main access lifts are cable cars and there are fast chairs scattered throughout each sector, but a lot of slow old lifts remain too.

QUEUES ★★★★☆
No problem
Generally there are few lift queues or crowds on the pistes. Queues can form for the cable car to Lagazuoi, which attracts as much business from the Alta Badia resorts as from Cortina.

TERRAIN PARKS ★★☆☆☆
Challenges for all
Socrepes has a 500m-long park for both beginners and intermediates, which has kickers, boxes, rails, and a wall ride. Helmets are compulsory.

SNOW RELIABILITY ★★★☆☆
Lots of artificial help
The snowfall record is erratic, depending on storms from the Adriatic to the south. But 95% of the pistes are covered by 'excellent' snowmaking, so cover is good if it is cold enough to make snow. As so often, it's the black runs that are most vulnerable when natural snow is short – several are south-facing, and liable to closure. Grooming is 'simply excellent'.

FOR EXPERTS ★★☆☆☆
Normally rather limited
A decent amount of natural snow is the key factor. Given that, you can find fresh tracks for days on end off-piste and good conditions on the few black pistes (some of which get rather too much sun).

There are short but genuinely black runs close to the lift line at the top of the Pomedes sector. The excellent Forcella Rossa from Tofana to Pomedes only just deserves to be black; but it faces south, so timing can be crucial. It goes through a gap in the rocks, and opens up to give wonderful views of Cortina way down in the valley below. Cortina's most serious piste challenge is Forcella Staunies at the top of the Cristallo area – a south-facing couloir that we have never found fully open (tougher than it looks from below, warns a reporter). This is also the launching point for some serious off-piste runs behind the hill, to the north. Locals speak highly of the ski touring possibilities, too.

There are some excellent red runs too, notably at Pomedes and Faloria.

Cortina d'Ampezzo

403

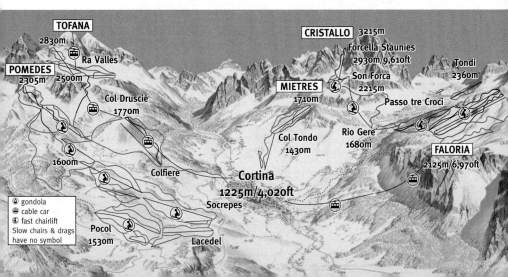

TOFANA 2830m
Ra Valles
POMEDES 2305m 2500m
Col Druscié 1770m
1600m
Colfiere
Pocol 1530m
Lacedel
Socrepes
Cortina 1225m/4,020ft

CRISTALLO 3215m
Forcella Staunies 2930m/9,610ft
Son Forca 2215m
Tondi 2360m
MIETRES 1710m
Passo tre Croci
Col Tondo 1430m
Rio Gere 1680m
FALORIA 2125m/6,970ft

◉ gondola
◎ cable car
◉ fast chairlift
Slow chairs & drags have no symbol

↑ Last winter, finally, we got to ski at least some of Forcella Staunies – in near-perfect conditions. The Faloria sector is in the middle distance
SNOWPIX.COM / CHRIS GILL

UK PACKAGES

Alpine Answers, Inghams, Momentum, Neilson, Oxford Ski Co, Ski Bespoke, Ski Solutions, Ski Weekend, Ski Yogi, Snow Finders, STC, White Roc, Zenith

FOR INTERMEDIATES ★★★★★
Fragmented and not extensive

Cortina is not a place for the avid mileage-hungry piste basher. But its slopes are varied and interesting.

The high, shady runs at the top of Tofana are short but worthwhile, and normally have good snow. If tempted to descend via the easy black Forcella Rossa, check out the snow conditions first. The reds at the top of the linked Pomedes area offer good cruising and some challenges. Again, be aware that the blacks can be hard or icy – in this case, late in the day in particular.

Faloria has a string of excellent although fairly short north-facing runs – we loved the Vitelli red run, round the back away from the lifts. And the Cristallo area has a long, easy red run served by a fast quad. The lower half of Forcella Staunies (shown in our picture above) is a lovely easy black.

It is well worth making the trip to Cinque Torri for fast cruising – usually with excellent snow on the front, north-facing side. The blue and red through the woods here are indistinguishable. Do not miss the great 'hidden valley' red run from the Lagazuoi cable car.

FOR BEGINNERS ★★★★★
Wonderful nursery slopes

There are points cards for the lifts, and the slopes, although a bus ride from the town, are near-perfect. The lower part of the Pomedes area, above

Lacedel and Socrepes, has some of the biggest and best nursery slopes and progression runs we have seen. Be aware that some isolated blue runs elsewhere in the area may be much less friendly.

FOR BOARDERS ★★★★★
Wide slopes and plenty of chairs

Despite its upmarket chic, Cortina is a good resort for learning to board. The Socrepes nursery slopes are wide, gentle and served by a fast chairlift. There are hardly any drag-lifts, so getting around is easy. Boarderline is a specialist snowboard shop that also organizes instruction. There are some nice trees and hits under the top chairlift at Cinque Torri.

FOR CROSS-COUNTRY ★★★★★
One of the best

Cortina has around 70km of trails suitable for all standards, mainly in the Fiames area, where there's a cross-country centre and a school. Trails include a 30km itinerary following an old railway from Fiames to Dobbiaco, and there is a beginner area equipped with snowmaking. Passo Tre Croci offers more challenging trails, covering 10km. A Nordic area pass is available.

MOUNTAIN RESTAURANTS ★★★★★
Good, but get in early

There are some excellent spots. Many can be reached by road or lift, and in some places skiers are in the minority.

SCHOOLS

Azzurra Cortina
t 0436 2694

Cristallo
t 0436 870073

Cortina
t 0436 2911

Dolomiti
t 0436 862264

Boarderline
t 0436 878261

Classes (Azzurra prices)
6 mornings (3hr)
€425

Private lessons
€55 for 1hr; each additional person €18

GUIDES

Guide Alpine
t 0436 868505

CHILDCARE

Snow play areas at Socrepes, Mietres and Pierosa

Ski school
From age 4

ACTIVITIES

Indoor Saunas, health spa, fitness centre, ice stadium, curling, museums, art gallery, cinema, concerts, observatory, planetarium

Outdoor Snowshoe tours, walking paths, tobogganing, ice climbing and trekking, snow kiting, snowmobiling, horse-drawn sleigh rides, snow biking, ice driving

Phone numbers
From abroad use the prefix +39 (and do **not** omit the initial '0' of the phone number)

TOURIST OFFICE

www.cortina.dolomiti.org

Prices are high in the swishest places. The piste map doesn't identify all restaurants, but the topo map on the reverse is more helpful.
Editors' choice Close to the top of Faloria, Capanna Tondi (0436 5775) does excellent food with table-service in a series of small, cosy rooms and on a terrace with a great view.
Worth knowing about Baita Son dei Prade above Pocol in the Pomedes sector is 'never too crowded, does wonderful lasagne', says an experienced reporter. Piè Tofana does ambitious food, but we weren't wowed by the results last season.

There are good restaurants at Cinque Torri. Rifugio Averau has recently had a makeover and looked very inviting when we visited. Rifugio Lagazuoi, at the top of the Passo Falzarego cable car, has great views.

SCHOOLS AND GUIDES ★★★☆☆
Mixed reports
We've had mixed reports of the Cortina school over the years – though we lack recent reports. The Guide Alpine offers off-piste and touring.

FOR FAMILIES ★★☆☆☆
Some good lift pass deals
There's a wide choice of lift pass deals for children and there are three snow gardens plus hotel-run nurseries. But don't count on good spoken English.

STAYING THERE

Make sure you pick up a copy of *Cortina Pocket* – a very useful guide to restaurants, bars, shops and the rest.

Hotels dominate the lodgings market but there are alternatives.
Chalets Inghams will be running the ideally located Parc Hotel Victoria as a chalet-hotel in 2013/14.
Hotels There's a big choice, from simple pensions to 5-star palaces (which we don't bother with).
★★★★Ancora (0436 3261) Elegant public rooms. On the central Corso Italia.
★★★★Park Faloria (0436 2959) Near ski jump, splendid pool, good food.
★★★★Poste (0436 4271) Central, on the Corso Italia. Large rooms, some with spa baths.
★★★Columbia (0436 3607) B&B hotel approved by a reader, not far from Tofana lift but a hike from town.
★★★Des Alpes (0436 862021) Way out of town. Simple but well run. Hot tub, sauna, steam.

★★★Menardi (0436 2400) Welcoming roadside inn, just out of the town.
★★★Olimpia (0436 3256) Comfortable B&B hotel in centre, near Faloria lift.
★★Montana (0436 862126) Good value, central B&B.
Apartments There are some chalets and apartments available to rent.
At altitude Rooms are available at several refuges – notably at Pomedes, at the renovated Averau at Cinque Torri and at Lagazuoi, where you can have breakfast watching the sunrise.

EATING OUT ★★★★★
Huge choice
There are lots of restaurants, with some variation on local traditional cuisine. Sadly, most of the better ones are a taxi ride out of town. The word is that the very smart El Toulà, in a beautiful old barn just on the edge of town, is now overpriced. Also on the edge, Da Beppe Sello is 'a little gem, with extraordinary salad entrées and a good meat choice'. Even further out: the Michelin-starred Tivoli, Meloncino al Camineto, Leone e Anna (Sardinian specialities), Rio Gere (game dishes) and Baita Fraina (pasta and meats).

In the centre there are plenty of modest places, including pizzerias – Croda Cafe claims to be the town's original, with wood-fired oven, and Birreria Vienna serves until midnight.

APRES-SKI ★★★☆☆
Lively in high season
Cortina is a lively social whirl in high season, with lots of well-heeled Italians staying up very late – but at other times it can be quiet, or 'very dull', to quote a January visitor.

The Lovat is one of several high-calorie teatime spots. There are some good wine bars, often doing excellent cheese and meats too: Enoteca, La Suite and LP26 have been tipped. Bar Sport is the place for grappa. Jambo is said to be 'heaving' later on.

OFF THE SLOPES ★★★★★
A classic resort
There's lots to do. There are popular walks in several sectors. There are lots of upmarket shops. Activities include swimming and skating. There is a planetarium, and an observatory at Col Druscié. There are regular ice hockey matches. The Country Club spa is tipped for its 'real Scan feel'. Trips to Venice are easy. You can visit First World War tunnels at Lagazuoi.

Courmayeur

A seductive old village on the sunny side of spectacular Mont Blanc, but with a flawed and very limited area of pistes

RATINGS

The mountains

Extent	★
Fast lifts	★★★★
Queues	★★★★
Terrain p'ks	★★
Snow	★★★★
Expert	★★★
Intermediate	★★★★
Beginner	★
Boarder	★★★
X-country	★★★
Restaurants	★★★★
Schools	★★★★
Families	★★

The resort

Charm	★★★★
Convenience	★
Scenery	★★★★
Eating out	★★★★
Après-ski	★★★★
Off-slope	★★★

RPI — 95

lift pass	£200
ski hire	£100
lessons	£90
food & drink	£115
total	**£505**

NEWS

2013/14: The new two-stage cable car to Punta Helbronner on Mont Blanc is still planned to open for 2014/15.

2012/13: The slow, inadequate Bertolini chairlift on the Val Veny side of the hill was upgraded to a fast quad. The cable car to Plan Checrouit now runs all evening. A new terrain park and airbag opened at 2000m.

+ Charming old village; car-free centre with stylish shops and bars

+ Stunning views of Mont Blanc

+ Some good off-piste and heli-skiing

+ Comprehensive snowmaking

+ Some great mountain restaurants

– Very small area of pistes; and lift-served off-piste reduced while new cable car up Mont Blanc being built

– Lots of drawbacks for beginners

– No really tough pistes

– No runs back to the village

Courmayeur is a great place for a short midweek break or for a day trip to escape bad weather in Megève and Chamonix – exactly what we used it for in 2013. Excellent restaurants both on and off the mountain plus village bars among the most civilized in the skiing world are factors, we admit.

The skiing is tricky to recommend for more than a day or two, though. Its pistes best suit competent intermediates, who are likely to have an appetite for mileage that Courmayeur will arouse but not satisfy.

THE RESORT

Courmayeur is a traditional old mountaineering village that has retained much of its character.

La Thuile is an easy drive or bus ride away; Aosta/Pila and Chamonix are not far, and Cervinia and Monterosa are reachable; all are covered by various lift passes.

VILLAGE CHARM ★★★★☆
Attractive and sophisticated
The village has a charming traffic-free core of cobbled streets and well-preserved old buildings. As the lifts close, the central Via Roma comes alive: people pile into the many bars, or browse the tempting delis and smart clothes shops (some now with doormen to stop celebrity-spotters, and some appointment-only at peak times, we're told); there's also a good bookshop. An Alpine museum and a statue of a long-dead mountain rescue hero add to the historical feel.

Away from the centre, there are pleasant woody suburbs but also a lot of conspicuous apartment blocks.

CONVENIENCE ★☆☆☆☆
Buses to the lifts
A huge cable car on the southern edge of the village will take you to and from Plan Checrouit, at the heart of the slopes. You cannot ski back to the village, but you can ski to the base of the alternative gondola from Dolonne (across the valley); parking is much

easier there, too. You can leave your gear up at Plan Checrouit – an attractive option if staying some distance from the cable car base station. Buses serve both lift stations but readers have found services 'inadequate'. Many hotels run shuttles that are welcomed by reporters.

Drivers can also go to Entrèves, up the valley, where there is a large car park at the cable car. Infrequent but timetabled buses go to La Palud, just beyond Entrèves, for the Monte Bianco cable car.

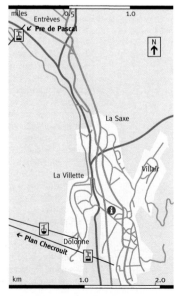

KEY FACTS

Resort	1225m
	4,020ft
Slopes	1210-2755m
	3,970-9,040ft
Lifts	18
Pistes	36km
	22 miles
Blue	27%
Red	59%
Black	14%
Snowmaking	70%

SCENERY★★★★☆
Mont Blanc rules

The high glacial slopes of the Mont Blanc massif overlook Courmayeur's slopes. The views from the high points at Cresta d'Arp and Cresta Youla, especially, are stunning.

THE MOUNTAINS

The slopes above the focal point of Plan Checrouit are mainly wide open, but there are also wooded areas, particularly on the back side of the hill. The piste map was improved a few years ago and now shows lift names and direction, but some reporters criticize piste signposting and marking.

EXTENT OF THE SLOPES ★☆☆☆☆
Small but quite challenging

Ever since this book started 19 years ago, we've been sceptical of the resort's claimed 100km of pistes. Two seasons ago, at last, it revealed that the true extent is 36km of pistes plus 64km of off-piste runs (whatever that means). 36km is even less than we would have guessed, and less than any other major resort in this book.

There are two distinct sectors, separated by a rocky ridge. The links between the two can be a bit confusing. Above Plan Checrouit, the east-facing **Checrouit** area, accessed mainly by the Checrouit gondola, catches the morning sun. The 20-person Youla cable car goes to the top of the pistes. A further tiny cable

car to Cresta d'Arp serves only long off-piste runs.

Most people follow the sun over to the north-west-facing slopes of **Val Veny** in the afternoon. These offer a mix of open and wooded slopes, with great views of Mont Blanc and its glaciers. The Val Veny slopes are also accessible by cable car from Entrèves, a few miles outside Courmayeur.

A little way beyond Entrèves a new cable car to Punta Helbronner, at the shoulder of **Mont Blanc,** is being built (completion 2014), and the top stage of the old cable car has closed. But from the second stage you can reach the famous Vallée Blanche run to Chamonix by climbing 120 steps (your skis are transported for you). Access to the Toula glacier run on the Italian side involves a bit of a climb on snow.

FAST LIFTS ★★★★☆
A decent network

The main access lifts are cable cars or a gondola. On the hill, with the old Bertolini chair on the Val Veny side now upgraded to a fast quad, there are now fast lifts in all the key spots.

QUEUES ★★★★☆
Much improved

These days, queues are generally not a problem unless conditions trigger a weekend influx. Queues to descend at the end of the day have been a problem, especially if the run to Dolonne is closed, but evening opening of the cable car should have put paid to that. On the back of the

LIFT PASSES

Prices in €

Age	1-day	6-day
under 14	31	132
14 to 64	44	220
65 plus	35	176

Free Under 8

Beginner Three free nursery lifts (but you have to pay for the access lifts to reach them)

Notes Covers Courmayeur and the Mont Blanc cable cars; 3- or 4-hour passes; weekly passes allow two days in another Aosta valley resort

Alternative passes Non-skier; Mont Blanc Unlimited (includes Chamonix valley and Verbier); Valle d'Aosta (covers Aosta Valley ski areas)

hill, Zerotta is a real bottleneck – we've waited 15 minutes here in March. It's worth waiting until late afternoon to ride the Youla cable car.

TERRAIN PARKS ★★☆☆☆
New and improved
A new park opened last season, served by the Aretù chairlift. It has a line of rails for beginners and children, another for intermediates and a line of kickers. There is also an airbag served by two differently-sized jumps.

SNOW RELIABILITY ★★★★☆
Good for most of the season
Courmayeur's slopes are not high – mostly between 1700m and 2250m. Those above Val Veny face north or north-west, so they keep their snow well, but the Plan Checrout side is too sunny for comfort in late season. There is snowmaking on most main runs, including the red run to the valley. So good coverage in early and mid-season is virtually assured – we've been there in a snow drought and enjoyed decent skiing entirely on man-made snow. Grooming is good – 'when it snowed eight inches overnight they sensibly concentrated on the blues

first'. On the other hand, it is quite unusual for an Italian resort to leave any pistes ungroomed.

FOR EXPERTS ★★★☆☆
Off-piste is the challenge
Courmayeur has few challenging pistes. The black runs on the Val Veny side are not severe, but moguls are allowed to develop. If you're lucky enough to find fresh powder, you can have fantastic fun among the trees.

Classic off-piste runs go from Cresta d'Arp, at the top of the lift network, in three directions: a clockwise loop via Arp Vieille to Val Veny, with close-up views of the Miage glacier; east down a deserted valley to Dolonne or Pré-St-Didier; or south through the Youla gorge to La Balme, near La Thuile.

A day trip to Chamonix is appealing, especially as some classic runs on Mont Blanc start from the French side.

There are also heli-drops, including a wonderful 20km run from the Ruitor glacier that ends near Ste-Foy in France – you take a taxi from there to La Rosière, ride the lifts back up from there and descend to La Thuile (then take another taxi back).

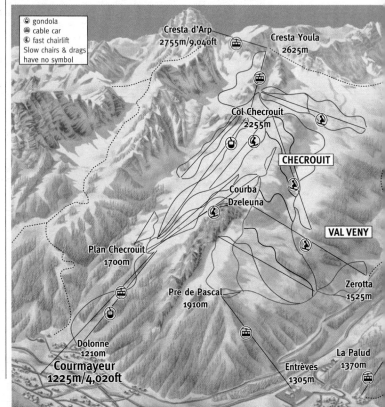

Courmayeur 1225m/4,020ft

GETTING THERE

Air Geneva 100km/
60 miles (1hr30);
Turin 150km/95 miles
(2hr)

Rail Pré-St-Didier
(5km/3 miles); regular
buses from station

SCHOOLS

Monte Bianco
t 0165 842477
Courmayeur
t 0165 848254

Classes (Monte
Bianco prices)
5 days (2hr per day)
€187
Private lessons
From €43 for 1hr;
additional person €13

GUIDES

Guides Courmayeur
t 0165 842064

CHILDCARE

Fun park Dolonne
9am-4.30
Mini club Biancaneve
(Monte Bianco school)
t 349 300 3132
Ages 0 to 10
Ski-tots (Mammolo)
(Monte Bianco school)
For 3 and 4 year olds

Ski schools
From age 5

FOR INTERMEDIATES ★★★★☆
Good reds, but limited extent
It's an intermediate's mountain, for sure, laced with interestingly varied, genuine red runs. But it is small; the avid piste-basher will ski it in a day. There are a few good long runs – it's 700m vertical from Col Checrouit to Zerotta, and an impressive 1400m vertical from Cresta Youla to Dolonne. On the steeper Val Veny side of the ridge there are challenges to be found – while the reds and blues cut across the mountain, a row of easy blacks go down more directly.

For the timid intermediate, on the other hand, the area is short of confidence-building blue runs. There is basically one long blue on each side of the ridge; that on the Val Veny side is better for the challenge-averse. Many of the reds, particularly up around Col Checrouit, and down to Plan Checrouit, do have the merit that they are generally wide, which helps a lot.

FOR BEGINNERS ★☆☆☆☆
Lots of drawbacks
Of course, you can learn to ski here, but you face obstacles. To get to the free beginner lifts (at Plan Checrouit, on the ridge above that and at the top of the Entrèves cable car) you have the hassle and cost of getting up the mountain. The best starting point is the Entrèves cable car, which takes you to a magic carpet, and easy longer runs on the Peindeint chair. There is a clear lack of other genuinely easy longer runs to progress to.

FOR BOARDERS ★★★☆☆
Mainly intermediate fun
Courmayeur's pistes suit intermediates well, and most areas are easily accessible by cable cars, chairs and gondolas (though the beginner slopes employ drags). For the more adventurous, there are off-piste routes. A terrain park opened last season.

FOR CROSS-COUNTRY ★★★☆☆
Beautiful trails
There are 30km of trails. The best are the five covering 20km at Val Ferret, served by bus.

MOUNTAIN RESTAURANTS ★★★★☆
A very good choice
The area is well endowed with establishments ranging from rustic little huts that do table-service of delicious pizza, pasta and other dishes, to snack bars and a large self-service place – but strangely they are not marked on the piste map.

Editors' choice We and readers have had excellent meals at Chiecco (338 7003035) by the drag-lift starting below Plan Checrouit – a small hut run by the very welcoming Anna; very varied menu, including fantastic chicken curry and wild boar stew; superb tiramisu. An old favourite of ours is Maison Vieille (337 230979), a cosy, rustic place with jolly service; but we and readers have been underwhelmed on recent visits – more reports please.

Worth knowing about Another favourite at Plan Checrouit is the Christiania (book a table downstairs to escape the crowds). Nearby, the Chaumière pizzeria is family-run, serving 'very good meals, especially the cheese board starter' on a 'sunny terrace with superb views'. Alpetta serves homemade pastas, burgers and 'nice apple crumble' and is 'great for families'. Reporters also like the Baita self-service for low prices and Bar du Soleil for more of those good views. Up at Col Checrouit, Chez Croux serves 'the best cakes and hot drinks on the mountain'. There is another clutch of worthwhile places in Val Veny: we enjoyed the smartly rustic Grolla for steaks and salads. The Petit Mont Blanc is also popular ('the roast suckling pig was fantastic').

SCHOOLS AND GUIDES ★★★★☆
Good private lessons
Past reports on private lessons with the Monte Bianco school have been fairly enthusiastic, though you can't count on good spoken English. The Courmayeur school has 'a more snowboardy and young funky image'. There is a thriving guides' association ready to help you explore the area's off-piste; it has produced a helpful booklet showing the main possibilities. We had a super day in 2011 with solo guide Gianni Carbone (www.giannicarbone.com), who was patient and reassuring. A 2012 visitor's Vallée Blanche guides were 'excellent'.

FOR FAMILIES ★★☆☆☆
Some facilities
There are children's playgrounds at Dolonne, Plan Checrouit and Val Veny, and a nursery at Plan Checrouit for children up to 10 years.

ACTIVITIES

Indoor Hotel swimming pools, sports centre (ice rink, climbing wall, fitness centre), tennis, museums, library

Outdoor Walking, snowshoeing

UK PACKAGES

Alpine Answers, Alpine Weekends, Crystal, Crystal Finest, Erna Low, Flexiski, Friendship Travel, Independent Ski Links, Inghams, Inspired to Ski, Interactive Resorts, Interski, Just Skiing, Mark Warner, Momentum, Mountain Beds, Ski Bespoke, Ski Club Freshtracks, Ski Expectations, Ski Line, Ski Solutions, Skitracer, Ski Weekend, Skiweekends.com, Ski Yogi, STC, Thomson, Tracks European Adventures, White Roc

Phone numbers
From abroad use the prefix +39 (and do **not** omit the initial '0' of the phone number)

TOURIST OFFICE

www.courmayeur.it
www.lovevda.it

STAYING THERE

There's a wide range of packages on offer (including some excellent weekend deals), mainly in hotels. Momentum Ski is an agent specializing in Courmayeur and can fix pretty much whatever you want here.

Chalets Mark Warner runs the central Cristallo as a chalet-hotel.

Hotels There are over 50 hotels, spanning the star ratings.

****Auberge de la Maison** (0165 869811) Small, atmospheric hotel in Entrèves; owned by the same family as Maison de Filippo (see 'Eating out').

****Cresta et Duc** (0165 842585) In the centre. Praised by a past reporter. Steam, sauna, hot tub.

****Villa Novecento** (0165 843000) A short walk from the centre. Elegant lobby, good food and breakfasts. Sauna, steam, hot tub.

***Bouton d'Or** (0165 846729) Small, friendly B&B hotel near main square, repeatedly recommended by a regular visitor – '3-star with friendly 5-star service; impossible to fault'.

***Courmayeur** (0165 846732) Near cable car. 'Very friendly; small rooms.'

***Pilier d'Angle** (0165 869760) Friendly, cosy hotel in Entrèves; rooms and self-contained chalets. Good restaurant and wellness centre.

***Camosci** (0165 842338) 800m from centre, minibus. '5-star welcome, charming, traditional, plentiful food.'

Apartments The 3-star Grand Chalet (0165 841448) is central with spacious apartments. Hot tub, steam and sauna are also available for non-residents.

At altitude If you're that keen to get going in the morning, this is probably not your ideal resort. But up the cable car at Plan Checrouit, the 1-star Christiania (0165 843572) has simple rooms; the 3-star Baita (0165 846542) is smarter.

EATING OUT ★★★★☆
Jolly Italian evenings

There is a great choice of places. A handy promotional booklet describes many of them (in English). We've been impressed by the traditional Italian cuisine of the smart Cadran Solaire. La Terrazza serves classic and local cuisine plus pizzas and is highly recommended, both by a local and a 2013 visitor ('superb – owners very accommodating, excellent set meal for 20 euros'). Reporters regularly recommend the Piazzetta ('very good

and inexpensive', 'extremely friendly'). The little Pizzeria du Tunnel is a bit of an institution, and is happily endorsed this year by two reporters – 'super food, attentive service' despite being over-busy at times. A new recommendation for 2013 is Ancien Casinò ('best pizza ever, and inexpensive – 100 euros for four with wine'). 2012 reporters recommended Le Vieux Pommier ('great atmosphere, serves a mixture of Italian and Savoyard fare') and Aria ('very friendly, an amazing wine list'). In Entrèves, the touristy but very jolly Maison de Filippo is rightly famous for its fixed-price, 36-dish feast. For a gourmet treat take a taxi to the Clotze in Val Ferret (same management as Chiecco – read 'Mountain restaurants').

APRES-SKI ★★★★☆
Stylish bar-hopping

Courmayeur has a lively evening scene – at weekends, at least – centred on stylish bars with comfy armchairs or sofas, often serving free canapés in the early evening. We like the Privé ('great cocktails', 'reasonable prices and good service') and the back room of the Caffè della Posta with its 'laden plates of goodies that arrive with each round'. It's 'not as expensive as you'd expect' and 'the people watching is superb'. Bar Roma is an old favourite – 'a big airy place complete with comfortable armchairs' – but seems to have dropped its antipasto buffet. A 2013 reporter enjoyed the 'great service and very good food' at Petit Bistro. The American Bar has good live music. Three new nightclubs opened for 2011/12 – Courmaclub ('relaxed rather than rowdy'), Jset and Shatush. Or try the branch of Shatush in Entrèves (free shuttle-bus service).

OFF THE SLOPES ★★★☆☆
Lots on for non-slope users

The resort attracts many non-skiing weekenders, who focus on showing off their togs and buying more of them – so there are some tempting shops. You can go by bus to Aosta, or up to Plan Checrouit where there are countless spots to meet friends for lunch. The huge sports centre is good (but has no pool). Don't miss a visit to the thermal baths at Pré-St-Didier – with over 40 spa 'experiences' including saunas and outdoor pools. The Parco Avventura (10km from town) has a 'great' ropes course.

Livigno

Lowish prices and highish altitude – a tempting combination,
especially when you add in a pleasant Alpine ambience

RATINGS

The mountains

Extent	★★
Fast lifts	★★★★
Queues	★★★★
Terrain p'ks	★★★★
Snow	★★★★
Expert	★★★
Intermediate	★★★
Beginner	★★★★
Boarder	★★★★
X-country	★★★★
Restaurants	★★★
Schools	★★★
Families	★★

The resort

Charm	★★★
Convenience	★★
Scenery	★★★
Eating out	★★★
Après-ski	★★★
Off-slope	★★

RPI 90

lift pass	£190
ski hire	£80
lessons	£85
food & drink	£115
total	**£470**

NEWS

2012/13: Heli-skiing was allowed for the first time – just for two weeks at the end of February. This may well be repeated.

KEY FACTS

Resort	1815m
	5,950ft
Slopes	1815-2795m
	5,950-9,170ft
Lifts	30
Pistes	115km
	71 miles
Blue	38%
Red	47%
Black	15%
Snowmaking	70%

➕ Reliable snow

➕ Large choice of beginners' slopes

➕ Impressive modern lift system

➕ Cheap by the standards of high, snow-sure resorts

➕ Lively, friendly, quite smart village with a good Alpine atmosphere

➕ Long, snow-sure cross-country trails

➖ Few tough pistes, and the resort's 'itineraries' are no such thing

➖ Bleak setting, susceptible to white-outs and lift closures

➖ Long transfers from some Italian airports (Innsbruck is quicker)

➖ Village is very long and straggling, with no buses later in the evening

➖ Nightlife can disappoint

Livigno's recipe of a fair-sized mountain, high altitude and fairly low prices is uncommon, and obviously attractive, and may be enough to get it on to your shortlist. But don't overlook the non-trivial drawbacks we list above.

We were excited to find, last season, that the resort had ditched its previous ban on off-piste skiing in favour of six freeride 'itineraries' on Mottolino. But we were misled: these are not itineraries in the usual sense – they are not supposed to be skied without guidance. Bizarrely, the 'itineraries' are basically a marketing device, designed to drum up business for the mountain guides.

THE RESORT

Livigno is set in a wide, remote valley near the Swiss border; the airport transfers are long and winding. The Alta Valtellina lift pass covers Bormio (about an hour's bus ride – free with the lift pass) and Santa Caterina (another 20 minutes). The Livigno pass gets you half-price on one day in St Moritz – an excursion not easily done from any other major resort.

VILLAGE CHARM ★★★★★
Pleasant enough
At the core of the resort is a single mainly pedestrian street, just over 1km long, lined by hotels, bars, specialist shops and supermarkets, with side streets linking to the parallel by-pass road. The buildings are small in scale and traditional in style, creating a pleasant atmosphere. Away from the central area, traffic can be intrusive.

CONVENIENCE ★★★★★
Where you gonna stay?
It's a long, spread-out place – over 4km end to end. The pedestrian core is the most attractive all-round location, but the three major lifts are out at the extremities. Unless you opt to stay near one of these, you will make heavy use of the free bus services. The main lines run every 10

minutes, but get overcrowded at peak times and stop at 8pm. The complex route map requires serious study, but visitors have found the services 'regular' and 'efficient'. Taxis (including minibuses for groups) are affordable.

SCENERY ★★★★★
High and probably white
Livigno's high position and long ridges provide attractive views from both sides of the valley – but it can feel bleak and isolated.

LIFT PASSES

Prices in €

Age	1-day	6-day
under 15	34	143
15 to 64	42	208
65 plus	34	143

Free Under 8

Beginner Points card

Notes Half-day passes and reduced Saturday passes; family reductions; 50% discount on day pass at St Moritz with a 3-day-plus pass

Alternative pass
Alta Valtellina pass covers Livigno, Bormio and Santa Caterina

THE MOUNTAINS

The slopes are on either side of the valley and are mainly above the treeline. It's not a good place in bad weather. Signposting is adequate, but the piste map does not identify runs. Night skiing is available on Thursdays.

EXTENT OF THE SLOPES ★★★★★
Widely spread
The slopes are more extensive than in many other budget destinations, but it's not a huge area and lots of the runs are very similar to one another.

At the north end of the village is the narrow **Costaccia** sector, reached by the two-stage Tagliede gondola (with the Cassana gondola and an adjacent six-pack offering alternative ways to the mid-station). From Costaccia, a long fast quad chairlift goes along the ridge towards the Carosello sector. The blue linking run back from Carosello to the top of Costaccia is flat in places and may involve energetic poling. **Carosello** is more usually accessed by the optimistically named Carosello 3000 gondola at the southern end of the village, which goes up, in two stages, to almost 2800m. Most runs return towards the village, but the Federia six-pack serves west-facing slopes on the back of the mountain.

The ridge of **Mottolino** is reached by a gondola or fast quad from Teola, across the valley from central Livigno. From the top, you can descend to fast quads on either side of the ridge, or take a very slow antique chair along the ridge.

We don't show on our map a link from the nursery drags at the bottom of Carosello to those below Costaccia; it's more of a walk than a run.

FAST LIFTS ★★★★★
A positive attraction
The lift system is impressively modern, with fast chairs and gondolas covering both sectors – though draglifts still serve the valley nursery slopes.

QUEUES ★★★★★
Few problems these days
Queues are generally not a problem. Delays can occur at the main gondolas at peak times, such as the Carosello 3000. A bigger problem is that winds can close the upper lifts, causing crowds lower down.

TERRAIN PARKS ★★★★★
Serious facilities
The main park behind Mottolino is an impressive freestyle zone for all levels. It also plays host to the World Rookie fest and River Jump contest – both on the Ticket to Ride calendar. It has kicker lines for all levels and is bordered by a big super-pipe, often used as a training ground by pros, and there are advanced rails in and around the jumps as well. There's also a huge airbag jump – perfect for trying out backflips and other advanced tricks.

Livigno's second park is at Carosello 3000. It also caters for all standards and includes another huge airbag jump. The two other parks – Amerikan, beside the Amerikan lift near the Carosello gondola, and the Del Sole area near the centre of town

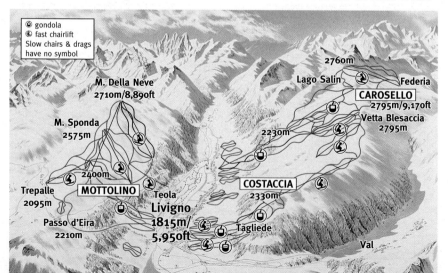

⛟ gondola
🚡 fast chairlift
Slow chairs & drags
have no symbol

M. Della Neve
2710m/8,890ft

2760m

Lago Salin

Federia

CAROSELLO
2795m/9,170ft

M. Sponda
2575m

2230m

Vetta Blesaccia
2795m

Trepalle
2095m

2400m

MOTTOLINO

Teola

COSTACCIA
2330m

Livigno
1815m/
5,950ft

Tagliede

Passo d'Eira
2210m

Val

↑ Two drawbacks of the place are clear in this shot – the linear nature of the village, and the very limited extent of the trees

APT LIVIGNO / MARTA MAGGIONI

APT LIVIGNO / MARTA MAGGIONI

GETTING THERE

Air Bergamo 190km/120 miles (3hr45); Brescia 225km/140 miles (4hr45); Innsbruck 180km/110 miles (3hr15); Zürich 190km/120 miles (3hr30)

Rail Tirano (48km/ 30 miles); Zernez (Switzerland, 28km/ 17 miles); regular buses from station, weekends only

– are aimed at novices and juniors.

New in 2012 was the Cable Park in the middle of the village near lift 20. There are rails, boxes and jumps of varying difficulty, but the area is flat: instead of using gravity, you are pulled along by a special cable system.

SNOW RELIABILITY ★★★★
Very good, given precipitation
Livigno's slopes are high (you can spend most of your time around 2500m) and, with snow-guns on the lower slopes of Mottolino and Costaccia, the season is long.

FOR EXPERTS ★★★
Off-piste confusion
There are several black runs on Mottolino, but they are of black steepness only in places, and regularly groomed. Having previously banned off-piste, the resort now promotes six freeride 'itineraries' on Mottolino; but don't be deceived – it turns out you need a guide for these routes, so they are not itineraries in the usual sense. We have suggested that this is confusing, and ought to be changed.

FOR INTERMEDIATES ★★★
Flattering slopes
Good intermediates will be able to have serious fun on the groomed blacks on Mottolino, as well as the wide choice of reds. The woodland black run from Carosello past Tea da Borch is narrow in places and can get mogulled and icy in the afternoon.

Moderate intermediates have virtually the whole area at their disposal. The long run beneath the Mottolino gondola is one of the best, and there is also a long, varied, under-used blue going less directly to the valley. Leisurely types have several long cruises available; the blue beneath the fast chair at the top of Costaccia is a splendid slope.

FOR BEGINNERS ★★★★
Excellent scattered slopes
There's a vast array of gentle, sunny, low-traffic nursery slopes rising from the village, with lifts concentrated in three areas – north, centre, south. For progression, there are longer blue runs at the top of Costaccia and Mottolino.

FOR BOARDERS ★★★★
Fun of all kinds
The pistes are in general big, wide, open and rolling motorways. The new freeride zones will be an obvious attraction for competent boarders. Beginners be warned: practically all the smaller lower slopes are serviced by drags. But the resort still attracts good numbers of beginners, and Madness is a specialist school.

FOR CROSS-COUNTRY ★★★★
Good snow, bleak setting
Long snow-sure trails (30km in total) follow the valley floor, making Livigno a good choice, provided you don't mind the bleak scenery. There is a specialist school, Livigno 2000.

SCHOOLS

Centrale
t 0342 996276
Azzurra
t 0342 997683
Livigno Italy
t 0342 996767
Livigno Galli Fedele
t 0342 970300
Madness Snowboard
t 0342 997792
New
t 0342 997801

Classes (Centrale prices)
6 2hr-days €115
Private lessons
€38 for 1hr; each additional person €10

CHILDCARE

Kinder Club Lupigno (Centrale)
t 0342 996276
From age 3
M'eating Point
t 0342 997408
From age 3
Pollicino
t 0342 997 408
From age 3mnth

Ski school
From age 4

ACTIVITIES

Indoor Aquagranda wellness park (swimming pool, sauna, fitness rooms), badminton, billiards
Outdoor Cleared paths, ice rink, snowshoeing, horse riding, tobogganing, dog sledding, go-karts on ice, snowmobiling, ice driving, ice climbing, paragliding

UK PACKAGES

Crystal, Inghams, Livigno Snow, Neilson, Skitracer, Thomson

Phone numbers
From abroad use the prefix +39 (and do **not** omit the initial '0' of the phone number)

TOURIST OFFICE

www.livigno.eu

MOUNTAIN RESTAURANTS ★★★★★
No more than adequate

Restaurants are not marked on the resort piste map. Our favourite, though not quite up to Editors' Choice standard, is the Berghütte, in a fine position close to the bottom of Costaccia; the food is simple but satisfying, the service efficient and friendly. Up the hill at Costaccia the upstairs restaurant 'has friendly table service and great pasta'. Carosello has a popular self-service place and a table-service wine bar and restaurant below doing 'outstanding' pasta. Tea da Borch, in the trees lower down, has a Tirolean-style atmosphere. On Mottolino, the huge M'eating Point at the top of the gondola has a self-service section that can be excessively busy but also a small, peaceful table-service section. Lower down there are rustic restaurants at Passo d'Eira and at Trepalle, on the back of the hill.

SCHOOLS AND GUIDES ★★★★★
Short but sweet classes

Past reports on the schools have generally been good, praising instruction and English. Classes are rated great value for money, but are mornings only (as is usual in Italy).

FOR FAMILIES ★★★★★
Not bad for Italy

The schools run classes for children from the age of four, and the Centrale school offers all-day non-skiing care for children from the age of three; the staff speak English. Beware the long, winding airport transfers.

STAYING THERE

Livigno has an enormous range of hotels and a number of apartments.
Hotels There is a wide choice.
★★★★Bivio (0342 996137) Welcoming chalet in centre with popular cellar bar. Good food à la carte. Pool and wellness area.
★★★★Camana Veglia (0342 996310) Charming old wooden chalet. Popular restaurant doing five-course gastro dinners, well placed in Santa Maria.
★★★★Intermonti (0342 972100) Modern with pool and other mod cons; on the Mottolino side of the valley.
★★★★Larice (0342 996184) Stylish little B&B well placed for Costaccia lifts.
★★★★Lac Salin (0342 996166) 'Modern, stylish, with an impressive spa,' says a 2013 report.

★★★Champagne (0342 996437) Pleasant B&B close to centre.
★★★Loredana (0342 996330) Modern chalet on the Mottolino side.
★★★Montanina (0342 996060) Very central, family-run, 'friendly staff'.
★★★Steinbock (0342 970520) Nice little place, far from major lifts.
★★Silvestri (0342 996255) Comfortable place in the San Rocco area.
Apartments Available locally and from tour operators.

EATING OUT ★★★★★
Value for money

Livigno's restaurants are mainly traditional, unpretentious places, many hotel-based. Over the years we've had countless recommendations for where to eat. The latest recommendations include Cantina, in the hotel Bivio ('excellent, with a fine choice of wines'), Paprika ('good flavour, good value') and Scala ('fish a speciality; flavour, service and ambience excellent').

APRES-SKI ★★★★★
Adequately lively

The scene is quieter than some people expect – and the best places are scattered about; but we haven't found it lacking life. At teatime, Tea del Vidal, at the bottom of Mottolino, is 'a great lively bar with good music' – and things also get lively at the Stalet bar at the base of the Carosello gondola ('very friendly and warm') and at the central umbrella bar. Nightlife gets going after 10pm. The Kuhstall under the Bivio hotel is an excellent cellar bar with live music, as is the Helvetia, over the road. At the southern end of the village, Daphne's is 'one of the few lively bars in Livigno', Miky's is 'vibrant and very busy', and Marco's is popular. Kokodi is the main disco.

OFF THE SLOPES ★★★★★
Some distractions

The newish thermal spa/wellness centre Aquagranda is no rival to Bad Gastein – a comparison one reader has made – but by other, more normal standards is OK, with indoor and outdoor swimming plus the usual range of relaxing facilities. Some visitors have enjoyed the dog sledding, and tobogganing is also popular. And you can go bowling and ice driving. Walks are uninspiring. There's duty-free shopping, of course – and trips to Bormio and St Moritz.

Madonna di Campiglio

A fashionable resort amid stunning scenery – a bit like Cortina, in other words, but with a more sensibly linked ski area

RATINGS

The mountains

Extent	★★★
Fast lifts	★★★★
Queues	★★★★
Terrain p'ks	★★★
Snow	★★★
Expert	★★
Intermediate	★★★★
Beginner	★★★
Boarder	★★★
X-country	★★★
Restaurants	★★★
Schools	★★★
Families	★★★

The resort

Charm	★★★★
Convenience	★★★
Scenery	★★★★
Eating out	★★★
Après-ski	★★★
Off-slope	★★

RPI 100

lift pass	£190
ski hire	£105
lessons	£95
food & drink	£130
total	**£520**

NEWS

2013/14: A new red piste, Namibino, is to open in the Cinque Laghi area.

2012/13: A new quad chair opened on the upper slopes of the Cinque Laghi sector, opening up two new pistes, a blue and a black that link with the Canalone Miramonti to create a new 1700m run that will be used for SuperG World Cup competitions.

➕ Splendid wooded setting in the dramatic Brenta Dolomites

➕ Pleasant, stylish village, with car-free centre and a tunnel bypass

➕ Extensive, varied slopes, including the linked areas of Folgarida, Marilleva and now Pinzolo

➕ Lots of long, easy runs

➖ Although it has a compact core, the resort spreads widely along the valley

➖ Tough pistes are few, and widely separated around a big area, and off-piste is formally banned

➖ Quiet from dinner time onwards

Madonna di Campiglio may come second to Cortina d'Ampezzo for smart shops and bars – and for scenic drama – but it is nevertheless a very attractive resort. A return visit in 2012 confirmed it as one of our Italian favourites.

What triggered our visit was the new lift link to the slopes of Pinzolo, opened in 2011. The link involves no skiing, but there is no denying that jumping on a gondola for a 16-minute ride is more appealing than waiting for buses, and we rate the new link highly. Pinzolo, like the other linked areas of Folgarida and Marilleva, adds considerably to the skiing, especially for confident skiers.

THE RESORT

Campiglio is a well-established, quite fashionable resort, set near the head of a heavily wooded valley. Although the clientele is mainly Italian, the resort seems now to be attracting Russian visitors in considerable numbers. The regional lift pass covers not only the several linked resorts but also others in the Val di Sole to the north, which are reachable by car or possibly bus, including Pejo and Passo Tonale (which gets its own chapter).

VILLAGE CHARM ★★★★
Smoothly traditional
Campiglio is mainly built in traditional Alpine style and has a towny, polished air, at least around the central, car-free Piazza Righi and nearby streets, where there are quite a few diverting shops. The village is bypassed by through-traffic. Near the centre is a small park, and a lake, used for skating. The place doesn't go to sleep in the day, and is quite lively in the early evening.

CONVENIENCE ★★★
Good links between sectors
The centre is fairly compact: the main lifts bracket many of the main hotels, and are a 5/10-minute walk apart. Skiing links between the main slope sectors work well. But the resort sprawls about 3km down the valley, and some hotels are widely spread; up

the valley is the outlying suburb of Campo Carlo Magno, where there are further major lifts and a sizeable car park as well as more hotels. The ski-bus service has not impressed reporters, and charges of 2 a day or 10 a week were introduced last season. Many hotels run shuttles.

SCENERY ★★★★
Splendid Dolomites
The resort has a splendid setting, with the dramatic cliffs of the Brenta group to the south-east.

THE MOUNTAINS

The upper slopes are open, the lower slopes attractively wooded. Many run classifications exaggerate difficulty. Some readers have found signposting not as clear as it could be.

EXTENT OF THE SLOPES ★★★
Plenty of variety
The extent of the pistes is not huge, but the slopes span large distances and give a great sense of travel.

Gondolas from close to the centre go west up to the **Pradalago** sector – which is linked via Monte Vigo to the distant slopes of **Folgarida** and **Marilleva** – and to **Cinque Laghi**, where at mid-mountain the new gondola link with **Pinzolo** starts. A bit further from the centre, another gondola goes east up to **Spinale**. The high **Grostè** sector can be reached from there or by yet another access gondola from the outlying Campo Carlo Magno where there is also a fast chairlift up to Pradalago.

The 300m Belvedere draglift, which normally offers an easy route from the centre to the blue home run to the Spinale gondola, has recently been closed by a local dispute.

FAST LIFTS ★★★★☆
Some weaknesses
Most of the key lifts are fast chairs and gondolas, but moving around the area you will still meet some slow lifts. Examples include several lifts around Monte Spolverino and Monte Vigo, on

Dos de la Pesa, on Monte Spinale and at Pinzolo. But at least the piste map helpfully distinguishes fast chairs.

QUEUES ★★★★☆
Not a big issue
Around Campiglio itself queues are rarely a problem except at ski school time in high season, when a 2012 visitor speaks of 10-minute waits. You may meet queues on the lifts around Monte Vigo and Monte Spolverino.

TERRAIN PARKS ★★★☆☆
Serious efforts
The Ursus park, at Grostè, includes boardercross, quarter-pipe, rails, boxes and kickers. There's a special boarders'

KEY FACTS

Resort	1520m
	4,990ft
Madonna, Folgarida, Marilleva, Pinzolo combined area	
Slopes	800-2505m
	2,620-8,220ft
Lifts	61
Pistes	150km
	93 miles
Blue	46%
Red	38%
Black	16%
Snowmaking	95%

LIFT PASSES

Prices in €

Age	1-day	6-day
under 8	21	105
8 to 15	29	146
16 to 64	42	209
65 plus	38	188

Free Under 8 if with family-paying adult

Notes Madonna only; daily extensions for Pinzolo, Folgarida-Marilleva

Alternative passes
Pinzolo pass; Skirama Adamello Brenta covers Madonna, Pinzolo, Marilleva-Folgarida, Passo Tonale, Ponte di Legno, Andalo, Pejo, Monte Bondone and Folgaria-Lavarone

SCHOOLS

Nazionale
t 0465 443243
Rainalter
t 0465 443300
Cinque Laghi
t 0465 441650

Classes (Nazionale prices)
6 2hr-mornings €165
Private lessons
From €42 for 1hr

---

pass for the area. There is also a beginner park in the Pradalago sector. A 2013 reporter approves.

SNOW RELIABILITY ★★★★★
Good snowmaking
Although many of the runs are sunny, they are at a fair altitude, and snowmaking is now claimed to cover 95% of the runs. As a result, snow reliability is reasonable, despite an erratic snowfall record. Reporters stress the immaculate grooming.

FOR EXPERTS ★★★★★
Relax and enjoy the view
As in many resorts in Italy, off-piste is formally banned, but the ban is often ignored. Finding ungroomed snow can be a bit of a challenge though – and this is not an area famed for reliable powder anyway. The trees around the Genziana chair at Pradalago are a good spot. There are black pistes dotted around – basically, one per sector – but they only just merit the classification. The lower part of Spinale Direttissima on the front of Monte Spinale is claimed to be 35°, which is a proper black. Few of the local reds present much challenge; it's worth checking out Pinzolo.

FOR INTERMEDIATES ★★★★★
A great area
Grostè and Pradalago have long, wide easy runs, and timid intermediates will love them, while confident skiers will need to seek out challenges. The long blue Pradalago Facile is a fabulous wide, scenic cruise. The nearby reds aren't a lot steeper, but the lovely, scenic black Amazzonia is quite testing. Grostè is both high and gentle, so has the feel of a glacier – but it is entirely rock. All four runs at the very top are of blue gradient, although two are marked red. Lower down, Lame is a decent red. Next-door Monte Spinale has easy slopes on the back, linking to Grostè, but much tougher stuff on the front (read 'For experts'). Spinale Diretta (not to be confused with Spinale Direttissima) is an excellent genuine red. Cinque Laghi, Campiglio's racing mountain, has something for everyone. The long Cinque Laghi is tricky at the top, but is then a lovely genuine blue run ending prettily in woods; the famous 2 Tre is a good, varied red, quite steep towards the bottom.

Keen intermediates should not fail

---

to explore the runs at Folgarida, Marilleva and Pinzolo. The Malghette red run on the way back from Monte Vigo is a favourite, with fabulous views across the valley; we'd be tempted to do laps on it if it were served by a faster lift.

FOR BEGINNERS ★★★★★
Get out of town
There are short drags near the village, but better nursery slopes up at Campo Carlo Magno, a bus ride out. The draglift here is not covered by the main lift pass, your expert friends should note. Progression to longer runs is easy – Pradalago is perfect.

FOR BOARDERS ★★★★★
Freeriders look elsewhere
The resort is popular with freestylers, and some major events have been held here.

FOR CROSS-COUNTRY ★★★★★
Respectable
There are 22km of pretty trails through the woods in a scenic setting up at Campo Carlo Magno.

MOUNTAIN RESTAURANTS ★★★★★
A fair selection
There are plenty of restaurants, all named on the piste map. Standards vary – there are plenty of routine cafeterias, but also table-service places with character doing good food, including mountaineering refuges.

One of the most promising table-service places is the little back room at Chalet Fiat at Spinale; the main self-service bit is stylishly done out, and has decent food, but finding a table can be a bit of a bunfight. Reader tips on Grostè: Boch, Stoppani ('gourmet-style but modest prices, very good service and atmosphere', 'wonderful views'), Graffer ('lovely position, very reasonable prices, efficient service') and Malga Montagnoli; on Pradalago: Viviani Pradalago ('superb – perfect service', 'traditional food, reasonable prices') and Cascina Zeledria ('delightful terrace, good service', 'cook your own on a hot rock').

SCHOOLS AND GUIDES ★★★★★
Insist on English
There are several schools – Nazionale is the main one. Language has been a problem in the past, but we are assured that Nazionale and Rainalter have English-speaking instructors.

↑ The car-free central area is a pleasant place to wander about in the evening, with some smart shopping

APT MADONNA DI CAMPIGLIO, PINZOLO, VAL RENDENA / C BARONI

CHILDCARE

Baita del Bimbo (Rainalter school)
t 0465 443300
Age 2 to 8

Ski schools
From age 4; half-days or full days (10am to 4pm)

MOMENTUM SKI

Weekend & a la carte ski holiday specialists

100% Tailor-made

Premier hotels & apartments

Flexible travel arrangements

020 7371 9111
WWW.MOMENTUMSKI.COM

FOR FAMILIES ★★★☆☆
Do your own thing
The ski schools take children from four. The Rainalter Ski School offers non-ski activities for children between two and eight years. But we wonder if English is reliably spoken. The central park is an attractive feature.

STAYING THERE

There is a wide choice of hotels – dozens of 4-star and 3-star places – and some self-catering.
Hotels
****Chalet del Brenta** (0465 443159) Newish, stylish place well south of the centre but strongly tipped by two readers this year – efficient shuttle, excellent food, 'very friendly staff, surprisingly good spa'.
****Lorenzetti** (0465 441404) At southern extremity not far from the new gondola for Cinque Laghi and Pinzolo, and with timetabled shuttles. Reporters agree the food is top notch, but rooms vary. 'Glorious views.'
****Maribel** (0465 443085) Stylish modern chalet out at Campo Carlo Magno – though not perfectly placed for the lift stations. Rooms and suites. Good wellness area.
****Oberosler** (0465 441136) 'Design' hotel (which in this case means bold

modern decor) right next to the Spinale gondola and return piste. We enjoyed staying here in 2012 – good food, helpful staff.
***Ariston** (0465 441070) On the town square, tastefully decorated and well run by an English-speaking Italian couple. 'Highly recommended.'
***Italo** (0465 441392) Simple, quiet place 300m from Spinale lift: 'Friendly, good food,' says a 2012 reporter.
***Sportivo** (0465 441101) Small B&B in pole position metres from the Pradalago gondola station.

EATING OUT ★★★☆☆
Some good options
There are around 20 restaurants in the resort. Bear in mind that some of the bars also offer food. Reader tips include Antico Focolare ('spectacular ravioli in creamy nut sauce'), Le Roi ('good location, cosy, excellent service, good food at reasonable prices') and, for a gourmet treat, the 'amazing' Da Alfiero in Piazza Palu at the south end of the park – 'luxury, good service and food, reasonable prices'.

APRES-SKI ★★★☆☆
Jolly enough at teatime
As the slopes close, people pile in to several central places – Cafe Campiglio, Nardis Cafe and Bar Suisse

GETTING THERE

Air Verona 150km/ 95 miles (3hr); Bergamo 160km/ 100 miles (3hr); Milan 200km/125 miles (3hr30)

Rail Trento (75km/ 45 miles)

ACTIVITIES

Indoor Pools and spas in hotels

Outdoor Ice skating, snowshoeing, ice climbing, dog sledding, paragliding

UK PACKAGES

Alpine Answers, Crystal, Crystal Finest, Erna Low, Flexiski, Momentum, Scott Dunn, Ski Club Freshtracks, Ski Expectations, Ski Solutions, Ski Yogi, Solos, STC, Zenith **Folgarida** Alpine Answers, Crystal, Erna Low, Rocketski, Solos, STC **Marilleva** STC, Zenith

Phone numbers From abroad use the prefix +39 (and do **not** omit the initial '0' of the phone number)

TOURIST OFFICE

www. campigliodolomiti.it

– a very welcoming cafe-bar on the main square. Ober One at Oberosler hotel, at the bottom of Spinale, is more 'conveniently placed but not so popular', which may be because of the music it pumps out. As dinner time approaches, everyone disappears. If some of them reappear later, it's to head for Des Alpes, Cliffhanger or Zangola (out of town). Cantina del Suisse (underneath Bar Suisse) has live music some evenings.

OFF THE SLOPES ★★☆☆☆
Take your Kindle
There's not a huge amount to do. Skating on the lake and snowshoeing are popular, and the local Alpine guides offer ice climbing.

LINKED RESORT – 1400m
MARILLEVA

Marilleva is a modern resort consisting of several 1960s-style, ugly but functional, low-rise concrete buildings (most of them well screened by trees, thankfully) built on a mid-mountain shelf at 1400m and reached by road or gondola from the lower part of the resort at 900m, on the valley floor.

The slopes above Marilleva are excellent, steep reds served by a gondola and a six-pack (with a few blues higher up the mountain), much better for adventurous intermediates than Campiglio's main Pradalago slopes. And they are shady, so the snow is usually the best in the area. There's also a genuine black run on Dos de la Pesa served by a slow two-stage chairlift. The Orti mountain restaurant offers 'good food, fantastic views, reasonable prices'.

LINKED RESORT – 1400m
FOLGARIDA

Folgarida is also purpose built and set above the floor of the Val di Sole, but it is beside the road over to Campiglio, and is much more traditional in style than Marilleva.

The resort spreads across the mountainside between two gondola stations, one right on the roadside at 1400m and the other some way off the road in a much more village-like area at 1300m. This part in particular feels more upmarket than Marilleva, with smart hotels and a few shops, but there are few other amenities. A 2011 reporter rates it excellent for families,

with 'friendly, helpful locals'. You may encounter some fur-clad patrons, or in January families from Eastern Europe. One enthusiastic past reporter judged the 4-star hotel Caminetto (0463 986109) 'almost perfect'.

The slopes down to Folgarida are gentler than those above Marilleva, though they include an easy black.

Midway between Marilleva and Folgarida, an eight-person gondola runs from the valley village of Daolasa up to Val Mastellina, below Monte Vigo, the top section serving a long, sweeping red with lovely views of the Val di Sole below.

LINKED RESORT – 770m
PINZOLO

Pinzolo is the main town of the Val Rendena, south-west of Campiglio, and 750m lower. The long (and long-planned) gondola link between the slopes of Pinzolo and Campiglio opened in 2011.

From Pinzolo, a gondola followed by a fast chair take you via a lively mid-mountain congregation area with nursery slopes to the area's high point of Doss del Sabion (2100m), where there are great close-up views of the Brenta massif.

It's quite a challenging area, mainly consisting of genuine blacks (groomed when we have visited) and genuine reds, some of them at the steep end of the spectrum. Most of the runs are quite short, the conspicuous exception being the excellent black/red run of almost 900m vertical to the valley station of a second gondola at Tulot, just outside the town. Start at Doss del Sabion and you can extend this to 1300m. Many of the slopes are shady, so keep snow well. The pistes are quiet; one recent reporter says: 'A delight! Empty runs.'

The Rifugio Doss del Sabion at the top has a calm little table-service room as an alternative to the often hectic terrace and self-service. There is a restaurant at mid-mountain, too.

PInzolo sells itself as a family resort, and has good childcare facilities at mid-mountain, but we would expect language problems in a resort little known in the UK.

There are plenty of guest houses and hotels, mainly 3-star but with some other options. One past reporter tipped the well-placed 4-star Quadrifoglio (0465 503600).

TVB TUX / JP PANKHAUSER

Monterosa Ski

One of Europe's best-kept secrets: three unspoiled and uncrowded valleys linked by pistes and fab off-piste terrain

TOP 10 RATINGS

Extent	★★
Fast lifts	★★★★★
Queues	★★★★
Snow	★★★★
Expert	★★★★
Intermediate	★★★★
Beginner	★★
Charm	★★★
Convenience	★★★
Scenery	★★★★

RPI 85

lift pass	£180
ski hire	£95
lessons	£65
food & drink	£100
total	**£440**

NEWS

2013/14: There are plans for a new snow park in the Champoluc area.

2012/13: A new restaurant, Baita Stella Alpina, opened on the Ostafa 1 piste in the Champoluc area.

420

- ➕ Fabulous off-piste and heli-skiing, for both intermediates and experts
- ➕ Slopes quiet on weekdays
- ➕ Comprehensive snowmaking
- ➕ Unspoiled valleys and villages
- ➕ Panoramic views at altitude
- ➕ Some great mountain restaurants
- ➕ Lovely long runs and a sensation of travel from place to place, but ...

- ➖ Virtually no choice of route when touring the three valleys on-piste, and a modest total extent
- ➖ Few challenges (or moguls) on-piste
- ➖ Unhelpful piste classification
- ➖ High winds can close links
- ➖ Few off-slope diversions
- ➖ Can be very busy at weekends
- ➖ Limited après-ski

Monterosa Ski's resorts – Champoluc, Gressoney la Trinité and Alagna – are popular with Italian weekenders and experts going off-piste, but are otherwise not widely known. They retain a friendly, small-scale, unspoiled ambience that we (and a growing band of readers) like a lot. In overall scale, this three-valley network matches the famed French one. But the Italian network is skeletal, quite unlike the full-bodied French one. The two areas are in different leagues.

Champoluc has been put on the UK map by one-resort operator Ski 2, which has built a great reputation here. This season, family specialist Esprit Ski arrives in the next valley; we expect they'll put Gressoney on the map, too.

There is one main village in each of the three valleys. Champoluc in the western Val d'Ayas and Gressoney in the central valley are both reached from the Aosta valley, to the south.

Day-trip outings to other resorts are hard work, but Cervinia, La Thuile, Courmayeur and Pila are reachable by car from these resorts. The Aosta Valley pass covers all of them.

Alagna is more remote and

isolated, and approached by a quite different route from the east.

All three villages are small-scale and pleasantly rustic, without being picture-postcard pretty. Like most Italian resorts, the villages really come to life only at weekends.

Monterosa Ski is surrounded by a string of peaks over 4000m, and some over 4500m; the panoramic views from restaurant terraces are fabulous.

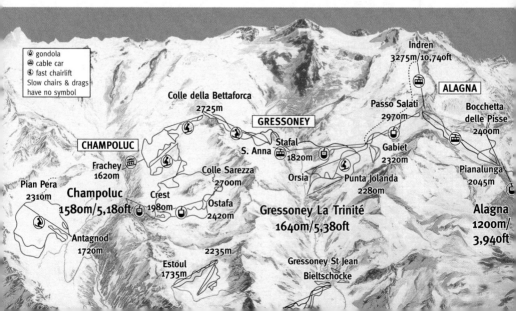

🚠 gondola
🚡 cable car
🚡 fast chairlift
Slow chairs & drags have no symbol

Indren
3275m/10,740ft

ALAGNA

Colle della Bettaforca
2725m

Passo Salati
2970m

Bocchetta delle Pisse
2400m

GRESSONEY

CHAMPOLUC

Stafal
S. Anna 1820m

Gabiet
2320m

Frachey
1620m

Colle Sarezza
2700m

Orsia

Punta Jolanda
2280m

Pianalunga
2045m

Pian Pera
2310m

Champoluc
1580m/5,180ft

Crest
1980m

Ostafa
2420m

Gressoney La Trinité
1640m/5,380ft

Alagna
1200m/
3,940ft

Antagnod
1720m

2235m

Gressoney St Jean

Estoul
1735m

Bieltschocke

Slopes	1200-3275m
	3,940-10,740ft
Lifts	23
Pistes	73km
	45 miles
Blue	17%
Red	72%
Black	11%
Snowmaking	97%

THE MOUNTAINS

Open slopes dominate, but there are also woodland runs lower down, particularly at Gressoney. The piste map and signposting are adequate. It's a shame that many runs that could be classified blue are red, leading to uncertainty for timid intermediates.

The attraction for experts and confident intermediates is the off-piste (the black pistes are mostly not steep), with great runs from the high points of the lift system and some excellent heli-drops. The Indren cable car accesses an excellent itinerary as well as more serious routes. Among the adventures we've enjoyed here was a heli-drop on Monte Rosa, skiing down to lifts out of Zermatt.

There is excellent intermediate piste skiing, with some notably long runs from the ridges to the villages. The run down to Alagna is 1760m vertical and 7km, for example.

Although the slopes span vast distances, and give a great sense of travel, they don't add up to a huge amount of skiing. The lift company has now quietly accepted our view that its claimed run lengths needed, more or

less, to be halved. The total for the linked area is now only 73km. Much larger totals are still in circulation.

The main three-valley network is very simple, with few variations: from each of the ridges, there is basically one way down each mountainside.

Champoluc and Gressoney have worthwhile local areas of pistes in addition to this three-valley system, but Alagna does not. The main lift system is vulnerable to bad weather, but both Champoluc and Gressoney have sheltered alternatives.

This is not a notably snowy area, but altitude helps, as does extensive snowmaking. Grooming is thorough – bumps on the pistes don't last long.

The lifts are virtually all chairs and gondolas; most of the important chairs are fast, though there are exceptions. Sunny weekends bring crowds, and one or two queuing problems in the Champoluc and Alagna valleys.

The mountain restaurants are generally simple, friendly and good value, but there are some notably good ones too. Pity most are not named on the piste map. Sadly, dear old favourite Rifugio Guglielmina, high above Alagna, burned down in 2011/12.

Monterosa Ski

Build your own shortlist: www.wheretoskiandsnowboard.com

Gressoney la Trinité 1640m

+ Centrally placed in the three valleys
+ Convenient if you pick your spot
+ Some good mountain restaurants

- Access to long easy runs involves lifts up and down the hill
- Slow lifts on lower local slopes

If you are planning daily excursions to Passo Salati to ski Alagna or to ride the Punta Indren cable car, Gressoney is the place to start. The big news this year is the opening of a chalet hotel by family specialist tour operator Esprit Ski.

Gressoney la Trinité is at the head of the long and beautiful Lys valley – a 40-minute drive from the Val d'Aosta. This is a resort of parts. The heart of the village is slightly away from the skiing, but there are skiers' satellites that have grown up at the lift bases: 500m away across the valley is the base station of a slow chairlift into the local slopes; there is a mini-resort conveniently clustered around the lift base, now almost as big as the village proper. The lifts for the other valleys go from a second mini-resort of Stafal, 5km away at the head of the valley.

Village charm Gressoney la Trinité is a quiet, neat little village, cobbled in the centre, with an old church and traditional wooden buildings – but also with many buildings closed up, in the winter at least. The satellites don't amount to much – a dense collection of hotels at the local lift base and a more spread-out one at Stafal.

Convenience The local lift base area is compact and convenient. Up at Stafal, walks to the lifts are a bit longer, but bearable from most lodgings.

THE MOUNTAINS

Slopes From Stafal, a cable car goes in one direction towards Colle Bettaforca and Champoluc, and a gondola goes in the other towards Passo Salati and Alagna. Down the valley at Gressoney, a chairlift accesses an area of wooded runs of 400m/500m vertical, with piste links across the mountainside to the lifts from Stafal to Passo Salati.

Down the valley beyond Gressoney St Jean, at Bieltschocke, is a small but worthwhile (700m vertical) area of slopes served by a chairlift.

Fast lifts The slow chairs in the woods at Gressoney are the main exceptions to a picture dominated by fast lifts.

Queues The queue-prone gondola from Stafal to Gabiet has been upgraded, but the one above it gets busy at times.

Terrain parks There's an 'excellent' park at Gabiet (Dream Park).

Experts Gressoney is well placed for access to Passo Salati and the cable car to Punta Indren, for off-piste runs. The only serious black run in the area is the short one from Punta Jolanda.

Intermediates On both sides of the valley there are fine, none-too-difficult reds above mid-mountain, with trickier runs lower down. The one on the Passo Salati side is classed as a black, but is not seriously steep.

Beginners There are nursery slopes with moving carpets at valley level at Gressoney itself and at Stafal. Then it's up the gondola to the short blue run at mid-mountain, or up to the top for the much longer blue runs to the mid-station of the cable car from Alagna.

Snowboarding There's a boardercross at Gabiet, at mid-mountain.

Cross-country There are decent trails: 23km around Gressoney St Jean.

Mountain restaurants On the local slopes, off the main system, there are two places we are itching to try. The welcoming, woody, table-service Punta Jolanda does 'great pasta' but also more serious dishes; lively bar, too. Lower down, Morgenrot is a reader favourite – 'good for a serious lunch', 'friendly service', 'excellent pasta'. Nearby, simple self-service Bedemie is 'great value'; the spag bol at 5 euros is the cheapest in the Alps. At mid-mountain on the main slope from P Salati, the stone-built Rif Gabiet this year celebrates its fifth consecutive recommendation by one reporter, for 'excellent, good-value pasta, polenta and cakes'. Oh, and 'best bombardinos on the mountain'. Keep it up, Julia!

Schools and guides The school at Stafal is said to be short of English-speaking instructors. The guides of Guide Monterosa have consistently got good reports – 'very professional but great fun', 'very good five days'.

Families Big news: family specialist Esprit is opening a chalet hotel here.

STAYING THERE

Chalets We know of no small chalets, but this year family specialist Esprit has taken over the hotel Valverde (in an excellent position at the village lift base) to operate it as a chalet hotel.

ESPRIT Ski

No.1 For Family Skiing
2013/14

Gressoney
& 14 more top resorts
in Switzerland, France, Austria and Italy with market-leading dedicated child care in every resort

ESPRIT FAMILY SAVERS
SAVE UP TO
£1,000
PER FAMILY!

★ We focus 100% on families, guaranteeing complete dedication to family needs

★ Up to £150 per couple Cash-Back, plus thousands of FREE child places

★ Dedicated Esprit Nurseries with qualified English-speaking nannies

★ Exclusive Esprit ski classes, with maximum 6 or 8 children per qualified instructor

★ Children's afternoon Activity Clubs and evening 'Cocoa Clubs' in every resort

★ Free evening Baby-Listening / Child Patrol Service available

★ Strict child care ratios and procedures based on 31 years' child care experience

NEW this season

THE VALVERDE ◆◆◆ PLUS
GRESSONEY

The latest addition to our Chalet Hotel portfolio is sure to become a sought-after choice with its own spa area, dedicated Esprit child care rooms, a chairlift right outside plus a piste running home to the back door.

✈ Gatwick, Heathrow, Southampton, Stansted, Bristol, Birmingham, Manchester, East Midlands & Edinburgh

For a free brochure call 01483 791900 or visit espritski.com

Hotels In the village, the Jolanda Sport (0125 366140) has had good reports. At the village lift base, the 3-star Dufour (0125 366139) earned glowing reports last year – 'charming owners, wonderful staff, excellent food'. At Stafal, the modern, stylish little Nordend (0125 366807) is in the same ownership. We enjoyed our stay here in 2013, eating at the good restaurant beneath. The Ellex is a chalet-style eco-place with 'a lovely lounge, smart bathrooms and a great spa'. The modern Chalet du Lys (0125 366806) offers good rooms and 'excellent' food.

Eating out The bar-restaurant underneath the hotel Nordend, known as the Core or Giovanni's, does excellent food, charmingly served.

Après-ski Gressoney is pretty quiet. At Stafal the bar under the Nordend is a 'great place for a beer' at teatime.

Off the slopes There's an ice rink and a sport hall plus big pool.

Champoluc 1580m

+ Relaxed, traditional-style village
+ Excellent beginner area at mid-mountain, but ...

- Progress to longer runs tricky
- Some tricky red runs
- Not notably convenient

Champoluc is at the western end of the three-valley network. Although it has drawbacks, it's an attractive all-round base. But what keeps many people going back is the warm welcome, and the service provided by UK tour operator Ski 2.

Champoluc is strung out along the street running from the centre past various hotels to the gondola base station, where a cluster of shops and bars forms a kind of distinct micro-resort. About 3km up the valley, a short funicular goes up from Frachey (with parking right at the base).

Down-valley from Champoluc are Antagnod and Brusson. Antagnod is a good alternative for bad weather days, and has some good off-piste.

Village charm There is a group of standard skiers' bars and restaurants at the lift base. The village as a whole lacks a real focus, but we and readers like the ambience – it seems like a pleasant summer mountain resort that happens also to have skiing.

Convenience The village is not compact or notably convenient, but everything is walkable. Some hotels are a 10-minute walk from the gondola base station. You can leave kit there. There is a 'hit and miss' bus service to and from Frachey.

THE MOUNTAINS

Slopes The gondola from Champoluc goes up to Crest, a mid-mountain nursery area with a further gondola and chairlift going on to Colle Sarezza. This area is linked to the runs above Frachey via a steep, narrow, bumpy red run, known by all and sundry as the Goat, because of the fine statue at the top; timid intermediates are better off starting at Frachey. From there, you ride lifts to Colle Bettaforca, for the descent to the Gressoney valley.

Fast lifts Most of the lifts are fast chairs and gondolas, but the link with Frachey involves slow chairs. You avoid these by starting at the funicular from the valley.

Queues Mostly blissfully queue-free. But there are two problems at Frachey. The Alpe Mandria chair above the funicular is a bottleneck, serving too many purposes, and gets queues at peak times even on weekdays. And the old double chair that forms the link to the home slopes of Champoluc cannot cope with afternoon demand.

Terrain parks There are plans to build a snow park for 2013/14.

Experts Read the introduction. In bad weather, head for the excellent Mandria forest area above Frachey.

Intermediates There is a good mix of varied pistes that suit confident intermediates. But Champoluc has drawbacks for timid intermediates – as well as the Goat run, the red descent to Champoluc (excellent if you can hack it) can be too much for many. Some people find it worth going down the valley to the separate Antagnod area to build confidence.

Beginners The high nursery slopes at Crest above Champoluc, served by two moving carpets, are excellent. For longer gentle runs, though, you need to go up the valley to Frachey. Or down the valley to Antagnod.

Snowboarding There's a boardercross at Gressoney.

Cross-country There are trails totalling 17km in Champoluc; but Brusson, down-valley, has the best trails in the area (30km) – 'Fantastic,' says a downhiller who gave it a go.

Gressoney la Trinité
Alpine Answers, Crystal, Crystal Finest, Erna Low, Esprit, Inghams, Momentum, Mountain Tracks, Ski Club Freshtracks, Skitracer, Ski Yogi, Snoworks, STC
Champoluc Alpine Answers, Crystal, Crystal Finest, Interski, Momentum, Ski 2, Ski Expectations, Ski Solutions, Ski Yogi, Snow Finders
Alagna Alpine Answers, James Orr Heliski, Ski Club Freshtracks, Ski Monterosa, Ski Weekend

Phone numbers
From abroad use the prefix +39 (and do **not** omit the initial '0' of the phone number)

www.monterosa-ski.com/en

Mountain restaurants There are three small, notably charming places on the lower slopes serving excellent food in beautifully renovated old buildings. Our favourites are l'Aroula and Rascard Frantze, above and below the Champoluc mid-station. Stadel Soussun above Frachey is possibly the most polished, but we've found service rather cool. Other reader tips include: the 'atmospheric' Belvedere, Ostafa ('good value, big portions'), the modern Campo Base ('the best hot chocolate'), Taconet ('great pies, tasty pasta, friendly') and Lo Retsignon ('charming rustic hut, smiling family, good prices, excellent burgers').

Schools and guides We have had mixed reports on the Italian ski schools – most recently about excellent private lessons. We have had good reports of the ski school run by Ski 2 ('good, friendly instructors').

Families UK tour operator Ski 2 operates all kinds of schemes to keep your children happy.

STAYING THERE

We've had good reports of Champoluc specialists Ski 2 ('great from pick-up to drop-off'). We know of no chalets.

Hotels For a small place, Champoluc has a good range of attractive hotels. In 2010 and 2013 we enjoyed the friendly, woody 4-star La Rouja (0125 308767). Another favourite of ours is the lovely 4-star Breithorn (0125 308734), despite some small rooms. This year readers favour the 3-star Champoluc (0125 308088), and not only for its perfect location next to the gondola: 'Owner and staff so pleased to make us comfortable.' Many have enjoyed the comfortable but rather formal 4-star Relais des Glaciers (0125 308182). The central 3-star Castor (0125 307117) has 'great atmosphere, good food, helpful, friendly staff'.

Comfortable lodgings up the hill are a local speciality. The Hôtellerie de Mascognaz (0125 308734), a satellite of the Breithorn, is a lovingly restored group of stone chalets in a very isolated spot reached by skidoo. Three mountain restaurants have charming rooms – Stadel Soussun (348 6527222), Rascard Frantze (0125 941065) and l'Aroula (347 0188095), where we had a wonderfully peaceful and comfortable stay in 2012.

Eating out Most restaurants are in hotels, but there are a few stand-alone places. Osteria Il Balivo is again tipped

('remarkable pork knuckle, dreamy puds'). But it is rather eclipsed by the Grange up at Frachey: 'Just brilliant; exceptional atmosphere, exemplary food, faultless service; owner insisted on driving us back to our hotel.'

Après-ski Atelier Gourmand is a 'cosy, rustic' place at the gondola base popular with readers for immediate après drinks or later aperitivos. The nearby Bistrot is popular too. And the hotel Glaciers' patisserie is 'well worth the walk'. Golosone is a small, atmospheric, distinctly Italian wine bar; and the West Road pub in the hotel California has karaoke some nights. Later on, Pachamama impressed one reader.

Off the slopes There are lovely walks up the valley. And an outdoor ice rink.

ALAGNA

Alagna is a small, remote village with a solid church and some lovely old wooden farmhouses built in the distinctive Walser style. But its local skiing is very limited; in bad weather there may be little or nothing to do. So it is difficult to recommend for a holiday booked well in advance.

The mountains above Alagna offer some of the most exciting off-piste routes in the whole area, including very steep couloirs.

In good weather, the splendid 7km (1760m vertical) descent from Passo Salati to Alagna is one of the highlights of the area. At the top, the black Olen piste (once rightly classified red) is a great blast. There is good, shady, easily accessible off-piste beside it. The tough red Alagna piste below it is equally rewarding – though the village is relatively low and sunny; the lower sections suffer as a result.

The gondola and (particularly) the cable car above it can build queues.

With the demise of Rif Guglielmina, the good mountain restaurants are all low down. At Pianalunga, Alpen Stop is tipped for pasta, cakes and 'superb veal escalope'. Just below it, La Baita is 'a very friendly family restaurant doing excellent pasta and polenta (eg with chamois)'. Much lower down, Shoppf Wittine is a cosy little hut, though with a bigger terrace and interior than appearances suggest. Friendly people, simple menu; most pastas meatless, but tagliatelle with sausage and onions was good.

Monterosa Ski

ADAMELLO SKI

Passo Tonale

An unusual and attractive combination of high, snow-sure slopes and low prices; now linked to lower, wooded Ponte di Legno

TOP 10 RATINGS

Extent	★★
Fast lifts	★★★★
Queues	★★★★
Snow	★★★★
Expert	★
Intermediate	★★★
Beginner	★★★★★
Charm	★★
Convenience	★★★
Scenery	★★★

RPI   75

lift pass	£170
ski hire	£70
lessons	£45
food & drink	£100
total	**£385**

NEWS

2013/14: Work will begin on a new gondola from Passo Paradiso to the top of the glacier, replacing the existing T-bars and chairlift.

2012/13: The resort's first six-pack was installed on the nursery slopes, replacing two T-bars. A covered travelator has been added next to this.

+ Good-value mid-market lodgings

+ Sunny but snow-sure slopes

+ Plenty of uncrowded, easy runs, immediately above the village

+ Link to Ponte di Legno adds attractive, steeper, treelined runs

− Not much locally for experts or keen intermediates

− Local slopes are above the treeline and are unpleasant in bad weather

− Linear village strung along the pass road is no beauty

Passo Tonale is a great place for beginners and timid intermediates on tight budgets. It's a more interesting destination for the more adventurous now that it is linked to the slopes of Ponte di Legno, over the pass to the west.

THE RESORT

Village charm The resort was developed mainly for skiing, along a road over a high pass; many of the buildings are in chalet style, but it lacks a focus, and traffic intrudes.
Convenience Tonale is fairly compact, with its hotels, shops, bars and restaurants spread along the bottom of the main slope area – so the nearest lift is generally not far away. The gondola to the glacier is outside the village, but you can ski to it.
Scenery The main slopes offer grand views of Presena, and Ponte di Legno slopes also offer good views.

THE MOUNTAINS

The Tonale slopes are entirely above the treeline, and bad weather can mean white-outs and closures. The linked slopes of Ponte di Legno are almost entirely wooded – a great combination. Thirty minutes east is Marilleva (free bus daily, except

Saturday), linked to Madonna di Campiglio. Buy the right pass and you get a day there included, or more.
Slopes Tonale's home slopes are limited in extent; one reader 'skied every run in half a day'. The broad, gentle, sunny area north of the pass road, served by a row of chairs and drags, is much the larger of the two sectors, but runs are short. The north-facing sector is steeper, narrower and taller. An eight-seat gondola leads to a double chairlift, and above that is the small Presena glacier, with two drags.
A blue/red run through the trees (mostly easy but with a short steeper section) descends almost 600m to a slow chair into the Ponte di Legno slopes; this is followed by an easy black run – you can avoid this by riding the gondola down to PdL.
Fast lifts The system is impressive – now eight fast chairs on the Tonale slopes, approaching a ★★★★ rating.
Queues In peak season, some lifts get busy at ski school time; the gondola

Build your own shortlist: **www.wheretoskiandsnowboard.com**

↑ The main slopes are directly above the village, which runs along the road over the pass to Ponte di Legno
ADAMELLO SKI

KEY FACTS

Resort	1885m
	6,180ft

Passo Tonale and Ponte di Legno combined area	
Slopes	1120-3015m
	3,670-9,890ft
Lifts	30
Pistes	100km
	62 miles
Blue	17%
Red	66%
Black	17%
Snowmaking	100%

UK PACKAGES

Crystal, Independent Ski Links, Neilson, Skitracer, STC, Thomson

Phone numbers
From abroad use the prefix +39 (and do **not** omit the initial '0' of the phone number)

TOURIST OFFICE

www.passotonale.it
www.adamelloski.com
www.valdisole.net

back from Ponte di Legno can be busy. But generally there are no problems.

Terrain parks Directly above the village is a small park with jumps, boxes and jibs, and a beginners' area.

Snow reliability In a normal season, the altitude and setting ensure good conditions. The sunny main slopes can suffer in late season, while the glacial south side fares better. Strong wind can be a problem, but the wooded slopes of Ponte di Legno offer shelter. The snowmaking is impressive.

Experts There isn't much for experts within the lift system. But in good conditions there are epic off-piste runs from the glacier, including the impressive 16km Pisgana run towards Ponte di Legno (a vertical of 1650m).

Intermediates The gentle south-facing slopes – many labelled red but of blue gradient – are great for building confidence. We enjoyed the 4.5km Alpino piste down a deserted valley to the village. Adventurous intermediates will enjoy the Presena area. The glacier runs are short and not steep. The black run beneath the gondola is easy but rewarding. The red runs at Ponte di Legno are excellent, and correctly classified. The blacks are not steep.

Beginners Excellent: the sunny slopes right by the village are ideal, with plenty of easy, wide blue runs to move on to, a couple of them quite long.

Snowboarding The gentle slopes and ability to get around mainly on chairlifts mean the area is good for beginner and intermediate boarders. The resort's second terrain park has been built on the Serodine piste.

Cross-country Not ideal. There are 8km of trails at Passo Tonale and 44km at Vermiglio (10km east).

Mountain restaurants Readers have generally been happy, particularly with the modest prices. Most places have table- and self-service sections. Tips include the village-level Baracca, the newish Rifugio Passo Paradiso and the Nigritella. At Ponte di Legno the rustic Valbione does excellent food.

Schools and guides A 2012 beginner reports good progress but confirms earlier reports of poor English.

Families The ski school takes kids from four, and it looks a good resort for skiing children. But there isn't much to do other than skiing.

STAYING THERE

Hotels There are around 30, most of them 3-stars, including the Sporting (0364 903781) where we had a pleasant short stay in 2012. Other recent visitors tip the 'great, friendly' Torretta (0364 903978) and the 'excellent' 4-star Miramonti (0364 900501) with pool and spa. Crystal's modern Paradiso (also with pool, spa) has repeatedly impressed reporters.

Apartments There are 1,400 beds in apartments, a few on the UK market.

Eating out Reporters seem content. Mainly hotel restaurants, including the 'good-value' Torretta ('best in town with a genuine pizza oven').

Après-ski It's not wild, but there are a few spots to try. Reader tips include El Bait and La Botte (both with free après snacks), the Magic Pub, Nico's Bar, Heaven (in Sport Hotel Vittoria) and the disco in the Miramonti (now called the Up Fun Park & Disco Pub) and the Paradiso disco.

Off the slopes There's not a lot to do off the slopes – snowmobiling, snowshoeing, skating.

Sauze d'Oulx

*A lively village beneath an attractive area of slopes forming part
of the extensive Milky Way; but non-trivial drawbacks persist*

RATINGS

The mountains

Extent	★★★★
Fast lifts	★★★
Queues	★★★
Terrain p'ks	★
Snow	★★
Expert	★★
Intermediate	★★★★
Beginner	★
Boarder	★★
X-country	★
Restaurants	★★★
Schools	★★
Families	★★

The resort

Charm	★★
Convenience	★★
Scenery	★★★
Eating out	★★★
Après-ski	★★★★
Off-slope	★

RPI   85

lift pass	£160
ski hire	£105
lessons	£75
food & drink	£110
total	**£450**

NEWS

2012/13: A new easy piste from Rif Mollino to Sportinia opened, completing the new alternative route to Sportinia.

- ➕ Extensive and uncrowded slopes – great intermediate cruising
- ➕ Mix of open and treelined runs is good for all weather conditions
- ➕ Entertaining nightlife
- ➕ Part of the Milky Way network, spreading across the border into France, but ...

- ➖ Full exploration of the Milky Way area really requires a car or taxis
- ➖ Erratic snow record and far from comprehensive snowmaking
- ➖ Lift system needs improvement
- ➖ Not great for novices or experts
- ➖ Steep walks around the village
- ➖ Weekend crowds in season

Skiers with long memories are inclined to dismiss Sauze as lager-lout territory. In the 1980s and maybe 1990s the tabloid newspapers mined a rich vein of young Brits behaving badly here. There are still lots of lively bars and shops festooned in English signs, and young Brits working in them, but it is a much more civilized place now, with the resort's Italian clientele more in evidence, especially at weekends (the Milky Way is Turin's closest major ski area). When we visit, we always seem to like the place more than we expect to.

But Sauze still has a problem: investment, lack of. It needs comprehensive snowmaking, and it needs new lifts. What the resort seems to be doing of late is reshuffling the lifts it already has, which doesn't quite do the trick.

THE RESORT

Sauze d'Oulx sits on a sloping mountain shelf facing north-west to the mountains bordering France.

It is a mid-sized resort – a big village rather than a town – but it spreads quite widely. Out of the bustle of the centre, there are secluded apartment blocks in quiet, wooded areas and a number of good restaurants also tucked away.

The Via Lattea (Milky Way) lift pass covers not only next-door Sestriere and Sansicario, easily reached by lift and piste, but also the more remote slopes of Claviere and Montgenèvre – much more easily reached by road.

VILLAGE CHARM ★★★★
Falling behind?
The village has an attractive old core, with narrow, cobbled streets and houses roofed with huge stone slabs.

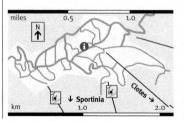

But most of the resort is modern and undistinguished, made up of block-like hotels relieved by the occasional chalet, spreading down the steep hillside from the slopes. There is little sign of investment in smart, woody hotels and apartments.

There is a central car-free zone, but at both ends of the day the rest of the village can be congested. The roads have few pavements and can be icy.

Despite the decline in lager sales, the centre is still lively at night; the late bars are usually quite full. Noise can be a problem in the early hours.

CONVENIENCE ★★★★
Uphill struggles
The Clotes chair, for the left-hand side of the network, is at the top of the village, up a short but steep hill. Some hotels are above this lift, and in good snow offer ski-in/ski-out convenience – but most are not. There is a moving carpet that cuts out part of the climb. The Sportinia chair, the most direct way to the heart of the slopes, is a strenuous and hazardous walk (often on slippery roads) further out. There is a free ski-bus service.

The smaller, lower village of Jouvenceaux is worth considering as a base, with a fast lift into the slopes and a good red run back down.

KEY FACTS

Resort	1510m	
	4,950ft	
Milky Way		
Slopes	1390-2825m	
	4,560-9,270ft	
Lifts		72
Pistes		400km
		249 miles
Blue		25%
Red		55%
Black		20%
Snowmaking		60%
Sauze d'Oulx-		
Sestriere-Sansicario		
Slopes	4,560-9,270ft	2825m
Lifts		41
Pistes		300km
		186 miles
Snowmaking		38%

SCENERY ★★★☆☆
Plenty of trees

The scenery is attractively woody, especially low down and along the Val di Susa. The sunny, open slopes higher up give wide panoramic views of the mountains bordering France.

THE MOUNTAINS

The higher slopes are open, the lower ones pleasantly wooded. Piste classifications change from year to year, and the signs on the ground don't always match the piste map. Pistes tend to be overclassified, with reds that should be blue and blacks that should be red. Piste marking may be absent. And signposting isn't great. Despite improvements, the Via Lattea piste map is still very difficult to follow – it doubtless makes an excellent marketing device but is a very poor skiing aid. Mad.

EXTENT OF THE SLOPES ★★★★☆
Big and varied enough for most

Sauze's local slopes are spread across a broad wooded mountainside above the resort, ranging from west- to north-facing. It is split by woods and ravines, and gives some sensation of travel as a result.

The main lifts are chairs, slow from the top of the village up to **Clotes** and fast from the western fringes to the

heart of Sauze's slopes at **Sportinia**, a sunny mid-mountain clearing in the woods, with a ring of restaurants and hotels, and a small nursery area. You can now get from Clotes to Sportinia via a single fast chair (Lago Nero – in fact the former Pian della Rocca chair realigned) and a short blue run. Progress towards Sestriere and other resorts is via the fast 'new' Rocce Nere chair, which uses the hardware of the former Triplex chair to replace the two ancient Rocce Nere chairs.

To leave the Sauze area you can take a steep draglift or ride a slow double chairlift to the high point of the system – the major junction of **Monte Fraiteve**. From here you can go south to **Sestriere**. There is a red piste all the way down, but the slope faces south; the bottom section is rarely open – expect to ride the gondola. Or you can go west on splendid broad, long runs to **Sansicario** – and on to a two-stage gondola near **Cesana Torinese** that links with **Claviere** and then **Montgenèvre**, in France.

FAST LIFTS ★★★☆☆
Few and far between

Fast lifts are in a minority. There are still a lot of drags and old, slow chairlifts. Things are improving slowly but serious investment is needed to update the lift system – above Sauze and on the return from Sansicario.

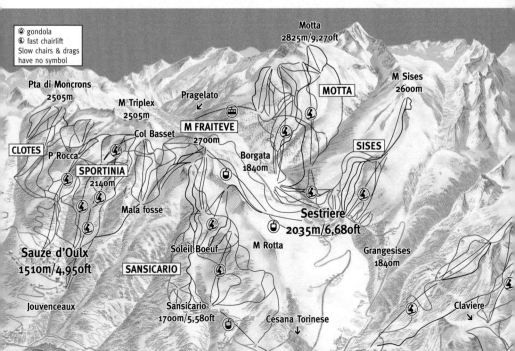

LIFT PASSES		
Via Lattea		
Prices in €		
Age	1-day	6-day
under 8	5	30
8 to 74	34	180
75+	15	90
Free No deals		
Beginner Restricted day pass (€24)		
Notes Covers lifts in Sauze d'Oulx, Sestriere, Sansicario, Cesana and Claviere; half-day passes		
Alternative pass International (covers all the above plus Montgenèvre)		

SNOWPIX.COM / CHRIS GILL

You can probably make out from this shot that the lift to Sportinia starts a good way above the village centre ↓

QUEUES ★★★☆☆
Weekend problems

There can be queues on weekends and holidays, when the hordes from Turin flock in. And crowds on the piste can be a problem then too. During the week the slopes are usually quiet – though recent changes around M Fraiteve have created serious congestion on the peak at busy times.

The rearrangement of existing lifts that seems to be the lift company's current way forward has solved some problems while creating others. Our regular reporter judges the net effect to be negative. Regulars will be glad to hear that the two ancient Rocce Nere chairs above Sportinia – painfully slow and prone to breakdown – have been replaced by a fast quad using the hardware of the Triplex lift. But this 'new' Rocce Nere lift is now the only way to M Fraiteve, so of course it builds queues – major ones at the February peak, we hear. The quad from the village to Clotes has long generated queues. Part of the new arrangement (with the Pian della Rocca chair realigned to finish above Sportinia) is that this now forms a relatively quick route to Sportinia. So it will attract more customers. So ... what these guys need is some serious lift network modelling software. Oh, and some investment.

A Christmas 2012 visitor also reports queues for the Tuassieres drag at the edge of the area, and the chair out of Sansicario.

TERRAIN PARKS ★☆☆☆☆
Maybe

The location and size of the park did change from year to year – but for the last few years it has been at Sportinia. Don't count on it though. There is a park at Sansicario too.

SNOW RELIABILITY ★★☆☆☆
Can be poor, affecting the links

The area is notorious for erratic snowfalls, suffering droughts with worrying frequency – though recent seasons have been pretty good. Snowmaking has been increased throughout the area (including the Sportinia nursery slopes) but coverage is still far from complete. Great efforts are made to keep runs open in poor conditions. Grooming is in general 'immaculate'.

FOR EXPERTS ★★☆☆☆
Head off-piste

There are black runs, but most of them do not deserve their classification. We're told the black Malafosse run is not fiercely steep, but is narrow and very isolated. There are quite a few off-piste opportunities within the lift network – between the pistes and down lift lines.

FOR INTERMEDIATES ★★★★☆
Splendid cruising terrain

The whole area is ideal for confident intermediates who want to clock up the kilometres. The less confident are not helped by the silly classification of many easy runs as red.

The Moncrons sector at the east of the area is served only by drags but offers some wonderful, uncrowded cruising, some of it above the treeline. In the central part of the slopes there are some good long descents – red 11 is about 1000m vertical.

At the higher levels, where the slopes are above the treeline, the terrain often allows a choice of route. Lower down are pretty runs through

SCHOOLS

Sauze Sportinia
t 0122 850218

Sauze d'Oulx
t 0122 858084

Sauze Project
t 0122 850654

Classes (Sauze Sportinia prices)
6 3hr-days €180

Private lessons
€37 for 1hr

the woods, where the main complication can be route-finding.

The long runs down to Jouvenceaux are splendid, flattering intermediate terrain, as are those below Sportinia.

The slopes above Sansicario are also excellent, including the amiable Olympic Women's Downhill and the particularly fine red run, away from the lifts, down to Pariol, the mid-station on the Cesana-Sansicario gondola. These runs are affected by the afternoon sun, though.

FOR BEGINNERS ★✶✶✶✶
Not a good choice
You might hope that a resort with cheap accommodation and gentle terrain would suit beginners, but in this case you would be disappointed. The main nursery area up at Sportinia has only a short moving carpet, and is reached by a chairlift. There is a day pass covering these plus two other lifts, but there is no suitable longer slope to progress to. There is a slope at village level with a free moving carpet, but the slope is too steep for complete beginners. The mornings-only classes (normal in Italy, of course) don't suit everyone. Once off the nursery slopes, the main problem is erratic piste classification.

FOR BOARDERS ★★✶✶✶
Too many drags
A recent reporter found little to interest adventurous boarders and 'far too many drags' – which is a serious drawback for novice riders too. But competent intermediates will enjoy cruising on the well-groomed pistes. Don't count on finding a terrain park.

FOR CROSS-COUNTRY ★✶✶✶✶
You're on your own
There are no prepared loops in Sauze.

MOUNTAIN RESTAURANTS ★★★✶✶
Some pleasant possibilities
There are about 15 restaurants locally. They are generally pleasant, but can get very busy; few are remarkable. Stupidly, only some are marked on the piste map. There are several places at Sportinia; most are routine self-service places but we know of two doing table-service. Having visited last season, we are happy to endorse the repeated praise from our regular reporter for the Rocce Nere ('excellent food and service'); and another reader's favourite this year was Monte Triplex ('very reasonable prices, and very quiet during the week'). Above Clotes, the 'cosy' Ciao Pais is again recommended, this time for its 'tasty carbonara'. The hotel Capricorno below it is the place for a serious table-service lunch; it is not cheap, and midweek in low season it can be deserted. Bar Basset below M Fraiteve offers 'friendly service' and 'excellent views on a sunny day'. The Fontaine at Jouvenceaux is good for 'a quiet drink and snack' and the Bar Mavie at Sansicario is tipped for 'excellent food, views and sunbathing'.

SCHOOLS AND GUIDES ★★✶✶✶
More reports, please
A 2011 visitor 'highly recommends' a private lesson with Roger Goodfellow of the Sauze d'Oulx school, who has been in Sauze for 30 years: 'We were of slightly different abilities but the lesson improved us all markedly.'

CHILDCARE

Ski school
From age 4

UK PACKAGES

Alpine Weekends, Crystal, Independent Ski Links, Inghams, Interactive Resorts, Neilson, Ski Club Freshtracks, Ski Line, Skitracer, Solos, STC, Thomson, Zenith
Sansicario Crystal, Thomson

GETTING THERE

Air Turin 90km/ 55 miles (1hr30)

Rail Oulx (5km/ 3 miles); frequent buses

ACTIVITIES

Indoor Sauna, solarium, massage

Outdoor Ice rink, snowshoeing, walking

Phone numbers
From abroad use the prefix +39 (and do **not** omit the initial '0' of the phone number)

TOURIST OFFICE

Sauze d'Oulx, Cesana Torinese (Sansicario)
www.turismotorino. org
www.vialattea.it
www.comune. sauzedoulx.to.it

FOR FAMILIES ★★★★★
Yes and no
All the schools take children from four years, and spoken English should be OK. But note our reservations about the resort for beginners. The moving carpet on the village nursery slope is a great aid to sledging.

STAYING THERE

All the major mainstream operators offer hotel packages here.
Chalets Neilson has a catered chalet here, and Inghams has taken over the 3-star Hermitage to run it as a chalet-hotel for the coming season.
Hotels Simple 2-star and 3-star hotels form the core, with a couple of 4-stars and some more basic places.
★★★★Relais des Alpes (0122 858585) 'Large rooms, food excellent with friendly restaurant staff.'
★★★★Torre (0122 859812) Cylindrical landmark 200m below the centre. Pool, spa, hot tub, sauna, steam.
★★★Gran Baita (0122 850183) Central place approved by a reader this year – 'location quiet but convenient, decor a bit dated but superior rooms huge, excellent lounge, friendly staff, decent dinners, great value'.
★★★Stella Alpina (0122 858731) Between main lifts. Well run by Anglo-Italian family: 'friendly'; 'quiet at night'; 'good Italian food'.
★★Albergo Martin (0122 858246) In Jouvenceaux. Basic, comfortable, with shuttle to the resort. 'Excellent value, helpful staff, good breakfast.'
★★Villa Cary (0122 850191) Praised for a seventh year by an annual visitor – 'ideal for people on a budget'.
Apartments Plenty are available, some through UK operators.
At altitude The 4-star Capricorno (0122 850273), up at Clotes, is the most attractive and expensive hotel in Sauze – a charming little chalet beside the piste, with only 10 bedrooms. Not quite in the same league are the places up at Sportinia – though reporters have enjoyed them.

EATING OUT ★★★★★
Caters for all tastes and pockets
Sauze has over 30 restaurants. Typical Italian banquets of five or six courses can be had in places such as the Cantun. In the old town there are several cutely rustic places. Del Falco offers fine wines and fine food; Paddy McGinty's does steaks. Sugo's is a great place for pasta and has 'a good atmosphere', and the Pizza House 'serves excellent pizza, good value'.

APRES-SKI ★★★★★
Suzy does it with more dignity
In most respects Sauze's bars now impress most reporters, young and old – 'classier than expected,' said one reporter this year. Choice is wide, with multiple happy hours, and free antipasti in some places. Our regular reporter picks out the Grotta for the cheapest beer (at well below UK prices); Max's Cafe ('busy for après and later') for its four-hour happy-hour; Mira ('probably the busiest') for sports TV – also tipped by another reporter for its friendly staff and happy-hour antipasti spread; Scatto Matto for its 'popular terrace and cocktail menu'; and the Scotch Bar in the hotel Stella Alpina, at the foot of the Clotes home run, for 'relaxed atmosphere and friendly welcome'. Other tips include the popular Assietta, with lots of entertainments later on; Il Lampione in the old town for a 'chilled out atmosphere and excellent beer'; Osteria dei Vagabondi for late-night live music; the intimate, atmospheric bar Moncrons, the Club (formerly Schuss Bar) and the Cotton Club, a wood-clad late-night bar with live bands. Banditos is the one identifiable nightclub, but our Sauze specialist repeatedly finds it closed.

OFF THE SLOPES ★★★★★
Go elsewhere
Shopping is limited, there are no gondolas or cable cars for pedestrians and there are few off-slope activities. Turin and Briançon are worth visiting.

LINKED RESORT – 1700m
SANSICARIO

Sansicario is ideally placed for exploration of the whole Milky Way. It is a modern, purpose-built, self-contained but rather soulless little resort, mainly consisting of apartments grouped around the small shopping precinct – but also spreading down the steep slope. The 46-room Rio Envers (0122 811937) is a comfortable, expensive 3-star hotel. The 4-star Majestic (085 83699) has a pool. Apartments to rent are 'hard to find but cheap'. Very little happens in the evening, but the Enoteca (wine bar) is 'excellent in all respects'.

Sella Ronda

Endless intermediate slopes amid spectacular scenery, and a choice of attractive valley villages with a distinctive local culture

TOP 10 RATINGS

Extent	★★★★★
Fast lifts	★★★★
Queues	★★★
Snow	★★★★
Expert	★★
Intermediate	★★★★★
Beginner	★★★★
Charm	★★★
Convenience	★★★
Scenery	★★★★★

RPI 105

lift pass	£230
ski hire	£95
lessons	£90
food & drink	£125
total	**£540**

NEWS

2013/14: A new six-pack is being built between Arabba and Passo Pordoi, going up to the Carpazza chair built last year – creating a new way to the lifts towards Marmolada. The kids' fun slope above San Cassiano is being expanded.

2012/13: In Arabba, a new six-seat chairlift, Carpazza, opened at mid-mountain below Porta Vescovo. In Corvara, the Boè gondola was upgraded. A new terrain park, PlaygroundSNOW, opened below Bioch.

Phone numbers
From abroad use the prefix +39 (and do **not** omit the initial '0' of the phone number)

TOURIST OFFICE

www.dolomitisuperski.com
www.sella-ronda.info

There are great views of the Sella group from the slopes of Alta Badia, between Corvara and San Cassiano →

+ Vast network of connected slopes – suits intermediates particularly well

+ Stunning, unique Dolomite scenery

+ Lots of mountain huts with good food as well as fab views

+ Relatively low prices

+ Extensive snowmaking – one of Europe's best systems – but ...

- They need it: natural snowfall is erratic in this southerly region

- Few tough pistes, and off-piste is very limited – in general, banned

- Mostly short runs with limited vertical (with notable exceptions)

- Crowds on the Sella Ronda circuit

- Some old draglifts and slow chairs

A few days in Corvara last February confirmed this as one of our absolute favourite destinations. The scenery is the thing: the Sella Ronda is an amazing circular network of lifts and pistes around the Gruppo del Sella – a mighty limestone massif. The spectacular Dolomite scenery is like something Disney might have conjured up for a movie or a theme park.

Sheer limestone cliffs rise out of gentle pasture land, which is where you ski mostly. The skiing is relaxing; the excitement comes from the views. This is one of the few destinations where we pray for sun; snowfalls would interfere with our scenery-gazing without bringing any real benefit – off-piste is off the agenda, and the snowmaking normally ensures reliably good pistes.

The scale of the area is some compensation for the lack of challenge; the distances you cover on skis are huge – in overall dimensions, the network beats even the famed Trois Vallées in France. There are three main resorts, each with its own slopes branching off from the main circuit: Corvara and Arabba are covered here, while Selva gets its own chapter. Another possible base, Canazei, is covered in the Val di Fassa chapter.

CHOOSING A BASE

For good skiers wanting challenges on hand, probably the best base is Selva – covered in the next chapter along with Santa Cristina and Ortisei, slightly further down the Val Gardena. Arabba is the other obvious option.

Corvara is the best all-round bet – well placed for access to Selva, Arabba, the Sella Ronda circuit, the Alta Badia area and Cortina (and the 'hidden valley' run). Colfosco is just next door. La Villa and San Cassiano are slightly off the Sella Ronda circuit.

The Dolomiti Superski pass covers dozens of resorts around this amazing region – read our new feature panel in this chapter. The lift system logs your lift rides – so you can go online to check your distance and vertical.

There are countless piste maps – a dozen Superski ones in all, plus locally produced ones for some resorts. The Alta Badia one, covering Corvara and neighbours, has the advantage of named mountain restaurants.

Arabba

➕ Some of the best steep pistes in the Sella Ronda area – shady too
➕ Quick access to Marmolada glacier

➖ Not a good base for novices, with more blacks than blues locally
➖ Off-slope activities are limited

Arabba is a small, quiet but fast-growing village appealing particularly to people looking for more challenging terrain than this region normally offers – but also immediate access to the Sella Ronda and Alta Badia sectors.

Village charm The village is small and traditional in style. There are some shops, bars and restaurants, but this is not a place for lively nightlife.
Convenience It's a small place, but staying in the older part can involve an uphill walk to reach the lifts, which provokes a few complaints from reporters. A newer area of hotels and chalets has developed higher up, well placed for the lifts and slopes, though perhaps not for bars.

Scenery Arabba is beautifully positioned between the stunning Gruppo del Sella and the glacial Marmolada massif, with great views at altitude in both directions.

THE MOUNTAIN

Arabba has a good mix of open and woodland slopes.
Slopes The two-stage double-cable gondola and the cable car beside it rise from the village almost 900m

You can ski around the huge Sella massif in either direction by following very clear coloured signs; it's easily managed in a day by even an early intermediate. The clockwise route is slightly quicker and offers more interesting slopes, but is much busier – so many reporters prefer the anticlockwise route, despite a tedious series of five lifts from Corvara. Some resort piste maps include a Sella Ronda map; most take something close to a bird's eye topographical view. (Bizarrely, at least one puts south at the top.) A very detailed topo map is available from the tourist offices (and some lift stations).

The runs total around 23km and the lifts around 14km. There is one bit where no skiing is possible: you ride the queue-prone Borest chair at Corvara both ways. The lifts take a total of about two hours (plus any queuing). We've done the circuit in just three and a half hours excluding diversions and hut stops; five or six hours is a realistic time when things are busy.

If you set out early and make good time, you can divert from the circuit, notably at Selva and Arabba. Less confident intermediates could explore the Alta Badia area, east of Corvara.

Not everyone likes it. You may find that 'it's a bit of a slog', 'too busy and crowded', 'over-hyped, and over-regimented' and 'not a relaxing business when it's busy'. And boarders should be aware that there are quite a few flat bits.

If you pick your time – low season or a Saturday, in good weather – and start early, we reckon it's well worth doing.

Sella Ronda

435

KEY FACTS

Sella Ronda
Linked network of Val Gardena, Alta Badia, Arabba, and of Canazei and Campitello in Val di Fassa

Slopes	1005-3270m
	3,300-10,730ft
Lifts	179
Pistes	433km
	269 miles
Blue	38%
Red	53%
Black	9%
Snowmaking	90%

SNOWPIX.COM / CHRIS GILL

← The slopes of Corvara and San Cassiano are mostly gentle blues, but an exception is red 16A

vertical to the high point at Porta Vescovo (2478m). From here a choice of runs return to the village or you can head off around the Sella Ronda circuit. The Porta Vescovo slopes west of Arabba (that is, on skier's left) are getting major investment – a new six-pack on the upper slopes last year, and another on the lower slopes this year. These are good slopes, so new lifts are welcome, but they also create a new access to the lifts towards Marmolada. From the mid-station of the gondola, chairs take you to Passo Padon and onwards to the Marmolada glacier. This is an excellent outing. The views from the top at 3270m are spectacular, and the 1500m vertical red run to Capanna Bill is splendid, with great snow on the top sections.

From the other side of the village, a fast quad gets you on the way to Burz, Passo di Campolongo and Corvara.
Fast lifts Key local lifts are fast, but there are slow lifts on the way to Marmolada.
Queues The outing to Marmolada can be troublesome on a busy day, with a bottleneck at the Sass de la Vegla double chair. There may be long waits for the Marmolada cable cars.
Terrain park There's a park in the Passo di Campolongo area.
Snow reliability Good snow is far from assured, but snowmaking is extensive and the main runs are high and shady.
Experts Arabba has steep slopes to rival those of Selva/Val Gardena. The north-facing blacks and reds from Porta Vescovo offer genuine challenges and there is some tempting off-piste terrain too – but read the off-piste feature panel in the margin.
Intermediates The local slopes suit adventurous intermediates best – most are quite challenging. But the easy Alta Badia area is nearby.
Beginners It is not a great choice for beginners. There is a nursery slope near the Burz chair, but beyond the Arabba local slopes things get tricky.
Snowboarding The slopes of Porta Vescovo offer some decent challenges. The nursery slope has a draglift.
Cross-country There are no trails here.
Mountain restaurants There's lots of choice, from rustic huts to larger places. Most are lively and welcoming, and many have great views, of course. The smart self-service Cesa da Fuoch

↑ The run to Corvara from Passo Gardena (part of the clockwise Sella Ronda) starts as an easy red and mellows into a lovely long, easy blue
SNOWPIX.COM / CHRIS GILL

at the mid-station has 'excellent and reasonable fresh-cooked pasta'; Rif Plan Boè, above Campolongo, has 'good food and service'. Below Marmolada, a visitor had a 'good-value' meal at Passo Fedaia, and Capanna Bill lower down is a cosy spot. Rifugio Fodom just below Passo Pordoi is 'great fun' with 'good food but dire Europop'.

Schools The local Arabba school offers group and private classes. We have no recent reports.

Families The ski school takes quite young children.

STAYING THERE

New accommodation has been built at the top end of the village, convenient for the lifts.

Chalets Ski Total has the dinky six-bed chalet Heidi and three slightly larger places. Inghams has three chalets sleeping 10 to 18 people.

Hotels There are about a dozen hotels. The favourite of one regular visitor is the 4-star Grifone (0436 780034) out at Passo di Campolongo – 'remote, but food and service superb; excellent bar and health club/pool'. In the village, the 3-star Portavescovo (0436 79139) and the 4-star Sporthotel (0436 79321) are possibilities.

Apartments Self-catering accommodation is available.

Eating out Restaurant choice is limited. The central hotels all have busy restaurants. Reporters consistently praise Miky's Grill in the hotel Mesdì ('good value', 'very good quality steaks and meat; mixed grill a speciality'). And reporters rate again Al Table as 'friendly and good value', serving everything from 'simple pasta and great pizzas to well-cooked steak'. The Stube Ladina in the Alpenrose hotel has been recommended in the past. For something a bit different, you can be ferried by snowmobile up the mountain to Rifugio Plan Boè for dinner and dancing. Or you might just arrive at 5pm and stay for the evening.

Après-ski The après-ski is limited. There are three bars and, according to recent reports, the central Bar Peter seems to be the focus – 'Very lively but quieter later on,' says a 2011 visitor. Reporters also mention the Stube in the Portavescovo hotel ('the closest thing in Arabba to a focal village bar, although it clears out at 8pm') and the Treina. Cosy hotel bars are other options in the village. The atmospheric Rifugio Plan Boè up the mountain is good for a last drink on the piste.

Off the slopes Off-slope diversions are few. There are some shops and cafes, and there's an ice rink. Snowmobiling and snowshoeing are available.

KEY FACTS	
Resort	1570m
	5,150ft
Slopes	1330-2530m
	4,360-8,300ft
Lifts	53
Pistes	130km
Snow-guns	392 guns

Corvara

☐ One of the best locations, where Alta Badia meets the Sella Ronda
☐ Pleasant, relaxed village
☐ Local slopes suit novices, but ...

■ Few challenges locally
■ Alta Badia still has plenty of drags and slow chairlifts

UK PACKAGES

Collett's, Inghams, Momentum, Ski Yogi, STC

Corvara rivals Selva from most points of view, the main exception being that of experts, who have to travel in search of challenges; for families and novices it takes some beating – though nearby Colfosco merits consideration too.

Village charm Although it's not notably cute, the place is lively and family-friendly, with a pleasant centre. There is some through-traffic, but it does not intrude hugely.

Convenience The main shops and some hotels cluster around a small piazza at the top end of the village, close to the Col Alto gondola; if you are based here nothing is more than a stroll away; but the rest of Corvara sprawls along the valley floor, so you may have some walking to do.

Scenery The setting is superb: there are impressive rock faces and spires all around the village, notably the distinctive, towering Sassongher.

THE MOUNTAIN

Corvara is well positioned, with village lifts heading off to reasonably equidistant Selva, Arabba and San

Cassiano. The local slopes are gentle and confidence-boosting.

Slopes Lifts go off in three directions. A long gondola heads south towards Boè and Arabba for the clockwise Sella Ronda circuit. Two successive fast quads head west towards Colfosco and the anticlockwise route around the circuit. The area around both lifts can get congested at peak times. A slow chair or a gondola from the heart of the village takes you to the slopes shared with San Cassiano and La Villa.

Fast lifts New fast lifts are gradually improving the area.

Queues You may hit long waits for the inescapable Borest chair between Corvara and Colfosco, but otherwise there are few problems.

Terrain park There is a terrain park above San Cassiano, easily reached from Corvara.

Sella Ronda

GOURMET SKIING

The Alta Badia – the area around La Villa, including Badia, San Cassiano, Corvara and Colfosco – has over recent years built up a gourmet culture. For many years, its top hotels have run excellent restaurants, but more recently the tourist office has been involving mountain restaurants, too.

For the last few seasons, a dozen mountain restaurant have served special dishes conceived by 'starred' chefs from resort restaurants in the area, plus their chums from around Europe. Both we and readers have enjoyed the results. This winter, things are changing. Some restaurants may continue to offer these dishes, but the emphasis is switching to a new idea, 'Slope Food'. This means appetizers or 'finger-food' rather than the main dishes of the old scheme.

At the heart of the scheme, as before, are the chefs from the three seriously good 'starred' restaurants in the Alta Badia area, all of which are in top hotels – the Rosa Alpina in San Cassiano, the Ciasa Salares in nearby Armentarola and hotel La Perla in Corvara.

TOURIST BOARD ALTA BADIA

The tourist office sponsors other foodie schemes too – for example, a series of mountain restaurants between La Villa and Santa Croce, above Badia, form a 'gourmet skitour' focusing on the local Ladin cuisine, detailed in a little brochure.

These schemes encourage variety and quality in mountain nosh; we approve. But we also hope some of the dishes from the original scheme do live on. A couple of years ago at I Tablà, for example, we had a superb dish – knuckle of pork in honey with thyme-scented polenta and chanterelles.

Build your own shortlist: www.wheretoskiandsnowboard.com

OFF-PISTE

Off-piste skiing is generally prohibited here – as in many Italian areas. This doesn't stop people doing it altogether. And it doesn't rule out some spectacular routes, away from the pistes, where you can safely go with guidance.

There are well-known routes on the Sella massif, reached via the cable car from Passo Pordoi. Fairly direct descents go back to the pass (the very sunny Forcella) or down Val Lasties towards Canazei. But the classic run is Val Mesdì, a long, shady couloir down to Colfosco, reached by hiking across the massif. Marmolada, the highest peak of the Dolomites, offers some big descents.

There is a mountain guides office in the centre of Corvara (www.altabadiaguides.com).

Snow reliability As in the rest of the Sella Ronda area, natural snowfall is erratic, but snowmaking and grooming are excellent.

Experts Very few of Corvara's slopes offer any real challenges. The short black above Boè is really no more than a red in gradient. The much longer wooded runs down to La Villa include a just-about-genuine black, adequately tricky when icy. Otherwise, you're off to Selva or Arabba. Look at the feature panel in the margin for off-piste info.

Intermediates There's a vast network of slopes ideal for cruising and confidence-boosting. On one side is the network of rolling hills shared with San Cassiano; on the other, above Colfosco, is the more dramatically set Val Stella Alpina, off the Sella Ronda circuit, plus the long, gentle runs from Passo Gardena – essentially one long nursery slope. The red back to the village underneath the Boè cable car that goes off towards Arabba is excellent – usually uncrowded and retains good snow. The adventurous can head for the steeper, wooded pistes going down to La Villa.

Beginners There's a decent nursery area and lots of easy runs to progress to on both sides of the village, making this one of the best bases in the Sella Ronda area for beginners.

Snowboarding Novices can make rapid progress on gentle slopes. A few awkward draglifts remain, but most can be avoided.

Cross-country This is one of the better bases in the area. The Alta Badia area offers 38km of trails, including a 10km valley loop on the way to Colfosco.

Mountain restaurants Despite hideous crowds, we had a good lunch last winter at a regular reader favourite – Rif Jimmy, in a fabulous position above Passo Gardena; but a reader going back a year on from a first visit was disappointed. The Edelweiss above Colfosco has an 'intimate, top-notch' table-service section. In the San Cassiano section we cover countless places between the two resorts.

Schools There's a local branch of the Alta Badia school – reports welcome.

Families A 2012 visitor found the school instructors 'very good' with the children in his party. The ski school's Kinderland takes children from the age of three.

STAYING THERE

The best location is near the main square at the top end of the village. We know of no catered chalets here.

Hotels There are some excellent 4-star hotels. La Perla (0471 831000) is one of our all-time favourites, offering superb food and service in a relaxed atmosphere and perfect position at the top of the village – ski down a few yards to the Col Alto gondola. Spa and small pool. Down at the other end of the village, Col Alto (0471 831100) is consistently praised from all points of view – rooms, service, food. We stayed last year in a very comfortable, stylish

THE 'HIDDEN VALLEY'

If you like runs in spectacular scenery well away from all signs of civilization, don't miss the easy red run from Lagazuoi, reached by cable car from Passo Falzarego. The pass is easily accessible from Armentarola, close to San Cassiano – shared taxis run a shuttle service (5 euros each) to the pass from here. There's also a bus from San Cassiano (but it is reported to be crowded and slow).

The run is one of the most beautiful we've come across, and delights most reporters. Views from the top of the cable car are splendid, and the run passes beneath sheer Dolomite cliffs and frozen waterfalls. The cable car has low capacity, so the run is never crowded. Make time to stop at the atmospheric Rifugio Scotoni near the end.

At the bottom, it's a long skate to a horse-drawn sled with ropes attached, which tows you back to Armentarola (for a couple of euros). This is more of a challenge than the run, and the risk of a pile-up if someone falls is of some concern. We favour the minibus alternative (there's a phone to summon it). At Armentarola there is a draglift up to the home run back to San Cassiano.

ALAN LIPTROT

↑ There are countless excellent mountain restaurants, such as Rifugio Lee at the mid-station of Santa Croce, above Badia

ALTA BADIA / FREDDY PLANINSCHECK

room in the new extension. Rooms in the annexe over the road are said to be huge. 'Superb' spa and 'huge' pool. Efficient shuttles to lifts, ski to the door (snow permitting). The Posta Zirm (0471 836175) next to the Col Alto gondola is 'one of the best', with 'very friendly staff, fantastic food'. Pool.

Eating out There's a reasonable choice. The Stüa de Michil restaurant in hotel La Perla has a Michelin star, and greatly impressed us – superb food and a warm atmosphere. Reader tips: La Fornella ('good food, great value'), La Stube, Pizzeria Caterina.

Après-ski The fashionable place to go at close of play these days seems to be L'Murin, a rustic outbuilding of hotel La Perla right on the home piste. The Icebar of the hotel Col Alto is 'very cool'. Other tips: the 'tiny, cosy' L'Got for a 'classic aperitivo'; the cellar of the hotel Posta Zirm ('lively later'); Toccami.

Off the slopes There's a covered ice rink, indoor tennis courts, an outdoor climbing wall and snowshoeing. The Posta Zirm pool is open to the public by reservation. There is a toboggan run up the road at Cherz.

San Cassiano

KEY FACTS

Resort	1540m
	5,050ft
Slopes	1330-2530m
	4,360-8,300ft
Lifts	53
Pistes	130km
Snow-guns	392 guns

UK PACKAGES

Alpine Answers, Carrier, Momentum, Mountainsun, Powder Byrne, Scott Dunn, STC

TOURIST OFFICE

www.altabadia.org

+ Local Alta Badia slopes are friendly, extensive and scenic
+ Small, quiet village with some notably good hotels

- Lifts and pistes are outside village
- Slightly off the Sella Ronda circuit
- Alta Badia still has plenty of drags and slow chairlifts

If you prefer San Cassiano to Corvara, it's likely to be because you particularly like one of its excellent hotels – or because you want a quiet time. In every other respect, Corvara has clear advantages.

Village charm It's a quiet, civilized resort, without much animation. It is bypassed by the road to Cortina.
Convenience Most hotels are close to the village centre – a five- or ten-minute walk from the gondola and slopes (but most of the better hotels have their own shuttle-buses).
Scenery The village is set in an attractive, tree-filled valley. The views from the slopes are superb.

THE MOUNTAIN
The local slopes adjoin the main Sella Ronda circuit.
Slopes A gondola starting just outside the village rises to Piz Sorega. From the top, fast chairs form the links with Corvara and La Villa, or you can head for Pralongia and the exceptionally long, gentle runs home. Most of the area has very gentle slopes, ideal for easy cruising.

LIFT PASSES

Dolomiti Superski

Prices in €

Age	1-day	6-day
under 16	35	178
16 to 64	50	254
65 plus	45	228

Free Under 8

Beginner No deals

Notes Includes all Sella Ronda resorts

Fast lifts Essentially well connected, but some old chairs and drags remain.

Queues Few problems, thanks to continual lift upgrades.

Terrain park You'll find boardercross, jumps, rails and humps.

Snow reliability The Dolomites have an erratic snowfall record, but snowmaking and grooming are excellent.

Experts Experts would be wise to stay elsewhere. There are steeper runs at La Villa, but it's a bit of a trek to other steep options at Selva or Arabba. Read the feature panel in the margin on the off-piste position.

Intermediates The slopes shared with Corvara are pretty much ideal if you love easy cruising on flattering, well-groomed runs. The red option back to the valley is a serious red though. There's relatively quick access to the famous 'hidden valley' run (described in our feature panel).

Beginners There are nursery slopes a short bus ride away at Armentarola, and at the top of the gondola – not ideal. But there are plenty of long, easy slopes to progress to.

Snowboarding Endless carving on quiet pistes and there's a terrain park.

Cross-country There are 25km of trails.

Mountain restaurants There are countless options on the slopes between San Cassiano and Corvara. The Alta Badia local piste map marks and names them clearly.

Most huts are woody and cosy in traditional style, but Las Vegas is a wild exception – cool, minimalist, with huge windows to make the most of the views. We have enjoyed a superb dinner here, and a 2012 lunch visitor 'loved it! Food excellent, especially the pasta.' Bamby gets two raves this year – 'the highlight, wonderful pasta', 'lovely cosy hut'. I Tablà is quite a plain little place but does excellent food – and readers repeatedly emphasize that it offers 'outstanding value'. Piz Arlara is again tipped for 'views, great friendly atmosphere and amazing food such as venison goulash'. Punta Trieste is again tipped for 'excellent pasta' (and live music). Capanna Nera is 'cosy, with great food, great service'.

Other reader tips include Club Moritzino ('fine wines, delicious cheeses, charming host'), Col Alt ('excellent venison') and Bioch.

Schools A snowboarder in a reporter's party 'had private lessons and the instructor was excellent', and a

MAKING THE MOST OF THE DOLOMITI SUPERSKI LIFT PASS

The Dolomiti Superski pass is a marvel. The one pass allows you to ski anywhere in this entire region, which includes several provinces and countless resorts. In Italy, of all places; it defies belief.

Of course, there is plenty to do around the Sella Ronda itself. But there are some tempting things to do elsewhere. First, make sure you don't overlook the skiing that is directly connected to the Sella Ronda – the outing to Marmolada from Arabba, and the Santa Croce area above Badia. Then there's the skiing above Ortisei – Seceda, linked by underground railway to the Ciampinoi slopes, and Alpe di Siusi on the other side of the town. Read the Selva chapter for more on these.

You will of course want to take in the 'hidden valley' run covered by another feature panel in this chapter. But while you are up at Passo Falzarego you can do a lot more. As well as the short slopes across the road at Col Gallina, you can ski down beside the road to the worthwhile Cinque Torri area, with lifts back forming a circular tour. And from there it is only a 10-minute ski-bus ride to the edge of Cortina's biggest area of slopes, the linked sectors of Pomedes and Tofana. Read the Cortina chapter to learn more. Obviously, it will all take a bit of planning unless you have a car or a taxi budget. But it makes a fabulous day out.

From Canazei you can explore other ski areas in the Val di Fassa (which gets its own chapter). From Badia you can get a free bus to Piccolino, where a gondola accesses the slopes of San Vigilio and Plan de Corones, and the world's biggest concentration of gondolas – 21 at the last count.

beginner 'progressed very quickly' – more reports welcome.

Families The school offers the usual arrangements for children and there are several kids' parks.

STAYING THERE

Hotels The Rosa Alpina (0471 849500) is a splendid place – genuine comfort, great food, good spa. Its three restaurants include the St Hubertus, which has two Michelin stars ('equal to some of the best in London, but also at least as expensive!' says a 2012 visitor). The Fanes (0471 849470) is a smart chalet-style place with indoor-outdoor pool and a spa. A reader this year tips the central Vajolet (0471 849483) – 'very friendly owners; excellent, varied, copious food'. You can stay up the mountain at the modern, trendy Las Vegas restaurant (0471 840138).

Eating out As well as the Rosa Alpina's two-star St Hubertus, two restaurants in the area have one Michelin star; one, the Siriola in the hotel Ciasa Salares, is in Armentarola, just up the road; for the other see Corvara. Las Vegas will take you up the mountain in a snowcat for dinner (you can ride back down or ski in front of the cat's headlights).

Après-ski It starts up the mountain with loud music at Las Vegas. Village nightlife is very limited.

Off the slopes There are some lovely walks amid the stunning scenery. There is a toboggan run from Piz Sorega to the village.

Other resorts

UK PACKAGES
Colfosco Inghams
Badia Collett's

TOURIST OFFICE
Colfosco, La Villa, Badia
www.altabadia.org

LINKED RESORT – 1645m

COLFOSCO

Colfosco (aka Kolfuschg – the German influence gets stronger as you move west towards Selva/Wolkenstein) is a smaller, quieter satellite of Corvara, 2km away. It has a fairly compact centre with a group of large hotels spread along the road from Corvara towards Passo Gardena and Selva, enjoying splendid views of the Gruppa del Sella.

On the snow Colfosco is connected to Corvara and the clockwise Sella Ronda circuit by the queue-prone two-way Borest chairlift. In the opposite direction, a gondola goes towards Passo Gardena. There are excellent nursery slopes and the runs back from Passo Gardena, after a red start, are easy, long blue cruises, making this a great base for novices.

The Kolfuschgerhof hotel (0471 836188) is 200m from the slopes (efficient shuttles) but a 'really nice family-run hotel with fantastic food, attentive staff'. But this year a regular visitor to this area trumps this report with a rave about the Cappella (0471 836183): 'One of the best ski hotels I have found, with the best food I have had on half-board.' Excellent ski-in/ski-out location, too.

Although it's a small place, there are some restaurants. Black Hill is a popular place for 'excellent wood-fired pizza'. Mathiaskeller is tipped for après beers and 'excellent risotto'. Otherwise it's 'a sleepy village'.

LINKED RESORT – 1435m

LA VILLA

Like San Cassiano, La Villa is a bit detached from the Sella Ronda circuit. It's a much busier place, with the road from Brunico running through it; but it is much more conveniently arranged, with lifts and pistes on both sides of the village, and nursery slopes dotted around. A 2011 visitor complained of inadequate rental shops, and poor spoken English both there and in the ski school. We've had repeated glowing reports on the hotel Antines (0471 844234) – 'one of the best, with an outstanding restaurant'; 'very friendly staff'. There is said to be a public swimming pool.

LINKED RESORT – 1325m

BADIA

This small roadside village (formerly known as Pedraces) is out on a limb beyond La Villa, so it's not a great base. But some will find it more interesting because there is a free bus link with Piccolino (20 minutes), where a gondola goes into the Plan de Corones/Kronplatz ski area. The village has its own one-run ski area with a fast quad and a slow double chair to Santa Croce (2045m) where there is a famous old rifugio with fabulous views (and a tiny church). At the mid-mountain lift station is one of our favourite restaurants, Rif Lee – sheltered terrace, excellent food, friendly service.

Selva / Val Gardena

Pleasant village amid spectacular Dolomite scenery, well placed for skiing on and off the vast Sella Ronda lift network

RATINGS

The mountains

Extent	★★★★★
Fast lifts	★★★★
Queues	★★★
Terrain p'ks	★★★
Snow	★★★★
Expert	★★★
Intermediate	★★★★★
Beginner	★★★
Boarder	★★★
X-country	★★★★★
Restaurants	★★★★★
Schools	★★★
Families	★★

The resort

Charm	★★★
Convenience	★★★
Scenery	★★★★★
Eating out	★★★
Après-ski	★★★
Off-slope	★★★

RPI   105

lift pass	£230
ski hire	£95
lessons	£90
food & drink	£125
total	**£540**

NEWS

2013/14: The capacity of the Dantercëpies gondola is to be increased, with more parking and better services at the base.

➕ A key resort of the Sella Ronda region, so good for snowmaking, extent, scenery, mountain huts

➕ Spectacular, dramatic setting

➕ Excellent local slopes, with big verticals by Sella Ronda standards

➕ Mix of open and wooded slopes

➕ Excellent nursery slopes

➖ Some of the minus points of the Sella Ronda region too, notably: erratic natural snowfall, crowds on the main Sella Ronda circuit

➖ Buses or taxis are needed for access to easy long runs to suit near-beginners, at Plan de Gralba

➖ Busy road through the village

Selva is one of three sizeable resorts near the head of Val Gardena (a name well known to ski racing fans) and one of the main bases for exploration of the unique Sella Ronda region described in the chapter before this one. Selva remains one of our favourite bases in the area, essentially because of the challenging local slopes, including two race courses through woods to the valley that are among the most satisfying runs in the area. Beginners and timid intermediates, though, are probably better off staying in Corvara or Colfosco, described in the Sella Ronda chapter.

THE RESORT

Selva is a long roadside village in a spectacular setting at the head of the Val Gardena.

For many years this area was part of Austria, and it retains a Tirolean charm. German is more widely spoken than Italian, and many visitors are German, too. Most places have two names: Selva is also known as Wolkenstein and the Gardena valley as Gröden. We do our bit for Italian unity by using the Italian place names here. The local language, Ladin, also survives – which means that some places have a third name. Not surprisingly, visitors find all this confusing. The valley is famed for wood carvings, which are on display (and sale) wherever you look.

At the end of this chapter we describe two other bases. Santa Cristina is the next village down the valley, and almost merges with Selva;

lifts from both villages meet on the steep racing hill of Ciampinoi. Further down the valley is Ortisei, the main town of Val Gardena, set beneath the distinct Alpe di Siusi area. Both bases have lifts to another distinct area, Seceda. Another possible base is the much lower village of Siusi (1005m), which has a gondola up to Alpe di Siusi.

VILLAGE CHARM ★★★★★
Pity about the traffic

The village has traditional Tirolean-style architecture and an attractive church, but is rather strung out along the main road and suffers a bit from through-traffic (and a lack of parking facilities) as well as a lack of central focus. Despite the World Cup fame of Val Gardena, Selva is a good-value, civilized, low-key resort – relaxed and family-friendly in many respects, once you get away from the intrusive through-road.

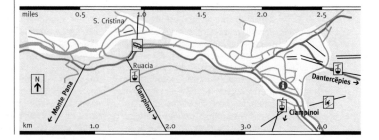

VAL GARDENA TOURIST OFFICE

↑ Ortisei is a handsome, polished town rather than a standard ski resort

VAL GARDENA TOURIST OFFICE

KEY FACTS

Resort	1565m
	5,130ft

Sella Ronda linked network: Val Gardena, Alta Badia, Arabba, and Canazei and Campitello in Val di Fassa

Slopes	1005-3270m	
	3,300-10,730ft	
Lifts		179
Pistes		433km
		269 miles
Blue		38%
Red		53%
Black		9%
Snowmaking		90%

Val Gardena-Alpe di Siusi only

Slopes	1005-2520m	
	3,300-8,270ft	
Lifts		78
Pistes		175km
		109 miles
Blue		30%
Red		60%
Black		10%
Snowmaking		95%

CONVENIENCE ★★★☆☆
Choose your spot with care

From the village, gondolas rise in two directions. The Ciampinoi gondola goes south from near the centre of the village to start the anticlockwise Sella Ronda route. The Dantercëpies gondola, for the clockwise Sella Ronda route, starts on the opposite side of the village and slightly above it, at the top of the nursery slopes (but accessible via a central chairlift and a short run down). The most convenient position to stay is near this chair or one of the gondolas. At various points there are lodgings on the snow.

There are local buses until early evening – 7 euros for a weekly card. They generate all sorts of complaints from reporters: lack of buses; not running to time; confusion between the public and the skiers' buses. There's a night bus between Selva and Ortisei. All the 4-star hotels run their own free shuttle-buses.

SCENERY ★★★★★
Pretty in pink

The village enjoys a fabulous setting under the impressive walls of Sassolungo, immediately above the slopes of Ciampinoi, and the Gruppo del Sella – a fortress-like massif 6km across that lies at the hub of the Sella Ronda circuit (described in a separate chapter). There are knockout views as you descend from Dantercëpies, for example, and from Alpe di Siusi.

THE MOUNTAINS

Selva's own slopes cover both sides of the valley. The lower slopes are wooded, with open slopes higher up.

The local piste map exists in several variations, which reporters find confusing. The maps show neither names nor numbers for the runs, which strikes us as insane. Piste signing provokes some criticism.

The Dolomiti Superski pass covers not only Selva and the Sella Ronda resorts but dozens of others. It's an easy road trip to Cortina.

EXTENT OF THE SLOPES ★★★★★
High-mileage excursions

The **Dantercëpies** gondola goes off eastwards to start the clockwise Sella Ronda circuit and serves lovely red runs back to Selva. On the other side of the valley, the **Ciampinoi** gondola goes south for the anticlockwise circuit via **Plan de Gralba** and accesses several shady pistes, leading back down to Selva and Santa Cristina, including the famous Downhill run.

In Santa Cristina, another gondola accesses Ciampinoi, and an underground train links the lift base to a gondola on the outskirts for the sunny **Seceda** area. In this sector, runs descend to Santa Cristina or to Ortisei – a red run of about 7km. And from Ortisei a gondola on the other side of the valley takes you to and from **Alpe di Siusi** – a gentle elevated area of

LIFT PASSES

Dolomiti Superski

Prices in €

Age	1-day	6-day
under 16	35	178
16 to 64	50	254
65 plus	45	228

Free Under 8

Beginner Points card

Senior Must be 65 before season starts

Notes Covers 1220km of piste and 450 lifts in the Dolomites, including all Sella Ronda resorts

Alternative pass Val Gardena-Alpe di Siusi

quiet, easy runs, cross-country tracks and walks. You can proceed from here to the backwater **Monte Pana** (which is connected to Ciampinoi) by bus, but it's a slow affair.

FAST LIFTS ★★★★☆
Getting better
The main access lifts are gondolas, and there are lots of fast chairs above them, so progress can be quick. But there are still a few slow chairs and drags – an irritant on Alpe di Siusi.

QUEUES ★★★☆☆
Still some problems
The gondolas out of the village are naturally busy at the morning peak, and the drags up to the Dantercëpies

gondola may hold you up, too. Other problems may arise on lifts that are part of the Sella Ronda circuit – Piz Seteur for example. Doing the circuit from Selva has the clear drawback that everyone ends up on the chain of lifts from Corvara at the end of the day, and facing 'morale-sapping' queues for each one in high season. The gondola out of Ortisei that takes you halfway to Seceda ensures that the cable car above it is over-busy in the mornings.

TERRAIN PARKS ★★★☆☆
Facilities spread around
There are parks, pipes and skier-cross courses in various spots. There is a mile-long park on Alpe di Siusi, with lines to suit all standards. Readers

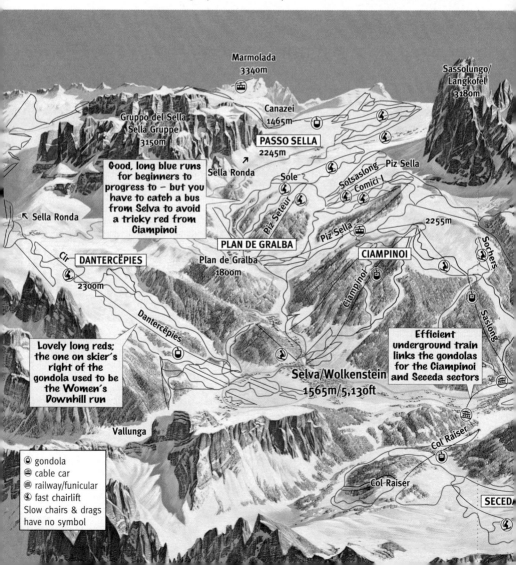

and their kids have loved the fun park at Piz Sella, which aims to entertain families and novices – it features a spiral tunnel and a jump over a car – but also has some challenges.

SNOW RELIABILITY ★★★★☆
Excellent when it's cold
The slopes are not high – there are few above 2200m and most are between 1500m and 2000m. Natural snowfalls are erratic, but the snowmaking is exceptionally good. During severe droughts we and readers have enjoyed excellent pistes here. The grooming is excellent too – 'unbelievable' is the latest comment. Problems arise only if it is too warm to make snow.

FOR EXPERTS ★★★☆☆
A few good runs
There are few challenges, essentially no moguls and a low likelihood of powder. There are few major off-piste routes because of the nature of the terrain, and off-piste is prohibited in places; read the off-piste panel in the Sella Ronda chapter.

The Val Gardena World Cup piste, the Saslong, is one of several steepish runs between Ciampinoi and both Selva and Santa Cristina. It is kept in racing condition, but it is open to the public much of the time – it's one of our favourite runs. There are also good reds down the same hills. The long red runs from Dantercëpies are entertaining, too.

Ideal area for early intermediates – very gentle pistes (almost flat in places), quiet, with superb scenery

Funicular built in 2010 offers a worthwhile alternative way to reach the Seceda cable car

Beautiful long run with a vertical drop of 1300m: not steep but quite narrow in places; wonderful views over the valley and through a very picturesque canyon

The Saslong World Cup Downhill piste is a wonderful, fast, rolling cruise that's especially good in January when it's not too crowded

Sassolungo/Langkofel 3180m
Punta d'Oro/Goldknopf 2210m
1940m
Fiè/Völs 880m
Mont de Seura 2115m
2000m
ALPE DI SIUSI
Siusi/Seis 1005m
Sorchels
Mont Seura
2100m
Castel Rotto/Kastel Ruth 1060m
1665m
MONTE PANA
Saslong
Alpe di Siusi
S Cristina/St Christina 1430m
Ortisei/St Ulrich 1235m/4,050ft
Rasciesa 2228m
Raiser
Furnes
SECEDA
Seceda 2520m

Resort news and key links: www.wheretoskiandsnowboard.com

FOR INTERMEDIATES ★★★★★
Fast cruising on easy slopes

There is a huge amount of skiing to do, in several areas.

Competent intermediates will love the red and black descents from Dantercëpies and Ciampinoi to Selva (but more timid intermediates may find them too steep and/or crowded).

The blue runs in the Plan de Gralba area are gentle, great for building confidence; the red run to get there from Ciampinoi is a real obstacle – it's steep and crowded and can be icy – so you might want to go by road.

The quiet red and black runs at Mont de Seura, above Monte Pana, are worth exploring.

The broad Alpe di Siusi above Ortisei is ideal for confidence-building. The red runs that dominate the map are rarely red in practice, and they are crowd-free. Runs are mostly of limited vertical, the main exception being the red from Punta d'Oro – 500m vertical.

The Seceda sector has good red and blue runs at altitude, and splendid runs to the valley – an easy blue/red to Santa Cristina and the beautiful red Cucasattel, passing through a natural gorge to Ortisei.

FOR BEGINNERS ★★★☆☆
Great slopes, but ...

The village nursery slopes below the Dantercëpies gondola are excellent – spacious, convenient. There are lots of gentle, long runs to progress to, but they are at Plan de Gralba and Alpe di Siusi, and reached by road.

FOR BOARDERS ★★★☆☆
Limited options

Selva attracts few boarders. There's little to challenge experts, and off-piste opportunities are limited, but the nursery slopes are good and there are lots of gentle runs to progress to. The main valley lifts are all gondolas or chairs. There are three terrain parks and a couple of half-pipes.

FOR CROSS-COUNTRY ★★★★★
Beautiful trails

There are 115km of trails, all enjoying wonderful scenery. The 12km trail up the Vallunga valley is particularly attractive, with neck-craning views all around. Almost half the trails have the advantage of being at altitude (so better snow as well as better views), running between Monte Pana and across Alpe di Siusi.

MOUNTAIN RESTAURANTS ★★★★★
A real highlight

There are countless huts, and many of them are lively and characterful, with helpful staff, good food and modest prices. They are not identified on the main resort piste map, but they are on the Sella Ronda map on the reverse.

In the Dantercëpies sector, readers have tipped the Panorama – a cosy, rustic suntrap at the foot of the drag near the top – and the Pastura.

In the Ciampinoi area the Rif Emilio Comici, set beneath the massive Sassolungo (arrive early if you want the sun), is repeatedly tipped, notably for 'great fresh fish'. Nearby Piz Sella

ALAN LIPTROT

Sassolungo and Sasso Piatto provide a spectacular backdrop to the lovely, amiable Alpe di Siusi area →

Selva Gardena – Ski Academy Peter Runggaldier (Ski Factory)
t 0471 795156

2000
t 0471 773125

Top School Val Gardena
t 0471 794099

Classes (Selva prices)
6 half-days €199

Private lessons
From €40 for 1hr

GUIDES

Val Gardena Mountain Guide Association
t 0471 794133

CHILDCARE

Selvi mini club
0471 795156
Ages 0 to 4

Casa Bimbo
0471 793013
From 0 to 3

Ski school
From age 4

---

is recommended for pizza. Down towards Plan de Gralba, Vallongia has a cool ice bar. Piz Seteur is a lively spot with an outdoor DJ, but also offers 'great food' in its table-service section. Baita Sole is a cute but simple place with good-value food. On the way down to Selva, Valentini makes a good last stop – 'always friendly'.

At Passo Sella, Rif Friedrich August has Highland cattle strolling around outside, and closely related steaks on sale inside.

In the Seceda sector there are countless options. Rif Odles is one reader's new favourite. On the run back to S Cristina, a regular visitor tips Baita Pramulin. Near the top of the long Cucasattel run, the tiny Curona is a favourite of several visitors ('friendly; best strudel'); nearer the bottom, Val d'Anna is another favourite – 'best pastries', 'friendly staff'.

Alpe di Siusi is said to have over 40 places to choose from. We have an enthusiastic report this year on Floralpina – 'Great place, excellent pasta, real sense of fun.' Our specialist reporter picks out Laurinhütte ('welcoming, excellent food, great views'), Zallinger Hütte ('charming – a great find'), Sanon Hütte ('fantastic views, cheerful service') and Mont Seuc, at the top of the gondola – 'Perfect for watching the cliffs turn red over a last drink.'

SCHOOLS AND GUIDES ★★★☆☆
No worries
The resort's main Selva Gardena school has been recommended by several readers, most recently in 2012. One visitor recommends the ski safari ('took us to places we would never have dreamed of getting to') but was unhappy with the large group size and range of ability on some days.

FOR FAMILIES ★★☆☆☆
It's all down to the detail
At first sight, in general, the village does not seem ideal for families. It's a sprawling place requiring use of not entirely efficient buses, with a busy through-road. But make the right arrangements, and you can have very successful family holidays here. An obvious first step is to look at chalet holidays with UK specialist operator Esprit. A 2012 visitor praised her son's Selva Gardena instructor arranged through Esprit: 'Good English, took his responsibilities very seriously.'

Chalets Crystal has three mid-sized catered chalets, and Total has three ranging from 8 beds to 26. Family specialist Esprit has four, ranging from the dinky two-bedroom Oskar to the big Wiesenheim with family suites.

Hotels There are about 20 4-star hotels in Selva, about 40 3-stars and numerous lesser hotels. It is not a small place. Few of the best are well positioned – though they generally operate shuttle-buses.

★★★★Aaritz (0471 795011) Best-placed 4-star, opposite the gondola.

★★★★Gran Baita (0471 795210) Large, luxurious sporthotel, with lots of mod cons including pool. A few minutes' walk from centre and lifts. 'Superb – huge rooms, wonderful facilities, far too much food, very pleasant waiters.'

★★★★Medzi (0471 795265) B&B hotel in good ski-in/out position. 'Good breakfast, very helpful owners.'

★★★★Mignon (0471 795092) Good value, close to lifts.

★★★★Oswald (0471 795151) One Californian reader's Alpine favourite. 'Good rooms, fantastic food, very helpful staff.' Has its own shuttle.

★★★★Savoy (0471 795343) Next to the 'slow but quiet' Ciampinoi chairlift. Approved again by our regular reporter – 'Very welcoming, great rooms, great food, lovely indoor/outdoor pool.'

★★★Miara (0471 794627) Next to the Ciampinoi gondola. 'Modern, quiet, with friendly helpful owners.'

Villa Seceda (0471 795297) A regular visitor reports that the recent renovation of this 'friendly' B&B near the nursery slopes has been a great success.

Apartments They are available, but we have no recent reader reports.

At altitude We had a report last year of a 'fabulous' stay at the hotel Sochers (0471 792101), on Ciampinoi.

EATING OUT ★★★☆☆
Adequate choice
The better restaurants are mainly based in hotels or, ironically, B&B guest houses. Current reader favourite – and 'popular with locals' – is La Bula ('went back three times – great food', 'staff who really care'). Other reader tips include: the slope-side hotel Freina ('superb seafood, excellent service'), the woody stube of the hotel des Alpes, for Tyrolean specialities, Rino ('huge and tasty pizza and

GETTING THERE

Air Verona 215km/
135 miles (2hr45);
Bolzano 55km/
35 miles (1hr);
Treviso 200km/
125 miles (3hr30);
Brescia 240km/150
miles (3hr30); Milan
340km/210 miles
(4hr30); Innsbruck
120km/75 miles
(1hr45)

Rail Chiusa (27km/
17 miles); Bressanone
(35km/22 miles);
Bolzano (40km/
25 miles); frequent
buses from station

UK PACKAGES

Alpine Answers, Crystal,
Crystal Finest, Esprit,
Independent Ski Links,
Interactive Resorts,
Momentum, Neilson,
Ski Solutions, Ski Total,
Skitracer, Ski Yogi,
Snow Finders, STC,
Thomson
Ortisei Crystal,
Inghams, Ski
Expectations, Thomson

ACTIVITIES

In Val Gardena:

Indoor Swimming
pool, sauna, bowling,
ice rink, climbing wall,
fitness centre, tennis,
bowling, museum,
chess

Outdoor Sleigh rides,
snowshoeing,
tobogganing, ice
climbing, ice rink,
paragliding, extensive
cleared paths

Phone numbers
From abroad use the
prefix +39 (and do **not**
omit the initial '0' of
the phone number)

TOURIST OFFICE

www.valgardena.it

carpaccio', 'great bruschetta'), the pizzeria of the hotel Sun Valley ('amazing'), Armin's Grillstube ('inexpensive and cosy cellar'), the Sal Fëur in the Garni Broi ('relaxed feel, generous portions').

APRES-SKI ★★★☆☆
Not without action

At close of play some of the mountain restaurants offer diversions. Piz Seteur, with its outdoor DJ, was as lively and fun as ever when we visited in 2012. The hotel Sochers is said to be good for a quiet drink. At the base, the Stua is a popular last stop – 'great place with delightful staff, great atmosphere and good prices' – and if you settle in for the evening, live music may arrive. The Kronestube has been tipped ('good atmosphere'). Café Mozart is 'a convivial place for a relaxed coffee'. Later on, the village streets are fairly quiet, but there are places to go. Goalies' Irish pub is 'good for a quiet drink' – it suits grown-ups with its classic rock music. The place to let your hair down is Luislkeller, tested thoroughly by this year's reporters – 'hopping, with great craic', 'really lively, difficult to get in', 'before we knew it, we were part of a party'. Yello's is a competitor. The serious nightclub is Dali, open until 3am, with dance music for 'a younger clientele'.

OFF THE SLOPES ★★★☆☆
Good variety

There are many spectacular walks, on Alpe di Siusi and Rasciesa, especially. There's a sports centre, snowshoeing, tobogganing and sleigh rides. 'We had our usual great night at the ice hockey,' says a repeat visitor. There are buses to Ortisei (if you don't fancy the lovely two-hour walk) and more distant Bolzano, with a museum featuring 5,000-year-old Oetzi the Ice Man, among many attractions. And there are coach excursions to Cortina and Verona. A group of hotels has formed Val Gardena Active, offering free excursions. Pedestrians can reach many good mountain restaurants.

LINKED RESORT – 1430m
SANTA CRISTINA

A few km down-valley from Selva, at the bottom of the race course from Ciampinoi, Santa Cristina is a pleasant village well worth considering as an alternative base. It has gondolas

towards Ciampinoi and Seceda (their base stations linked by an underground railway), and a slow chairlift up to a ring of nursery slopes at Monte Pana (but no piste back). There is accommodation up here, too. There's a good range of hotels in the village from 5-star down, and countless B&Bs.

LINKED RESORT – 1235m
ORTISEI

Ortisei is an attractive, prosperous market town with a life of its own apart from tourism. It's full of lovely buildings, pretty churches, smart shops and tempting cafes, and has an interesting museum, a large hot-spring swimming pool and an ice rink. The valley road follows the river, bypassing the centre. The local slopes offer an astonishing six toboggan runs – one from Rasciesa 6km long and accessed by funicular – as well as vast amounts of easy skiing. If you plan to spend time on the Sella Ronda circuit beyond Selva, plan on using the ski-buses.

The gondola to the Seceda slopes is easily reached from the centre by a 300m-long series of moving walkways and escalators. Alternatively, you can reach the top of that gondola, and the start of the Seceda cable car, by riding the Rasciesa funicular and descending a red piste. The gondola for Alpe di Siusi is a similar distance out, across the river – a footbridge from the centre is the best approach, going over the valley road too. Note that to move from one area to another involves quite a walk.

The nursery area, school and kindergarten are also over the river, along with a fair range of accommodation. The fine public indoor pool and ice rink are also here.

There are hotels and self-catering accommodation to suit all tastes and pockets, and many good restaurants, mainly specializing in local dishes. The 3-star hotel Dolomiti Madonna (0471 796207) was recommended in 2011 despite its location at the very end of the town – 'delightful evening meals'. The 5-star Adler (0471 775001) is tipped this year for its 'excellent food and outstanding staff'; another visitor prefers the 5-star Gardena (0471 796315): 'Outstanding food, nicer guest rooms, unbeatable ski guide and fewer people.' Après-ski is quite jolly, and many bars keep going till late.

SESTRIERE TOURIST OFFICE

Sestriere

Altitude is the main attraction of this, Europe's first purpose-built resort; some would say it's the only attraction

TOP 10 RATINGS

Extent	★★★★
Fast lifts	★★★
Queues	★★★
Snow	★★★★
Expert	★★★
Intermediate	★★★★
Beginner	★★★
Charm	★
Convenience	★★★
Scenery	★★★

RPI   90

lift pass	£160
ski hire	£105
lessons	£90
food & drink	£110
total	**£465**

NEWS

2012/13: Two new easy pistes opened: from Anfiteatro to Pragelato and from Anfiteatro to Borgata. A Club Med opened in Pragelato in December 2012.

PISTE MAP

Sestriere is covered on the Sauze d'Oulx map

SNOWPIX.COM / CHRIS GILL

We found the run from M Fraiteve open last February, when we bagged this shot – M Motta is on the left and M Sises is on the right →

+ Local slopes suitable for most levels, with some tougher runs than in the next-door resorts

+ Part of the extensive Milky Way area, with Sauze d'Oulx and Sansicario only one lift away

+ Snowmaking covers all but one or two marginal slopes, but ...

– It needs to, given the local snowfall

– Full exploration of the Milky Way area really requires a car or taxis

– The village is a bit of an eyesore

– For a purpose-built resort, not conveniently arranged

– Weekend and peak-period queues

– Little après-ski during the week

Sestriere was built for snow – high, with north-west-facing slopes. Sadly, the snowfalls in this corner of Italy are notoriously erratic; but extensive snowmaking means you should be fairly safe here. The place makes a great weekend away for the residents of Turin. As a holiday destination for residents of Tunbridge Wells, it doesn't have such a strong case.

THE RESORT

Sestriere was the first purpose-built resort in the Alps, developed by Fiat's Giovanni Agnelli in the 1930s.

Village charm The resort sits on a broad, sunny and windy col. Neither the site nor the village, with its rows of apartment blocks, looks very hospitable. The satellite of Borgata, a gentle blue run to the east and 100m lower, is quiet and traditional in style.

Convenience The village is not huge, and some lodgings are very close to the snow; but some are quite distant from the lifts, or the bars. There are non-free buses. Borgata is a linear place with its lifts at one end, at the

foot of the piste from Sestriere.

Scenery The slopes give extensive views across the part-wooded Milky Way to the peaks of the French border.

THE MOUNTAINS

The local skiing is on shady slopes, mainly open with some woodland, facing the village. Sestriere is at one extreme of the big Franco-Italian Milky Way area – though the slopes around the border are best reached by road. (Tour ops organize coach outings.)

The piste map and piste signing combine to form a small nightmare, especially on M Motta; good luck! Piste classification is erratic, and tends to exaggerate difficulty.

449

KEY FACTS

| Resort | 2035m |
| | 6,680ft |

Milky Way

Slopes	1390-2825m
	4,560-9,270ft
Lifts	66
Pistes	400km
	249 miles
Blue	25%
Red	55%
Black	20%
Snowmaking	60%

Sestriere-Sauze
d'Oulx-Sansicario

Slopes	1390-2825m
	4,560-9,270ft
Lifts	41
Pistes	300km
	186 miles
Snowmaking	38%

UK PACKAGES

Alpine Answers, Alpine Weekends, Club Med, Crystal, Inghams, Momentum, Neilson, Ski Line, Skitracer, STC, Thomson

Phone numbers
From abroad use the prefix +39 (and do **not** omit the initial '0' of the phone number)

TOURIST OFFICE

www.turismotorino.
org
www.vialattea.it
www.comune.
sestriere.to.it

Slopes The local slopes, served by drags and chairs, are in two main sectors: Sises, directly in front of the village, and Motta, above Borgata; Motta is more varied and bigger, with more vertical. From a car park west of the village a gondola goes up over the opposite mountainside to M Fraiteve, for access to Sauze d'Oulx, Sansicario and the rest of the Milky Way. There are blue runs back from M Fraiteve – sunny, and not reliably open. You may face a long walk from the end of the piste to the lifts or your lodgings.

Fast lifts The main lifts are modern fast ones, but there are still too many slow, old ones, both here and over in Sansicario and Sauze.

Queues The main lifts can have queues on sunny weekends. We lack high-season reports, but we would expect the double chair back from Sauze to be a regular problem. At M Fraiteve the confined summit area can get seriously congested. There may be long queues for the gondola down.

Terrain parks A terrain park is now built by the Baby lift.

Snow reliability The Italian part of the Milky Way gets notoriously unreliable snowfalls, but Sestriere has extensive snowmaking. Add in altitude and orientation, and you can count on good cover on the pistes. Don't expect powder, though. Grooming is 'comprehensive', and 'excellent'.

Experts There are things to do – steep pistes served by the drags at the top of both sectors, three now designated as mogul fields. Given good snow, there is some decent off-piste; don't count on it, though. Outings to snowy Montgenèvre may be more rewarding.

Intermediates Both sectors also offer something for confident intermediates – Motta especially – but they don't add up to a lot, so plan on multiple visits to other linked resorts.

Beginners There are good nursery slopes directly in front of the village served by draglifts, but you need a lift pass (a special day pass covers five lifts). There are easy longer runs to progress to locally, and over in Sauze.

Snowboarding The draglifts are largely avoidable except above Sansicario. There's a specialist snowboard school.

Cross-country There are three loops covering about 10km.

Mountain restaurants Not all places are marked on the resort piste map. We haven't made it to the place, but the woody Raggio di Sole, on skier's right at M Motta, sounds like the best bet ('tasty, filling local dishes; happy, helpful staff'). Alpette, directly above the village, is tipped for 'simple lunches, or bombardinos as the lifts close and the sun goes down'.

Schools and guides There are four schools: the main ones are the Nazionale and Vialattea.

Families The two main schools have mini-clubs for children aged three and four and offer lessons for children from the age of five.

STAYING THERE

Most accommodation is in apartments.

Hotels There are a dozen hotels, mostly 3-star or 4-star. The 3-star Biancaneve (0122 755177) has 'great food, good service'. Crystal operates the ideally positioned hotel du Col ('very friendly, lovely food'); go for rooms on the snow not the road side. Just out of the village is the swanky Ròseo (0122 7941), formerly Principi di Piemonte. Out at Borgata, we found a warm welcome at the Banchetta (0122 70307), a traditional, family-run hotel with old photos on the walls and very good food in the dining room. The Village Resort Spa in Pragelato reopened as a Club Med in 2012.

Apartments The Villagio Olimpico apartments built for the 2006 Olympics are reasonably central.

Eating out There are plenty of options. Current reader favourite ('so impressed we went a second night') is Last Tango – 'fab wild boar carpaccio, pork in mustard, and violet sorbet'. We can recommend the pizzas at Pinky, and a reader tips Kandahar for its cheeseburgers. If you don't mind a drive, Antica Spelonca in Borgata has been tipped; it's in a cute vaulted cellar.

Après-ski The quietness of the place during the week disappoints some visitors. Pinky is a cafe-style bar that was packed with Brits at close of play last time we visited. The bar of the hotel du Col is popular too. Readers also tip Black Pepper – 'very lively, lovely cocktails'. Tabata is the main club, with a cool bar upstairs and big disco below.

Off the slopes There's more to do than most visitors realize. There are some smart shops, a fitness centre, an ice rink, a sports centre and pool, and other diversions such as dog sledding. Outings are possible to nearby Pragelato and also to Turin – only 100km away by road.

La Thuile

A spread-out resort with a mix of ancient and modern parts and extensive, easy, snow-sure slopes linked with La Rosière in France

NEWS

2013/14: A new B&B, Il Cillegio, and a new restaurant, Lo Tatà, are to open.

2012/13: The Chaz Dura chair was refurbished. A new B&B, Rifugio Lilla, opened.

➕ Fair-sized area linked to La Rosière in France

➕ Strikingly crowd-free slopes

➕ Excellent beginner and easy intermediate slopes

➖ The tough runs are low down, and most low, woodland runs are tough

➖ The French link is exposed to bad weather, and the return is slow

➖ Not the place for lively après-ski

La Thuile has a lot going for it. And if you are limited to school holidays and have had enough of the peak-season crowds over the hill in France, it could be just the job – provided a quiet village appeals to you as much as quiet slopes.

THE RESORT

La Thuile is based on an old mining village that has been expanded and restored. The attractive centre, with shops, bars and restaurants, is at the entrance, with newer developments fairly widely spread. The modern Planibel complex, at the base of the lifts, looks a bit like a French purpose-built resort. The pass includes two days in other Val d'Aosta resorts, and free buses run to nearby Courmayeur, making this an easy outing.

Village charm The village centre is attractive, but many people find the Planibel complex rather soulless.

Convenience The main village is a little way from the lift base, and most accommodation is served by a regular free bus. The Planibel complex is right by the main lift, with a few other hotels nearby.

Scenery The scenery is varied, with open bowls and lower wooded slopes overlooked by the nearby Mont Blanc massif. Good views into France.

THE MOUNTAINS

La Thuile has quite extensive slopes linked to those of La Rosière via slopes above the Petit St Bernard pass – a good area, but poorly represented on the stupidly over-ambitious piste map. The piste signposting is better. Many runs marked red deserve no more than a blue rating. Strong winds can close high lifts, including the link.

Slopes A gondola out of the village takes you to Les Suches and an alternative chair to 100m below it. Shady black runs go back down directly to the village through the trees, and a couple of reds take more roundabout routes. Chairs take you up to Chaz Dura for access to a variety of gentle bowls and slightly more testing slopes on the back of the ridge. From there two chairs go up to the link with La Rosière. Immediately above the lift base is the small Maison Blanche area.

Fast lifts The key lifts are fast chairs and a gondola.

Queues Short queues may form at the gondola first thing, but not at the chair. There are no problems once you are up the hill. Reporters regularly comment on the lack of queues, and a 2012 comment is typical: 'Not a single queue all week. Yippee.'

Terrain parks The Wazimu park is in the Les Suches area.

Snow reliability Most of La Thuile's slopes are north- or east-facing and above 2000m, so the snow keeps well. There's also a decent amount of snowmaking; grooming is 'excellent'. The snow was in fine condition when we were there in hot April 2012 sunshine and experienced ice and slush elsewhere on the same trip.

Experts The black pistes down through the trees from Les Suches are serious

Chaz Dura
2580m

Col de
Fourclaz

2610m /
8,560ft

Arnouvaz
Cerellaz

Les
Suches
2200m

↙ La Rosière

La Thuile
1440m / 4,720ft

ⓖ gondola
④ fast chairlift
Slow chairs & drags have no symbol

KEY FACTS

Resort	1440m
	4,720ft

Espace San Bernardo
(La Rosière and La
Thuile)

Slopes	1175-2610m
	3,850-8,560ft
Lifts	38
Pistes	160km
	99 miles
Green	10%
Blue	31%
Red	40%
Black	19%
Snowmaking	25%

UK PACKAGES

Alpine Answers, Crystal,
Inghams, Interski, Just
Skiing, Momentum,
Neilson, Ski Bespoke,
Ski Club Freshtracks,
Ski Solutions, Skitracer,
STC, Thomson

Phone numbers
From abroad use the
prefix +39 (and do **not**
omit the initial '0' of
the phone number)

TOURIST OFFICE

www.lathuile.net

SNOWPIX.COM / CHRIS GILL
The old village centre
is a shuttle ride away
from the lift base –
but there are also
lodgings right by the
lifts ↓

stuff, as are two steepish blacks at
Maison Blanche. The black slopes
down to the pass are easier – only
just genuine – but there is also plenty
of good off-piste here; fast quads
mean you can do quick circuits in this
area. Don't hope for moguls on-piste.

Heli-lifts are available. The Ruitor
glacier offers a 20km run to Ste-Foy in
France, a short taxi ride from La
Rosière for the lifts for La Thuile.

Intermediates The slopes above Les
Suches consist almost entirely of
gentle blue and red runs, ideal for
cruising and carving but free of
challenges. There are also good long
reds through the trees back to the
resort. The red runs on the back side
of the top ridge, down towards the
Petit St Bernard pass, are less gentle.
The pass road forms the San Bernardo
red to the village, dropping 600m in
11km; avoid in fresh snow.

The skiing in La Rosière is more
testing – mostly genuine red runs,
sometimes with moguls, and with
snow more affected by sun. The route
back starts with a genuine red, and
involves long, exposed draglifts.

Beginners There are no free lifts, but a
day pass (5 euros) allows use of the
moving carpet on the village nursery
slope. There is also a nursery area up
at Les Suches and long, easy blues
above there, ideal for progression. You
ride the gondola down.

Snowboarding These are great slopes
for learning. There are no draglifts,
unless you go to La Rosière. For the
more experienced there are great tree
runs, good freeriding and some good
carving runs. But there are some
frustratingly flat sections too.

Cross-country La Thuile has three
loops of varying difficulty on the valley
floor, adding up to 11km of track.

Mountain restaurants Generally not
great by Italian standards, but marked

on the piste map. We liked the
ambience of the Off Shore, a small hut
with an eclectic mix of 1960s/70s
memorabilia and music and nautical/
Asian/African themes – simple food
that you order at the bar. Maison
Carrel off run 30 is a table-service
place with floor-to-ceiling windows
that has a history of good reviews
from readers; we've had both good
and disappointing meals there. Newish
Chalet de Cantamont has quickly
found favour with readers, who have
also tipped Foyer and Riondet.

Schools and guides A 2012 visitor
found the 'teaching was effective, but
there were some language issues'.

Families There is a nursery area, with
mini-club and snow garden. The village
kindergarten and the Planibel hotel
club both take children from 4 to 12.
Over fives can join ski school.

STAYING THERE

Hotels The 4-star Planibel (0165
884541) has the obvious attraction of
its prime location at the lift base (plus
pools, sauna, steam room and gym)
and is 'really good for families', but it
is very impersonal. In sharp contrast,
we were very impressed last winter by
the 4-star Miramonti (0165 883084), in
the old village (shuttle on demand) –
smartly renovated in traditional style,
with excellent food and service. It has
a swanky spa. Chalet Eden (0165
885050), a short walk from the lifts, is
a 4-star eco-hotel with a big spa,
strongly tipped last year ('very large
room, gourmet meals, lots of open
fires').The 3-star B&B hotel du Glacier
(0165 884137), a short walk above the
lifts, has had rave reviews, mainly
thanks to its energetic owner Susanna.

Apartments The Planibel apartments
are now 'looking a little worn', but
they are spacious and good value.

Eating out Reader tips include the
Grotta ('friendly, good pizza, pasta,
fondue'), Pizzeria Dahü ('good value'),
Coppapan ('steaks to die for'), Coq
Maf ('best steak in 37 years of skiing')
and Pepita Café ('good food, friendly
service and good value').

Après-ski Nightlife is quiet. The Konver
is open until late and has a regular DJ.

Off the slopes Not great. There are few
shops; the Planibel has a pool, open
late afternoon; there are walks, but
information is 'poor'; there's also dog
sledding and a climbing wall.
Pedestrians can ride the gondola, but
can't reach the best lunch spots.

Val di Fassa

Two resorts linked in to the Sella Ronda circuit, and several much smaller separate areas well worth exploring for a day or two

The Val di Fassa runs from the town of Moena to an abrupt end at the massive twin obstacles of the Gruppo Sella and glacial Marmolada. The valley's biggest resort, Canazei, is at the south-west corner of the famous Sella Ronda circuit (which has its own chapter). Campitello, 2km down the valley, also has a lift into the circuit. A separate network links Alba (up the valley) to Pozza di Fassa (down the valley). And there are separate areas at Vigo di Fassa and Carezza.

Canazei is a sizeable, bustling, pretty, roadside village of narrow streets, rustic buildings, traditional-style hotels and little shops, set at 1460m beneath a heavily wooded mountainside.

The village itself is slightly off the main Sella Ronda circuit, but its main slopes form part of it. A 12-person gondola (powerful, but queue-prone) rises 465m to Pecol, at the foot of the slopes of Belvedere. These are linked in one direction to the slopes of Passo Pordoi and Arabba, and in the other to Passo Sella and Col Rodella (above Campitello), and then on to Selva. A red run returns to Canazei, but it gets the afternoon sun and is often closed.

The Belvedere slopes are open and sunny, with modest verticals of about 450m. Almost all are graded red; this exaggerates their difficulty, but rules the resort out for timid intermediates and beginners. There is a nursery slope in the valley, next to the village.

The grand 4-star Schloss Hotel Dolomiti (0462 601106) in the centre is one of the oldest hotels: 'Very Italian, good food and lots of choice; stylish and historic,' says a 2012 visitor. The 4-star Perla (0462 602453), also central, is praised by a 2011 visitor for 'great food and value, amazing spa'.

There are numerous restaurants, and the après-ski is surprisingly animated. The Giardino delle Rose and Osteria, at the bottom of the home run, and the Paradis (a converted barn – 'great fun') are popular at close of play. The 'friendly' International bar and ice cream parlour is quieter. La Stua di Ladins serves local wines.

Off-slope entertainment consists of beautiful walks and shopping. There's also a pool, sauna and Turkish baths.

Neighbouring **Campitello** (1445m) is a pleasant, unremarkable village, smaller, quieter and cheaper than Canazei, and still unspoiled. A cable car starting just outside the village rises 1000m up to Col Rodella and the slopes above Passo Sella. At the start of the day this lift can build queues even in January, and in high season they can be 'massive' – get the bus up to Canazei's gondola. There are no pistes to the resort. There is a nursery slope, on the opposite side of the village from the cable car.

A reporter this year enjoyed the 4-star hotel Stella Montis, up a steep hill outside the village (has a shuttle): 'Excellent, good food, first-class spa.' Après-ski these days is reported to be rather quiet.

About 2km up the valley from Canazei, a cable car just beyond **Alba** goes up to a small area of slopes (six lifts, 15km of runs) above Ciampac, which is linked around the back of the low peak of Crepa Negra to another small area of slopes (seven lifts, 17km of runs and 'excellent' mountain huts) above **Pozza di Fassa**, which is down-valley from Canazei and Campitello.

Over the road from Pozza another small area of slopes (six lifts, 16km of runs) links Pera to **Vigo di Fassa**. A road from there leads west to **Carezza** (or Passo Costalunga) where another area of slopes (16 lifts, 40km of runs, 20+ huts!) links with Nova Levante.

453

SWISS FRANC

Back in the winter of 2007 we were getting 2.4 Swiss francs for £1. When we went to press for this edition the rate was 1.35 francs, which makes everything almost 80% more pricey in terms of £s than six years ago. Things were even worse in September 2011 when the rate hit around 1.2 francs to £1; the Swiss authorities got so worried about the franc's strength that they decided to peg the Swiss franc to the euro so that it would not continue to rise.

Switzerland is home to some of our favourite resorts. Only two resorts in this book are awarded ★★★★ for both resort charm and spectacular scenery – the essentially traffic-free Swiss villages of Mürren and Wengen. Many other Swiss resorts are not far behind in the charm and scenery stakes. Many resorts have impressive slopes, too – including some of the biggest, highest and toughest runs in the Alps – as well as a lot of good intermediate terrain. For fast, queue-free lift networks, Swiss resorts are not known as pacesetters – too many historic cable cars and mountain railways for that. But the real bottlenecks are steadily disappearing. And there are compensations – the world's best mountain restaurants, for one, and pretty reliable accommodation, too.

Until recently, one of the drawbacks of Switzerland was that smoking was allowed in public areas. But now nearly every canton that matters has banned smoking except in dedicated smoking rooms, and all hotels, restaurants and bars have smoke-free areas.

There's no doubt that Switzerland is expensive. That is largely because of the strength of the Swiss franc – see the panel in the margin. Our price survey shows that food and drink now costs way more than in any other skiing country – only two non-Swiss resorts (Courchevel in France and Beaver Creek in the US) are pricier than the cheapest Swiss resort. Overall holiday costs (when you add in the cost of lifts, ski hire and lessons) are less than most North American resorts but way above the European norm. Until the exchange rate improves, most people will simply go elsewhere.

Many Swiss resorts have a special relationship with the British, who invented downhill skiing in its modern form in Wengen and Mürren by persuading the locals to run their mountain railways in winter, to act as ski lifts, and by organizing the first downhill races. An indication of the continuing strength of the British presence in these resorts is that Wengen has an English church.

TRADITIONAL YEAR-ROUND RESORTS

While France is the home of the purpose-built resort, Switzerland is the home of the mountain village that has transformed itself from traditional farming community (or health retreat) into year-round holiday resort. Many of Switzerland's most famous mountain resorts are as popular in the summer as in the winter, or more so. This creates places with a more lived-in feel to them and a much more stable local community.

Many villages are still dominated by a handful of families lucky or shrewd enough to get involved in the early development of the area. This has its downside as well as advantages. The ruling families have been able to stifle competition and bar newcomers from taking a slice of their action. Alternative ski schools – to compete with the traditional, nationally organized school, ensuring continuing pressure to raise standards – were slower to come in than in other Alpine countries, for example. But this grip has at last been weakened.

The quality of service throughout Switzerland is generally high.

SWISS RAIL PASSES

These are the main options – there are others. On any of the passes listed, children under 16 accompanied by at least one parent travel free.

Swiss Pass *Covers unrestricted travel on most of the Swiss railway network, buses and postal buses during the period of validity – 4, 8, 15 or 22 days; or one month. Prices: 4 days from £187; 8 days from £269*

* Includes panoramic rail routes as well as trams and buses in 38 towns

* 50% discount on the price of using most of the mountain railways

* Free entrance to about 400 museums

* 15% discount for two and more adults travelling together

Swiss Transfer Ticket *Permits travel between the Swiss border or airport and your destination, out and back, by the most direct route. Valid for one month. You can use two different airports. Prices: from £92*

Swiss Flexi Pass *Permits unrestricted travel across Switzerland, like the Swiss Pass, on 3, 4, 5 or 6 days of your choice during a one-month period of validity. On days when you choose to use the card, you just write the date on the card. On days when you choose not to use up one of the 3, 4, 5 or 6 days, the pass gets you a discount of 50%. There's 15% discount for two and more adults travelling together. Prices: 3 days from £179; 6 days from £286*

Swiss Card *An extension of the Transfer Ticket. As well as travel to and from your destination, you get a 50% discount on all rail, bus and boat fares during the one-month period of validity – and on some cable car fares. Prices: from £134*

SWISS-IMAGE.CH / CHRISTOF SONDEREGGER

The food is almost universally of good quality and much less stodgy than in neighbouring Austria. Even the standard rustic dish of rösti is haute cuisine compared to Austrian sausages. And in Switzerland you get what you pay for: the cheapest wine, for example, is not cheap, but it is reliable.

Perhaps surprisingly for such a traditional, rather staid skiing nation, Switzerland has gone out of its way to attract snowboarders. Davos may hit the headlines mainly when it hosts huge economic conferences, but yards from the conference hall there are dudes getting big air on the Bolgen slope's training kickers. Little-known Laax claims one of Europe's best terrain parks and firmly targets its marketing at the youth and freestyle markets as well as families.

Switzerland, like Italy, doesn't have much time for tree-huggers who object to the impact of helicopters on wildlife. Heli-skiing is not unrestricted, but it is available – indeed, in Zermatt at peak times choppers are taking off from the helipad every few minutes. In Austria heli-skiing is confined to Lech-Zürs and in France it is largely confined to the retrieval of clients from valley bottoms – you can't be deposited on a peak.

GETTING AROUND BY TRAIN

The Swiss railway network is famously extensive and reliable. The trains run like clockwork to the advertised timetable – if you think a Swiss train is late, make sure your watch is right before you complain. (There is, however, some truth in the cynical view that the trains are able to run on time because the timetables incorporate long stops at stations.)

The rail network is a perfectly viable means of reaching many resorts. There are often linking services that run to the top of the mountain, doubling as ski lifts, too. And if a resort is not on the rail network, there will usually be efficient bus services to take you from the nearest station.

GETTING AROUND BY CAR

Access to practically all Swiss resorts is fairly straightforward when approaching from the north – just pick your motorway. But many of the high passes that are perfectly sensible ways to get around the country in summer are closed in winter, which can be inconvenient if you are moving around from one area to another.

There are very useful car-carrying trains in various places; they can cut out huge amounts of driving. One key link is between the Valais (Crans-Montana, Zermatt etc) and Andermatt via the Furka tunnel, and another is from Andermatt to the Grisons (Laax, Davos etc) via the Oberalp pass – closed to road traffic in winter but open to trains except after very heavy snowfalls. Another rail tunnel that's very handy is the Lötschberg, linking Kandersteg in the Bernese Oberland with Brig in the Valais. The recently opened Lötschberg Base Tunnel is lower, longer and faster, but it takes only passenger and freight trains.

St Moritz is more awkward to get to than other major resorts. The main road route is over the Julier pass. This is normally kept open, but at 2285m it is naturally prone to heavy snowfalls that can shut it for a time. Fallbacks are car-carrying rail tunnels under the Albula pass and the Vereina tunnel from near Klosters.

These car-carrying rail services are generally painless. Often you

can just turn up and drive on. But carrying capacities are obviously limited. Some services (eg Oberalp) carry only a handful of cars, and booking is vital. Others (eg Furka, Lötschberg, Vereina) are much bigger operations with much greater capacity – but that's a reflection of demand, and at peak times there may be long queues – particularly for the Furka tunnel from Andermatt, which Zürich residents use to get to the big Valais resorts. There is a car-carrying

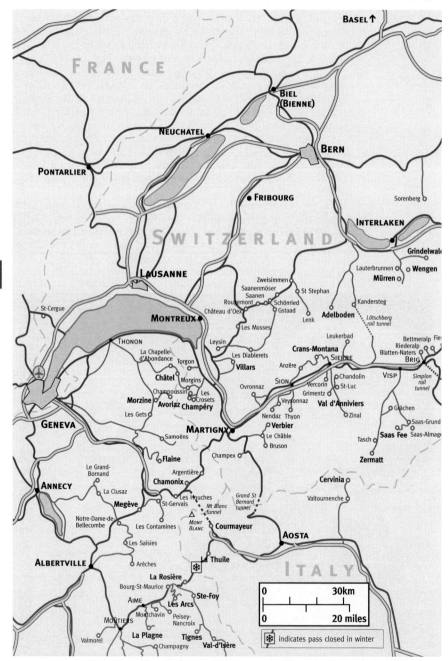

rail tunnel linking Switzerland with Italy – the Simplon. But most routes to Italy are kept open by means of road tunnels. Read the Italy introduction for more information.

To use Swiss motorways you have to buy an annual permit to stick on your windscreen. These cost 40 francs, are sold at the border and are valid for 14 months – from 1 December to 31 January.

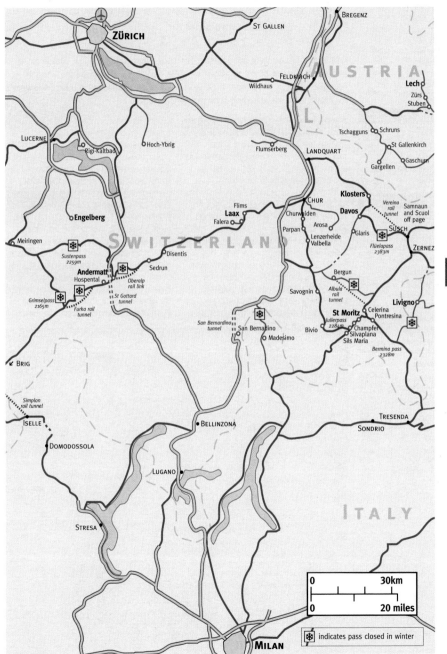

indicates pass closed in winter

Adelboden

Traditional village with plenty to do off the snow – and with extensive, varied and scenic slopes, some also accessible from Lenk

TOP 10 RATINGS

Extent	★★★
Fast lifts	★★★
Queues	★★★
Snow	★★★
Expert	★★
Intermediate	★★★
Beginner	★★★★
Charm	★★★★
Convenience	★★
Scenery	★★★★

RPI	125
lift pass	£210
ski hire	£140
lessons	£105
food & drink	£190
total	**£645**

NEWS

2013/14: A new hybrid 6/8-seat chondola is due to replace the existing Hahnenmoos gondola for December 2013.

2012/13: A blue run from Sillerenbühl to Aebi opened, down an otherwise entirely red mountainside.

KEY FACTS

Resort	1355m
	4,450ft
Slopes	1070-2360m
	3,510-7,740ft
Lifts	57
Pistes	185km
	115 miles
Blue	44%
Red	45%
Black	11%
Snowmaking	60%

+ Chalet-style mountain village in a splendid setting

+ Good off-slope facilities

+ Some pleasantly uncrowded slopes linked to Lenk, but ...

– The slopes are fragmented and widely spread; access can be slow

– Not a place for bumps but there are plenty of off-piste opportunities

– Quiet, limited nightlife

Adelboden is not quite your classic postcard-pretty village, but it comes close, and offers a good blend of attractions. We have found our primitive German brought into play here more than is usual in Switzerland, but the resort is keen to attract more visitors, and it merits consideration.

THE RESORT

Adelboden is a traditional village tucked away on a sunny mountainside at the head of a long valley. Its major sector of slopes is linked to the slopes in the village of Lenk, to the west. The Jungfrau resorts (Wengen, Mürren etc) to the east are within day-trip range.
Village charm The village is built more or less entirely in chalet style, and the long, main street (not car-free, but nearly so) is lined with chalets housing shops. It's a pity many of them have racks of cheap goods out in front.
Convenience The village is fairly compact, but getting to and from the slopes usually involves quite a bit of hassle, or at least time. Buses to Engstligenalp are included with the lift pass; those to Elsigen-Metsch are not.
Scenery There are fine panoramas from the village and from the slopes.

THE MOUNTAINS

Adelboden's slopes are split into five varied sectors, widely spread. The main sector stretches across to Lenk, where a sixth area is reached by bus.
Slopes Village lifts access three of the sectors. A small cable car/gondola hybrid goes up to Tschentenalp, with an itinerary back to the village. An even smaller lift goes down to Oey,

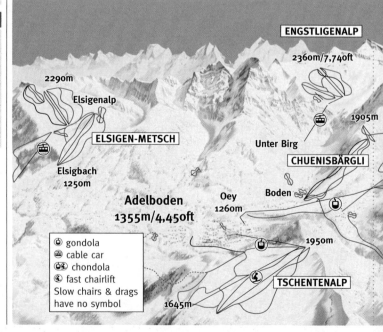

ENGSTLIGENALP
2360m/7,740ft

2290m

Elsigenalp

ELSIGEN-METSCH

1905m

Unter Birg

CHUENISBÄRGLI

Elsigbach
1250m

Adelboden
1355m/4,450ft

Oey
1260m

Boden

1950m

⊙ gondola
🚠 cable car
⛟ chondola
🚡 fast chairlift
Slow chairs & drags
have no symbol

1645m

TSCHENTENALP

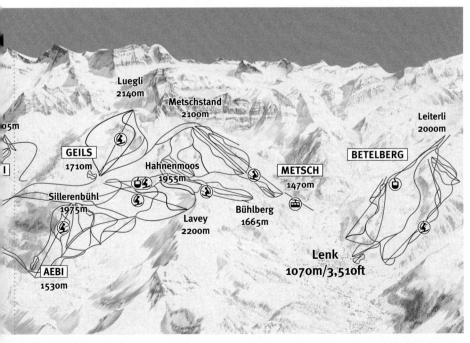

UK PACKAGES

PowderBeds, Ski
Solutions, Solos

Phone numbers
From elsewhere in
Switzerland add the
prefix 033; from
abroad use the prefix
+41 33

TOURIST OFFICE

www.adelboden.ch

ADELBODEN TOURIST OFFICE

From Tschentenalp
you get good views of
the wooded slopes of
Chuenisbärgli and the
high, snowy bowl of
Engstligenalp ↓

where a proper gondola goes up to Chuenisbärgli and then on to the major sector (taking 15 minutes in total), which has three sub-sectors – Geils, Aebi and Metsch (above Lenk). There is a pretty run home to Oey.

Engstligenalp, a flat-bottomed high-altitude bowl, is reached by a cable car 4km south of the resort; Elsigen-Metsch is 5km away to the north-east.

Fast lifts The main lifts are fast, but there are still a fair few slow ones.

Queues The main access gondolas get busy at peak times. The new Hahnenmoos chondola, due to open in December 2013, should help reduce non-trivial queues at Geils. The Bühlberg chair at Metsch can have queues. The little lift linking Oey to the centre is a real bottleneck; public and hotel buses offer a way round it.

Terrain parks The Gran Masta Park has jumps, big air, rails, snack bar and chill-out zone. There's a boardercross run, and skiercross out at Elsigen.

Snow reliability Most slopes are above 1500m, so reliability is reasonable, especially at north-facing Tschentenalp and Luegli. Snowmaking is extensive, and grooming is good.

Experts The black pistes generally merit the rating, at least in parts, and are great fun unless you crave bumps – they are groomed regularly. Off-piste possibilities are good and don't get tracked out quickly; the Lavey and Luegli chairs in the Geils bowl access routes to Adelboden and Lenk. Engstligenalp has off-piste potential.

Intermediates All five areas deserve exploration. There is a lot of ground to be covered in the main sector; at Geils and Aebi the runs are mainly excellent wide reds, but on the sunny Metsch side there is great blue cruising. Quiet Tschentenalp is worth a visit.

Beginners There are good nursery slopes in the village and at the foot of nearby sectors. But progress to longer runs requires a bit of planning.

Snowboarding There are still lots of draglifts. Two specialist schools.

Cross-country There are trails along the valley to Engstligenalp where there is a high-altitude, snow-sure circuit.

Mountain restaurants There are plenty of pleasant spots.

Schools and guides A 2013 visitor thought the Swiss school 'great'.

Families Several hotels offer childcare. One 2013 visitor said: 'There are many flat areas where you have to push the kids.'

STAYING THERE

There is locally bookable self-catering, and some 30 pensions and hotels.

Hotels The central 4-star Beau-Site (673 2222) offers 'excellent breakfast, helpful staff; worth paying for a better room upstairs'. The 3-star Waldhaus Huldi (673 8500) is a welcoming pair of chalets in a peaceful location, approaching 100 years in the same family ownership. The Cambrian (673 8383) has also had good reports.

Eating out The Bären has 'good prices, excellent food'; the Kreuz does 'delicious pizza and meringue'.

Après-ski There are several tea rooms and bars to head for at close of play, including some in central hotels. The village seems pretty quiet later on.

Off the slopes The leisure arena offers various diversions. Some hotel pools are open to the public. There's a bowling alley, and there are several toboggan runs of up to 5km. Some mountain restaurants are reachable on foot for lunchtime meetings, and there are well-marked paths. Lift passes are available for walkers.

Andermatt

A slow-paced, old-fashioned resort with great steep, high, snowy terrain on- and off-piste; but major changes are imminent

TOP 10 RATINGS

Extent	★★
Fast lifts	★★
Queues	★★
Snow	★★★★
Expert	★★★★
Intermediate	★★
Beginner	★
Charm	★★★★
Convenience	★★★
Scenery	★★★

RPI 115

lift pass	£190
ski hire	£100
lessons	£130
food & drink	£180
total	**£600**

NEWS

2013/14: Four magic carpets will be installed to improve access to other lifts and restaurants. If permission is given, a new six-seater chair will replace the T-bar from Oberalppass towards Sedrun. The first hotel in the resort's big new development, the Chedi Andermatt, is planned to open in December.

+ Attractive, traditional village
+ Excellent snow record
+ Some good steep pistes, off-piste terrain and ski-touring opportunities

– Not great for beginners, or mileage-hungry intermediates
– Limited off-slope diversions
– Busy at weekends

Little old Andermatt may soon be overwhelmed by the construction of what amounts to a new village next to the original; the first of countless luxury hotels and apartments opens in December 2013. For the moment, at least, the appeal of the tall, steep, snowy, largely off-piste Gemsstock is undiminished, but plans to expand the skiing include major new lifts on the Gemsstock, and more pistes. To enjoy the place in its traditional form, don't delay.

THE RESORT

Andermatt gets a lot of weekend business, but at other times can seem deserted. East–west links with the Grisons and the Valais rely on car-carrying trains. The lift pass also covers Sedrun – 20 minutes away and a popular excursion (see the Directory) – and linking trains to Oberalppass.

Village charm The town is quietly attractive. Charming wooden houses and handsome churches line the main street that runs from the central river bridge to the cable car. The new development of about 500 apartments, 25 chalets and 6 hotels is being built on the outskirts, past the station.

Convenience The centre is compact, but the lifts are on opposite sides of the town. A minibus shuttle runs half-hourly in high season, but in low season may run at weekends only.

Scenery The local Gemsstock peak is well defined and higher than its neighbours, with rugged steep terrain.

THE MOUNTAINS

Andermatt's local skiing is split over two unlinked mountains, both limited in extent. Most slopes are above the trees and piste marking is slack – bad news in a resort prone to white-outs.

Slopes A two-stage cable car from the edge of the village serves the open, steep, north-facing Gemsstock. Across town is the gentler, sunny Nätschen area. There is confusion over the extent of the pistes. We believe our new figure, a modest 86km, is for the existing Andermatt/Sedrun slopes.

Fast lifts The Gemsstock cable car and the chair to Gütsch in the Nätschen sector are the only fast lifts.

463

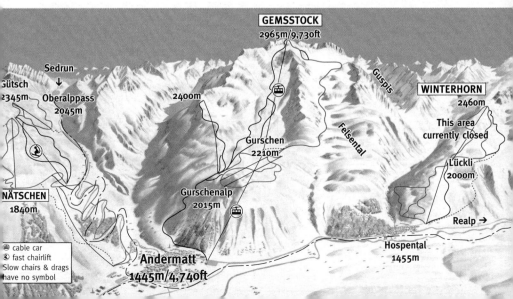

GEMSSTOCK
2965m/9,730ft

Sedrun ↓

Gütsch
2345m

Oberalppass
2045m

2400m

Guspis

WINTERHORN
2460m

This area currently closed

Gurschen
2210m

Felsental

Lückli
2000m

NÄTSCHEN
1840m

Gurschenalp
2015m

Realp →

Hospental
1455m

Andermatt
1445m/4,740ft

⬤ cable car
⬤ fast chairlift
Slow chairs & drags have no symbol

KEY FACTS

Resort	1445m
	4,740ft
Slopes	1445-2965m
	4,740-9,730ft
Lifts	20
Pistes	86km
	54 miles
Blue	22%
Red	46%
Black	32%
Snowmaking	36%

UK PACKAGES

Alpine Answers, PowderBeds, Ski Club Freshtracks, Ski Safari, Ski Solutions, Ski Weekend

Phone numbers
From elsewhere in Switzerland add the prefix 041; from abroad use the prefix +41 41

TOURIST OFFICE

www.andermatt.ch

Queues The Gemsstock cable car can generate queues, even in low season. **Terrain parks** Gemsstock has one. **Snow reliability** The area has a justified reputation for reliable snow. Nätschen gets a lot of sun. Piste grooming is generally good. **Experts** It is most definitely a resort for experts. The north-facing bowl beneath the top Gemsstock cable car is a glorious, long, steep slope (about 900m vertical), usually with excellent snow, down which there are countless off-piste routes, an itinerary and a piste. Outside the bowl, Sonnenpiste is a fine, open red run away from the lifts, with more off-piste opportunities. From Gurschen to the village there is a black run, not steep but often tricky. Routes outside the bowl go down the Felsental or Guspis valleys towards Hospental, or steeply into the deserted Untertal, to the east (ending in a bit of a walk). Nätschen has black pistes, and off-piste terrain, including worthwhile itinerary routes. **Intermediates** Intermediates needn't be put off Gemsstock: the Sonnenpiste

can be tackled, and at mid-mountain there are some short blues and an easy but longer black (served by a tricky draglift). Nätschen is well worth a visit, as are the red runs of Sedrun. **Beginners** Not ideal; but the lower half of Nätschen has a long, easy blue run. **Snowboarding** The cable car accesses some great freeride terrain. **Cross-country** There are 28km of loops along the valley. **Mountain restaurants** Inadequate. The over-busy Gurschen hut has a table-service section. You can picnic at Gurschen and at Nätschen huts. **Schools and guides** The Swiss ski school, Andermatt Xperience and Bergschule Uri/Mountain Reality are the options, and Snowlimit is a specialist snowboard school. For a guide, plan ahead: one reader this year had to hire one from Chamonix. **Families** Family passes are available.

STAYING THERE

Andermatt's accommodation is mostly in cosy 2- and 3-star hotels. The 5-star Chedi opens in December 2013. **Hotels** River House (887 0025) is a stylish, upmarket B&B in a 250-year-old building, with eight individually designed rooms. And see 'Eating out'. Gasthaus Sternen (887 1130) is an attractive central chalet. The 3-star Sonne (887 1226), towards the Gemsstock lift, is a lovely old place. A reporter rates the Schweizerhof (887 1189) good value: 'Very cheap, large rooms, decent breakfast.' **Apartments** The hotel Monopol (887 1575) has apartments. **Eating out** The restaurant at the River House has been well supported (meat and fish dishes with a 'modern twist'). Café Toutoune (cafe, restaurant and lounge bar) is smart, with a veggie/Mediterranean bias. Gasthaus Sonne is a more traditional alternative. **Après-ski** We like the cosy bar Alt Apothek at River House for tea and cake (live music later on). Other possibilities include the Curva at the hotel Monopol and the Spycher. The Piccadilly pub and Dancing Gotthard liven up at weekends. **Off the slopes** There's a toboggan run at Nätschen. The fitness centre at the hotel Drei König is open to the public. There are 20km of footpaths.

SNOWPIX.COM / CHRIS GILL

← What Andermatt is all about for many visitors: the steep, snowy, shady, uncrowded front face of Gemsstock

Champéry

Picture-postcard village that few UK tour operators feature these days, with access to the Portes du Soleil circuit

TOP 10 RATINGS

Extent	★★★★★
Fast lifts	★
Queues	★★★★
Snow	★★
Expert	★★★
Intermediate	★★★★
Beginner	★★
Charm	★★★★
Convenience	★
Scenery	★★★★

RPI   125

lift pass	£210
ski hire	£140
lessons	£105
food & drink	£190
total	**£645**

NEWS

2012/13:
Construction work started on the hotel du Parc, a new 4-star. It's due to be ready for 2014/15.

KEY FACTS

Resort	1050m
	3,440ft

Portes du Soleil	
Slopes	950-2275m
	3,120-7,460ft
Lifts	195
Pistes	650km
	404 miles
Green	12%
Blue	43%
Red	36%
Black	9%
Snowmaking	
	900 guns

Swiss side only	
Slopes	1050-2275m
	3,440-7,460ft
Lifts	34
Pistes	100km
	62 miles

It's a very appealing village, and we've known it have more snow on the streets than this →

- + Charmingly rustic mountain village
- + Access to Portes du Soleil circuit
- + Quiet, relaxed – yet plenty to do off the slopes

- − Lift system is antiquated
- − Local slopes suffer from the sun
- − No runs back to the village
- − Not good for beginners

Champéry is great for intermediate skiers looking for a quiet time in a lovely place – if you can live with the negatives. With exchange rates as they are, readers are not flocking here; if you do go, a report would be welcome.

THE RESORT

Champéry is on the Swiss side of the Portes du Soleil region, with fairly quick links to Avoriaz in France, and to the valley between Avoriaz and Châtel.
Village charm The village is friendly and relaxed, with classic old wooden chalets and some more substantial buildings; a charming spot.
Convenience Champéry's slopes are mainly high above the village, reached by a cable car that starts at the railway station, down a steepish hill, away from the main street. The village spreads over quite an area, but there is a free shuttle-bus.
Scenery The resort sits beneath the dramatic ridge of the Dents du Midi – impressive both from the village and the slopes.

THE MOUNTAINS

Champéry's slopes are open and sunny with the exception of two long runs to the valley which are partly wooded.
Slopes You reach the edge of the bowl of Planachaux via the village cable car or a fast six-seat chairlift from Grand Paradis, a short, free bus ride from Champéry. If snow is good, there are a couple of pistes back to Grand Paradis – one curling well away from the lift system – but no pistes back to Champéry. With a couple of lift rides you can get up to the French border.
Fast lifts Although there are now two fast chairlifts up to the French border, from Les Crosets, elsewhere on the Swiss slopes ancient draglifts and slow chairs prevail. Plans to modernize the system seem to have stalled.

Queues If snow is poor, expect end-of-day queues for the cable car down to the village. Few other problems.

Terrain parks The Superpark is a good terrain park at Les Crosets. It has everything you could want. There are also three beginners' parks: the micro park at the Grand Conche chair, the Village Kids at the base and another at the Planachaux chair. There are other (excellent) parks in Avoriaz.

Snow reliability The Swiss side of the mountain roughly faces south-east. More snowmaking would be good.

Experts The Swiss Wall, on the Champéry side of Pas de Chavanette, has a reputation for great steepness which is not justified; but it is a classic black (formally now an itinéraire), long and bumpy, and it provides great amusement when riding the chairlift that rises over it. The other blacks from the border ridge are worthwhile, too.

There's plenty of off-piste terrain. And at four points on the ridge the piste map has arrows indicating 'unmarked freeride itineraries'. We don't get this variation on the usual itinerary concept. It is basically saying 'There are some popular off-piste routes starting somewhere around here', and there would be less scope for confusion if they said just that.

Intermediates Confident intermediates have the whole Portes du Soleil at their disposal. Locally, the runs home to Grand Paradis are good when the snow conditions allow. Les Crosets is a junction of several fine runs. There are slightly tougher pistes from Mossettes and Pointe de l'Au, leisurely cruising above Champoussin, and delightful tree-lined meanders from La Foilleuse to Morgins. From Col des Portes du Soleil a long blue run goes down a quiet, wooded valley to Morgins; but after a good descent to the rustic Tovassière restaurant the run is a path, dropping a mere 200m in 4km.

Beginners Far from ideal. The Planachaux runs, where lessons are held, are steepish and small (as well as remote from the village), and some of the local blue runs could be red.

Snowboarding Not ideal for beginners (see above), and there are several draglifts (some quite steep). There are good terrain parks in Les Crosets and Avoriaz for intermediates and experts, though, and some good powder areas.

Cross-country It's advertised as 7km – not a lot – with 4km floodlit every night, but the snow is unreliable.

Mountain restaurants There are about 15 between Champéry and Morgins, marked but not named on the piste map. A regular visitor reckons they are all table-service, which simplifies things for us. Chez Coquoz near the Planachaux chair offers a warm welcome, a 'modern Swiss menu' and a knockout Valais wine list. The tiny Lapisa on the way to Grand Paradis is delightfully rustic – they make cheese and smoke meat on the spot.

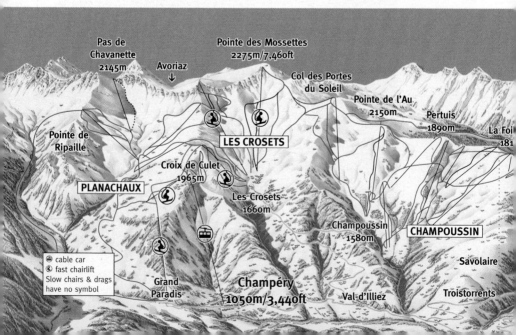

Phone numbers
From elsewhere in
Switzerland add the
prefix 024; from
abroad use the prefix
+41 24

TOURIST OFFICES

Champéry
www.champery.ch
**Les Crosets /
Champoussin / Val-
d'Illiez**
www.valdilliez.ch
Morgins
www.morgins.ch

Schools and guides We get few reports. At least the Swiss school faces healthy competition from the Freeride Co and Redcarpet Snowsport School.
Families Champéry wouldn't be high on our shortlist for a family trip, given the lack of slopes at village level.

STAYING THERE

Hotels There's a handful of modest hotels, with an unusual number outside the star system. A regular visitor to the resort supports earlier recommendations of the 3-star Beau Séjour (479 5858); other past tips are the National (479 1130) and the rustic Auberge du Grand Paradis (479 1167), which is out at, er, Grand Paradis.
Apartments Erna Low and Ski Independence have some smart, modern, spacious apartments with good views in The Lodge, a new development below the village.
Eating out Mitchell's is stylish and modern, and we had a good meal there on our last visit. Michelin-starred Le Centre, operating in a 'perfectly restored' 18th-century chalet, has been relaunched as C21, still offering a choice of proper meals or tapas-style dishes. You can 'have your steak cooked on an open fire' at the 'atmospheric' Vieux Chalet. Other reader tips are the bar of the hotel National ('hearty food'), the Farinet, Le Pub and the 'great bistro' Cafe Nord, downstairs from the 'more sophisticated' Atelier Gourmand.

Après-ski Mitchell's, with big sofas and a fireplace, is 'fun and lively' and popular at teatime. There are a few bars; the Bar des Guides in the hotel Suisse suits grown-ups. The Crevasse and Farinet are nightclubs.
Off the slopes Walks are pleasant, and the railway allows lots of excursions. There's ice climbing on a frozen waterfall and snowshoeing. The Palladium is a big ice sports centre with various other facilities, including a pool and tennis.

LINKED RESORT – 1660m
LES CROSETS

A good base for a quiet time and slopes on the doorstep. The 3-star Télécabine hotel (479 0300) has 'basic rooms but extremely helpful staff, and the five-course dinner is delicious'. Mountain Lodge (UK: 0845 127 1750) is a smart chalet-style hotel that impressed a caller this year and was rated 'fantastic' by a visitor in 2010.

LINKED RESORT – 1580m
CHAMPOUSSIN

A good family choice – no through traffic, on the slopes – is the 3-star Alpadze Lou Kra (pool, sauna, steam, gym – 476 8300). Chez Gaby is tipped for 'Valais specialities'.

LINKED RESORT – 1350m
MORGINS

Over the hill and close to Châtel in France, Morgins is a fairly scattered, but attractive, quiet resort with a gentle nursery slope right in the village. The hotel Reine des Alpes (477 1143) is well thought of, as is the 'cosy' Buvette des Sports restaurant.

DOWN-VALLEY VILLAGE – 950m
VAL-D'ILLIEZ

About 4km down the valley from Champéry, and in a similar position facing the Dents du Midi, Val-d'Illiez has no lifts or slopes, but makes a viable base – there are buses and trains up to Champéry. Down in the valley bottom is the Thermes Parc thermal spa. The hotel du Repos (477 1414) is comfortable, woody and British-run; it is in a central position, opposite the station, with a piano bar, a bar/bistro and a trattoria as well as a dining room.

La Foilleuse
1815m

Super
Châtel

Châtel

Pas de
Morgins

MORGINS

N

olaire

rrents

Morgins
1350m/4,430ft

Crans-Montana

An increasingly stylish big-town base with a fabulous panoramic view and sun-soaked slopes

TOP 10 RATINGS

Extent	★★★
Fast lifts	★★★★
Queues	★★★
Snow	★★
Expert	★★
Intermediate	★★★★
Beginner	★★★
Charm	★★
Convenience	★★
Scenery	★★★★

RPI   140

lift pass	£240
ski hire	£155
lessons	£120
food & drink	£215
total	**£730**

NEWS

2013/14: The Chetzeron mountain restaurant will open a further 12 luxury rooms plus a private dining and conference room. The 5-star Crans Ambassador hotel has reopened with 60 extra bedrooms following a refurbishment. The Momentum Ski Festival and City Ski Champs will be held here again – from 13 to 16 March 2014.

2012/13: All pistes have been numbered, both on the slopes and on the piste map. The 5-star Royal hotel reopened after refurbishment.

MOMENTUM SKI

Weekend & a la carte ski holiday specialists

100% Tailor-made

Premier hotels & apartments

Flexible travel arrangements

020 7371 9111
WWW.MOMENTUMSKI.COM

- ➕ Large, varied piste area
- ➕ Splendid setting and views
- ➕ Excellent, gentle nursery slopes
- ➕ Very sunny slopes, but ...
- ➖ Snow is badly affected by the sun
- ➖ Large, busy, urban resort
- ➖ May need a car or buses
- ➖ Few challenges except off-piste

We love the views, the local scenery and some of the mountain restaurants and smart lodgings in Crans-Montana. It's just a shame that the place is more like a city than a rustic village and that the slopes face south – the strong sunshine that's so lovely in dark December days can spoil the snow from mid-season on.

THE RESORT

Set on a broad shelf facing south across the Rhône valley, Crans-Montana is really two towns, their centres a mile apart and their fringes merging. The resort is reached by road or by a funicular railway from Sierre. There are also places to stay at the other base stations, a mile east at Les Barzettes (aka Les Violettes, the name of the hill above) and further out at Aminona. Outings to, for example, Saas-Fee and Verbier are possible.

Village charm Both Crans and Montana are emphatically towns rather than villages, with little traditional Alpine character and a lot of traffic. But the wooded setting softens the urban feel a bit. Crans is the more upmarket part, with fancy shops, several 5-star hotels and a pedestrian-friendly centre.

Convenience The towns spread widely away from their respective gondola stations and many visitors need to use cars or the free half-hourly shuttle-bus.

Scenery The panoramic views over the Rhône valley to the peaks bordering Italy are breathtaking.

THE MOUNTAINS

There's a pleasant mix of open and wooded runs with few challenges. At last, the runs were numbered on the piste map and new signs installed on the ground for last season. Virtually all the runs are red, but many are gentle and wide enough to be blue.

Slopes The slopes are spread over a broad mountainside, with lifts from four valley bases. Gondolas from Crans and Montana meet at Cry d'Er – an open bowl descending into patchy forest. A third gondola accesses the next sector, Les Violettes. A six-pack from the mid-station here links with

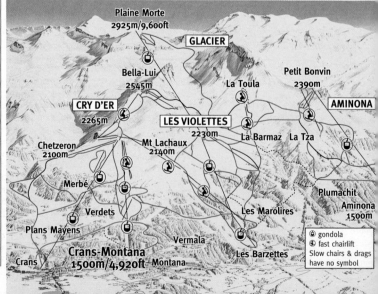

Plaine Morte 2925m/9,600ft

GLACIER

Bella-Lui 2545m

La Toula

Petit Bonvin 2390m

CRY D'ER 2265m

LES VIOLETTES 2230m

La Barmaz   La Tza

AMINONA

Chetzeron 2100m

Mt Lachaux 2140m

Merbé

Plumachit
Aminona
1500m

Verdets

Les Marolires

Plans Mayens

Vermala

Crans

Crans-Montana
1500m/4,920ft   Montana

Les Barzettes

🚠 gondola
🚡 fast chairlift
Slow chairs & drags
have no symbol

It's a large, spread out resort with no semblance of rustic charm →

CRANS-MONTANA TOURISME

KEY FACTS

Resort	1500m
	4,920ft
Slopes	1500-2925m
	4,920-9,600ft
Lifts	28
Pistes	140km
	87 miles
Blue	39%
Red	50%
Black	11%
Snowmaking	21%

UK PACKAGES

Alpine Answers, Carrier, Inghams, Momentum, Mountain Beds, Oxford Ski Co, PowderBeds, Ski Line, Ski Safari, Ski Solutions, Skitracer, Ski Weekend

Phone numbers
From elsewhere in Switzerland add the prefix 027; from abroad use the prefix +41 27

TOURIST OFFICE

www.crans-montana.ch

Cry d'Er. Above Les Violettes, a jumbo gondola goes up to the Plaine Morte glacier. The fourth sector is served by a gondola from Aminona. Some runs down to the valley are narrow paths.

Fast lifts A few slow lifts remain; the slow chair up from La Barmaz to Les Violettes is a particularly weak point.

Queues None on our recent visits.

Terrain parks A park with features for all levels, plus a beginner park, half-pipe and boardercross are at Cry d'Er.

Snow reliability The runs on the Plaine Morte glacier are very limited, and nearly all the other slopes get a lot of direct sun. There is snowmaking on the main runs but the condition of the snow depends heavily on the weather. Some runs to resort level have often been closed on our visits.

Experts There are few steep pistes and the only decent moguls are on the short slopes at La Toula. There's plenty of off-piste, particularly beneath La Toula, La Tza and Chetzeron – the best place to go in a storm. There are more adventurous routes outside the lift network – Les Faverges is a beautiful, easy valley bringing you to Aminona.

Intermediates There's a lot to do, including some notably long runs. The 12km run from Plaine Morte to Les Barzettes starts with top-of-the-world views and powder, and finishes among pretty woods. The Piste Nationale downhill course is a good fast cruise.

Beginners There are excellent nursery areas at resort level (on the golf course) and at mid-mountain but no special beginner passes.

Snowboarding Despite the resort's mature image, boarding is popular. Avalanche Pro is a specialist shop and school. There are few draglifts.

Cross-country There are around 20km of trails, plus a glacier trail (with limited opening).

Mountain restaurants A special section of the piste map marks 23 huts. Our traditional favourite is Merbé, but we have lately fallen for the smart, cool Chetzeron – all steel, glass, wood and stone, with good food at prices no higher than elsewhere. At Violettes, the cute Cabane CAS is another favourite, serving traditional meals and with great views over the valley. A local recommends Pépinet which he tells us is Roger Moore's favourite.

Schools and guides We have no recent reports of the schools, but past reports have been mainly positive.

Families This doesn't strike us as a natural family resort.

STAYING THERE

Hotels and apartments are plentiful. Crans Luxury Lodges (480 3508) are five nearly new slope-side chalets above Les Barzettes, combining chalet-style privacy with deep comfort and hotel service. We loved them.

Hotels There are some very swanky lodgings. We love two dinky little places – 5-star LeCrans (486 6060), way above the town, with chalet-style suites, and Relais & Châteaux Pas de l'Ours (485 9333) – chic but welcoming, on the edge of town.

Eating out There is a big variety of places, from French to Lebanese to Thai. Among the best is the Bistrot in the Pas de l'Ours hotel.

Après-ski At close of play, Dutch-run bar/restaurant Zérodix at the Crans lift base is the happening place. After that, New Haven and Monk'is (also a club) have been recommended.

Off the slopes There are swimming pools in hotels, two ice rinks, dog sledding, tubing, tobogganing, snowshoeing, 65km of walks, a cinema, casino and model train museum. Sierre and Sion are close.

Build your own shortlist: www.wheretoskiandsnowboard.com

Davos

A grey urban sprawl at the centre of a glorious Alpine playground
(for skaters and langlaufers as well as downhillers)

RATINGS

The mountains

Extent	★★★★
Fast lifts	★★★★
Queues	★★★
Terrain p'ks	★★★★
Snow	★★★★
Expert	★★★★
Intermediate	★★★★★
Beginner	★★
Boarder	★★★★★
X-country	★★★★★
Restaurants	★★★
Schools	★★★
Families	★★

The resort

Charm	★★
Convenience	★★
Scenery	★★★★
Eating out	★★★
Après-ski	★★★
Off-slope	★★★★★

RPI 135

lift pass	£240
ski hire	£125
lessons	£130
food & drink	£210
total	**£705**

NEWS

2012/13: A new 4-star Hilton Garden Inn opened.

470

➕ Very extensive slopes

➕ Some superb, long, and mostly easy pistes away from the lifts, with trains to bring you back to base

➕ Lots of accessible off-piste terrain, with several marked itineraries

➕ Good cross-country trails

➕ Plenty to do off the slopes

➖ Davos is a huge, busy place with dreary block-style buildings, lacking ski-resort atmosphere

➖ Five separate areas of slopes

➖ Lots of T-bars on outlying mountains

➖ The only piste back to town from the main Parsenn area is a black

One of your editors learned to ski in Davos, so it has a special place in our affections. Many return visits have confirmed the appeal of its slopes, which are both distinctive and extensive, and have revealed its considerable off-piste potential. But the town/city (it could never be called a village) does not get any easier to like. Davos may be the more convenient base for access to most of the mountains it shares with Klosters, but Klosters has the welcoming, intimate feel of a ski resort, and Davos does not.

THE RESORT

Davos is set in a high, broad, flat-bottomed valley, with its lifts and slopes either side. Arguably it was the very first place in the Alps to develop its slopes. The railway up the Parsenn was one of the first built for skiers (in 1931), and the first draglift was built on the Bolgen nursery slopes in 1934. You can reach the resort by train, but the trip from Zürich airport involves two changes. The Davos Express coach transfer service is a recommended alternative.

Davos shares its slopes with the famously royal resort of Klosters, which has its own chapter. Trips are possible by car or rail to St Moritz (via the Vereina rail tunnel) and Arosa, and by road to Laax-Flims and Lenzerheide.

VILLAGE CHARM ★★
City in the mountains
The resort is more like a city than a village, and is plagued by traffic. It started life as a health resort and many of its massive luxury hotels were built as sanatoriums. Sadly, that's just what they look like and ski resort ambience is notably lacking. It is now well known for its conference and sporting facilities too.

CONVENIENCE ★★
Take the train
The resort has two main centres, Dorf and Platz, about 2km apart. Transport is good, with an 'excellent' bus service around the town as well as the railway linking Dorf and Platz to Klosters and other villages. It's a good idea to arm yourself with timetables. Easiest access to the main Parsenn area is from Dorf, via the funicular railway; Platz is better placed for Jakobshorn, the sports facilities, smarter shopping and the evening action.

SCENERY ★★★★
Pick your viewpoint
It's an area of grand, wide views across the broad, deep, wooded valleys from one sector of the slopes to another, and to high peaks beyond.

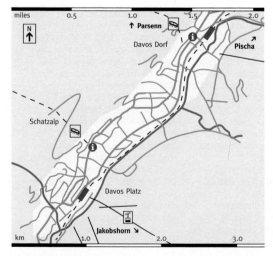

miles
0.5
1.0
1.5
2.0
↑ Parsenn
Davos Dorf
Pischa
Schatzalp
Davos Platz
Jakobshorn ↘
km
1.0
2.0
3.0

LIFT PASSES

Davos/Klosters

Prices in francs

Age	1-day	6-day
under 13	27	130
13-17	46	227
18 plus	66	324

Free under 6

Senior If 65+ (women 64+), 10% reduction on passes of 3+ days

Beginner No deals

Notes Does not cover Schatzalp; day pass is for Parsenn

Alternative passes Individual areas; pedestrian single tickets

THE MOUNTAINS

Most of the pistes are above the treeline – there are few in the woods and most are genuine blacks. Piste classification is questionable; many blue and red runs are of similar pitch. The piste map generally looks clear, but tries to cover too much ground in a small space – at some points it is simply misleading and distances are unclear. Signposting is generally fine, but reporters have complained that the long runs to Küblis and Serneus are poorly marked.

EXTENT OF THE SLOPES ★★★★
Vast and varied

You could hit a different mountain around Davos nearly every day for a week. The out-of-town areas tend to be much quieter than the ones directly accessible from the resort.

The Parsennbahn funicular from Davos Dorf takes you to mid-mountain, where a choice of a six-pack or a further funicular takes you on up to the major lift junction of Weissfluhjoch, at one end of the **Parsenn**. The only run back to town is a sunny black that can have poor snow (the alternative runs to Klosters are shadier). At the other end of the wide, open Parsenn bowl is Gotschnagrat, reached by cable car from the centre of Klosters. There are exceptionally long intermediate runs down to Klosters and other villages (see feature panel later in chapter).

Across the valley, **Jakobshorn** is reached by cable car or chairlift from Davos Platz; this is popular with snowboarders but good for skiers too. **Rinerhorn** and **Pischa** are reached by bus or (in the case of Rinerhorn) train.

A few years ago the little **Schatzalp-Strela** area above Platz – which had been closed for several years – partly reopened; however, it is not covered by the main lift pass.

Beyond the main part of Klosters, a gondola goes up from Klosters Dorf to the sunny, scenic **Madrisa** area.

FAST LIFTS ★★★★
Key ones are fine but ...

The main lifts from the valley are mostly gondolas or cable cars. Higher up, Jakobshorn is very well served for fast chairs and Parsenn reasonably so (hence the 4-star rating). But the upper lifts on Madrisa, Rinerhorn and Pischa are entirely T-bars except for one slow double chair on Madrisa.

QUEUES ★★★
Few problems

Davos has improved its key lifts and generates relatively few complaints. But there can still be lengthy queues at the cable car out of Klosters and the Totalp chair on the mountain at Parsenn at peak times and weekends. Crowded pistes have raised concern – in the Parsenn sector around Weissfluhjoch especially. In contrast, the Jakobshorn is said to be quiet.

TERRAIN PARKS ★★★★
Head for Jakobshorn

The focus of the action is the big Jatz Park on Jakobshorn. At 2300m, with snowmaking to be sure, it's open from mid-November to the very end of the

Davos is a popular spot for cross-country and has 123km of trails along the main valley and going into side valleys ➔

season, and is looked after by a small dedicated team. Four lines (including kickers from 2m to 18m, rainbow rail, down rails and a spine feature with wall ride and tyre bonk) provide something for everyone, although it's clear the better features are geared towards higher-end riders. Jakobshorn is also home to a super-pipe – one of Europe's largest; it is floodlit three evenings a week. There's also a small park on Rinerhorn (at the Trainer lift) and a kicker at Pischa (next to the Mitteltäli lift). There are boardercross courses on Parsenn and Madrisa.

SNOW RELIABILITY ★★★★☆
Good, but not the best
Davos is high by Swiss standards. Its mountains go respectably high, too.

Not many of the slopes face directly south, but Pischa does suffer from excessive sun. Snow reliability is generally good higher up. Snow-guns cover several of the upper runs on the Parsenn, most on the Jakobshorn, and the home runs from the Parsenn to Davos Dorf and Klosters. Piste grooming is generally good; but the super-long runs to the valley can become a bit neglected.

FOR EXPERTS ★★★★☆
Plenty to do, given snow
The appeal of this area for experts depends to a considerable degree on the snow conditions. Although there are challenges to be found at altitude, most of the rewarding runs descend through the woods to valley level, and

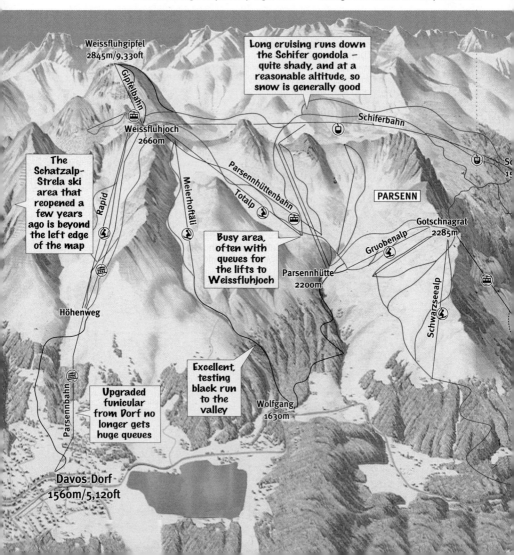

Weissfluhgipfel
2845m/9,330ft

Long cruising runs down
the Schifer gondola –
quite shady, and at a
reasonable altitude, so
snow is generally good

Gipfelbahn

Schiferbahn

Weissfluhjoch
2660m

Parsennhüttenbahn

Meierhoftäli

Totalp

PARSENN

The Schatzalp-Strela ski area that reopened a few years ago is beyond the left edge of the map

Rapid

Gotschnagrat
2285m

Busy area, often with queues for the lifts to Weissfluhjoch

Gruobenalp

Parsennhütte
2200m

Schwarzseealp

Höhenweg

Parsennbahn

Excellent testing black run to the valley

Upgraded funicular from Dorf no longer gets huge queues

Wolfgang,
1630m

Davos Dorf
1560m/5,120ft

PISCHA
2485m

Flüelatal

JAKOBSHORN
2590m/8,500ft

Dischmatal

Teuf
1700m

Dörfji
1800m

Jschalp
1930m

Clavadeler Alp
2005m

Davos Dorf
1560m/5,120ft

Davos Platz
1540m/5,050ft

Sertigtal

Mühle
1615m

Nüllisch Grat
2490m

Juonl
2390m

RINERHORN

Juonlimeder
1970m

Glaris
1460m

gondola
cable car
railway/funicular
fast chairlift
Slow chairs & drags
have no symbol

Exceptionally long, easy
runs through the woods
below the Schifer gondola
– a great way to end the
day, with lively huts to
stop at en route

Known as a family-
friendly area, but
worth a visit by
anyone – experts
included

Rätschenjoch
2600m

Küblis
810m

Saas

Schifer
1560m

Schaffürggli
2395m

nagrat
85m

Serneus
990m

Klosters' cable car is
queue-prone in the
mornings – more of a
problem for those
based here than those
based in Davos

MADRISA
1890m

Madrisabahn

Golschnabahn

Klosters Dorf
1125m

Beautiful long run away
from lifts; the lower black
section isn't difficult in
good snow conditions (it
used to be red)

Schlappin

Klosters
1190m/3,900ft

gondola
cable car
railway/funicular
fast chairlift
Slow chairs & drags
have no symbol

↑ The Parsenn is by far the biggest of Davos's five separate ski areas

DESTINATION DAVOS KLOSTERS

ACTIVITIES

Indoor Swimming pools, solarium, climbing wall, tennis, squash, badminton, wellness centre, sauna, massage, ice rink, horse-riding school, golf driving range, cinema, casino, galleries, museums, libraries

Outdoor Over 111km of cleared paths, ice climbing, ice rinks, curling, snowshoeing, tobogganing, hang-gliding, paragliding

GETTING THERE

Air Zürich 165km/ 105 miles (2hr30); Friedrichshafen 150km/95 miles (2hr30)

Rail Stations in Davos Dorf and Platz

are not reliable for snow. The black pistes include some distinctive, satisfying descents. The Meierhoftälli run to Wolfgang is a favourite – quite steep and narrow. The run from Parsennhütte to Wolfgang is less challenging; it probably owes its black status to one short tricky section.

There are also some off-piste itineraries – runs that are supposedly marked but not patrolled. At one time, these runs were a key attraction for adventurous skiers not wanting to pay for guidance, but over the decade to 2005 no fewer than 10 of them disappeared from the map, including the infamous Gotschnawang run down the top stage of the Klosters cable car and its less fearsome neighbours, Drostobel and Chalbersäss. Many of these abandoned runs have had piste status at some time in the past, and are not difficult to follow if you know what you are doing. Two of the most satisfying itineraries that remain are long ones from the top of Jakobshorn, both with decent restaurants at the end. The start of the run to Mühle is not obvious, which has led more than one reporter into difficulty; once found, the run is reportedly nowhere steeper than a tough red. The run to Teufi is more often closed: it goes first down a steep 200m gully, but thereafter is easier.

There is also excellent 'proper' off-piste terrain, for which guidance is more clearly needed. Reporters have enjoyed heading away from the pistes above Serneus and Küblis. The long descent from Madrisa to St Antönien, north of Küblis, is popular, not least for the views along the way. And there are some short tours to be done. Arosa can be reached with a bit of

help from a train or taxi, and is due to be linked to Lenzerheide for 2013/14 – forming a linked ski area with 225km of slopes. From Madrisa you can make easy circular tours to Gargellen in Austria.

FOR INTERMEDIATES ★★★★★
A splendid variety of runs
For intermediates this is a great area. There are good cruising runs on all five mountains, so you would never get bored in a week. This variety of different slopes, taken together with the wonderful long runs to the Klosters valley, makes it a compelling area with a unique character.

As well as the epic runs described in the feature panel there is a beautiful away-from-the-lifts run to the valley from the top of Madrisa back to Klosters Dorf via the Schlappin valley (it starts off red and becomes an easy black).

The Jakobshorn has some genuine challenges, notably by the Brämabüel chairlift. Rinerhorn and Pischa have more gentle terrain.

FOR BEGINNERS ★★★★★
Platz is the more convenient
There are no free lifts but each sector offers day or half-day passes. The Bolgen nursery slope beneath the Jakobshorn is adequately spacious and gentle, and a bearable walk from the centre of Platz. Dorf-based beginners face more of a trek out to Bünda though – unless staying at the hotel of the same name. There are easy runs to progress to, spread around all the sectors. The Parsenn sector probably has the edge, with long, easy intermediate runs in the main Parsenn bowl, as well as in the valleys down from Weissfluhjoch.

FOR BOARDERS ★★★★★
Epic
Davos is a Mecca for keen snowboarders. And Jakobshorn is the favoured mountain for many of them, with its top-notch park and super-pipe. It's also a great area to learn on. Rinerhorn has trees galore and pistes like roller-coaster rides – but be aware that all except the access lifts here and at Pischa are T-bars. Parsenn has a boardercross and night riding, and is host to international freeride competitions on the face beneath the Weissfluhgipfel, but watch out for the flats on the runs down to the Schifer

SCHOOLS

Swiss Davos
t 416 2454

Top Secret
t 413 7374

Pat. Skilehrer Rageth
t 416 3901

Snow & You
t 079 636 7030

Snow Doc Davos
t 078 716 1417

Swissfreeride
t 079 429 2684

Synergy Snowsports
t UK 0141 416 3525

Classes
(Swiss prices)
6 4hr-days 375 francs

Private lessons
Half day 220 francs
for 1-2 persons

---

gondola. And if you have a family in tow, the kids can stay out of trouble in the small terrain park at Rinerhorn. Synergy Snowsports is a specialist school. There are several cheap hotels geared to boarders, notably the Bolgenhof near the Jakobshorn, the Snowboardhotel Bolgenschanze and the Snowboarders Palace.

FOR CROSS-COUNTRY ★★★★★
Long, scenic valley trails
Davos is a popular spot for langlauf, and it's not difficult to see why. It has a total of 123km of trails – classic and skating – running along the flat main valley and reaching well up into the side valleys of Sertigtal, Dischmatal and Flüelatal that lead away south-east. There is a cross-country ski centre on the outskirts of the town. Trails are free.

MOUNTAIN RESTAURANTS ★★★☆☆
Stay high or go low
Most high-altitude restaurants are dreary self-service affairs – but there are good table-service exceptions. Overall, reader reports are mixed.

Weissfluhgipfel is a long-standing favourite; it changed hands a few years ago but a regular reporter says the cooking is still 'at the same excellent level'. The prices remain high, too. A 2013 reporter says the Berghaus Schifer is 'worthy of a mention' for the staff who are 'particularly friendly'. The Gotschnagrat is 'friendly, with decent mountain fare'.

The Totalp bar is recommended 'for a marginally cheaper meal'. There are compelling places lower down in the Parsenn sector. Readers enjoy the Höhenweg at the Parsennbahn mid-station for 'excellent pizzas' and 'quick service, even when busy'. There are several rustic 'schwendis' in the woods on the way down to the Klosters valley: the Serneuser warmed us on a cold day in January 2013. Some stay open until after sunset – and sell wax torches to light your way home.

On Jakobshorn the Jatzhütte is unusual, with changing decor such as mock palm trees, parrots and pirates – and serves 'delicious soups'. Châlet Güggel is also tipped: 'excellent', 'rustic charm and efficient service'.

On Pischa, the Mäderbeiz at Flüelamäder is an 'extremely pleasant' and spacious woody hut. And on Rinerhorn, try the Hubelhütte.

There are two picnic rooms: at the Weissfluhjoch on Parsenn and at the Jatzmeder on Rinerhorn.

SCHOOLS AND GUIDES ★★★☆☆
Decent choice
There are several options but we lack recent reports – more would be welcome. Top Secret limits groups to a maximum of eight. Guiding outfit Swissfreeride specializes in all-inclusive off-piste weeks. Synergy Snowsports provides enthusiastic guiding and instruction by Brits. Snow Doc Davos opened a couple of years ago, mainly offering guiding.

THE PARSENN'S SUPER-RUNS

The runs from Weissfluhjoch that head north, on the back of the mountain, make this area special for many visitors. The pistes that go down to Schifer and then on to Küblis and Serneus, and the one that curls around to Klosters, are a fabulous way to end the day, given good conditions. The run to Saas used to be a red piste but is now marked as an ungroomed and unpatrolled route.

The other runs are classified red. They are not steep, but the latter parts can be challenging because of the snow conditions – they get heavily skied, they are not reliably groomed, and by the end you are at low altitudes. Signposting is not always good, either. What marks these runs out is their sheer length (10-12km) and the resulting sensation of travel they offer – plus a choice of huts in the woods at Schifer and lower down on the way to Klosters. You can descend the 1100m vertical to Schifer and take the gondola back up. Once past there, you're committed to finishing the descent.

If you are based in Davos, the return journey is by train (included in the lift pass).

ALAN SHEPHERD

CHILDCARE

Kinderland Pischa
t 079 660 3168
Age from 3
TOPSI kindergarten
t 413 4043
Age from 30mnth
Babysitter list
At tourist office

Ski school
From age 4

UK PACKAGES

Alpine Answers, Alpine Weekends, Carrier, Headwater, Inghams, Luxury Chalet Collection, Momentum, Neilson, Oxford Ski Co, PowderBeds, Ski Bespoke, Ski Club Freshtracks, Ski Safari, Ski Solutions, Ski Weekend, Skitracer, Switzerland Travel Centre, White Roc

Phone numbers
From elsewhere in Switzerland add the prefix 081; from abroad use the prefix +41 81

TOURIST OFFICE

www.davos.ch

FOR FAMILIES ★★★★★
Not ideal

There are plenty of amusements, but Davos is a rather spread-out place in which to handle a family. The kids' ski schools operate a themed slope at Bolgen. The Top Secret school runs the TOPSI ski kindergarten. Kinderland Pischa offers childcare, and there is a snow garden on Rinerhorn. But Madrisa Land at Klosters is a more comprehensive facility.

STAYING THERE

Although most beds are in apartments, hotels dominate the UK market.
Hotels A dozen 4-stars and about 30 3-stars form the core. The tourist office runs a central booking service.
★★★★★Flüela (410 1717) The more atmospheric of the 5-star hotels, in central Dorf. Pool.
★★★★National (415 1010) Five minutes from centre of Davos Platz. 'Good service and five-course dinners.'
★★★★Sheraton Waldhuus (417 9333) Convenient for langlaufers. Quiet, modern, tasteful. Pool and spa facility. 'Bucolic setting, ideal for families.'
★★★★Sunstar Park (836 1215) In Platz, 500m from station and Jakobshorn cable car. Pool, sauna, spa.
★★★★Waldhotel (415 1515) In Platz. 'Looked after really well; beautiful pool,' says a recent visitor.
★★★Davoserhof (417 6777) Our favourite. Small, old, beautifully furnished, excellent food; in Platz.
★★★Ochsen (417 6777) Good value; near the train station in Platz.
★★★Panorama (413 2373) In central Platz. Pool, sauna.
★★★Sunstar Family (413 2373) In Platz near Sunstar Park. Games room, kids' club, pool, sauna.
★★Alte Post (417 6777) Traditional place in central Platz.
Fiftyone Designer hotel. Room only; internet bookings only.

EATING OUT ★★★★★
Wide choice, mostly in hotels

In a town this size, you need to know where to go. For a start, get the tourist office's pocket guidebook. The more ambitious restaurants are mostly in hotels. The Hotel Seehof now has an executive chef who moved from the Walserhof Klosters, which had a Michelin star under him. There are two good Chinese places, in the hotels Europe and Grischa. Go to the Carretta

in Platz for pizza and pasta, and the small and cosy Gentiana for fondues and gamey dishes (with an upstairs stübli). Excursions out of town are popular. The Höhenweg (at the mid-station of the Parsenn funicular) is open some evenings, but you pay to ride the funicular.

APRES-SKI ★★★★★
Generally quiet

At tea time, mega-calories are consumed at the Weber and the Schneider. The Scala (hotel Europe) has a popular outside terrace. Nightlife is generally quiet. The rustic little Chämi bar is lively and popular with locals. The smart Ex Bar attracts a mixed age group. Nightclubs tend to be sophisticated, expensive and lacking atmosphere during the week. The pick are Cabanna, Cava Davos and Rotliechtli. Bolgenschanze and Bolgen-Plaza attract lots of boarders. There's a casino.

OFF THE SLOPES ★★★★★
Great, apart from the buildings

Looks aside, Davos has lots to offer the non-skier. The towny resort has shops and other diversions, and transport along the valley and up on to the slopes is good – though the best of the mountain restaurants are well out of range.

The sports facilities are excellent. Europe's biggest natural ice rink is supplemented by indoor and outdoor artificial rinks, Spectator events include speed skating as well as ice hockey. The Eau-là-là leisure centre incorporates pools and wellness facilities. There's a Bowling-Bar-Bistro in Platz, and a climbing wall in the Färbi sports hall.

There are lots of walks on the slopes, around the lake and along the valleys (special map available). There's tobogganing on Rinerhorn and Schatzalp (both floodlit) and from the mid-station of the cable car back to Klosters, but the best in the area is the 8.5km run from Madrisa right down to Saas.

A reporter recommends the 'extraordinarily scenic, cheap and easy' day trips by train to St Moritz, Scuol (for the spa) and Preda-Bergün for the 6km toboggan run. Another praises the local museums and galleries.

Engelberg

A high, distinctive mountain with some classic off-piste runs, above a solid valley town dominated by an ancient monastery

TOP 10 RATINGS

Extent	★★
Fast lifts	★★★
Queues	★★
Snow	★★★
Expert	★★★★
Intermediate	★★★
Beginner	★★
Charm	★★
Convenience	★
Scenery	★★★★

RPI	120
lift pass	£210
ski hire	£100
lessons	£125
food & drink	£180
total	**£615**

NEWS

2012/13: The Titlis Cliff Walk – a 100m long suspension bridge – opened at the top of the mountain.

KEY FACTS

Resort	1050m	
	3,440ft	
Slopes	1050-3030m	
	3,440-9,940ft	
Lifts		25
Pistes		82km
		51 miles
Blue		33%
Red		57%
Black		10%
Snowmaking		70%

+ Reliable snow on high, shady slopes

+ Some classic off-piste runs

+ Big vertical of almost 2000m

– Fragmented slopes, some poor links

– Ski-bus needed from most lodgings

– Limited pistes, mostly above trees

Quick access from Zürich airport and abundant lodgings make Engelberg great for short breaks (for which we find the towny nature of the resort is worth putting up with). And Titlis is a compelling mountain, particularly for experts.

THE RESORT

The resort was named after the 12th-century Benedictine monastery (Engelberg means the mountain of the angel) that dominates the town as you look down from the lifts.

Village charm The place is more of a town than a village. Its grand Victorian hotels have been joined by chalet-style buildings and concrete blocks. There is one traffic-free cobbled street.

Convenience It's a free shuttle-bus, sometimes over-busy, or longish walks to the lifts from most hotels.

Scenery There's lots of visual drama from the high, glacial slopes.

THE MOUNTAINS

The mainly treeless, shady slopes of Titlis rise almost 2000m above the town. The separate slopes of Brunni are sunnier and gently wooded. The slopes are numbered on the mountain and until 2012/13 were numbered on the piste map too; but they omitted them last season – crazy.

Slopes The pistes in the main area are limited and fragmented by the glaciers

and rugged terrain. There are two main sectors: Titlis-Stand and Jochpass. A gondola (plus an old funicular, which rarely runs) goes up to Trübsee, whence two successive cable cars go up to Stand and then Klein Titlis – the latter rotating 360° on the way. From Trübsee, you can also head for Jochpass via a two-way chairlift to Alpstübli. At Jochpass the top is served by a fast six-pack. The much smaller Brunni area is served by a cable car on the other side of town.

Fast lifts High-capacity cable cars and gondolas provide the main access.

Queues Big queues form for the gondola from town at weekends and in peak season (half-hour waits are reported; quicker to use the funicular if it's running, says a regular visitor). The old Engstlenalp double chair below Jochpass can have queues too. Pistes can also get busy.

Terrain parks The park is at Jochpass and is smaller than it used to be.

Snow reliability The high, north-facing slopes of Titlis and Jochpass keep their snow well and have a long season. Piste grooming is 'very good'.

477

Klein Titlis
3030m/9,940ft

Jochstock
TITLIS 2565m

Fürenalp
1840m

2450m

Stand
2430m

Jochpass
2205m

Schonegg
2040m

Laub

Engstlenalp

Alpstübli

Trübsee
1800m

Brunnihütte
1860m

Ristis
1605m

Obertrübsee

BRUNNI

Klostermatte

Engelberg
1050m/3,440ft

Gerschnialp
1260m

Untertrübsee

Key:
🚠 gondola
🚡 cable car
🚋 railway/funicular
🚡 fast chairlift
Slow chairs & drags have no symbol

↑ The rugged terrain makes for a scenic backdrop but means that pistes are limited and fragmented
SIMON MEDLEY

Phone numbers
From elsewhere in Switzerland add the prefix 041; from abroad use the prefix +41 41

TOURIST OFFICE

www.engelberg.ch

Experts There is lots of superb off-piste. The classic Laub run is 1000m vertical down a hugely wide, consistently steep face with great views of town. We enjoyed even more the less popular 2000m vertical Galtiberg run from the top, which ends among streams and trees, with a bus back to town – guide essential. The off-piste from the top of the Jochpass area to Engstlenalp has been recommended and the terrain at the top of Titlis looks great but is not without danger. There are few black pistes; the itinerary from Titlis to Stand is steep and often mogulled.

Intermediates Most runs are steep reds, and there are few easy cruises. The Jochpass area is often quieter than Titlis, with enjoyable blue and red runs, including lovely long ones down to the valley station (especially nice in the mornings when they are quiet).

Beginners There's a good isolated beginner area at Gerschnialp, smaller areas at Trübsee and Untertrübsee. You have to use lifts to and from these slopes (limited passes are available); and there are few longer easy runs to progress to – all far from ideal. Some beginners go to Brunni.

Snowboarding The beginner area is served by draglifts, so it's not ideal. But there is excellent freeriding if you hire a guide. Beware of the flat start to the runs down from Jochpass.

Cross-country A 2013 reporter's friend was 'very impressed' with the 40km trails and loops (some at altitude).

Mountain restaurants An impressive choice. Our favourite, and that of reporters, is Skihütte Stand, a woody table-service place beside the cable car to Titlis: 'super atmosphere' and 'good main courses'. Jochpass serves the 'best alpen macaroni'. Try

Untertrübsee for 'perfect' rösti with bacon and eggs. The Trübsee hotel 'is a good place to meet non-skiers'.

There are picnic rooms at Stand and Toporama at Titlis.

Schools and guides There is a choice of four schools. The local guiding outfit is Outventure.

Families Globi's Winterland at Brunni is best for families, with play areas and lifts. The Swiss ski school takes kids from age three, the kindergarten from two. Some hotels offer childcare; the tourist office has details of babysitters.

STAYING THERE

Hotels The 3-star Edelweiss (639 7878) is 'excellent for families with young children'. The 3-star Schweizerhof (637 1105) is centrally located with 'good food and service, spacious rooms'. The Ski Lodge (637 3500) is popular – but avoid rooms above the bar. The Alpenclub (637 1243) is a central guest house and the Ramada Treff (639 5858) is 'gorgeously furnished and the spa is quite something'.

Eating out There is a huge variety of restaurants – more than 50 – from traditional Swiss to Tex-Mex (at the Yucatan), Chinese (Moonrise), and Indian (Chandra at the Terrace hotel). We had splendid chicken/veal dishes at the hotel Central; large portions, very well presented. The Ski Lodge is 'one of the best' (gourmet duck, salmon). The Schweizer Haus 'is worth the 15-minute stroll from town'.

Après-ski The liveliest venue is the Chalet (bottom of the gondola) which has a popular happy hour. A 2013 visitor found the previously lively Yucatan (main square) 'quiet, even at happy hour'. The Ski Lodge bar is 'pleasant'. For dancing, try Eden or the Spindle nightclub.

Off the slopes The 12th-century monastery and its cheese-making factory and shop are worth a visit. It's worth going up the cable cars for the views, the suspension bridge and the ice grotto. There are many walking and snowshoeing trails, tubing, sledging and a sports centre. Up the valley, a gondola goes up to Fürenalp for walking, tobogganing, snowshoeing. Lucerne is a possible train trip.

UK PACKAGES

Alpine Answers, Chalet Espen, Flexiski, Inntravel, Momentum, Mountain Beds, PowderBeds, Ski Club Freshtracks, Ski Independence, Ski Monterosa, Ski Safari, Ski Solutions, Skitracer, Ski Weekend, STC, White Roc

Grindelwald

Traditional mountain village set beneath the towering Eiger and with an old cog railway still the main way up to the slopes

RATINGS

The mountains

Extent	★★★
Fast lifts	★★★★
Queues	★★
Terrain p'ks	★★★
Snow	★★
Expert	★★
Intermediate	★★★★
Beginner	★★★
Boarder	★★★
X-country	★★
Restaurants	★★★
Schools	★★★
Families	★★

The resort

Charm	★★★★
Convenience	★★
Scenery	★★★★★
Eating out	★★★
Après-ski	★★★
Off-slope	★★★★

RPI   125

lift pass	£230
ski hire	£115
lessons	£110
food & drink	£185
total	**£640**

NEWS

2012/13: A new six-pack replaced the Wixi chair in the Wengen sector. A new skiercross was built on First. And on some slopes there are special photo spots and places where you can check your speed. You can also be filmed and view the video on the Jungfrau website later.

+ Dramatically set, beneath the north face of the Eiger

+ Lots of long intermediate runs

+ Pleasant old village with long mountaineering history

+ Fair amount to do off the slopes, including splendid walks

– Slow, queue-prone trains and gondola to access the main slopes

– Few challenging pistes for experts

– A long trek to visit Mürren

– Natural snow-cover unreliable (but substantial snowmaking now)

– Village gets little midwinter sun

For stunning views from the resort and the slopes, there are few places to rival Grindelwald. The village is nowhere near as special as Mürren or Wengen, just over the hill, but it does provide direct access to Grindelwald's own First slopes.

The main access lifts are appalling, taking half an hour to ride even if you don't have to queue (for the gondola) or wait (for the train). Grindelwald regulars accept all this as part of the scene. We're not Grindelwald regulars.

THE RESORT

Grindelwald is a long village set along a road that runs across a hillside facing the towering north wall of the Eiger, which means that the resort gets very little sun in January. Its main slopes are shared with Wengen; and there is a separate area of sunny slopes on First. Getting to the tougher, higher slopes of Mürren on snow and lifts is a lengthy business (around three hours to the top). Trips to other resorts are not very easy.

VILLAGE CHARM ★★★★
Not quite in the Wengen league
The central buildings are mainly in traditional chalet style, in keeping with its long mountaineering history. And the station and cog railway add to the olde-worlde charm. The village can feel very jolly at times (eg during the snow carving festival in January, when huge sculptures are created). Although the road through goes nowhere, traffic on it can be intrusive.

CONVENIENCE ★★
Not a strong point
The most convenient places to stay are in the centre near the main station or at Grund, departure point of the main access lifts and arrival point of the main home piste, about 80m vertical lower. If you stay in the centre, you can also take the train up, but you need to catch it back up from Grund on the way home too. Staying near the centre means the gondola up to the First area is a walkable distance. At the foot of First are nursery slopes, ski school and kindergarten. Buses link the lift stations – 'very efficient and regular, even when the roads are covered in snow', says a recent visitor.

SCENERY ★★★★★
Unrivalled
The mountains in these parts are legendary among climbers – from all over the slopes there are superb views, not only of the Eiger but also of the Wetterhorn and other peaks.

THE MOUNTAINS

The major area of slopes is shared with Wengen and offers a mix of a few wooded runs and much more extensive open slopes. The smaller First area is mainly open. Several areas are designated as wildlife reserves, where you may well spot chamois. Piste marking and the piste map are poor; reporters find the Männlichen slopes, in particular, confusing.

Map: miles 0.5 — 1.0 — 1.5 — 2.0; ↑ First; N↑; Männlichen; Grund; Kleine Scheidegg; km 1.0 — 2.0 — 3.0

KEY FACTS

Resort	1035m
	3,400ft

Jungfrau region	
Slopes	945-2970m
	3,100-9,740ft
Lifts	45
Pistes	213km
	132 miles
Blue	33%
Red	49%
Black	18%
Snowmaking	50%

First-Männlichen-Kleine-Scheidegg	
Slopes	945-2500m
	3,100-8,200ft
Lifts	34
Pistes	170km
	106 miles

GETTING THERE

Air Zürich 160km/ 100 miles (2hr45); Bern 70km/45 miles (1hr30); Basel 165km/105 miles (2hr30)

Rail Station in resort

EXTENT OF THE SLOPES ★★★
Broad and mainly gentle
The area shared with Wengen spreads broadly beneath the Eiger. From Grund, near the western end of town, you can get to **Männlichen** by an appallingly slow two-stage gondola, or to **Kleine Scheidegg** by an equally slow cog railway (with some trains starting in the centre of town). The slopes of the separate south-facing **First** area are reached by a long, slow gondola starting a walk or short bus ride east of the centre.

FAST LIFTS ★★★★
Better high up
Getting up into the main area from the village is seriously slow, but new fast chairlifts continue to improve the area higher up – most recently, the six-pack to Eigergletscher and the Wixi six-pack, built for 2012/13.

QUEUES ★★
Can be dreadful at the bottom
These days visitors generally find few problems once they are on the mountain, but the train and the Männlichen gondola at Grund can be crowded at peak periods. Queues for the gondola can be very bad in high season, especially on Saturdays – this is the obvious entry point for residents of Bern attracted by the special family pass deals on Saturdays. And the gondola goes very slowly, too.

TERRAIN PARKS ★★★
First has it all
The White Elements Pro Park on First next to the Bärgelegg lift has 850m of rails, boxes, kickers and jumps, with lines for different abilities. There is also a beginner park at Oberjoch at the top of First and a new skiercross near the top of the Schilt lift.

SNOW RELIABILITY ★★
Improved snowmaking helps
Grindelwald's low altitude means that natural snow is often in short supply or in poor condition. First is a bit higher than the Männlichen area, and may have better snow in midwinter; but it is sunny, and less snow-sure as spring approaches. Snowmaking has been increased recently and the resort claims that more than 65% of its slopes are now covered. When we were there last, it had not snowed for a few weeks and a warm Föhn wind had melted a lot of snow, but most slopes were in good condition. Piste maintenance gets mixed reviews.

FOR EXPERTS ★★
Few on-piste challenges
The area is quite limited for experts, but there is some fine off-piste if the snow is good. Heli-trips are organized. We and readers have enjoyed the splendid Bort Direct black run on First. This turns into a downhill route between Bort and town and is quite tough, especially when the snow has suffered from the sun.

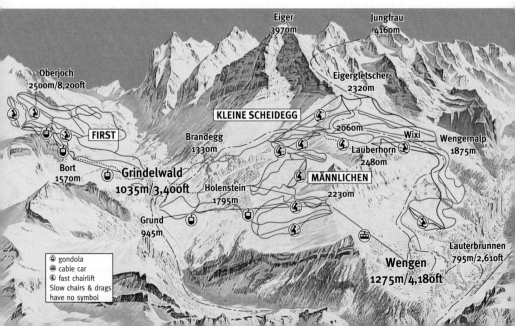

Scenery doesn't come much more spectacular than this: the Eiger on the left, the Mönch on the right and the Jungfrau out of shot →

JUNGFRAU REGION MARKETING AG

FOR INTERMEDIATES ★★★★
Ideal intermediate terrain
In good snow, First makes a splendid intermediate playground, though the general lack of trees makes the area less friendly than the larger Kleine Scheidegg-Männlichen area. Nearly all the runs from Kleine Scheidegg are long blues or gentle reds – great cruising terrain. On the Männlichen there's a choice of gentle runs down to the mid-station of the gondola – and in good snow, down to the bottom. For tougher pistes, head for the top of the Lauberhorn lift and the runs to Kleine Scheidegg, or to Wixi (following the World Cup downhill course). The north-facing run from Eigergletscher served by the Eigernordwand six-pack often has the best snow late in the season.

FOR BEGINNERS ★★★
Depends where you go
The Bodmi nursery slope at the bottom of First is scenic but not particularly convenient. Snow quality can also suffer from the sun and the low altitude, and fast skiers and tobogganers racing through are off-putting. Kleine Scheidegg has a better, higher beginner area and splendid long runs to progress to, served by the railway. There are no free lifts, but a points card is available.

FOR BOARDERS ★★★
Best for intermediates
Intermediates will enjoy the area most, while experts will hanker for Mürren's steep, off-piste slopes. First is the main boarders' mountain, not only because of the two terrain parks but also because of the open freeride terrain near the top. There are still a few draglifts but most are avoidable.

FOR CROSS-COUNTRY ★★
Okay but shady
There are 15km of prepared tracks. Almost all of this is on the valley floor, so it's shady in midwinter and may have poor snow later on.

MOUNTAIN RESTAURANTS ★★★
Wide choice
There are lots, all clearly marked on the piste map. Read the Wengen chapter for additional options. Brandegg, on the railway, is regularly recommended ('fritters hit the spot', 'still very good', 'legendary doughnuts'). Other reader tips include: the Genepi on First ('tasty kebabs'); and Berghaus Aspen just above Grund ('best-ever rösti'). On First we enjoyed Bort, where the old building houses a restaurant built in contemporary style. One reader loved the tiny Alpweg, not for the food but for a welcoming, local atmosphere – 'where the locals break out into song and yodelling'.

There are two picnic rooms: at the middle-station Schreckfeld on First; and at the Männlichen top station.

SCHOOLS AND GUIDES ★★★
Good reports
A recent visitor says of the Swiss school: 'I've always had good experiences with this school and its various instructors at all levels.' The Privat school offers off-piste guiding.

FOR FAMILIES ★★
Lacks convenience
It's not a convenient place for families (see 'For beginners'). Snowli Children's Club based at Bodmi (First) takes kids from three years old and operates a bus from the village. Snowli Club Sunshine is a nursery and play area at the top of Männlichen.

CHILDCARE

Snowli Club Sunshine
t 854 1280
From 6mnth

Snowli Club Bodmi
t 854 1280
From age 3

Felix Ski Paradies
t 853 1288
From age 3

Ski schools
From age 3 or 4

ACTIVITIES

Indoor Sports centre
(pool, sauna, steam,
fitness), ice rink,
curling, rope park,
museum

Outdoor 100km of
cleared paths, ice
rink, tobogganing,
snowshoeing, snow
biking, 'First flyer' zip
rider, paragliding

UK PACKAGES

Alpine Answers, Crystal,
Crystal Finest, Elegant
Resorts, Inghams,
Momentum, Mountain
Beds, Neilson, Powder
Byrne, PowderBeds, Ski
Club Freshtracks,
Skitracer, Ski Weekend,
STC, Switzerland Travel
Centre, Thomson, White
Roc

Phone numbers
From elsewhere in
Switzerland add 033;
from abroad use the
prefix +41 33

TOURIST OFFICE

www.grindelwald.com

STAYING THERE

Hotels There's a 5-star, eight 4-stars
and plenty of more modest places.
*****Grand Regina (854 8600) Big and
imposing; right next to the station.
Pool and spa.
****Belvedere (888 9999) Over 100
years old, comfortable, family-run,
friendly, close to the station. Pool,
steam, sauna, hot tub.
****Eiger (854 3131) 'Spacious rooms,
superb service, great wellness area.'
****Schweizerhof (854 5858) Close to
the station. Pool.
****Sunstar (854 7777) Near First
gondola. Comfortable rooms, big
wellness complex, conference facilities.
***Derby (854 5461) Modern; next to
station.
***Gletschergarten (853 1721) Out
past First gondola. 'Friendly, good
English spoken, four-course meals.'
***Hirschen (854 8484) Family-run; by
nursery slopes. Good food.
***Wetterhorn (853 1218) Cosy, simple
chalet way beyond the village, with
great views of the glacier.
Apartments The Eiger hotel has
apartments.
At altitude Berghaus Bort (853 1762),
at the First gondola mid-station, has
proper rooms and dormitories.

EATING OUT ★★★☆☆
Hotel based

There's a wide choice of good hotel
restaurants such as the Hirschen,
Challistübli in the Kreuz & Post,
Schmitte in the Schweizerhof, and the
Alte Post. Hotel Spinne has the
candlelit Rôtisserie, and Onkel Tom's
Hütte is an Italian. A reporter
recommends the Steinbock ('good
food, reasonable prices, pizza cooked
in wood oven, busiest place in town').

APRES-SKI ★★★☆☆
Getting livelier

Tipirama (a wigwam at Kleine
Scheidegg) is a fun place immediately
after skiing 'if not too cold',
sometimes with DJs and live bands;
you can catch the train down. There
are various (mainly open air) bars to
stop in on the way down to Grund. The
liveliest are the Rancher (on run
22), attracting a young crowd;
Holzerbar (on run 21) and the Aspen
hotel (just below). In town, the terrace
of the C&M Café und Mehr is good for
coffee and cake. Later on, there's live
music in several bars and hotels, such
as the Challibar (hotel Kreuz & Post);
but it isn't a place for bopping until
dawn. The Espresso bar in the Spinne
hotel seems to be the liveliest and the
Gepsi Bar in the Eiger hotel is 'a
continual favourite'. Later on, people
head for the Mescalero (in the Spinne)
and Plaza (in the Sunstar) clubs.

OFF THE SLOPES ★★★★☆
Plenty to do, easy to get around

There are many cleared paths with
magnificent views and a special (but
pricey) pedestrian lift pass. Many of
the mountain huts are accessible to
pedestrians. A trip to Jungfraujoch is
spectacular (see the feature panel),
and train trips are easy to Interlaken
and Bern. Tobogganing is big here; the
69km of runs include what is claimed
to be Switzerland's longest (15km) but
it starts a 2hr30 walk from the top of
the First gondola. First also has the
First Flyer – a zip-wire affair – free if
you have a ski pass. There's ice
hockey and curling to watch, an
indoor rope park and an excellent
sports centre with pool. Scenic flights
around the spectacular peaks from
Männlichen are popular.

THE JOURNEY TO THE TOP OF EUROPE

*From Kleine Scheidegg you can take a train
through the Eiger to the highest railway
station in Europe – Jungfraujoch at 3450m.
The journey is a bit tedious – you're in a
tunnel except when you stop to look out at
magnificent views from two galleries carved
into the sheer north face of the Eiger. At the
top is a big restaurant complex, an 'ice
palace' carved out of the glacier and fabulous
views of the Aletsch glacier (a UNESCO
World Heritage Site). The cost in 2012/13
was 58 francs with a Jungfrau lift pass for
three days or more.*

JUNGFRAU REGION MARKETING AG

Klosters

*Ski the extensive slopes of Davos from a traditional village base –
with Davos traffic happily banished to a bypass some years ago*

TOP 10 RATINGS

Extent	★★★★
Fast lifts	★★
Queues	★★
Snow	★★★★
Expert	★★★★
Intermediate	★★★★★
Beginner	★★★
Charm	★★★★
Convenience	★★
Scenery	★★★★

RPI · 130

lift pass	£240
ski hire	£105
lessons	£120
food & drink	£210
total	**£675**

NEWS

2013/14: The Wynegg hotel, an old favourite with British guests, is due to reopen in December after refurbishment by new owners hoping to appeal to a younger clientele.

+ Extensive slopes shared with Davos

+ Some lovely long intermediate runs

+ Lots of accessible off-piste terrain

+ Some cute mountain restaurants

+ Pleasant traditional village bypassed by the valley traffic

− The slopes are spread over six widely separated areas

− Preponderance of T-bars is a problem for some visitors

− Queue-prone cable car

− May be too quiet for some visitors

In a word association game, 'Klosters' might trigger 'Prince of Wales'. The resort has even named its queue-prone cable car after him. Don't be put off: Klosters is not particularly exclusive, and makes an attractive alternative to towny Davos, with which it shares its slopes.

THE RESORT

Klosters is a sizeable village with a relaxed Alpine atmosphere.

Village charm Klosters Platz is the main focus – a collection of upmarket, traditional-style hotels around the railway station. Traffic for Davos and the Vereina rail tunnel takes a bypass – an improvement still much appreciated by old hands like us.

Convenience The cable car up the wooded slopes of Gotschna starts in the heart of Platz. The village spreads along the valley road, fading into the countryside; then you come to the even quieter village of Klosters Dorf, and the gondola to Madrisa. Local train and bus services are good.

Scenery The contrast between steeply wooded valleys and high, craggy peaks is impressive.

THE MOUNTAINS

Most of the runs are on open slopes above steeper woodland.

Slopes A cable car from the railway station in Platz takes you to the Gotschnagrat end of the Parsenn area shared with Davos. These slopes are dealt with in the Davos chapter. A gondola from Dorf takes you up to the scenic Madrisa area, which we deal with here. There's also a little slope at Selfranga (floodlit some evenings), a suburb of Platz.

Fast lifts Apart from the gondola, it's T-bars and one slow chair on Madrisa.

Queues Queues for the Gotschna cable car can be a problem at weekends and peak times, but visitors report that they found no queues elsewhere.

Terrain parks Madrisa has a boardercross course.

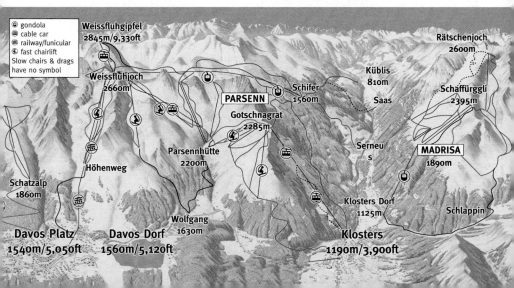

Key:
- ⊙ gondola
- ⊜ cable car
- ⊜ railway/funicular
- ⊙ fast chairlift
- Slow chairs & drags have no symbol

Weissfluhgipfel 2845m/9,330ft
Weissfluhjoch 2660m
PARSENN
Gotschnagrat 2285m
Parsennhütte 2200m
Höhenweg
Schatzalp 1860m
Schifer 1560m
Küblis 810m
Saas
Serneus
Rätschenjoch 2600m
Schafürggli 2395m
MADRISA 1890m
Klosters Dorf 1125m
Schlappin
Wolfgang 1630m
Davos Platz 1540m/5,050ft
Davos Dorf 1560m/5,120ft
Klosters 1190m/3,900ft

KEY FACTS

Resort	1190m
	3,900ft
Slopes	810-2845m
	2,660-9,330ft
Lifts	59
Pistes	320km
	199 miles
Blue	23%
Red	42%
Black	35%
Snowmaking	40%

UK PACKAGES

Alpine Answers, Carrier, Elysian Collection, Flexiski, Independent Ski Links, Inghams, Kaluma, Luxury Chalet Collection, Momentum, Neilson, Oxford Ski Co, Powder Byrne, PowderBeds, PT Ski, Pure Powder, Ski Bespoke, Ski Club Freshtracks, Ski Expectations, Ski Independence, Ski Safari, Ski Solutions, Skitracer, Ski Weekend, Snow Finders, STC, Supertravel, Switzerland Travel Centre, White Roc

Phone numbers

From elsewhere in Switzerland add 081; from abroad use the prefix +41 81

TOURIST OFFICE

www.klosters.ch

Snow reliability It's usually good higher up. A 2013 reporter thought the grooming on the Parsenn was better than that on Madrisa.

Experts The lift-served off-piste possibilities are the main appeal, on Madrisa as elsewhere in the region – and on 'family-friendly' Madrisa it doesn't get skied out so quickly.

Intermediates Madrisa is not huge, but it is all excellent intermediate terrain. The black run to the valley is not difficult unless conditions make it so.

Beginners There is a slope between Dorf and Platz, plus Selfranga; but Madrisa's higher slopes are more appealing. Be aware that Madrisa closes before the area as a whole. There are no special lift-pass deals.

Snowboarding Local slopes are good, but more boarders stay in Davos.

Cross-country There are 35km of free trails and lots more up at Davos; a Nordic ski school offers lessons.

Mountain restaurants For the Parsenn read the Davos chapter. On Madrisa the woody Erika at Schlappin offers 'excellent atmosphere and food' and we enjoyed the rustic Zügenhüttlibar.

Schools and guides Swiss and Saas are well regarded: 'Helpful, perceptive and encouraging,' says a recent visitor of Saas. Adventure Skiing has been praised for private guiding: 'Knew the area well and was safety conscious.'

Families Madrisa Land adventure park has lots to offer children, and access is free to kids under six years old. The kindergarten there takes children from birth to six years. There is also an indoor playroom and the Saaseralp restaurant has a special play area. The ski schools offer classes to children from the age of three.

STAYING THERE

Hotels For most people, central Platz is the best location. There's the smart Chesa Grischuna (422 2222) but the readers' favourite is the 4-star Alpina (410 2424) – again recommended this year for 'good food and location'. Other possibilities are the Wynegg (422 1340) and 3-star Rustico (410 2288) – which have both changed hands recently (so reports needed, please) – and the 4-star Silvretta Park Hotel (423 3435). In Dorf the Sunstar Albeina (423 2100) is in a 'lovely location and is very comfortable'.

Apartments Apartments are available through local agencies.

Eating out Good restaurants abound, but there are few cheap and cheerful places. Top of the range has been the Walserhof but the chef has changed recently. Other possibilities are Casanna at Platz, Chesa Grischuna (varied menu and good wines), Al Berto and Fellini (both for pizza).

Après-ski Gaudy's umbrella bar at the foot of the slopes is the focal point at the end of the day. In the village, the Chesa Grischuna has a pianist. Bär's at Piz Buin opened last season and is popular all day long. The Casa Antica is a small disco.

Off the slopes Klosters is an attractive base for walking (there's a special map available) and cross-country skiing. Tobogganing is popular – there is an exceptional 8.5km run from Madrisa to Saas. There is an ice rink, and some hotel pools are open to the public. A new gramophone and radio museum opened in 2012. Read the Davos chapter for ideas for train outings.

Laax

Contrasting villages beneath high, wide, sunny slopes shared by well-heeled families and trendy young freestylers

SWISS-IMAGE / MOUNTAIN MARKETING AG

TOP 10 RATINGS

Extent	★★★★
Fast lifts	★★★★★
Queues	★★★★
Snow	★★★
Expert	★★★
Intermediate	★★★★★
Beginner	★★★★
Charm	★★★
Convenience	★★★
Scenery	★★★

RPI 130

lift pass	£240
ski hire	£100
lessons	£135
food & drink	£190
total	**£665**

NEWS

2012/13: A six-pack from Lavadinas replaced an old double that started lower down at Alp Ruschein. Another new six-pack now goes from Treis Palas to Crap Masegn. And 15km of new runs were built to go with these two lifts.

+ Extensive, varied slopes ideal for intermediates, shared with Flims
+ Generally efficient lift system, but with some long ride times
+ Some of Europe's best terrain parks

− Sunny orientation can spoil snow
− Bus rides or long walks from some lodgings to the lifts
− Most convenient lodgings are in bases we find difficult to like

Laax and neighbouring Flims share a ski area that is, in terms of piste km, one of Switzerland's biggest. It used to be marketed as Flims (and still is in the summer) but now calls itself Laax in the winter – part of its (successful) attempt to change its image to appeal to the youth, snowboard and freestyle markets as well as its traditional well-heeled family clientele. It has invested heavily in terrain parks, half-pipes, indoor freestyle facilities and organizing high-profile events. Most reporters like the skiing but not the slope-side bases.

THE RESORT

The resort has three separate main bases a few km apart by road: Laax, Flims and Falera. Laax and Flims are themselves resorts of parts. Laax Dorf is the original rustic village, a couple of km from a much newer big, busy lift base/hotel/parking complex, now called Laax. Flims Dorf is a traditional resort at the foot of the slopes; Flims Waldhaus is a leafy suburb.

Village charm Laax Dorf is pleasantly traditional, with quiet suburbs set around a lake. Laax is modern, more youth-oriented, and 'all grey rock with flat roofs and lacks any Alpine charm', as a recent reporter put it. Flims Dorf is unremarkable, spread along the road through it (though a bypass takes the through-traffic). Flims Waldhaus is wooded and more appealing with upscale secluded hotels. Falera, once a quiet hamlet, has been much expanded in traditional style.

Convenience It depends where you stay. The smart hotels in Waldhaus run courtesy buses and there are 'quick and efficient' free ski-buses.

Scenery There are great panoramic views from the top of the glacier but lower down the views are less spectacular.

485

WEISSE ARENA GRUPPE, LAAX

The ski area's sunny slopes have great intermediate pistes plus plenty of off-piste →

KEY FACTS

Resort	1100m
	3,610ft
Altitude	1100-3020m
	3,610-9,910ft
Lifts	29
Pistes	235km
	146 miles
Blue	29%
Red	32%
Black	39%
Snowmaking	16%

THE MOUNTAINS

The slopes are mostly open but there are also some quite long woodland runs. The piste map includes 'freeride runs' (dotted on our map), which are avalanche-controlled and patrolled just like pistes. Many of the black runs could really be classified red.

Slopes There are long gondolas into the slopes from both Flims Dorf and Laax (plus a cable car of exceptional length from Laax) and a fast quad chair from Falera. Above mid-mountain, there is a complex web of lifts and runs. The glacier is limited; but it accesses a superb long run to Lavadinas.

Fast lifts The system is impressive with most lifts being fast chairs, gondolas and cable cars. The two new six-packs for 2012/13 moved Laax firmly into our ★★★★★ category.

Queues There may be queues for the village lifts at peak times and for the glacier drags. High winds can close the upper lifts and put pressure on the lower ones.

Terrain parks Laax is one of the top resorts in Europe for freestylers and has four parks in the Crap Sogn Gion area, catering for every standard from beginner to pro-rider, where many high-profile competitions are held (including the British freestyle championships before 2013, when they moved to Tignes). Between them, they have 56 obstacles, 15 kickers, an airbag and two pipes (super- and mini-) plus an 'excellent' freestyle slope to Curnius. The glacier has an early season park, too. An indoor Freestyle Academy at the base in Laax offers tuition.

Snow reliability Upper runs are fairly snow-sure. The lower ones can suffer from sun, even early in the season, and some can close (the runs from Cassons and the glacier are also prone to closure); key ones have snowmaking but more is needed.

Experts The black pistes present few challenges, but the freeride runs add a lot of excellent terrain – timing your descents can be crucial, though, to avoid rock-hard moguls. There is a huge amount of good off-piste terrain, notably from La Siala and Cassons.

Intermediates A superb area. Reporters are often surprised by the extent, length and variety of the slopes. The bowl below La Siala is huge and gentle. For the more confident, there are plenty of reds and some easy blacks. The sheltered Grauberg valley is a good area for long and fast runs. The long black run from the glacier is one of our favourites and is steep only at the top. The Downhill piste from Crap Sogn Gion is also excellent. Some

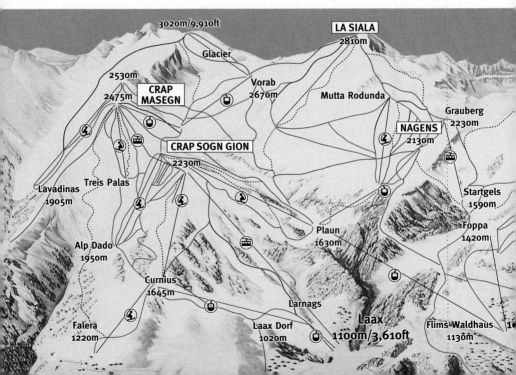

UK PACKAGES

Alpine Answers, Erna Low, Momentum, Powder Byrne, PowderBeds, Ski Club Freshtracks, Ski Expectations, Ski Safari, Skitracer, Ski Weekend, Snow Finders, Switzerland Travel Centre, Zenith **Flims** Alpine Answers, Independent Ski Links, Momentum, PowderBeds, Powder Byrne, Ski Solutions, Skitracer, Ski Weekend, Switzerland Travel Centre, White Roc

Phone numbers
From elsewhere in Switzerland add the prefix 081; from abroad use the prefix +41 81

TOURIST OFFICE

Flims, Laax and Falera
www.laax.com

of the freeride runs are great for trying off-piste, but others are steep.

Beginners There are beginner areas at village level (which can suffer from the sun) and at Crap Sogn Gion and good easy runs to progress to. A beginner day pass was available on certain lifts in all three base areas last season.

Snowboarding Hugely popular. Apart from the top terrain parks, there's good freeriding. Many linking pistes have flat/uphill stretches though – plan carefully.

Cross-country There are 55km of trails.

Mountain restaurants The piste map classifies them into Easy (seems to mean self-service)/Cosy/Exquisite and they are marked but not named. There's a separate 'Gastro Guide' piste map which also describes them – an excellent idea. The two 'Exquisites' we hear most about are Alpenrose at Startgels (good views, fine grills and Italian specials) and Tegia Larnags (a 'charming' farmhouse with typically Swiss dishes). Tegia Curnius is a popular self-service ('excellent rösti'). Also tipped: Tegia Miez ('simple, rustic, excellent local meats'), Foppa ('excellent schnitzel and ravioli') – both table-service – and Nagens (self-service but 'fantastic pasta').

You can eat a picnic inside at Cafe NoName (Crap Sogn Gion) on the lower floor only and on the terrace

there (great views of the terrain park) and at Vorab.

Schools and guides The school is run by the lift company, USA-style. We've had glowing reports of children's instruction, and a recent reporter says they kept 'an eye on things very effectively' after his grandson had a few problems. Another reporter had 'excellent private instruction with an extremely friendly instructor with excellent English'.

Families There are 'Wonderlands' at all three resort bases.

STAYING THERE

Hotels At Laax the 4-star 'design hotel' Signina (927 9000) is part of Rocksresort (see 'Apartments') and has 'excellent staff, good breakfasts, pool, wonderful indoor tennis courts'. The 4-star Laaxerhof (920 8200) is almost ski-out/in and has good-sized rooms, pool and sauna; its stubli has been praised. Laax Dorf offers the charming little Posta Veglia (921 4466).

In Flims Dorf the cheap and cheerful Arena (911 2400) – with 'cool rooms, friendly and helpful staff, good restaurant and the best bar in town – suits boys' trips' (see 'Après-ski').

In Flims Waldhaus the Sunstar (928 1800) is over 100 years old and has been praised for its food and staff. Cresta (911 3535) has 'excellent food, service and top spa facilities'. The Adula (928 2828) is similarly praised by a regular visitor.

Apartments At Laax, Rocksresort is uber-cool but the architecture is not to everyone's taste – and you can use the facilities of the Signina hotel. The tourist office has a list of apartments.

Eating out In Laax, Rocksresort places include Nooba ('excellent Asian food, friendly staff'), and the smart Grandis (fine wines and BBQ specialities). In Laax Dorf the Posta Veglia has a lovely old stube, with a plainer room behind. In Flims, a regular recommends both à la carte restaurants of the hotel Adula.

Après-ski There are busy bars at the lift bases at close of play. Later on, clubs at the hotel Arena and the Riders Palace at Laax throb until late.

Off the slopes There's a big sports centre on the edge of Flims, with ice rink and ice hockey, and 100km of 'really excellent' marked walks. Shopping is limited. Outings to historic Chur are easy.

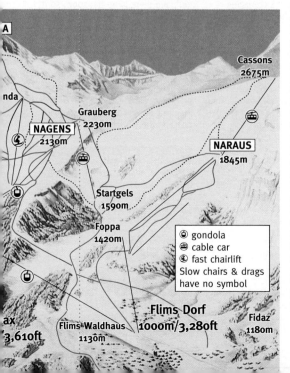

Cassons 2675m

nda

Grauberg 2230m

NAGENS 2130m

NARAUS 1845m

Startgels 1590m

Foppa 1420m

gondola
cable car
fast chairlift
Slow chairs & drags have no symbol

Flims Dorf 1000m/3,280ft

Fidaz 1180m

Flims Waldhaus 1130m

ax 3,610ft

Mürren

The dinky, car-free mountain village where the British invented downhill ski racing; stupendous views from one epic run

RATINGS

The mountains

Extent	★
Fast lifts	★★★★★
Queues	★★★
Terrain p'ks	★★
Snow	★★★
Expert	★★★
Intermediate	★★★
Beginner	★★★
Boarder	★★
X-country	★
Restaurants	★★
Schools	★★★
Families	★★★

The resort

Charm	★★★★★
Convenience	★★★
Scenery	★★★★★
Eating out	★★
Après-ski	★★
Off-slope	★★★

RPI   125

lift pass	£230
ski hire	£120
lessons	£105
food & drink	£185
total	**£640**

NEWS

2012/13: The sports centre was renovated and a wellness centre and new cafeteria added.

+ Tiny, charming, traditional village, with 'traffic-free' snowy paths

+ Stupendous scenery, best enjoyed descending from the Schilthorn

+ Good sports centre

+ Good snow high up, even when the rest of the region is suffering

- Extent of local pistes very limited, no matter what your level of expertise

- Lower slopes can be in poor condition

- Quiet, limited nightlife

Mürren is one of our favourite resorts. There may be other mountain villages that are equally pretty, but none of them enjoys views like those from Mürren across the deep valley to the rock faces and glaciers of the Eiger, Mönch and Jungfrau: simply breathtaking. Then there's the Schilthorn run – 1300m vertical with an unrivalled combination of varied terrain and glorious views.

But our visits are normally one-day affairs; those staying for a week are likely to want to explore the extensive intermediate slopes of Wengen and Grindelwald, across the valley. And that takes time.

It was in Mürren that the British more or less invented modern skiing. Sir Arnold Lunn organized the first ever slalom race here in 1922. Some 12 years earlier his father, Sir Henry, had persuaded the locals to open the railway in winter so that he could bring the first winter package tour here. Sir Arnold's son Peter was a regular visitor for 95 years, until his death in November 2011.

THE RESORT

Mürren is one of a trio of resorts set amid the fabulous scenery of the Jungfrau group. It has an amazing position, set on a shelf high above the valley floor, across from Wengen, and can be reached only by cable car from Stechelberg or from Lauterbrunnen (via Grütschalp, where you change to a train). To get to Wengen, you go down to Lauterbrunnen by lift or piste, and catch the cog railway up. You can then ski to Grindelwald, but getting to the First area on the far side of Grindelwald is a long trek.

VILLAGE CHARM ★★★★★
Picturesque and peaceful
You can't fail to be struck by Mürren's beauty and tranquillity. Paths and narrow lanes weave between little wooden chalets and a handful of bigger hotel buildings – all normally blanketed by snow.

Mürren's traffic-free status is being somewhat eroded; there are now a few delivery vehicles. But it still isn't plagued by electric carts and taxis in the way that many other traditional 'traffic-free' resorts are. Even Wengen seems busy by comparison.

CONVENIENCE ★★★
Small enough not to matter
The village is tiny by general resort standards. But it's 1km from end to end, and there is no transport, so it pays to plan your end-of-day return to the village with a bit of care.

SCENERY ★★★★★
Glorious panorama
The views from the village and from the Schilthorn are magnificent. The grandeur of the Eiger, Mönch and Jungfrau across the valley as you descend the slopes is outstanding.

THE MOUNTAINS

Despite its small size, Mürren's ski area is interestingly varied. The lower slopes are below the treeline, but in practice it is an inhospitable area when the weather is bad.

EXTENT OF THE SLOPES ★
Small but interesting
Mürren's slopes aren't extensive. But there is something for everyone, including a vertical of some 1300m to the village. There are three connected areas. On the lower slopes, **Schiltgrat** is served by a fast quad chair at the

---

miles   0.5

↑ down to Lauterbrunnen

Allmendhubel

Schilthorn ←

N ↑

↓ down to Stechelberg

km   0.5   1.

KEY FACTS

Resort	1650m
	5,410ft

Jungfrau region

Altitude	945-2970m
	3,100-9,740ft
Lifts	45
Pistes	213km
	132 miles
Blue	33%
Red	49%
Black	18%
Snowmaking	40%

Mürren-Schilthorn only

Slopes	1650-2970m
	5,410-9,740ft
Lifts	17
Pistes	54km
	34 miles

GETTING THERE

Air Zürich 155km/ 95 miles (3hr); Bern 65km/40 miles (2hr); Basel 160km/ 100 miles (2hr45)

Rail Lauterbrunnen; transfer by mountain railway and cable car

south end of the village. A short funicular goes from the middle of the village to the nursery slope at **Allmendhubel** – linked by red run and then chairlift to the slightly higher **Maulerhubel**. Runs go down from here to Winteregg and a newish fast quad.

Then there are the higher slopes reached by cable car to **Birg**. Below Birg, the fast Riggli chair serves a shady slope, and lower down two more chairs serve sunnier slopes. A further cable car goes up to the Schilthorn and its revolving restaurant – check out the feature panel. In good snow you can ski from here (via a short chairlift) right down to Lauterbrunnen – almost 16km and 2175m vertical; below Winteregg, it's mostly narrow paths. Every January the Inferno race for amateurs is run over this route (without using the chairlift).

FAST LIFTS ★★★★★
Mostly OK
There's a draglift and a few slow chairs but most lifts are fast chairs and cable cars – plus a funicular.

QUEUES ★★★☆☆
Generally not a problem
Mürren doesn't get as crowded as Wengen and Grindelwald, except on

sunny Sundays. But there can be queues for the cable cars to Birg and Schilthorn; the top stage has only one cabin, so if you don't get on you have to wait for it to go up and back.

TERRAIN PARKS ★★☆☆☆
One on the lower slopes
There is a terrain park on the lower slopes of Schiltgrat, with jumps, a couple of pipes and chill-out bar area.

SNOW RELIABILITY ★★★☆☆
Good on the upper slopes
The Jungfrau region does not have a good snow record – but we've always found Mürren has the best snow in the area. When Wengen-Grindelwald (and Mürren's lower slopes) have problems, the slopes up at Birg often have packed powder snow. The runs from below Engetal to Allmendhubel and parts of the lower slopes have snowmaking, as does the woodland path on down to Lauterbrunnen.

FOR EXPERTS ★★★☆☆
An attractive cocktail
The run from the top of the Schilthorn starts with a steep but not terrifying slope, in the past generally mogulled but now more often groomed. It flattens into a schuss to Engetal,

LIFT PASSES

Jungfrau

Prices in francs

Age	1-day	6-day
under 16	31	157
16 to 19	50	251
20 to 61	62	314
over 62	56	283

Free Under 6 (if with parent)

Beginner Points card

Notes Covers trains between villages and Grindelwald ski-bus; day pass is for Mürren-Schilthorn area only; 6-day-plus pass allows one day in Zermatt

Alternative passes Grindelwald and Wengen only; Mürren only; non-skier pass

ACTIVITIES

Indoor Alpine Sports Centre: swimming pool, sauna, solarium, steam bath, massage, fitness room

Outdoor Ice rink, curling, tobogganing, cleared paths, snowshoeing, paragliding

below Birg. Then there's a wonderful, wide run with stunning views over the valley. Below the Engetal lifts you hit the Kanonenrohr (gun barrel). This is a shelf with solid rock on one side and a steep drop on the other – protected by nets; it is wider than it once was, and is now not seriously scary. After an open slope and scrappy zigzag path, you arrive at the 'hog's back' and can descend towards the village on either side of Allmendhubel.

There are steep mogul runs at Birg and Schiltgrat and quite a lot of off-piste potential, notably runs into the Blumental – from Schiltgrat (the north-facing Blumenlucke) and from Birg (sunnier Tschingelchrachen). And there are more adventurous runs from the Schilthorn top station.

FOR INTERMEDIATES ★★★★★
Limited, but Wengen nearby
Keen piste-bashers will want to make a few trips to the long cruising runs of Wengen-Grindelwald. The blue runs up at Engetal, below Birg and served by the Riggli chair, are good easy cruises and normally have good snow. The best easy cruising run on the lower slopes is the north-facing blue down to Winteregg. The reds on the other low slopes can get mogulled, and snow conditions can be poor.

Competent, confident intermediates can consider tackling the Schilthorn.

FOR BEGINNERS ★★★★★
Not ideal, but adequate
The main nursery slopes at Allmendhubel, up the funicular, are a

little on the steep side, but secluded and quiet. You pay via points cards. From there, you have easy blue runs to graduate to in each of the sectors; since construction of the chairlift link from Maulerhubel to Allmendhubel, getting back from Maulerhubel to the village poses no difficulty.

FOR BOARDERS ★★★★★
Tough going for intermediates
The major lifts are snowboard-friendly cable cars and chairlifts. The terrain above Mürren is suitable mainly for good freeriders – it's steep, with a lot of off-piste. Intermediates will find the area tough and limited; nearby Wengen is gentler and larger.

FOR CROSS-COUNTRY ★★★★★
Forget it
There's a 12km loop along the Lauterbrunnen valley but snow is unreliable.

MOUNTAIN RESTAURANTS ★★★★★
Nothing outstanding
You'll want to visit the Schilthorn even if it's only for a drink – see the feature panel. Other reader tips include the cosy Schilthornhütte, at Obere Hubel, and the rustic, secluded Suppenalp lower down in the Blumental – but it gets no sun in January. Gimmelen is famous for its apple cake, but is self-service (which a 2012 visitor found slow). The Schiltgrathüsi, near blue run 23, is 'good value' and 'a lovely coffee stop', say reporters. The restaurant at Birg offers table-service. Winteregg is 'good and not expensive'.

SNOWPIX.COM / CHRIS GILL

This is one of our favourite runs in the world: down from the Schilthorn with stunning views of the Eiger, Mönch and Jungfrau over the Lauterbrunnen valley →

Piz Gloria revolves once an hour, displaying a fabulous 360° panorama of peaks and lakes. We don't find the ambience very tempting, but reporters have enjoyed the 'amazingly tasty' and 'surprisingly good-value' meals. You can enjoy the views from the terrace, and can also take in a 15-minute film show including clips from the famous Bond movie featuring the place. What you must not miss, if you are half-competent on skis or board, is the fabulous black run from here, more or less to village level, described under 'For Experts'.

JUNGFRAU MARKETING AG

SCHOOLS
Swiss
t 855 1247

Classes
5 half-days (2hr) 180 francs
Private lessons
From 140 francs for 2hr for 1-2 people

CHILDCARE
Kinder Paradis
t 856 8686
Ages 3 to 8
Babysitter list
Available from tourist office

Ski school
From age 3

UK PACKAGES
Inghams, Momentum, Mountain Beds, PowderBeds, Ski Line, Ski Solutions, STC, Switzerland Travel Centre
Lauterbrunnen Ski Miquel

Phone numbers
From elsewhere in Switzerland add the prefix 033; from abroad use the prefix +41 33

TOURIST OFFICE
www.mymuerren.ch
www.muerren.ch

SCHOOLS AND GUIDES ★★★☆☆
No recent reports
We lack recent reports. But the school has a long tradition of teaching Brits.

FOR FAMILIES ★★★☆☆
Attractive
Mürren is attractive for a quiet family holiday, not least because of the relaxed, safe and snowy village, and the free facilities (read 'Off the slopes'). There is a nursery slope with a rope tow. Children as young as three can now have lessons.

STAYING THERE

Hotels There are fewer than a dozen.
****Eiger (856 5454) Chalet style; next to station. Widely recommended for good blend of efficiency and charm. Good food; pool.
***Alpenruh (856 8800) Attractively renovated chalet next to the cable car.
***Jungfrau (856 6464) Perfectly placed for families, in front of the baby slope and close to the funicular.
**Alpenblick (855 1327) Simple, small, modern chalet near the station.
Apartments There are plenty of chalets and apartments in the village for independent travellers to rent.
At altitude We have a good report of a stay at Suppenalp (855 1726): 'Good atmosphere, friendly host, excellent dinner, basic facilities, incredibly creaky – they issue earplugs.'

EATING OUT ★★☆☆☆
Mainly in hotels
The main alternative to hotels is the rustic Stägerstübli – a bar as well as a restaurant, and popular with locals, serving regional dishes. The Jägerstübli in the hotel Bellevue is recommended for 'amazing' veal stew. The Edelweiss,

and Alpenruh have been recommended in the past.

APRES-SKI ★★☆☆☆
Not entirely devoid of life
The tiny Stägerstübli is cosy, and the place to meet locals. The Bliemlichäller disco in the Blumental hotel caters for kids, the bar in the Eiger for a more mixed crowd.

OFF THE SLOPES ★★★☆☆
Tranquillity plus diversions
There is a very good sports centre, which was renovated last year with new spa facilities. The pool and ice rink are free to those staying in Mürren with a guest card. The toboggan run from Allmendhubel to the village is popular. There are lots of prepared walking trails. Parapenting is very popular. Excursions to Bern and Interlaken are easy. Skiers can easily return to the village to meet non-skiers for lunch, and non-skiers can ascend the cable cars to the Schilthorn – though at a price.

LAUTERBRUNNEN

This is a good budget base, with a bit of resort atmosphere and access to both Wengen (until late) and Mürren. We've happily stayed at two hotels – the 3-star Schützen (855 3026) and 2-star Oberland (855 1241), also praised for its food; the 3-star Silberhorn (856 2210) is again highly recommended by a 2013 visitor for its 'convenience right by the lifts for both Mürren and Wengen and very good, price-competitive' four-course dinners. There are bars in the hotels Horner, Steinbock and Silberhorn. Ski Miquel's chalet hotel Rosa is said to be good.

Saas-Fee

Some of the highest skiing in the Alps, plus a cute old village at the base; great for an early/late break

RATINGS

The mountains

Extent	★★
Fast lifts	★★★★
Queues	★★★★
Terrain p'ks	★★★★
Snow	★★★★★
Expert	★★
Intermediate	★★★★
Beginner	★★★★★
Boarder	★★★★
X-country	★★★
Restaurants	★★★
Schools	★★★★
Families	★★★★

The resort

Charm	★★★★★
Convenience	★★
Scenery	★★★★
Eating out	★★★★
Après-ski	★★★★
Off-slope	★★★★

RPI 135

lift pass	£250
ski hire	£105
lessons	£135
food & drink	£205
total	**£695**

NEWS

The planned new eight-person gondola from the car park at the edge of the village via the nursery slope area to Spielboden and on to Längfluh and maybe to the top of the mountain has been delayed. Work is now planned to start in summer 2014.

2012/13: More snowmaking was installed in the Längfluh area.

- ➕ Most runs are at exceptionally high altitude, and snow-sure
- ➕ Great for early intermediates
- ➕ Traditional, car-free village, with clear attractions for families
- ➕ Dramatic setting amid high peaks and glaciers
- ➕ Good off-slope facilities

- ➖ Small area of slopes
- ➖ Mainly easy runs, with little to amuse experts (glacier limits off-piste exploration)
- ➖ Many visitors face some long walks around the village
- ➖ Shady and cold for much of winter
- ➖ Bad weather can shut the slopes

Saas-Fee is one of our favourite places – a sort of miniature Zermatt without the conspicuous consumption. As well as the charm factor there's the super-reliable snow: you spend most of your days here at an altitude – between 2500m and 3500m – that is unrivalled in the Alps. It's a compelling combination.

We tend to drop in here for a day or two at a time, so the limited extent and challenge of the slopes is not a worry; if we were here for a week, we'd soon be taking trips to Saas-Grund and even Zermatt. But if you don't mind skiing the same flattering slopes every day, Saas-Fee takes some beating.

THE RESORT

Saas-Fee is a traditional mountain village of narrow streets, lined by old chalets and free of cars, which made a recent visitor feel 'safe allowing the children to wander through the streets'. It's not completely free of traffic, though: electric taxis and trucks are not the nuisance that they are in Zermatt, but do provoke complaints.

The worthwhile slopes of Saas-Almagell and Saas-Grund are not far away, and you can buy a lift pass that covers them and the linking buses. Trips to Zermatt are time-consuming but possible, and with a six-day pass the day pass for Zermatt costs just 30 francs. Some tour ops arrange trips.

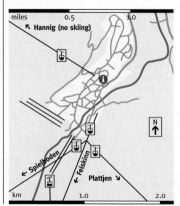

miles 0.5 1.0
↖ Hannig (no skiing)
N ↑
← Spielboden ← Felskinn Plattjen →
km 1.0 2.0

VILLAGE CHARM ★★★★★
Unpretentious rural idyll

Despite expansion, Saas-Fee still feels like a village, with cow sheds still in evidence. It doesn't have much of a central focus, but we'll forgive that; it's a charming place just to stroll around and relax in – at least when the spring sun is beating down (it's chilly in midwinter). There are some smart hotels (plus many more modest ones) and good bars and restaurants.

CONVENIENCE ★★
A hike maybe

Although it's a small village, it's about 2km long, and the main slopes and most of the lifts are at one end. There are free but limited public mini-buses and a road-train, and the bigger hotels run their own taxis. But most people, most of the time, just walk everywhere. The biggest lift – the Alpin Express gondola – starts from a more central location (that you can ski back to). And you can store your gear near the lifts, which helps.

SCENERY ★★★★
The Pearl of the Alps

Saas-Fee has stunning views up to a ring of 4000-metre peaks – on a sunny day the restaurant terraces by the nursery slopes at the south end of the village are a magnet. Higher up, the views are even better.

KEY FACTS

Resort	1800m
	5,910ft
Slopes	1800-3500m
	5,910-11,480ft
Lifts	21
Pistes	100km
	62 miles
Blue	25%
Red	50%
Black	25%
Snowmaking	70%

LIFT PASSES

Saas-Fee

Prices in francs

Age	1-day	6-day
under 16	35	172
17 to 18	59	292
19 to 64	69	344
65 plus	66	327

Free Under 10

Beginner Pass for village lifts only

Notes Covers whole valley (Saas-Fee, Saas-Grund, Saas-Almagell and Saas-Balen)

Alternative passes
Passes for each of the Saastal ski areas; single and return tickets on main lifts; also afternoon passes

THE MOUNTAINS

The upper slopes are largely gentle, while the lower mountain, below the glacier, is steeper and rockier, needing good snow-cover. There is very little shelter in bad weather: during and after heavy snowfalls you may find yourself limited to the nursery area.

Take it easy when climbing out of the top lift station at 3500m: some people can't handle the thin air.

Some of the red runs on the glacier would be better classified as blue.

Saas-Fee is one of the leading resorts for ski touring: the extended Haute Route from Chamonix via Zermatt ends here.

EXTENT OF THE SLOPES ★★
A glacier runs through it

There are two routes up to the main **Felskinn** area. The 30-person Alpin Express gondola, starting across the river from the centre of the village, takes you there via a mid-station at Morenia. The alternative is a short drag across the nursery slope at the south end of the village, and then the Felskinn cable car.

From Felskinn, the Metro Alpin underground funicular hurtles up to **Allalin**. From below here, two draglifts access the high point of the area.

Also from the south end of the village, a gondola leaves for Spielboden. This is met by a cable car that takes you up to **Längfluh**.

Between Felskinn and Längfluh is an off-limits glacier area with huge crevasses. A very long draglift from Längfluh takes you to a point where you can get down to the Felskinn area. These two sectors are served mainly by draglifts, and you can get down to the village from both.

Another gondola from the south end of the village goes up to the small area of slopes on **Plattjen**.

FAST LIFTS ★★★★
Too many T-bars

The area is a strange mixture of powerful fast lifts and a lot of 'ghastly long and cold T-bars', as a recent reporter put it; there are only two chairlifts. Blame the glaciers, on which it's tricky to build chairlifts. Our rating may look mysterious, but over half the lifts are fast, which puts Saas-Fee comfortably into the 4-star range.

QUEUES ★★★★
No recent problems to report

We had no problems with queues on our recent February and March visits, and have no reports from readers of particular problems in the last couple of seasons. Crowds on the home run from Morenia can be an issue at the end of the day.

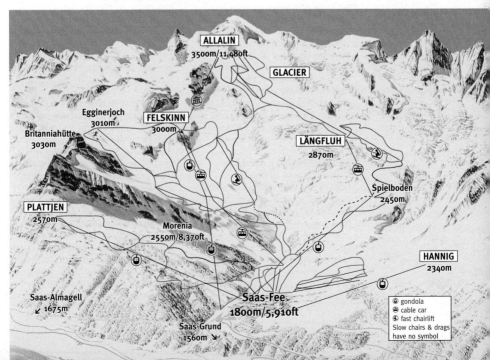

ALLALIN
3500m/11,480ft

GLACIER

Egginerjoch
3010m

FELSKINN
3000m

Britanniahütte
3030m

LÄNGFLUH
2870m

Spielboden
2450m

PLATTJEN
2570m

Morenia
2550m/8,370ft

HANNIG
2340m

Saas-Almagell
1675m

Saas-Fee
1800m/5,910ft

Saas-Grund
1560m

	gondola
	cable car
	fast chairlift
Slow chairs & drags have no symbol	

↑ Looking down
Plattjen to the
southern end of the
village and the gentle
beginner slopes up
the other side

SNOWPIX.COM / CHRIS GILL

GETTING THERE

Air Sion 75km/
45 miles (1hr45);
Geneva 225km/
140 miles (3hr30);
Zürich 250km/
155 miles (4hr);
Milan 200km/
125 miles (3hr30)

Rail Brig (38km/
24 miles) or Visp;
regular buses from
station

TERRAIN PARKS ★★★★
Well developed

The 42 Crew (www.42crew.ch), which
runs the show here, is renowned for
building great parks. The big Morenia
park has a plethora of kickers, rails
and boxes and lines for different
ability levels. Shapers are constantly
changing the rail and box lines to
keep the park creative as well as
adding interesting obstacles. There
used to be a world-class half-pipe too
– but it wasn't built last season and
there are no plans for it for 2013/14
either. There's a park for beginner
freestylers at the foot of the mountain
near the nursery slopes; you'll find
plenty of entry-level jumps and rails
here. In summer, the park moves up to
the glacier and you will often see pro
riders honing their skills there.

SNOW RELIABILITY ★★★★★
A question of altitudes

Most of Saas-Fee's slopes face north
and many are above 2500m, making
this one of the most reliable resorts
for snow in the Alps. The glacier is
open most of the year. Lower down,
on the runs back to the resort, snow
quality and cover can be more patchy,
but snowmaking seems adequate.
Grooming is done 'very well'.

FOR EXPERTS ★★
Not a lot to keep your interest

There is not much steep stuff – the
handful of short, sharp pitches dotted
around the area just merit their black
classification. The slopes around the
top of Längfluh can provide good
powder, and there are usually moguls
above Spielboden. There is excellent
tree skiing on Plattjen but it requires
serious depths of snow to cover the
very rocky terrain. On the main sector,
the glacier puts limits on the off-piste
even with a guide – crevasse danger is
extreme. But there are extensive
touring possibilities.

FOR INTERMEDIATES ★★★★
Great for gentle cruising

For early intermediates and those not
looking for much of a challenge, Saas-
Fee is ideal. For long cruises and
usually excellent snow, head for Allalin
– from here down as far as Längfluh in
one direction and Morenia in the
other, you get gentle reds leading to
even gentler blues.

The reds from mid-mountain down
to the village are a bit more
challenging, notably from Längfluh and
Spielboden. They have steepish, tricky
sections and can have poor snow, and
the blues here are mainly narrow
paths – timid intermediates might
prefer to take a lift down from mid-
mountain. The descents all the way

from Allalin to the village offer a leg-testing 1700m vertical.

Don't ignore the rather neglected Plattjen area, which is basically of red-run gradient.

FOR BEGINNERS ★★★★★
A great place to start

There's a superb, large, out-of-the-way nursery area at the edge of the village, as snow-sure as any you will find. Those ready to progress can head for the gentle blues between Felskinn and Morenia and the red runs (which are of only blue gradient really) on the glacier. A useful beginners' pass covers all the short village lifts.

FOR BOARDERS ★★★★☆
Year-round fun

Saas-Fee has backed snowboarding from its inception and provides year-round riding. The terrain suits intermediates and beginners best; there's little to satisfy experts and the glacier limits freeriding, but carvers will find wide, well-groomed pistes to shred down. The main access lifts are gondolas, cable cars and a funicular, but nearly all the rest are T-bars. The high altitude and the glacier mean the resort is a favourite for early-season and summer riding.

FOR CROSS-COUNTRY ★★★☆☆
Good local trail and lots nearby

There is a nice short (6km) trail at the edge of the village and 26km down in the Saas valley.

MOUNTAIN RESTAURANTS ★★★☆☆
Huge improvements

Saas Fee's mountain restaurants used to be mediocre at best. But in the past few years two have been taken over by the resort's two top hotels and improved beyond recognition. The piste map gives details and phone numbers for these and several others.
Editors' choice The Vernissage Berghaus Plattjen (just down from the top of Plattjen), in the Ferienart hotel stable, has great Alpine atmosphere, delicious hearty food, excellent service and wonderful glacier views from a tiny terrace. We look forward to trying the Spielboden hut, which was taken over and refurbished a couple of seasons ago by the Fletschorn hotel (where the food has a Michelin star). Reporters say it is 'superb' and 'very good quality, if expensive'; a local says 'it is the best mountain restaurant, with Berghaus Plattjen closely following; you can have a bowl of a really fantastic soup, or you could have a wonderful three-course lunch'.
Worth knowing about Before the two above appeared, our favourite was the cosy Gletschergrotte, slightly off the run from Spielboden (watch for signs on the left) – 'amazing views and food' and 'good cake in the afternoon' says a 2013 reporter, but 'be prepared for a wait'. Of the self-service restaurants, the one at Längfluh has a great view of the glacier and its crevasses from its large terrace and at Morenia you can get 'fresh bolognese sauce on well-cooked pasta and lovely goulash soup', says a 2013 visitor.

For something different, a 15-minute trek from the pistes at Felskinn brings you to Britanniahütte, a real climbing refuge with great views; understandably, food is simple.

There's a room in the Morenia where you can eat your packed lunch.

WORLD'S HIGHEST REVOLVING LUNCH?

If you fancy 360° views during lunch, head up to Threes!xty, the world's highest revolving restaurant at Allalin, which was refurbished a couple of seasons ago and where you can get a different vista with starters, mains and pud. Only the bit of floor with the tables on it revolves; the stairs stay put (along with the windows – watch your gloves). The other two revolving cafes in the Alps are also in Switzerland – at Mürren and Leysin – and we rate the views there better. But it's an amusing novelty that most visitors enjoy. To reserve a table next to the windows phone 957 1771.

SAAS-FEE TOURISM / SWISS-IMAGE.CH

SCHOOLS

Swiss
t 957 2348
Eskimos
t 957 4904
Optimum Snowsports
t 957 2039

Classes
5 3hr-days 199 francs
(no full day lessons)
Private lessons
From 80 francs for 1hr

CHILDCARE

GoSulino (Hotel Alphubel)
t 283 3674 4057
From age 6mnth
Wallo (Hotel Ferienart)
t 958 1900
From age 6mnth
Swiss
t 957 2348
Ages 3 to 6

Ski school
From age 7

ACTIVITIES

Indoor Bielen leisure centre: swimming, hot tub, steam bath, solarium, sauna, tennis, badminton; museums
Outdoor Cleared paths, ice rink (skating, curling, snow bowling), ice climbing, tubing, tobogganing, snowshoeing, 'Feeblitz' bobsleigh

Phone numbers
From elsewhere in Switzerland add the prefix 027; from abroad use the prefix +41 27

TOURIST OFFICE

www.saas-fee.ch

SCHOOLS AND GUIDES ★★★★
Good reports
We have had consistently good reports in the last few seasons on Eskimos ('excellent, with young and friendly instructors' says a 2013 reporter) and British-run Optimum Snowsports ('private lessons highly recommended' was a 2013 comment). The Swiss school has also been praised in past reports.

FOR FAMILIES ★★★★
Safely suitable
The village and its gentle nursery slopes form a good environment for families and the kids' fun park proved a 'great introduction' for one toddler. Several hotels have an in-house kindergarten. Two hotels offer day care and there's also a babysitting service at the Ferienart hotel. Child-friendly operator Esprit has a chalet hotel here.

STAYING THERE

Chalets We had two glowing 2013 reports on Ski Total's 50-bed chalet hotel Ambassador ('incredibly friendly and helpful staff', 'fantastic food and lots of it'). It's in a prime spot, over the street from the nursery slopes with hot tub, pool and sauna. Haus Jessica run by Alpine Life is 'the best catered chalet in the village by some margin', said a 2012 reporter; hot tub, sauna/ steam room. See also 'For families', above.
Hotels There are over 50.
★★★★★Ferienart (958 1900) Central top hotel. Superb blend of comfort, service and relaxed style with a great wellness area. Half-board food about the best we've had. Beware of rooms with bath in the bedroom if that's not your thing.
★★★★Allalin (958 1000) 'Large rooms, outstanding food, fantastic staff.'
★★★★Saaserhof (958 9898) Near lifts. Reputation for good service and food.
★★★★Sunstar Hotel Beau-Site (958 1560) On main street. 120 years old, individually designed rooms/suites, small but stylish spa, cosy restaurant.
★★★Elite (958 6060) Central, 'basic but comfortable' rooms. 'Family were utterly charming and helpful, food excellent,' says a 2013 visitor.
★★★Bristol (958 1212) Good location right by the nursery slopes.
★★★Europa (958 9600) Near the Hannig gondola. 'Clean, comfortable'; 'good food'; 'gorgeous wellness facilities'.
★★★Waldesruh (958 6464) Close to the

Alpin Express and 'family-friendly'.
Fletschhorn (957 2131) Upmarket, elegant (Relais & Chateaux) chalet in the woods. A trek from the village and lifts, but they'll drive you, of course; great food.
Hohnegg (957 2268) Small, more rustic alternative to the Fletschhorn, in a similarly remote spot.
Apartments Two 2012 reporters recommended Chalet Feekatz, which has six bedrooms ('beautiful, a 10-minute walk from centre'). Perla apartments have also been tipped.

EATING OUT ★★★★
Good variety
Gastronomes will want to head for the Michelin-starred and expensive Fletschhorn – endorsed by a 2012 reporter. We like the woody Bodmen, which has great food and a varied menu. As well as its main Cäsar Ritz restaurant, the hotel Ferienart runs the Mandarin (Asian) and Del Ponte (Italian). Don Ciccio's is 'child-friendly' and 'serves authentic Italian food'. The Vieux Chalet (for fondue and raclette), hotel Tenne (good rösti) and the Dom Bar ('great value burger and chicken and chips') have been recommended.

APRES-SKI ★★★★
Lively bars and clubs
At close of play, the SnowPoint umbrella bar at the foot of the slopes and the terraces of Zur Mühle and the Black Bull in the main street are always buzzing. Later on, Nesti's ('small but the best place' says a 2013 reporter) and the Fee Pub are lively. The Dom Bar has live music every night. Popcorn ('real party place'), Metropol, Poison and Night-Life are other popular clubs. A 2013 visitor warns that if your revelries are too noisy between 10pm and 8am, you're at risk of a fine.

OFF THE SLOPES ★★★★
A mountain for pedestrians
The Hannig mountain is dedicated to walking, snowshoeing, paragliding and 'good fun' tobogganing. The leisure centre has a 25m pool, indoor tennis and a sunbed area. The Feeblitz 'roller-coaster-style' ride is good fun. The museums are interesting and if you like ice caves, don't miss the world's largest. The tourist office organizes walks every week. There are tours and tastings at a local brewery.

St Moritz

One of a kind: a panoramic high-altitude playground with as much happening off the slopes as on them

RATINGS

The mountains

Extent	★★★★★
Fast lifts	★★★★
Queues	★★★
Terrain p'ks	★★★★
Snow	★★★★
Expert	★★★★
Intermediate	★★★★
Beginner	★★
Boarder	★★★★
X-country	★★★★★
Restaurants	★★★
Schools	★★★
Families	★★

The resort

Charm	★★
Convenience	★
Scenery	★★★★
Eating out	★★★★
Après-ski	★★★
Off-slope	★★★★★

RPI	155
lift pass	£270
ski hire	£140
lessons	£150
food & drink	£235
total	**£795**

NEWS

2013/14: Once again visitors will be able to buy lift passes for 25 francs a day if they stay at least two nights in one of the 100 hotels in St Moritz that are participating in the scheme. In July 2014 a new sports centre is due to open with indoor and outdoor pools, a wellness area, a fitness centre, outdoor sports centre and restaurants.

2012/13: Four places on the red Paradiso slope on Corviglia have been set aside for Yoga on Snow, where visitors can practise yoga on their own or, once a week, with a teacher from the Suvretta school.

➕ Wonderful panoramic scenery

➕ Extensive intermediate slopes

➕ High, and fairly snow-sure

➕ Off-slope activities second to none (and a whole mountain dedicated to non-skiing activities)

➕ Some good mountain restaurants, some with magnificent views

➖ A sizeable town, with little traditional Alpine character and some big block buildings

➖ Several unlinked mountains

➖ Runs on home mountain mostly fairly easy and lacking variety

➖ Can be pricey, as you'd expect from such a fashionable resort

St Moritz is Switzerland's definitive 'exclusive' winter resort: glitzy, fashionable and, above all, the place to be seen – a place for an all-round winter holiday, with an unrivalled array of wacky diversions such as cricket on snow, and countless festivals. It has long been popular with upper-crust Brits, who come for the sledging. Well, OK: for the world-famous Cresta Run. But, like all such self-consciously smart resorts, it makes a perfectly good destination for anyone. We were there in 2012 and loved the place, as usual.

The town of St Moritz is a bit of a blot on the landscape; but that landscape is truly spectacular. Our skiing here is regularly interrupted by the need to stand and gaze, and once installed on a terrace we take some shifting.

THE RESORT

St Moritz is at the heart of the upper Engadin – the remote, high valley of the En, which becomes the Austrian Inn (as in Innsbruck). The valley bottom is filled by a chain of lakes, one of which separates the two parts of St Moritz. On a steep hillside above the lake, St Moritz Dorf is the fashionable main town. Beside the lake is the more ordinary spa resort, St Moritz Bad. The skiing is in several separate sectors; only one, Corviglia, is reachable directly from the resort.

In winter the lake is used for eccentric activities including horse and greyhound racing, show jumping, polo, golf and even cricket. And there's a whole mountain (Muottas Muragl) set aside for not skiing – see 'Off the slopes'. The upper Engadin is superb for walking and cross-country skiing, which is very big here; the Engadin Ski Marathon attracts over 11,000 entries.

The home slopes are shared with Celerina, down the valley (see the end of the chapter). And there are other possible bases along the valleys.

There is a fabulously scenic railway from Zürich, but it's quicker to drive. A car is handy around the resort, too: the bus service is covered by the lift pass but it gets crowded at peak times

and a car greatly speeds up visits to the more distant mountains. Trips are possible to Davos and other resorts, including Austrian and Italian ones; you get a half-price pass in Livigno, for example. There is a strong Italian flavour to the area – lots of Italian visitors, workers, food and wine.

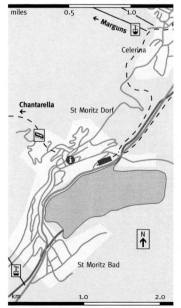

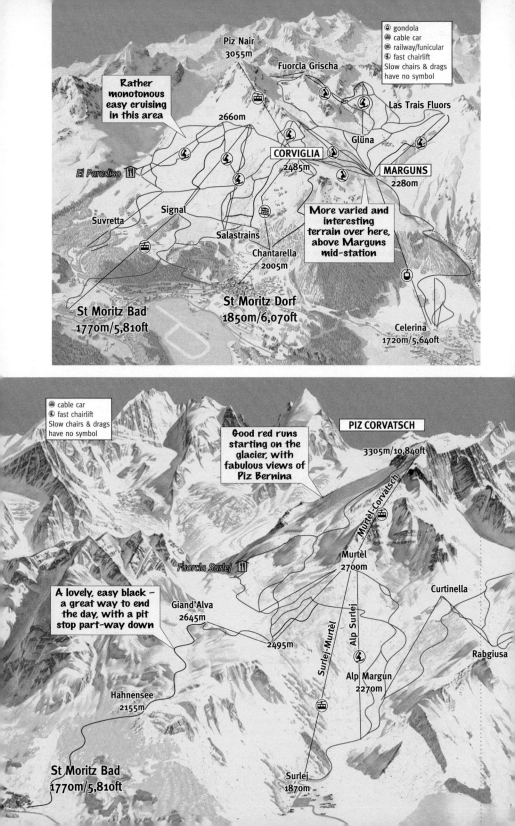

Build your own shortlist: www.wheretoskiandsnowboard.com

KEY FACTS

Resort	1770m
	5,810ft
Slopes	1730-3305m
	5,680-10,840ft
Lifts	56
Pistes	350km
	217 miles
Blue	20%
Red	70%
Black	10%
Snowmaking	30%

For Corviglia only

Slopes	1730-3055m
	5,680-10,020ft
Lifts	22
Pistes	100km
	62 miles

VILLAGE CHARM ★★☆☆☆
Urban glitz instead

In the main resort towns there is little traditional Alpine character; St Moritz is very much a glitzy town rather than a cute village. St Moritz Dorf has two main streets – lined with boutiques selling Rolex, Cartier, Hermes etc – a few side lanes and a small main square. St Moritz Bad is less urban, and less prestigious. Many buildings in both parts of the resort are block-like.

CONVENIENCE ★☆☆☆☆
Bad is good – or better, at least

It's a perfectly convenient resort if you are content to ski Corviglia, stay in central Dorf and ride the funicular, or stay on the edge of Bad and use the Signal cable car. But both parts of the resort spread widely away from these lifts, and to ski other mountains transport is needed. For keen skiers, Bad is the better base – you can ski back to it from both local sectors. If this is all too much for you, the local heli-skiing outfits will drop you at the top of the lifts. It's that kind of place.

SCENERY ★★★★☆
Fabulous panoramas

The lake-filled valley, with 4000m peaks on the Italian border, provides mesmerizing views from Corviglia, and the close-up views of Piz Bernina from Corvatsch are stunning.

THE MOUNTAINS

There are three separate areas of slopes, covered on three very clear piste maps; our maps show only the two main areas (Corviglia and Corvatsch) close to St Moritz. The terrain is varied, with lots of long, wide, well-groomed runs – practically all on open slopes above the trees. Every Friday, from 7pm to 2am, the 4.2km piste down from the middle station on Corvatsch is floodlit.

EXTENT OF THE SLOPES ★★★★★
Three separate areas

The resort claims 350km of slopes but this may be an exaggeration and they are certainly fragmented. From St Moritz Dorf a two-stage railway goes up to **Corviglia**, a lift junction at the eastern end of a sunny and rather monotonous area of slopes facing east and south over the main valley. The peak of Piz Nair, reached from here by cable car, separates these slopes from the less sunny and more varied ones in the wide bowl above **Marguns** – and gives fabulous views across the valley to Piz Bernina. From Corviglia you can (snow permitting) head down easy paths to Dorf and Bad; at Salastrains, just above Dorf, are nursery slopes, restaurants and two hotels. There is also a red run from Marguns to Celerina.

From Surlej, a few miles from St Moritz, a two-stage cable car takes you to the north-facing slopes of **Corvatsch**, which reach glacial heights. From the mid-station at Murtèl you have a choice of reds to Stüvetta Giand'Alva and Alp Margun. From the latter you can work your way to **Furtschellas**, also reached by cable car from Sils Maria. If you're lucky with the snow, you can end the day with the splendid Hahnensee run, from the northern limit of the Corvatsch lift system at Giand'Alva down to St Moritz Bad – a black-classified run that is of red difficulty for 95% of its 6km length. It often opens around noon, when the snow softens. It's a five-minute walk from the end of the run

Interesting, varied intermediate terrain on this side of the sector

Furtschellas 2800m

Val Fex

nella

Rabgiusa

FURTSCHELLAS 2310m

Excellent winding run to the valley – best done early in the day on good snow with no crowds

Sils-Furtschellas

Sils Maria 1795m ↘

LIFT PASSES

Upper Engadin

Prices in francs

Age	1-day	6-day
under 13	24	122
13 to 17	49	243
18 plus	73	365

Free under 6

Senior no deals

Beginner no deals

Notes
Covers Corviglia, Corvatsch, Diavolezza-Lagalb and Zuoz, the Engadin bus services and stretches of the Rhätische Bahn railway; 1-day price is for Corviglia only

Alternative passes
Half-day and day passes for individual areas; 'family spots' passes

to the cable car to Corviglia.

The third area is about 20km from St Moritz (50 minutes by bus) and consists of two peaks above car parks on opposite sides of the Bernina pass road to Italy. **Diavolezza** (2980m) has excellent north-facing pistes of 900m vertical, down its cable car. **Lagalb** (2960m) is a smaller area with quite challenging slopes – west-facing, 850m vertical – served by a smaller cable car. From late February these cable cars run until 5pm.

FAST LIFTS ★★★★
Plenty of options
St Moritz has invested heavily in upgrading lifts, especially on Corviglia and Marguns, where there are fast chairs all over the place. Corvatsch still has some T-bars, though. The area as a whole has a lot of modest-sized cable cars – both for getting out of the resort and for access to peaks.

QUEUES ★★★
Not much of a problem
Queues for the cable cars are not unknown but recent reporters have had no problems.

TERRAIN PARKS ★★★★
World-class facilities
The park on Corviglia was designed with female pro skiers and boarders and advanced riders in mind, and is home to some of the biggest contests for women. There are three lines, the hardest including a big 12m tabletop jump, plus a brilliant 400m easy line. There are many rails and boxes of all sizes, and a boardercross course. The Freestyle Park on Corvatsch has big

jumps, an air bag, rails, half-pipe and boardercross; the World Freeride Tour visits there (30 Jan to 2 Feb 2014).

SNOW RELIABILITY ★★★★
Improved by good snowmaking
This corner of the Alps has a rather dry climate, but the altitude means that any precipitation is likely to be snowy. The top runs at Corvatsch are glacial and require good snow depths to be safe. There is snowmaking in each sector, and grooming is excellent.

FOR EXPERTS ★★★★
Dispersed challenges
Few of the black runs are genuinely steep; those at Lagalb and Diavolezza are the most challenging. But there is good off-piste terrain, and it doesn't get tracked out. There is an excellent north-facing slope immediately above Marguns, for example, and tough routes from Piz Nair and the Corvatsch summit. More serious expeditions can be undertaken – eg the Roseg valley from Corvatsch.

Out at Diavolezza, a very popular and spectacular off-piste glacier route goes off the back beneath Piz Bernina to Morteratsch. There's a 30-minute plod at first, then it's downhill, with splendid views. It is not difficult, but may take you close to crevasses; we wouldn't do it without a guide. On the front of the mountain, the Gletscher chair accesses an excellent shady run down Val d'Arlas. At Lagalb, there's off-piste down the back towards La Rosa (again, a guide is needed).

There are a few firms offering heli-drops on Fuorcla Chamuotsch, for runs back to the Engadin valley.

Air Zürich 220km/
135 miles (3hr15);
Friedrichshafen
210km/130 miles
(2hr45); Upper
Engadine airport
5km/3 miles

Rail Mainline station
in resort

Indoor Golf range,
tennis, squash, health
spa, casino, cinema,
museums, galleries

Outdoor 150km of
cleared paths, ice
rink, curling, ice
climbing, snow-
shoeing, sleigh rides,
tobogganing, para-
gliding, bobsleigh
rides, Cresta Run,
snow kiting, horse
riding

FOR INTERMEDIATES ★★★★★
Good but flattering

St Moritz is great for intermediates.
Most pistes on Corviglia are very well
groomed, easyish reds that could well
have been classified blue – ideal
cruising terrain, or monotonous,
depending on your view. The Marguns
bowl is more interesting, including
some easy blacks and the pleasant Val
Schattain run away from the lifts.

The Corvatsch-Furtschellas area is
altogether more varied, interesting and
challenging, as well as higher and
wider. There are excellent red runs in
both parts of the area, including the
runs from the Corvatsch glacier, which
give fabulous views, and descents to
the two valley stations – particularly
the Furtschellas one. Do these in the
morning, and at the end of the day
return to St Moritz Bad via the lovely
Hahnensee run – an easy black. There
isn't much easy skiing at Corvatsch;
some of the blues (eg the lower bit of
19) should be red.

Diavolezza is mostly intermediate
stuff, too. There is an easy open slope
at the top, served by the Gletscher
chair, and a splendid long intermediate
run back down under the lift. The link
to Lagalb requires use of parts of a
black run, but it is of red gradient.
(Plans to improve this link seem to
have stalled.) Lagalb has more
challenging pistes – two reds and a
genuine black.

FOR BEGINNERS ★★★★★
Not ideal

Beginners start up at Salastrains or
Corviglia, or slightly out of town at
Suvretta. Celerina has good, broad
nursery slopes at village level and a
child-friendly lift. But progression from
the nursery slopes to longer runs is
rather awkward – there are few blue
runs without a difficult section. Nor
are there any free lifts, or particularly
helpful special passes.

FOR BOARDERS ★★★★★
Very welcoming

The terrain in St Moritz is boarder-
friendly. Freeride tours are available
through the ski schools and the best
freeride terrain is on Diavolezza and
Corvatsch, but there are several
draglifts on Corvatsch. Apart from
those, most of St Moritz's lifts are
chairs, gondolas, cable cars and trains;
beginners will enjoy the rolling blue
runs, and intermediates will relish the
red runs. The great thing for freeriders
is that terrain can stay untracked for
days after a snowfall. There are good
parks on both Corviglia and Corvatsch.
Playground in Paradise is a specialist
board shop.

FOR CROSS-COUNTRY ★★★★★
Excellent

This is one of the premier regions in
the Alps, with 200km of trails, some
floodlit, amid splendid scenery and
with fairly reliable snow. 'Fantastic,'
says a 2013 visitor. Another reporter
recommends lessons at the Langlauf
Centre near the hotel Kempinski. But
the best bases are outside St Moritz,
along the valleys.

MOUNTAIN RESTAURANTS ★★★★★
Some special places

Mountain restaurants are plentiful, and
include some of the most glamorous
in Europe. Not surprisingly, prices can
be high. The piste maps have pictures
and phone numbers of the restaurants.
Editors' choice El Paradiso (833 4002),
secluded at the extreme southern end
of Corviglia, has it all: breathtaking
views from the big terrace, a tastefully
renovated, slightly trendy interior,
great service and top-notch food.
Fuorcla Surlej (842 6303, though we
doubt they'll take a reservation), on
the Fuorcla run from the Corvatsch
glacier, could not be more different: a
remote refuge serving basic food,
sometimes very slowly. But the view of
Piz Bernina and Piz Roseg from the
snowy ramshackle 'terrace' is stunning.
Worth knowing about On Corviglia, the
top lift station houses several
restaurants run under the umbrella
title of Mathis Food Affairs, including
the famously swanky Marmite. Not our
cup of tea, but a trusted reporter last
year recorded his 'best ever skiing
lunch' here. The more atmospheric
Chasellas is also recommended,
particularly for strudel. Lej da la Pêsch,
behind Piz Nair, is a cosy spot, better
for a snowy day than a sunny one. On
the Corvatsch side, the cosy, rustic
Alpetta has been tipped in the past,
and the varied menu looked good to
us on a recent visit. Hahnensee, on
the run of that name to Bad, is a
splendid place to pause in the sun.

There are two picnic rooms: at the
Lagalb cable-car base and in the
Marguns restaurant building.

501

SCHOOLS

Swiss
t 830 0101

Suvretta
t 836 6161

Classes (Swiss prices)
3 3hr-days 280 francs

Private lessons
From 100 francs for
1hr

CHILDCARE

Schweizerhof Hotel
t 837 0707
From age 3

**Palazzino – in
Badrutt's Palace Hotel**
t 837 1000
Ages 3 to 12

Kempinski Hotel
t 838 3838

Salastrains kids' park
t 830 0101
Run by Swiss school

Ski school
Ages from 5

UK PACKAGES

Alpine Answers, Alpine
Weekends, Carrier, Club
Med, Elegant Resorts,
Flexiski, Inghams,
Jeffersons, Luxury Chalet
Collection, Momentum,
Neilson, Oxford Ski Co,
Powder Byrne,
PowderBeds, Scott
Dunn, Ski Bespoke, Ski
Independence, Ski Line,
Ski Safari, Ski Solutions,
Skitracer, Ski Weekend,
STC, Supertravel,
Switzerland Travel Centre

SCHOOLS AND GUIDES ★★★☆☆
Internal competition

There are two main schools, Swiss and
Suvretta. Past reports on both have
been positive but a 2013 visitor said
the Swiss instructor provided by Club
Med should have demoted some in
her group to a lower class. Other
hotels have private instructors, too.

FOR FAMILIES ★★☆☆☆
Choose a hotel with a nursery

There's a kindergarten and children's
restaurant at Salastrains, and we'd be
inclined to stay up there if you can
afford it. Some hotel nurseries are
open to non-residents.

STAYING THERE

There is a 'very comfortable' Club Med
with 'excellent food', which has its
own restaurants on the main slope
sectors. The tourist office can provide
a list of apartments.

Hotels From Switzerland's highest
concentration of 5-stars, we allow
ourselves one.

★★★★★Kempinski (838 3838)
Unfashionable but spacious location in
Bad. 'The only 5-star where I felt
vaguely relaxed,' says a young but
widely experienced reporter.

★★★★Crystal (836 2626) Austere-looking
central place with contrasting
traditional rooms, and interesting art
in public areas. Wellness.

★★★★Monopol (837 0404) Good value
(for St Moritz); in centre of Dorf.
Repeatedly approved by readers. Good
spa facilities.

★★★★Nira Alpina (838 6969) Fairly new
'design' hotel right by the Corvatsch
cable-car station in Surlej. 'Great food,
fab bar; faultless.'

★★★★Schweizerhof (837 0707) 'Relaxed'
hotel in central Dorf, five minutes from
the Corviglia lift. Après-ski hub.

★★★★Margna (836 6600) Near railway
and bus stations. 'Staff could not have
been more helpful,' says a reporter.

★★★Laudinella (836 0000) In Bad. Cool
decor; seven varied restaurants.
'Comfortable rooms, helpful staff.'
Fitness facilities limited and not free.

★★★Nolda (833 0575) One of the few
chalet-style buildings, close to the
cable car in Bad.

★★★Sonne (838 5959) Generous rooms
in Bad, not far from the lake.

Landhotel Meierei (838 7000) Relaxing
traditional country hotel in a quiet
setting across the lake.

At altitude The 3-star Salastrains (830
0707) is on the lower slopes of
Corviglia and has great views. Muottas
Muragl (842 8232), at over 2500m on
the non-skiing mountain, was fully
renovated a couple of years ago and
has even better views.

EATING OUT ★★★★☆
Mostly chic and expensive

A lot of restaurants here are very
pricey. We liked the three smooth,
expensive restaurants in the Chesa
Veglia (an ancient 'rustic' outpost of
Badrutt's hotel). A top world-class
restaurant is Bumanns Chesa Pirani, a
fine old house out of town in La Punt.
We had an excellent dinner in 2012 at
the charming, polished hotel Bellavista
in Surlej. Of course you can eat more
cheaply, and that often means eating
basic Italian. The hotels Laudinella and
Sonne, in Bad, both have wood-fired
pizza ovens, approved of by a reader.
The Laudinella has six other
restaurants too. For something
completely different ... La Baracca is a

THE CRESTA RUN

*No trip to St Moritz is really complete
without a visit to the Cresta Run. It's the
last bastion of Britishness (until recently,
payment had to be made in sterling) and
male chauvinism (women need an
invitation from a club member). Any adult
male can pay around £350 for five rides
(helmet and lunch at the Kulm hotel
included). You lie on a toboggan (called a
'skeleton') and hurtle head-first down a
sheet ice gully from St Moritz to Celerina.
Watch out for Shuttlecock corner – that's
where most of the accidents happen.*

ENGADIN ST MORITZ / SWISS-IMAGE.CH / JR LARRAMAN

The frozen lake is an important part of St Moritz's attraction for the many visitors who don't hit the slopes →
ENGADIN ST MORITZ / SWISS-IMAGE.CH / MAX WEISS

big shed in the car park of the Signal cable car doing simple but thoroughly good food in a canteen-like setting.

An evening up at Muottas Muragl, between Celerina and Pontresina, offers spectacular views, a splendid sunset and dinner.

APRES-SKI ★★★☆☆
Caters for all ages
There's a big variety of après-skiing age groups here. The fur coat count is high – people come to St Moritz to be seen. For tea and good cakes head for Hanselmann's. The Roo bar terrace outside the hotel Hauser is a popular après drinking spot.

Bobby's Pub attracts a young crowd, as does the loud music of the Stübli, one of the bars in the hotel Schweizerhof: the others are the Mulibar with dancing, and the chic Piano Bar. The Cresta, at the Steffani, is popular with the British, while the Cava below it is louder, livelier and younger. We don't get many reports on the late-night scene, but the Diamond Club has been mentioned. The jazz night at the Kulm is 'great for people watching', says a 2013 reporter. The two most popular discos are Vivai (expensive), and King's at Badrutt's Palace (even more expensive; jackets and ties required). If you need to splash even more cash, try the casino.

OFF THE SLOPES ★★★★★
Excellent variety of pastimes
Even if you lack the bravado for the Cresta Run, there is lots to do. In midwinter the snow-covered lake provides a playground for events such as polo, horse racing and cricket, but then activities are limited as the lake starts to thaw. There's an annual 'gourmet festival', with chefs from all over the world. The Engadin museum is said to be 'very interesting'. And the shopping is simply 'incredible' if your plastic remains flexible.

There are 150km of well-marked walking trails, which a reporter loved (a map is available). Muottas Muragl is a mountain set aside for not skiing – with funicular access to snowshoeing, tobogganing and an igloo village – all with stunning panoramic views.

Some hotels run special activities, such as a curling week. Other options are para-gliding and indoor tennis. Several reporters rave about the views from the Bernina Express train to Italy, with 'amazing bends and scenery'. Another visitor highly recommends a trip by train to Scuol for the 'fabulous spa with great facilities'. There's an 'excellent' public pool in Pontresina.

LINKED RESORT – 1730m
CELERINA
At the bottom end of the famous Cresta Run, Celerina is an appealing base if you want a quiet time – it is unpretentious and villagey, but lacks a central focus (and has very few shops). It has good access to the Corviglia/Marguns sector – a gondola to Marguns. It spreads quite widely, with a lot of second homes, many owned by Italians (the upper part is known as Piccolo Milano). There are some appealing small hotels – reporters like Chesa Rosatsch (837 0101) – and a couple of bigger 4-stars. The modern Inn Lodge (834 4795) has rooms and dormitories. The food at the Chesa Rosatsch has been recommended. The Freestyle School focuses on park practice.

Phone numbers
From elsewhere in Switzerland add the prefix 081; from abroad use the prefix +41 81

TOURIST OFFICES

St Moritz
www.stmoritz.ch

Celerina
www.engadin.
stmoritz.ch/celerina/

Val d'Anniviers

Exceptionally cute, unspoiled villages beneath high, snow-sure slopes. Sounds perfect? Well, there are some drawbacks ...

TOP 10 RATINGS

Extent	**
Fast lifts	*
Queues	****
Snow	****
Expert	****
Intermediate	***
Beginner	***
Charm	*****
Convenience	**
Scenery	****

RPI   115

lift pass	£190
ski hire	£100
lessons	£120
food & drink	£185
total	**£595**

NEWS

2013/14: Grimentz-Zinal: a new 125-person cable car linking Grimentz village to the heart of the Zinal ski area is due to open.

2012/13: Grimentz: the capacity of the gondola from the village was increased by 20%.

Vercorin: A 10-person gondola replaced an old four-seater from the village. More snowmaking was installed.

Chandolin: The red run off the Tsapé chairlift has been enlarged and improved.

KEY FACTS

Resorts	1340-2000m	
	4,400-6,560ft	
Slopes	1340-3000m	
	4,400-9,840ft	
Lifts	45	
Pistes	220km	
	137 miles	
Blue	36%	
Red	52%	
Black	12%	
Snowmaking	14%	

➕ Charming unspoiled villages
➕ Four varied ski areas (two newly linked for 2013/14)
➕ Excellent, extensive off-piste
➕ Reliable snow-cover
➕ No crowds, few queues

➖ Most lifts are T-bars; few fast chairs
➖ Very quiet villages; dead, even
➖ Almost entirely open slopes
➖ Each area has limited pistes
➖ If you plan to ski them all, best to have a car

In some ways, Val d'Anniviers is in a bit of a time warp. There is plenty of modern accommodation and some modern lifts in key spots, including a new cable car for the 2013/14 season linking two of the four ski areas for the first time. But most of the villages have unspoilt rustic cores with old wooden houses and narrow lanes; and you spend a lot of time on the slopes riding draglifts and not much riding fast chairs (there are only four in the whole valley). Approach the area with the right attitude and you'll probably find it all quite a refreshing change from big-name resorts with high-speed everything.

The Val d'Anniviers runs almost due south from the Rhône valley at Sierre and the road up to the resorts is narrow and has in places been carved out of sheer rock faces.

The main villages have lots of old wooden houses and barns, narrow paths and lanes and few shops. Some more modern development has taken place around these old villages, but it is generally tasteful and low-rise.

There are five villages. On the morning-sun side of the valley, the slopes of Zinal are linked to those of Grimentz by a long, isolated black run and a new cable car back for the 2013/14 season — forming the biggest linked ski area in the valley with 110km of pistes. On the afternoon-sun side, the slopes of Chandolin and St Luc are linked at high and low altitude, and share 75km of pistes. Vercorin is a smaller separate area with just 35km of pistes and is rather isolated from the other areas.

Except at Vercorin, nearly all the slopes are above the treeline and there's a lot of skiing above 2400m, which usually means good snow. All of the individual areas are small, but they add up to a decent amount.

Free buses link the villages and lift bases. Getting between Grimentz–Zinal and St Luc–Chandolin takes about an hour and you have to change buses in the little town of Vissoie. Getting to Vercorin takes much longer and involves a change in Sierre — best to have a car if you plan trips there.

1650m / 2000m
ST LUC / CHANDOLIN

These are the sunniest of the main ski resort villages, a few km apart, and they share a well-linked area of slopes. St Luc also has the attraction of a fabulous, characterful old hotel. A funicular goes up from the edge of St Luc and a fast chair from the edge of Chandolin. Both are served by the free ski-buses. The slopes face west to south-west, so the snow suffers from the sun. Apart from Chandolin's fast quad, there is only one other chair – the other 10 lifts are all drags.

The pistes suit beginners and intermediates best; though there are two black runs, five short itinerary routes (including one that we reckon is the steepest marked run in the Alps) and a gnarly freeride area where competitions are held. There are some testing reds, but in general the slopes are gentle, easy cruising territory. A highlight is the long, easy red run of 1230m vertical from Bella Tola at 3000m, away from all the lifts down to a bar and ski-bus stop – a great way to end the day. There's a good beginner area and a terrain park near the top of the St Luc funicular.

There are some good mountain restaurants with fine views. Above Chandolin the tiny Illhorn has a limited menu but a cosy panelled room (and fab pear tart); the Tsapé is a smart, stark place, high-up, with good local cuisine; above St Luc, the Bella Tola is a traditional, basic table-service hut.

Both Chandolin and St Luc are fairly spread out. But St Luc has a cute, compact old centre with a small outdoor après-ski bar. The 4-star hotel Bella Tola (475 1444) is just a few strides from here. Built in 1859, it has been beautifully renovated by its current owners, with a fine spa, sunny terrace, and good restaurant. We enjoyed staying there hugely. The owners recently renovated and opened the smaller Grand Chalet Favre.

1670m
ZINAL

This small village near the head of the valley doesn't have the charm of the other villages. But its local slopes have stunning views of high peaks including the Matterhorn. And the new cable car back from Grimentz means the two resorts now share the biggest area of linked slopes in the valley.
A modern cable car goes to Sorebois at 2440m, the hub of the ski area. Most of the slopes face roughly east and keep their snow well.

The runs are mainly short (some only 200m or 300m vertical) but include some good reds – our favourites are those from Combe Durand at the edge of the ski area, served by a steepish draglift that also accesses a freeride area. The one fast chairlift serves wide and gentle blue runs, ideal for novices. The two short black runs are really of red steepness. There is a longer red run (with a black variant on the lower part) back to the village. And there's great off-piste in bowls between the pistes (and, with a guide, off the back of the ski area to the Moiry dam and on to Grimentz).

From the top of the area, Piste du Chamois is a real highlight – a long, mainly easy black run of almost 1300m vertical down a shady deserted bowl with lots of accessible off-piste, ending with a woodland path to Grimentz to catch the new cable car back.

Zinal is popular with families and there's a good beginner area and children's snow garden.

On weekends and holidays the Sorebois self-service ('decent, reasonable-value food') offers an 'all you can eat' buffet downstairs.

Zinal has a handful of hotels. The central 2-star Pointe de Zinal (475 1164) does excellent food and the 2-star Le Trift (475 1466) is 'comfortable with adequate but small rooms and good food'. There are also a couple of catered chalets.

1570m
GRIMENTZ

Grimentz has a richly deserved reputation for its extensive off-piste. And it has a small area of varied pistes above its very cute old village. For 2013/14 its attraction as a base will be transformed by the new cable car to the Zinal ski area – making the joint area the biggest in the valley.
The village is spread out on quite a steep slope and a lot of new building has been going on. Here (more than in the other villages except Chandolin)

Selected chalets in Val d'Anniviers

MOUNTAIN HEAVEN *www.mountainheaven.co.uk*   T **0151 625 1921**

Mountain Heaven has a wonderful selection of chalets and apartments in Grimentz, all with WIFI and ranging from two to five bedrooms. They can be booked on either a self-catered or a catered basis. We are financially bonded and offer all-inclusive prices with no hidden extras.

Included in our portfolio are Le Lievre, a stunning apartment right by the piste, Chalet Mélèze, a detached chalet with a commanding position, Les Vieux Chalets no 2 & 7, which are right in the village centre, and Sur Les Pistes, an apartment situated on the piste itself.

HIGH QUALITY ACCOMMODATION ↑

Combe Durand

Corne de Sorebois
2895m

2440m

ZINAL

Piste du Chamois

Zinal
1670m/5,48oft

288om

Mottec

GRIMENTZ

Bella Tola
3000m/
9,84oft

Grimentz
1570m/5,150ft

2130m

Roc d'Orzival
2855m

2770m

St-Jean

Tignousa
218om

St-Luc
1650m/5,41oft

2470m

ST LUC-CHANDOLIN

Vissoie

Mt Major
2375m

Illhorn
2600m

Chandolin
2000m/6,56oft

VERCORIN

Vercorin
1340m/4,40oft

Chalais

gondola
cable car
railway/funicular
fast chairlift
Slow chairs & drags
have no symbol

Sierre
56om/1,84oft

To
Geneva
→

↑ There's great scenery up the time-warp valley of Val d'Anniviers – the village of Grimentz is seen in this pic, with its slopes up to the right

SNOWPIX.COM / CHRIS GILL

Phone numbers
From elsewhere in Switzerland add the prefix 027; from abroad use the prefix +41 and omit the initial '0'

TOURIST OFFICES

Val d'Anniviers
www.sierre-anniviers.ch

Grimentz
www.grimentz.ch

St Luc
www.saint-luc.ch

Vercorin
www.vercorin.ch

Zinal
www.zinal.ch

Chandolin
www.chandolin.ch

there is a separation between the cute old centre – lots of tiny old barns and narrow paths – and the skiers' accommodation. Much of this is conveniently close to the gondola up to Bendolla at 2130m – but some is less conveniently placed on the opposite side of the old village.

Bendolla has a good, roped-off beginner area and snow garden for kids, and above it are two main sectors. On the right as you look up are easy blue and red runs. On the left are steeper and quieter runs, including the long Piste Lona, which goes from the top to almost the bottom of the mountain (1300m vertical), right at the edge of the ski area; it deserves its black classification and is interestingly varied. The main run to the village is quite steep too, but you can ride the gondola down.

The real attraction for experts is the extensive off-piste. There are lots of options, including over 1500m vertical down to Vercorin, returning from there to the village of St Jean, a bus ride from Grimentz. We had a great day skiing off-piste in the trees with a guide from the International ski school in poor visibility on our 2013 visit and have received positive past reports on them – especially for teaching kids. The Swiss school is endorsed by a 2013 visitor – 'our daughters enjoyed themselves and for the first time our youngest was keen to do more'.

Our favourite mountain restaurant is the rustic Etable du Marais below Grands Plans where we had good rösti and pasta dishes. We've also had good pasta at the self-service Orzival. The functional main Bendolla

restaurant is mainly self-service ('Lengthy wait, poor food,' said a recent reporter, but 'good portions') with a small table-service section where we have had an enjoyable meal.

As the lifts close, Chez Florioz on the piste just above the village is the place for a drink. The best restaurants are probably those in the main hotels. But we have also enjoyed an excellent meal at Arlequin (a pizzeria). Bar le Country is a lively sports bar.

We have had comfortable stays and good food at the two 3-star hotels – the Alpina (476 1616), almost opposite the gondola, and the less convenient Cristal (475 3291). The 'comfortable' 2-star Becs de Bosson is recommended by a 2012 visitor.

UK tour operator Mountain Heaven has some smart chalets and apartments, which can be rented on a catered or self-catered basis. A satisfied 2013 reporter who stayed in their Sur Les Pistes apartment said: 'Perfect location, very good accommodation, well priced.'

1340m

VERCORIN

The smallest area of slopes (we skied virtually all the pistes in 90 minutes), and isolated from other resorts.

The pretty village of Vercorin, perched on a shelf overlooking the Rhône valley, is reached by a winding road or by a cable car from Chalais, just outside Sierre. This is followed by a free ski-bus to a revamped two-stage gondola. The slopes suit intermediates best and were deserted when we were there in January 2013.

Verbier

Big, chalet-style resort that attracts powder hounds from all over the world – and big-spending night owls from Geneva

508

RATINGS

The mountains

Extent	★★★★★
Fast lifts	★★★★
Queues	★★★
Terrain p'ks	★★★
Snow	★★★
Expert	★★★★★
Intermediate	★★★
Beginner	★★
Boarder	★★★
X-country	★
Restaurants	★★★
Schools	★★★★★
Families	★★★

The resort

Charm	★★★
Convenience	★★
Scenery	★★★★
Eating out	★★★★
Après-ski	★★★★★
Off-slope	★★★

RPI 140

lift pass	£260
ski hire	£140
lessons	£120
food & drink	£215
total	**£735**

KEY FACTS

Resort	1500m
	4,920ft

4 Valleys area	
Slopes	1500-3330m
	4,920-10,930ft
Lifts	92
Pistes	412km
	256 miles
Blue	39%
Red	44%
Black	17%
Snowmaking	13%

Verbier, Bruson and Tzoumaz/Savoleyres sectors only (covered by Verbier pass)

Slopes	1500-3025m
	4,920-9,920ft
Lifts	34
Pistes	195km
	121 miles
Blue	43%
Red	29%
Black	28%
Snowmaking	
	114 guns

+ Extensive, challenging slopes with a lot of off-piste and long bump runs

+ Upper slopes offer a real high-mountain feel, plus great views

+ Sizeable, animated village in a sunny, panoramic setting

+ Lively, varied nightlife

+ Much improved lift system, piste grooming and signposting, but …

− Piste map and piste naming still have a long way to go

− Some overcrowded pistes and areas

− The 4 Valleys network is much less wonderful than it looks on paper

− Sunny lower slopes will always be a problem, even with snowmaking

− Some long walks/rides to lifts

− Expensive bars and restaurants

For serious off-piste routes and for mogul fields, Verbier is one of the world's cult resorts. For vibrant nightlife, too, it is difficult to beat. At first, with its claimed 410km of pistes, Verbier also seems to rank alongside the French mega-networks as a dream resort for keen piste-bashers. But if the French 3 Vallées floats your boat, you may be sorely disappointed by the Swiss 4 Vallées. The network is an inconveniently sprawling affair, with lots of tedious links and the Schrahe report (read our feature on piste extent at the front of the book) has confirmed our long-held view that the piste extent here is much less than is claimed. Verbier's local pistes leave a lot to be desired, too: in comparison with the slopes of somewhere like Courchevel, they are distinctly limited and a good intermediate could cover them in a day. This is partly because many of the runs that could and should be black pistes are classified as unpatrolled itinéraires.

But on the plus side, the Bruson ski area is set to become much easier to reach this season – you'll just ride the gondola down to Le Châble and catch another up the other side to the heart of the Bruson area (which has a lot going for it).

THE RESORT

Verbier enjoys an impressive setting on a wide, sunny balcony facing spectacular peaks. It's a fashionable, informal, very lively place that teems with cosmopolitan visitors. Most are younger than visitors to other big Swiss resorts.

The resort is at one end of a long, strung-out series of interconnected slopes, optimistically branded the 4 Valleys and linking Verbier to Nendaz, Veysonnaz, Thyon and other resorts. These other resorts have their own pros and cons. All are much less lively in the evening than Verbier, and appreciably cheaper places to stay. Some are more sensible bases for those who plan to stick to pistes rather than venture off-piste – the Veysonnaz–Thyon sector, in particular, is much more intermediate-friendly than Verbier. As bases for exploration of the whole 4 Valleys, only tiny Siviez is much of an advance on Verbier. You

can also stay down in the valley village of Le Châble, which has a gondola up to Verbier and on into the slopes, and from 2013/14 will have a gondola up to Bruson. More on all these places at the end of the chapter.

Chamonix and Champéry are within reach by car. So are small resorts near Orsières about 45 minutes away – Champex-Lac, La Fouly and Vichères-Liddes (covered in our resort directory at the back of the book). But a car can

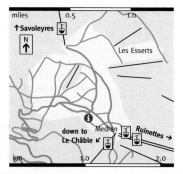

miles 0.5 1.0

↑ Savoleyres

N ↑

Les Esserts

down to Le Châble ↙ Medran Ruinettes →

km 1.0 2.0

NEWS

2013/14: A new gondola from Le Châble is due to link to the heart of the Bruson ski area. So you'll be able to ride gondolas all the way from Verbier rather than have to catch a bus at Le Châble and then a slow chairlift into the Bruson area.

A new 5-star hotel – W Verbier – is due to open in December, along with a number of upmarket shops, bars and restaurants in a new development at Médran.

2012/13: A new 4-star hotel, the Cordée des Alpes, opened, as did a new mountain restaurant, La Vache, part owned by celebs such as singer James Blunt and rugby player Lawrence Dallaglio. A new ice rink opened in the town square at La Tzoumaz.

---

be a bit of a nuisance in Verbier itself. Parking is tightly controlled; your lodging may not have enough space for all guests' cars, which means a hike from the free parking at the sports centre or paying for parking.

Danni Sports was praised by a recent reporter: 'Extremely helpful and friendly, good choice of equipment for hire, and they do a half-price ski-service happy hour mid-week.'

VILLAGE CHARM ★★★
Busy upmarket chalet town
The resort is an amorphous sprawl of chalet-style buildings. Most of the shops and hotels (but not chalets) are set around the Place Centrale and along the sloping streets stretching both down the hill and up it to the main lift station at Médran, 500m away. At close of play this street, in particular, is buzzing with après-ski activity. These central areas get unpleasantly packed with cars at busy times, especially weekends when lots of people are coming and going, which rather detracts from the ambience.

CONVENIENCE ★★
Pick your spot
It's a sprawling resort where most people suffer some inconvenience. But most people just get used to using the free buses, which run on several routes until 8pm. They're generally efficient, but some areas have quite an infrequent service.

The Médran lift station is a walkable distance from the Place

Centrale, so staying between the two has attractions. If nightlife is not a priority, staying somewhere near the upper fringes of the village may mean that you can almost ski to your door. Skiing from the door is less likely. More chalets are built each year, with many newer properties inconveniently situated along the road to the lift base for the secondary Savoleyres area, about 1.5km from Médran. A very convenient new development at Médran will open in 2013/14.

SCENERY ★★★★
A circle of Alpine peaks
Verbier is surrounded by stunning Alpine scenery; from the top of Mont-Fort there are impressive views in all directions, including Mont Blanc to the west and the Matterhorn to the east.

THE MOUNTAINS

Essentially this is high-mountain terrain. There are wooded slopes directly above the village, but the runs here are basically just a way home at the end of the day. There is more sheltered woodland skiing in other sectors of the 4 Valleys – particularly above Veysonnaz.

The piste signposting has been improved, and the piste map now has some (but not all) runs named – but in type too small to read. What's more, the piste names are still not posted on the mountain. So it's less of a shambles than it was, but still a shambles. And readers still complain.

VERBIER ST-BERNARD
The Savoleyres area is a good place for intermediates – it's much less busy than the main area and usually has good snow →

EXTENT OF THE SLOPES ★★★★★
Smaller than claimed

We have been saying since the first edition of this book 19 years ago that Verbier's and the 4 Valleys' pistes are very limited compared with the French mega resorts. Now the Schrahe report (see our piste extent feature at the front of the book) has confirmed it; it says the 4 Vallées (excluding Bruson) has 164km of pistes compared with a claimed 362km (plus 48km at Bruson). And those km are very spread out.

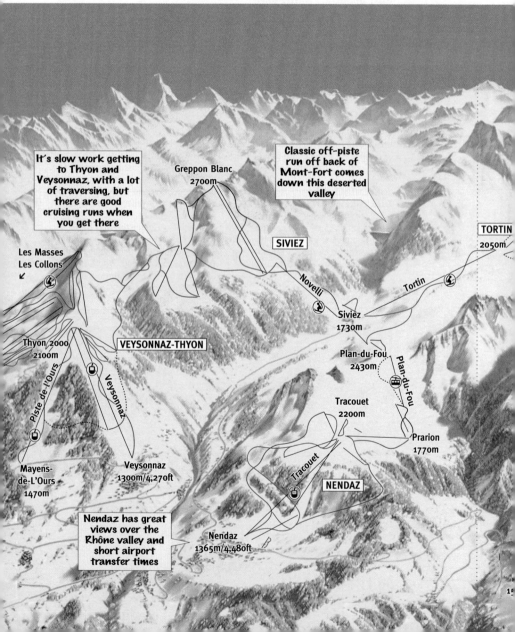

In the local Verbier sector, **Savoleyres** is a small area effectively isolated from the major network, reached by a gondola from the north-west end of the village. This area is underrated and generally underused. It has open, sunny slopes on the front side, and long, pleasantly wooded, shadier runs on the back. You can take a catwalk across from Savoleyres to the foot of Verbier's main slopes.

The main slopes are served by lifts from Médran, at the opposite end of the village. Two gondolas rise to Les Ruinettes and then a gondola and chairlift continue on to **Les Attelas**. From Les Attelas a small cable car goes up to Mont-Gelé, for steep off-piste runs only. Heading down instead, you can go back westwards to Les Ruinettes, south to La Chaux or north to Lac des Vaux. From Lac des Vaux chairs go to Les Attelas and to Chassoure, the top of a wide, steep and shady off-piste mogul field going down to **Tortin**, with a gondola back.

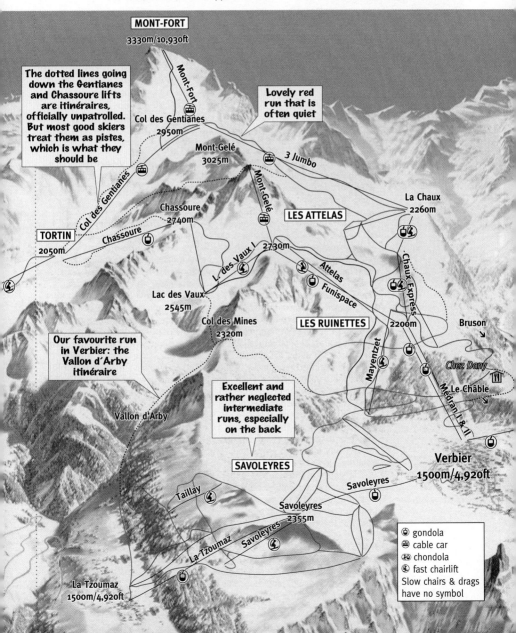

MONT-FORT
3330m/10,930ft

The dotted lines going down the Gentianes and Chassoure lifts are itinéraires, officially unpatrolled. But most good skiers treat them as pistes, which is what they should be

Col des Gentianes
2950m

Lovely red run that is often quiet

Mont-Gelé
3025m

3 Jumbo

Mont-Gelé

La Chaux
2260m

Chassoure
2740m

LES ATTELAS

TORTIN
2050m

Chassoure

2730m

L. des Vaux I

Chaux Express

Lac des Vaux
2545m

Attelas

Funispace

Col des Mines
2320m

LES RUINETTES

Bruson

Our favourite run in Verbier: the Vallon d'Arby itinéraire

Mayentzet

2200m

Chez Dany

Le Châble

Médran I & II

Excellent and rather neglected intermediate runs, especially on the back

Vallon d'Arby

SAVOLEYRES

Verbier
1500m/4,92oft

Savoleyres

Taillay

Savoleyres
2355m

Savoleyres

La Tzoumaz

La Tzoumaz
1500m/4,92oft

◎ gondola
🚡 cable car
🚠 chondola
🚄 fast chairlift
Slow chairs & drags have no symbol

Verbier has some of the best off-piste in the world. Here, we pick out just a few of the runs on offer. See 'For experts' for the status of itinéraires; for the other runs here you should hire a guide.

The Col des Mines and Vallon d'Arby itinéraires, accessible from Lac des Vaux, are relatively easy, though there may be some unnerving moments on the traverse to the point where they split. The first is a long, open slope back to Verbier and the latter a very beautiful run in a steep-sided valley down to La Tzoumaz. The Eteygeon itinéraire from Greppon Blanc above Siviez is 'wonderfully varied and should not be missed', says a reporter; it ends up on a road and you catch a bus back to Les Masses.

Stairway to Heaven starts with a steep climb from near Col des Gentianes. Then you drop over the

ridge into a deserted valley, and it's a long, relatively easy ski down to Tortin. The Mont-Gelé cable car offers some of the most amazing terrain accessible anywhere by lift, with long runs down to Siviez on steep but open slopes. Or go down the opposite side of the mountain through the steep rock face towards Lac des Vaux (not a route for the faint hearted). The many couloirs from Les Attelas can also be fantastic. We love the runs off the back of Mont-Fort (except for the long walk out past Lac de Cleuson); it's a vast bowl and you can find fresh powder long after a snowfall; you end up at Siviez. And try the tree skiing in Bruson (see the end of the chapter).

VERBIER ST BERNARD / FRANCOIS PERRAUDIN

You can also ride a chondola from Les Ruinettes to the sunny, easy slopes of La Chaux. At the bottom of these slopes a jumbo cable car goes up to **Col des Gentianes** and the glacier area. The lovely, often quiet, red run back down to La Chaux is one of our favourites. A second, much smaller cable car goes up from Gentianes to the **Mont-Fort** glacier. From the top, there's only a long, steep black run back down. From Gentianes you can head down on another off-piste route to Tortin; the whole north-facing run from the top to Tortin is almost 1300m vertical. A cable car returns to Col des Gentianes.

Below Tortin is the gateway to the rest of the 4 Valleys, **Siviez**. From here, a ridiculously outdated chair goes off into the long, thin **Nendaz** sector. A fast quad heads the other way towards **Veysonnaz–Thyon**, via a couple of drags and a lot of catwalks. Allow plenty of time to get to and from these remote corners.

The slopes of **Bruson**, across the valley from Verbier, will be easier to reach this year with a new gondola from Le Châble and are described briefly at the end of this chapter.

FAST LIFTS ★★★★☆
Locally fine
The main access lifts are gondolas and chairs. Further afield, more upgrades are needed to improve links throughout the 4 Valleys (especially between Siviez and Veysonnaz–Thyon, where draglifts are the norm).

QUEUES ★★★☆☆
Not the problem they were
Queues have been greatly eased by investment in powerful new lifts and have barely been a problem for reporters over the past few years. There may be queues at Médran if Sunday visitors fill the gondola from Le Châble, but they shift quickly.

Queues still occur for outdated lifts in the outlying 4 Valleys resorts, and the quad at Siviez gets busy at peak times and if the weather is poor. Bruson may have queues at its old lifts if the new gondola from Le Châble is popular – reports wanted, please.

TERRAIN PARKS ★★★☆☆
Expert and beginner options
The Swatch Snowpark, Verbier's main freestyle area, is at La Chaux. It has separate lines for varying levels: blue, red and black. Features are varied, with kickers, boxes and rails of all types and a giant airbag. Freestyle coaching (check www.snowschool.ch) is available.

SNOW RELIABILITY ★★★☆☆
Improved snowmaking
The slopes of the Mont-Fort glacier always have good snow, naturally. The runs to Tortin are normally snow-sure,

LIFT PASSES

4 Valleys/Mont-Fort

Prices in francs

Age	1-day	6-day
under 14	35	178
14 to 19	55	284
20 to 64	69	355
65 plus	55	284

Free Under 6; over 77
Beginner Limited pass 30 francs
Notes Covers Verbier, Mont-Fort, Bruson, La Tzoumaz, Nendaz, Veysonnaz and Thyon including ski-buses; part-day passes; family reductions

Alternative passes
Verbier only; La Tzoumaz/Savoleyres only; Bruson only

too. But nearly all of this terrain is steep and mogulled, and much of it is formally off-piste. Most of Verbier's main local slopes face south or west and are below 2500m – so they can be in poor condition at times. Snowmaking covers the whole main run down from Les Attelas to Médran at the top of the village. The slopes of La Chaux, the nursery slopes and some of the Savoleyres sector are also well served. At Veysonnaz–Thyon snowmaking now covers 80% of the area. We have been very impressed with its use on the runs down to Mayens-de-L'Ours and to Veysonnaz. Piste grooming is good.

FOR EXPERTS ★★★★★
The main attraction

Verbier has some superb tough slopes, many of them off-piste and needing a guide – see feature panel. There are few black pistes; most steep runs are instead classified as itinéraires and 'marked, not maintained, not controlled'. They are said to be closed if unsafe, but this information is not made public – and if they are not patrolled, you should not ski them alone. We'd like to see these runs given black piste status, so you know clearly where you stand. The black pistes that do exist are mostly indistinguishable from nearby reds. The front face of Mont-Fort is an exception: a long mogul field, with a choice of gradient from steep to intimidatingly steep. The World Cup run (Piste de l'Ours) at Veysonnaz is a steepish, often icy red, ideal for really speeding down when in good nick. The two most popular itinéraires to

Tortin are both excellent in their different ways. The one from Chassoure starts with a rocky traverse at the top and is then normally one huge, steep, wide mogul field. The north-facing one from Gentianes is longer, less steep, but feels much more of an adventure (keep left for shallower slopes and better snow).

From 2013/14 the Bruson slopes will be much more accessible (see 'News'); the main attraction for experts here is great tree skiing (see end of chapter).

FOR INTERMEDIATES ★★★☆☆
Be willing to travel

Many mileage-hungry intermediates find Verbier disappointing. The intermediate slopes in the main area are concentrated between Les Attelas and the village, above and below Les Ruinettes, plus the little bowl at Lac des Vaux and the sunny slopes at La Chaux. This is all excellent and varied intermediate territory, but there isn't much of it; and it is used by the bulk of the visitors staying in one of Switzerland's largest resorts. So it is often crowded, especially the lovely sweeping red from Les Attelas to Les Ruinettes. There is excellent easy blue run skiing at La Chaux, including a 'slow skiing' piste.

The under-used Savoleyres area has good intermediate pistes, usually better snow and fewer people. It is also a good hill for mixed abilities, with variations of many runs. There is a blue run linking this sector to the Médran lift base, but the way down to that link from the top is not easy.

The easier access to Bruson this season means that area will be worth

SCHOOLS

Swiss
t 775 3363

Fantastique
t 771 4141

Adrenaline
t 771 7459

Altitude
t 771 6006

New Generation
t +33 479 010318
0844 770 4733 (UK)
www.skinewgen.com

European Snowsport
t 771 6222

Powder Extreme
t 076 479 8771
020 8123 9483 (UK)

Fresh Tracks
t 079 388 3729

Warren Smith Ski Academy
t 01525 374757 (UK)

Classes
(Swiss prices)
5 half-days 280 francs

Private lessons
From 195 francs for
2hr for 1 or 2 people

GUIDES

Bureau des guides
t 775 3370

a visit too. The Veysonnaz–Thyon and Nendaz sectors are also worth exploring (those not willing to take on the itinéraires can ride the lifts down).

FOR BEGINNERS ★★
OK but not ideal
There are sunny nursery slopes close to the middle of the village and at Les Esserts, at the top of it. These are fine provided they have snow, and they are well equipped with snowmaking. Day passes covering these two areas cost 30 francs in 2012/13 (15 francs for children). For progression, a local Verbier pass is available. Progression to longer runs is not straightforward, but there are easy blues at La Chaux and on the back of Savoleyres.

FOR BOARDERS ★★★
Extreme freeride heaven
Verbier has become synonymous with extreme snowboarding and is generally seen as a freeriders' resort, with powder, cliffs, natural hits and trees all easily accessible. The final event of the Freeride world tour (see www. freerideworldtour.com) is held here every March on the Bec des Rosses. There is a lot of steep and challenging terrain to be explored with a guide, but the pistes and itinéraires will provide most riders with plenty to think about. Chairlifts and gondolas serve the main area, with no drags. The area is far from ideal for beginners and timid intermediates, who should stick to the lower blue runs and Savoleyres. The terrain park is good.

FOR CROSS-COUNTRY ★
Little on offer
There's a 4km loop in Verbier, 10km at Les Ruinettes–La Chaux and 8km down the valley in Champsec and Lourtier.

MOUNTAIN RESTAURANTS ★★★
Improving, at last
Most restaurants are surprisingly uninspiring for such an upmarket resort. But a few new openings have improved things recently.
Editors' choice In the main area, the rustic Chez Dany (771 2524) is a classic old chalet in the forest on the itinéraire on the southern fringe of the area; we had another enjoyable lunch there in 2013.
Worth knowing about Near the top of Attelas, La Vache – run by the team that runs the Farinet in town and part owned by celebs including singer

James Blunt and rugby player Lawrence Dallaglio – opened last season, offering reasonably priced (for Verbier) pizzas, pastas, soups and salads. Service can be slow, but the men's loos are worth a visit (check out the Lawrence Dallaglio cubicle). Another new place, built to look like a giant igloo with an aluminium exterior, opened at Col des Gentianes – reports, please. The Dahu, at the bottom of the La Chaux chair, opened two seasons ago with table- and self-service sections; we stopped by for a drink and enjoyed the light, airy ambience – good pizzas, we're told.

Some reader favourites are far-flung. Among the most frequently recommended are the Chottes between Siviez and Veysonnaz–Thyon ('large terrace; potage paysanne a favourite') and the Caboulis on the run down to Veysonnaz ('very good soup'). At Les Collons the Cambuse has 'excellent food and is not too expensive'. At Siviez, Chez Odette has changed hands but it is 'essentially unchanged, with good food and big helpings', says a recent visitor.

Closer to home, there are some nice places on Savoleyres, though most rarely generate reports. The Croix de Coeur at the top is an attractive 15-sided building with great views from the terrace and 'very pleasant' table-service of good food. Don't overlook the rustic Marmotte and the Namasté lower down, or the Sonalon, on the fringe of the village.

Back in the main sector, the restaurants at Les Ruinettes were smartened up a few years ago: the Cristal offers fine dining under the former chef of Chalet d'Adrien, but visitors say the self-service restaurant is 'poor' and 'uninspiring'. The Olympique at Les Attelas includes a good table-service restaurant. The Cabane Mont-Fort is a proper mountain refuge off the run to La Chaux from Col des Gentianes: 'one of the best for atmosphere' but gets packed. Chalet Carlsberg has a good position at La Combe and has impressed us with fast and efficient service. Carrefour, near the top of the nursery slopes, does 'great food, worth a visit'. Mayen, accessible from both the main Verbier slopes and the Col des Mines, has 'great views' and 'very good table service'.

There are two picnic rooms: at Les Ruinettes and at Savoleyres.

SCHOOLS AND GUIDES ★★★★★
Good reports

There's no shortage of schools to choose between. New Generation, well established and a reader favourite in several top French resorts, has its first Swiss branch in Verbier. We were very impressed with our mountain guide from Adrenaline. We have had good reports of Altitude: 'booked 3hr off-piste lessons and were the only two in the group'. European Snowsports has been praised for competitive pricing of private lessons. British instructor Warren Smith runs his Ski Academy here (five-day courses that you have to book in advance), and Powder Extreme specializes in off-piste. We have skied with both outfits and thought them good.

FOR FAMILIES ★★★☆☆
Good for childcare

The nursery slopes are central, and the Swiss school's facilities are good. There are considerable reductions on the lift pass price for families. The possibility of leaving very young babies at the Schtroumpfs nursery is valuable. Nanny services are offered by Chalet Services Verbier.

STAYING THERE

There are surprisingly few apartments and B&Bs, though there are inexpensive B&Bs in Le Châble. Hotels are pricey for their gradings.

Chalets Verbier is the chalet holiday capital of Switzerland, with some very luxurious places. Ski Verbier has an impressive portfolio at the top of the market. Ski Total has the luxurious Montpelier chalet hotel – with pool, sauna and steam room, and endorsed again by 2013 reporters ('couldn't fault it, good rooms, food excellent', 'exceptional views from south-facing rooms') – plus a separate penthouse apartment on the top floor of Montpellier, with use of the pool etc, and a smart new chalet with a steam room. Skiworld has two central chalets, one large with jacuzzi and sauna. Inghams has a chalet hotel in the main square and a separate chalet.

Hotels Two 5-stars, five 4-stars, ten 3-stars and a few simpler places.

★★★★★W Verbier (079 173 6541) Due to open December 2013 right by the slope and gondola at Médran, with spa, gym and pool. Michelin star chef will produce 'locally inspired' menus.

★★★★★Chalet d'Adrien (771 6200) Relais & Chateaux. A beautifully furnished low-rise 29-room chalet, with top-notch cooking. In a peaceful setting next to the Savoleyres lift, with great views. Neat spa/gym/pool.

★★★★Nevaï (775 4000) Modern, minimalist, trendy, next to Farm Club (same ownership). Après-ski bar.

★★★★Vanessa (775 2800) Central, with spacious apartments as well as rooms.

★★★Farinet (771 6626) Central, British-owned, with a focal après-ski bar.

★★★Poste (771 6681) Midway between centre and Médran; pool. Some rooms small. 'Pleasant atmosphere.'

★★★Rotonde (771 6525) Much cheaper; well positioned between centre and Médran; some budget rooms.

Apartments There are surprisingly few on the UK market. Ski Expectations has a conveniently located, Swiss-owned four-bedroom chalet and studio apartment. Ski Verbier has some nice-looking places.

EATING OUT ★★★★☆
Plenty of choice

There is a wide range of restaurants; many are listed in a free pocket guide.

The 5-star Chalet d'Adrien is one of the best gourmet places in town

ALPINEANSWERS.CO.UK

GREAT CHALET
HOLIDAYS SINCE 1992

020 7801 1080
ABTA & ATOL PROTECTED

UK PACKAGES

Alpine Answers, Alpine Weekends, Belvedere Travel, Bramble Ski, Crystal, Crystal Finest, Elegant Resorts, Erna Low, Flexiski, Independent Ski Links, Inghams, Interactive Resorts, Jeffersons, Kaluma, Luxury Chalet Collection, Momentum, Mountain Beds, Oxford Ski Co, Peak Ski, Powder White, PowderBeds, Ski Bespoke, Ski Expectations, Ski Freedom, Ski Independence, Ski Line, Ski Safari, Ski Solutions, Ski Total, Skitracer, Ski Verbier, Ski Weekend, Skiworld, Snow Finders, Snoworks, STC, Supertravel, Thomson, V-Ski, VIP, White Roc **Nendaz** Alpine Answers, Erna Low, Lagrange, Mountain Beds, Peak Ski, Ski Club Freshtracks, Ski Independence, Ski Solutions, Skiworld, STC, Ted Bentley **Veysonnaz** Erna Low, Luxury Chalet Collection, Oxford Ski Co, Peak Ski

GETTING THERE

Air Geneva 160km/100 miles (2hr15)

Rail Le Châble (7km/ 4 miles); regular buses to resort or gondola

(one Michelin star). The pop-up Pot Luck, serving fusion tapas below the Farinet was so popular last season that they want to continue for 2013/14. We've had good (but pricey) meals in the Nevaï and Cordée des Alpes hotels and in the Rouge Restaurant and Club (which a reader praises for its wide-ranging menu and 'lovely pumpkin soup'), and enjoyed sushi at the Nomad. We've also had good meals in the stylish, quiet and sophisticated Millénium, which is 'the place to go for top-quality venison and steaks'.

Down the price scale somewhat, the small Ecurie in hotel Ermitage has a 'traditional atmosphere' and does 'very good' food. For Swiss specialities, try the Relais des Neiges ('quieter than many; excellent food'), the Caveau, Vieux Verbier, by the Médran lifts, and Esserts, by the nursery slopes. The ever-popular Fer à Cheval is known for its pizzas, but other dishes are also very good ('superb steak tartare'). Downstairs in the Pub Mont Fort you can get good-value gastropub food. Borsalino, near the centre of town, and Al Capone, out near the Savoleyres gondola, have been recommended for pizzas.

You can be ferried by snowmobile up to Chez Dany or the Marmotte for a meal, followed by a torchlit descent.

APRES-SKI ★★★★★
Throbbing but expensive

On the slopes, popular stops include the Rocks bar at Ruinettes, Chalet Carlsberg and the yurts of 1936. In town, the Offshore Coffee Bar at Médran is ever popular for people-watching, milk shakes and cakes. The Apres Ski Bar at the Farinet (with happy hour from 4pm to 5pm and live bands) and the Big Ben pub are lively. The Nevaï hotel has live music on its terraces, and the Rouge at the bottom of the golf course is packed, thanks to its popular sun deck and resident DJs.

Then if you're young, loud and British, it's on to the Pub Mont Fort – there's a widescreen TV for live sport. The Nelson and Fer à Cheval ('great atmosphere from après through to the small hours') are popular with locals. The absolutely central Farinet has won awards for its après-ski and was revamped last year to combine the lounge and cocktail bar and increase the sofa area. It rocks until the early hours to live bands and DJs shipped in from Ibiza regularly ('packed with

people dancing on the tables and bar – an iconic après-ski place').

After dinner the Pub Mont Fort is again popular (the shots bar in the cellar is worth a visit). Crock No Name is a cool cocktail bar often with a blues band or a DJ. T-Bar is 'packed' for live rugby and football, and 'best on live music nights'.

The Farm Club is seriously pricey – and on Friday and Saturday packed with rich Swiss paying 220 francs for bottles of spirits. The Casbah and Coup d'Etat are other clubs.

OFF THE SLOPES ★★★★★
A few things to do

Verbier has an excellent sports centre (with pool, saunas, hot tubs), dog sledding between Les Ruinettes and La Chaux and some nice walks. Montreux is an enjoyable train excursion from Le Châble, and Martigny is worth a visit for the Roman remains and art gallery. Reporters have recommended the spa complex at Lavey-les-Bains. Various mountain restaurants are accessible to pedestrians – a walkers' pass covers most of the local lifts. There are popular long toboggan runs on Savoleyres.

LINKED RESORT – 1365m
NENDAZ

Nendaz is little known in Britain but is a major resort, with over 17,000 beds (practically all in apartments). Most of the resort is modern, built in traditional chalet style, and there are great views across the Rhône valley.

It's a sizeable and sprawling place, and the centre is busy with traffic. The local bus services are reliable, but get oversubscribed at peak times. There are 100km of walks, an ice rink, fitness centre, climbing wall, squash courts.

A 12-person gondola takes you to the top of the local slopes at Tracouet. This is a splendid, sunny little shelf with gentle slopes and long, shady red and blue runs back down to Nendaz. But getting to and from the rest of the 4 Valleys can be a slow business, and key links on the way have no snowmaking and can be closed. Getting back involves taking an itinéraire (or riding a cable car down) followed by a black run – too tricky for many intermediates. Many people prefer to drive/bus to Siviez, and start/ finish skiing there.

ACTIVITIES

Indoor Sports centre
(swimming pool, ice
rink, curling, squash,
sauna, solarium,
steam bath, hot tub),
museums, galleries

Outdoor Cleared
walking paths, ice
karting, paragliding,
snowshoeing, dog
sledding, tobogganing

Skiworld has two good-looking
chalets almost opposite the gondola,
one with sauna and outdoor hot tub.
Two small 3-star hotels, both about
five minutes' walk from the lift, have
been tipped by readers. The 'basic but
pleasant' Mont-Fort (288 2616) is
'friendly' with a 'cool urban' bar. The
Déserteur (288 2455) provided 'almost
perfect service'. There's also a plentiful
supply of apartments.

There's quite a wide choice of
restaurants, offering Tex-Mex, pizzas,
Thai and sushi, as well as steaks and
local mountain food. Chez Edith, a tiny
restaurant on the way to Siviez, has
been recommended.

LINKED RESORT – 1730m
SIVIEZ

Siviez, a small huddle of buildings in
an isolated spot, is effectively a
junction of the slopes of Verbier,
Nendaz and Veysonnaz–Thyon. It is the
best base from which to explore the
whole 4 Valleys lift network, though
lodging is limited almost entirely to
apartments. There are daytime buses
to/from Nendaz. The long and gentle
blue run through the sheltered valley
from Tortin is super beginner
progression territory. It is also an
excellent base for doing the tough
skiing of Verbier – you can end the
day with a descent of 1600m vertical
from Mont-Fort; no noise in the
evenings; perfect.

LINKED RESORT – 1300m
VEYSONNAZ

Veysonnaz is a small, family resort,
sunny in the afternoon, at the foot of
an excellent, long red slope from the
ridge above Thyon. A second excellent
(though often icy) red, regularly used

for major races, descends to the
isolated lift base of Mayens-de-L'Ours.

The resort is spread widely across
and down the hillside, with extensive
views across the Rhône valley. The
original attractive old village, complete
with church, is two hairpin bends
below Veysonnaz Station, the lift base
and the main focus of the place for
the visitor. The link up to Thyon is an
eight-seat gondola, but progress from
there towards Verbier is a slow
business. Taking a car means you can
drive to Siviez for much quicker access
to the Verbier slopes. Shuttle-buses
serve the lifts, but they are not super-
frequent and do not run on Saturdays.

Veysonnaz Station has the essential
facilities – half a dozen bars and cafes,
four restaurants, a disco or two and a
wellness centre with swimming pool
and spa facilities (closed Saturdays).
There are adequate shops, including a
butcher and baker.

Accommodation is mainly in
apartments – substantial chalet-style
buildings dotted along the road the lift
base is on. There are plenty of smaller
chalets, too. There are two 3-star
hotels next to the gondola station: the
Chalet Royal (208 5644) has 'stunning
views', though not from all rooms, and
'generally good' food. The Magrappé
(208 5700) has 'a bit of atmosphere'
and is more the focus of lively après-
ski. There are some B&Bs.

There are two schools: Swiss and
Neige Aventure. And there is a
children's day care centre on the
mountain. A 5km cross-country trail
has great views.

LINKED RESORT – 2100m
THYON 2000

Thyon 2000 is a purpose-built
collection of plain, medium-rise
apartment blocks just above the
treeline at the hub of the Veysonnaz–
Thyon sector of the 4 Valleys. The
apartments are a bit of a blot on the
landscape, but some of them at least
are of a high standard, according to a
reporter. It has the basics of resort life
– supermarket, newsagent, a couple of
restaurants (the Luge pizzeria is rated
'excellent, with friendly atmosphere
and reasonable prices' by a recent
visitor), an indoor pool, a disco. A free
shuttle-bus runs to Les Collons.
There's a fair-sized terrain park and
boardercross, children's snow garden
and a kindergarten, as well as a ski

school. The slopes are ideal for families and beginners, with two nursery lifts close to the accommodation. The lift network shared with Les Collons and Les Masses is elderly and slow (though gradually being improved). Snowmaking is extensive.

LINKED RESORT – 1800m
LES COLLONS

Some 300m below Thyon, at the foot of a broad, east-facing slope, Les Collons is nothing more than a couple of strings of chalet-style buildings spread along two roads following the hillside, 50m vertical apart; a lot of building has been going on recently.

Three draglifts go up towards Thyon from the upper level of the resort, and a chairlift from the lower level takes you above Thyon. There's 6km of cross-country. A free shuttle-bus runs to Thyon.

Most accommodation is in apartments, but there are also a couple of modest hotels – including the 3-star Cambuse (281 1883) just below one of the lift bases. There are a few bars and restaurants, plus a 1km toboggan run through the woods above the village. Prepared walking trails add up to a modest 8km.

LINKED RESORT – 1515m
LES MASSES

Half-a-dozen hairpins down the mountainside from Les Collons, Les Masses is no more than a hamlet at the base of the double chairlifts that form the southern limit of the Thyon–Veysonnaz slopes. The home run is a red. Accommodation is in apartments. There is a grocery and a bar/ restaurant.

LINKED RESORT – 1500m
LA TZOUMAZ

This tiny hamlet sits in a quiet valley on the shady, wooded side of Verbier's Savoleyres slope sector. There are a handful of small hotels, shops and restaurants, forming a very quiet place to stay and ski this underrated sector. A free bus serves the lifts. A newish gondola and a couple of fast chairs serve most of the slopes here. The 10km toboggan run back to the base area is one of the longest in the region; we're told by the tourist office

that it is a professional run and not suitable for children under seven; helmets are recommended.

LINKED RESORT – 820m
LE CHÂBLE

Le Châble is a village in the valley, set off the main road to Italy at the bottom of the hairpin road up to Verbier. Beside the main road is a huge car park and a queue-free gondola to Verbier that goes on (without changing cabins) to Les Ruinettes – access to the slopes can be just as quick from here as from Verbier, and the gondola runs till 7.30pm. Buses run later. From 2013/14 another gondola is due to open to take you to the heart of the slopes of the Bruson area. Le Châble is on the rail network (the station is near the gondolas), and is also convenient for drivers who want to visit other resorts. There are several modest hotels, of which the 2-star Giétroz (776 1184) is the pick.

LINKED RESORT – 1100m
BRUSON

Bruson is a small village on a shelf just above Le Châble, across the valley from Verbier. From 2013/14 its ski area will be reachable by a new gondola from Le Châble that cuts out the need to take a bus followed by a slow old chairlift. The slopes above the new gondola are served by a triple chair up to a ridge, on the far side of which is a short draglift serving a tight little bowl. In addition to the intermediate pistes served by these lifts there are large areas of off-piste terrain – including tremendous skiing in the woods between well-spaced trees that is reminiscent of Canadian heli-skiing – quite steep in places though. And the front side of the mountain is mainly north-east facing, so it keeps its snow well. The off-piste down the back towards Orsières is good; you return by train. When we were there on a Saturday in January last season it was all delightfully quiet and a great contrast with Verbier's busy slopes; whether it will remain that way with the new access gondola remains to be seen (reports, please). It would be a good place to go when it's snowing and there are white-out conditions on most of Verbier's slopes.

Phone numbers
From elsewhere in Switzerland add the prefix 027; from abroad use the prefix +41 27

TOURIST OFFICES

Verbier / Le Châble (Bruson) / La Tzoumaz
www.verbier-st-bernard.ch
Nendaz / Siviez
www.nendaz.ch
Veysonnaz
www.veysonnaz.ch
Thyon 2000 / Les Collons / Les Masses
www.thyon-region.ch

Villars

Traditional year-round resort with local low-altitude slopes, a cog railway and a much needed but far-flung glacier

TOP 10 RATINGS

Extent	★★★
Fast lifts	★★
Queues	★★★
Snow	★★
Expert	★★
Intermediate	★★★
Beginner	★★★★
Charm	★★★
Convenience	★★
Scenery	★★★

RPI	120
lift pass	£220
ski hire	£105
lessons	£110
food & drink	£190
total	**£625**

NEWS

2012/13: A SuperPass lift pass was launched. It covers 420km of runs in 17 ski areas including those in this chapter, Leysin and Les Mosses and the Gstaad area. Children under nine now ski free.

- ➕ Pleasant, year-round resort
- ➕ Fairly extensive intermediate slopes
- ➕ Distant access to glacier slopes

- ➖ Unreliable local snow-cover
- ➖ Short runs on the upper slopes
- ➖ Little to amuse experts on piste

Villars is popular with second-home owners because of its closeness to Geneva airport. For many keen skiers, its low altitude and far from snow-sure slopes will rule it out. But for a varied family holiday it has its attractions.

THE RESORT

Villars sits on a sunny hillside looking across the Rhône valley to the Portes du Soleil. Its home slopes link to those of Les Chaux, above the delightfully rustic village of Gryon. You can get a whole area pass covering Les Diablerets (linked by lifts and pistes) plus Leysin and Les Mosses (easy outings by rail or road). It also covers Glacier 3000, the small glacier area beyond Les Diablerets. A new SuperPass was introduced in 2012/13 including Gstaad. Getting to and from the glacier is a long, slow business – from Les Diablerets you need to catch a bus to the glacier lift or walk 10 mins to the Isenau area to ski down to it. Outings to Verbier are possible.

Village charm Villars is more a town than a village, with sprawling suburbs of chalets and several international schools. The focus is a longish, traffic-filled but pleasant street.

Convenience A slow cog railway goes from the main street up to the slopes around Bretaye. A gondola at the other end of town is quicker. It's best to stay near one of these or at a hotel with a shuttle-bus, but there are ski-buses.

Scenery The scenery is more dramatic than you might expect.

THE MOUNTAINS

There's a good mix of wooded and open slopes. But the piste map and signing could be improved.

Slopes The cog railway goes up to the col of Bretaye, which has intermediate slopes on either side. To the east, open slopes go to La Rasse and the link to Les Chaux. There used to be another piste to La Rasse down from Chaux Ronde, but this is now an itinerary; it has a tricky section at the top that is often closed. There's an alternative blue run from Bretaye. From Les Chaux there are runs to Barboleuse above Gryon, with a

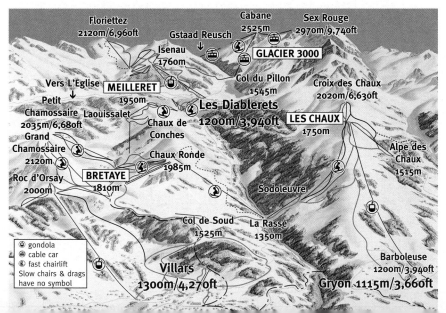

gondola
cable car
fast chairlift
Slow chairs & drags have no symbol

Floriettez 2120m/6,96oft
Cabane 2525m
Sex Rouge 2970m/9,740ft
Gstaad Reusch
Isenau 176om
GLACIER 3000
Col du Pillon 1545m
Vers L'Eglise
MEILLERET 1950m
Croix des Chaux 2020m/6,630ft
Petit Chamossaire 2035m/6,68oft
Laouissalet
Chaux de Conches
Les Diablerets 1200m/3,940ft
LES CHAUX 1750m
Grand Chamossaire 2120m
Chaux Ronde 1985m
Alpe des Chaux 1515m
Roc d'Orsay 2000m
BRETAYE 1810m
Sodoleuvre
Col de Soud 1525m
La Rasse 1350m
Barboleuse 1200m/3,940ft
Villars 1300m/4,27oft
Gryon 1115m/3,66oft

↑ Villars is a sprawling resort but is prettily set with splendid views over the Rhône valley to the Portes du Soleil

VILLARS TOURISM

KEY FACTS

Resort	1300m
	4,270ft

Villars, Gryon and Les Diablerets (excludes Glacier 3000)

Slopes	1115-2120m
	3,660-6,960ft
Lifts	34
Pistes	100km
	62 miles
Blue	37%
Red	53%
Black	10%
Snowmaking	20%

Phone numbers
From elsewhere in Switzerland add the prefix 024; from abroad use the prefix +41 24

TOURIST OFFICE

www.villars.ch

gondola back up. The gondola from Villars takes you to Roc d'Orsay, from where you can head for Bretaye or back to Villars. A long, slow, two-way chairlift links to Les Diablerets. The glacier area has very gentle slopes at the top, but there is a splendid run down the Combe d'Audon (which used to be red but is now undeservedly classified black on the piste map) with a dramatic cliff face rising up on the right. You can descend to the valley, or part way down catch a fast chair which serves a splendid red run.

Fast lifts Fast lifts exist, but so do old chairs and drags.

Queues The lifts at Bretaye get busy mainly at peak times. The buses and train can get overcrowded.

Terrain parks There's one at Chaux Ronde and a smaller one at Diablerets.

Snow reliability Low altitude and sunny slopes mean snow reliability isn't good – though on such gentle, grassy terrain, deep snow-cover isn't needed. Recent snowmaking on the runs back to town and at La Rasse are welcome improvements; but plans for more seem to have stalled.

Experts Little on-piste challenge but some good off-piste with a guide.

Intermediates The local slopes offer a good variety. Les Chaux has some steeper slopes and a lovely long cruisy blue to Barboleuse. The run from Meilleret to Les Diablerets is a delightful long cruise that can be deserted first thing in the morning.

Beginners The nursery slope behind the station is free to use. There is another at Gryon. There are gentle but often crowded runs at Bretaye.

Snowboarding There are a few tricky draglifts but good intermediate slopes.

Cross-country There are 50km of trails; those up the valley past La Rasse are long and pretty. There are more in the depression beyond Bretaye.

Mountain restaurants They are often oversubscribed. We hear most about Lac des Chavonnes (a short walk below Petit Chamossaire) and the Col de Soud for 'very good food, a real sun trap'. The Golf Club does 'delicious tartiflette'. Above Gryon, we like the relatively quiet Des Chaux at Les Chaux and Refuge Frience (it's a walk back to the T-bar though). The Etable is a converted farmhouse at Sodoleuvre above La Rasse. There are picnic rooms at the top of the Roc d'Orsay gondola and at Les Chaux.

Schools and guides Past reports have been positive.

Families La Trottinette non-ski nursery takes children up to six.

STAYING THERE

Hotels We've enjoyed staying at the 4-star central Golf (496 3838) – big rooms, spa facilities. Nearby is the 3-star Alpe Fleurie (496 3070). The 4-star Eurotel Victoria (495 3131) is near the gondola and 'almost ski-in'.

Eating out Cookie, out past Barboleuse, does traditional and Asian-fusion food. Francis does 'good pizza' and the Sporting serves traditional dishes/grills.

Après-ski The rustic Buvette d'Arrivée on the home run above the top of town is popular at close of play, as is the Sporting. Try the Moon Boot Lounge for cocktails.

Off the slopes Activities include paragliding, snowshoeing, skating, tobogganing and swimming. There are 'excellent' walks and rail trips.

UK PACKAGES

Alpine Answers, Alpine Weekends, Bramble Ski, Carrier, Club Med, Independent Ski Links, Momentum, Neilson, PowderBeds, Ski Bespoke, Ski Expectations, Ski Independence, Ski Line, Ski Safari, Ski Solutions, Ski Weekend, Skitracer, Switzerland Travel Centre, Tracks European Adventures

SNOWPIX.COM / CHRIS GILL

Wengen

A charming old village, stunning scenery, an old cog railway and gentle intermediate slopes make for a relaxing and leisurely holiday

521

RATINGS

The mountains

Extent	★★★
Fast lifts	★★★★
Queues	★★★
Terrain p'ks	★
Snow	★★
Expert	★★
Intermediate	★★★★
Beginner	★★★
Boarder	★★
X-country	★
Restaurants	★★★
Schools	★★★
Families	★★★★

The resort

Charm	★★★★★
Convenience	★★★
Scenery	★★★★★
Eating out	★★
Après-ski	★★
Off-slope	★★★★

RPI 125

lift pass	£230
ski hire	£110
lessons	£115
food & drink	£185
total	**£640**

NEWS

2012/13: The Wixi double chair was upgraded to a six-pack with covers. On some slopes there are special photo spots and places where you can check your speed. You can also be filmed and view the video on the Jungfrau website later.

+ Some of the most spectacular scenery in the Alps

+ Small, traditional, nearly traffic-free Alpine village

+ Lots of long, gentle runs, ideal for leisurely intermediates

+ Nursery slopes in heart of village

+ Calm, unhurried atmosphere

+ Good resort for families and groups that include non-skiers. It's easy to get around on mountain railways

– Limited terrain for experts and adventurous intermediates

– Natural snow unreliable (but substantial snowmaking now)

– Trains to slopes are slow and there are still a few old lifts

– Getting to/from Grindelwald's First area can take hours

– Subdued in the evening, with little variety of nightlife

Given the charm of the village, the friendliness of the locals and the drama of the scenery, it's easy to see why many people love Wengen – including large numbers of Brits who have been going for decades. It's great for a relaxing time, for those who don't take their skiing too seriously, for families and for mixed groups of intermediates and non-skiers.

Keen piste-bashers should not underestimate the drawbacks. If you're used to modern mega-resorts, you'll find Wengen a huge contrast, and may have difficulty adjusting. But the spectacularly scenic Jungfrau region is one that every keen skier should experience; and to experience all of it Wengen, centrally placed between Mürren and Grindelwald, is the best base.

THE RESORT

Wengen is one of three resorts close together in the Jungfrau region. It is set on a sloping shelf above the Lauterbrunnen valley, opposite Mürren, and reached only by a cog railway, which carries on up to Kleine Scheidegg and the slopes shared with Grindelwald. Access to Mürren involves a train down to Lauterbrunnen, a cable car up and then another train (or a bus from Lauterbrunnen to a different two-stage cable car to Mürren). Access to the First area of Grindelwald is an even longer process, including skiing down to Grindelwald and crossing town. The Jungfrau lift pass covers all of this. Outings further afield aren't really worth the effort.

VILLAGE CHARM ★★★★★
Almost traffic-free
The village was a farming community long before skiing arrived; it is still tiny, but dominated by sizeable hotels, mostly of Victorian origin. So it is not exactly chocolate-box pretty, but it is charming and relaxed, and almost traffic-free. There are electric hotel

taxi-trucks and a few ordinary, engine-driven taxis. (Why, we wonder?)

The short main street is the hub. Lined with chalet-style shops and hotels, it also has the ice rink and village nursery slopes right next to it.

CONVENIENCE ★★★
Compact, but hilly in parts
Wengen is small, so location isn't as crucial as in many resorts. But those who don't fancy a steepish morning climb should avoid places down the hill, below the station. The ridge where the slopes of Wengen meet those of Grindelwald is reached either by train or – much quicker – by cable car. Both stations are central. There are hotels on the home piste, convenient for the slopes.

SCENERY ★★★★★
Three of the best are here
The views across the valley are stunning. They get even better higher up, when the famous trio of peaks comes fully into view – the Mönch (Monk) in the centre protecting the Jungfrau (Maiden) on the right from the Eiger (Ogre) on the left.

KEY FACTS

Resort	1275m
	4,180ft

Jungfrau region	
Slopes	945-2970m
	3,100-9,740ft
Lifts	45
Pistes	213km
	132 miles
Blue	33%
Red	49%
Black	18%
Snowmaking	40%

First-Männlichen-Kleine Scheidegg only	
Slopes	945-2500m
	3,100-8,200ft
Lifts	34
Pistes	170km
	106 miles

LIFT PASSES

Jungfrau

Prices in francs

Age	1-day	6-day
under 16	31	157
16 to 19	50	251
20 to 61	62	314
over 62	56	283

Free Under 6 (if with parent)

Beginner Points ticket

Notes Covers trains between villages and Grindelwald ski-bus; day pass is for First-Kleine Scheidegg-Männlichen area only; 6-day-plus pass allows one day in Zermatt

Alternative passes Grindelwald and Wengen only; Mürren only; non-skier pass

THE MOUNTAINS

Although Wengen is famous for the fearsome Lauberhorn Downhill course – the longest and one of the toughest on the World Cup circuit – its slopes are best suited to early intermediates. Most of the Downhill course is now open to the public and the steepest section (the Hundschopf jump) can be avoided by an alternative red route. Most of Wengen's runs are gentle blues and reds, ideal for cruising.

Piste marking and piste map are poor; reporters find the Männlichen slopes, in particular, confusing.

EXTENT OF THE SLOPES ★★★☆☆
Picturesque playground
Most of the slopes are on the Grindelwald side of the mountain. From the railway station at Kleine Scheidegg you can head straight down to Grindelwald or work your way across to the top of the Männlichen. This area is served by a drag and several chairlifts, and can be reached directly from Wengen by the cable car. There are a few runs back down towards Wengen from the top of the Lauberhorn, but there's really only one below Wengernalp.

FAST LIFTS ★★★★☆
OK except for the train
The fast cable car and slow train are the main access lifts; new fast chairs replacing old lifts have improved things higher up; the most recent was the Eigernordwand six-pack from below Kleine Scheidegg (on the Grindelwald side) to Eigergletscher, and the Wixi six-pack, which replaced an old double chair in 2012/13.

QUEUES ★★★☆☆
Village crowds, better higher up
Both the train and the cable car can be crowded at peak periods – '40 minutes to an hour queue at the cable car at 9.30am,' said a February 2013 reporter. It is best to avoid travelling up at the same time as the ski school. Queues up the mountain have been alleviated a lot in the past few years by the installation of fast chairs, and reporters have experienced few problems in midweek. But weekends can be busy, especially on the Grindelwald side of the hill – the obvious entry point for residents of Bern attracted by the special family pass deals on Saturdays.

TERRAIN PARKS ★☆☆☆☆
A fair trek
There isn't one. The nearest parks are at First and Mürren – each a fair trek.

SNOW RELIABILITY ★★☆☆☆
Improved snowmaking helps
Most slopes are below 2000m, and the few runs on the Wengen side of the ridge are sunny; the long blue run back to the village is particularly vulnerable. But a lot of snowmaking has been added recently, and some 60% of the slopes in the Kleine Scheidegg-Männlichen area are now covered. When we were last there, it had not snowed for a few weeks and a warm Föhn wind had melted a lot of snow, but most slopes were in good condition. Piste maintenance gets mixed reviews.

FOR EXPERTS ★★☆☆☆
Few challenges
Wengen is quite limited for experts. The only genuine black runs in the area are parts of the Lauberhorn World Cup Downhill and a couple of pistes from Eigergletscher towards Wixi. There are some decent off-piste runs from under the north face of the Eiger and the Eigernordwand lift helps with access to these. More adventurous runs from the Jungfraujoch become possible later in the season (see the Grindelwald chapter for more about going to the Jungfraujoch). For more challenges it's well worth going to nearby Mürren, around an hour away. Heli-trips are organized if there are enough takers.

FOR INTERMEDIATES ★★★★☆
Wonderful if the snow is good
Wengen and Grindelwald share superb easy-intermediate slopes. Nearly all are long blue or gentle red runs (though there are genuine reds too); read the Grindelwald chapter. The run back to Wengen is a relaxing end to the day, although it can be crowded and the snow can be patchy.

For tougher pistes, head for the top of the Lauberhorn chair and then the runs to Kleine Scheidegg, or to Wixi (following the start of the Downhill course). You could also try the shady run from Eigergletscher, which often has the best snow late in the season. Or head for Mürren – well worth doing for adventurous intermediates for a day or two during a week's stay.

FOR BEGINNERS ★★★★★
Not ideal

There's a nursery slope in the centre of the village – convenient and gentle, but it gets afternoon sun and at this modest altitude the snow can suffer. There's a beginners' area at Wengernalp and some short beginner lifts up at Kleine Scheidegg, but of course to use these you have to take the train down as well as up, or tackle the blue run down to the village, which can be tricky, with some flat sections. None of these areas offers free lifts, but there are alternatives to buying a full lift pass (there is a points card). There are plenty of good, long, gentle runs to progress to on the slopes above Grindelwald, reached either by train to Kleine Scheidegg or cable car to Männlichen.

FOR BOARDERS ★★★★★
Best for beginners

Wengen is not a bad place for gentle boarding – the nursery area is not ideal, but beginners have plenty of slopes to progress to, with lots of long blue and red runs served by the train and chairlifts. Getting from Kleine Scheidegg to Männlichen means an unavoidable draglift, though. And the slope back to Wengen is narrow and almost flat in places, so you may have to scoot. For the steepest slopes and best freeriding, experts will want to head for Mürren.

FOR CROSS-COUNTRY ★★★★★
There is none

There's no cross-country in Wengen itself, which seems a shame given the nature of the resort. There are 12km of tracks down in the Lauterbrunnen valley, where the snow is unreliable.

MOUNTAIN RESTAURANTS ★★★★★
Plenty of variety

Editors' choice The Jungfrau hotel at Wengernalp (855 1622) is an old favourite of ours – and of reporters: beautiful views from the terrace; the menu is limited, but the rösti is excellent. You also get magnificent views from the narrow balcony of Wengen's highest restaurant, Eigergletscher.

Worth knowing about The station buffet at Kleine Scheidegg has received repeated endorsements ('good rösti', 'efficient'), but a 2013 reporter found the service 'rushed, bordering on rude'. Recent reporters have enjoyed the busy Eigernordwand restaurant ('great goulash soup in a bread bowl'). The Allmend, near the top of the Innerwengen chair and the train stop, has wonderful views but 'no atmosphere – even at the end of the day'. Far better, in the opinion of two reporters last year, is Mary's Cafe at the bottom of the Lauberhorn ('really good lunch', 'best snack of the week'). The Vorsaasstube below the gondola mid-station on Männlichen

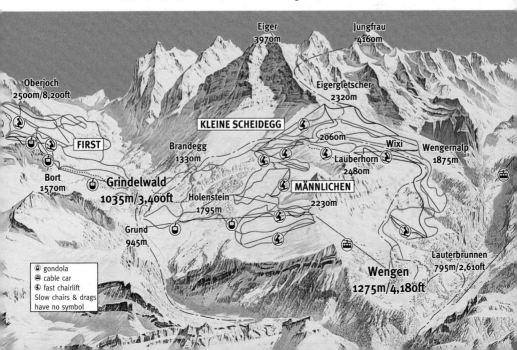

↑ Wengen is a charming traffic-free village with nursery slopes right in the centre

JUNGFRAU REGION MARKETING AG

SCHOOLS
Swiss
t 855 2022

Swiss Kleine Scheidegg
t 079 311 1474

Privat
t 855 5005

Altitude
t 853 0040

Classes
(Swiss prices)
6 3hr-days 275 francs

Private lessons
From 149 francs for 2hr

CHILDCARE
Playhouse
t 856 8585
From 1mnth to 8yr

Snowli Club Sunshine
t 854 1280
From 6mnth

Ski school
From age 3

gets the thumbs up this year. There is a picnic room at the Männlichen top station. For restaurants above Grindelwald, read that chapter.

SCHOOLS AND GUIDES ★★★☆☆
Reports please
We have no reports again this year. Guides are available for heli-trips and off-piste.

FOR FAMILIES ★★★★☆
A family favourite
It is an attractive and reassuring village for families. The nursery slope is in the centre and there are two kindergartens. There is a list of babysitters available at the tourist office. The train gives easy access to higher slopes.

STAYING THERE

Most accommodation is in hotels. There is only a handful of catered chalets (none especially luxurious). Self-catering apartments are few, too.
   Staying down in Lauterbrunnen will halve your accommodation costs and give faster access to Mürren.
Hotels There are about two dozen hotels, mostly 4-star and 3-star, with a handful of simpler places.
★★★★Beausite Park (856 5161) The best in town reputedly: 'very well run with charming staff, good food'. Good pool, steam, sauna, massage. Situated at the top of the nursery slopes.
★★★★Caprice (856 0606) Small, smartly

furnished, chalet-style, just above the railway. Sauna and massage.
★★★★Regina (856 5858) Grand Victorian hotel with piano bar, sun terrace, spa and fitness room – 'tremendous food and service though drinks are expensive'.
★★★★Silberhorn (856 5131) Comfortable, modern and central. 'Great views, quality five-course meals, and attractive spa.'
★★★★Sunstar (856 5200) Family-friendly, modern, on main street right opposite the cable car. 'Extremely welcoming, good rooms, pool a bit cool' is the verdict of a 2012 visitor.
★★★★Wengener Hof (856 6969) No prizes for style or convenience, but recommended for peace, helpful staff, spacious rooms with good views and 'exceptional food'.
★★★Alpenrose (855 3216) Long-standing British favourite; eight minutes' climb to the station.
★★★Belvédère (856 6868) Some way out, buffet-style meals, family-friendly, spacious rooms and grand art nouveau public rooms. 'Stylish and comfortable, lovely staff, good food.'
★★★Falken (856 5121) Further up the hill. Another British favourite.
Apartments The hotel Bernerhof's decent Résidence apartments are well positioned just off the main street, and the hotel facilities are available for guests to use.
At altitude You can stay at two points up the mountain reached by the railway: the expensive Jungfrau hotel

GETTING THERE

Air Zürich 155km/
95 miles (3hr); Bern
65km/40 miles (2hr);
Basel 160km/100
miles (2hr45)

Rail Station in resort

UK PACKAGES

Alpine Answers, Club
Med, Crystal, Crystal
Finest, Inghams,
Momentum, Neilson,
PowderBeds, Ski Club
Freshtracks, Ski Line,
Ski Solutions, Skitracer,
STC, Switzerland Travel
Centre, Thomson

ACTIVITIES

Indoor Swimming
pools (in hotels),
sauna, solarium,
whirlpool, massage
(in hotels)

Outdoor Ice rink,
curling, 100km of
cleared paths,
tobogganing,
paragliding,
snowshoeing

Phone numbers
From elsewhere in
Switzerland add the
prefix 033; from
abroad use the prefix
+41 33

TOURIST OFFICE

www.wengen.ch

(855 1622) at Wengernalp – with fabulous views – and at Kleine Scheidegg, where there are rooms in the big Bellevue des Alpes (855 1212) and dormitory space above the Grindelwaldblick restaurant (855 1374) and the station buffet.

EATING OUT ★★☆☆☆
Mainly hotel-based
Most restaurants are in hotels and offer good food and service. The Silberhorn offers varied and 'excellent' meals. The Bernerhof has good-value traditional dishes. The little hotel Hirschen offers speciality steaks. The hotel Regina's food is 'excellent but they won't serve tap water'. There's no shortage of fondues in the village, and several bars do casual food. Da Sina is a steakhouse and pizzeria. Cafe Gruebi is the place for cakes.

APRES-SKI ★★☆☆☆
It depends on what you want
People's reactions to Wengen's après-ski scene vary widely, according to their expectations and their appetites.

If you're used to raving in Kitzbühel or Les Deux-Alpes, you'll rate Wengen dead, especially for young people. If you've heard it's dead, you may be pleasantly surprised to find that there is a handful of small bars that do good business both early and late in the evening.

On the mountain, the outdoor Läger Bar, next to the Männlichen chair, is good for 'sitting in a deckchair in the sun'. Tipirama (a wigwam at Kleine Scheidegg) is a fun place immediately after skiing 'if not too cold', sometimes with DJs and live

bands; you can catch the train down. We've had mixed reviews of the Start Bar on the Lauberhorn ('tasty pancakes' but 'very unfriendly service'). The Wäsch bar at the Bumps section of the home run is a popular final-run stop-off.

In the village the tiny, 'pleasant' Pickel Bar is popular at the end of the day. The small, traditional Tanne is also recommended. Sina's, a little way out of the centre, next to the Club Med, 'is probably the best night time bar with DJ and karaoke'. The 'lively' Rocks Bar, with its plasma screens showing Sky Sports, has 'the best Guinness'. There are discos and live music in some hotels.

OFF THE SLOPES ★★★★☆
Good for a relaxing time
With its unbeatable scenery and pedestrian-friendly trains and cable car (there's a special – but pricey – pass for pedestrians), Wengen is a superb resort for those who want a relaxing holiday. It's easy for mixed parties of skiers and non-skiers to meet up for lunch on the mountain. There are some lovely walks ('paths are superbly signposted'), and ice skating, tobogganing ('well worth doing') and curling ('great fun') are popular. Several hotels have health spas. The cinema often shows films in English.

Excursions to Interlaken and Bern are possible by train, as is the trip up to the Jungfraujoch (see the Grindelwald chapter). From Männlichen there are scenic flights giving splendid close-up views of the mountains and glaciers, either by helicopter or much cheaper small plane.

THE BRITISH IN WENGEN

There's a very strong British presence in Wengen. Many Brits have been returning for years to the same rooms in the same hotels in the same week, and treat the resort as a sort of second home. There is an English church with weekly services, and a British-run ski club, the DHO (Downhill Only) – so named when the Brits who colonized the resort persuaded the locals to keep the summer railway running up the mountain in winter, so that they would no longer have to climb up in order to ski down again. That greatly amused the locals, who until then had regarded skiing in winter as a way to get around on snow rather than a pastime to be done for fun. The DHO is still going strong.

JUNGFRAU REGION MARKETING AG

Zermatt

A magical combination of just about everything you could hope to find in a ski resort, both on and off the slopes

RATINGS

The mountains

Extent	★★★★
Fast lifts	★★★★★
Queues	★★★
Terrain p'ks	★★★
Snow	★★★★
Expert	★★★★
Intermediate	★★★★
Beginner	★★
Boarder	★★★
X-country	★
Restaurants	★★★★★
Schools	★★★
Families	★★

The resort

Charm	★★★★
Convenience	★★
Scenery	★★★★★
Eating out	★★★★★
Après-ski	★★★★★
Off-slope	★★★★

RPI   140

lift pass	£270
ski hire	£140
lessons	£120
food & drink	£210
total	**£740**

NEWS

2013/14: The Sunnegga funicular is being upgraded, with bigger carriages and more of them. Snowmaking capacity is being increased.

2012/13: More snowmaking was added from Furi to town. Work started on a new run back to town from Sunnegga to replace the existing narrow path low down. The 4-star Alex Schlosshotel reopened after a refit.

➕ Wonderful, high, extensive slopes

➕ Spectacular high mountain scenery

➕ Charming although rather sprawling old village, largely traffic-free

➕ Reliable snow at altitude

➕ World's best mountain restaurants

➕ Nightlife to suit most tastes

➕ Lots to do off the slopes, from walking to shopping

➕ Linked to sunny Cervinia in Italy

➕ Extensive helicopter operation

➖ You may face long walks, crowded buses or pricey taxi rides

➖ Far from ideal for novices, despite recent efforts to improve matters

➖ High prices for everything, including lift pass (one of Europe's priciest)

➖ Slow train up to Gornergrat

➖ Some lift queues at peak periods

➖ Annoying electric taxis in 'car-free' streets detract from ambience

➖ Few options to ski in bad weather; can be really windy or cold too

Our verdict is short and simple: you must try Zermatt before you die. There is nowhere else to match it. Its drawbacks are non-trivial but, for us and for virtually all our reporters, these pale into insignificance compared with its attractions. Editor Watts has taken countless holidays here. Enough said.

THE RESORT

Zermatt started life as a simple farming village, developed as a mountaineering centre in the 19th century, then became a winter resort. Summer is still as big as winter here.

The village is car-free, but not traffic-free – electric buggies operating either as hotel shuttles or as public taxis zip around the streets. Residents can drive up to Zermatt, but the rest of us must park at Täsch (or more distant Visp) and arrive by train. At Täsch there's a big car park (14.50 francs a day) and you can wheel luggage trolleys on and off the trains.

Zermatt mainly attracts a well-heeled international clientele; the clientele is also relatively, er, mature for what is quite a sporty resort.

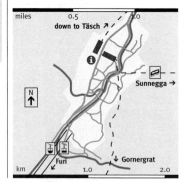

VILLAGE CHARM ★★★★
Old and new in harmony

The resort is a mixture of ancient chalets and barns, grand 19th-century hotels and modern buildings, most in traditional style but some decidedly funky. The oldest, most charming part of the village has narrow lanes and old wooden barns with slate roofs, many of them supported on stone 'legs'. But modern-day Zermatt sprawls along both sides of the river with a lot of new building at both ends and up the mountainsides that rise steeply on each side.

Arriving at the station, it all seems very towny, especially if there is no snow on the ground. The centre doesn't have the relaxed, rustic feel of other car-free Swiss resorts, such as Wengen and Saas-Fee. The main street running away from the station is lined with luxury hotels, restaurants, banks and glitzy shops. The electric taxis are intrusive, especially at busy times.

CONVENIENCE ★★
Lifts at opposite ends

The village is small enough to get around on foot in the evenings, but not in ski boots and carrying skis. There is a free ski-bus service; but it is inadequate at peak times, especially from the Matterhorn area at the end of the day. Electric taxis are pricey.

You arrive at a fair-sized square at

↑ Almost there ... last and possibly noisiest of the many possible stops on the home run from the glacial Matterhorn sector is Hennu Stall

SNOWPIX.COM / CHRIS GILL

KEY FACTS

Resort	1620m
	5,310ft

Zermatt only

Slopes	1620-3820m
	5,310-12,530ft
Lifts	33
Pistes	200km
	124 miles
Blue	16%
Red	61%
Black	23%
Snowmaking	70%

Zermatt-Cervinia-Valtournenche combined

Slopes	1525-3820m
	5,000-12,530ft
Lifts	54
Pistes	360km
	224 miles
Blue	21%
Red	61%
Black	18%
Snowmaking	61%

the north end of the resort, where you find ranks of electric taxis and hotel shuttles and horse-drawn sleighs.

The cog railway to the Gornergrat sector starts from near the main station. The Sunnegga underground funicular for the Rothorn sector is a few minutes' walk away, but the lifts to Furi and the other sectors (and the link to Cervinia) are over 1km away.

Staying near the lifts to Furi gives swift access to three of the four sectors. But a more central location can combine proximity to the Gornergrat and Sunnegga railways, and to most of the resort's shops, bars and restaurants.

Some accommodation is up the steep hill across the river in Winkelmatten, which has its own reliable bus service.

SCENERY ★★★★★
On a grand scale

Zermatt's emblematic, unmistakable Matterhorn is not visible from central parts of the village – if you want the famous view from your balcony, stay on the east side of the village, or at the south end – but once you are on the slopes its unreal profile dominates the views wherever you go. And the cable car trip up to the Klein Matterhorn opens up vast panoramas, as well as close-up glacier views.

THE MOUNTAINS

Practically all of the slopes are above the treeline – a run served by the Sunnegga funicular is the main exception, and once you pass below the Patrullarve chair this is mainly a path to the village.

A single piste map covers both Cervinia and Zermatt fairly clearly, and lists recommended 'ski safari' routes of either 10,500m or 12,500m vertical. Runs are numbered on the map and the ground (though only at the start). The map names runs, but not lifts.

In each sector there are runs, marked in yellow on the resort map and dotted on ours, called 'itineraries'. We'll call them itineraries. These runs are not patrolled, but this is not explained – a dangerous state of affairs. (The Cervinia map is clearer – it labels them as 'fuoripista', or off-piste, and 'freeride'.) Don't ski these runs alone, particularly late in the day.

On Thursdays, you can get first tracks from Trockener Steg. For 33 francs you can take the lift at 7.40am, about an hour ahead of the herd, ski deserted pistes for a while, then have a buffet breakfast at the Restaurant Les Marmottes. We prefer our daily routine of taking the 8am train to Gornergrat, to enjoy deserted pistes before the hordes get out of bed.

Build your own shortlist: **www.wheretoskiandsnowboard.com**

Once a month there are moonlight descents from Rothorn with the ski patrol, including a fondue at the restaurant at the top, at a cost of 70.50 francs.

Over recent years, service has improved to a high standard: polite and helpful lift staff; big boards at the bottom of each sector indicating which lifts and pistes are open in all sectors; useful announcements in English on the train and some cable cars; and free tissues at most lift stations.

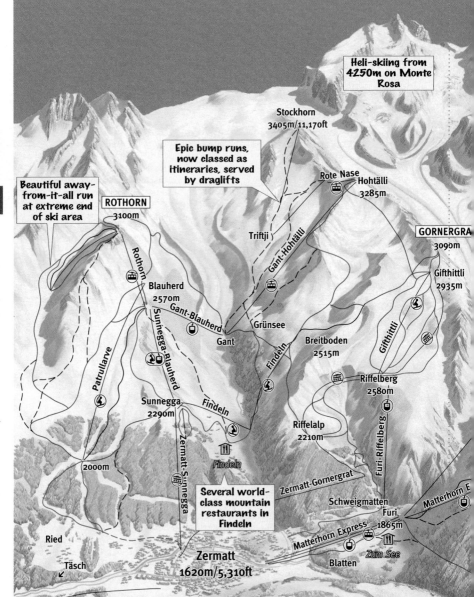

Heli-skiing from 4250m on Monte Rosa

Stockhorn 3405m/11,170ft

Epic bump runs, now classed as itineraries, served by draglifts

Rote Nase — Hohtälli 3285m

Beautiful away-from-it-all run at extreme end of ski area

ROTHORN 3100m

Triftji

Gant-Hohtälli

GORNERGRA 3090m

Rothorn

Blauherd 2570m

Gant-Blauherd

Grünsee

Gant

Gifthittli 2935m

Findeln

Breitboden 2515m

Gifthittli

Sunnegga-Blauherd

Patrullarve

Riffelberg 2580m

Findeln

Sunnegga 2290m

Riffelalp 2210m

Furi-Riffelberg

2000m

Zermatt-Sunnegga

Findeln

Several world-class mountain restaurants in Findeln

Zermatt-Gornergrat

Schweigmatten

Furi 1865m

Matterhorn E

Ried

Matterhorn Express

Zum See

Täsch

Zermatt 1620m/5,310ft

Blatten

EXTENT OF THE SLOPES ★★★★☆
Beautiful and varied

Zermatt's slopes divide naturally into four main sectors. The resort likes to identify more sectors on its maps.

The **Rothorn** sector is reached by an underground funicular (being increased in capacity this year) to Sunnegga, starting by the river, not far from the centre of the village. The main nursery area is just below Sunnegga, reached from there by a miniature funicular system. A hybrid chondola goes from Sunnegga to Blauherd, where a cable car goes up to Rothorn.

The second main area, **Gornergrat**, is reached from Zermatt by cog railway trains that take 30 or 40 minutes to the top – arrive at the station early to get a seat (best on the right-hand side to enjoy the fabulous views). We love getting the 8am train with the lifties and restaurant staff. It arrives at the top just as they drop the rope to open the pistes, and you have the slopes to yourself for an hour or two.

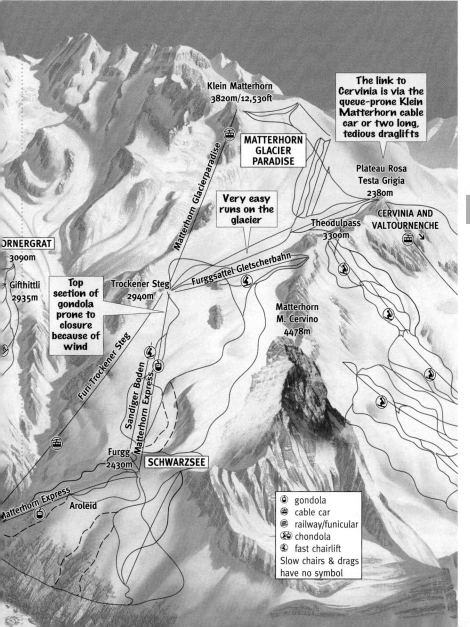

Klein Matterhorn
3820m/12,530ft

MATTERHORN GLACIER PARADISE

The link to Cervinia is via the queue-prone Klein Matterhorn cable car or two long, tedious draglifts

Plateau Rosa
Testa Grigia
2380m

Matterhorn Glacierparadise

Very easy runs on the glacier

Theodulpass
3300m

CERVINIA AND VALTOURNENCHE

GORNERGRAT
3090m

Gifthittli
2935m

Top section of gondola prone to closure because of wind

Trockener Steg
2940m

Furggsattel Gletscherbahn

Matterhorn
M. Cervino
4478m

Furi-Trockener Steg

Sandiger Boden

Matterhorn Express

Furgg
2430m

SCHWARZSEE

Matterhorn Express

Aroleid

- ⊚ gondola
- ⊞ cable car
- ⊛ railway/funicular
- ⊛⊚ chondola
- ④ fast chairlift
- Slow chairs & drags have no symbol

LIFT PASSES

Zermatt

Prices in francs

Age	1-day	6-day
under 16	38	186
16 to 19	64	315
20 to 64	75	371
65 plus	71	349

Free Under 9

Beginner Wolli Pass covering nursery area at Sunnegga

Notes
Covers Swiss side of the border; half-day passes and single-ascent tickets on some lifts

Alternative passes
International for Zermatt and Cervinia; International-Aosta for Zermatt and Cervinia plus 2 days in Val d'Aosta; Peak Pass for pedestrians

The Rothorn and Gornergrat sectors, separated by the Findel valley, are linked by pistes and itineraries descending to two lift stations.

The Matterhorn Express gondola from the south end of the village goes first to Furi (where you can change to another gondola to go to Riffelberg, for Gornergrat) and on to the small but worthwhile **Schwarzsee** area. The same gondola goes on up to Trockener Steg, focal point of the fourth sector, the super-high **Matterhorn Glacier Paradise**. This can also be reached by a jumbo cable car from Furi – quicker if you time it right, and less affected by wind. Above Trockener Steg another cable car makes a spectacular ascent to Klein Matterhorn. At the top, you walk through a long tunnel to the highest piste in Europe. From the glacier there are two ways to Cervinia.

There are pistes back to the village from all sectors – though some can be closed or tricky due to poor snow conditions (and crowds).

FAST LIFTS ★★★★★
Now top-notch
All Zermatt's four sectors are well-connected by fast chairs, gondolas, big cable cars or mountain railways. There are of course slow lifts in places, but most can be avoided. The low speed of the Gornergrat train is just something you have to accept.

QUEUES ★★★★★
Main problems being solved
Zermatt has improved its lift system hugely in recent years, eliminating major bottlenecks. Again, all this year's reporters are generally positive, but a couple of problems remain.

There may be queues to get up to the Matterhorn sector, and the gondola to Trockener Steg is prone to closure in high winds, putting pressure on the alternative cable car in these conditions. The Klein Matterhorn cable car often has serious queues in good weather (up to an hour mid-morning; quieter in the afternoon). One regular reporter recommends jumping these queues occasionally by splashing out for a 20-minute bottom-to-top heli-lift incorporating a close-up tour of the Matterhorn – 'fantastic; one of the highlights of my life'. But it is now hugely expensive.

A real bottleneck is Gant in the Findel valley – notably the old, slow gondola to Blauherd. Half-hour waits are common here in high season. There are plans to construct a piste from Gant down the valley to the Findeln chairlift so that the gondola can be retired, maybe in 2014.

The Sunnegga underground funicular is being upgraded to carry more people this year.

The top section of piste from Hohtälli can get dangerously busy.

TERRAIN PARKS ★★★★★
Things are getting better
Gravity Park, next to the Furggsattel six-seat chair was redone for 2012 with a variety of jumps, rails, a half-pipe and big rollers. One reporter this year said the park was 'well received, but less funky than Verbier', while another notes: 'It is far away and very cold if the weather is at all bad.' In the summer, the park moves up to Plateau Rosa where a six-man crew shape the 600m park daily. A nicely integrated 120m-long super-pipe sits next to an array of kickers, rails, a quarter-pipe, wall ride, mail box and tree jib.

SNOW RELIABILITY ★★★★★
Generally good
Zermatt has rocky terrain and a relatively dry climate. But it also has some of the highest slopes in Europe. As well as the glacier, two other sectors go over 3000m, and there are loads of runs above 2500m, many of which are north-facing.

On repeated March visits we have been impressed by the snowmaking, in all four sectors, on pistes from above 3000m down to resort level. Piste grooming is generally excellent.

FOR EXPERTS ★★★★★
Head off-piste
There is some great off-piste when conditions are right, and the off-piste itineraries include some excellent runs – read our feature panel. But Zermatt

Zermatt offers a wide variety of off-piste runs for all abilities, from off-piste beginner to expert. And if the runs reached from the lift system aren't enough, heli-skiing is available (and popular).

Zermatt's 'itineraries' (explained under 'The mountains') open up a lot of terrain to explore without needing guidance. If you love long mogul pitches, those on the Stockhorn are the stuff of dreams. Being north-facing and high, this area keeps good snow long after a new snowfall (but it needs deep snow, and does not normally open until February, or even March). The itineraries carry on down below the Triftji T-bar to Gant, but snow quality can deteriorate on this lower part. There are excellent itineraries in other sectors, too – though again they generally need good snow-cover to be really enjoyable. Our own favourites include the two wonderful runs from Rothorn (16 and 17), with spectacular views. A recent visitor particularly liked 10 from Blauherd to Findeln. The runs in the Schwarzsee sector – 58, 59 and 60 – are steeper, shadier and narrower than most.

Away from the marked runs, there are marvellous off-piste possibilities from the top lifts in each sector, but they are dangerous, because of rocky and glacial terrain; guidance is essential. Stockhorn is a great starting point; descending towards Gant, one special run goes down 'the lost valley'; going in the other direction, there is an excellent descent to the Gornergletscher, ending at Furi. Be warned: getting off the glacier may involve narrow rocky paths above long drops, or side-stepping down steep slopes, depending on snow levels (we've encountered both). In the Schwarzsee sector there are many good slopes, including 'innru waldieni', right under the Matterhorn, reached from the Hörnli T-bar.

Zermatt is the Alps' biggest heli-skiing centre; at times the helipad has choppers taking off every few minutes. There are only a few drop points. The classic run is from over 4250m on Monte Rosa and descends over 2300m vertical through wonderful glacier scenery to Furi; note our warning above.

doesn't get huge snowfall, so you can't always count on good conditions, particularly early in the season. The handful of black runs are not worthy of their classification; the one with the steepest pitches (Blauherd-Patrullarve) is also very wide.

FOR INTERMEDIATES ★★★★☆
Mile after mile of beautiful runs
Zermatt is ideal for adventurous intermediates. Many of the blue runs tend to be at the difficult end of their classification. Reds vary unhelpfully: some are quite tough; some ought to be blue. Few are really what you might call 'cruising' runs.

Among our favourites in the Gornergrat sector are the very beautiful reds down lift-free valleys from both Gornergrat (Kelle) and Hohtälli (White Hare) to Breitboden – we love these first thing in the morning, before anyone else is on them. The steepest part of Kelle is classified black, but an easier red variant bypasses it. From Breitboden you can go on down to Gant, or to the mid-station of the Findeln chairlift, or to Riffelalp on a run that includes a narrow wooded path with a sheer cliff and magnificent views to the right.

On the Rothorn sector, the 5km Kumme/Tufternkumme run – from Rothorn itself to the Patrullarve chair – also gets away from the lift system

and has an interesting mix of straight-running and mogul pitches (but it gets a lot of sun and lacks snowmaking).

In the Matterhorn Glacier Paradise sector the reds served by the fast quad chair from Furgg are gloriously set at the foot of the Matterhorn. The Furggsattel chair from Trockener Steg serves more pistes with stunning views, notably the Matterhorn piste – blue in gradient for most of its great length, but classified red because of a short, steep pitch near the end that causes problems for many skiers.

For timid intermediates, the best runs are the blues from Blauherd on Rothorn, and above Riffelberg on Gornergrat, and in good weather the super-high runs between Klein Matterhorn and Trockener Steg. Of these, the Riffelberg area often has the best combination of good snow and easy cruising, and is understandably popular with the ski schools.

In the Matterhorn Glacier Paradise sector most of the runs, though marked red on the piste map, are very flat and include the easiest slopes Zermatt has to offer, as well as the best snow. Even an early intermediate can make the trip to Cervinia, via Theodulpass rather than the more challenging run from Plateau Rosa.

Beware the black run from Furgg to Furi at the end of the day. It is not steep, but gets chopped up, mogulled in places and very crowded. A much more relaxed alternative is the scenic Weisse Perle run from Schwarzsee (the Stafelalp variant is even more scenic but has a short uphill section). The final red run from Furi to the village gets unpleasantly crowded.

runs is awkward – the slopes as a whole are very challenging for near-beginners, which includes fast learners who are ready to quit the nursery slopes after a couple of days. Of course, you can learn to ski here, but given a choice we would go elsewhere.

FOR BEGINNERS ★★✩✩✩
Still far from ideal
These days the resort makes an effort to cater for beginners – there are beginner areas dotted around on all four sectors, and a main one has been developed (with three moving carpets and two rope tows) at Leisee, just below Sunnegga, reached from there by a short funicular. There is now a half-price pass to get you to and from that area, which is a step forward. But some readers judge this small area inadequate. And progression to longer

FOR BOARDERS ★★★✩✩
Some good angles
The slopes are best for experienced freeriders and there's a terrain park above Trockener Steg. There are adequate beginner areas, complete with moving carpet lifts, where we've seen many beginner snowboarders. The main lifts are boarder-friendly: train, funicular, gondolas, cable cars and fast chairs. There aren't too many flat bits, but a reader identifies runs 52 and 69 as problems. Stoked is a specialist school.

THE WORLD'S BEST MOUNTAIN RESTAURANTS ★★★★★

The choice of restaurants is enormous, the standard (and prices) high. We list here only a selection. It is best to book – as a reader notes this year, this is not a resort where it is always easy to just stop for a bite when you are hungry. Restaurants are marked on the piste map, but only isolated places are explicitly named. The tourist office restaurant directory has photos, and clues about the style of food, but does not indicate prices. Beware: some places don't take cards.

Below Sunnegga, at Findeln, are several attractive, expensive, rustic restaurants sharing a great Matterhorn view. A return visit confirms Chez Vrony (967 2552) as one of our favourites, endorsed this year by several readers; service can be stretched but is reliably friendly, and the food excellent. They added 45 seats last season, some on an additional third floor. Readers also recommend the nearby Adler (967 1058), with its outdoor BBQ ('delicious food', 'impeccable service'), Findlerhof (967 2588) ('wonderful pasta with mussels') and Paradies (967 3451).

Further up the Findel valley, in splendid isolation, Fluhalp (967 2597) is another favourite; excellent food and service, often with live music on the huge terrace – enthusiastically endorsed by three readers this year. Up at Blauherd, Blue Lounge is a cool modern bar with lots of sofas, serving tapas and 'great burgers' to jazz and other music. Lower down, Tufternalp famously does 'slabs of bread and cheese on a terrace with a great view'; see if you can get a smile out of the 'distinctly grumpy' old blokes who run it.

At Trockener Steg we love the Ice Pizzeria (967 1812) – a smart, modern table-service place with great views; delicious pizzas, as readers agree. The higher Gandegghütte (079 607 8868) has stunning views and good, simple food; but no milk, so no hot choc. Over at Schwarzsee, the Stafelalp (967 3062) is a reader favourite – glorious position, 'interesting food,' 'great service'.

At Furi, restaurant Furri (966 2777) offers 'a really friendly welcome and good food' and the 'always welcoming' Simi (967 2695), tucked away a bit lower down, does 'great grills on its open fire'. Just above Furi, Aroleid (967 2658) is recommended for rösti, and hotel Silvana (966 2800) is 'spacious, with good food, decent value'. Below Furi are countless places to pause on the way home. Zum See (967 2045) is a charming old hut, and among the best restaurants on the mountain. Blatten (967 2096) serves 'one of the best strudels'.

SNOWPIX.COM / CHRIS GILL

Views that exclude the Matterhorn and restaurants are rare; this is Furgg, below the glacier →
KERRY LEWIS

SCHOOLS

Swiss (Matterhorn)
t 966 2466
Stoked
t 967 7020
Summit
t 967 0001
European Snowsport
t 967 6787
Adventure
t 967 5020
Almrausch
t 967 0808
AER
t 967 7067
Prato Borni
t 967 5115

Classes (Swiss prices)
5 days (10am to 3.30
with lunch break) 350
francs
Private lessons
170 francs for 2hr for
1 or 2 people

GUIDES

Alpin Center
t 966 2460

CHILDCARE

Kinderparadies
t 967 7252
Ages from 3mnth
Kidactive
t 077 405 3957
**Kinderclub Pumuckel
(Hotel Ginabelle)**
t 966 5000
Ages from 30mnth
Schwarzsee (Stoked)
t 967 7020
Ages from 30mnth
**Nico Kids Club
(Schweizerhof hotel)**
t 966 0000
Ages from 2 to 8
Snowli Village (Swiss)
t 966 2466
Ages 4 to 5
Private babysitters
List at tourist office

Ski school
Ages 6 to 14

FOR CROSS-COUNTRY ★☆☆☆☆
Down the valley
There are 17km of trails from Täsch to Randa (but don't count on good snow at these altitudes).

SCHOOLS AND GUIDES ★★★☆☆
Competition paying off
The main Swiss school – once a real embarrassment – seems to have improved since competing schools were permitted, and our most recent reports have been positive. Of the other schools, Summit and European Snowsport are staffed mainly by Brits. We've had mixed reports on Summit recently – some criticisms of beginner lessons, but enthusiasm for an intermediate class. Stoked snowboard school is made up of young instructors, some of whom are British and all of whom speak good English. Again, we have had mixed reports. The two reports we have had on Prato Borni have been very positive.

FOR FAMILIES ★★☆☆☆
Good hotel nurseries
The prices, the general inconvenience of the place and the challenges facing beginners and near-beginners all work against families. But, as our margin panel shows, there are plenty of facilities for children and we don't doubt that they are thoroughly well run. The tourist office has a list of babysitters. And families do have successful holidays here, some repeatedly. 'Choose your location with care,' says one reader. Another notes that the number of hotels offering family suites is a plus-point.

STAYING THERE

Chalets Several operators have places here; many of the most comfortable are in apartment blocks. Ski Total has a remarkable portfolio – at the last count 13 properties – mostly with six or eight beds, a couple with more and some with sauna, steam room or hot tub. Skiworld has five chalet-apartments, including three very smart modern ones in the same building. Inghams has four chalets sleeping from 6 to 16, plus a chalet hotel. Supertravel has a handful of places.
Hotels There are over 100 hotels, mostly traditional-style 3-stars and 4-stars, but taking in the whole range. What distinguishes Zermatt is the number of 'hip' places, some of which are listed below.
*****Mont Cervin (966 8888) Biggest in town and entirely renovated in 2012. Pool etc. We enjoyed a stay here in 2013 – it's now a perfect blend of tradition and modern style.
*****Omnia (966 7171) Designer hotel, minimalist, central, reached by a lift in the rock, smart fitness centre.
****Alex (966 7070) Close to train stations. An old favourite, though no recent reports. Large pool, sauna.
****Beau Site (966 6868) Grand place over the river with Matterhorn views. Traditional.
****Cervo (968 1212) Hip place with rooms, suites, chalets for up to 10. At the end of the piste from Sunnegga.
****'Europe (966 2700) Superb place over the river from the church, with fab modern rooms in new extension. We stayed here in 2011.

****Matterhorn Focus** (966 2424) Super-stylish B&B designed by Heinz Julen, right by the Matterhorn lifts.

****Mirabeau** (966 2660) Heartily tipped by two reporters in 2011 – 'outstanding food, friendly staff, excellent spa – made our holiday'.

****Monte Rosa** (966 0333) Well-modernized original Zermatt hotel in centre; full of climbing mementos. 'Wonderful,' says a 2011 report.

****Sonne** (966 2066) In quiet setting; 'superb' spa. 'Great food, and the staff couldn't do enough for us.'

****Sunstar Style** (966 5666) Recent addition to the Sunstar group and

renovated in 2012. Modern decor. Pool, spa.

****Walliserhof** (966 6555) Good past reports, and recommended this year – 'convenient, very friendly, good food, spacious rooms'. Mini-spa.

***Alpenroyal** (966 6066) 'Good value, comfortable, staff friendly, good food.'

***Continental** (966 2840) Central and great value; fantastic food and friendly staff – we stayed here in 2013.

Atlanta (966 3535) Good past reports, and tipped this year for 'excellent value, great staff, rooms and food'. Good position, too.

*Bahnhof** (967 2406) Basic place with various forms of accommodation. No meals, but 'very clean, well equipped kitchen for self-catering'.

Apartments There are lots. We have repeatedly enjoyed staying in the amazingly cheap apartments of the hotel Ambassador (966 2611), with free use of pool and sauna, but they are overdue for a refurb.

At altitude There are several hotels on the hill, and they are not your regular mountain refuges. The pick is the 5-star Riffelalp Resort (966 0555), at the first stop on the Gornergrat railway, with pool, spa and its own evening trains. Highly recommended – luxurious, but 'not at all stuffy'. We fancy staying a couple of nights at the Kulmhotel Gornergrat (966 6400) at the top of the mountain – the highest hotel in Switzerland.

EATING OUT ★★★★★
Huge choice

There are over 100 restaurants to choose from: top-quality haute cuisine, through traditional Swiss food, Chinese, Japanese and Thai, to egg and chips. There is even a McDonald's. The tourist office produces a directory, with photos. One reader reckons that you pay a lot less in restaurants at the south end of the village, well away from the centre.

At the top end of the market, the Mont Cervin's Ristorante Capri was awarded a Michelin star in 2011. One regular visitor tips the cool hotel Cervo ('exceptional – excellent food, very smart, nice small dining rooms, impeccable service'), Heimberg ('continues to be fab'), Omnia ('Bond-like experience – wonderful decor, interesting food and wine') and Chez Gaby ('great grilled food, prawns, etc').

At more modest prices, we've enjoyed the Schwyzer Stübli (local

SNOWPIX.COM / CHRIS GILL

Better than your average park bench view; this is from Schwarzsee ↓

UK PACKAGES

Alpine Answers, Alpine Weekends, Carrier, Crystal, Crystal Finest, Elegant Resorts, Elysian Collection, Erna Low, Flexiski, Independent Ski Links, Inghams, Interactive Resorts, Kaluma, Lagrange, Luxury Chalet Collection, Momentum, Mountain Beds, Mountain Exposure, Mountain Tracks, Neilson, Oxford Ski Co, PowderBeds, Powder Byrne, Pure Powder, Scott Dunn, Ski Bespoke, Ski Club Freshtracks, Ski Expectations, Ski Independence, Ski Line, Ski Monterosa, Ski Safari, Ski Solutions, Ski Total, Skitracer, Skiweekends.com, Skiworld, Snow Finders, STC, Supertravel, Switzerland Travel Centre, Thomson, VIP, White Roc, Zenith

GETTING THERE

Air Geneva 240km/ 150 miles (4hr); Zürich 265km/ 165 miles (4hr30); Sion 80km/ 50 miles (2hr)

Rail Station in resort

ACTIVITIES

Indoor Hotel saunas and swimming pools (some open to public), climbing wall, museums, cinema

Outdoor Ice rinks, curling, 50km cleared paths, snowshoeing, tobogganing, helicopter flights, ice climbing, paragliding

Phone numbers
From elsewhere in Switzerland add the prefix 027; from abroad use the prefix +41 27

TOURIST OFFICE

www.zermatt.ch

specialities and live Swiss music and dancing), good-value Mexican and Swiss dishes at the Weisshorn and decent Thai food at Rua Thai. Sparky's pub/restaurant has been praised for its 'basic but nourishing food', which includes vegetarian options, stews and curries. The Pipe serves interesting Asian/African fusion dishes but we lack reports since it relocated in 2010. 'Absolutely rammed' Grampi's has been tipped repeatedly for 'very good simple food, good service'.

Other reader tips include: Klein Matterhorn for fish/pasta; Schäferstube ('some of the best lamb dishes in the village'); Stockhorn ('generous portions, delicious venison'); and the dear old Whymper-Stube.

APRES-SKI ★★★★★
Something for everybody
There's a good mix of sophisticated and informal fun, though it helps if you have deep pockets. Promenading the main street checking out expensive clothes and watches is a popular early-evening activity.

There are lively places to pause on your final descent. On the way back from Rothorn, Othmar's Skihütte and Olympia Stübli have great views, and the funky Cervo where the piste ends has a popular outdoor bar with live music. Caffè Snowboat (near the Sunnegga funicular) is a small, modern place that looks like, er, a boat with a deck and lounge bar. On the way back from Furi there are lots of options, some described under 'Mountain restaurants'. Very near the end of the run, Hennu Stall blasts out loud music and attracts huge crowds – live bands play most days.

For a lively bar through the evening you won't beat the revamped Papperla Pub. The long-established North Wall doesn't get many mentions in reports but still seems to be the season-worker favourite. Potters Bar (geddit?) is a relaxed British pub.

There are plenty of quieter places. The Vernissage is our favourite – unusual, stylish and modern, with the projection room for the cinema built into the upstairs bar and displays of art elsewhere; 'great ambience and decor'. Elsie's famous wood-panelled bar continues to please our more mature readers ('much enjoyed for its cosy traditional ambience and excellent wine'); it gets seriously busy early and late. Reader tips include Brit-run Sparky's ('best priced beer in town'), the Little Bar (crowded if there are 10 people in) and the cosy/ cramped Hexen. Of the hotel bars, the Alex has comfy sofas, good service and a pool table and the Pollux is 'reliably good'.

Later on, the hotel Post complex has something for everyone, from a quiet, comfortable bar (Papa Caesar's) to a lively disco (Broken), live music (Pink) and various restaurants. The T-Bar draws a young crowd for dancing and bands. At Grampi's ('very lively later in the evening'), there is a disco below. The Schneewittchen nightclub (at the Papperla) is very popular.

OFF THE SLOPES ★★★★☆
Considerable attractions
Zermatt is an attractive place to spend time. As well as expensive jewellery and clothes shops, there are interesting places selling food, wine, books and art. It is easy (but costly) for pedestrians to get around on the lifts and meet others for lunch, and there are some splendid walks (70km) – a special map is available.

If the weather is good, the Klein Matterhorn cable car is an experience not to be missed: there is a small self-service restaurant at the top as well as a viewing platform and an ice cave, with 'incredible carvings'. Be aware that the air is thin up there, though.

The Matterhorn Museum in the village is well worth a visit. You can take a helicopter trip around the Matterhorn (see 'Queues'). There is a cinema, and free village guided tours. For an icy experience, visit (or stay at) the Igloo above Riffelberg. It's easy to visit various Swiss cities by rail.

DOWN-VALLEY VILLAGE – 1450m

TÄSCH

Täsch, where visitors must leave their cars, is just a 12-minute train ride from Zermatt, so it makes a viable base. There are several 3-star hotels charging half the Zermatt price. The Täscherhof (966 6262) and Walliserhof (966 3966) ('nice and friendly, very good chef') have been recommended by reporters. Täsch is very quiet in the evening, but it's no problem to spend evenings in Zermatt – trains run until 12.30am Monday to Wednesday, and hourly all night from Thursday to Sunday. And taxis can operate up to the edge of Zermatt.

Most people who give it a try find America is pretty seductive, despite the relatively small sizes of its ski areas. What got the US started in the UK market was its (generally) reliable snow, and that remains a key factor. Other factors are the relatively deserted pistes, the high quality of accommodation, the excellent and varied resort restaurants, the high standards of service and courtesy, and the immaculate piste grooming. Depending on the resort, you may also be struck by the cute Wild West ambience and the superb quality of the snow. Of course, US skiing does have disadvantages, too. Not least of which is the cost – long-haul air fares have risen and local prices are high (all US resorts fall into our red category – the most expensive – for their RPI and eight out of the ten priciest resorts in the book are American).

We have organized our US chapters in regional sections – California, Colorado, Utah, Rest of the West and New England.

Most American resorts receive serious amounts of snow – typically in the region of 6m to 12m (or 250 to 500 inches, as they measure it there) in a season; that's around double the 3m to 6m that resorts like Chamonix, St Anton and Val d'Isère in Europe average. It tends to arrive in more frequent falls than in Europe, too, so your chances of hitting fresh snow are appreciably higher. And most resorts have serious snowmaking facilities that are used well – laying down a base of snow early in the season rather than patching up shortages later. There are wide differences in quantity and quality of snowfall, both between individual resorts and between regions.

The classification of pistes (or trails, to use the local term) is different from that in Europe. Red runs don't exist. The colours used are combined with shapes. Green circles correspond fairly closely to greens in France and easy blues in the rest of Europe. American blue squares correspond to blues and easy reds in Europe; the tougher ones are sometimes labelled as double squares, or as blue-black squares. Then there are black-diamond runs, which is where things get interesting. Single diamonds correspond fairly closely to European blacks and really tough reds. But then there are

PATROLLED AND AVALANCHE-CONTROLLED OFF-PISTE

One of the great attractions of North American resorts to us is that they have patrolled and avalanche-controlled ungroomed terrain that would be classified as off-piste in Europe. Each resort has a 'ski area boundary'; this may be marked by signs on the trees bordering the trails or there may be a rope running right round the ski area boundary. The 'boundary' may be moved depending on snow conditions, and anywhere within the boundary is known as 'in-bounds' and is patrolled and avalanche controlled. In-bounds terrain includes areas between marked and groomed trails and often big areas of ski-anywhere bowls or steep couloirs (or chutes, to use the local term). In Europe such terrain is normally off-piste, and we recommend you ski it only with a qualified local guide; in North America it is safe to ski it without that expense. North America also has what it calls backcountry, which is the area outside the ski area boundary (and which you are often forbidden to access except through gates placed at various points on the boundary). This is not controlled or patrolled and should be treated like European off-piste and skied only with a guide.

ASPEN / SNOWMASS / DANIEL BAYER

← Don't worry: most US slopes aren't this steep. These are some of Aspen Highlands' double-black-diamond runs – steeper than almost any pistes you'd get in Europe

multiple diamonds. Double-diamond runs are seriously steep – usually steeper than the steepest pistes in the Alps. A few resorts have wildly steep 'extreme' double diamonds, or triple diamonds.

The most obvious drawback to the US is that many resorts have slopes that are very modest in extent compared with major Alpine areas. But usually there are other resorts nearby – so if you are prepared to travel a bit, you won't get bored. Roads are good, and car hire is relatively cheap (watch out for extra insurance charges, though). But if snow is expected, you will need a 4WD or snow chains (you'll have to buy them – we've yet to find a US rental company that will provide them). It's also true that in many resorts the mountains are slightly monotonous, with countless similar trails cut through the forest. You don't usually get the spectacular mountain scenery and the distinctive high-mountain runs of the Alps. But the forest runs do offer good visibility in bad weather, and unlike in Europe, it's normal to be able to ski in among the trees themselves (or glades as they call them) – great fun in fresh snow.

GREAT GROOMING AND DESERTED SLOPES
Piste grooming is taken very seriously – most US resorts set standards that only the best Alpine resorts seem to be able to match. Every morning you can expect to step out on to perfect 'corduroy' pistes. But this doesn't mean that there aren't moguls – far from it. It's just that you get moguls where the resort says you can expect moguls, not everywhere.

The slopes of most US resorts are blissfully free of crowds – a key advantage that becomes more important as the pistes of Europe become ever more congested. If you want to ski quickly and safely with less fear of collisions, head for the States.

Ski schools offer consistently high standards but, unlike in Europe, people don't sign up for a week, only for one or two lessons as they feel the need. Most resorts offer free guided tours of the ski area once or twice a day (usually carried out by volunteers who get a free lift pass in return); and many have 'mountain hosts' on hand to help you find your way. Piste maps are freely available at lift stations, and signposting is generally exemplary.

Lifts are generally efficient, and queues are orderly and short, partly because spare seats are religiously filled with the aid of cheerful, conscientious attendants who ask 'How are you today?' or urge you to 'Have a nice day' every time you get on a lift. You'll also find that Americans on chairlifts with you will be keen to talk to you on the way – weird to Europeans, but we like it. First-time visitors are surprised that some chairlifts in the States do not have safety bars; even on a chair that has a bar, you will find Americans curiously reluctant to use it, and eager to raise it as soon as the top station is in view. They worry about being trapped, not falling off. The lifts close irritatingly early – as early as 3pm in some cases (and some upper lifts might start closing as early as 1.30pm). That may explain another drawback of America – the dearth of decent mountain restaurants. The norm is a monster (but crowded) self-service refuelling station – designed to minimize time off the slopes.

US resort towns vary widely in style and convenience, from cute restored mining towns to purpose-built monstrosities. Two important things the resorts have in common are high-quality, spacious accommodation and restaurants that are reliably good and varied in cuisine. Young people should be aware that the rigorously

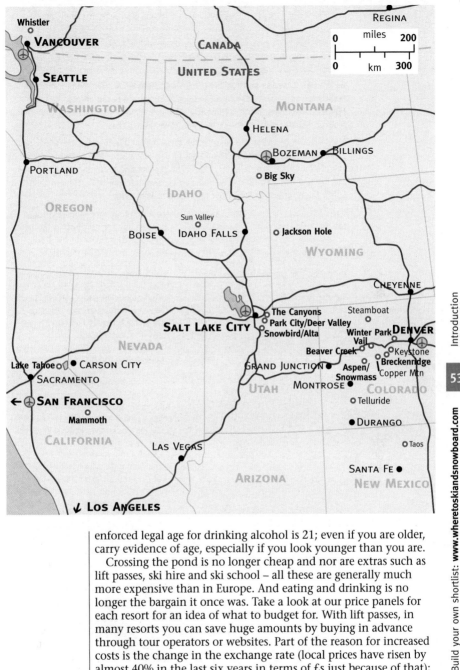

enforced legal age for drinking alcohol is 21; even if you are older, carry evidence of age, especially if you look younger than you are.

Crossing the pond is no longer cheap and nor are extras such as lift passes, ski hire and ski school – all these are generally much more expensive than in Europe. And eating and drinking is no longer the bargain it once was. Take a look at our price panels for each resort for an idea of what to budget for. With lift passes, in many resorts you can save huge amounts by buying in advance through tour operators or websites. Part of the reason for increased costs is the change in the exchange rate (local prices have risen by almost 40% in the last six years in terms of £s just because of that); and maybe increased costs is one reason why we are now receiving fewer reader reports on US resorts than we used to.

In the end, your reaction to skiing and snowboarding in America may depend on your reaction to America. If repeated exhortations to have a nice day wind you up – or if you like to ride chairlifts in silence – you'd better stick to the Alps. We love skiing there.

California? It means surfing, beaches, wine, Hollywood, Disneyland and San Francisco cable cars. Nevada means gambling. But this region also has the highest mountains in the continental USA and some of America's biggest winter resorts, usually reliable for snow from November to May.

Most visitors head for the Lake Tahoe area, mapped below. Spectacularly set high in the Sierra Nevada 320km east of San Francisco, Lake Tahoe is ringed by skiable mountains containing 14 downhill resorts and 7 cross-country centres – the highest concentration of winter sports resorts in the USA. Then, a long way south (more often reached from LA), there is Mammoth.

Each of the three major 'destination' resorts – Heavenly and Squaw Valley, at opposite ends of Lake Tahoe, and Mammoth, way off our map to the south – is covered in its own chapter following this page. The other main Lake Tahoe resorts (shown on our map) each have an entry in the resort directory at the back of the book. Many are well worth visiting for a day or two, especially the four second-division resorts – Alpine Meadows (next door to Squaw and now in the same ownership with a shared pass), Kirkwood, Northstar and Sierra-at-Tahoe. We have also enjoyed Sugar Bowl and Mount Rose.

Californian resorts often have the deepest accumulations of snow in North America, which Rockies powder connoisseurs are inclined to brand as wet 'Sierra Cement'. The snow can be heavy. But mostly the snow is fine, at least by Alpine standards – we've had truly fabulous powder days in all the major resorts here.

Californian resorts don't have the traditional mountain-town ambience that can add an extra dimension to holidays in other parts of the States, particularly Colorado. The recently developed car-free plaza in South Lake Tahoe called Heavenly Village and the pedestrian Village at Mammoth – both linked to the slopes above by gondola – haven't achieved a great deal in this respect. But Squaw Valley and Northstar have both developed more substantial base villages.

You could visit all the Tahoe resorts by car (best to have a 4WD) from a single base at Heavenly or somewhere thereabouts; but a two-centre holiday also including some time at the north end of the lake would be better. A six-pack of lift tickets covering seven resorts around the lake is available (go to www.skilaketahoe.com).

The drives from major airports are non-trivial. Consider taking onward flights to Reno (for Tahoe) and Mammoth Yosemite.

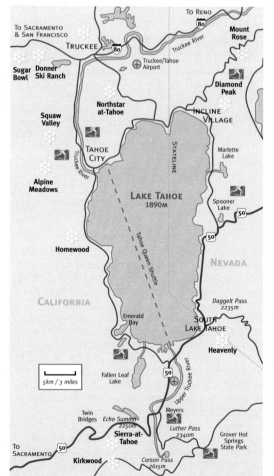

Heavenly

Heavenly is unique: one of America's biggest mountains, with fabulous lake and 'desert' views, above a tacky casino town

RATINGS

The mountains

Extent	★★★
Fast lifts	★★★★
Queues	★★★★
Terrain p'ks	★★★★★
Snow	★★★★
Expert	★★★
Intermediate	★★★★
Beginner	★★★★
Boarder	★★★★
X-country	★★
Restaurants	★
Schools	★★★★
Families	★★

The resort

Charm	★
Convenience	★
Scenery	★★★★
Eating out	★★★★
Après-ski	★★★
Off-slope	★★★

RPI 165

lift pass	£350
ski hire	£125
lessons	£195
food & drink	£170
total	**£840**

NEWS

2013/14: Activities at Adventure Peak are being expanded to include two rope courses, a canopy tour and a zipline centre.

2012/13: A half-pipe was built for the first time in five years. Booyah's, a sports and burger bar, opened in Lakeview Lodge, at the top of the cable car from California Lodge.

- ➕ Spectacular views of Lake Tahoe and Nevada from slopes
- ➕ Fair-sized mountain that offers a sensation of travelling around
- ➕ Large areas of widely spaced trees – fabulous in fresh powder
- ➕ Some serious challenges for experts
- ➕ Other worthwhile resorts reachable
- ➕ Good snow and snowmaking
- ➕ Unique nightlife in town at base

- ➖ Town at base, South Lake Tahoe, is a messy, traffic-ridden place
- ➖ No trail back to central SLT
- ➖ Lifts vulnerable to wind closure
- ➖ Pronounced step from easy groomed blues to mogulled blacks
- ➖ If natural snow is poor, most of the challenging terrain may be closed
- ➖ Mountain restaurants dire
- ➖ Very little traditional après-ski

With a top height of 3060m and vertical of 1060m, Heavenly is the highest and biggest of the resorts around famously deep, pure and beautiful Lake Tahoe. It has the best lake views, too. But anyone drawn by the scenic setting is likely to be dismayed by the barren base town of South Lake Tahoe, straddling busy US Highway 50. You could stay out of town, close to one of the other lift bases.

And the skiing? If your taste is for easy Alpine blacks or tough reds, just be sure you are ready to step up to ungroomed stuff – you'll find the blues tame.

THE RESORT

South Lake Tahoe, on the shore of the lake, is primarily a summer resort. It straddles the California-Nevada border, and its economy is based on gambling, which Nevada permits. The central Stateline area is dominated by a handful of high-rise hotel-casinos on the Nevada side of the line.

These brash but comfortable hotels offer good-value rooms (subsidized by the gambling), swanky restaurants and various entertainments. Picking your way between the slot machines in ski gear, carrying skis or board, is weird.

Near the casino area is the small Heavenly Village, purpose-built around the main lift base. There are other lift base areas (with lodgings) on both the

On the back side of the hill, the views are of parched Nevada – officially classified as a desert ➔

KEY FACTS

Resort	1900m
	6,230ft
Slopes	2000-3060m
	6,570-10,040ft
Lifts	29
Pistes	4,800 acres
Green	20%
Blue	45%
Black	35%
Snowmaking	73%

California and Nevada sides of the hill.

Other resorts around the lake are easily visited, and lift passes that cover several areas are available. A car is handy to explore them (although buses, some free, are available) and to get to many of the best restaurants, but parking can be expensive.

The obvious gateway airport is San Francisco, but Reno is much closer, and the road up less likely to be affected by snow.

VILLAGE CHARM ★☆☆☆☆
The highway rules
From a distance the casinos look like a classic American downtown area, which you'd expect to be full of shops and bars. But there's hardly any of that – just the seriously busy and pedestrian-hostile Highway 50. The rest of the town spreads for miles along the road – dozens of low-rise hotels and motels (some quite shabby), stores, wedding chapels and so on. The general effect is less dire than it might be, thanks to the camouflage of tall trees. Heavenly Village provides a downtown après-ski focus (basically just one bar), but is otherwise not a great success.

CONVENIENCE ★☆☆☆☆
Gamble on the gondola?
The central area close to Heavenly Village and the gondola looks the obvious place to stay, despite the lack of trails down to it. Some of the casino-hotels are within five minutes' walk of the gondola, but others are a hike away. There are lodgings close to the other lift bases – California Lodge, up a heavily wooded slope 2km out of town, and the more remote Nevada bases, Boulder Lodge and Stagecoach Lodge. And there are cheaper places literally miles from a lift, used largely by people with cars. There are free shuttle-buses. You can ski down to all these other bases.

SCENERY ★★★★☆
Splendid panoramas
The views over Lake Tahoe, ringed by snow-capped mountains, are spectacular. The casinos are a conspicuous part of those views from the lower slopes, though not from above mid-mountain; Ridge Run is good for lake views. In the other direction is arid Nevada – sufficiently arid to be classified as desert, though the Sahara it ain't.

THE MOUNTAIN

Practically all of Heavenly's slopes are cut through forest, but in many areas the forest is not dense and there is excellent tree skiing. The trail map gives a good indication of the density of trees. As elsewhere in the US, this 'off-piste' terrain is 'patrolled', but only by hollering – ineffective if you are unconscious; don't ski the trees alone.

Two days a week, am and pm, there are free and 'excellent' mountain tours led by forest rangers.

EXTENT OF THE SLOPES ★★★☆☆
Interestingly complex
The mountain is complicated, and getting from A to B requires more careful navigation than is usual on American mountains. Quite a few of the links between different sectors involve long, flat tracks.

There is a clear division between the California side of the mountain (above South Lake Tahoe) and the Nevada side. If lift closures leave you on the wrong side, it's not a big deal – the bus rides don't take long.

The gondola from South Lake Tahoe goes to one end of the California side. There is no skiing back to the town. At the other end of this side, the steep lower slopes are served by the Aerial Tramway (cable car) and Gunbarrel fast chair from California Lodge. The much more extensive upper slopes are served by four fast chairs, one going up to the Skyline trail to the Nevada side.

The Nevada side is more fragmented, but the central focus is East Peak Lodge. Above it is an excellent intermediate area, served by two fast quad chairs, with a downhill extension served by the Galaxy chair. From the fast Dipper chair back up, you can access the open terrain of Milky Way Bowl, leading to the seriously steep chutes of Mott and Killebrew Canyons, served by the Mott Canyon chair. Below East Peak Lodge are runs down to Nevada's two bases, Stagecoach and Boulder – the latter often quiet because its chairs are slow.

FAST LIFTS ★★★★☆
California does it better
Most people can spend practically all their time on fast chairs. The Mott Canyon chair is slow, but that's a niche market. The main weaknesses are the slow chairs up from Boulder Lodge.

QUEUES ★★★★
Gondola up and down

The gondola can have queues to go up and particularly to go down – and because of this you'll see signs advising you to get back to the gondola ridiculously early. Pay no attention – have a beer or two at the top while waiting for the queue to dissipate. Or forget the gondola and head for one of the other bases, and jump on a shuttle. A couple of recent visitors have found queues for the slow Groove chair and the Sky Express at the end of the day when people are returning to base. Another reported crowds around the lifts from East Peak Lodge on the Nevada side. Some lifts, including the gondola, also seem prone to closure because of wind. Most reporters have had few other problems, often commenting on uncrowded slopes.

TERRAIN PARKS ★★★★★
Splendid for all abilities

Heavenly has something for everyone – all sensibly located on the California slopes. Progression Park, at Adventure Peak near the top of the gondola, is part of the new kids' adventure zone; it has small rails, gentle jumps and boxes designed to help youngsters explore.

Groove Park, at the top of the lifts up from California Lodge, has beginner/intermediate features such as small jumps and boxes for riders wanting to move to the next level. Ante Up Park under the Tamarack chair is intended for advanced and intermediates. High Roller Park, near the top of the Canyon chair, serves expert riders. A half-pipe (5.5m high and 135m long) was built here in 2012/13, the first in Heavenly for five years. There is a large double-jump line – with jumps exceeding 20m in length – as well as large boxes, rails, wall rides and recycled features that often elevate 1–3m off the snow.

SNOW RELIABILITY ★★★★
Fewer worries for intermediates

Heavenly averages an impressive 360 inches per year, but the weather here is much less consistent than further inland, and 2011/12 was an especially poor year for snow. When snow is poor and temperatures are cold enough, intermediates can still have a good time thanks to impressive snowmaking and grooming. But much of the challenging ungroomed terrain

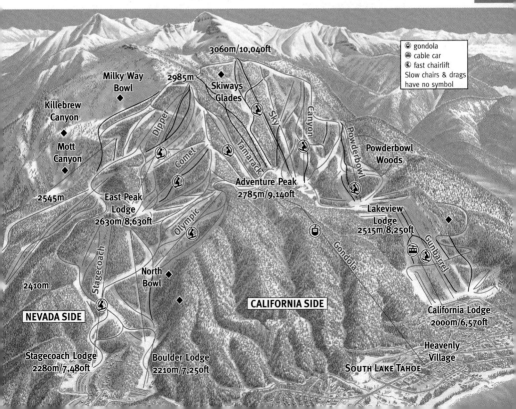

gondola
cable car
fast chairlift
Slow chairs & drags have no symbol

3060m/10,040ft

Milky Way Bowl

2985m

Skiways Glades

Killebrew Canyon

Mott Canyon

Sky

Canyon

Powderbowl

Powderbowl Woods

Dipper

Comet

Tamarack

2545m

East Peak Lodge
2630m/8,630ft

Adventure Peak
2785m/9,140ft

Olympic

Lakeview Lodge
2515m/8,250ft

2410m

Stagecoach

North Bowl

Gondola

Gunbarrel

NEVADA SIDE

CALIFORNIA SIDE

California Lodge
2000m/6,570ft

Stagecoach Lodge
2280m/7,480ft

Boulder Lodge
2210m/7,250ft

SOUTH LAKE TAHOE

Heavenly Village

↑ Pinacles is a single black diamond run on the California side, with some areas of friendly tree skiing off to the sides

TANYA BOOTH

GETTING THERE

Air San Francisco 320km/200 miles (3hr45); Reno 90km/55 miles (1hr30); South Lake Tahoe, 15min

ACTIVITIES

Indoor Casinos, spas, galleries, cinema, museums

Outdoor Lake cruises, snowmobiling, snowshoeing, tobogganing, gondola rides, helicopter tours, tubing, ski biking, sleigh rides, dog sledding, hot springs, small ice rink, ballooning

---

can be closed when snow is poor. Lake Tahoe TV provides updates on snow conditions each day.

FOR EXPERTS ★★★☆☆
Some specific challenges
The black runs under the California base lifts – including the Face and Gunbarrel (often used for mogul competitions) – are seriously steep. We've seen lots of people struggling on the top-to-bottom icy bumps. Many of the single diamonds higher up are at the easy end of the range. Ellie's, at the top of the mountain, may offer continuous moguls too, but was groomed and a great fast cruise when we last skied it. Skiways Glades and the Pinnacles, to skier's right of that, offer friendly, widely spaced trees. Lower down, a trusted reader raves about Maggie's Canyon.

On the Nevada side there are some excellent single-diamond glade areas too – notably to skier's left of the slow North Bowl chair. And there is some really steep stuff. Milky Way Bowl provides a gentle single-diamond introduction to the double-diamond terrain beyond it: the chutes in the otherwise densely wooded Mott and Killebrew Canyons are seriously steep

---

and narrow. They are accessed through roped gateways, and are not to be underestimated. The Mott Canyon chair is slow, but you may not mind. Good natural snow is needed for the Canyons to be enjoyable (or open).

FOR INTERMEDIATES ★★★★☆
Lots to do
The California side offers a progression from the relaxed cruising of the long Ridge Run, starting right at the top of the mountain, to more challenging blues dropping off the ridge towards Sky Deck. More confident intermediates will want to spend time on the Nevada side, where there is more variety of terrain, more carving space and some great longer cruises down to the lift bases. But really strong intermediates looking for challenges need to be prepared to step up to the tree runs – maybe starting with Powderbowl Woods or The Pines – or to the blacks, which are often mogulled.

FOR BEGINNERS ★★★★☆
An excellent place to learn
There are excellent beginner areas at the top of the gondola, at California Lodge and at Boulder Lodge. On the California side there are gentle green runs to progress to at the top of the cable car. Package deals of tuition and lift ticket are worth looking into.

FOR BOARDERS ★★★★☆
Perfect playground – nearly
Heavenly has several terrain parks, and the resort's naturally varied terrain makes a perfect playground for advanced freeriders. Intermediates will have fun too, especially if there's powder in the trees. And there are good areas for beginners. But beware: there are many flat spots where you'll have to scoot. Boardinghouse at Heavenly Village is the local snowboard-only shop.

FOR CROSS-COUNTRY ★★☆☆☆
A separate world
Heavenly does not provide cross-country skiing – it is available at Kirkwood.

MOUNTAIN RESTAURANTS ★☆☆☆☆
Dire – but new one helps
The on-mountain catering is grossly inadequate, especially in bad weather. However, a new restaurant, Tamarack Lodge, opened at the top of the

Build your own shortlist: **www.wheretoskiandsnowboard.com**

SCHOOLS

Heavenly
t 001 303 504 5870

Classes
Half-day learn-to-ski package (includes equipment and pass) from $147

Private lessons
From $435 for 3hr for up to 2 people

CHILDCARE

Day Care Center
t 530 542 6912
Ages 6wk to 6yr

Ski school
Ages 4 to 13 (boarding 5 to 13)

UK PACKAGES

Alpine Answers, AmeriCan Ski, American Ski Classics, Crystal, Crystal Finest, Erna Low, Independent Ski Links, Momentum, Ski Independence, Ski Line, Ski Safari, Ski Solutions, Skitracer, Skiworld, Supertravel, Virgin Snow

Phone numbers
Different area codes are used on the two sides of the stateline; for this chapter, therefore, the area code is included with each number

From distant parts of the US, add the prefix 1. From abroad, add the prefix +1

TOURIST OFFICE

www.skiheavenly.com

gondola in 2011, and reporters are united in welcoming it: 'a great improvement', 'fairly standard food but quality fine, and the place is large and comfortable'. A new sports bar, Booyah's, opened last season in Lakeview Lodge, offering 'exotic burgers and brews'. The other options are outdoor decks serving BBQs and pizzas (hugely unenjoyable in a blizzard, as we can testify) and grossly overcrowded cafeterias.

SCHOOLS AND GUIDES ★★★★
Small groups if you're lucky
A recent reporter sums up the general view well: 'Excellent tuition for all levels, with everyone progressing well; the beginners were skiing black-diamond tree runs by the end of the week.' Groups are generally small.

FOR FAMILIES ★★
Head for Adventure Peak
Heavenly offers various children's programmes and facilities. A kids' ski school building and adventure zone opened at Adventure Peak in 2011/12, and Adventure Peak is home to family activities such as tubing too.

STAYING THERE

Accommodation in the South Lake Tahoe area is abundant and ranges from the huge casinos to small motels.
Hotels Of the main casino hotels, Harrah's (775 588 6611) and Harveys (775 588 2411) are the closest to the gondola.
★★★★Embassy Suites (530 544 5400) Luxury suites close to the gondola. Breakfast and après cocktails included.
★★★★MontBleu Resort (775 588 3515) 'Cheap rooms; can be noisy at night.'
★★★Inn by the Lake (530 542 0330) 'Posh motel', less convenient but 'big rooms, nice view'. Hot tub, pool.
★★★Lakeland Village (530 544 1685) Wide range of lodgings. A 2011 reporter rated his townhouse there 'very large and comfortable'.
★★★Stardust Lodge (800 262 5077) Rooms and suites over the road from the gondola, tipped by two readers this year – 'lovely apartments, friendly, great hot tub, convenient'.
★★★Station House Inn (530 542 1101) A Best Western; 'comfortable and well maintained'; 'excellent choice of full cooked breakfasts'.
★★★3 Peaks Resort (530 544 4131) Convenient, with large rooms. Pool.

★★★Timber Cove Lodge (530 541 6722) Bland but well run, with lake views from some rooms.
Apartments Plenty of choice.

EATING OUT ★★★★
Good value and choice
There's a huge variety, at least if you are prepared to drive (and not drink). The casino hotels' all-you-can-eat buffets offer great value and variety, and there are 'gourmet' choices too – try 19 Kitchen and Bar on the 19th at Harveys. This year's reader tips include the 'excellent' Applebees. LewMarNel's at the Station House Inn serves good fish, pasta, steak and veal ('delicious filet mignon'). The Stateline Brewery does 'excellent pub fare'. MacDuff's Public House, near the Inn by the Lake, is billed as a Scottish pub and has a wood-fired pizza oven and pub grub. Other recent reporter tips include Fresh Ketch at Tahoe Keys Marina and Evan's American Gourmet Cafe. Heidi's serves a 'vast' breakfast, or try Nikki's Chaat Cafe (Indian), the Blue Angel or the Driftwood Cafe.

APRES-SKI ★★★
From bars to baccarat
For years there has been a bit of late-afternoon action to the top of the gondola, to provide an alternative to simply queuing for the lift down. But now there's an organized party: 'Unbuckle at Tamarack runs from 3.30pm to 5.30pm daily, featuring live DJs, half-priced drinks and food specials with the Heavenly Angel dancers exclusively on Fridays and Saturdays,' they say. Fire+Ice at the foot of the gondola (with an outdoor seating area with open fires and heaters) gets busy. Whiskey Dick's, on the main highway, has regular live music. Later on, the casinos have shows, occasionally with top-name entertainers, as well as endless opportunities for throwing your money away gambling.

OFF THE SLOPES ★★★
Quite a bit to entertain
If you want to get away from the bright lights, try a boat trip or a hot-air balloon ride. Pedestrians can use the cable car or the gondola to share the lake views. Adventure Peak at the top of the gondola has tubing, snow biking tobogganing and a zipline. There's ice skating and lots of snowshoe trails.

Mammoth Mountain

A big, sprawling mountain above a car-oriented, sprawling but pleasantly woody resort, a five-hour drive from Los Angeles

RATINGS

The mountains

Extent	★★★
Fast lifts	★★★★
Queues	★★★★
Terrain p'ks	★★★★★
Snow	★★★★
Expert	★★★★
Intermediate	★★★★
Beginner	★★★★
Boarder	★★★★★
X-country	★★★★
Restaurants	★
Schools	★★★★
Families	★★★★

The resort

Charm	★★
Convenience	★★
Scenery	★★★
Eating out	★★★★★
Après-ski	★★★
Off-slope	★

RPI   160

lift pass	£330
ski hire	£135
lessons	£220
food & drink	£140
total	**£825**

NEWS

2013/14: June Mountain, under the same ownership as Mammoth and a scenic 30-minute drive away, is to reopen after being closed last season. The area will be covered by the Mammoth lift pass.

2012/13: Yet another terrain park – Unbound Playground – opened. In The Village a new restaurant and bar, Underground Lounge, opened, and elsewhere a new fine-dining restaurant, Campo, opened.

- ➕ One of North America's bigger ski hills, with something for everyone
- ➕ Mix of open Alpine-style bowls and classic American wooded slopes
- ➕ Impressive snowfall record
- ➕ Uncrowded slopes most of the time
- ➕ Mightily impressive terrain parks
- ➕ Good views by US standards

- ➖ Mammoth Lakes is a rather straggling place with no focus, where life revolves around cars
- ➖ Most, though not all, lodgings are miles from the slopes
- ➖ Weekend crowds in high season
- ➖ Wind can be a problem

Mammoth may not be mammoth in Alpine terms – from end to end, it's less than one-third of the size of Val d'Isère/Tignes, in area more like one-sixth. But in American terms it's a decent size, with enough to keep most visitors happy.

These days there is something resembling a village to stay in – The Village, a typically careful Intrawest confection of lodgings, restaurants and shops. But most people stay elsewhere – in hotels, condos and houses spread around the vast wooded area of Mammoth Lakes – and never go near it. Pick your location carefully, and you can walk to a lift; get a car, and you open up lots of options.

THE RESORT

The mountain is set above Mammoth Lakes, a small year-round resort that spreads over a wide area of woodland and is close to Yosemite National Park (local entrance road closed in winter). The drive up from Los Angeles takes around five hours (more in poor conditions). You pass through the Santa Monica mountains close to Beverly Hills, then the San Gabriel mountains and Mojave Desert (with the world's biggest jet-plane parking lot) before reaching the Sierra Nevada.

The place is almost entirely geared to driving, with no discernible centre – hotels, restaurants and little shopping centres are scattered along the four-lane highway called Main Street and Old Mammoth Road, which crosses it.

Two lift bases are both a mile or two from most of the hotels and condos. The major one is Canyon Lodge, with a big day lodge and hotels and condos in the area below it. A green run (very flat in parts) from here goes down to The Village, a car-free approximation to a village with a gondola back up to Canyon Lodge.

The minor base is Eagle Lodge (aka Juniper Springs, which strictly is the name of the adjacent condos).

A road skirts the mountain to two other lift base areas: Mill Cafe, and Main Lodge, a mini-resort with a big day lodge. You can stay here, in the Mammoth Mountain Inn.

It's welcome news that June Mountain, half an hour away from Mammoth, will be open again this coming season after a year's closure. The slopes were spectacularly under-used, and we shall be interested to see how the lift company goes about making the operation viable.

VILLAGE CHARM ★★
Good first impressions
The resort buildings are generally timber-clad in traditional style – even the McDonald's is tastefully designed – and are set among trees. So although it may be short on village ambience, the place has a pleasant enough appearance – particularly when under several feet of snow. The Village is car-free, and neatly designed.

CONVENIENCE ★★
Canyon Lodge is closest
Even ignoring outlying parts, Mammoth Lakes is spread over an area roughly two miles square, so location obviously matters. If you stay at one of the lift bases, you'll have only a short walk to a lift. But out at Main Lodge you'll be four miles from the 50+ restaurants in Mammoth Lakes. With its gondola link to Canyon Lodge, The Village is also a fairly convenient base.

The Village at Mammoth is the nearest thing to a recognizable village in a resort geared to car-driving visitors →

MAMMOTH MOUNTAIN

KEY FACTS

Resort	2425m
	7,950ft
Slopes	2425-3370m
	7,950-11,050ft
Lifts	28
Pistes	3,500 acres
Green	25%
Blue	40%
Black	35%
Snowmaking	33%

'Fantastic, reliable, frequent and free' shuttle-buses run on several colour-coded routes serving the lift bases. Less frequent night buses run until midnight. But a car is useful.

SCENERY ★★★
Hint of the Alpine
The resort has a wooded setting below open Alpine-style ridges. From the top there are great views north-east into Nevada, and of the jagged Minarets.

THE MOUNTAIN

The 28 lifts access an impressive area, suitable for all abilities. The highest runs are open, the lower ones sheltered by trees, with lightly wooded slopes at mid-mountain that are great on a stormy day.

Finding your way around is not easy at first. All the chairlifts are numbered (the traditional practice), and many are also named (a relatively new practice), but the trails are rather ill defined, and signposting on the mountain could be better. The resort trail map uses six grades of difficulty instead of the usual four, of which we approve. The free tours by mountain hosts are 'excellent'.

EXTENT OF THE SLOPES ★★★
Lots for everyone
As you can see from our star ratings, Mammoth is good for every ability of skier and boarder. But it's not huge – using the data discussed in our feature on piste extent, it falls right on the borderline between our ** and *** extent ratings.

From **Main Lodge** the two-stage

Panorama gondola goes via McCoy Station right to the top. From here, there are countless ways down the front of the mountain that range from steep to very steep – or vertical if the wind has created a cornice, as it often does. Or you can go off the back of the hill, down to **Outpost 14**, whence Chair 14 or Chair 13 brings you back to lower points on the ridge. The third option is to follow the ridge, which curls around and eventually brings you down to the Main Lodge area – though you might not realize that from the trail map. This route brings you past an easy area served by a double chair, and a very easy area served by the Discovery fast quad.

McCoy Station can also be reached using the Stump Alley fast chair from **Mill Cafe**, on the road up from town. The fast Gold Rush quad, also from Mill Cafe, takes you into the more heavily wooded eastern half of the area. This has long, gentle runs served by lifts up from **Canyon Lodge** and **Eagle Lodge** and seriously steep stuff as well as some intermediate terrain served by lifts 25 and 22 and some excellent tree skiing.

FAST LIFTS ★★★★
Where it counts
The main access lifts from every base are fast chairs or gondolas. But there are still several slow old lifts. The Outpost area is the least well served for fast lifts. Usefully, the trail map lists the ride time of every lift.

QUEUES ★★★★
Normally quiet slopes
Mammoth's lifts and slopes are usually

LIFT PASSES

Mammoth Mountain

Prices in US$

Age	1-day	6-day
under 13	30	180
13 to 18	73	366
19 to 64	94	472
65 plus	80	402

Free Under 7, over 80

Beginner Pass for four chairs $57

Notes Prices are for booking online 14 days in advance; ticket window prices are more expensive; afternoon pass available

very quiet, with very few queues: 'Queues? What queues?' says a 2012 visitor. But on fine peak-season weekends hordes of people may arrive from Los Angeles, and the lifts can struggle to cope. Which explains why one of the privileges of membership of the exclusive Mammoth Black club is that you get lift priority.

TERRAIN PARKS ★★★★★
Difficult to beat

'Absolutely awesome,' is the summary of a 2013 reporter. Mammoth's world-class Unbound Terrain Parks number no fewer than nine, all looked after with 'artistic proficiency'. There are over 50 jumps, 100 jibs and three half-pipes in over 100 acres of freestyle territory. Easiest are the Eagle Park at Eagle Lodge (with easy rollers), Disco Park at Main Lodge (with small low-to-the-snow rails and boxes) and the Wonderland Park by Chair 7 (with a mini-pipe and micro-scale rails, boxes and mini-jumps). For intermediate to advanced riders South Park, Jibs Galore (Chair 4) and Forest Trail Park (Chair 6) are playgrounds offering a bewildering choice of rails and kickers. Alternatively, take on the X-Course boardercross (Chair 4). Main Park, situated off Chair 6 above Main Lodge, is huge; everything here is up to pro standard. Kickers range from 18m to 24m long and border the famous super-duper pipe (170m long, with 7m walls) that looms over the car park and dwarfs the super-pipe beside it; it is cut daily. Main Park is serviced by a fast chairlift, allowing for a full lap

time of only eight minutes. Downtown Collection is a series of rails. The newest park is Unbound Playground. It's designed to prepare you for bigger, more advanced parks.

SNOW RELIABILITY ★★★★
A long season

Mammoth has an impressive snow record – an annual average of 350 inches, which puts it ahead of major Colorado resorts. Its slopes are appreciably higher than those of the Tahoe resorts, and it has an ever-expanding array of snow-guns, so it enjoys a long season – it sometimes has slopes open on 4 July. The mountain faces roughly north-east; the relatively low and slightly sunny slopes down to Eagle Lodge are affected by warm weather before others. Strong winds are not uncommon on the upper mountain, and the snow quality can be affected. But you may find powder is just shifted down the hill. Visitors continue to report 'excellent' grooming.

FOR EXPERTS ★★★★
Some very challenging terrain

The steep double-diamond chutes strung across the width of the mountain top provide wonderful opportunities for experts. Fortunately for the rest of us, there are three or four broad single-diamond slopes, requiring rather less bottle.

There is lots of challenging terrain lower down, too, much of it lightly wooded and therefore good to ski in bad conditions; Chair 5, Chair 22 (the

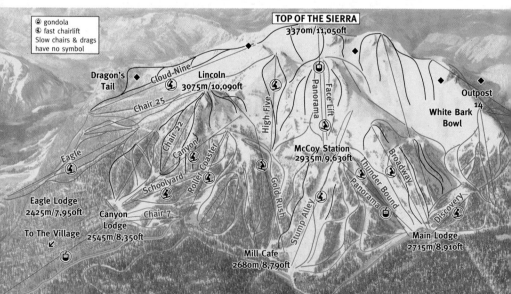

↑ Steep open slopes at the top, gentle, woodland runs at the bottom, and a mixture between the two
MAMMOTH MOUNTAIN

top of which is higher than the very top of Heavenly) and Broadway are often open in bad weather when the top is firmly shut, and their more sheltered slopes may in any case have the best snow. There are plenty of good slopes over the back, too.

Many of the steeper trails are short by Alpine standards (typically under 400m vertical), but despite this we've had some great powder days here.

FOR INTERMEDIATES ★★★★☆
Lots of great cruising

Although there are exceptions, most of the lower mountain, below the treeline, is intermediate cruising territory and generally flattering.

Some of the mountain's longest runs – blue-blacks served by the Cloud Nine Express and Chair 25 – are ideal for good intermediates. There are also some excellent, fairly steep woodland trails down to Mill Cafe. Most of the long runs above Eagle Lodge, and some of the shorter ones above Canyon Lodge, are easy cruises. There is a variety of terrain, including lots of gentle stuff, on skier's left of the area.

FOR BEGINNERS ★★★★☆
Good, gentle slopes

Chair 7 and the Schoolyard Express chair (at the Canyon Lodge base) and Discovery Chair (at Main Lodge) serve quiet, gentle green runs – perfect terrain for novices. These lifts, plus two others, are included in a beginner lift pass. Excellent instruction and top-notch piste maintenance usually make progress speedy, delighting reporters.

FOR BOARDERS ★★★★★
Great parks and terrain

Regularly voted one of the best snowboard resorts in the USA by *Transworld Snowboarding* magazine readers, Mammoth has encouraged snowboarding since its early days: 'We felt like we were being welcomed home here!' said a 2012 reporter. A huge amount has been spent on the terrain parks, and this tends to overshadow just how good the mountain's natural terrain really is. Largely serviced by hassle-free fast chairs and gondolas, this is a snowboarder's heaven with terrain to suit every ability level. Lower Road Runner is reportedly the only unbearably flat trail. Specialist shops include Wave Rave and P3.

FOR CROSS-COUNTRY ★★★★☆
Very popular

Two specialist centres, Tamarack (31km) and Sierra Meadows (ungroomed), provide lessons and tours. A past reporter enjoyed 'gorgeous vistas gliding through the forest around lakes'. And there are lots of ungroomed tracks, including some through the pretty Lakes Basin area.

MOUNTAIN RESTAURANTS ★☆☆☆☆
Back to base ...

The already limited lunch options on the hill have been narrowed further, we regret to report. The pleasant table-service Parallax at mid-mountain is now open only to members of the exclusive Mammoth Black club. We have cut our rating to ★ as a result.

Build your own shortlist: www.wheretoskiandsnowboard.com

SCHOOLS
Mammoth Mountain
t 760 934 2571

Classes
Half-day (2.5hr) $140
Private lessons
From $498 for 3hr

CHILDCARE
Mammoth Childcare
t 760 934 2571
Newborn to 6yr

Ski school
Ages 3 to 13

GETTING THERE
Air Los Angeles
494km/305 miles
(5hr); Reno
275km/170 miles
(4hr15)

ACTIVITIES
Indoor Spa, art
gallery, arts centre,
cinema, theatre

Outdoor Ice rink, dog
sledding, tubing,
snowmobiling,
snowshoeing

UK PACKAGES
AmeriCan Ski, American
Ski Classics,
Independent Ski Links,
Momentum, Ski
Independence, Ski Line,
Ski Safari, Ski
Solutions, Skitracer,
Skiworld, Snow Finders,
Supertravel, Virgin
Snow

Phone numbers
From distant parts of
the US, add the prefix
1 760; from abroad,
add the prefix +1 760

TOURIST OFFICE
www.mammoth
mountain.com

McCoy Station, the plebs' facility at mid-mountain, offers a wide choice. Top of the Sierra is small and 'very functional' but has 'views to die for'. A fair-weather option is the primitive outdoor BBQ at Outpost 14. Mill Cafe is at a lift base, but gets a mention for its welcoming atmosphere, and for operating the Little Mill snowcat that drives around the hill selling food.

Mammoth says you can eat your packed lunch in any of its places. Try that in the Parallax.

SCHOOLS AND GUIDES ★★★★
More reports needed
We have no recent reports. But there are 'workshops' with a maximum of four guests and three-day 'camps' (eg terrain park, all mountain, moguls).

FOR FAMILIES ★★★★
Family favourite
Mammoth is keen to attract families. The focal points are the Mammoth Childcare centres at the Inn and at The Village, with comprehensive facilities for children up to six years old. Kids from age three can have ski lessons, and there are four Kids Adventure zones with fun features for skiers and boarders, two non-skiing Play Zones and a tubing park with its own lift.

STAYING THERE

There's a good choice of hotels (none very luxurious or pricey) and condos. The condos tend to be out of town, near the lifts or on the road to them. **★★★★Westin Monache Resort** (934 0400) Condo hotel near The Village gondola: restaurant, hot tubs, pool. **★★★Alpenhof Lodge** (934 6330) Comfortable and central; shuttle-bus stop and plenty of restaurants nearby. **★★★Mammoth Mountain Inn** (934 2581) Good value, but way out of town at Main Lodge. **★★★Sierra Nevada Lodge** (934 2515) Central; recently renovated. Spa. Our 2012 reporter was so taken he went back again this year: 'Nice rooms, really friendly staff, good value.' **Apartments** The Village Lodge is close to many restaurants and shops; Juniper Springs Resort is near the Eagle base; both are of high quality. Other comfortable options are the Seasons 4 condos (close to The Village), the 1849 Condos (Canyon Lodge area) and the nearby Mammoth Ski and Racquet Club.

EATING OUT ★★★★★
Outstanding choice
Mammoth has 50+ restaurants offering a wide choice from typical American to Japanese. There's a local menu guide covering many but not all.

The chalet-style Lakefront in the Tamarack Lodge is one of the best, with great views and excellent food with a French theme (not cheap though). Rafters and the Red Lantern Chinese in the Sierra Nevada Lodge both have 'excellent cuisine and are good value for money, especially in happy hour when prices are reduced', says a recent reporter who also rates the Mogul for 'the best steak in town' and Jimmy's Taverna for 'high-quality Greek food and fish dishes at reasonable prices'. We've had excellent dinners at Skadi (fine dining) and Whiskey Creek (also a saloon). Giovanni's is good for pizza and pasta. Slocums is a popular steakhouse. Angels has typical American family food – burgers, steaks, ribs. Chart House is a chain place doing seafood and steaks.

Other possibilities include Shogun for Japanese or Gomez's for Tex-Mex. For a hearty breakfast, try the Breakfast Club. The Side Door cafe is an appealing eatery in The Village. The Parallax at McCoy Station opens for snowcat dinners up the mountain.

APRES-SKI ★★★
Lively at weekends
At the close of play, the Yodler at Main Lodge is the liveliest spot – an old chalet (brought from Switzerland, they claim). Tusks at Main Lodge and the Dry Creek bar in the Mammoth Mountain Inn across the road are other choices. Lakanuki in The Village is a 'Hawaiian-style bar that attracts a younger crowd'. Nightlife revolves around a handful of bars that liven up at weekends: Whiskey Creek (stays open late), Grumpy's sports bar and quieter Slocums.

OFF THE SLOPES ★
Mainly sightseeing
Outdoor activities include skating, tubing, snowmobiling, snowshoeing, thermal hot springs and pleasant drives. Mono Lake and the WW2 centre at Manzanar on the road to Los Angeles have been recommended. There is factory shopping nearby, too. But overall, Mammoth isn't a great place for non-skiers.

Squaw Valley

The site of the 1960 Olympics has a lot to offer novices and experts, and the little purpose-built village is worth a few days' stay

TOP 10 RATINGS	
Extent	★★★
Fast lifts	★★★
Queues	★★★★
Snow	★★★★
Expert	★★★★
Intermediate	★★
Beginner	★★★★
Charm	★★★
Convenience	★★★★
Scenery	★★★

RPI	150
lift pass	£340
ski hire	£115
lessons	£175
food & drink	£150
total	**£780**

KEY FACTS

Resort	1890m
	6,200ft
Slopes	1890-2760m
	6,200-9,050ft
Lifts	30
Pistes	3,600 acres
Green	25%
Blue	45%
Black	30%
Snowmaking	17%

TANYA BOOTH

The main bowl; you may be able to pick out the Gold Coast lift station more or less in the middle ↓

Pros
+ Lots of challenging terrain
+ Impressive snow record
+ Superb beginner slopes
+ Convenient 'village' at the base

Cons
− Not for mile-hungry intermediates
− Lifts prone to closure by wind
− Limited range of village amenities

When Intrawest built a neat little base 'village' a decade ago, Squaw became a more attractive place to stay. But the village is small, and the ski area won't suit everyone – in particular, keen piste-bashers who like cruising groomed runs will find it limited. We would always combine it with a visit to Heavenly.

But Squaw now shares ownership and its lift pass with Alpine Meadows, a very worthwhile resort only 10 minutes away, which means there is quite a lot to do locally, without venturing far afield.

A few years ago, Squaw's founder and owner died, and a 'renaissance' is under way; crucially, runs are now marked and classified for difficulty, on both the mountain and the trail map. Squaw is now much more accessible as a result. Many other improvements are under way, too.

THE RESORT

Squaw is the major resort at the north end of Lake Tahoe. Since construction of the car-free Village, staying here has become more attractive; but it is still also popular as a day trip from South Lake Tahoe and Heavenly. There are shuttle-buses. There are other lodgings around the valley, and at Tahoe City. The lift pass also covers neighbouring Alpine Meadows (a 10-minute ride by half-hourly free shuttle-buses).

Village charm The Village is very small but works well, and older buildings next to it are not unpleasant. Improvements are being made, too.

Convenience The Village is at the base of the main lifts. The self-contained, luxurious, conference-oriented Resort at Squaw Creek hotel, well outside the Village, has its own chairlift into one end of the network.

Scenery There are fabulous views of Lake Tahoe from Squaw Peak.

THE MOUNTAINS

One of the attractions of the area is that the slopes are lightly wooded. Until recently the resort was stupidly unhelpful about navigation. Only from 2011/12 have trails been shown on the mountain map and signposted on the ground.

Slopes A gondola and a big cable car rise 600m to the twin stations of Gold Coast and High Camp (linked by the Pulse gondola). Above them is a wide area of beginner slopes, and beyond that the three highest peaks of the area, with lifts of modest vertical; much the biggest is Squaw Peak's Headwall six-pack: 535m.

From High Camp you can descend into a steep-sided valley from which the Silverado chair is the return.

Two other peaks are accessed directly from the village. A fast quad serves steep KT-22; a slow triple goes to rather neglected Snow King.

Squaw's cable car runs until 7pm on Friday and Saturday evenings (and on every evening during holiday times) to serve the floodlit slopes (including

CALIFORNIA

552

2013/14: Further investment in terrain park features, snowmaking, signage and grooming is planned. The Village at Squaw Valley condos are to be renovated.

2012/13: A triple chair was replaced by a six-pack, Big Blue Express, for quicker access to the Belmont terrain park and the Granite Chief, Silverado and Shirley Lake areas. A rope tow was installed to allow easy access to the Belmont park. Squaw joined the Mountain Collective, a small group of widely spread western resorts offering an attractive lift-pass deal.

UK PACKAGES

AmeriCan Ski, American Ski Classics, Crystal, Independent Ski Links, Interactive Resorts, Momentum, Ski Independence, Ski Safari, Ski Solutions, Skitracer, Supertravel, Virgin Snow

Phone numbers
From distant parts of the US, add the prefix 1 530; from abroad, add the prefix +1 530

TOURIST OFFICE

www.squaw.com

a 5km run to the base area), and terrain parks and the dining facilities at High Camp.

Fast lifts There are fast lifts in each sector, but also slow old chairs.

Queues There are few problems usually, but the weather and weekend invasions are key factors.

Terrain parks Riviera park offers intermediate and expert jump lines, a night-accessible pipe with 5.5m walls, and big jib features. The Gold Coast park is constantly updated with innovative features. The Belmont park offers small to medium features. Last season Squaw brought back the Mainline park, which includes a superpipe and large jumps. There are other parks when conditions permit, and parks designed for kids and novices.

Snow reliability An impressive 450 inches on average, plus snowmaking.

Experts The possibilities for experts on KT-22, Squaw Peak, Granite Chief and the Silverado valley are huge, with lots of steep chutes and big mogul fields; many extreme skiing and boarding movies are made here.

Intermediates Blue-run skiers have a choice of some lovely cruises in the Emigrant and Snow King sectors and a 5km top-to-bottom run. But there is not much more groomed cruising, so keen piste-bashers will find the area limited. There is, however, lots of steep blue and easy black terrain to test your deep-snow or mogul skills.

Beginners The Papoose nursery area has a gentle slope served by a double chairlift – a special beginner package, with lift pass, is available. There's a superb choice of easy runs to progress to at altitude, notably at High Camp.

Snowboarding This is one of the most snowboarder friendly resorts around. The higher areas are full of steep and deep gullies, cliff drops, kicker building spots and tree runs, and the parks are kept in excellent shape.

Cross-country There are 18km of groomed trails at Squaw Creek.

Mountain restaurants Uninspiring, except in terms of views.

Schools and guides As well as group lessons, the school runs specialist workshops – eg Chutes and Hikes, Vintage Squaw – on certain dates.

Families Squaw offers slope-side convenience and a children's on-slope play area at the Papoose base. Squaw Kids takes children from three years.

STAYING THERE

Hotels The PlumpJack Inn (583 1576) is our favourite – comfortable, stylish, central. The Resort at Squaw Creek (583 6300) offers luxury rooms, an outdoor pool and hot tubs, and 'fantastic buffet breakfasts'.

Apartments The Village has well-appointed ski-in/ski-out condos.

Eating out The PlumpJack Inn has an excellent restaurant. More routine places include the Auld Dubliner pub ('good Guinness stew'), Fireside (pizza/pasta) and Mamasake (sushi). You can eat up at High Camp.

Après-ski The Olympic House has several venues. In the Village, the places above mostly function as bars, too: Auld Dubliner has live music on a Friday, but is 'dead during the week'. Uncorked at Squaw Valley is a wine bar with live music and wine tastings.

Off the slopes High Camp has an ice rink and other activities. The Trilogy Spa offers a range of treatments.

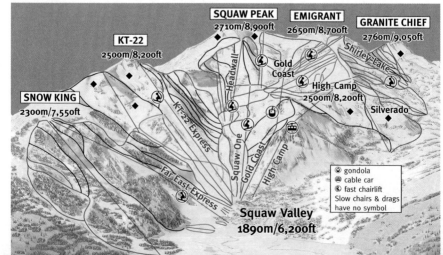

SQUAW PEAK
2710m/8,900ft

EMIGRANT
2650m/8,700ft

GRANITE CHIEF
2760m/9,050ft

KT-22
2500m/8,200ft

Shirley Lake

Gold Coast

High Camp
2500m/8,200ft

Headwall

SNOW KING
2300m/7,550ft

Silverado

KT-22 Express

Squaw One

Gold Coast

High Camp

Far East Express

gondola
cable car
fast chairlift
Slow chairs & drags have no symbol

Squaw Valley
1890m/6,200ft

Colorado

Colorado is the most popular American destination state for UK visitors, and justifiably so: it has the most alluring combination of attractive resorts, slopes to suit all abilities and excellent, reliable snow – dry enough to justify its 'champagne powder' label. It also has direct scheduled BA flights to Denver, an easy drive or shuttle transfer from some of the resorts (unless it's snowing). But you may be able to save money by taking an indirect flight – and if you are going to a resort far from Denver, this makes sense because you can fly into a nearer airport.

Resorts such as Breckenridge, Vail and Winter Park are around a two-hour transfer from Denver. But Aspen and Snowmass are around four to five hours, and places such as Crested Butte and Telluride even more. For these more remote places you might want to consider an indirect flight, changing to a plane that lands at a nearby airport: Aspen, for example, has its own airport a few minutes from town. Even for Vail, you may prefer to change planes and fly into Eagle airport, only 45 minutes away.

Colorado has amazingly dry snow. Even when the snow melts and refreezes, the moisture seems to be magically whisked away, leaving it soft and powdery. Even the artificial snow is of a quality you'll rarely find in Europe. And like most North American rivals, Colorado resorts generally have excellent, steep, ungroomed areas that you can ski safely without a guide.

The resorts vary enormously. If you want cute restored buildings from the mining boom days of the late 19th century, try the dinky old towns of Telluride and Crested Butte or the much bigger Aspen. Other resorts (such as Aspen's modern satellite, Snowmass) major on convenience. Some (such as Vail and Beaver Creek) deliberately pitch themselves upmarket, with lots of glitzy, expensive hotels, while others (such as Breckenridge and Winter Park) are much more down to earth.

You could consider renting a car and touring several resorts – maybe cutting costs by staying in valley towns rather than resorts. One regular reporter did a 2013 tour staying in Avon near Beaver Creek and Vail and Frisco near Breckenridge, Keystone, Copper Mountain and Arapahoe Basin.

Six major resorts get write-ups in this section. The others with blue circles on the map have entries in the resort directory at the back of the book – of these, Steamboat, Copper Mountain, Keystone, Crested Butte, Telluride and Durango have proper resort villages, while the others cater mainly for day visitors.

Many Colorado resorts are at an extremely high altitude. As a result, visitors arriving straight from sea level are at risk of altitude sickness, which can spoil your trip. We always try to start in one of the lower resorts – or do a night in Denver to acclimatize.

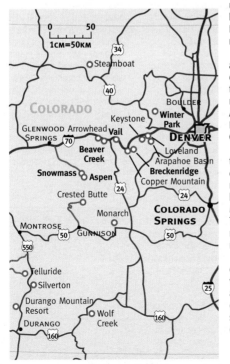

Aspen

Don't be put off by the ritzy image – with a fun, historic town and quiet, extensive slopes, this is America's best resort

RATINGS

The mountains

Extent	★★
Fast lifts	★★★★
Queues	★★★★
Terrain p'ks	★★★★★
Snow	★★★★★
Expert	★★★★★
Intermediate	★★★★★
Beginner	★★★★★
Boarder	★★★★
X-country	★★★★
Restaurants	★★★
Schools	★★★★★
Families	★★

The resort

Charm	★★★★
Convenience	★★
Scenery	★★★
Eating out	★★★★★
Après-ski	★★★★
Off-slope	★★★★

Our extent rating excludes Snowmass. Including Snowmass would rate ★★★★

RPI	190
lift pass	£400
ski hire	£205
lessons	£235
food & drink	£155
total	**£995**

NEWS

2012/13: Free 'Yoga for skiers' classes started at the Sundeck at the top of Aspen Mountain; three days a week from 9.30am to 10.30am. Little Nell's pop-up champagne bar is back on Aspen Mountain. The 5-star Jerome hotel was refurbished and a spa added.

➕ Notably uncrowded slopes

➕ Attractive, characterful old town, with lots of restaurants and shops

➕ Excellent Aspen Highlands and Snowmass just up the road

➕ Convenient airport on edge of town

➕ Extensive slopes to suit every standard, but ...

➖ Slopes split over four separate mountains (including Snowmass), served by efficient, free buses

➖ Expensive, and tending to become more so as cheap places disappear

➖ A bit isolated – no other major resorts within easy day-trip distance

Aspen is our favourite American resort. It has everything we look for – well, everything except convenience. Our affection depends heavily on the presence of Aspen Highlands, a little way down the valley, and on Snowmass, considerably further down the valley (covered in a separate chapter). So most days you have to ride a bus; that doesn't worry us, and doesn't seem to worry readers who report on the place – most people who try it are captivated, and can't wait to go back.

Many rich and some famous guests jet in here, and for connoisseurs of cosmetic surgery the bars of the top hotels can be fascinating places. And the place does seem to be drifting even further upmarket, with ever fewer funky bars and ever more international-brand shops. But, like all other 'glamorous' ski resorts, Aspen is actually filled by ordinary holidaymakers. Don't be put off.

THE RESORT

In 1892 Aspen was a booming silver-mining town, with 12,000 inhabitants, six newspapers and an opera house. But the town's fortunes took a nosedive when the silver price plummeted in 1893, and by the 1930s the population had shrunk to 700 or so, and the handsome Victorian buildings had fallen into disrepair. Development of the skiing started on a small scale in the late 1930s. The first lift was opened shortly after the World War 2, and Aspen hasn't looked back.

Aspen Mountain is right above the town, its access lifts starting yards from the main street. And there are three other ski areas nearby (all covered by the ski pass). Around 3km from Aspen are Buttermilk and Aspen Highlands. Buttermilk has the Inn at Aspen hotel at the base. Highlands has a limited amount of lodgings (including the very smart Ritz Carlton Club).

Snowmass, 14km away, is a proper resort in its own right – with great attractions as a base for families, in particular – and has its own chapter.

VILLAGE CHARM ★★★★
Smart old town

Aspen's historic centre – with a typical American grid of streets – has been preserved to form the core of the most fashionable ski town in the Rockies, and one of the most charming. There's a huge variety of restaurants, bars, swanky shops and galleries.

A mixture of developments spreads out from the centre, ranging from the homes of the super-rich through surprisingly modest hotels and motels to mobile homes for the workers. Though the town is busy with traffic, it moves slowly, and pedestrians effectively have priority in much of the central area.

KEY FACTS

Resort		2425m
		7,950ft

Aspen Mountain

Slopes		2425-3415m
		7,950-11,210ft
Lifts		8
Pistes		675 acres
Green		0%
Blue		48%
Black		52%
Snowmaking		31%

Aspen Highlands

Slopes		2450-3560m
		8,040-11,680ft
Lifts		5
Pistes		1,028 acres
Green		18%
Blue		30%
Black		52%
Snowmaking		11%

Buttermilk

Slopes		2400-3015m
		7,880-9,900ft
Lifts		8
Pistes		470 acres
Green		35%
Blue		39%
Black		26%
Snowmaking		23%

Total with Snowmass

Slopes		2400-3815m
		7,880-12,510ft
Lifts		42
Pistes		5,535 acres
Green		10%
Blue		45%
Black		45%
Snowmaking		12%

CONVENIENCE ★★★★★
Better by bus

Aspen is very unusual in being a cute old town with a major lift close to the centre: the gondola to the top of Aspen Mountain is only yards from some of the top hotels. Downtown Aspen is quite compact by American resort standards, but it spreads far enough to make the free ski-bus a necessity for some visitors staying less centrally. You also need buses to get to the other mountains, of course. Generally, they work well. But they can get crowded, and you may need to keep an eye on the timetables.

SCENERY ★★★★★
Beautiful Bells

The views from the upper part of Highlands are the best – the famous and distinctive Maroon Bells that appear on countless postcards. Buttermilk enjoys great views too.

THE MOUNTAINS

Most of the slopes are in the trees. All the mountains have free guided tours at 10.30, given by excellent volunteer ambassadors. At Highlands there is a special Highland Bowl tour on Wednesdays at noon. The ratio of acres to visitor beds is high, and the slopes are usually blissfully uncrowded. Signposting could be better where runs merge.

EXTENT OF THE SLOPES ★★★★★
Widely dispersed

Each of the four mountains is worth a visit. Much the most extensive mountain in the area is at Snowmass – see separate chapter. Note that our extent rating excludes Snowmass; including it would give ★★★★.

Once you are up the gondola, a series of chairs serves the ridges of **Aspen Mountain**. In general, there are long cruising blue runs along the valley floors and short, steep blacks down from the ridges.

Buttermilk is the smallest, lowest and least challenging mountain, accessed by a fast quad from the fairly primitive main base lodge. The runs fan out from the top in three directions – back to the base, down to Tiehack and down to West Buttermilk (with fast quads back from all three).

Aspen Highlands consists essentially of a single ridge served by three fast quad chairs, with easy and intermediate slopes along the ridge itself and steep black runs on the flanks – very steep ones at the top. And beyond the lift network, a free snowcat ride leads to Highland Bowl, where gates access a splendid open bowl of entirely double-black gradient.

FAST LIFTS ★★★★★
Serving bottom to top

Each mountain has a few key fast chairs or a gondola up to the top.

A great view of downtown Aspen with the gondola up Aspen Mountain starting a stroll from much of the lodging →

Aspen offers special experiences for small numbers of skiers or riders.

First Tracks *The first skiers to sign up each day get to ride the gondola up Aspen Mountain at 8am the next morning and get first tracks on perfect corduroy or fresh powder. Well worth doing. Free, but numbers are limited! When we did it, we took our time over the descent, to let the start-of-day queue at the bottom dissipate, but we're told you now ski in a guided group at a set pace.*

Powder Tours *Spend the day finding untracked snow in a guided group in 1,500 acres of backcountry beyond Aspen Mountain, with a 12-passenger heated snowcat as your personal lift. You're likely to squeeze in about 10 runs in all. You break for lunch at an old mountain cabin. It costs about $400 per person.*

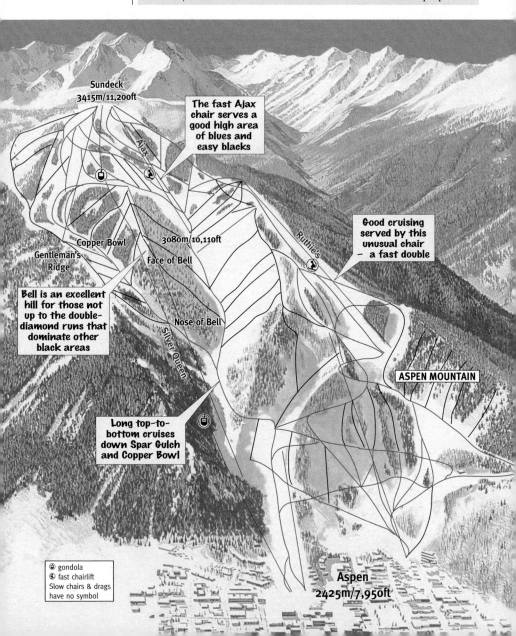

Sundeck
3415m/11,200ft

The fast Ajax chair serves a good high area of blues and easy blacks

Ajax

Good cruising served by this unusual chair – a fast double

Ruthie's

Copper Bowl
Gentleman's Ridge

3080m/10,110ft

Face of Bell

Bell is an excellent hill for those not up to the double-diamond runs that dominate other black areas

Nose of Bell

Silver Queen

ASPEN MOUNTAIN

Long top-to-bottom cruises down Spar Gulch and Copper Bowl

gondola
fast chairlift
Slow chairs & drags
have no symbol

Aspen
2425m/7,950ft

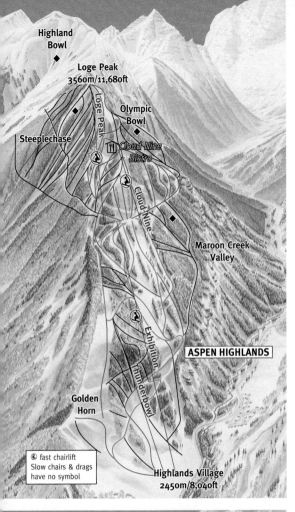

Highland
Bowl
◆

Loge Peak
356om/11,68oft

Olympic
Bowl

Steeplechase

🕚 *Cloud Nine
Bistro*

Loge Peak

Cloud Nine

◆

Maroon Creek
Valley

Exhibition

Thunderbowl

ASPEN HIGHLANDS

Golden
Horn

④ fast chairlift
Slow chairs & drags
have no symbol

Highlands Village
245om/8,04oft

ASPEN HIGHLANDS

West Summit
3015m/9,900ft

Cliffhouse
2955m/9,690ft

West Buttermilk

Tiehack ④

Summit

BUTTERMILK

West
Buttermilk
2655m/
8,710ft

Tiehack
2450m/
8,04oft

④ fast chairlift
Slow chairs & drags
have no symbol

Panda
Hill

Main
Buttermilk
2400m/788oft

QUEUES ★★★★
Few problems

Major queues are rare on any of the mountains – you may hit a few during the college spring break in March. At Aspen Mountain, the gondola can still have delays at peak times. You can use the slow Shadow Mountain chair, instead, with a short uphill walk to reach it. Aspen Highlands is almost always queue-free, even at peak times. The lift out of Main Buttermilk sometimes gets congested.

TERRAIN PARKS ★★★★★
X Games standard

Aspen has two pipe and park mountains – Snowmass (see separate chapter) and Buttermilk. Buttermilk Park is famous as the home of the Winter X Games, and stretches over 3km from the top to the bottom of the mountain – it is said to be the longest in the world. It has over 100 features, the X Games slope-style course and a world-class super-pipe that's over 150m long with 6.7m walls.

SNOW RELIABILITY ★★★★★
Rarely a problem

Aspen's mountains get an annual average of 300 inches of snow – not in the front rank, but not far behind. In addition, all areas have substantial snowmaking. Immaculate grooming adds to the quality of the pistes, and the light traffic can only help.

FOR EXPERTS ★★★★★
Buttermilk is the only soft stuff

There's plenty to choose from – all the mountains except Buttermilk offer lots of challenges, and it is relatively easy to find untouched powder in the many gladed areas.

Aspen Mountain has a formidable array of double black diamond runs. From the top of the gondola, Walsh's, Hyrup's and Kristi are on a lightly wooded slope and link up with Gentleman's Ridge and Jackpot to form the longest black run on the mountain. A series of steep glades drops down from Gentleman's Ridge. The central Bell ridge has less extreme single diamonds on both its flanks, including some delightful lightly wooded areas. On the opposite side of Spar Gulch is another row of double blacks, collectively called the Dumps, because mining waste was dumped here.

At Highlands there are challenging runs from top to bottom of the

LIFT PASSES

Four Mountain Pass

Prices in US$

Age	1-day	6-day
under 13	79	360
13 to 17	105	516
18 to 64	114	570
65 plus	105	516

Free Under 7: $5 for unlimited period

Senior Over 70: $419 for unlimited period

Beginner Included in price of lessons

Notes Includes shuttle-bus between the areas. 6-day prices are online 7 days in advance (window prices are higher). Savings if you purchase in advance through certain UK tour operators

mountain. Consider joining a guided group as an introduction to the best of them. Highland Bowl, beyond the top lift, is superb in the right conditions: a big open bowl with access gates reached by hiking (but there are usually free snowcat rides to cut out the first 20-minute walk). The trail map usefully gives key facts for each run – orientation and average and steepest pitch, from a serious 38° to a terrifying 48°.

Left of the bowl, the Steeplechase area consists of a number of parallel natural avalanche chutes, and their elevation means the snow stays light and dry. The Olympic Bowl area on the opposite flank of the mountain has great views of the Maroon Bells and some serious moguls. The Thunderbowl chair from the base serves a nice varied area that's often underused.

FOR INTERMEDIATES ★★★★★
Grooming to die for
Most intermediate runs on Highlands are concentrated above the mid-mountain Merry-Go-Round restaurant, many served by the Cloud Nine fast quad chair. But there are other good slopes – don't miss the vast, neglected expanses of Golden Horn, on the eastern limit of the area.

Aspen Mountain has its fair share of intermediate slopes, but they tend to be tougher than on the other mountains. Copper Bowl and Spar Gulch, running between the ridges, are great cruises but can get crowded. Upper Aspen Mountain, at the top of the gondola, has a dense network of well-groomed blues served by the Ajax

fast chair. The unusual Ruthie's chair – a fast double, apparently installed to rekindle the romance that quads have destroyed – serves more cruising runs.

Buttermilk offers good, easy slopes to practise on, and can be extraordinarily quiet. And good intermediates should be able to handle the relatively easy black runs – when groomed, these are a real blast. Buttermilk is also a great place for early experiments off-piste.

Read the Snowmass chapter too.

FOR BEGINNERS ★★★★★
Can be a great place to learn
Buttermilk is superb. West Buttermilk has beautifully groomed, gentle, often deserted runs, served by a quad. The easiest slopes of all, though, are at the base of the Main Buttermilk sector – on Panda Hill. Despite its macho image and serious double-diamond terrain, Highlands boasts the highest concentration of green runs in Aspen, served by the fast Exhibition chair.

FOR BOARDERS ★★★★
Loads of scope
There is a huge amount of terrain to explore, which will satisfy all levels of boarder – especially when you include Snowmass (see our separate chapter). The hills are free of draglifts and have few flat sections. Buttermilk is the least testing of the mountains, with gentle carving runs and freeriding – but also has a huge terrain park.

FOR CROSS-COUNTRY ★★★★
Backcountry bonanza
There are 90km of groomed trails between Aspen and Snowmass in the

SCHOOLS

Aspen
t 923 1227

Classes
Full day (5hr) $144
Private lessons
$680 for full day for
up to 5 people

CHILDCARE

Childcare
t 923 1227
Ages 8wk to 4yr
**Cubs on Skis, Pandas
and Grizzlies**
t 923 1227
Various different
groups for ages
30mnth to 4yr, 3 to 4
and 5 to 6
Babysitting services
Several

Ski school
Ages 7 to 12

GETTING THERE

Air Aspen 6km/
4 miles (15min); Eagle
110km/70 miles
(1hr45); Denver
360km/225 miles
(4hr45)
Rail Glenwood Springs
(65km/40 miles)

UK PACKAGES

Alpine Answers,
AmeriCan Ski, American
Ski Classics, Carrier,
Crystal, Crystal Finest,
Elegant Resorts, Erna
Low, Flexiski, Frontier,
Independent Ski Links,
Interactive Resorts,
Momentum, Oxford Ski
Co, PowderBeds, Scott
Dunn, Ski Bespoke, Ski
Club Freshtracks, Ski
Expectations, Ski
Independence, Ski Line,
Ski Safari, Ski
Solutions, Skitracer,
Skiworld, Snow Finders,
Supertravel, Virgin
Snow

Roaring Fork valley – the most extensive cross-country network in the US. And the Ashcroft Ski Touring Center maintains around 35km of trails around Ashcroft, a mining ghost town. The Pine Creek Cookhouse (925 1044) does excellent food and is accessible only by ski, snowshoe or horse-drawn sleigh. Aspen is at one end of the famous Tenth Mountain Division Trail, heading 370km north-east almost to Vail, with 12 huts for overnight stops.

MOUNTAIN RESTAURANTS ★★★
Good by American standards
Surprisingly, Highlands and Snowmass (see separate chapter) have good table-service places and Aspen Mountain doesn't.
Editors' choice At Highlands, Cloud Nine bistro (544 3063) is the nearest thing in the States to a cosy Alpine hut, with excellent food – thanks to an Austrian chef. Not wildly expensive, either – $40 for two courses (daily changing set menu). We had delicious elk stew here on our last visit.
Worth knowing about On Aspen Mountain there's the Sundeck self-service – about as good as an American self-service restaurant gets – light and airy with great views across to Highland Bowl. Bonnie's self-service is another option: 'fantastic white chilli bean soup', 'hearty stews and burgers'. On Highlands, the recently refurbished mid-mountain Merry-Go-Round self-service has 'a comfortable bar area', where one recent reporter enjoyed 'one of the best pastas ever'.
On Buttermilk the mountaintop Cliffhouse specializes in a Mongolian barbecue stir-fry, and Bumps (self-service) offers a 'good range'. You can picnic at The Cafe West, Top of West warming hut, Bottom of Tiehack warming hut and No Problem Cabin.

SCHOOLS AND GUIDES ★★★★★
One of the best?
Aspen's school is highly regarded, and group classes are usually small and of a high standard. 'Maximum of three people in our lessons and the same instructor for the three days,' says a reporter. Another praises the free 'Inside Tracks' programme being run by the school exclusively for Limelight Lodge guests. You get a day skiing with a pro, who will act as a guide as well as give you pointers on your technique.

FOR FAMILIES ★★
Choice of nurseries
Aspen caters well for families, with Buttermilk the focus for lessons. Children are bussed to and from the mountain's impressive Fort Frog, and the kids' trail map is a great idea. But Snowmass has clear advantages for young families.

STAYING THERE

Hotels There are places for all budgets, including very grand places such as the Hyatt and St Regis on which we never get reports. Most smaller hotels provide a good free après-ski cheese and wine buffet.
★★★★★Jerome (920 1000) Step back a century: Victorian authenticity combined with modern-day luxury. Refurbished for 2012/13 season with new spa. Several blocks from the gondola.
★★★★★Little Nell (920 4600) Stylish, modern hotel right by the gondola, with popular bar. Fireplaces in every room, outdoor pool, hot tub, sauna. Smart condos, too.
★★★★Lenado (925 6246) Smart modern B&B with open-fire in lounge, individually designed rooms, hot tub.
★★★Aspen (925 3441) Spacious, basic rooms; pool, hot tub; 10 minutes' walk to gondola. Near bus stop.
★★★Aspen Mountain Lodge (925 7650) Small, friendly, in a quiet location. 'Very friendly, helpful staff.'
★★★Limelight Lodge (925 3025) Modern style, central. Pool, tubs. Recommended by a 2012 visitor 'on just about every count': 'great rooms, good breakfasts, pretty good location'.
★★★Molly Gibson Lodge (925 3434) Pool, hot tub. Opposite hotel Aspen. 'Excellent value for money,' says a 2012 visitor. 'Comfortable with big breakfasts.' But 'run of the mill; wouldn't return', says a 2013 visitor.
★★★The Sky (925 6760) Hip, swanky New York-style hotel in great location by gondola.
★★Mountain Chalet (925 7797) Cosy lodge five minutes from gondola. Pool, sauna, steam and fitness centre.
★★St Moritz Lodge (925 3220) Aspen's youth hostel. A reporter remarks: 'Not many hostels have a heated pool and complimentary happy hour! Super-friendly guests and staff.'
Apartments The standards here are high, even in US terms. Many of the smarter developments have their own

free shuttle-buses. The Gant, Aspen Square and Aspen Meadows Resort have been recommended.

EATING OUT ★★★★★
Dining dilemma

Aspen has an excellent blend of upmarket places and cheaper options. Some giveaway magazines include menu guides, and there are listings at www.eataspen.com. Every year brings a raft of closures and new ventures; we welcome your reports.

Top of the range places include: Il Mulino (an outpost of a classy Italian restaurant in New York) in the Little Nell residences; Syzygy, Piñons and Element 47 (in the Little Nell hotel) – all with innovative American cooking; Matsuhisa (Japanese fusion); and the Rustique Bistro, Brexi Brasserie ('lovely food, but a bit dark') and Cache Cache (all French). Steakhouse 316 is a small 'boutique' steakhouse in 1920s' style: 'Pricey, but fantastic steaks! Great service.' The tiny Wild Fig has 'a varied, Mediterranean-influenced menu'. The underground Zocalito offers Latin American cuisine: 'absolutely delicious' was one reporter's view. The main dining room at the Jerome hotel is 'very good, very glamorous', says a 2013 visitor.

You can eat more cheaply at a lot of the smart places by eating at the bar – basically, you get smaller portions and can't book, which of course may suit you. We did this very happily on our last visit at Jimmy's (American), L'Hostaria and Campo de Fiori (both Italian).

Mid-market and cheaper choices include: Little Annie's ('massive portions', 'a meat feast'), Asie (Asian fusion – 'astonishingly good' dumplings); Hickory House for Ribs ('an Aspen institution – very busy and generous helpings'); Brunelleschi's ('good Italian food', 'excellent service', 'very family friendly'); Cantina ('friendly service and good Tex Mex'); Red Onion (saloon/grill – 'large portions'); Su Casa (Mexican – 'central; good value'); Ute City (American style bistro – 'varied menu, great value').

APRES-SKI ★★★★
Lots of options

In the late afternoon, we've known Cloud Nine on Highlands to turn into a very un-American Austrian-style après-ski venue – booze-fuelled dancing on the tables in ski boots. A few bars at the bases get busy – notably Out of Bounds at Highlands and Ajax Tavern ('very lively upmarket crowd') in Aspen. The Terrace Bar at the Little Nell is a great place for gazing at facelifts; 39 Degrees at the Sky hotel has a chic atmosphere.

Later on, wine connoisseurs could try Victoria's Espresso & Wine Bar. Many of the restaurants are also bars – Jimmy's (spectacular stock of tequila), for example. The J-bar of the Jerome hotel dates back to 1889 and has a traditional feel ('great place to stop for a pre-dinner drink or two'). Aspen Billiards adjoining the fashionable Cigar Bar is an upscale venue for playing pool. The local microbrewery, The Aspen Brewing Company, is in the centre of Aspen.

For music and dancing, head for Belly Up ('good selection of live music') or the Regal Watering Hole. Or you can get a week's membership of the famous Caribou club.

OFF THE SLOPES ★★★★
Silver service

Aspen has lots to offer, especially if your credit card is in good shape. There are literally dozens of art galleries, as well as the predictable clothes and jewellery shops. There are plenty of shops selling affordable stuff. And 'one of the best bookshops I have ever seen', says a 2013 visitor. Glenwood Springs is worth a visit for its hot-spring outdoor pool. The Aspen Recreation Center at Highlands has a huge swimming complex and an indoor ice rink. Hot-air ballooning is possible. Some mountain restaurants are accessible to pedestrians.

Beaver Creek

Exclusive and very pricey modern resort with quiet, varied slopes. Good for a pampered stay or a day trip from Vail

TOP 10 RATINGS

Extent	★★★
Fast lifts	★★★★★
Queues	★★★★★
Snow	★★★★★
Expert	★★★★
Intermediate	★★★★
Beginner	★★★★★
Charm	★★
Convenience	★★★★
Scenery	★★★

RPI   180

lift pass	£350
ski hire	£175
lessons	£235
food & drink	£185
total	**£945**

NEWS

2013/14: The restaurant at Red Tail Camp will be replaced by a new 500-seat restaurant, more than doubling the existing capacity.

2012/13: A new women's downhill race course was built in the Birds of Prey area, which added 17 acres of new terrain, including a black run. Free two-hour women-only mountain tours have started. They're at 10am on Tuesdays to Fridays.

VAIL RESORTS INC

The village is small, smart and traffic-free – with heated pavements and escalators up to the slopes ➔

- **+** Slopes generally quiet on weekdays
- **+** Mountain has it all, from superb novice runs to daunting moguls
- **+** Fast chairlifts all over the place
- **+** Compact, traffic-free village centre

- **–** Lacks any Wild West atmosphere
- **–** Very expensive
- **–** Table-service mountain restaurants are member-only
- **–** Not much going on at night

'Not exactly roughing it' is the strangely coy slogan of Vail's kid sister resort, discreetly underlining its status as about the smoothest resort in the US. We don't find the exclusive resort village particularly appealing, but the mountain certainly is. As a budget base, consider staying down in Avon.

THE RESORT

Beaver Creek, 16km to the west of Vail, was developed in the 1980s and is unashamedly exclusive. The lift system spreads across the mountains to Bachelor Gulch, a small collection of relatively new condos and houses and a Ritz-Carlton hotel, and to Arrowhead, a slope-side hamlet that is less pricey than Beaver Creek. Below here is the valley town of Avon, where a 2013 reporter happily stayed much more cheaply than is possible in Beaver Creek or Vail. There are free car parks in Avon for day visitors (parking in the resort itself is expensive and limited) and you can take a free shuttle to the village or a fast chair up to Bachelor Gulch. A gondola links the Riverfront area of Avon to this chair.

Day trips to Vail, Breckenridge and Keystone (all covered by the lift pass) and Copper Mountain are possible.
Village charm The village centres on a small, smart, modern pedestrian area with upmarket shops, open-air ice rink and heated pavements.
Convenience There are top-quality hotels and condos right by the slopes, and escalators up from the centre.
Scenery The scenery is pleasantly woody rather than dramatic.

THE MOUNTAINS

All the slopes are below the treeline, though there are some more open areas. Free two-hour mountain tours are operated every day at 10am. At the top of most main lifts is a big piste map board (and lights showing which runs have been groomed – a great idea that we haven't seen before). They take their 'slow skiing zones' seriously here too – with big banners across the piste warning that skier speed is monitored.
Slopes The slopes immediately above Beaver Creek divide into two sectors, each accessed by a fast quad chair – one centred on Spruce Saddle, the other on Bachelor Gulch (which links to Arrowhead). Between these are Grouse Mountain and Larkspur Bowl, again with fast quads. Off to the left is another sector, with a fast quad.
Fast lifts Nearly all key lifts are fast chairs; beginners have a gondola.
Queues Not normally a problem.
Terrain parks Park 101 is a small beginners' park, Zoom Room has intermediate-level features, and Rodeo has big hits for advanced riders.

KEY FACTS

Resort	2470m
	8,100ft
Slopes	2255-3485m
	7,400-11,440ft
Lifts	25
Pistes	1832 acres
Green	19%
Blue	43%
Black	38%
Snowmaking	37%

UK PACKAGES

Alpine Answers, AmeriCan Ski, American Ski Classics, Crystal, Crystal Finest, Elegant Resorts, Frontier, Independent Ski Links, Momentum, Oxford Ski Co, PowderBeds, Ski Bespoke, Ski Independence, Ski Line, Ski Safari, Ski Solutions, Skitracer, Skiworld, STC, Supertravel

Central reservations phone number
496 4900

Phone numbers
From distant parts of the US, add the prefix 1 970; from abroad, add the prefix +1 970

TOURIST OFFICE

www.beavercreek.com

There's a 110m-long half-pipe, off Barrel Stave. Parkology is a park and pipe programme for kids.

Snow reliability An impressive snow record (average 325 inches) and snowmaking mean you can relax. But Grouse Mountain can have thin cover (some call it Gravel Mountain).

Experts There is plenty of satisfying steep terrain. In the Birds of Prey and Grouse Mountain areas most runs are long, steep and mogulled, but the downhill race course pistes are groomed periodically, making great fast cruises. Grouse and Stone Creek Chutes have great steep glades.

Intermediates There are marvellous long, quiet, cruising blues everywhere you look, including top-to-bottom runs with a vertical of 1000m.

Beginners There are excellent nursery slopes at resort level – served by a short gondola – and a further large area at altitude. And there are plenty of easy long runs to progress to.

Snowboarding Good riders will love the excellent gladed runs and perfect carving slopes. The resort is great for beginners, too.

Cross-country There's a splendid, mountain-top network of tracks at McCoy Park (over 32km), reached via the Strawberry Park lift.

Mountain restaurants Spruce Saddle at mid-mountain is the main place – a food court in an airy log building; but it can get very busy. Red Tail Camp is being rebuilt and expanded for 2013/14. But for table-service you have to head down to a base area; the swanky on-mountain cabins are

member-only at lunchtime.

Schools and guides We lack recent reports, but don't doubt that the school is excellent.

Families Small World Play School looks after non-skiing kids from two months to six years from 8.30 to 4pm. At the top of the Buckaroo gondola are adventure trails and a tubing park.

STAYING THERE

The resort lodging is pricey and luxurious. As a budget option, consider staying down in Avon.

Hotels Lots of upmarket places, such as the Ritz-Carlton and Park Hyatt. The Osprey, Charter and Pines Lodge combine hotel facilities with luxury condo convenience.

Apartments Slope-side condos include Elkhorn Lodge, Oxford Court, St James Place, Bear Paw and SaddleRidge.

Eating out SaddleRidge is plush and packed with photos and Wild West artefacts. Toscanini, the Golden Eagle Inn, Dusty Boot (in St James Place), and Beaver Creek Chophouse have been recommended. You can take a sleigh ride to dine at swanky Beano's or Zach's cabins on the slopes. Or try the numerous restaurants in Avon (buses run to and from there until 10pm): the Blue Plate was recommended by a 2013 reporter ('good duck and schnitzel').

Après-ski Try the Coyote Cafe and McCoy's (live bands) and the 8100 Mountainside Bar at Park Hyatt.

Off the slopes Smart shops and galleries, an ice rink, ballooning, dog sledding, snowshoeing and concerts.

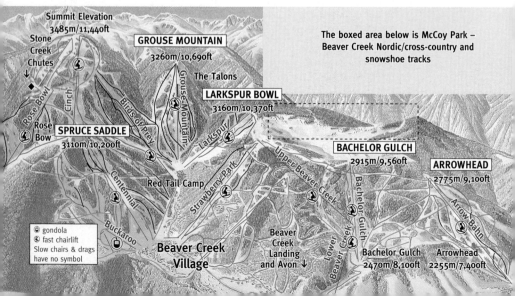

Breckenridge

A sprawling resort with a cute 'Wild West' core, beneath a wide, varied mountain; increasing amounts of slope-side accommodation

RATINGS

The mountains

Extent	★★★
Fast lifts	★★★★
Queues	★★★★
Terrain p'ks	★★★★★
Snow	★★★★★
Expert	★★★★
Intermediate	★★★★
Beginner	★★★★★
Boarder	★★★★★
X-country	★★★★
Restaurants	★★
Schools	★★★★★
Families	★★★★

The resort

Charm	★★★
Convenience	★★★
Scenery	★★★
Eating out	★★★★★
Après-ski	★★★
Off-slope	★★★

RPI   165

lift pass	£320
ski hire	£155
lessons	£215
food & drink	£150
total	**£840**

NEWS

2013/14: A new area, Peak 6, with 400 acres of lift-served and 143 acres of hike-to terrain, is due to open. The area will be served by a new six-pack and a quad chair and will increase the resort's terrain by over 25%.

KEY FACTS

Resort	2925m 9,600ft
Slopes	2925-3915m 9,600-12,840ft
Lifts	31
Pistes	2,901 acres
Green	14%
Blue	31%
Black	55%
Snowmaking	24%

➕ Slopes have something for all abilities – good for mixed groups

➕ Cute Victorian Main Street, with mainly sympathetic new buildings

➕ Plenty of lively bars and restaurants

➕ Shared lift pass with four other worthwhile resorts nearby

➕ Efficient lifts mean few queues

➕ Some slope-side accommodation

➕ Short transfer from Denver, but ...

➖ At 2925m the village poses a risk of altitude sickness if you go there directly from the UK

➖ Very prone to high winds, affecting mainly the high, advanced slopes

➖ On-piste terrain not very extensive, with few long runs

➖ Lack of good, central hotels

➖ Main Street is a thoroughfare and always busy with traffic

Breckenridge has a lot going for it. The Main Street is attractive and lively, with Wild West roots and lots of places to eat and drink. The slopes have something for everyone, provided the ungroomed top slopes are open. But the downsides are serious. Some areas have modern, rather characterless buildings that contrast starkly with most of Main Street. The top slopes are too often closed by wind. And the groomed trails are limited and very similar to each other. Those keen on mileage and variety should plan to visit other resorts (covered by the lift pass) by car or bus too; they'll find Breck limited for a week's stay.

Heed our warning about altitude sickness. At almost 3000m this is the highest resort to get a full chapter in this book – and the altitude you sleep at is a key factor. Like many readers, Editor Gill has been affected by altitude sickness here, and now always spends time in a lower resort before hitting Breckenridge; a couple of nights in Denver is an alternative way to cut the risk.

THE RESORT

Breckenridge was founded in 1859 and became a booming gold-mining town. Old clapboard buildings line much of Main Street, and the streets nearby have been well renovated. Small shopping malls and other buildings have been added in similar style. But there are some (rather out-of-place) modern buildings too, especially around the base of Peak 9.

The resort is in the same ownership as Vail, Beaver Creek and Keystone. A multi-day lift ticket covers all these plus Arapahoe Basin. All of them plus Copper Mountain can be reached by bus (free to Keystone and Arapahoe Basin; paid-for to the others).

VILLAGE CHARM ★★★
A festive treat
The town centre is lively in the evening – particularly at weekends – with lots of people strolling around the shops on their way to or from the 100-plus restaurants and bars in and around the busy main street.

Christmas lights and decorations remain throughout the season, giving the town a festive air. This is enhanced by festivals such as Ullr Fest – honouring the Norse God of Winter – and snow sculpture championships.

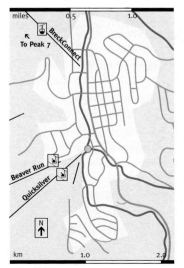

CONVENIENCE ★★★
Slope life or nightlife

There is a lot of slope-side lodgings, including smart recent developments at the bases of Peaks 7 and 8. But there is also some inconveniently distant from both Main Street and the lift base stations. Hotels and condos are spread over a wide area and linked by regular, free shuttle-buses (less frequent in the evening – worth staying centrally if you plan to spend much time in Main Street). There are two supermarkets – a smaller one near the centre of town and a larger one on the outskirts (a long walk if you don't have a car).

SCENERY ★★★
Peak after peak

This is high country; on a clear day above the treeline there are extensive views of Colorado's highest summits – many of which reach over 4000m.

THE MOUNTAINS

The slopes are mainly cut through the forest, but there is quite a lot of steeper skiing above the treeline (prone to closure by high winds).

The resort used to have some runs classified as blue-black. They have now scrapped these and made them single black diamond – a real backward step because the old blue-blacks (mainly on Peak 10) are still great intermediate cruises and the new black classification may put people off trying them.

EXTENT OF THE SLOPES ★★★
Growing but fragmented

There are five sectors, linked by lift and piste. Two fast chairlifts go from one end of the town up to **Peak 9**, one accessing mainly green runs on the lower half of the hill, the other mainly blue runs higher up. From there you can get to **Peak 10**, with black runs (including former blue-blacks) served by one fast quad.

The **Peak 8** area – tough stuff at the top, easier lower down – can be reached by a fast quad from Peak 9. The base lifts of Peak 8 can also be reached by the slow Snowflake lift from the suburbs, or by gondola from a car park on the fringes of town. The six-pack serving **Peak 7** can be accessed from Peak 8 and from the gondola's mid-station. **Peak 6** is due to open with two new lifts for 2013/14.

The higher open slopes on Peaks 7 and 8 are accessed by a T-bar – a rarity in these parts – reachable from either base, and by the Imperial fast quad at the top of the Peak 8 lift network. The resort claims a top height of 3960m, but that involves a hike of 45m vertical at the very top.

FAST LIFTS ★★★★
Good coverage

Breckenridge's gondola and ten fast chairlifts cover all five sectors and provide good access from either end of town – the slow Snowflake chair to Peak 8 in between is an obvious exception, which will be an irritant if you are based nearby.

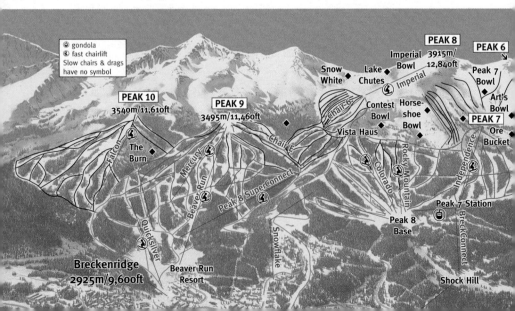

↑ A lot of buildings reflect the style of the town's gold-mining heritage

LIFT PASSES

Prices in US$

Age	1-day	6-day
under 13	59	300
13 to 64	100	468
65 plus	90	408

Free Under 5

Beginner Included in price of lessons

Notes 3-day-plus pass covers Breckenridge, Keystone and Arapahoe Basin, plus 3 days (of a 6-day pass) at Vail and Beaver Creek; prices are online rates for early Feb purchased 14 days in advance of trip; window rates in resort are considerably higher; international visitors will get best prices by pre-booking through a UK tour operator (it is not necessary to buy a complete holiday package to obtain these prices)

QUEUES ★★★★
Peak times possibly

A 2013 reporter encountered 20-minute queues on Presidents weekend but no queues midweek. Outside peak periods, reporters confirm there are few problems. There may be queues for the old Chair 6 on a powder day and the slow Snowflake chair that gives access to Peak 8 for thousands of condo-dwellers.

TERRAIN PARKS ★★★★★
Five to choose from

The main focus is Peak 8, with three parks for different ability levels. Freeway is one of the best parks in North America and the largest of Breck's park, featuring a series of big jumps, obstacles and a super-pipe. Next to it, Park Lane offers a variety of challenging features. And Trygves has gentle jumps and rollers for beginner freestylers. On Peak 9 are two more parks: Bonanza is a beginner progression park, and Gold King bridges the gap between Bonanza and Park Lane. See www.breck1080.com.

SNOW RELIABILITY ★★★★★
Normally ample quantities

With its high altitude, Breckenridge boasts a good natural snow record – annual average 300 inches. That is supplemented by substantial snowmaking (used mainly early in the season to form a good base). There are a lot of east- and north-east-facing slopes, which hold snow well. But high winds can remove or spoil the snow, notably on exposed upper runs (on lower runs too in 2013, said a reporter).

FOR EXPERTS ★★★★
Lots of short but tough runs

A remarkable 55% of the runs are classified black – that's a higher proportion than famous 'macho' resorts such as Jackson Hole, Taos and Snowbird. And a good proportion are classified as 'expert' (double diamond) or 'extreme' terrain. But most runs are short – most of the key lifts offer verticals of around 300m.

Peak 8 is at the core of the tough skiing. The lightly wooded slopes served by Chair 6 are a good place to start – picturesque and not too steep. Below, steeper runs lead further down to the junction with Peak 9. Above, the Imperial quad accesses huge amounts of above-the-treeline terrain and longer runs. You can hike up to the double-diamond Imperial Bowl, and the 'extreme' Lake Chutes and Snow White areas. Or you can traverse round the back towards Peak 7 and double-diamond runs in the bowl (we had a great time in fresh snow there on our last visit); the T-bar on Peak 8 accesses the lower parts of these runs (single diamonds) and the double-diamond Horseshoe and Contest bowls. On the lower, wooded part of Peak 8 is a worthwhile area of single diamonds.

Peak 9's wooded North Slope under Chair E is excellent – shady, sheltered and steep – we've had great runs down Devil's Crotch, Hades and Inferno. Peak 10 has easy black runs (former blue-blacks) down the central ridge, but more challenging stuff on both flanks. To skier's left is a lovely, lightly wooded area called The Burn.

ACTIVITIES

Indoor Recreation centre on outskirts (accessible by bus): pool, gym, tennis, climbing wall; spas, ice rink, theatre, cinema, museums, galleries

Outdoor Horse-drawn sleigh rides, dog sledding, snowmobiles, ice rink, snowshoeing, tobogganing

GETTING THERE

Air Denver 165km/ 105 miles (2hr15)

VAIL RESORTS / AARON DODDS

The main Freeway terrain park regularly hosts top competitions. And there are four easier parks too ↓

FOR INTERMEDIATES ★★★★
Nice cruising, limited extent
Breckenridge has some good blue cruising runs for all intermediates. But dedicated piste-bashers are likely to find the runs short and limited in variety. Peak 9 has the easiest slopes. It is nearly all gentle, wide, blue runs at the top and almost flat, wide, green runs at the bottom. And the ski patrol is supposed to enforce slow-speed skiing in certain areas.

Peak 10 has a number of easy, normally groomed, black runs that used to be classified blue-black, such as Crystal and Centennial, which make for good fast cruising. Peaks 7 and 8 both have blues on trails cut close together in the trees, which feel very similar and offer little variety. Adventurous intermediates can also try some of the high bowl runs and more gentle gladed runs such as Ore Bucket glades on the fringe of Peak 7 and the runs beneath Chair 6 on Peak 8.

FOR BEGINNERS ★★★★★
Excellent
The bottom of Peak 9 has a big, virtually flat area and some good, gentle nursery slopes. There's then a good choice of green runs to move on to. Beginners can try Peak 8 too, with another selection of green runs and a choice of trails back to town. There is a special beginner package available (see 'Schools and guides').

FOR BOARDERS ★★★★★
One of the best
Breckenridge is pretty much ideal for all standards of boarder and hosts several major US snowboarding events. Beginners have ideal nursery slopes and greens to progress to. Intermediates have good cruising runs, all served by chairs. The powder bowls at the top of Peaks 7 and 8 make great riding and can be accessed via the Imperial quad, so avoiding the awkward T-bar. Boarders of all levels will enjoy the choice of excellent terrain parks. Nearby Arapahoe Basin is another area for hardcore boarding in steep bowls and chutes.

FOR CROSS-COUNTRY ★★★★
Specialist centre in woods
The Nordic Center is set in the woods between the town and Peak 8 and served by shuttle-bus. It has 32km of trails and 15km of snowshoeing trails.

MOUNTAIN RESTAURANTS ★★
Improved by more base options
Of the self-service places above base level, Ten Mile Station, where Peak 9 meets 10, is the place we gravitate to. Both it and the dreary Vista Haus on Peak 8 are food-court operations and get nightmarishly busy at weekends. Peak 9 restaurant serves 'reasonable' food, says a reporter. Sevens is a table-service restaurant at the Peak 7 base. The Ski Hill Grill at the base of Peak 8 has a smart decor with lots of stone and a 'good variety' of self-service food (including Asian fusion).

SCHOOLS

Breckenridge
t 453 3272

Classes
Day (4.5hr) $155
Private lessons
$495 for 3hr for up to
3 people

CHILDCARE

Child Care Centers
t +1 888 576 2754
Age 8wk to 3yr
Summit Sitters
t 513 4445
Mountain Sitters
t 512 261 5053

Ski school
Ages 3 to 13

UK PACKAGES

Alpine Answers,
AmeriCan Ski, American
Ski Classics, Crystal,
Crystal Finest, Erna
Low, Flexiski, Frontier,
Independent Ski Links,
Inghams, Interactive
Resorts, Momentum,
Oxford Ski Co,
PowderBeds, Ski
Bespoke, Ski
Expectations, Ski
Independence, Ski Line,
Ski Safari, Ski
Solutions, Skitracer,
Skiworld, Snow Finders,
STC, Supertravel,
Thomson, Virgin Snow
Frisco AmeriCan Ski

Phone numbers
From distant parts of
the US, add the prefix
1 970; from abroad,
add the prefix +1 970

TOURIST OFFICE

www.breckenridge.
com

SCHOOLS AND GUIDES ★★★★★
Usual high US standard
We lack recent reports but past ones have been positive. The beginner package includes lessons, equipment rental and lift pass, and the school's special clinics include telemark.

FOR FAMILIES ★★★★
Excellent facilities
Past reports on the children's school and nursery have been full of praise. The Mountains of Discovery Program aims to combine teaching and fun on the slopes (for kids aged three to 13).

STAYING THERE

Chalets Skiworld has a four-bedroom house built in traditional clapboard style near Main Street and with an outdoor hot tub. Crystal features a smart six-bedroom log cabin in the woods with hot tub near Peak 8 (run privately rather than Crystal-operated).
Hotels There's a noticeable lack of good places close to Main Street.
★★★★DoubleTree by Hilton (547 5550) (Formerly Great Divide, renovated in 2012.) A short walk to the slopes and a bearable walk to Main Street.
★★★★Lodge & Spa at Breckenridge (453 9300) Stylish luxury spa resort set out of town among 32 acres, with great views. Private shuttle-bus.
★★★★Barn on the River (453 2975) B&B on Main Street. Hot tub.
★★★Beaver Run (453 6000) Huge, slope-side resort complex with 520 spacious rooms. Pools, hot tubs.
Apartments There is a huge choice. Mountain Thunder Lodge (near the gondola and the supermarket), Hyatt Main Street Station (near the Quicksilver lift) and One Ski Hill Place at Peak 8 are recommended at the luxury end. A regular visitor tips The Village at Breckenridge and River Mountain Lodge (for quality, value and location), also Trails End, Corral, One Breckenridge Place and Saddlewood. Der Steiermark is a cheaper option.

EATING OUT ★★★★★
Over 100 restaurants
There's a wide range, from typical US food to fine dining. At peak times they get busy, and many don't take bookings. The Breckenridge Dining Guide (available online) lists the full menu of most places.
    Recent visitors confirmed the attractions of the Hearthstone (modern

American cuisine in a beautiful 100-year-old house): 'Excellent food, decor and atmosphere good.' For no-nonsense grills-and-fries in a pub ambience, we've enjoyed both the Brewery (famous for mega 'appetizers', such as buffalo wings, and splendid beers) and the Kenosha steakhouse. Reader tips: Whale's Tail (mainly, but not only, seafood), Mi Casa (Mexican), South Ridge (predominantly fish), Downstairs at Eric's (burgers and pizzas), Michael's (Italian), Steak & Rib ('bit of an institution; stacks of photos and memorabilia') and Spencer's, at Beaver Run resort (steaks and seafood). The Blue Moose does killer breakfasts.

APRES-SKI ★★★
The best in the area ...
There's not much teatime animation at the lift bases. The Maggie, at the base of Peak 9, 'has music on the terrace but doesn't stay open much beyond 5pm'. Park Avenue Pub, just off Main Street, and the Brewery were lively on our recent visits. Later on we've enjoyed the Gold Pan saloon (reputedly the oldest bar west of the Mississippi); reader tips include the Liquid Lounge and Fatty's. Cecilia's serves good cocktails; Burke and Riley's is an Irish bar; Downstairs at Eric's is a disco sports bar, and Three2oSouth has live bands.

OFF THE SLOPES ★★★
Pleasant enough
Breckenridge is a pleasant place to wander around, with souvenir and gift shops plus a museum. Silverthorne (about 30 minutes away by free bus) has bargain factory outlet stores.

NEARBY TOWN – 2765m

FRISCO

Staying in Frisco makes sense for those touring or on a tight budget. It's a pleasant small town with bars, restaurants and good-value lodgings and linked to resorts by a free bus. A 2013 reporter liked the Lake Dillon Lodge (668 5094) – pool, hot tub, good breakfasts. Hotel Frisco (668 5009) is on Main Street. Restaurants include Tuscato (Italian), Blue Spruce Inn ('fantastic steaks and ambience'), the Boatyard (pizzas), Food Hedz World Cafe ('good duck and steak') and Ollie's ('Wednesday $2 burger night is great value').

Breckenridge

Build your own shortlist: www.wheretoskiandsnowboard.com

Snowmass

Aspen's modern satellite – with impressively varied and extensive slopes, and a smart new fledgling Base Village

TOP 10 RATINGS

Extent	★★★
Fast lifts	★★★★★
Queues	★★★★
Snow	★★★★★
Expert	★★★★★
Intermediate	★★★★★
Beginner	★★★★★
Charm	★★
Convenience	★★★★
Scenery	★★★★

Our extent rating is for Snowmass alone. Including the other Aspen mountains would make it ★★★★

RPI	190
lift pass	£400
ski hire	£205
lessons	£235
food & drink	£150
total	**£990**

568

UK PACKAGES

Alpine Answers, AmeriCan Ski, American Ski Classics, Crystal, Ski Independence, Ski Safari, Supertravel

+ Varied mountain, with the biggest vertical in the US – 1340m

+ Aspen accessible by free bus. Aspen airport only a few minutes away

+ Uncrowded slopes

+ Lots of slope-side lodgings

− Limited dining, shopping and nightlife

− Diversions of Aspen town are a bus ride away

The slopes of Snowmass are a key part of the attraction of nearby Aspen as a destination. As a base, Snowmass has obvious appeal for families wanting easy cruising on their doorstep; its appeal is starting to broaden as more shops and restaurants open at the new Base Village – but progress is slow.

THE RESORT

Snowmass is a modern, purpose-built resort, with low-rise buildings set next to the gentle home slope. Within these buildings is Snowmass Village Mall. Further down the hill is a new Base Village, the development of which has been slowed by the current recession.
Village charm The new Base Village has added a bit of style to what is a rather plain modern resort.
Convenience Much of the lodging is ski-in/ski-out, and Snowmass Village Mall has a small cluster of shops and restaurants. Efficient free bus services (crowded at times) link Snowmass with Aspen's mountains and town – the one to Aspen runs to 2am.
Scenery The views from the high-points are long but not dramatic.

THE MOUNTAIN

Most of the slopes are in the forest; higher ones are only lightly wooded.
Slopes Snowmass is big by US standards – almost 8km across, with the biggest vertical in the US. Chairlifts and a gondola diverge from the base to go up to two high-points at either end of the ski area – Elk Camp and Sam's Knob. Links higher up go to the two sectors in the middle, High Alpine and Big Burn, where a draglift goes to the high-point on The Cirque. The Two Creeks base is nearer Aspen.
Fast lifts Most key lifts are fast. But there are still a couple of long, slow chairs that can be cold in midwinter.
Queues Any problems can usually be avoided. The home slope gets busy.
Terrain parks Snowmass has a super-

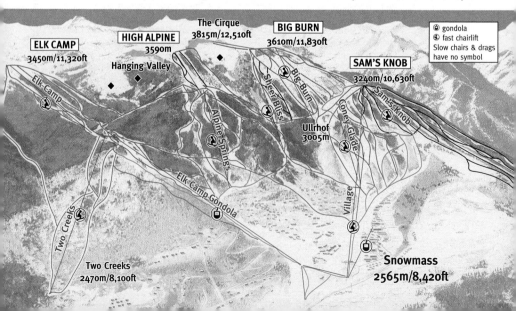

ELK CAMP
3450m/11,320ft

HIGH ALPINE
3590m

Hanging Valley

The Cirque
3815m/12,510ft

BIG BURN
3610m/11,830ft

SAM'S KNOB
3240m/10,630ft

🚠 gondola
🚡 fast chairlift
Slow chairs & drags have no symbol

Ullrhof
3005m

Two Creeks
2470m/8,100ft

Snowmass
2565m/8,420ft

NEWS

2012/13: Three new gladed black runs opened in 230 acres off to the left of our piste map on terrain that was formerly backcountry. At the top of the Elk Camp gondola $13 million has been spent on building a bigger restaurant to replace Cafe Suzanne. The former Silvertree Hotel has been transformed into the Westin Snowmass Resort.

KEY FACTS

Resort	2565m
	8,420ft
Snowmass only	
Slopes	2470-3815m
	8,100-12,510ft
Lifts	21
Pistes	3,332 acres
Green	6%
Blue	47%
Black	47%
Snowmaking	7%

See Aspen chapter for statistics on other mountains

Phone numbers
From distant parts of the US, add the prefix 1 970; from abroad, add the prefix +1 970

TOURIST OFFICE

www.aspen
snowmass.com

pipe and three parks: Lowdown (beginner) with half-pipe, Little Makaha (intermediate) and Snowmass (expert), with about 90 features including jibs, rails, boxes and jumps.

Snow reliability With 300 inches a year plus snowmaking, it's good.

Experts There's great terrain, although the steep runs tend to be short. Consider joining a guided group as an introduction. Our favourite area is around the Hanging Valley Wall and Glades – beautiful scenery and steep wooded slopes. The other seriously steep area is The Cirque, reached by draglift from Big Burn to the area's highest point. From here, the Headwall is not terrifyingly steep, but there are also narrow, often rocky, chutes – Gowdy's is one of the steepest. Try the new gladed black runs mentioned under 'Intermediates' too.

Intermediates Excellent – this is the best mountain in the Aspen area for intermediates (and by far the biggest). Highlights include: the top slopes on Big Burn – a huge, varied, lightly wooded area, including the Powerline Glades for the adventurous; long, top-to-bottom cruises from Elk Camp and High Alpine; regularly groomed single-black runs from Sam's Knob. Then there are glorious runs set in the forest starting a short hike from the top of Elk Camp: these are around 5km long, end at Two Creeks and include a long-time favourite, the blue Long Shot, and three gladed black runs that were new for last season and classified black only because of a narrow and quite steep traverse out.

Beginners In the heart of the resort is a broad, gentle beginners' run. An even easier slope (and less busy) is Assay Hill, at the bottom of Elk Camp. There's also a beginner area served by three lifts at the top of the Elk Camp gondola. From Sam's Knob there are long, gentle cruises back to the resort.

Snowboarding A great mountain, whatever your boarding style.

Cross-country Excellent trails between here and Aspen – see Aspen chapter.

Mountain restaurants There are three table-service places: Gwyn's High Alpine (established over 30 years), Lynn Britt Cabin (old log cabin, elegant table settings) and Sam's Smokehouse (newish, big windows, great views) – all do good food. Self-service options include Elk Camp and Up 4 Pizza. You can picnic at the Wapiti Wildlife Center at the top of Elk Camp and in the warming huts at the top of Sam's Knob, Big Burn and High Alpine.

Schools and guides We've had mixed reports. A recent visitor had two different teachers with 'no real enthusiasm or feedback', but his son had the same teacher throughout – 'very enthusiastic, good feedback'.

Families Snowmass is a family-friendly resort. The Treehouse adventure centre at Base Village is a very impressive facility and there are special trails and trail maps for children.

STAYING THERE

Most accommodation is self-catering.
Hotels The focal hotel, the Silvertree, was transformed into the plush Westin Snowmass Resort (923 8200) for 2012/13. A recent visitor raves about the Stonebridge Inn (923 2420): 'Excellent bar/restaurant; awesome outdoor pool and hot tubs.' The luxury Viceroy (923 8000) is at Base Village.
Apartments Capitol Peak and Hayden Lodge are luxury condos at Base Village. Tamarack Townhouses and Crestwood Condos are popular. A recent visitor found the Timberline condos 'OK', with 'attentive staff'.
Eating out The Eight K restaurant in the Viceroy is highly recommended by a recent reporter, especially the 'chef's tables' where the atmosphere is 'more laid back'. Il Poggio is recommended for Italian. Base Camp has reasonable prices and Buchi is a Japanese place.
Après-ski Try Base Camp (live music), Venga Venga Cantina & Tequila Bar or, at Base Village, Sneaky's Tavern.
Off the slopes Snowshoe trails, snowcat rides, dog sledding plus swimming at the Recreation Center.

Vail

A vast, swanky resort with some very swanky hotels at the foot of one of the biggest (but also busiest) ski areas in the States

RATINGS

The mountains

Extent	★★★★
Fast lifts	★★★★★
Queues	★★
Terrain p'ks	★★★★★
Snow	★★★★★
Expert	★★★★
Intermediate	★★★★★
Beginner	★★★
Boarder	★★★
X-country	★★★
Restaurants	★★
Schools	★★★★
Families	★★★★

The resort

Charm	★★★
Convenience	★★★
Scenery	★★★
Eating out	★★★★★
Après-ski	★★★
Off-slope	★★★

RPI 180

lift pass	£350
ski hire	£175
lessons	£235
food & drink	£170
total	**£930**

KEY FACTS

Resort	2500m
	8,200ft
Slopes	2475-3525m
	8,120-11,570ft
Lifts	31
Pistes	5,289 acres
Green	18%
Blue	29%
Black	53%
Snowmaking	9%

+ One of the biggest areas in the US – especially great for confident intermediates

+ The Back Bowls are big areas of treeless terrain – unusual in the US

+ Fabulous area of ungroomed, wooded slopes at Blue Sky Basin

+ Largely traffic-free resort centres, very pleasant in parts – but ..

– Resort is a vast sprawl

– Slopes can be crowded by American standards, with serious lift queues

– Inadequate mountain restaurants

– Blue Sky Basin and the Back Bowls may not be open in early season; warm weather can close the Bowls

– Expensive, with lots of luxury lodgings but few budget options

We always enjoy skiing Vail; it's a big mountain with a decent vertical, and Blue Sky Basin's 'adventure' skiing is a key attraction. But it is far from being our favourite American mountain. In an American resort you expect the runs to be pretty much crowd-free – and in any resort you expect 20-minute lift queues to be a thing of the past. In these respects, Vail disappoints – the new Mountaintop Express six-pack may cut queues, but it won't cut crowds.

When the budget runs to a swanky billet in Vail Village or the new Lionshead area, we're happy enough with the resort, too; it is a pleasant place to wander around. But we're not enthusiastic about Vail Village's pseudo-Tirolean style, and the rest of the huge resort lacks character. In the end, we reckon Vail can't compete with more distinctively American resorts based on old mining or cowboy towns.

THE RESORT

Vail is an enormous resort, stretching almost four miles along the I-70 freeway running west from Denver. Beaver Creek, 16km away, is covered by the lift pass and is easily reached by bus. Breckenridge and Keystone – both owned by Vail Resorts and covered by the lift pass – and Copper Mountain are other possible excursions.

VILLAGE CHARM ★★★
No real identity
Standing in the centre of Vail Village, surrounded by chalets and bierkellers, you could be forgiven for thinking you

were in the Tirol – which is what Vail's founder, Pete Seibert, intended back in the 1950s. But this is now just one part of a huge resort, and the rest is built mostly in anonymous (but smart) modern style.

CONVENIENCE ★★★
There's always the bus
The vast village has a free and efficient bus service ('always on time'), – frequent from Lionshead to Golden Peak, less frequent to the outskirts. But the most convenient – and expensive – places to stay are in the mock-Tirolean Vail Village or at Lionshead – an area that has some very smart lodgings to match Vail

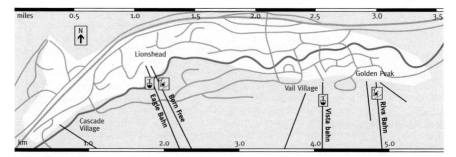

2013/14: A new six-pack is planned to replace the Mountaintop quad at Mid-Vail; it will increase capacity by 33% and should help to reduce queues here, but we doubt it will eliminate them. A double chair on the nursery slopes at Golden Peak is due to be replaced by a triple.

2012/13: A gondola (with heated seats and Wi-Fi) replaced the Vista Bahn chair from Vail Village to Mid-Vail, increasing capacity by 40%. The 10th – a restaurant at Mid-Vail – is now open for dinner.

SNOWPIX.COM / CHRIS GILL

Blue Sky Basin is great fun: normally dry powdery snow and lots of runs through the trees – some widely spaced, others tight ↓

Village – and both have gondolas out. There is a lot of accommodation further out – some on the far side of the I-70.

SCENERY ★★★
Rolling Colorado

Like most Colorado resorts, Vail is set among rather softly contoured mountains with forest reaching to the top of the slopes. From the top you can see for miles.

THE MOUNTAINS

You get a real sense of travelling around Vail's mountains – something missing in many smaller American resorts. Run classification exaggerates the difficulty of some slopes – some of the blacks, in particular. Several runs are partly classified blue, partly black, which means fewer surprises if you pay close attention to the map. Compared with most American resorts the runs are usually crowded – nothing like as bad as in Europe but not as pleasant as elsewhere. There are free mountain tours at 10.30am and separate tours of Blue Sky Basin at 11am every day. The slopes have yellow-jacketed patrollers who stop people speeding recklessly.

EXTENT OF THE SLOPES ★★★★
Something for everyone

Vail's 5,289 acres of lift-linked slopes make it one of the biggest ski areas in the US. The slopes can be accessed via three main lifts. From Vail Village, a gondola goes up to the major mid-mountain focal point, Mid-Vail; from Lionshead, the Eagle Bahn gondola goes up to the Eagle's Nest complex; and from the Golden Peak base area just to the east of Vail Village, the Riva Bahn fast chair goes up towards the Two Elk area.

The front face of the mountain is largely north-facing, with well-groomed trails cut through the trees. At altitude the mountainside divides into three bowls – Mid-Vail in the centre, with Game Creek to the south-west and the area below Two Elk Lodge to the north-east. Lifts reach the ridge at three points, all giving access to the **Back Bowls** (mostly ungroomed and treeless) and through them to **Blue Sky Basin** (mostly ungroomed and wooded, with a 'backcountry' feel).

FAST LIFTS ★★★★★
Plenty of them

There are lots of fast lifts on both sides of the mountain. All three of Blue Sky Basin's lifts are fast chairs.

QUEUES ★★
Can be bad

The front side of Vail has had some of the longest lift lines we've hit in the US, especially at weekends because of the influx from nearby Denver. A 2013 visitor took weekend lessons to jump the queues. And even on a mid-

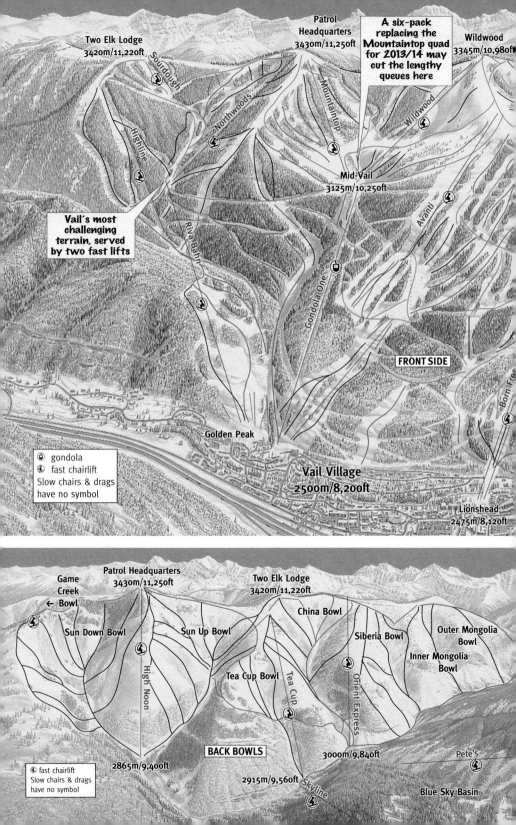

Two Elk Lodge
3420m/11,220ft

Patrol
Headquarters
3430m/11,250ft

A six-pack
replacing the
Mountaintop quad
for 2013/14 may
cut the lengthy
queues here

Wildwood
3345m/10,980ft

Sourdough

Northwoods

Mountaintop

Wildwood

Highline

Mid-Vail
3125m/10,250ft

Avanti

Vail's most
challenging
terrain, served
by two fast lifts

Riva Bahn

Gondola One

FRONT SIDE

Born Free

Golden Peak

gondola
fast chairlift
Slow chairs & drags
have no symbol

Vail Village
2500m/8,200ft

Lionshead
2475m/8,120ft

Game
Creek
← Bowl

Patrol Headquarters
3430m/11,250ft

Two Elk Lodge
3420m/11,220ft

China Bowl

Sun Down Bowl

Sun Up Bowl

Siberia Bowl

Outer Mongolia
Bowl

Inner Mongolia
Bowl

High Noon

Tea Cup Bowl

Tea Cup

Orient Express

BACK BOWLS

2865m/9,400ft

3000m/9,840ft

Pete's

2915m/9,560ft

Skyline

Blue Sky Basin

fast chairlift
Slow chairs & drags
have no symbol

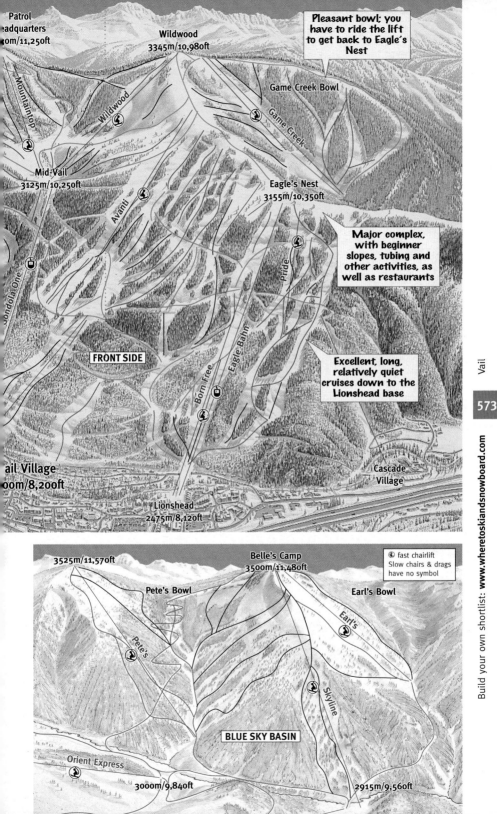

Patrol
eadquarters
om/11,25oft

Wildwood
3345m/10,98oft

Pleasant bowl: you
have to ride the lift
to get back to Eagle's
Nest

Game Creek Bowl

Game Creek

Mountaintop

Wildwood

Mid-Vail
3125m/10,25oft

Avanti

Eagle's Nest
3155m/10,35oft

Major complex,
with beginner
slopes, tubing and
other activities, as
well as restaurants

Pride

FRONT SIDE

Gondola One

Born Free

Eagle Bahn

Excellent, long,
relatively quiet
cruises down to the
Lionshead base

ail Village
oom/8,200ft

Cascade
Village

Lionshead
2475m/8,12oft

3525m/11,57oft

Belle's Camp
3500m/11,48oft

fast chairlift
Slow chairs & drags
have no symbol

Pete's Bowl

Earl's Bowl

Earl's

Pete's

Skyline

BLUE SKY BASIN

Orient Express

3000m/9,84oft

2915m/9,56oft

LIFT PASSES

Colorado

Prices in US$

Age	1-day	6-day
under 13	74	342
13 to 64	106	510
65 plus	96	450

Free Under 5

Beginner Included in price of lessons

Notes 3+ day passes cover Vail, Beaver Creek, Breckenridge, Keystone and Arapahoe Basin; prices are online rates for early February purchased 14 days in advance of trip; window rates in resort are considerably higher; international visitors will get best prices by pre-booking through a UK tour operator (it is not necessary to buy a complete holiday package to obtain these prices)

UK PACKAGES

Alpine Answers, AmeriCan Ski, American Ski Classics, Carrier, Crystal, Crystal Finest, Elegant Resorts, Erna Low, Flexiski, Frontier, Independent Ski Links, Interactive Resorts, Momentum, Oxford Ski Co, PowderBeds, Scott Dunn, Ski Bespoke, Ski Expectations, Ski Independence, Ski Line, Ski Safari, Ski Solutions, Skitracer, Skiworld, Snow Finders, STC, Supertravel, Thomson, Virgin Snow

December visit we hit big queues. Mid-Vail is a bottleneck that is difficult to avoid; 20-minute waits are common (and 45 minutes is not unheard of). The planned six-pack replacement for the Mountaintop Express may help – reports please. The Northwoods chair and the Eagle Bahn gondola are other hot spots.

TERRAIN PARKS ★★★★★
Three to choose between

There are three parks. Beginner and intermediate freestylers will want to explore the Bwana and Pride parks, located under the Eagle Bahn gondola on Bwana run. Here, a selection of small to medium-sized jumps and boxes gradually become more challenging as you progress through each park.

More advanced riders will be best served at the Golden Peak Terrain Park. Located halfway down the Riva Bahn chairlift, the park is home to various high-profile events and is often in the top ten in terrain park lists and polls. Last season there were nine jumps ranging up to 15m in length, and 30 jibs, boxes and rails. It also has two super-pipes.

SNOW RELIABILITY ★★★★★
Excellent, except in the Bowls

As well as an exceptional natural snow record (average 348 inches), Vail has extensive snowmaking, normally needed only in early season. Grooming is excellent. Both the Back Bowls and Blue Sky Basin usually open later in the season than the front of the mountain. Blue Sky is largely north-facing (and wooded) and keeps its snow well. But the Bowls are sunny, and in warm weather snow can deteriorate to the point where they are closed or only a traverse is kept open to allow access to Blue Sky Basin; for the best snow, head skier's right from the top of the Game Creek chair, where the sun has least effect because the runs are east-facing.

FOR EXPERTS ★★★★
Lots of variety

Vail's Back Bowls are vast areas, served by four chairlifts and a short draglift. You can go virtually anywhere you like in the half-dozen identifiable bowls, trying the gradient and terrain of your choice. There are interesting, lightly wooded areas, as well as the open slopes that dominate the area. Some 87% of the runs in the Back Bowls are classified black but are not particularly steep, and they have disappointed some expert reporters, who seek more challenge and variety.

Blue Sky Basin has much better snow than the Back Bowls and some great adventure runs in the trees – some widely spaced, some very tight, some on relatively gentle terrain, some quite steep. All the runs funnel into the same run-out so you can't get lost.

On the front face there are some genuinely steep double black diamond runs, which usually have great snow; they are often mogulled, but they are sometimes groomed to make wonderful fast cruising. The fast Highline lift – on the extreme east of the area – serves three black runs. Prima Cornice, served by the Northwoods Express, is one of the steepest runs on the front of the hill.

If the snow is good, try the backcountry Minturn Mile – you leave the ski area through a gate in the Game Creek area to descend a powder bowl and finish on a path by a river – ending up at the atmospheric Saloon. Go with a local guide.

FOR INTERMEDIATES ★★★★★
Ideal territory

The majority of Vail's front face is great intermediate terrain, with easy cruising runs. Above Lionshead, especially, there are excellent, long, relatively quiet blues – Bwana, Born Free and Simba all go from top to bottom. Game Creek Bowl, nearby, is excellent, too. Avanti, underneath the chair of the same name, is a nice cruise.

As well as tackling some of the easier front-face blacks, intermediates will find plenty of interest in the Back Bowls. Some of the runs are groomed and several are blue, including Silk Road, which loops around the eastern edge, with wonderful views. Some of

SCHOOLS

Vail
t 496 4800

Classes
Full day $150
Private lessons
From $775 for 1 day
for up to 6 people

CHILDCARE

Child Care Centers
t 496 4800
Ages 2mnth to 6yr

Ski school
Ages 3 to 15

Mock-Tirolean Vail
Village is one of the
most convenient (and
expensive) places to
stay ↓

the unpisted slopes are ideal for
learning to ski powder. Confident
intermediates will also enjoy Blue Sky
Basin's clearly marked blue runs and
the easier ungroomed runs there
(Cloud 9 is a lovely gentle area of
groomed glades; In the Wuides is a bit
steeper but still lovely).

FOR BEGINNERS ★★★
Good but can be crowded
There are fine nursery slopes at resort
level and at altitude, and easy longer
runs to progress to. But they can be
rather crowded.

FOR BOARDERS ★★★
Big isn't always best
The terrain is about as big as it comes
in America. Beginners will enjoy the
front side's gentle groomed pistes (but
not the crowds), good for honing skills
and serviced by fast chairlifts. But
beware of flat areas, especially at the
top of the Wildwood and Northwoods
lifts, and cat tracks. The back bowls
will keep most expert and intermediate
riders busy for days. Blue Sky Basin is
definitely worth checking out, with its
acres of natural trails, gladed trees
and cornices. There are three terrain
parks too.

FOR CROSS-COUNTRY ★★★
Go for Golden
Vail's cross-country areas (17km) are at
the foot of Golden Peak and at the
Nordic Center on the golf course.
There are 10km of snowshoe trails too.

MOUNTAIN RESTAURANTS ★★
Surprisingly poor
Vail's mountain restaurants are
disappointing for such a big, upscale
resort. The major self-service
restaurants can be unpleasantly
crowded from 11am to 2pm.

There are only two table-service
places. Bistro Fourteen at Eagle's Nest
is in an airy room and does decent
food. The 10th at Mid-Vail opened a
couple of seasons ago and looks good
– reports, please.

Of the self-service places, Two Elk
is huge and airy and many visitors
find it satisfactory, but it can get
unpleasantly crowded. Try Wildwood
for BBQs and Buffalo's for soup and
sandwiches. You can take your own
food and cook it on free BBQs at
Belle's Camp at the top of Blue Sky
Basin (take your own booze too).

SCHOOLS AND GUIDES ★★★★
Generally excellent, but...
The school has an excellent reputation
and reports are usually wholly
positive. But a 2013 reporter had a
mixed experience: 'Snowboard lesson
was fantastic, hiked to get untracked
powder. Brill, brill, brill.' But his wife's
lesson was 'dreadful – she asked for a
change of instructor for day two but
was told that wasn't possible', and his
nine-year-old was taught by 'an older
gentleman with no enthusiasm'. More
reports, please.

You can sign up for lessons on the
mountain. Full day Adventure Sessions
offer guided instruction for
intermediates and experts.

FOR FAMILIES ★★★★
Good all round
The main children's centre is at Golden
Peak and takes kids aged three to 15;
the nursery takes kids from two
months to six years. There are
splendid areas with adventure trails
and themed play zones, such as the
Magic Forest and Chaos Canyon.
There's even a special kids' cafe area
at Mid Vail. There are kids'
snowmobiles and trampolines at
Adventure Ridge.

Vail

Build your own shortlist: www.wheretoskiandsnowboard.com

↑ Game Creek Bowl is a great place for intermediates to play – the piste in the middle of this pic is the aptly named Showboat
SNOWPIX.COM / CHRIS GILL

GETTING THERE

Air Eagle 55km/ 35 miles (45min); Denver 195km/ 120 miles (2hr15)

ACTIVITIES

Indoor Athletic clubs and spas

Outdoor Tubing, ski biking, snowmobiling, snowshoe excursions, bungee trampolining

Central reservations phone number
t 496 4500

Phone numbers
From distant parts of the US, add the prefix 1 970; from abroad, add the prefix +1 970

TOURIST OFFICE

www.vail.com

STAYING THERE

There's a big choice of packages to Vail and it's easy to organize your own visit too, with regular airport shuttle services.

Chalets Skiworld has a couple of smart chalets with outdoor tubs in East Vail.

Hotels Vail's hotels are nearly all upmarket and expensive (becoming even more so with the opening in recent years of the luxurious Ritz-Carlton, Four Seasons and Solaris hotels). Other top-rank places include the Vail Cascade (with its own lift into the slopes), the plushly Bavarian Sonnenalp, and the brilliantly convenient Lodge at Vail (right by the gondola in Vail Village). Other slightly more affordable places include:

****Manor Vail Resort At Golden Peak. Suites with sitting area, fireplace, kitchen, terrace. Hot tub and pools.

****Marriot Mountain Resort At Golden Peak. Spa, pool, hot tub.

***Evergreen Lodge Between village and Lionshead. More affordable than others. Outdoor pool, sauna and hot tub. Sports bar.

Apartments There's a wide range of condos, from standard to luxury. The Racquet Club at East Vail has lots of amenities. At Vail Village, Mountain Haus is central and high quality. Vail Cascade Resort and Spa is good value, including breakfast and use of the hotel's leisure facilities. And Manor Vail might be a preferred family choice – it's beside the children's ski school. Good value places at Lionshead include Village Inn Plaza, Vantage Point, the Antlers, Enzian, Westwind and Vail 21.

EATING OUT ★★★★★
Endless choice

Whatever kind of food you want, Vail has it – but most of it is expensive.

Fine-dining options include Elway's (in the Lodge), the Tour (modern French) and Ludwig's (in the Sonnenalp). For Alpine ambience try Pepi's (in the hotel Gramshammer) or the Alpenrose. You can take gondolas up to The 10th at Mid-Vail or to Eagle's Nest and then be driven by snowcat to the Game Creek Club for dinner (it's a private members' club at lunchtimes).

For more moderate prices, we've found Blu's 'contemporary American' food satisfactory; Billy's Island Grill does steaks and seafood ('good service and menu'); and Campo de Fiori is an excellent Italian. The Chophouse at Lionshead serves seafood and steaks. Reader recommendations include: Sweet Basil (modern American) and Lancelot (steaks), both in Vail Village; May Palace (Chinese) and Nozawa (Asian) in West Vail; also Matsuhisa (Asian, in the Solaris hotel), Montauk (seafood), Los Amigos (Mexican), Russell's (steak), Vendetta's and Pazzo's (both pizzas).

APRES-SKI ★★★★★
Fairly lively

Lionshead is quiet in the evenings; but Garfinkel's has a DJ, sun deck and happy hour. The Red Lion in Vail Village has live music, big-screen TVs and huge portions of food. The George models itself on an English-style pub. Pepi's is popular, and Los Amigos is lively at four o'clock. The Tap Room is a relaxed woody bar.

You can have a good night out at Adventure Ridge at the top of the gondola. As well as restaurants and bars, there's lots to do on the snow.

OFF THE SLOPES ★★★★★
A lot to do

Getting around on the free bus is easy, and there are lots of activities. The factory outlets at Silverthorne are a must if you can't resist a bargain. Pedestrians can get to Eagle's Nest or Mid-Vail for lunch by gondola. The National Mining Museum in Leadville, a 35-minute drive away, is recommended.

Winter Park

A radical alternative to the run of Colorado resorts, for those more interested in snow and space than in après-ski amusements

NEWS

2012/13: A new tubing hill opened. Willie's Adventure club is a new evening programme for children aged two months to 14 years.

STEPHEN ASHLEY

Most accommodation is in spacious condos a shuttle-bus ride from the slopes; but you can stay in The Village right by the slopes too →

➕ The best snowfall record of all Colorado's major resorts

➕ Good terrain for all abilities

➕ Quiet on weekdays

➕ Leading resort for teaching people with disabilities to ski and ride

➕ Largely free of inflated prices and ski-resort glitz

➖ 'Village' at the lift base is still very limited and dead in the evening

➖ Town is a bus ride away and lacks the usual shops and restaurants

➖ Trails tend to be either easy cruises or stiff mogul fields

➖ Some tough terrain liable to closure by bad weather

Winter Park's ski area – developed for the recreation of the citizens of nearby Denver, and still owned by the city – is world class. When Intrawest (developers of resorts such as Whistler) got involved a few years ago, there was the prospect of a world-class resort being developed at the base, too. But things have stalled, and expansion plans now seem to have been put on hold.

For the present, there's only a small, very quiet 'village' at the base, and most lodging, shops and restaurants are a bus ride away.

THE RESORT

Winter Park started life in the 19th century: when the Rio Grande railway was built, workers climbed the slopes to ski down. One of its mountains, Mary Jane, is named after a legendary 'lady of pleasure' who is said to have received the land as payment for her favours. The resort (at 2745m) is one of the highest to get a chapter in this book (only Breckenridge is higher) so there is a risk of altitude sickness if you go straight there from the UK. And the approach road from Denver is seriously high – crossing the Continental Divide at Berthoud Pass (3450m) – and Alpine in character, with very un-American hairpin bends. Don't plan on driving over in the dark. Having a car makes day trips to Denver and to resorts such as Copper Mountain, Breckenridge (see separate chapter) and Keystone possible.

You can stay at The Village at the base of the slopes or in the town of Winter Park, linked by shuttle-bus.

VILLAGE CHARM ★★
Old or new?
Most accommodation is in spacious condos scattered around either side of

US highway 40, the road through the town of Winter Park. Drive into the town at night, and the neon lights make it seem like a real ski resort town – but in the cold light of day it's clear that the place doesn't amount to much. It even lacks a proper supermarket – the nearest is a drive or free bus ride away at Fraser.

Stylish lodgings have been developed at or near the foot of the slopes, to form a very small car-free mini-resort known as The Village at Winter Park. Confusingly, an area between the mountain and the town is known as Old Town.

CONVENIENCE ★★★★★
Walk or ride
If you stay in The Village, you are right by the slopes. Shuttle-buses run between town and the lift base, and hotels and condos also have shuttles.

SCENERY ★★★★★
See the Continental Divide
You are almost on the Continental Divide here, with views of the rolling hills in the other direction from the top of Parsenn Bowl.

THE MOUNTAINS

There's a good mix of terrain that suits all abilities – when it's all open. There are guided tours at 10am and 1pm. Route finding can be tricky in places.

EXTENT OF THE SLOPES ★★★★★
Interestingly divided
Winter Park's ski area is big by US standards. There are five distinct, but well-linked, sectors. From the main base, a fast quad takes you to the peak of the original **Winter Park** mountain. From there, you can descend in all directions.

Some runs lead back towards the main base and over to the **Vasquez Ridge** area on skier's left, served by the Pioneer fast quad.

Or you can descend to the base of **Mary Jane** mountain, where four chairs up the front face serve tough runs; other chairs serve easier terrain on the flanks. Going down the back of Mary Jane you can head for the **Parsenn Bowl**, riding the Panoramic Express chair for intermediate terrain above and in the trees. From Parsenn, conditions permitting, you can hike for

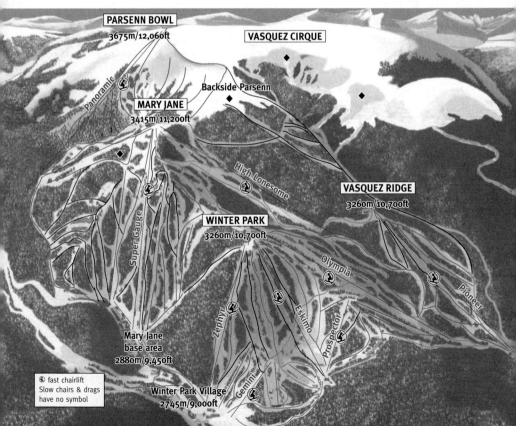

PARSENN BOWL
3675m/12,066ft

VASQUEZ CIRQUE

Panoramic

Backside Parsenn

MARY JANE
3415m/11,200ft

High Lonesome

VASQUEZ RIDGE
3260m/10,700ft

Super Gauge

WINTER PARK
3260m/10,700ft

Olympia

Pioneer

Zephyr

Eskimo

Prospector

Mary Jane
base area
2880m/9,450ft

Gemini

Winter Park Village
2745m/9,000ft

④ fast chairlift
Slow chairs & drags
have no symbol

LIFT PASSES

Prices in US$

Age	1-day	6-day
under 13	51	241
13 to 64	89	408
65 to 69	81	383

Free Under 6

Seniors Age 70+, season ticket is $350

Beginner Included in price of lessons

Notes These are advance-purchase prices; window ticket prices are considerably higher; special deals for disabled skiers

ACTIVITIES

Indoor Fitness clubs, hot tubs (in hotels), museum

Outdoor Ice rink, snowshoeing, ski bikes, snowcat tours, tubing, sleigh rides

---

up to half an hour to access advanced and extreme terrain at **Vasquez Cirque**. You can return to Parsenn Bowl using the Eagle Wind chair, saving a long run-out to the base of the Vasquez Ridge area and the Pioneer lift.

FAST LIFTS ★★★★
Adequately covered
Fast chairs have gradually replaced old lifts, though a few slow ones remain.

QUEUES ★★★★
Quiet during the week
During the week the mountain is generally very quiet; however, the Zephyr Express can get busy at peak times and there are often weekend crowds and queues ('Half an hour for the Zephyr; up to 10 minutes up the mountain,' says a 2013 visitor).

TERRAIN PARKS ★★★★★
Parks for all standards
All six parks were upgraded a few seasons ago. The flagship Rail Yard park – with 30 features including big jumps, jibs, boxes, a host of variously shaped rails and quarter-, half- and super-pipes – is enough to challenge most experts. It runs down much of the front of Winter Park mountain for 1.3km. Halfway down it crosses a bridge so that those on the Village Way green run can cross the park safely. At the bottom are the huge features of Dark Territory, open to special pass holders only (you need to pay $20, sign a waiver and watch a safety video to get the pass). For those who prefer smaller hits, there are the Re-Railer and Gangway parks for intermediates nearby. There's also the beginner-intermediate Ash Cat on the Jack Kendrick green run plus the Starter park under Prospector Express and the Bouncer park in The Village – both for beginners. Check them out at www.rlyrd.com.

SNOW RELIABILITY ★★★★★
Among Colorado's best
Winter Park's position, close to the Continental Divide, gives it an average yearly snowfall of 330 inches – higher than most major Colorado resorts. Snowmaking covers a lot of Winter Park mountain's runs.

FOR EXPERTS ★★★★
Some hair-raising challenges
Mary Jane has some of the steepest mogul fields, chutes and hair-raising

---

challenges in the US. On the front side is a row of long black mogul fields that are quite steep enough for most of us. There are some good genuine blacks on Winter Park mountain, too.

Some of the best terrain is open only when there is good snow and/or weather – so it's especially unreliable early in the season. The fearsome chutes of Mary Jane's back side – all steep, narrow and bordered by rocks – need a lot of snow, are marked as 'Extreme Terrain' on the trail map and are accessed by a control gate. Parsenn Bowl has superb blue/black gladed runs and black diamond gladed runs on the back side down to the Eagle Wind chair. Vasquez Cirque, the least reliably open area, has excellent ungroomed expert terrain but not much vertical before you hit the forest.

FOR INTERMEDIATES ★★★★
Choose your challenge
From pretty much wherever you are on Winter Park mountain and Vasquez Ridge you can choose a run to suit your ability. Most blue runs are well groomed every night, giving you perfect early morning cruising on the famous Colorado corduroy pistes. Black runs, however, tend not to be groomed, and huge moguls form. If bumps are for you, try Mary Jane's front side. If you're learning to love them, the blue/black Sleeper enables you to dip in and out.

Parsenn Bowl has grand views and several gentle cruising pistes as well as more challenging ungroomed terrain. There are blue and blue-black runs and glades here, offering a nice range of gradients. It's also an ideal place to try powder for the first time. But when it's actually snowing you are better off riding lower lifts, sticking to the powdery edges of treelined runs for better visibility. The blue-black Hughes is a great thrash home at close of play.

FOR BEGINNERS ★★★★★
About the best we've seen
Discovery Park is a 25-acre dedicated area for beginners, reached by a high-speed quad and served by two more chairs. As well as a nursery area and longer green runs, it has an adventure trail through trees. Sorensen Park learning zone at the base area is good too. There are lots of long green runs, but some are perilously close to flat.

SCHOOLS

Winter Park
t 1 800 729 7907

National Sports Center for the Disabled
t 726 1518
Special programme for disabled skiers and snowboarders

Classes
Day (5.5hr) from $99
Private lessons
$389 for 3hr for 1 to 3 people

CHILDCARE

Wee Willie's
t 1 800 420 8093
Ages 2mnth to 6yr

Ski school
Takes ages 3 to 14

GETTING THERE

Air Denver 165km/ 105 miles (2hr15)

Rail Denver, Sat and Sun only

UK PACKAGES

Alpine Answers, AmeriCan Ski, American Ski Classics, Crystal, Erna Low, Independent Ski Links, Interactive Resorts, Momentum, Ski Independence, Ski Safari, Ski Solutions, Skitracer, Skiworld, Snow Finders, Supertravel, Thomson, Virgin Snow

Central reservations
Toll-free number (from within the US)
1 800 979 0332

Phone numbers
From distant parts of the US, add the prefix 1 970; from abroad, add the prefix +1 970

TOURIST OFFICE

www.winterparkresort.com

FOR BOARDERS ★★★★★
Beware the moguls and flats
There is some great advanced and extreme boarding terrain and a high probability of fresh powder to ride. And the terrain parks are great. The resort is also good for beginners and intermediates, with excellent terrain for learning. But there are quite a few flat spots to beware of, and a lot of the steep runs have huge moguls, which many boarders find tricky. Beginners can meet their instructors and learn about the sport prior to taking a lesson if they go to the Burton Experience Snowboarding Lounge at Winter Park Resort Rentals.

FOR CROSS-COUNTRY ★★★★★
Lots of it nearby
There are several areas nearby (none actually in the resort) with over 200km of groomed trails plus backcountry tours and generally excellent snow.

MOUNTAIN RESTAURANTS ★★★★★
Some good facilities
The highlight is the Lodge at Sunspot, at the top of Winter Park mountain. This wood and glass building has a welcoming bar with a roaring log fire and table- and self-service sections ('good soups') – but it gets very busy. Lunch Rock Cafe at the top of Mary Jane has 'excellent views', does quick snacks and has a deli counter. And there is a self-service ('reasonable prices' but 'overcrowded') at Snoasis, by the beginner area. Otherwise, it's down to the bases. The Club Car at the base of Mary Jane offers table-service and a varied menu. You can eat your own packed lunch at Moffat Market (at the base) and Mary Jane Market (at The Village).

SCHOOLS AND GUIDES ★★★★★
No recent reports
We have no reason to doubt the school is up to the usual high US standards. Two variations on standard classes are 3-hour Max Four Lessons (which start at 11.45 and limit group size to four) and Adult Full Day Group Lessons that include lunch.

FOR FAMILIES ★★★★★
Some of the best
Wee Willie's Child Care at the base area houses day-care facilities, taking kids from two months to six years, and is the meeting point for children's classes, which have their own areas.

STAYING THERE

Chalets Skiworld has a lovely log-cabin chalet with outdoor hot tub: 'The best we've ever stayed in – very spacious, Wi-Fi, bus stop outside,' says a visitor.
Hotels There are a couple of hotel/ condo complexes with restaurants and pools near, but not in, The Village.
***Iron Horse Resort Outdoor pool and hot tubs, steam room.
***Vintage Hotel Linked by the car park bucket lift to The Village. Good value and comfortable, but a reporter said that the bar closed at 9pm. Outdoor pool and tub.
Apartments The Zephyr Mountain Lodge, Fraser Crossing and Founders Pointe are swish places in The Village. There are a lot of comfortable condos in or on the way to town. Reader tips: Beaver Village, Sawmill Station, Red Quill, Meadowridge, Crestview Place.

EATING OUT ★★★★★
A real weakness
There isn't the range of places you get in most 'destination' resorts. For fine dining you have to drive 13km to Devil's Thumb Ranch. Get hold of the giveaway Grand County menu guide. In town, reporters are keen on Deno's (seafood, steaks etc and '600 different wines'), New Hong Kong (Chinese), Gasthaus Eichler (German-influenced food), Carlos and Maria's (Tex-Mex), Fontenot's (seafood and Cajun), Hernando's (pizza/pasta) and Lime ('good Mexican food'). At The Village Cheeky Monk does pub grub – 'excellent sausage and mash'.

APRES-SKI ★★★★★
If you know where to go ...
At close of play, there's action in The Village at the Derailer Bar, Cheeky Monk (a huge selection of Belgian beers) and Doc's Roadhouse ('great atmosphere') and at the Club Car at the base of Mary Jane. Later on, Deno's and the Winter Park Pub in town are the main hot spots. Moffat Station microbrewery has good beer.

OFF THE SLOPES ★★★★★
Mainly the great outdoors
Past reporters have enjoyed floodlit tubing at Fraser – and in 2012/13 a new tubing hill opened at the base. There's also ice skating at the base and snowmobiling to the Continental Divide. Factory outlet stores are 90 minutes away at Silverthorne.

Utah

'The Greatest Snow on Earth' is Utah's marketing slogan. And it's not far from the truth: some Utah resorts do get huge amounts of snow – usually light, dry powder. If you like the steep and deep, you should at some point make the pilgrimage here. And if you like an après-ski beer or two, don't be put off by the image of a 'dry' Mormon state – getting alcohol has never been a problem (and the laws were greatly relaxed in 2009, anyway). But boarders beware: two of its top resorts don't allow snowboarding.

The biggest dumps fall at Alta (which bans boarding) and Snowbird. Their average of 500 inches of snow a year (twice as much as some Colorado resorts) has made them the powder capitals of the world.

Park City, over the hill from Alta but 45 minutes away by road, is the main 'destination' resort of the area and a sensible holiday base; as well as its own slopes it has upmarket Deer Valley (which also bans boarding) right next door, and Canyons only a short drive away. Although all these resorts are close together – you can ski off-piste from Park City to Alta – Park City and neighbours get 'only' 300 to 350 inches of snow. We have separate chapters on these five resorts.

Of course, you're not guaranteed fresh powder. Alta and Snowbird may

TOURIST OFFICE

Ski Utah
www.skiutah.com

get less than 300 inches over a season; or they may get over 700 inches. Be careful what you wish for: In 2008, we spent a week in Park City when it virtually never stopped snowing. Every day we had fresh, knee-high powder. We never made it to Alta or Snowbird: the access road to them was often closed by avalanche danger. But we had a great time skiing the other three resorts.

Other resorts worth visiting (covered in the resort directory at the end of the book) include **Brighton** and **Solitude**, in the valley that separates Park City from Alta. The snow here, which is almost a match for Alta/Snowbird in quantity, gets tracked out less quickly because the resorts attract far fewer experts. The main claim to fame of **Sundance** is that it's owned by Robert Redford; it averages 320 inches of snow. It was unknown **Snowbasin** (400 inches), well to the north, that hosted the Olympic downhill events in 2002. **Powder Mountain** (500 inches), a bit further north, is aptly named. As well as lift-served slopes there are 3,000 acres of guided snowcat-skiing.

Until 2009 the sale and consumption of alcohol was tightly controlled in Utah, the Mormon state. Until then, to get a drink in bars and clubs you had to jump through various hoops. These rules have now been scrapped. There are still differences between bars and restaurants, but effectively you don't need to worry about them, and as long as you are over 21 (and have ID to prove it) you should have no problem getting alcoholic drinks between 10am and midnight or 1am. The amount of spirits allowed in a drink has been increased as well.

You normally fly in to Salt Lake City, which means changing planes somewhere en route – a bit of a drag.

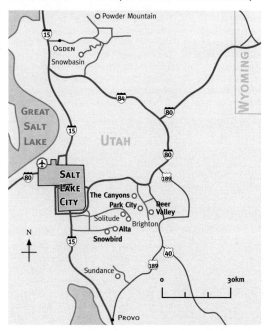

Alta

Cult powder resort linked to Snowbird but with less brutal architecture and a friendlier, old-fashioned feel

TOP 10 RATINGS

Extent	★★★
Fast lifts	★★★★
Queues	★★★
Snow	★★★★★
Expert	★★★★★
Intermediate	★★★
Beginner	★★★
Charm	★★
Convenience	★★★★
Scenery	★★★

RPI 155

lift pass	£300
ski hire	£195
lessons	£160
food & drink	£145
total	**£800**

NEWS

2012/13: Alta joined the Mountain Collective, a small group of widely spread western resorts offering an attractive lift-pass deal. A new eco-friendly building was built at Wildcat Base, including ticket office, admin offices and toilets.

KEY FACTS

Resort	2600m
	8,530ft

See Snowbird for Alta/Snowbird area

Alta only
Slopes	2600-3215m
	8,530-10,550ft
Lifts	11
Pistes	2,200 acres
Green	25%
Blue	40%
Black	35%
Snowmaking	Some

- ✚ Phenomenal snow and steep terrain mean cult status among experts
- ✚ Linked to Snowbird, making one of the largest ski areas in the US
- ✚ Ski-almost-to-the-door convenience
- ✚ No snowboarding allowed

- ▬ 'Resort' is just a scattering of lodges, so not much goes on off the slopes
- ▬ Limited groomed runs for intermediates
- ▬ No snowboarding allowed

Alta and linked Snowbird are the powder capitals of the world, and add up to a great area for adventurous skiers. Alta has a friendlier, funkier feel than Snowbird, which gets its own chapter a few pages on.

THE RESORT

Alta sits at the craggy head of Little Cottonwood Canyon, 2km beyond Snowbird and less than an hour's drive from downtown Salt Lake City. Both the resort and the approach road are prone to avalanches and closure: visitors can be confined indoors.
Village charm Where once there was a bustling and bawdy mining town, there is now just a dozen lodges plus several parking areas.
Convenience Life revolves around the two lift base areas – Albion and Wildcat – linked by a rope tow along the valley floor. All the lodges are convenient for the lifts.
Scenery Alta is recognized for its impressively rugged scenery and challenging, sparsely wooded ridges.

THE MOUNTAINS

Most of Alta's slopes are lightly wooded. Alta does not differentiate between single and double black diamond trails – regrettable, we think.

Slopes The dominant feature of the terrain is the steep end of a ridge that separates the area's two basins. To the left, above Albion Base, the slopes stretch away over easy green terrain towards the blue and black runs from Point Supreme and from the top of the Sugarloaf quad (also the access lift for Snowbird). To the right, above Wildcat Base, is a more concentrated bowl with blue runs down the middle and blacks either side, served by the fast two-stage Collins chair. The two sectors are linked at altitude.
Fast lifts Fast chairs depart from each base; another one links to Snowbird.
Queues The slopes are normally uncrowded and queues rare. But it is said to be difficult to board the Collins chair at the mid-station at times because of the number of people skiing to the base and boarding there.
Terrain parks There isn't one.
Snow reliability The quantity and quality of snow and the northerly orientation put Alta in the top rank. The average is 500 inches; totals for

ALTA SKI AREA
Lightly wooded slopes are the norm, except at the top; groomed slopes are not →

UK PACKAGES

American Ski Classics,
Momentum, Skitracer

the last three seasons were 700+, 390, and last season 450 inches.

Experts Alta has long held cult status among experts. There are dozens of steep slopes and chutes. But finding the best spots is tricky without local guidance and quite a lot of traversing is involved.

Intermediates There isn't a lot of groomed terrain (more in Snowbird). But adventurous intermediates happy to try powder can have a good time.

Beginners Albion has a nursery area and gentle lower slopes, with a beginner lift pass covering three lifts.

Snowboarding Boarding is banned, but it's allowed in Snowbird, and guided snowcat boarding is available nearby.

Cross-country 5km of groomed track.

Mountain restaurants There's one in each sector. Watson Shelter on the Wildcat side is light and airy with big windows, self- and table-service sections and a small coffee bar; we enjoyed the table-service Collins Grill here – interesting menu (eg creole soup, snails and prawns en croûte). Alf's on the Albion side is a standard self-service.

Schools and guides The ski school specializes in powder lessons – though there are regular classes, too.

Families Day care for children from six weeks to nine years is available at the Children's Center at Albion Base.

Phone numbers
From distant parts of
the US, add the prefix
1 801; from abroad,
add the prefix +1 801

TOURIST OFFICE

www.alta.com

STAYING THERE

None of the hotels is luxurious in US terms, but most fill up with repeat visitors and, unusually for the US, offer half-board (ie dinner included).

Hotels We enjoyed our 2012 stay at the venerable Alta Lodge (742 3500): comfortable rooms, an atmospheric bar. It has developed a cult following by operating a bit like a catered chalet, serving dinner at shared or private tables. Saunas, indoor hot tubs. Rustler Lodge (742 2200) is more luxurious, with a big outdoor pool, but impersonal. The comfortable, modern and conveniently located Goldminer's Daughter (742 2300) and the basic Peruvian Lodge (742 3000) are cheaper. The Snowpine Lodge (742 2000) was the first lodge to be built in the Canyon (in 1938), is convenient and has a sauna and outdoor hot tub.

Eating out It is possible, but eating in is the normal routine.

Après-ski This rarely goes beyond a few drinks in one of the hotel bars. The Goldminer's Daughter Saloon is the main après-ski bar for day visitors; the upstairs lounge has sofas, an open fire and huge floor-to-ceiling windows.

Off the slopes There are few options other than snowshoeing, the Cliff Lodge spa down the road at Snowbird or a sightseeing trip to Salt Lake City.

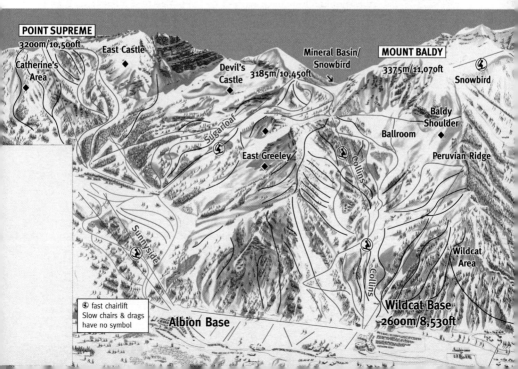

POINT SUPREME
3200m/10,50oft
Catherine's Area
East Castle
Devil's Castle
Mineral Basin/ Snowbird
3185m/10,45oft
MOUNT BALDY
3375m/11,07oft
Snowbird
Baldy Shoulder
Ballroom
Peruvian Ridge
Sugarloaf
East Greeley
Collins
Sunnyside
Collins
Wildcat Area
fast chairlift
Slow chairs & drags
have no symbol
Albion Base
Wildcat Base
2600m/8,53oft

Canyons

One of the five biggest ski areas in the US, with a small purpose-built resort at the base, just outside Park City

CANYONS / HUGHES MARTIN

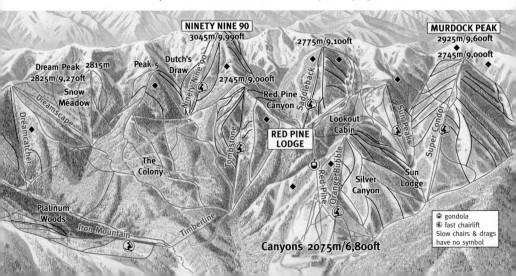

TOP 10 RATINGS

Extent	★★★
Fast lifts	★★★
Queues	★★★★
Snow	★★★★
Expert	★★★★
Intermediate	★★★★
Beginner	★★
Charm	★★
Convenience	★★★★
Scenery	★★★

RPI 170

lift pass	£350
ski hire	£195
lessons	£180
food & drink	£150
total	**£875**

NEWS

2013/14: Vail Resorts – operator of Beaver Creek, Breckenridge and Heavenly among other resorts, as well as Vail – has taken over operation of the resort.

2012/13: The Sunrise Lodge, offering suites and studios, opened at the base of the Sunrise lift.

+ Relatively extensive area of slopes
+ Modern lift system with few queues
+ Easy access to Park City and Deer Valley ski areas
+ Can stay at the base, but ...

− Village is limited
− Snow on the many south-facing slopes is affected by sun
− Many runs are short
− Few green runs

Canyons has the potential to become the most extensive ski area in the US and already claims it is among the five biggest. Anyone having a holiday in adjacent Park City should plan to visit – there are good bus services. Whether you would want to stay here is another question.

THE RESORT

Canyons has been transformed over the past decade or so. The area of the slopes has more than doubled, and a small car-free village built at the base.
Village charm The village has lodgings and a few shops, restaurants and bars. But it doesn't add up to much – you can stroll round it in 10 minutes or so.
Convenience Staying at the base is convenient for the Canyons ski area. There are buses from the base of the access lift direct to Park City and its ski area; Deer Valley requires one change. A 2013 visitor found the bus services quick and convenient.
Scenery A series of broad, long ridges are separated by valleys and most of the area is fairly densely wooded.

THE MOUNTAINS

Canyons claims that its slopes spread over nine mountains. It is certainly a complicated and extensive area.

'Excellent' free mountain tours start daily at 10.30, and not-free First Tracks tours runs twice a week – early-morning tours led by Olympic skiers.
Slopes Red Pine Lodge, at the heart of the slopes, is reached by an eight-seat gondola from the village. A fast quad reaches a higher point. From the top of both lifts you can move in either direction across a series of ridges and valleys. Runs come off both sides of each ridge and generally face north or south. Most runs are quite short (less than 500m vertical), with some long, quite flat run-outs.
Fast lifts The core of the lift system either side of Red Pine Lodge consists of fast quads, but the Dream Peak sector has no fast lifts.
Queues We found no queues on our February 2012 visit.
Terrain parks There are three parks, accessed from the Saddleback and Sun Peaks chairs. Painted Horse is the park to progress in, Transitions has

Map labels

NINETY NINE 90
3045m/9,990ft

MURDOCK PEAK
2925m/9,600ft

2775m/9,100ft

2745m/9,000ft

Dream Peak 2815m
2825m/9,270ft

Peak 5

Dutch's Draw

2745m/9,000ft

Snow Meadow

Dreamscape

Ninety Nine 90

Red Pine Canyon

Saddleback

Sun Peak

Super Condor

Lookout Cabin

RED PINE LODGE

Tombstone

Dreamcatcher

The Colony

Red Pine

Orange Bubble

Silver Canyon

Sun Lodge

Platinum Woods

Iron Mountain

Timberline

Canyons 2075m/6,800ft

gondola
fast chairlift
Slow chairs & drags
have no symbol

↑ There's more to the base village than is shown in this shot; but not much more

CANYONS RESORT / ROB BOSSI

KEY FACTS

Resort	2075m
	6,800ft
Slopes	2075-3045m
	6,800-9,990ft
Lifts	19
Pistes	4,000 acres
Green	10%
Blue	44%
Black	46%
Snowmaking	6%

UK PACKAGES

AmeriCan Ski, American Ski Classics, Frontier, Independent Ski Links, Ski Safari, Skitracer

Central reservations

Call 1 866 604 4171 (toll-free from within the US)

Phone numbers
From distant parts of the US, add the prefix 1 435; from abroad, add the prefix +1 435

TOURIST OFFICE

www.canyonsresort.com

five large jumps and two wall rides, and Elwoods is a natural zone. There is also a Burton Riglet Park, aimed at infants. There are six natural half-pipes (marked on the trail map).

Snow reliability Snow here is not the best in Utah. The average snowfall of 350 inches is a match for Park City and more than Deer Valley. But the south-facing slopes suffer in late season. Snowmaking is very limited.

Experts There is steep terrain all over the mountain. We particularly liked the north-facing runs off Ninety Nine 90, with steep double black diamond runs plunging down through the trees. We had a great time here on our last visit, after fresh snow. A short hike from the top accesses some fine powder runs even days after a snowfall. There is also lots of double-diamond terrain on Murdock Peak (a 20-minute hike from the Super Condor lift). Runs off the Peak 5 chair are more sheltered. And there's heli-skiing too.

Intermediates There are groomed blue runs for intermediates on all the main sectors except Ninety Nine 90. Some are quite short, but you can switch from valley to valley for added interest. From the Super Condor and Tombstone fast chairs there are excellent double blue square runs. The Dreamscape area can be quiet, and is great for early experiments in powder.

Beginners There are good areas with moving carpets up at Red Pine Lodge. But the run you progress to is rather short and gets very busy.

Snowboarding Except for the flat runouts from many runs, it's a great area, with lots of natural hits. Canis Lupus is a mile-long natural half-pipe.

Cross-country None in resort. The Park City golf course has 20km and Soldier Hollow near Homestead Resort 26km.

Mountain restaurants Red Pine Lodge is a large, attractive building with a busy cafeteria, table-service restaurant and big deck. Reporters have found the Sun Lodge quieter. The smart table-service Lookout Cabin has wonderful views from huge windows, and we had excellent game stew there in 2012. Cloud Dine specializes in salads and sandwiches. The Dreamscape and Tombstone Grill snack huts offer simple food outdoors. People can bring their own lunch into any of the self-service places.

Schools and guides No recent reports; but as well as the usual classes, there are special clinics and the chance to join former Olympic skiers for a day of racing or powder training. Children's classes are for ages 4 to 14.

Families There's day care in the Grand Summit Hotel for children from six weeks to six years, and at the school for ages two and three years.

STAYING THERE

Hotels The Waldorf Astoria is the best, set below the village and served (until 5.30pm) by its own gondola. We stayed at the Grand Summit in 2012, but our standard King room was disappointing in various respects. Silverado Lodge is the other main hotel. All have pools and hot tubs.

Apartments The Hyatt Escala Lodge (with pool and hot tubs) and Westgate Resort and Spa are pricey and luxurious. Of the cheaper places Timberwolf condos have been praised; other options include Bear Hollow, Hidden Creek, Red Pine and Sundial.

Eating out We had a great meal (excellent fillet steak and buffalo osso bucco) at The Farm – the best place in town. Red Tail Grill does Tex-Mex, and Bistro offers 'modern American' kosher food. Red Pine Lodge at the top of the gondola does a BBQ on Saturdays, with a C&W band and dancing.

Après-ski It's generally pretty quiet. The Umbrella Bar is the main focus as the lifts close.

Off the slopes There's a great zipline tour that we enjoyed (two short training wires followed by a minute-long whizz above a deep canyon), snowshoeing, snowmobiling, dog sledding, horse-drawn sleigh rides and a factory outlet mall and Salt Lake City and Park City nearby.

Canyons

Build your own shortlist: www.wheretoskiandsnowboard.com

Deer Valley

Top of the Ivy League of US ski resorts: it promises, and delivers, the best ski and gastronomic experience – we love it

TOP 10 RATINGS

Extent	★★
Fast lifts	★★★★
Queues	★★★★
Snow	★★★★
Expert	★★★
Intermediate	★★★★
Beginner	★★★★
Charm	★★★
Convenience	★★★★
Scenery	★★★

RPI 175

lift pass	£350
ski hire	£195
lessons	£215
food & drink	£150
total	**£910**

NEWS

2012/13: A high-speed quad called Mountaineer Express replaced the slow Deer Crest chair on Little Baldy Peak. The deck paving at Empire Canyon Lodge is now heated.

KEY FACTS

Resort	2195m	
	7,200ft	
Slopes	2000-2915m	
	6,570-9,570ft	
Lifts		21
Pistes	2,026 acres	
Green		24%
Blue		43%
Black		33%
Snowmaking		33%

UK PACKAGES

AmeriCan Ski, American Ski Classics, Frontier, Momentum, Oxford Ski Co, Ski Independence, Ski Safari, Skitracer

+ Good snow, and good terrain including tree skiing

+ Brilliant free powder tours

+ Many fast lifts and no queues

+ Good restaurants and lodgings

+ Snowboarding is banned

– Relatively expensive

– Small area of slopes

– Mostly short runs

– Quiet at night, though Park City is right next door

– Snowboarding is banned

Deer Valley prides itself on pampering its guests, with valets to unload your skis, gourmet dining, immaculately groomed slopes, limited numbers on the mountain – and no snowboarding. Park City ski area is right next door – nothing more than a fence separates the two – and any skier visiting the area should try both. For most people, Park City town is the obvious base; but there are some seductive hotels here at mid-mountain Silver Lake.

THE RESORT

Just a mile from the end of Park City's Main Street, Deer Valley is overtly upmarket – famed for the care and attention lavished on the slopes and the guests. But it is unpretentious.
Village charm The Silver Lake area is something of a mid-mountain focus.
Convenience Most lodgings are right on the slopes.
Scenery From Bald Mountain there are extensive views to Park City and the Jordanelle reservoir. And the views of the reservoir on the run down to the Jordanelle gondola are spectacular.

THE MOUNTAINS

The slopes are varied and interesting. Deer Valley's reputation for immaculate grooming is justified, but there is also a lot of exciting tree skiing – and some steep bump runs, too. There are free mountain tours for different standards. We have been on two three-hour black-diamond tours, and they were both brilliant, taking us through fresh powder in the trees that we would never have found on our own. Reporters praise these tours, too.
Slopes Two chairs take you up Bald Eagle Mountain, just beyond which is the mid-mountain focus of Silver Lake Lodge. You can ski from here to the isolated Little Baldy Peak, served by a gondola and a fast quad chairlift, with mainly easy runs to serve property developments there (though a local loves skiing these first thing because they are immaculately groomed and deserted, with great views). But the

main skiing is on three linked peaks beyond Silver Lake Lodge – Bald Mountain, Flagstaff Mountain and Empire Canyon. The top of Empire is just a few metres from the runs of the Park City ski area but crossing the fence that divides the two is banned.
Fast lifts Fast quads rule; the three main peaks have nine.
Queues Waiting in lift lines is not something that Deer Valley wants its guests to experience, so it limits the number of lift tickets sold. But it has built four lifts ending at the same place at the top of Flagstaff – resulting in hordes of people trying to go in different directions (insane – and not what you'd expect in Deer Valley).
Terrain parks There isn't one.
Snow reliability Excellent, and there's plenty of snowmaking too.
Experts Despite the image of luxury there is excellent expert terrain on all three main mountains, including fabulous glades, bumps, chutes and bowls. And the snow doesn't get skied out quickly. The Ski Utah Interconnect Tour to Alta starts here (read about this in the Park City chapter).
Intermediates There are lots of superbly groomed blue runs.
Beginners There are nursery slopes at Silver Lake Lodge as well as the base, and gentle green runs to progress to.
Snowboarding Boarding is banned.
Cross-country There are 20km of trails on the Park City golf course and 26km at Soldier Hollow near Homestead Resort plus lots of backcountry scope.
Mountain restaurants The best in Utah, with attractive wood-and-glass self-

↑ The slopes in the centre of this shot are those of Deer Valley. The slopes and the town on the extreme right are Park City. But no, they're not linked

DEER VALLEY

Central reservations
Call 645 6538

Phone numbers
From distant parts of the US, add 1 435; from abroad, add the prefix +1 435

TOURIST OFFICE
www.deervalley.com

service places at Silver Lake (we had delicious lamb stew and turkey chilli), Empire Canyon and the base lodge. You can eat your own packed lunches at all three. For table-service, try the Stein Eriksen Lodge, Goldener Hirsch or Royal Street Cafe at Silver Lake.

Schools and guides The ski school is doubtless excellent; book in advance.

Families The Children's Center accepts children from two months to 12 years.

STAYING THERE

A car is useful for visiting other nearby Utah resorts, though Deer Valley, Park City and Canyons are all linked by efficient shuttle-buses.

Hotels The St Regis Resort, Montage Deer Valley, Stein Eriksen Lodge and Goldener Hirsch are some of the plushest hotels in any ski resort.

Apartments There are many luxury apartments and houses to rent. Reader tips include Ridgepoint, Royal Plaza and The Woods at Silver Lake – and Aspenwood and Boulder Creek at Snow Park (cheaper).

Eating out Of the gourmet restaurants, Mariposa is the best. We enjoyed the all-you-can-eat Seafood Buffet (it's not just seafood) and a 'Fireside Dining' evening at Empire Canyon Lodge: four courses, each one served at a different fireplace. It's held four nights a week.

Après-ski Edgar's Beers & Spirits Lounge at the base area is the main après-ski venue, with live music at weekends. For more choice, it's not far to Main Street in Park City.

Off the slopes Park City has lots of shops and galleries etc. Salt Lake City has concerts, sights and shopping. Balloon rides, snowmobiling and snowshoeing are popular.

Deer Valley

587

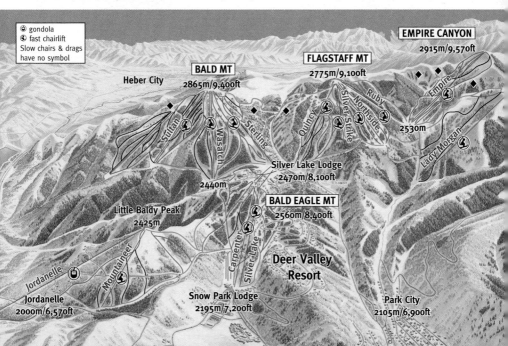

gondola
fast chairlift
Slow chairs & drags have no symbol

EMPIRE CANYON 2915m/9,570ft

FLAGSTAFF MT 2775m/9,100ft

BALD MT 2865m/9,400ft

Heber City

Empire

2530m

Sultan
Wasatch
Sterling
Quincy
Silver Strike
Northside
Ruby
Lady Morgan

Silver Lake Lodge 2470m/8,100ft

2440m

Little Baldy Peak 2425m

BALD EAGLE MT 2560m/8,400ft

Carpenter
Silver Lake
Mountaineer

Deer Valley Resort

Jordanelle

Jordanelle 2000m/6,570ft

Snow Park Lodge 2195m/7,200ft

Park City 2105m/6,900ft

SNOWPIX.COM / CHRIS GILL

Park City

With its cute and lively Main Street, the most attractive base for skiing three very worthwhile areas on one lift pass

RATINGS

The mountains

Extent	★★★
Fast lifts	★★★
Queues	★★★★
Terrain p'ks	★★★★★
Snow	★★★★
Expert	★★★★
Intermediate	★★★★
Beginner	★★★★
Boarder	★★★★
X-country	★★★
Restaurants	★★
Schools	★★★★
Families	★★

The resort

Charm	★★★
Convenience	★★
Scenery	★★★
Eating out	★★★★★
Après-ski	★★★
Off-slope	★★★

RPI — 170

lift pass	£350
ski hire	£195
lessons	£185
food & drink	£150
total	**£880**

NEWS

2012/13: The capacity and energy efficiency of the snow-guns was upgraded.

KEY FACTS

Resort	2105m
	6,900ft
Slopes	2105-3050m
	6,900-10,000ft
Lifts	16
Pistes	3,300 acres
Green	17%
Blue	52%
Black	31%
Snowmaking	15%

PARK CITY MOUNTAIN RESORT

Sadly, Jupiter Peak itself is not lift-served, but you can hike up from McConkey's six-pack or from the higher Jupiter chair away to the right →

➕ Entertaining, historic Main Street

➕ Lots of bars and restaurants make nonsense of Utah's Mormon image

➕ Easy to ski Deer Valley and Canyons as well as the Park City slopes

➖ Resort is an enormous, charmless sprawl, with most lodgings a drive from Main Street and the slopes

➖ Runs tend to be rather short

➖ Still too many slow chairlifts

Staying in Park City has clear attractions, particularly if you are based near the centre to make the most of lively Main Street. It makes an excellent base for touring all of Utah's main resorts.

Park City Mountain Resort (covered in this chapter) is just one of three local ski areas covered by the Three Resort Pass (available through some UK tour operators but not locally – buy before you go) and easily reached by frequent free buses. Deer Valley is separated from the Park City slopes only by a fence between two pistes, and by separate ownership – all very strange, to European eyes. Canyons is a little further away. Then there are the famously powdery resorts of Snowbird and Alta, less than an hour away; you need a separate lift pass for them. These four resorts all have their own chapters.

THE RESORT

Park City is about 45 minutes by road from Salt Lake City. It was a silver-mining boom town, and at the turn of the 19th century it boasted a population of 10,000, a red-light area, a Chinese quarter and 27 saloons.

VILLAGE CHARM ★★★
A colourful past
Careful restoration has left the town with a splendid historic centrepiece in Main Street, now lined by a colourful selection of bars, restaurants, galleries and shops, many quite smart, but there are touristy souvenir places too. New buildings have been tastefully designed to blend in smoothly. But

most lodging is in the sprawling and characterless suburbs, a drive or bus ride from Main Street. Traffic levels can be bad, especially at weekends.

CONVENIENCE ★★
Depends on your base
The slow Town chairlift goes up to the slopes from Main Street, but the main lifts are on the fringes at Resort Base; there are lodgings out there but most are a bus ride away.

Deer Valley, Canyons and Park City are linked by free shuttle-buses that reporters praise, which also go around town until fairly late – but we've found it a pain to wait for buses in the evenings. A car is useful to avoid this, and for visiting Alta/Snowbird.

LIFT PASSES

Prices in US$

Age	1-day	6-day
under 13	65	330
13 to 64	102	540
65 plus	66	336

Free Under 7

Beginner Lower Mtn ticket ($62) covers First Time and 3 Kings lifts only

Notes Prices quoted are advance-purchase prices

Alternative pass
Three Resort (Park City, Canyons, Deer Valley) International Pass available only to international visitors and in advance of holiday departure

---

If you're not hiring a car, pick a location that's handy for Main Street and the Town chair or the free bus.

SCENERY ★★★☆☆
Gently undulating ridges
In contrast to Park City's sprawling mass, the rounded mountain ridges have a modest and gentle presence.

THE MOUNTAINS

Park City Mountain Resort consists mostly of blue and black trails cut through the trees, with easier runs running along the ridges and the valleys between. The more interesting terrain is in the lightly wooded bowls and ridges at the top. The trail map marks several black 'Signature Runs' that are groomed every night ('A great blast first thing,' says a 2012 reporter) – and a few 'Adventure Alley' blue runs among the trees ('great fun').

Reporters have enjoyed the free mountain history tours of the slopes that look at the area's silver-mining heritage and take place at 1pm. There are also free intermediate and advanced tours of the slopes at 10am. A long intermediate run, a beginner run and the Three Kings terrain park are floodlit for night skiing till 9pm.

It is much cheaper to buy lift passes in advance than on the spot. Signposting is clear.

EXTENT OF THE SLOPES ★★★☆☆
Bowls above the woods
The ski area is bigger than Deer Valley but smaller than Canyons. Most of the easy and intermediate runs lie between Summit House and the base area, and are spread along the sides of a series of interconnecting ridges. Virtually all the steep terrain is above Summit House in a series of ungroomed bowls, and accessed by the McConkey's six-pack and the old, slow Jupiter double chair.

FAST LIFTS ★★★☆☆
Not up to usual US standards
Two fast chairlifts whisk you up from Resort Base and others beyond take you to Summit House. But there are still too many slow lifts serving the upper mountain and some of the best steep slopes.

QUEUES ★★★★☆
Peak period crowds
It can get pretty crowded (on some trails as well as the lifts) at weekends ('massive, well-managed queues on Saturday') and in high season. You can pay extra for a Fast Tracks pass to jump queues on six main lifts.

TERRAIN PARKS ★★★★★
Among the best in the world
There are three terrain parks here to suit all levels. The vast number of kickers, rails and pipes are maintained daily, and rank among the best in the world. See www.irideparkcity.tv. Neff Land is a great entry-level park, Three Kings is for all abilities and floodlit for night riding till 9pm, and King's Crown is the park for pros, with the biggest jumps and features. The Eagle super-pipe was used for the 2002 Winter Olympics and today is consistently one of the best pipes in the world. Intermediate level kids aged 11 to 15 can join three-day 'I Ride Park City' freestyle camps to learn park and all-mountain skills.

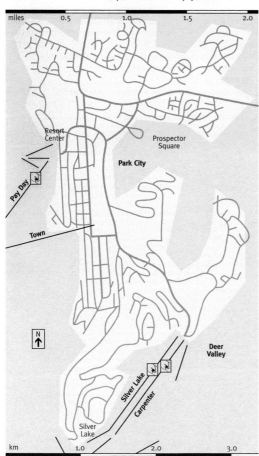

Build your own shortlist: www.wheretoskiandsnowboard.com

GETTING THERE

Air Salt Lake City
55km/35 miles
(45mins)

SNOW RELIABILITY ★★★★☆
Not quite the greatest on Earth

Utah is famous for the quality and quantity of its snow. Park City's record doesn't match those of Snowbird and Alta, but an annual average of 360 inches is still impressive, and ahead of most Colorado figures. When it falls it is 'well managed'. Snowmaking covers about 15% of the terrain.

FOR EXPERTS ★★★★☆
Lots of variety

There is a lot of excellent steep terrain at the top of the lift system. It is all marked as double diamond on the trail map, but many runs deserve only a single-diamond rating.

McConkey's Bowl is served by a six-pack and offers a range of open pitches and gladed terrain; we've had some great runs here on each of our visits. The slow, old Jupiter lift accesses the highest bowls, which include some serious terrain – with narrow couloirs, cliffs and cornices – as well as easier wide-open slopes. We had some enjoyable runs through fresh snow in lightly wooded terrain by heading to the right at the top of the lift, then skiing down without hiking. But if you are prepared to hike, you can find fresh powder most of the time – turn left for West Face, Pioneer Ridge and Puma Bowl, right for Scott's

Bowl and the vast expanse of Pinecone Ridge, stretching for miles down the side of Thaynes Canyon.

Lower down, the side of Summit House ridge, serviced by the slow Thaynes and Motherlode chairs, has some little-used black runs, plus a few satisfying trails in the trees. There's a zone of steep runs towards town from further round the ridge. And don't miss Blueslip Bowl near Summit House – so called because in the past when it was out of bounds, ski company employees caught skiing it were fired, and given their notice on a blue slip.

Skiers (no snowboarders, due to some long flat run-outs) should consider doing the Ski Utah Interconnect Tour – see the feature panel opposite. Park City Powder Cats offers snowcat skiing and Wasatch Powderbird Guides heli-skiing.

FOR INTERMEDIATES ★★★★☆
OK for a day or two

There are blue runs served by all the main lifts, apart from Jupiter. The areas around the King Con high-speed quad and Silverlode six-pack have a dense network of great (but fairly short) cruising runs. There are also more difficult trails close by, for those looking for a challenge. The 'Signature Runs' and 'Adventure Alleys' (see first para under 'The Mountain' above) are

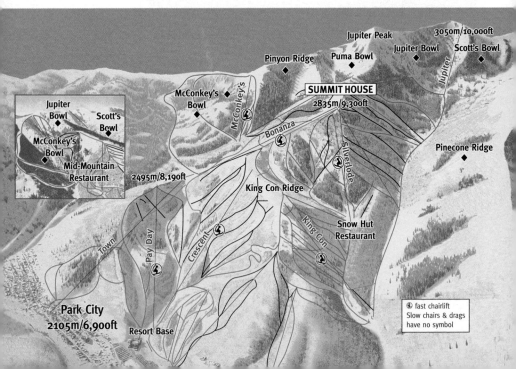

Park City
2105m/6,900ft

Resort Base

Jupiter Peak
3050m/10,000ft
Jupiter Bowl
Scott's Bowl
Pinyon Ridge
Puma Bowl

SUMMIT HOUSE
2835m/9,300ft

McConkey's Bowl

Jupiter
Bowl
Scott's Bowl
McConkey's Bowl
Mid-Mountain Restaurant
2495m/8,190ft

Pinecone Ridge

Bonanza

Silverlode

King Con Ridge

Snow Hut Restaurant

Town

Pay Day

Crescent

King Con

⬆ fast chairlift
Slow chairs & drags
have no symbol

SCHOOLS

Park City
t 1 800 227 2754

Classes
One 3hr lesson $102
Private lessons
From $385 for 3hr

CHILDCARE

Guardian Angel
t 435 640 1229
Babysitting service
Kid's Clubhouse
t 940 1607
Ski Town Sitters
Babysitter finder
service
Signature Programs
(run by ski school)
t 1 800 227 2754
Ages 3½ to 5

Ski school
Ages 6 to 14

good ideas and worth trying.

But there are few long, fast cruising runs – most trails are around 1–2km, and many have long, flat run-outs. The Pioneer and McConkey's chairlifts are off the main drag and serve some very pleasant, often quiet runs. The runs under the Town lift have great views of the town. Mileage-hungry intermediates should explore other nearby resorts, too.

FOR BEGINNERS ★★★★
A good chance for fast progress
An excellent area for beginners. The 'Never Ever' deal offers first-timers a half-day taster lesson including a lift pass and equipment rental. In the beginner area, novices start on moving carpets; classes graduate up the hill quite quickly, and there's a good, gentle and wide 'easiest way down' – the three-and-a-half-mile Home Run – all the way from Summit House. It's easy enough for most to manage after only a few lessons. The Town chair can be ridden down.

FOR BOARDERS ★★★★
Plenty of scope
It was not until 1996, when Park City won its Olympic bid, that the resort lifted its ban on snowboarding. Since then it has steamrollered ahead to attract boarders by building some of the best terrain parks in the world. And there's some great ungroomed terrain as well: the higher bowls offer treelined powder runs and great kicker-building spots. Beginners will have no trouble on the lower slopes.

FOR CROSS-COUNTRY ★★★
Some trails; lots of backcountry
There are prepared trails on the Park City golf course (20km), next to the downhill area, and at Soldier Hollow near Homestead Resort (25km), just out of town. There is lots of scope for backcountry trips.

MOUNTAIN RESTAURANTS ★★
Standard self-service stuff
The Mid-Mountain Lodge is a picturesque 19th-century mine building that was heaved up the mountain to its present location near the bottom of Pioneer chair. The food is standard self-service fare, but most reporters prefer it to the alternatives ('had a really good lunch of chicken tenders with fries there'). The Summit House has chilli, pizza, soup and good views from a big deck; Snow Hut is a log building that often has an outdoor grill; Viking Yurt is a coffee house in a tent halfway down the Bonanza chairlift; Snowed Inn has 'the cheapest food on the mountain'. There are more options down at Resort Base – the Pig Pen Saloon 'does a very good sandwich and beer'.

SCHOOLS AND GUIDES ★★★★
Good past reports
We lack recent reports, but past reviews have been very positive.

FOR FAMILIES ★★
Well organized
There are a number of licensed carers. The ski school takes children from age three and a half. Book in advance.

THE SKI UTAH INTERCONNECT TOUR

Good skiers prepared to do some hiking should consider this excellent guided backcountry tour that runs four days a week from Deer Valley to Snowbird. (Three days a week it runs from Snowbird, but only as far as Solitude.) When we did it (a few years back, starting from Park City) we got fresh tracks in knee-deep powder practically all day. After a warm-up run to weed out weak skiers, we went up the top chair, through a 'closed' gate in the area boundary and skied down a deserted, prettily wooded valley to Solitude. After taking the lifts to the top of Solitude we did a short traverse/walk, then down more virgin powder towards Brighton. After more powder runs and lunch back in Solitude, it was up the lifts and a 30-minute hike up the Highway to Heaven to north-facing, treelined slopes and a great little gully down into Alta. How much of Alta and Snowbird you get to ski depends on how much time is left. The price ($295) includes two guides, lunch, lift tickets and transport home.

SNOWPIX.COM / CHRIS GILL

↑ Editor Watts would insist on checking out the impressive terrain parks himself

PARK CITY MOUNTAIN RESORT / ROB MATHIS

ACTIVITIES

Indoor Silver Mountain Sports Club and Spa (pools, hot tubs, sauna, steam room, gym); other fitness clubs, spa treatments, bowling, cinema, museum, galleries

Outdoor Ice skating, snowmobiles, sleigh rides, hot-air ballooning, dog sledding, tubing, snowshoeing, winter fly fishing, Alpine Coaster

Phone numbers
From distant parts of the US, add the prefix 1 435; from abroad, add the prefix +1 435

TOURIST OFFICE

www.
parkcitymountain.com
www.visitparkcity.com

STAYING THERE

We prefer to stay near Main Street and its bars and restaurants, but most accommodation is in the sprawling suburbs. These, such as Kimball Junction, are relatively cheap and convenient if you have a car.
Hotels There's a wide variety, from typical chains to individual little B&Bs.
*****Park City (200 2000) Swanky all-suite place on outskirts. Pool, sauna, hot tub.
****Silver King (649 5500) De luxe hotel/condo complex at base of the slopes, with indoor-outdoor pool.
****Washington School House (649 3800) Historic old inn, recently renovated, in a great location near Main Street.
***Best Western Landmark Inn (649 7300) At Kimball Junction. Pool.
***Park City Peaks (649 5000) 'Large, dated rooms, great value, friendly staff, good breakfast', indoor-outdoor pool and 'outdoor hot tub you could boil a lobster in', but out of town. We stayed here and thought it adequate.
***Yarrow (649 7000) Adequate charmless base, a 15-minute walk from Main Street. Pool, hot tub.
Apartments There's a big range. The Town Lift condos near Main Street and Park Avenue condos are both modern and comfortable, the latter with a pool and hot tubs. Silver Cliff Village is adjacent to the slopes and has spacious units and access to the facilities of the Silver King Hotel. Other ski-in/ski-out recommendations from reporters are the Lodge at the Mountain Village, Silver Star and Snow Flower. Blue Church Lodge is a well-converted 19th-century Mormon church with luxury condos and rooms.

EATING OUT ★★★★★
Lots of choice
There are over 100 restaurants. Our favourites are Wahso (Asian fusion; excellent food, but slow service on the occasion of our 2012 visit), 350 Main (new American – 'very good and excellent service') and Riverhorse (in a grand, high-ceilinged first-floor room with live music). Zoom is the old Union Pacific train depot, now a trendy restaurant owned by Robert Redford (past reports have been mixed though). Chez Betty (American/French) is small with excellent food – but expensive.

For more basic food we like the atmospheric No Name Saloon and enjoyed their signature buffalo burgers and draft beers on our 2012 visit. Squatters is a good microbrewery a bit out of town. Other reporter tips include Baja Cantina (Mexican), Legends (American), Fuego Bistro & Pizzeria, Bangkok Thai, Bandit's Grill ('basic but satisfying', 'great cowboy food'), the Eating Establishment (fish), and Butcher's Chop House. Bear in mind the option of upscale dining at next-door Deer Valley.

APRES-SKI ★★★
Plenty around
As the slopes close, Legends is the place to head for at Resort Base. After that, go to Main Street. The Wasatch Brew Pub makes its own ale. O'Shuck's and No Name Saloon are lively, and there's usually live music and dancing at weekends.

For clubs, try the Jupiter Bowl at the bowling alley and Cisero's.

OFF THE SLOPES ★★★
Some things of interest
At the resort there's a roller coaster style toboggan ride on rails, tubing and a zipline. Backcountry snowmobiling, balloon flights and trips to Nevada for gambling are popular. There is a bowling alley. You can learn to ski jump or try the Olympic bob track at the Olympic Park down the road – 'worth the effort'. Robert Redford's Sundance Film Festival is held each January. There are lots of shops and galleries. There's discount shopping at a factory outlet mall at Kimball Junction. Salt Lake City is easily reached and has some good concerts, shopping and Mormon heritage sites.

Snowbird

A powder-pig paradise linked to neighbouring Alta; with big concrete and glass base buildings that remind us of Flaine

TOP 10 RATINGS

Extent	★★★
Fast lifts	★★★★★
Queues	★★★
Snow	★★★★★
Expert	★★★★★
Intermediate	★★★
Beginner	★★
Charm	★
Convenience	★★★★★
Scenery	★★★

RPI	155
lift pass	£270
ski hire	£195
lessons	£200
food & drink	£145
total	**£810**

NEWS

2013/14: The Gad 2 double chairlift is to be replaced by a fast quad.

2012/13: The Little Cloud double chairlift was replaced by a fast quad.

SNOWBIRD

The appeal of Snowbird is simple: it's the snow ↓

➕ Unrivalled quantity and quality of powder snow, combined with fabulous ungroomed slopes

➕ Link to Alta makes it one of the largest ski areas in the US

➕ Slopes-at-the-door convenience

➖ Limited groomed intermediate runs, but more than at Alta

➖ Tiny, claustrophobic resort 'village'

➖ Stark concrete architecture

➖ Very quiet at night

There can be few places where nature has combined the steep with the deep better than at Snowbird and next-door Alta. The resorts' combined area is one of the top powder-pig paradises in the world (at least for skiers – boarders are banned from Alta). So it is a shame that Snowbird's concrete, purpose-built 'base village' is so lacking in ski resort ambience.

THE RESORT

Snowbird lies 40km from Salt Lake City in Little Cottonwood Canyon – just before Alta. Both the resort and (particularly) the approach road are prone to avalanches and closure: visitors are sometimes confined indoors for safety.

Village charm The resort buildings are mainly block-like and lack any semblance of charm.

Convenience The resort area and the slopes are spread along the road on the south side of the narrow canyon. The focal Snowbird Center (lift base/ shops/restaurants) is towards the eastern, up-canyon end. All lodgings are within walking distance, and most are ski-in/ski-out. There are shuttle-buses, with a service to Alta.

Scenery Snowbird's setting is rugged and rather Alpine. Hidden Peak's lofty heights give impressive views.

THE MOUNTAINS

Snowbird's link with Alta (see separate chapter) forms one of the largest ski areas in the US. The stats show Snowbird and Alta's ski areas to be of fairly similar size, but Snowbird's feels much bigger to us. There are free mountain tours at 9.30 and 10.30 each day. The nursery slopes are floodlit three evenings a week.

Slopes The north-facing slopes rear up from the edge of the resort. Six access lifts are ranged along the valley floor, the main ones being the 125-person cable car (the Aerial Tram) to Hidden Peak, the Peruvian Express quad and the Gadzoom fast quad. To the west, in Gad Valley, there are runs ranging from very tough to very easy. Mineral Basin, behind Hidden Peak, has 500 acres of terrain for all abilities, but can be badly affected by sun.

Fast lifts All the key lifts are fast, and with new fast quads this year and last, our rating goes to ★★★★★ this year.

Queues The big problem has always been the cable car, with queues of up to an hour at times. But the Peruvian Express chair provides an alternative way to the top (via a long tunnel at the top with a moving carpet that leads to Mineral Basin and then the Mineral Basin Express chair).

Terrain parks There is one aimed at beginners and intermediates with rails and jumps.

Snow reliability Like Alta, Snowbird averages 500 inches of snowfall a year – twice as much as some Colorado resorts and around 50% more than the nearby Park City area. The snowfall in the last three seasons was 700+, 380

593

KEY FACTS

Resort	2470m
	8,100ft

For Snowbird and Alta combined area

Slopes	2365-3350m
	7,760-11,000ft
Lifts	24
Pistes	4,700 acres
Green	25%
Blue	37%
Black	38%
Snowmaking	12%

Snowbird only

Slopes	2365-3350m
	7,760-11,000ft
Lifts	11
Pistes	2,500 acres
Green	27%
Blue	38%
Black	35%
Snowmaking	21%

UK PACKAGES

Alpine Answers, AmeriCan Ski, American Ski Classics, Independent Ski Links, Momentum, Ski Independence, Ski Safari, Skitracer, Skiworld

Phone numbers
From distant parts of the US, add the prefix 1 801; from abroad, add the prefix +1 801

TOURIST OFFICE

www.snowbird.com

and last season 420 inches. There's snowmaking in busy areas too.

Experts The trail map is liberally sprinkled with double black diamonds, and some of the gullies off the Cirque ridge – Silver Fox and Great Scott, for example – are exceptionally steep and frequently neck-deep in powder. Lower down lurk the bump runs, including Mach Schnell – a great run straight down the fall line through trees. There is wonderful ski-anywhere terrain in the bowl beneath the high Little Cloud chair, and the Gad 2 lift opens up attractive tree runs (and is the best place to be in a white-out). Fantastic go-anywhere terrain under the High Baldy traverse is controlled by gates. Mineral Basin has more expert terrain. Backcountry tours and heli-skiing are also offered.

Intermediates The winding Chip's Run provides the only comfortable route from the top back to town. There's good cruising in Mineral Basin – take the narrow Path to Paradise traverse for a wide blue-black and head up the Baldy Express lift for the easiest cruises. For adventurous intermediates wanting to try powder skiing, the bowl below the Little Cloud lift is a must. There are some challenging runs through the trees off the Gad 2 lift. The groomed runs don't add up to a lot but there's more than in Alta.

Beginners There is a nursery slope next to Cliff Lodge and a special lift pass is available ($22), plus the Mountain Learning area part-way up the hill. But progression to longer runs is not easy. Go and learn elsewhere.

Snowboarding Competent freeriders will have a wild time in Snowbird's powder, though there are some flat spots to beware of. Be aware that Alta bans boarders.

Cross-country No prepared trails (though there are in next-door Alta).

Mountain restaurants It's the Mid-Gad Lodge self-service or back to one of the bases – try the table-service Forklift and Rendezvous.

Schools and guides The school has a good reputation, though we lack recent reports.

Families Camp Snowbird takes children aged 12 and under. The 'kids ski free' programme allows children (six and under) to ski for free with an adult ($15 a day in 2011/12 for the Tram). Baby Thunder is a gentle family area.

STAYING THERE

Hotels There are several lodges and smaller condo blocks. Cliff Lodge (a huge concrete building shown in our last edition) and The Lodge at Snowbird are both convenient and have pools and hot tubs, but they lack charm – and we lack recent reports.

Eating out Cliff Lodge and Snowbird Center are the focal points, with various options, including the 'fine dining' Aerie in the Cliff Lodge.

Après-ski Après-ski is a bit muted. The Tram Club and El Chanate Cantina are lively as the slopes close, but don't expect them to be later on.

Off the slopes There's not much to do apart from snowshoeing, snowmobiling and visiting Salt Lake City and the spas in various lodges.

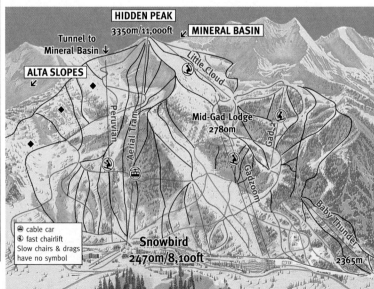

HIDDEN PEAK
3350m/11,000ft
MINERAL BASIN
Tunnel to Mineral Basin ↓
Little Cloud
ALTA SLOPES
Mid-Gad Lodge
2780m
Peruvian
Aerial Tram
Gad 2
Gadzoom
Baby Thunder
cable car
fast chairlift
Slow chairs & drags have no symbol
Snowbird
2470m/8,100ft
2365m

Rest of the West

This section contains detailed chapters on just two resorts – Jackson Hole in Wyoming and Big Sky in Montana. Below are notes on these and various other resorts in different parts of the great chain of mountains that stretches from Washington in the north to New Mexico in the south.

TANYA BOOTH

Big Sky: the base area isn't up to much, but the slopes are extensive, varied and deserted ↓

The resorts of Washington state and Oregon are covered in our resort directory at the end of this book. We visited Oregon a couple of seasons back; our exploration was hampered by poor early-season snow, but if you want to try somewhere largely undiscovered by fellow Brits, it is worth considering. The major resorts are **Mt Hood** (which has three separate areas of slopes: Mt Hood Meadows, Mt Hood Skibowl and Timberline) and **Mt Bachelor.** These get extended entries in the resort directory.

Sun Valley, Idaho, was America's first purpose-built resort, developed in the 1930s by the president of the Union Pacific Railway. It quickly became popular with the Hollywood movie set and has managed to retain its stylish image and ambience; it has one of our favourite luxury hotels. Also in Idaho is the USA's newest purpose-built resort – **Tamarack**, two hours

north of Boise. The company developing the resort went bankrupt in 2009, but it has operated four days a week for the past couple of seasons, and season passes for 2013/14 were on sale when we went to press.

Jackson Hole in Wyoming is a resort with an impressive snow record and equally impressive steep slopes. Jackson town has a touristy Wild West cowboy atmosphere. Check out the separate chapter. A 90-minute drive from Jackson over the Teton pass (slower if you go by excursion bus) brings you to **Grand Targhee**, which gets even more snow. The slopes are usually blissfully empty, and are much easier than at Jackson. The main Fred's Mountain offers 1,500 acres and 610m vertical accessed from a central fast quad. One-third of smaller Peaked Mountain is accessed by a fast quad, while the rest – around 500 acres – is used for guided snowcat-skiing.

About four hours north of Jackson, just inside Montana, is **Big Sky**, which has one of the biggest verticals in the US and together with neighbouring **Moonlight Basin**'s linked terrain is the biggest ski area in the US. When we visited, we were very impressed – particularly by the lack of crowds. Check out the Big Sky chapter. From Big Sky you might also visit **Bridger Bowl**, a 90-minute drive away. It boasts broad, steep, lightly wooded slopes that offer wonderful powder descents after a fresh snowfall.

A long way south of all these resorts, **Taos** in New Mexico is the most southerly major resort in America, and because of its isolated location it is largely unknown on the international market. There's a small chalet-style base village with a handful of lodges; the adobe town of Taos, home to many famous artists and writers over the years, is 30km down the road. There's some good terrain for all standards, but the ski area is best known for steep, challenging terrain, some of which you hike to.

Big Sky

One of America's biggest linked ski areas, with extraordinarily quiet slopes; unappealing modern resort village, though

RATINGS

The mountains

Extent	★★★★
Fast lifts	★★
Queues	★★★★★
Terrain p'ks	★★★★
Snow	★★★★★
Expert	★★★★
Intermediate	★★★★
Beginner	★★★★★
Boarder	★★★★
X-country	★★★★
Restaurants	★
Schools	★★★★
Families	★★★★

The resort

Charm	★★
Convenience	★★★★
Scenery	★★★
Eating out	★★★
Après-ski	★
Off-slope	★★

RPI 155

lift pass	£360
ski hire	£135
lessons	£185
food & drink	£120
total	**£800**

NEWS

2013/14: Huntley Lodge and Mountain Mall are due to be revamped and new shops should open including a new grocery and deli. Five more snow-guns are planned.

2012/13: A burrito shack opened at the top of the Swift Current lift. Ten snow-guns were added.

- ➕ Linked ski area much the same size as Vail; big vertical by US standards
- ➕ By far the quietest slopes you will find in a major resort, anywhere
- ➕ Among the cheapest resorts in the US for food and drink
- ➕ Excellent snow record
- ➕ Some comfortable slope-side accommodation, but ...

- ➖ Many condos are spread widely away from the lift base
- ➖ Base area lacks charm
- ➖ Resort amenities are limited, with little choice of nightlife
- ➖ Tiny top lift accessing the most testing terrain is prone to queues
- ➖ Getting there from the UK involves at least one stop and plane change

Big Sky is renowned for its powder, steeps and big vertical. Since the resort buried the hatchet with next-door Moonlight Basin and agreed a joint lift pass, they have been able to boast one of the biggest linked ski areas in the US.

They should also be boasting the world's least crowded slopes – we and our reporters have been astonished by the lack of people. Big Sky gets an average of 2,000 people on its slopes – that's about two acres each. We have no idea how they make this arrangement work financially. We're happy to take advantage of it while it lasts. But if ambling around in the evening soaking up the mountain village atmosphere is part of your holiday, forget it.

THE RESORT

Big Sky is set amid the wide open spaces of Montana, one hour from Bozeman airport (which reporters are very impressed with). The resort has been purpose-built at the foot of the slopes and the main focus of development is Mountain Village, at the lift base. Bridger Bowl ski area is an easy day trip by car.

VILLAGE CHARM ★★
Some way to go

Mountain Village is a hotchpotch of buildings in different styles set vaguely around a traffic-free central plaza and bordered by car parks and service roads. There are a few hotels, a handful of bars and restaurants, a variety of shops and some slope-side condos. The French-style underground Mountain Mall has shops and access to many of the bars and restaurants and some of the lodging.

CONVENIENCE ★★★★
Generally fine

There is quite a bit of lodging at or close to the lift base. Some outlying condos and houses are served by lifts to the slopes, but most rely on the 'comparatively poor' free bus services; a car is a better idea.

SCENERY ★★★
The lone ranger

Lone Mountain is Big Sky's signature peak, its distinctive summit rising over 1000m above the village and Andesite Mountain's wooded slopes. From the top, there are panoramic views of Montana and Yellowstone.

THE MOUNTAINS

Taking Big Sky and Moonlight Basin's slopes together, they cover a big area (5,532 acres), with long runs for all abilities. There are free mountain tours at both Big Sky and Moonlight. Despite the marketing hype about the linked area, for many people it makes sense to decide which area to ski when, and buy tickets accordingly, rather than buy a joint pass for the duration of your stay. The piste maps are separate. Recent visitors complain of poor signposting, especially for some black runs and gladed blues.

EXTENT OF THE SLOPES ★★★★
Big – the name's right

Lone Mountain provides the resort's poster shot, with some seriously steep, open upper slopes. From Mountain Village a fast quad goes to mid-mountain. From there you can get to the Lone Peak triple chair, which

The Mountain Village is small and more or less all in this photo. The Summit (on the right) is the best hotel →

TANYA BOOTH

KEY FACTS

Resort	2285m
	7,500ft

Big Sky only

Slopes	2070-3400m
	6,800-11,160ft
Lifts	21
Pistes	3,832 acres
Green	14%
Blue	26%
Black	60%
Snowmaking	10%

Big Sky and Moonlight Basin combined

Slopes	2070-3400m
	6,800-11,160ft
Lifts	26
Pistes	5,532 acres

LIFT PASSES

Big Sky only

Prices in US$ inc tax

Age	1-day	6-day
under 11	50	300
11 to 18	71	426
18 to 69	92	519
70 plus	81	486

Free Under 6; also under 11 with lessons

Beginner First half-day lesson includes a base area pass

Notes Prices include 3% tax. Discounts if purchased with lodging; half-day pass available

Alternative pass
Big Sky-Moonlight Basin Interconnect covers Moonlight Basin too

takes you up to the Lone Peak Tram – two 15-person gondola cabins, operated as if they were a cable car. This leads to the top and fabulous 360° views. The Dakota triple chairlift serves Lone's south face and its steep bowls and glades. But a couple of reporters have found the area prone to closure due to avalanche risk. Lone Mountain's lower slopes are wooded and varied, as are those of **Andesite Mountain**, which has less vertical but three of the five fast lifts, including one from Mountain Village. From various points on Lone Mountain you can head down to the **Moonlight Basin** slopes, which start with a slow chair from Moonlight Lodge. Runs from the top of that lead to the Six Shooter fast chair, which, together with the slow Lone Tree quad, serves nearly all Moonlight's wooded, largely easy intermediate terrain. The Headwaters lift at the top serves expert-only runs.

FAST LIFTS ★★
Needs some more
There are five fast quad chairs, but many of the chairs are still old triples and doubles.

QUEUES ★★★★★
Only for the Tram
The tiny Tram continues to attract queues on powder days and in peak season ('15 minutes,' says a 2013 visitor). Queues are rare otherwise: 'Even on a Saturday morning powder day, the most we stood in line was two minutes,' says a 2012 visitor.

TERRAIN PARKS ★★★★
Plenty of choice
Swifty Park on Lone Peak has large jumps, rails and boxes for advanced

riders. There is a natural half-pipe near the Lone Peak triple chair and an intermediate park, Swifty 2.0, near the village. There is a beginner park by the Explorer chair. Moonlight has the Zero Gravity park under the Six Shooter chair, and a beginner park near the base.

SNOW RELIABILITY ★★★★★
No worries here
Snowfall averages 400+ inches – more than most resorts in Colorado. Grooming is 'exceptional' too.

FOR EXPERTS ★★★★
Enough to keep you amused
All of the terrain accessed from the Tram is single or double black diamond. The steepest runs are the Big Couloir on the Big Sky side and the North Summit Snowfield on the Moonlight side. For Big Sky, you are required to have a partner to ski with, an avalanche transceiver and a shovel; for Moonlight, it is highly encouraged. We'd recommend a guide, too. There are easier ways down, though – Liberty Bowl is easiest. Marx and Lenin are a little steeper. The Dakota Territory has 212 acres of black-diamond glades, chutes and high bowls, to skier's right of Liberty Bowl – served by a triple chairlift. Lower down, the Lone Peak Triple, Challenger and Shedhorn chairs also serve good steep terrain. There are some excellent gladed runs, especially on Andesite. In the Moonlight sector the Headwaters is the biggest challenge – but it gets windblown and you may have to pick your way through rocks at the top. The further you hike to skier's left the steeper the couloirs. There are some good gladed runs lower down.

ACTIVITIES

Indoor Solace Spa (massage, beauty treatments), fitness centres in hotels

Outdoor Snowmobiles, snowshoeing, sleigh rides, tubing, fly fishing, ziplines, high ropes course, snowcat tours, visiting Yellowstone National Park

FOR INTERMEDIATES ★★★★
Great deserted cruising

The bulk of the terrain on both mountains is of intermediate difficulty (including lots of easy blacks). The main complaint we have is that they don't seem to groom any blacks – with no people, they would be fabulous when groomed. But there is lots of excellent blue-run cruising served by fast chairs and with few others on the runs: Ramcharger, Southern Comfort and Thunder Wolf on Andesite, Swift Current on Lone Mountain, and Six Shooter in the Moonlight sector. Several wide, gentle bowls offer a good introduction to off-piste. And there are some good easy glade runs, such as Singlejack on Moonlight and The Congo on Andesite. In general the groomed blues at Moonlight are easier than those at Big Sky, especially the ones served by the Lone Tree chair. Adventurous intermediates could try Liberty Bowl from the top of the Tram; but be prepared for a rocky, windswept traverse between wooden barriers at the top to access the run.

FOR BEGINNERS ★★★★★
Ideal – lots of lovely greens

Go to Big Sky rather than Moonlight. There's a good, well-developed nursery area at the base of the Explorer chair with a separate Explorer pass. There is a Learn to Ski taster half or full day including lesson, equipment rental and Explorer pass. There are long, deserted greens to progress to from those lifts and on Andesite.

Andesite has great cruising runs, although the vertical isn't huge

ANDESITE
268om/8,8ooft

Southern Comfort

Ramcharger

Thunder Wolf

Mountain Village
2285m/
7,5ooft

207om/6,8ooft
Lone Moose Meadows

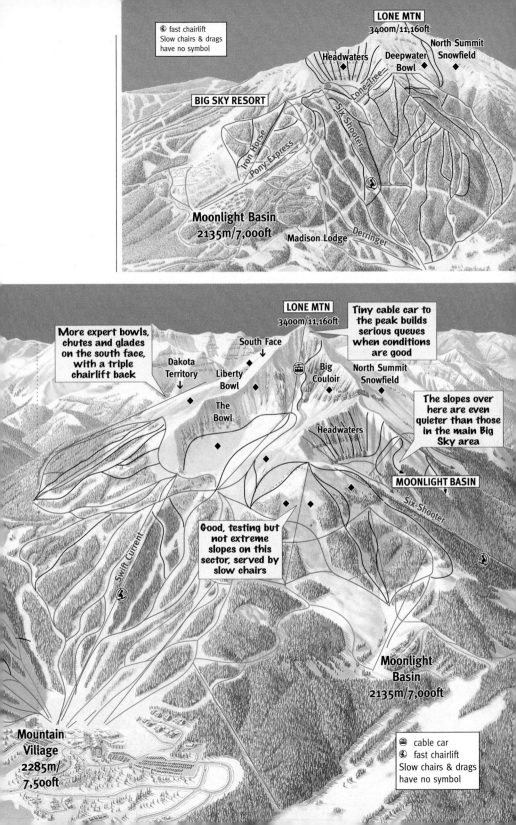

Top map:

LONE MTN
3400m/11,16oft

Headwaters

Deepwater Bowl

North Summit Snowfield

④ fast chairlift
Slow chairs & drags have no symbol

BIG SKY RESORT

Lone Tree

Six Shooter

Iron Horse

Pony Express

Moonlight Basin
2135m/7,000ft

Madison Lodge

Derringer

Bottom map:

LONE MTN
3400m/11,16oft

More expert bowls, chutes and glades on the south face, with a triple chairlift back

South Face ↓

Tiny cable car to the peak builds serious queues when conditions are good

Dakota Territory ↓

Liberty Bowl ↓

Big Couloir

North Summit Snowfield

The Bowl

The slopes over here are even quieter than those in the main Big Sky area

Headwaters

MOONLIGHT BASIN

Six-Shooter

Good, testing but not extreme slopes on this sector, served by slow chairs

Swift Current

Moonlight Basin
2135m/7,000ft

Mountain Village
2285m/7,500ft

🚡 cable car
④ fast chairlift
Slow chairs & drags have no symbol

SCHOOLS

Big Sky
t 995 5743

Classes
Half day (2.5hr) $80
(inc 3% tax)
Private lessons
From $268 for 2hr

CHILDCARE

Lone Peak Playhouse
t 993 2220
Ages 6mnth to 8yr

Ski school
Ages 4 to 14

GETTING THERE

Air Bozeman 70km/
45 miles (1hr15)

UK PACKAGES

AmeriCan Ski, American
Ski Classics, Ski
Bespoke, Ski
Independence, Ski
Safarii

Central reservations
Call 995 5000; toll-
free number (from
within the US) 1 800
548 4486

Phone numbers
From distant parts of
the US, add the prefix
1 406; from abroad,
add the prefix +1 406

TOURIST OFFICE

Big Sky
www.bigskyresort.com
Moonlight Basin
www.moonlightbasin.
com

FOR BOARDERS ★★★★
Something for everyone
The terrain has lots of variety, with few flats. Experts will enjoy the steeps and the glades, freestylers the good terrain parks, and novices the easy cruising runs served by chairlifts. Instruction is 'excellent'.

FOR CROSS-COUNTRY ★★★★
Head for the Ranch
There are 85km of 'excellent' trails at Lone Mountain Ranch ('helpful staff'), and more at West Yellowstone.

MOUNTAIN RESTAURANTS ★
Back to base for lunch?
The Shedhorn Grill is a yurt (tent) on the south side of Lone Mountain, doing simple meals. Then there's the Black Kettle on the front of Lone Mountain – soup and snacks – and the Burrito Shack at the top of the Swift Current chairlift.

SCHOOLS AND GUIDES ★★★★
Good reputation
The Big Sky school has a good reputation. Britain's best ever Olympic downhiller Martin Bell lives here and runs a couple of two-day clinics during the season. Visitors have praised the beginner snowboard classes: 'Exceptionally happy with the quality of the instruction.'

FOR FAMILIES ★★★★
Usual high US standard
Lone Peak Playhouse in the slope-side Snowcrest Lodge will take kids to and from ski school. Children five years and under ski free with an adult. There's a Kids' Club in the Huntley Lodge and snow garden at the base of the mountain.

STAYING THERE

Hotels There's not much choice.
★★★★Summit (548 4486) Best in town; central, slope-side, good rooms, outdoor hot pool, with good views.
★★★Huntley Lodge (548 4486) Big Sky's original hotel; central, part of Mountain Mall, outdoor pool, hot tubs, saunas. 'Unacceptable inter-room noise; ask for an upper floor,' complains a 2012 reporter.
★★★The Lodge at Big Sky (995 7858) Five minutes' walk to slopes; a shuttle at peak times. Indoor pool, indoor/outdoor hot tubs. 'Large rooms, friendly staff, but basic food.'

★★★Rainbow Ranch (995 4132) Five miles south of resort. Luxury riverside rooms and cabins. Recommended.
Apartments The good-value Stillwater condos have been recommended, along with Village Center, Arrowhead, Snowcrest, Big Horn, Black Eagle and, way out of town, Powder Ridge ('fantastic accommodation', 'beautiful' said two 2013 reporters) and Lone Moose. Check location carefully.

EATING OUT ★★★
A fair choice for a small place
Two 2013 visitors recommend M R Hummers ('cheerful staff, good atmosphere'), Whiskey Jack's (burgers, Tex-Mex) and The Cabin ('excellent gourmet style food – elk and bison'). Tips from earlier years include: Lone Peak Brewery ('excellent eatery'), Andiamo ('stylish, fresh pasta in big portions'). Down in the valley, Rainbow Ranch is good for fine dining, Buck's T-4 has a log cabin decor and is popular with locals, and a reporter enjoyed 'good steaks and burgers' at the Corral. Moonlight dinners and live music are held at a backcountry yurt.

APRES-SKI ★
Limited
Nightlife is generally quiet but there are a few bars to try, most with regular live music. Chet's bar has pool. The Carabiner in the Summit and Whiskey Jack's are popular. The Black Bear can be lively, says a reporter.

OFF THE SLOPES ★★
Mainly the great outdoors
There's snowmobiling, snowshoeing, sleigh rides, a floodlit tubing hill, ziplines, snowcat tours, visiting Yellowstone National Park (highly recommended by reporters), treatments at the Solace Spa; the Huntley Lodge pool and spa is open to all for a fee.

MOONLIGHT BASIN

There's not much at the Moonlight base except a few condos and cabins and the impressive Moonlight Lodge – spacious and log-built, with high ceilings and beams. The bar at the Lodge is lively as the slopes close and it has the Jack Creek Grille for dinner. We had an enjoyable dinner a drive away at the Headwaters Grille, at the Madison base area.

Jackson Hole

Touristy 'Wild West' town 12 miles from big, exciting slopes, and a small, modern base village with a famous après-ski saloon

RATINGS

The mountains

Extent	★★★
Fast lifts	★★★★
Queues	★★★
Terrain p'ks	★★★
Snow	★★★★
Expert	★★★★★
Intermediate	★★
Beginner	★★★
Boarder	★★★
X-country	★★★★
Restaurants	★★
Schools	★★★★
Families	★★★★

The resort

Charm	★★★
Convenience	★★★★
Scenery	★★★
Eating out	★★★★★
Après-ski	★★★★
Off-slope	★★★

RPI   160

lift pass	£370
ski hire	£145
lessons	£190
food & drink	£120
total	**£825**

+ Tough expert-only terrain and one of the US's biggest verticals

+ Jackson town has an entertaining Wild West ambience

+ Unspoiled, remote location

+ Excellent snow record

+ Some unique off-slope diversions

+ The airport is only minutes away

− The town is 30 minutes by bus from the slopes, though the lift base has attractive places to stay

− Low altitude and sunny orientation mean snow can deteriorate quickly

− Groomed cruising is in relatively short supply

− Getting there from the UK involves at least one stop and plane change

Our last editorial visit confirmed that Jackson Hole's metamorphosis is almost complete. When we first visited in the early 1990s, you went for its gnarly mountain, shedloads of snow and big vertical – simple as that. It had few facilities at the base or on the mountain and an antiquated lift system. The place attracted hardcore expert skiers, many of them regulars or locals.

But ownership changed and there was a new vision. Now there's a modern (though still inadequate) cable car, a gondola, three fast chairs serving easy and intermediate terrain, a bunch of upscale hotels at the base, a table-service restaurant on the mountain – and many more beginners, intermediates and families around as a result. Some old stagers hate the change; we love it.

THE RESORT

The town of Jackson, with its wooden sidewalks, cowboy saloons and pool halls, sits on the edge of Jackson Hole – a high, flat valley surrounded by mountain ranges in Wyoming. Jackson gets many more visitors in summer than in winter, thanks to the nearby national parks. The slopes are a short

drive away. At the base is Teton Village, which has developed a lot over the past few years, with an increased choice of bars, restaurants and hotels – some notably upscale.

A popular excursion by car or daily bus is over the Teton pass to the smaller resort of Grand Targhee, which gets even more snow. Read the Rest of the West intro.

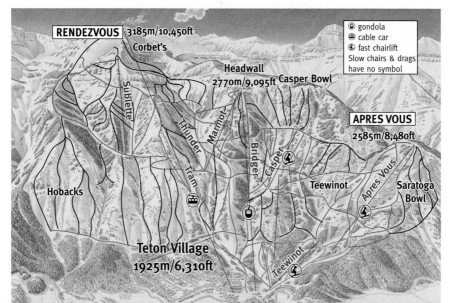

RENDEZVOUS 3185m/10,450ft
Corbet's
Headwall 2770m/9,095ft Casper Bowl
APRES VOUS 2585m/8,480ft
Teewinot
Saratoga Bowl
Hobacks
Sublette
Thunder
Marmot
Bridger
Casper
Apres Vous
Tram
Teton Village 1925m/6,310ft
Teewinot

⊙ gondola
⊜ cable car
④ fast chairlift
Slow chairs & drags have no symbol

NEWS

2012/13: The Casper triple chairlift was replaced by a fast quad. Two new restaurants opened in Teton Village and a wine bar in Jackson town.

KEY FACTS

Resort	1925m
	6,310ft
Slopes	1925-3185m
	6,310-10,450ft
Lifts	12
Pistes	2,500 acres
Green	10%
Blue	40%
Black	50%
Snowmaking	8%

JACKSON HOLE MOUNTAIN RESORT

Ungroomed powder – that's what people have traditionally come to Jackson for. But the resort is now attracting more families and intermediates too ↓

VILLAGE CHARM ★★★☆☆
Cowboy or convenient
To amuse summer tourists Jackson town strives to maintain its Wild West flavour, with saloons with swing doors, country and western music and dancing, and cowboys in stetsons around. It has lots of clothing and souvenir shops, plus upmarket galleries aimed at second-home owners. In winter it's all a bit quiet, but still quite amusing and pleasant. The efficient town bus and friendly and helpful locals are praised by reporters. Teton Village is modern and quite pleasant.

CONVENIENCE ★★★★☆
Stay at the slopes
From Jackson, getting to the slopes means a $3 30-minute bus ride or a slightly quicker drive followed by payment of $15 to park close to the mountain ($5 further away). Our preferred option is to stay at the base and take the bus into town for the occasional night out.

SCENERY ★★★☆☆
You can see forever
You get great long views across the wide plain of Jackson Hole from the slopes, which rise abruptly from the valley floor.

THE MOUNTAINS

Most of the slopes are below the treeline, but most of the forest is not dense. The piste map identifies only a handful of chutes as double-diamond experts-only runs, and we'd say the classification is pretty accurate; but some visitors reckon the toughest single diamonds would be double diamonds elsewhere. There are free mountain tours at 9.30am and 1pm.

EXTENT OF THE SLOPES ★★★☆☆
One big mountain, one small
The main lifts out of Teton Village are the Bridger gondola and the Tram (US-speak for cable car). The Tram takes you up 1260m to the summit of **Rendezvous** mountain – an exceptional vertical for the US. It can be very cold and windy at the top, even when it's warm and calm below. To the right looking up, fast quads access **Apres Vous** mountain, with half the vertical of Rendezvous and mostly much gentler runs. Between these two, the Bridger gondola goes up over a broad mountainside split by gullies, and gives speedy access to the slow Thunder and Sublette chairs – serving some of the steepest terrain on Rendezvous – and the fast Casper chair, from which you can traverse over to the Apres Vous area. The newish Marmot double chair from the base of Thunder quad makes moving across the mountain without returning to the bottom easier.
　　Snow King is a separate area right by Jackson town. Locals use it at lunchtime and in the evenings (it's partly floodlit).

FAST LIFTS ★★★★☆
Few at mid-mountain
Fast lifts access both mountains; slow chairs rule on the upper part of Rendezvous, but a reader points out that they rise steeply, and permit a lot of vertical in a day.

QUEUES ★★★☆☆
Only for the Tram
The Tram holds only 100 people, and many locals do laps on it all day long. So it generates queues – we waited 20 minutes on our last visit, and a more recent visitor waited 30 minutes. Queues elsewhere on Rendezvous are rare, but if wind closes the Tram, the result is '20-minute queues all over Apres Vous'. One reader's tip to avoid

LIFT PASSES

Prices in US$

Age	1-day	6-day
under 15	56	324
15 to 64	94	540
65 plus	75	432

Free Under 6 (Eagle's Rest and Teewinot lifts only)

Beginner Ticket for Eagle's Rest and Teewinot lifts ($29)

Notes Prices are online advance purchase; ticket window prices are higher; afternoon ticket available

Alternative passes
Grand Targhee; Snow King Mountain

---

queuing on powder days is to head for Apres Vous and 'great first tracks in the Saratoga Bowl' (though the Teewinot chair you need to get there can be busy these days).

TERRAIN PARKS ★★★☆☆
Six plus a pipe

In addition to two terrain parks on the lower mountain with features from beginner through to advanced, there are four Burton Stash parks featuring wooden and natural obstacles. Plus there's a half-pipe; and Dick's Ditch is a 450m-long natural half-pipe.

SNOW RELIABILITY ★★★★☆
Deep snow, strong sun

The claimed average of 460 inches of snow is much more than the average for most Colorado (and some Utah) resorts. But the base elevation is low for the Rockies, and the slopes are fairly sunny – they basically face south-east (Apres Vous more south). The steep lower slopes, like the Hobacks, may be in poor shape, or even shut, and the higher slopes can be affected too – on our last visit they were frozen solid because of very low temperatures after a melt. The flanks of some ridges have a more northerly orientation, and a reporter says that Saratoga Bowl keeps its snow well. Locals claim that you can expect powder roughly half the time. Don't assume early-season conditions will be good.

FOR EXPERTS ★★★★★
Best for the brave

For the good skier or boarder who wants challenges without the expense of off-piste guides, Jackson is one of the world's best resorts. Rendezvous mountain offers virtually nothing but black slopes. The routes down the main Rendezvous Bowl are not particularly fearsome; but some of the alternatives are. Go down the East Ridge at least once to stare over the edge of the notorious Corbet's Couloir. It's the jump in that's special; the slope you land on is a mere 50°, they say.

Below Rendezvous Bowl, the wooded flanks of Cheyenne Bowl offer serious challenges, at the steep end of the single black diamond spectrum. If instead you take the ridge run that skirts this bowl to the right, you get to the Hobacks – a huge area of open and lightly wooded slopes, gentler than those higher up, but still black and usually with big moguls; check snow conditions before embarking on these – there's no turning back.

Corbet's aside, most of the steepest slopes are more easily reached from the slightly lower quad chairs. From the Sublette chair, you have direct access to the short but seriously steep Alta chutes, and to the less severe Laramie Bowl beside them. Or you can track over to Tensleep Bowl – pausing to inspect Corbet's from below – and on to the less extreme (and less chute-like) Expert Chutes, and the single-black Cirque and Headwall areas. Casper Bowl often has good powder, and the Crags is an area of bowls, chutes and glades reached by hiking – both are accessed through gates. Thunder chair serves steep, narrow, fairly shady chutes. Again, the lower part of the mountain here offers lightly wooded single diamond slopes.

The gondola serves some good, underused expert terrain, particularly to skier's left of the lift, including the glades of Woolsey and Moran Woods. Even Apres Vous has serious, usually quiet, single blacks in Saratoga Bowl.

The gates into the backcountry access over 3,000 acres of amazing terrain, which should be explored only with guidance. You can stay out overnight at a backcountry yurt (tent). There are some helicopter operations.

FOR INTERMEDIATES ★★☆☆☆
Exciting for some

They have tried hard to improve the intermediate terrain, with fast lifts and much more grooming than in the old days. There are good cruising runs on the front face of Apres Vous, from the Casper chair and top-to-bottom quite gentle blues from the gondola. But they don't add up to a great deal of mileage, and you shouldn't consider Jackson unless you want to tackle ungroomed runs. It's then important to get guidance on steepness and snow conditions. A good number of blues are identified on the trail map as more difficult, and many of these are less frequently groomed too – these are the places to get the hang of powder. The steepest single blacks are steep, intimidating when mogulled and fearsome when hard. The daily grooming map is worth consulting, but falling snow will mean moguls form.

SCHOOLS

Jackson Hole
t 1 800 450 0477

Classes
Full day $125
Private lessons
Half day (3hr) from
$420

CHILDCARE

Kids Ranch
t 1 800 450 0477
Ages 6mnth to 6yr

Ski school
Ages 7 to 14

JACKSON HOLE MOUNTAIN RESORT
The iconic Jackson Hole Tram takes you up 1260m, an exceptional vertical for the US. And many locals just do laps on the Tram all day ↓

FOR BEGINNERS ★★★★★
Fine, up to a point
There are good broad, gentle beginner slopes and a lift pass covering the two chairs that serve them. The progression to the blue Werner run off the Apres Vous chair is gradual enough and the mid-mountain blues from the Casper chair are reached via the chairs from the beginner area. But few other runs will help build confidence.

FOR BOARDERS ★★★★★
Steep and deep thrills
Jackson Hole is a cult resort for expert snowboarders. It's not bad for novices either. But intermediates not wishing to venture off the groomed runs will find the resort limited. Six terrain parks and a half-pipe provide the freestyle thrills. There are some good snowboard shops, including the Hole-in-the-Wall at Teton Village.

FOR CROSS-COUNTRY ★★★★★
Plenty of scenic choices
The Saddlehorn Nordic Center at Teton has 17km of trails and organizes trips into the National Parks.

MOUNTAIN RESTAURANTS ★★★★★
Bridger blossoms
The complex at the top of the Bridger gondola has a coffee shop and fast food pizza area downstairs and a light and airy self-service with good views upstairs serving fresh stir-fry Asian dishes as well as standard fare; and there's also the Couloir table-service restaurant. We enjoyed the Couloir – sit near the entrance for great views over the valley and town through floor-to-ceiling windows and further in

for views of the Headwall and Corbet's through smaller windows. The food is good but not gourmet – burgers, salads, upmarket sandwiches, pasta. Corbet's Cabin has 'great waffles', and the restaurant at the base of the Casper chairlift does a wide range of self-service food. There are simple snack bars at four other points on the mountain. There are some excellent places at the base.

SCHOOLS AND GUIDES ★★★★★
Learn to tackle the steeps
The school is highly regarded and has generated favourable reports. As well as the usual lessons, there are also special Camps on certain dates (pre-booking required). The four-day Steep and Deep Camp was 'carefully matched to ability, good value and a maximum five in each group'.
Rendezvous Backcountry Tours has been recommended for exploring the backcountry from Teton Pass.

FOR FAMILIES ★★★★★
Adventures on the Ranch
There were lots of kids around having fun on our last visit. The 'Kids' Ranch' facilities are good, including regular pizza parties in the evenings. There's a fun kids' version of the trail map.

STAYING THERE

Teton Village is our preferred option now it has comfortable hotels. You can catch the bus to town for a night out – the last one back is around 11pm. Some town hotels are far from central. **Hotels** Because winter is low season, town hotel prices are low.

GETTING THERE

Air Jackson 20km/ 15 miles (45mins)

UK PACKAGES

Alpine Answers, AmeriCan Ski, American Ski Classics, Elegant Resorts, Frontier, Independent Ski Links, Inghams, Momentum, Oxford Ski Co, Scott Dunn, Ski Bespoke, Ski Independence, Ski Line, Ski Safari, Ski Solutions, Skitracer, Skiworld

ACTIVITIES

Indoor Fitness centres, spas (in hotels), concerts, wildlife art and other museums

Outdoor Snowmobiles, snowshoeing, sleigh rides, dog sledding, paragliding, snow kite boarding

Phone numbers
From distant parts of the US, add the prefix 1 307; from abroad, add the prefix +1 307

TOURIST OFFICE

www.jacksonhole.com

TETON VILLAGE
*****Four Seasons Resort (732 5000) Stylish luxury, with art on the walls, superb skier services, health club, an exceptional outdoor pool; perfect position just above the base.
****Snake River Lodge & Spa (732 6000) Smartly welcoming and comfortable, with fine spa facilities.
****Terra (739 4000) Smart, boutique 'eco' hotel, rooftop 'infinity' hot tub, pool. Spa. Nice breakfast cafe. No bar.
****Teton Mountain Lodge & Spa (734 7111) Very comfortable. Good pool, fitness centre, hot tub, spa.
***Alpenhof (733 3242) Tirolean-style, with varied rooms. Good food, lively bar. Pool, sauna, hot tub, spa.
*Hostel (733 3415) Basic, good value and recommended by a reporter.

JACKSON TOWN
****Rusty Parrot Lodge (733 2000) Stylish, small, with a rustic feel. Hot tub, spa.
****Wort (733 2190) Central, above Silver Dollar Bar. Hot tub. Comfortable.
***Lodge at Jackson Hole (739 9703) Western-style on outskirts. Big rooms. Free breakfast. Indoor/outdoor pools, spa, hot tub. Shuttle to the slopes.
***Parkway Inn (733 3143) Central. 'Decent sized rooms. Friendly. Highly recommended.' Free breakfast. Pool, sauna, hot tubs. Shuttle to the slopes.
**49'er Inn and Suites (733 7550) Central, good value, free breakfast and shuttle.
**The Lexington (733 2648) Fairly central. Pool, hot tubs, free breakfast and shuttle.

BETWEEN THE TWO
*****Amangani Resort (734 7333) Hedonistic luxury in isolated position way above the valley.
****Spring Creek Ranch (733 8833) Exclusive retreat; cross-country on hand. Hot tub, spa, shuttle.
Apartments There is lots of choice at Teton Village and better-value places a mile or two away. Surprisingly little in and around Jackson town. Love Ridge and Snow King are 'good value'.

EATING OUT ★★★★★
A wide range of options
Jackson offers a range of excellent dining options. To check out menus, get hold of the local dining guide.

At Teton Village Il Villaggio Osteria at the hotel Terra has a good choice of Italian and seafood dishes. The Couloir at the top of the gondola opens on Thursday and Friday nights with a four-course gourmet menu for $95 – we had great foie gras and bison.

In Jackson town there is a big choice. We loved the Asian/Japanese-fusion dishes to share at The Kitchen. The Cadillac Grille (steaks, burgers, seafood) is 'great for families'. Blue Lion is small and serves seafood and meat dishes. The Million Dollar Cowboy Bar's basement steakhouse has had good reports. The Snake River brew-pub – not to be confused with the expensive Snake River Grill – has a 'great, happy atmosphere' and good beers. Other suggestions: the Merry Piglets (Mexican), Bubba's BBQ, Thai Me Up and Bon Appe Thai ('Real Thai chefs; great pad Thai noodles').

APRES-SKI ★★★★
Amusing saloons
The renowned Mangy Moose is the focus of après-ski activity at Teton Village – a big, happy place, often with live music – though it closed at 10pm mid-week during our last stay. In town, the Silver Dollar Bar (with 2,032 silver dollars inlaid in the counter) was packed with locals dancing to live country music at 8pm on the Saturday night. Round the corner the big Million Dollar Cowboy Bar, featuring saddles as bar stools, gets lively later and also has live music and dancing. The Rancher is an upstairs bar with pool and live music and attracts a younger crowd. Town Square Tavern also has pool and often live music. Out of town, the Stagecoach Inn at Wilson is famously lively on Sunday nights.

OFF THE SLOPES ★★★
'Great' outdoor diversions
Yellowstone National Park is 100km to the north. You can tour the park by snowcat or snowmobile with a guide; numbers are now restricted to reduce pollution. Some visitors really enjoy the park; we were underwhelmed – largely because of the noise and fumes from the snowmobiles and driving everywhere in convoy. The National Elk Refuge, with the largest elk herd in the US, is next to Jackson and across the road from the National Museum of Wildlife Art. Reporters recommend both – and walks beside the Snake river, spotting eagles and moose. In town there are some 40 galleries and museums plus Western arts and crafts shops. Shopping and restaurant discounts can be gained by joining the Jackson Hole Ski Club ($30).

New England

You go to Utah for the deepest snow, to Colorado for the lightest powder and swankiest resorts, to California for big mountains and relatively low prices. You go to New England for ... well, for what? Extreme cold? Rock-hard artificial snow? Mountains too limited to be of interest beyond New Jersey? Yes and no: all of these preconceptions have some basis, and in the end the East can't compete with the West. But they don't give the full picture.

Yes, it can be cold: one of our reporters recorded –27°C, with wind chill producing a perceived –73°C. Early in the season, people routinely wear face masks to prevent frostbite. It can also be warm – another reporter had a whole week of rain that washed away the early-season snow. The thing about New England's weather is that it varies – rather like old England's. The locals' favourite saying is: 'If you don't like the weather, wait two minutes.'

Many of the resorts get impressive amounts of natural snow over the season – in some years. But New England doesn't usually get much deep powder to play in. And snowmaking plays a big part in the resorts' operations. They have big snow-gun installations, designed to ensure a long season and to help the slopes to recover after a thaw. They were the pioneers of snowmaking technology; and 'farming' snow, as they put it, is something they do superbly well.

The mountains are not huge in terms of trail mileage, although Killington in particular packs in more than you would think. But several have verticals of over 800m (on a par with Colorado resorts such as Keystone), and most have over 600m (matching Breckenridge), and are worth considering for a short stay, or even for a week if you like familiar runs. For more novelty, a road trip is the obvious solution.

Most resorts suit snowboarders well, and many have numerous and serious terrain parks.

You won't lack challenge – most of the double-black-diamond runs are seriously steep. And you won't lack space: most Americans visit over weekends, which means deserted slopes on weekdays – except at peak holiday periods.

It also means the resorts are keen to attract long-stay visitors, so UK package prices are low. But the big weekend and day-trip trade also means few New England resorts have developed atmospheric resort villages – just a few condos and a hotel, maybe, with places to stay further out geared to visitors with cars.

New England is easy to get to from Britain – a flight to Boston, then perhaps a three- or four-hour drive to your resort. And there are some pretty towns to visit, with their clapboard houses and big churches. You might also like to consider spending a day or two in Boston – one of America's most charming cities. Or have a shopping spree at the factory outlet stores that abound in New England.

We cover two of the most popular resorts on the UK market, Killington and Stowe, briefly on the opposite page. But there are many other small areas, too, shown on the map and covered in our directory at the back of the book.

606

Killington

+ New England's biggest ski area
+ Excellent nursery slopes
+ Lively après-ski and nightlife
– Widely spread lodgings, with no proper resort village
– Terminally tedious for non-skiers

Killington caters mainly for weekend visitors who drive in from the east-coast cities. There is no resort village in the usual sense.

Most of Killington's hotels and restaurants are spread along a five-mile approach road; the car is king. But there's also a free day-time shuttle-bus The lift pass includes Pico – a separate little mountain next door.

The ski area spreads over a series of wooded peaks, with an impressive number of lifts and runs crammed into a modest area. Amazingly, the Schrahe report (read our piste extent feature) reveals that they total 124km. Killington Base is the main focus, with chairlifts radiating to three of the peaks. Crowds can be a problem at weekends. It's a complex mountain, but the map and signing are fine. It has a good snow record (average 250 inches) and lots of snowmaking.

There are no less than six terrain parks including Burton's The Stash, an all-natural park with more than 50 features, as well as two pipes.

There are a handful of genuine double-diamond fall-line runs to suit experts, steepest on Bear Peak. There are also lots of easy cruising blue and green runs all over the slopes. The resort is excellent for complete beginners too: the Snowshed base home slope is really one vast nursery slope. The Snowshed base lodge has several eating options.

Most hotels are a drive or bus ride away, but there is a wide choice of places to stay and dine. The Grand Resort at Snowshed is a swanky 4-star, newly renovated. Try the Santa Fe Steakhouse ('good seafood too') or Peppino's for Italian. Killington has a well-deserved reputation for a vibrant après-ski scene, led by the famous Wobbly Barn – with live music.

Off the slopes? There's a new tubing park plus sleigh rides and snowmobiling, but do take a car.

Stowe

+ Classic, cute Vermont town
+ Queue-free except at weekends
+ Great children's facilities
– Slopes a bus ride from town
– Slow chairlifts in main area
– Lacks après-ski animation

Stowe is one of New England's cutest towns, its main streets lined with dinky clapboard shops and restaurants. The slopes have something for everyone.

The small slopes of Mount Mansfield, Vermont's mainly wooded highest peak, are a 15-minute drive away. There's a good, free, day-time shuttle-bus service, but a car is useful.

The slopes span two main sectors, Mansfield and Spruce Peak, linked by gondola at base level. Up the mountain the Four Runner chair was replaced by a fast quad in 2011/12. The area is largely queue-free during the week. Snowmaking is extensive, with a big investment last season.

The main slopes are dominated by the famous Front Four – a row of double-black-diamond runs, with genuine challenges for experts. But there is plenty of easier stuff, too. The nursery slopes at Spruce Peak are excellent, and there are splendid long green runs to progress to. There are six terrain parks, and the resort is popular with snowboarders. Children's

facilities are excellent, too. There are a couple of decent eateries. The Cliff House, at the top of the gondola, has table-service ('a great spot').

Much of the lodging is along the road between the town and the slopes – though you can now stay at the swanky Stowe Mountain Lodge, right by the lifts. Elsewhere, the Green Mountain Inn is a reader favourite. There are restaurants of every kind in the town; the Whip in Green Mountain Inn ('always good'), Frida's ('solid Tex-Mex') and Piecasso pizzeria are reader recommendations. Nightlife is fairly muted, but the Matterhorn is 'a Stowe institution not to be missed' and the Den (Mansfield Lodge) 'still rocks'.

Stowe is a pleasant place to spend time off the slopes – at least if you like shopping. There is snowmobiling and dog sledding too. Ben & Jerry's ice cream factory is just down the road.

Canada

In many ways Canada combines the best that the US has to offer – good service, a warm welcome, relatively quiet slopes, good lift systems with lots of fast lifts, frequent dumps of snow, great grooming and a high standard of accommodation – with more spectacular scenery. It also has the advantage that you can get direct flights to its main airports without having to change planes and go through customs part-way through your journey. But it is no longer cheap – long-haul air fares have risen and local prices are high (all Canadian resorts fall into our red category – the most expensive – for their RPI).

Canadian resorts generally have a lot of skiing among the trees – great for visibility during the substantial snowfalls they get ↓

If Canada – well, western Canada at least – has one central attraction, it is snow. In an average year, you can expect frequent and abundant falls to provide the powder you dream of. And, as in the US, there is lots of steep terrain within resort area boundaries, which is therefore avalanche protected and safely skiable without guidance. And there is lots of skiing among the trees – something that is rare in Europe and is great fun, especially in fresh snow or when it's snowing. If you really want untracked powder and are feeling flush, there is nothing to beat western Canada's amazing heli-skiing and snowcat-skiing operations.

The east is completely different: expect snow and extremes of weather much like New England's. The main attraction of Québec for us is the French culture and ambience, plus the advantage of a shorter flight time. In both east and west, lifts close much earlier than in Europe – as early as 3pm in some cases (and some upper lifts might start closing as early as 1.30pm).

The Canadian people are another attraction. They share the American service culture but have a sincerity in putting it into practice that we (and our reporters) appreciate. In the west you'll also find spectacular scenery quite unlike what you generally find in the US. You may also see an impressive range of wildlife, especially in the Rockies and the interior of British Columbia; if this sounds good, you might change your mind if you are driving at night and suddenly see an elk on the middle of the road in your headlights – take care.

The resorts obviously vary. But most have purpose-built villages (much more tastefully done than the French monstrosities of the 1960s and 70s) at the foot of the slopes – Banff and Lake Louise are notable exceptions because they are in a National Park where building is severely restricted. Whistler's village is now huge but many of the others are tiny. A couple – notably Fernie and Revelstoke – have small working towns nearby with decent restaurants and places to stay.

NOT AS CHEAP AS IT WAS

Canada is not as cheap a ski destination as it was. There used to be cheap charter flights that the big tour operators organized to keep package holiday prices down but these were dramatically reduced several seasons ago. And local prices for lift passes, ski school and equipment rental are all much more expensive than in Europe. And eating and drinking is no longer the bargain it once was. Take a look at our price panels for each resort for an idea of what to budget for. In many resorts you can save money by buying lift passes in advance through tour operators or websites. Part of the reason for increased costs is the change in the exchange rate (local prices have risen by 45% in the last six years in terms of £s just because of that) – and, not surprisingly, the number of reports we're getting on Canadian resorts has fallen since then. But it's still cheaper than the US and people who go skiing in Canada generally love it.

Note that the legal age for buying and consuming alcohol is 18 in Alberta and Québec and 19 in British Columbia. The law is strictly enforced, so carrying your passport as evidence of age is a good idea even if you are well over the required age.

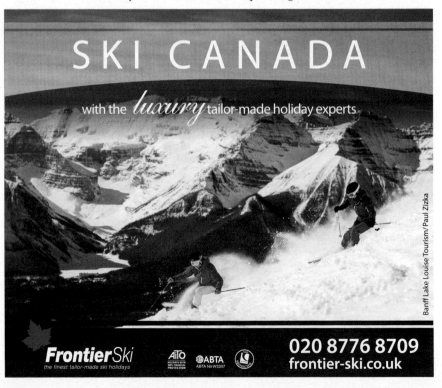

Western Canada

For international visitors to Canada, the main draw is the west. It has fabulous scenery, good snow and a wonderful sense of the great outdoors. The big names of Whistler, Banff and Lake Louise capture most of the British market, but there are lots of good smaller resorts that the more intrepid visitors are now exploring. You can have a great trip by renting a car and combining two or more of these, perhaps with a couple of days on virgin powder served by helicopters or snowcats as well.

The three big resorts mentioned above and six of the smaller ones get their own write-ups in this section.

Whistler is plenty big enough to amuse you for a whole holiday. Most visitors to Banff or Lake Louise, a half-hour drive apart, will spend time at both (and could also fit in day trips to Kicking Horse and Panorama).

But none of the others has enough terrain to keep a keen piste-basher amused for a week or ten days without skiing the same runs a lot. So we'd suggest that if you want variety, you combine two or more on one holiday. Even if you don't want to drive, it is easy to combine, say, Sun Peaks with Whistler, Big White or Silver Star (and the latter two with each other) using regular buses.

Places that don't get a full chapter that you might also consider include Jasper (which you can reach via the spectacular Icefields Parkway drive from Lake Louise), Apex, Red Mountain, Panorama and Kimberley – these all have entries in the resort directory at the back of the book.

We once spent two weeks driving from Whistler to Banff, calling in at lots of smaller resorts on the way. It was a fantastic trip; for eight days in the middle it did not stop snowing, and the variety of slopes and resorts made for great contrasts. In 2013 we combined Fernie, Kicking Horse, Revelstoke and Whistler.

If you fancy a day or two snowcat-skiing, there are lots of possibilities, including great operations near Fernie (see chapter). Revelstoke has both cat- and heli-skiing.

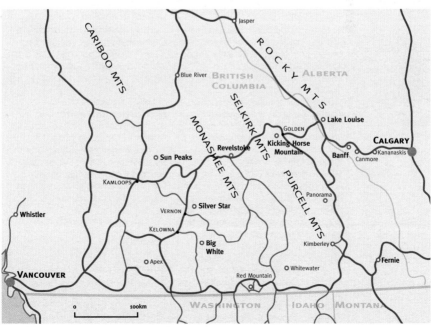

Banff

A major summer resort amid spectacular National Park scenery, with varied ski areas – including Lake Louise – nearby

RATINGS

The mountains

Extent	★★★
Fast lifts	★★★★
Queues	★★★★
Terrain p'ks	★★★★
Snow	★★★★
Expert	★★★★
Intermediate	★★★★
Beginner	★★★
Boarder	★★★★
X-country	★★★★
Restaurants	★★★
Schools	★★★★
Families	★★★★

The resort

Charm	★★★
Convenience	★
Scenery	★★★★
Eating out	★★★★★
Après-ski	★★★
Off-slope	★★★★★

RPI 160

lift pass	£360
ski hire	£125
lessons	£175
food & drink	£170
total	£830

612

NEWS

2012/13: On Sunshine, a moving carpet was fitted at the Wawa chair to shorten queues, new features were added to the terrain parks and the Chimney Corner Lounge at Sunshine Mountain Lodge was refurbished and extra seating added.

- Spectacular high-mountain scenery – quite unlike the Colorado Rockies
- Lots of touristy shops, restaurants and bars
- Good-value lodging because winter is the area's low season
- Excellent snow at main local area, Sunshine Village, but ...

- It's a 20-minute bus ride then a long gondola ride away
- You'll probably want to ski Lake Louise too, 45 minutes away
- Most lifts/runs are of limited vertical
- Can be very cold (–30ºC or less)
- Banff lacks ski resort atmosphere, though it's not an unattractive town

Banff is nothing like your typical ski resort. We enjoy its restaurants and bars, but not the daily commuting to Sunshine Village or Lake Louise (which gets its own chapter). Even the small local hill, Norquay, is a bus ride out of town.

The alternative is to stay a few nights mid-mountain at Sunshine Village and a few at Lake Louise. Lake Louise also has the advantage of being much closer to Kicking Horse, which makes a great day trip for powderhounds.

THE RESORT

Banff is a big summer tourist town, with two ski areas nearby. Mt Norquay is a tiny area of slopes overlooking the town. Sunshine Village – whose base station is 20 minutes' drive from Banff – is a much bigger mountain; despite the name, it's not a village (it has just one hotel at mid-mountain), nor is it notably sunny (sitting on the Continental Divide, it has an excellent snow record).

Most visitors buy a three-area pass that also covers the resort of Lake Louise, 45 minutes' drive away – dealt with in a separate chapter. Bus excursions are available to the more distant resorts of Panorama and Kicking Horse (the latter especially worthwhile) and the smaller (and closer) resort of Nakiska, and day trips for heli-skiing are offered locally.

VILLAGE CHARM ★★★
Pleasantly touristy
Banff consists basically of a long main street connecting the 'downtown' area – a small network of side roads built in grid fashion, lined with clothing and souvenir shops aimed at summer visitors – with a large area of hotel and condo lodgings. The buildings are low-rise, and some are wood-clad. The town is pleasant enough, but it's essentially a modern tourist town, without the character of the classic American cowboy or mining towns.

CONVENIENCE ★
Sprawling town, outlying slopes
Banff is a sprawling place, and many of the lodgings (even on the main Banff Avenue) can be quite a way from the downtown area. A car can be helpful here, especially in cold weather. But there are plentiful taxis.

To get to the slopes, bus services for each mountain (free with the Tri-area lift pass) pick up from many of the main hotels – but getting from your hotel to the lift base can take much longer than by car because of the number of stops, though the buses 'run like clockwork', says a 2013 visitor. At Sunshine when you arrive there is a long access gondola to ride.

SCENERY ★★★★
Distinctive and dramatic
Banff National Park offers spectacular scenery – that's what brings the millions of summer visitors – and the town's setting is dramatic. Sunshine's Lookout mountain, right on the Continental Divide, gives panoramic views into British Columbia.

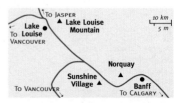

Norquay, Sunshine and Lake Louise

Slopes	1630-2730m
	5,350-8,950ft
Lifts	26
Pistes	7,748 acres
Green	23%
Blue	39%
Black	38%
Snowmaking	24%

Norquay only

Slopes	1630-2135m
	5,350-7,000ft
Lifts	5
Pistes	190 acres
Green	20%
Blue	36%
Black	44%
Snowmaking	85%

Sunshine only

Slopes	1660-2730m
	5,440-8,950ft
Lifts	12
Pistes	3,358 acres
Green	20%
Blue	55%
Black	25%
Snowmaking	2 guns –
early season only	

LIFT PASSES

Tri-area lift pass

Prices in C$

Age	1-day	6-day
under 13	31	207
13 to 17	63	474
18 to 64	87	533
65 plus	66	474

Free Under 6
Beginner Lift, lesson and rental package
Notes Day pass is for Sunshine only; 3-day-plus pass covers all lifts and transport between Banff, Lake Louise, Norquay and Sunshine Village; prices include 5% tax

SKI BANFF-LAKE LOUISE-SUNSHINE / SEAN HANNAH

Sunshine Village, with the Sunshine Mountain Lodge on the left, the Day Lodge beyond it and the access gondola in the distance →

THE MOUNTAINS

The Sunshine Village slopes are mostly above the treeline, although there is a wooded sector – served by the second section of the gondola – and some lightly wooded slopes higher up.

Mt Norquay is a much smaller area of quiet, wooded slopes. But it's worth a visit, especially in bad weather or as a first-day warm-up.

Each area (and Lake Louise) has its own trail map, and there's another that shows all three areas. The signposting at the top of each lift is praised, but at Sunshine it is difficult to follow some trails after that ('Signs are small and difficult to spot,' says a reporter).

There are good, free mountain tours led by friendly volunteer hosts.

EXTENT OF THE SLOPES ★★★★★
Lots of variety
The main slopes of **Sunshine Village** are not visible from the base station: you ride a gondola to Sunshine Village itself, with a mid-station at the base of Goat's Eye Mountain. Goat's Eye is served by a fast quad rising 580m – much the most serious lift on the mountain. Although there are some blue runs, this is basically a black mountain, with some genuine double diamonds (including extreme terrain in the Wild West area – see 'For experts').

Further up at Sunshine Village, lifts fan out in all directions, with short runs back from Mount Standish and longer ones from Lookout Mountain. From the top here you can access the more extreme terrain of Delirium Dive – see 'For experts'.

The 2.5km green run to the

gondola base is a pretty cruise. Go down while the lifts are still running, and you can take the Jackrabbit chair to cut out a flat section. Delay your descent and you'll avoid the close-of-play crowds. The Canyon trail is a fun alternative for more advanced skiers and riders. The lower part is marked black; it's just a bit narrow and twisty in places. The final option is to ride the gondola down; many people do.

The slopes at **Norquay** are served by a row of five parallel lifts and have floodlit trails twice a week.

FAST LIFTS ★★★★★
Most sectors well served
At Sunshine, most sectors of the slopes have fast chairs. The main weakness is the Wawa chair, which had a new moving carpet fitted for 2012/13 to speed up loading. Norquay is so small that lift speed is hardly an issue, but it does have one fast chair.

QUEUES ★★★★★
Sunshine can get busy
Many visitors are day-trippers from cities such as Calgary – so the slopes are fairly quiet during the week. Public holidays and weekends at Sunshine have provoked past complaints of long queues. But queues generally move quickly, and there are effective singles lines you can use if in a hurry. On busy weekends, we're told the trick is to arrive at the gondola by 9am.

TERRAIN PARKS ★★★★★
Fun on both areas
At Sunshine, the terrain park on Lookout Mountain covers an impressive 12 acres. The park is

Banff

613

divided into three: Rogers has a wide selection of obstacles and jumps from S to XL; Grizzly has L and XL rails, jumps and boxes; and Springhill has S and M features. Experts should not miss the Norquay park, which has an airbag and is littered with gap jumps, tabletops, rails and boxes. The park is floodlit twice a week from January to March.

SNOW RELIABILITY ★★★★
Excellent

Sunshine Village used to claim '100% natural snow', a neat reversal of the usual snowmaking hype. Now it has two snow-guns, which are used on the lower part of the run out to the bottom of the gondola and in the ski school beginner area, at the beginning of the season only. So in a poor snow season, some black runs can remain rocky (especially those on Goat's Eye), but the blues are usually fine. 'Three times the snow' is still a Sunshine claim – a sly comparison between the impressive average snowfall here (360 to 400 inches, depending on the source) and the modest 180 inches at Lake Louise and 120 inches on Norquay. But we're told the Sunshine figures relate to Lookout, and that Goat's Eye gets less snow than this. At Norquay there is snowmaking on all green and blue pistes. Late-season snow on Sunshine is usually good (we've had great April snow there).

FOR EXPERTS ★★★★
Pure pleasure

Sunshine has plenty of open runs of genuine black steepness above the treeline on Lookout, but Goat's Eye is much more compelling. It has a great area of expert double black diamond trails and chutes, both above and below the treeline. But the slopes are rocky and need good cover, and the

Goat's Eye has some great steep terrain – single and double black diamond runs and an extreme zone. But it's very rocky and windswept and needs a lot of snow to be enjoyable

GOAT'S EYE
2600m/8,530ft

Goat's Eye

Deliriu Dive
◆◆

Wild West
◆◆

1660m/5,440ft

2020m/6,630ft

Wolverine

Gondo

If it's snowing hard, visibility is usually best on the easy runs in the trees around here and on the long run down to the bottom of the gondola

Ⓖ gondola
④ fast chairlift
Slow chairs & drags have no symbol

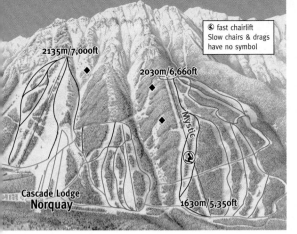

2135m/7,000ft

2030m/6,66oft

Mystic

Cascade Lodge
Norquay

1630m/5,35oft

challenging novelty here is a pitch known as the Waterfall run – because you do actually ski down over a snow-covered frozen waterfall. But a lot of snow is needed to cover the waterfall and prevent it reverting to ice. Also try the Shoulder on Lookout Mountain; it is sheltered, tends to accumulate powder and has been deserted whenever we've been there (probably because access to it involves a long traverse that can be tricky and is poorly marked).

A popular backcountry route follows the back of the Wawa ridge, through a river valley ('great fun – tight turns in the trees of the river bed'); a guide is essential, of course.

Real experts will want to get to grips with Delirium Dive on Lookout Mountain's north face and the Wild West area on Goat's Eye (with some narrow chutes and rock bands). For both you must have a companion, an

top can be windswept. The double diamond runs at skier's left reportedly hold their snow better than the rest of the mountain.

There are short, not-too-steep black runs on Mount Standish. One more

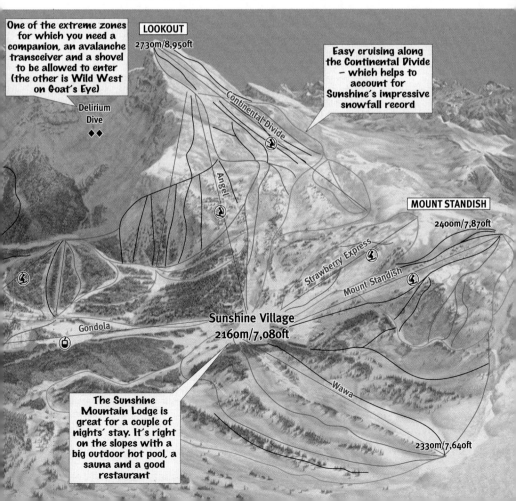

One of the extreme zones for which you need a companion, an avalanche transceiver and a shovel to be allowed to enter (the other is Wild West on Goat's Eye)

LOOKOUT
2730m/8,95oft

Delirium
Dive
◆◆

Continental Divide

Angel

Easy cruising along the Continental Divide – which helps to account for Sunshine's impressive snowfall record

MOUNT STANDISH
2400m/7,87oft

Strawberry Express

Mount Standish

Sunshine Village
216om/7,08oft

Gondola

Wawa

The Sunshine Mountain Lodge is great for a couple of nights' stay. It's right on the slopes with a big outdoor hot pool, a sauna and a good restaurant

2330m/7,64oft

avalanche transceiver, probes and a shovel – and a guide is recommended. It is best to book in advance and rent your equipment in Banff (you can't in Sunshine). We tried Delirium in a group with the ski patrol, who provided equipment, and the scariest part was the walk in, along a narrow, icy path with a sheer drop (protected by a flimsy-looking net).

Norquay's two main lifts give only 400m vertical, but both serve black slopes, and the North American chair accesses a couple of serious double diamond runs.

Heli-skiing is available from bases outside the National Park in British Columbia – roughly two hours' drive.

FOR INTERMEDIATES ★★★★
Ideal runs
Half the runs on Sunshine are classified as intermediate. Wherever you look there are blues and greens – and some of the greens are as enjoyable (and pretty much as steep) as the blues.

We particularly like the World Cup Downhill run, from the top of Lookout to the Village. All three chairs on Mount Standish are excellent for building confidence, provided you choose a sensible route down. The slow Wawa chair gives access to the Wawa Bowl and Tincan Alley ('great first blues'). This area also offers some shelter from bad weather.

There's a delightful wooded area under the second stage of the gondola served by the Jackrabbit and Wolverine chairs. The blue runs down Goat's Eye are good cruises too, some of them with space to indulge in fast carving.

The Mystic Express at Norquay serves a handful of quite challenging treelined blues and a couple of blacks that are sometimes groomed.

FOR BEGINNERS ★★★
Pretty good terrain
Most beginners start with a package that includes a lift pass, equipment hire and tuition. Sunshine has a good nursery area at the Village, served by a moving carpet. And there are great long green runs to progress to, served by the fast Strawberry Express chair.

Norquay has a good small nursery area with a moving carpet and gentle greens to progress to, served by the Cascade chair.

Banff is not the ideal destination for a mixed party of beginners and more experienced friends. The beginners are likely to want familiar surroundings, while the more experienced will want to travel.

FOR BOARDERS ★★★★
A good base
Boarders will feel at home in Banff, and there is some excellent freeriding terrain. Natural features are part of the appeal, with ledges, jumps and tree gaps aplenty. But Sunshine has some flat areas to beware of (such as the green run to the base – see 'Extent of the slopes'), and the blue traverse on Goat's Eye is tedious. A trip to Lake Louise's Powder Bowls is a must for freeriders.

There are specialist snowboard shops in Banff: Rude Boys, Rude Girls and Unlimited Skate & Snow.

FOR CROSS-COUNTRY ★★★★
High in quality and quantity
It's a good area for cross-country. There are trails near Banff, around the Bow River, and on the Banff Springs golf course. But the best area is around Lake Louise. Altogether, there are around 80km of groomed trails within Banff National Park.

MOUNTAIN RESTAURANTS ★★★
Quite good
With a mini-resort at mid-mountain, Sunshine offers better options than usual in North America. Our favourite is the welcoming Chimney Corner Lounge in the Sunshine Mountain Lodge with a big open fire – endorsed by reporters ('Tasty and good value,' said a recent visitor) and revamped for 2013. The Day Lodge offers different styles of catering on three floors – the table-service Lookout Lounge has great views and does a buffet.

At Norquay, the big, stylish, timber-framed Cascade Lodge is excellent – it has table- and self-service restaurants.

SCHOOLS AND GUIDES ★★★★
Some great ideas
Each mountain has its own school. But recognizing that visitors wanting lessons won't want to be confined to just one mountain, the resorts have organized an excellent Club Ski Program – three-day courses starting on Sundays and Thursdays that take you to Sunshine, Norquay and Lake Louise on different days, offering a mixture of guiding and instruction. Reporters are full of praise for these.

SCHOOLS

Ski Big 3
t 760 7731

Banff-Norquay
t 762 4421

Sunshine Village
t 1 877 542 2633

Classes (Big 3 prices)
3 days' guided tuition
of the three areas
C$314 incl. tax

Private lessons
Half day (3hr) C$398,
incl. tax, for up to 5
people

CHILDCARE

Tiny Tigers (Sunshine)
t 705 4000
Ages 19mnth to 6yr

Kid's Place (Norquay)
t 760 7709
Ages 19mnth to 6yr

Childcare Connection
t 760 4443
Childminding in guest
accommodation

Ski school
Ages 6 to 12

UK PACKAGES

Alpine Answers,
AmeriCan Ski, American
Ski Classics, Canadian
Affair, Crystal, Crystal
Finest, Elegant Resorts,
Frontier, Independent
Ski Links, Inghams,
Momentum, Neilson,
Oxford Ski Co,
PowderBeds, Ski
Bespoke, Ski
Independence, Ski Line,
Ski Safari, Ski
Solutions, Skitracer,
Skiworld, Snow Finders,
Supertravel, Thomson,
Virgin Snow

Phone numbers
From distant parts of
Canada, add the
prefix 1 403; from
abroad, add the prefix
+1 403

TOURIST OFFICE

www.skibanff.com
www.banffnorquay.
com
www.SkiBig3.com

FOR FAMILIES ★★★★
Excellent choices

There are various school and activity programmes for all ages. We've had good reports of the schools in the past – new reports please. All three resorts offer childcare. The Tiny Tigers Ski and Play Program at Sunshine introduces youngsters to the slopes.

STAYING THERE

A huge amount of accommodation is on offer, with lots of varied hotels.
Hotels Summer is peak season here, with generally lower prices in winter.
★★★★★Fairmont Banff Springs (762 2211) A late-19th-century, castle-style property outside town (no shuttle-bus – you have to use taxis). It's a town in itself – 2,000 beds, 40 shops, several restaurants and bars, a nightclub and a superb spa (which costs extra).
★★★★Banff Caribou Lodge (762 5887) On the main street, slightly out of town. Wood-clad, individually designed rooms (some small). 'Massive' hot tub; spa. Repeatedly praised by reporters ('fantastic service', 'good food').
★★★★Banff Park Lodge (762 4433) Best-quality, central hotel, with hot tub, steam room and indoor pool.
★★★★Fox (760 8500) On the main street. Hotel rooms and suites, with a restaurant, fitness area and an unusual 'cavern' style hot pool.
★★★★Rimrock (762 3356) Spectacularly set out of town, with great views and a smart health club. Luxurious.
★★★Buffalo Mountain Lodge (762 2400) Slightly out of town but in a beautiful location. 'Excellent food.' Hot tub.
★★★Irwin's Mountain Inn (762 4566) Good value; on Banff Avenue.
★★Homestead Inn (762 4471) Central, with cheap, good-sized rooms.
Apartments The Banff Rocky Mountain Resort is set in the woods on the edge of town, with indoor pool and hot tubs. Douglas Fir resort is a bit out of town but has a free shuttle and is popular with families; lots of facilities such as adults' and kids' swimming pools and a giant indoor playground.
At altitude The Sunshine Mountain Lodge (705 4000) makes a very welcoming, comfortable base at Sunshine Village. Luggage is transported while you ski. Rooms vary in size and include luxury loft rooms. Big outdoor hot pool. Sauna. Good restaurant. Guests can get on the slopes half an hour early.

EATING OUT ★★★★★
Lots of choice

Banff boasts over 100 restaurants, from McDonald's to the fine dining restaurant in the Banff Springs hotel.

The award-winning Maple Leaf Grille offers fine seafood and steak dishes, and over 600 different wines. We've enjoyed the designer-cool Saltlik – good game, steak and fish.

Of the dozens of places that readers recommend, popular spots are Melissa's (central, 'varied menu and good ambience'), Athena ('excellent large pizzas – good value for money'), Giorgio's (beef, fish, Italian), Café de Paris ('tasty wild boar') and Magpie & Stump (aka Maggers – Tex-Mex, with Wild West decor). Old Spaghetti Factory is a good family choice. Try Bison for steaks, fish and live music. And for burgers and ribs try Keg, Bumper's, Wild Bill's or Tony Roma's.

APRES-SKI ★★★
Night on the town is best

There's little teatime après-ski because the town is a drive from the slopes. Mad Trapper's Saloon at the top of the Sunshine gondola is the place to be during the close-of-play happy hour.

In town later, the two main live music venues are the Rose & Crown and Wild Bill's. The Banff Avenue Brewing Company is the local microbrewery. The Elk and Oarsman has a lively sports bar and the St James's Gate is the local Irish pub. There are a couple of good nightclubs.

OFF THE SLOPES ★★★★★
Lots to do

Banff has lots to do off the slopes. Outdoor activities include skating, snowshoeing, dog sledding and snowmobiling. Ice canyon walks are popular – notably Johnson Canyon – and there's wildlife to see.

Shopping and soaking in the spas and hot springs are popular – the Red Earth Spa at the Caribou Lodge has the works. There are sightseeing tours and several museums – a 2013 visitor recommends the Whyte Museum of the Canadian Rockies and the Banff Park Museum. Many reporters have enjoyed evenings in Calgary watching the ice hockey. A recent reporter enjoyed a good day out in Canmore. Banff is quite near one end of the Columbia Icefields Parkway, a three-hour drive to Jasper through national parks – one of the world's most beautiful drives.

Big White

It's a big village by Canadian standards and it's certainly white. There are few places to match it for learning to ski powder

TOP 10 RATINGS

Extent	★★★
Fast lifts	★★★★
Queues	★★★★★
Snow	★★★★★
Expert	★★★
Intermediate	★★★★
Beginner	★★★★
Charm	★★
Convenience	★★★★
Scenery	★★★

RPI 145

lift pass	£320
ski hire	£130
lessons	£135
food & drink	£170
total	**£755**

KEY FACTS

Resort	1755m
	5,760ft
Slopes	1510-2320m
	4,950-7,610ft
Lifts	16
Pistes	2,765 acres
Green	18%
Blue	54%
Black	28%
Snowmaking	
	In terrain park

+ Great for learning to ski powder

+ Slopes quiet except at weekends

+ Convenient, purpose-built village with high-quality condos and a traffic-free centre; good for families

+ Lots of non-skiing snow-based activities at Happy Valley

− Visibility can be poor, especially on the upper mountain, because of snow, cloud or freezing fog

− Few off-slope diversions, and it's isolated without a car

− Limited après-ski

'It's the snow' says the Big White slogan. And as slogans go, it's spot on. If you want a good chance of skiing powder on reasonably easy slopes, put Big White high on the shortlist. If you want a suntan (or lively après-ski, or extensive steep terrain), look elsewhere; but if you are an intermediate looking to learn to ski powder or try gladed skiing, there can be few better places. Consider combining it with another BC resort such as Silver Star or Sun Peaks for variety.

THE RESORT

Big White is a purpose-built resort that has more visitor beds than any other BC resort except Whistler. It's less than an hour from Kelowna airport.
Village charm The resort is rather spread out but attractively built in wood and stone, with a family-friendly traffic-free centre.
Convenience Much of the place is ski-in/ski-out of smart modern condos.
Scenery Trees fill the views wherever you look; and near the top of the mountain the trees usually stay white all winter and are known as 'snow ghosts'; they make visibility tricky in a white-out but are great fun to ski between on clear days.

THE MOUNTAINS

Much of the terrain is heavily wooded. But the trees thin out towards the summits, leading to almost open slopes in the bowls at the top. There's at least one green option from the top of each lift, but the one from Gem Lake is narrow and can be tricky and busy. In general, the easiest slopes are on the right as you look at the mountain (including some very easy glade skiing) and get steeper the further left you go.
Slopes Chairs run from points below village level to above mid-mountain, serving the main area of wooded beginner and intermediate runs above and beside the village. A T-bar and

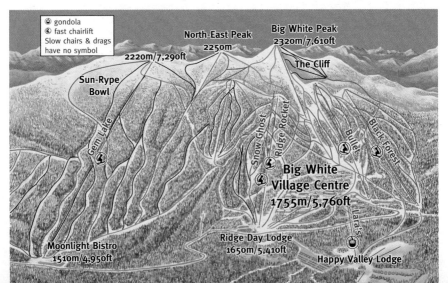

↑ The centre of the resort is small, attractive, traffic-free and family-friendly
BIG WHITE SKI RESORT

Big White

619

Build your own shortlist: www.wheretoskiandsnowboard.com

NEWS

2013/14: Cross-country, snowshoe and dog sledding trails and walking paths are due to be upgraded.

2012/13: Some 5km of new cross-country trails were created. High Performance coaching sessions for skiing and boarding were introduced. The lodge at the foot of the Gem Lake chair is now The Moonlight Bistro and the Ridge Day Lodge has also been renovated. There are now climbing clinics on the ice tower and snowshoe tours for all ages and abilities.

four chairs serve the higher slopes. Quite some way across the mountainside is the Gem Lake fast chair, serving a range of long top-to-bottom runs; with its 710m vertical, this lift is in a different league from the others.

'Snow hosts' (highly praised by reporters) run free guided ski tours starting at 10.30 every morning. The signposting and piste map and classification are good ('excellent', says a recent visitor). There is night skiing Tuesday to Saturday evenings on four slopes.

Fast lifts The lifts from the village and the Gem Lake lift are all fast. But the other upper lifts are tediously slow.

Queues Queues are very rare.

Terrain park Served by a double chair and snowmaking, the excellent Telus park includes three 9m jumps, rails and hits for all levels, large-diameter tube rails, a half-pipe and a boardercross, and is highly praised by reporters. The park is open for night riding Thursday to Saturday.

Snow reliability Big White has a reputation for great powder; average snowfall is about 300 inches, which is similar to many Colorado resorts. On each of our three visits it snowed practically non-stop, the powder was excellent and we hardly saw the sun.

Experts The Cliff area at the top right of the ski area is of serious double-black-diamond pitch; the runs are short, but you can ski them repeatedly using the Cliff chair. Sun-Rype bowl at the opposite edge of the ski area is

more forgiving ('Excellent place to ski deep powder,' says a reporter). There are some long blacks off the Gem Lake chair and several shorter ones off the Powder and Falcon chairs. There are plenty of glades to explore – and bump runs too.

Intermediates The resort is excellent for cruisers and families, with long blues and greens all over the hill. Good intermediates will enjoy the easier blacks and some of the gladed runs too. There is marvellous easy skiing among the trees in the Black Forest area (which we loved when it was snowing) and among the snow ghosts (see 'Scenery'), which we loved when it was clear. Some of the blues off the Gem Lake chair are quite steep, narrow and challenging.

Beginners There's a good dedicated beginner learning area at Happy Valley and lots of long easy runs to progress to. Every day three slopes are designated slow zones, gated and patrolled.

Snowboarding There's some excellent beginner and freeriding terrain with boarder-friendly chairlifts and few flat areas to worry about.

Cross-country A reporter enjoyed the 25km of 'great open spaces and wooded routes'. She found trail maps good but some of the signage poor. There are free guided tours daily at 10.30am.

Mountain restaurants There aren't any – it's back to the bottom for lunch. You can eat a packed lunch at any of the day lodges.

Central reservations
Call 765 8888; toll-free (within Canada)
1 800 663 2772
Phone numbers
From distant parts of
Canada, add the
prefix 1 250; from
abroad, add +1 250

TOURIST OFFICE

www.bigwhite.com

School and guides We have received rave reviews from reporters for both skiing and snowboarding lessons for both adults and children. One six-year-old had only one other child in his group lessons and made rapid progress on black moguls and in the trees.

Families The excellent day care centre takes children from 18 months to five years; it has a list of babysitters too.

STAYING THERE

A good range of accommodation is featured by specialist tour operators such as Frontier Ski and Ski Independence.

Hotels Chateau Big White is our reporters' favourite: 'excellent location', 'room was huge', 'cosy fires'; ask for a room facing away from the village to avoid late-night noise. The White Crystal Inn receives better reviews than the Inn at Big White.

Apartments Condo standards are high. Stonebridge and Towering Pines are both central, ski-in/ski-out, with big, well-furnished rooms and private hot tubs on the balconies. Other reporter tips include Black Bear and (a bit less luxurious) Eagles and Whitefoot Lodge.

Eating out The best restaurants here have a great selection of local Okanagan wines (there are over 130 wine producers in the valley). We had a superb meal at the 6 Degrees bistro, sharing delicious dishes (tapas-style); endorsed by a 2013 reporter; not cheap. We've also had good meals in the Kettle Valley Steakhouse at Happy Valley. Reporters also recommend the 'charming' upstairs restaurant at Snowshoe Sam's and the 'excellent' Globe ('imaginative food, served tapas-style'). The BullWheel is a family place with handmade burgers. The Blarney Stone Irish Tavern will be replacing former favourite Carvers in the Inn at Big White for 2013/14 – it will be run by the people that own the Globe; reports please.

Après-ski In general, après-ski is fairly quiet. But the ground floor of Snowshoe Sam's has a DJ and live entertainment.

Off the slopes Happy Valley is a great area for families, with ice skating, snowmobiling, snow biking, tubing, dog sledding, sleigh rides, 15km of snowshoeing trails and an 18m ice climbing tower. There are two spas and a shopping shuttle to Kelowna.

Fernie

Lots of snow and lots of steeps – one of our favourites, with a choice of convenient base lodging or a valley town

+ Good snow record, with less chance of rain than at Whistler

+ Blissfully quiet much of the time

+ Great terrain for those who like it steep and deep; good for confident intermediates too

+ Snowcat operations nearby

+ Some good on-slope accommodation available, but ...

− Mountain resort is very limited

− Access to many excellent runs is via slow lifts and long traverses

− Not a huge amount of groomed cruising to do

− After a dump it can take time to make the bowls safe (and to get the groomed trails groomed again)

− One basic mountain restaurant

Fernie has long had cult status among the residents of Calgary. Before the recession and exchange rate changes started to bite, we also got a good flow of reports from enthusiastic British visitors impressed by the adventurous nature of the skiing – it's mostly ungroomed, and much of it is steep, with a lot of lightly wooded slopes (not common in Europe). Despite all that, it's now quite a good resort for novices, too. Keen but cautious intermediates unhappy about giving the powder a go are the ones who may want to look elsewhere.

Fernie town, a couple of miles from the lift base, has few of the usual tourist trappings, but makes an amusing change from the ski resort norm.

THE RESORT

Fernie Alpine Resort is set a little way up the mountainside from the flat Elk Valley floor and a couple of miles from the little town of Fernie. Outings to Kimberley are possible; a coach goes weekly, taking about 90 minutes.

VILLAGE CHARM ★★ ☆☆☆
Unpretentious small town
A slope-side resort has grown from very little in recent years, but there's still not much there except convenient lodging and a few restaurants, bars and sports shops. It is quiet at night. There's much more going on in the nearby town, named after William Fernie – a prospector who discovered coal here and triggered a boom in the early 1900s. Much of the town was destroyed by fire in 1908, but some buildings survived.

Fernie town is primarily a place for locals, not tourists, but there are some lively bars, decent places to eat and a reasonable range of shops. It is down to earth rather than charming, and reporters' reactions to it vary: some like staying in a 'real' town while others are put off by the highway that runs through it, quite close to the centre. Most stress the friendliness of the locals.

CONVENIENCE ★★★★
Base lodging or bus ride
There is accommodation at the resort and in town. Buses between town and mountain run hourly and cost C$3 one way, stopping at some of the bigger hotels on the way. They run until 2am

on Friday and Saturday nights. A reporter found drivers 'happy to be flagged down'.

SCENERY ★★★☆☆
The rocky ridges are impressive
Fernie's two main peaks, Grizzly and Polar, are part of the steep-sided Lizard Range. They provide an impressively rocky backdrop. There are good views across the Elk Valley too.

THE MOUNTAINS

Fernie's 2,500 acres pack in a lot of variety, from superb green terrain at the bottom to ungroomed chutes, open bowls and huge numbers of steep runs in the trees. Quite a few runs go directly down the fall line.

Over the years we've been visiting, both the trail map and the on-mountain signposting have been improved hugely, to the point where you can find your way around most of the time with confidence. But, as we found last winter, it is still quite easy to be misled by the map in certain areas, and we still think you'll get the best out of the area with some sort of local guidance. Without it, you can end up in tight trees on slopes of double-diamond steepness. The map employs some ludicrously small type.

EXTENT OF THE SLOPES ★★★☆☆
Bowl after bowl
What you see when you arrive at the lift base is a trio of impressive mogul slopes towering above you. These excellent black runs exemplify one of the weaknesses of Fernie's lift system:

to get to them you must ride lifts way off to the left or right, and then make long traverses to get to the start of the runs proper – a slow business.

The slow Deer chair serves green runs at the foot of these black slopes, but goes no further.

On the right, riding the slow Elk quad followed by the fast Great Bear quad takes you to the ridge where **Lizard Bowl** meets **Cedar Bowl**. You can traverse across the head of both of these open/lightly wooded bowls and descend pretty much wherever you like, though both have trails marked on the map. At the far side of Cedar Bowl are steeper runs among tighter trees from Snake Ridge. The Haul Back T-bar brings you out of Cedar to ride the Boomerang chair. This serves a mini-bowl between Lizard and Cedar.

Off to the left, the Timber Bowl fast quad chair gives access to **Siberia Bowl** and the lower part of **Timber Bowl**. But for access to the higher slopes of Timber Bowl and to **Currie Bowl** you must take the slow White Pass quad. A long traverse from the top gets you to the steeper slopes on the flanks of Currie (our favourite area). On the way, you pass the new slow triple chair, which accesses the open and mainly steep runs from **Polar Peak**, the highest runs in the ski area. If you descend Currie Bowl you have to go all the way to the lift base, and it takes quite a while to get back up. The new chair takes the skiing 210m higher than the White Pass chair, and the run from Polar Peak to the base is over 1000m vertical.

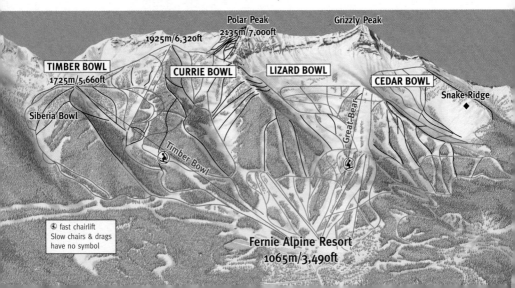

Polar Peak
2135m/7,000ft
1925m/6,320ft
Grizzly Peak

TIMBER BOWL
1725m/5,660ft

CURRIE BOWL

LIZARD BOWL

CEDAR BOWL

Snake Ridge ◆

Siberia Bowl

Timber Bowl

Great Bear

ⓐ fast chairlift
Slow chairs & drags
have no symbol

Fernie Alpine Resort
1065m/3,490ft

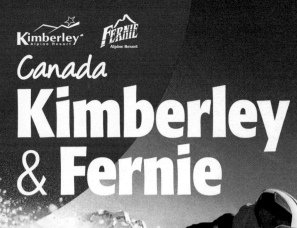

There are long views over the town of Fernie from the slopes – this is from Polar Peak, looking across Lizard Bowl →

LIFT PASSES

Prices in C$

Age	1-day	6-day
under 13	27	163
13 to 17	59	352
18 to 64	84	504
65 plus	67	403

Free Under 6

Beginner Rental, limited pass and tuition deals

Notes Prices include taxes; half-day pass available

GETTING THERE

Air Calgary 340km/210 miles (4hr15)

Free mountain tours are available twice a day, but they only scratch the surface.

FAST LIFTS ★★☆☆☆
A poor show
There are only two fast chairs, serving opposite ends of the mountain. And only one of them goes up from the resort base area. Slow chairs and a draglift elsewhere make getting around a slow process. You spend time traversing to many of the descents, as well as riding lifts. But keen intermediates can rack up the miles doing laps in Siberia and Timber bowls on the fast Timber Bowl chair and in Lizard on the fast Great Bear quad.

QUEUES ★★★★☆
Not usually a problem
Queues are generally rare unless there are weekend crowds from Calgary or heavy snow keeps part of the mountain closed. The slopes are usually very quiet – last March we skied lots of runs more or less alone.

TERRAIN PARKS ★★☆☆☆
Just a rail park
There is no proper park, but there is a patrolled rail park beside the Great Bear Express – you'll need a special pass (C$5 per day) and must sign a waiver to use it.

SNOW RELIABILITY ★★★★☆
A key part of the appeal
Fernie has an excellent snow record – with an average of 360 inches per year, it's better than practically anywhere in Colorado. But the altitude is modest: rain is not unknown, and in warmer weather the lower slopes can suffer. Too much snow can be a problem, with the high bowls prone to closure; the headwalls hold a lot of snow and require a lot of bombing to be made safe. Snowmaking has been increased over recent years and now covers most of the base area.

On our most recent visits we've been impressed by the quality of the groomed runs, despite less than ideal weather; we put it down to the very low levels of traffic. As a whole, the area faces roughly north-east; but many runs are on the flanks of the ridges, facing south-east, so the sun can affect things in late season.

FOR EXPERTS ★★★★★
Wonderful with guidance
The combination of heavy snowfalls and abundant steep terrain with the shelter of trees makes this a superb mountain for good skiers, so long as you know where you are going. If you don't, consider getting guidance. It has taken us half a dozen visits to get to know the mountain reasonably well.

There are about a dozen identifiable faces offering genuine black or double-black slopes, each of them with several alternative ways down and all worth exploring. Pay attention to the diamonds: the doubles are the genuine article.

The new Polar Peak area is of limited vertical but serious double-diamond gradient; there is one single diamond run, but even this can have a tricky entry. You can hike up to a gated double-diamond area where

SCHOOLS

Fernie Telus
t 423 2406

Classes
C$68 for half-day
(2hr) (incl. taxes)

Private lessons
From C$131 (incl.
taxes) for 1.5hr

CHILDCARE

Resort Kids
t 423 2430
Age 18mnth to 6yr

Ski school
Ages 6 to 12

---

transceivers (and great care) are required.

There are a few areas where you can do laps fairly efficiently, but mostly you have to put up with a cycle of long traverse–descent–run-out–lift–lift on each lap (with an extra lift to get to the Polar Peak area).

There are backcountry routes you can take with guidance (some include an overnight camp) and snowcat operations in other nearby mountains – read the feature panel overleaf. A regular reporter especially enjoyed exploring Fish Bowl, a short hike outside the resort boundary from Cedar Bowl. (Read 'Schools and guides.')

FOR INTERMEDIATES ★★
Getting better
In recent years Fernie has made great strides to broaden its appeal. These days, the resort grooms quite a wide range of runs, including some great blue cruisers down all the bowls – but there are also quite a few blacks that get regularly groomed. And the lack of crowds makes fast skiing on these runs a real pleasure. But the groomed stuff doesn't add up to much when you compare it to many other resorts with the same sort of acreage, and after a big dump in particular the grooming takes time. if you are not happy to try some of the easier ungroomed terrain you may find the place a bit limited. For the adventurous willing to give the powder a go, though, Fernie can be fab.

FOR BEGINNERS ★★★★
Surprisingly, pretty good
There's a good nursery area served by two lifts (a moving carpet and a drag), and the lower mountain served by the Deer and Elk chairs has lots of wide, smooth trails to gain confidence on.

FOR BOARDERS ★★★
Fine if you're good
Fernie is a fine place for good boarders (and there are a lot of local experts here). Lots of natural gullies, hits and endless off-piste opportunities – including some adrenalin-pumping tree runs and knee-deep powder bowls – will keep freeriders of all abilities grinning from ear to ear. But there's a lot of traversing involved to get to many of the best runs – hard work in fresh snow and bumpy later. The main

board shops, Board Stiff and Edge of the World, are in downtown Fernie. It's not a brilliant place for freestylers – there's just a rail park, for which you'll need a special pass.

FOR CROSS-COUNTRY ★★★
Some possibilities
There are 10km of trails in the forest adjacent to the resort. In the Fernie area as a whole there are around 50km of tracks.

MOUNTAIN RESTAURANTS ★
One tiny sit-down hut
Lost Boys Cafe is a tiny self-service place in a fine position with great views at the top of Timber Bowl with a basic, limited menu. It gets busy even when the mountain isn't. Bear's Den at the top of the Elk chair is an open-air fast-food kiosk. Naturally, most people eat at the base area. The ancient no-frills Day Lodge at the Griz Lodge serves soups, burgers and daily specials. Look at 'Eating out' to see other options – we usually head for the Corner Pocket.

SCHOOLS AND GUIDES ★★★★
Highly praised
Reporters have praised the school, which seems to achieve rapid progress. A recent visitor was very happy with his 'really brilliant' private lessons, but also noted that class sizes are often very small, making group lessons very good value.

There are several programmes to help you get the best out of the mountain. The Steep and Deep camp has had good feedback; it is a two-day programme (C$329) where you get technique tips while exploring steep terrain – a great way to get to know at least some of the mountain. We've had good sessions being guided by some of their instructor-guides. 'First Tracks' (from C$269 for three people) is a two-hour private lesson that gets you up the mountain at 8am, before the lifts are open to others.

FOR FAMILIES ★★★★
Good day care centre
There's a day care centre in the Cornerstone Lodge. Once a week there's a craft night for children aged 6 to 12. And there's an adventure park with cut-outs of bears and wolves. The ski school offers a 'family' private lesson option for up to two adults and three kids.

Build your own shortlist: www.wheretoskiandsnowboard.com

Good skiers who relish off-piste should consider treating themselves to some cat-skiing, where you ride snowcats instead of lifts; there are several operations in this area. We've had two or three fabulous days at Island Lake Lodge (423 3700), which does all-inclusive packages in a luxury lodge (spacious rooms, big lounge, hot tubs, bar, excellent food) 10km from Fernie, reached only by snowcat, amid 7,000 acres of spectacular bowls and ridges. It has 26 rooms and three cats. In a day you might do 10 to 14 powder runs averaging 500m vertical, taking in all kinds of terrain from gentle open slopes to some very Alpine adventures. You can do single days on a standby basis. Fernie Wilderness Adventures (877 423 6704) has three cats accessing 5,000 acres.

SNOWPIX.COM / CHRIS GILL

ACTIVITIES

Indoor Aquatic Centre (pool, hot tub, steam), fitness centre, climbing wall, spas, cinema, museum, gallery, library, brewery tour

Outdoor Walking, snowmobiling, ice rink, curling, dog sledding, sleigh rides, snowshoe excursions, zipline

Central reservations phone number
Call 1 403 209 3321

Phone numbers
From distant parts of Canada, add the prefix 1 250; from abroad, add the prefix +1 250

TOURIST OFFICE

www.skifernie.com

STAYING THERE

Chalets Canadian Powder Tours has one with an outdoor hot tub in town.
Hotels There's a wide choice.
****Best Western Plus Fernie Mountain Lodge** Next to the golf course near town. Pool, hot tub, fitness room. But a 30-minute bus ride to the slopes.
****Lizard Creek Lodge** Best ski-in/ski-out condo hotel, with good rooms and a grand, high-ceilinged lounge; spa, outdoor pool and hot tub. Good food (read 'Eating out'). We've enjoyed staying here a couple of times.
***Alpine Lodge** B&B on edge of resort. 'Homely and welcoming.'
***Cornerstone Lodge** Modern condo hotel.
***Griz Inn Sport Hotel** Condo hotel at foot of slopes. Pool.
***Park Place Lodge** On highway; easy walk to centre of town, lively pub; pool and hot tub in main lobby.
***Slopeside Lodge** Formerly Wolf's Den. At base of slope. Basic but convenient. Hot tub.
Apartments Timberline Lodges are very comfortable condos a shuttle-ride from the lifts. Snow Creek Lodge is another option.

EATING OUT ★★★★★
Better choice in town
At the base, Lizard Creek Lodge offers 'generous portions – lamb shank particularly good'. The Corner Pocket is an airy modern place at the Griz Inn, simply furnished, with quite a wide-ranging menu, good service and excellent food. Yamagoya in the Alpine Lodge does Japanese ('good to eat some lighter food for a change', 'wonderful ice cream'); there's another branch in town. Kelsey's (part of a chain) serves standard and reliable steaks, burgers, pasta and pizza.

In the town of Fernie, there are quite a few options, though some places we have liked in the past have closed. Last winter we enjoyed an excellent simple dinner at the jolly, busy Brick House (all BC wines though, which means pricey). Picnic, which we enjoyed on our previous visit, has changed hands. We also enjoyed various Asian cuisines at Curry Bowl. A 2011 visitor recommends the Indian food at Tandoor & Grill in the out-of-town Stanford hotel.

APRES-SKI ★★★★★
Have a beer
When the lifts close head for the Griz Bar above the Day Lodge. During the week, the mountain resort bars are pretty quiet later on. In town, the bars of the Royal hotel are popular with locals, as is the Park Place Lodge Pub, (with pool, table-football and big-screen TVs).

OFF THE SLOPES ★★★★★
Get out and about
The Arts Station has two galleries, a theatre and craft studios, and there is a walking tour of historic Fernie – you buy a C$5 self-guided booklet from the visitor information centre or retailers. Watching the local ice hockey team, the Ghostriders, is 'well worth doing – good fun', says a reporter. There's a pool at the Aquatic Centre in town. But the main diversion is the great outdoors.

Kicking Horse

One of Canada's newest resorts: only a few lifts, but great powder at the top, and a small village at the base

TOP 10 RATINGS	
Extent	★★★
Fast lifts	★★★
Queues	★★★★
Snow	★★★★
Expert	★★★★
Intermediate	★★
Beginner	★★★
Charm	★★
Convenience	★★★★
Scenery	★★★

RPI	155
lift pass	£310
ski hire	£135
lessons	£175
food & drink	£180
total	**£800**

+ Great terrain for experts and some for adventurous intermediates

+ Big vertical served by a gondola

+ Splendid mountain-top restaurant

− Resort village still small and quiet

− Gondola needs a mid-station to make the most of the mountain

− Few groomed intermediate runs

Kicking Horse was developed from a small local hill in 2000, when a long gondola was built to two high, powder-filled bowls – previously heli-skiing country. There were great ambitions to turn it into a major resort. But things moved much more slowly than was planned, and the original owner eventually sold out in December 2011 to a company that owns five other Canadian resorts including Fernie. Let's hope they can make a go of things because the mountain has huge potential, and both the lift system and the small resort village at the base need to be expanded to make the place worth a week's stay. Meanwhile, it's best for a short stay, or a day trip if you're staying in Banff or Lake Louise.

THE RESORT

Eight miles from the logging town of Golden, Kicking Horse still has only two main lifts and a tiny base village. Daily Powder Express buses run from Banff and Lake Louise – the 2012/13 cost was C$99, including a lift pass.

Village charm The small resort village at the lift base has several lodges, a few restaurants and bars, a ski shop and a general store. The town of Golden has no real appeal.

Convenience Fine if you stay at the mountain, and why not?

Scenery The scenery is not without drama – especially from the top.

THE MOUNTAINS

The lower two-thirds of the hill is wooded, with trails cut in the usual style. The upper third is a mix of open and lightly wooded slopes spread over four separate bowls, with scores of ways down for experts through the open terrain, chutes and trees.

Slopes The eight-seat gondola to Eagle's Eye takes you to the top in one stage of 1150m vertical. It serves three bowls and CPR Ridge. To the left as you ride the gondola is Bowl Over. Or take the narrow Milly Goat Traverse along a ridge towards Super Bowl, which opened three seasons ago – but the last part of this 'traverse' is a hike up to Terminator Peak or an easier walk/skate around the back. To the right of the gondola is Crystal Bowl; you can do laps here on the slow chair to the slightly higher peak of Blue Heaven, which also accesses Feuz Bowl. From Bowl Over, Super Bowl and Feuz Bowl – and also from below the chair in Crystal Bowl – you have to make the full descent to the base as there is no mid-station on the gondola. Two chairlifts near the base serve the lower runs that formed the

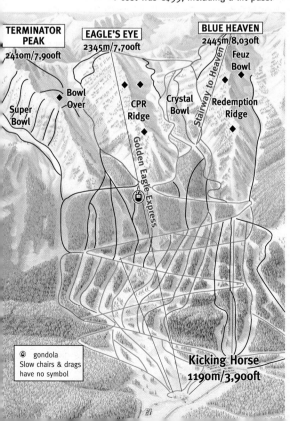

TERMINATOR PEAK
2410m/7,900ft

EAGLE'S EYE
2345m/7,700ft

BLUE HEAVEN
2445m/8,030ft

Feuz Bowl

Super Bowl

Bowl Over

CPR Ridge

Crystal Bowl

Stairway to Heaven

Redemption Ridge

Golden Eagle Express

Kicking Horse
1190m/3,900ft

⊙ gondola
Slow chairs & drags have no symbol

SNOWPIX.COM / CHRIS GILL

NEWS

2012/13: More grooming was introduced along and from Redemption Ridge to allow intermediates access to more terrain such as Feuz Bowl. The tubing park was moved to the beginner area.

KEY FACTS

Resort	1190m
	3,900ft
Slopes	1190-2445m
	3,900-8,030ft
Lifts	5
Pistes	2,825 acres
Green	20%
Blue	20%
Black	60%
Snowmaking	Some

UK PACKAGES

Alpine Answers, AmeriCan Ski, American Ski Classics, Canadian Affair, Frontier, Independent Ski Links, Momentum, Neilson, Ski Independence, Ski Safari, Ski Solutions, Skitracer, Skiworld

Central reservations
Call 439 5425
Phone numbers
From distant parts of Canada, add the prefix 1 250; from abroad, add the prefix +1 250

TOURIST OFFICE

www.kickinghorse
resort.com

original ski area here. There are free mountain tours twice a day.

Fast lifts Just the gondola.

Queues We've had reports of serious weekend queues for the gondola. During the week, though, it's quiet.

Terrain park There wasn't one in 2012/13.

Snow reliability The top slopes average 250 to 300 inches a year and usually have light, dry powder. But the lower ones may have crud and thin cover and average only 100 inches a year; and with most of the runs, you have to descend the lower slopes every time – a real drawback.

Experts From the top, you can go right into the gentle Crystal Bowl via an easy piste, or via serious chutes from CPR Ridge; or go left down pleasantly wooded single-diamond slopes into Bowl Over; or head to Super Bowl. The Stairway to Heaven chair serves further single-diamond wooded slopes. Feuz Bowl offers various challenges, not all of genuine double-diamond steepness, and gets tracked out less quickly. The lower half of the mountain has short black runs cut through the woods, some with big moguls. There is heli-skiing nearby.

Intermediates Adventurous types will have a fine time learning to play in the powder from Blue Heaven down to Crystal Bowl. Most of it is open, but you can head off into trees if you want to. There is very little groomed cruising, other than a top-to-bottom 10km winding green run and a few blues. The new owners are in the process of creating more groomed intermediate terrain, but for now timid intermediates should go elsewhere.

Beginners The beginner area at the base is fine, with easy slopes (but

maybe poor snow) on the lower mountain for progression.

Snowboarding Freeriders will love this powder paradise.

Cross-country Dawn Mountain has loops of 30km including skating trails.

Mountain restaurants The Eagle's Eye at the top of the gondola is Canada's best mountain restaurant – it offers excellent food and service in stylish log-cabin surroundings with splendid views. The Heaven's Door yurt (tent) in Crystal Bowl serves snacks; many people lunch at one of the lodges at the base.

Schools and guides A reporter took a group lesson, which 'was worth every cent – a lot of fun and we learned a lot'; she also enjoyed the free tours.

Families The school teaches children from the age of three.

STAYING THERE

There are smart, quite large condo-style lodges on the slopes. But we'd choose to stay in one of three much more captivating family-run places (each with about 10 rooms and outdoor hot tubs) a short walk away – described below.

Hotels The log-built Vagabond Lodge features a fabulous first-floor living room and comfortable, traditional-style rooms. Copper Horse Lodge has spacious but more austere rooms in modern styles. Winston Lodge (formerly Highland Lodge; now under new ownership) has handmade wooden furniture, a welcoming sitting room with floor-to-ceiling stone fireplace and a cosy, woody saloon. In Golden, a reader has enjoyed staying at the Auberge Kicking Horse B&B.

Apartments The Whispering Pines and the Selkirk Townhomes have been recommended.

Eating out Eagle's Eye at the top of the gondola opens on Friday and Saturday evenings ('excellent food but prices to match'). The Saloon in Winston Lodge does burgers, steaks, pizzas etc. Corks in Copper Horse Lodge has been recommended. In Golden, Kicking Horse Grill, Eleven22 and the out-of-town Cedar House are rated.

Après-ski Quiet. In Golden the Mad Trapper and Taps are lively bars.

Off the slopes There is snowmobiling, snowshoeing, tubing and an ice rink; plus a wolf centre near Golden.

Lake Louise

Stunning views and the biggest ski area in the Banff region, with some good places to stay but no real village

RATINGS

The mountains

Extent	★★★
Fast lifts	★★★★
Queues	★★★★
Terrain p'ks	★★★★
Snow	★★★
Expert	★★★★
Intermediate	★★★★
Beginner	★★★
Boarder	★★★
X-country	★★★★★
Restaurants	★★
Schools	★★★★
Families	★★★★

The resort

Charm	★★★
Convenience	★
Scenery	★★★★
Eating out	★★
Après-ski	★★
Off-slope	★★★★

RPI 165

lift pass	£360
ski hire	£125
lessons	£175
food & drink	£180
total	**£840**

NEWS

2013/14: In December 2013 the resort will host the FIS Snowboard Cross World Cup for the first time.

2012/13: The beginners' area was remodelled and the T-bar replaced by three moving carpets. A new tube park opened and the terrain park got an airbag.

➕ Spectacular high-mountain scenery, in a largely unspoilt wilderness

➕ Large ski area by local standards

➕ Snowy slopes of Sunshine Village within reach (see Banff chapter)

➕ Excellent very scenic cross-country

➖ 'Village' is just a few hotels and shops, quiet in the evening

➖ Slopes a drive or bus ride away

➖ Snowfall record modest

➖ Can be very cold, and the chairlifts have no covers

If you care more for scenery than for après-ski action, Lake Louise is worth considering for a holiday. We've seen a few spectacular mountain views, and the view from the Fairmont Chateau Lake Louise hotel of the Victoria Glacier across frozen Lake Louise is as spectacular as they come: simply stunning.

Even if you prefer the more animated base of Banff, you'll want to make expeditions to Lake Louise during your holiday. It can't compete with Sunshine Village for quantity of snow, but it's an interesting mountain. And from the slopes you get a distant version of that stunning view.

THE RESORT

Lake Louise is small, but it's a resort of three distinct parts. First, there's the splendid lake itself overlooked by the huge Fairmont Chateau Lake Louise hotel. Then there's Lake Louise 'village' – a spacious collection of hotels, condos, petrol station, liquor store and a few shops a couple of miles away in the valley bottom. Finally, a mile or two across the valley, there's the lift base station.

Sunshine Village and Norquay ski areas (covered in our Banff chapter) are 45 minutes away by road. Buses (covered by the Tri-area lift pass) run only two days a week to each (on the days the ski school Club Ski Program goes there), so having a car helps. Bus trips also run to the more distant resorts of Kicking Horse and Panorama, subject to demand, and there are heli-skiing day trips.

VILLAGE CHARM ★★★
Low key and relaxed
The 'village' has no focus other than a small shopping mall, but it's a quiet and relaxing place. Up at the lake, it's all about the setting: the scenery

provides the charm, and somehow the scale of the giant hotel seems perfectly appropriate.

CONVENIENCE ★
Lake or village, not slopes
Most lodging is around the 'village'. Buses run every half hour to the ski area. Staying up at the Chateau, or near it, just means a slightly longer bus ride. Taxis are said to be 'ridiculously expensive'.

SCENERY ★★★★
Splendid lakes and mountains
Lake Louise itself is in a spectacular setting beneath the Victoria Glacier. Tom Wilson, who discovered it in 1882, declared: 'As God is my judge, I never in all my exploration have seen such a matchless scene.' Neither have we. It can be appreciated from many of the rooms of the Fairmont Chateau Lake Louise hotel on the lake shore, and there are grand views from the ski area of other peaks and glaciers, including Canada's Matterhorn lookalike, Mount Assiniboine.

THE MOUNTAINS

There's an attractive mixture of high, open slopes, low trails cut through forest and gladed slopes between the two. There are good, free guided tours at 10am and 1.15pm. Louise is known for fiercely low temperatures; we've luckily escaped them on recent visits.

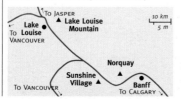

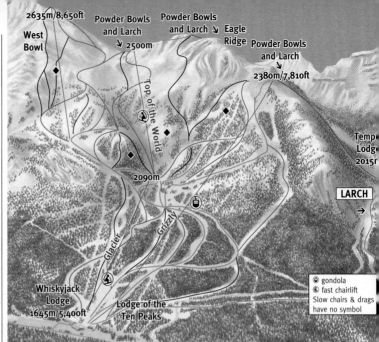

KEY FACTS

Resort	1645m
	5,400ft

Sunshine, Norquay
and Lake Louise

Slopes	1630-2730m
	5,350-8,950ft
Lifts	26
Pistes	7,748 acres
Green	23%
Blue	39%
Black	38%
Snowmaking	24%

Lake Louise only

Slopes	1645-2635m
	5,400-8,650ft
Lifts	9
Pistes	4,200 acres
Green	25%
Blue	45%
Black	30%
Snowmaking	40%

EXTENT OF THE SLOPES ★★★☆☆
A wide variety

The Lake Louise ski area is a fair size by North American standards but is quite modest by Alpine standards; a good intermediate could ski the groomed trails in a day or two. A recent reporter complained of the terrain park taking up too much of the lower mountain and 'limiting the options for regular skiers'.

From the base area you have a choice of a fast quad to mid-mountain, followed by a six-pack to the top centre of the **Front Side** (or South Face), or a gondola direct to a slightly lower point off to the right side. From both, as elsewhere, there's a choice of green, blue or black runs (good for a group of mixed abilities who want to keep meeting up). In poor visibility,

the gondola is a better option, as the treeline goes almost to the top there. Or you can stay on the lower part of the mountain using the chairs. From mid-mountain on the left, the long Summit draglift takes you to the high point of the area.

From here or the top chair you can go over the ridge and into the **Powder Bowls** – almost treeless, shady and mainly steep (though there are easy ways round the steep parts). From the top of the gondola, the Ptarmigan area is more wooded. From below the bowls you can take the Paradise lift back to the top again or go on down to Temple Lodge, base station of the Ptarmigan chair to the main mountain and a fast chair to the separate **Larch** area (just off our map). Its lift-served vertical is a modest 375m, but the

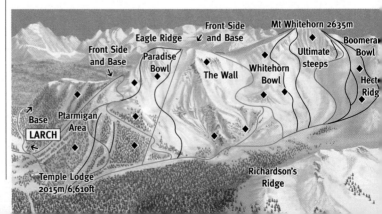

Tri-area lift pass

Prices in C$

Age	1-day	6-day
under 13	31	207
13 to 17	66	474
18 to 64	87	533
65 plus	66	474

Free Under 6

Beginner Lift, lesson and rental package

Notes Day pass is for Lake Louise only; 3-day-plus pass covers all lifts and transport between Banff, Lake Louise, Norquay and Sunshine Village; prices include 5% tax

SNOWPIX.COM / CHRIS GILL

The small Larch sector has pretty wooded runs for all ability levels ↓

sector has pretty wooded runs for all abilities. From Temple Lodge there's a long green path back to the base area. A 2013 visitor found the signposting 'confusing: I'd start on a green but end up on a black diamond'.

FAST LIFTS ★★★★
Beware the cold rides
There is gondola and fast chair access to most of the slopes on the Front Side, and to Larch. The few slow lifts serve steep slopes where your descent may take some time, so the lift ride time is bearable. This is a famously cold resort, and reporters regularly complain of extremely cold rides.

QUEUES ★★★★
Not during the week
Queues are rarely a problem midweek. But half of the area's visitors come for the day from cities such as Calgary, so there can be queues for some lifts at weekends and public holidays ('up to 45 minutes for the gondola on the Saturday'). Busy pistes and lift breakdowns can be a problem too.

TERRAIN PARKS ★★★★
Better every year
After a brief absence in 2008, the terrain park is improving year on year. The 2013 park had 32 features set out in clearly defined areas including progression and XL jumps, plus a skier/boardercross and, new for last season, an airbag. The Snowboard Cross World Cup will be held here in December 2013.

SNOW RELIABILITY ★★★
Usually OK
Lake Louise gets around 180 inches a year on the Front Side, which is not a lot, and nowhere near as much as Sunshine Village down the road (see the Banff chapter). The Front Side faces south-west, which is not good; but the Powder Bowls face north-east, and Larch north. Snowmaking covers 40% of the pistes. Grooming is fine.

FOR EXPERTS ★★★★
Widespread pleasure
There are plenty of steep slopes – but bear in mind that powder is less likely here than in many other Canadian resorts. On the Front Side, as well as a score of marked black-diamond trails in and above the trees, there is the alluring West Bowl, reached from the Summit drag – a wide, open expanse of snow outside the area boundary to be explored with a guide.

Inside the boundary, the Powder Bowls area on the Back Side offers countless black mogul/powder runs, though there is no great variation in character. From the Summit drag, you can drop into The Ultimate Steeps area if it is open, directly behind the peak – a row of exceptional chutes almost 1km long. Starting from the blue Boomerang trail, you can also access much tamer, wide, open slopes in Boomerang Bowl.

The Top of the World six-pack takes you to the very popular Paradise Bowl/ Eagle Ridge area, also served by its own triple chair on the Back Side –

Lake Louise

SNOWPIX.COM / CHRIS GILL

The views of high peaks across the valley from the ski hill are spectacular. This is Mt Temple, the highest mountain in the area ↓

there are endless variants here, ranging from comfortably steep single diamonds to very challenging double diamonds. The seriously steep slope served by the Ptarmigan quad chair has great gladed terrain and is a good place to escape the crowds and find good snow.

The Larch area has some steep double-diamond stuff in the trees. And with good snow-cover, the open snowfields at the top are great for those with the energy to hike up.

Heli-skiing day trips are available to bases outside the National Park in British Columbia.

FOR INTERMEDIATES ★★★★
Some good cruising
Almost half the runs are classified as intermediate. But from the top of the Front Side the blue runs down are little more than paths in places, and there are very few blues or greens in the Powder Bowls. Once you get part-way down the Front Side the blues are much more interesting. And when groomed, the Men's and Ladies' Downhill black runs are great fast cruises on the lower half of the mountain. Juniper, in the same area, is a varied cruise. Meadowlark is a

beautiful treelined single black run to the base area, curling away from the lifts – to find it from the Grizzly Express gondola, first follow the Eagle Meadows green. The Larch area has some short but ideal intermediate runs – and reporters have enjoyed the natural lumps and bumps of the aptly named blue, Rock Garden ('never had so much fun; really away from it all').

The adventurous should try the blue Boomerang run – which starts with a short side-step up from the top of the Summit drag – and also some of the ungroomed terrain in the Powder Bowls reachable from that run.

FOR BEGINNERS ★★★
Some long greens
Lake Louise offers first-timers a package that includes a beginner pass with tuition and equipment rental. There is a decent nursery area near the base served by three moving carpets. You progress to the gentle, wide Wiwaxy (a designated 'learning area'), Pinecone Way and the slightly more difficult Deer Run or Eagle Meadows. The greens in the Powder Bowls and in the Larch area are worth trying for the views, though some do contain slightly steep pitches and can get busy ('Our beginner was very nervous trying the Saddleback Bowl,' said one past reporter).

FOR BOARDERS ★★★
Something for everyone
Lake Louise is a great mountain for freeriders, with plenty of challenging terrain in the bowls and glades. Beginners will have fun on the Front Side's blue and green runs. But beware of the vicious Summit button lift (top left looking at the trail map). Also avoid the long, very gentle green run through the woods from Larch back to base. This is flat in places and a nightmare for boarders. Freestylers will enjoy the varied terrain park.

FOR CROSS-COUNTRY ★★★★★
High in quality and quantity
It's a very good area for cross-country, with around 80km of groomed trails in the National Park – plenty of scenic stops needed. There are 14km of excellent trails in the local area and at Lake Louise itself. An alternative is the secluded Emerald Lake Lodge, 40km away and with some lovely trails.

SCHOOLS

Ski Big 3
t 760 7731
Lake Louise
t 522 1333

Classes (Big 3 prices)
3 days guided tuition
of the three areas
C$314 incl. tax
Private lessons
Half day (3hr) C$398,
incl. tax, for up to 5
people

CHILDCARE

Lake Louise Daycare
t 522 3555
Ages 18 days to 6yr

Ski school
Ages 6 to 12

UK PACKAGES

Alpine Answers,
AmeriCan Ski, American
Ski Classics, Canadian
Affair, Crystal, Crystal
Finest, Elegant Resorts,
Frontier, Independent
Ski Links, Inghams,
Momentum, Neilson,
Oxford Ski Co,
PowderBeds, Ski
Bespoke, Ski
Independence, Ski Line,
Ski Safari, Ski
Solutions, Skitracer,
Skiworld, Snow Finders,
Supertravel, Thomson,
Virgin Snow

Phone numbers
From distant parts of
Canada, add the
prefix 1 403; from
abroad, add the prefix
+1 403

TOURIST OFFICE

www.skilouise.com
www.SkiBig3.com

MOUNTAIN RESTAURANTS ★★★★★
Good base facilities

There is only one proper mountain hut in winter. The Temple Lodge near the bottom of Larch and the Ptarmigan chair is a rustic-style building with 'very good' table-service and 'reasonable' self-service restaurants, but it can get unpleasantly crowded.

Most people eat at the base, where there are big-scale but 'soulless' facilities. The Northface Bistro in the Whiskyjack Lodge offers fixed-price, 'high-quality' buffet lunches and 'good-value' breakfasts. The Lodge of the Ten Peaks is a hugely impressive log-built affair with various 'fairly efficient' eating, drinking and lounging options.

SCHOOLS AND GUIDES ★★★★★
All reports positive

All past reports are positive, for both adults' and children's classes and a 2013 visitor is enthusiastic: 'The school is well run and the instructors are extremely professional. Probably the friendliest group of instructors we have ever come across. Excellent.' See the Banff chapter for details of the excellent three-day, three-mountain Club Ski Program.

FOR FAMILIES ★★★★★
Good facilities

The resort has good school and childcare facilities that have been praised by reporters. Parents are lent free pagers too. The Minute Maid Wilderness Adventure Park is a kids' learning area at the base. The school gets good reviews and offers a fun programme for teenagers.

STAYING THERE

You might like to consider a two-centre holiday, combining Lake Louise with, say, Banff or Kicking Horse.
Hotels Summer is the peak season here. Prices are much lower in winter.
★★★★★Fairmont Chateau Lake Louise (522 3511) Huge old place with 550 rooms, seven restaurants and stunning views over frozen Lake Louise to the glacier beyond; shops, pool, hot tub, spa, steam room.
★★★★Post (522 3989) Small, relaxed, comfortable Relais & Châteaux place in the village, with excellent restaurant (huge wine list), pool, hot tub, steam room. Avoid rooms on railway side. 'Beautifully furnished; friendly, helpful.'
★★★Deer Lodge (522 3991) Charming old hotel next to the Chateau. Small rooms, but helpful staff and good food. Roof-top hot tub.
★★★Lake Louise Inn (522 3791) Cheaper option in the village, with pool, hot tub and steam. One recent reporter has stayed there nine times.
Apartments Some are available but local shopping is limited. The Baker Creek Chalets (522 3761) are a popular retreat for a traditional 'log cabin, log fire, isolation and wildlife' experience.
At altitude Skoki Lodge (522 1347) is a charming log cabin, 11km on skis from Temple Lodge. Built in the 1930s.

EATING OUT ★★★★★
Limited choice

The Post hotel's restaurant has repeatedly impressed us and reporters with its ambitious food and excellent service. The Chateau has the top-notch Fairview Dining Room and the 'really good' Glacier Saloon ('sea chowder soup and bison pie both excellent'). Readers also like the Timberwolf Cafe (Italian) at the Lake Louise Inn, the Mountain restaurant (pasta, burgers) and Village Grill (Western/Chinese menu) for cheaper options.

APRES-SKI ★★★★★
Lively at teatime, quiet later

At close of play there is some action in the main base lodge, but the hub is the Kokanee Kabin, which has live music most weekends, a terrace and an outdoor fire. Later on, things are fairly quiet. Try the Glacier Saloon, in Chateau Lake Louise, the Explorer's Lounge in the Lake Louise Inn or the Outpost Pub in the Post hotel.

OFF THE SLOPES ★★★★★
Beautiful scenery

Lake Louise makes a lovely, peaceful place to stay for someone who does not intend to hit the slopes but enjoys the great outdoors. The lake itself makes a stunning setting for walks, snowshoeing, cross-country skiing and ice skating. Reporters highly recommend the dog sledding and the Wilson Icefield discovery tour – a helicopter flight, snowshoe walk and lunch ('BBQ with superb steaks'). There are lots of attractions around the Banff area too (see Banff chapter).

Lake Louise is near one end of the Columbia Icefields Parkway, a three-hour drive to Jasper through national parks – one of the world's most beautiful drives.

Revelstoke

Recently developed resort with a ready-made reputation for steep terrain and deep snow; shame it's so remote and isolated

TOP 10 RATINGS

Extent	★★★
Fast lifts	★★★★★
Queues	★★★★★
Snow	★★★★
Expert	★★★★★
Intermediate	★★
Beginner	★★
Charm	★★
Convenience	★★★
Scenery	★★★★

RPI 150

lift pass	£320
ski hire	£150
lessons	£135
food & drink	£170
total	**£775**

KEY FACTS

Resort	510m
	1,680ft
Slopes	510-2225m
	1,680-7,300ft
Lifts	5
Pistes	3,121 acres
Green	7%
Blue	45%
Black	48%
Snowmaking	at base

634

+ Fabulous steep, ungroomed terrain and an impressive snow record

+ North America's biggest vertical, with some epic black runs going from top to bottom

+ Great cat- and heli-skiing next door

+ Fine views over the Columbia valley

− Not much intermediate groomed terrain

− No snowmaking on main slopes

− Very remote location – awkward to get to from the UK

− Resort base village still tiny, and Revelstoke town a drive away

Revelstoke has long been known as a heli-skiing base, but it's only in the last few years that it has become a ski resort for the rest of us. A gondola and two fast chairs have transformed its little local ski hill into a serious resort with a vertical of over 1700m – the biggest in North America.

The resort claims over 3,000 acres of terrain – more than many Canadian and American rivals (notably Fernie and Jackson Hole) – but the quantity of defined trails is not huge. More than most places, this is a resort where you need to be happy in the trees to spend a long stay here. You might want to combine it with Kicking Horse and/or Lake Louise, both on the way from Calgary airport.

THE RESORT

Revelstoke is remote. Getting there from the UK involves two flights to get to Kelowna or Kamloops followed by a three-hour drive. Or it's a drive of five hours from Calgary, or six hours from Vancouver – and that's assuming good weather.

There is an embryonic village at the base of the slopes – one smart condo-hotel, a restaurant, a coffee shop, a wine bar, a sports shop. Five minutes down the hill, there's a wider choice of lodging and restaurants in Revelstoke itself, a working town between the dammed Columbia river and the Trans-Canada Highway.

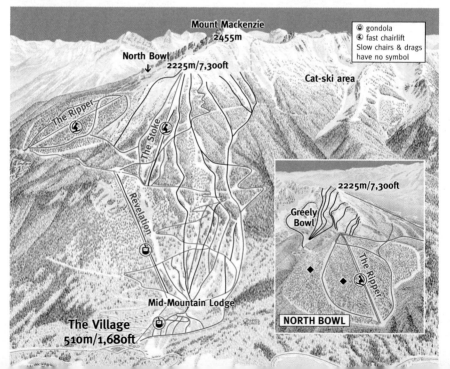

2013/14: The green runs from mid-mountain to the base are to be improved; more snowmaking will be installed. Two new blue runs and two new tree-skiing areas are planned.

2012/13: The blue run Tumbelina, from mid-mountain to the base, was regraded to provide easier progression from the beginner area.

REVELSTOKE

The town has some cute backwaters, but overall it is not in the Breckenridge/Aspen league ↓

Village charm At the lift base, the Village is quite polished, but it is not yet a village. The town developed on the back of forestry, mining and the railroad. There are some 'historic' brick and wooden buildings, but overall it is a rather plain, 'down to earth' place.

Convenience The Village could not be more convenient: the access gondola is mere yards from your door. Town shuttle-buses are regular and reliable, but Village residents going out on the town in the evening are reliant on the hotel shuttle ($20 a trip, regardless of number of people) or taxis.

Scenery There are wide views from the upper slopes over the Columbia valley and snow-capped mountains beyond.

THE MOUNTAINS

A two-stage gondola takes you from the Village to mid-mountain, from which you can reach both the fast quads. The trail map marks black runs, but does not use single/double diamond classification. Be prepared for extreme cold (we once got −41°C with wind chill on a December visit).

Slopes The lift-served terrain puts Revelstoke among the biggest Canadian resorts (leaving massive

Whistler aside). As we've said, the quantity of defined trails is not huge, but there are top-to-bottom runs of exceptional length, three of them classified black. There are 5,000 acres of cat-skiing next door, and vast amounts of heli-skiing on hand.

Fast lifts All three main lifts are fast.

Queues We have no reports of queues, and both we and readers have often skied trails alone.

Terrain parks There is a small rail park.

Snow reliability They claim 360 to 540 inches a year; an average mid-range figure of 450 is up there with the best. But warm weather is not unknown, and the lower slopes can suffer (and may be closed). There's snowmaking only on the beginner area at the base.

Experts Experts are in their element here. On skier's left, there are long top-to-bottom black runs, which are often groomed. On skier's right, reached by traversing and possibly hiking from the top chairlift, is entirely ungroomed North Bowl. This has excellent steep open slopes at the top giving way to gentler woods at the bottom; for many of us the major challenge, though, is access through the band of cliffs at the top. There are

Tourism BC/Eric Berger

↑ Long, wide views to the west across the Columbia valley and the town of Revelstoke
DAVE WATTS

UK PACKAGES

AmeriCan Ski, American Ski Classics, Canadian Affair, Frontier, Luxury Chalet Collection, Momentum, Oxford Ski Co, Pure Powder, Ski Bespoke, Ski Club Freshtracks, Ski Safari, Ski Solutions, Skiworld

Phone numbers
From distant parts of Canada add the prefix 1 250; from abroad use the prefix +1 250

TOURIST OFFICE

www.revelstoke
mountainresort.com

about 10 identified ways in, ranging from merely tricky Meet the Neighbours to (reportedly) much more scary options. In between are several big areas of glades with nicely spaced trees. And there are further wide areas of glades served by the Ripper chair, below North Bowl.

The ski school runs affordable day and half-day Inside Tracks groups, to show you terrain to suit your ability – exactly what you need on this hill.
Intermediates Most blues are steepish and suit adventurous intermediates best. The Ripper chair accesses the easiest blues. And there's a 15km-long blue/green run from top to bottom. But the intermediate groomed terrain doesn't add up to much (the claimed 45% gives a misleading impression).
Beginners A magic carpet serves a small beginner area at the bottom, and there are long, winding green runs from mid-mountain and the very top.
Snowboarding There's fabulous freeriding but lots of flats, especially getting to and from North Bowl.
Cross-country 26km of groomed trails.
Mountain restaurants The self-service Mid Mountain Lodge serves decent food but gets packed. You can eat your own food here. For table-service, it's down to the smart Rockford restaurant at the base.
Schools and guides The ski school aims to help people progress from groomed runs to the backcountry.
Families This is far from an ideal family resort.

STAYING THERE

Hotels In 2013 we enjoyed Sutton Place (814 5000), at the Village – an excellent hotel with exceptionally smart, well-equipped rooms, a good pool and hot tubs. There are various options in and around the town. We've also enjoyed the friendly Courthouse Inn (837 3369) – great breakfast. A reporter this year tips Swiss Chalet motel (837 4650) – 'small but immaculate rooms, excellent value with free breakfast'. Probably the best downtown option is the Regent (837 2107), which dates from the 1920s. Reporters have also enjoyed the Inn on the River (837 3262), with a panoramic rooftop hot tub, and slightly out of town the Hillcrest (837 3322) – Selkirk-Tangiers Heliski base – and the Best Western Plus (837 2043).
Eating out At the Village, the Rockford is a smooth modern place doing grills and wok dishes. In town, 112 at the Regent is polished and intimate, with good gourmet food at tables or at the bar. Woolsey Creek is another gourmet option. In contrast, the Village Idiot is a lively pub-style joint doing good burgers and gigantic pizzas. Kawakubo has a super-high reputation for sushi.
Après-ski The Rockford at the lift base is popular. Good downtown bars are the Village Idiot and the Last Drop (sofas; in Powder Springs Inn) and River City (music, pool; in the Regent).
Off the slopes The Aquatic Centre offers pools, hot tubs, saunas.

Silver Star

Car-free, purpose-built village designed to resemble a Victorian-era mining town, with slopes for all standards

637

TOP 10 RATINGS

Extent	★★★
Fast lifts	★★★★
Queues	★★★★★
Snow	★★★★
Expert	★★★★
Intermediate	★★★
Beginner	★★★★
Charm	★★★
Convenience	★★★★★
Scenery	★★★

RPI 145

lift pass	£310
ski hire	£130
lessons	£135
food & drink	£170
total	**£745**

NEWS

2013/14: There are plans to expand the gladed areas on both Vance and Putnam Creeks.

2012/13: An all-inclusive lift ticket, My1Pass, was introduced. As well as downhill skiing, it allows unlimited access to the cross-country and snowshoe trails plus the tubing park and ice skating. A new four-lane bowling alley – Pinheads – opened.

KEY FACTS

Resort	1610m
	5,280ft
Slopes	1155-1915m
	3,790-6,280ft
Lifts	12
Pistes	3,065 acres
Green	20%
Blue	50%
Black	30%
Snowmaking	none

- **+** Cute, colourful village
- **+** Very family-friendly
- **+** Some good runs for all abilities
- **+** Excellent cross-country skiing
- **−** Tiny village; very quiet at night
- **−** Limited choice of accommodation (but some high-quality condos)
- **−** Ski area not huge

This quiet, family-friendly resort has a tiny traffic-free centre resembling a 19th-century mining town. The ski area has slopes to suit everyone but it is small, so we suggest you combine a stay here with one at another BC resort such as Big White, Sun Peaks, Revelstoke or Whistler.

THE RESORT

Silver Star is a small, purpose-built resort right on the slopes.

Village charm The village has brightly painted Victorian-style buildings with wooden sidewalks and faux gas lights. It's a bit Disneyesque but works well.

Convenience The centre is compact and car-free. Ski-in/ski-out chalets are dotted in the trees too.

Scenery The views from Silver Star's summit are over gently rolling hills.

THE MOUNTAINS

The mountain has trees going right to the top and four main linked sectors.

Slopes The Vance Creek area has mainly easy intermediate runs served by the Comet six-pack, which starts below the village. From there you can ski down to the Silver Woods high-speed quad, which serves an area of mainly intermediate slopes and glades. The top of the Comet chair links to the Attridge area, which has a mix of easy runs and short steep

blacks served by its own slow chairs too. It also links to the Putnam Creek sector on the back side, which has lots of steep blacks and easier blues, all served by a fast quad.

Fast lifts There's one for each sector.

Queues 'No queues,' says a recent visitor. We skied here on a busy Saturday and waited a few minutes for the Comet chair at peak times but the trails were still delightfully deserted.

Terrain parks The 16-acre Rockstar park on Vance Creek is excellent for experts and intermediates, and the Kiddie park for beginners is beside it. There's a boardercross in the Silver Woods area.

Snow reliability Silver Star gets an average of 276 inches a year – not in the top flight but not far off.

Experts Putnam Creek has a dense network of single and double black diamond runs plunging through the trees, many of them mogul runs. The runs to the left as you ride up the chair are north-facing and keep their snow well. There are some good short

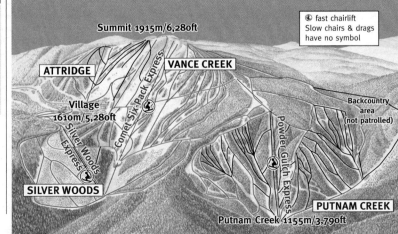

Resort news and key links: **www.wheretoskiandsnowboard.com**

↑ The brightly painted buildings are a bit Disneyesque but the concept works really well

SILVER STAR MOUNTAIN RESORT

UK PACKAGES

AmeriCan Ski, American Ski Classics, Canadian Affair, Frontier, Momentum, Ski Independence, Ski Line, Ski Safari, Ski Solutions, Skiworld

Central reservations
Call 558 6083; toll-free (within Canada)
1 800 663 4431

Phone numbers
From distant parts of Canada, add the prefix 1 250; from abroad, add +1 250

TOURIST OFFICE

www.skisilverstar.com

blacks in the Attridge area, too. Heli-skiing can be organized.

Intermediates Vance Creek has mainly easy cruising runs. Silver Woods has lovely, gentle runs cut through the trees and easy blues among the trees themselves. Putnam Creek also has excellent blue cruising. Good intermediates will appreciate the groomed black runs (they groom at least two each night – look on the boards for which ones).

Beginners There's a good nursery slope area by the village with a moving carpet and long easy green runs to move on to.

Snowboarding Intermediates will enjoy the blue runs and glades. But the steep bump runs in Putnam Creek are tough on a snowboard. And there are some flat areas (including the way to Putnam Creek).

Cross-country They claim 'The Best Nordic Skiing in North America' and there's over 100km of trails in the area.

Mountain restaurants The small atmospheric table-service Paradise Camp on Putnam Creek is popular and serves good stews and soups.

Schools and guides A 2013 visitor's children 'improved by leaps and bounds; the instructors made the lessons fun'; and the two parents were able to 'tidy up our skills. I'd return to Silver Star for the ski school alone.'

Families Star Kids takes children aged 18 months to six years; reporters have sent us glowing reports.

STAYING THERE

It is mainly specialist North American operators that come here, such as Frontier Ski and Ski Independence.

Hotels A recent reporter liked the Bulldog Hotel ('fairly basic rooms, fun bulldog pictures on the wall'). The Vance Creek, Lord Aberdeen and Pinnacles are the other main options. The Samesun Backpackers Hostel has both regular and dorm rooms.

Apartments We stayed in a huge, luxurious condo with private hot tub in the Snowbird Lodge, and loved it – as did a 2012 visitor. Snowbird and Firelight Lodge (ask for a condo overlooking the skating pond and tubing hill) are the best in town – both ski-in/ski-out. Other recommendations include Chilcoot Lodge, Creekside, Grandview and Pinnacles.

Eating out Reporters' favourite is the Bulldog Grand Cafe (Asian-influenced food and 'ribs that melt in your mouth'). Other tips: the Silver Grill Steak & Chop House for fine dining ('good food, friendly service'), Long John's Pub with silver-mining theme decor, Isidore's ('Swiss with a twist'), Bugaboos for breakfast.

Après-ski It's very quiet. But the Saloon, Den and Lord John's Pub may be lively and have live entertainment.

Off the slopes There's a natural ice rink on a lake, tubing, snowshoeing, snowmobiling, bowling and sleigh rides; the first three are free with a lift pass (as is cross-country skiing).

SUN PEAKS RESORT

Sun Peaks

Attractive car-free village at the foot of three linked mountains with varied slopes, including some unusual easy groomed glade runs

TOP 10 RATINGS	
Extent	★★★
Fast lifts	★★
Queues	★★★★★
Snow	★★★★
Expert	★★★
Intermediate	★★★★
Beginner	★★★★
Charm	★★★
Convenience	★★★★
Scenery	★★★

RPI	150
lift pass	£320
ski hire	£130
lessons	£150
food & drink	£170
total	**£770**

NEWS

2013/14: There are plans to groom some double-black-diamond runs regularly as well as single blacks.

2012/13: A new glade was created, Delta's Return on Mt Morrisey. Two new restaurants opened: the Voyageur in the Kookaburra Lodge (traditional Canadian food) and Oya (Japanese).

+ Great terrain for early intermediates

+ Excellent glades

+ Slopes very quiet during the week

+ Good for families

− Village may be too small and quiet for some tastes

− Ski area modest by Alpine standards

Sun Peaks has sprung from the drawing board since the mid-1990s. It has a friendly, attractive small village and a fair amount of varied terrain – enough for three or four days, say. We suggest combining it with resorts such as Whistler, Silver Star or Big White on a two- or three-centre trip.

THE RESORT

Until 1993 Sun Peaks was Tod Mountain, a local hill for the residents of nearby Kamloops. Since then the ski area has been expanded, and a small (smaller than many reporters expect), attractive resort village has developed. There are regular transfers to other resorts such as Whistler – making a two-centre trip easy. Day trips to Revelstoke are organized.

Village charm The low-rise pastel-coloured buildings have a vaguely Tirolean feeling to them. It's a pleasant place to stroll around and very family-friendly. The traffic-free main street is lined with lodgings, restaurants and shops, including a smart art gallery, a chocolate shop and a few coffee bars.

Convenience Much of the accommodation is ski-in/ski-out.

Scenery The slopes are pleasantly wooded and Mt Tod's modest summit gives views over gently rolling terrain.

THE MOUNTAINS

There are three linked mountains, but the links to and from Mt Morrisey from the other two are roundabout and flattish. Free guided tours are run twice a day (9.15am and 1pm), and you can ski for free with Nancy Greene (former Olympic champion, Canada's Female Athlete of the 20th Century and a Canadian senator) when she's in town. Don't miss it – she's great fun. At the top of each main lift there is a board showing which pistes in that area have been groomed. Each day at least one single-black-diamond piste is groomed and some double blacks should be groomed for 2013/14.

Slopes With almost 3,700 acres of skiable terrain, Sun Peaks is the second biggest ski area in British Columbia (Whistler is the biggest) – but it's not big by Alpine standards.

One lift goes from the centre of the village to mid-mountain on the resort's original ski hill, Mt Tod. This has mainly black runs, but there are easier blues and greens, too. Many of Mt Tod's steepest runs are served only by the slow Burfield quad, which takes over 20 minutes to get to the top and is frequently the subject of complaint by reporters (there's a mid-station that allows you to ski the top runs only). The Sundance area – also reached from the village centre – has mainly blue and green cruising runs. Both Sundance and Tod have some great gladed areas to play in (12 of them, plus a new one on Mt Morrisey last season, all marked on the trail map).

Mt Morrisey is reached by a long green run from the top of Sundance and has a delightful network of easy blue runs with trees left uncut in the trails, effectively making them

639

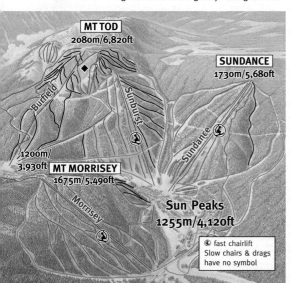

MT TOD
2080m/6,820ft

SUNDANCE
1730m/5,680ft

Burfield

Sunburst

Sundance

1200m/
3,930ft **MT MORRISEY**
1675m/5,490ft

Morrisey

Sun Peaks
1255m/4,120ft

🚡 fast chairlift
Slow chairs & drags
have no symbol

↑ The traffic-free main street is small-scale, family-friendly and a pleasant place to stroll around

SUN PEAKS RESORT / ADAM STEIN

KEY FACTS

Resort	1255m
	4,120ft
Slopes	1200-2080m
	3,930-6,820ft
Lifts	11
Pistes	3,678 acres
Green	10%
Blue	58%
Black	32%
Snowmaking	3%

UK PACKAGES

AmeriCan Ski, American Ski Classics, Canadian Affair, Erna Low, Frontier, Independent Ski Links, Ski Bespoke, Ski Independence, Ski Line, Ski Safari, Ski Solutions, Skitracer, Skiworld, Snow Finders, Virgin Snow

Phone numbers
From distant parts of Canada, add the prefix 1 250; from abroad, add the prefix +1 250

TOURIST OFFICE

www.sunpeaksresort.com

groomed glade runs that even early intermediates can try.

Fast lifts The three distinct sectors are each served by a high-speed quad. The other lifts are painfully slow.

Queues Weekdays are usually very quiet; it's only at peak weekends that you might find short queues.

Terrain parks The park has advanced, intermediate and beginner areas, plus snowmaking. But there is no half-pipe.

Snow reliability Sun Peaks gets an average snowfall of 220 inches a year: not in the top league but better than some. The snow can suffer on the lower part of Mt Tod's south-facing slopes, especially later in the season.

Experts Mt Tod has most of the steep terrain, and you can ski some good (but short) steep and gladed runs without descending to the bottom by riding the Burfield quad from its mid-station and the Crystal and Elevation chairs. Some of the blacks on Mt Morrisey (such as Static Cling) have steep mogul sections, too.

Intermediates This is great terrain for early intermediates: there are the easy and charming groomed glades of Mt Morrisey, lovely swooping blues on Sundance and the long 5 Mile run from Mt Tod. More adventurous intermediates can also tackle the easier glades (such as Cahilty) and blacks (such as Peek-A-Boo).

Beginners There are nursery slopes right in the village centre, with long easy greens to progress to.

Snowboarding Boarders can explore the whole mountain. But there are flat greens to and from Mt Morrisey.

Cross-country 30km of groomed trails and 14km of backcountry trails.

Mountain restaurants The Sunburst Lodge is the only option and gets busy; its cinnamon buns are highly recommended. The Umbrella Cafe at the Morrisey base serves hot soup and sandwiches. And it's easy to return to a village restaurant for lunch – Mountain High Pizza is 'great value'; Bento's Day Lodge has basic hot food and drinks; you can eat your own packed lunch there too.

Schools and guides Past reports have been good, but we lack recent ones. As well as standard lessons, there are Super Groups (maximum of three people), women-only lessons, and freestyle programmes for children and teenagers (ages 6 to 12 and 13 to 18).

Families The Sundance Kids Centre takes children from 18 months and the ski school children from three years.

STAYING THERE

Hotels Nancy Greene's Cahilty Lodge is a comfortable ski-in/ski-out base, and you get the chance to ski with her and husband Al Raine (former Canadian ski team coach and now mayor of Sun Peaks). The ski-in/ski-out Delta Sun Peaks Resort (outdoor pool and hot tub) in the village centre is regularly recommended. We've enjoyed staying at both. Fireside Lodge and the family run Heffley Boutique Inn have been recommended too.

Apartments Delta Residences are luxurious, ski-in/ski-out and central. Crystal Forest and McGillivray Creek condos have been tipped – some have private hot tubs. Other well-positioned condos include Forest Trails, Snow Creek Village and Timberline Village.

Eating out For a small resort, there's a good choice of restaurants. Reader tips include Powder Hounds, Steakhouse ('top-quality ribs and steaks, but need to book'), Bella Italia, and Mantles in the Delta Sun Peaks. Cahilty Creek Bar and Grill and Black Garlic Bistro (Asian fusion) are other options, and Voyageur and Oya were new last season.

Après-ski It's quiet. Bottom's and Masa's are the main après-ski bars. Morrisey's in the Delta is supposed to be like a British pub. At weekends MackDaddy's nightclub in the Delta can get lively. There are fondue evenings with torchlit descents.

Off the slopes There's skating, tubing, tobogganing, snowmobiling, bungee trampolining, dog sledding, sleigh rides, snowshoeing and swimming.

Whistler

North America's biggest mountain, with terrain to suit every standard and a big, purpose-built, largely car-free village

RATINGS

The mountains

Extent	★★★★
Fast lifts	★★★★★
Queues	★★
Terrain p'ks	★★★★★
Snow	★★★★
Expert	★★★★★
Intermediate	★★★★★
Beginner	★★★
Boarder	★★★★★
X-country	★★★
Restaurants	★★
Schools	★★★★★
Families	★★★★

The resort

Charm	★★★
Convenience	★★★★
Scenery	★★★
Eating out	★★★★★
Après-ski	★★★★
Off-slope	★★★

RPI	170
lift pass	£370
ski hire	£155
lessons	£170
food & drink	£180
total	**£875**

KEY FACTS

Resort	675m
	2,210ft
Altitude	650-2285m
	2,140-7,490ft
Lifts	37
Pistes	8,171 acres
Green	18%
Blue	55%
Black	27%
Snowmaking	8%

➕ North America's biggest, both in area and vertical (1610m)

➕ Excellent combination of high open bowls and woodland trails

➕ Good snow record

➕ Almost Alpine scenery

➕ Attractive modern village, purpose-built with car-free central areas

➕ Good range of village restaurants and lively après-ski

➖ Proximity to Pacific Ocean means a lot of cloudy weather, and rain at resort level is not unusual

➖ Inadequate lift system; queues can be a big problem at peak times

➖ Overcrowded runs also a problem

➖ Mountain restaurants are overcrowded and mostly no more than functional

➖ Resort restaurants over-busy, too

Whistler is unlike any other resort in North America. In some respects – the scale, the high bowls and glaciers, the scenery, the crowds – it is more like an Alpine resort. But like most resorts on the western side of North America, it offers the advantages of excellent snow and a lot of woodland runs as well.

All things considered, the mountain is about the best that North America has to offer, and for us a visit here is always a highlight of the season. But we'll admit that we are generally lucky with the weather, and haven't had to put up with much rain at resort level – a real hazard. And we try to time our visits to avoid peak periods and weekends, and therefore the worst of the crowds.

THE RESORT

Whistler Village sits at the foot of its two mountains, Whistler and Blackcomb, a scenic 113km drive from Vancouver on Canada's west coast.

Whistler started as a locals' ski area in 1966 at Creekside. Whistler Village, a 10-minute bus ride away, was developed in the late 1970s; Upper Village – around the base of Blackcomb Mountain and a 10-minute walk from Whistler Village – was started in the 1980s.

VILLAGE CHARM ★★★
High rise but tasteful

The three main centres are all traffic-free. The architecture is varied and, for a purpose-built resort, quite tasteful – but it is all a bit urban, with lots of blocks approaching 10 storeys high. There are also many chalet-style apartments on the hillsides. Some reporters find the central Village Square area noisy in the early hours.

CONVENIENCE ★★★★
Take your pick

The Peak 2 Peak gondola opened in 2008 and made Whistler Village, Upper Village and Creekside all equally convenient places to stay – from all,

you can easily access both mountains by taking a maximum of three lifts.

Whistler Village – by far the biggest and liveliest – has a gondola to each mountain. A pedestrian bridge over an access road links the main centre to newer Whistler Village North (further from the lifts), making a huge car-free area of streets lined with shops, condos, bars and restaurants.

Upper Village is much smaller and quieter. So is Creekside, which was revamped and expanded for the 2010 Winter Olympics.

There is a free bus between central Whistler and Upper Village, but it can be just as quick to walk. Some lodging

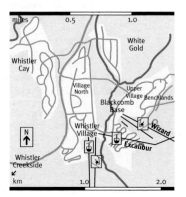

NEWS

2013/14: At last Whistler will get its first six-pack; one is planned to replace the notoriously queue-prone Harmony chair near the top of Whistler mountain, increasing the carrying capacity by 50%. The slow Crystal chair on Blackcomb is due to be replaced by a fast quad, increasing capacity by 65%; the new Crystal chair will end at the same place as the old one but start lower down, making existing little-used runs much more attractive to ski and significantly cutting the long run out from the Blackcomb Glacier and Spanky's Ladder runs.

2012/13: The ski school introduced a new programme – a day's skiing or snowboarding with an Olympian.

LIFT PASSES

Prices in C$

Age	1-day	6-day
under 13	53	274
13 to 18	89	466
19 to 64	104	548
65 plus	89	466

Free Under 7

Beginner Lift and lesson deal

Notes Prices include sales tax. 1-day price is window price; 6-day price is online advance-purchase price

is a long way from the centre and means taking buses (not free) or taxis. Some hotels have free buses, which will take you to and pick you up from restaurants and nightlife.

SCENERY ★★★
Almost Alpine
There are splendid views of the deep Fitzsimmons Creek valley from both mountains, and especially from the Peak 2 Peak gondola, which goes right across it – the views from the two cabins with glass floors are particularly spectacular. The upper slopes give good views to coastal sounds, high open bowls, glaciers and ridges.

THE MOUNTAINS

The mountains offer an excellent combination of high, open bowls and sheltered forest runs.

Many reporters enthuse about the mountain host service and the 'go slow' patrol – some find the latter over-zealous, but crowded slopes, especially on the runs home, mean they're often needed; we approve.

Signposting is excellent. But every year some reporters complain about inaccuracies on the trail map; most seem to be happy with it though. A separate Wonder Routes map has suggested tours for different ability levels, families and panoramic views.

One thing that annoys most people is the crazily early closing times of the lifts – 3pm or 3.30pm till late February, with the top lifts closing even earlier.

EXTENT OF THE SLOPES ★★★★
The biggest in North America
Whistler and Blackcomb together form the biggest area of slopes, with the longest runs, in North America.

Whistler Mountain is accessed from Whistler Village by a two-stage, 10-person gondola that rises over 1100m to Roundhouse Lodge at mid-mountain. Or you can use two fast quads (which reporters say don't always run).

Runs down through the trees fan out from the gondola: cruises to the Emerald and Big Red chairs and longer runs to the gondola mid-station.

From Roundhouse you can see the jewel in Whistler's crown – magnificent open bowls, served by the fast Peak and Harmony chairs. The bowl beyond Harmony is served by the Symphony fast quad. The bowls are mostly

go-anywhere terrain for experts, but there are groomed trails, so anyone can appreciate the views. Roundhouse is the departure point of the Peak 2 Peak gondola to Blackcomb.

A six-seat gondola from Creekside also accesses Whistler Mountain.

Access to **Blackcomb** from Whistler Village is by an eight-seat gondola, followed by a fast quad. From the base of Blackcomb you take two consecutive fast quads up to the main Rendezvous restaurant – departure point of the Peak 2 Peak gondola. From Rendezvous, on skier's right is great cruising terrain and the Glacier Express quad up to the Horstman Glacier area; on skier's left are steeper slopes, the terrain park and the traverse over to the 7th Heaven chair. The 1610m vertical from the top of 7th Heaven to the base is the biggest in North America. A T-bar from the Horstman Glacier brings you (with a short hike) to the Blackcomb Glacier in the next valley – away from all lifts.

Fresh Tracks is a deal that allows you to ride up Whistler Mountain (at extra cost) from 7.15am, have a buffet breakfast and get on the slopes early – very popular with many reporters. We prefer to ski first on deserted runs and breakfast later – check what time breakfast ends (9am on our March 2013 visit). Free guided tours of each mountain are offered at 11.15am.

FAST LIFTS ★★★★★
Can't cope with the crowds
While the resort has more fast lifts than any other in North America, the lift system is antiquated compared with the Alps and can't handle the crowds (see 'Queues'). Gondolas provide the main access, with lots of fast quads after that – but only this season is the resort's first six-pack due and there are no eight-seaters, which are becoming common in Europe.

QUEUES ★★
A big problem
Whistler has become a victim of its own success. At peak holiday periods and weekends when people pour in from Vancouver, queues can be horrendous. There are displays of waiting times at different lifts, which readers generally find useful.

Some reporters have signed up with the ski school just to get lift priority. Others have visited Vancouver at the weekend to avoid the crowds.

There's a clear rating system in place, based on size (S, M, L, XL). On Blackcomb, novices should begin in the Big Easy Terrain Garden. It features small rails and rollers to help you get a feel for airtime and improve your control. The M-L Choker Park is vast, but is usually the busiest. With many step-up jumps, hips, tabletops, rails and boxes, this park will suit intermediate to advanced riders. Very confident freestylers should hit the XL Highest Level Park. The obstacles are huge and you have to wear a helmet. On Whistler mountain, the Habitat Park by the Emerald chair has something for everyone, from beginner boxes to medium jumps and jibs and 15m+ XL tabletops.

SNOW RELIABILITY ★★★★
Excellent at altitude
Snow conditions at the top are usually excellent – the snowfall averages over 400 inches a year (that's way more than most Colorado resorts). And three out of the last four seasons have been among the snowiest ever for the resort, with well over 500 inches recorded. But because the resort is low and close to the Pacific, the bottom slopes can have poor snow or slush – leading people to 'download' from the mid-stations, especially in late season. Reporters are mixed about piste maintenance this year with one complaining: 'Why have a blue to the valley at Creekside and not groom it? I saw novices struggling at the end of the day. The black was easier.'

FOR EXPERTS ★★★★★
Few can rival it
Whistler Mountain's bowls are enough to keep experts happy for weeks. Each has endless variations, with chutes and gullies of varied steepness and width. The biggest challenges are around Flute, Glacier, Whistler and West Bowls – you can go anywhere in these high, wide areas.

Blackcomb's steep slopes are not as extensive as Whistler's, but some are more challenging. From the top of the 7th Heaven lift, traverse to Xhiggy's Meadow for sunny bowl runs. If you're feeling brave, go in the opposite direction and drop into the extremely steep chutes down towards Glacier Creek, including the infamous 41° Couloir Extreme (which can have massive moguls at the top), Secret Bowl and the very steep Pakalolo

The routes out of Whistler Village in the morning can be busy (we had one report of a queue of more than 200 metres for the Blackcomb gondola). Creekside is less of a problem, but gets long queues at weekends. Some of the chairs higher up also produce long queues (even the singles lines took 10 minutes or so on our March 2013 visit); the Emerald and Peak chairs are bottlenecks – one reporter noted a 45-minute wait for the Peak chair on a Sunday in January. The worst queues have been for the Harmony chair but this should be improved by the new six-pack planned for 2013/14. Another issue is that some of the higher lifts, especially the Peak chair, are prone to open late on powder days while the ski patrol finish their avalanche control. Crowds on the slopes, especially the runs home, can be annoying, too.

TERRAIN PARKS ★★★★★
World class for all abilities
While both mountains have parks, freestylers tend to head to Blackcomb, which is home to the Olympic-standard Nintendo Super Pipe (with walls almost 7m high and shaped daily), the Mini Pipe with 4.5m high walls, a boardercross course ('a good laugh with friends') and three terrain parks.

couloir. Our favourite runs are the less frequented but also seriously steep bowls reached by a short hike up Spanky's Ladder, after taking the Glacier Express lift. You emerge after the hike at the top of a huge deserted area with several ways down; best to have a guide.

Both mountains have challenging trails through trees. The Peak to Creek area offers 400 acres below Whistler's West Bowl to Creekside.

There's also backcountry guiding, cat-skiing and heli-skiing available by the day. A recent reporter had 'two incredible days' with Powder Mountain cat-skiing. Other reporters used Coast Range mountain guides ('top-quality guides and superb skiing') and found the heli-skiing 'expensive but a great experience'. We recommend the two-day Extremely Canadian clinic (see 'Schools and guides') for getting the most out of the in-bounds steeps and their one-day Backcountry Adventures.

One of our favourite runs is behind the mountain away from all the lifts on the Blackcomb glacier – almost 1000m vertical to the new Crystal chair

Fabulous, usually deserted, ungroomed slopes are reached by climbing Spanky's Ladder and dropping over the back

Great blue and green cruising, but beginners should beware of some steeper sections on the greens

New chair for 2013/14 will make runs here more attractive to ski and cut long run out from Blackcomb glacier

The Peak 2 Peak gondola means you no longer have to ski to the village to switch between mountains

BLACKCOMB

Horstman Hut 2285m/7,490ft

Blackcomb Glacier

7th Heaven

Horstman Glacier

Rendezvous Lodge 1860

Crystal Hut

Glacier

Jersey Cream 1645m

Solar Coaster

Peak 2 Peak

Crystal Ridge

Glacier Creek

Excelerator

1290m

Wizard

Excalibur

Blackcomb Base

ⓖ gondola
ⓕ fast chairlift
Slow chairs & drags have no symbol

FOR INTERMEDIATES ★★★★★
Ideal and extensive terrain

Both mountains are an intermediate's paradise. In good weather, good intermediates will enjoy the easier slopes in the high bowls. One of our favourite intermediate runs is down the Blackcomb Glacier, from the top of the mountain; the tedious run out should be a lot shorter for 2013/14 due to the planned opening of the new Crystal chair almost 1000m below. This 5km run, away from all lifts, starts with a two-minute walk up from the top of the Showcase T-bar. Don't be put off by the 'Experts only' sign. You drop over the ridge into a wide bowl and traverse the slope to get to gentler gradients – descend too soon and you'll get a shock in the very steep double-diamond Blowhole.

The blue runs served by the 7th Heaven chair start above the treeline and end in it – some can get bumpy in parts. Lower down, including from the new Crystal chair, there are lots of

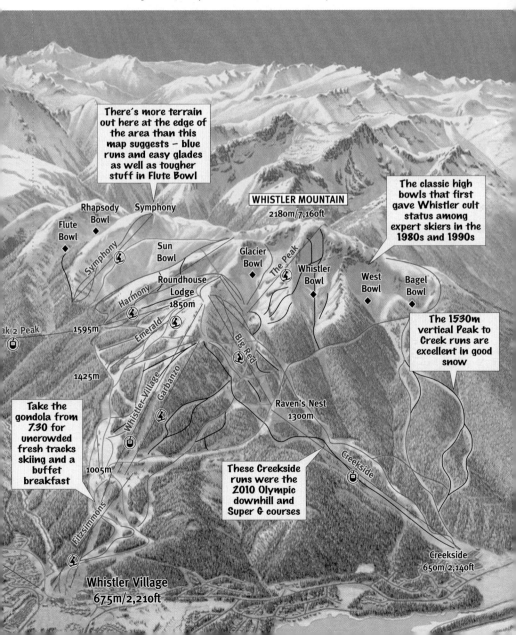

There's more terrain out here at the edge of the area than this map suggests – blue runs and easy glades as well as tougher stuff in Flute Bowl

WHISTLER MOUNTAIN
2180m/7,160ft

The classic high bowls that first gave Whistler cult status among expert skiers in the 1980s and 1990s

Rhapsody Bowl

Symphony

Flute Bowl ◆

Symphony

Sun Bowl

Glacier Bowl ◆

The Peak

Whistler Bowl

West Bowl

Bagel Bowl

Roundhouse Lodge 1850m

Harmony

Emerald

ak 2 Peak   1595m

Big Red

The 1530m vertical Peak to Creek runs are excellent in good snow

1425m

Whistler-Village

Garbanzo

Raven's Nest 1300m

Creekside

Take the gondola from 7.30 for uncrowded fresh tracks skiing and a buffet breakfast

1005m

These Creekside runs were the 2010 Olympic downhill and Super G courses

Fitzsimmons

Creekside 650m/2,140ft

Whistler Village 675m/2,210ft

ACTIVITIES

Indoor Sports arena (ice rink, pool, gym, squash), tennis, spa and health clubs, climbing wall, art galleries, museums, library, cinema

Outdoor Flightseeing, snowshoeing, snowmobiling, sno-limo (chauffeur-driven motorized sled), walking, snowcat tours, dog sledding, tubing, sleigh rides, bungee jumping, ziplining, bobsleigh

perfect cruising runs through the trees – ideal for bad weather days.

On Whistler Mountain, the ridges and bowls served by the Harmony and Symphony chairs have lots to offer – not only groomers but also excellent terrain for experiments off-piste. Symphony in particular has some very gentle and usually uncrowded terrain and widely spaced trees to play in. The Saddle run from the top of the Harmony Express lift is a favourite with many of our reporters, though it can get busy. The blue Highway 86 path, which skirts West Bowl from the Peak to Creek trail, has beautiful views over a steep valley and across to the rather phallic Black Tusk mountain. The 7km-long Peak to Creek blue run is good too, but it's rarely all groomed – check before setting off. The green Burnt Stew Trail has great views, and accesses lots of easy off-piste terrain.

Lower down the mountain there is a vast choice of groomed blue runs, with a series of fast chairs to bring you back up to the top of the gondola. It's a cruiser's paradise – especially the aptly named Ego Bowl. A great long run is the fabulous Dave Murray Downhill all the way from mid-mountain to the finish at Creekside – used as the 2010 Olympic men's downhill course. Although it is classed black, it's a wonderful fast and varied cruise when it has been groomed.

FOR BEGINNERS ★★★★★
OK if the sun shines
Whistler has excellent nursery slopes by the mid-station of the gondola, as does Blackcomb at the base. Both have facilities higher up too. There is a lift pass, lesson and rental deal on certain dates (see 'Schools and guides'), but no free lifts. The map has easy runs and slow zones marked.

On Whistler, there are some gentle runs from the top of the gondola. Their downside is other people speeding past. On Blackcomb, there are green runs from top to bottom. The top parts are very gentle, with some steeper pitches lower down.

In general, greens can be trickier than in many North American resorts – steeper, busier and, on the lower mountain, in less good condition.

Another serious reservation is the weather. Beginners don't get a lot out of heavy snowfalls, and might be put off by rain.

The base of Blackcomb mountain, with Merlin's on the left and Fairmont Chateau Whistler on the right →

WHISTLER BLACKCOMB / PAUL MORRISON

FOR BOARDERS ★★★★★
Epic – winter and summer

Whistler has world-class terrain parks as well as epic terrain for freeriders: bowls with great powder and awesome steeps, steep gullies, tree runs, and shedloads of natural hits, wind lips and cliffs. There are mellow groomed runs ideal for beginners and intermediates, too, and the lifts are generally snowboard-friendly; there are T-bars on the glacier, but they're not vicious. The resort has as high a reputation for summer snowboarding and camps on the glacier as for its winter boarding, and the summer Camp of Champions is hugely popular. Specialist snowboard shops include Showcase and Katmandu Boards.

FOR CROSS-COUNTRY ★★★★★
Picturesque but low

There are over 28km of cross-country tracks around Lost Lake, starting by the river on the path between Whistler and Blackcomb. But it is low altitude, so conditions can be unreliable. A specialist school, Cross-Country Connection (905 0071) offers lessons and rental. Keen cross-country merchants can go to the Whistler Olympic Park and its 90km of trails (around 20 minutes away by car).

MOUNTAIN RESTAURANTS ★★★★★
Overcrowded

The main restaurants sell decent food but are charmless self-service stops with long queues; most get incredibly crowded. They're huge, but not huge enough. 'Seat-seekers' are employed to find you space, but success is not guaranteed. The piste map advises eating lunch before 11.30 (sorry?) or after 1pm. Blackcomb has the 500-seat Rendezvous and 775-seat Glacier Creek. Whistler has the gigantic (2,080-seat) Roundhouse.

Editors' choice Christine's (938 7437) table-service restaurant in the Rendezvous building on Blackcomb is the place to book for a decent lunch. We had a delicious bouillabaisse and 'flight' of four different Okanagan wines with tasting notes there.

Worth knowing about On Whistler, Steep's Grill (905 2379) in the Roundhouse is the table-service place ('Good food and views,' says a 2013 visitor), but we much prefer Christine's for both ambience and food.

There are other smallish (self-service) places, but they're still packed at normal times, and may be closed in early and late season. On Blackcomb are two tiny huts with great views – Crystal Hut ('amazing waffles') and Horstman Hut ('excellent goulash and mulled wine'). On Whistler, Raven's Nest is small and friendly, and does soups, sandwiches and BBQs; the Chic Pea ('cinnamon rolls to die for') and Harmony Hut are other options.

You can eat your own picnic at the Roundhouse or Rendezvous.

SCHOOLS AND GUIDES ★★★★★
A great formula

The school limits the number in an adult group to a maximum of four. And they also run Discover Whistler Days at some periods outside high season when you get a discount (30% in 2012/13) off the normal cost of lessons – and rentals and lift pass for beginners. A recent reporter who took private lessons says, 'In a day we progressed from doing greens and

SCHOOLS

Whistler/Blackcomb
t 967 8950

Extremely Canadian
t 1 800 938 9656

Classes
Full day from C$194
(max 4 in class)

Private lessons
Half day (3hr) C$471

GUIDES

Whistler Guides
t 938 9242

WHISTLER BLACKCOMB / ROBIN O'NEILL

Roundhouse Lodge on Whistler mountain isn't very round. But it is the arrival point of the Whistler Village gondola and the Peak 2 Peak gondola ↓

occasional blues to taking on blacks.' The school also runs special programmes such as 4-day Ski Camps, which combine instruction with guiding – with the same instructor and group daily (unusual for North America); these Camps seem to have replaced the Ski Esprit groups, which many of our reporters have enjoyed. The three-day Dave Murray Camps, which include race training, are 'superb for strong intermediates to experts', says a reporter.

The Extremely Canadian two-day camps run three times a week and are for those who want guiding (with a bit of coaching) in Whistler's steep and deep terrain and are a great way of finding the best steep terrain. We have been with them several times and have been impressed. A recent reporter said, 'A well-spent C$400, whether you want to increase your skills/confidence or just ski some great terrain.'

Extremely Canadian started Backcountry Adventures day trips last season. Backcountry day trips or overnight touring are also available with Whistler Alpine Guides Bureau.

FOR FAMILIES ★★★★
Impressive

Blackcomb's base area has the slow-moving Magic chair to get children part-way up the mountain. Whistler's gondola mid-station has a splendid kids-only area. A reporter found the staff 'friendly, instilling confidence'. The school now uses the Flaik GPS real-time tracking system so that each child's exact location is known at all times. There's a Magic Castle on Blackcomb and a Family Zone and Tree Fort on Whistler. One reporter enthused about 'climb and dine': kids combine dinner with three hours of climbing at The Core.

STAYING THERE

Whistler has every kind of lodging you might want. Ski Independence and Frontier Ski offer an impressive range of hotels and apartments in and around the resort.

Hotels There is a wide range, including a lot of top-end places.

*****Fairmont Chateau Whistler (938 8000) Well run, luxurious, at the foot of Blackcomb. We and reporters love it. Excellent spa with pools and tubs.

*****Four Seasons (935 3400) Luxury hotel five minutes' walk from Blackcomb base, but with ski valet service at the base. Unremarkable public areas but good food. Good fitness/spa facilities.

*****Westin Resort & Spa (905 5000) Luxury all-suite hotel at the foot of Whistler mountain. We enjoyed our 2013 stay there except the pool and hot tubs were always so crowded we didn't use them.

CHILDCARE

Whistler Kids
t 1 800 766 0449
Ages 18mnth to 4yr

Ski school
Ages 3 to 12

UK PACKAGES

Alpine Answers, AmeriCan Ski, American Ski Classics, Canadian Affair, Carrier, Cold Comforts Lodging, Crystal, Crystal Finest, Elegant Resorts, Erna Low, Flexiski, Frontier, Independent Ski Links, Inghams, Interactive Resorts, Kaluma, Momentum, Neilson, Oxford Ski Co, PowderBeds, Scott Dunn, Ski Bespoke, Ski Expectations, Ski Independence, Ski Line, Ski Safari, Ski Solutions, Skitracer, Skiworld, Snow Finders, STC, Supertravel, Thomson, Virgin Snow

GETTING THERE

Air Vancouver 135km/85 miles (2hr15)

Phone numbers
From distant parts of Canada, add the prefix 1 604; from abroad, add the prefix +1 604

TOURIST OFFICE

www.whistler
blackcomb.com
www.tourismwhistler.
com

****Crystal Lodge** (932 2221) In Whistler Village. Pool/sauna/hot tub. Discounts in several restaurants and shops in building.
****Glacier Lodge** (905 4607) In Upper Village. Large rooms, 'good value'.
****Pan Pacific Mountainside** (905 2999) Luxury, all-suite, at Whistler Village base. Pool/steam/hot tub.
****Sundial Boutique** (932 2321) In Whistler Village; one- and two-bedroom suites. Rooftop hot tubs.
****Summit Lodge & Spa** (932 2778) In Whistler Village. Pool/sauna/hot tub, 'free hot drinks in lobby'.
***Lost Lake Lodge** (580 6647) Out by the golf course; studios and suites. Pool/hot tub.
***Tantalus Resort Lodge** (932 4146) In Whistler Village; targets families and groups. Hot tub/sauna.
***Whistler Village Inn & Suites** (932 4004) Central, side-by-side buildings. Relatively cheap, but 'tired old decor and furnishings', says a 2013 reporter. Pool/hot tub/sauna.
Apartments There are plenty of spacious, comfortable condominiums. Price tends to be dictated by location – ski-in/ski-out condos are pricier than those a shuttle-ride from the lifts.

EATING OUT ★★★★★
Good but crowded
Reporters are enthusiastic about the range, quality and value of places to eat, but there aren't enough restaurant seats to meet demand. You have to book well ahead (which may mean months ahead in some cases), or resign yourself to queuing for one of the places that doesn't take bookings.

At the top of the market, the Rimrock Cafe near Whistler Creek specializes in seafood and game and has several different small areas that make it feel more intimate than many Whistler restaurants; we have eaten very well there (most recently in 2013, when we booked three weeks ahead).

In Whistler Village, we've enjoyed Araxi ('Top quality for a special occasion; recommend the scallops and chorizo and the venison,' says a recent reporter), Il Caminetto di Umberto (a classy Italian) and 21 Steps (mid-market place up, er, 21 steps, where we enjoyed several delicious small plates on our 2013 visit). The pricey Ric's Grill and cheaper Keg are both parts of chains but do good seafood and steak. Mid-market places include: Quattro and Old Spaghetti Factory

('Real value,' says a 2012 reporter) for Italian, Bocca ('casual, good bar food, excellent service'), Three Below ('reasonably priced; great banana in puff pastry with caramel'), and Earl's ('burgers, ribs, good microbeers'). Others to try are Sushi Village and Teppan (both Japanese), Mongolie (Asian) and Kypriaki Norte (Greek). In Village North, Hy's Steakhouse ('good food and service, free garlic bread') and the lively Brewhouse are good for steaks and ribs (we enjoyed the Brewhouse in 2013). There are plenty of budget places, including Fat Tony's ('tasty pizzas') and the après-ski bars below. You can also take a snowcat to the Crystal Hut for fondue, music and the history of Whistler.

APRES-SKI ★★★★☆
Something for most tastes
Whistler is very lively. We get most reviews on the Garibaldi Lift Company, which is still 'buzzing from 4pm onwards, with good live music'. Other tips are the Brewhouse (where a model train runs all the way round the interior), Longhorn (with a terrace), Dubh Linn Gate Irish pub ('fun', 'good food, live entertainment') and Tapley's. Merlin's is the focus at Blackcomb base, with sports TV, quiz nights and music ('great party atmosphere'). Dusty's at Creekside has good beer, loud music, but 'very slow service at lunchtime', says a 2013 reporter.

Later on, Buffalo Bill's is lively. Tommy Africa's, Maxx Fish, Moe Joe's and Garfinkel's are the main clubs.

OFF THE SLOPES ★★★☆☆
Quite a lot to do
Meadow Park Sports Centre has fitness facilities. There are several luxurious spas and an eight-screen cinema. Reporters recommend walks around the lake and the climbing wall at The Core. Ziptrek Ecotours offers tours on ziplines and suspension bridges through the forest between Whistler and Blackcomb mountains – 'great fun' says a reporter. You can also do ATV/snowmobile trips and dog sledding. A 2013 visitor raves about the bobseigh run at the Sliding Centre ('for adrenaline junkies'). The free Sunday evening Fire & Ice show is popular. Excursions to Squamish (for eagle watching) and to Vancouver are easy. And non-slope users can get around the mountain easily (and take the Peak 2 Peak gondola for great views).

Eastern Canada

For us the main attraction of skiing or riding in eastern Canada is the French culture and language that are predominant in the province of Québec. It really feels like a different country from the rest of Canada. And the resorts are only a 6-hour flight from the UK, compared with a 10-hour flight for western Canada.

Be prepared for variable snow conditions, including rock-hard pistes and ice; and be prepared for extreme cold in early and midwinter. But cold weather means the extensive snowmaking systems can be effective for a long season. Don't go expecting light, dry powder – if that's what you want, go west.

UK PACKAGES

Tremblant Alpine Answers, American Ski Classics, Crystal, Crystal Finest, Erna Low, Frontier, Independent Ski Links, Inghams, Neilson, Ski Bespoke, Ski Independence, Ski Safari, Ski Solutions, Skitracer, Skiworld, STC, Thomson, Virgin Snow

For people heading on holiday for a week or more, eastern Canada really means the province of Québec, its capital, Québec City, and the main destination resort Tremblant (covered below) nearer Montreal. French culture and language dominate the region. Notices, menus, trail maps and so on are usually printed in both French and English. Many ski area workers are bilingual or only French-speaking. And French cuisine abounds.

Slopes in all resorts are small, both in extent and vertical. The weather is very variable, so the snow – though pretty much guaranteed by snowmaking – varies greatly in quality.

Québec City makes a good base for access to several ski areas. Old Québec, at the city's heart, is North America's only walled city and is a World Heritage site. Within the city walls are narrow, winding streets and 17th- and 18th-century houses. It is situated right on the banks of the St Lawrence river. In January/February there is a famous two-week carnival, with an ice castle, snow sculptures, dog-sled and canoe races, parades and balls. But most of the winter is low season, with good-value rooms available in big hotels.

Stoneham is the closest ski area to Québec City, around 20 minutes away. The biggest and most varied resort is Mont-Ste-Anne 30 minutes away. Le Massif is around an hour away – a cult area with locals. These three resorts have extended entries in the resort directory at the back of the book.

650

KEY FACTS

Resort	265m
	870ft
Slopes	230-875m
	750-2,870ft
Lifts	14
Pistes	654 acres
Snow-guns	71%

TOURIST OFFICE

www.tremblant.ca

Tremblant

➕ Charming, purpose-built core village
➕ Some good runs for all abilities

➖ Very limited in extent
➖ Weekend queues and crowds

Tremblant is eastern Canada's leading destination ski resort, about 90 minutes' drive from Montreal.

The Intrawest core village is purpose-built in the cute style of old Québec, with buildings in vibrant colours and narrow, cobbled, traffic-free streets; it feels very French. There is a regular, free ski-bus and a local town service.

The slopes are pleasantly wooded. A heated gondola from the village takes you to the top of the so-called South Side. From here you can drop over the back onto the North Side. Most lifts are fast chairs. At weekends there can be queues, but they tend to move quickly. Half the runs are blacks; most are at the easier end of their grading, but there are bump runs and glades. There is good intermediate cruising, an excellent nursery area with long, easy greens to progress to and terrain parks aimed at advanced, intermediate beginner freestylers; plus a children's adventure area. There's over 80km of cross-country.

Many people return to town for lunch, but the Grand Manitou at the top of the gondola has good views and decent food. The Refuge on the Soleil sector of the South Side is 'more charming but has a very limited menu'. Of the hotels, the Fairmont Tremblant is the most luxurious. There are ample condos. Restaurants and bars are plentiful. Try the Forge Grill or Ya'ooo Pizza Bar. The Shack brews its own beer. Off the slopes there is an 'expensive' pool complex, snowshoeing, skating, tubing and a casino. Visiting Montreal is popular.

Spain

RPI	100
lift pass	£200
ski hire	£130
lessons	£95
food & drink	£105
total	**£530**

UK PACKAGES

Baqueira-Beret Crystal Finest, Neilson, Scott Dunn, Ski Miquel
Formigal Crystal, Skitracer, Thomson, White Roc, Zenith
Sierra Nevada Crystal, Thomson

+ Vibrant Spanish culture gives a different experience from the Alps
+ Low prices for food and drink
+ Few crowds outside peak times

− Access can be difficult, with lengthy drives to reach Pyrenean resorts
− Still lots of old lifts, but improving

Spanish resorts vary enormously, so it's difficult to generalize. Nearly all the main ones, though, are benefiting from recent investment. The three we feature here have respectably sized and varied terrain that compares favourably with many smaller Alpine resorts.

The relatively low cost and the relaxed ambience of eating, partying and posing are key parts of the appeal of Spanish skiing. The majority of resorts are in the Pyrenees, and the villages are built more for convenience than charm. But they do offer a wide range of lodging set in some of the Pyrenees' most stunning scenery.

There is a group of worthwhile resorts in the west, between Pau and Huesca. Formigal is now the largest, and making a steady comeback on the wider market. Candanchu and Astún nearby are popular on the Spanish market. The downside is access, which can be tricky from France if snowfall closes key mountain passes. There are long drives up from Spanish airports, too, but weekly charter flights to Huesca have cut some transfer times.

In the south of Spain is the high resort of Sierra Nevada – a quite different experience and close to the coast. A two-centre trip is possible.

The other main group of resorts is just east of Andorra and includes La Molina and Masella (Alp 2500). These have brief descriptions in the resort directory at the back of the book.

KEY FACTS

Resort	1500m
	4,920ft
Slopes	1500-2510m
	4,920-8,230ft
Lifts	33
Pistes	120km
Snow-guns	608 guns

TOURIST OFFICE

www.baqueira.es

Baqueira-Beret

+ Compact modern resort
+ Lots of good intermediate slopes

− Main village lacks atmosphere
− Still some old, slow lifts

Baqueira's village is not inspiring, but the resort has a well-linked and developing ski area that appeals to intermediates. Fine for beginners too.

Baqueira was purpose-built in the 1960s and has its fair share of drab high-rise blocks. The central area is clustered below the road that runs through to the high pass of Port de la Bonaigua, while the main lift base is just above it. The village is small enough for location not to be too much of an issue. And there are big car parks with shuttles to the lift base.

The slopes are split into three distinct but well-connected areas – Baqueira, Beret and Bonaigua – with long, intermediate runs, practically all of them on open, treeless slopes. Most are above 1800m with extensive snowmaking; but afternoon sun is a problem in spring. Some slopes were remodelled to improve grooming for 2012/13. There are fast chairs dotted around, including a long six-pack.

Experts will find few on-piste challenges, but there is extensive off-piste and five ungroomed itinerary runs (including Escornacrabes, which both our recent reporters said was not for the faint-hearted). There are good nursery slopes with moving carpets at Beret, and at the top of the gondola – the blues there are on the tough side though. Queues are rarely of major concern. The Brit-run BB Ski School is praised, including for off-piste guiding. The huts disappoint and lack variety, but Pla de Beret and Bonaigua ('good pizza') have table-service, and a reporter tips the San Miguel tapas bar at Bonaigua and the small bar at Tanau 1700 for 'hearty mountain soups and stews'.

There are good-quality hotels: the 5-star AC Baqueira (a Marriott) is 'the best'. But the best restaurants and bars are down the valley. Some hotels have pools and spas, but there is little else to amuse non-skiers.

KEY FACTS

Resort	1550m
	4,920ft
Slopes	1500-2250m
	5,090-7,380ft
Lifts	21
Pistes	137km
Snow-guns	22%

TOURIST OFFICE

www.aramon.co.uk
www.formigal.com

When quality
and value
matter,
do more with

zenith
·holidays·

0203 137 7678

zenithholidays.co.uk

ABTA
ABTA No.Y1542

Formigal

- Sizeable, varied area for all abilities
- Linked valleys give sense of travel
- Traffic congestion in resort
- Wind-prone slopes, lacking trees

Formigal has the largest ski area in the Spanish Pyrenees, and varied terrain. Recent investment is slowly attracting more British visitors – reports welcome.

The resort is on the Spanish–French border at the Col de Portalet, which can be closed in heavy snowfall and prevent direct access from France.

The village – of purpose-built apartment blocks and smart hotels – is on the east side of the Tena valley. The central street is pleasant enough, with an attractive clocktower and a replica church as its focus, but it is spoiled by heavy traffic.

There are excellent free shuttles to and from the slopes, which span the west side of the valley and spread over four side-valleys. Most slopes are treeless, prone to wind and north- or south-facing. Grooming is good and snowmaking extensive. Queues are rare outside holiday periods. Sextas is the nearest of the four bases to the village, with an eight-seat chair. All four have big car parks and US-style day lodges including big self-service cafeterias. There are fast chairs linking the lower parts of each valley, and runs for all standards from the tops.

Experts have three freeride areas, plus heli-skiing. Many of the black runs could be red, though. The nursery slopes are excellent. There are good intermediate runs; the gentle blue Rio from Cantal to Sextas is ideal for the more timid. The only tree-lined run is a remote lovely cruise, quiet because access is by a long, slow chair.

Confident skiers can ride a snowcat above Portalet, which accesses remote runs and freeride terrain to Anayet. The huge terrain park is one of the best we've seen, and there's a kids' mini-park and boardercross. We enjoyed good Italian food at the Cantal Trattoria. The school has a good reputation. Families are well catered for with 'slow ski zones', family zones and an Indian 'village'.

There is a choice of 3- and 4-star hotels (the Aragon Hills and Abba Formigal have pools and spas), lots of apartments and over 30 restaurants, from Spanish to pizzerias. We had good gourmet food at the Vidocq. Après-ski is low-key, but the Marchica bar at Sextas is lively at close of play. Later on, there are two discos, the popular Cueva, and the Tralala.

Off-slope activities include dog sledding, floodlit tobogganing and snowmobile outings up to a mountain hut. Thermal baths are nearby.

KEY FACTS

Resort	2100m
	6,890ft
Slopes	2100-3300
	6,890-10,830ft
Lifts	29
Pistes	105km
Snow-guns	350 guns

TOURIST OFFICE

www.sierranevada.es

Sierra Nevada

- Reasonably good snow record
- Fine beginner slopes
- Exposed, and prone to wind
- Crowds at weekends

Despite its southerly position near Granada, Sierra Nevada is a high, modern resort with a modest area of slopes. It gets its own weather, of course.

Pradollano is the hub, a stylish modern base with shops, restaurants and bars set around traffic-free open spaces. Most of the accommodation is in older, less smart buildings along a steeply winding road.

From town, two gondolas go up to the mid-station at Borreguiles, and a two-stage fast quad goes up above there. There are four identifiable sectors, well linked, with a good range of intermediate and easy runs but not a lot for experts. Snowmaking was increased this year. There are excellent nursery slopes at mid-mountain (where a new moving carpet was installed this year), and a terrain park with an FIS standard half-pipe. There are also good views from the mountain of the plains and towns – and on a clear day across the Med to Africa. Weekends can be busy, and queues may develop for some of the older lifts, especially the chair up the village slope. The home run can get crowded too. Sierra Nevada can have good snow years when the Alps has bad, and vice versa. Most slopes face north-west, but some get the afternoon sun. And when the wind blows, as it does, the slopes close; there are no trees.

The Sol y Nieve hotel – with spa and good kids' facilities – was recommended by a recent reporter.

Finland

- ✚ Good for families and beginners
- ✚ Ideal terrain for cross-country
- ✚ Reliable snow well into spring
- ✚ Chance of seeing Northern Lights

- ▬ Can be bitterly cold (and dark in the early season)
- ▬ Small ski areas lacking challenge
- ▬ Draglifts are the norm

For skiers with no appetite for the hustle and hassle of Alpine resorts in high season – especially families, perhaps – escaping to the white silence of Lapland can be an attractive alternative. Finland has the lion's share of Lapland, and we started getting more reports on it – but they've more or less dried up. The resorts are small but rapidly developing both their ski areas and their facilities.

The Arctic landscape of flat and gently rolling forest, countless lakes and the occasional treeless hill is a paradise for cross-country skiing.

It also offers good beginner and intermediate downhilling, albeit on a small scale. None of the areas has significant vertical by Alpine standards, and in some cases it is seriously limited. The resorts usually open a few runs in late November. For two months in midwinter the sun does not rise – at least, not at sea level. Most areas have floodlit runs. The mountains do not open fully until mid-February, when a normal skiing day is possible and Finnish schools have holidays that usually coincide with ours – making it a busy time. Finland comes into its own at the end of the season, with friendlier temperatures and long daylight hours. Easter is extremely popular, and the slopes are crowded. If you're lucky, you may see the Northern Lights – one March visitor saw them three times ('a great sight').

Conditions are usually hard-packed powder or fresh snow from the start of the season to the end (early May).

The temperature can be extremely variable, yo-yoing between 0°C and –30°C several times in a week. Fine days are the coldest, but the best for skiing: it may be 10 to 15 degrees warmer on the slopes than at valley level. 'Mild' days of cloud and wind are worse, and face masks are sold.

The staple Finnish lift is the T-bar; chairs and gondolas are rare. Pistes are wide and well maintained, as are nursery slopes. The Finns are great boarders and consider their terrain parks far superior to those in the Alps; super-pipes are increasingly common. There are few mountain restaurants

– but you are never far from the base, with its self-service restaurants. The ski areas also have shelters or 'kotas' – log-built teepees with an open fire and a smoke hole – where you can warm up and cook your own food.

Ski school is good, with English widely spoken. All ski areas have indoor playrooms for small children, but they may be closed at weekends.

Excursions are common and generally very popular – husky sledding, snowmobile safaris, a reindeer sleigh ride and tea with the Lapp drivers in their tent. Reporters are generally very enthusiastic about these off-slope adventures.

Hotels are self-contained resorts, large and practical rather than stylish, typically with a shop, a cafe, a bar with dance floor, and a pool and sauna with outdoor cooling-off area. Hotel supper is typically served no later than seven, sometimes followed by a children's disco or dancing to a live band.

Finns usually prefer to stay in cabins, and tour operators offer the compromise of staying in a cabin but taking half-board at a nearby hotel. Cabins vary, but are mostly well equipped, with a sauna and drying cupboard as standard.

The main resorts are Levi and Ylläs, respectively 17km north and 50km west of Kittilä, which has charter flights from Britain. They are described here. Three other resorts worth considering are: Ruka, 80km south of the Arctic Circle, close to Kuusamo airport and the Russian border; Pyhä, 150km north-east of Rovaniemi; and Iso-Syöte, Finland's southernmost fell region. These are covered in our resort directory at the back of the book.

653

UK PACKAGES
Ylläs Inghams, Inntravel, Skiworld
Levi Inghams, Skiworld

Phone numbers
From abroad use the prefix +358 and omit the initial '0' of the phone number

KEY FACTS	
Resort	255m
	840ft
Slopes	255-715m
	840-2,350ft
Lifts	29
Pistes	53km
Snow-guns	40 guns

TOURIST OFFICE

www.yllas.fi

Ylläs

➕ Best for novices and Nordic fans
➕ Few queues and reliable late snow

➖ Slopes a bus ride from the villages
➖ Bars and restaurants not a highlight

Ylläs is Finland's largest resort; it's a quiet family area with an increasing choice of accommodation dotted around its two villages.

Ylläs mountain has two main bases, both 4km from the mountain. The minor one is Ylläsjärvi near the Sport Resort Ylläs base; the major one is Äkäslompolo near the Ylläs-Ski base. Development is taking place at both, and closer to the slopes too.

It is Finland's largest downhill ski area – but still has only 53km of pistes on two broad flanks with runs that suit novices best. Second- and third-week skiers will rapidly conquer the benign black runs. Grooming is 'good'. Past reports of the ski school have been positive. And there's a mountain-top restaurant.

The area has 330km of cross-country trails, 38km of which are floodlit, transforming it from awkward sprawl to doorstep ski resort of limitless scope. There are also 15 cafes along the tracks. From the lift base trails fan out around the mountain, across the frozen lake and away through the endless forest.

The Äkäs cabins at Äkäslompolo have been recommended, as has the 'comfortable' Saaga hotel at Sport Resort Ylläs, which has 'gym, pool, kids' pool, sauna, steam and hot tub and a useful drying cabinet in the bedrooms'.

Eating out is slowly improving, with four restaurants at the Taiga base (Sport Resort Ylläs) opening a few seasons ago. These include a pizzeria. Established favourites in town include more upmarket Poro for traditional fish and meat dishes. Julie's suits families better (pizza and burgers). Tower is new this year at Äkäslompolo.

Off-slope activities include snowmobiling (410km of tracks), dog sledding, reindeer safaris, snowshoeing and ice fishing.

KEY FACTS	
Resort	205m
	670ft
Slopes	205-530m
	670-1,740ft
Lifts	26
Pistes	44km
Snow-guns	20%

TOURIST OFFICE

www.levi.fi

Levi

➕ Lodging convenient for slopes
➕ Airport transfer only 15 to 20 mins

➖ Not ideal for beginners
➖ Can be very windy

Levi's convenience is its key appeal for visitors. There are good hotels and plentiful off-slope diversions too. Midwinter can be bleak on the hill though.

Levi is a small, purpose-built village of hotels, apartments and cabins at the foot of its slopes.

The runs are mostly intermediate (only one green and three black). A gondola and a six-pack take you up from the village base, but apart from another gondola serving the World Cup slope, the other lifts are drags. They can be bleak and exposed in bad weather, but the area usually has a long season. Seventeen slopes have snowmaking, which was increased this year with more planned for 2013/14, and 17 are floodlit. The main terrain park is 'excellent' with boxes, rails, a spine, plus big and small lines, half-pipe and super-pipe. There are several mountain restaurants (including the Okta in the Panorama hotel). Cross-country trails total 230km. Vilpuri Kids' Land has lifts and tobogganing areas, plus day care.

Levi's biggest hotel is the Spa Levitunturi (016 646301), with a bowling alley and huge spa facility – including 17 pools and nine saunas. The hotel Levi Panorama (336 3000) is at the top of the mountain, reached by gondola. The Sokos hotel (016 3215 500) and the Levilehto apartments (403 120200) have been recommended (though the latter are 'a 10-minute walk to the slopes').

There are dozens of places to eat – King Crab House is new this year. The Hullu Poro (Crazy Reindeer) complex has impressed reporters and has several restaurants including fine dining, traditional Finnish, Asian and a steakhouse – its Reindeer lounge bar was renovated this year. Of the handful of bars, Oliver's Corner is supposedly lively. Off-slope activities include snowmobiling, reindeer and husky safaris, snowshoeing, ice fishing and skating on the frozen lake. You can also visit a reindeer park and a husky park.

Norway

- ➕ One of the best places in Europe for serious cross-country skiing
- ➕ The home of telemark – plenty of opportunities to learn and practise
- ➕ Freedom from the glitz and ill-mannered lift queues of the Alps
- ➕ Impressive terrain parks
- ➕ Usually reliable snow conditions throughout a long season

- ➖ Very limited downhill areas
- ➖ Very basic mountain restaurants
- ➖ Booze is prohibitively taxed
- ➖ Scenery more Pennine than Alpine
- ➖ Après-ski that is either deadly dull or irritatingly rowdy
- ➖ Short daylight hours in midwinter
- ➖ Highly changeable weather
- ➖ Limited off-slope activities

For downhillers who fancy a change from the usual ski-resort glitz, Norway could be just the place. Families with young children, in particular, will have no trouble finding junk food to please the kids – the mountain restaurants serve little else. For us, any one of our first three ➖ points is reason to pause. Add together all the negatives, and you can count us out. One fan, scraping his personal barrel, pointed out that he can be in Lillehammer four hours after taking off from Edinburgh. Four hours after taking off from Gatwick, we can be in Megève or Chamonix. Hmmm, tricky call ...

This year we detect a small surge of interest in Norway in the UK travel trade, with more tour operators entering the fray in several resorts.

There is a traditional friendship between Norway and Britain, and English is widely spoken.

For the Norwegians and Swedes, skiing is a weekend rather than a special holiday activity, and not an occasion for extravagance. So at lunchtime they haul sandwiches out of their backpacks as we might while walking the Pennine Way, and in the evening they cook in their apartments. Don't expect tempting restaurants.

The Norwegians have a problem with alcohol. Walk into an après-ski bar at 5pm on a Saturday and you may find young men already inebriated. And this is despite incredibly high taxes on booze. Restaurant prices for wine are ludicrous, and shop prices may be irrelevant – Hemsedal has no liquor store. Other prices are generally not high by Alpine standards.

Cross-country skiing comes as naturally to Norwegians as walking; and even if you're not very keen, the fact that cross-country is normal, and not a wimp's alternative to 'real' skiing, gives Norway a special appeal. Here, cross-country is both a way of getting about the valleys and a way of exploring the hills. What distinguishes

Norway for the keen cross-country skier is the network of long trails across the gentle uplands, with refuges along the way where backpackers can pause for refreshment or stay overnight. More and more Norwegians are taking to telemarking, and snowboarding is very popular – local youths fill the impressive terrain parks at weekends. For downhill skiing, the country isn't nearly so attractive. Despite the fact that it is able to hold downhill races, Norway's Alpine areas are of limited appeal. The most rewarding resort is Hemsedal, covered on the next page.

The other downhill resorts most widely known are Geilo and Voss, on the railway line from Bergen to Oslo. Tryvann is just 20 minutes from the centre of Oslo, on a spur of the underground system, and popular with the locals. Lillehammer is well known too, of course – host of the 1994 Olympics; but it's a lakeside town not a downhill ski resort (the Alpine races were held some distance away). Other main resorts are Trysil, on the border with Sweden, Beitostølen in the Jotunheimen National Park, and Oppdal. All are covered in the directory at the back of the book.

KEY FACTS

Resort	640m
	2,100ft
Slopes	670-1450m
	2,200-4,760ft
Lifts	24
Pistes	47km
Snow-guns	45%

NEWS

2013/14: The first stage of a new development on the slopes – shops and restaurants – is to open. There will be three terrain parks, plus a park just for kids.

2012/13: Lift opening was extended by an hour. Accommodation at Skarsnuten was linked to the slopes by new paths.

UK PACKAGES

Crystal, Crystal Finest, Ski Safari, Thomson

Phone numbers
From abroad use the prefix +47

TOURIST OFFICE

www.hemsedal.com
www.skistar.com/hemsedal

HEMSEDAL.COM/NILS-ERIK BJØRHOLT

There's a lot of telemarking goes on, but it's not obligatory
↓

Hemsedal

+ Convenient slope-side lodging
+ Some quite challenging slopes
+ Excellent children's nursery slopes

– Not much of a village
– Weekend queues
– Exposed upper mountain

Hemsedal is both an unspoiled valley and a village, the latter also referred to as Trøym and Sentrum ('Centre') – but you can also stay at the lift base or higher up in the slopes, a mile or so away.

Hemsedal is a three-hour drive from Oslo and geared mainly to weekenders arriving by car or coach. But there is a ski-bus linking all parts and floodlit paths to/from the centre. The lift pass also covers smaller Solheisen, up the valley. Geilo is an hour away.

Sentrum is a bus ride from the slopes and little more than a small area of low-rise apartments/hotels, shops, a garage, a bank and a couple of cashpoints. There's a developing area of lodgings close to the base. You can also stay further up the hill where there are several areas of more or less ski-in/ski-out lodgings.

Hemsedal's slopes pack a lot of variety into a small space. Fast lifts serve a high proportion of the slopes, though a few awkward drags remain. There can be weekend crowds and queues for the main access lifts. Otherwise it is quiet. A third park is being added to the two good existing parks, the mini park for kids and the boardercross. Snowmaking covers 45% of the slopes. There is quite a bit to amuse experts: several black pistes and wide areas of gentler off-piste terrain served by drags. Mileage-hungry piste-bashers will find Hemsedal's runs very limited. There are quite a few red and blue runs to play on, and splendid long green runs

– but they get a lot of traffic. There is floodlit skiing several nights a week. Beginners have a separate, gentle nursery area. The resort caters well for families, with day care offered for children aged six months to eight years; the kids' nursery slopes at the lift base are now very well developed.

There are 120km of prepared cross-country trails in the valley and forest, and (in late season) 90km at altitude.

The best hotel is the Skogstad (320 55000) in Sentrum – comfortable, with a spa; but its bar and nightclub may be noisy at weekends. The hotel Skarsnuten (320 61700), on the hill, is stylishly modern. But apartments dominate. The chalet-style Alpin Lodge by the nursery slopes includes 30 apartments, restaurants and shops.

The dining choices are OK; the Big Horn at Fjellandsby is a popular steakhouse, and there's the Lodgen bar and restaurant (Mediterranean cuisine) at the Alpin Lodge; plus more places in town.

Après-ski starts at the Skistua (Skisenter), which also has live music at the weekends. The bars and clubs get rowdy at weekends and holidays, but can be very quiet midweek.

Off-slope diversions include bowling, tobogganing, dog sledding, ice climbing and snowmobiling.

Sweden

+ Snow-sure from December to May
+ Unspoiled, beautiful landscape
+ Uncrowded pistes and lifts
+ Super Nordic and off-slope activities

- Limited challenging downhill terrain
- Small areas by Alpine standards
- Lacks dramatic Alpine scenery
- Short days during the early season

Sweden appeals most to those who want an all-round winter holiday in a different environment and culture. Standards of accommodation, food and service are good, and the people are welcoming, lively and friendly, but most of the downhill areas are limited in size and challenge.

Holidaying in Sweden is a completely different experience from a holiday in the Alps. Although virtually everyone speaks good English, menus and signs are often written only in Swedish. The food is delightful, especially if you like fish and venison. And resorts are very family-friendly. It is significantly cheaper than neighbouring Norway, but reporters still complain that eating and drinking is very expensive.

Days are very short in early season. But from early February the lifts usually work from 9am to 4.30pm and by March it is light until 8.30pm. Most resorts have some floodlit pistes.

On the downside, downhill slopes are limited in both challenge and extent, and the lift systems are dominated by T-bars. There's lots of cross-country and backcountry skiing.

Après-ski is taken very seriously – with live bands from mid- to late afternoon. There is plenty to do off the slopes: snowmobile safaris, ice fishing, dog-sled rides, ice climbing, saunas galore and visiting local Sami villages.

The main resort is Åre, described below. Others include Sälen (big but fragmented) and Vemdalen. These two, plus Riksgränsen, Björkliden (both above the Arctic Circle) and tiny Ramundberget are covered in our directory at the back of the book.

KEY FACTS

Resort	380m
	1,250ft
Slopes	380-1275m
	1,250-4,180ft
Lifts	47
Pistes	100km
Snow-guns	70%

UK PACKAGES
Neilson, Ski Safari

TOURIST OFFICE
www.skistar.com

Åre

+ Good for intermediates and novices
+ Excellent children's facilities

- High winds can affect snow and lifts
- Few expert challenges

Sweden's biggest ski area, with lots to do off the slopes as well as on. Not great for keen skiers but good for families wanting a change from the Alps.

The centre of this small lakeside town has old, pretty, coloured wooden buildings and some larger modern additions. Lodgings are spread out along the valley.

There are two separate areas of slopes linked by a ski-bus. The main area has fast lifts to the top (including a funicular, gondola, chondola, cable car, and from 2013/14 three six-packs). A fast chair accesses the separate Duved area with a new quad replacing a T-bar for 2013/14. But nearly all other lifts are drags. Queues are rare.

The slopes offer mainly beginner and intermediate tree-lined terrain, with two windswept bowls above that are prone to closure. Experts will find the slopes limited, especially if the high bowls are closed. But there is a lot of off-piste. For intermediates there are steep, sometimes icy, black and red runs back to town, and lots of pretty blue runs through the trees. You get a real sense of travelling around on the main area. Beginners have good facilities in both sectors. There are three terrain parks and 58km of groomed cross-country trails. The ski school has a good reputation, and children have special areas. Kids under seven get free lift passes if wearing helmets. Mountain huts are good.

The best central hotel is the charming old Diplomat Åregården. There are ample apartments and cabins. And you can spend the night in an igloo up the mountain. There are lots of restaurants, from Japanese to pizza. Après-ski is lively, with the Tott, Fjällgården and Åregården busy from 3pm. Off-slope diversions are plentiful.

Bulgaria

RPI	55
lift pass	£140
ski hire	£45
lessons	£40
food & drink	£70
total	£295

+ Costs very low by Alpine standards
+ Good ski schools
+ Lively bars and nightlife

- Poor snow record, though snowmaking has been improved
- Small ski areas
- Cheap booze attracts 18–30 crowds

Bulgaria best suits novices and early intermediates looking for a jolly time at bargain-basement prices. Bansko's arrival on the scene in 2004 raised the bar for the country's other main resorts, which are now starting to catch up.

Bulgaria has traditionally been a place for a cheap and cheerful holiday. It is well worth considering if you are a beginner or early intermediate on a budget and want a lively time, fuelled by cheap booze. Don't expect sophistication or big ski areas. A keen piste-basher could ski even the biggest resort in a matter of hours.

But the ski schools have an excellent reputation. And Bansko has some good hotels and a modern lift system. Even Pamporovo now has a six-pack. The scenery and culture provide a very different holiday experience from the Alps.

KEY FACTS

Resort	1300m
	4,270ft
Slopes	1300-2560m
	4,270-8,400ft
Lifts	12
Pistes	58km
Snow-guns	75 guns

TOURIST OFFICE

www.borovets-bg.com

UK PACKAGES

Borovets Balkan Holidays, Crystal, Independent Ski Links, Neilson, Skitracer, Thomson
Bansko Balkan Holidays, Crystal, Neilson, Skitracer, Thomson
Pamporovo Balkan Holidays, Crystal, Independent Ski Links, Skitracer, Thomson

Borovets

+ Lively, convenient village
+ Some good intermediate slopes

- Not ideal for beginners
- Nightlife can be tacky

Borovets is a mixture of large, modern hotels and small bars, clubs and restaurants. The slopes suit intermediates best.

Most people come here on packages and stay in big hotels with their own bars, restaurants and shops within them. There is also a large selection of quirkier and lively small bars, shops and eating places lining 'The Strip', as a 2012 reporter describes the 300m long street, counting 'at least 26'. He goes on: 'There must be over 40 if you include the back streets. Borovets is now the Benidorm of skiing, with touts outside most bars trying to get you in; it's a shanty-town mix of wooden huts plus big hotels.' And a 2011 reporter complained of 'dogs roaming the streets'. Nevertheless, the resort's beautiful woodland setting gives a degree of Alpine-style charm.

A long, slow gondola rises over 1000m in 25 minutes to reach both the short, easy slopes of Markoudjika and the longer, steepish Yastrebets pistes. The runs are best for good intermediates, and include some longish reds. The resort is not ideal for novices: nursery slopes are crowded, and the step from easy blues to testing reds is a big one. There is night skiing and 35km of cross-country.

Queues form for the gondola at peak times ('45 minutes', says a recent reporter) and for the nursery draglifts. The gondola is also said to be prone to closure by wind. Grooming is erratic. The ski schools are praised – a 2012 reader says of the school attached to the Samokov Hotel: 'I progressed from complete beginner to red runs in a week; my instructor regularly spent more than the allotted time with the group.'

Most reporters stay at the Samokov or the Rila: noise can be a problem at the latter, say reporters; and a 2012 guest found the latter 'a good basic hotel but a bit tired; the self-service buffet meals were always cold'. Recent visitors found the Lion 'clean, tidy, with friendly staff' and thought the villas at the Iglika Palace were 'basic, but quiet and comfortable'. Food shopping is limited.

The Black Cat restaurant has 'good food, service and a lively open fire'. There are plenty of lively bars with 'dancing girls and live music'. Buzz is said to be one of the liveliest, and there's a night club in the Rila hotel. A 2012 reporter recommended Katy's Pub 'with a guitarist in the attic' and Mamacita's Mexican restaurant and bar. There are also 'adult' bars, but they are away from the main streets, and advertising is now said to be banned, though there are plenty of touts.

Tour operator reps organize pub crawls, folklore evenings etc. Excursions to the Rila monastery or to Sofia by coach are interesting.

DAVID MAXWELL-LEES

The Bansko lift system is pretty slick, with lots of fast chairs ↓

Bansko

- ➕ Lots of fast lifts on the mountain
- ➕ Atmospheric town centre
- ➕ Friendly, helpful locals
- ➖ Long, queue-prone access gondola
- ➖ Few off-slope diversions
- ➖ Some unfinished buildings evident

Bansko is an old valley town in the scenic Pirin National Park, catapulted into the 21st century in 2004 by the construction of modern lifts and smart lodgings. Reporters like what they find, and some go back repeatedly.

The area near the base of the access gondola to the slopes has a lot of modern hotels, apartments, bars and restaurants. Some are ski-in, and many others run shuttle-buses to the lift.

The older part of town looks no great beauty on the outskirts, but the central square reveals a quiet and charming heart, and there are few outward signs of commercial tourism.

The slopes are reached by an eight-seat gondola to Bunderishka, for which there are long queues in the morning ('can take hours'). Some people start queuing well before the lift opens. An alternative is to pay for a VIP card, we're told. A planned

additional gondola is on hold. Queues further up the hill are rare.

There is an easy blue piste back to the town, with snowmaking and floodlighting. Most lifts are fast chairs, and successive ones take you up mainly north-facing slopes to the high point of the area. You can ski down reds or blues to Shiligarnika, or a red followed by the Tomba black to Bunderishka. Some of these are quite long and challenging. Reporters judge the piste classification accurate. A reporter notes that small variations on the pistes and skiable trees beside them make the area add up to more skiing than you might expect. There is

Bulgaria

There are mountain restaurants, but the food is rather basic →
DAVID MAXWELL-LEES

a small terrain park.

The nursery slopes near the top of the gondola are good, with little through-traffic. The main school – Ulen – is 'excellent', says a 2013 visitor. Children have a snow garden, and the kindergarten takes infants.

Reporters find the grooming good, but a 2012 visitor complains about lack of piste marker poles. Snow is more reliable than the Bulgarian norm.

Mountain huts are mostly self-service, and the food 'basic'. A 2012 reporter advises: 'The lift company runs all the on-piste places, but a short stroll through the woods will take you to independent hotels with good-value fresh food.'

Hotels near the gondola station (the obvious place to stay) include the swanky Florimont with its own casino; the 5-star Kempinski Grand Arena ('spa to die for') – its Tepanyaki Japanese restaurant is 'a special experience'; and the MPM Sport ('spacious, with a good spa'). The Emerald has 'superb rooms, friendly staff and tasty, hot food'. The Lion has 'spacious, spotlessly clean rooms and a pool, steam and sauna'.

There are some smart bars near the lift. Staying there, you are a short taxi-ride from the town and its many mehanas (traditional inns) with roaring fires, real Bulgarian food and good wine. And there are lots of lively bars – readers' tips include Harry's bar behind the Victoria restaurant ('a good buzz'), the Flora in the Emerald hotel ('happy hour from noon till midnight with two-for-one drinks; open till 5am'), Diamonds and Amigos.

Other activities include paragliding, skating, snowmobiling and bowling.

KEY FACTS

Resort	1650m
	5,410ft
Slopes	1450-1935m
	4,760-6,350ft
Lifts	15
Pistes	37km
Snow-guns	90%

TOURIST OFFICE
www.
pamporovoresort.com

Pamporovo

+ Pretty, tree-lined slopes
+ Good, low-cost choice for novices

- Limited extent and short runs
- Poor piste maintenance

Pamporovo is a purpose-built village, in a pretty woodland area a short shuttle-bus ride from its easy slopes that suit beginners best.

The resort is strictly for beginners and near-beginners, with mostly easy and short runs. Others will find the limited area rather inadequate. The 37km of slopes are pretty and sheltered, with pistes cutting through pine forest. Some beginners find the runs rather too narrow, and our most recent reporter complained of grooming 'only one day in the week, which made it difficult for beginners'. There's a half-pipe and a decent-sounding terrain park. Snow reliability is poor, but snowmaking covers 90% of the slopes. There are plenty of mountain huts, though they are not enticing.

Past reports have praised the ski schools but we lack recent reports. There are 25km of cross-country trails.

A reporter recommends the hotel Finlandia ('comfortable; friendly staff; plentiful but plain food').

Romania

RPI	45
lift pass	£90
ski hire	£45
lessons	£45
food & drink	£50
total	**£230**

UK PACKAGES

Poiana Brasov Balkan Holidays

Phone numbers
From abroad use the prefix +40 and omit the initial '0' of the phone number

TOURIST OFFICE

www.poiana-brasov.com

Poiana Brasov is set on a prettily wooded plateau ↓

- ➕ Cheap packages, and very low prices on the spot
- ➕ Interesting excursions and friendly local people
- ➕ Good tuition from keen instructors

- ➖ Primitive facilities, especially mountain restaurants and toilets
- ➖ Uninspiring food
- ➖ Very limited slopes

Romania sells mainly on price. On-the-spot prices, in particular, are very low. Provided you don't have unreasonably high expectations, you'll probably come back from Poiana Brasov content. It allows complete beginners to try a ski holiday at the minimum cost, and to have a jolly time in the evenings without adding substantially to that cost.

Romania's main resort – and the only one featuring in any UK package programme – is **Poiana Brasov** (1030m) in the Carpathian mountains. It is a short drive above the city of Brasov, about 120km (on alarmingly rough, slow roads) north-west of the capital and arrival airport, Bucharest.

The resort is purpose-built, and has the air of a spacious, pleasant holiday camp. But it is not designed for the convenience of skiers: some serious-sized hotels are right by the lifts, but most are scattered about a pretty, wooded plateau, served by regular buses and cheap taxis.

The slopes are extremely limited – 24km of pistes in total. They consist of decent intermediate tree-lined runs with a decent vertical of about 825m, roughly following the line of the main cable car and gondola, plus an open nursery area at the top. In 2011/12 four new slopes (two blues and two reds) opened, accessed by a new quad and a six-pack. There are some nursery lifts at village level, which are used when snow permits. Night skiing is also available. The resort gets weekend crowds from Brasov and Bucharest, and queues can result, but during the week there are few problems.

A key part of the resort's appeal is the friendly and effective teaching from enthusiastic instructors.

Hotel standards are higher than you might expect. The linked 3-star Bradul and 4-star Sport hotels (0268 407330) are handy for the lower nursery slopes and for one of the cable cars. Guests in both have use of the Sport's spa facilities. A swanky Radisson hotel with over 180 rooms and smart spa facility is due to open early in 2014.

Après-ski revolves around the hotel bars and nightclubs – plus outings to rustic barns for BBQs with gypsy music and to the bars and restaurants in the nearby town of Brasov. With cheap beer and very cheap spirits on tap, things can be quite lively. Off-slope facilities are limited: there are two good-sized pools (in hotels) and bowling. An excursion to nearby Bran Castle (Count Dracula's lair) is also popular.

Slovenia

RPI	70
lift pass	£140
ski hire	£55
lessons	£75
food & drink	£90
total	**£360**

UK PACKAGES

Kranjska Gora Balkan Holidays, Crystal, Thomson
Bled (for Vogel) Balkan Holidays, Crystal, Thomson

TOURIST OFFICES

www.slovenia.info
Bled
www.bled.si

KRANJSKA GORA TOURIST OFFICE

Kranjska Gora enjoys a pretty and properly Alpine setting ↓

+ Low prices
+ Beautiful, varied scenery
+ Good beginner slopes and lessons

− Limited, mostly easy slopes
− Still lots of slow, antiquated lifts
− Mountain huts not a highlight

Slovenia offers lower prices and fewer crowds than the Alps, attracting economy-minded visitors from neighbouring Italy and Austria as well as Britain and the Netherlands. The ski areas are limited and still a bit antiquated, though making obvious investments. Most suit novices well.

Slovenia – which is bordered by Italy, Austria and Croatia – has 30 or so ski areas, the main ones concentrated in the Julian Alps in the west, dominated by its highest mountain, Mt Triglav; all are small and some are tiny. None is likely to keep the adventurous piste-basher amused for a week; but you can have an enjoyable trip touring by car or by combining several resorts from one base. EasyJet (from Stansted) and Adria (from Gatwick) fly to Ljubljana.

The season is shorter than in the Alps (except at Kanin) and the resorts low. Most slopes are below 2000m.

Prices are low, and there is a positive feel – and a warm and hospitable welcome. Standards of service and accommodation have improved – the hotels may not be particularly attractive, but many are new or modernized, complete with pools, spas and often free Wi-Fi.

Getting around is relatively easy, and most ski areas are within a 40-minute drive of each other on good roads. And the main resorts are within a two-hour bus ride of Ljubljana. Bled, with its beautiful lake and fairly lively nightlife, is an attractive base. It has just one steepish slope. But other resorts nearby include Kranjska Gora and lesser known Krvavec, Kanin, Vogel and Kobla (the only ski area in Slovenia reachable by train).

The other main group of resorts centres on Maribor to the east, a quite different area of low-slung wooded ridges. But it has the biggest ski area in the country at 43km.

The Ski Pass Slovenia covers all resorts in Slovenia.

Most resorts fit best into the intermediate category but differ on their suitability for novices. Experts will find few black runs, but there is good off-piste when conditions permit. Lift systems are improving and queues are rare. Most Slovenians visit at weekends; midweek the slopes can be deserted. A common feature of many areas is an access lift with no runs back to valley level. One drawback for us is the lack of quality lunches: snacks and picnics are the norm, so hearty menus and cute huts are rare. Ski schools are of a high quality and cheap, with good spoken English. Other winter activities are big in Slovenia, too, so there is plenty to do off the slopes.

KEY FACTS

Resort	1450m
	4,760ft
Slopes	1450-1970m
	4,760-6,460ft
Lifts	11
Pistes	30km
Snow-guns	95%

TOURIST OFFICE

www.rtc-krvavec.si

Krvavec

➕ Convenient for short breaks
➕ Quiet slopes midweek
➕ Jolly, family atmosphere

➖ Lacks proper resort base
➖ Short, mainly south-facing runs
➖ Not ideal for novices

Krvavec has been voted Slovenia's best ski area and is just 8km from Ljubljana airport. There's no central village, but then most visitors are locals on day trips from the city.

Krvavec has some of the country's steepest slopes, including five black runs. It is a lively place, especially at weekends. Most visitors are families on day trips. Bled is 40 minutes by daily bus (free with the lift pass). There is no resort, but there is one hotel on the slopes and some lodging in nearby Cerklje. The local lift pass also covers Rogla, near Maribor.

A gondola goes up to the slopes, which span three partly wooded hills from a high point of 1970m. The lifts include a six-pack and a quad; queues are rare. The pistes get a lot of sun, though snowmaking is extensive and grooming good. There's a good nursery slope and children's area, complete with moving carpet, but few easy blues to progress to. The mid-mountain Plaza has picnic spots and snack bars. Kriska Planina is an Alpine-style hut. Snowshoeing is popular, and you can try airboarding and tobogganing – floodlit on Friday and Saturday evenings.

KEY FACTS

Resort	810m
	2,660ft
Slopes	810-1295m
	2,660-4,250ft
Lifts	18
Pistes	20km
Snow-guns	Some

TOURIST OFFICE

www.kr-gora.si

Kranjska Gora

➕ Good for novices and families
➕ Convenient, good, slope-side hotels

➖ Slopes limited in extent, variety, length and vertical
➖ Still some old lifts, and gets busy

Despite limited slopes (most other areas are bigger), Kranjska Gora is offered by more UK tour operators than any other Slovenian resort. It's a good-value, pretty and compact resort that is popular with families. Since the centre is fairly small, most facilities are near the slopes, too.

Kranjska Gora is close to the Austrian and Italian borders. Day trips to ski in resorts over the borders are possible.

The 20km of wide, tree-lined pistes rise to 1295m and best suit very unadventurous intermediates and novices – though there is a World Cup slalom black run. The slopes above Podkoren are quiet and gentle. There are four quads, but still lots of draglifts. And getting around involves tedious traversing. Queues are rare despite busier slopes here. Snow reliability is poor, but snowmaking covers most pistes, and more is planned for 2013/14. There is a terrain park and a children's area with a moving carpet. Cross-country trails total 40km. It is back to base for lunch, but Bedanc is a good self-service beside chair 7.

Hotels are plentiful and of a high standard, most with pools and spas. For slope-side convenience, the Lek, Prisank and Larix are best. The Alpina is popular with families. We liked the Kompas, with good breakfast buffet and pool. For eating out try the Kotnik and Via Napoli (hotel Prisank) pizzerias, and the Ostarija for finer dining. Ice skating, night tobogganing and snowshoeing are popular.

Kanin

KEY FACTS	
Resort	460m
	1,510ft
Slopes	1140-2290m
	3,740-7,510ft
Lifts	9
Pistes	30km
Snow-guns	Some

TOURIST OFFICE

www.boveckanin.si

+ Splendid Dolomite-like scenery
+ High, reliably snow-sure slopes
+ Long runs down Italian side

− More remote than the other areas
− Upper mountain bleak and exposed
− Bovec quiet at night

Adventure capital Bovec has an isolated position in the splendid Soca Valley; its ski area Kanin is a cross-border resort with uncrowded intermediate slopes.

Kanin, linked to Sella Nevea in Italy, is Slovenia's highest ski area, with the biggest vertical (1150m). The link is by a red piste and a jumbo cable car to return. There are 30km of largely intermediate terrain, and a shared lift pass that also covers the Arnoldstein area in Austria. The resort enjoys a long season and reliable snow.

Bovec has an attractive centre, with a few shops, hotels and restaurants. The Kanin hotel is comfortable with a super pool and spa centre. The smaller Mangart is a modern place, with suites and dormitories. There are free ski-buses to the lift station.

A long gondola from the edge of town rises to 2200m, from where chairs (including two quads) and a draglift serve two short, easy blues up top and longer red runs back to the gondola mid-station or towards Italy. Kanin is not ideal for beginners though; the blues are high and exposed. Intermediates have a choice of genuine red runs – the two down to Sella Nevea are north-facing and sheltered, and interrupted only by one chairlift. There are off-piste routes to be explored, though much of the limestone terrain is pitted with hollows and holes that make it hazardous.

Mountain huts are limited. Bovec Sports offers lots of activities, and the Triglav National Park centre (Slovenia's only National Park) is worth a visit.

Vogel

KEY FACTS	
Resort	570m
	1,870ft
Slopes	1535-1800m
	5,040-5,910ft
Lifts	8
Pistes	18km
Snow-guns	None

TOURIST OFFICES

www.vogel.si
www.bohinj.si/kobla

+ Beautiful lake setting, pretty runs
+ Good choice of huts

− Bus ride from most lodging
− Limited in extent and challenge

Vogel overlooks stunning Lake Bohinj, part of the Triglav National Park. It's tiny, but is the main ski area within commuting distance of Bled.

Vogel has the best conditions and prettiest slopes in the area. Buses arrive daily from Bled; but there are small hotels and restaurants near the base and in villages along the lakeside (served by free ski-bus).

The 18km of partly wooded slopes are reached by a cable car up from the valley. A fast quad serves a mid-mountain area, with a single-seat chair to the high point at 1800m (great views). Pistes served by another chair and three drags include a lovely gentle blue. There is a separate nursery slope, a children's area and a terrain park. When conditions permit, a long red run returns to the bottom cable car station via a quiet, pretty valley. Several of the huts are nicer than the Slovenian norm.

For a change of scene Kobla, with 24km of wide, wooded runs, is a short bus ride away at Bohinjska Bistrica – the railway terminus. The 5-star Bohinj Park hotel is eco-friendly, with pool, cinema and bowling. Next door is a huge aqua park. Near Vogel, the 3-star Zlatarog is comfortable.

Maribor-Pohorje

KEY FACTS	
Resort	325m
	1,070ft
Slopes	325-1330m
	1,070-4,360ft
Lifts	21
Pistes	43km
Snow-guns	95%

TOURIST OFFICE

www.maribor-
pohorje.si

+ Good access, close to the city
+ Gentle, sheltered slopes for novices

− Mostly short runs
− Few challenges except the FIS run

Slovenia's second city, Maribor, is 6km from its local slopes – where there's also limited lodging. There's little vertical to be achieved, but some varied terrain.

This is the country's biggest ski area, twice the size of better-known Kranjska Gora.

The lifts include a six-pack and a gondola to Pohorje summit. There's night skiing, and snowmaking covers 95% of the area. There are 27km of cross-country trails. The area lift pass also covers Kranjska Gora. The Pohorje school offers a wide range of classes. There are several atmospheric old inns serving good, Hungarian-influenced food. The 4-star Arena and 3-star Videc hotels are slope-side.

Scotland

- ✚ Easy to get to from northern Britain
- ✚ It is possible to experience perfect snow and very satisfying skiing
- ✚ Decent, cheap accommodation and good-value packages
- ✚ Midweek it's rarely crowded
- ✚ Lots to do off the slopes

- ▬ Weather is extremely changeable and sometimes vicious
- ▬ Snowfall is erratic
- ▬ Slopes limited; runs mainly short
- ▬ Queuing can be a problem
- ▬ Little ski resort ambience and few memorable mountain restaurants

Scottish skiing conditions are unpredictable, to say the least. If you live nearby and can go at short notice when things look good, the several ski areas are a tremendous asset. But booking a holiday here as a replacement for your usual week in the Alps is just too risky.

Most of the slopes in most of the areas suit intermediates best. But all apart from The Lecht also offer one or two tough or very tough slopes.

For novices who are really keen to learn, Scotland could make sense, especially if you live nearby. You can book instruction via one of the excellent outdoor centres, many of which also provide accommodation. The ski schools at the resorts themselves are also very good.

Snowboarding is popular, and all of the resorts have some special terrain features, but maintaining these facilities in good nick is problematic. When the conditions are right, the natural terrain is good for freeriding.

CairnGorm Mountain is the best-known resort, with 11 lifts and 30km of runs. Aviemore is the main centre (with a shuttle-bus to the slopes) – the 'friendly' Dunroamin Guest House is praised this year. The slopes are accessed by a funicular from the main car park up to Ptarmigan at 1100m.

Nevis Range is the highest Scottish resort, with slopes reaching 1190m. It has 11 lifts plus a long six-seat access gondola. The 20km of groomed runs are on the north-facing slopes of Aonach Mor. There are many B&Bs and hotels in and around Fort William, 10 minutes away by bus.

Glenshee is the largest ski area, with 40km of runs spread out over three minor parallel valleys served by 23 lifts. It has some natural quarter-pipes. In 2012/13 a new double chairlift opened to access the Cairnwell cafe and the slopes in that area. Glenshee is primarily a venue for day-trippers, though there are hotels, hostels and B&Bs in the area.

Glencoe is one well-travelled reporter's 'favourite resort for scenery'. Its seven lifts and 20km of runs lie east of moody Glen Coe itself. A double chairlift and a drag up to the main slopes, including the nursery area. There are freeriding opportunities and a challenging descent on Flypaper, the resort's steepest run. 'Great-value, cosy' cafe at the base. The isolated Kings House Hotel is 2km away.

The Lecht is largely a novices' area, with 13 lifts and 20km of runs on the gentle slopes beside a high pass, with a series of parallel lifts and runs above the car parks. With a maximum vertical of only 200m, runs are short. There's extensive snowmaking, a terrain park, and a day lodge at the base. The village of Tomintoul is 10km away.

FURTHER INFORMATION

The VisitScotland organization runs an excellent website at: ski.visitscotland.com

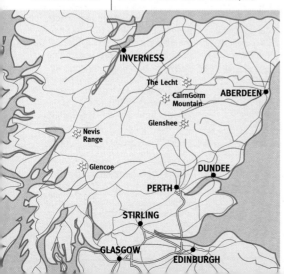

INVERNESS

The Lecht

CairnGorm Mountain   ABERDEEN

Glenshee

Nevis Range

Glencoe   DUNDEE

PERTH

STIRLING

GLASGOW   EDINBURGH

Japan

- ➕ Reliable deep powder snow in Hokkaido resorts, lift-served
- ➕ Fabulous food
- ➕ Polite and gracious locals
- ➕ Night skiing is the norm, allowing a long ski day if you want one

- ➖ Pricey and lengthy trip; 6,000 miles and 24 hours door to door
- ➖ Lack of off-slope diversions
- ➖ Snowfall can go on for weeks in Hokkaido resorts
- ➖ Main hotels vast, modern, charmless

Although it is roughly the same size as the British Isles, Japan has hundreds of ski resorts. And places on the northern island of Hokkaido have developed something like cult status with keen skiers and riders from Australia. The reason is simple: humongous, frequent and reliable falls of powder snow.

You fly in to Sapporo (about three hours by bus to the resorts), via Tokyo or Osaka. Ski Independence says a week in Niseko and a two-night stopover in Tokyo on the way home would cost around £2,300.

Few of the locals speak English but we were struck by how friendly, charming, polite and helpful they all were. The food is delicious – and the menus often have photos to help you.

Hokkaido has a well-deserved reputation for powder snow, which usually falls almost constantly from December to the end of February. Skiing waist-deep powder is normally an everyday occurrence. You go for that, not for the piste skiing. The slopes are not steep and some people are disappointed by that; but there is tremendous skiing among nicely spaced trees. And there are surprisingly different attitudes to skiing off-piste in the different resorts. In Niseko it is allowed except in two dangerous areas and there are also gates into the backcountry. In Rusutsu there are signs everywhere (in English as well as Japanese) saying off-piste is prohibited – but the authorities turn a blind eye to it and nearly everyone skis off-piste in the trees. In Furano there are signs saying it is prohibited (except in a special Premium Zone) and we hear that it is strictly policed and offenders can be arrested.

On our 2013 visit we were unlucky with the weather – it was warm and either foggy or windy most of the time. That meant avalanche danger was high and so out-of-bounds skiing was out of the question most of the time. But nearly all reporters have been luckier. Getting the most out of the off-piste means hiring a guide. We used Hokkaido Powder Guides one day when we were in Furano – we went to the tiny resort of Kamui and they found us the legendary waist deep powder at last. And a 2013 reporter in Niseko was very happy with Black Diamond Tours.

Niseko is made up of three areas of slopes – Grand Hirafu (Hirafu and Hanazono), Annupuri and Niseko Village. All except Hanazono open until

UK PACKAGES
Niseko Crystal, Crystal Finest, James Orr Heliski, Mountain Tracks, Oxford Ski Co, Ski Independence, Ski Safari, Skitracer, Skiworld
Rusutsu Crystal, Ski Independence, Ski Safari, Skitracer
Furano Ski Independence, Ski Safari, Skiworld
Hakuba Ski Safari, Skiworld

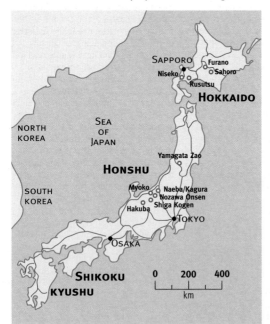

← There are lots of resorts on the main island of Honshu – only the better-known ones are shown on our map. But the best snow is on Hokkaido

Tree skiing is a highlight and allowed here in Niseko but not in some other Japanese resorts →
TANYA BOOTH

More information
To really get to grips with the resorts on offer in Japan, spend some time delving into this site:
www.snowjapan.com

8pm or 8.30 thanks to one of the world's largest – and most heavily used – night skiing operations. The three are linked, but not as efficiently as you might wish. There are some modern lifts, but also lots of old chairs – including three ancient singles.

The biggest and most popular area, Grand Hirafu, has an eight-seat gondola from the base and a smart day lodge and restaurant.

There are modern rather isolated ski-in/ski-out hotels (but little else) at the Annupuri and Niseko Village bases. We (and a reporter) stayed happily at the Green Leaf in Niseko Village in 2013 – lovely onsen (see below), good buffet food, friendly staff. The Hilton Niseko Village has spectacular views from most rooms and its own onsen.

Or you can stay in the little town of Hirafu which has varied architecture – ancient and modern; a bit ramshackle but with a very friendly feel with lots of small bars and restaurants serving excellent traditional Japanese food as well as burgers and the like, many quite lively and busy. A reader enjoyed the Hao Hao ramen house. We enjoyed the almost entirely Tamashii bar – full of Australians, with music, dancing, pool and dartboards. There are some good modern apartments alongside traditional pensions and lodges. Beware of the pavements – they were icy and treacherous when we were there and reporters warn of them.

Free shuttle-buses run between the lift bases every 40 minutes, but they were oversubscribed on our visit and they stop at 8.30pm. Taxis from Hirafu to Niseko Village cost 3,000 yen.

Rusutsu is about half an hour from Niseko, and makes a viable day trip. The slopes, over three interlinked mountains, are slightly more limited but have a much better lift system (four gondolas and seven fast chairs). The snow here can be as good as in Niseko (though it doesn't fall in quite the same quantity), and it doesn't get tracked out so quickly. But they blast out pop music from speakers on the lift pylons which spoils the charm of the surroundings. The vast Rusutsu Resort Hotel complex is the only place to stay and is quite bizarre to western eyes – with a huge summer roller coaster and big wheel outside. Inside there are surreal touches such as life-size dummies playing jazz and a huge carousel for kids to ride. None of the bars open till 5pm so there is a distinct lack of après-ski. There's a wide choice of restaurants serving good Japanese food.

Furano offers a tad more vertical than Niseko, over two linked sectors, but the ski area is half the size, the slopes are easy and there are a lot of old lifts. It is four to five hours from Niseko and Rusutsu, so not within day-trip range. But you can visit other nearby resorts such as Kamui and also go with a guided group to the lift-served but ungroomed Asahidake mountain (a live volcano, around an hour away). The New Furano Prince is a vast modern, isolated hotel at the foot of the slopes and a 10-minute bus ride from town.

The largest ski area in Japan is on the main island of Honshu: **Shiga Kogen**, comprising 21 interlinked resorts and a huge diversity of terrain. It was the site of several major events in the 1998 Winter Olympics. **Hakuba** is a group of nine resorts accessing more than 200 runs.

THE ONSEN EXPERIENCE

Onsen are complexes of hot baths to soak in, showers and communal volcanic thermal pools; they are a key part of Japanese culture and a major part of après-ski. All onsen are basically set up in the same way: men and women shower and bathe in their separate areas. Then, if they wish, they can congregate to soak and have a drink in a communal thermal pool, which more often than not will be outside and surrounded by snow.

REFERENCE SECTION

SKI BUSINESSES

This is a list of ski businesses including all the holiday operators and ski travel agents we know about.

247 Recruit
Ski jobs and training directory
Tel 08452 247 450

360 Sun and Ski
Family holidays in Les Carroz, French Alps
Tel +33 450 903180

Absolute Alps Holidays
Catered chalet in Châtel
Tel 0844 774 0608

Absolutely Snow
Holidays to France, Andorra and Norway
Tel 01244 439801

Action Outdoor Holidays
All-inclusive holidays in the French Alps
Tel 0845 890 0362

ActivityBreaks.com
Flexible breaks and group specials
Tel 028 9140 4080

Adventure Base Ltd
Accommodation in Morzine, Méribel and Chamonix
Tel 0845 527 5612

L'Aiglon de Morzine
Apartments in Morzine

Alpine Action
Catered chalets in Méribel and La Tania
Tel 01273 466535

Alpine Answers
Ski travel agent + tailor-made holidays
Tel 020 7801 1080

Alpine Club
Chalets in St-Martin-de-Belleville
Tel +33 778 845710

Alpine Elements
Holidays in France and Austria
Tel 020 3642 3431

Alpine Encounters
Chalet hotel in Morzine
Tel +33 450 790842

Alpine Guru
Chalets and hotel agency
Tel 0203 004 8750

Alpine Inspirations
Self-catered chalets in Les Gets
Tel 0845 474 7901

Alpine Life
Catered chalet in Saas-Fee
Tel 07801 982645

Alpine Weekends Ltd
Weekends in the Alps
Tel 020 8944 9762

Alps Accommodation
Accommodation in Samoëns and Morillon
Tel +33 450 985056

Alpsholiday
Farmhouse apartments in Serre-Chevalier
Tel +33 492 204426

Altitude Holidays
Ski travel agent
Tel 01243 781019

AmeriCan Ski
North America specialist plus France
Tel 01892 779900

American Ski Classics
Holidays in major North American resorts
Tel 020 8607 9988

Ardmore Educational Travel
Group and school trips
Tel 01628 826699

Avery Crest
Luxury catered chalets in Méribel
Tel 07518 582147

Balkan Holidays
Bulgaria, Slovenia and Romania holidays
Tel 0845 130 1114

Belvedere Travel
Catered chalets in Méribel and self-catered in Verbier
Tel 01264 738257

Bigfoot Chamonix
Holidays in the Chamonix Valley
Tel 0870 300 5874

Borderline
Apartments, chalets and hotels in Barèges
Tel +33 562 926895

Boutique Chalet Company
Chalet in Morzine
Tel 020 3582 6409

Bramble Ski
Chalets in Verbier, Villars and St Anton
Tel 020 7060 0824

CanadaTravelSpecialists.com
Canadian holiday specialist
Tel 0808 256 2609

Canadian Affair
Flights and holidays in Canada
Tel 020 7616 9999

Canadian Powder Tours Chalet Holidays
Chalet holidays in Western Canada
Tel +1 250 423 3019

Carrier
Upmarket chalets and hotels in the Alps, the USA and Canada
Tel 0161 491 7670

Catered Ski Chalets
Ski travel agent
Tel 020 3080 0202

Chalet Bezière
Chalet in Samoëns
Tel +33 450 905181

ChaletBook Limited
Accommodation agency in the Portes du Soleil
Tel 0845 680 6802

Chalet Chez Bear
Chalet in Serre-Chevalier
Tel 00 33 614 384794

Chalet Chocolat
Self-catered chalet in Morzine
Tel 01872 580814

The Chalet Collection
Agent for chalet holidays in the French and Swiss Alps
Tel 020 8144 8102

Chalet Le Dragon
Chalet in La Chapelle d'Abondance
Tel +33 450 172913

Chalet Entre Deux Eaux
Chalet in Morzine
Tel +33 450 37 47 55

Chalet Espen
Chalet in Engelberg
Tel +41 41 637 2220

Chaletfinder.co.uk
Ski travel agent
Tel 0161 408 0441

Chalet la Forêt
Self-catered chalet in Chamonix
Tel 07545 575277

The Chalet Group
Agent for owner-run chalets in Europe

Chalet Kiana
Self-catered chalet in Les Contamines
Tel 07968 123470

Chalet One
Catered chalet in Ste-Foy
Tel 07899 911855

Chamonix.uk.com
Apartment holidays in central Chamonix
Tel 01224 641559

Le Chardon Mountain Lodges Val d'Isère
Luxury chalets in a private hamlet in Val d'Isère
Tel 0131 209 7969

Chez Michelle
Self-catering apartment in Samoëns
Tel 01372 456463

Chez Serre Chevalier
Flexible chalet, apartment and hotel trips to Serre-Chevalier
Tel 020 8144 1351

Chill Chalet
Chalet in Bourg-St-Maurice (Paradiski)
Tel 020 8144 2287

Classic Ski Limited
Holidays for 'mature' skiers/ beginners
Tel 01590 623400

Club Europe Schools Skiing
Schools trips to Europe
Tel 0800 496 4996

Club Med
All-inclusive holidays in 'ski villages'
Tel 0845 367 0670

Cold Comforts Lodging
Whistler specialist
Tel 0800 881 8429

Collett's Mountain Holidays
Holidays in the Dolomites
Tel 01799 513331

Collineige
Chamonix valley specialist
Tel 01483 579242

Connick Ski
Chalet with in-house ski school in Châtel
Tel +33 450 732212

Consensio Holidays
Luxury chalets in the Trois Vallées, Val d'Isère, Les Gets
Tel 020 3393 0833

Contiki Holidays
Holidays for 18–35s
Tel 0845 075 0990

The Corporate Ski Company
Event management company
Tel 020 8542 8100

Cosmos
Holidays in Europe
Tel 0971 902 5838

Crystal Ski
Major mainstream operator
Tel 0871 231 2256

Crystal Finest
Ski holidays to Europe and North America
Tel 0871 971 0364

Directski.com
Holidays in Europe
Tel 0800 358 0448

Elegant Resorts
Luxury ski holidays
Tel 01244 897333

Elevation Holidays
Holidays in the Austrian Alps
Tel 01622 370570

Elysian Collection
Luxury chalets in Zermatt and Klosters
Tel +353 1 524 1314

Erna Low
Self-catering apartments in the Alps
Tel 0845 863 0525

Esprit Ski
Families specialist in Europe
Tel 01483 791900

EurekaSki Ltd
Chalet and apartment agent in Serre-Chevalier and La Grave
Tel +33 679 462484

Exodus
Cross-country skiing holidays
Tel 0845 869 9170

Family Friendly Skiing
Family specialist in La Tania – in-house nannies
Tel +33 450 327121

Family Ski Company
Family skiing holidays in France
Tel 01684 540333

Ferme de Montagne
Chalet hotel in Les Gets
Tel 0844 669 8652

Flexiski
Weekends and corporate events in Europe
Tel 020 8939 0864

Friendship Travel
Holidays for singles 25 to 60
Tel 0871 200 2035

Frontier Ski
Holidays in Canada and the USA
Tel 020 8776 8709

Go Montgenevre
Holidays in Montgenèvre
Tel +33 688 358473

Headwater Holidays
Cross-country skiing holidays
Tel 0845 527 7061

High Mountain Holidays
Holidays in Chamonix
Tel 01993 775540

Holiday in Alps
Self-catered accommodation in St Gervais and Les Contamines
Tel 01327 828239

Host Savoie
Catered chalets and apartments in Morzine
Tel 07714 508395

Hugski Holidays
Catered chalet in Les Gets
Tel 07738 550151

Huski
Catered and self-catered chalet holidays in Chamonix
Tel 0800 520 0935

Ice and Fire
Catered chalets in La Plagne (Paradiski)
Tel 07855 717997

Ifyouski.com
Ski travel agent
Tel 020 7471 7733

Iglu.com
Ski travel agent
Tel 020 8542 6658

Independent Ski Links
Ski tour op and travel agent
Tel 01964 533905

I Need Snow
Ski travel agent
Tel 020 8123 7817

Inghams
Major mainstream operator
Tel 01483 791111

Inntravel
Mainly cross-country skiing and snowshoeing trips
Tel 01653 617920

Inspired to Ski
Holidays with tuition in France and Italy
Tel 020 8133 4131

Interactive Resorts
Agent specializing in catered chalets worldwide
Tel 020 3080 0200

Interhome
Self-catered apartment and chalet rentals in Europe
Tel 020 8877 6370

Interski
Family/group holidays with tuition in the Aosta valley
Tel 01623 456333

Jagged Horizons
Corporate trips to the Alps
Tel 020 8123 7817

James Orr Heliski
Heliskiing packages in Canada, Alaska, Italy and Japan
Tel 01799 516964

Jeffersons Private Jet Holidays
Luxury holidays by private jet
Tel 020 8746 2496

Just Skiing
Courmayeur specialist plus La Thuile
Tel 01202 479988

Kaluma Ski
Tailor made corporate and private holidays in the Alps
Tel 01730 260263

Kwik Travel
Ski travel agent
Tel 0800 655 6518

Lagrange Holidays
Accommodation only, self-drive and rail packages primarily to France
Tel 020 7371 6111

Le Ski
Chalets in Courchevel, Val d'Isère and La Tania
Tel 01484 548996

Ski businesses

669

Build your own shortlist: **www.wheretoskiandsnowboard.com**

Live the Season
Seasonal and long-term holiday accommodation in Europe and Canada
Tel 0203 286 5959

Livigno Snow Holidays
Holidays to Livigno
Tel +39 340 393 5474

Luxury Chalet Collection
Luxury chalets in the Alps
Tel 01993 899429

Mark Warner
Chalet hotel holidays in big-name resorts
Tel 0844 273 6777

Marmotte Mountain Adventure
Chalets in Chamonix Valley
Tel +33 682 891523

Meriski
Chalet specialist in Méribel
Tel 01285 648518

MGS Ski Limited
Hotel and apartments in Val Cenis
Tel 01603 742842

Momentum Ski
Specialists in ski weekends and tailor-made holidays
Tel 020 7371 9111

Mountain Exposure
Chalets and apartments in Saas Fee and Zermatt
Tel 0845 425 2001

Mountain Beds
Accommodation agents and Verbier specialists
Tel 01502 471960

Mountain Heaven
Catered and self-catered accommodation in France and Switzerland
Tel 0151 625 1921

Mountain Lodge
Chalet hotel in Les Crosets, Portes du Soleil
Tel 0845 127 1750

Mountain Lodge Adventures
Chalet in St-Martin-de-Belleville
Tel +33 479 817718

Mountainsun Ltd
Chalets in Europe – short breaks and week-long trips
Tel 01273 257008

Mountain Tracks
Off-piste, hut-to-hut touring and avalanche awareness
Tel 020 8123 2978

Mountain Wave Travel
Ski packages and accommodation
Tel 01964 550741

Neilson
Major mainstream operator
Tel 0845 070 3460

Nick Ski
Catered chalet in La Tania
Tel +33 673 436769

The Oxford Ski Company
Ski travel agency
Tel 01993 899420

Peak Pursuits
Catered chalet in St-Martin-de-Belleville
Tel 01322 866726

Peak Retreats
Holidays to traditional French Alps resorts
Tel 0844 576 0170

Peak Ski
Chalets in Verbier
Tel 01442 832629

PGL Ski
School group specialist and holidays for teenagers
Tel 0844 371 0101

Pierre & Vacances
8,000+ ski apartments in France
Tel 0870 026 7145

Pilaski
Holidays in Pila, Aosta Valley
Tel 01478 613561

PowderBeds
Hotels and apartments in Europe and North America
Tel 0845 180 5000

Powder Byrne
Luxury holidays in European resorts
Tel 020 8246 5300

Powder N Shine
Luxury chalets in Reberty (Les Menuires)
Tel 0845 163 7596

Powder White
Holidays in big-name resorts
Tel 020 8877 8888

Première Neige
Catered/self-catered holidays in Ste-Foy
Tel 0131 510 2525

PT Ski
Holidays in Klosters
Tel 020 7736 5557

Pure Powder
Powder skiing in Canada, Alaska, Chile and Europe
Tel 020 7736 8191

Purple Ski
Chalet holidays in Méribel
Tel 01885 488799

Ramblers Holidays
Mostly cross-country skiing holidays
Tel 01707 331133

Reach4theAlps
Holidays in the French Alps
Tel 0845 680 1947

Richmond World Holidays
Christian holidays
Tel 020 3004 2661

Ride & Slide
Chalets in Morzine
Tel +33 450 388962

Rocketski.com
Club hotels and chalets in Austria, France and Italy
Tel 01273 810777

Rude Chalets
Holidays in Morzine, Avoriaz and Chamonix
Tel 0870 068 7030

Scott Dunn Ski
Luxury chalet and hotel holidays in the Alps and N America
Tel 020 8682 5050

Select Chalets
Chalets in Hochkönig
Tel 01444 848680

Silver Ski
Chalet holidays in France
Tel 01622 735544

Simon Swaffer
Apartment in La Plagne
Tel 07919 170227

Simon Butler Skiing
Holidays in Megève with ski instruction
Tel 01483 212726

Simply Alpine
Agent for accommodation in Europe and N America
Tel 023 9279 8901

Simply Val d'Isère
Specialist agent for Val d'Isère
Tel 0845 021 0222

Ski 2
Specialists in Champoluc (Monterosa)
Tel 01962 713330

Ski Addiction
Chalets/hotels in the Portes du Soleil
Tel +33 607 979736

Skialot
Chalet in Châtel
Tel 0780 156 9264

Ski Amis
Catered chalet and self-catered holidays in the French Alps
Tel 020 3411 5439

Ski Basics
Catered chalets in Méribel
Tel 01225 731312

Ski Beat
Catered chalets in the French Alps
Tel 01243 780405

Ski Bespoke
Tailor-made holidays in the Alps and N America
Tel 01243 200202

Ski Blanc
Chalet holidays in Méribel
Tel 020 8502 9082 / +33 622 056416

Ski Bluebird
Chalet holidays in Courchevel
Tel 0808 134 9903

SkiBound
School trips
Tel 01273 244570

Skibug
Catered chalets in La Plagne
Tel 0845 260 7573

Ski Club Freshtracks
Group holidays for Ski Club of Great Britain members
Tel 020 8410 2022

Ski Collection
French 3- and 4-star self-catering apartment specialist
Tel 0844 576 0175

Ski Cuisine
Chalets in Méribel
Tel 01702 589543

Ski Dazzle
Chalet holidays in Les Trois Vallées
Tel +33 479 001725

Ski Deep
Self-catered chalets in La Tania and Le Praz
Tel +33 479 081905

Ski Etoile
Accommodation in Montgenèvre
Tel 01225 290998

Ski Europe
Ski travel agent
Tel 01350 728869

Ski Expectations
Small travel agency specializing in ski holidays
Tel 01799 531888

Ski Famille
Family properties in the Alps
Tel 0845 644 3764

Ski France
Packaged and tailor-made holidays in France
Tel 01273 358538

Ski Freedom
Catered and self-catered chalets in Verbier and Champéry
Tel +41 27 767 1505

Ski Hame
Catered chalets in Méribel and La Tania
Tel 01875 320157

Ski Hiver
Chalets in Paradiski
Tel 020 8144 4160

Ski Ici
Low-carbon holidays to French resorts
Tel 07779 006689

Ski-in.co.uk
Self-catered apartment in Serre-Chevalier
Tel 01630 672540

Ski Independence
USA, Canada, Japan, France, Switzerland and Austria
Tel 0131 243 8097

Skiing Austria
Agent for accommodation in Austria
Tel 020 8123 7817

Ski Inspired
Holidays in Baqueira-Beret and Formigal
Tel 01903 233323

Ski La Cote
Self-catered chalet in the Portes du Soleil
Tel 01482 668357

Ski Line
Ski travel agent + chalets in Europe and North America
Tel 020 8313 3999

Ski Magic
Chalet holidays in La Tania
Tel 0844 993 3686

SkiMcNeill.com
Ski travel agent
Tel 028 9066 6699

Ski Miquel Holidays
Small but eclectic programme
Tel 01457 821200

Ski Monterosa Ltd
Monterosa (Alagna) specialist
Tel 020 7361 0086

Ski Morgins Holidays
Self-catered and B&B holidays in Morgins
Tel +41 79 279 3463

Ski Morzine
Accommodation in Morzine
Tel 0845 370 1104

Skiology.co.uk
Catered chalets in Les Carroz and Morzine
Tel 07894 758535

Ski Olympic
Chalet holidays in France
Tel 01302 328820

Ski Peak
Specialist in Vaujany
Tel 01428 608070

SkiPlan Travel Service
Schools programme
Tel 0871 222 6565

Ski Power
Chalets in La Tania and hotel in Les Deux-Alpes
Tel 01737 306029

Ski Safari
Multi-resort safaris
Tel 01273 224060

Ski Soleil
Chalet and apartments in Montchavin (La Plagne)
Tel 020 3239 3454

Ski Solutions
Ski travel agent + tailor-made holidays
Tel 020 7471 7700

Ski Supreme
Holidays to France and to Pila (Italy)
Tel 0845 194 7541

Ski Surf
Ski travel agent
Tel 020 8736 0735

Ski Total
Quality chalet holidays in Europe
Tel 01483 791933

Skitracer
Ski travel agent
Tel 020 8600 1650

Ski Travel Centre
Ski travel agent
Tel 0845 601 8993

Ski-Val
Catered chalets in Val d'Isère and St Anton
Tel 01822 611200

Ski Verbier
Specialists in Verbier chalets
Tel 020 7401 1101

Ski Weekend
Tailor-made short breaks, chalet holidays and event management
Tel 01392 878353

Ski Weekender
Weekends in La Clusaz, Le Grand Bornand and the Grand Massif
Tel 0845 557 5983

Skiweekends.com
Weekends and short breaks to the Alps
Tel 08444 060600

Skiworld
Catered chalets, hotels and self-catering apartments in Europe, USA and Canada
Tel 0844 493 0430

Ski Yogi
Hotels and catered chalets agent in Italy
Tel 01799 531886

SkiZinal
Catered/self-catering chalets in Zinal (Val d'Anniviers)
Tel 020 8144 7575

Sloping Off
Schools holidays
Tel 01273 648200

Sno
Travel agent
Tel 020 8133 8899

Snowbizz
Family ski specialist in Puy-St-Vincent
Tel 01778 341455

Ski businesses

671

Build your own shortlist: www.wheretoskiandsnowboard.com

Ski & Board Holidays

Europe • North America • South America
Chalets • Hotels • Apartments

Snow Finders Aspen House 12 Kings Head Place
Market Harborough LE16 7JT Tel: 01858 466888
Fax: 01858 466788 www.snowfinders.com

ABTA
J5552

Snowcard Insurance Services Ltd
Winter sports insurance
Tel 0844 826 2699

Snowchateaux
Catered chalet holidays in Paradiski and Tignes
Tel 0800 066 4996

Snowcoach
Holidays to France
Tel 01727 866177

SnowCrazy
Chalets in the French Alps
Tel 0845 260 2910

Snowed Inn Chalets
Catered chalets in Serre-Chevalier
Tel 020 3514 2394

Snow Finders
Travel agent + tour operator to Europe and N America
Tel 01858 466888

Snowfocus
Catered chalet with childcare in Châtel
Tel 01392 479555

Snowhounds
Ski travel agent
Tel 01243 788487

Snowlife
Catered chalet in La Clusaz
Tel 01534 863630

Snoworks Ski Courses
Performance ski courses and adventure skiing
Tel 0844 543 0503

Snowpod
Hosted apartments with a twist in Tignes
Tel 07881 725062

Snowscape
Weekly and flexible trips to Austria
Tel 08453 708570

Snowslippers
Trips to Austria for schools, universities and groups
Tel 07837 093989

Snowstar Holidays
Agent for accommodation in Tignes
Tel 020 8133 8411

Snowy Pockets
Chalet/apartment holidays in France and Switzerland
Tel +41 79 833 3608

Solos
Singles' holidays
Tel 0844 815 0005

La Source
Accommodation in Villard-Reculas (Alpe-d'Huez)
Tel 01707 655988

Stanford Skiing
Megève specialist
Tel 01603 477471

Star Ski Chalets
Catered chalets in Morzine
Tel +33 679 181401

STC Ski
Europe and North America, specializing in Austria
Tel 01483 771222

Sugar Mountain
Chalet in Morzine
Tel +33 450 749033

Summit Retreats
Ski travel agent
Tel 01985 850111

Supertravel
Upmarket European and North American holidays
Tel 020 7962 9933

Susie Ward Alpine Holidays
Upmarket accommodation in Châtel
Tel +33 450 734087

Switzerland Travel Centre
Specialists in Swiss resorts
Tel 020 7420 4934

Ted Bentley Chalet Holidays
Self-catered holidays in Nendaz
Tel 01934 820854

Thomson Ski
Major mainstream operator
Tel 0871 971 0578

Tracks European Adventures
Customized tours in the Alps
Tel +41 24 498 1347

TravelSAC
Ski travel agent
Tel 01323 842599

V-Ski
Self-catered chalets in Verbier
Tel +41 79 431 9228

Val d'Isère A La Carte
Specialists in Val d'Isère hotel/self-catering holidays
Tel +33 629 894457

VIP
Chalets in the Alps
Tel 0844 557 3119

Virgin Snow
Holidays to America and Canada
Tel 0844 557 4321

Wake Up and Ski
Accommodation in France
Tel 020 7118 3818

White Roc
Tailor-made hotel/self-catering holidays
Tel 020 7792 1188

YSE
Chalet holidays in Val d'Isère
Tel 0845 122 1414

Zenith Holidays
Holidays in the Alps and Pyrenees with flexible transport arrangements
Tel 0203 137 7678

RESORT DIRECTORY / INDEX

This is an index to the resort chapters in the book; you'll find page references for about 400 resorts that are described in those chapters (note that if the resort you are looking up is covered in a chapter devoted to a bigger resort, the page reference will be to the start of the chapter, not to the exact page on which the minor resort is described). You'll also find here brief descriptions of around 1,000 other resorts, most of them smaller than those we've covered in full.

Key

⛷ *Lifts*
⛷ *Pistes*
🎿 *UK tour operators*

49 Degrees North USA
Inland area with best snow in Washington State, including 120-acre bowl reserved for powder weekends.
1195m; slopes 1195–1760m
⛷ 5 ⛷ 780 acres

Abetone Italy
Resort in the exposed Apennines, less than two hours from Florence and Pisa.
1400m; slopes 1200–1940m
⛷ 25 ⛷ 70km

Abtenau Austria
Sizeable village in Dachstein-West region near Salzburg, on large plain ideal for cross-country.
710m; slopes 710–1190m
⛷ 7 ⛷ 12km

Achenkirch Austria
Unspoiled, low-altitude Tirolean village close to Niederau and Alpbach. Beautiful setting overlooking a lake.
930m; slopes 930–1800m
⛷ 30 ⛷ 50km

Adelboden 460

Les Aillons-Margériaz France
Traditional village near Chambéry. Nicely sheltered slopes.
1000m; slopes 1000–1900m
⛷ 21 ⛷ 40km

Alagna 420
Small resort on the east fringe of the Monterosa Ski area.

Alba 453
Pretty village in Val di Fassa.

Alberschwende 192
Village in Bregenzerwald.
720m ⛷ 8 ⛷ 18km

Albiez-Montrond France
Authentic old French village in Maurienne valley with panoramic views. Own easy slopes and close to other ski areas.
1500m; slopes 1500–2200m
⛷ 13 ⛷ 67 hectares

Alleghe Italy
Dolomite village near Cortina in a pretty lakeside setting close to numerous areas.
1000m
⛷ 24 ⛷ 80km

Les Allues 287
Rustic village on the road up to Méribel.

Alpbachtal-Wildschönau – Ski Juwel Austria
Exceptionally pretty and friendly old village near the head of a valley, looking south across it to the slopes of Wiedersbergerhorn. It is now forms the Ski Juwel area with Wildschonau, best known in Britain as the area that includes the smaller resort of Niederau, although its major resort in skiing terms is Auffach. A two-stage gondola is all it has taken to link Alpbach and Auffach, and the linked area offers an appealing mix of small, friendly villages and fairly extensive intermediate slopes.
1000m; slopes 670–2025m
⛷ 47 ⛷ 128km
🎿 Alpine Answers, Crystal, Inghams, Ski Solutions, STC, Thomson, Zenith

Alpe-d'Huez 206

Alpe-du-Grand-Serre France
Small resort close to Grenoble, off road to Alpe-d'Huez and Les Deux-Alpes. 800m vertical, split between a broad open bowl above the treeline and a worthwhile sheltered sector below it. Mainly blue and red slopes served by draglifts.
1370m; slopes 1370–2185m
⛷ 14 ⛷ 55km

Alpendorf Austria
Outpost of St Johann im Pongau, at one end of an extensive three-valley lift network linking via Wagrain to Flachau – all part of the Salzburger Sportwelt area. Good intermediate runs.
850m; slopes 800–2185m
⛷ 64 ⛷ 200km

Alpenglow USA
Alaskan ski resort.
762m; slopes 2500–3900m
⛷ 4 ⛷ 320 acres

Alpenregion Bludenz 195

Alpika Service 35
One of the venues for the Sochi Winter Olympics in 2014.

Alpine Meadows USA
Squaw Valley's neighbour – and covered on the same lift pass – with similar, lightly wooded terrain, an impressive snow record and runs of all classifications, but a modest total vertical; excellent beginner slopes and mostly uncrowded. The resort boundary is open – expeditions require guidance. There's no resort in the European sense, but there's lots of lodgings close by in lakeside Tahoe City.
2085m; slopes 2085–2635m
⛷ 13 ⛷ 2400 acres

Alps Resort South Korea
Korea's most northerly, snow-reliable resort, about five hours from Seoul. ⛷ 5

Alta 582

Alta Badia 433
Part of the Sella Ronda circuit.

Radstadt-Altenmarkt Austria
Unspoiled village, well placed just off the Salzburg-Villach autobahn for numerous resorts including snow-sure Obertauern and those in the Salzburger Sportwelt.
855m; slopes 855–1570m
⛷ 8 ⛷ 20km

Alto Campoo Spain
Barren, desolate place near Santander, with undistinguished slopes, but magnificent wilderness views.
1650m; slopes 1650–2130m
⛷ 13

Alt St Johann Switzerland
Old cross-country village with Alpine slopes connecting into Unterwasser area near Liechtenstein.
900m; slopes 900–2260m
⛷ 17 ⛷ 60km

Alyeska USA
Alaskan area 60km from Anchorage, with luxury hotel.
75m; slopes 75–1200m
⛷ 9 ⛷ 785 acres
🎿 Frontier, Skiworld

Aminona 468
Purpose-built resort in Crans-Montana network.

Andalo Italy
Trentino village not far from Madonna.
1050m; slopes 1035–2125m
⛷ 16 ⛷ 60km
🎿 Rocketski

Andelsbuch 192
Village in Bregenzerwald.
615m ⛷ 8 ⛷ 15km

Andermatt 463

Andorra la Vella 88
Andorra's capital.

Angel Fire USA
Intermediate area near Taos, New Mexico. Height usually ensures good snow.
2620m; slopes 2620–3255m
⛷ 5 ⛷ 455 acres

Les Angles 322

Ankogel Austria
Limited but varied area in the Hohe Tauern region in Carinthia; close to the Molltal Glacier and Slovenia. Mostly red and black runs; longest is 7km. Lift status a short drive from Mallnitz village.
1300m; slopes 1300–2635m
⛷ 7 ⛷ 35km

Annaberg-Lungötz Austria
Peaceful village near Filzmoos in a pretty setting, sharing a sizeable area with Gosau.
775m; slopes 775–1620m
⛷ 33 ⛷ 65km

Annupuri 666
Interlinked area in Niseko, Japan.

Antagnod Italy
Day-trip area near Champoluc, above Aosta valley. Great views to Monte Rosa. No village, but family oriented with quiet nursery slopes and handful of runs.
1710m; slopes 1710–2305m
⛷ 4 ⛷ 14km

Anthony Lakes USA
Small area in Oregon with one chair and two beginner lifts.
2165m; slopes 2165–2435m
⛷ 3 ⛷ 21 trails

Anzère Switzerland
Sympathetically designed modern resort on a sunny balcony near Crans-Montana, with uncrowded slopes suited to leisurely intermediates. Lots of old, slow lifts but the area is very much a family resort, with village nursery slopes and spa centre. Little to challenge experts except the 5km Pas de Maimbre black run, an itinerary and some gentle off-piste. There's a terrain park. For a small place there is a reasonable choice of restaurants and bars. Lots of marked walks and a 3km toboggan run.
1500m; slopes 1500–2420m
⛷ 11 ⛷ 52km
🎿 Lagrange, Mountain Beds

Barboleuse 519
Quiet base for skiing the Villars slopes.

Bardonecchia Italy
Sizeable railway town set in an attractive valley near the entrance to the Fréjus road tunnel; overlooked until the 2006 Turin Winter Olympics brought investment and raised its profile as a good-value intermediate destination. What it lacks in classic mountain charm, it gains in a fairly extensive area of slopes on two separate mountains linked by free bus. There are plenty of hotels, and the former Olympic village residence has spacious apartment accommodation. The resort's easy road and rail links mean it is popular with weekenders from Turin, but otherwise fairly quiet during the week with plenty of leisurely cruising on uncrowded pistes – worth considering as a base for touring other nearby French and Italian resorts too. Snow reliability isn't particularly great though and, coupled with the large number of awkward draglifts, may deter some visitors.
1310m; slopes 1290–2695m
🚠 23 ⛷ 100km
🚌 Alpine Answers, Crystal, Erna Low, Neilson, Thomson

Barèges 322

Bariloche (Catedral) Argentina
The place to stay when skiing Cerro Catedral, this was once a quaint lakeside town, but is now a substantial resort – including the Llao Llao Resort and Spa. The slopes at Cathedral are 20 minutes by shuttle-bus.
slopes 1030–2180m
🚠 39 ⛷ 103km

Les Barzettes 468
Smaller base along the road from Crans-Montana.

Bayrischzell Germany
Bavarian resort south of Munich and close to Austrian border.
800m; slopes 1090–1563m
🚠 25 ⛷ 40km

Bear Mountain USA
Southern California's main area, in the beautiful San Bernardino National Forest region. Full snowmaking.
slopes 2170–2685m
🚠 12 ⛷ 195 acres

Bears Town South Korea
Modern resort with runs cut out of thick forest. Biggest resort near Seoul (only an hour's drive), so it can get very crowded. English-language website at www.bearstown.com. 🚠 9

Bear Valley USA
Resort in northern California, between Lake Tahoe and Yosemite.
2010m; slopes 2010–2590m
🚠 10 ⛷ 1280 acres

Beaulard Italy
Little place just off the road between Sauze d'Oulx and Bardonecchia.
1215m; slopes 1215–2120m
🚠 6 ⛷ 20km

Beaver Creek 561

Beaver Mountain USA
Small Utah area north of Salt Lake City, too far from Park City for a day trip.
2195m; slopes 2195–2680m
🚠 3 ⛷ 525 acres

Beitostølen Norway
Small family resort in southern Norway (east of Bergen), with lots of cross-country in the region.
900m 🚠 9 ⛷ 25km
🚌 Crystal, Inntravel, Ski Safari, Thomson

Belleayre Mountain USA
State-owned resort near Albany, New York State. Cheap but old lifts and short runs.
775m; slopes 775–1015m
🚠 7 ⛷ 170 acres

Bellwald Switzerland
Traditional Rhône valley resort near Fiesch, Riederalp and Bettmeralp. Part of the Goms Valley region.
1600m; slopes 1600–2560m
🚠 5 ⛷ 30km

Ben Lomond Australia
Small intermediate/beginner area in Ben Lomond National Park, Tasmania, 260km from Hobart.
1450m; slopes 1460–1570m
🚠 6 ⛷ 14 hectares

Berchtesgaden Germany
Pleasant old town close to Salzburg, known for its Nordic skiing but with several little Alpine areas nearby.
550m

Bergün Switzerland
Traditional, quiet, unspoiled, virtually traffic-free little family resort on the rail route between Davos and St Moritz. 5km toboggan run.
1375m; slopes 1400–2550m
🚠 3 ⛷ 23km

Berkshire East USA
Resort in Massachusetts, southern New England, near the Mohawk Trail.
slopes 165–525m
🚠 5 ⛷ 200 acres

Berwang Austria
Quiet village in a spacious valley close to Lermoos. It claims the most skiing of the region too (36km) – though many runs are short and easy. The Zugspitz Arena lift pass, to which our figures relate, covers these and the other resorts of the valley. The

village enjoys a splendid winter-wonderland setting, with lifts rising on two sides. There is a good mix of sunny and shady slopes, shared with Bichlbach; some of these give over 500m vertical to the lift station. There are good cross-country loops at altitude, plenty of huts and a long toboggan run.
1340m; slopes 990–2960m
🚠 52 ⛷ 147km
🎿 Ski Bespoke

Bessans France
Old cross-country village near Modane well placed for touring Maurienne valley resorts.
1710m; slopes 1740–2200m
🚠 2 ⛷ 3km

Besse France
Charming old village built out of lava, with purpose-built slope-side satellite Super-Besse. Beautiful extinct-volcano scenery.
1050m; slopes 1300–1850m
🚠 23 ⛷ 43km

Bethel USA
Pleasant, historic town very close to Sunday River, Maine. Attractive alternative to staying in the resort.

Le Bettex 274
Small base above St-Gervais, with links to Megève.

Bettmeralp Switzerland
Central village of the sizeable Aletsch area near Brig, high above the Rhône valley, amid spectacular glacial scenery. Reached by cable cars from the valley.
1950m; slopes 1925–2870m
🚠 35 ⛷ 100km

Beuil-les-Launes France
Alpes-Maritimes resort closest to Nice. Medieval village which shares area with Valberg.
1460m; slopes 1400–2011m
🚠 26 ⛷ 90km

Bezau 192
Bregenzerwald village.
620m 🚠 8 ⛷ 15km

Biberwier Austria
Village near Lermoos, with mainly shady local slopes more or less spilt equally into red and blue runs. Makes a quiet base from which to access the rest of the Zugspitz Arena (to which our figures relate). The main lift from the valley is a six-pack, and there are quiet nursery slopes at the base – with a very long moving carpet. There is a terrain park, half-pipe and boardercross course. There are a couple of pleasant restaurants and bars. Like Lermoos, the village benefits from a tunnel to remove traffic from the centre.
990m; slopes 990–2960m
🚠 52 ⛷ 147km

Bichlbach Austria
Smallest of the Zugspitz Arena villages, sharing slopes with Berwang. Austria's first chondola lift starts here. An unspoiled base for visiting the rest of the area.
1080m; slopes 990–2960m
🚠 52 ⛷ 147km

Bielmonte Italy
Popular with day trippers from Milan. Worthwhile on a bad-weather day.
1200m; slopes 1200–1620m
🚠 9 ⛷ 20km

Big Powderhorn USA
Area with the most 'resort' facilities in south Lake Superior region – and the highest lift capacity too. The area suffers from winds.
370m; slopes 370–560m
🚠 10 ⛷ 250 acres

Big Sky 596

Big White 618

Bischofshofen Austria
Working town and mountain resort near St Johann im Pongau, with very limited local runs and the main slopes starting nearby in Muhlbach (Hochkönig area).
545m; slopes 545–1000m
🚠 1 ⛷ 2km

Bivio Switzerland
Quiet village near St Moritz and Savognin, with easy slopes.
1770m; slopes 1780–2560m
🚠 4 ⛷ 40km

Björkliden Sweden
538m vertical. Feb-to-May Arctic Circle area. Ultra snow-reliable. You can even ski in caves – beautiful ice formations. Magnificent Lapland views.
🚠 5 ⛷ 15km 🚌 Ski Safari

Björnrike Sweden
20 minutes from Vemdalsskalet (same pass). 385m vertical.
🚠 9 ⛷ 15km

Black Mountain USA
New Hampshire area with lodging in nearby Jackson.
🚠 4 ⛷ 143 acres

Blatten Switzerland
Mountainside hamlet above Naters, beside the Rhône near Brig. Small but tall Belalp ski area, with larger Aletsch area nearby.
1320m; slopes 1320–3100m
🚠 9 ⛷ 60km

Bled 662
Lakeside base in Slovenia.

Blue Cow Australia
Part of Perisher resort, Australia's highest and expanding ski area. Accessible only by tube train. Nearest town – Jindabyne. Six hours from Sydney.
1890m; slopes 1605–2035m
🚠 47 ⛷ 3075 acres

Build your own shortlist: **www.wheretoskiandsnowboard.com**

Champex-Lac Switzerland
Lakeside hamlet tucked away
in the trees in Ski St-Bernard
area near Verbier. A quiet,
unspoiled base from which to
visit Verbier's area. Small area
of slopes due to open again
after being closed by a fire.
1480m; slopes 1480–2220m
🚡4 🚠 15km

Champfèr 497
Lakeside hamlet between St
Moritz and Silvaplana.

Champoluc 420
Unspoiled village at one end
of the Monterosa Ski area.

Champorcher Italy
Small village south of Aosta
valley with narrow ski
area, mostly red runs on open
slopes, with one black
through the trees to the lift
base at Chardonney.
1430m; slopes 1430–2500m
🚡5 🚠 21km

Champoussin 465
Quiet village with links to the
rest of the Champéry slopes.

Chamrousse France
Functional family resort near
Grenoble, with good,
sheltered slopes. Chairlifts
and a cable car from three
bases serve largely beginner
and intermediate slopes.
1650m; slopes 1400–2250m
🚡19 🚠 90km
✉ Crystal, Erna Low,
Lagrange, PowderBeds, Ski
Collection, Ski France, Ski
Independence, Thomson, Zenith

Chandolin 504
Village in the Val d'Anniviers.

Chantemerle 331
One of the villages making up
Serre-Chevalier.

Chapa Verde Chile
60km north-east of Rancagua
and 145km from Santiago.
1200m; slopes 1200–2500m
🚡4 🚠 1200 hectares

Chapelco Argentina
Small ski area with full
infrastructure of services 19km
from sizeable town of San
Martin de Los Andes.
Accommodation in hotels
11km from the slopes.
slopes 1250–1980m
🚡10 🚠 140 hectares

La Chapelle-d'Abondance 243
Unspoiled village 5km down
the valley from Châtel.

Charlotte Pass Australia
Oldest and most remote
resort in NSW, on a charming
Alpine pass near Mt
Kosciusko. Reached only by
snowcat from Perisher. Scenic
chalets and five lifts. Nearest
town Jindabyne. 6.5 hours
from Sydney.
1765m; slopes 1850–2000m
🚡5 🚠 123 acres

Chastreix Sancy France
Small family ski area near
Mont Dore and Super-Besse.
Limited but varied terrain. All
draglifts.
1400m
🚡7 🚠 16km

Château d'Oex Switzerland
Pleasant French-speaking
valley town sharing a lift pass
with neighbouring, but
unconnected, Gstaad. Good
rail links to other sectors. Low
slopes. Famous for its Alpine
Balloon festival.
950m; slopes 890–1630m
🚡8 🚠 30km

Châtel 243

Le Chatelard France
Small resort in remote Parc
des Bauges between Lake
Annecy and Chambéry.

Le Chazelet France
Tiny hamlet 5km above La
Grave, useful on bad weather
days.
1800m; slopes 1800–2300m
🚠 6km

Chiesa Italy
Attractive beginners' resort
with a fairly high plateau of
easy runs above the resort.
1000m; slopes 1700–2335m
🚡16 🚠 50km

Le Chinaillon France
Chalet-style village at lift base
above Le Grand-Bornand.
1300m; slopes 1000–2100m
🚡29 🚠 90km ✉ PowderBeds

Chiomonte Italy
Tiny resort on the main road
east of Bardonecchia and
Sauze d'Oulx. A good half-day
trip from either.
745m; slopes 745–2210m
🚡6 🚠 10km

Chsea Algeria
Largest of Algeria's skiable
areas, 135km south-east of
coastal town of Alger in the
Djur Djur mountains.
1860m; slopes 1860–2510m 🚡2

Chur–Brambruesch Switzerland
Chur's local ski area, a cable
car and gondola ride from the
town.
595m; slopes 1170–2200m
🚡6 🚠 25km

Churwalden Switzerland
Hamlet on fringe of
Lenzerheide-Valbella area,
linked via a slow chair. Four
short local runs served by a
quad and steep drag.
1230m; slopes 1230–2865m
🚡35 🚠 155km

Claviere 297
Village linked to Montgenèvre
and the Milky Way ski area.

La Clusaz France
Genuine mountain village near
Geneva that exudes rustic and
Gallic charm. Attracts a lot of
weekend visitors, so can be
crowded. Buses also link with
Le Grand Bornand. Together
they offer over 200km slopes
– covered by the area lift
pass. The local slopes sprawl
over five attractively wooded
and varied sectors. All are
below 2500m, so snow
conditions are unreliable; but
there is a lot of snowmaking.
Good steep blacks and bumps
on La Balme (the highest
sector), as well as decent off-
piste when conditions permit.
There are challenging but
wide blues, as well as gentle
cruises and nursery slopes up
the mountain. But there are
still a lot of old chairs and
drags. There's a park and
pipe, plentiful rustic huts, and
a few lively bars.
1100m; slopes 1100–2600m
🚡53 🚠 220km
✉ Absolutely Snow, Alpine
Answers, Classic Ski, Crystal,
Crystal Finest, Independent Ski
Links, Lagrange, Peak Retreats,
Pierre & Vacances,
PowderBeds, Ski Famille, Ski
France, Ski Solutions, Ski
Weekend, Ski Weekender,
Skiweekends.com, Snowlife,
STC, Zenith

Les Coches 310
Purpose-built village, linked
to the La Plagne ski area.

Cogne Italy
One of Aosta valley's larger
villages. Main resort in the
Gran Paradiso national park.
Worth a visit from nearby Pila.
Limited, mostly red slopes.
Major cross-country centre,
with 70km trails.
1535m; slopes 1530–2250m
🚡4 🚠 9km

Colfosco 433
Smaller, quieter satellite of
Corvara in the Sella Ronda.

Colle di Tenda Italy
Dour, modern resort that
shares a good area with much
nicer Limone. Not far from
Nice.
1400m; slopes 1120–2040m
🚡33 🚠 80km

Colle Isarco Italy
Brenner Pass area – and the
bargain-shopping town of
Vipiteno is nearby.
1095m; slopes 1095–2720m
🚡5 🚠 15km

Le Collet-d'Allevard France
Ski area of sizeable summer
spa Allevard-les-Bains in
remote region east of
Chambéry-Grenoble road.
1450m; slopes 1450–2140m
🚡11 🚠 35km

Collio Italy
Tiny area of short runs in a
remote spot between lakes
Garda and d'Iseo.
840m; slopes 840–1715m 🚡14

Les Collons 508
Near Thyon 2000 in the
Verbier area.

Combloux 274
Quiet, unspoiled alternative to
linked Megève.

Les Contamines France
Largely unspoiled but
sprawling chalet resort close
to Megève and Chamonix,
with a fair-sized intermediate
area and a good snow record
for its height. The main access
lift is a shuttle-bus ride from
the centre, with a few
lodgings at its base. Most of
the slopes are above the
treeline and on both sides of
the Col du Joly – from where a
long red run descends over
1000m vertical. There's a good
mix of blue and red runs, and
substantial off-piste
opportunities. Complete
beginners are better off
elsewhere though. Reports of
the school are mixed too. The
village is quiet with few
amenities, but there are other
sporting activities.
1160m; slopes 1160–2485m
🚡24 🚠 120km
✉ Alpine Answers, Chalet
Kiana, Classic Ski, Holiday in
Alps, Lagrange, Peak Retreats,
Ski Expectations, Ski France

Copper Mountain USA
Modern, but pleasant
purpose-built village with
some of Colorado's best
terrain. And good value by
regional standards.
Worthwhile outing from
nearby resorts such as Vail.
The Village at Copper is the
main base, with smart condo
lodging and fast chairs into
the slopes. Two other bases
are served by free shuttle-
buses and with easier terrain
above them. The slopes
spread across two main
peaks, Union and Copper,

with an attractive mix of open and wooded areas. There is lots of expert terrain in the upper bowls, some seriously steep. There are top-to-bottom greens and excellent nursery slopes. The terrain park is well regarded. Queues are rarely a problem outside peak weekends. Limited off-slope diversions. Reports of the school are favourable. Nightlife livens up at weekends.
2925m; slopes 2925–3765m
⛷ 22 ✦ 2465 acres
🚐 *Alpine Answers, AmeriCan Ski, American Ski Classics, Erna Low, Independent Ski Links, Momentum, Ski Independence, Ski Safari, Skitracer, Skiworld, Supertravel*

Le Corbier France
A no-compromise functional resort centrally placed in the Sybelles area. The resort is purpose-built and compact, as well as being traffic-free – so it suits families very well. Nearly all of the lodging is slope-side apartments, some in a traditional style. There are bars and restaurants, but evenings are generally very quiet. Lifts link directly to St-Jean-d'Arves and La Toussuire, as well as a higher level connection to St-Sorlin. But progress can be slow – only seven fast chairs in the whole area. One belongs to Le Corbier and serves local slopes. The gentle terrain is mostly north-east facing and makes ideal cruising, if rather lacking in variety – though there's a black run from the top. Beginners have good slopes at resort level.
1550m; slopes 1100–2620m
⛷ 72 ✦ 310km
🚐 *Erna Low, Lagrange, Pierre & Vacances, Rocketski, Ski France*

Cordon France
Traditional little family resort near Megève. 'Ideal for a relaxing ski before catching an early evening flight,' says a 2013 visitor.
870m; slopes 1000–1600m
⛷ 6 ✦ 11km

Corno alle Scale Italy
Small resort in the Emilia Romagna region of the Apennines.
1355m; slopes 1355–1945m
⛷ 9 ✦ 36km

Coronet Peak New Zealand
Closest area to Queenstown (20 minutes). Good mix of bowls, chutes, varied level pistes. Biggest vertical is 462m. Relies on large snowmaking facility for good snow-cover. Splendid views.
1230m; slopes 1230–1650m
⛷ 7 ✦ 690 acres

Corrençon-en-Vercors France
Charming, rustic village at foot of Villard-de-Lans ski area. Good cross-country, too.
1160m; slopes 1145–2170m
⛷ 25 ✦ 125km

Cortina d'Ampezzo 401
Corvara 433
Courchevel 248
Courmayeur 406
Cranmore USA
Area in New Hampshire with attractive town/resort of North Conway. Easy skiing. Good for families.
150m; slopes 150–515m
⛷ 9 ✦ 190 acres

Crans-Montana 468
Crested Butte USA
One of the cutest old Wild West towns in Colorado, and the steep, gnarly terrain enjoys cult status among experts. It's a small area, but it packs in an astonishing mixture of perfect beginner slopes, easy cruising runs and expert terrain. Snowfall is modest by Colorado standards, but for those who like steep, ungroomed terrain, if the snow is good, it's idyllic. You can stay there or at the mountain, a couple of miles away, with its modern resort 'village'.
2860m; slopes 2775–3620m
⛷ 15 ✦ 1547 acres
🚐 *AmeriCan Ski, American Ski Classics, Ski Safari*

Crest-Voland France
Attractive, unspoiled traditional village near Megève and Le Grand Bornand with wonderfully uncrowded intermediate slopes linked to Les Saisies and beyond to Praz sur Arly, as part of the Espace Diamant region – to which our figures relate.
1035m; slopes 1000–2070m
⛷ 84 ✦ 179km

Crissolo Italy
Small, remote day-tripper area, south-west of Turin. Part of the Monviso ski area.
1320m; slopes 1745–2340m
⛷ 4 ✦ 20km

La Croix-Fry France
On the pass to La Clusaz. Couple of hotels and good gentle slopes.
1480m

Les Crosets 465
Micro-resort above Champéry in the Portes du Soleil.

Crystal Mountain USA
Area in glorious Mt Rainier National Park, near Seattle. Good, varied area given good snow/weather, but it's often wet. Lively at weekends.
1340m; slopes 1340–2135m
⛷ 9 ✦ 2300 acres

Cuchara Valley USA
Quiet little family resort in southern Colorado, some way from any other ski area.
2800m; slopes 2800–3285m
⛷ 4 ✦ 250 acres

Cutigliano Italy
Sizeable village near Abetone in the Apennines. Less than two hours from Florence and Pisa.
1125m; slopes 1125–1850m
⛷ 9 ✦ 13km

Cypress Mountain Canada
Vancouver's most challenging area, 20 minutes from the city and with 40% for experts. Good snowfall record but rain is a problem.
920m; slopes 910–1445m ⛷ 5

Daemyeong Vivaldi Resort
South Korea
One of the less ugly Korean resorts, 75km from Seoul.
⛷ 10

La Daille 366
Ugly apartment complex at the entrance to Val d'Isère.

Daisen Japan
Western Honshu's main area, four hours from Osaka.
800m; slopes 740–1120m ⛷ 21

Damüls 192
Village in Bregenzerwald.
1430m; slopes 700–2010m
⛷ 31 ✦ 105km

Davos 470
Deer Mountain USA
South Dakota area close to 'Old West' town Deadwood and Mount Rushmore.
1825m; slopes 1825–2085m
⛷ 4 ✦ 370 acres

Deer Valley 586
Les Deux-Alpes 258
Les Diablerets Switzerland
Spacious chalet resort towered over by the Diablerets massif, with two areas of local slopes, plus Glacier 3000. A high-speed quad followed by a slow chair lead up to the red runs of the Meilleret area and the link to Villars. A gondola in the centre of town takes you to Isenau, a mix of blues and reds served by draglifts. From Isenau there's a red run down to Col du Pillon and the cable car to and from the glacier. On Glacier 3000, you'll find blue runs at over 3000m, stunning views and the long, black Combe d'Audon – a wonderful, usually quiet, run away from all the lifts with sheer cliffs rising up on both sides. Snow reliability away from the glacier is not great – especially on sunny Isenau.
1150m; slopes 1115–3000m
⛷ 44 ✦ 130
🚐 *Alpine Answers, Independent Ski Links, Lagrange, Momentum, Neilson, PowderBeds, Ski Club*

Freshtracks, Switzerland Travel Centre, Tracks European Adventures

Diamond Peak USA
Quiet, pleasant, intermediate area on Lake Tahoe, with lodging in Incline Village five minutes' drive away. Its narrow area consists of a long ridge served by one fast chair; there are great lake views from the run along the ridge and from the terrace of Snowflake Lodge. There are black runs off the ridge, but nothing seriously steep.
2040m; slopes 2040–2600m
⛷ 6 ✦ 655 acres

Dienten Austria
Quiet, tiny, picturesque village with a handful of traditional hotels and guest houses east of Saalbach and at the heart of the large, low-altitude Hochkönig area that spreads over a series of gentle peaks linking Maria Alm to Mühlbach.
1070m; slopes 800–1900m
⛷ 33 ✦ 150km

Dinner Plain Australia
Attractive resort best known for cross-country skiing. Shuttle to Mt Hotham for Alpine slopes. Four hours from Melbourne.
1520m; slopes 1490–1520m

Discovery Ski Area USA
Pleasant area miles from anywhere except Butte, Montana, with largely intermediate slopes but double-black runs on the back of the mountain – and the chance of seriously good snow. Fairmont Hot Springs (two huge thermal pools) nearby.
1975m; slopes 1760–2485m
⛷ 8 ✦ 2200 acres

Disentis Switzerland
Unspoiled old village in a pretty setting on the Glacier Express rail route near Andermatt. Scenic area with long runs.
1125m; slopes 1150–2830m
⛷ 10 ✦ 60km

Dobbiaco Italy
One of several little resorts in the South Tyrol near the Austrian border; a feasible day out from the Sella Ronda. Toblach is its German name.
1250m; slopes 1250–1610m
⛷ 5 ✦ 15km
🚐 *Exodus, Headwater*

Dodge Ridge USA
Novice/leisurely intermediate area north of Yosemite. The pass from Reno is closed in winter, preventing crowds.
2010m; slopes 2010–2500m
⛷ 12 ✦ 815 acres

Dolonne 406
Quiet suburb of Courmayeur.

Build your own shortlist: **www.wheretoskiandsnowboard.com**

Donnersbachwald   Austria
Small area in the Dachstein-Tauern region.
950m; slopes 950–1990m
🚡4 ⛷ 25km

Donner Ski Ranch   USA
One of California's first ski resorts, still family owned and operated.
2140m; slopes 2140–2370m
🚡6 ⛷ 460 acres

Dorfgastein   104
Quieter, friendlier alternative to Bad Gastein.

Doucy-Combelouvière   France
Quiet hamlet tucked away in the trees at the foot of Valmorel's slopes, linked by easy green pistes, a fast chair and draglifts into the main sector.
1250m 🚠 *Lagrange*

Dundret   Sweden
Lapland area 100km north of the Arctic Circle with floodlit slopes open through winter when the sun barely rises.
slopes 475–825m
🚡7 ⛷ 15km

Durango Mountain ResortUSA
Not a resort to cross the Atlantic to visit – it's a small area even by US standards. Directly above the resort is a steepish slope with a slow double chair off to the right serving gentle green runs. All link to the shady slopes that form the main part of the area, served by a row of three chairs with a vertical of not much over 350m. Snowcat skiing is said to operate from the top. The heart of the resort is Purgatory Village, a modern, purpose-built affair. Evening options in the 'village' are extremely limited. The city of Durango is worth visiting.
2680m; slopes 2680–3300m
🚡11 ⛷ 1200 acres

Eaglecrest   USA
Close to Yukon gold rush town Skagway. Family resort famous for its ski school.
365m; slopes 365–790m
🚡3 ⛷ 640 acres

Eben im Pongau   Austria
Part of Salzburger Sportwelt Amadé area that includes nearby St Johann, Wagrain, Flachau and Zauchensee.
855m; slopes 855–2185m
🚡100 ⛷ 350km

Egg   192
Village in Bregenzerwald.
565mm; slopes 1100–1400m
🚡6 ⛷ 10km

Ehrwald   Austria
Pleasant village with easy access to three small and varied ski areas, notably the Zugspitze glacier. Access to the slopes there is by cable car a couple of miles outside the resort at Obermoos. There are gentle nursery slopes and good open intermediate

terrain – including a couple of genuine reds. Most are of limited extent. There's a half-pipe and three restaurants. Après-ski is fairly lively. The Zugspitz Arena lift pass covers all three sectors, plus the other resorts of the valley.
1000m; slopes 990–2960m
🚡52 ⛷ 147km 🚠 Ski Famille

El Colorado / Farellones   Chile
Scattering of accommodation around a base station 40km east of Santiago, sharing Valle Nevado's ski area (to which our figures relate).
slopes 2430–3670m
🚡43 ⛷ 113km

Eldora Mountain   USA
Day-visitor resort with varied terrain (including plenty of steep stuff) close to Denver Boulder (45min by regular scheduled bus). All forest trails, but with some good glade areas. Crowded at weekends.
2795m; slopes 2805–3230m
🚡12 ⛷ 680 acres

Elk Meadows   USA
Area south of Salt Lake City, more than a day trip from Park City.
2775m; slopes 2745–3170m
🚡6 ⛷ 1400 acres

Ellmau   107

Elm   Switzerland
One hour from Zürich, at the head of a quiet, isolated valley. Good choice of runs including a long black to the valley.
1020m; slopes 1000–2105m
🚡6 ⛷ 40km

Encamp   Andorra
Traffic-choked town, with a gondola link to the Pas de la Casa slopes. Popular for its nightlife and low prices.

Enego   Italy
Limited weekend day-trippers' area near Vicenza and Trento.
1300m; slopes 1300–1445m
🚡7 ⛷ 30km

Engelberg   477

Entrèves   406
Cluster of hotels at the lift up to Courmayeur's slopes.

Escaldes   Andorra
Central valley town, effectively part of Andorra la Vella.

Estoul   Italy
Village in the Aosta valley up a side valley near Brusson. Sunny, easy red slopes.
1800m; slopes 1800–2235m
🚡2 ⛷ 9km

Etna   Italy
Scenic, uncrowded, short-season area on the volcano's flank, 20 minutes from Nickolossi.
1800m; slopes 1800–2350m
⛷ 5km

Evolène   Switzerland
Charming rustic village in the Val d'Hérens. Small ski area in unspoiled, attractive setting south of Sion. Area lift pass gives access to the 4 Valleys.
1370m; slopes 1405–2680m
🚡7 ⛷ 42km

Faak am See   Austria
Limited area, one of five overlooking town of Villach.
560m; slopes 560–800m
🚡1 ⛷ 2km

Fai della Paganella   Italy
Trentino village near Madonna that shares its slopes with Andalo.
1000m; slopes 1035–2125m
🚡16 ⛷ 60km

Fairmont Hot Springs   Canada
Major luxury spa complex ideal for a relaxing holiday with some gentle skiing thrown in.
🚡2 ⛷ 60 acres

Faistenau   Austria
Cross-country area close to Salzburg and St Wolfgang. Limited Alpine slopes.
785m; slopes 785–1000m
🚡3 ⛷ 3km

Falcade   Italy
Trentino village south of the Sella Ronda with lifts up to slopes at San Pellegrino.
1150m; slopes 1150–2245m
🚡19 ⛷ 75km

Falera   485
Village with access to ski area shared by Flims and Laax.

Le Falgoux   France
One of the most beautiful old villages in France, set in the very scenic Volcano National Park. Several ski areas nearby.
930m; slopes 930–1350m

Falkertsee   Austria
Base area rather than a village, with bleak, open slopes in contrast to nearby Bad Kleinkirchheim.
1850m; slopes 1690–2310m
🚡5 ⛷ 15km

Falls Creek   Australia
Alpine-style modern family resort, 5 hours from Melbourne, near Mt Hotham. Fair-sized area of short intermediate runs. Access by snowcat to Mt McKay's steep slopes. Lavish day resort nearby.
1600m; slopes 1500–1780m
🚡14 ⛷ 1115 acres

La Feclaz   France
One of several little resorts in the remote Parc des Bauges. Popular cross-country ski base. *1165m*

Feldberg   386
Small resort in the Black Forest. 🚡31 ⛷ 55

Fernie   621

Fieberbrunn   Austria
Atmospheric and friendly Tirolean village, sprawling along the valley floor for 2km, but mostly set back from the road and railway. Its small but attractive area of wooded slopes is a bus ride away. One sector consists mainly of blue runs, the other mainly of easy reds, many below the treeline. Across a valley are separate lifts going up to the high point of 2020m on Hochhörndl – gondola down to 1284m accesses some good off-piste here. The resort is boarder-friendly, with a popular terrain park. Accommodation in the village is in hotels, and there is also lodging at the lift station.
800m; slopes 830–2020m
🚡11 ⛷ 43km
🚠 Crystal, Ski Club Freshtracks, Snowscape, Thomson

Fiesch   Switzerland
Traditional Rhône valley resort near Brig, with a lift up to Fiescheralp (2220m) part of the lovely Aletsch area; includes Bettmeralp to Riederalp.
1050m; slopes 1925–2870m
🚡35 ⛷ 100km

Fiescheralp   Switzerland
Mountain outpost of Fiesch, down in the Rhône valley. At one end of the beautiful Aletsch area extending across the mountain via Bettmeralp to Riederalp.
2220m; slopes 1925–2870m
🚡35 ⛷ 100km

Filzmoos   Austria
Charming, unspoiled, friendly village with leisurely slopes that are ideal for novices. Good snow record for its height. Quiet pistes, good grooming and decent nursery slopes.
1055m; slopes 1055–1645m
🚡8 ⛷ 32km
🚠 Inghams, Skitracer, STC

Fiss   Austria
Nicely compact, quiet, traditional village sharing an extensive, sunny area with bigger Serfaus.
1435m; slopes 1200–2750m
🚡70 ⛷ 190km
🚠 Ski Bespoke

Flachau   Austria
Quiet, spacious village in a pretty setting at one end of an extensive three-valley lift network linking via Wagrain to Alpendorf. Central to an impressive lift system. On the Salzbuger Sportwelt lift pass.
925m; slopes 800–2185m
🚡64 ⛷ 200km
🚠 Ski Bespoke, STC

Flachauwinkl   Austria
Tiny ski station beside Tauern autobahn. Centre of an extensive three-valley lift

network linking Kleinarl to Zauchensee. Near similarly sized Flachau. All these resorts are covered by the Salzburger Sportwelt ski pass.
930m; slopes 800–2185m
🚡 *15* 🎿 *65km*

Flaine 264

Flims 485
Long-established resort sharing an area with Laax.

Flumet France
Surprisingly large traditional village, the main place from which to ski the Espace Diamant area, linked through to Les Saisies/ Crest Voland. Near Megève.
1000m; slopes 1000–2070m
🚡 *84* 🎿 *179km* 🚌 *Lagrange*

Flumserberg Switzerland
Collective name for the villages sharing a varied area an hour south-east of Zürich. Part of the wider Heidiland region. Mostly red and black runs, served by good network of fast lifts.
425m; slopes 1220–2220m
🚡 *16* 🎿 *65km*

Folgaria Italy
Sizeable area east of Trento.
1165m; slopes 1185–2005m
🚡 *22* 🎿 *74km*
🚌 *Solos, STC, Zenith*

Folgarida 415
Small Trentino village linked to Madonna di Campiglio.

Foncine-le-Haut France
Major cross-country village in the Jura Mountains with extensive trails.
🚌 *Lagrange*

Fonni Gennaragentu Italy
Sardinia's only 'ski area' – and it's tiny. 🚡 *1* 🎿 *5km*

Font-Romeu 322

Foppolo Italy
Relatively unattractive but user-friendly village, a short transfer from Bergamo.
1510m; slopes 1610–2160m
🚡 *9* 🎿 *47km*

Forca Canapine Italy
Limited area near the Adriatic and Ascoli Piceno. Popular with weekend day-trippers.
1450m; slopes 1450–1690m
🚡 *11* 🎿 *20km*

Formazza Italy
Cross-country base with some downhill slopes.
1280m; slopes 1275–1755m
🎿 *8km*

Formigal 651

Formigueres France
Small downhill and cross-country area in the Neiges Catalanes. There are 110km cross-country trails.
slopes 1700–2350m
🚡 *8* 🎿 *19km*

Le Fornet 366
Rustic old hamlet 3km up the valley from Val d'Isère.

Forstau Austria
Secluded hamlet above Radstadt–Schladming road. Very limited area (Fageralm) with old lifts, but nice and quiet.
930m; slopes 930–1885m
🚡 *7* 🎿 *14km*

La Fouly Switzerland
Small area in Ski St-Bernard area near Verbier, with west-facing slopes, 10km of cross-country trails and a floodlit toboggan run. Good base for ski touring. Hotel Edelweiss serves excellent food.
1600m; slopes 1600–2200m
🚡 *3* 🎿 *20km*

La Foux-d'Allos France
Purpose-built resort that shares a good intermediate area with Pra-Loup (Val d'Allos ski area).
1800m; slopes 1800–2600m
🚡 *51* 🎿 *180km* 🚌 *Zenith*

Frabosa Soprana Italy
One of numerous little areas south of Turin, well placed for combining winter sports with Riviera sightseeing.
850m; slopes 860–1740m
🚡 *7* 🎿 *40km*

Frisco 563
Small town down the valley from Breckenridge.

Frontignano Italy
Best lift system in the Macerata region, near the Adriatic Riviera.
1340m; slopes 1340–2000m
🚡 *8* 🎿 *10km*

Fucine Italy
Old Trentino valley village near Marilleva/Folgarida.
980m

Fügen Austria
Unspoiled Zillertal village with road up to satellite Hochfügen – part of fair-sized Ski Optimal area, along with Kaltenbach.
550m 🚌 *Crystal, Lagrange, Skiweekends.com, STC*

Fulpmes 189
Village in the Stubai valley.

Furano 666
Resort on Hokkaido island, Japan.

Fusch Austria
Cheaper, quiet place to stay when visiting Zell am See. Across a golf course from Kaprun and Schuttdorf.
805m; slopes 805–1050m
🚡 *2* 🎿 *5km*

Fuschl am See Austria
Attractive, unspoiled, lakeside village close to St Wolfgang and Salzburg, 30 minutes from its slopes. Best suited to part-time skiers who want to sightsee as well. *670m*

Gålå Norway
Base for downhill and cross-country skiing, an hour's drive north of Lillehammer.
930m; slopes 830–1150m
🚡 *7* 🎿 *20km* 🚌 *Inntravel*

Gallio Italy
One of several low resorts near Vicenza and Trento. Popular with weekend day-trippers.
1100m; slopes 1100–1550m
🚡 *11* 🎿 *50km*

Galtür 116
Charming traditional village near Ischgl.

Gambarie d'Aspromonte Italy
Italy's second most southerly ski area (after Mt Etna). On the 'toe' of the Italian 'boot' near Reggio di Calabria.
1310m; slopes 1310–1650m 🚡 *3*

Gantschier Austria
No slopes of its own but particularly well placed for visiting all the Montafon areas. *700m*

Gargellen Austria
Quiet, tiny and secluded village tucked up a side valley in the Montafon area, with a small but varied piste network of blues and reds on Schafberg that is blissfully quiet. For experts there is lots of off-piste terrain plus ski routes, and there is a special day tour of Madrisa (Klosters). Snowmaking on the valley pistes is good, and you can ski to the door of some hotels.
1425m; slopes 1425–2300m
🚡 *8* 🎿 *33km*

Garmisch-Partenkirchen 388

Gaschurn Austria
A pleasant village in the Montafon area, bypassed by the valley traffic, with a gondola to the Nova area of slopes – the valley's largest, with 114km of pistes.This is generally the most challenging area in the valley, with many red runs, and blues that are not entirely easy. Most of the slopes are above the treeline, typically offering a very modest 300m vertical. There is lots of off-piste potential, including steep (and quite dangerous) slopes down into the central valley. Snowmaking covers almost half the area, including runs down to the valley. The NovaPark terrain park features a half-pipe and boardercross course. There are lots of mountain restaurants. It also links to the Hochjoch ski area (see St Gallenkirch).
1000m; slopes 655–2395m
🚡 *61* 🎿 *219km*
🚌 *Ski Bespoke*

Gaustablikk Norway
Small snow-sure Alpine area on Mt Gausta in southern Norway with plenty of cross-country. 🎿 *15km*

Gavarnie France
Traditional village and fair-sized ski area, with the longest green run in the Pyrenees. Grand views of the Cirque de Gavarnie.
1400m; slopes 1850–2400m
🚡 *11* 🎿 *45km*

Gazprom Laura 35
One of the venues for the Sochi Winter Olympics in 2014.

Geilo Norway
Small, quiet, unspoiled community on the railway line from Bergen, on the coast, to Oslo. It provides all the basics of a resort – a handful of cafes and shops around the railway station, a dozen hotels more widely spread around the wide valley, children's facilities and a sports centre. Geilo is a superb cross-country resort. It's very limited for downhillers, and none of the runs is very difficult, but it does claim to have Scandinavia's only super-pipe.
800m; slopes 800–1180m
🚡 *18* 🎿 *35km*
🚌 *Absolutely Snow, Crystal, Crystal Finest, Headwater, Inntravel, Neilson, Ski Safari, Thomson*

Gérardmer France
Sizeable lakeside resort in the northerly Vosges mountains near Strasbourg, with plenty of amenities. Limited downhill slopes nearby include one of almost 4km. Extensive ski de fond trails in the area.
665m; slopes 750–1150m
🚡 *20* 🎿 *40km* 🚌 *Lagrange*

Gerlitzen Austria
Carinthia's central ski area. A worthwhile outing from Bad Kleinkirchheim. Gondola ride from the valley near Villach, with good views and varied but short runs.
500m; slopes 1000–1910m
🚡 *15* 🎿 *26km*

Gerlos 140
Village in the Zillertal Arena.

Gerlosplatte Austria
Inexpensive but fairly snow-sure area above the village of Krimml, linked to Königsleiten, Gerlos and Zell am Ziller to form a fair-sized intermediate area.

Les Gets 270

La Giettaz 274
Tiny village between La Clusaz and Megève.

Gitschtal / Weissbriach Austria
One of many little areas near Hermagor in eastern Austria, close to Italian border.
690m; slopes 690–1400m
🚡 *4* 🎿 *5km*

Glaris Switzerland
Hamlet base station for the uncrowded Rinerhorn section of the Davos slopes.
1460m; slopes 1460–2490m
🚡5 🚠 30km

Glencoe 665
Scottish ski resort.
305m; slopes 305–1110m
🚡7 🚠 20km

Glenshee 665
Scottish ski resort.
610m; slopes 610–1070m
🚡22 🚠 40km

Going 107
Small area near Ellmau, linked to the huge SkiWelt area.

Goldegg Austria
Year-round resort famous for its lakeside castle. Limited slopes but Wagrain (Salzburger Sportwelt) and Grossarl (Gastein valley) are nearby.
825m; slopes 825–1250m
🚡4 🚠 12km

Golden Canada
Small logging town, the place to stay when visiting Kicking Horse resort 15 minutes away. Also the launch pad for Purcell heli-skiing.

Golte Slovenia
Ski area in the East Karavanke mountains, above Mozirje. Gondola to the slopes from Zekovec village. Mostly advanced runs.
🚡7 🚠 18km

Gore Mountain USA
One of the better areas in New York State. Near Lake Placid, sufficiently far north to avoid worst weekend crowds. Intermediate terrain.
455m; slopes 455–1095m
🚡9 🚠 290 acres

Göriach Austria
Hamlet with trail connecting into one of the longest, most snow-sure cross-country networks in Europe. *1250m*

Gornaya Karusel 35
One of the venues for the Sochi Winter Olympics in 2014.

Gortipohl Austria
Traditional village in the pretty Montafon valley.
920m; slopes 900–2395m
🚡61 🚠 243km

Gosau Austria
Family-friendly resort, with straggling village. Plenty of pretty, if low, runs. Fast lifts mean queues are rare. Snow-sure Obertauern and Schladming are within reach.
755m; slopes 755–1800m
🚡37 🚠 80km 🚋 Crystal

Göstling Austria
One of Austria's easternmost resorts, between Salzburg and Vienna. A traditional village in a wooded setting.
530m; slopes 530–1880m
🚡8 🚠 18km

Götzens Austria
Valley village base for Axamer Lizum and Mutters, near Innsbruck. Gondola from village to Mutteralm and red run back down.
870m; slopes 830–2100m
🚡4 🚠 15km
🚋 Inghams, Lagrange

Gourette-Eaux-Bonnes France
Most snow-sure resort in the French Pyrenees. Very popular with local families, so best avoided at weekends.
1400m; slopes 1400–2400m
🚡14 🚠 30km

Grächen Switzerland
Charming chalet-village reached by tricky access road off the approach to Zermatt. A small area of open slopes, mainly above the trees and of red-run difficulty, reached by two gondolas – one to Hannigalp (2115m), the main focus of activity with a very impressive children's nursery area. The village has almost a score of hotels, mostly 3-star; most of the accommodation is in chalets and apartments.
1615m; slopes 1615–2865m
🚡9 🚠 42km

Le Grand-Bornand France
Covered by the Aravis lift pass, and much smaller and even more charming than La Clusaz. The slopes can be accessed from either the outskirts of the village or from the satellite village of Le Chinaillon. There are worthwhile shady black runs on Le Lachat, and on the lower peak of La Floria. There are plenty of good cruising blue and red intermediate runs, and also good beginner slopes. And there are extensive cross-country trails in the Vallée du Bouchet and towards Le Chinaillon.
1000m; slopes 1000–2100m
🚡29 🚠 90km
🚋 AmeriCan Ski, Erna Low, Lagrange, Peak Retreats, PowderBeds, Ski France, Ski Independence, Ski Weekender, Zenith

Grand Targhee 595
Powder skiing paradise an hour from Jackson Hole.
2439m; slopes 2260–3005m
🚡5 🚠 2100 acres

Les Granges 216
Hamlet at the mid-station of the funicular up from Bourg to Les Arcs.

Grangesises Italy
Small satellite of Sestriere, with lifts up to the main slopes.

Granite Peak USA
One of the oldest areas in the Great Lakes region, and now one of the largest. New base

village. Good selection of black runs on the upper mountain.
🚡7 🚠 400 acres

Grau Roig 95
Mini-resort between Pas de la Casa and Soldeu.

La Grave 272

Great Divide USA
Area near Helena, Montana, best for experts. Mostly bowls; plus near-extreme Rawhide Gulch.
1765m; slopes 1765–2195m
🚡6 🚠 720 acres

Gresse-en-Vercors France
Resort south of Grenoble. Sheltered slopes worth noting for bad-weather days.
1250m; slopes 1600–1750m
🚡13 🚠 18km

Gressoney-la-Trinité 420
Village in Monterosa Ski area.

Gressoney-St-Jean Italy
Larger and lower of the two villages in the central valley of the Monterosa Ski area. Good for cross-country as well as downhill. Varied slopes and well-equipped nursery area.
1390m; 🚠 7km
🚋 Alpine Answers

Grimentz 504
Village in the Val d'Anniviers.

Grindelwald 479

Grossarl 104
Secluded village in the Gastein valley.

Grossglockner area Austria
Two linked areas near Heiligenbliut, above the villages of Kals and Matrei. Remote position west of Bad Gastein. Uncrowded, fairly extensive slopes. Some long, varied runs.
1000m; slopes 1000–2620m
🚡15 🚠 110km

Grosskirchheim Austria
Area near Heiligenblut, not linked but access to 55km slopes.
1025m; slopes 1025–1400m

Grouse Mountain Canada
The Vancouver area with the largest lift capacity. Superb city views from mostly easy slopes; night skiing.
880m; slopes 880–1245m
🚡11 🚠 120 acres

Grünau Austria
Spacious riverside village in a lovely lake-filled part of eastern Austria. Nicely varied area, but very low.
525m; slopes 620–1600m
🚡15 🚠 40km

Gryon 519
Village below Villars.

Gstaad Switzerland
Despite its exclusive reputation, an attractive, traditional village where anyone could have a relaxing holiday. Of the four sectors, the largest is above

Saanenmöser and Schönried, reached by train. Snow-cover can be unreliable except on the Glacier des Diablerets, 15km away. Few runs challenge experts. Black runs rarely exceed red or even blue difficulty. There is off-piste potential. Given good snow, this is a superb area for intermediates, with long, easy descents in the major area. The nursery slopes at Wispile are adequate, and there are plenty of runs to progress to. Time lost on buses or trains is more of a problem than queues.
1050m; slopes 950–3000m
🚡53 🚠 220km
🚋 Alpine Answers, Momentum, Oxford Ski Co, Powder Byrne, PowderBeds, Ski Bespoke, Ski Independence, Ski Weekend, STC, Switzerland Travel Centre, White Roc

Gunstock USA
One of the New Hampshire resorts closest to Boston, popular with families. Primarily easy slopes. Lovley Lake Winnisquam views.
275m; slopes 275–700m
🚡8 🚠 220 acres

Guthega Australia
Australia's most challenging and diverse resort (at Perisher). Comfortable accommodation in the resort's only commercial lodge. Free shuttle from Jindabyne. 6.5 hours from Sydney.
1640m; slopes 1605–2035m
🚡47 🚠 3075 acres

Guzet France
Charming cluster of chalets set in a pine forest at Guzet 1400. Three main sectors offer slopes for all levels.
1400m; slopes 1100–2100m
🚡14 🚠 40km

Hafjell Norway
Main ski area for Lillehammer.
🚡12 🚠 33km 🚋 Neilson

Haider Alm Italy
Area in the Val Venosta in the South Tyrol close to Nauders. Malda Haider is its Italian name. 🚡5 🚠 20km

Hakuba 666
European-style resort four hours from Tokyo.

Harper Mountain Canada
Small, family-friendly resort in Kamloops, British Columbia.
1100m; slopes 1100–1525m
🚡3 🚠 400 acres

Harrachov Czech Republic
Closest resort to Prague, with enough terrain to justify a day trip. No beginner area.
650m; slopes 650–1020m
🚡4 🚠 8 runs

Hasliberg Switzerland
Four rustic hamlets on a sunny plateau overlooking Meiringen and Lake Brienz.

Two of them are the bottom stations of a varied intermediate area. *1050m*

Haus   **164**
Village next to Schladming.

Haystack   USA
Minor satellite of Mount Snow, in Vermont, but with a bit more steep skiing.
580m; slopes 580–1095m
⛷ 26 ⛰ 540 acres

Heavenly   **541**

Hebalm   Austria
One of many small areas in Austria's easternmost ski region near Slovenian border. No major resorts in vicinity.
1350m; slopes 1350–1400m
⛷ 6 ⛰ 11km

Heiligenblut   Austria
Picturesque village in beautiful surroundings at the foot of the Grossglockner, west of Bad Gastein. Quiet, mainly red runs in two main areas. Lifts include three gondolas and a fast chair.
1300m; slopes 1300–2910m
⛷ 12 ⛰ 55km

Heiterwang   Austria
Small lakeside village with access to Berwang's slopes in the Zugspitz Arena. Bus ride to the lift station. Couple of local downhill slopes and popular cross-country venue.
995m ⛷ 2 ⛰ 2km

Hemlock Resort   Canada
Area 55 miles east of Vancouver towards Sun Peaks. Mostly intermediate terrain and with snowfall of 600 inches a year. Lodging is available at the base area.
1000m; slopes 1000–1375m
⛷ 4 ⛰ 350 acres

Hemsedal   **655**

Heremence   Switzerland
Quiet, traditional village in unspoiled attractive setting south of Sion. Verbier's slopes are accessed a few minutes' drive away at Les Masses.
1250m

Hermagor   Austria
Main village base for the Nassfeld ski area in Carinthia.
600m; slopes 610–2000m
⛷ 30 ⛰ 100km

High 1 Resort   South Korea
Small ski area at the High 1 leisure complex, 250km from Seoul by train. ⛰ 21km

Hinterglemm   **158**
One of the villages making up Saalbach-Hinterglemm.

Hintermoos   Austria
Tiny village east of Saalbach and part of the large, low-altitude Hochkönig area that spreads impressively over a series of gentle peaks linking Maria Alm to Mühlbach.
slopes 800–1900m
⛷ 33 ⛰ 150km

Hintersee   Austria
Easy slopes very close to Salzburg. Several long top-to-bottom runs and lifts so size of the ski area is greatly reduced if the snowline is high.
745m; slopes 750–1470m
⛷ 9 ⛰ 40km

Hinterstoder   Austria
A very quiet valley village – neat but not overtly charming – spread along the road up the dead-end Stodertal in Upper Austria. The local Höss slopes are pleasantly wooded, less densely at the top, with splendid views. It's a small area, but has a worthwhile vertical of 1250m, and 450m above mid-mountain. A gondola from the main street goes up to the flat-bottomed bowl of Huttereböden (1400m), where there are very gentle but limited nursery slopes and lifts up to higher points. Most of the mountain is of easy red steepness. The run to the valley is a pleasant red with one or two tricky bits where it takes a quick plunge; it has effective snowmaking.
600m; slopes 600–1860m
⛷ 14 ⛰ 36km

Hinterthal   Austria
One of five villages in the varied Hochkönig area that spreads over a series of gentle peaks from Maria Alm to Mühlbach. The village is small – little more than a few four-star hotels and chalets, shops and bars – but it connects well with the main area via a newish gondola. There are good nursery slopes and some challenging reds.
990m; slopes 800–1900m
⛷ 33 ⛰ 150km
✉ *Elevation Holidays, STC*

Hintertux / Tux valley   **110**

Hippach   **140**
Hamlet near a crowd-free lift into Mayrhofen's main area.

Grand Hirafu   **666**
Interlinked area in Niseko, Japan.

Hittisau   **192**
Village in Bregenzerwald.
800m; slopes 800–1600m
⛷ 5 ⛰ 9km

Hochfügen   Austria
High-altitude ski-station outpost of Fügen, part of Ski Optimal area linked with Kaltenbach. Best suited to intermediates.
1500m; slopes 560–2500m
⛷ 35 ⛰ 155km

Hochgurgl   **146**
Quiet village with connection to Obergurgl's slopes.

Hochkönig   Austria
Varied area that spreads over four linked mountains from Maria Alm via Hinterthal and Dienten to Mühlbach.
800–1070m; slopes 800–1900m
⛷ 33 ⛰ 150km

Hochpillberg   Austria
Hamlet with fabulous views towards Innsbruck and an antique chairlift into varied terrain above Schwaz with good vertical of 1000m. Wonderfully safe for children; all accommodation within two minutes of lift.
1300m; slopes 1300–2100m
⛷ 5 ⛰ 10km

Hochsölden   **168**
Satellite above Sölden.

Hoch-Ybrig   Switzerland
Purpose-built complex only 64km south-east of Zürich, with facilities for families.
1050m; slopes 1050–1830m
⛷ 12 ⛰ 50km

Hochzillertal   Austria
Along with Hochfugen forms the large Ski Optimal area above the valley village of Kaltenbach. Best suited to intermediates – but there is plenty of potential for off-piste too.
1500m; slopes 560–2500m
⛷ 35 ⛰ 155km

Holiday Valley   USA
Family resort in New York State, an hour's drive south-east of Buffalo.
slopes 485–685m
⛷ 12 ⛰ 270 acres

Hollersbach   Austria
Hamlet near Mittersill, over Pass Thurn from Kitzbühel, with a gondola up to the Resterhöhe above Pass Thurn.
805m; slopes 805–1000m
⛷ 2 ⛰ 5km

Homewood   USA
Uncrowded area near Tahoe City with the most sheltered slopes in the vicinity. Apart from one fast quad, most slopes are served by slow chairlifts, and the views are as much of an attraction as the slopes. Set right on the western shore of the lake, so access is quick and easy. The notably quiet slopes include plenty of short black pitches as well as cruisers.
1900m; slopes 1900–2400m
⛷ 7 ⛰ 1260 acres

Hoodoo Ski Bowl   USA
Small area in Oregon with short runs and limited vertical of around 300m. Some 65km from Bend (see Mount Bachelor).
1420m; slopes 1420–1740m
⛷ 5 ⛰ 800 acres

Hopfgarten   **173**
Small chalet village with lift link into the SkiWelt area.

Horseshoe Resort   Canada
Toronto region resort with high-capacity lift system and 100% snowmaking. The second mountain – The Heights – is open to members only.
310m; slopes 310–405m
⛷ 7 ⛰ 60 acres

Les Houches   **233**
Varied area at the entrance to the Chamonix valley.

Hovden   Norway
Big, modern luxury lakeside hotel in wilderness midway between Oslo and Bergen. Cross-country venue with some Alpine slopes.
820m; slopes 820–1175m
⛷ 5 ⛰ 14km

La Hoya   Argentina
Small uncrowded resort 15km from the town of Esquel.
slopes 1350–2150m
⛷ 9 ⛰ 22km

Huez   **206**
Charming old hamlet on the road up to Alpe-d'Huez.

Hunter Mountain   USA
Popular New Yorkers' area so it gets very crowded at weekends.
485m; slopes 485–975m
⛷ 14 ⛰ 230 acres

Hüttschlag   Austria
Hamlet in a dead-end valley with lifts into the Gastein area at nearby Grossarl.
1020m; slopes 1020–1220m ⛷ 1

Hyundai Sungwoo Resort
South Korea
Modern high-rise resort, 140km from Seoul. Host to the 2009 World Snowboard Championships. ⛷ 9

Idre Fjäll   Sweden
Collective name for four areas 490km north-west of Stockholm.
slopes 590–890m
⛷ 30 ⛰ 28km

Igls   Austria
Almost a suburb of Innsbruck – the city trams run out to the village – but it is a small resort in its own right. Its famous downhill race course is an excellent piste.
900m; slopes 900–2245m
⛷ 9 ⛰ 7km
✉ *Crystal, Lagrange, STC*

Iizuna   Japan
Tiny area 2.5 hours from Tokyo.
slopes 1080–1480m ⛷ 7

Incline Village   USA
Large village on northern edge of Lake Tahoe – it is a reasonable stop-off if you are touring.

Indianhead   USA
South Lake Superior area with the most snowfall in the region. Winds are a problem.
395m; slopes 395–585m
⛷ 12 ⛰ 195 acres

Inneralpbach Austria
Small satellite of Alpbach,
3km up the valley. *1050m*

Innerarosa Switzerland
The prettiest part of Arosa,
with lifts into the slopes and
a quiet, 'gentle' children''s
area. *1800m*

Innichen Italy
Small resort in South Tyrol.
San Candido in Italian.
1175m; slopes 1175–1580m
⛷4 ⛴ *15km*

Innsbruck Austria
Lively and interesting former
Olympic city at Alpine
crossroads, surrounded by
small areas, each ideal for a
day trip. Among them is the
Stubai glacier. Area pass
available.
575m; slopes 800–3210m
⛷90 ⛴ *300km*
📧 *Skiweekends.com*

Interlaken Switzerland
Large lakeside summer resort
at entrance to the valleys
leading to Wengen,
Grindelwald and Mürren.
📧 *Crystal, Neilson*

Ischgl 116
**Ishiuchi Maruyama-Gala-
Yuzawa Kogen** Japan
Three resorts with a shared
lift pass 90 minutes from
Tokyo by bullet train and
offering the largest ski area in
the central Honshu region.
255m; slopes 255–920m ⛷52

Isola 2000 France
A compact purpose-built
resort 90km from Nice, which
makes it great for short
breaks and very convenient.
The doorstep snow, high
slopes and an improving
range of amenities make it
equally appealing to families
and beginners; there are
some excellent nursery slopes
near the base. But the core of
the resort village isn't pretty:
mostly block-like and tatty
apartment buildings. The
slopes spread across three
main sectors, with varied runs
suiting confident
intermediates best; most are
above the treeline and often
sunny, but the resort's
southerly aspect means that
the area can have masses of
snow when it is in shorter
supply elsewhere in the
French Alps. And most slopes
keep their snow well.
2000m; slopes 1840–2610m
⛷22 ⛴ *120km*
📧 *Erna Low, Lagrange, Pierre
& Vacances, PowderBeds, Ski
Collection, Ski France, Ski
Solutions, Zenith*

Iso Syöte Finland
Finland's most southerly fell
region, 150km south of the
Arctic Circle but receiving the
most snow in the country. A
family-friendly resort that suits

beginners and intermediates
best, since there are only two
black runs. But there are two
freeride areas. Most runs are
short, with the longest 1200m
and a maximum vertical of
less than 200m. And all the
lifts are drags. There's a
terrain park, expanded
children's nursery area, tubing,
tobogganing, and igloo hotel.
Cross-country is big here, with
120kms of trails. There's a
choice of hotels and cabins.
430m; slopes 240–430m
⛷9 ⛴ *21km*
📧 *Crystal, Thomson*

Itter 173
Next to Söll.

Jackson USA
Classic New England village,
and a major cross-country
base. A lovely place from
which to ski New Hampshire's
Alpine areas.

Jackson Hole 601
Jasná Slovakia
Largest ski area in Slovakia, in
the Low Tatras mountains. Big
children's area, terrain park,
night skiing. Several tough
'freeride zones'.
slopes 1240–2005m
⛷14 ⛴ *21km* 📧 *Zenith*

Jasper Canada
Set in the middle of Jasper
National Park, this low-key,
low-rise little town appeals
more to those keen on
scenery and wildlife (and
cross-country skiing) rather
than piste miles. Could
combine a stay with Whistler,
Banff or Lake Louise. Snowfall
is modest by North American
standards and there is lots of
steep terrain that needs good
snow to be fun. Keen piste-
bashers will cover all the
groomed runs in half a day.
There are excellent nursery
slopes. Visitors have
commented on few crowds
and queues. There are 300km
of cross-country trails. Most
accommodation is out of town
or on the outskirts and the
local slopes are a 30-minute
drive.
1695m; slopes 1695–2610m
⛷8 ⛴ *1675 acres*
📧 *American Ski Classics,
Canadian Affair, Crystal, Crystal
Finest, Frontier, Independent
Ski Links, Inghams, Momentum,
Neilson, Ski Independence, Ski
Safari, Ski Solutions, Skiworld,
Virgin Snow*

Jay Peak USA
Vermont resort near Canadian
border with best snowfall
record in the east. Tree-lined
intermediate/advanced slopes
– as many classified black as

blue. Experts also have access
to hike-in/out terrain in West
bowl.
550m; slopes 550–1205m
⛷8 ⛴ *385 acres*
📧 *American Ski Classics, Ski
Safari, Virgin Snow*

Jochberg 123
Straggling village, 8km from
Kitzbühel.

La Joue-du-Loup France
Slightly stylish little purpose-
built place a few km north-
west of Gap. Shares a fair-
sized intermediate area with
Superdévoluy. A ski-in/ski-out,
family-oriented resort; all
accommodation in good-value
apartments and chalets; good
choice of affordable
restaurants. Easily reached
using budget flights to
Marseille.
1450m; slopes 1450–2450m
⛷22 ⛴ *100km*
📧 *Lagrange, Ski Collection*

Jouvenceaux 428
Less boisterous base near
Sauze d'Oulx.

Jukkasjärvi Sweden
Centuries-old cross-country
resort with unique ice hotel
rebuilt every December.

June Mountain USA
Small area a half-hour drive
from Mammoth and in same
ownership. Closed during the
2012/13 but due to be open
for the 2013/14 season.
2300m; slopes 2300–3090m
⛷8 ⛴ *500 acres*

Juns 110
Small village between
Lanersbach and Hintertux.

Kals am Grossglockner Austria
Remote valley village north of
Lienz. Now linked to Matrei.
1325m; slopes 975–2620m
⛷15 ⛴ *110km*

Kaltenbach Austria
One of the larger, quieter
Zillertal areas, with plenty of
high-altitude slopes, mostly
above the treeline.
560m; slopes 560–2500m
⛷35 ⛴ *155km*

Kamui Ski Links Japan
Small area on Hokkaido with
excellent powder reputation
and access to it allowed more
than in many other resorts.
Easy day trip from Furano.
slopes 150–750m ⛷6

Kananaskis Canada
Small area near Calgary, nicely
set in woods, with slopes at
Nakiska.
slopes 1525–2465m
⛷12 ⛴ *605 acres* 📧 *Frontier*

Kandersteg Switzerland
Good cross-country base set
amid beautiful scenery near
Interlaken. Easy, but limited,
slopes. Popular with families.
1175m; slopes 1175–1900m
⛷7 ⛴ *14km*
📧 *Headwater, Inntravel,
Neilson*

Kanin 662
Kappl Austria
A 15-minute bus ride down
the valley from Ischgl, and
worth a visit. Both the village
and the slopes are family-
oriented, and delightfully
quiet compared with Ischgl.
The village, with a couple of
dozen hotels and guest-
houses, sits on a shelf 100m
above the valley floor. The
slopes – served by an access
gondola from the roadside
and fast quads above it –
offer plenty of variety, with
several tough reds. Most of
the slopes are open, but the
run down the gondola offers
some shelter for bad-weather
days.
1260m; slopes 1180–2690m
⛷9 ⛴ *40km*
📧 *Interactive Resorts*

Kaprun 198
Classic Austrian charmer near
Zell am See.

Les Karellis France
Resort with slopes that are
more scenic, challenging and
snow-sure than those of
better-known Valloire, nearby.
1600m; slopes 1600–2550m
⛷15 ⛴ *60km*

Kastelruth Italy
German name for Castelrotto.

Kasurila Finland
Siilinjarvi ski area popular
with boarders. ⛷5

Katschberg Austria
Cute hamlet above the road
pass from Styria to Carinthia,
by-passed by Tauern
motorway. Non-trivial area of
high intermediate slopes.
Popular with families.
1640m; slopes 1065–2220m
⛷16 ⛴ *70km* 📧 *Neilson*

Keystone USA
Sprawling condo-dominated
resort below three varied
mountains; the nearest thing
to a proper village is a handy
development near the
gondola. Evenings are quiet,
with limited restaurants/bars.
The lift pass covers
Breckenridge and nearby
Arapahoe Basin. Fast lifts link
all three mountains, including
varied terrain including
ungroomed steep bowls,
forest glades and cat skiing.
There's a beautifully groomed
network of treelined blues
and greens, and good nursery
slopes. Reporters praise the
school for small classes.
There's a huge terrain park

and super-pipe, floodlit skiing and tubing. A favourite hut is the table-service Alpenglow Stube.
2830m; slopes 2830–3780m
🚡 20 🚠 3148 acres
✉ Alpine Answers, AmeriCan Ski, American Ski Classics, Erna Low, Independent Ski Links, PowderBeds, Ski Independence, Ski Safari, Skitracer, Snow Finders

Kicking Horse   **627**

Killington   **606**

Kimberley   Canada
Mining town turned twee mock Austro-Bavarian/English Tudor resort scenically set 2 hours from Banff. The terrain offers a mix of blue and black runs (and occasional green) and a vertical of 750m. The mainly forested runs are spread over two rather bland hills. There are only a few short double diamonds, but classification tends to understate difficulty, and many of the single diamonds are quite challenging. It has a reputation for good powder, although it doesn't get huge amounts by the standards of this region.
1230m; slopes 1230–1980m
🚡 5 🚠 1800 acres
✉ AmeriCan Ski, Frontier, Inghams, Ski Safari, Skiworld

Kirchberg   **123**
Lively town close to Kitzbühel.

Kirchdorf   Austria
Attractive village a bus ride from St Johann in Tirol, with good local beginner slopes.
640m; ✉ Crystal, Thomson

Kirkwood   USA
Renowned for its powder, and has a lot to offer experts and confident intermediates, but it's limited for intermediates who are not happy to tackle black runs. It makes a great outing from South Lake Tahoe, though heavy snowfall may close the high-level passes to get there. Deep snow is part of the attraction, often reportedly better than Heavenly.
2375m; slopes 2375–2985m
🚡 14 🚠 2300 acres

Kitzbühel   **123**

Kleinarl   Austria
Secluded traditional village up a pretty side valley from Wagrain, part of the three-valley lift network linking Flachauwinkl to Zauchensee – our figures relate to this area.
1015m; slopes 800–2185m
🚡 15 🚠 65km

Kleinwalsertal   **386**
Area in the German Alps.

Klippitztörl   Austria
One of many little areas in Austria's easternmost ski region near Slovenian border.
1550m; slopes 1460–1820m
🚡 6 🚠 25km

Klösterle   **195**
Valley village in the Alpenregion Bludenz.
1100m; slopes 1100–2300m
🚡 10 🚠 39km

Klosters   **483**

Kobla   **662**
Slovenian village a bus ride from Vogel.

Kolasin 1450   Montenegro
Small ski area on Bjelasica Mountain above the town of the Kolasin, where you stay.
1450m 🚡 5 🚠 20km

Kolsass-Weer   Austria
Pair of Inn-side villages with low, inconvenient and limited slopes.
555m; slopes 555–1010m
🚡 3 🚠 14km

Königsleiten   **140**
Quiet resort sharing area with Gerlos in the Zillertal Arena.

Konjiam   South Korea
Purpose-built resort 40 minutes north of Seoul. The slopes suit beginners best, and offer the area's longest run at 1.8km. The base village has over 400 condos, a restaurant and spa. Popular with families.
🚡 3 🚠 11 runs

Kopaonik   Serbia
Modern, sympathetically designed family resort in a pretty setting.
1770m; slopes 1110–2015m
🚡 23 🚠 60km

Koralpe   Austria
Largest and steepest of many gentle little areas in Austria's easternmost ski region near the Slovenian border.
1550m; slopes 1550–2050m
🚡 10 🚠 25km

Korea Condo   South Korea
A single condo complex built some way from the three slopes. 🚡 2

Kössen   Austria
Village near St Johann in Tirol with low, scattered and limited local slopes.
600m; slopes 600–1700m
🚡 9 🚠 25km

Kötschach-Mauthen   Austria
One of many little areas near Hermagor in eastern Austria, close to the Italian border.
710m; slopes 710–1300m
🚡 4 🚠 7km

Kranjska Gora   **662**

Krimml   Austria
Sunny area, high enough to have good snow usually. Shares regional pass with Wildkogel resorts (Neukirchen).
1075m; slopes 1640–2040m
🚡 9 🚠 33km

Krippenstein   Austria
A mainly freeride resort on Dachstein glacier near Salzburg. Cable car from Obertraun in the valley. 30km off-piste routes and 11km long blue/red run. Shares lift pass with Annaberg-Gosau region.

Krispl-Gaissau   Austria
Easy slopes very close to Salzburg. Several long top-to-bottom lifts mean the size of the area is greatly reduced if the snow line is high.
925m; slopes 750–1570m
🚡 11 🚠 40km

Kronplatz   Italy
Distinctive ski area in South Tyrol, with amazingly efficient lifts from Brunico and San Vigilio di Marebbe. Plan de Corones is its Italian name.
1200m; slopes 1200–2275m
🚡 32 🚠 114km
✉ Mountainsun

Krvavec   **662**

Kühtai   Austria
A collection of comfortable hotels beside a high road pass only 25km from Innsbruck – higher than equally snow-sure Obergurgl or Obertauern, but cheaper than either. Covered also by the standard Innsbruck pass. A modern gondola, three fast quads and a handful of drags serve red cruisers of about 500m vertical on either side of the road, plus some token black runs; not ideal for novices – few easy blues to graduate to. Very quiet in the week, but liable to weekend crowds if lower resorts around Innsbruck are short of snow. Limited mountain huts. Quiet in the evening, but for its size a reasonable selection of hotels.
2020m; slopes 800–2620m
🚡 12 🚠 44km
✉ Crystal, Inghams, STC

Kusatsu Kokusai   Japan
Attractive spa village with hot springs, three hours from Tokyo.
slopes 1250–2170m 🚡 13

Laax   **485**

Le Lac Blanc   France
Mini-resort with six-pack in the northerly Vosges mountains near Strasbourg. Extensive ski de fond trails.
830m; slopes 830–1235m
🚡 9 🚠 14km

Laces   Italy
Village in the Val Venosta in the South Tyrol covered by the Ortler Skiarena pass.

Lachtal   Austria
Second largest ski resort in the Styrian region NE of Salzburg.
1600m; slopes 1600–2100m
🚡 8 🚠 29km

Ladis   Austria
Smaller alternative to Serfaus and Fiss, with lifts that connect into the same varied ski area.
1200m; slopes 1200–2750m
🚡 70 🚠 190km

Lagunillas   Chile
83km south-east of Santiago.
🚠 494 acres

Le Laisinant   **366**
Tiny hamlet down the valley from Val d'Isère.

Lake Louise   **629**

Lake Tahoe   USA
Collection of 14 ski areas spectacularly set on California–Nevada border – Heavenly and Squaw Valley best known in Britain.
✉ AmeriCan Ski, Crystal Finest, Snow Finders

Lamoura   France
One of four villages that makes up the Les Rousses area in the Jura.
1120m; slopes 1120–1680m
🚡 40 🚠 40km

Landeck–Zams   Austria
Small ski area in the Tirol region.
780m; slopes 816–2210m
🚡 7 🚠 22km

Lans-en-Vercors   France
Village close to Villard-de-Lans and 30km from Grenoble. Highest slopes in the region; few snowmakers.
1020m; slopes 1400–1805m
🚡 16 🚠 24km

Lanslebourg   **363**
One of the villages that make up Val Cenis.

Lanslevillard   **363**
One of the villages that make up Val Cenis.

Laterns   Austria
Small, low altitude resort in the Vorarlberg near Friedrichshafen. Two fast chairs serve mainly red runs and some ski routes.
900m; slopes 900–1785m
🚡 6 🚠 27km

Lauchernalp-Lötschental   Switzerland
Small but tall and challenging slopes reached by cable car from Wiler in the secluded, picturesque, dead-end Lötschental, north of Rhône valley. Glacier runs above 3000m.
1970m; slopes 1420–3110m
🚡 6 🚠 33km

Lauterbrunnen   **488**
Valley town with rail connection up to Mürren.

on one side and more modern development on the other, but with a good choice of mid-priced hotels. The slopes have an almost equal share of blue and red runs that make great intermediate territory, though there are a few notable challenges – including the classic Canalone ski route. For a resort with a respectable altitude and a generally quiet and queue-free mountain, it is worth considering.
1550m; slopes 1550–2945m
↙ 12 ↗ 60km
✉ *Momentum*

Madonna di Campiglio 415
Mad River Glen USA
Cult resort, co-operatively owned, with some tough ungroomed terrain, a few well-groomed intermediate trails and antique lifts. Snowboarding is banned.
485m; slopes 485–1110m
↙ 4 ↗ 115 acres

La Magdelaine Italy
Close to Cervinia, and good on bad-weather days.
1645m; slopes 1645–1870m
↙ 4 ↗ 4km

Maishofen Austria
Cheaper place to stay when visiting equidistant Saalbach and Zell am See. *765m*

Malbun Liechtenstein
Quaint user-friendly little family resort, 16km from the capital, Vaduz. Limited slopes and short easy runs.
1600m; slopes 1595–2100m
↙ 6 ↗ 21km

Malcesine Italy
Large summer resort on Lake Garda with a fair area of slopes, served by a revolving cable car.
1430m; slopes 1430–1830m
↙ 8 ↗ 12km

Malga Ciapela Italy
Resort at the foot of the Marmolada glacier massif, with a link into the Sella Ronda. Cortina is nearby.
1445m; slopes 1445–3270m
↙ 8 ↗ 18km

Malga Haider Italy
Small area in Val Venosta, close to Austrian border. Haideralm is its German name. ↙ 5 ↗ 20km

Mallnitz Austria
Village in a pretty valley close to Slovenia, with two varied areas providing a fine mix of wooded and open runs. Closest is Ankogel. The snow-sure Molltal Glacier is nearby, above Flattach.
1200m ↙ 15 ↗ 88km

Mammoth Mountain 546
Manigod France
Small valley village, sharing quiet, wooded slopes with La Clusaz – over the Col de la Croix-Fry. *1100m* ↗ 132km

Marble Mountain Canada
Tiny area in the Humber Valley on Newfoundland. Good snow record by east coast standards. Splendid base lodge, and some slope-side lodging. Blomidon Cat Skiing operates nearby.
85m; slopes 10–545m
↙ 5 ↗ 175 acres ✉ Frontier

Les Marecottes Switzerland
Small area in Ski St-Bernard area near Verbier and 15 minutes from Martigny. Good views. Popular with families and freeriders.
1100m; slopes 1720–2200m
↙ 4 ↗ 25km

Maria Alm Austria
Charming unspoiled village at one end of the varied Hochkönig area that spreads over a series of gentle peaks via Hinterthal and Dienten to Mühlbach. Maria Alm, though small, is one of the two largest villages in the area, and the most animated in the evening; it's a pretty place with a splendid old church boasting the highest spire in Salzburgerland. The Hochkönig area is best for adventurous intermediates, but for beginners there is a good local nursery slope. Experts can explore the ungroomed ski routes and excellent off-piste. Snowboarders may find there are too many draglifts. Maria Alm also has its own small local area of slopes. There are 40km of cross-country trails in the area.
800m; slopes 800–1900m
↙ 33 ↗ 150km
✉ Interactive Resorts, Rocketski, Select Chalets

Mariapfarr Austria
Village at the heart of one of the longest, most snow-reliable cross-country networks in Europe. Sizeable Mauterndorf-St Michael Alpine area and Obertauern area are nearby. *1120m* ↙ 5 ↗ 30km

Mariazell Austria
Traditional Styria village with an impressive basilica. Limited slopes.
870m; slopes 870–1265m
↙ 5 ↗ 11km

Maribor-Pohorje 662
Marilleva 415
Small Trentino resort linked with Madonna di Campiglio.

Le Markstein France
Long-standing small resort in the northerly Vosges region near Strasbourg, which has hosted World Cup slalom races. Extensive Nordic trails.
slopes 770–1270m ↙ 10

Masella Spain
Friendly Pyrenean village linked with the slopes of La Molina to form the Alp 2500 area. Weekend crowds.
1600m; slopes 1600–2535m
↙ 31 ↗ 121km

La Massana Andorra
Pleasant valley town linked by gondola to the Arinsal/Pal slopes and fairly convenient for trips to Arcalis.
slopes 1550–2563m
↙ 31 ↗ 63km

Les Masses 508
A hamlet below Les Collons in the Verbier ski area.

Le Massif Canada
One of several small but developing areas near historic Québec City, dramatically set in a UNESCO World Bio Reserve overlooking the St Lawrence river; the views of the ice floes from the summit lodge are stunning. The varied but limited tree-lined slopes offer Eastern Canada's biggest vertical at 770m – including a couple of steep double-black-diamond runs and some good intermediate cruising.
35m; slopes 35–805m
↙ 6 ↗ 406 acres
✉ AmeriCan Ski, Frontier, Ski Safari

Matrei in Osttirol Austria
Large market village south of Felbertauern tunnel. Mostly high slopes, linked to Kals on the other side of the hill.
1000m; slopes 975–2620m
↙ 15 ↗ 110km ✉ Zenith

Maurienne Valley France
A great curving trench with over 20 winter resorts, from pleasant old valley villages to convenience resorts purpose-built in the 1960s.

Mauterndorf Austria
Village near Obertauern with tremendous snow record.
1120m; slopes 1075–2360m
↙ 10 ↗ 35km

Maverick Mountain USA
Montana resort with plenty of terrain accessed by few lifts. Cowboy Winter Games venue – rodeo one day, ski races the next.
2155m; slopes 2155–2800m
↙ 2 ↗ 500 acres

Mayens de Riddes Switzerland
Hamlet at the base of lifts on the back of Verbier's Savoleyres sector, more often referred to as La Tzoumaz. *1500m*

Mayens-de-Sion Switzerland
Tranquil hamlet off the road up to Les Collons – part of the Verbier area. *1470m*

Mayrhofen 140

Méaudre France
Small resort near Grenoble with good snowmaking to make up for its low altitude.
1000m; slopes 1000–1600m
↙ 10 ↗ 18km

Megève 274
Meiringen Switzerland
An old town in the broad Haslital valley, a good outing from the nearby Jungfrau resorts or Interlaken and 90 minutes' drive from Zürich or Bern. High-speed lifts take you into the slopes, which are on a broad, sunny mountainside spread across two main sectors. The area is particularly suitable for beginners and confident intermediates – experts will find little to challenge them and early intermediates will find a lack of blue runs. The area is popular with boarders but there are some flat sections. There's a good choice of mountain restaurants, and the resort is great for families with kids' snow gardens, special restaurants and fun areas. There's a choice of hotels and plenty of apartments; most of the restaurants are hotel-based. Après-ski is lively up the mountain but quiet and relaxed in town later on. There's plenty to do off the slopes – including visiting the Sherlock Holmes museum, of course.
600m; slopes 1060–2435m
↙ 14 ↗ 60km

Melchsee-Frutt Switzerland
Limited, but high and snow-sure bowl above a car-free village. Family-friendly.
1920m; slopes 1080–2255m
↙ 10 ↗ 32km

Mellau 192
Village in Bregenzerwald.
700m; slopes 700–2000m
↙ 31 ↗ 105km

Les Menuires 281
Merano 2000 Italy
Small ski area just outside Merano, with main lift base at Falzeben above Avelengo/Hafling.
2000m; slopes 2000–2240m
↙ 7 ↗ 40km

Méribel 287
Métabief-Mont-d'Or France
Twin villages in the Jura region, not far from Geneva.
900m; slopes 880–1460m
↙ 22 ↗ 42km

Methven New Zealand
Nearest town/accommodation to Mt Hutt, and helicopter base for trips to Arrowsmith range – good for intermediates as well as advanced.

Mieders 189
Village in the Stubai valley.

Mijoux France
Pretty wooded slopes between Dijon and Geneva. Lélex nearby.
1000m; slopes 900–1680m
29 50km

Mission Ridge USA
Area in dry region that gets higher-quality snow than other Seattle resorts but less of it. Good intermediate slopes.
1390m; slopes 1390–2065m
6 300 acres

Misurina Italy
Tiny village near Cortina. A cheap alternative base.
1755m; slopes 1755–1900m
4 13km

Mittenwald 386
Cute town in the Bavarian Alps. *915m*

Mittersill Austria
Valley-junction village south of Pass Thurn. A gondola runs from Hollersbach up to the Resterhöhe sector above Pass Thurn.
790m; slopes 1265–1895m
15 25km

Moena Italy
Large village between Cavalese and Sella Ronda resorts, ideally located for touring the Dolomites area.
1200m; slopes 1200–2500m
8 35km

La Molina Spain
Cheap, basic resort near Andorra, sharing a fair-sized, varied area with Masella to form Alp 2500.
1400m; slopes 1400–2535m
31 121km

Mölltal Glacier Austria
Little-known high glacier slopes above Flattach on the other side of the Tauern tunnel from Bad Gastein. Varied runs and fast lifts. Worthwhile excursion when the snowline is high. Summer skiing available.
2570m; slopes 695–3120m
8 53km

Molveno Italy
Lakeside village on the edge of the Dolomites, with a couple of lifts – but mostly used as a base to ski nearby Andalo.

Monarch USA
Wonderfully uncrowded area, a day trip from Crested Butte. Great powder. Good for all but experts.
3290m; slopes 3290–3645m
5 800 acres

Monesi Italy
Southernmost of the resorts south of Turin. Close to Monaco and Nice.
1310m; slopes 1310–2180m
5 38km

Le Monêtier 331
Quiet little village with access to Serre-Chevalier's slopes.

La Mongie 322

Montafon Austria
The 40km-long Montafon valley contains eleven resorts and four main lift systems. The valley is well worth a look. The biggest is the Nova area (linking Gaschurn and St Gallenkirch) and this is now linked to the Hochjoch area and Schruns. Gargellen and Golm are smaller ski areas in the valley.
655-1425m; slopes 655–2395m
61 219km
Crystal, Crystal Finest

Montalbert 310
Traditional village with access to the La Plagne network.

Mont Blanc Canada
Small locals' hill near Tremblant, with only 300m of vertical and no resemblance to the Franco-Italian item.
7 36

Montchavin 310
Attractive village on the fringe of La Plagne.

Mont-de-Lans 258
Low village near Les Deux-Alpes.

Le Mont-Dore France
Attractive traditional small town, the largest resort in the stunningly beautiful volcanic Auvergne region near Clermont-Ferrand.
1050m; slopes 1350–1850m
17 42km

Monte Bondone Italy
Trento's local hill.
1300m; slopes 1185–2090m
5 20km

Monte Campione Italy
Tiny purpose-built resort, spread thinly over four mountainsides; 80% snowmaking helps to offset the low altitude.
1100m; slopes 1200–2010m
16 80km

Monte Livata Italy
Closest resort to Rome, popular with weekenders.
1430m; slopes 1430–1750m
8 8km

Monte Piselli Italy
Tiny area with the highest slopes of the many little resorts east of Rome.
2100m; slopes 2100–2690m
3 5km

Monte Pora Italy
Tiny resort near Lake d'Iseo and Bergamo. Several other little areas nearby.
1350m; slopes 1350–1880m
11 30km

Monterosa Ski 420

Mont Gabriel Canada
Montreal area with runs on four sides of the mountain, though the south-facing sides rarely open. Two short but renowned double-black-diamond bump runs. 9

Montgenèvre 297

Mont Glen Canada
Least crowded of the Montreal areas, so a good weekend choice.
680m; slopes 680–1035m
4 110 acres

Mont Grand Fonds Canada
Small area sufficiently far from Québec not to get overrun at weekends.
400m; slopes 400–735m 4

Mont Habitant Canada
Very limited area in the Montreal region but with a good base lodge. 3

Mont Olympia Canada
Small, two-mountain area near Montreal, one mostly novice terrain, the other best suited to experts. 6

Mont Orford Canada
Cold, windswept lone peak (no resort), worth a trip from nearby Montreal on a fine day.
slopes 305–855m
8 180 acres

Mont-Ste-Anne Canada
Quebec City's biggest and most varied local ski area. Wide choice of amenities at the base. The slopes are limited, but the vertical is a decent 625m. A gondola goes to the top, from where slopes span north and south sides of the mountain. The views are spectacular. Over a third of the area is classified black or double black, so it's a good place for experts. The Beast (double-black diamond) has one of the steepest pitches in the east at 65%. But there are decent intermediate trails too, adequate nursery slopes and an easy top-to-bottom green run. The Dual mountain lift pass is valid at Stoneham.
175m; slopes 175–800m
11 526 acres
AmeriCan Ski, Frontier, Ski Safari

Mont-St-Sauveur Canada
Perhaps the prettiest resort in Canada, popular with Montreal (60km) day trippers and luxury condo owners.

Mont Sutton Canada
Varied area with some of the best glade skiing in eastern Canada, including some for novices. Quaint Sutton village nearby.
9 175 acres

Moonlight Basin 596
Quiet area of slopes linked to Big Sky, Montana.

Morgins 465
Resort on the Swiss side of the Portes du Soleil circuit.

Morillon 264
Valley village in the Flaine network.

Morin Heights Canada
Area in the Montreal region with 100% snowmaking. Attractive base lodge. 6

Morzine 302

Les Mosses Switzerland
Peaceful scenic resort and area, best for a day trip from Villars or Les Diablerets. There's a terrain park, a few chalet-style hotel-restaurants, shops and a rather fine church. There are only draglifts to access the mainly red and blue runs. Prides itself on the number of activities on offer – such as ice-diving, a natural ice rink and an international dog-sled track.
1500m; slopes 1500–2200m
14 60km

Mottaret 287
Purpose-built but reasonably attractive part of Méribel.

Mottarone Italy
Closest slopes to Lake Maggiore. No village – just a base area.
1200m; slopes 1200–1490m
25km

Les Moulins Switzerland
Village down the road from Château d'Oex with its own low area of slopes, part of the big Gstaad lift-pass area.
890m; slopes 890–3000m
58 250km

Mount Abram USA
Small, pretty, tree-lined area in Maine, renowned for its immaculately groomed easy runs.
295m; slopes 295–610m
5 170 acres

Mountain High USA
Best snowfall record and highest lift capacity in Los Angeles vicinity – plus 95% snowmaking. Mostly intermediate cruising.
2010m; slopes 2010–2500m
12 220 acres

Mount Ashland USA
Arty town in Oregon renowned for Shakespeare performances. Tiny ski area best for experts run by local charity.
1935m; slopes 1935–2285m
4 200 acres

Mount Bachelor USA
Extinct volcano in Oregon with a big ski area and runs on all sides. Higher elevation means better chance of good snow than many other resorts in north-west USA and average annual snowfall of 370 inches is more than any major Colorado resort. Good cruising and beginner terrain lower down and plenty to occupy experts, including tree-lined blacks and steep terrain on the south-facing slopes. No lodging at the base; stay 30 mins away at Sunriver Resort – a big lodge with bar, restaurant, chalet lodging and

excellent spa – or in Bend, an attractive small town served by free shuttles.
1920m; slopes 1755–2765m
⛷ 13 ⛷ 3680 acres
✉ *American Ski Classics, Ski Safari*

Mount Baker   USA
Almost on the coast near Seattle, yet one of the top resorts for snow (averages 600 inches a year). Plenty of challenging slopes. Known for spectacular avalanches.
1115m; slopes 1115–1540m
⛷ 9 ⛷ 1000 acres

Mount Baldy   Canada
Tiny area, but a worthwhile excursion from Big White. Gets ultra light snow – great glades/powder chutes.
slopes 1705–2150m
⛷ 2 ⛷ 150 acres

Mount Baldy   USA
Some of the longest and steepest runs in California. Only an hour's drive from Los Angeles so a day trip is feasible, but 20% snowmaking and antiquated lifts are major drawbacks.
1980m; slopes 1980–2620m
⛷ 4 ⛷ 400 acres

Mount Baw Baw   Australia
Small but entertaining intermediate area in attractive woodland, with great views. Closest area to Melbourne (150km).
1450m; slopes 1450–1560m
⛷ 7 ⛷ 35 hectares

Mount Buffalo   Australia
Site of Australia's first ski lift. Plateau area best suited to beginners. Short season. On-mountain accommodation four hours from Melbourne.
1400m; slopes 1455–1610m
⛷ 8 ⛷ 66 acres

Mount Buller   Australia
Three hours from Melbourne and Victoria's largest ski area. Proper resort village, with with a 360-degree network of short runs on its isolated massif. Luxury hotel and spa.
1600m; slopes 1600–1790m
⛷ 22 ⛷ 80km

Mount Dobson   New Zealand
Mostly intermediate slopes in a wide, treeless basin near Mt Cook, with good snow-cover. Accommodation in Fairlie, 40 minutes away.
1610m; slopes 1610–2010m
⛷ 3 ⛷ 990 acres

Mount Falakro   Greece
Area two hours' drive from Salonica in northern Greece; almost as big as Parnassos, uncrowded and with good views. Has a fast quad.
1720m ⛷ 8 ⛷ 22km

Mount Hood Meadows   USA
The biggest and most varied ski area on Mt Hood in Oregon served by 11 lifts including five fast quads.

Good beginner area, intermediate cruising, single black diamond runs in the centre of the main ski area and a big area of double black diamond runs roped off and entered through gates. Up to six terrain parks, depending on snow conditions. No accommodation at the base – stay at Timberline (see separate entry) half an hour away or Government Camp (near Mt Hood Skibowl, which also gets its own entry) 20 minutes away.
1635m; slopes 1375–2225m
⛷ 11 ⛷ 2150 acres
✉ *Ski Safari*

Mount Hood Skibowl   USA
Small area of mainly tough gladed runs, offering the steepest and most extreme slopes in the Mount Hood area. Claims to be America's largest night skiing area with a lot of runs open up to 10/11pm nightly. Two floodlit terrain parks, tubing hills, snow bikes and snowmobiles. Just below Timberline ski area; stay there or in Government Camp at the foot of Skibowl's slopes, a sizeable settlement with a choice of lodgings and restaurants. Other local ski area is Mt Hood Meadows.
1075m; slopes 1075–1530m
⛷ 7 ⛷ 960 acres

Mount Hotham   Australia
Australia's highest ski village. Built on a ridge above the slopes. Intermediate and advanced skiing. Good snow record. Nearest town Bright, four hours from Melbourne.
1750m; slopes 1450–1845m
⛷ 13 ⛷ 30km

Mount Hutt   New Zealand
Steepest, most snow-sure area in NZ, with ocean views, but prone to bad weather; 100km from Christchurch, a tricky drive up from Methven.
slopes 1405–2085m
⛷ 4 ⛷ 365 hectares

Mount Lemmon   USA
Southernmost area in North America, close to famous Old West town Tombstone, Arizona. Reasonable snowfall.
2500m; slopes 2500–2790m
⛷ 3 ⛷ 70 acres

Mount McKay   Australia
Australia's steepest skiing accessed from Falls Creek, with genuine black-diamond terrain and snowcats. *1600m*

Mount Pilio   Greece
Pleasant slopes cut out of dense forest, only 15km from the holiday resort of Portaria above town of Volos.
1500m ⛷ 3

Mount Rose   USA
Much the highest base elevation in the Tahoe area – a good 600m above the lake – and with an annual snowfall average of 400 inches. The Chutes is a shady bowl mainly of serious double-diamond gradient on the front face of the slopes. But there are blue and easy black runs to the base and a wider, gentler, lightly wooded area. The slopes have a lot to offer, especially if staying in Heavenly – where the groomed stuff may be too dull and the ungroomed stuff too challenging.
2520m; slopes 2410–2955m
⛷ 6 ⛷ 1200 acres

Mount Shasta Ski Park   USA
Californian resort 300 miles north of San Francisco.
⛷ 4 ⛷ 425 acres

Mount Snow   USA
A one-peak resort, with a long row of lifts on the front face (two fast quads among them) serving easy and intermediate runs of just over 500m vertical. Separate area of black runs on the north face – including a couple of short but serious double blacks – served by a triple chair and a six-pack. And on the opposite side a small area of intermediate runs above Carinthia base, accessed by a third fast quad. Reputed to have some of the best terrain parks in the east. Lodgings at the base include a Grand Summit hotel.
580m; slopes 580–1095m
⛷ 19 ⛷ 590 acres
✉ *American Ski Classics, Ski Safari*

Mount Spokane   USA
Little intermediate area near Spokane (Washington State).
1160m; slopes 1160–1795m
⛷ 5 ⛷ 350 acres

Mount St Louis / Moonstone   Canada
Premier area in Toronto region, spread over three peaks. Very high-capacity lift system and 100% snowmaking. ⛷ 13 ⛷ 175

Mount Sunapee   USA
Area in New Hampshire closest to Boston; primarily intermediate terrain.
375m; slopes 375–835m
⛷ 10 ⛷ 230 acres

Mount Vermio   Greece
Oldest ski base in Greece. Two areas in central Macedonia 60km from Thessaloniki. Barren but interesting slopes.
slopes 1420–2000m ⛷ 7

Mount Washington Resort   Canada
Scenic area on Vancouver Island with lodging in the base village. Impressive snowfall record but rain is a problem.
1110m; slopes 1110–1590m
⛷ 6 ⛷ 970 acres ✉ *Frontier*

Mount Washington Resort   USA
One of several small resorts in New Hampshire scattered along the Interstate 93 highway. The slopes are on a single mountain face but highly rated, particularly by families, who relish the top-to-bottom easy trails on the main peak, Mt Rosebrook. There is a good mix of terrain, with West Mountain consisting mainly of double-diamond slopes. Snowmaking is comprehensive. There's a terrain park, half-pipe and boardercross. There are a few places to stay near the base, with the grand old Mount Washington hotel five minutes away.
480m; slopes 480–940m
⛷ 8 ⛷ 435 acres

Mount Waterman   USA
Small Los Angeles area where children ski free. The lack of much snowmaking is a drawback.
2135m; slopes 2135–2440m
⛷ 3 ⛷ 210 acres

Mühlbach   Austria
Sprawling village along the main road at one end of the Hochkönig area that spreads over a series of gentle peaks via Dienten to Maria Alm. The Hochkönig area is best for adventurous intermediates, but for beginners there is a good local nursery slope. Experts can explore the ungroomed ski routes and the excellent off-piste. Snowboarders may find there are too many draglifts. There are 40km of cross-country trails in the area.
855m; slopes 800–1900m
⛷ 33 ⛷ 150km

Mühltal   Austria
Small village halfway between Niederau and Auffach in the Wildschönau. No local skiing of its own.
780m; slopes 830–1905m
⛷ 25 ⛷ 70km

Muhr   Austria
Village by Katschberg tunnel well placed for visiting St Michael, Bad Kleinkirchheim, Flachau and Obertauern.
1110m

Muju Resort   South Korea
Largest area in Korea and with a fair amount of lodging. Though it is the furthest resort from Seoul (four hours south) it is still overcrowded.
⛷ 14

Mürren   488
Mutters   Austria
Charming rustic village near Innsbruck, at the foot of long slopes of 900m vertical that extend along the Götzens valley to Axamer Lizum. Good for families and beginners.
830m; slopes 830–2340m
⛷ 4 ⛷ 15km

Myoko Suginohara Kokusai
  Japan
A series of small resorts two or three hours from Tokyo, which together make up an area of extensive slopes with longer, wider runs than normal for Japan. ⛷ 15
⛷ Ski Safari

Naeba   Japan
Fashionable resort with lots of accommodation two hours north of Tokyo. Crowded slopes.
900m; slopes 900–1800m ⛷ 30

Nakiska   Canada
Small area of wooded runs between Banff and Calgary, with emphasis on downhill speed. Unreliable snow, but state-of-the-art snowmaking and pancake-flat grooming.
1525m; slopes 1525–2260m
⛷ 5 ⛷ 230 acres

Nasserein   180
Quiet suburb of St Anton.

Nassfeld Ski Arena   Austria
Carinthia's biggest: scenic and sunny area on the Italian border. Good intermediate slopes. Stay in Tröpolach, by the gondola, or larger Hermagor, further east.
1500m; slopes 610–2195m
⛷ 30 ⛷ 110km
⛷ Interactive Resorts, Ski Line, STC

Nauders   Austria
Spacious, traditionally Tirolean village tucked away only 3km from the Swiss border and almost on the Italian one. Its slopes start 2km outside the village (free shuttle-bus) and are mainly high and sunny intermediate runs spread over three areas. Lots of snowmaking. Not ideal for experts, though there is a lot of off-piste terrain. Not ideal for complete beginners either – the village nursery slopes are some way out. There are five cross-country trails amounting to 40km in all.
1400m; slopes 1400–2850m
⛷ 24 ⛷ 120km

Nax   Switzerland
Quiet, sunny village in a balcony setting overlooking the Rhône valley. Own little

area and only a short drive from Veysonnaz. Handful of red and blue runs.
1300m ⛷ 6 ⛷ 35km

Nendaz   508
A sizeable family resort linked in to the Verbier ski area.

Neukirchen   Austria
Quiet, pretty resort sharing slopes with Bramberg. Fairly snow-sure plateau at the top of its mountain.
855m; slopes 855–2150m
⛷ 15 ⛷ 50km
⛷ Crystal

Neustift   189
Village in the Stubai valley.

Nevegal   Italy
Weekend place near Belluno, south of Cortina.
1030m; slopes 1030–1650m
⛷ 14 ⛷ 30km

Nevis Range   665
Scottish ski resort.
90m; slopes 655–1220m
⛷ 11 ⛷ 35km

Niederau   Austria
Chalet-style village, the main resort in the Wildschönau part of Ski Juwel, and a favourite with beginners and early intermediate skiers. Quite spread out, but few hotels are more than five minutes' walk from a main lift.
830m
⛷ Crystal, Independent Ski Links, Inghams, Neilson, Skitracer, STC, Thomson

Niederdorf   Italy
Cross-country village in South Tyrol. Villabassa is its Italian name.

Niseko   666
Resort on Hokkaido island, Japan.

Niseko Village   666
One of Niseko's three interlinked areas.

Nockberge Innerkrems Austria
Area just south of Katschberg tunnel.
1500m; slopes 1500–2020m
⛷ 10 ⛷ 33km

Nordseter   Norway
Cluster of hotels in deep forest north of Lillehammer. Some Alpine facilities but best for cross-country.
850m; slopes 1000–1090m
⛷ 2 ⛷ 2km

Norefjell   Norway
Norway's toughest run, a very steep 600m drop. 120km north-west of Oslo.
185m; slopes 185–1185m
⛷ 10 ⛷ 23km
⛷ Absolutely Snow, Ski Safari

La Norma   France
Traffic-free, purpose-built resort near Modane and Val Cenis.
1350m; slopes 1350–2750m
⛷ 18 ⛷ 65km
⛷ AmeriCan Ski, Erna Low, Peak Retreats, Ski France

Norquay   612
Banff's quiet local hill.

North Conway   USA
Attractive factory-outlet-shopping town in New Hampshire close to Attitash and Cranmore ski areas.
⛷ Virgin Snow

Northstar-at-Tahoe   USA
Classic US-style mountain, with runs cut through dense forest and a pleasant base village that is still growing. The whole area is very sheltered and good for bad-weather days. A gondola and a fast quad go up to a lodge at Big Springs, only 160m above the village. From this point three fast chairs radiate to serve a broad bowl with some short steep pitches at the top, with easier blue runs lower down and around the ridges. From the ridge you can access the Backside, a steeper bowl with a central fast quad chair serving a row of easy black runs. Lookout Mountain has more black runs and a modest vertical of 390m.
1930m; slopes 1930–2625m
⛷ 19 ⛷ 3000 acres
⛷ American Ski Classics, Ski Safari, Ski Solutions, Skiworld, Supertravel, Virgin Snow

Nôtre-Dame-de-Bellecombe
  France
Pleasant 'very French' village spoiled by the busy road. Inexpensive base from which to visit Megève, though it has fair slopes of its own. Queues and slow lifts can be a problem now it is linked to Les Saisies. Free bus to/from Crest Voland.
1150m; slopes 1035–2070m
⛷ 84 ⛷ 175km
⛷ AmeriCan Ski, Erna Low, Lagrange, Peak Retreats

Nova Levante   Italy
Village close to Bozen/Bolzano with lifts up to small network around Passo di Costalunga.
1200m ⛷ 16 ⛷ 40km

Nozawa Onsen   Japan
Spa village with good hot springs three hours from Tokyo. The runs are cut out of heavy vegetation.
500m; slopes 500–1650m ⛷ 21
⛷ Ski Safari

Nub's Nob   USA
One of the most sheltered Great Lakes ski areas (many suffer fierce winds). 100% snowmaking; weekend crowds from Detroit. Wooded slopes suitable for all abilities.
275m; slopes 275–405m
⛷ 8 ⛷ 245 acres

O2Resort   South Korea
Built up the mountain in Gangwon province and with Korea's best snow. Slopes suit all levels and include a 3.2km

long run. Facilities include: condos, youth hostel, fitness centre, spa and restaurants.
1420m ⛷ 16runs

Oberammergau   386
Village in the Bavarian Alps.
835m

Oberau   Austria
Pretty village in the Ski Juwel (Alpbachtal-Wildschönau) area – but least convenient for the slopes.
935m ⛷ Inghams, Neilson

Obereggen   Italy
Tiny resort close to Bozen/Bolzano with modest area of slopes also accessible from Predazzo in Val di Fiemme.
1550m; slopes 1550–2200m
⛷ 6 ⛷ 10km

Obergurgl   146
Oberjoch–Hindelang   Germany
Small, low-altitude resort, particularly good for beginners.
850m; slopes 1140–1520m
⛷ 12 ⛷ 32km

Oberlech   131
Car- and crowd-free family resort alternative to Lech.

Oberndorf   Austria
Quiet hamlet with beginners' area and a chair connecting it to St Johann's undemanding ski area. *700m*

Oberperfuss   Austria
Small village west of Innsbruck, with tall but limited slopes. On the Innsbruck lift pass.
820m; slopes 820–2000m
⛷ 5 ⛷ 17km

Obersaxen-Mundaun-
Lumnezia   Switzerland
Several quiet villages above Ilanz, in the Vorderrhein Valley, near Laax. Sizeable area of mainly red and blue runs on four linked mountains. The main lifts are fast chairs.
1300m; slopes 1200–2310m
⛷ 18 ⛷ 120km

Oberstaufen   Germany
Three small areas: Steibis; Thulkirchdorf and Hochgrat. Within an hour of Friedrichshafen.
600m; slopes 860–1880m
⛷ 30 ⛷ 45km

Oberstdorf   386
Town in the German Alps near the Austrian border.
815m; slopes 800–2220m
⛷ 31 ⛷ 30km

Obertauern   152
Ochapowace   Canada
Main area in Saskatchewan, east of Regina. It doesn't get a huge amount of snow but 75% snowmaking helps.
⛷ 4 ⛷ 100 acres

Ohau New Zealand
Some of NZ's steepest slopes, with great views of Lake Ohau 9km away (where you stay). 320km south of Christchurch.
1500m; slopes 1425–1825m
⛄ 3 ⛷ 310 acres

Okemo USA
Worthwhile and nicely varied intermediate area above the old Vermont town of Ludlow. Family oriented, with good child care. Comprehensive snowmaking and highly rated grooming.
345m; slopes 345–1020m
⛄ 18 ⛷ 624 acres
📨 *American Ski Classics*

Oppdal Norway
One of the larger Norwegian resorts, but very far north. Many runs are quite short.
715m; slopes 715–1020m
⛄ 17 ⛷ 60km

Orcières-Merlette France
High, convenient family resort a few km north-east of Gap, Merlette being the ugly, purpose-built ski station above the village of Orcières (1450m). Snow-sure beginner area. Slopes have a good mix of difficulty spread over several mountain flanks, and expanded to open a cable car up to almost 3000m on Roche Brune.
1850m; slopes 1850–2725m
⛄ 28 ⛷ 100km
📨 *Lagrange, Ski Collection, Ski France*

Ordino Andorra
Rustic valley village near La Massana, on the way up to Andorra's best snow at Arcalis.

Orelle 376
Village in the Maurienne with access to Val Thorens.

Oropa Italy
Little area just off the Aosta–Turin motorway. An easy change of scene from Courmayeur.
1180m; slopes 1200–2390m
⛷ 15km

Les Orres France
Friendly modern resort with great views and varied intermediate terrain, but the snow is unreliable, and it's a long transfer from Lyon.
1550m; slopes 1550–2720m
⛄ 23 ⛷ 62km
📨 *Crystal, Lagrange, Ski Collection, Ski France*

Orsières Switzerland
Traditional winter resort near Martigny. Close to Grand St Bernard resorts, including Champex-Lac. Well-positioned base from which to visit Verbier and the Chamonix valley. *900m*

Ortisei 442
Market town in Val Gardena.

Oslo Norway
Capital city with cross-country ski trails in its parks. Alpine slopes and lifts in Nordmarka region, just north of city boundaries.

Otre il Colle Italy
Smallest of many little resorts near Bergamo.
1100m; slopes 1100–2000m
⛄ 7 ⛷ 7km

Ötz Austria
Village at the entrance to the Ötz valley with an easy/intermediate ski area of its own and access to the Sölden, Kuhtai (sharing a lift pass) and Niederau areas.
820m; slopes 820–2200m
⛄ 11 ⛷ 34km

Oukaimeden Morocco
Slopes 75km from Marrakech with a surprisingly long season.
2600m; slopes 2600–3260m
⛄ 7 ⛷ 15km

Ovindoli Italy
Small area in Abruzzo, east of Rome, claiming the distinction of Europe's longest magic carpet lift. The town is about 3km from the slopes. Shares a lift pass with equally small Campo Felice, nearby.
1375m; slopes 1470–2055m
⛄ 11 ⛷ 30km

Ovronnaz Switzerland
Pretty village set on a sunny shelf above the Rhône valley, with a good pool complex. Limited area but Crans-Montana and Anzère are close.
1350m; slopes 1350–2080m
⛄ 8 ⛷ 30km

Owl's Head Canada
Steep mountain rising out of a lake, in a remote spot bordering Vermont, away from weekend crowds.
⛄ 7 ⛷ 90 acres

Oz-en-Oisans 206
Old village with satellite at the lifts into Alpe-d'Huez.

Pajarito Mountain USA
Los Alamos area laid out by nuclear scientists. Atomic slopes too – steep, ungroomed. Open Fridays, weekends and holidays. Fun day out from Taos.
2685m; slopes 2685–3170m
⛄ 6 ⛷ 220 acres

Pal 90
Prettily wooded mountain linked with slopes of Arinsal.

Palandöken Turkey
Varied skiing area, transformed by three big hotels, overlooking the Anatolian city of Erzurum.
slopes 2150–3100m ⛄ 4

Pampeago Italy
Trentino area convenient for a trip from Milan.

Pamporovo 658

Panarotta Italy
Smallest of the resorts east of Trento. At a higher altitude than nearby Andalo, so worth a day out from there.
1500m; slopes 1500–2000m
⛄ 6 ⛷ 7km

Panorama Canada
Home to one of North America's biggest verticals (1220m), with something for everyone on its quiet, wooded mountain. Small, purpose-built place at the foot of the slopes and on two levels. The upper 'village' is centred on a hot-pool complex, while the mostly condo accommodation in the lower area. The slopes rise steeply above the resort, but steepest at the top – with genuine blacks and two expert bowls (Taynton and Extreme Dream). Excellent terrain for adventurous intermediates too. More limited for novices. Heli-ski trips are available. There's a big park, pipe and floodlit mini-park. The school is 'very professional' and facilities for families good.
1160m; slopes 1180–2400m
⛄ 9 ⛷ 2847 acres
📨 *American Ski Classics, Canadian Affair, Crystal, Frontier, Ski Independence, Ski Safari, Ski Solutions, Skiworld, Snow Finders*

Panticosa Spain
Charming old Pyrenees spa village near Formigal with limited but varied slopes.
1500m; slopes 1500–2220m
⛄ 16 ⛷ 35km

Paradiski 308

Park City 588

Parnassos Greece
Biggest and best-organised area in Greece, 180km from Athens and with surprisingly good slopes and lifts.
slopes 1600–2300m
⛄ 9 ⛷ 14km

Parpan Switzerland
Pretty village linked to the large intermediate area of Lenzerheide.
1510m; slopes 1230–2865m
⛄ 35 ⛷ 155km

Partenen Austria
Traditional village in a pretty setting at the end of the Montafon valley. The slopes start at Gaschurn, and there are lots more in the vicinity.
1100m; slopes 700–2300m
⛄ 25 ⛷ 100km

La Parva Chile
Only 50km east of Santiago and condoville for the capital's elite. A collection of apartments occupied mostly at weekends, linked with Valle Nevado and El Colorado (no area pass).
2750m; slopes 2430–3630m
⛄ 43 ⛷ 113km

Pas de la Casa 92

Passo Costalunga Italy
Dense network of short lifts either side of the road over a pass, close to Val di Fassa, with links up from Nova Levante.

Passo Lanciano Italy
Closest area to Adriatic. Weekend crowds from nearby Pescara when the snow is good.
1305m; slopes 1305–2000m
⛄ 13

Passo Rolle Italy
Small group of lifts either side of the road over a high pass just north of San Martino di Castrozza.

Passo San Pellegrino Italy
Smallish ski area south of the Sella Ronda, with lifts each side of the pass road and links with the valley village of Falcade.
1920m; slopes 1150–2245m
⛄ 19 ⛷ 75km

Passo Tonale 426

Pass Thurn 123
Road-side lift base for one of Kitzbühel's ski areas.

Passy-Plaine-Joux France
Small, quiet village 25km from Chamonix. Draglifts serve woody slopes best suited to novices.
1340m ⛄ 6 ⛷ 12km

Pebble Creek USA
Small area on Utah-Jackson Hole route. Blend of open and wooded slopes.
1920m; slopes 1920–2530m
⛄ 3 ⛷ 600 acres

Pec Pod Snezku Czech Republic
Collection of hamlets spread along the valley road leading to the main lifts and the very limited ski area.
770m; slopes 710–1190m
⛄ 10 ⛷ 9km

Peisey 216
Small village linked to Les Arcs.

Peisey-Vallandry 216
Group of villages linked to Les Arcs and Paradiski area.

Pejo Italy
Trentino spa resort near Madonna. New cable car now serves slopes to 3000m.
1400m; slopes 1400–3000m
⛄ 7 ⛷ 15km

Penitentes Argentina
180km from Mendoza. Accommodation at the base.
⛄ 10 ⛷ 300 hectares

Perelik Bulgaria
Development aiming to link Pamporovo with Mechi Chal.

Perisher / Smiggins Australia
Expanding resort with slopes on seven mountains, which between them offer plenty of short, intermediate runs. 30km from Jindabyne town, six hours from Sydney.
1640m; slopes 1680–2035m
🚡 47 🎿 3075 acres

Pescasseroli Italy
One of numerous areas east of Rome in L'Aquila region.
1250m; slopes 1250–1945m
🚡 6 🎿 25km

Pescocostanzo Italy
One of numerous areas east of Rome in L'Aquila region.
1395m; slopes 1395–1900m
🚡 4 🎿 25km

Pettneu Austria
Snow-sure beginners' resort with an irregular bus link to nearby St Anton.
1250m; slopes 1230–2020m
🚡 4 🎿 15km

Petzen Austria
One of many little areas in Austria's easternmost ski region near the Slovenian border.
600m; slopes 600–1700m
🚡 5 🎿 16km

Peyragudes France
Small Pyrenean resort with its ski area starting high above.
1600m; slopes 1600–2400m
🚡 17 🎿 60km
🚌 Lagrange, Ski Collection

Pfelders Italy
Resort near Merano in the South Tyrol covered by the Ortler Skiarena pass.
🚡 4 🎿 5km

Pfunds Austria
Picturesque valley village with no slopes but quick access to several resorts in Switzerland and Italy, as well as Austria.
970m

Phoenix Park South Korea
Golf complex with 12 trails in winter. Two hours (140km) from Seoul.
slopes 650–1050m 🚡 9

Piancavallo Italy
Uninspiring yet cSochiuriously trendy purpose-built village, an easy drive from Venice.
1270m; slopes 1270–1830m
🚡 17 🎿 45km

Piani delle Betulle Italy
One of several little areas near the east coast of Lake Como.
730m; slopes 730–1850m
🚡 6 🎿 10km

Piani di Artavaggio Italy
Small base complex rather than a village. One of several little areas near Lake Como.
875m; slopes 875–1875m
🚡 7 🎿 15km

Piani di Bobbio Italy
Largest of several tiny resorts above Lake Como.
770m; slopes 770–1855m
🚡 10 🎿 20km

Piani di Erna Italy
Small base development – no village. One of several little areas above Lake Como.
600m; slopes 600–1635m
🚡 5 🎿 9km

Piau-Engaly France
User-friendly St-Lary satellite in one of the best Pyrenean areas.
1850m; slopes 1420–2530m
🚡 17 🎿 65km 🚌 Lagrange

Piazzatorre Italy
One of many little areas in the Bergamo region.
870m; slopes 870–2000m
🚡 5 🎿 25km

Pichl 164
Hamlet outside Schladming.

Pico USA
Low-key little family area (no resort village) close to Killington.
605m; slopes 605–1215m
🚡 9 🎿 160 acres

Piesendorf Austria
Cheaper, quiet place to stay when visiting Zell am See. Tucked behind Kaprun near Niedernsill.
780m 🚡 3 🎿 3km

Pievepelago Italy
Much the smallest and most limited of the Apennine ski resorts. Less than two hours from Florence and Pisa.
1115m; slopes 1115–1410m
🚡 7 🎿 8km

Pila Italy
Modern, purpose-built, car-free resort that's popular with families and school groups and is set above the old Roman town of Aosta – a 15-minute gondola ride away or reached by a 30-minute drive on a winding road. Chairlifts (some fast, most slow) and a cable car fan out to serve a fair-sized and interesting mix of well-groomed, snow-sure slopes. The treeline is high, at about 2300m, and most runs are below it, making this an excellent bad-weather resort. From the top heights there are grand views to Mont Blanc in the west and the Matterhorn in the east. There are runs for all standards, but mostly they are reds. The few blacks, above the treeline at the top of the area, don't amount to much, but there is quite a bit of off-piste. There are two short beginner lifts, but progression to longer runs means using a central run, which when the resort is busy is unpleasant. Like so many other Aosta Valley resorts, Pila is pretty quiet during the week but can be hectic at

weekends – and it does attract lots of British school groups.
1800m; slopes 1800–2750m
🚡 12 🎿 70km
🚌 Crystal, Erna Low, Interski, Pilaski, Ski Solutions, Ski Supreme, Ski Yogi, STC, Thomson

Pinzolo 415
Trentino resort near Madonna.

Pitztal Austria
Long valley with good glacier area at its head, accessed by underground funicular.
1680m; slopes 880–3440m
🚡 12 🎿 68km 🚌 Zenith

Pla-d'Adet France
Limited purpose-built complex at the foot of the St-Lary ski area (the original village is further down the mountain).
1680m; slopes 1420–2450m
🚡 32 🎿 80km
🚌 Lagrange

La Plagne 310

Plan de Corones Italy
Distinctive ski area in South Tyrol, with amazingly efficient lifts from Brunico and San Vigilio di Marebbe. Better known by its German name, Kronplatz.
1200m; slopes 1200–2275m
🚡 32 🎿 103km

Plan-Peisey 216
Small development with link to Les Arcs.

Plose Italy
Varied area close to Bressanone, with the longest run in the South Tyrol.
560m; slopes 1065–2500m
🚡 11 🎿 40km

Poiana Brasov 661
Cheap, informal resort in Romania.
1020m; slopes 1020–1775m
🚡 10 🎿 12km

Pomerelle USA
Small area in Idaho on the Utah–Sun Valley route.
2430m; slopes 2430–2735m
🚡 3 🎿 300 acres

Pontechianale Italy
Highest, largest area in a remote region south-west of Turin. Day-tripper place.
1600m; slopes 1600–2760m
🚡 8 🎿 30km

Ponte di Legno 426
Attractive sheltered alternative to Passo Tonale.

Pontresina Switzerland
Small, sedate, sunny village with one main street, rather spoiled by the sanatorium-style architecture. All downhill skiing involves travel by car or bus, except the single long piste on Pontresina's own hill, Languard. It's cheaper to stay here than St Moritz.
1805m; slopes 1730–3305m
🚡 54 🎿 350km

Port-Ainé Spain
Small but high intermediate area in the Spanish Pyrenees near Andorra. Lifts include a six-pack; eponymous 3-star hotel at base.
1975m; slopes 1650–2440m
🚡 8 🎿 44km

Port del Comte Spain
High resort in the forested region of Lleida, north-west of Barcelona. The slopes spread across three linked sectors: El Sucre, El Hostal and El Estivella.
slopes 1700–2400m
🚡 15 🎿 40km

Porté Puymorens France
Little-known Pyrenean area close to Pas de la Casa in Andorra.
slopes 1600–2470m
🚡 12 🎿 45km

Porter Heights New Zealand
Closest skiing to Christchurch (one hour). Open, sunny bowl offering mostly intermediate skiing – with back bowls for powder.
1340m; slopes 1340–1950m
🚡 5 🎿 200 acres

Portes du Soleil 321

Portillo Chile
Luxury hotel 150km north-east of Santiago. Quiet snow-sure slopes used for training by US national ski team. Suits experts best.
2880m; slopes 2450–3310m
🚡 14 🎿 1200 acres
🚌 Momentum, Scott Dunn, Skiworld

Powderhorn USA
Area in west Colorado perched on the world's highest flat-top mountain, Grand Mesa. Sensational views. Day trip from Aspen.
2490m; slopes 2490–2975m
🚡 4 🎿 300 acres

Powder King Canada
Remote resort in British Columbia, between Prince George and Dawson City. As its name suggests, it has great powder. Plenty of lodging.
880m; slopes 880–1520m
🚡 3 🎿 160 acres

Powder Mountain USA
Massive Utah area sprawled over six ridges, an hour and a quarter's drive from Salt Lake City. An ample 2,800 acres of its terrain is lift served, a mix of mainly north-facing slopes with enough green, blue and black runs to satisfy all abilities. You access the rest by snowcat or snowmobile tow, buses and hiking. It is the abundance of intermediate freeride terrain that makes it special. You can also stay in Ogden, 32km away.
2100m; slopes 2100–2740m
🚡 7 🎿 7000 acres

Pozza di Fassa 453
Pretty village in Val di Fassa.

Pragelato Italy
Inexpensive base, linked by
cable car to Sestriere. Its own
area is worth a try for half a
day.
1535m; slopes 1535–2700m
🚡 6 ↟ 50km

Prägraten am Grossvenediger
Austria
Traditional mountaineering/ski
touring village in lovely
setting south of Felbertauern
tunnel. The Alpine ski slopes
of Matrei are nearby.
1310m; slopes 1310–1490m
🚡 2 ↟ 30km

Prali Italy
Tiny resort east of Sestriere –
a worthwhile half-day trip.
1450m; slopes 1450–2500m
🚡 7 ↟ 25km

Pralognan-la-Vanoise France
Unspoiled traditional village
overlooked by spectacular
peaks. Champagny (La
Plagne) and Courchevel are
close by.
1410m; slopes 1410–2355m
🚡 14 ↟ 30km
✉ Erna Low, Lagrange, Ski
France

Pra-Loup France
Convenient, purpose-built
family resort with an
extensive, varied intermediate
area linked to La Foux-d'Allos
(Val d'Allos region).
1500m; slopes 1500–2600m
🚡 51 ↟ 180km
✉ Lagrange, Ski Collection,
Ski France

Prati di Tivo Italy
Weekend day-trip place east
of Rome and near the town of
Teramo. A sizeable resort by
southern Italy standards.
1450m; slopes 1450–1800m
🚡 6 ↟ 16km

Prato Nevoso Italy
Purpose-built resort with
rather bland slopes. Part of
Mondolé ski area with
Artesina.
1500m; slopes 1500–1950m
🚡 25 ↟ 90km

Prato Selva Italy
Tiny base development (no
village) east of Rome near
Teramo. Weekend day-trip
place.
1370m; slopes 1370–1800m
🚡 4 ↟ 10km

Le Praz 248
Lowest of the Courchevel
resorts.

Les Praz 233
Quiet hamlet near Chamonix.

Praz-de-Lys France
Little-known snow-pocket area
near Lake Geneva that can
have good snow when nearby
resorts (eg La Clusaz) do not.
1450m; slopes 1240–1965m
🚡 23 ↟ 60km
✉ Pierre & Vacances

Praz-sur-Arly France
Traditional village in a pretty,
wooded setting just down the
road from Megève. Sharing
slopes with Notre Dame de
Bellecombe and beyond to
Crest Voland / Les Saises, to
form the Espace Diamant.
1035m; slopes 1035–2070m
🚡 84 ↟ 175km
✉ Ski France

Predazzo Italy
Small, quiet place between
Cavalese and the Sella Ronda
resorts, with lift into modest
area of slopes above
Obereggen.
1015m; slopes 995–2205m
🚡 8 ↟ 17km

Premanon France
One of four resorts that make
up Les Rousses area in Jura
region.
1050m; slopes 1120–1680m
🚡 40 ✉ Lagrange

La Presolana Italy
Large summer resort near
Bergamo. Several other little
areas nearby.
1250m; slopes 1250–1650m
🚡 6 ↟ 15km

Les Prodains 226
Village at the foot of the cliffs
on which Avoriaz sits.

Pucón Chile
Ski area on the side of the
active Villarrica volcano in
southern Chile, 800km south
of Santiago. Lodgings are at
Pucón village, 30 minutes
away from the slopes.
1200m; slopes 1200–2440m
🚡 9 ↟ 20 runs

Puigmal France
Resort in the French Pyrenees
with accommodation in
nearby villages.
1830m; slopes 1830–2700m
🚡 12 ↟ 34km

Puy-St-Vincent France
Modern apartment complex
above an old village south of
Briançon; convenient access
to an area of slopes that are
limited in extent but offer a
decent vertical and a lot of
variety, including a bit of
steep stuff. Most
accommodation is in self-
catering apartments at the
foot of the slopes. It is a
relatively inexpensive place
and makes an attractive
choice for a family not hungry
for piste miles.
*1400–1600m; slopes 1250–
2700m* 🚡 12 ↟ 75km
✉ Erna Low, Lagrange, Ski
Collection, Ski France,
Snowbizz, Zenith

Pyhä Finland
Expanding resort 150km
north-east of Rovaniemi. Much
of the area is in a National
Park, with the 14 slopes on
two sides of a part-wooded
hill. Vertical is only 280m and
there's no steep terrain but

good off-piste. The best
powder runs are on both
sides of a long T-bar on the
north side. Most pistes open
for floodlit skiing. There's a
well-developed terrain park,
hosting regular competitions.
220m 🚡 8
✉ Inghams, Skiworld

The Pyrenees 322

Pyrenees 2000 France
Tiny resort built in a pleasing
manner. Shares a pretty area
of short runs with Font-
Romeu. Impressive
snowmaking.
2000m; slopes 1750–2250m
🚡 32 ↟ 52km

Québec City Canada
French-speaking capital and
old city with a number of ski
areas a short drive away.
✉ AmeriCan Ski, Crystal

Queenstown New Zealand
South Island's outdoor
adventure capital, in a
stunning lakeside setting. Two
local resorts: the Remarkables
and Coronet Peak. Treble
Cone and Cardrona are easily
reached by car. Typically
commercialized but lively and
relaxed, and where most
people stay. The slopes are a
30-40 minute drive away. The
Remarkables appeals mainly
to families and beginners,
while Coronet Peak is more
satisfying to intermediates.
Both resorts have challenges
for experts too.
310m; slopes 1170–1650m
🚡 8 ↟ 280 hectares

Radium Hot Springs Canada
Summer resort offering an
alternative to the purpose-
built slope-side resort of
Panorama.
slopes 975–2155m
🚡 8 ↟ 300 acres

Radstadt Austria
Unspoiled medieval town near
Schladming, with its own
small area and the Salzburger
Sportwelt slopes accessed
from nearby Zauchensee or
Flachau.
855m; slopes 855–2185m
🚡 100 ↟ 350km

Ragged Mountain USA
Family-owned ski area in New
Hampshire.
🚡 9 ↟ 200 acres

Rainbow New Zealand
Northernmost ski area on
South Island. Wide, treeless
area, best for beginners and
intermediates. Accommodation
at St Arnaud.
1440m; slopes 1440–1760m
🚡 5 ↟ 865 acres

Ramsau am Dachstein Austria
Charming village overlooked
by the Dachstein glacier.
Renowned for cross-country, it

also has Alpine slopes locally,
on the glacier and at
Schladming.
1200m; slopes 1100–2700m
🚡 18 ↟ 30km

Ramundberget Sweden
Small, quiet, ski-in/ski-out
family resort with very limited
pistes but lots of cross-
country. ↟ 22km

Rasos de Peguera Spain
The only resort in the
Barcelona province. 14km
from Berga. Ten pistes, mostly
red classified.

Rauris 155

Ravascletto Italy
Resort in a pretty wooded
setting near Austrian border,
with most of its terrain high
above on an open plateau.
920m; slopes 920–1735m
🚡 12 ↟ 40km

Reallon France
Traditional-style village, with
splendid views from above
Lac de Serre-Ponçon.
1560m; slopes 1560–2115m
🚡 6 ↟ 20km

Red Lodge USA
Picturesque Old West Montana
town. Ideal for a combined
trip with Big Sky or Jackson
Hole.
1800m; slopes 2155–2860m
🚡 8 ↟ 1600 acres

Red Mountain Canada
Up there with the likes of
Fernie as a cult resort for
expert skiers who can handle
its steep terrain, wide glades
and powder-filled bowls.
While not big in European
terms, it packs a lot of tough
stuff into its two mountains. If
that's your scene, get there
quickly as the ski area has
been developing. But it's still
the black and double-black
stuff that is the real
attraction; it's marked on the
map, but not on the mountain
– so a guide may be
necessary to explore it fully.
There are long-term plans for
a proper resort village at the
base, but the small old
mining town of Rossland is
just 3km away.
1185m; slopes 1185–2075m
🚡 6 ↟ 1685 acres
✉ AmeriCan Ski, American Ski
Classics, Frontier, Ski
Independence, Ski Safari

Red River USA
New Mexico western town –
complete with stetsons and
saloons – with intermediate
slopes above.
2665m; slopes 2665–3155m
🚡 7 ↟ 290 acres

Reichenfels Austria
One of many small areas in
Austria's easternmost ski
region near the Slovenian
border.
810m; slopes 810–1400m

Reinwald Italy
Resort near Merano in the South Tyrol covered by the Ortler Skiarena pass.

Reit im Winkl Germany
Southern Bavarian resort, straddling the German–Austrian border. Winklmoos ski area is best suited to intermediates.
750m; slopes 750–1800m
🚡 7 🎿 40km

The Remarkables
New Zealand
Three bleak basins with great views of 'remarkable' jagged alps, 45 minutes from Queenstown. Popular with families and beginners, but some tougher terrain too. Big terrain park.
1580m; slopes 1580–1945m
🚡 6 🎿 545 acres

Rencurel-les-Coulumes France
One of seven little resorts just west of Grenoble. Unspoiled, inexpensive place to tour. Villard-de-Lans is the main resort.

Reschenpass Austria
Area in the Tirol right on the Swiss border; includes Schöneben and Haider Alm in Italy. Nauders is the main resort.
1520m 🚡 7 🎿 28

Rettenberg Germany
Small resort near Austrian border.
750m; slopes 820–1650m
🚡 15 🎿 40km

Reutte Austria
500-year-old market town with many traditional hotels, and rail links to nearby Lermoos.
855m; slopes 855–1900m
🚡 9 🎿 19km

Revelstoke 634

Rhêmes Notre Dame Italy
Unspoiled village in the beautiful Rhêmes valley, south of Aosta. Courmayeur and La Thuile within reach. Handful of hotels and tiny amount of downhill – including two black runs.
1725m; slopes 1625–3605m
🚡 4 🎿 5km

Riederalp Switzerland
Pretty, car-free village high above the Rhône valley near Brig; part of the Aletsch Arena. Cable car or gondola from the valley village of Mörel. Quiet, friendly, uncrowded slopes.
1925m; slopes 1050–2870m
🚡 35 🎿 100km

Riefensberg 192
Village in Bregenzerwald.
780m 🎿 14km

Rigi-Kaltbad Switzerland
Resort on a mountain rising out of Lake Lucerne, with superb all-round views, accessed by the world's first mountain railroad.
1440m; slopes 1195–1795m
🚡 4 🎿 9km

Riihivuori Finland
Small area with 'base' at the top of the mountain. 20km south of the city of Jyväskylä.
🚡 5

Riksgränsen Sweden
Unique Arctic Circle Alpine area not open until late February. You can use the slopes under the midnight sun (lift-served) from mid-May to June. 20 hours by train from Stockholm.
600m; slopes 600–910m
🚡 6 🎿 21km 🚌 Ski Safari

Riscone Italy
Dolomite village sharing a pretty area with San Vigilio. Good snowmaking. Short easy runs.
1200m; slopes 1200–2275m
🚡 35 🎿 40km

Rittner Horn Italy
Resort near Merano in the South Tyrol covered by the Ortler Skiarena pass.
🚡 3 🎿 15km

Rivisondoli Italy
Sizeable mountain retreat east of Rome, with one of the better lift systems in the vicinity.
1350m; slopes 1350–2050m
🚡 7 🎿 16km

Roccaraso Italy
Clearly largest of the resorts in Abruzzo, east of Rome, with lodgings in the town of Roccaraso and at three lift bases on the mountain.
1280m; slopes 1325–2140m
🚡 24 🎿 110km

Rohrmoos 164
Suburb of Schladming, with vast area of nursery slopes.

La Rosière 325

Rosa Khutor 35
One of the venues for the 2014 Sochi Winter Olympics.

Rossland Canada
Remote little town 5km from cult powder paradise Red Mountain.

Rougemont Switzerland
Cute rustic hamlet just over the French/German language border near Gstaad, with local slopes and links to Gstaad's Eggli sector.
990m; slopes 950–3000m
🚡 58 🎿 250km

Les Rousses France
Group of four villages – Les Rousses, Premanon, Lamoura and Bois d'Amont – in the Jura mountains, 50km from Geneva airport.
1120m; slopes 1120–1680m
🚡 40 🎿 40km 🚌 Lagrange

Ruka Finland
80km south of the Arctic Circle, close to Kuusamo airport and the Russian border, in a region known for abundant and enduring snow. Lively, upbeat resort with a newly developed pedestrian village. Good but widely spread cabin lodging served by the ski bus. Slopes on two sides of a single low hill, with a mix of open and forest terrain, most floodlit and with snowmaking. None is particularly steep and the vertical very modest – but there is a new FIS racing piste. There's a terrain park and boardercross course. The cross-country scope is vast: 500km, of which 40km are floodlit.
200m
🚡 20 🎿 20km
🚌 Crystal, Crystal Finest, Skiworld, Thomson

Russbach Austria
Secluded village tucked up a side valley and linked into the Gosau-Annaberg-Lungotz area. The slopes are spread over a wide area.
815m; slopes 780–1620m
🚡 33 🎿 65km

Rusutsu 666
Resort on Hokkaido, Japan.

Saalbach-Hinterglemm 158

Saalfelden Austria
Town ideally placed for touring eastern Tirol. Lift networks of Maria-Alm and Saalbach are nearby.
745m; slopes 745–1550m
🚡 3 🎿 3km

Saanen Switzerland
Cheaper and more convenient alternative to staying in Gstaad – but much less going on.
slopes 950–3000m
🚡 58 🎿 250km

Saanenmöser Switzerland
Small village with rail/road links to Gstaad. Scenic and quiet local slopes, with good mountain restaurants.
1270m; slopes 950–3000m
🚡 58 🎿 250km

Saas-Almagell Switzerland
Compact village up the valley from Saas-Grund, with good cross-country trails and walks, and a limited Alpine area.
1670m; slopes 1670–2400m
🚡 7 🎿 12km

Saas-Fee 492

Saas-Grund Switzerland
Sprawling valley village below Saas-Fee, with a separate small but high Alpine area.
1560m; slopes 1560–3200m
🚡 8 🎿 35km

Saddleback USA
Small area between Maine's premier resorts. High slopes by local standards.
695m; slopes 695–1255m
🚡 5 🎿 100 acres

Sahoro Japan
Ugly, purpose-built complex on snowy northern Hokkaido island, with a limited area.
610m; slopes 610–1030m
🚡 8 🎿 15km 🚌 Club Med

Les Saisies France
Traditional-style cross-country venue, surrounded by varied four-mountain Alpine slopes. Now part of Espace Diamant. Easy runs, but some lift queues at peak times.
1650m; slopes 1035–2070m
🚡 84 🎿 175km
🚌 AmeriCan Ski, Classic Ski, Erna Low, Lagrange, Peak Retreats, PowderBeds, Ski Collection, Ski France, Ski Independence

Sälen Sweden
Well-developed family resort with extensive lift system, and some good off-piste for experts.
550m; slopes 550–950m
🚡 101 🎿 144km

Salt Lake City USA
Underrated base from which to ski Utah. 30 minutes from Park City, Deer Valley, The Canyons, Snowbird, Alta, Snowbasin. Cheaper and livelier than the resorts.
🚌 AmeriCan Ski

Salzburg-Stadt Austria
A single, long challenging run off the back of Salzburg's local mountain, accessed by a spectacular lift-ride from a suburb of Grodig. 425m

Samedan Switzerland
Valley town, just down the road from St Moritz. A run heads back to base from Corviglia-Marguns.
1720m; slopes 1730–3305m
🚡 54 🎿 350km

Samnaun 116
Shares large ski area with Ischgl.

Samoëns 329

San Bernardino Switzerland
Pretty resort south of the road tunnel, close to Madesimo.
1625m; slopes 1600–2525m
🚡 8 🎿 35km

San Candido Italy
Resort on the border with Austria on the road to Lienz. Innichen is its German name.
1175m; slopes 1175–1580m
🚡 4 🎿 15km

San Carlos de Bariloche
Argentina
Year-round resort, with five areas nearby and the place to stay when skiing Cerro Catedral – 20 minutes away by bus. Once a quaint lakeside town, but now a substantial resort.
slopes 1030–2180m
⛷ 39 ⛷ 103km

San Cassiano 433

Sandia Peak USA
The world's longest lift ride ascends from Albuquerque. Mostly gentle slopes; children ski free.
slopes 2645–3165m
⛷ 7 ⛷ 100 acres

San Grée di Viola Italy
Easternmost of resorts south of Turin, surprisingly close to the Italian Riviera.
1100m; slopes 1100–1800m
⛷ 30km

San Martin de los Andes
Argentina
Sizeable town with accommodation, 19 km from the Chapelco ski area.

San Martino di Castrozza Italy
Trentino village south of Val di Fassa.
1465m; slopes 1465–2610m
⛷ 20 ⛷ 50km

Sansicario 428
Small, stylish resort in the Milky Way near Sauze d'Oulx.

San Simone Italy
Tiny development north of Bergamo, close to unappealing Foppolo area.
2000m; slopes 1105–2300m
⛷ 9 ⛷ 45km

Santa Caterina Italy
Pretty, user-friendly village near Bormio, with a snow-sure novice and intermediate area.
1740m; slopes 1740–2725m
⛷ 8 ⛷ 25km

Santa Cristina 442
Quiet village in Val Gardena.

Santa Fe USA
Interesting area only 15 miles from beautiful Santa Fe town. A tree-filled bowl with a good variety of terrain crammed into its small area. Ideal stopover en route from Albuquerque airport to Taos.
3145m; slopes 3155–3680m
⛷ 7 ⛷ 550 acres

Santa Maria Maggiore Italy
Resort south of the Simplon Pass from the Rhône valley, and near Lake Maggiore.
820m; slopes 820–1890m
⛷ 5 ⛷ 10km

San Vigilio di Marebbe /
Kronplatz Italy
Pretty village in South Tyrol with lifts on two mountains, one being the quite impressive Plan de Corones / Kronplatz.
1200m; slopes 1200–2275m
⛷ 32 ⛷ 116km

San Vito di Cadore Italy
Sizeable, alternative place to stay to Cortina. Negligible local slopes, though.
1010m; slopes 1010–1380m
⛷ 9 ⛷ 12km

Sappada Italy
Isolated resort close to the Austrian border below Lienz.
1215m; slopes 1215–2050m
⛷ 17 ⛷ 21km

Sappee Finland
Resort within easy reach of Helsinki, popular with boarders and telemarkers. Lake views. ⛷ 7

Sarnano Italy
Main resort in the Macerata region near Adriatic Riviera. Valley village with ski slopes accessed by lift.
540m
⛷ 9 ⛷ 11km

Le Sauze France
Fine area near Barcelonnette, sadly remote from airports.
1400m; slopes 1400–2440m
⛷ 23 ⛷ 65km

Sauze d'Oulx 428

Savognin Switzerland
Pretty village with a good mid-sized area; a good base for the nearby resorts of St Moritz, Davos/Klosters and Laax.
1200m; slopes 1200–2715m
⛷ 10 ⛷ 80km ⛷ Crystal

Scheffau 107
Rustic village not far from Söll.

Schia Italy
Very limited area of short runs – the only ski area near Parma. No village.
1245m; slopes 1245–1415m
⛷ 7 ⛷ 15km

Schilpario Italy
One of many little areas near Bergamo.
1125m; slopes 1125–1635m
⛷ 5 ⛷ 15km

Schladming 164

Schnalstal Italy
Valley and high ski area, in the Dolomites near Merano. Val Senales is its Italian name.
3210m; slopes 2110–3210m
⛷ 12 ⛷ 35km

Schöneben Italy
Area in the Val Venosta in the South Tyrol, close to Austrian border and Nauders.
1520m
⛷ 7 ⛷ 28km

Schönried Switzerland
A cheaper and quieter resort alternative to staying in Gstaad.
1230m; slopes 950–3000m
⛷ 58 ⛷ 250km

Schoppernau 192
Village in Bregenzerwald.
860m; slopes 860–2060m
⛷ 8 ⛷ 44km

Schröcken 192
Bregenzerwald village near Lech.
1260m; slopes 1260–2100m
⛷ 15 ⛷ 66km

Schruns Austria
Pleasant little working valley town with a car-free centre at the heart of the Montafon region, with access to both the Hochjoch area (see St Gallenkirch) from a cable car near the centre of town and the Golm ski area (a few km away). At Golm four chairs and a drag serve easy blue and red slopes above the trees. A six-pack goes to the top of the area, linked via a ski tunnel to slopes on the back of the hill, including the Diabolo black run (the steepest in the valley). Snowmaking covers many of the upper slopes and the run to the valley. Ernest Hemingway ensconced himself in Schruns in 1925/26, and his favourite drinking table in the hotel Taube can be admired. Après-ski is not the big deal it is in many Austrian resorts, but a few places get quite lively. There's a big sports centre.
700m; slopes 655–2395m
⛷ 61 ⛷ 219km

Schüttdorf 198
Ordinary dormitory satellite of Zell am See, with easy access to the shared ski area. Kids' area and nursery slopes at the base.

Schwarzach im Pongau
Austria
Riverside village with rail links. There are limited slopes at Goldegg; Wagrain (Salzburger Sportwelt) and Grossarl (Gastein valley) are also nearby.
600m ⛷ 4 ⛷ 12km

Schwarzenberg 192
Village in Bregenzerwald.
700m; slopes 1145–1465m
⛷ 9 ⛷ 24km

Schwaz Austria
Valley town beside the Inn with a lift into varied terrain shared with the village of Pill and its mountain outpost, Hochpillberg.
540m; slopes 540–2030m
⛷ 6 ⛷ 10km

Schweitzer USA
Excellent family-friendly resort in northern Idaho, 85 miles from Spokane (Washington state) and 45 miles from Canada.
1220m; slopes 1229–1950m
⛷ 10 ⛷ 2900 acres

Schwemmalm Italy
Resort near Merano in the South Tyrol covered by the Ortler Skiarena pass.
⛷ 5 ⛷ 18km

Scopello Italy
Low area close to the Aosta valley, worth considering for a day trip in bad weather.
slopes 690–1700m
⛷ 6 ⛷ 35km

Scuol Switzerland
Year-round spa resort close to Austria and Italy, with an impressive range of terrain.
1225m; slopes 1225–2780m
⛷ 15 ⛷ 80km

Searchmont Resort Canada
Ontario area with modern lift system and 95% snowmaking. Fine Lake Superior views.
275m; slopes 275–485m
⛷ 4 ⛷ 65 acres

Sedrun Switzerland
Sizeable roadside village east of the Oberalp Pass, and covered along with Andermatt by the Gotthard Oberalp lift pass. The most extensive piste skiing in the area. There's a good choice of red runs, a rewarding black and a 'freeride' route, plus plenty of scope for off-piste. At Milez there's a terrain park and family restaurant area. Spa centre.
1450m; slopes 1450–2350m
⛷ 10 ⛷ 50km

Seefeld Austria
Classic winter holiday resort, well designed in traditional Tirolean style, with a large pedestrian-only centre and lots of upmarket hotels (including three 5-stars). Lots of people come here to enjoy the superb cross-country trails and off-slope activities rather than the downhill skiing, but there are two main downhill sectors on the outskirts – Gschwandtkopf and Rosshütte – the latter served by fast lifts. Both areas have intermediate runs of decent vertical; Rosshütte is more extensive, with a cable car across to the separate peak of Härmelekopf, and some worthwhile challenges for experts. There's a good long red run back to village level and a gentle nursery area too. But overall the terrain is far too limited to keep most kids entertained for a week's stay. You can always make excursions to Innsbruck, not far away and easily reached by train, or to the Stubai and Zugspitze glaciers.
1200m; slopes 1200–2065m
⛷ 30 🚡 48km
✉ *Crystal, Inghams, Momentum, Neilson, STC, Thomson*

See im Paznaun Austria
Small family-friendly area in the Paznaun Valley, near Ischgl, with rustic old village set quietly 100m above the valley floor and main road.
1050m; slopes 1050–2300m
⛷ 8 🚡 33km

Le Seignus-d'Allos France
Close to La Foux-d'Allos (which shares large area with Pra-Loup) and has own little area, too.
1400m; slopes 1400–2425m
⛷ 13 🚡 47km

Seis Italy
German name for Siusi.

Sella Nevea Italy
Limited but developing resort in a beautiful setting on the Slovenian border, and now linked to Bovec-Kanin. Summer glacier nearby.
1140m; slopes 1190–2300m
⛷ 12 🚡 30km

Sella Ronda 433

Selva / Val Gardena 442

Selvino Italy
Closest resort to Bergamo.
960m; slopes 960–1400m
⛷ 9 🚡 20km

Selwyn Snowfields Australia
Popular with beginners and families. Six hours from Sydney. Good lift system and cheaper passes than the major Oz resorts.
1520m; slopes 1490–1615m
⛷ 10 🚡 111 acres

Semmering Austria
Long-established winter sports resort set in pretty scenery, 100km from Vienna, towards Graz. Mostly intermediate terrain.
1000m; slopes 1000–1340m
⛷ 5 🚡 14km

Semnoz France
Small, family and beginner focused resort above Lake Annecy with views of the lake and Mont Blanc.
1705m ⛷ 11 🚡 18

Les Sept-Laux France
Improving family resort near Grenoble. Modern lift system – 90% of lifts having been replaced in recent years. Pretty slopes.
1350m; slopes 1350–2400m
⛷ 21 🚡 120km ✉ *Zenith*

Serfaus Austria
Virtually unknown in the UK, but it is a charming village of chalet-style buildings set on a sunny shelf and kept largely traffic-free by an underground railway to the lifts. Most of the accommodation is in hotels, frequented by well-heeled German families. It shares with Fiss and Ladis a broad area of high slopes, with long runs spanning several ridges – well-suited to mixed-ability parties and especially good for families. The vast kids' facilities at mid-mountain level and ample nursery slopes are key attraction. A lack of English speakers may be a drawback though.
1430m; slopes 1200–2830m
⛷ 70 🚡 212km
✉ *Crystal, Ski Bespoke, Ski Club Freshtracks, STC*

Serrada Italy
Very limited area near Trento.
slopes 1250–1605m ⛷ 5

Serre-Chevalier 331

Sesto Italy
Dolomite village off the Alta Val Pusteria, surrounded by pretty little areas. Sexten is its German name.
1310m; slopes 1130–2200m
⛷ 31 🚡 50km

Sestola Italy
Apennine village a short drive from Pisa and Florence with its pistes, some way above, almost completely equipped with snowmakers.
900m; slopes 1280–1975m
⛷ 23 🚡 50km

Sestriere 449

Seven Springs Mountain USA
Pennsylvania's largest resort.
slopes 220–2995m
⛷ 18 🚡 494 acres

Sexten Italy
Dolomite village off the Hochpustertal, surrounded by pretty little areas. Sesto is its Italian name.
1310m; slopes 1130–2200m
⛷ 31 🚡 50km

Shames Mountain Canada
Remote spot inland from coastal town of Prince Rupert and with impressive snowfall record. Deep powder.
670m; slopes 670–1195m
⛷ 3 🚡 183 acres

Shawnee Peak USA
Small area near Bethel and Sunday River renowned for its night skiing. Spectacular views. Mostly groomed cruising.
185m; slopes 185–580m
⛷ 5 🚡 225 acres

Shemshak Iran
Most popular of the three mountain resorts within easy reach of Tehran (60km).
3600m; slopes 2550–3050m
⛷ 7

Shiga Kogen 666
Largest area in Japan.

Showdown USA
Intermediate area in Montana forest north of Bozeman. 50km to the nearest hotel.
2065m; slopes 2065–2490m
⛷ 4 🚡 640 acres

Sierra-at-Tahoe USA
A Colorado-style resort, with runs cut on densely wooded slopes. It claims an impressive average of 420 inches of snow. The slopes are spread over two flanks of Huckleberry Mountain. The fronts of both offer good intermediate cruising plus some genuine single-diamond blacks. The backside of Huckleberry has easier blue and green slopes. This is a natural day trip for those staying in South Lake Tahoe.
2210m; slopes 2025–2700m
⛷ 14 🚡 2000 acres

Sierra Nevada 651

Sierra Summit USA
Sierra Nevada area accessible only from the west. 100% snowmaking.
2160m; slopes 2160–2645m
⛷ 8 🚡 250 acres

Silbertal Austria
Low secluded village in the Montafon valley, linked to Schruns. A good base for touring numerous areas.
890m; slopes 700–1450m
⛷ 3 🚡 6km

Sillian Austria
A gondola and two fast quads serve this varied area in Austria's Hochpustertal region.
1100m ⛷ 6 🚡 45km

Sils Maria 497
Lakeside village linked to the St Moritz Corvatsch slopes.

Silvaplana 497
Pretty village near St Moritz.

Silver Mountain USA
Northern Idaho area near delightful resort town of Coeur d'Alene. Best for experts, but plenty for intermediates too.
1215m; slopes 1215–1915m
⛷ 6 🚡 1500 acres

Silver Star 637

Silverthorne USA
Factory outlet town on main road close to Keystone and Breckenridge. Good budget base for skiing those resorts plus Vail and Beaver Creek.
✉ *AmeriCan Ski*

Silverton USA
Expert-only area in southern Colorado that used to be heli-ski country. Served by one lift. Avalanche transceiver, shovel and probe compulsory.
3170m; slopes 3170–3750m ⛷ 1

Sinaia Romania
Dreary main-road town with a modest, open area of slopes. Recent investment in new lifts, included a gondola.
795m; slopes 795–2030m
⛷ 10 🚡 20km

Sipapu USA
Great little New Mexico area, with mostly treelined runs. Snow unreliable, but 70% snowmaking. Nice day out from Taos when conditions are good.
slopes 2500–2765m
⛷ 4 🚡 70 acres

Siusi 442
Village west of the Sella Ronda circuit; Seis in German.

Siviez 508
A quieter, cheaper base for Verbier's Four Valleys circuit.

Sixt-Fer-a-Cheval 264
Village near Samoëns.

Sjusjøen Norway
Cluster of hotels in deep forest close to Lillehammer. Some Alpine facilities but better for cross-country.
885m; slopes 1000–1090m
⛷ 2 🚡 2km
✉ *Exodus, Inntravel*

Ski Apache USA
Apache-owned area south of Albuquerque noted for groomed steeps. Panoramic views. Nearest lodging in charming Ruidoso.
2925m; slopes 2925–3505m
⛷ 11 🚡 750 acres

Ski Cooper USA
Small area close to historic Old West town of Leadville. Good ski/sightseeing day out from nearby Vail, Beaver Creek and Copper Mountain.
slopes 3200–3565m ⛷ 4

Ski Windham USA
Two hours from New York City and second only to Hunter for weekend crowds. Decent slopes by eastern standards. *485m; slopes 485–940m*
⛷ 7 ⛷ 230 acres

Smugglers' Notch USA
French-style purpose-built family resort with sympathetic instructors, comprehensive childcare, child-friendly layout and long, quiet, easy runs. There are varied and satisfying slopes, spread over three hills, with a worthwhile vertical of 800m. It's a great area for beginners, but mileage-hungry intermediates should go elsewhere. Snowboarding is encouraged, and there are three impressive terrain parks and an Olympic-size super-pipe. *315m; slopes 315–1110m*
⛷ 8 ⛷ 1000 acres

Snowbasin USA
Underrated hill, usually with very good snow. No base village, but a worthwhile day out from Park City. The crowd-free slopes cover a lot of pleasantly varied terrain. This is a great mountain for experts – the Grizzly Downhill course drops 885m and is already claimed to be a modern classic. Between the race course and the area boundary is a splendid area of off-piste wooded glades and gullies. Middle Bowl is great terrain for the adventurous, with a complex network of blues and blacks. You have to stay in the town of Ogden on the Salt Lake plain in the backwater of Huntsville. *1965m; slopes 1965–2850m*
⛷ 11 ⛷ 3000 acres

Snowbird 593

Snowbowl (Arizona) USA
One of America's oldest areas, near Flagstaff, Arizona, atop an extinct volcano and with stunning desert views. Good snowfall record. *2805m; slopes 2805–3505m*
⛷ 5 ⛷ 135 acres

Snowbowl (Montana) USA
Montana area renowned for powder, outside lively town of Missoula. Intermediate pistes plus 700 acres of extreme slopes. Grizzly Chute is the ultimate challenge. *1520m; slopes 1520–2315m*
⛷ 4 ⛷ 1400 acres

Snowmass 568

Snow Park New Zealand
Dedicated terrain park across the valley from Cardrona. Features galore, including new 7m pipes. Budget lodging at the base. *1530m* ⛷ 1

Snow Summit USA
San Bernardino National Forest ski area near Palm Springs. Lovely lake views. 100% snowmaking. High-capacity lift system for weekend crowds. *2135m; slopes 2135–2500m*
⛷ 12 ⛷ 230 acres

Snow Valley USA
Area quite near Palm Springs. Fine desert views. High-capacity lift system copes with weekend crowds better than nearby Big Bear. *2040m; slopes 2040–2390m*
⛷ 11 ⛷ 230 acres

Sochi 35
Host of the 2014 Winter Olympic Games.

Solda Italy
The other side of the Stelvio Pass from Bormio. Very long airport transfers. Sulden is German name. *1905m; slopes 1905–2625m*
⛷ 10 ⛷ 40km

Sölden 168

Soldeu 92

Soldier Mountain USA
Family resort in Central Idaho; backcountry snowcat tours. *slopes 1770–2195m*
⛷ 4 ⛷ 670 acres

Solitude USA
Smart, car-free mini-village linked with Brighton in the valley next to Alta and Snowbird. Most (not all) of the slopes are easy or intermediate, including a wide area served by the one fast quad. When open, the top lift accesses lots of steeps in Honeycomb Canyon, on the back of the hill, with a short quad to bring you back to the front face. Headwall Forest and Eagle Ridge also have good blacks. The resorts' boundaries are open, and there are good backcountry adventures to be had. *2490m; slopes 2435–3200m*
⛷ 13 ⛷ 2250 acres
📖 *American Ski Classics, Ski Safari*

Söll 173

Solvista USA
Child-oriented resort close to Winter Park. Low snowfall record for Colorado. *2490m; slopes 2490–2795m*
⛷ 5 ⛷ 250 acres

Sommand France
Purpose-built base that shares area with Praz-de-Lys. *1420m; slopes 1200–1800m*
⛷ 22 ⛷ 50km

Sonnenkopf 195
Ski area above Klösterle in the Alpenregion Bludenz. *slopes 1100–2300m*
⛷ 9 ⛷ 30km

Sorenberg Switzerland
Popular weekend retreat between Berne and Lucerne, with a high proportion of steep, low runs. *1165m; slopes 1165–2280m*
⛷ 16 ⛷ 50km

South Lake Tahoe USA
Tacky base for skiing Heavenly, with cheap lodging, traffic and gambling.

Spindleruv Mlyn
Czech Republic
Largest Giant Mountains region resort but with few facilities serving several little low areas. *715m; slopes 750–1310m*
⛷ 16 ⛷ 25km

Spital am Pyhrn Austria
Small village near Hinterstoder in Upper Austria, a bus ride from its limited intermediate slopes at Wurzeralm. *650m; slopes 810–1870m*
⛷ 8 ⛷ 20km

Spittal an der Drau Austria
Historic Carinthian town with a limited area at Goldeck starting a lift-ride above it. A good day trip from Bad Kleinkirchheim or from Slovenia. *555m; slopes 1650–2140m*
⛷ 8 ⛷ 30km

Spitzingsee Germany
Beautiful small lake (and village) an hour from Munich. ⛷ 18 ⛷ 25km

Splugen Reinwald
Switzerland
Small intermediate area south of Chur. *1485m; slopes 1455–2215m*
⛷ 6 ⛷ 30km

Sportgastein 104
Remote, high ski area at the top of the Badgastein valley.

Squaw Valley 551

Stafal 420
Isolated village with access to the Monterosa Ski area.

St Andra Austria
Valley-junction village ideally placed for one of the longest, most snow-sure cross-country networks in Europe. Close to the Tauern pass and to St Michael. *1045m*

St Anton 180

Starhill Resort South Korea
Purpose-built resort formerly called Cheonmasan, 30km north-east of Seoul. ⛷ 8

Stari Vrh Slovenia
About 30 minutes from Ljubljana airport. Runs include a never-groomed black, three interesting reds and a winding blue virtually from top to bottom. *slopes 580–1200m*
⛷ 5 ⛷ 12km

Stary Smokovec Slovakia
Spa town in the High Tatras mountains, with three small areas – Tatransky Lomica is the biggest. Funicular railway and snowmaking facilities. *1480m; slopes 1000–1500m*
⛷ 8 ⛷ 4km

St Cergue Switzerland
Limited resort in the Jura mountains, less than an hour from Geneva and good for families with young children. *1045m; slopes 1045–1680m*
⛷ 16 ⛷ 21km

St Christoph 180
Small village on Arlberg pass above St Anton.

St-Colomban-des-Villards
France
Small resort in next side valley to La Toussuire. Series of drags link to the rest of the area, with a pretty run to return. *1100m*

Steamboat USA
A few miles from the old cattle town of Steamboat Springs, and famed for its powder snow. Huge investment continues to equip the slope-side base with modern lodging, shops and restaurants. The slopes are compact but varied, with pretty treelined runs rising to 3220m; many of them are ideal for novices. Fast chairs serve each area. The main attraction for experts is the glades, but also the steep chutes and bowls on the backside of the area. Much of the mountain is ideal cruising terrain, although there is limited vertical to be achieved. The nursery slopes at the base are excellent, revamped recently. And family facilities are splendid. Steamboat town has countless hotels, condos and restaurants. *2105m; slopes 2105–3220m*
⛷ 18 ⛷ 2965 acres
📖 *Alpine Answers, American Ski Classics, Crystal, Crystal Finest, Erna Low, Independent Ski Links, Momentum, Ski Bespoke, Ski Independence, Ski Line, Ski Safari, Ski Solutions, Skitracer, Skiworld, Supertravel, Thomson*

Ste-Foy-Tarentaise 341

Steinach Austria
Pleasant market town with small area of slopes in picturesque surroundings, just off the autobahn up to the Brenner Pass, south of Innsbruck. *1050m; slopes 1050–2200m*
⛷ 6 ⛷ 25km

Stevens Pass USA
A day trip from Seattle, and accommodation 60km away in Bavarian-style town Leavenworth. Mostly intermediate slopes, with long expert runs on backside. Busy at weekends Jan to March.
1235m; slopes 1235–1785m
🚡 14 🚠 1125 acres

St-François-Longchamp France
Sunny, gentle slopes, with a couple of harder runs. Linked to Valmorel.
1400m ⛴ Erna Low, Lagrange

St Gallenkirch Austria
Village in the Montafon strung along the main road and spoiled by traffic. A gondola goes up to Valisera on the west ridge of the Nova ski area (see Gaschurn) and a blue run comes back down to the gondola base. From the 2011/12 season a new gondola from the same area as the old one goes up the opposite side of the valley to Grasjoch on the Hochjoch ski area – but there is no piste back. Hochjoch is a fair-sized area of easy blue runs, with occasional red alternatives. Apart from the new gondola and one eight-pack, the lifts are slow chairs and drags. The blue/red run from Kreuzjoch down to Schruns is a notable 12km long and 1700m vertical (and includes a section through the longest ski tunnel in the world – 473m). Snowmaking covers almost half the runs.
900m; slopes 900–2370m
🚡 27 🚠 100km

St-Gervais 274
Small town sharing its ski area with Megève.

St Jakob am Arlberg Austria
Quiet St Anton village, beyond Nasserein. Depends on shuttle-bus to the slopes.
1295m

St Jakob in Defereggen Austria
Unspoiled traditional village in a pretty, sunny valley close to Lienz and Heiligenblut, and with a good proportion of high-altitude slopes.
1400m; slopes 1400–2525m
🚡 7 🚠 52km

St Jakob in Haus Austria
Snowy village with its own slopes (Buchensteinwand). Fieberbrunn, Waidring, St Johann are nearby.
855m; slopes 855–1500m
🚡 8 🚠 19km
⛴ Inntravel

St-Jean-d'Arves France
Small, scattered community with 'friendly locals', in the Sybelles area. The original old village, with the usual ancient church, is set across the valley from the slopes,

which are at the mid-mountain hamlet of La Chal. Here, where a tasteful development of chalet-style buildings has been expanding, there are nursery slopes and the lift link to and piste back from Le Corbier. Not the best base to exploit the whole area, given the slow chair to Le Corbier, but a bus goes to St-Sorlin-d'Arves.
1550m ⛴ Peak Retreats, Ski France, Thomson

St Jean d'Aulps France
Small village in Portes du Soleil area, with its own interesting slopes.

St-Jean-de-Sixt France
Traditional hamlet, a cheap base for La Clusaz and Le Grand-Bornand (3km to both).
960m

St-Jean-Montclar France
Small village at the foot of thickly forested slopes. Good day out from nearby Pra-Loup.
1300m; slopes 1300–2500m
🚡 18 🚠 50km ⛴ Zenith

St Johann im Pongau Austria
Bustling, lively working town with its own small area. An extensive three-valley lift network starts 4km away at Alpendorf, linking via Wagrain to Flachau – all part of the Salzburger Sportwelt ski pass area.
650m; slopes 800–2185m
🚡 64 🚠 200km ⛴ Crystal

St Johann in Tirol Austria
Friendly valley town, an attractive place for beginners and leisurely part-timers – keen piste-bashers will ski all the local slopes in a day and need to go on to explore nearby resorts covered by the Kitzbüheler Alpenskipass as well. There is nothing here to challenge an expert. The main access lift is a 10-minute walk from the centre. It gets more snow than neighbouring Kitzbühel and the SkiWelt, and also has substantial snowmaking. Given good snow, St Johann is one of the best cross-country resorts in Austria – trails total 275km. The Park hotel is near the gondola and recommended by a reader.
650m; slopes 690–1700m
🚡 18 🚠 60km
⛴ Crystal, Ski Line, Skitracer, Snowscape, STC, Thomson

St Lary Espiaube 322
Satellite of St-Lary-Soulan in the Pyrenees.

St-Lary-Soulan 322

St Leonhard in Pitztal Austria
Village beneath a fine glacier in the Oetz area, accessed by underground funicular.
1250m; slopes 880–3440m
🚡 12 🚠 68km

St Luc 504
Village in the Val d'Anniviers.

St Margarethen Austria
Valley village near Styria/Carinthia border, sharing slopes with higher Katschberg.
1065m; slopes 1065–2210m
🚡 16 🚠 70km

St Martin bei Lofer Austria
Traditional cross-country village in a lovely setting beneath the impressive Loferer Steinberge massif. Alpine slopes at Lofer.
635m; slopes 640–1745m
🚡 10 🚠 46km

St-Martin-de-Belleville 344

St Martin in Tennengebirge Austria
Highest village in the Dachstein-West region near Salzburg. It has limited slopes of its own but nearby Annaberg has an interesting area.
1000m; slopes 1000–1350m
🚡 4 🚠 5km

St-Maurice-sur-Moselle France
One of several areas near Strasbourg. No snowmakers.
550m; slopes 900–1250m
🚡 8 🚠 24km

St Michael im Lungau Austria
Quiet, unspoiled village in the Tauern pass snowpocket with an uncrowded but disjointed intermediate area. Close to Obertauern and Wagrain.
1075m; slopes 1065–2220m
🚡 16 🚠 70km

St Moritz 497

St-Nicolas-de-Véroce 274
Small hamlet in the Megève network.

St-Nicolas-la-Chapelle France
Small village close to larger Flumet, in the Val d'Arly.
1000m; slopes 1000–1600m
🚡 10 🚠 40km

St-Nizier-du-Moucherotte France
Unspoiled, inexpensive resort just west of Grenoble with no lifts of its own. Villard-de-Lans is the main resort.

Stoneham Canada
The closest resort to Québec City, around 20 minutes away. It also has its own small base 'village', with condo accommodation and an impressive lodge that has its own lively après-ski bar, restaurant and spas. But night owls should probably head for the city as the evenings are generally quiet in resort. Like most resorts in this region, the ski area is small. The slopes spread across three linked peaks, with mainly sheltered intermediate and beginner pistes. It suits families well and has a special nursery area equipped with a moving carpet. A key

attraction is the resort's four terrain parks and half-pipe, regularly revamped and chosen to host the 2013 Snowboard World Championships.
210m; slopes 210–630m
🚡 7 🚠 326 acres
⛴ Frontier, Ski Safari

Stoos Switzerland
Small, unspoiled village an hour from Zürich. Weekend crowds. Splendid views of Lake Lucerne.
1300m; slopes 500–1935m
🚡 7 🚠 35km

Storlien Sweden
Small family resort amid magnificent wilderness scenery, one hour from Trondheim, 30 minutes from Åre.
600m; slopes 600–790m
🚡 7 🚠 16km

Stowe 606

St-Pierre-de-Chartreuse France
Locals' weekend place near Grenoble. Unreliable snow.
900m; slopes 900–1800m
🚡 14 🚠 35km

Stratton USA
Something like the classic Alpine arrangement of a village at the foot of the lifts: a smart, modern development with a car-free shopping street. The slopes are mostly easy and intermediate, with some blacks and some short double-black pitches, spread widely around the flanks of a single peak, served by modern lifts. Stratton calls itself the 'snowboarding capital of the east', with no fewer than five terrain parks. The Suntanner Park has a super-pipe.
570m; slopes 570–1180m
🚡 14 🚠 660 acres

Strobl Austria
Close to St Wolfgang in a beautiful lakeside setting. There are slopes at nearby St Gilgen and Postalm.
545m; slopes 545–1510m
🚡 7 🚠 12km

St-Sorlin-d'Arves France
A refreshing contrast to the stark, functional resorts of Le Corbier and La Toussuire, with which it shares the extensive Les Sybelles ski area. And the resort accesses some of the most interesting slopes. The village is a picturesque collection of traditional buildings, alongside a more modern development that spreads out along the main road and has attracted some major tour operators. The local slopes form the biggest single sector of the linked network, with lifts serving two distinct mountains. Some of the most varied slopes in the

whole area are here, and
reached by fast quads to Les
Perrons – which also has
some of the best off-piste
opportunities. There are
leisurely cruising runs on La
Balme.
1600m ▭ *AmeriCan Ski, Erna
Low, Lagrange, Peak Retreats,
Ski France, Ski Independence,
Thomson*

St Stephan   Switzerland
Unspoiled old farming village
at the foot of the largest
sector of slopes in the area
around Gstaad.
1000m; slopes 950–3000m
⛷ *58* ⛷ *250km*

Stubai valley   **189**

Stuben   **180**
Small, unspoiled village linked
to St Anton.

St Veit im Pongau   Austria
Spa resort with limited slopes
at Goldegg; Wagrain
(Salzburger Sportwelt) and
Grossarl (Gastein valley) are
nearby.
765m ⛷ *4* ⛷ *12km*

St-Veran   France
Said to be the highest 'real'
village in Europe, and full of
charm. Close to Serre-
Chevalier and the Milky Way.
Snow-reliable cross-country
skiing.
2040m; slopes 2040–2800m
⛷ *15* ⛷ *30km*

St Wolfgang   Austria
Charming lakeside resort near
Salzburg, some way from any
slopes, best for a relaxing
winter holiday with one or
two days on the slopes.
540m; slopes 665–1350m
⛷ *9* ⛷ *17km*
▭ *Crystal, Skitracer, STC,
Thomson*

Sugar Bowl   USA
Exposed area north of Lake
Tahoe with highest snowfall in
California, best for experts.
Lodging in Truckee but Squaw
Valley nearby.
2100m; slopes 2100–2555m
⛷ *8* ⛷ *1500 acres*

Sugarbush   USA
Dynamic resort in upper
Vermont, with two mountains
linked by fast chair, and
something resembling a
village at the foot of one of
them. Good range of runs,
including some real
challenges.
480m; slopes 450–1245m
⛷ *16* ⛷ *508 acres*
▭ *Ski Safari*

Sugarloaf   USA
Developing Maine resort, 5
hours from Boston, with the
Eastern US's best open
terrain.
430m; slopes 405–1290m
⛷ *15* ⛷ *1410 acres*
▭ *American Ski Classics*

Sulden   Italy
The other side of the Stelvio
Pass from Bormio. Very long
airport transfers. Solda is its
Italian name.
1905m; slopes 1905–2625m
⛷ *10* ⛷ *40km*

Summit at Snoqualmie   USA
Four areas – Summit East,
Summit Central, Summit West
and Alpental – with interlinked
lifts. Damp weather and wet
snow are major drawbacks.
slopes 915–1645m
⛷ *24* ⛷ *2000 acres*

Sun Alpina   Japan
Collective name for three ski
areas four hours away from
Tokyo. ⛷ *21*

Sundance   USA
Robert Redford-owned,
tastefully designed family
resort set amid trees in snow-
sure Utah. It's a small, narrow
mountain but the vertical is
respectable, the setting is
spectacular and there is
terrain to suit all abilities. The
lower mountain is easy-
intermediate, the upper part
steeper. There are 17km of
cross-country trails, of varying
difficulty.
1860m; slopes 1860–2515m
⛷ *4* ⛷ *450 acres*

Sunday River   USA
One of the more attractive
resorts in the East, four hours
from Boston, for intermediate
intermediate cruisers. The
slopes spread across eight
peaks, but it's a small area.
Only four of the chairs are
fast quads but queues are not
a problem – midweek, the
resort is very quiet. Cross-
country is big around here.
245m; slopes 245–955m
⛷ *16* ⛷ *743 acres*
▭ *American Ski Classics, Ski
Independence, Ski Safari*

Sunlight Mountain ResortUSA
Quiet, small area 10 miles
south of Glenwood Springs.
Varied terrain with some
serious glades.
2405m; slopes 2405–3015m
⛷ *3* ⛷ *470 acres*

Sun Peaks   **639**

Sunrise Park   USA
Arizona's largest area,
operated by Apaches. Slopes
are spread over three
mountains; best for novices
and leisurely intermediates.
2805m; slopes 2805–3500m
⛷ *12* ⛷ *800 acres*

Sunshine Village   **612**
One-hotel mountain station in
Banff's ski area.

Sun Valley   **595**
Purpose-built resort in Idaho.
1750m; slopes 1750–2790m
⛷ *17* ⛷ *2054 acres*

Suomu   Finland
A lodge (no village) right on
the Arctic Circle with a few
slopes but mostly a ski-
touring place.
140m; slopes 140–410m ⛷ *3*

Superbagnères   France
Little more than a particularly
French-dominated Club Med;
best for a low-cost, low-effort
family trip to the Pyrenees.
Said to have good off-piste if
the snow is good.
1880m; slopes 1440–2260m
⛷ *16* ⛷ *35km* ▭ *Lagrange*

Super-Besse   France
Purpose-built resort amid
spectacular extinct-volcano
scenery. Shares area with the
spa town of Mont-Dore.
Limited village.
1350m; slopes 1300–1850m
⛷ *22* ⛷ *43km*
▭ *Lagrange, Lagrange*

Superdévoluy   France
Purpose-built but friendly
family resort in a remote spot
near Gap, with huge
apartment blocks plus
traditional chalets. Sizeable
intermediate area shared with
more appealing La Joue-du-
Loup.
1450m; slopes 1450–2450m
⛷ *22* ⛷ *100km*
▭ *Erna Low, Ski Collection*

Super Espot   Spain
Small area on the eastern
edge of the Aigues Tortes
National Park, close to the
valley town of Sort.
slopes 1500–2500m
⛷ *8* ⛷ *28km*

Supermolina   Spain
Dreary, purpose-built satellite
of Pyrenean resort of La
Molina, with a reasonable
sized area of its own and
linked to the slopes of
Masella to form an area called
Alp 2500.
1700m; slopes 1600–2535m
⛷ *31* ⛷ *121km*

Les Sybelles   France
A group of linked ski resorts
in the Maurienne massif,
forming an impressively large
network.
slopes 1100–2620m
⛷ *72* ⛷ *310km*

Tahko   Finland
Largest resort in southern
Finland. Plenty of intermediate
slopes in an attractive,
wooded, frozen-lake setting.
⛷ *9*

Tahoe City   USA
Small lakeside
accommodation base for
visiting nearby Alpine
Meadows and Squaw Valley.

Talisman Mountain Resort
                             Canada
One of the best areas in the
Toronto region, but with a
relatively low lift capacity.
100% snowmaking.
235m; slopes 235–420m ⛷ *8*

Tamsweg   Austria
Large cross-country village
with rail links in snowy region
close to Tauern Pass and St
Michael. *1025m*

La Tania   **347**

Taos   **595**
Isolated resort in New Mexico.
2805m; slopes 2805–3600m
⛷ *14* ⛷ *1294 acres*

Tärnaby-Hemavan   Sweden
Twin resorts in north Sweden,
offering downhill, cross-
country and heliskiing. Own
airport. *slopes 465–1135m*
⛷ *13* ⛷ *44km*

El Tarter   **92**
Relatively quiet, convenient
alternative to Soldeu.

Tarvisio   Italy
Interesting, animated old
town bordering Austria and
Slovenia. A major cross-
country base with fairly
limited Alpine slopes.
750m; slopes 750–1860m
⛷ *12* ⛷ *15km*

Täsch   **526**
The final road base on the
way to car-free Zermatt.

Tauplitz   Austria
Traditional village at the foot
of an interestingly varied area
north of Schladming. Few
queues and decent lift
system, including some fast
chairs.
900m; slopes 900–2000m
⛷ *18* ⛷ *40km*

Telluride   USA
An isolated resort in south-
west Colorado, but a
beautifully renovated old
mining town with great Wild
West charm and fairly
dramatic mountain scenery.
It's a friendly, small-scale
resort, with a smartly
developing slope-side base
above it. Both have lifts into
the ski area. Mountain Village
has new luxury hotels and spa
facilities. The slopes are
limited in overall extent, but
quite varied and with recently
expanded expert terrain. Most
runs are below the treeline,
but the top lifts and bowls
give great views. Queues are
rarely a problem. Experts have
some truly challenging terrain
to play such as the Gold Hill
Chutes, while there are
splendid blue and greens runs
for intermediates and
beginners too – but it's not a
resort for keen piste bashers.
There are three terrain parks.
Nightlife revolves around the
bars.
2665m; slopes 2660–3830m
⛷ *18* ⛷ *2000 acres*
▭ *Alpine Answers, AmeriCan
Ski, American Ski Classics,
Elegant Resorts, Momentum,
Ski Bespoke, Ski Independence,
Ski Safari, Ski Solutions,
Skiworld*

Temù Italy
Sheltered hamlet near Passo Tonale. Worth a visit in bad weather.
1155m; slopes 1155–1955m
⛷4 ⛬5km

Tengendai Japan
Tiny area three hours by train and bus from Tokyo. One of Japan's best snow records, including occasional powder.
920m; slopes 920–1820m ⛷4

Termas de Chillán Chile
Ski and spa resort 400km south of Santiago. Base village has lodgings or you can stay at Las Trancas a few minutes' drive away.
1650m; slopes 1600–2700m
⛷9 ⛬46km ⛺ Momentum

Termignon 363
Rustic village 6km from Lanslebourg and the linked slopes of Val Cenis.

Terminillo Italy
Purpose-built resort 100km from Rome with a worthwhile area when its lower runs have snow-cover.
1500m; slopes 1500–2210m
⛷15 ⛬40km

Teton Village 601

Thollon-les-Mémises France
Attractive base for a relaxed holiday. Own little area and close to Portes du Soleil.
1000m; slopes 1600–2000m
⛷19 ⛬50km

Thredbo Australia
Oz's best, six hours from Sydney; with uncharacteristically long (and, in places, testing) runs, snowmaking, lots of accommodation and active nightlife.
1365m; slopes 1365–2035m
⛷14 ⛬480 acres

Three Valleys
La Thuile 451
Thyon 2000 508
Mid-mountain resort above Veysonnaz in the Verbier area.
Tignes 351

Timberline (Palmer Snowfield) USA
Fair-sized area of largely intermediate slopes served by six lifts including four fast quads on Mt Hood in Oregon.
1800m; slopes 1510–2600m
⛷6 ⛬1430 acres

Toblach Italy
Small resort in South Tyrol. Dobbiaco is its Italian name.
1250m; slopes 1250–1610m
⛷5 ⛬15km

Togari Japan
One of several areas close to the 1998 Olympic site. Nagano, 2hr30 from Tokyo.
slopes 400–1050m ⛷9

Torgnon Italy
Small village off the road up to Cervinia, good for bad-weather days. Some good cross-country loops.
1500m; slopes 1500–1965m
⛷7 ⛬6km

Torgon Switzerland
Old village in a pretty wooded setting, with a connection to the Portes du Soleil. Still some steep draglifts.
1150m; slopes 950–2300m
⛷197 ⛬650km

Le Tour 233
Charming hamlet at the head of the Chamonix valley.

La Toussuire France
Highest and most central of the Sybelles resorts, and convenient base for exploring the whole area. The centre has fairly dreary buildings, of apartments and hotels spreading widely from the car-free centre. But the local slopes have three of the seven fast chairs in the area, so access to Pte de L'Ouillon and the rest of the linked network is fairly quick. Two drags were installed in 2009 to reduce queues here too. Above the resort is a wide bowl with drags and chairs all around. Locally, the pistes are short cruisers with few challenges – but judged by a reporter as the most varied and snow-sure in the area. A splendid longer run goes to Les Bottières. There are gentle nursery slopes and good, easy progression runs. Eating out is relatively inexpensive for France, but nightlife is dull.
1700m ⛷72 ⛬310km
⛺ Erna Low, Lagrange, PowderBeds, Ski Collection, Ski France, STC

Trafoi Italy
Quiet, traditional village in the Val Venosta in the South Tyrol covered by the Ortler Skiarena pass.
1570m; slopes 1570–2550m
⛷4 ⛬10km

Treble Cone New Zealand
Plenty of good skiing opened up by two main lifts. Varied open terrain suitable for all levels. Great powder bowls. Nearly 2 hours from Queenstown.
1260m; slopes 1260–1960m
⛷4 ⛬550 hectares

Tremblant 650

Trentino Italy
Fabulously scenic area of the Dolomites, with a great many small ski areas that you won't have heard of, as well as a few large ones that are better known – Madonna di Campiglio chief among them.

Troodos Cyprus
Ski area on Mt Olympus, a 70-minute drive from Nicosia. Pretty, wooded slopes and fine views.
slopes 1730–1950m
⛷4 ⛬5km

Tröpolach Austria
Small village at base of access gondola for Nassfeld ski area.
610m; slopes 610–2195m
⛷30 ⛬110km

Trysil Norway
Extensive area, some distance from the town, spread around the conical Trysilfjellet, with some good, long runs of up to 4km. On the border with Sweden.
350m; slopes 350–1100m ⛷24
⛺ Absolutely Snow, Ski Safari

Tryvann Norway
Small area close to Oslo and popular with ocals. Vertical of 380m – are served by two drags and two chairs, one of them fast. ⛷6

Tschagguns Austria
Village the Montafon valley – effectively a suburb of Schruns.
700m; slopes 700–2100m
⛷13 ⛬32km

Tsugaike Kogen Japan
Sizeable resort four hours from Tokyo, three hours from Osaka. Helicopter service to the top station.
800m; slopes 800–1700m ⛷26

Tulfes Austria
Hamlet on mountain shelf close to Innsbruck, with small main area above the trees and long runs back to base.
920m; slopes 920–2305m
⛷7 ⛬22km

Turoa New Zealand
On the south-western slopes of Mt Ruapeha, with NZ's biggest vertical. Shares lift pass with Whakapapa. Mix of open, gentle and steeper runs. Good scope for off-piste.
slopes 1600–2320m
⛷23 ⛬2590 acres

Turracherhöhe Austria
Tiny, unspoiled resort on a mountain shelf, with varied intermediate slopes above and below it. A good outing from Bad Kleinkirchheim.
1765m; slopes 1400–2205m
⛷14 ⛬38km

Tyax Mountain Lake Resort Canada
Heli-skiing operation in the Chilcotin mountains – transfers from Whistler or Vancouver.

La Tzoumaz 508
Hamlet in Verbier's ski area.

Uludag Turkey
Surprisingly suave, laid-back, well-equipped, purpose-built resort near Bursa, south of Istanbul.
1750m; slopes 1750–2322m
⛷14 ⛬15km

Unken Austria
Traditional village hidden in a side valley. Closest slopes to Salzburg.
565m; slopes 1000–1500m
⛷4 ⛬8km

Untergurgl 146
Valley-floor alternative to staying in Obergurgl.

Unternberg Austria
Riverside village with trail connecting into one of the longest, most snow-sure cross-country networks in Europe. St Margarethen slopes close by. *1030m*

Unterwasser-Toggenburg Switzerland
Old but not especially attractive resort 90 minutes from Zürich. Fabulous lake and mountain views. The more challenging half of the Toggenburg area shared with Wildhaus.
910m; slopes 900–2260m
⛷17 ⛬60km

Uttendorf-Weiss-See Austria
Astute alternative to crowded Kaprun when the snowline is high.
805m; slopes 1485–2600m
⛷8 ⛬23km

Vail 570

Valbella Switzerland
Convenient but ordinary village sharing large intermediate Lenzerheide area.
1540m; slopes 1230–2865m
⛷35 ⛬155km

Valberg France
Large Alpes-Maritimes resort (bigger than better-known Isola 2000) close to Nice.
1650m; slopes 1430–2100m
⛷26 ⛬90km

Val Cenis Vanoise 363
Val d'Anniviers 504
Val di Fassa 453
Val d'Illiez 465
Peaceful, unspoiled village near Champéry.
Val d'Isère 366
Val Ferret Switzerland
Old climbing village near Martigny, with spectacular views. Own tiny area.
1600m ⛷3 ⛬20km

Valfréjus France
Small and unusual modern resort on a narrow, shady shelf in the Maurienne valley – built in the woods, with the slopes higher up above the treeline. The focus is Plateau d'Arrondaz, with steep, open slopes above, offering

genuine bumpy blacks with excellent snow (snowmaking on the lower runs is urgently required, though). There's a natural terrain park, and good off-piste is available above the main plateau. The nursery slopes are at mid-mountain and village levels. Recent investment in new lifts.
1550m; slopes 1550–2740m
🚠 *8* 🏂 *65km*
🚡 *Erna Low, Lagrange, PowderBeds, Ski Collection, Ski France*

Val Gardena 442
Valley area of Selva, Ortisei and Santa Cristina.

Valgrisenche Italy
Small, peaceful village on the southern side of the Aosta valley. Established heli-ski centre – about 20 drop points on the local peaks. A couple of intermediate runs, nursery area and a few cross-country loops.
1665m; slopes 🚠 *4* 🏂 *12km*

Vallandry 216
Satellite of Les Arcs.

Valle Nevado Chile
Developing purpose-built resort 46km east of Santiago. Varied, intermediate terrain.
3025m; slopes 2860–3670m
🚠 *14* 🏂 *2225 acres*
🚡 *Momentum, Skiworld*

Valloire France
A compelling combination of an old mountain village with extensive slopes, branded as Galibier Thabor, and shared with the more modern two-part resort of Valmeinier. The village is the best known of the Maurienne valley resorts and retains a quiet, rustic charm of narrow streets, shops and restaurants set around a lively market square. The slopes spread widely across three sunny sectors, served by two gondolas out of the village, and are particularly good for intermediates wanting lots of gentle cruising and a sense of travel. Experts will find the challenges limited, although there is some decent off-piste opportunity towards Valmeinier.
1430m; slopes 1430–2600m
🚠 *31* 🏂 *150km*
🚡 *AmeriCan Ski, Crystal, Erna Low, Lagrange, Peak Retreats, Pierre & Vacances, PowderBeds, Ski France, Ski Independence*

Vallorcine 233
Backwater on road between Chamonix and Switzerland.

Vallter 2000 Spain
Small resort on the far eastern fringes of the Pyrenees, close to the Costa Brava.
slopes 1960–2535m
🚠 *10* 🏂 *420 acres*

Valmeinier France
Quiet, old mountain village with a modern purpose-built satellite where most people stay. Shares with Valloire the most extensive slopes in the Maurienne region, spreading widely over three mostly sunny sectors.
1500–1800m; slopes 1430–2600m 🚠 *31* 🏂 *150km*
🚡 *Erna Low, Lagrange, Pierre & Vacances, PowderBeds, Ski Collection, Ski France, Ski Ici, Ski Independence, Snowcoach*

Valmorel France
The main resort in the Grand Domaine ski area, sharing slopes with St-François and Longchamp. The purpose-built village is prettily designed with a traffic-free centre, though lodging is broadly scattered among six 'hamlets' – mainly of simple hotels and apartments. The slopes offer a fair-sized area of varied skiing, with runs criss-crossing a number of minor valleys. Most are blue runs. Fast chairs serve the key links, but there are lots of slow drags. So, queues can be evident at peak times. The area appeals mainly to intermediates, and beginners. Few slopes are challenging, and there are good gentle greens for progression. Children are well catered for too. Nightlife is generally quiet and there is little off-slope diversion, although the soupe-side cafe-bars are 'jolly'.
1400m; slopes 1250–2550m
🚠 *46* 🏂 *152km*
🚡 *Alpine Answers, Club Med, Crystal, Erna Low, Inghams, Interactive Resorts, Lagrange, Peak Retreats, Pierre & Vacances, PowderBeds, Ski France, Ski Independence, Ski Line, Ski Solutions, Ski Supreme, Skitracer*

Val Senales Italy
Top-of-the-mountain hotel, the highest in the Alps, in the Dolomites near Merano.
3210m; slopes 2110–3210m
🚠 *12* 🏂 *35km*

Val Thorens 376

Valtournenche 395
Cheaper alternative to Cervinia.

Vandans Austria
Sizeable working village well placed for visiting all the Montafon areas. A gondola goes up directly from here into the Golm area.
655m; slopes 655–2085m
🚠 *9* 🏂 *30km*

Vars / Risoul 383

Vasilitsa Greece
Resort in northern Greece, in the Pindos range, offering intermediate skiing.
1780m 🚠 *8*

Vaujany 206
Tiny village in the heart of the Alpe-d'Huez ski area.

Las Vegas Ski Resort USA
Tiny area formerly known as Lee Canyon, cut from forest 50 minutes' drive north-west of Las Vegas.
2595m; slopes 2595–2855m
🚠 *4* 🏂 *200 acres*

Velka–Raca Slovakia
Small resort near Oscadnica, with a modern lift system, including a 'chondola'.
630m; slopes 630–1050m
🚠 *6* 🏂 *14km*

Vemdalen Sweden
Twin areas of Björnrike and Vemdalsskalet (same pass) 20 minutes apart. 385m vertical.
🚠 *18* 🏂 *28km*

Vemdalsskalet Sweden
20 minutes from Björnrike (same pass). 385m vertical. Said to have hottest après-ski in Sweden.
🚠 *18* 🏂 *28km*

Venosc France
Captivating tiny village of cobbled streets, ancient church and craft shops with fast gondola to Les Deux-Alpes. 🚡 *Peak Retreats*

Vent Austria
High, remote Oztal village known mainly as a touring base, with just enough lift-served skiing to warrant a day trip from nearby Obergurgl.
1900m; slopes 1900–2680m
🚠 *4* 🏂 *15km*

Ventron France
Small village near La Bresse in the northerly Vosges mountains near Strasbourg, with more ski de fond than downhill terrain.
630m; slopes 900–1110m
🚠 *8* 🏂 *15km*

Verbier 508

Vercorin 504
Cluster of chalets in the Val d'Anniviers.

Verditz Austria
One of several small, mostly mountain-top areas overlooking the town of Villach.
675m; slopes 675–2165m
🚠 *5* 🏂 *15km*

Vex Switzerland
Major village in unspoiled, attractive setting south of Sion. Verbier slopes accessed nearby at Mayens-de-l'Ours.
900m

Veysonnaz 508
Little old village within Verbier's Four Valleys network.

Vichères–Liddes Switzerland
Small area in Ski St-Bernard area near Verbier that is popular with families. Good

off-piste down to near La Fouly to be explored with a guide.
1350m; slopes 1600–2270m
🚠 *4* 🏂 *15km*

Vic-sur-Cère France
Charming village with fine architecture, beneath Super-Lioran ski area. Beautiful extinct-volcano scenery.
680m; slopes 1250–1850m
🚠 *24* 🏂 *60km*
🚡 *Lagrange*

Viehhofen Austria
Cheaper place to stay when visiting Saalbach. 3km from the Schönleiten gondola, and there's a run back to the village from the Asitz section.
860m 🚠 *1*

Vigla-Pisoderi Greece
The longest run in Greece (over 2km), in an unspoiled setting 18km from the town of Florina in the north.
1600m 🚠 *5*

Vigo di Fassa 453
Best base for the Val di Fassa.

La Villa 433
Quiet Sella Ronda village.

Villabassa Italy
Cross-country village in South Tyrol. Niederdorf is its German name.

Villach-Dobratsch Austria
One of several small, mostly mountain-top areas overlooking the town of Villach.
900m; slopes 980–2165m
🚠 *8* 🏂 *15km*

Villar-d'Arêne France
Tiny area on main road between La Grave and Serre-Chevalier. Empty, immaculately groomed, short easy runs, plus a couple of hotels.
1650m

Villard-de-Lans France
Unspoiled, lively, traditional village west of Grenoble. Snow-sure, thanks to snowmaking.
1050m; slopes 1145–2170m
🚠 *25* 🏂 *125km*

Villard-Reculas 206
Rustic village on periphery of Alpe-d'Huez ski area.

Villaroger 216
Rustic hamlet with direct links up to Arc 2000.

Villars 519

Villeneuve 331
One of the villages making up the resort of Serre-Chevalier.

Vipiteno Italy
Bargain-shopping town close to Brenner Pass.
960m; slopes 960–2100m
🚠 *12* 🏂 *25km*

Virgen Austria
Traditional village in a beautiful valley south of the Felbertauern tunnel. Slopes at Matrei.
1200m; slopes 975–2620m
🎿 15 ⛷ 110km

Vitosha Bulgaria
Limited area of slopes and a few widely scattered hotels, 22km from Sofia, leading to crowds at weekends. The slopes are north-facing and have a decent snow record.
1810m; slopes 1515–2290m
🎿 12 ⛷ 29km

Vogel 662

Vorarlberg 191

Vorarlberg – Alpenregion Bludenz 195

Vorarlberg – Bregenzerwald 192

Vorderlanersbach 110
Village with access to Mayrhofen's ski area.

Voss Norway
Well-equipped winter sports resort attractively set on a lake, with relatively limited Alpine slopes.
6om; slopes 150–945m
🎿 10 ⛷ 40km
⛴ Ski Safari

Vuokatti Finland
Small mountain in a remarkable setting, surrounded on three sides by lots of little lakes. Good activity base. 🎿 8

Wagrain Austria
A towny little resort at the centre of a lift system that is typical of many in Salzburgerland – spreading widely across several low, partly wooded ridges. Flachau and Alpendorf/St Johann are at its extremities, and all these resorts are covered by Salzburger Sportwelt lift pass that our figures relate to. It's pleasant without being notably charming, and though it's a compact place the main lift bases are still a good walk apart. The slopes – wooded at the bottom, open higher up – are practically all easy/intermediate stuff, but cover a huge area almost 15km across. The lift system is impressive, with a lot of fast chairs and gondolas. Despite the altitude, most of the upper slopes are fairly open. Some get too much sun for comfort, and snow reliability is not a strong point.
850m; slopes 850–2000m
🎿 10 ⛷ 35km ⛴ STC

Waidring Austria
Quiet valley village north of Kitzbühel. Mainly gentle open and north-facing slopes, also

accessible from Germany. Impressive lift system, but still prone to weekend queues.
780m; slopes 1230–1860m
🎿 10 ⛷ 35km

Waiorau Snow Farm New Zealand
Specialist cross-country base just over an hour from Queenstown. Spectacular views. Overnight huts.
1500m

Wald im Pinzgau Austria
Cross-country village surrounded by Alpine areas – Gerlos, Krimml and Neukirchen – and with Pass Thurn also nearby.
885m 🎿 50 ⛷ 160km

Wanaka New Zealand
Quiet, diffuse village in beautiful lakeside mountain setting close to four ski areas; the nearest is Treble Cone.

Warth 192
Bregenzerwald village near Lech.
1500m; slopes 1260–2100m
🎿 15 ⛷ 66km

Waterville Valley USA
Compact New Hampshire area with runs dropping either side of a broad, gentle ridge rising 615m above the lift base. A couple of short but genuine double-black-diamond mogul fields, but most of the slopes are intermediate. The village is a Disneyesque affair a couple of miles away down on the flat valley bottom.
6oom; slopes 600–1215m
🎿 12 ⛷ 255 acres

Watles Italy
Village in the Val Venosta in the South Tyrol covered by the Ortler Skiarena pass.
🎿 3 ⛷ 18km

Weinebene Austria
One of many gentle little areas in Austria's easternmost ski region near the Slovenian border. No major resorts in the vicinity.
1580m; slopes 1560–1835m
🎿 7 ⛷ 22km

Weissbach bei Lofer Austria
Traditional resort between Lofer and Saalfelden. No slopes of its own, but it's well placed for touring the Tirol. Kitzbühel, Saalbach, St Johann and Zell am See are nearby.
665m

Weissensee Naggeralm Austria
Little area in eastern Austria and the location of Europe's largest frozen lake, which is used for all kinds of ice sports, including ice-golf.
930m; slopes 930–1400m
🎿 5 ⛷ 6km

Weisspriach Austria
Hamlet on snowy pass near Obertauern that shares its area with Mauterndorf and St Michael.
1115m; slopes 1115–2050m
🎿 13 ⛷ 47km

Wengen 521

Wentworth Canada
Long-established Nova Scotia area with largest accessible acreage in the Maritime Provinces. Harsh climate ensures good snow-cover despite low altitude.
55m; slopes 55–300m
🎿 6 ⛷ 150 acres

Werfen Austria
Traditional village spoiled by the Tauern autobahn, which runs between it and the slopes. Good touring to the Dachstein West region.
620m

Werfenweng Austria
Hamlet with the advantage over the main village of Werfen of being away from the autobahn and close to the slopes. Best for novices.
1000m; slopes 1000–1835m
🎿 9 ⛷ 25km ⛴ Thomson

Whakapapa/Turoa New Zealand
NZ's largest area, on a volcano close to Turoa with similarly superb views and shared pass. The Grand Chateau is a lovely old hotel in the tiny village 6km away.
1630m; slopes 1630–2320m
🎿 23 ⛷ 2590 acres

Whistler 641

Whitecap Mountains Resort USA
Largest, snowiest area in Wisconsin, close enough to Lake Superior and Minneapolis to ensure winds and weekend crowds.
435m; slopes 435–555m
🎿 7 ⛷ 500 acres

Whiteface Mountain USA
Varied area in New York State 15km from attractive lakeside resort of Lake Placid. 93% snowmaking ensures good snow-cover. Plenty to do off the slopes.
365m; slopes 365–1345m
🎿 10 ⛷ 211 acres
⛴ American Ski Classics

Whitefish Mountain Resort USA
Resort set close to the Canadian border and to Montana's Glacier National Park, this place has revamped its image in recent years. Lots of redevelopment has taken place, both on and off the slopes. Its 3,000 acres embrace a wide range of slopes that are not only impressively snowy but also blissfully devoid of people. There's easy cruising in dense

forest around the base area, and steeper stuff higher up on 'gladed' slopes. There are two good terrain parks. There's lodging at the base and you can stay in the small town of Whitefish, a few miles away.
1360m; slopes 1360–2135m
🎿 13 ⛷ 3000 acres
⛴ Ski Safari

White Pass Village USA
Closest area to Mt St Helens. Remote and uncrowded during the week, with a good snowfall record. Some genuinely steep, expert terrain, as well as intermediate cruising.
1370m; slopes 1370–1825m
🎿 5 ⛷ 635 acres

Whitewater Canada
Renowned for powder (40% off-piste), food and weekend party atmosphere. Accommodation in the historic town of Nelson or a great day out from nearby Red Mountain.
1640m; slopes 1640–2040m 🎿 3
⛴ Frontier

Wildcat Mountain USA
New Hampshire area infamous for bad weather, but one of the best areas on a nice day. Lodging in nearby Jackson and North Conway.
slopes 600–1250m
🎿 4 ⛷ 225 acres

Wildhaus Switzerland
Undeveloped farming community in stunning scenery near Liechtenstein; popular with families and serious snowboarders. Shares its slopes with Unterwasser.
1050m; slopes 900–2260m
🎿 17 ⛷ 60km

Wildschönau – Ski Juwel Austria
Dramatic-sounding name adopted by a group of small resorts in the Tirol – Niederau, Oberau and Auffach. It now forms the Ski Juwel area with Alpbach – a two-stage gondola is all it has taken to link Alpbach and Auffach, and the linked area offers an appealing mix of small, friendly villages and fairly extensive intermediate slopes.
830m; slopes 670–2025m
🎿 47 ⛷ 128km

Willamette Pass USA
Set in national forest near beautiful Crater Lake, Oregon. Small area of varied slopes. An average of 430 inches of snow a year – that's up there with Utah.
1560m; slopes 1560–2035m
🎿 6 ⛷ 550 acres

Williams USA
Tiny area above the main place to stay for the Grand Canyon.
slopes 2010–2270m
🎿 2 ⛷ 50 acres

Willingen   Germany
Resort in Sauerland, east of
Düsseldorf. ⛟ 8

WindhamMountain   USA
Boutique resort in the Catskill
Mountains 2.5 hours from
New York.
455m; slopes 455–945m
⛟ *10* 🏂 *269 acres*

Windischgarsten   Austria
Large working village in Upper
Austria with cross-country
trails around and downhill
slopes at nearby Hinterstoder
and Spital am Pyrhn. *600m*

Winterberg   Germany
Resort in Sauerland, east of
Düsseldorf. ⛟ 24

Winter Park   **577**

Wolf Creek   USA
Remote area on a pass of the
same name, with 'the most
snow in Colorado' – 465
inches a year. One-third of the
terrain is standard American
trails through the trees; two-
thirds is 'wilderness', served
by a single lift. Great stop en
route between Taos and
Telluride. Stay in Pagosa
Springs to the west, or South
Fork to the east.
3140m; slopes 3140–3630m
⛟ *6* 🏂 *1600 acres*

Wolf Mountain   USA
Utah cross-country area close
to Salt Lake City. Powder
Mountain and Snowbasin are
nearby Alpine areas.
⛟ *3* 🏂 *100 acres*

Xonrupt   France
Cross-country venue only 3km
from nearest Alpine slopes at
Gérardmer.
715m 🚌 *Lagrange*

Yangji Pine Resort
                             South Korea
Modern resort an hour (60km)
south of Seoul, with runs cut
out of dense forest. Gets very
crowded. ⛟ 6

Ylläs   **653**

Yong Pyong Resort
                             South Korea
200km east of Seoul, close to
the east coast, also known as
Dragon Valley. The self-
contained purpose-built resort
village is centred on 200-room
Dragon Valley Hotel. Modern
lifts serve a small, mainly
wooded slope area, with
snowmaking on all its runs.
750m; slopes 750–1460m
⛟ *15* 🏂 *20km*

Zakopane   Poland
An interesting old town 100km
south of Kraków on the
Slovakian border. Mostly
intermediate slopes, branded
as 14 small and fragmented
sectors. Reported to have
renovated its 70-year-old
cable car.
830m; slopes 1000–1960m
⛟ *60* 🏂 *60km*

Zao   Japan
Big area with unpredictable
weather, four hours from
Tokyo by train. Known for
'chouoh' – pines frozen into
weird shapes. Hot springs.
780m; slopes 780–1660m ⛟ *42*

Zauchensee   Austria
Purpose-built resort part of
big three-valley lift network
linking it via Flachauwinkl to
Kleinarl – which our figures
relate too. Also on the
Salzburger Sportwelt ski pass.
'Attractive, compact village,
shops limited to ski kit, no
nightlife, dining only in hotels,
relatively easy family-friendly
skiing'.
855m; slopes 800–2185m
⛟ *15* 🏂 *88km*

Zell am See   **198**

Zell im Zillertal   **140**
Sprawling valley town with
slopes on two mountains.

Zermatt   **526**

Zillertal   Austria
Valley of ten ski resorts, of
which the most well known is
Mayrhofen.

Zinal   **504**
Village in the Val d'Anniviers.

Zug   **131**
Tiny village with Lech's
toughest skiing.

Zugspitz Arena   Austria
The name of Germany's
highest mountain, and part of
Austria's Zugspitz Arena over
the border – a collection of
small, gentle but low ski
areas, with pretty villages.
990-1340m; slopes 990–2960m
⛟ *55* 🏂 *148km*

Zuoz   Switzerland
An unspoiled village in a
sunny setting just down the
valley from St Moritz, with
gentle slopes at village level
and some more challenging
runs higher up.
1715m; slopes 1720–2465m
⛟ *5* 🏂 *15km*
🚌 *Inntravel*

Zürs   **131**
High village on road to Lech.

Zweisimmen   Switzerland
Limited but inexpensive base
for slopes around Gstaad,
with its own delightful little
easy area too.
965m; slopes 950–3000m
⛟ *58* 🏂 *250km*

Build your own shortlist: **www.wheretoskiandsnowboard.com**